D0600159

53RD EDITION

KOVELS'® ANTIQUES & COLLECTIBLES PRICE GUIDE 2021

WITHDRAWN

San Diego Public Library

BLACK DOG
& LEVENTHAL
PUBLISHERS
NEW YORK

Copyright © 2020 Terry Kovel and Kim Kovel
The Kovels® is a registered trademark of Kovels Antiques, Inc.

Cover design by Carlos Esparza and Katie Benezra

Front cover photographs, from left to right:
Mocha, Pitcher, Cat's Eye, Blue Engine-Turned Bands;
Furniture, Cupboard, Corner, Federal, Maple, Cherry;
Toy, Taxi, Black, Yellow, Tin, Windup

Back cover photographs, top to bottom:
Tiffany, Lamp, Banded Dogwood, Leaded Glass Shade, Bronze;
Schneider, Vase, Air Trap, Cranberry, Opal Splatter;
Purse, Suede & Fur, Quilted, Black, Goldtone CC Logo;
Advertising, Box, Display, Shredded Wheat, Factory

Spine:
Indian, Bracelet, Navajo, Cuff, Turquoise Cabochons

Authors' photographs © Kim Ponsky (top) and Alex Montes de Oca (bottom)

Cover copyright © 2020 by Hachette Book Group, Inc.

Hachette Book Group supports the right to free expression and the value of copyright.
The purpose of copyright is to encourage writers and artists to produce the creative works that enrich our culture.

The scanning, uploading, and distribution of this book without permission is a theft of the author's intellectual property.
If you would like permission to use material from the book (other than for review purposes), please contact
permissions@hbgusa.com. Thank you for your support of the author's rights.

Black Dog & Leventhal Publishers
Hachette Book Group
1290 Avenue of the Americas
New York, NY 10104

www.hachettebookgroup.com
www.blackdogandleventhal.com

First Edition: September 2020

Black Dog & Leventhal Publishers is an imprint of Perseus Books, LLC, a subsidiary of Hachette Book Group, Inc.
The Black Dog & Leventhal Publishers name and logo are trademarks of Hachette Book Group, Inc.

The publisher is not responsible for websites (or their content) that are not owned by the publisher.
The Hachette Speakers Bureau provides a wide range of authors for speaking events.
To find out more, go to www.HachetteSpeakersBureau.com or call (866) 376-6591.

Print book interior design by Sheila Hart Design/Hartsart

LCCN: 2020940575
ISBN: 978-0-7624-9746-1

Printed in the United States of America

WALSWORTH
10 9 8 7 6 5 4 3 2 1

BOOKS BY RALPH AND TERRY KOVEL

American Country Furniture, 1780–1875

A Directory of American Silver, Pewter, and Silver Plate

Kovels' Advertising Collectibles Price List

Kovels' American Antiques 1750–1900

Kovels' American Art Pottery

Kovels' American Collectibles 1900–2000

Kovels' American Silver Marks, 1650 to the Present

Kovels' Antiques & Collectibles Fix-It Source Book

Kovels' Antiques & Collectibles Price Guide (1968–2009)

Kovels' Bid, Buy, and Sell Online

Kovels' Book of Antique Labels

Kovels' Bottles Price List (1971–2006)

Kovels' Collector's Guide to American Art Pottery

Kovels' Collector's Guide to Limited Editions

Kovels' Collectors' Source Book

Kovels' Depression Glass & Dinnerware Price List (1980–2004)

Kovels' Dictionary of Marks— Pottery and Porcelain, 1650 to 1850

Kovels' Guide to Selling, Buying, and Fixing Your Antiques and Collectibles

Kovels' Guide to Selling Your Antiques & Collectibles

Kovels' Illustrated Price Guide to Royal Doulton (1980, 1984)

Kovels' Know Your Antiques

Kovels' Know Your Collectibles

Kovels' New Dictionary of Marks— Pottery and Porcelain, 1850 to the Present

Kovels' Organizer for Collectors

Kovels' Price Guide for Collector Plates, Figurines, Paperweights, and Other Limited Edition Items

Kovels' Quick Tips: 799 Helpful Hints on How to Care for Your Collectibles

Kovels' Yellow Pages: A Resource Guide for Collectors

The Label Made Me Buy It: From Aunt Jemima to Zonkers— The Best-Dressed Boxes, Bottles, and Cans from the Past

BOOKS BY TERRY KOVEL AND KIM KOVEL

Kovels' Antiques & Collectibles Price Guide (2010–2021)

INTRODUCTION

Kovels' Antiques & Collectibles Price Guide 2021 has current, reliable price information and makers' marks. The book has 11,500 prices, 3,000 new color photographs, more than 730 categories, hundreds of dated marks, plus an all-new center section on "Collecting Trends: Iconic Designers of Twentieth-Century Lighting."

We are frequently asked questions like "How old is my grandmother's dish?" Each of the 730 categories includes an introductory paragraph with history, locations, explanations, and other important information to help identify unknown pieces, and some include information about reproductions. We update these introductory paragraphs every year to indicate new owners, new distributors, or new information about production dates. This year we made updates to over 40 paragraphs, many that tell of the sale or closing of a company. This guide includes more than 500 marks. Even more dated marks can be found online at Kovels.com. You will also find more than 200 added facts of interest and tips about care and repair. Each photograph is shown with a caption that includes the description, price, and source, and information about the seller of the piece is listed at the end of the book. The book has color tabs and color-coded categories that make it easy to find listings, and it uses a modern, readable typestyle. All antiques and collectibles priced here were offered for sale during the past year, most of them in the United States, from June 2019 to June 2020. Other prices came from sales that accepted bids from all over the world. Almost all auction prices given include the buyer's premium since that is part of what the buyer paid. Very few include local sales tax or extra charges for things such as phone bids, online bids, credit cards, storage, or shipping.

Most items in our original 1968 price book were made before 1860, so they were more than a century old. Today in *Kovels' Antiques & Collectibles Price Guide*, we list pieces made as recently as 2010. There is great interest in furniture, glass, ceramics, and design made since 1950 in the midcentury modern style and pieces made after the 1980s.

The 2021 edition is 600 pages long and crammed full of prices and photographs. We try to include a balance of prices and do not include too many items that sell for more than $5,000. By listing only a few very expensive pieces, you can realize that a great paperweight may cost $10,000, but an average one is only $25. Nearly all prices are from the American market for the American market. Only a few European sales are reported. These are for items that may be of interest to American collectors. We don't include prices we think result from "auction fever," but we do list verified bargains.

There is an index with cross-references. Use it often. It includes categories and much more. For example, there is a category for Celluloid. Most celluloid will be there, but a toy made of celluloid may be listed under Toy as well as indexed under Celluloid. There are also cross-references in the listings and in the category introductions. But some searching must be done. For example, Barbie dolls are in the Doll category; there is no Barbie category. And when you look at "doll, Barbie," you find a note that "Barbie" is under "doll, Mattel, Barbie" because Mattel makes Barbie dolls and most dolls are listed by maker.

Wherever we had extra space on a page, we filled it with tips about the care of collections and other useful information. Don't discard this book. Old *Kovels'* price guides can be used in the coming years as a reference source for identifying pictures and price changes and for tax, estate, and appraisal information.

The prices in this book are reports of the general antiques market. As we said, every price in the book is new. We do not estimate or "update" prices. Prices are either realized prices from auctions or completed sales. We have also included a few that are asking prices, knowing that a buyer may have negotiated a lower price. We do not pay dealers, collectors, or experts to estimate prices. If a price range is given, at least two identical items were offered for sale at different prices. Price ranges are found only in categories such as Pressed Glass, where identical items can be identified. Some prices in *Kovels' Antiques & Collectibles Price Guide* may seem high and some low because of regional variations, but each price is what you could have paid for the object somewhere in the United States. Internet prices from individual sellers' ads or listings are avoided. Because so many noncollectors sell online but know little about the objects they are describing, there can be inaccuracies in descriptions. Sales from well-known Internet sites, shops, and sales, carefully edited, are included.

If you are selling your collection, do not expect to get retail value unless you are a dealer. Wholesale prices for antiques are 30 to 40 percent of retail prices. The antiques dealer must make a profit or go out of business. Internet auction prices are less predictable; because of an international audience or "auction fever," prices can be higher or lower than retail.

Time has changed what we collect, the prices we pay, what is "best," and what has dropped in price. There are also laws about endangered species, not a concern when we started, and many changes in tax laws, estate problems, and even more and better reproductions and fakes that make buying more difficult. But there are many more ways to buy and sell. When we started, it was house sales, flea markets, and a few formal antiques shows and auctions. Now, computers and the Internet have made it possible for anyone to buy and sell any day of the week, in every price range. This year there were shows canceled because of the coronavirus, a number of auction houses merging, and many more auction bidders. Almost every auction is online as well as available by phone to buyers around the world. And there are frequently live bidders at the more expensive sales. But many auctions end up with unsold pieces, some offered for sale at a set price after the auction. Even eBay is selling only part of the offered antiques. And there are thousands of places to look for prices!

READ THIS FIRST

This is a book for the buyer and the seller. It is an organized, illustrated list of average pieces, not million-dollar paintings and rare Chinese porcelains. Everything listed in this book was sold within the last 12 months. We check prices, visit shops, shows, and flea markets, read hundreds of publications and catalogs, check Internet sales, auctions, and other online services, and decide which antiques and collectibles are of most interest to most collectors in the United States. We concentrate on average pieces in any category. Prices of some items were very high because a major collection of top-quality pieces owned by a well-known collector, expert, or celebrity was auctioned. Fame adds to the value. Many catalogs now feature the name, picture, and biography of the collector and advertise the auction with the collector's name in all the ads. This year there were major sales of one-owner collections of bottles, target balls, Tiffany, iconic Max Ingrand lighting, a Canadian Modernist collection, Shaker furniture and household items, Christmas decorations and gifts, Memphis furniture, Japanese kimonos, Mexican silver jewelry, half-dolls, Boehm bird sculptures, Rookwood pottery, carnival glass, and the advertising archives of a tire company. Our favorite was a collection we have reported on over the years of pressing and other types of household irons put together by, of course, David and Sue Irons. The sales were well advertised and prices were high. Some of these high prices are reported. The most important bottle auctions are run by major bottle auction companies that feature only bottles, including American flasks. Some of these high prices are also reported, along with less expensive inkwells, bitters bottles, and more.

The largest thing listed this year is a 38-star American flag commemorating Colorado's statehood

(1877 to 1889). It has stars made of cotton fabric machine-sewn to wool bunting. The flag is large—284 inches by 143 inches—and it sold for $625. There was also some yardage of a black horsehair fabric with diaperwork made in the 1900s. It is 434 inches by 28 inches and sold for $410. The smallest is a ⅞-inch carved shell button with a brass portrait of Jupiter. It was only $24. Also sold was a jelly belly (a clear rounded glass jewel) pin shaped like a fly. The 1-inch pin sold for $120.

The least expensive entry was a crown bottle cap for Royal Crown Cola. The yellow, red, white, and green plastic-lined cap had a printed slogan "R C Cola with a Twist." It was $2.

There are always some strange and even weird things listed in our price books. We have listed artificial legs several times, usually the plain wooden stump that is pictured in stories of pirates of earlier days. This year we list a molded plywood splint for a leg of a wounded soldier in World War II that was made by Charles and Ray Eames. It was in its original paper wrapper. The 42- by 8-inch splint sold for $688, just a little more than a similar one sold for last year. The idea of molding plywood led the Eameses to create a new type of furniture when the war ended that is still being made. There was also a World War I (1918) gas mask with its original pouch marked C.W. Steverson, 87th Division A.E.F. (American Expeditionary Force), It was 10 inches by 10 inches and sold for $266. But the most eye-catching item was a decorative piece called "Ridiculous bench," a piece of recent design. It's hand-painted with faux marbling, checks, dots, gold leaf, Scottish tartan paper, and flower transfers over a hardwood frame. The bench has gold-lustered ceramic feet and glass beaded fringe. It is 52 by 28 by 21 inches and can be used as a small table or a bench. Part of a decorating style that is still being made by Mackenzie-Childs: the pre-owned bench was offered at auction with a $600 to $800 estimate but sold for $3,500. A new one costs $4,995.

RECORD-SETTING PRICES

BOTTLES

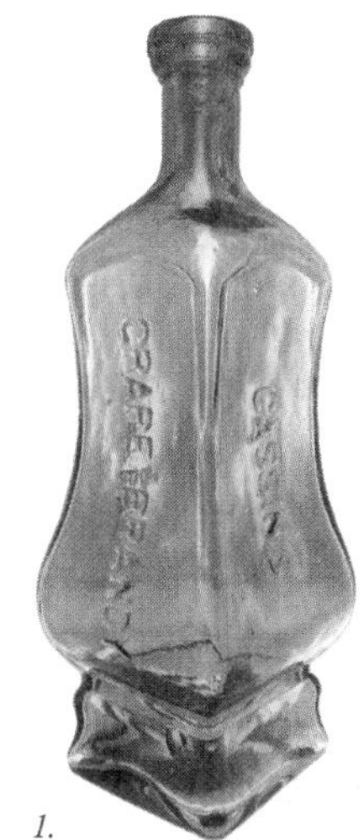

1.

Cassin's Grape Brandy Bitters Bottle (image 1): $155,000 for the 150-year old bluish-teal color Cassin's Grape Brandy Bitters bottle, 1867–1868, with applied top; its shape resembles a cello. Sold December 8, 2019, by American Bottle Auctions, Sacramento, California.

CLOCKS & WATCHES

Patek Philippe watch (image 2): $31,000,000 for the "Only One" Patek Philippe Grandmaster Chime wristwatch made in stainless steel, Ref. 6300A-010 with 2 dials in rose gold and black ebony, reversible case, patented reversing mechanism, featuring 20 complications with no fewer than 5 chiming modes, "The Only One" appears at 12 o'clock, black alligator leather strap, handstitched, fold-over clasp, 47.7mm diameter, 16.07mm thickness. Sold November 9, 2019, by Christie's, Geneva, Switzerland.

2.

COINS

Lincoln cent 1955 double die obverse (image 3): $124,875 for the 1955 double struck Lincoln penny, rated PCGS MS-65+. Approximately 40,000 error coins were stuck and some were mixed in with the

3.

4.

regular pennies for release; it was decided it was too much trouble to separate them out. Sold March 1, 2020, by GreatCollections.com, an online auction, Irvine, California.

Walking Liberty 1938 half dollar (image 4): $81,562 for the proof 1938 Walking Liberty half dollar, graded Proof-68+. Sold April 26, 2020, by GreatCollections.com, an online auction, Irvine, California.

FURNITURE

5.

Most expensive piece of Spanish furniture (image 5): $447,000 for a royal Spanish brass-inlaid and ormolu-mounted commode, tulipwood, ebony, padauk, kingwood, and marquetry, marble top, 2 long drawers, carved black flower sprays, c.1765–1775, 37 x 52 x 22 in. Sold October 29, 2019, by Christie's, New York.

JEWELRY

Any jewel sold in an online auction (image 6): $1,340,000 for a diamond & emerald Tutti Frutti bracelet by Cartier, resembling meandering vines with old European single-cut diamonds, carved emeralds, rubies, sapphires, and emerald bead accents, highlighted with calibre-cut onyx & black enamel, signed Cartier, c.1930, 7 in. Sold April 28, 2020, by Sotheby's, New York.

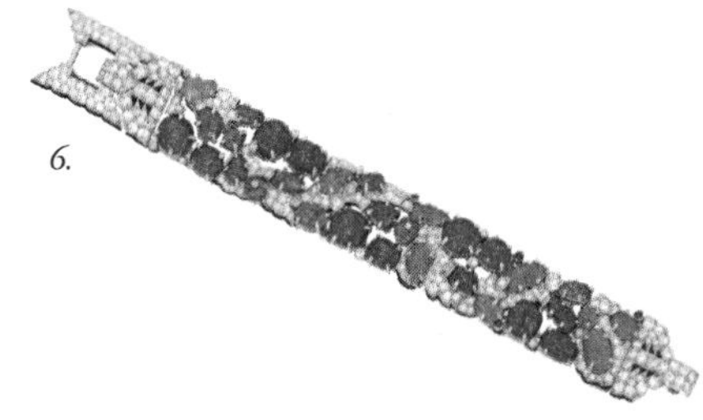
6.

LAMPS & LIGHTING

Tiffany aquatic fish lamp (image 7): $193,600 for a leaded glass Tiffany lamp with rippling seaweed, five swimming fish made of mottled gold glass with red and green glass eyes on a bronze pumpkin base, 17 ½ in. h., shade 16 in. dia. Sold September 14, 2019, by Fontaine's Auction Gallery, Pittsfield, Massachusetts.

7.

MISCELLANEOUS

Working Enigma cipher machine (image 8): $800,000 for a fully operational four-rotor (M4) Kriegsmarine Enigma cipher machine, seized from the Bauaufsicht Der Kriegsmarine in Trondheim, Norway, in 1945. Made in 1942. Sold December 17, 2019, by Sotheby's, New York.

8.

Superman cape sold at auction, most expensive (image 9): $193,750 for the bright red cape with yellow "S" symbol outlined in black and stitched to the back of the cape worn by Christopher Reeve in the movie *Superman* (Warner Bros., 1978). In January 1979, the cape was awarded as first prize for answering 25 questions correctly in a contest by DC Comics. Sold December 16, 2019, by Julien's Auctions, Los Angeles, California.

9.

PAINTINGS & PRINTS

Medieval painting, most expensive (image 10): $26,600,000 for the medieval painting titled *Christ Mocked* attributed to the 13th-century Italian painter Cimabue, found hanging in the kitchen of an elderly woman in northern France, 10 x 8 in. Sold October 27, 2019, by Actéon Auction, Senlis, France.

Any work by Monet (image 11): $110,700,000 for the 1890 Claude Monet painting *Meules*, from the artist's Haystacks series, oil on canvas, signed and dated 91, 28 ⅝ x 36 ¾ in. Sold May 14, 2019, Sotheby's, New York.

10.

11.

12.

PAPER

Comic book art piece, American published (image 12): $5,400,000 for Frank Frazetta's *Egyptian Queen* comic book cover art, appearing on the cover of *Eerie* magazine No. 23 in 1969. Sold May 16, 2019, by Heritage Auctions, Dallas, Texas, auction held in Chicago.

13.

Concert poster, most expensive sold at auction (image 13): $137,500 for a 1966 concert poster from The Beatles' performance at New York's Shea Stadium on August 23, 1966, yellow cardboard with black and white photograph of the Fab Four, printed by Murray Poster Printing Co., 18 x 24 in. Sold April 4, 2020, by Heritage Auctions, Dallas, Texas.

Previously sold: 2004—$132,736; November 2019—$125,000

14.

15.

16.

Marvel comics Star Wars interior-page art (image 14): $33,748 for a *Star Wars* No. 3 comic book original art, drawn by Howard Chaykin and inked by Steve Leialoha, Marvel, Sept. 1977, signed by both artists, Marvel copyright stamp. Sold November 6, 2019, by Hake's Auctions, York, Pennsylvania.

Marvel comic book, most expensive (image 15): $1,260,000 for a copy of Marvel Comics No. 1, 1939, graded 9.4, features the first appearance of The Human Torch, Ka-Zar, Angel, and Sub-Mariner. Sold November 21, 2019, by Heritage Auctions, Dallas, Texas.

Captain America No. 1 comic book (image 16): $915,000 for Captain America No. 1 comic book that marked the debut of the Marvel superhero, 1941. Sold August 1, 2019, by Heritage Auctions, Dallas, Texas.

17.

Nintendo Pokémon "Pikachu Illustrator" card (image 17): $224,250 for the Nintendo Pokémon "Pikachu Illustrator" Trainer Promo Hologram trading card, put out in 1998 (PSA 9) and given to the winners as a prize of a CoroCoro Comic Illustration contest for Pokémon, created specifically for the contest. Sold October 23, 2019, by Weiss Auctions, Lynbrook, New York.

POTTERY & PORCELAIN

Face vessel, America & Ohio stoneware (image 18): $177,000 for a stoneware face cooler, two-toned slip brushed in cobalt oxide and Albany slips, lizard handles, turtle-form spout, and decorated on the front with a hand modeled applied clay face, by William Wilbur, Ironton, Ohio, c.1870, 25 in. h. Sold July 20, 2019, by Crocker Farm, Inc., Sparks, Maryland.

George Ohr vessel (image 19): $100,000 for the George E. Ohr glazed earthenware vessel with an in-body twist, irregular shaped rim, cone-shaped protruding center, ocher and gunmetal sponged-on and

18. 19. 20. 21.

speckled glaze, incised "Ohr" signature inside rim, 1898–1910, 12 ½ x 6 x 6 ½ in. Sold January 18, 2020, by Rago Arts and Auction Center, Lambertville, New Jersey.

Stoneware, record for New York State pottery / 2nd highest auction result for American stoneware (image 20): $480,000 for a stoneware water cooler with incised cobalt blue street scene of Broadway in Manhattan, by W.H. Farrar, 1846, 7 gallon, 26 in. Sold May 1, 2020, by Crocker Farm, Inc., Sparks, Maryland.

Record for the form (image 21): $56,250 for the Betty Woodman "Divided Aegean Pillow Pitcher," multicolored glazed earthenware, pillow-shaped body, and twisted handle, signed, 1985, 21 x 25 x 18 ½ in. Sold September 21, 2019, by Rago Arts and Auction Center, Lambertville, New Jersey.

SPORTS

22.

Babe Ruth game-worn jersey (image 22): $5,640,000 for the 1928–1930 Babe Ruth New York Yankees game-worn gray road jersey, "Ruth" stitched in the collar. Sold June 15, 2019, by Hunt Auctions, LLC, Exton, Pennsylvania.

Nike "Moon Shoe" sneakers (image 23): $437,500 for a pair of Nike Waffle Racing Flat "Moon Shoes," nylon, leather/suede, rubber, size 12 ½, designed by track coach and Nike cofounder Bill Bowerman for the U.S. 1972 Olympic trials, using his wife's waffle iron as a mold for the rubber sole. Sold July 23, 2019, by Sotheby's, New York.

23.

Nike "Air Jordan" sneakers, most expensive (image 24): $560,000 for Michael Jordan's Nike "Air Jordan" autographed leather sneakers, game worn in 1985, Sold May 17,

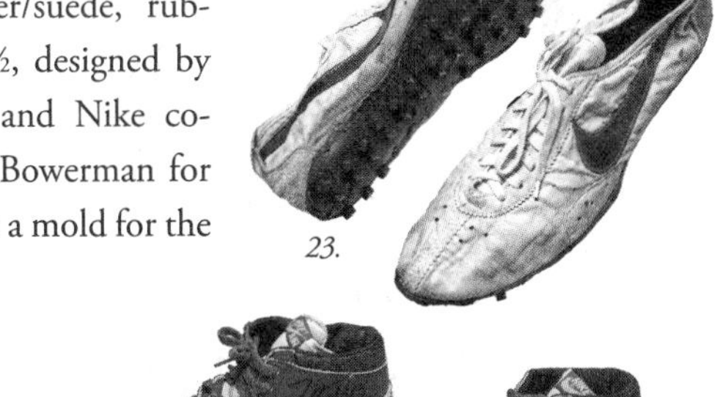

24.

2020, by Sotheby's, New York. Surpassed the previous record of $437,500 for the Nike "Moon Shoe" sneakers sold in July 2019 by Sotheby's.

25.

Honus Wagner baseball card (image 25): $1,353,625 for a Honus Wagner 1909–1911 T206 Sweet Caporal 150/25 PSA 2 Good. Sold October 11, 2019, by Mile High Card Co., Castle Rock, Colorado.

26.

Game-worn jersey (image 26): $2,580,000 for Lou Gehrig's 1937 New York Yankees road jersey. This is the highest price paid for a game-worn jersey not worn by Babe Ruth. Sold August 17, 2019, by Heritage Auctions, Dallas, Texas.

27.

Piece of sports memorabilia (image 27): $8,806,500 for the original Olympic Games manifesto, written in 1892 by Pierre de Coubertin, original Olympic Committee founder, a 14-page handwritten document outlining why he wanted to bring back the Ancient Greek tradition of Olympic competition. Sold December 18, 2019, by Sotheby's, New York.

28.

Derek Jeter rookie card 1993 (image 28): $180,000 for the 1993 Derek Jeter foil rookie card No. 279, PSA 10 gem mint. Sold January 11, 2020, by Memory Lane Inc., Tustin, California.

29.

Heisman Trophy (image 29): $504,000 for the Heisman Trophy won by University of Texas running back Ricky Williams in 1998. Sold October 30, 2019, by Heritage Auctions, Dallas, Texas.

New York Yankees promotional nodder (image 30): $90,000 for the 1961–1962 oversized promotional New York Yankees nodder, in the white with blue pinstripes uniform, made in Japan, 14 in. Sold October 30, 2019, by Heritage Auctions, Dallas, Texas.

30.

TOYS, DOLLS & BANKS

Video game at auction (image 31): $75,000 for the sealed video game Mega Man ("Dr. Wright" first release)—Carolina Collection Wata 9.4 A+, 1987, marking the first appearance of the character Mega Man. Sold November 22, 2019, by Heritage Auctions, Dallas, Texas.

31.

Video game item (image 32): $360,000 for a Nintendo PlayStation Super NES CD-ROM prototype console produced by Sony and Nintendo before their partnership ended, including a single controller, c.1992. Sold March 6, 2020, by Heritage Auctions, Dallas, Texas.

32.

Figural Mickey Mouse toy (image 33): $64,575 for a figural five-finger Mickey Mouse toy, tin lithograph, made in Germany by Saalheimer & Strauss, windup, Mickey dances back and forth, cut-out pie eyes go up and down, his mouth opens and closes, 9 in. h. Sold March 11, 2020, by Morphy Auctions, Denver, Pennsylvania.

Star Wars toy (image 34): $112,926 for the Star Wars *Empire Strikes Back* prototype of a Boba Fett L-slot action rocket-firing figure, 3 ¾ in. Displayed at the 1979 Toy Fair in New York City, intended to be part of Kenner's licensed toy line but never making it to mass production. Sold July 11, 2019, by Hake's Auctions, York, Pennsylvania.

33.

Star Wars toy (image 35): $185,850 for the Star Wars *Empire Strikes Back* prototype of a Boba Fett J-slot rocket-firing action figure, 3 ¾ in., c.1979. There are two variants of the figure, the monotone blue L-slot figure and the full-color J-slot; the loose missile was deemed hazardous to children, and neither variant ever made it into full production. Sold November 6–7, 2019, by Hake's Auctions, York, Pennsylvania.

34.

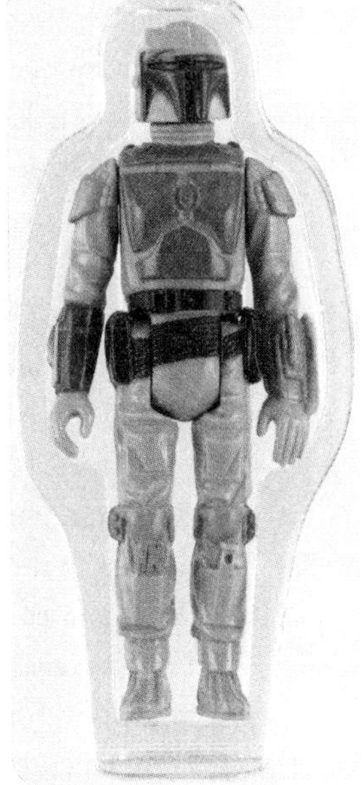

35.

HOW TO USE THIS BOOK

There are a few rules for using this book. Each listing is arranged in the following manner: CATEGORY (such as silver), OBJECT (such as vase), DESCRIPTION (as much information as possible about size, age, color, and pattern). Some types of glass, pottery, and silver are exceptions to this rule. These are listed CATEGORY, PATTERN, OBJECT, DESCRIPTION, PRICE. All items are presumed to be in good condition and undamaged, unless otherwise noted. In most sections, if a maker's name is easily recognized, such as Gustav Stickley, we include it near the beginning of the entry. If the maker is obscure, the name may be near the end.

- To save space, dollar amounts do not include dollar signs, commas, or cents at the end so $1,234.00 is written 1234.
- You will find silver flatware in either Silver Flatware Plated or Silver Flatware Sterling. There is also a section for Silver Plate, which includes coffeepots, trays, and other plated hollowware. Most solid or sterling silver is listed by country, so look for Silver-American, Silver-Danish, Silver-English, etc. Silver jewelry is listed under Jewelry. Most pottery and porcelain is listed by factory name, such as Weller or Wedgwood; by item, such as Calendar Plate; in sections like Dinnerware or Kitchen; or in a special section, such as Pottery-Art, Pottery-Contemporary, Pottery-Midcentury, etc.
- Sometimes we make arbitrary decisions. Fishing has its own category, but hunting is part of the larger category called sports. We have listed historic guns in "weapons" and toy guns in the toy category. It is not legal to sell weapons without a special license, so guns are not part of the general antiques market. Air guns, BB guns, rocket guns, and others are listed in the Toy section. Everything is listed according to the computer alphabetizing system.
- We made several editorial decisions. A butter dish is listed as a "butter." A salt dish is called a "salt" to differentiate it from a saltshaker. It is always "sugar and creamer," never "creamer and sugar." Where one dimension is given, it is the height; if the object is round, it's the diameter. The height of a picture is listed before width. Glass is clear unless a color is indicated. We never call glass "crystal." A crystal is a natural shape of a mineral.
- Some antiques terms, such as "Sheffield" or "Pratt," have two meanings. Read the paragraph headings to know the definition being used. All category headings are based on the vocabulary of the average person, and we use terms like "mud figures" even if not technically correct. Some categories are known by several names. Pressed glass is also called pattern glass or EAPG (Early American Pattern Glass). We use the name "pressed glass" because much of the information found in old books and articles uses that name.
- This book does not include price listings for fine art paintings, antiquities, stamps, coins, or most types of books. Comic books are listed only in special categories like Batman, but original comic art is listed in Comic Art, and cels are listed in Animation Art.
- Prices for items pictured can be found in the appropriate categories. Look for the matching entry with the abbreviation "illus." The color photograph will be nearby.
- Thanks to computers, the book is produced quickly. The last entries are added in June; the book is available in September. But humans find prices and check accuracy. We read everything at least five times, sometimes more. We edit more than 20,000 entries down to the 11,500 entries found here. We correct spelling, remove incorrect data, write category paragraphs, and decide on new categories. We proofread copy and prices many times, but there may be some

misspelled words and other errors. Information in the paragraphs is updated each year, and this year more than 40 updates and additions were made.

- Prices are reported from all parts of the United States, Canada, Europe, and Asia, and converted to U.S. dollars at the time of the sale. The average rate of exchange on June 1, 2020, was $1.00 to about $1.36 Canadian, €0.90 (euro), and £0.80 (British pound). Meltdown price for silver was $18.46 per ounce in June. Prices are from auctions, shops, Internet sales, shows, and even some flea markets. Every price is checked for accuracy, but we are not responsible for errors. We cannot answer your letters asking for price information, or where to sell, but please write if you have any requests for categories to be included or any corrections to the paragraphs or prices. You may find the answers to your other questions at Kovels.com or in our newsletter, *Kovels On Antiques & Collectibles.*
- When you see us at shows, auctions, house sales, flea markets, or even the grocery store, please stop and say hello. Don't be surprised if we ask for your suggestions. You can write to us at P.O. Box 22192, Beachwood, OH 44122, or visit us at our website, Kovels.com.

TERRY KOVEL AND KIM KOVEL
July 2020

ACKNOWLEDGMENTS

The world of antiques and collectibles is filled with people who share knowledge and help, tell stories of record prices, amazing sales, online activities, and news, and make books like this possible. Dealers, auction galleries, antiques shops, serious collectors, clubs, publications, and even museum experts have given advice and opinions, sent pictures and prices, and made suggestions for changes. Thank you to all of them! Each picture is labeled with the name of the source. We list a phone number, postal address, and Web address at the end of the book, so you can learn more about any pictured piece. We also include the names of many of the people or places that reported some prices. Anyone who sells collectibles and antiques must buy them, so you may want to contact a source listed here.

And we want to give special thanks to the staff at Kovels'. They deserve the most credit. They helped gather the 11,500 prices, 3,000 pictures, marks, tips on care of collections, and hotlines (bits of information too important to ignore), put it all together, and made it work. This year it was completed during the days we were all following the pandemic rules and we had to invent new ways to share responsibilities.

Special thanks to Hachette Book Group, our publisher.

Our thanks to the Hachette staff:

- Lisa Tenaglia, our editor who has worked with us for ten years, who makes sure the book gets finished on time. She is also our advocate and problem solver.
- Lillian Sun, senior production manager, Melanie Gold, senior production editor, and the others at Hachette who do all the things we never see that create the quality of the finished product.
- Kara Thornton, publicity manager, who worries about getting stories in newspapers, magazines, book reviews, social media, TV talk shows, and the many online sites that are interested in collecting.
- Betsy Hulsebosch, director of marketing, who creates the modern online advertising and explanations.
- Katie Benezra, associate art director, who knows how to be sure the art is at its best.
- Mary Flower, Robin Perlow, and Cynthia Schuster Eakin, copyeditors, who seem to find every typo, mislabeled picture, and misspelled name. They make sure the names and dates of every royal family, period of furniture, historic event, the spelling of the Chinese dynasties, and the most misspelled name of them all—Wedgwood—are correct.
- Sheila Hart, who has worked on many editions of the book—redesigning the pages to look great, and adapting the layout each time we change the content, adding things such as pages of marks, number of prices, and more color pictures. She also does the layout and design of the special features such as the record prices and the yearly fact-filled insert. Somehow she has solved the problem of getting all 11,500 prices and all 3,000 pictures in position in alphabetical order near one another so readers can see both on the same page.

And to those on the Kovels' staff who work on both the digital and print versions of this book:

- Janet Dodrill, our art director, who somehow can keep track of all of the pictures and permissions for the items shown in this book as well as extra pictures used for our columns and other publications. She then uses her superior photo-editing skills to improve the look and the quality of the pictures by outlining the objects, checking the color, and even working magic with close-ups of details.
- Our in-house price staff, Mozella Colon, Elizabeth Burroughs-Heineman, Beverly Malone, and Renee McRitchie, who know the vocabulary needed to get prices from all parts of the country and turn them into the proper form to sort into the book.
- Cherrie Smrekar, who takes time from her job running our newsletter to help with prices, tips, hotlines, record prices, and other special features of the book.
- Liz Lillis, the Kovels' staff copyeditor, writer, and researcher, who not only knows all the dates

and names but tells us where the commas and periods go and solves other grammar problems. She also writes online publicity for the book and our homepage.

- Gay Hunter, who is the official boss of the price book production, tracks the prices and pictures in and out, suggests sources for prices at sales and shows, records where and when it was sold, and what the seller said about it. She records the work of the others doing the book prices or paragraphs or reports, runs spell-checks on each document, and knows all of our special codes and dating systems. She makes sure we are getting a variety of prices, especially the new ones we seem to see each year when we add new categories (a new category this year is Jacob Petit). But most of all, she keeps us meeting the book deadlines by reminding us all year that we are way behind.
- And Alberto Eiber, the expert who makes sure we are accurate with articles and reports of the recent things we include that are now called "Design" by art and auction gallery dealers. He also writes about the twentieth-century and contemporary designers.

CONTRIBUTORS

The world of antiques and collectibles is filled with people who have answered our every request for help. Dealers, auction houses, and shops have given advice and opinions, supplied photographs and prices, and made suggestions for changes. Many thanks to all of them:

Photographs and information were furnished by: Abington Auction Gallery, Actéon Auction, Ahlers & Ogletree Auction Gallery, Alderfer Auction Company, American Bottle Auctions, AntiqueAdvertising.com, Apple Tree Auction Center, Auction Team Breker, Austin Auction Gallery, Belhorn Auction Services, Bertoia Auctions, Blackwell Auctions, Bourgeault-Horan Antiquarians & Associates, LLC, Brinkman Auctions, Bruneau & Co. Auctioneers, Brunk Auctions, Bunch Auctions, Bunte Auction Services, California Historical Design, Case Antiques, Charleston Estate Auctions, Charlton Hall Auctions, Christie's, Clars Auction Gallery, Conestoga Auction Company, Copake Auction, Cordier Auctions, Cottone Auctions, Cowan's Auctions, Crescent City Auction Gallery, CRN Auctions, Crocker Farm, Inc., Discogs.com, DuMouchelles, Eldred's, Fontaine's Auction Gallery, Forsythes' Auctions, Freeman's Auctioneers & Appraisers, Garth's Auctioneers & Appraisers, Glass Works Auctions, GreatCollections.com, Hake's Auctions, Hartzell's Auction Gallery Inc., Heritage Auctions, Hudson Valley Auctions, Humler & Nolan, Hunt Auctions, LLC, Jeffrey S. Evans & Associates, Julien's Auctions, Kamelot Auctions, Leland Little Auctions, Hindman Auctions, Locati Auctions, Long Auction Co., Los Angeles Modern Auctions, Medina Antique Mall, Memory Lane Inc., Michaan's Auctions, Mile High Card Company, Milestone Auctions, Morphy Auctions, Nadeau's Auction Gallery, Neal Auction Company, New Orleans Auction Galleries, Palm Beach Modern Auctions, Phillips, Pook & Pook, Quittenbaum Kunstauktionen GmbH, Rago Arts and Auction Center, Rich Penn Auctions, Richard D. Hatch & Associates, Richard Opfer Auctioneering, Inc., Ripley Auctions, Roland Auctioneers & Valuers, Schmitt Horan & Co., Seeck Auctions, Selkirk Auctioneers & Appraisers, Skinner, Inc., Sotheby's, Soulis Auctions, Stair Galleries, Stevens Auction Co., Strawser Auction Group, Susanin's Auctioneers & Appraisers, Theriault's, Thomaston Place Auction Galleries, Toomey & Co. Auctioneers, Treadway, Tremont Auctions, Weiss Auctions, Whitely's Auctioneers, Willis Henry Auctions, Witherell's, Wm Morford Auctions, Wolfs Gallery, Woody Auction, World Auction Gallery, and Wright.

To the others who knowingly or unknowingly contributed to this book, we say thank you Aspire Auctions, Blueberry Hill Galleries, Bright Star Antiques, Burchard Galleries, Fox Auctions, Hill Auction Gallery, Homestead Auctions, J. James Auctioneers & Appraisers, Jackson's International Auctioneers & Appraisers, Jasper52, Keystone Auctions LLC, Martin Auction Co., Potteries Specialist Auctions, Quinn's Auction Galleries, Rachel Davis Fine Arts, Replacements, Ltd., RSL Auction, Ruby Lane, and Sloans & Kenyon.

A. WALTER

A. Walter made pate-de-verre glass under contract at the Daum glassworks from 1908 to 1914. He decorated pottery during his early years in his studio in Sevres, where he also developed his formula for pale, translucent pate-de-verre. He started his own firm in Nancy, France, in 1919. Pieces made before 1914 are signed *Daum, Nancy* with a cross. After 1919 the signature is *A. Walter Nancy.*

Bowl, Lid, Bugs, Yellow, Signed, Henri Berge, c.1920, 5 x 7 In. .... *illus* 5000
Box, Lid, Cicadas, Turned-Up Sides, Blue, Flat Lid, Handle, Yellow Flowers, 9 In. 3750
Dish, Scarabs On Rock, Asymmetric Shape, Mottled Red & Brown, 3 x 11 In. 8400
Dish, Scarabs, Flower Band, Mottled Blue Ground, Oval, 6 ½ x 3 ¾ In. 960
Dish, Thistle, Yellow Shaded To Green To Brown, Marked, H. Berge, 2 x 4 ½ In. 938
Figurine, Young Woman, Sitting, Bent Over Her Knees, Yellow Green, P. Duberry, 7 x 9 In. 5000
Jar, Lid, Mistletoe, Shades Of Blue, Round, Squat, c.1900, 2 ½ In. 813
Paperweight, Lizards, Spotted, Yellow Orange Base, 3 In. 1800
Paperweight, Young Bird, Brown, Henri Berge, 4 ¾ x 3 ½ In. 594
Vase, Grapes, Vines, Leaves, Mottled Blue Ground, Tapered, Spread Foot, 6 ½ x 3 In. 1150

A. Walter, Bowl, Lid, Bugs, Yellow, Signed, Henry Berge, c.1920, 5 x 7 In.
$5,000

Freeman's Auctioneers & Appraisers

Thought of the Day:
"The things people discard tell more about them than the things they keep." Really? We saw this saying in a magazine and aren't sure we agree.

ABC PLATES

ABC plates, or children's alphabet plates, were most popular from 1780 to 1860 but are still being made. The letters on the plate were meant as teaching aids for children learning to read. The plates were made of pottery, porcelain, metal, or glass. Mugs and other items were also made with alphabet decorations. Many companies made ABC plates. Shown here are marks used by three English makers.

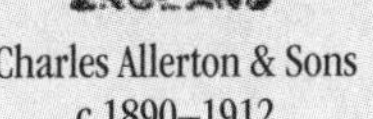

Charles Allerton & Sons
c.1890–1912

Enoch Wood & Sons
1818–1846

William E. Oulsnam & Sons
c.1880–1892

Plate, Niagara, From The Edge Of The American Side, Raised Letters, 1800s, 7 In. 75
Plate, Organ Grinder & 3 Children, Raised Letters, 1800s, 6 In. 49

ABINGDON POTTERY

Abingdon Pottery was established in 1908 by Raymond E. Bidwell as the Abingdon Sanitary Manufacturing Company. The company started making art pottery in 1934. The factory ceased production of art pottery in 1950.

Cookie Jar, Hippo, Sitting, Flowers, Cream Ground, Marked, 8 In. .... *illus* 196
Vase, Green, Star Shape, Raised Stars & Clouds, 7 x 7 ½ In. 22
Vase, Pink Satin Glaze, V-Shape Top, 9 x 9 In. 45
Vase, White, Fan Shape, Bow, Marked, 5 x 3 In. 30

Abingdon, Cookie Jar, Hippo, Sitting, Flowers, Cream Ground, Marked, 8 In.
$196

Belhorn Auction Services

ADAMS

Adams china was made by William Adams and Sons of Staffordshire, England. The firm was founded in 1769 and became part of the Wedgwood Group in 1966. The name *Adams* appeared on various items through 1998. All types of tablewares and useful wares were made. Other pieces of Adams may be found listed under Flow Blue and Tea Leaf Ironstone.

Adams, Bowl, Dark Blue, Jasperware, Ray Base, Garland Trim, Silver Plate Rim, 5 x 9 ½ In.
$115

Richard D. Hatch & Associates

This is an edited listing of current prices. Visit **Kovels.com** to check thousands of prices from previous years and sign up for free information on trends, tips, reproductions, marks, and more.

ADAMS

Adams, Plate, Rabbit & Frog Border, Adam's Rose, Stick Spatter Center, 9 ¼ In.
$148

Conestoga Auction Company

Advertising, Bin, Beech-Nut Chewing Tobacco, Tin Lithograph, Yellow, Red, Countertop, 8 x 10 x 8 In.
$507

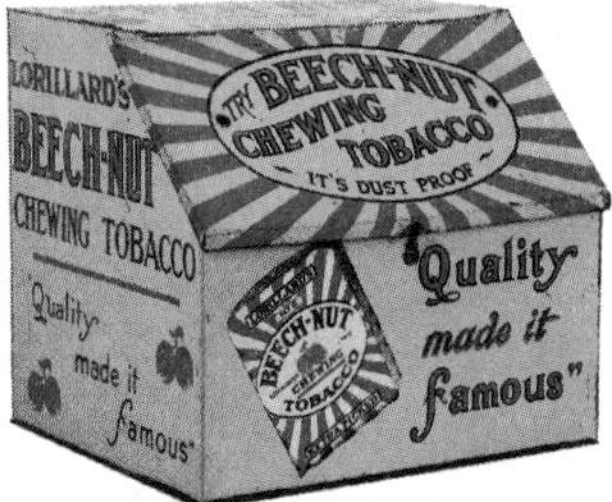

AntiqueAdvertising.com

Advertising, Bin, Coffee, Jersey, Pine, Slant Lid, Red Paint, Black Stenciling, 1880s, 31 x 22 x 17 In.
$420

Garth's Auctioneers & Appraisers

Dr. Kellogg's Breakfast
Although he invented granola and Corn Flakes, Dr. John Harvey Kellogg ate seven graham crackers for breakfast everyday.

William Adams & Co.
1905–1917

William Adams & Sons
1917–1965

Adams under Wedgwood
1966–1975

Bowl, Dark Blue, Jasperware, Ray Base, Garland Trim, Silver Plate Rim, 5 x 9 ½ In. ......*illus* 115
Eggcup, Double, Brentwood, Blue Shamrocks, 3 ¾ In. 18
Eggcup, Double, Multicolor Flowers, Yellow Trim, 3 ¾ In. 21
Plate, Landing Of Columbus, Blue, White, Transferware, 1800s, 10 In. 95
Plate, Rabbit & Frog Border, Adam's Rose, Stick Spatter Center, 9 ¼ In. ....*illus* 148
Platter, Yellow & Blue Flowers, White Ground, 8-Sided, c.1920, 12 x 9 In. 59
Sugar & Creamer, Wheat, Footed, Creamy White, c.1800........ 102

ADVERTISING

Advertising containers and products sold in the old country store are now all collectibles. These stores, with crackers in a barrel and a potbellied stove, are a symbol of an earlier, less hectic time. Listed here are many advertising items. Other similar pieces may be found under the product name, such as Planters Peanuts. We have tried to list items in logical places, so enameled tin dishes will be found under Graniteware, auto-related items in the Auto category, paper items in the Paper category, etc. Store fixtures, cases, signs, and other items t hat have no advertising as part of the decoration are listed in the Store category. The early Dr Pepper logo included a period after "Dr," but it was dropped in 1950. We list all Dr Pepper items without a period so they alphabetize together. Some collectors call enameled iron or steel signs "porcelain signs." For more prices, go to kovels.com.

Ashtray, Black, Painted, Dog Design, Cast Iron, Staunton Paint & Wallpaper Co., 4 x 3 In. 85
Ashtray, Match Holder, Abbottmaid De-Lux Ice Cream, Lamberton China, 5 ¾ In. 175
Banner, Circus, Eeka Vs. Jungle Killers, Man, Snakes, Trees, Fred Johnson, 1940s, 80 x 111 In. 2160
Banner, Dartmouth Chocolates, Smith & Sons, Canvas, Matted, Frame, 23 x 53 In. 276
Banner, Mayo's Plug, Light & Dark, Rooster, Matted, Frame, 35 x 23 x 1 In. 510
Barrel, Richardson Root Beer, Wood Stave, Stainless Steel Hoops, 2 Spigots, 25 x 15 In. 180
Bin, Beech-Nut Chewing Tobacco, Tin Lithograph, Yellow, Red, Countertop, 8 x 10 x 8 In. *illus* 507
Bin, Coffee, Jersey, Pine, Slant Lid, Red Paint, Black Stenciling, 1880s, 31 x 22 x 17 In. ...*illus* 420
Bin, Coffee, King Bee, Slant Hinged Lid, Wood, Stenciled, 26 x 18 x 13 ¾ In. 677
Bin, H.R. Doste & Co., Pure Pepper, Polar Bear, Medallion, Red, 12 x 9 ½ x 14 In. 403
Bin, Lion Coffee, Pine, Slant Lid, Red, Late 1800s-Early 1900s, 33 ½ x 21 x 21 In. 263
Bin, Rough Rider Coffee, O'Donohue Coffee Co., Teddy Roosevelt Portrait, 18 x 15 x 15 In. 390
Bin, Sweet Cuba Fine Cut Tobacco, Tin Lithograph, Countertop, 8 x 8 x 10 In. ....*illus* 210
Bin, Tea, Finest Oolong, Steel, Black, Silver, Gold, Oriental Landscape, 19 x 18 x 22 In. 207
Bin, Tea, Norton Bros., Chicago, Tin, Painted Chinese Scene, Porcelain Knob, 16 In. 144
Bottles are list in the Bottle category.
Bottle Openers are listed in the Bottle Opener category.
Box, see also Box category.
Box, Arbuckles Roasted Coffees, Rectangular, Wooden, 16 x 29 ½ x 19 In. ....*illus* 210
Box, Display, Shredded Wheat, Factory, Original Niagara Falls Product, 12 x 14 x 8 In. ...*illus* 40
Broadside, La Voiture Du Progress Mathis, Blue Ground, White & Yellow Text, 1931, 38 x 51 In.. 211
Cabinet, Diamond Dyes, Fairy, 10 Cent, Vignettes, Wells & Richardson, 31 x 24 x 10 In. ..*illus* 622
Cabinet, Diamond Dyes, Governess, Oak Case, Embossed Tin Panel, c.1910, 29 x 22 x 9 In....... 819
Cabinet, Diamond Dyes, Mansion, 5 Children Playing, Stairs To House, 24 x 16 x 8 In. 570
Cabinet, Dr. Daniels' Veterinary Medicines, Tin, Embossed, Oak, 1800s, 21 x 6 x 26 ¾ In. *illus* 1180
Cabinet, Dy-O-La Dyes, Southern Gum, Tin Lithograph Door, c.1900, 11 x 13 ¾ x 8 ½ In. *illus* 252
Cabinet, Spool, Clark's O.N.T. Spool Cotton, 2 Drawers, George A. Clark Sole Agent 196
Cabinet, Spool, J. & P. Coats, Garage Door, Knob Handle, Oak Case, 23 x 20 ¾ In. 840

Advertising, Bin, Sweet Cuba Fine Cut Tobacco, Tin Lithograph, Countertop, 8 x 8 x 10 In.
$210

AntiqueAdvertising.com

Mail Pouch Ads on Barns
Mail Pouch tobacco used signs painted on barns as huge ads from the beginning of the twentieth century until the 1990s.

Advertising, Box, Arbuckles Roasted Coffees, Rectangular, Wooden, 16 x 29 ½ x 19 In.
$210

Rich Penn Auctions

Advertising, Box, Display, Shredded Wheat, Factory, Original Niagara Falls Product, 12 x 14 x 8 In.
$40

Soulis Auctions

Advertising, Cabinet, Diamond Dyes, Fairy, 10 Cent, Vignettes, Wells & Richardson, 31 x 24 x 10 In.
$622

Soulis Auctions

Advertising, Cabinet, Dr. Daniels' Veterinary Medicines, Tin, Embossed, Oak, 1800s, 21 x 6 x 26 ¾ In.
$1,180

Copake Auctions

Advertising, Cabinet, Dy-O-La Dyes, Southern Gum, Tin Lithograph Door, c.1900, 11 x 13 ¾ x 8 ½ In.
$252

Garth's Auctioneers & Appraisers

Advertising, Cabinet, Tobacco, P. Lorillard & Co., Walnut, Burl Veneers, Glass, c.1883, 43 x 34 x 19 In.
$1,534

Leland Little Auctions

Advertising, Can, Billy Beer, Tin
$3

Medina Antique Mall

TIP
Do not hide a key outside the house, not even in a key-holding stone. Burglars are smart.

Advertising, Case, Display, J.P. Primley's, Chewing Gum, Glass Front, Gold Leaf, 10 x 18 ½ x 12 In.
$540

Morphy Auctions

Advertising, Case, Display, Torrey's Best Razor Strops, Wood Case, c.1900, 28 x 13 x 13 In.
$438

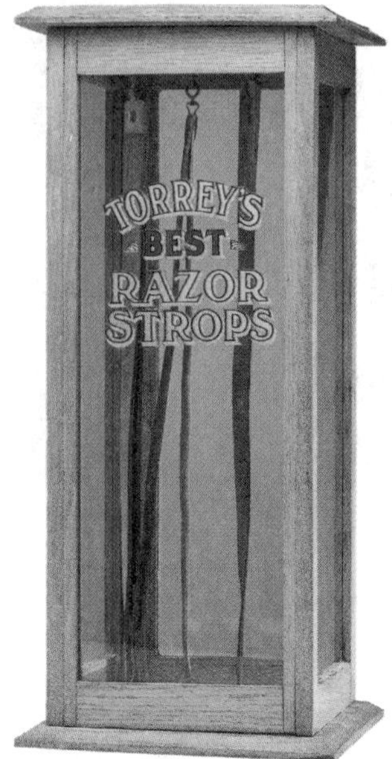

Cowan's Auctions

Cover the Earth from Cleveland
The Sherwin-Williams famous logo with the slogan "Cover the Earth" shows a globe covered with dripping paint. But if you look carefully, you will see the paint is not pouring on the North Pole; it is pouring on Cleveland, Ohio, the city where the paint company began in 1866.

Advertising, Case, Gunther's Beer, Cardboard, Laminated, 17 x 11 In.
$62

Richard Opfer Auctioneering, Inc.

Advertising, Cooler, Dr Pepper, Metal, Mint Green Paint, Casters, Front Opening, 30 x 17 ½ In.
$600

Rich Penn Auctions

Advertising, Cooler, Moxie, Wood, Tin Man, Horse, Car, 32 x 21 ⅜ x 32 In.
$3,000

Morphy Auctions

Advertising, Crate, Fox Branch U.S. Bakery Crackers, Man Sleeping Under Tree, Wood, 13 x 20 x 14 In.
$210

Morphy Auctions

Advertising, Crate, Hershey's, Wood, Metal Edges, 12 Glass Milk Bottles, 10 ½ In.
$59

Conestoga Auction Company

Advertising, Dispenser, Cigarette, Mechanical, Metal Crane Finial, Wood Box, Early 1900s, 7 In.
$207

Leland Little Auctions

Advertising, Dispenser, Mission Orange, Porcelain Base, Pink Glass Jar, Embossed, 1920s, 13 In.
$271

Leland Little Auctions

Cabinet, Spool, Willimantic, Cotton, Six Cord, Soft Finish, Wood, 4 Drawers, 15 x 25 In. 500
Cabinet, Tobacco, P. Lorillard & Co., Walnut, Burl Veneers, Glass, c.1883, 43 x 34 x 19 In. *illus* 1534
Cake Crock, Lid, S.S. Pierce Co., Boston Brookline, Stoneware, Blue, Salt Glaze, 6 x 9 In. 472
Calendars are listed in the Calendar category.
Can, Billy Beer, Tin *illus* 3
Can, Niggerhair, Smoking Tobacco, Tin Lithograph, Bail Handle, Lid, 6 ½ In. 277
Canisters, see introductory paragraph to Tins in this category.
Cards are listed in the Card category.
Case, Aldek Scaffolds, Aluminum Pieces, Photos, Salesman's Sample, 19 x 18 In. 340
Case, Display, Adam's Pepsin Tutti-Frutti, Ornate, Wooden, 17 ⅜ x 12 ⅝ x 6 ½ In. 390
Case, Display, J.P. Primley's, Chewing Gum, Glass Front, Gold Leaf, 10 x 18 ½ x 12 In. *illus* 540
Case, Display, Kopp's Kidney Pills, 3 Tiers, Oak, Glass, Slide-Out Drawer, 14 x 21 x 24 In. 300
Case, Display, Torrey's Best Razor Strops, Wood Case, c.1900, 28 x 13 x 13 In. *illus* 438
Case, Display, Waterman's Ideal Fountain Pens, Wood, Glass, Decal, 12 x 21 x 18 In. 300
Case, Gunther's Beer, Cardboard, Laminated, 17 x 11 In. *illus* 62
Change Receiver, see also Tip Tray in this category.
Cigar Box, Chevrolet, Used Car Committee Of 1937, Wood, Carved, 12 x 3 In. 510
Cigar Cutter, Fritz Emmet Cigars, Town Crier, Top Hat, Mechanical, John McKinley, c.1885, 7 ½ x 5 In. 180
Clocks are listed in the Clock category.
Coaster, Drink Hires Root Beer, Health & Cheer, Hires Boy, Stoneware, Mettlach, 1900 4800
Cooler, Cott, Quality Beverage, Ginger Ale, Lid, Swing Handle, White Ground, 17 x 13 x 19 In. 94
Cooler, Dr Pepper, Good For Life, White, Green, Metal Handle, 14 x 12 ¾ In. 450
Cooler, Dr Pepper, Metal, Mint Green Paint, Casters, Front Opening, 30 x 17 ½ In. *illus* 600
Cooler, Moxie, Wood, Tin Man, Horse, Car, 32 x 21 ⅜ x 32 In. *illus* 3000
Crate, Anheuser-Busch Inc., Eagle Logo, Stencils, Wood, St. Louis, 1976, 18 x 12 x 13 In. 59
Crate, Fox Branch U.S. Bakery Crackers, Man Sleeping Under Tree, Wood, 13 x 20 x 14 In. *illus* 210
Crate, Hershey's, Wood, Metal Edges, 12 Glass Milk Bottles, 10 ½ In. *illus* 59
Crock, H.J. Heinz, Keystone Pickling & Preserving, Blue Incised, Stoneware, 5 ½ In. 153
Dispenser, Candy, Hershey's, 1 Cent, Glass, Brown, Key, 19 x 7 In. 480
Dispenser, Cardinal Cherry, Green Cherries, Embossed, Blue Ground, Gold Leaf, 13 x 9 x 9 In. 3000
Dispenser, Carnation Malted Milk, Green Porcelain, Etched Glass Cylinder, Hamilton Beach, 18 In. 660
Dispenser, Cigarette, Mechanical, Metal Crane Finial, Wood Box, Early 1900s, 7 In. *illus* 207
Dispenser, Cigarette, Piedmont, Lighter, Cutter, Cast Iron Body, Wood Base, 1912, 4 x 8 x 7 In. 330
Dispenser, Dr. Swett's Root Beer, 5 Cents, Barrel, Gold Bands, Pump, 15 In. 1169
Dispenser, Fowler's Cherry Smash, Always Drink, Yellow Letters, Pump, 15 In. 1125
Dispenser, Hires Root Beer,, Drink Hires, Hourglass Shape, 1920s, 14 x 7 In. 1465
Dispenser, Mission Orange, Porcelain Base, Pink Glass Jar, Embossed, 1920s, 13 In. *illus* 271
Dispenser, Orange Crush, Soda Fountain, Black Cast Metal Base, Glass Bottle, 13 ½ In. 264
Dispenser, Orangeade Syrup, Spigot & Lid, Glass Top & Base, 14 In. 170
Display, American Beauty, Glass, Electric Iron Inside, 24 x 11 ½ In. 480
Display, Clark's Teaberry Gum, Box, Vaseline Glass, Chromed Hinge, 2 ¾ x 6 x 4 In. *illus* 396
Display, Columbian Packages, Rotating, Wood, Cast Iron Base, 38 x 9 ½ x 9 ½ In. 450
Display, Dog, Boston Terrier, Bryant Pup, Papier-Mache, Old King Cole, 20 x 11 In. *illus* 450
Display, Hatchet, Roofer's, Estwing, Unbreakable Tools, Molded Fiberglass, 37 ½ x 13 In. *illus* 192
Display, Kewpie Garter, Tin, Painted, 12 x 8 x 7 In. 300
Display, Laird's Apple Jack, Brandy Distillers, Sailor, Life Preserver, Chalkware, 13 ½ x 11 ¾ In. 360
Display, Michelin Man, Painted, Plastic, Wall Mount, Metal Bracket, 1960s, 18 In. *illus* 117
Display, Munsing Wear, Figural, Die Cut, Tin Lithograph, Countertop, 14 ½ x 8 x 3 In. *illus* 3186
Display, Plaster Ice Cream Cone, Eat It All, Chocolate Dip, 23 x 10 In. 1080
Display, Shults Bread, Oak, Glass Case, Red Lettering, Wood Tray, c.1915, 35 x 27 x 21 In. 322
Display, Tru-Lax, Nurse, Ask For Products, Laxative, Tin Lithograph, 14 x 14 x 12 ½ In. 240
Display, Victorinox, Swiss Army Knife, Moving Tools, Electric, Thomson-Leed, 1990s, 29 In. 480
Dolls are listed in the Doll category.
Door Push, Colonial Is Good Bread, Steel, Blue Ground, White, Blue, Embossed, 2 ¾ x 25 In. 367
Door Push, Orange Crush, Come In Drink, Tin, Marked 8-20 Made In USA, 1920, 12 x 3 In. 660
Door, Screen, Green, Buy Bond Bread, Stays Fresher Days Longer, 32 x 80 ½ In. 148
Figure, Antique Bourbon, Boxer, Pail, Towel, Painted, Round Base, 4 In. 450
Figure, Big Boy, Hamburger On Platter, Red & White, Cast Metal, 39 x 18 In. *illus* 1440
Figure, Blatz Beer, Bottle Man Carrying Tray, Beer Mug, Sign, Metal, 18 In. *illus* 156

Advertising, Display, Clark's Teaberry Gum, Box, Vaseline Glass, Chromed Hinge, 2 ¾ x 6 x 4 In.
$396

Soulis Auctions

Advertising, Display, Dog, Boston Terrier, Bryant Pup, Papier-Mache, Old King Cole, 20 x 11 In.
$450

Milestone Auctions

Advertising, Display, Hatchet, Roofer's, Estwing, Unbreakable Tools, Molded Fiberglass, 37 ½ x 13 In.
$192

Soulis Auctions

Popular Brands
Some brands are more popular with collectors than others. Coca-Cola, McDonald's restaurants, and M&Ms are tops. Others are Planters Peanuts, Anheuser-Busch, Budweiser, Kentucky Fried Chicken, and soft drinks like Pepsi-Cola, and Hires Root Beer.

Advertising, Display, Michelin Man, Painted, Plastic, Wall Mount, Metal Bracket, 1960s, 18 In.
$117

Thomaston Place Auction Galleries

Advertising, Display, Munsing Wear, Figural, Die Cut, Tin Lithograph, Countertop, 14 ½ x 8 x 3 In.
$3,186

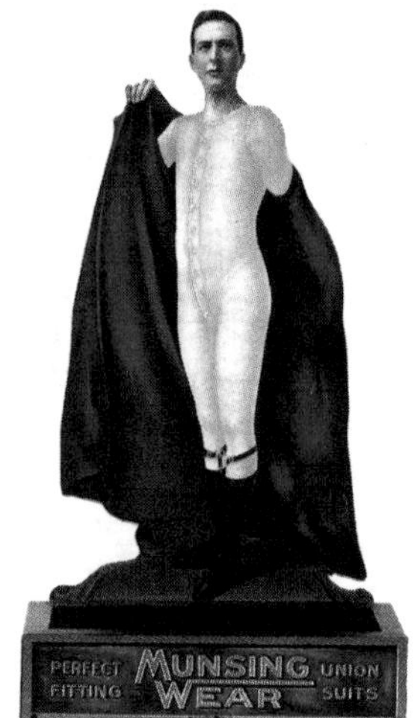

Wm Morford Auctions

Advertising, Figure, Big Boy, Hamburger On Platter, Red & White, Cast Metal, 39 x 18 In.
$1,440

Morphy Auctions

Advertising, Figure, Blatz Beer, Bottle Man Carrying Tray, Beer Mug, Sign, Metal, 18 In.
$156

Milestone Auctions

Advertising, Figure, Curlee Clothes, Man, Standing, Rubber, Black Base, Painted, 1950s, 17 ½ In.
$124

Soulis Auctions

Advertising, Figure, Dutch Master Cigar, Indian Chief, Full Dress, Peace Pipe, Resin, 19 In.
$168

Milestone Auctions

Advertising, Flagon, Greybeard, Mitchell Brothers, Stoneware, 1880s, ¼ Gal., 7 ½ In.
$30

Woody Auctions

Advertising, Icebox, J.B. Van Sciver Co., Oak, Camden, N.J., Salesman's Sample, 11 x 7 ½ x 5 In.
$450

Morphy Auctions

Advertising, Jar, Heinz Apple Butter, Multicolor Stone Lithograph Label, Original Closure, 8 x 4 In.
$177

AntiqueAdvertising.com

Advertising, Jug, Heinz Tomato Ketchup, Fruits & Vegetables, Stoneware, Bail Handle, 9 ½ x 7 In.
$578

AntiqueAdvertising.com

Advertising, Label, Peacock Brand, Flowers, Painted, Ruddock, Trench & Co., 1900s, 10 x 11 In.
$61

Witherell's

Advertising, Label, Scout Brand, Chinese Super Flash Firecrackers, Made In China, 3 x 2 ¾ In.
$413

AntiqueAdvertising.com

Advertising, Mirror, Hires Rootbeer, Put Roses In Your Cheeks, Girl, Oval, c.1905, 3 x 1 ¾ In.
$300

Morphy Auctions

Advertising, Mixer, Malt, Hamilton Beach, Soda Fountain, Green Porcelain, 3 Heads, 20 x 13 In.
$240

Rich Penn Auctions

Advertising, Model, Delta Passenger Jet, Stand, Damron Worldwide Trading, c.1970s, 9 x 13 x 17 In.
$254

Soulis Auctions

Advertising, Pail, Peter Rabbit Peanut Butter, Rabbits, Frogs, Tin Lithograph, Newton Tea, 4 x 3 In.
$378

AntiqueAdvertising.com

Advertising, Pail, Sanders Satin Candies, Handle, Tin Lithograph, Children, Forest Animals, 5 ½ x 5 In.
$102

Soulis Auctions

Advertising, Shoe, Skechers, Figural, Sneaker, Blue, Yellow, 32 In.
$24

Copake Auctions

Advertising, Sign, A Nation's Choice, Teddy Roosevelt, Tin Lithograph, Beveled, 19 x 13 In.
$555

AntiqueAdvertising.com

Advertising, Sign, American Locksmith, Tin Padlock, Bracket, Painted Black, Key, Early 1900s, 23 x 22 In.
$500

Garth's Auctioneers & Appraisers

Advertising, Sign, Buster Brown Bread, Golden Sheaf Bakery, Embossed, Tin Lithograph, Frame, 24 x 32 In.
$743

AntiqueAdvertising.com

Advertising, Sign, Continental Insurance Co., Minuteman, Tin, Self-Framed, c.1915, 30 In.
$1,230

Rich Penn Auctions

Advertising, Sign, Cook's Brewing Co., Hand Holding 2 Bottles, Tin Lithograph, Oval, 17 x 14 In.
$679

Wm Morford Auctions

Advertising, Sign, Dr Pepper, King Of Beverages, Lion, Paper, Lithograph, c.1910, 13 x 18 In.
$2,214

Rich Penn Auctions

Advertising, Sign, Duke Tobacco, Young Beauties, 2-Sided, Pine, 3-Part Screen, c.1890, 57 x 52 In.
$2,950

Leland Little Auctions

Tin Trays
The tin advertising tray was first used in the 1880s and is still popular.

Advertising, Sign, Ebbert, In The Shade Of The Old Apple Tree, Wagon, Tin, Self-Framed, 37 x 25 In.
$1,260

Milestone Auctions

Advertising, Sign, Electric Bitters, Dr. King's, Dogs, Monkey Playing Poker, Cardboard, 9 x 12 In.
$378

AntiqueAdvertising.com

Figure, Curlee Clothes, Man, Standing, Rubber, Black Base, Painted, 1950s, 17 ½ In. .....*illus* 124
Figure, Dutch Master Cigar, Indian Chief, Full Dress, Peace Pipe, Resin, 19 In. ....*illus* 168
Figure, Oertels, Polar Bear, Holding Beer Bottle, Chalkware, 14 ½ In. 324
Flagon, Greybeard, Mitchell Brothers, Stoneware, 1880s, ¼ Gal., 7 ½ In. ....*illus* 30
Grader, J.D. Adams & Co., Leaning Wheel, Salesman's Sample, c.1910, 10 x 8 ½ x 22 ½ In....... 6900
Horseshoe, N. Lewis, 99 Williams St., New Bedford, Mass., Iron, 6 x 5 x 1 In.......... 79
Humidor, Belinda Havana, Cuban Cigar, Wood, c.1930, 6 ¾ x 25 x 19 ⅞ In.......... 1404
Ice Cream Maker, Horlick's Malted Milk Co., Peerless Iceland, Salesman's Sample, 7 x 7 x 5 In. 330
Icebox, J.B. Van Sciver Co., Oak, Camden, N.J., Salesman's Sample, 11 x 7 ½ x 5 In. ....*illus* 450
Jar, Eskimo Pie, Real Ice Cream Covered In Chocolate, Eskimos, Tin, Metal, 15 x 7 In. 720
Jar, Heinz Apple Butter, Multicolor Stone Lithograph Label, Original Closure, 8 x 4 In. ....*illus* 177
Jar, Thompson's Malted Milk, Porcelain, Lid, c.1920s, 10 x 7 ½ x 7 ½ In. 540
Jug, Heinz Tomato Ketchup, Fruits & Vegetables, Stoneware, Bail Handle, 9 ½ x 7 In. .....*illus* 578
Jug, White Rose Rye Whiskey, Embossed, Stoneware, Blue, Gray, 7 ½ x 4 ½ In.......... 136
Label, Marguerite Brand, Earl Fruit Company, Floral, Multicolor, c.1890-1906, 10 x 11 In....... 61
Label, Moulton & Greene, California Oranges, Our Favorite Brand, Early 1900s, 10 x 11 In...... 61
Label, Peacock Brand, Flowers, Painted, Ruddock, Trench & Co., 1900s, 10 x 11 In. ....*illus* 61
Label, Scout Brand, Chinese Super Flash Firecrackers, Made In China, 3 x 2 ¾ In. ....*illus* 413
Letter Opener, Mountain States Telephone & Telegraph, Brass, 8 In. 58
Letter Opener, Prudential Insurance, Bronze, 1890s, 7 ½ In. 59

Advertising mirrors of all sizes are listed here. Pocket mirrors range in size from 1 ½ to 5 inches in diameter. Most of these mirrors were given away as advertising promotions and include the name of the company in the design.

Mirror, Hires Rootbeer, Put Roses In Your Cheeks, Girl, Oval, c.1905, 3 x 1 ¾ In. ....*illus* 300
Mirror, Runkel's Cocoa, Highest Grade, Girl Holding Box, Oval, 3 In. 270
Mirror, Sweet Wheat Chewing Gum, 2 Children, Gum Of Quality, Round, 1 ¾ In.......... 570
Mirror, White, Mack Truck, Celluloid, Circular, 2 ½ In. 600
Mixer, Malt, Hamilton Beach, Soda Fountain, Green Porcelain, 3 Heads, 20 x 13 In. ......*illus* 240
Model, Delta Passenger Jet, Stand, Damron Worldwide Trading, c.1970s, 9 x 13 x 17 In. ..*illus* 254
Mug, Dr. Swett's Original Root Beer, Man With Moustache, Embossed, 6 In.......... 128
Mug, Drink Hires Root Beer, Hires Boy, Squat, Villeroy & Boch, c.1905, 4 In. 92
Pail, Peter Rabbit Peanut Butter, Rabbits, Frogs, Tin Lithograph, Newton Tea, 4 x 3 In. ..*illus* 378
Pail, Sanders Satin Candies, Handle, Tin Lithograph, Children, Forest Animals, 5 ½ x 5 In. *illus* 102
Pail, Sunny Boy Peanut Butter, Red & White, Boy, Sandwich, Tin Lithograph, Bail Handle, 1 Lb. 200
Pen Stand, Northwestern Gibraltar Spring Wheat, Figural Sack, Mauser Mill Co., 4 ½ x 6 In.. 79
Rack, Gunther's Beer, 4 Shelves, Painted & Decal Metal, 50 x 19 In. 1107
Rack, Zeno Gum, Tin, Embossed, Key, 21 x 11 x 11 In. 2160
Radiator, Sapolin, Papier-Mache, Painted, Marked, Salesman's Sample, 10 x 4 ½ In.......... 256
Salt & Pepper Shakers are listed in the Salt & Pepper category.
Scales are listed in the Scale category..........
Shoe, Skechers, Figural, Sneaker, Blue, Yellow, 32 In. ....*illus* 24
Sign, A Nation's Choice, Teddy Roosevelt, Tin Lithograph, Beveled, 19 x 13 In. ....*illus* 555
Sign, A.E. Hutchison Trimmings & Notions, Green & Yellow, 15 ¾ x 73 In. 708
Sign, Abbey 10 Cents Cigar, Tin, Faux Grain, Molded Frame, A Revelation, Early 1900s, 28 x 22 In. 354
Sign, American Brewing Co. Lager, Factory, Gold, Silver Font, Frame, 30 x 42 In. 3900
Sign, American Locksmith, Tin Padlock, Bracket, Painted Black, Key, Early 1900s, 23 x 22 In. .*illus* 500
Sign, Belvidere Barber Shop, Double Sided, Wood, c.1900, 20 x 25 ½ In. 375
Sign, Bitter Campari, Pierrot Inside Orange Peel, L. Cappiello, 1921, 38 x 27 In. 5760
Sign, Budweiser Classic Draught, On Tap, Neon, Light-Up, 20 ½ x 31 In. 270
Sign, Buffalo Lager, Toast Of The Coast, Buffalo Brewing Co., Sacramento, Metal, 8 x 17 In..... 510
Sign, Buster Brown Bread, Golden Sheaf Bakery, Embossed, Tin Lithograph, Frame, 24 x 32 In. ...*illus* 743
Sign, C.L. Centlivre Brewing Co., Lithograph, Brick Factory, Street, Founder, c.1893, 33 x 46 In. 600
Sign, Cafe Bar, Krug & Co., Reims, Red Ground, Ornate, Molded Base, 1843, 33 x 48 x 4 In...... 2925
Sign, Camel Cigarettes, Display, Cardboard, Die Cut, Model in Red Gown, 1950s, 30 x 17 ½ In. 41
Sign, Canby's Tulare, Oval, Enamel, Yellow Ground, Red & Black Lettering, 15 x 23 In. 212
Sign, Carling's Red Cap Canadian Ale, Tin Lithograph, c.1950, 14 ⅞ x 6 ⅞ In. 201
Sign, Chocolat, Frigor, F.L. Caillers, Eskimo Holding Large Box, 1936, 59 x 45 In. 767

Advertising, Sign, Federal Brewing Co., Factory, Street Scene, Lithograph, 1902-07, 31 x 25 In.
$2,100

Milestone Auctions

Advertising, Sign, Grapette Soda, Bottle Cap Shape, Crimped Edge, Stout Sign Co., c.1950, 38 In. Diam.
$1,695

Soulis Auctions

Advertising, Sign, H & H Pneumatic Bust Forms, Nature's Only Rival, Tin Lithograph, 23 x 15 In.
$2,950

Wm Morford Auctions

A

Advertising, Sign, Hall's Distemper, For Healthy Homes, Sissons Brothers & Co. Ltd., Frame, 31 x 71 In.
$363

Fontaine's Auction Gallery

Printing Colors
Raised printing was often used on tin containers for tobacco or food made from about 1895 to 1900. Black and one other color were used on lithographed packaging in the 1890s, but four-color lithography was not used until about 1930.

Advertising, Sign, Hats Cleaned Shoes Shined, Wood, 2-Sided, Signed, Duffy, c.1900, 42 x 31 In.
$6,000

Eldred's

Advertising, Sign, Heinz Grape Fruit Marmalade, Slogan, Cardboard, Printer's Proof, Frame, 16 x 19 In.
$425

AntiqueAdvertising.com

Sign, Colgate's Ribbon Dental Cream, Child Brushing Teeth, Trifold, 25 Cents, 20 x 35 x 3 In.. 1200
Sign, Continental Insurance Co., Minuteman, Tin, Self-Framed, c.1915, 30 In. ....*illus* 1230
Sign, Cook's Brewing Co., Hand Holding 2 Bottles, Tin Lithograph, Oval, 17 x 14 In. ....*illus* 679
Sign, Devoe Paints & Varnishes, Indian, Tin Lithograph, 2-Sided, c.1900, 25 x 15 In................ 3904
Sign, Dr Pepper, King Of Beverages, Lion, Paper, Lithograph, c.1910, 13 x 18 In. ....*illus* 2214
Sign, Drink Braems Bitters, For Appetite, Aluminum, Cardboard Back, 1906, 13 ½ x 7 In. 59
Sign, Drink Gunther Quality Brews, Healthful & Refreshing, Cardboard, 27 ½ x 22 In............ 461
Sign, Duke Tobacco, Young Beauties, 2-Sided, Pine, 3-Part Screen, c.1890, 57 x 52 In. ....*illus* 2950
Sign, Ebbert, In The Shade Of The Old Apple Tree, Wagon, Tin, Self-Framed, 37 x 25 In. .*illus* 1260
Sign, Electric Bitters, Dr. King's, Dogs, Monkey Playing Poker, Cardboard, 9 x 12 In. ....*illus* 378
Sign, Emerson's Bromo Seltzer, Collection Of 83 Popular Songs, Frame, 12 x 14 ½ In. 53
Sign, F.W. Woolworth Co., Glass, Gold Lettering, Brass Frame, 10 ½ x 57 In............................. 780
Sign, Federal Brewing Co., Factory, Street Scene, Lithograph, 1902-07, 31 x 25 In. ....*illus* 2100
Sign, Frontier Gun Club, Metal, Green Ground, White Lettering, 25 x 36 In. 354
Sign, Fruit Bowl Beverage, Flange, Embossed Tin, 2-Sided, 1940s, 14 x 18 In............................ 354
Sign, GE Radios, Natural Color Tone Radios, Electric, Spinner, Round, 13 In............................ 420
Sign, Genuine Regal China Handcrafted, White, Blue, 7 In.. 69
Sign, Gold Dust, Twins, Tin Lithograph, Meek & Beach Co., Frame, c.1905, 25 ½ x 38 In. 4500
Sign, Grapette Soda, Bottle Cap Shape, Crimped Edge, Stout Sign Co., c.1950, 38 In. Diam. *illus* 1695
Sign, H & H Pneumatic Bust Forms, Nature's Only Rival, Tin Lithograph, 23 x 15 In. ......*illus* 2950
Sign, H.C. Judkins, Wood, Painted, Red & Gilt Lettering, 1800s, 5 ½ x 50 ½ In. 148
Sign, Hall's Distemper, For Healthy Homes, Sissons Brothers & Co. Ltd., Frame, 31 x 71 In. *illus* 363
Sign, Hamilton-Brown Shoe Co., Woman, Sitting On Chair, Frame, 35 x 27 ½ x 1 ½ In........... 420
Sign, Harrisons' Town & Country, Ready Mixed Paints, Wood, Brush, c.1915, 4 ½ x 77 In. 236
Sign, Hats Cleaned Shoes Shined, Wood, 2-Sided, Signed, Duffy, c.1900, 42 x 31 In. ....*illus* 6000
Sign, Heinz Grape Fruit Marmalade, Slogan, Cardboard, Printer's Proof, Frame, 16 x 19 In. *illus* 425
Sign, Hier, Man & Woman, Mangling Machine, Enamel, White, Black German Text, 23 x 15 In. 113
Sign, Hires, Drink Hires In Bottles, Girl, Haskill Coffin, Frame, 1920s, 29 x 22 In.................... 480
Sign, Huntsman, Finest Ales, Man On Horseback, Arched Top, Painted, Wood, 23 ¾ x 36 In. ... 184
Sign, It's Hoods Ice Cream For Health, Rich In Flavor, Tin, 2-Sided, 1910s, 18 x 24 In. .....*illus* 720
Sign, King Bourbon, Lion, Tin Lithograph, Chas. W. Shonk Co., Wood Frame, 49 x 37 In. *illus* 2700
Sign, Kings Beer & Ale, Fit For A King, Light-Up, Counter, c.1900, 12 x 8 In.............................. 1035
Sign, Kis-Me Gum, Victorian Woman, Glitter Collar, Germany, c.1900, 26 In. ....*illus* 430
Sign, Lifebuoy Soap, Soap In Tub, Chromolitho, Paper, Frame, c.1915, 23 x 13 In. 263
Sign, London & Lancashire Fire Insurance, Reverse On Glass, England, 1861, 26 ½ x 22 In. ... 182
Sign, Massa-Chew-Setts, Wood, Black Lettering, White Ground, 1900s, 6 ½ x 36 In. ....*illus* 330
Sign, Member Pennsylvania State Hotel Association, Yellow, Round, 18 In................................ 158
Sign, Miller, High Life Beer, 3 Bottles, Champagne Bucket Style, Plastic, 16 In.......................... 57
Sign, Miss Blanche Cigarettes, Elegant Woman, Puffs Of Smoke, Art Deco Fabrics, 1920, 36 In. 2880
Sign, N. Leaf, House & Sign Painter, Painted, Wood, 15 ¾ x 26 In... 767
Sign, Nesbitt's Orange, Embossed, Tin, Black Border, Painted, Matthews Co., 1946, 17 x 53 In. 1921
Sign, Nobility Chocolates, Crowd, Display Case, That's The Kind, Self-Framed, 23 x 28 In. *illus* 2726
Sign, Noma Lights, Mazda Lamps, Wood, Back-Lit Glass Beads, 56 In. 4500
Sign, Old Dutch Beer, Man Rolling Barrels, Masonite, 9 x 7 In. ....*illus* 132
Sign, Old Dutch Cleanser, 10 Cents, Enamel, 32 x 22 In. 700
Sign, Orange-Julep, It's Julep Time, Die Cut Cardboard, Frame, 20 x 17 In. ....*illus* 98
Sign, Pabst Blue Ribbon, Cardboard, Old Time Car & Driver, Street Scene, 48 x 95 In. 264
Sign, Palmer Foundry, Wood, Green Ground, Massachusetts, 1910s, 20 ½ x 30 In...................... 180
Sign, Pan-American Orangeade, J. Hungerford Smith, Wood Frame, c.1901, 32 x 20 In............ 1920
Sign, Patrick Henry Beer, Tin Over Cardboard, Self-Framed, Henry Giving Speech, 13 x 17 In. 168
Sign, People's Store Dry Goods Shoes & Groceries, Wood, Painted, 54 ½ x 38 In...................... 501
Sign, Poll-Parrot Shoes For Boys & Girls, Embossed Cardboard, Easel, 15 x 10 In. ....*illus* 295
Sign, Renner's Hi-Power Malt Tonic, Tin Over Cardboard, Painted, 10 x 9 In. 300
Sign, Ro's, Red, Blue Ground, White Lettering, 2-Sided, Frame, 1900s, 27 x 49 ½ In. 431
Sign, Royal Crown Cola, 6 Bottles, Take Home A Carton, 25 Cents, Green, 16 x 28 ½ x 2 In. 1020
Sign, Royal Crown Cola, Drink, Embossed, Metal, Marked MCA 1961, Self-Framed, 40 x 62 In. 360
Sign, Royal Crown Cola, Relax & Enjoy, Tin, 2-Sided, Marked A-M 12-40, 1940, 24 x 16 In. 960
Sign, Ruler, A Good Rule, Use, Diamond Edge, Tools, Painted, 72 x 6 In.................................... 502
Sign, Sealtest Ice Cream, Chocolate Malt, Sundae, Embossed, Frame, c.1957, 11 x 29 In. .*illus* 663

Advertising, Sign, It's Hoods Ice Cream For Health, Rich In Flavor, Tin, 2-Sided, 1910s, 18 x 24 In.
$720

Eldred's

Advertising, Sign, King Bourbon, Lion, Tin Lithograph, Chas. W. Shonk Co., Wood Frame, 49 x 37 In.
$2,700

Morphy Auctions

Advertising, Sign, Kis-Me Gum, Victorian Woman, Glitter Collar, Germany, c.1900, 26 In.
$430

Rich Penn Auctions

Advertising, Sign, Nobility Chocolates, Crowd, Display Case, That's The Kind, Self-Framed, 23 x 28 In.
$2,726

AntiqueAdvertising.com

Advertising, Sign, Old Dutch Beer, Man Rolling Barrels, Masonite, 9 x 7 In.
$132

Milestone Auctions

TIP
Advertising collectors should check every address, phone number, name, and price information that is on a label, a sticker, or the container. They will help with the research to determine the age of the product.

Advertising, Sign, Massa-Chew-Setts, Wood, Black Lettering, White Ground, 1900s, 6 ½ x 36 In.
$330

Eldred's

Advertising, Sign, Orange-Julep, It's Julep Time, Die Cut Cardboard, Frame, 20 x 17 In.
$98

Rich Penn Auctions

Advertising, Sign, Poll-Parrot Shoes For Boys & Girls, Embossed Cardboard, Easel, 15 x 10 In.
$295

AntiqueAdvertising.com

Advertising, Sign, Sealtest Ice Cream, Chocolate Malt, Sundae, Embossed, Frame, c.1957, 11 x 29 In.
$663

Soulis Auctions

Advertising, Sign, Smokettes 5 Cent Cigar, Powell Smith & Co., c.1900, 20 x 37 x 1 In.
$248

Charleston Estate Auctions

Advertising, Sign, Thos. J. Bucknell Optician, Convex, Reverse Painted Glass, c.1910, 20 In.
$826

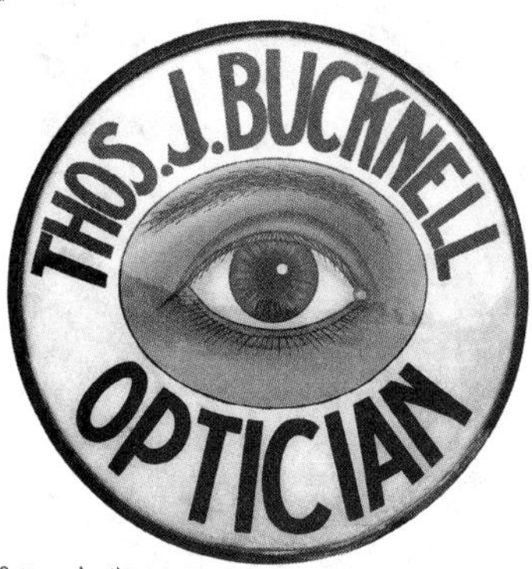

Cottone Auctions

Advertising, Sign, Way-Bel, Rooms, Tourists, Wooden, Painted, 2-Sided, Iron Hooks, 17 ½ x 20 In.
$311

Hartzell's Auction Gallery Inc.

Advertising, Sign, Welcome Aboard!, Silver Bar, Embossed Foil, Frame, 1950s, 12 x 29 In.
$345

Blackwell Auctions

Advertising, Sign, Welcome Soap, 2 Women, Paper Litho, Fabric Dresses, Frame, 31 x 16 In.
$553

Rich Penn Auctions

Advertising, Sign, Where Pure Schlitz, Is Brewed, Alfred Von, Frame, 1903, 45 x 33 ½ x ¾ In.
$3,900

Morphy Auctions

Advertising, Sign, Wrigley's Spearmint Chewing Gum, Painted Plywood, 1900s, 36 x 6 x 9 In.
$523

Skinner, Inc.

Advertising, Stand, Display, 2-Tone Leather Button Shoes, Hanan & Son, Early 1900s, 21 In.
$210

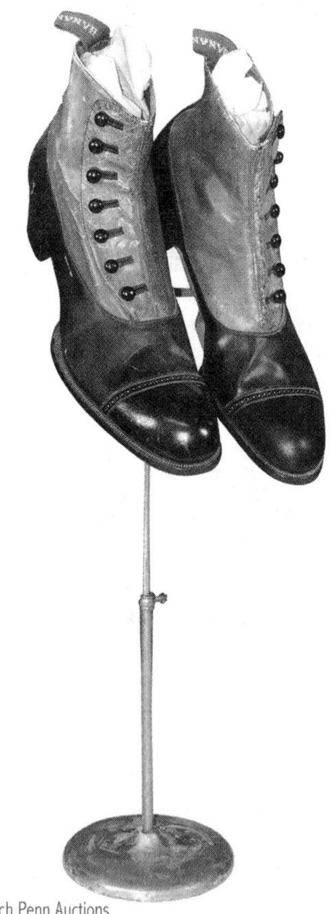

Rich Penn Auctions

Advertising, Statue, Schlitz Beer, Woman Holding Globe, Plastic, Light-Up Globe, 45 In.
$300

Milestone Auctions

Advertising, Tin, Biscuit, Huntley & Palmers, Hey Diddle Diddle, 7 x 4 ½ x 5 ¾ In.
$102

Hartzell's Auction Gallery Inc.

Advertising, Tin, Great Atlantic & Pacific Tea Co., Grandmother, Branch, Lithograph, 11 x 7 In.
$448

AntiqueAdvertising.com

Advertising, Tin, Peterson's Salted Nuts, Cleveland, Oh., Lithograph, 10 Lb., 11 x 8 In.
$189

AntiqueAdvertising.com

Advertising, Tin, Roly Poly, Mayo's Tobacco, Singing Waiter, Lithograph, 7 In.
$177

Cottone Auctions

TIP

Never wash a tobacco "felt." The small flannel flags and pictures that were packed with cigarettes in the early 1900s lose value if washed.

Advertising, Tin, Anti-Stiff, Strengthens The Muscles, Athlete, Gina Type Lithography, 2 x 3 In.
$448

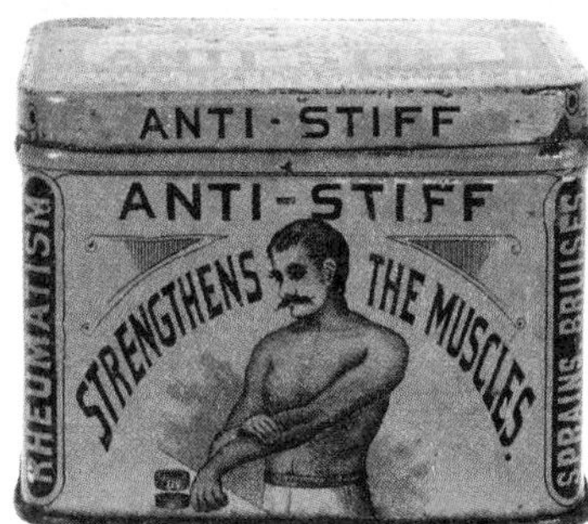

AntiqueAdvertising.com

Advertising, Tin, Lucky Strike Cigarettes, Green, Red, Logo, 1 Lb.
$20

Medina Antique Mall

Advertising, Tin, Royal Ceylon Java, Elephant, Lithograph, Yellow, Black, 1 Lb., 5 x 4 ⅜ In.
$738

Wm Morford Auctions

Advertising, Tip Tray, Chum's Whiskey, Scranton Distributing Co., Man, Drink In Hand, Dog, 4 In.
$260

AntiqueAdvertising.com

Advertising, Toilet, Shank Co. Toilet Bowls, Porcelain, Salesman's Sample, 4 x 3 x 4 In.
$70

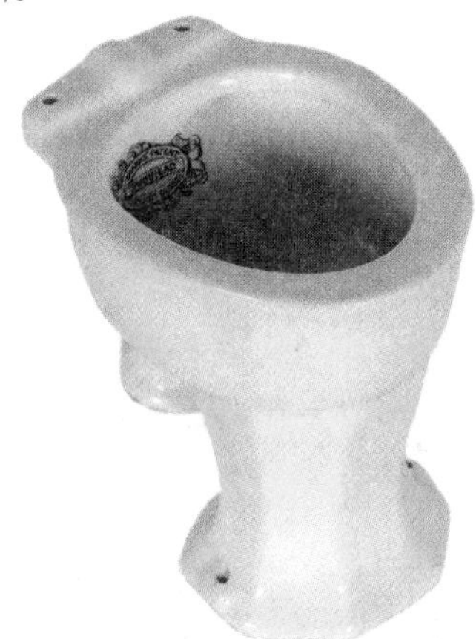

AntiqueAdvertising.com

TIP

Trade card collectors should be careful about how the cards are displayed. Don't use photo albums with plastic envelopes and a sticky cardboard backing (sometimes called "magnetic" albums). The cards will stick and the backs will be ruined. But pure pharmacy acetone, carefully dripped under the corner of the card, will help free it with minimal damage. Do not use nail polish remover.

Advertising, Trade Card, Humpty Dumpty Mechanical Bank, Shepard Hardware, 5 ⅜ x 3 ½ In.
$295

AntiqueAdvertising.com

Advertising, Tray, Hires Root Beer, Boy, Red, Black, Tin, c.1905, 13 ½ x 13 ½ In.
$1,200

Morphy Auctions

Advertising, Tray, Portsmouth Bottled Beer, Woman With Tiger, Flowers, Metal, 13 ½ In.
$1,080

Milestone Auctions

Advertising, Tray, Rainier Beer, Girl On Horse, Boy Standing By, Tin Lithograph, 13 x 10 ½ In.
$1,770

Wm Morford Auctions

Advertising, Tray, Velvet Ice Cream, Kewpie Characters, Neapolitan Ice Cream, Tin Lithograph, 13 x 13 In.
$354

AntiqueAdvertising.com

Advertising, Tray, Zipp's Cherri-O, Bird, Drinking From Glass, H.D. Beach Company, 12 In.
$570

Milestone Auctions

Sign, Smokettes 5 Cent Cigar, Powell Smith & Co., c.1900, 20 x 37 x 1 In. ....*illus* 248
Sign, Standard Oil Credit Card, Boy, Boxing, Wood, Iron Curb Stand, 2-Sided, 55 x 28 x 30 In. 720
Sign, Stop & Save, At The Sign Of The Scottie, Holding Bone, Ford, Canvas, Pole, 25 x 17 In. 283
Sign, Street, Graham Road, Metal, Bradley-Garvey Co., Frame, 26 x 4 In. 123
Sign, Subway, Interborough, Uptown, Enamel, Blue, White Font, L.D. Helke, 72 x 12 In. 480
Sign, Sun Drop Gold-En Girl Cola, Embossed, Metal, Self-Framed, 12 x 28 In. 480
Sign, Thos. J. Bucknell Optician, Convex, Reverse Painted Glass, c.1910, 20 In. ....*illus* 826
Sign, Viceroy, Smoother, Filter Tip Cigarette, King Size, 1954, 15 ¾ x 27 ¾ x 28 In. 181
Sign, Way-Bel, Rooms, Tourists, Wooden, Painted, 2-Sided, Iron Hooks, 17 ½ x 20 In. ....*illus* 311
Sign, Welcome Aboard!, Silver Bar, Embossed Foil, Frame, 1950s, 12 x 29 In. ....*illus* 345
Sign, Welcome Soap, 2 Women, Paper Litho, Fabric Dresses, Frame, 31 x 16 In. ....*illus* 553
Sign, Where Pure Schlitz, Is Brewed, Alfred Von, Frame, 1903, 45 x 33 ½ x ¾ In. ....*illus* 3900
Sign, Whiskey, Rooney's Malt, We Challenge Them All, Rooster, Tin, Chas W. Shonk Co., 24 x 20 In. 2040
Sign, Whistle, Soda, Elves, Embossed Metal, Stout Sign Co., Self-Framed, 1947 738
Sign, Whitman's Chocolates, Cardboard, Die Cut, Messenger, c.1942, 38 x 24 In. 415
Sign, Wm. Redfern & Bro. Saddlery, Suppliers Of All Equestrian Needs, Wood, 1950s, 26 x 36 In. 360
Sign, World's Best Coffee, Neon, Cup Shape, Red & Blue, 36 x 35 In. 344
Sign, Wrigley's Spearmint Chewing Gum, Painted Plywood, 1900s, 36 x 6 x 9 In. ....*illus* 523
Signal, Syracuse Plows, Blue, White, Black, Louis H. Booster, Swayze Adv. Co., 6 x 24 ¾ In. 150
Stand, Display, 2-Tone Leather Button Shoes, Hanan & Son, Early 1900s, 21 In. ....*illus* 210
Statue, Schlitz Beer, Woman Holding Globe, Plastic, Light-Up Globe, 45 In. ....*illus* 300
Thermometers are listed in the Thermometer category. ....

Advertising tin cans or canisters were first used commercially in the United States in 1819 and were called tins. Today the word *tin* is used by most collectors to describe many types of containers, including food tins, biscuit boxes, roly poly tobacco containers, gunpowder cans, talcum powder sprinkle-top cans, cigarette flat-fifty tins, and more. Beer Cans are listed in their own category. Things made of undecorated tin are listed under Tinware.

Tin, Anti-Stiff, Strengthens The Muscles, Athlete, Gina Type Lithography, 2 x 3 In. ....*illus* 448
Tin, Biscuit, Huntley & Palmers, Hey Diddle Diddle, 7 x 4 ½ x 5 ¾ In. ....*illus* 102
Tin, Great American & Pacific Tea Co., Grandmother, Branch, Lithograph, 11 x 7 In. .....*illus* 448
Tin, Lucky Strike Cigarettes, Green, Red, Logo, 1 Lb. ....*illus* 20
Tin, Peterson's Salted Nuts, Cleveland, Oh., Lithograph, 10 Lb., 11 x 8 In. ....*illus* 189
Tin, Roly Poly, Mayo's Tobacco, Singing Waiter, Lithograph, 7 In. ....*illus* 177
Tin, Royal Ceylon Java, Elephant, Lithograph, Yellow, Black, 1 Lb., 5 x 4 ⅜ In. ....*illus* 738
Tin, Slant Lid, Drop Handle, M.C. Vitie & Price Biscuit Mfr., 4 x 4 ½ x 6 In. 29

Advertising tip trays are decorated metal trays less than 5 inches in diameter. They were placed on the table or counter to hold either the bill or the coins that were left as a tip. Change receivers could be made of glass, plastic, or metal. They were kept on the counter near the cash register and held the money passed back and forth by the cashier. Related items may be listed in the Advertising category under Change Receiver.

Tip Tray, Chum's Whiskey, Scranton Distributing Co., Man, Drink In Hand, Dog, 4 In. ...*illus* 260
Toilet, Shank Co. Toilet Bowls, Porcelain, Salesman's Sample, 4 x 3 x 4 In. ....*illus* 70
Trade Card, Humpty Dumpty Mechanical Bank, Shepard Hardware, 5 ⅜ x 3 ½ In. ....*illus* 295
Tray, Beer, Falstaff Princess, Holding Glass, Tin, Circular, c.1910, 16 In. 50
Tray, Drink Dr Pepper King Of Beverages, Red & Black Letters, Glass, Round, 6 In. 904
Tray, Drink Zipp's Cherri-O, 5 Cents, Robin, Green Leaves, c.1915-20, 12 x 12 x 1 In. 660
Tray, Frank's, Pale Dry Ginger Ale, 5 Full Glasses, Bottle, 1895, 13 x 10 ½ In. 45
Tray, Hires Boy, Join Health & Cheer, Circular, Green Back Side, Mettlach, c.1900, 5 In. 1695
Tray, Hires Root Beer, Boy, Red, Black, Tin, c.1905, 13 ½ x 13 ½ In. ....*illus* 1200
Tray, Portsmouth Bottled Beer, Woman With Tiger, Flowers, Metal, 13 ½ In. ....*illus* 1080
Tray, Rainier Beer, Girl On Horse, Boy Standing By, Tin Lithograph, 13 x 10 ½ In. ....*illus* 1770
Tray, Stegmaier Brewing, Factory, Wilkes-Barre, Pa., Tin Lithograph, 12 In. 51

Never Too Much Shopping
Have a bad day? Psychologists have proved that shopping is one way to combat depression. Cheer up. Rummage through some antiques for sale. You can even stay at home and look online. Collecting can make you happy.

Agata, Tumbler, Green, Gilt Ruffled Band, New England Glass, c.1890, 3 ¾ In.
$150

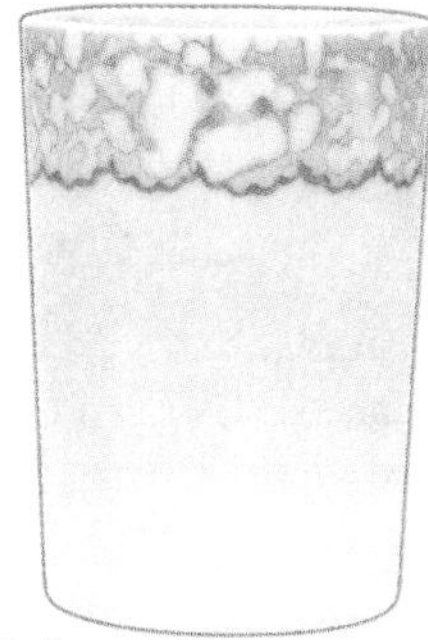

Woody Auctions

Akro Agate, Smoking Stand, Light-Up, Star Dome, Chrome Base, Lighter, Ashtray, 29 x 13 ½ In.
$210

Rich Penn Auctions

Alabaster, Sculpture, The Silence, Die Stille, Woman, Bending Down, Gilt Bronze Skirt, M. Getze, 17 In.
$510

Michaan's Auctions

Aluminum, Tray, Lithograph Transfer Print, Corkscrew, Pipe, Playing Card, Key, Fornasetti, 24 x 10 In.
$1,750

Palm Beach Modern Auctions

Amber Glass, Salt Cellar, Opalescent, Yellow Interior, Metal Stand, 2 In.
$142

Strawser Auction Group

Tray, Tip, see Tip Trays in this category.
Tray, Velvet Ice Cream, Kewpie Characters, Neapolitan Ice Cream, Tin Lithograph, 13 x 13 In. *illus* 354
Tray, Zipp's Cherri-O, Bird, Drinking From Glass, H.D. Beach Company, 12 In. *illus* 570
Trivet, Cast Iron, Mfd. For John Randles Inc., 8 In. 147
Wall Hanging, The Newest Hotpoint Super Iron, Wood Frame, Under Glass, 20 x 16 In. 113

AGATA

Agata glass was made by Joseph Locke of the New England Glass Company of Cambridge, Massachusetts, after 1885. A metallic stain was applied to New England Peachblow, which the company called Wild Rose, and the mottled design characteristic of agata appeared. There are a few known items made of opaque green with the mottled finish.

Toothpick Holder, Amber Stain, Cylindrical, 2 ½ In. 188
Tumbler, Green, Gilt Ruffled Band, New England Glass, c.1890, 3 ¾ In. *illus* 150

AKRO AGATE

Akro Agate glass was founded in Akron, Ohio, in 1911 and moved to Clarksburg, West Virginia, in 1914. The company made marbles and toys. In the 1930s it began making other products, including vases, lamps, flowerpots, candlesticks, and children's dishes. Most of the glass is marked with a crow flying through the letter *A*. The company was sold to Clarksburg Glass Co. in 1951. Akro Agate marbles are listed in this book in the Marble category.

Smoking Stand, Light-Up, Star Dome, Chrome Base, Lighter, Ashtray, 29 x 13 ½ In. *illus* 210

ALABASTER

Alabaster is a very soft form of gypsum, a stone that resembles marble. It was often carved into vases or statues in Victorian times. There are alabaster carvings being made even today.

Bust, Caesar Augustus, c.1875, 17 In. 960
Bust, Napoleon, Removable Socle, Round Base, 17 ¾ In. 500
Bust, Parsifal, Knight In Wagner's Opera, Signed, Hertel, 12 ⅝ In. 406
Cassolette, Louis XVI Style, Gilt, Bronze Mounted, Tripod Base, c.1800, 7 ¾ In., Pair 563
Figurine, Buffalo Chief, Carved Stone, Mounted, Larry Decoteau, 13 x 10 In. 192
Figurine, Grecian, Nude, Holding Cup Aloft, Bronze, Marble, Signed, Heinrich, 14 x 6 x 5 In. 1250
Group, 3 Cherubs, Playing Guitar, 1800s, 15 x 19 x 10 ½ In. 313
Lamp, Classical Style, Urn Shape, Plinth Base, Continental, 21 In. 1732
Lamp, Neoclassical Woman, Pink Dress, Flowers, Marble Base, Electric, c.1930, 45 In. 242
Pedestal, White, Parcel Gilt, Bronze, Beaded Top, Mounted, c.1800s, 45 In. 1000
Rooster, Carved, Mounted, Black Wood, Signed, Robert Laurent, 10 x 12 ½ x 2 ½ In. 8190
Sculpture, Paperboy, Shouting, Holding Newspapers, Spiral Twist Pedestal, 62 x 14 In. 1625
Sculpture, The Silence, Die Stille, Woman, Bending Down, Gilt Bronze Skirt, M. Getze, 17 In. *illus* 510

ALUMINUM

Aluminum was more expensive than gold or silver until the 1850s. Chemists learned how to refine bauxite to get aluminum. Jewelry and other small objects were made of the valuable metal until 1914, when an inexpensive smelting process was invented. The aluminum collected today dates from the 1930s through the 1950s. Hand-hammered pieces are the most popular.

Pan, Square, Lid, 2 Handles, Don Drumm, 9 In. 35
Tray, Lithograph Transfer Print, Corkscrew, Pipe, Playing Card, Key, Fornasetti, 24 x 10 In. *illus* 1750

AMBER, *see Jewelry and Stone categories.*

AMBER GLASS

Amber glass is the name of any glassware with the proper yellow-brown shading. It was a popular color just after the Civil War and many pressed glass pieces were made of amber glass. Depression glass of the 1930s–1950s was also made in shades of amber glass. Other pieces may be found in the Depression Glass, Pressed Glass, and other glass categories. All types are being reproduced.

Bowl, Footed, Blown, Fluted Rim, 1800s, 4 5/8 x 9 3/4 In. 1037
Lamp, Oil, Stained, Clear Glass Shade, Cut Edges, 15 1/2 In., Pair 142
Salt Cellar, Opalescent, Yellow Interior, Metal Stand, 2 In. .... *illus* 142
Vase, Panel, Bohemian Flashed, Engraved, Flowers, 9 3/4 In. 90

AMBERINA

Amberina, a two-toned glassware, was originally made from 1883 to about 1900. It was patented by Joseph Locke of the New England Glass Company but was also made by other companies and is still being made. The glass shades from red to amber. Similar pieces of glass may be found in the Baccarat, Libbey, Plated Amberina, and other categories. Glass shaded from blue to amber is called *Blue Amberina* or *Bluerina*.

Bowl, Square, Silver Plate Base, Girl, Dog, Hobbs, Brockunier & Co., c.1884, 9 1/2 x 2 1/2 In. *illus* 410
Canoe, Button& Daisy, Scalloped Rim, Hobbs, 3 1/2 x 8 In. .... *illus* 180
Cruet, Spout & Handle, Stopper, Glaze, Footed, 6 1/2 In. .... *illus* 213
Salt & Pepper, Baby Thumbprint, Black Lid, Enamel, Flowers, 3 1/2 In. 112
Vase, Stork, Capturing Snake, Bulrushes, New England Glass Works, c.1885, 4 1/2 x 2 In. 1180
Vase, Swirl, Enamel, Flowers & Leaves, 7 x 3 1/2 In. .... *illus* 84
Vase, Trumpet Shape, Crimped, Swirled & Folded Rim, Dome Foot, 17 1/2 In., Pair 396
Vase, Trumpet Shape, Mounted, Silver Frame, Flowers, Stepped Base, 5 3/4 In. 77

AMERICAN DINNERWARE, *see Dinnerware.*

AMERICAN ENCAUSTIC TILING COMPANY

American Encaustic Tiling Company was founded in Zanesville, Ohio, in 1875. The company planned to make a variety of tiles to compete with the English tiles that were selling in the United States for use in fireplaces and other architectural designs. The first glazed tiles were made in 1880, embossed tiles in 1881, faience tiles in the 1920s. The firm closed in 1935 and reopened in 1937 as the Shawnee Pottery.

Tile, Plaque, Cherubs By The Fire, Green, Majolica, 6 In., Pair 92
Tile, Schooner, Blue, Yellow, Glazed, c.1925, 24 x 12 In., 2 Piece .... *illus* 1625

AMETHYST GLASS

Amethyst glass is any of the many glasswares made in the dark purple color of the gemstone amethyst. Included in this category are many pieces made in the nineteenth and twentieth centuries. Very dark pieces are called *black amethyst*.

Jardiniere, Gilt Bronze, Oval, Pierced Surround, Griffins, Wreaths, 1810s, 3 x 7 x 4 In. 550
Vase, Enamel, Flowers, Brass Rim & Base, Tripod Base, 14 1/2 x 5 In., Pair .... *illus* 403

AMPHORA *pieces are listed in the Teplitz category.*

ANDIRONS *and related fireplace items are included in the Fireplace category.*

Amberina, Bowl, Square, Silver Plate Base, Girl, Dog, Hobbs, Brockunier & Co., c.1884, 9 1/2 x 2 1/2 In.
$410

Jeffrey S. Evans & Associates

Amberina, Canoe, Button & Daisy, Scalloped Rim, Hobbs, 3 1/2 x 8 In.
$180

Woody Auctions

Amberina, Cruet, Spout & Handle, Stopper, Glaze, Footed, 6 1/2 In.
$213

Strawser Auction Group

TIP

Protect your wooden floors by keeping dirt out of the house. Use floor mats inside and outside the doors.

Amberina, Vase, Swirl, Enamel, Flowers & Leaves, 7 x 3 ½ In.
$84

Woody Auctions

TIP

Don't like to haggle over prices? Just write the price you will offer on a small card and give it to the dealer to consider. Or ask the dealer to write down the lowest acceptable price. Probably a good ploy for very expensive antiques or art.

American Encaustic, Tile, Schooner, Blue, Yellow, Glazed, c.1925, 24 x 12 In., 2 Piece
$1,625

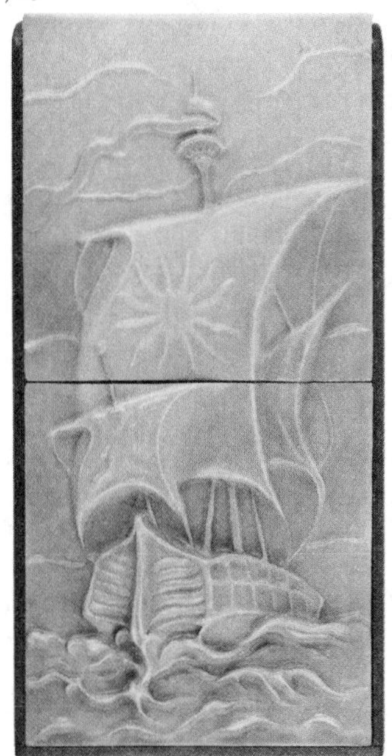

Rago Arts and Auction Center

Amethyst Glass, Vase, Enamel, Flowers, Brass Rim & Base, Tripod Base, 14 ½ x 5 In., Pair
$403

Stevens Auction Co.

Anna Pottery, Flask, Pig, Incised Railroad Map, Peoria House, Chas. H. Dean, 3 ½ x 7 ½ In.
$4,063

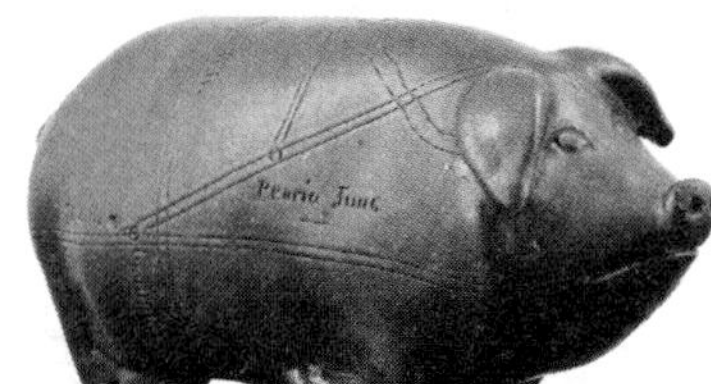

Palm Beach Modern Auctions

Architectural, Caryatid, Cast Iron, Neo-Egyptian, Black Patina, 35 x 8 x 6 ½ In., Pair
$215

Stair Galleries

Architectural, Bathtub, Copper Exterior, Zinc Interior, Painted, 65 x 27 x 25 In.
$375

Hudson Valley Auctions

ANIMAL TROPHY

Animal trophies, such as stuffed animals (taxidermy), rugs made of animal skins, and other similar collectibles made from animal, fish, or bird parts, are listed in this category. Collectors should be aware of the endangered species laws that make it illegal to buy and sell some of these items. Any eagle feathers, many types of pelts or rugs (such as leopard), ivory, rhinoceros horn, and many forms of tortoiseshell can be confiscated by the government. Related trophies may be found in the Fishing category. Ivory items may be found in the Scrimshaw or Ivory categories.

Antelope, Pronghorn Rack, Skull, Sable, 30 x 17 In. 344
Deer, 8-Point Antlers, Shoulder Mount, Taxidermist's Eyes, 38 x 14 x 21 In. 156
Deer, Molded Fur, Facial Details, Multicolor, Cast Iron, Zinc, Late 1800s, 20 In. 2091
Deer, Skull Mount, Red-Tail Stag, Rack Specimen, Carved Wood Plaque, 49 x 38 x 25 In. 813
Elephant Foot, Footstool, Zebra Hide Upholstered Seat, 22 In. 1750

ANIMATION ART

Animation art collectibles include cels that are painted drawings on celluloid needed to make animated cartoons shown in movie theaters or on TV. Hundreds of cels were made, then photographed in sequence to make a cartoon showing moving figures. Early examples made by the Walt Disney Studios are popular with collectors today. Original sketches used by the artists are also listed here. Modern animated cartoons are made using computer-generated pictures. Some of these are being produced as cels to be sold to collectors. Other cartoon art is listed in Comic Art and Disneyana.

Cel, Dilbert, Shipper, Man With Walkman, Scott Adams, 10 ½ x 12 ½ In. 31
Cel, Dumbo In Washtub, Disney, Multicolor, 9 x 10 In. 1003
Cel, Jumbo & Dumbo, Pink Hat, Disney, 9 ½ x 12 In. 2478
Cel, Pinocchio, Disney, Wood Frame, Stencil, 8 x 7 ½ In. 2478
Cel, Teenage Mutant Ninja Turtles, Captured In Net, 1980s, 10 ½ x 12 ½ In. 63
Cel, Wendy Darling, Peter Pan, Watercolor, c.1953, 12 ½ x 15 ½ In. 307
Cel, Woody Woodpecker, Sitting In Big Chair, Signed, Walter Lanz, 15 x 16 In. 120
Drawing, Butterfly Stompers, Beatles, Yellow Submarine, Pencil, 1968, 12 x 16 In. 118
Drawing, Judy & George Jetson, Aerocar, Pencil, c.1962, 10 ½ x 12 ½ In. 770
Drawing, Pluto, Army Mascot, Lead Pencil, Initials BDT, 1942, 10 x 11 ¾ In. 348
Drawing, Zazu, Lion King, Concept, Mixed Media, c.1994, 11 x 14 In. 118
Story Board, Happy Household, Flintstones, Pencil, 5 Sheets, 9 Panels Each 242

ANNA POTTERY

Anna Pottery

Anna Pottery was started in Anna, Illinois, in 1859 by Cornwall and Wallace Kirkpatrick. They made many types of utilitarian wares, bricks, drain tiles, and giftware. The most collectible pieces made by the pottery are the pig-shaped bottles and jugs with special inscriptions, applied animals, and figures. The pottery closed in 1894.

Flask, Pig, Incised Railroad Map, Peoria House, Chas. H. Dean, 3 ½ x 7 ½ In. .... *illus* 4063
Inkwell, Frog, Stoneware, Impressed Kirkpatrick, Anna Ill, 1800s, 3 ¾ x 4 In. 6100

ARCHITECTURAL

Architectural antiques include a variety of collectibles, usually very large, that have been removed from buildings. Hardware, backbars, doors, paneling, and even old bathtubs are now wanted by collectors. Pieces of the Victorian, Art Nouveau, and Art Deco styles are in greatest demand.

Bathtub, Copper Exterior, Zinc Interior, Painted, 65 x 27 x 25 In. .... *illus* 375
Bracket, Limewood, Cherub Bust, Figural, Fruit Pendant, Scroll, c.1800, 34 x 7 x 4 ¼ In. 200

Architectural, Door, Walnut, Wrought Iron, Carved, Flowers, Leaves, c.1930, 56 x 15 x 1 In., Pair
$594

Kamelot Auctions

Architectural, Element, American Indian Portrait, Stylized Headdress, Zinc, Late 1800s, 32 x 41 x 14 In.
$1,560

Garth's Auctioneers & Appraisers

Architectural, Hanger, Wood, Wall Mounted, 5 Hooks, 14 x 4 x 15 In.
$40

Hartzell's Auction Gallery Inc.

Architectural, Model, Cathedral, Wood, Glass Windows, Gray Paint, 1900s, 15 1/2 x 23 1/2 In.
$121

Bruneau & Co. Auctioneers

Architectural, Monument, White Metal, Wood Case, Salesman's Sample, c.1890, 28 In.
$875

Garth's Auctioneers & Appraisers

Architectural, Overdoor, Mahogany, Carved, King Saul & David, Harp, Late 1800s, 19 x 55 x 3 In.
$1,287

Thomaston Place Auction Galleries

Architectural, Panel, Giltwood, Carved, 3 Tiers, Deities, Temple, Flowers, c.1900, 31 x 19 In.
$688

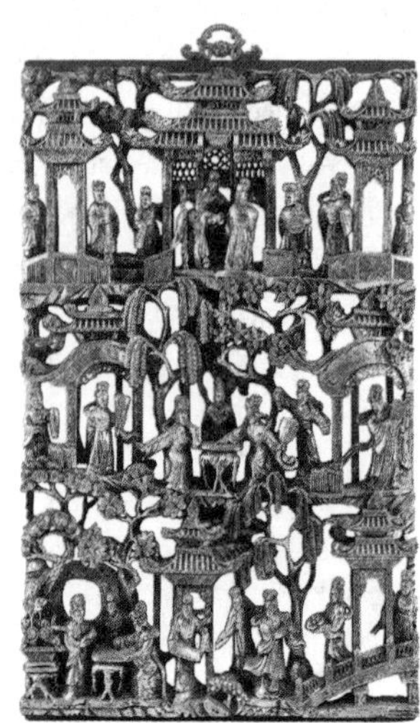

Eldred's

Architectural, Windmill, Wooden Wheel, Cast Iron Hood, Salesman's Sample, 1800, 21 1/2 x 12 x 4 In.
$3,000

Morphy Auctions

Art Deco, Figure, Nude Woman, Kneeling, 2 Bowls, Ceramic, Gudrun Baudisch, 1925-30, 6 3/4 In.
$1,495

Richard D. Hatch & Associates

Caryatid, Cast Iron, Neo-Egyptian, Black Patina, 35 x 8 x 6 ½ In., Pair ....*illus* 215
Column, Interior Flat Pilasters, Applied Lithograph, John Sherer, 77 ½ In., Pair...................... 531
Corbel, Mahogany, Carved, Red Varnish, Continental, 1900s, 15 x 13 x 8 In............................. 125
Door, Pond Lily, Leaded Glass, Painted, Wood, Art Nouveau Style, 1900s, 63 ¾ x 17 In., Pair.... 2500
Door, Walnut, Wrought Iron, Carved, Flowers, Leaves, c.1930, 56 x 15 x 1 In., Pair ....*illus* 594
Doorknocker, Iron, Oblong, Flower Basket, Cream Ground, 4 x 3 In. 34
Downspout, Copper, Gargoyle, Green, Patina, Outstretched Wings, Star Feet, 1800s, 27 In...... 1464
Element, American Indian Portrait, Stylized Headdress, Zinc, Late 1800s, 32 x 41 x 14 In. *illus* 1560
Element, Owl, Pressed Copper, 2 Parts, c.1930, 17 ½ x 9 ½ In.. 492
Element, Square, Molded, Floral Center, Late 1800s, 3 x 4 ¾ x 4 ¾ In. 98
Element, Urn Shape, Black, Painted, Ball Finial, Flared Gilt Base, Wood, 1900s, 31 x 12 In...... 96
Element, Wooden, Carved, Dragons, Man's Face, 54 ½ In. 118
Faucet, Bathtub, Telephone Shape, Shower, Stamped MWB, London, Brass, 1900s, 15 x 8 x 7 In. 207
Finial, Copper, 4 Flowers, Turned, Painted Wood Base, c.1900, 32 In... 1169
Fragment, Confucian Scholar, Seated, Stone, Carved, 1600s-1700s, 13 ½ x 7 ¾ x 5 In............ 1404
Fragment, Red Painted Board, White Heart, Blue Star Symbols, 1800s, 26 ½ x 56 ½ In. 738
Gate, 4 Sections, Scrollwork, Repeating Kidney Shapes, Center Hinged, Iron, 73 x 97 In.......... 800
Hanger, Wood, Wall Mounted, 5 Hooks, 14 x 4 x 15 In. ....*illus* 40
Indicator, Elevator Floors, 22 Floors, Dial Number, Arrow, Bronze, Art Deco, 14 In................. 60
Louver, Fan Shape, Wooden, Green Paint, 1800s, 21 x 75 In... 570
Mantel, Federal, Pine, Fluted Pilaster, Shaped Bracket, Gray, 1810s, 53 x 55 ½ In................... 500
Mantel, Louis XVI Style, Carved Marble, Serpentine Top, 1800s, 47 x 59 x 11 ¾ In. 2875
Mantel, Oak, Quartersawn, Griffin, Square Column, Claw Feet, 96 x 60 x 15 In........................ 363
Mantel, Wood, Carved, Figures Both Side, Flowers, 2 Putti, 86 x 17 x 53 In............................... 1770
Model, Cathedral, Wood, Glass Windows, Gray Paint, 1900s, 15 ½ x 23 ½ In. ....*illus* 121
Monument, White Metal, Wood Case, Salesman's Sample, c.1890, 28 In. ....*illus* 875
Obelisk, Rosso Antico, Lateran, Marble, Slate Base, c.1700, 22 x 4 ½ x 4 ½ In......................... 2706
Overdoor, Mahogany, Carved, King Saul & David, Harp, Late 1800s, 19 x 55 x 3 In. ....*illus* 1287
Overmantel Mirror, Giltwood, Rectangular Flat Top, Square Foot, 1830s, 24 x 59 In............. 281
Panel, Aesthetic, Walnut, Carved, Gilt, Birds, Trees, c.1880-84, 19 ½ x 48 ½ In....................... 2340
Panel, Bronze Cast, Angel Head, Wings, Geometric Frame, Renaissance, 1800s, 12 x 11 In. 936
Panel, Giltwood, Carved, 3 Tiers, Deities, Temple, Flowers, c.1900, 31 x 19 In. ....*illus* 688
Screens are listed in the Fireplace and Furniture categories...
Shutters, Wood, Monumental, Green Paint, France, 1800s, 121 x 12 In., 8 Piece...................... 1062
Staircase, Model, Wood, Mounted, Round Base, 14 ½ In.. 325
Tile, Terra-Cotta, Octagonal, Turkeys, White Glaze, 24 x 24 x 5 In., 3 Piece............................. 113
Wall Bracket, Baroque, Walnut, Carved, Cartouche Shape Top, Wire Hangers, 1700s, 12 x 21 x 10 In. 480
Windmill, Wooden Wheel, Cast Iron Hood, Salesman's Sample, 1800, 21 ½ x 12 x 4 In. .*illus* 3000

AREQUIPA POTTERY

Arequipa Pottery was produced from 1911 to 1918 by the patients of the Arequipa Sanatorium in Marin County, north of San Francisco. The patients were trained by Frederick Hurten Rhead, who had worked at Roseville Pottery.

Vase, Olla Shape, Semimatte Strawberry Glaze, Carved Eucalyptus Leaves, 4 x 6 in. 1020
Vase, Stylized Leaves, Blue, Green, Squeezebag, Marked 2084, F.H. Rhead, 6 x 3 in. 4062
Vase, Turquoise, Stylized Leaves, Squeezebag, Marked 2128, F.H. Rhead, 8 x 3 in. 15000

ARITA

Arita is a port in Japan. Porcelain was made there from about 1616. Many types of decorations were used, including the popular Imari designs, which are listed under Imari in this book.

Plate, Round, Blue, White, Geometric, Footed, Japan, 1 ½ x 8 ¼ In. 118

ART DECO

Art Deco, or Art Moderne, a style started at the Paris Exposition of 1925, is characterized by linear, geometric designs. All types of furniture and decorative arts,

Art Deco, Vase, Multicolor, White Ground, Flared Rim, France, 12 In.
$197

Skinner, Inc.

Art Nouveau, Epergne, Centerpiece, Woman, Spelter, Cranberry, Opalescent, Metal Base, 25 x 11 In.
$270

Woody Auctions

This is an edited listing of current prices. Visit **Kovels.com** to check thousands of prices from previous years and sign up for free information on trends, tips, reproductions, marks, and more.

Art Nouveau, Hand Mirror, 9K Gold, Tortoise, Mounted, Charles Henry Dumenil, c.1876, 10 ½ In.
$1,250

Hindman Auctions

Art Nouveau, Sculpture, Bronze, 2 Women Dancing, Embossed, La Danse Des Nymphes, 16 ½ In.
$177

Bunch Auctions

Art Nouveau, Tray, Vide Poche, Bronze, Josef Ofner, c.1920, 8 In.
$221

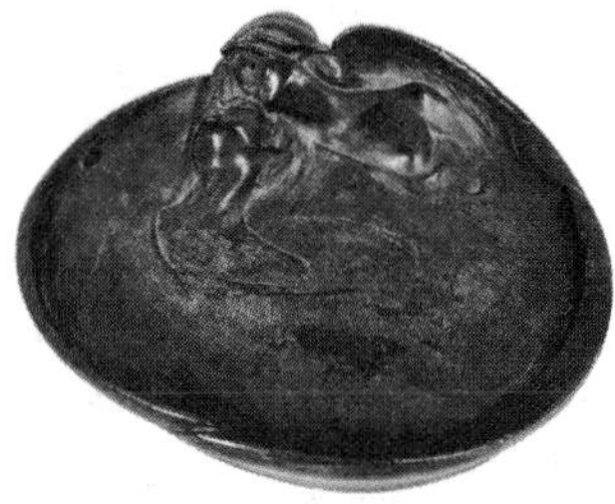

Skinner, Inc.

jewelry, book bindings, and even games were designed in this style. Additional items may be found in the Furniture category or in various glass and pottery categories, etc.

Ashtray, Semicircular, Impressed Mark, Chester Nicodemus, 4 ½ In. 23
Bust, Young Girl, Marble, Snow Cap, Mounted, M. Pedrini, Italy, 14 ½ In. 300
Figure, Nude Woman, Kneeling, 2 Bowls, Ceramic, Gudrun Baudisch, 1925-30, 6 ¾ In. ..*illus* 1495
Lamp, Woman, Seated, Nude, Electric, Nuart Creation, 8 ½ x 4 ½ x 8 In. 148
Sculpture, Cat & Ball, Painted, Wood & Glass, Rectangular Base, 5 ¾ x 6 ¾ In. 62
Vase, Multicolor, White Ground, Flared Rim, France, 12 In. ....*illus* 197
Vase, Wheel Carved, Etched Orange Flowers, Vine, Frosted Ground, 7 x 7 ½ x 7 ½ In. 1800

ART GLASS, *see Glass-Art category.*

ART NOUVEAU

Art Nouveau is a style of design that was at its most popular from 1895 to 1905. Famous designers, including Rene Lalique and Emile Galle, produced furniture, glass, silver, metalwork, and buildings in the new style. Ladies with long flowing hair and elongated bodies were among the more easily recognized design elements. Copies of this style are being made today. Many modern pieces of jewelry can be found. Additional Art Nouveau pieces may be found in Furniture or in various glass and porcelain categories.

Epergne, Centerpiece, Woman, Spelter, Cranberry, Opalescent, Metal Base, 25 x 11 In. ...*illus* 270
Hand Mirror, 9K Gold, Tortoise, Mounted, Charles Henry Dumenil, c.1876, 10 ½ In. .....*illus* 1250
Sculpture, Bronze, 2 Women Dancing, Embossed, La Danse Des Nymphes, 16 ½ In. ......*illus* 177
Tray, Vide Poche, Bronze, Josef Ofner, c.1920, 8 In. ....*illus* 221

ART POTTERY, *see Pottery-Art category.*

ARTS & CRAFTS

Arts & Crafts was a design style popular in American decorative arts from 1894 to 1923. In the 1970s collectors began to rediscover Mission furniture, art pottery, metalwork, linens, and light fixtures from this period. The interest has continued. Today everything from this era is collectible, including jewelry, graphics, and silverware. Additional items may be found in the Furniture category and other categories.

Screen, Winter Scene, Painted, 4 Panels, C. Williams, 1931, 61 x 76 In. 1230
Tray, Dresser, Copper, Sterling Silver Shark, Graziella Laffi, Peru, 4 ½ x 3 ½ In. 102
Vase, Ephraim, 2 Opposing Dragonflies, Blue Matte, Scott Draves, 9 ⅞ x 5 In. 207

AURENE *pieces are listed in the Steuben category.*

AUSTRIA *is a collecting term that covers pieces made by a wide variety of factories. They are listed in this book in categories such as Royal Dux or Porcelain.*

AUTO

Auto parts and accessories are collectors' items today. Gas pump globes and license plates are part of this specialty. Prices are determined by age, rarity, and condition. Collectors say "porcelain sign" for enameled iron or steel signs. Packaging related to automobiles may also be found in the Advertising category. Lalique hood ornaments are listed in the Lalique category.

Banner, Cloth, Wiper Service, Trico Station, Orange, 83 x 35 In. 1140
Can, Gargoyle Motoroil, Embossed, White, Screw Top Lid, Socony, 5 Gal., 24 In. 132
Can, Havoline Oil, Indian Refining, Square, Metal, 5 Gal., 14 x 9 ½ In. 240
Can, Texaco, Motor Oil, Red & White, 9 ½ In. 51
Car Topper, Farmers Automobile Insurance, Agent Office, Glass Sign, Metal Base, 15 x 11 In. . 690

Carburetor, Kingston, 4 Ball, Brass, Used On Ford Model T, 1912-13, 7 In. 120
Clock, Mercedes 220, Spring Driven, 8-Day, Silver Metal Case, c.1955, 4 In. Diam. 204
Clock, Monroe Shocks & Struts, Molded Plastic, Light-Up, 20 ½ In. 108
Credit Card Machine, Texaco, Orange & Green, Key, Small 240
Eco Tireflator, Air Meter, Gulf Gasoline, Hose, Orange, 57 x 11 x 12 In. 3000
Figure, Fisk Tires, Time To Retire Boy, Fiberglass, Holding Tire, 84 x 64 In. .... *illus* 4200
Flag, Indianapolis Speedway, Checkered, Black, White, Frame, 17 ½ x 17 ½ In. 81
Flask, Packard, Super 8, Cap, Stainless, Round, 5 ½ In. 96
Gas Pump Globe, Atlantic Gasoline, Red, White Ground, Blue Lettering, Round Base, 21 In. 767
Gas Pump Globe, Gulf, Copper Screw Base, Cast Globe, Orange, White, Blue, 18 In. 3000
Gas Pump Globe, Lion Oil, Milk Glass, Red, Black, White, 2-Sided, 16 ½ x 13 ½ In. .... *illus* 1130
Gas Pump Globe, M.F.A. Gasoline, Reverse Painted, Glass Lens, Red, White, Blue, 17 x 13 In. 226
Gas Pump Globe, Shell, Clamshell Lens, Metal Body, Yellow, White, 15 In. .... *illus* 2700
Gas Pump Globe, Texaco, Globe Body, Milk Glass, Lens, 13 ½ In. 780
Gas Pump Sign, Texaco, Gasoline, Marine White, Enamel, Green, Black, 15 x 10 In. 2400
Gas Pump, Bowser Phillips 66, Buckeye Brass Nozzle, Metal Face Plate, 73 x 26 In. .... *illus* 1140
Gas Pump, Gulf Diesel, Logo Plate, Porcelain Face, Nozzle & Hose, 22 x 16 x 52 In. .... *illus* 900
Gas Pump, Johnson Gasolene, Tokheim 300, Hose, Nozzle, Orange, Black, 58 In. .... *illus* 1680
Hood Ornament, Bronze, Nickel Plate, Silver, Wood Base, Art Deco, c.1925, 5 x 2 In. 420
Hood Ornament, Pegasus, Stover Racine, Emory P. Seidel, 5 ½ x 7 x 2 ½ In. .... *illus* 424
Hood Ornament, Super Chief, Plastic, Chromed, Multicolor, Box, 5 x 4 ½ In. 360
Lamp, New The Spirit Of Texaco, White, Scalloped Slag Glass Shade, 24 In. 120
Lantern, Neverout, Red Lenses, Brass, Applied Handle, Early 1900s, 9 In. .... *illus* 168
License Plate, Maine, 8113, Mounted, Holes, 1915, 14 ½ x 5 ½ In. .... *illus* 132
Lubester, Lion Head Motor Oil, Standard Oil Service, Indiana, Marked M & E, 55 x 10 x 23 In. 210
Lubester, Veedol Motor Oil, Tin, Tide Water Associated Oil Co., 53 x 22 x 10 In. 270
Parking Meter, Stand, Silver & Black, Round Top & Base, Duncan Industries, 51 In. .... *illus* 168
Poster, Mercedes, Art Nouveau Women, Car, Schreiber, 1912, 43 x 29 In. 22800
Poster, Pierce Arrow, Car Silhouette, Art Deco Arrows, R. Louis, 1929, 25 x 39 In. 14400
Poster, Texaco, News Report, Cardboard, Wood Frame, 28 x 19 In. 72
Rack, Castrol, Motor Oil, Quart Can, Tin, 3 Shelves, Green, 46 x 24 In. 360
Rack, Gulflube, Motor Oil, 20 Quart Cans, 4 Shelves, Metal, Blue, 21 x 46 x 4 In. 480
Rack, Map, Shell, Road Maps, Wood, Tin, Yellow, 20 x 13 In. .... *illus* 960
Rack, Phillips 66 Motor Oil, 3 Tiers, Wire, Black & Red, 26 x 19 x 39 In. 108
Radiator, Ford, Model T, Brass, Made In USA, 25 x 23 ½ In. .... *illus* 240
Sign, Agency For Otto, Gas & Gasoline Engines, Porcelain, White, Blue, 8 x 10 In. 3600
Sign, Approved Packard Service, Porcelain, 2-Sided, Round, Blue, White, Red, 60 In. 3658
Sign, B.F. Goodrich, Tires & Batteries, Metal, Blue Ground, White Letters, 26 ½ x 60 In. 240
Sign, Champion Spark Plugs, Tin, Black, White, Red, Framed Edge, 72 x 36 In. 348
Sign, Chicago Motor Club, Roof Top, Glass Panel, Metal Bracket, 2-Sided, 14 x 7 ½ In. ...*illus* 3120
Sign, Delco Dry Charge Battery, Tin, 2-Sided, 28 x 20 In. 390
Sign, Delco, America's No. 1 Battery, Die Cut, Tin, 23 x 19 In. 570
Sign, Edison Mazda Lamps, Tin Over Cardboard, Woman, Lightbulbs, 22 x 11 In. .... *illus* 450
Sign, Exxon, Mobil Dealer, Hanging, Mounted, Bracket, 2-Sided, 52 x 2 x 32 In. .... *illus* 240
Sign, Firestone, Logo, Orange Ground, White Text, Metal, 72 x 13 ½ In. 132
Sign, Ford & Fordson, Blue Ground, White Text, Enamel, 27 x 58 In. 1921
Sign, Gas, 17 Cents, Oil, 2-Sided, Reverse Painted, Light-Up, Wood Frame, 21 x 19 x 7 In.. *illus* 363
Sign, Goodyear Balloon Tires, Tire Around Globe, Enamel, 1930s, 40 x 46 In. .... *illus* 880
Sign, Goodyear, Tire, Die Cut, Porcelain, Flange, 34 x 21 ½ In. 2280
Sign, Hudson-Essex, Motor Cars, Black Ground, Reverse Painted, 9 ¾ x 23 ¾ In. 325
Sign, John Lewis Motor Company, Wood Frame, Black Lettering, 35 x 46 ¾ In. 210
Sign, Kelly Tires, Kelly Girl Logo, Tin, 1930s, 42 x 30 ½ In. .... *illus* 5610
Sign, McCurry Oil Co., Pegasus, White Plastic Lens, Tin, Light-Up, Frame, 15 x 12 x 5 ½ In. 537
Sign, North Star Gasoline, Porcelain, Stars, White, Blue, Red, Round, 60 In. 1680
Sign, OK Tires, Die Cut, Attendant With Logos, Tin, 1960s, 60 x 37 In. .... *illus* 715
Sign, Pennzoil Lubrication Service, Shaped Metal Sheet, Brass Rivets, 1950s, 16 x 32 In. 307
Sign, Pennzoil, Tin, 3 Colors, Embossed Lettering, Vertical, Wood Frame, 57 ½ x 10 x 1 In. 2034
Sign, Polarine Motor Oil, The Perfect Motor Oil, Triangle, Red, White, 28 x 60 In. 625
Sign, Red Indian Motor Oils, Rack, Enamel, Red, White, 21 x 14 In. 1020
Sign, Refiners, Pioneer Distributors, Enamel, Ethyl Gasoline Corp., Round, 30 In. 978
Sign, Richfield Ethyl, 1920s Style, Glass Globe, White Ground, Red Text, 2-Sided, 16 In. 59

Auto, Figure, Fisk Tires, Time To Retire Boy, Fiberglass, Holding Tire, 84 x 64 In.
$4,200

Morphy Auctions

Auto, Gas Pump Globe, Lion Oil, Milk Glass, Red, Black, White, 2-Sided, 16 ½ x 13 ½ In.
$1,130

Soulis Auctions

Auto, Gas Pump Globe, Shell, Clamshell Lens, Metal Body, Yellow, White, 15 In.
$2,700

Morphy Auctions

Auto, Gas Pump, Bowser Phillips 66, Buckeye Brass Nozzle, Metal Face Plate, 73 x 26 In.
$1,140

Rich Penn Auctions

Auto, Gas Pump, Gulf Diesel, Logo Plate, Porcelain Face, Nozzle & Hose, 22 x 16 x 52 In.
$900

Alderfer Auction Company

Auto, Gas Pump, Johnson Gasolene, Tokheim 300, Hose, Nozzle, Orange, Black, 58 In.
$1,680

Morphy Auctions

Auto, Hood Ornament, Pegasus, Stover Racine, Emory P. Seidel, 5 ½ x 7 x 2 ½ In.
$424

Fontaine's Auction Gallery

Auto, Lantern, Neverout, Red Lenses, Brass, Applied Handle, Early 1900s, 9 In.
$168

Milestone Auctions

Auto, License Plate, Maine, 8113, Mounted, Holes, 1915, 14 ½ x 5 ½ In.
$132

Milestone Auctions

Auto, Parking Meter, Stand, Silver & Black, Round Top & Base, Duncan Industries, 51 In.
$168

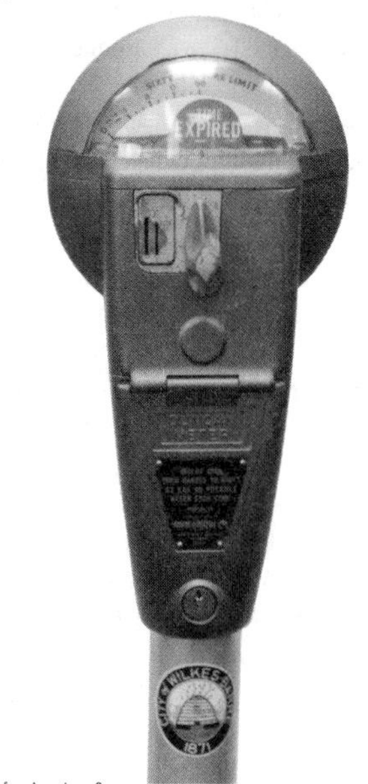

Alderfer Auction Company

Auto, Rack, Map, Shell, Road Maps, Wood, Tin, Yellow, 20 x 13 In.
$960

Morphy Auctions

Auto, Radiator, Ford, Model T, Brass, Made In USA, 25 x 23 ½ In.
$240

Rich Penn Auctions

Auto, Sign, Chicago Motor Club, Roof Top, Glass Panel, Metal Bracket, 2-Sided, 14 x 7 ½ In.
$3,120

Milestone Auctions

Auto, Sign, Edison Mazda Lamps, Tin Over Cardboard, Woman, Lightbulbs, 22 x 11 In.
$450

Milestone Auctions

Auto, Sign, Exxon, Mobil Dealer, Hanging, Mounted, Bracket, 2-Sided, 52 x 2 x 32 In.
$240

Alderfer Auction Company

The Famous Rolls
The Rolls-Royce automobile was created by Charles Stewart Rolls (1877–1910) and Frederick Henry Royce (1863–1933) in 1903. Mr. Rolls died when his airplane fell apart in mid-air.

Auto, Sign, Gas, 17 Cents, Oil, 2-Sided, Reverse Painted, Light-Up, Wood Frame, 21 x 19 x 7 In.
$363

Fontaine's Auction Gallery

Auto, Sign, Goodyear Balloon Tires, Tire Around Globe, Enamel, 1930s, 40 x 46 In.
$880

Brinkman Auctions

Auto, Sign, Kelly Tires, Kelly Girl Logo, Tin, 1930s, 42 x 30 ½ In.
$5,610

Brinkman Auctions

Auto, Sign, OK Tires, Die Cut, Attendant With Logos, Tin, 1960s, 60 x 37 In.
$715

Brinkman Auctions

Auto, Steering Wheel, Sports Car, Mahogany, Aluminum, Engraved, Signed, Nardi, 15 In.
$439

Thomaston Place Auction Galleries

Auto, Traffic Light, 4-Way Intersection, 13 Lenses, Yellow Painted, Hanger, 53 In.
$840

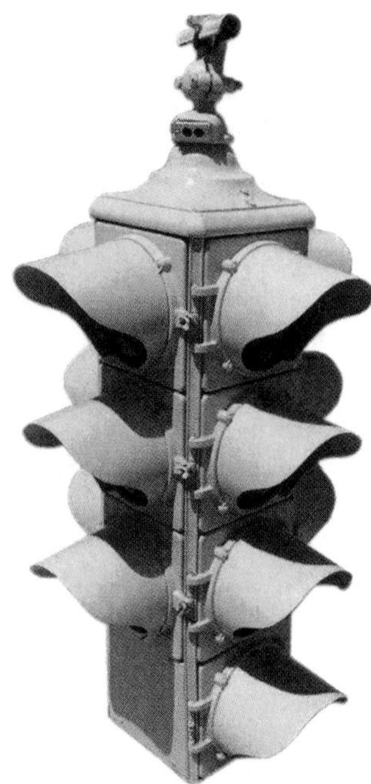

Milestone Auctions

Baccarat, Box, Diamond Point, Hinged Lid, Brass Mounted, 4 x 3 x 3 In.
$416

Neal Auction Company

Baccarat, Box, Green Cut To Clear, Hinged Lid, Tooled Brass Mounts, 4 ½ x 5 ½ In.
$960

Neal Auction Company

Baccarat, Caviar Dish, Flared, Silver Mount, Glass Insert, Acid Stamp, 6 ¾ In.
$185

Stair Galleries

Baccarat, Goblet, Tsar, Cobalt Cut To Clear, Diamond & Palm Leaf, Ring Stem, Signed, 14 In.
$1,840

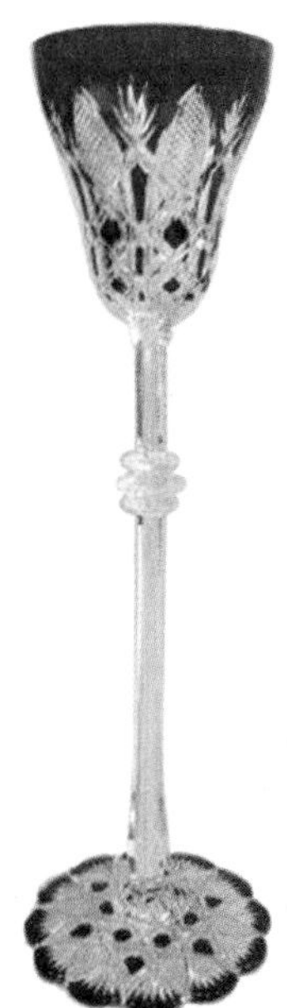

Richard D. Hatch & Associates

Baccarat, Knife Rest, Frosted Figural Babies' Heads At Ends, 2 x 3 ⅞ In., Pair
$117

Jeffrey S. Evans & Associates

Sign, Richfield, Ethyl, Enamel, Lollipop Shape, 62 x 28 In. 4200
Sign, Shell, Ladies, Die Cut, Orange, Red Text, Border, Enamel, 2 ½ x 10 ¾ In. 450
Sign, Simpson Premium Products, Super A, Red, Blue, White, 54 x 120 In. 1062
Sign, Sinclair Opaline Motor Oils, Porcelain, Vertical, White, Red, 60 x 15 In. 1920
Sign, Station, Gulf, Molded Plastic, Metal, Light-Up, 28 In. 360
Sign, Texaco, Red Border, 2-Sided Porcelain, 54 x 87 In. 1250
Sign, White Swan Service Station, Nothing Wrong There, Woman, Man, Dog, Car, Frame, 11 x 13 In. 192
Sign, Winstun Gasoline & Motor Oils, Porcelain, Red, Blue, White, Round, 23 ½ In. 2160
Spotlight, Bennett & Morse Pathfinder, Applied Back Handle, Early 1900s, 10 In. 168
Steering Wheel, Sports Car, Mahogany, Aluminum, Engraved, Signed, Nardi, 15 In. *illus* 439
Tire Cover, Ford, Spare, 15-Inch Section, Orange Peel In Paint, 26 x 28 In. 180
Tire Cover, Tone's Old Golden Coffee, High Vacuum Container, Conserves Flavor, 28 In. 509
Tire Meter, Eco, Model 38, Clock Face, Metal, 54 x 9 In. 1800
Tire Pump, Eco Tireflator, Wall Mount Bracket, Light-Up, Electric, Bennett 1080
Traffic Light, 4-Way Intersection, 13 Lenses, Yellow Painted, Hanger, 53 In. *illus* 840
Traffic Light, 3 Lights, Hanging, Yellow Paint, Embossed, Econolight, 10 x 14 x 38 In. 144
Traffic Light, Electric, 3 Lenses, Metal Case, Green, Yellow, Red, 36 In. 246
Traffic Light, Red, Yellow, Green, Cast Iron, Green Paint, Eagle Signal Corp., 75 x 16 In. 1320
Window Display, Chevrolet, Tie Lights Up, Neon, Metal Frame, 1939, 20 x 15 In. 570

AUTUMN LEAF

Autumn Leaf pattern china was made for the Jewel Tea Company beginning in 1933. Hall China Company of East Liverpool, Ohio, Crooksville China Company of Crooksville, Ohio, Harker Potteries of Chester, West Virginia, and Paden City Pottery, Paden City, West Virginia, made dishes with this design. Autumn Leaf has remained popular and was made by Hall China Company until 1978. Some other pieces in the Autumn Leaf pattern are still being made. For more prices, go to kovels.com.

Butter, Cover, 1960s 29
Cake Plate, Pedestal, 9 ½ In. 65
Casserole, Stackette Set, Lid, 1950s, 8 ½ x 7 ⅞ In. 95
Dutch Oven, c.1935, 5 x 8 In. 40
Pitcher, Handle, Gold Trim, 5 ¾ In. 26
Plate, Silver Trim, 9 In., 4 Piece 37

AVON *bottles are listed in the Bottle category under Avon.*

AZALEA

Azalea dinnerware was made for Larkin Company customers from about 1915 to 1941. Larkin, the soap company, was in Buffalo, New York. The dishes were made by Noritake China Company of Japan. Each piece of the white china was decorated with pink azaleas.

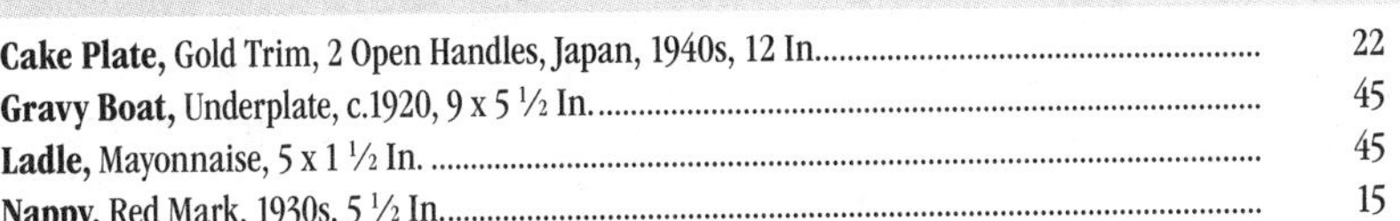

Cake Plate, Gold Trim, 2 Open Handles, Japan, 1940s, 12 In. 22
Gravy Boat, Underplate, c.1920, 9 x 5 ½ In. 45
Ladle, Mayonnaise, 5 x 1 ½ In. 45
Nappy, Red Mark, 1930s, 5 ½ In. 15

BACCARAT

Baccarat glass was made in France by La Compagnie des Cristalleries de Baccarat, located 150 miles from Paris. The factory was started in 1765. The firm went bankrupt and began operating again about 1822. Cane and millefiori paperweights were made during the 1845 to 1880 period. The firm is still working near Paris making paperweights and glasswares.

Bowl, Gilt, Bronze Mounted, Crystal, Handle, Late 1800s, 12 x 14 ½ x 11 ½ In. 600

Baccarat, Paperweight, Clear, Cut Face, Mushroom, Blue, Opal Torsade, Millefiori, France, 1800s, 2 ⅝ In.
$527

Jeffrey S. Evans & Associates

Baccarat, Paperweight, Gridel, Moth Cane, Silhouettes, Horse, Goat, Elephant, Rooster, 1848, 3 In.
$1,020

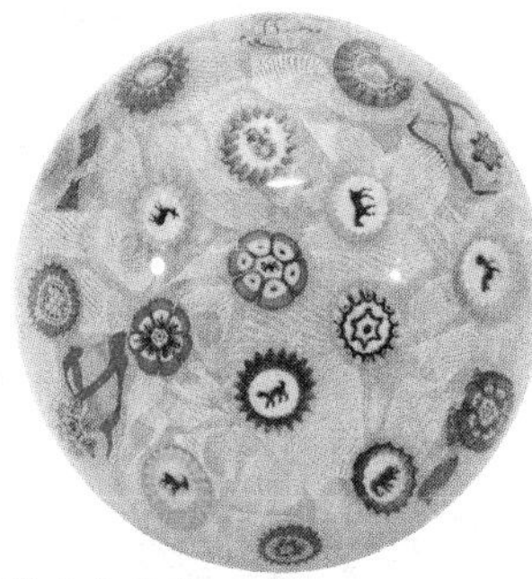

Alderfer Auction Company

TIP
Install motion detector lights to guard your yard at night.

Baccarat, Vase, Edo, Etched Peonies, Rectangular, Kenzo Takada, 12 ¾ x 10 x 8 In.
$1,750

Abington Auction Gallery

Bank, Bulldog, Seated, Tin, Cream Ground, Saalheimer & Strauss, 5 x 3 x 2 In.
$3,000

Morphy Auctions

Bank, Cadet, Blue Uniform, Holding Sword, Cast Iron, Hubley, 5 ½ In.
$100

Bertoia Auctions

Bank, Dutch Boy, Seated On Crate, Spelter, 4 ½ In.
$1,300

Bertoia Auctions

Bowl, Glass, Wave-Like Lines, Swirl Effect, Janson, 7 x 15 ¾ In. 625
Box, Diamond Point, Hinged Lid, Brass Mounted, 4 x 3 x 3 In. ....*illus* 416
Box, Glass & Bronze, Floral Swags, Beveled, Lift-Off Lid, Oval, 6 x 8 In. 460
Box, Green Cut To Clear, Hinged Lid, Tooled Brass Mounts, 4 ½ x 5 ½ In. ....*illus* 960
Candlestick, Glass, Clear, Sculptural, Castor & Pollux, Salvador Dali, c.1970, 11 ½ In., Pair... 492
Caviar Dish, Flared, Silver Mount, Glass Insert, Acid Stamp, 6 ¾ In. ....*illus* 185
Decanter, Harmonie, Stopper, Marked, Logo, 12 ½ x 3 ½ In. 303
Figurine, Angel, Hands Clasped To Her Chest, Signed, France, 6 x 3 x 2 In. 112
Figurine, Giraffe, Lying Down, Clear, 4 ½ In. 150
Figurine, Panther, Crouching, Black, Etched Circular Logo, 10 x 3 x 3 ½ In. 395
Goblet, Tsar, Cobalt Cut To Clear, Diamond & Palm Leaf, Ring Stem, Signed, 14 In. ....*illus* 1840
Ice Bucket, Ribbed, Cylindrical, 2 Handles, Screwed On, 9 In. 388
Knife Rest, Frosted Figural Babies' Heads At Ends, 2 x 3 ⅞ In., Pair ....*illus* 117
Lamp Base, Etched Flowers, Pink & Frosted, 13 ¾ x 4 ½ In., Pair 263
Paperweight, Clear, Cut Face, Mushroom, Blue, Opal Torsade, Millefiori, France, 1800s, 2 ⅝ In. .. *illus* 527
Paperweight, Figurine, Pig, 5 ½ In. 118
Paperweight, Garland, Millefiori, Arrowhead Cane, Green & Red Star Cane, 1800s, 3 In. 1500
Paperweight, Gridel, Moth Cane, Silhouettes, Horse, Goat, Elephant, Rooster, 1848, 3 In. .. *illus* 1020
Perfume Bottle, Opaque, Pink, Brass Top, 4 ½ In. 120
Punch Bowl, Swirl Design, Molded, Undertray, Early 1900s, 6 x 12 x 19 ⅜ In. 400
Sherbet, Harcourt, Cut Panel, Gold Rim, Stem, Footed, 5 x 3 ¾ In., 10 Piece 750
Tumbler, Old Fashioned, Michelangelo, Etched Scrolls, France, 1950s, 4 x 4 In., 10 Piece 510
Vase, Cut, Gold Enamel Leaves, 19 x 5 In. 375
Vase, Edo, Etched Peonies, Rectangular, Kenzo Takada, 12 ¾ x 10 x 8 In. ....*illus* 1750

BADGES

Badges have been used since before the Civil War. Collectors search for examples of all types, including law enforcement and company identification badges. Well-known prison or law enforcement badges are most desirable. Most are made of nickel or brass. Many recent reproductions have been made.

Burns International Security Services Inc., Captain, Gold Metal, Pinback, 2 x 2 In. 30
Chauffeur, Minnesota, State Seal, 1941, 2 In. Diam. 38
Employee, Republic Steel, Buffalo, N.Y., Art Deco, 2 In. 44
Fire, Walsenburg, Colorado, 2 In. 95
Greyhound Bus Lines, Leave The Driving To Us, Pinback, 1960s, 2 ¾ x 2 ½ In. 125
Mexico Federal Police, Brass, Star Shape, 3 x 3 In. 109
Police, City Of New York, Excelsior, 2 ½ x 2 ¼ In. 249
Police, Pittston, Nickel, c.1910, 2 ½ x 2 ½ In. 345
Reading Co., Railway Police, 1930s, 2 ½ In. 275
Security, Wells Fargo Services, Brass, Copper, Enamel, 3 x 2 In. 50
Taxi Driver, 1408, Buffalo, N.Y., c.1950, 2 x 1 ½ In. 65
Teamsters, A.F. Of L., Steward, Brass, 1950s, 1 ¾ x 1 ½ In. 20
Texas Ranger, Co. A, Star, Sterling Silver, 1 ¼ In. 55

BANKS

Banks of metal have been made since 1868. There are still banks, mechanical banks, and registering banks (those that show the total money deposited on the face of the bank). Many old iron or tin banks have been reproduced since the 1950s in iron or plastic. Some old reproductions marked *Book of Knowledge, John Wright*, or *Capron* may be listed. Pottery, glass, and plastic banks are also listed here. Mickey Mouse and other Disneyana banks are listed in Disneyana.

Baseball & 3 Bats, Official League Ball, Silver Ball, Red Bats, Cast Iron, Hubley, 5 In. 1320
Baseball Player, Holds Bat, Painted, Cast Iron, A.C. Williams, 5 ½ In. 390
Basket, World's Fair Columbian, 1492-1892, Cast Iron, Woven, 4 In. 510
Battleship, Maine, White Paint, Cast Iron, J. & E. Stevens, 10 In. 3900
Bear & Honey Pot, Hubley, 6 ½ In. 210

B

Bear On Hind Legs, Cast Iron, John Harper, 6 In. 150
Building, Bank, Equitable Savings & Loan, Cast Iron, 11 x 8 x 6 In. 600
Building, Bank, Pearl Street Bank, 4 Story, Silver Paint, Cast Iron, 4 ½ In. 300
Building, Bank, State Bank, Arched Double Doors & Windows, 3 Steps, Cast Iron, 6 In. 100
Building, Bank, State Bank, Arched Front Door Opens, Cast Iron, Kenton, c.1900, 8 In. 780
Building, Bungalow, Cottage With Porch, Cast Iron, Grey Iron Casting, c.1920, 3 ½ In. 210
Building, Church, Yellow, Orange Door, Green Roof, Cast Iron, Kyser & Rex, 1882, 5 ½ In. 4200
Building, House With Bay Windows, 3 Trefoils In Peak, Painted, Stepped Base, 5 ½ In. 5100
Building, House With Bay Windows, Cast Iron, 4 In. 7800
Building, Palace, Center Steeple, 2 Chimneys, Gold Trim, Cast Iron, Ives, 8 In. 660
Building, Palace, Gold Trim, Cast Iron, Ives, c.1885, 7 ½ x 8 In. 5400
Building, Palace, Spire, Stairs To Balcony, Painted Red Brick, Ives, c.1885, 8 x 8 In. 760
Building, Tabernacle, Salt Lake City, Utah, Oval, Electroplated, Keyless Lock Co., 5 In. 480
Building, Villa, Church, Kyser & Rex, Gold Trim, Cast Iron, 1882, 6 In. 153
Bulldog, Seated, Tin, Cream Ground, Saalheimer & Strauss, 5 x 3 x 2 In. *illus* 3000
Cadet, Blue Uniform, Holding Sword, Cast Iron, Hubley, 5 ½ In. *illus* 100
Clock With Movable Hands, Incised Greek Key & Scrolls, Cast Iron, Judd, c.1890, 5 ½ In. 540
Clock, Cast Iron, Red Paint, Fluted Column, Gilt Face, Dent, Early 1900s, 6 x 2 ¾ In. 254
Cow, Red, Cast Iron, A.C. Williams, c.1920, 5 ½ In. 420
Devil, 2 Faces, Red Paint, Cast Iron, A.C. Williams, 4 In. 1680
Doghouse, Ornate, Chained Dog, Silver, Germany, 1859, 3 ¾ In. 240
Duck, Green Paint, Red Speckled Head, Round, Squat, Cast Iron, Kenton, 5 In. 840
Dutch Boy, Seated On Crate, Spelter, 4 ½ In. *illus* 1300
Electric Railroad Car, Conductor At End, Cast Iron, Shimer, c.1893, 8 In. 1680
Fish, Glass Eyes, Key, Trap, Cast Lead, 2 x 5 x 1 ¾ In. *illus* 570
Hippo, Cast Iron, 5 ½ In. 4800
Indian Family, 3 Busts, Man, Woman, Child, Harper, 1905, 6 In. 1080
Indian, 2 Faces, Yellow Feather Headdress, Cast Iron, A.C. Williams, 4 ½ In. 1440
Indian, Old Honesty, 5 Cent, Square Base, Painted, 13 ½ In. *illus* 1560
Indiana Silo, Anderson, Ind., 3 ½ x 2 In. 900
Key, Golden Brown, Cast Iron, William J. Somerville, 1905, 5 ½ In. 390
Mammy, Red Handkerchief, White Apron, Wooden Spoon, c.1910 546

Mechanical banks were first made about 1870. Any bank with moving parts is considered mechanical. The metal banks made before World War I are the most desirable. Copies and new designs of mechanical banks have been made in metal or plastic since the 1920s. The condition of the paint on the old banks is important. Worn paint can lower a price by 90 percent.

Mechanical, Artillery, Officer, Cast Iron, J. & E. Stevens, c.1892, 6 x 8 ¾ In. *illus* 660
Mechanical, Bad Accident, Green, Red, Blue, Yellow, Cast Iron, J. & E. Stevens, 1875, 6 ½ x 10 In. 540
Mechanical, Bird On Roof, Cast Iron, J. & E. Stevens, 4 ¾ x 3 ½ x 6 In. 1080
Mechanical, Bonzo, Verse, Saalheimer & Strauss, 1920s, 7 In. *illus* 1100
Mechanical, Chief Big Moon, Cast Iron, J. & E. Stevens, 1875, 6 x 9 ½ In. 1200
Mechanical, Circus Ticket Collector, Black Coat, Barrel, Salafian Brothers, 1930s *illus* 900
Mechanical, Clown On Globe, Yellow Base, J. & E. Stevens 720
Mechanical, Creedmoor, Soldier Shooting Rifle, Cast Iron, J. & E. Stevens, c.1877, 6 ½ x 10 In. 300
Mechanical, Eagle & Eaglets, Cast Iron, J. & E. Stevens, 6 In. *illus* 413
Mechanical, Frog On Round Base, Lattice, Gold, Black, Cast Iron, J. & E. Stevens, 1880s, 4 x 4 ½ In. 344
Mechanical, Frogs, Two, Grass Base, Green, Cast Iron, J. & E. Stevens, 8 ½ x 3 x 4 In. 738 to 1140
Mechanical, I Always Did 'Spise A Mule, Jockey, Red Base, Cast Iron, J. & E. Stevens, c.1890, 8 x 10 In. 702
Mechanical, Indian Shooting Bear, J. & E. Stevens, Cromwell, c.1907, 10 In. 1711
Mechanical, Jonah & The Whale, Cast Iron, Shepard Hardware, c.1890, 5 x 10 In. *illus* 660
Mechanical, Magic Bank, Cashier Behind Door, Painted, CastIron, J. & E. Stevens 390
Mechanical, Magician, Red Table, Stepped Base, Painted, Cast Iron, 8 In. *illus* 1599
Mechanical, Mary Roebling, Trenton Trust, 75th Anniversary, Grey Iron Casting 1140
Mechanical, Mason, 2 Workers, Build Red Brick Wall, Shepard Hardware 1320
Mechanical, Mosque, Goldtone, Onion Dome, Finial, Square Base, H.L. Judd, 1880s 510
Mechanical, Organ Grinder, Bear, House, Fence, Cast Iron, Kyser & Rex, c. 1890, 5 ½ x 4 ¾ In. 4980
Mechanical, Organ, Monkey, Dog, Cat, Cast Iron, Kyser & Rex, 1882, 8 x 5 ½ x 4 In. *illus* 270

Bank, Fish, Glass Eyes, Key, Trap, Cast Lead, 2 x 5 x 1 ¾ In.
$570

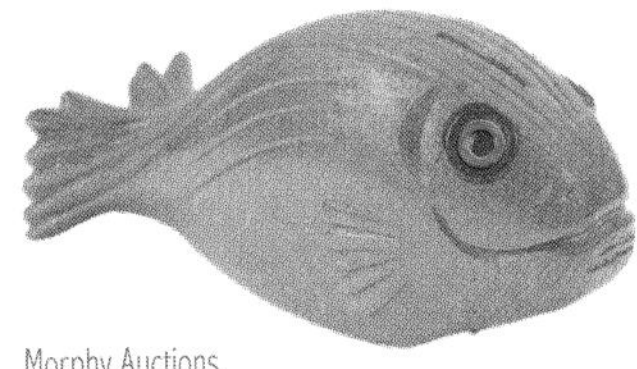

Morphy Auctions

Bank, Indian, Old Honesty, 5 Cent, Square Base, Painted, 13 ½ In.
$1,560

Rich Penn Auctions

Bank, Mechanical, Artillery, Officer, Cast Iron, J. & E. Stevens, c.1892, 6 x 8 ¾ In.
$660

Eldred's

TIP
Never repaint an old bank. It lowers the resale value.

Bank, Mechanical, Bonzo, Verse, Saalheimer & Strauss, 1920s, 7 In.
$1,100

Bertoia Auctions

Bank, Mechanical, Circus Ticket Collector, Black Coat, Barrel, Salafian Brothers, 1930s
$900

Milestone Auctions

Bank, Mechanical, Eagle & Eaglets, Cast Iron, J. & E. Stevens, 6 In.
$413

Copake Auctions

Bank, Mechanical, Jonah & The Whale, Cast Iron, Shepard Hardware, c.1890, 5 x 10 In.
$660

Alderfer Auction Company

Bank, Mechanical, Magician, Red Table, Stepped Base, Painted, Cast Iron, 8 In.
$1,599

Richard Opfer Auctioneering, Inc.

Bank, Mechanical, Organ, Monkey, Dog, Cat, Cast Iron, Mechanical, Crank, Kyser & Rex, 1882, 8 x 5 ½ x 4 In.
$270

CRN Auctions

Bank, Mechanical, Owl, Turns Head, Cast Iron, Painted, 7 ½ In.
$461

Richard Opfer Auctioneering, Inc.

Bank, Mechanical, Paddy & The Pig, Cast Iron, Original Paint, J. & E. Stevens, c.1882, 8 ½ x 7 In.
$406

Eldred's

Bank, Mechanical, Rabbit, Standing, Ball, Cast Iron, Novelty Works, c.1880, 5 ¾ In.
$420

Eldred's

Bank, Mechanical, Trick Dog, Shepard Hardware, c.1888
$500

Bertoia Auctions

Bank, Three Little Pigs House, Big Bad Wolf, Tin, Orange Roof, Red Chimney, Chein, 3 In.
$132

Milestone Auctions

Bank, Yellow Cab, Orange, Black, White Tires, Cast Iron, Arcade, 4 x 8 In.
$360

Rich Penn Auctions

Barber, Cabinet, Shaving Mug, Oak, Glass Door, 36 Spaces, Drawer, c.1900, 80 x 41 x 23 In.
$600

Garth's Auctioneers & Appraisers

Barber, Chair, Chrome, Metallic Gold Vinyl, Armrest, Koken, 51 In.
$492

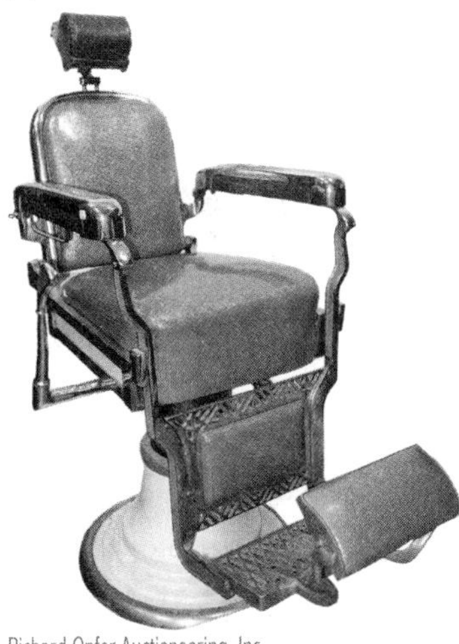

Richard Opfer Auctioneering, Inc.

Barber, Chair, White Porcelain, Leather, Koken, 48 ½ x 27 x 40 In.
$840

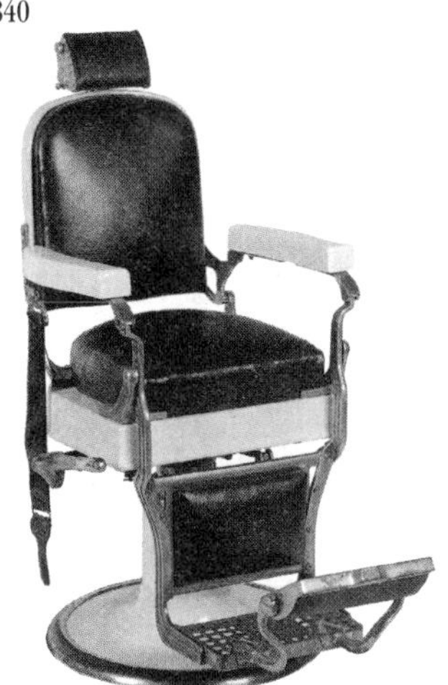

Morphy Auctions

Barber, Pole, Glass Cylinder, Red, White & Blue Stripes, Matte Aluminum Caps, Electric, 26 x 19 In.
$240

Witherell's

Barber, Pole, Iron, Painted, Enamel, Glass Cylinder, Globe Finial, James Barker Inc., c.1930, 42 In.
$2,925

Thomaston Place Auction Galleries

Barber, Pole, Translucent Glass Dome, Red, White & Blue Stripes, Mounted, c.1900, 31 x 8 In.
$246

Skinner, Inc.

Barber, Pole, Wood, Turned, Painted, Red, White, Cannonball Finial, 1800, 54 In.
$266

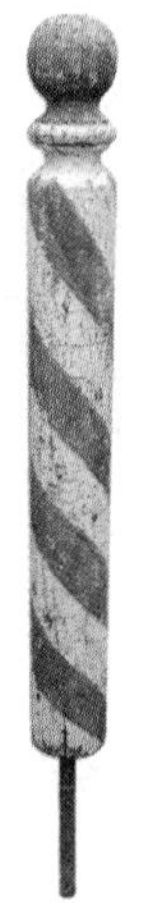

Copake Auctions

Barber, Sink, Porcelain Over Cast Iron, Round Bowls, Reeded Pedestal Base, 46 x 24 x 23 In., Pair
$847

Fontaine's Auction Gallery

Barber, Towel Sterilizer, Sun, Copper Dome, Access Hatch, Interior Holder, Early 1900s, 59 In.
$1,408

Cowan's Auctions

Barometer, Thermometer, Sheraton, Inlaid Shells, Round Face, England, c.1700, 38 x 10 In.
$115

Selkirk Auctioneers & Appraisers

Barometer, Wheel, Crosta Gobbi & Co., Rosewood, Inlaid, Silvered Dial, Engraved, 43 In.
$545

Fontaine's Auction Gallery

Basket, Berry, Woven, Pinched Handle, 1800s, 10 ½ In.
$1,830

Pook & Pook

Mechanical, Owl, Perched, Cast Iron, Orange & Yellow Paint, Vindex, c.1930, 4 In. 420
Mechanical, Owl, Turns Head, Cast Iron, Painted, 7 ½ In. .... *illus* 461
Mechanical, Owl, Turns Head, White Owl, On Branch, J. & E. Stevens.......... 3000
Mechanical, Paddy & The Pig, Cast Iron, Original Paint, J. & E. Stevens, c.1882, 8 ½ x 7 In. ...*illus* 406
Mechanical, Presto, Cast Iron, Ball Finial, Painted, 4 ½ In. 185
Mechanical, Rabbit In Cabbage, Ears Rise, Painted, Cast Iron, Kilgore.......... 840
Mechanical, Rabbit, Standing, Ball, Cast Iron, Novelty Works, c.1880, 5 ¾ In. .... *illus* 420
Mechanical, Rooster, Coin In Tail, Head Moves, Kyser & Rex, 1880-90.......... 2040
Mechanical, Rooster, Red & Black, Cast Iron, Kyser & Rex, 6 x 5 ½ x 2 ½ In. 720
Mechanical, Southern Comfort, Man Shooting Bottle, Cast Iron, 8 ½ In. 192
Mechanical, Speaking Dog, Cast Iron, Shepard Hardware, Buffalo, 1885, 6 ½ x 7 In. 330
Mechanical, Tammany, Boss Tweed, Cast Iron, J. & E. Stevens, 1873, 6 x 3 ½ x 4 In. 703
Mechanical, Teddy & The Bear, Painted, Cast Iron, J. & E. Stevens 1020
Mechanical, Trick Dog, Shepard Hardware, c.1888.......... *illus* 500
Mechanical, Trick Pony, Painted, Rectangular Base, Cast Iron, 8 In. 615
Mechanical, Uncle Remus, Cast Iron, Kyser & Rex, 4 x 5 ½ x 3 ½ In. 390
Mechanical, William Tell, Cast Iron, J. & E. Stevens, Late 1800s, 7 x 10 ½ In. 450
Minuteman, Holds Rifle, Brown Paint, Cast Iron, Hubley, 6 In. 420
Radio, Crosley, Arched, Cast Iron, Electroplated, Kenton, 1931, 4 ½ In. 300
Red Goose School Shoes, Goose, Cast Iron, Red, Black, A.C. Williams, 1915, 4 In. 390
Register, Cash Register, Junior, Scrolls, Crosshatched Top, J. & E. Stevens, 4 In. 360
Register, Dime, Airplane, Keep 'Em Flying, Tin, 8-Sided, 2 ½ In. 150
Register, Mosque, Onion Dome Turns, Kyser & Rex, 1890 1200
Register, Penny, Bucket, Hinged Handle, Gold-Painted Bands, Cast Iron, Kyser & Rex, 3 In. 120
Safe, Arched Door, Filigree, Cast Iron, Kyser & Rex, 4 ½ In. 240
Safe, Globe, Hinged Door, Copper Flashed, 3 Ball & Claw Feet, Kenton, 5 ½ In. 1140
Safe, Japanese, Embossed Dragon, Trees, 2 Interior Drawers, Key, Cast Iron, 5 ½ In. 135
Safe, National, 2 Doors, Front Dial, American Eagle, Cast Iron, 5 ¾ x 4 x 3 ¾ In. 311
Safe, Old Homestead, Combination Lock On Door, Cast Iron, Shimer, 4 ½ In. 660
Sundial, Fluted Pedestal Base, Cast Iron, Yellow Paint, Arcade, 4 ½ In. 1320
Three Little Pigs House, Big Bad Wolf, Tin, Orange Roof, Red Chimney, Chein, 3 In. ....*illus* 132
Turkey, Brown, Red Head & Neck, Cast Iron, A.C. Williams, 4 ½ In. 300
Water Wagon, Train Car, Tank, 4 Wheels, 5 In. 2280
Yellow Cab, Orange, Black, White Tires, Cast Iron, Arcade, 4 x 8 In. .... *illus* 360

BARBER

Barber collectibles range from the popular red and white striped pole that used to be found in front of every shop to the small scissors and tools of the trade. Barber chairs are wanted, especially the older models with elaborate iron trim.

Cabinet, Shaving Mug, Oak, Glass Door, 36 Spaces, Drawer, c.1900, 80 x 41 x 23 In. ....*illus* 600
Chair, Child, Copper, Cast Iron, Red Upholstered Seat, Twisted Wire Legs, 1910s, 40 ½ In. 396
Chair, Chrome, Metallic Gold Vinyl, Armrest, Koken, 51 In. .... *illus* 492
Chair, White Porcelain, Leather, Koken, 48 ½ x 27 x 40 In. .... *illus* 840
Pole, Glass Cylinder, Red, White & Blue Stripes, Matte Aluminum Caps, Electric, 26 x 19 In. *illus* 240
Pole, Iron, Painted, Enamel, Glass Cylinder, Globe Finial, James Barker Inc., c.1930, 42 In. ..*illus* 2925
Pole, Lamp, Red, White & Blue Paint, Electrified, Cast Iron Base, Late 1900s, 54 In. 138
Pole, Red, White, Blue, Gilt Finial, Iron Bracket, Early 1900s, 86 In. 3240
Pole, Red, White, Central Blue Stripe, Gold Cannonball Finial, Black Base, c.1900, 62 In. 1989
Pole, Shave & Haircut, 25 Cents, Porcelain, Cast Iron, Orange, Red, Black, 42 x 18 x 16 In. 1140
Pole, Translucent Glass Dome, Red, White & Blue Stripes, Mounted, c.1900, 31 x 8 In. ....*illus* 246
Pole, Wood, Turned, Painted, Ball Finial, Medial Rings, Red, White, Blue, c.1880, 77 In. 1180
Pole, Wood, Turned, Painted, Red, White & Blue, Gilt Ball Top, Mounted, c.1930, 90 ½ In. 1440
Pole, Wood, Turned, Painted, Red, White, Blue, c.1900, 60 ½ In. 3281
Pole, Wood, Turned, Painted, Red, White, Cannonball Finial, 1800, 54 In. .... *illus* 266
Rack, Mug, Pine, Finials On Top, 6 Open Shelves, Brass Rods, 1910s, 46 x 85 x 8 In. 300
Sink, Porcelain Over Cast Iron, Round Bowls, Reeded Pedestal Base, 46 x 24 x 23 In., Pair .*illus* 847
Towel Sterilizer, Sun, Copper Dome, Access Hatch, Interior Holder, Early 1900s, 59 In. .*illus* 1408

Lightship Nantucket Baskets

Most people are familiar with Nantucket baskets made by crew members who worked on lightships (boats that served as floating lighthouses) off the coast of Nantucket. The most valuable baskets were made in the late 19th century by a known designer, have a unique shape, and are in great condition.

Basket, Buttocks, Splint, Woven, Arched Wood Handle, Red, 1800s, 7 x 13 ½ In.
$308

Skinner, Inc.

Basket, Gathering, Woven, Footed, Round, Brown, 1900s, 9 ½ x 23 In.
$88

Eldred's

Basket, Market, White Oak, Split, Red Dye, 2 Lock Handle, Signed Bessie Long, 18 x 21 x 13 In.
$500

Brunk Auctions

Basket, Nantucket, Round, Turned Wood Base, Incised, Diane Webb Mackey, 1990, 3 x 8 In.
$240

Eldred's

TIP
Splint baskets should have an occasional light shower. Shake off the excess water. Dry the basket in a shady spot.

Basket, Nantucket, Straight-Sided, Swing Arm, Signed, 1900s, 3 In.
$461

Skinner, Inc.

Basket, Oval, Reed, Woven, 2 Handles, Wood Frame, 25 ½ In.
$53

Thomaston Place Auction Galleries

BAROMETER

Barometers are used to forecast the weather. Antique barometers with elaborate wooden cases and brass trim are the most desirable. Mercury column barometers are also popular with collectors. It is difficult to find someone to repair a broken one, so be sure your barometer is in working condition.

Banjo, Ebonized Wood, Carved, Turned, Arched Top, Drop Finials, Belgium, 1900, 18 In. 15239
Banjo, George III, Mahogany, Inlaid, Hygrometer, Convex Mirror, Early 1800s, 38 x 9 In. 350
Banjo, Mahogany, Bronze Rooster, Thermometer, Levasseur, France, 1800s, 39 x 11 In. 400
Banjo, Mahogany, Silvered Dials, Thermometer, J. Curotti, England, c.1880, 39 In. 1385
Banjo, Oak, Porcelain Dial, Leafy Scrolls, Aneroid Thermometer, Victorian, c.1890, 35 x 11 In. . 240
Black Forest, Wood, Carved, Thermometer, Leaves, 18 x 9 ½ In. 207
Giltwood, 2 Cherubs, Dial Marked, Ecoffier Opticien Toulouse, Late 1800s, 38 x 21 x 8 In. 600
Stick, J. Hicks, Oak Case, Central Thermometer, London, c.1900s, 35 ½ In. 300
Stick, Mahogany Veneer, Pine Case, Label Barometer Paris, Maal, England, 1800s, 37 In. 175
Stick, Marine, Eimer & Amend, New York, 42 x 4 In. 148
Stick, Rosewood, Mercury, Hygrometer, Brass Bezel & Gimbal, Hinged Door, 1800s, 37 ½ x 4 In. ... 1872
Stick, Spencer Browning & Co., Mahogany, Brass, Gimbal, Ivory Scale, England, 36 ½ In. 819
Thermometer, Carved Oak, Classical Details, American, Late 1800s, 36 In. 156
Thermometer, Louis XV, Green Enamel, Gilt Inlay, Ormolu, c.1880, 57 x 19 In. 1800
Thermometer, Sheraton, Inlaid Shells, Round Face, England, c.1700, 38 x 10 In. ....*illus* 115
Wheel, Crosta Gobbi & Co., Rosewood, Inlaid, Silvered Dial, Engraved, 43 In. ....*illus* 545
Wheel, Hardwood Case, Painted, Broken Arch Top, Steel Dial, Thermometer, 44 In. 132
Wheel, Jas. Field Hertford, Thermometer, Hygrometer, 38 In. 92

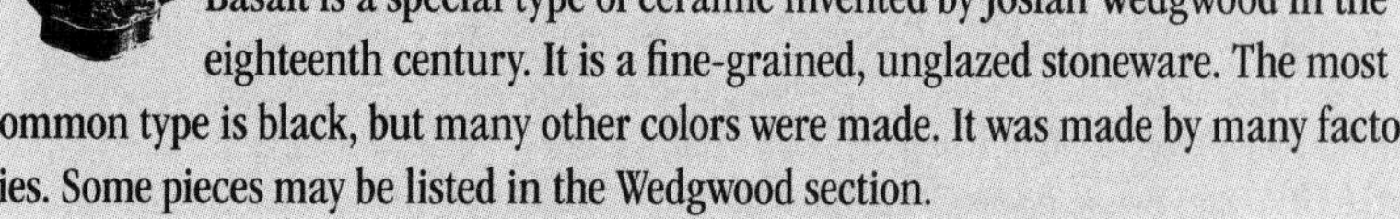

BASALT

Basalt is a special type of ceramic invented by Josiah Wedgwood in the eighteenth century. It is a fine-grained, unglazed stoneware. The most common type is black, but many other colors were made. It was made by many factories. Some pieces may be listed in the Wedgwood section.

Bust, Zingara, Black, Circular Socle, Bentley, c.1775, 7 ¾ In. 615
Cassolette, Black, Leaves, Molded Handles, Stepped Plinth, Wedgwood & Bentley, c.1775, 7 In. 923
Plaque, Roundel, 2 Classical Men, Flutes, Frame, Wedgwood & Bentley, c.1775, 14 ½ In. 5535
Vase, Black, Leopard Handles, Square Plinth, Wedgwood & Bentley, c.1775, 16 ⅝ In. 8610

BASEBALL *collectibles are in the Sports category. Baseball cards are listed under Baseball in the Card category.*

BASKET

Baskets of all types are popular with collectors. American Indian, Japanese, African, Nantucket, Shaker, and many other kinds of baskets may be found in other sections. Of course, baskets are still being made, so a collector must learn to judge the age and style of a basket to determine its value. Also see Purse.

Berry, Woven, Pinched Handle, 1800s, 10 ½ In. ....*illus* 1830
Buttocks, Red Body, Black Rim, Handle, Splint, Late 1800s, 6 ½ x 8 In. 1845
Buttocks, Splint, Woven, Arched Wood Handle, Red, 1800s, 7 x 13 ½ In. ....*illus* 308
Buttocks, Woven, Split Hickory, Bentwood Handle, Miniature, 1800s, 1 ½ x 1 In. 173
Buttocks, Woven, Wood Handle, Bent Hickory Handle, Half Eye Of God Binding, 9 x 8 In. 104
Carrying, Conical, Geometric Banded, Rawhide Strips Rim & Foot, c.1940, 11 x 15 In. 360
Double Top, Rectangular, 2 Hinged Lids, Bentwood Handle, Late 1800s, 5 x 8 x 4 ½ In. 135
Egg, White Oak, Rib Type, Woven Splint, Handle, Appalachian, 1950s, 9 ½ x 8 x 10 In. 322
Gathering, Oval, Woven Splint, 2 Handles, 9 x 23 x 16 In. 153
Gathering, Splint, Hand Holes, 1800s, 12 x 26 x 18 In. 59
Gathering, Woven, Bulbous Body, 2 Iron Handles, 12 In. 30
Gathering, Woven, Footed, Round, Brown, 1900s, 9 ½ x 23 In. ....*illus* 88
Hanging, Pine, Painted, Ocher Grain, Carved, Late 1800s, 22 x 15 ¾ In. 244

Basket, Rectangular, Blue Splints, Lid, Red, Yellow, Late 1800s, 9 ½ x 14 x 7 In.
$3,998

Skinner, Inc.

Basket, Woven, Shell, Round Top, 1800s, 4 x 9 ¾ In.
$1,440

Eldred's

Basket, Splint Feather, Lid, Apple Green Surface, Painted, 1800s, 34 In.
$3,416

Pook & Pook

Batman, Toy, Batmobile, Tin Lithograph, Blinking Light, Jet Engine Noise, Box, c.1967, 3 ¾ x 9 ¾ In.
$565

Soulis Auctions

Bauer, Ring, Cake Stand, Pedestal, Turquoise, 5 x 11 ¾ In.
$130

Strawser Auction Group

Bavaria, Plate, Amorosa, Portrait Center, Maroon & Gold Border, c.1920, 9 ¾ In.
$30

Woody Auctions

Basket, Splint, Picnic, Hinged Lid, Leather Handle, Painted, Late 1800s, 9 ½ x 13 x 8 ½ In.
$2,214

Skinner, Inc.

Beehive, Plaque, Woman, Classical Dress, Hand Painted, Gilt Frame, 22 x 15 x 22 In.
$1,210

Fontaine's Auction Gallery

Beehive, Urn, Lid, Pedestal, Painted, Young Woman Portrait, Red Ground, c.1910, 35 x 11 In.
$1,500

Woody Auctions

Beehive, Urn, Lid, Portrait, Lustrous Green Ground, Gold, Royal Vienna, Late 1800s, 20 ½ In.
$2,337

Skinner, Inc.

Key, Leather, Oval Shape, Arched Handle, Stitched, 1850s, 3 x 8 ½ In. 1112
Market, White Oak, Split, Red Dye, 2 Lock Handle, Signed Bessie Long, 18 x 21 x 13 In. ..*illus* 500
Melon, Round, Arched Handle, Leather Lining, 2 x 2 In. 2583
Nantucket Style, Swallow's Nest Shape, Swing Handle, Sherry Tinney, 1900s, 11 x 9 ¾ In. 125
Nantucket, Ebonized Carved Whale, Lid, Swing Handle, Jose Formoso Reyes, c.1940, 6 x 9 In. 3281
Nantucket, Egg, Swing Handle, Wood Base, Maureen Reed, 1983, 3 x 3 ¼ In. 439
Nantucket, Lid, Swing Handle, Carved, Mounted Seagull, Ebony Plaque, Stephen Gibbs, 11 In. 1800
Nantucket, Lightship, Stave, Wrapped Rim, Arched Swing Handle, c.1900, 10 x 4 ¾ x 10 In. ... 439
Nantucket, Oval, Lid, Swing Handle, Applied Seagull, Whalers Crafts, 1965, 8 ½ In. 780
Nantucket, Purse, Carved Gull Lid, Swing Handle, Signed Jose Reyes, 1940s, 6 In. 1968
Nantucket, Purse, Wood Handle, Farnum, 1978, 10 x 6 ½ x 6 ½ In. 130
Nantucket, Round, Turned Wood Base, Incised, Diane Webb Mackey, 1990, 3 x 8 In. ......*illus* 240
Nantucket, Straight-Sided, Swing Arm, Signed, 1900s, 3 In. ....*illus* 461
Nantucket, Swing Arm, Oval, Bentwood Handles, Jose Formoso Reyes, 1950s, 5 x 13 x 10 In. .. 923
Nantucket, Swing Handle, Single-Wrap Rim, Wood Base, Jose Reyes, Early 1900s, 8 x 12 ½ In. . 360
Nantucket, Swing Handle, Single-Wrap Rim, Wood Ears, Turned Base, c.1890, 4 ½ x 6 In. 406
Nantucket, Woven, Oval, Swing Handle, c.1900, 4 ½ x 10 ½ In. 540
Oval, Reed, Woven, 2 Handles, Wood Frame, 25 ½ In. ....*illus* 53
Oval, Rye Straw, Lid, Pennsylvania, Late 1800s, 16 ½ x 14 In. 610
Purse, Hand Painted, Buildings, Purple Gingham Lining, Sabra Stockdale, 1975, 7 x 10 x 7 In. 72
Rectangular, Blue Splints, Lid, Red, Yellow, Late 1800s, 9 ½ x 14 x 7 In. ....*illus* 3998
Rye Straw, Bent Handle, Red, Green, Squat, 1850s, 3 x 8 ½ In. 60
Rye Straw, Iron Bail Handle, Bunghole At Bottom, Pennsylvania, 1800s, 15 ½ In. 1464
Splint Feather, Lid, Apple Green Surface, Painted, 1800s, 34 In. ....*illus* 3416
Splint, 2 Lids, Oak, Picnic Style, Rectangular, Bentwood Frame, Early 1900s, 11 x 11 x 7 In. ... 89
Splint, Hanging, 2 Tiers, Stepped Back, Green Dot, Late 1800s, 20 x 11 x 6 In. 185
Splint, Picnic, Hinged Lid, Leather Handle, Painted, Late 1800s, 9 ½ x 13 x 8 ½ In. ....*illus* 2214
Splint, Rectangular, Flower Stamping, Red, Blue, Yellow, Late 1800s, 6 x 14 x 14 In. 400
Splint, White Oak, Bottle, Woven, Cylinder, Side Handle, James W. Cook, c.2003, 10 In. 164
Splint, Wide & Narrow Oak, Bentwood Handle, Wrapped Rim, Market, c.1915, 13 x 16 x 8 In. .. 154
Square, Ash, Splint, Lid, Blue, 1800s, 8 x 10 ½ x 11 In. 2829
Storage, Woven Coil, Rye Straw, Cylinder, Late 1800s-Early 1900s, 10 ¾ x 13 In. 70
Wash, Woven, 2 Handles, Brown, 17 x 36 x 26 In. 147
Woven, Farm, Round, Rim, Kicked-Up Bottom, 11 x 3 ½ In. 45
Woven, Mustard Yellow, Painted, Wood Handle, Frederick Wilky Leeds, 1800s, 23 In. 187
Woven, Oak Berry, Yellow, Red, Green, Dyed Splints, 4 ½ In. 147
Woven, Shell, Round Top, 1800s, 4 x 9 ¾ In. ....*illus* 1440
Woven, Splint, Stationary Handle, Blue, Ohio, 1850s, 13 x 14 ½ x 13 In. 480
Woven, Square Bottom, Bent Fixed Handle, Red Stained Finish, 7 x 6 In. 94

BATCHELDER

BATCHELDER
LOS ANGELES

Batchelder products are made from California clay. Ernest Batchelder established a tile studio in Pasadena, California, in 1909. He went into partnership with Frederick Brown in 1912 and the company became Batchelder and Brown. In 1920 he built a larger factory with a new partner. The Batchelder-Wilson Company made all types of architectural tiles, garden pots, and bookends. The plant closed in 1932. In 1936 Batchelder opened Batchelder Ceramics, also in Pasadena, and made bowls, vases, and earthenware pots. He retired in 1951 and died in 1957. Pieces are marked *Batchelder Pasadena* or *Batchelder Los Angeles*.

Corbel, Arts & Crafts, Scroll, Flower, Blue Slip, 1930s, 8 x 5 In., Pair 125
Tile, Double Peacock, Flowers, Blue Background, c.1910, 5 ½ x 5 ½ In. 720
Tile, Flower, Banded Border, Blue Glaze, 1909-32, 2 ¾ x 2 ¾ In. 60
Tile, Lion, Green Glaze, 1909-32, 3 ⅞ x 3 ⅞ In. 115
Tile, Mayan, Face, Hieroglyphics, Stoneware, 1910-30, 3 Piece 256
Tile, Stylized Flower In Pot, 1920s, 7 ¾ x 5 ¾ In. 660
Tile, Stylized Peacock, c.1915, 3 ¾ x 3 ¾ In. 360

BATMAN

Batman and Robin are characters from a comic book created by Bob Kane. Batman first appeared in a 1939 issue of *Detective Comics*. The first Batman comic book was published in 1940. In 1966, the characters became part of a popular television series. There have been radio and movie serials that featured the pair. The first full-length movie was made in 1989.

Comic Book, Jokermobile & Joker Cover, No. 37, DC Comic, Oct.-Nov. 1946, 13 x 8 In. 4719
Comic Book, Silver Age Riddler, 1st Appearance, No. 171, DC Comic, May 1965, 13 x 8 In. 206
Cookie Jar, Batman, Black, Blue, 1997, 12 x 10 ½ In. 90
Glass, Super Series, Pepsi, Yellow, Blue, Gray, 1976, 6 In. 28
Toy, Batcraft, Battery Operated, Flashing Light, Louis Marx, 1966 2000
Toy, Batmobile, Tin Lithograph, Blinking Light, Jet Engine Noise, Box, c.1967, 3 ¾ x 9 ¾ In. *illus* 565

BATTERSEA

Battersea enamels, which are enamels painted on copper, were made in the Battersea district of London from about 1750 to 1756. Many similar enamel boxes, old and new, are mistakenly called Battersea.

Box, Oval, Lid, Castle, Colonial Man, Trees, Blue & Red Stripes, 1 x 1 ⅝ x 1 ½ In. 260
Candlestick, Cobalt Blue, Gilt, Birds & Fruit, Removable Bobeches, 10 x 5 In., Pair 400
Candlestick, Flowers, Multicolor, White Ground, Removable Bobeche, 1760s, 11 In. 246
Candlestick, Light Blue, Gilt Scrollwork, Flower Cartouches, c.1780, 9 ½ In., Pair 1188
Pin, Cloak, Air Balloon, Black & White, Brass Mounts, c.1780, 1 ¾ x 1 x 2 In. 1200
Salt, 3 Pastoral Scenes, Pink, Gilt, 3 Footed, 1 ⅜ x 2 ⅝ In. 492

BAUER

Bauer pottery is a California-made ware. J.A. Bauer bought Paducah Pottery in Paducah, Kentucky, in 1885. He moved the pottery to Los Angeles, California, in 1910. The company made art pottery after 1912 and introduced dinnerware marked *Bauer* in 1930. The factory went out of business in 1962 and the molds were destroyed. Since 1998, a new company, Bauer Pottery Company of Los Angeles, has been making Bauer pottery using molds made from original Bauer pieces. The pottery is now made in Highland, California. Pieces are marked *Bauer Pottery Company of Los Angeles.* Original pieces of Bauer pottery are listed here. See also the Russel Wright category.

La Linda, Gravy Boat, Yellow, Marked, c.1939 48
Monterey, Coffee Server, Cobalt Blue, Wooden Handle, 1940s, 8 Cup, 6 x 3 In. 120
Monterey, Plate, Green, Marked, 1940s, 9 In. 33
Ring, Ball Pitcher, Yellow, c.1930, 6 ½ x 6 In. 150
Ring, Cake Stand, Pedestal, Turquoise, 5 x 11 ¾ In. .... *illus* 130
Ring, Candlestick, Blue, Spool Delph, 1920s, 2 x 2 ½ In., Pair 300
Vase, Yellow Matte Glaze, Art Deco, 5 x 5 In. 60

BAVARIA

Bavaria is a region in Europe where many types of porcelain were made. In the nineteenth century, the mark often included the word *Bavaria*. After 1871, the words *Bavaria, Germany*, were used. Listed here are pieces that include the name *Bavaria* in some form, but major porcelain makers, such as Rosenthal, are listed in their own categories.

Bowl, Cobalt Blue, Classical Scene, Gold Stencil, 10 ½ In. 60
Plate, Amorosa, Portrait Center, Maroon & Gold Border, c.1920, 9 ¾ In. .... *illus* 30

BEADED BAGS *are included in the Purse category.*

Beehive, Urn, Pedestal, Classical Scene, Green & Yellow Trim, Gilt, Marked, 12 In.
$108

Woody Auctions

Beehive, Vase, Woman, Brunette, Gold Headband, Pink Ground, Early 1900s, 15 ½ In.
$497

Jeffrey S. Evans & Associates

Bell, Brass, Spinning, Hotel Front Desk, Silvertone Metal, Marble Base, 6 ¾ In.
$92

Apple Tree Auction Center

Bell, Bronze, Roman Centurion, Emil Huddy, 1976, 7 ½ In.
$81

Apple Tree Auction Center

Bell, Bronze, School, Yoke, Clapper, Cast By Chaplain-Fulton Mfg., Pittsburgh, 1912, 26 In.
$2,990

Apple Tree Auction Center

Bell, Bronze, Schoolmarm, Marked, Blake Valleau, 6 In.
$69

Apple Tree Auction Center

BEATLES

Beatles collectors search for any items picturing the four members of the famous music group or any of their recordings. The condition is very important and top prices are paid for items in mint condition. The Beatles first appeared on American network television in 1964. The group disbanded in 1971. Ringo Starr and Paul McCartney are still performing. John Lennon died in 1980. George Harrison died in 2001.

Album, Help, LP, Vinyl, c.1965, 12 In. 50
Bracelet, Presentation, ID Engraved Ognir Ratts, Chain Link, 14K Gold, 1978, 7 In. 1280
Compact, Round, Full Size, Powder Puff, 1960s, 3 In. 275
Model, Ringo Starr, Wildest Skins In Town, Box, 1964, 6 x 9 ½ In. 221
Postcard, Variety Club Great Britain, Hearts in Boxes, 1963 18
Poster, Yellow Submarine, Graphics, Characters, King Features-Suba Films, 12 ½ x 20 In. 158
Toy, Yellow Submarine, Die Cast, 2 Beatles In Front, 2 Beatles In Back, 1969, 5 x 2 In. 250
Wig, Brush, Portraits, Wow The Beatles Are Here, Red, 10 x 12 In. 131

BEEHIVE

Beehive, Austria, or Beehive, Vienna, are terms used in English-speaking countries to refer to the many types of decorated porcelain bearing a mark that looks like a beehive. The mark is actually a shield, viewed upside down. It was first used in 1744 by the Royal Porcelain Manufactory of Vienna. The firm made what collectors call Royal Vienna porcelains until it closed in 1864. Many other German, Austrian, and Japanese factories have reproduced Royal Vienna wares, complete with the original shield or beehive mark. This listing includes the expensive, original Royal Vienna porcelains and many other types of beehive porcelain. The Royal Vienna pieces include that name in the description.

Imperial and Royal Porcelain Manufactory
Vienna, Austria
1749–1827

Bourdois & Bloch
Paris, France
c.1900

Waechtersbach Earthenware Factory
Schlierbach, Hesse, Germany
1921–1928

Ewer, Woman & Cupid, Curled Wavy Rim, Handle, Cream Ground, Ruby, Leafy Gold, 22 In. 1029
Group, Royal Vienna, Courtship Scene, Dog, Austria, 1800s, 10 In. 192
Group, Three Graces, 3 Nude Women, Purple & Yellow Rose Garland, 16 ½ x 13 ¾ In. 5760
Plaque, Woman, Classical Dress, Hand Painted, Gilt Frame, 22 x 15 x 22 In. .... *illus* 1210
Stein, Courting Couple, Hinged Lid, Gilt, Landscape, Royal Vienna, 6 ½ In. 440
Urn, Lid, Pedestal, Painted, Young Woman Portrait, Red Ground, c.1910, 35 x 11 In. .... *illus* 1500
Urn, Lid, Portrait, Lustrous Green Ground, Gold, Royal Vienna, Late 1800s, 20 ½ In. .... *illus* 2337
Urn, Lid, Vienna Style, Cobalt Blue, Gold Tapestry Ground, F. Kohl, c.1900, 8 In. 175
Urn, Mother & 3 Children, Woman, Cupid, Gilt Square, 2 Handles, 17 ½ In. 1200
Urn, Pedestal, Classical Scene, Green & Yellow Trim, Gilt, Marked, 12 In. .... *illus* 108
Vase, Potpourri, Cylindrical, Fluted Legs, Claw Feet, Hand Painted, Forstner, 18 x 7 In. 968
Vase, Woman, Brunette, Gold Headband, Pink Ground, Early 1900s, 15 ½ In. .... *illus* 497
Vase, Woman, Green Gown, Red Rose, Art Nouveau Style, Gilt, Enamel, Proscholett, 9 ¾ In. ... 484

BEER BOTTLES *are listed in the Bottle category under Beer.*

BEER CAN

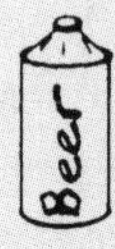

Beer cans are a twentieth-century idea. Beer was sold in kegs or returnable bottles until 1934. The first patent for a can was issued to the American Can Company in September of that year, and Gotfried Kruger Brewing Company,

Newark, New Jersey, was the first to use the can. The cone-top can was first made in 1935, the aluminum pop-top in 1962. Collectors should look for cans in good condition, with no dents or rust. Serious collectors prefer cans that have been opened from the bottom.

Black Hawk Premium Beer, American Indian Silhouette, 1950s, 12 Oz. 152
Burger Brau, Cone Top, Cincinnati, c.1940.......... 196
Crown Darby, Flat Top, Westminster Brewery, 1950s.......... 40
Dutch Club Beer, Cone Top, Pittsburgh Brewing Co., Cap, 1930s, 12 Oz. 544
Falstaff, Cone Top, Gold & Red, c.1930, 6 In. 52
Fox Head 400, Flat Top, Red Fox Head, Fox Head Brewing Co., 12 Oz. 96
Gotham Fine Beer, Cone Top, Skyline, 1940s, 12 Oz.......... 1697
Holihan's Light Ale, Pull Top, Mint Green, 12 Oz. 125
Kingsbury, Aristocrat of Beer, Crowntainer, Cap.......... 82
Menominee Champion Light Beer, Cone Top, Cap, 1950s, 12 Oz. 468
Pabst Export Beer, Flat Top, c.1935, 12 Oz.......... 322
Paul Bunyan Beer, Flat Top, 1950s, 12 Oz. 410
Schlitz Lager, Cone Top, Beer That Made Milwaukee Famous, Cap, 1930s.......... 1117
Stoney's, Cone Top, Pilsener Beer, Jones Brewing Co., 6 In. 400
Yuengling Beer, Cone Top, Banner & Shield, Cap, c.1950, 12 Oz.......... 468

BELL

Bell collectors collect all types of bells. Favorites include glass bells, figural bells, school bells, and cowbells. Bells have been made of porcelain, china, or metal through the centuries.

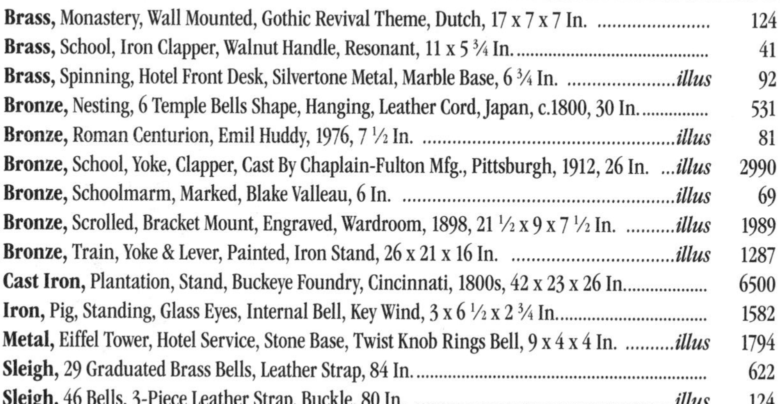

Brass, Monastery, Wall Mounted, Gothic Revival Theme, Dutch, 17 x 7 x 7 In. 124
Brass, School, Iron Clapper, Walnut Handle, Resonant, 11 x 5 ¾ In. 41
Brass, Spinning, Hotel Front Desk, Silvertone Metal, Marble Base, 6 ¾ In. ....*illus* 92
Bronze, Nesting, 6 Temple Bells Shape, Hanging, Leather Cord, Japan, c.1800, 30 In. 531
Bronze, Roman Centurion, Emil Huddy, 1976, 7 ½ In. ....*illus* 81
Bronze, School, Yoke, Clapper, Cast By Chaplain-Fulton Mfg., Pittsburgh, 1912, 26 In. ...*illus* 2990
Bronze, Schoolmarm, Marked, Blake Valleau, 6 In. ....*illus* 69
Bronze, Scrolled, Bracket Mount, Engraved, Wardroom, 1898, 21 ½ x 9 x 7 ½ In. ....*illus* 1989
Bronze, Train, Yoke & Lever, Painted, Iron Stand, 26 x 21 x 16 In. ....*illus* 1287
Cast Iron, Plantation, Stand, Buckeye Foundry, Cincinnati, 1800s, 42 x 23 x 26 In. 6500
Iron, Pig, Standing, Glass Eyes, Internal Bell, Key Wind, 3 x 6 ½ x 2 ¾ In. 1582
Metal, Eiffel Tower, Hotel Service, Stone Base, Twist Knob Rings Bell, 9 x 4 x 4 In. ....*illus* 1794
Sleigh, 29 Graduated Brass Bells, Leather Strap, 84 In. 622
Sleigh, 46 Bells, 3-Piece Leather Strap, Buckle, 80 In. ....*illus* 124

BELLEEK

Belleek china was made in Ireland, other European countries, and the United States. The glaze is creamy yellow and appears wet. The first Belleek was made in 1857 in the village of Belleek, County Fermanagh, in what is now Northern Ireland. In 1884 the name of the company became the Belleek Pottery Works Company Ltd. The mark changed through the years. The first mark, black, dates from 1863 to 1891. The second mark, black, dates from 1891 to 1926 and includes the words *Co. Fermanagh, Ireland.* The third mark, black, dates from 1926 to 1946 and has the words *Deanta in Eireann.* The fourth mark, same as the third mark but green, dates from 1946 to 1955. The fifth mark (second green mark) dates from 1955 to 1965 and has an *R* in a circle added in the upper right. The sixth mark (third green mark) dates from 1965 to 1981 and the words *Co. Fermanagh* have been omitted. The seventh mark, gold, was used from 1981 to 1992 and omits the words *Deanta in Eireann.* The eighth mark, used from 1993 to 1996, is similar to the second mark but is printed in blue. The ninth mark, blue, includes the words *Est. 1857,* and the words *Co. Fermanagh Ireland* are omitted. The tenth mark, black, is similar to the ninth mark but includes

Bell, Bronze, Scrolled, Bracket Mount, Engraved, Wardroom, 1898, 21 ½ x 9 x 7 ½ In.
$1,989

Thomaston Place Auction Galleries

Bell, Bronze, Train, Yoke & Lever, Painted, Iron Stand, 26 x 21 x 16 In.
$1,287

Thomaston Place Auction Galleries

Bell, Metal, Eiffel Tower, Hotel Service, Stone Base, Twist Knob Rings Bell, 9 x 4 x 4 In.
$1,794

AntiqueAdvertising.com

Bell, Sleigh, 46 Bells, 3-Piece Leather Strap, Buckle, 80 In.
$124

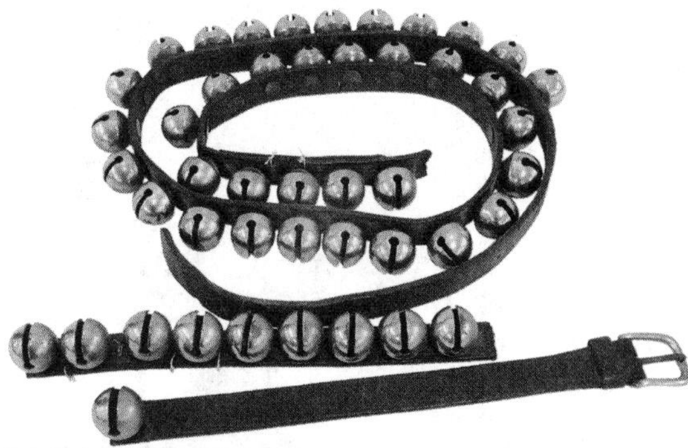

Hartzell's Auction Gallery Inc.

Look at the B

The word *Belleek* with the capital letter *B* can be used as part of a mark or description only by the Irish pottery in Fermanagh, Ireland. Other potteries used the word *belleek* in marks before 1929, when a lawsuit ruled it was a copyrighted name. Now the word sometimes is used generically (with a small *b*) to describe the mother-of-pearl-like glaze. See more information about Belleek at Kovels.com.

Belleek, Basket, Lid, Flowers Finial, 4 Strands, 2 Pads, Rope Shape Handle, 6 ½ x 13 In.
$540

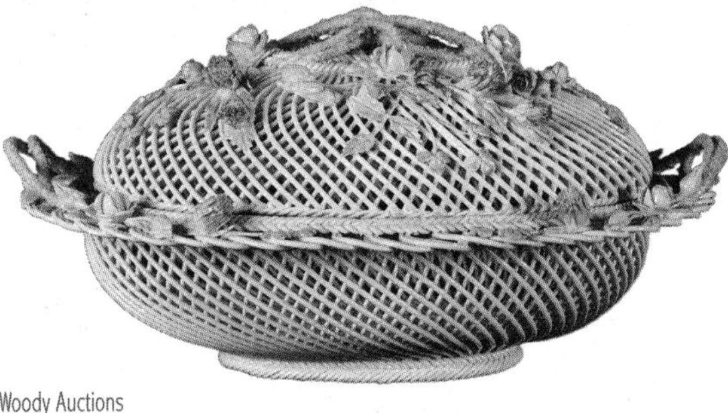

Woody Auctions

Belleek, Basket, Woven, Lid, Flowers & Clover, 4 Strands, 5 x 8 In.
$509

Soulis Auctions

Belleek, Teapot, Lid, Shell & Shamrock Pattern, Green Leaves, Harp Handle, 7 ¾ x 8 ¾ In.
$72

Woody Auctions

Bennington, Figurine, Lion, Facing Left, Coleslaw Mane, Flint Enamel, 1849-58, 7 x 10 In.
$1,200

Bourgeault-Horan Antiquarians & Associates, LLC

Bennington, Jug, Stoneware, Cobalt Blue, Bird, On Tree Trunk, J. & E. Norton, 1850-59, 3 Gal.
$1,560

Bourgeault-Horan Antiquarians & Associates, LLC

the words *Millennium 2000* and *Ireland*. It was used only in 2000. The eleventh mark, similar to the millennium mark but green, was introduced in 2001. The twelfth mark, black, is similar to the eleventh mark but has a banner above the mark with the words *Celebrating 150 Years*. It was used in 2007. The thirteenth trademark, used from 2008 to 2010, is similar to the twelfth but is brown and has no banner. The fourteenth mark, the Classic Belleek trademark, is similar to the twelfth but includes Belleek's website address. The Belleek Living trademark was introduced in 2010 and is used on items from that giftware line. All pieces listed here are Irish Belleek. The word *Belleek* is now used only on pieces made in Ireland even though earlier pieces from other countries were sometimes marked *Belleek*. These early pieces are listed in this book by manufacturer, such as Ceramic Art Co., Lenox, Ott & Brewer, and Willets.

Belleek Pottery Co.
1863–1891

Ceramic Art Co.
1894–1906

Willets Manufacturing Co.
1879–1912+

Basket, Lid, Flowers Finial, 4 Strands, 2 Pads, Rope Shape Handle, 6 ½ x 13 In. ....*illus* 540
Basket, Woven, Lid, Flowers & Clover, 4 Strands, 5 x 8 In. ....*illus* 509
Figurine, Irish Wolfhound, Seated, Oblong Base, 1988, 7 ½ x 7 In. 60
Teapot, Lid, Shell & Shamrock Pattern, Green Leaves, Harp Handle, 7 ¾ x 8 ¾ In. ....*illus* 72
Vase, Multicolor, Flowers, Glazed, Green Mark, 11 In. 240

BENNINGTON

Bennington ware was the product of two factories working in Bennington, Vermont. Both the Norton Company and Lyman Fenton & Company were out of business by 1896. The wares include brown and yellow mottled pottery, Parian, scroddled ware, stoneware, graniteware, yellowware, and Staffordshire-type vases. The name is also a generic term for mottled brownware of the type made in Bennington.

Figurine, Lion, Facing Left, Coleslaw Mane, Flint Enamel, 1849-58, 7 x 10 In. ....*illus* 1200
Footbath, Flint Enamel, Scalloped Ribs, 1848-58, 7 ½ x 16 ½ In. 600
Jar, Cobalt Blue Deer, Flat Rolled Rim, Handles, J. & E. Norton, 1860s, 11 x 10 In. 2214
Jug, Cobalt Blue Leaves, Handle, Impressed, E. & L.P. Norton, Stoneware, 1950s, 11 ½ In. 132
Jug, Cobalt Blue, Flower, Bulbous Body, Handle, Stoneware, J. & E. Norton, 1800s, 12 In. 266
Jug, Stoneware, Bird, On Grapevine, Edmand & Co., Massachusetts, c.1860, 3 Gal. 720
Jug, Stoneware, Cobalt Blue, Bird, On Tree Trunk, J. & E. Norton, 1850-59, 3 Gal. ....*illus* 1560

BERLIN

Berlin, a German porcelain factory, was started in 1751 by Wilhelm Kaspar Wegely. In 1763, the factory was taken over by Frederick the Great and became the Royal Berlin Porcelain Manufactory. It is still in operation today. Pieces have been marked in a variety of ways.

Figurine, Boy, Basket, Wheat Sheaf, White, Blue Scepter Mark, 4 ½ In., Pair 52
Soup Service, Tureen, Lid, 10 Plates, Blue Flowers, Blue Scepter Mark, 9 In. 1200
Tureen, Lid, Putto Finial, Oval, Birds, Butterflies, Blue Mark, c.1900, 10 x 11 ¾ In., Pair 505
Vase, Lid, Men On Horseback, Yellow, Red, Gilt, Handles, Footed, 1800s, 14 x 8 ½ In., Pair....... 2900

BESWICK

Beswick started making pottery in Staffordshire, England, in 1894. The pottery became John Beswick Ltd. in 1936. The company became part of Royal Doulton Tableware, Ltd.in 1969. Production ceased in 2002 and the John Beswick brand

TIP
Get an automatic dialer on you bedside phone and program the police number so you can simply push a button for help.

Bicycle, American Star, High Wheel, Patented By George Pressey, 1880s, 42-In. Wheel
$5,605

Copake Auctions

Bicycle, Hawthorne, Flyer, Flat Tank, Rear Rack, Comet Speedometer, 1929, 19-In. Frame
$3,540

Copake Auctions

Bicycle, Iver Johnson, Diamond, Safety, Hard Tires, Lovell Arms Co., 1890s, 30-In. Wheels
$6,490

Copake Auctions

This is an edited listing of current prices. Visit **Kovels.com** to check thousands of prices from previous years and sign up for free information on trends, tips, reproductions, marks, and more.

Bicycle, Lamp, Union Lamp Co., Green, Ruby Opalescent Jewels, Alcohol Burner, Reflector, 7 ½ In.
$2,280

Rich Penn Auctions

Bicycle, Seat, Black, Padded Leather, Persons, Worcester, Mass., 10 x 8 ½ In.
$215

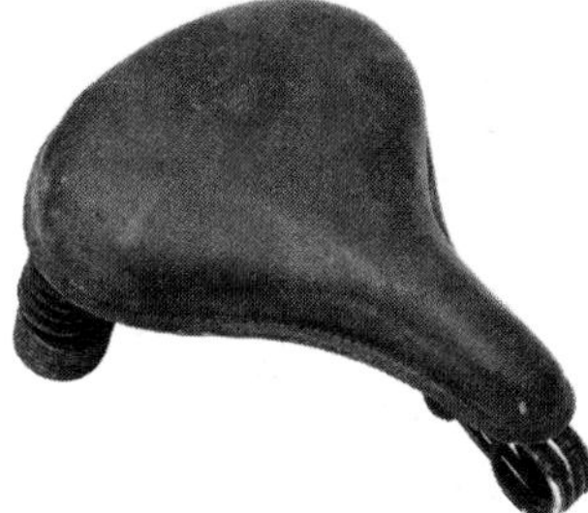

Hartzell's Auction Gallery Inc.

Bicycle, Sign, Pirelli Bicycle Tires, Tin Lithograph, Self-Framed, 1930s, 27 x 19 In.
$2,530

Brinkman Auctions

was bought by Dartington Crystal in 2004. Figurines, vases, and other items are being made and use the name Beswick. Beatrix Potter figures were made from 1948 until 2002. They shouldn't be confused with Bunnykins, which were made by Royal Doulton.

Bowl, Gardenia Ware, Tulips, Green, Yellow Pink, 1930s, 9 ¾ In. 48
Figurine, Dog, Basset Hound, Black, Tan, White, Raised Tail, 5 x 7 ½ In. 50
Figurine, Horse, Brown, White Nose, Head Down, 6 ¾ x 8 ½ In. 75
Vase, Forest, Shrubs, Rabbit, Relief, Brown Matte, Foot Ring, 1936, 9 In. 98
Vase, Urn Shape, Footed, Handles, Blue Flowers, 5 In. 59
Vase, Wood Effect, Footed, c.1952, 11 In. 138

BETTY BOOP

Betty Boop, the cartoon figure, first appeared on the screen in 1930. Her face was modeled after the famous singer Helen Kane and her body after Mae West. In 1935, a comic strip was started. Her dog was named Pudgy. Although the Betty Boop cartoons ended by 1938, there was a revival of interest in the Betty Boop image in the 1980s and new pieces are being made.

Clock, Wall, Flirty Eye, Flashing, Pudgy Pendulum, Tezuka, c.1935, 13 x 6 In. 339
Cookie Jar, Betty Stirring, White Chef Hat, Cookies Across Apron, 12 In. 42
Figurine, Plaster, Matte, Gold Glitter Dress & Shoes, Gold Pedestal, c.1930, 14 In. 150
Valentine Card, Baby, Beach, I'm Piling Up Affection For You My Valentine, 1938 6
Wall Pocket, Betty Boop & Dog Bimbo, Porcelain, Lusterware, 1930s 85
Watch, Leopard Print Top, Black Skirt, Puppy, Black Band, Goldtone, 1989 45

BICYCLE

Bicycles were invented in 1839. The first manufactured bicycle was made in 1861. Special ladies' bicycles were made after 1874. The modern safety bicycle was not produced until 1885. Collectors search for all types of bicycles and tricycles. Bicycle-related items are also listed here. Many posters have been reproduced.

American Star, High Wheel, Patented By George Pressey, 1880s, 42-In. Wheel .... *illus* 5605
AMF Roadmaster, Pleasure Liner, Black, White, Red Grip, 45 x 45 In. 147
Hawthorne, Flyer, Flat Tank, Rear Rack, Comet Speedometer, 1929, 19-In. Frame .... *illus* 3540
Iver Johnson, Diamond, Safety, Hard Tires, Lovell Arms Co., 1890s, 30-In. Wheels .... *illus* 6490
Lamp, Union Lamp Co., Green, Ruby Opalescent Jewels, Alcohol Burner, Reflector, 7 ½ In. *illus* 2280
Poster, 31st Peace Race, 1948-78, Berlin, Prague, Warsaw, Cyclist, 1977, 38 In. 720
Poster, Cleveland Cycles, Native American Cyclist, Logo, 1898, 58 x 43 In. 2400
Poster, Cycles Papillon, Bruxelles, Woman On Bicycle On Butterfly, 1896, 55 In. 2640
Poster, Orient Cycles, Lead The Leaders, Cyclist, E. Penfield, 1895, 40 In. 16800
Poster, Rudge, 16 Rue Halevy, Paris, 3 Men On Tandem Bike, 50 x 36 In. 2160
Poster, Victor, Art Nouveau Woman & Flower Border, Bradley, 1895, 40 x 13 In. 9600
Seat, Black, Padded Leather, Persons, Worcester, Mass., 10 x 8 ½ In. .... *illus* 215
Sign, French Cycle Co., Lithograph, Motorbike, Bellenger, 1937, 15 x 23 ½ In. 144
Sign, Pirelli Bicycle Tires, Tin Lithograph, Self-Framed, 1930s, 27 x 19 In. .... *illus* 2530
Tandem, Barnes, White Flyer, 2 Seats, Rear Lap Bell, 1896 .... *illus* 4130
Tricycle, Iver Johnson, Original Paint, Bell, 1920s-30s, Child's, 27 In. .... *illus* 295
Velocipede, Boneshaker, Cast Iron, Wood, 2 Spoke Wheels, Red, 1880s, 49 In. .... *illus* 3042

BING & GRONDAHL

Bing & Grondahl is a famous Danish factory making fine porcelains from 1853 to the present. Underglaze blue decoration was started in 1886. The annual Christmas plate series was introduced in 1895. Dinnerware, stoneware, and other ceramics are still being made today. The figurines remain popular. The firm has used the initials *B & G* and a stylized castle as part of the mark since 1898. The company became part of Royal Copenhagen in 1987.

Bicycle, Tandem, Barnes, White Flyer, 2 Seats, Rear Lap Bell, 1896
$4,130

Copake Auctions

The Safety Bicycle
In the beginning, bicycles had tall or high wheels. In the late 1800s, the "safety bicycle" was developed in which the rider's feet could reach the ground, making it easier to stop. A safety bike also was chain-driven and an ancestor of the modern bicycle. The Overman Wheel Co. in Massachusetts was the first U.S. manufacturer of safety bikes.

Bicycle, Tricycle, Iver Johnson, Original Paint, Bell, 1920s-30s, Child's, 27 In.
$295

Copake Auctions

Bing & Grondahl, Figurine, Polar Bear, Hand Painted, Glaze, No. 1954, Niels Nielsen, 17 In.
$590

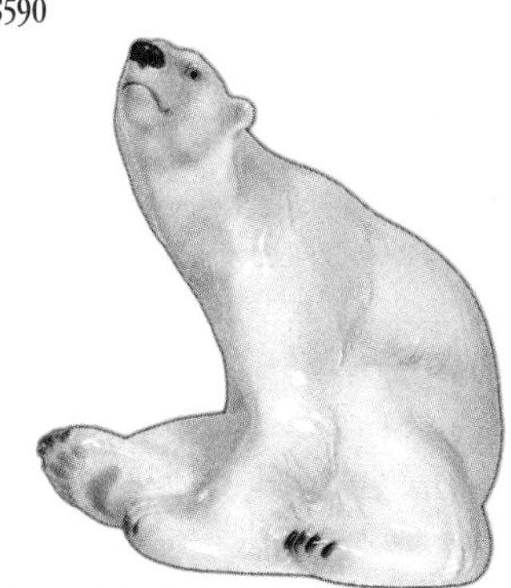

Ahlers & Ogletree Auction Gallery

Bicycle, Velocipede, Boneshaker, Cast Iron, Wood, 2 Spoke Wheels, Red, 1880s, 49 In.
$3,042

Jeffrey S. Evans & Associates

Binoculars, Mother-Of-Pearl, Opera Glasses, Cobalt, Enamel, Silver Star, Le Fils Paris, 1800s, 6 x 2 x 2 In.
$140

Cordier Auctions

Binoculars, T.J. Williams, Brass, Etched, Lignum Vitae Focus Knob, c.1910, 5 In., Pair
$180

Eldred's

TIP
Storing collectibles now and hoping they'll go up in value later may or may not be a good idea. Storing pottery, glass and metal in a dry attic or basement is usually OK, but not if the rooms get very hot (over 90 degrees) or very cold (below freezing). Furniture can dry out or rot in climates you don't enjoy yourself. Linens attract insects. Be wary of plastic bags that could melt in high heat. Plastic jewelry, toys and purses can melt or disintegrate over time; heat destroys plastic. Rented storage should be air-conditioned and heated, but it's expensive. If you don't have room or the right conditions for storage, it might be better to sell-even at low prices.

Birdcage, Walnut, Arcades, Dome, Removable Zinc-Lined Trays, Georgian, 1800s, 38 x 32 x 14 In.
$1,320

Brunk Auctions

TIP

Binoculars should be checked by looking into the big end to be sure there are no cracks, chips, or even fungus. These problems may not change the view, but they will lower the price.

Black, Button, Booker T. Washington, Muskogee Negro Business League, 1914, 1 ¼ In.
$2,875

Cowan's Auctions

B. & G.
Bing & Grondahl
1895+

Bing & Grondahl
1915+

Bing & Grondahl
1983+

Dish, Sea Gull, Shell Form, Ribbed, Blue Shell Handle, Gold Trim, 6 In., 4 Piece 188
Figurine, Cat, Arched Back, Ears Back, Mouth Open, White Glaze, 6 x 8 ⅜ In. 563
Figurine, Danish Fisherwoman, Headscarf, Basket On Back, 11 In. 25
Figurine, Eagle, Perched, Brown Glaze, 9 In. 250
Figurine, Grizzly Bear, Brown Glaze, Textured Fur, Marked, 20 x 13 In. 1140
Figurine, Hamlet, Ophelia, 9 In., Pair 156
Figurine, Penguin, Blackfoot, Glossy Black & White Glaze, 10 In. 63
Figurine, Polar Bear, Hand Painted, Glaze, No. 1954, Niels Nielsen, 17 In. .... *illus* 590
Group, Young Boy & Girl Dancing, Cobalt Blue Suit On Boy, Marked, 8 In. 25
Tea Set, Sea Gull, 4 Cups & Saucers, Teapot, Elongated Neck, Marked, 9 Piece 125
Tureen, Delft Style, Blue Flowers, Pedestal Base, Fish Handles, 9 x 13 In. 63
Tureen, Lid, Sea Gull, Raised Scales, Round, Handles, Seahorse Finial, 8 x 10 In. 188
Vase, White Dogwood Blossom, Cobalt Blue Ground, Swollen, 8 ¾ x 5 In. 38

BINOCULARS

Binoculars of all types are wanted by collectors. Those made in the eighteenth and nineteenth centuries are favored by serious collectors. The small, attractive binoculars called opera glasses are listed here.

Carl Zeiss, 8x56, Low Light, Neck Strap, Case, West Germany, 9 ½ x 5 ½, 1970s 1169
Focal, 2.5x25, Folding, Pocket, 1940s, 4 In. 43
Mother-Of-Pearl, Opera Glasses, Cobalt, Enamel, Silver Star, Le Fils Paris, 1800s, 6 x 2 x 2 In. *illus* 140
Nash Kelvinator, 6x30, Neck Strap, Leather Case, 1943 95
National Instrument Corps, 5x40, Leather Case 42
Sears, 10x50, Wide Angle, Neck Strap 13
T.J. Williams, Brass, Etched, Lignum Vitae Focus Knob, c.1910, 5 In., Pair .... *illus* 180

BIRDCAGE

Birdcages are collected for use as homes for pet birds and as decorative objects of folk art. Elaborate wooden cages of the past centuries can still be found. The brass or wicker cages of the 1930s are popular with bird owners.

Bamboo, Dome Shape, Hanging Hook, Carved, Figural Scene, Bracket Feet, Chinese, 23 x 13 In. 1125
Metal, Dome Top, Door, Square, Victorian, 35 x 14 In. 71
Walnut, Arcades, Dome, Removable Zinc-Lined Trays, Georgian, 1800s, 38 x 32 x 14 In. *illus* 1320
Wood, Square, Splayed Shape, 4 Scroll Supports, Bird Feeder, Metal Hook, Chinese, 8 In. 400
Wood, Wire, Hanging, Dome Roof, 10 x 10 x 22 In. 35

BISQUE

Bisque is an unglazed baked porcelain. Finished bisque has a slightly sandy texture with a dull finish. Some of it may be decorated with various colors. Bisque gained favor during the late Victorian era when thousands of bisque figurines were made. It is still being made. Additional bisque items may be listed under the factory name.

Bust, Woman, Gilt, Crown Hairpiece, Lace, Butterfly, Rose, 20 x 9 In. 480
Figurine, Cigar & Match Holder, Black Man, Sitting On Basket, Painted, 10 ¾ In. 79

BLACK AMERICANA

Black Americana has become an important area of collecting since the 1970s. F & F is the mark used on plastic made by Fiedler & Fiedler Mold & Die Works, Inc. in the 1930s and 1940s. Objects that picture a black person may also be listed in this book under Advertising, Sign; Bank; Bottle Opener; Cookie Jar; Doll; Salt & Pepper; Sheet Music; Toy; etc.

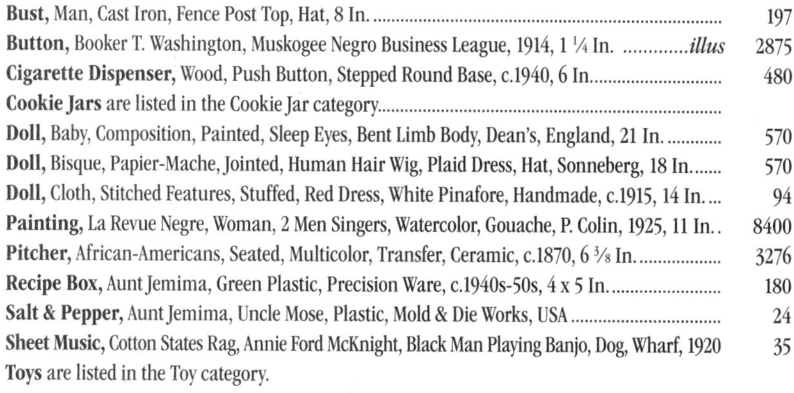

Bust, Man, Cast Iron, Fence Post Top, Hat, 8 In. 197
Button, Booker T. Washington, Muskogee Negro Business League, 1914, 1 ¼ In. .... *illus* 2875
Cigarette Dispenser, Wood, Push Button, Stepped Round Base, c.1940, 6 In. 480
Cookie Jars are listed in the Cookie Jar category. ....
Doll, Baby, Composition, Painted, Sleep Eyes, Bent Limb Body, Dean's, England, 21 In. 570
Doll, Bisque, Papier-Mache, Jointed, Human Hair Wig, Plaid Dress, Hat, Sonneberg, 18 In. 570
Doll, Cloth, Stitched Features, Stuffed, Red Dress, White Pinafore, Handmade, c.1915, 14 In. 94
Painting, La Revue Negre, Woman, 2 Men Singers, Watercolor, Gouache, P. Colin, 1925, 11 In. 8400
Pitcher, African-Americans, Seated, Multicolor, Transfer, Ceramic, c.1870, 6 ⅜ In. 3276
Recipe Box, Aunt Jemima, Green Plastic, Precision Ware, c.1940s-50s, 4 x 5 In. 180
Salt & Pepper, Aunt Jemima, Uncle Mose, Plastic, Mold & Die Works, USA 24
Sheet Music, Cotton States Rag, Annie Ford McKnight, Black Man Playing Banjo, Dog, Wharf, 1920 35
Toys are listed in the Toy category.

BLENKO GLASS COMPANY

Blenko Glass Company is the 1930s successor to several glassworks founded by William John Blenko in Milton, West Virginia. In 1933, his son, William H. Blenko Sr., took charge. The company made tablewares and vases in classical shapes. In the late 1940s it hired talented designers and made innovative pieces. The company made a line of reproductions for Colonial Williamsburg. It is still in business and is best known today for its decorative wares and stained glass.

Ashtray, Kidney Shape, Blue To Yellow, 1960s, 6 x 2 In. 79
Bottle, Decanter, Green, Black Stopper, 14 ½ In. .... *illus* 144
Champagne Bucket, Top Hat Shape, Clear, Blue Band, 1970s, 12 x 11 x 8 In. 89
Tray, Cheese, Mouse Shape, Clear, Tail Shape Handle, c.1952, 10 x 3 In. 26
Vase, Blue Round, 2 Handles, 1937, 7 x 7 In. 227
Vase, Bud, Green, Crackle, Round, Pontil, c.1950, 4 x 4 In. 103
Vase, Red, Trumpet Shape, Signed, 23 In. .... *illus* 88
Vase, Trumpet Shape, Blue Rim & Base, Late 1900s, 15 In. .... *illus* 25

BLOWN GLASS, *see Glass-Blown category.*

BLUE GLASS, *see Cobalt Blue category.*

BLUE ONION, *see Onion category.*

BLUE WILLOW, *see Willow category.*

BOCH FRERES

Boch Freres factory was founded in 1841 in La Louviere in eastern Belgium. The pottery wares resemble the work of Villeroy & Boch. The factory closed in 1985. M.R.L. Boch took over the production of tableware but went bankrupt in 1988. Le Hodey took over Boch Freres in 1989, using the name Royal Boch Manufacture S.A. It went bankrupt in 2009.

Lamp, 2-Light, White Shade, Bronze Base, c.1925, 27 In. 135
Vase, 4 Stags, Crackle Glaze, Charles Catteau, 1920s, 12 In. .... *illus* 540
Vase, Biches Bleues, Oval, Deer, Crackle Ground, Leafy Border, c.1925, 12 In. 431
Vase, Black Ground, Multicolor, Flared Rim, Leon Lambillotte, c.1927, 12 x 8 In. 367
Vase, Crows, Charles Catteau, 8 x 7 In. 1000

Blenko, Bottle, Decanter, Green, Black Stopper, 14 ½ In.
$144

Ripley Auctions

Blenko, Vase, Red, Trumpet Shape, Signed, 23 In.
$88

Hudson Valley Auctions

Blenko, Vase, Trumpet Shape, Blue Rim & Base, Late 1900s, 15 In.
$25

Skinner, Inc.

TIP
If you got mud on the carpet when you came in from gardening, scoop off any loose mud then sprinkle the stain with salt. Let it dry and then vacuum.

Boch Freres, Vase, 4 Stags, Crackle Glaze, Charles Catteau, 1920s, 12 In. $540

Eldred's

Boch Freres, Vase, Penguins, Black & Mint Green, Crackle Ground, Footed, c.1925, 9 In. $2,091

Skinner, Inc.

Boehm, Eagle Of Freedom, Commemorative Mark, 1976, 15 In. $496

Ahlers & Ogletree Auction Gallery

Vase, Keramis, Iridescent, 4 Handles, Floral, Metallic Glaze, Black Slip, 17 In. 1200
Vase, Penguins, Black & Mint Green, Crackle Ground, Footed, c.1925, 9 In. ....*illus* 2091
Vase, Penguins, Black & White, Egg Shape, Flared Rim, Charles Catteau, 1920s, 12 In. 720
Vase, Repeating Owls, Glazed Stoneware, Charles Catteau, 1926, 12 x 7 ½ In. 2875

BOEHM

Boehm is the collector's name for the porcelains of Edward Marshall Boehm. In 1953 the Osso China Company was reorganized as Edward Marshall Boehm Inc. In the early days of the factory, dishes were made, but the elaborate and lifelike bird figurines are the best-known ware. Edward Marshall Boehm, the founder, died in 1969, but the firm continued to design and produce porcelain. The Museum of American Porcelain Art bought the assets, including the molds and trademarks, in 2015. The museum is located in South Euclid, Ohio, a suburb of Cleveland. The Boehm Showroom in Trenton, New Jersey, has exclusive use of the molds and trademarks. It also does restoration work and has some retired figures for sale.

Boehm Porcelain, LLC 1952–1954

Boehm Porcelain, LLC 1959–1970

Boehm Porcelain, LLC 1971+

Bookends, Owl, Perched, White, Glass Eyes, Signed, Book Shape Base, 9 ½ x 4 x 3 ½ In. 124
Crested Flycatcher, Perched, Leafy Branch, Marked, 1900s, 18 ½ In. 250
Eagle Of Freedom, Commemorative Mark, 1976, 15 In. ....*illus* 496
Eagle, Bisque, Script Mark, Fluted Column, 15 x 11 x 12 In. 700
Giant Panda, 1975, 13 ½ In. ....*illus* 434
Marsh Harrier With Water Lilies, Flying, Yellow Blossoms, Black, Marked, 1900s, 26 ½ In. 625
Orchids, White Cattleya, Leaves, Signed, 7 ½ In. 210
Patriotic Eagle, American Flag, Spread Wings, Holding, Signed, 23 x 11 In. ....*illus* 660
Varied Buntings, 21 ¼ x 15 In. 434
Wood Thrushes, Male Bird Perched Above Blooming Flowers, Porcelain, 1980s, 16 In. 90
Yellow Bellied Sapsucker, 13 In. ....*illus* 558

BOHEMIAN GLASS, *see Glass-Bohemian*

BOOKENDS

Bookends have probably been used since books became inexpensive. Early libraries kept books in cupboards, not on open shelves. By the 1870s bookends appeared, especially homemade fret-carved wooden examples. Most bookends listed in this book date from the twentieth century. Bookends are also listed in other categories by manufacturer or material. All bookends listed here are pairs.

Bird, Woodpecker, Perched, Wood, Carved, Painted, Early 1900s, 8 In. 488
Book Shape, Onyx, Bronze, Cold Painted, Marked ANR Charles Austria, 6 x 4 ¾ x 3 In. 300
Bronze, J.L. Lambert, Track Related, Griffoul Newark, c.1925, 7 In. 98
Bronze, Slag Glass, Sliding, Patinated Green Frame, Bradley & Hubbard, c.1900, 3 ¾ x 13 In. *illus* 182
Bulldog, Standing, Bronze, Naturalistic Base, Stylized Tree, Impressed Austria, 4 x 5 In. 1023
Cats, Seated, Bronze, Hand Hammered Back, Arts & Crafts, 5 ½ x 3 ½ In. ....*illus* 452
Cats, Stretching, Bronze, Brown Glaze, Art Deco, 5 ½ x 3 ¼ x 7 In. 593
Cross Shape, Paper, Flower Spray, Lithograph, Pax Christi, c.1950, 5 ½ x 2 ½ In. 5
Deer, Steel, Standing, Art Deco, Karl Hagenauer, Austria, 4 x 3 ½ x 3 ½ In. 216
Horse Standing By Stall Door, Cast Metal, Bronze Color, Pair, 6 In. 75
Shoes Shape, Wood, Square Base, Stamped, Imprinted 8B, 9 ½ x 6 In. 88
Wood, Fruit & Leaves, Carved, Painted, Green, Red, 6 ½ x 7 In. 41

B

Boehm, Giant Panda, 1975, 13 ½ In.
$434

Ahlers & Ogletree Auction Gallery

Boehm, Patriotic Eagle, American Flag, Spread Wings, Holding, Signed, 23 x 11 In.
$660

Alderfer Auction Company

Boehm Yellow Bellied Sapsucker, 13 In.
$558

Ahlers & Ogletree Auction Gallery

Bookends, Bronze, Slag Glass, Sliding, Patinated Green Frame, Bradley & Hubbard, c.1900, 3 ¾ x 13 In.
$182

Bruneau & Co. Auctioneers

Bookends, Cats, Seated, Bronze, Hand Hammered Back, Arts & Crafts, 5 ½ x 3 ½ In.
$452

Hartzell's Auction Gallery Inc.

Bottle, Bitters, Dr. J.F. Nolman's Original Spring, Label, Sloping Collar, Pontil
$181

American Bottle Auctions

Bottle, Bitters, Dr Wonser's U.S.A. Indian Root, Aqua, Double Rolled Collar
$25,300

American Bottle Auctions

Bottle, Bitters, Drake's Plantation, Cabin, 6 Log, Amber, Squat Sloping Collar
$147

American Bottle Auctions

BOOKMARK

Bookmarks were originally made of parchment, cloth, or leather. Soon woven silk ribbon, thin cardboard, celluloid, wood, silver, tortoiseshell, and metals were used. Examples made before 1850 are scarce, but there are many to be found dating before 1920.

Brass, Enamel, Art Deco, Step Design, Ford Building, Chicago Fair, 1934 65
Copper, Racehorse, Jockey, 3 ⅝ In. 28
Enamel, Silvertone, Flowers, Green, Plum, Leaves, France, 3 In. 58
Metal, 18K Gold Plated, Monkey, Holding Banana, Taiwan, 1970s, 2 ⅞ In. 10
Silk, Burgundy, Madonna & Child, Embroidery, c.1890, 8 ¾ x 2 In. 32
Silver, Oval, Deep Blue Tassel, c.1980, 2 x 2 ½ In. 199
Sterling Silver, Applied Rooster, Hammered, 3 In. 59
Sterling Silver, Aztec Figure, Stamped, ADC, Mexico, 2 In. 69
Sterling Silver, Corner Style, Chased Flowers, Gorham, 1982, 2 x 2 In. 34
Sterling Silver, Mother-Of-Pearl Handle, Trowel Shape, 1890s, 3 In. 139
Wood, Man In Night Clothes, Sleeping Cap, Painted, Red & Gray, 1940s, 1 x 4 In. 95

BOSSONS

Bossons

Bossons character wall masks (heads), plaques, figurines, and other decorative pieces of chalkware were made by W.H. Bossons, Limited, of Congleton, England. The company was founded in 1946 and closed in 1996. Dates shown are the date the item was introduced.

Wall Figure, Gypsy Girl, Tamarind, Bright Red & Yellow Dress, c.1955, 4 x 2 ½ In. 288
Wall Mask, Austrian Man, Tyrolean Smoking Pipe, 1977, 5 ½ x 3 ½ In. 27
Wall Mask, Desert Hawk, Man & Hawk, Signed, 1961, 6 x 7 In. 55
Wall Mask, Sir Winston Churchill, Blue Bowtie, 1966, 6 ¾ x 4 In. 40

BOSTON & SANDWICH CO. *pieces may be found in the Sandwich Glass category.*

BOTTLE

Bottle collecting has become a major American hobby. There are several general categories of bottles, such as historic flasks, bitters, household, and figural. ABM means the bottle was made by an automatic bottle machine after 1903. Pyro is the shortened form of the word *pyroglaze*, an enameled lettering used on bottles after the mid-1930s. This form of decoration is also called ACL or applied color label. Shapes of bottles often indicate the age of the bottle. For more prices, go to kovels.com.

Calabash flask
1840-1870

Teakettle ink
1830-1885

Case gin bottle
1650-1920

Apothecary, Stoppers, Glass, Early 1900s, 24 x 12 x 12 In., Pair 960
Apothecary, Syr. Phosph Co., Label Under Glass, Cobalt Blue, Cylindrical, Stopper, 6 ¾ In. 72

Avon started in 1886 as the California Perfume Company. It was not until 1929 that the name Avon was used. In 1939, it became Avon Products, Inc. Avon has made many figural bottles filled with cosmetic products. Ceramic, plastic, and glass bottles were made in limited editions from 1965 to 1980. There was a limited-edition bottle collecting frenzy and prices rose. By 2018 the bottle prices were back to a very low level.

Barber, Amethyst, White Enamel, Mary Gregory, Girl With Sprig, Ribbed, Shaped Neck, 8 In. 120
Barber, Cobalt Blue, Silver Band, 7 In., Pair 48

Barber, Orange & White, Swirl, 13 In.	96
Beer, Geo. Ch. Gemenden, Savannah, Ga., Lager, Lime Green, Squat, Blob Top, 6 ¾ In.	108
Beer, T. Maher, Savannah, Ga., Porter & Ale, Emerald Green, Squat, 6 ½ In.	450
Bininger, A.M. & Co., Old London Dock Gin, Green, c.1870, 8 ¾ In.	1080
Bininger, Clock, Regulator, 19 Broad St., N.Y., Yellow Amber, Flask, Double Collar, 6 In.	510
Bitters, A.D. Atkinson, Chirayta, Norvo Tonic Elixir, Aqua, c.1850, 8 ⅞ In.	1200
Bitters, Arabian, An Old & Reliable Tonic, Amber, Arched & Indented Panels, 9 ½ In.	600
Bitters, Bouvier Buchu, Amber, Sloping Collar, Louisville, Ky., 10 ½ In.	108
Bitters, Brady's Family, Amber, Sloping Collar, 9 ½ In.	84
Bitters, Dingens Napoleon Cocktail, Buffalo, Green, Drum Form, Lady's Leg Neck, 10 In.	12000
Bitters, Dr. Ball's Vegetable Stomach, Northboro, Mass., Aqua, Pontil, 7 In.	288
Bitters, Dr. J.F. Nolman's Original Spring, Label, Sloping Collar, Pontil ... *illus*	181
Bitters, Dr. John Bull's Compound Cedron, Louisville, Ky., Yellow Amber, 9 ¾ In.	276
Bitters, Dr. Planett's, Aqua, Sloping Collar, Pontil, 9 ⅞ In.	600
Bitters, Dr Wonser's U.S.A. Indian Root, Aqua, Double Rolled Collar ... *illus*	25300
Bitters, Drake's Plantation, Cabin, 6 Log, Amber, Squat Sloping Collar ... *illus*	147
Bitters, Drake's Plantation X, Patented 1862, 4 Log, Red Amber, 10 In.	120
Bitters, Drake's Plantation X, Patented 1862, Cabin, 6 Log, Amber, Pink Tint, 10 In.	7200
Bitters, English Female, Dromgoole, Louisville, Ky., Blue Aqua, Sloping Collar, 8 ½ In.	300
Bitters, Excelsior Herb, J.V. Mattison, Semi-Cabin, Amber, Flattened Collar, 10 ¼ In.	570
Bitters, G.C. Segur's Golden Seal, Springfield, Mass., Aqua, Sloping Collar, 8 ½ In.	240
Bitters, Globe Tonic, Semi-Cabin, Yellow Amber, Indented Panels, Sloping Collar, 9 ¾ In.	780
Bitters, Greeley's Bourbon Whiskey, Barrel, Dark Amber, Applied Mouth, 1860-80, 9 ½ In. . *illus*	938
Bitters, Greeley's Bourbon, Barrel, Copper Puce, Flattened Collar, 1865-75, 9 ⅛ In.	390
Bitters, Greeley's Bourbon, Barrel, Olive Topaz, Flattened Collar, 1865-75, 9 ¼ In.	2640
Bitters, Greer's Eclipse, Louisville, Ky., Yellow Amber, Indented Panels, 8 ¾ In.	156
Bitters, Holtzermann's Patent Stomach, Cabin, Amber, Sloping Collar, c.1870, 9 ¼ In.	1020
Bitters, J.W. Colton's Nervine, Strengthening, Orange Amber, Flattened Lip, 8 ⅜ In.	300
Bitters, Jackson's Aromatic Life, Deep Olive, Indented Panels, 1855-65, 9 In.	3300
Bitters, Keystone, Barrel, Amber, Sloping Collar, 1865-75, 9 ⅞ In.	390
Bitters, Moulton's Oloroso, Trade Mark, Pineapple, Blue Aqua, Ribbed Neck, 11 ¼ In.	960
Bitters, National, Ear Of Corn, Golden Amber, Neck Ring, Label ... *illus*	678
Bitters, National, Ear Of Corn, Patent 1867, Yellow Amber, Double Collar, 12 ½ In.	228
Bitters, National, Ear Of Corn, Yellow Topaz, Double Collar, 12 ⅛ In.	1440
Bitters, Old Sachem & Wigwam Tonic, Barrel, Peach Topaz, Flattened Lip, 9 ¼ In.	480
Bitters, Olive Amber, Cylindrical, Lady's Leg Neck, Ring Mouth, Pontil, 12 In.	132
Bitters, Oswego, Amber, Rounded Shoulder, Label, Squared Lip ... *illus*	113
Bitters, Pepsin Calisaya, Dr. Russell Med Co., Grass Green, Sloping Collar, 8 In.	84
Bitters, Pepsin, Golden Gate Medicine Co., Orange Amber, Sloping Collar, 1905 ... *illus*	7910
Bitters, Prune Stomach & Liver, Best Cathartic, Blood Purifier, Amber, Sloping Collar .... *illus*	124
Bitters, Quaker, Dr. Flint's, Providence, R.I., Aqua, Label With Quaker Man, 9 ¼ In.	2760
Bitters, Royal Pepsin Stomach, Lion & Unicorn, Amber, Double Ring Collar, 7 ½ In.	276
Bitters, Saint Jacob's, Amber, Case, Sloping Collar, Ohio, 8 ¾ In.	240
Bitters, Schroeder's, Louisville, Ky., Amber, Lady's Leg Neck, 9 ⅛ In.	192
Bitters, Seaworth, Cape May, New Jersey, Lighthouse, Amber, 1880-90, 6 ½ In.	10200
Bitters, Seaworth, Cape May, New Jersey, Lighthouse, Aqua, Sloping Collar, 11 ¼ In.	26400
Bitters, Suffolk, Philbrook & Tucker, Pig, Amber Shaded To Yellow, 10 In.	2400
Bitters, Tyler's Standard American, Red Amber, Sloping Collar, 9 ⅜ In.	300
Bitters, Uncle Tom's Log, Clear, Cylindrical, Textured Log, Tooled Lip, 3 ¾ In.	204
Bitters, Wait's Liver & Kidney, Amber, Label, Contents ... *illus*	192
Bitters, Yellow Olive, Smoky Tone, Barrel, 1865-75, 9 ¼ In.	330
Black Glass, Ale, Cylindrical, Deep Olive Green, Sloping Double Collar, c.1840, 8 ⅜ In.	48
Black Glass, Cylindrical, Dip Mold, Deep Olive Green, Applied Lip, 1780-1800, 9 In.	84
Black Glass, Mallet, Dark Olive Amber, String Lip, Pontil, England, 1740-50, 8 ½ In.	204
Coca-Cola bottles are listed in the Coca-Cola category.	
Cologne, Ball Shape, Cane Circles, Fan Highlights, Ray Cut Base, 5 ¼ In.	90
Cologne, Brazilian Pattern, Ball Shape Stopper, 6 In.	180
Cologne, Cobalt Blue, Diamond Diaper Band, 3-Piece Mold, Flattened Lip, 5 ½ In.	204
Cordial, J.N. Kline & Co., Aromatic Digestive, Wreath, Cobalt Blue, Teardrop, 5 ½ In.	180

Bottle, Bitters, Greeley's Bourbon Whiskey, Barrel, Dark Amber, Applied Mouth, 1860-80, 9 ½ In.
$938

Eldred's

Bottle, Bitters, National, Ear Of Corn, Golden Amber, Neck Ring, Label
$678

American Bottle Auctions

Bottle, Bitters, Oswego, Amber, Rounded Shoulder, Label, Squared Lip
$113

American Bottle Auctions

Bottle, Bitters, Pepsin, Golden Gate Medicine Co., Orange Amber, Sloping Collar, 1905
$7,910

American Bottle Auctions

Bottle, Bitters, Prune Stomach & Liver, Best Cathartic, Blood Purifier, Amber, Sloping Collar
$124

American Bottle Auctions

Bottle, Bitters, Wait's Liver & Kidney, Amber, Label, Contents
$192

American Bottle Auctions

Cosmetic, Bogle's Hyperion Fluid For The Hair, Aqua, Sloping Shoulders, 7 ¾ In. 36
Cosmetic, Nathan Jarvis Orris Tooth Wash, Boston, Aqua, Oval, Rolled Lip, 5 In. 144
Cosmetic, Professor Mott's Magic Hair Invigorator, Price 25 Cents, Aqua, 6 ⅜ In. 360
Cosmetic, Storrs Chemical Hair Invigorator, Aqua, Inward Rolled Lip, 5 ⅜ In. 180
Cure, Dr. L.E. Keeley's Double Chloride Of Gold, For Drunkenness, Tested, 5 ½ In. 252
Cure, Dr. L.E. Keeley's Double Chloride Of Gold, For Tobacco Habit, Infallible, 5 ¾ In. 216
Decanter, Diamond Diaper Band, Sunburst, Olive Amber, Pontil, Tooled Lip, 7 In. 570
Decanter, Diamond Diaper, Fluted Bottom, Square, 3-Piece Mold, Pontil, Stopper, 6 ½ In. 390
Decanter, Diamond Diaper, Fluted Bottom, Square, Emerald Green, Flared Lip, Keene, 8 In. 300
Decanter, Etched Glass, Silver Overlay, Stopper, c.1900, 9 In. 144
Demijohn, Blown, Molded, Olive Green, Applied Mouth, 1800s, 20 x 13 In. 117
Demijohn, Clear, Painted, Merlot, Bulbous, Sloping Collar, 21 In. 177
Demijohn, Green, Hand Blown, 1800s, 26 x 18 In. .... *illus* 148
Demijohn, Green, Squat, Sloping Collar, Pontil, 1800s, 19 x 14 In. .... *illus* 325
Demijohn, Yellow Olive Amber, Bullet Head Form, Sloping Collar, 1830-50, 13 x 5 In. 300
Figural, Book, Departed Spirits, Mottled Glaze, Bennington Pottery, 5 ½ In. 204
Fire Grenade, Hazelton's High Pressure Chemical Fire Keg, Barrel, Amber, 11 In. 510
Fire Grenade, MC Fire Extinguisher, Price $2.00, 12-Sided, Amber, Partial Label, 11 In. 252
Flask, 16 Vertical Ribs, Milk Glass, Elongated Form, Pontil, Tooled Lip, 7 ½ In. 360
Flask, 16 Vertical Ribs, Straw Yellow, Tooled Lip, Pocket, Kent, O., 1820-30, 5 ¼ In. 132
Flask, 20 Vertical Ribs, Pale Green, Rolled Lip, Pocket, 1810-25, 4 In. 264
Flask, Aqua, Embossed, M. Geary Liquor Dealer Woodstock, Va., c.1880, 7 ½ In. 380
Flask, Chestnut, Blue Aqua, Outward Rolled Lip, 1820-40, 7 ⅝ In. 204
Flask, Chestnut, Vertical Ribs, Red Amber, Tooled Lip, Pontil, Zanesville, 1815-35, 6 In. 180
Flask, Columbia & Eagle, Aqua, Pontil, Sheared & Tooled Mouth, Pt. 240
Flask, Cornucopia & Urn, Teal Blue, Sheared & Tooled Lip, Pontil, Pt. 720
Flask, Double Eagle, Forest Green, String Lip, Qt. 228
Flask, Double Eagle, Light Apple Green, Vertical Ribs, Pontil, 1840-50, Pt. 660
Flask, Double Eagle, Olive Amber, Sheared & Tooled Mouth, Pt. 252
Flask, Eagle & Willington, Deep Olive Yellow, Double Collar, Pt. 360
Flask, Eagle & Willington, Olive Green, Sheared & Tooled Lip, Pontil, ½ Pt. 600
Flask, Eagle, Amber, Rounded Shoulders, Ring Mouth, ½ Pt. 120
Flask, For Pike's Peak, Prospector, Eagle, Aqua, Ring Mouth, ½ Pt. 60
Flask, Half Barrel, A Merry Christmas, Happy New Year, Woman & Glass, Amber, 6 In. 720
Flask, Half Barrel, Dr. N. Wilson, Deep Red Amber, Sloping Collar, 7 ¼ In. 108
Flask, Half Pint, Amber, 24 Ribs, Zanesville, c.1830, 4 ¾ In. 519
Flask, Horseman & Hound, Golden Amber, Double Collar, Pt. 510
Flask, Hunter & Fisherman, Calabash, Peach Amber, Sloping Collar, Qt. 192
Flask, Hunter & Fisherman, Calabash, Strawberry Puce, Tapered Collar, Pontil, Qt. 330
Flask, Hunter & Fisherman, Calabash, Teal, Tapered Collar, Pontil, 1855-65, Qt. 450
Flask, Jenny Lind & Glasshouse, Calabash, Aqua, Pontil, Sloping Collar, Qt. 84
Flask, Jenny Lind & Glasshouse, Calabash, Blue Aqua, Vertical Ribs, Applied Lip, Qt. 780
Flask, Jenny Lind & Glasshouse, Calabash, Emerald Green, Sloping Collar, 1855-65, Qt. 3300
Flask, Jenny Lind & Lyre, Blue Aqua, Sheared & Tooled Lip, 1855-60, Pt. 660
Flask, Kossuth & Frigate, Calabash, Aqua, Pontil, Double Collar, Qt. 1080
Flask, Masonic & Eagle, Old Amber, Pontil, Sheared & Tooled Mouth, Pt. 252
Flask, Masonic & Seeing Eye, Forest Green, Sheared & Tooled Lip, Pontil, 1840-50, Pt. 1920
Flask, Masonic Arch & Eagle, Green, Sheared & Tooled Lip, Pontil, Keene, Pt. 720
Flask, Masonic Arch & Frigate, Green Aqua, Sheared & Tooled Lip, Pontil, 1820-30, Pt. 510
Flask, Melon Ribs, 20 Vertical, Bottle Green, Bulbous, Pontil, Sheared Mouth, 6 ½ In. 216
Flask, Our Choice, Cleve & Steve, G. Cleveland & A. Stevenson Busts, Half Barrel, ½ Pt. 300
Flask, Pitkin Type, 26 Broken Ribs, Swirled To Left, Old Yellow Amber, Sheared, 4 ⅞ In. 264
Flask, Pitkin Type, 30 Broken Ribs, Swirled To Right, Light Blue Green, 5 ½ In. 390
Flask, Pitkin Type, 36 Broken Ribs, Swirled To Right, Olive Green, 1790-1810, 6 ⅝ In. 450
Flask, Pitkin Type, Swirled Ribs, Oval, Sloping Shoulder, 6 ¾ In. 75
Flask, Scroll, Aqua, Iron Pontil, Sheared & Tooled Mouth, Pt. 480
Flask, Scroll, Blue Aqua, Corset Waist, Sheared & Tooled Mouth, Pontil, Pt. 216
Flask, Scroll, Blue Aqua, Pinched Waist, Sheared & Tooled, Pittsburgh, Pt. 660
Flask, Scroll, Blue Aqua, Pinched Waist, Sheared & Tooled, Pontil, Pt. 480

Item	Price
Flask, Scroll, Deep Blue Aqua, Green Tint, Ring Mouth, ½ Pt.	84
Flask, Scroll, Deep Ice Blue, Sheared, Pontil, Qt.	300
Flask, Scroll, Deep Yellow Olive Amber, Applied Neck Ring, Pontil, c.1845, Qt.	660
Flask, Scroll, Hearts & Flowers, Blue Aqua, Sheared & Tooled Mouth, Pontil, Qt.	216
Flask, Scroll, Yellow Amber, Olive Tone, Applied Ring Mouth, 1840-50, Pt.	1920
Flask, Sheaf Of Grain & Tree, Calabash, Emerald Green, Double Collar, 1855-65, Qt.	360
Flask, Sheaf Of Grain, Westford Glass Co., Aqua, Ring Mouth, Pt.	96
Flask, South Carolina Dispensary, Palmetto Tree, Aqua, Strapside, ½ Pt.	240
Flask, Stag & Willow Tree, Aqua, Inward Rolled Lip, Pontil, ½ Pt.	660
Flask, Success To The Railroad, Horse Pulling Cart, Dark Olive Amber, Sheared, Pt.	276
Flask, Success To The Railroad, Horse Pulling Cart, Olive Amber, Sheared, Coventry, Pt.	360
Flask, Success To The Railroad, Horse Pulling Cart, Yellow Amber, Pt.	192
Flask, Success To The Railroad, Olive Green, Sheared & Tooled Mouth, Pt.	360
Flask, Sunburst, Golden Yellow Old Amber, Sheared & Tooled Mouth, ½ Pt.	960
Flask, Sunburst, Olive, Amber, c.1830, 7 ½ In. *illus*	1037
Flask, Sunburst, Yellow Amber, Olive Tone, Sheared & Tooled Lip, 1815-35, ½ Pt.	780
Flask, Teardrop, Milk Glass, Cased Red Herringbone Pattern, Tooled Lip, 7 ⅞ In.	144
Flask, Traveler's Companion & Sheaf Of Grain, Deep Red Amber, Tapered Collar, Qt.	228
Flask, Union, Clasped Hands & Eagle, Calabash, Red Amber, Double Collar, Qt.	330
Flask, Union, Clasped Hands & Eagle, Ice Blue, Ring Mouth, Qt.	132
Flask, Washington & Eagle, Aqua, Sheared & Tooled Lip, Qt.	180
Flask, Washington & Taylor, Blue Green, Sheared Mouth, Pontil, Bridgeton, Pt.	390
Flask, Washington & Taylor, Yellow Lime Green, Sheared Lip, Pontil, Qt.	3600
Flask, Washington & Tree, Calabash, Aqua, Double Collar, Qt.	144
Flask, Whiskey, Columbus On A Barrel, Raised Bust, Rooster, Amber, ½ Pt., 5 In.	510
Food, Oil, Amber, Graduated Measure Marks, Pinched & Ruffled Top, Stopper, Paris, 9 In.	84
Fruit Jar, Cunninghams & Co., Pittsburgh, Deep Cornflower Blue, Outward Rolled Lip, Qt.	840
Fruit Jar, Flaccus Bros., Steer's Head, Wheeling, W.Va., Cylindrical, ABM Lip, 6 ¾ In.	48
Fruit Jar, Gilberds Jar, 5-Point Star, Aqua, Ground Lip, 1883-90, ½ Gal.	216
Fruit Jar, Golden Amber, Cylindrical, Applied Wax Seal Ring, 1875-85, Qt.	84
Fruit Jar, Mason's CFJCo Patent Nov 30th 1858, Yellow Green, Zinc Screw Lid, Qt.	192
Fruit Jar, Mason's Patent Nov 30th 1858, Citron, Glass Lid, Zinc Screw Band, Midget	2520
Fruit Jar, Mason's Patent Nov 30th 1858, Shaded Yellow Green, Zinc Lid, ½ Gal.	510
Fruit Jar, Myers Test Jar, Aqua, Sheared & Ground Lip, Metal Cap, Brass Yoke, Qt.	330
Fruit Jar, S.B. Dewey Jr., No. 65 Buffalo St., Rochester, N.Y., Aqua, Squared Collar, Qt.	570
Fruit Jar, Van Vliet Jar Of 1881, Aqua, Glass Lid, Wire & Cast Iron Clamp, Thumbscrew, Pt.	840
Gin, Case, Olive Amber, Applied Lip, Pontil, Dutch, 11 ¼ In.	192
Gin, Tan King Hoey, Samarang, Seal, TKH, Deep Olive Amber, Indonesia, c.1880, 11 ⅝ In.	108
Globular, Green Aqua, Bulbous, Applied Lip, Pontil, 1815-25, 8 ½ In.	180
Globular, Yellow Amber, Olive Tone, Applied Lip, 1790-1810, Miniature, 3 ¼ In.	1920
Globular, Yellow Olive, Amber Tone, String Lip, Pontil, c.1800, 11 In.	420
Ink, Carter's, 6-Sided, Quatrefoils, Cobalt Blue, 2 ⅞ In.	240
Ink, Carter's, Cathedral, Cobalt Blue, 6 Panels, CA-RT-ER On Base, c.1930, 6 ¼ In.	192
Ink, Carter's, Cathedral, Cobalt Blue, 6 Panels, CA-RT-ER On Base, c.1930, 9 ⅞ In.	96
Ink, Carter's, Cylindrical, Shaded Green, Applied Mouth, Pinched Spout, 7 ⅞ In.	144
Ink, Cottage, Blue Aqua, Tooled Mouth, 2 ⅝ In.	144
Ink, David's, Turtle, Golden Amber, Sheared & Ground Lip, 1 ¾ In.	288
Ink, Dog, Sitting, Figural, Clear, Metal Hinged Collar, 1895-1920, 3 ⅞ In.	72
Ink, Fine Black, Made & Sold By J.L. Thompson, Yellow Olive, Flattened Lip, Master, 6 In.	600
Ink, Geometric, Diamond Point, Dark Olive Green, 3-Piece Mold, Disc Mouth, 1815-35, 2 In.	240
Ink, Geometric, Diamond, Olive Green, 3-Piece Mold, Disc Mouth, c.1825, 1 ½ In.	204
Ink, Harrison's Columbian, Blue Aqua, 12-Sided, Double Collar, Master, 7 ¼ In.	330
Ink, Harrison's Columbian, Blue Aqua, Paneled, Double Collar, 9 ¼ In.	3900
Ink, Harrison's Columbian, Cobalt Blue, Inward Rolled Lip, 2 In.	660
Ink, Hover, Cylindrical, Olive Green, Flared Lip, 4 ½ In.	72
Ink, Hover, Cylindrical, Shaded Blue Green, Double Collar, Pinched Spout, Master, 7 ½ In.	144
Ink, J. & I.E.M., Turtle, Apple Green, Paneled Base, 1 ⅝ In.	330
Ink, J. & I.E.M., Turtle, Cobalt Blue, Sheered & Ground Lip, 1 ¾ In.	780
Ink, J. & I.E.M., Turtle, Light Citron, Paneled Base, 1 ¾ In.	510

Bottle, Demijohn, Green, Hand Blown, 1800s, 26 x 18 In.
$148

Leland Little Auctions

Bottle, Demijohn, Green, Squat, Sloping Collar, Pontil, 1800s, 19 x 14 In.
$325

Copake Auctions

Bottle, Flask, Sunburst, Olive, Amber, c.1830, 7 ½ In.
$1,037

Pook & Pook

Bottle, Ink, Teakettle, Opal, Opaque White, Gilt, 10-Sided, Flower Sprays, 1850-90, 3 x 3 In.
$263

Jeffrey S. Evans & Associates

Bottle, Olive Green, Squat, Applied String Lip, 1700s, 6 ⅝ In.
$197

Skinner, Inc.

Bottle, Snuff, Glass, Warriors On Horseback, Painted, Black, Chinese Characters, 1900s, 2 ⅝ x 2 In.
$23

Thomaston Place Auction Galleries

Ink, J.A. Williamson Chemist, Banner, Cylindrical, Aqua, Pinched Spout, Master, 9 ½ In. 60
Ink, Miller's Writing & Copying Fluid, Star, Oval Label Panel, Teal, Master, 9 ¾ In. 510
Ink, S.O. Dunbar, Taunton, Mass., Aqua, Sloping Collar, Master, 8 ¼ In. 84
Ink, Stafford's, Cylindrical, Blue Green, Tooled Mouth, Pour Spout, Master, 9 ¾ In. 84
Ink, Teakettle, 8-Sided, Amethyst, Brass Cap, 2 ⅜ In. 3300
Ink, Teakettle, 8-Sided, Cobalt Blue, Alternating Vertical Ribs, Sheared & Ground Lip, 2 In. 228
Ink, Teakettle, 8-Sided, Yellow Amber, Brass Neck Ring, Hinged Cap, 1 ¼ In. 420
Ink, Teakettle, Barrel, Cobalt Blue, Sheared Lip, Brass Neck Ring, Hinged Cap, 2 ¼ In. 1140
Ink, Teakettle, Cut Glass, Clear, 8-Sided, Brass Hinged Cap, c.1880, 2 ½ In. 510
Ink, Teakettle, Opal, Opaque White, Gilt, 10-Sided, Flower Sprays, 1850-90, 3 x 3 In. ......*illus* 263
Ink, Umbrella, 8-Sided, Cornflower Blue, 1840-60, 2 ½ x 2 ¼ In. 702
Ink, Zieber & Co., Excelsior, 12-Sided, Emerald Green, Applied Flattened Lip, 5 ⅞ In. 2160
Jug, Label Under Glass, Victorian Girl, Clear, Sheared Mouth, Handle, Screw Cap, 6 In. 420
Medicine, Birney's Febrifuge, Aqua, Sloping Collar, 6 ¼ In. 450
Medicine, C. Brinkerhoff's Health Restorative, Price 1 Dollar, Olive Amber Tone, 7 ⅜ In. 840
Medicine, Carter's Spanish Mixture, Grass Green, Double Collar, 8 ¼ In. 660
Medicine, Chadwick's Compound Vegetable Liniment, Aqua, Double Collar, 5 ¼ In. 228
Medicine, Daily's Pain Extractor, Louisville, Ky., Deep Blue Aqua, Rolled Lip, 5 ½ In. 228
Medicine, Dr. Clark, N. York, Deep Blue Green, Straight Sides, Tapered Collar, 9 ¼ In. 840
Medicine, Dr. Cooper's Ethereal Oil For Deafness, Aqua, Inward Rolled Lip, 2 ⅝ In. 540
Medicine, Dr. Duncan's Expectorant, Green Aqua, Outward Rolled Lip, 6 ¼ In. 390
Medicine, Dr. Foord's Pectoral Syrup, New York, Aqua, Sloping Collar, 6 In. 192
Medicine, Dr. G.W. Roback's Scandinavian Blood Purifier, Purely Vegetable, Aqua, 8 ¾ In. 108
Medicine, Dr. H.W. Jackson, Druggist, Vegetable Home Syrup, Yellow Olive, 4 ½ In. 3300
Medicine, Dr. Hawk's Universal Stimulant, Aqua, Cylinder, Flattened Rim, 3 ⅞ In. 120
Medicine, Dr. Hooker's Cough & Croup Syrup, Aqua, Pontil, 5 ½ In. 144
Medicine, Dr. Pinkham's Emmenagogue, Blue Aqua, Sloping Collar, 6 In. 168
Medicine, Dr. Wistar's Balsam Of Wild Cherry, Cincinnati, Sapphire Blue, 8-Sided, 6 ¼ In. 660
Medicine, E. Queru's Cod Liver Oil Jelly, Aqua, Wide Mouth Jar, Rolled Lip, c.1850, 6 In. 108
Medicine, G.W. Merchant, Chemists, Lockport, N.Y., Blue Green, Cylindrical, 7 In. 252
Medicine, G.W. Merchant, Lockport, N.Y., Green, Sloping Collar, c.1850, 5 In. 288
Medicine, Gouley's Fountain Of Health, Baltimore, Fountain, Aqua, Cylindrical, 9 ¾ In. 156
Medicine, Graefenberg Co. Children's Panacea, New York, Blue Aqua, Rolled Lip, 4 In. 144
Medicine, Graefenberg Co. Dysentery Syrup, New York, Aqua, Sloping Collar, 5 ¾ In. 144
Medicine, H. Lake's Indian Specific, Blue Aqua, Shaped Neck, Ring Mouth, 8 ¼ In. 510
Medicine, Hoover & Bryant, New Albany, Ind., Blue Aqua, Rolled Lip, 4 ¼ In. 480
Medicine, McLean's Volcanic Liniment Oil, Aqua, Sloping Shoulders, 6 ⅛ In. 180
Medicine, Phelps's Arcanum, Worcester, Mass., Olive Amber, Recessed Panels, 8 ½ In. 2760
Medicine, Reed & Cutler Druggists, Boston, Aqua, Cylindrical, Rounded Shoulders, 7 ¾ In. 144
Medicine, Rohrer's Expectoral Wild Cherry Tonic, Amber, Roped Corners, 10 ¼ In. 1800
Medicine, Swaim's Panacea, Philada., Light Apple Green, Double Collar, Pontil, 8 ⅜ In. 780
Medicine, Vaughn's Vegetable Lithontriptic Mixture, Buffalo, Blue Aqua, Indented Panels, 8 In. 300
Medicine, W.W. Clark's Infallible Worm Syrup, Phila., Aqua, Inward Rolled Lip, 4 In. 60
Medicine, Winchester's Kentucky Liniment, Aqua, Cylindrical, Rolled Lip, 4 ⅞ In. 276
Milk, Standard Dairy Farm Co., Shanghai, Chinese Letters, ABM, Qt. 48
Mineral Water, A. Dearborn & Co., New York, Cobalt Blue, Blob Top, 7 ⅜ In. 240
Mineral Water, A. Hain & Son, Lebanon, Pa., Cobalt Blue, Blob Top, 7 ¼ In. 120
Mineral Water, A.D. Schnackenberg & Co., Brooklyn, Yellow Amber, Sloping Collar, Pt. 48
Mineral Water, Adirondack Spring Co., Whitehall, N.Y., Green, Sloping Double Collar, Pt. 84
Mineral Water, Blount Spring Natural Sulphur Water, Alabama, Cobalt Blue, 7 ⅝ In. 252
Mineral Water, C. Cleminshaw, Troy, N.Y., Deep Cobalt Blue, Blob Top, 7 ⅛ In. 132
Mineral Water, Congress & Empire Spring Co., C, Emerald Green, Double Collar, Pt. 84
Mineral Water, Darien Mineral Springs, Tifft & Perry, Darien Center, N.Y., Blue Aqua, Pt. 288
Mineral Water, Deep Rock Spring, Oswego, N.Y., Blue Aqua, Double Collar, Pt. 156
Mineral Water, Gettysburg Katalysine Water, Emerald Green, Sloping Double Collar, Qt. 96
Mineral Water, Geyser Spring, Saratoga, State Of New York, Teal, Double Collar, Pt. 120
Mineral Water, Guilford Mineral Spring Water, Vt., Blue Green, Double Collar, Qt. 120
Mineral Water, John H. Gardner & Son, Sharon Springs, N.Y., Green, Double Collar, Pt. 276
Mineral Water, Kissingen Water, Hanbury Smith, Olive Amber, Applied Collar, Cork & Wire, Pt. 96

Mineral Water, Lynch & Clarke, New York, Deep Olive Amber, Sloping Double Collar, Pt. 300
Mineral Water, Minnequa Water, Bradford Co., Pa., Blue Aqua, Double Collar, Pt. 264
Mineral Water, Pavilion & United States Spring Co., Saratoga, N.Y., Olive Green, Pt................ 108
Mineral Water, S. Smith, Auburn, N.Y., Cobalt Blue, Tenpin, Blob Top, 8 1/4 In. 180
Mineral Water, Saratoga Red Spring, Emerald Green, Double Collar, Pt.................................. 144
Mineral Water, Teller's, Detroit, Cobalt Blue, Tenpin, Sloping Collar, 7 3/4 In........................... 216
Nursing, 14 Vertical Ribs, Elongated Form, Light Green, Tooled Lip, 6 1/4 In. 228
Olive Green, Squat, Applied String Lip, 1700s, 6 5/8 In. ....*illus* 197
Pepper Sauce, Cathedral, 6-Sided, Aqua, Sloping Double Collar, 8 3/4 In. 84
Perfume bottles are listed in the Perfume Bottle category. ....
Pickle, Barrel, 7-Up Green, Bulbous, Pontil, Tooled Lip, 9 3/4 In... 60
Pickle, Cathedral, 4-Sided, Blue Green, Outward Rolled Lip, 11 3/4 In. 330
Pickle, Cathedral, 4-Sided, Shaded Green, Outward Rolled Lip, 11 1/2 In... 240
Pickle, Cathedral, Deep Yellow Amber, Outward Rolled Lip, Willington, 8 1/4 In. 8400
Pickle, Heinz Bros. & Co., Gherkins, Iron Cross In Shield, Pittsburgh, Label, 6 1/4 In. 84
Pickle, W.K. Lewis, Boston, Blue Aqua, 5 Lobed Panels, Outward Rolled Lip, 10 1/2 In. 1320
Poison, Embossed Poison, Transfer, Swift's Arsenate Of Lead, Stoneware Crock, Handle, 6 In. 132
Sarsaparilla, Ayer's Concentrated Compound Extract, Lowell, Mass., Double Collar, 7 3/4 In. .. 330
Sarsaparilla, Bristol's Extract, Buffalo, Light Citron, Arched Indented Panels, 6 In. 450
Sarsaparilla, Bristol's, Buffalo, Aqua, Sloping Collar, Pontil, 1840-60, 5 5/8 In........................ 216
Sarsaparilla, Dr. Guysott's Yellow Dock, Blue Aqua, Oval, Sloping Collar, 10 In. 450
Sarsaparilla, John Bull's Extract, Louisville, Ky., Aqua, Sloping Collar, 9 1/2 In. 450
Sarsaparilla, John Bull's King Of Pain, New York, Light Green Aqua, Sloping Collar, 5 In. 132
Sarsaparilla, Old Dr. J. Townsend's, New York, Cornflower Blue, Tapered Collar, 9 3/8 In. 1320
Sarsaparilla, Old Dr. J. Townsend's, New York, Shaded Amber, Sloping Collar, 9 1/2 In. 3600
Sarsaparilla, Sand's Genuine, New York, Aqua, Double Collar, c.1850, 10 1/8 In. 360
Sarsaparilla, Turner's, Buffalo, N.Y., Blue Aqua, Sloping Collar, c.1860, 12 1/4 In...................... 1020
Seal, Brynker, Wine, Dark Olive Amber, Cylindrical, Double Collar, 1840-50, 11 3/4 In. 60
Seal, F.J.O., Wine, Olive Green, Cylindrical, Double Collar, England, c.1845, 10 1/2 In................ 390
Seal, Nathans Bros 1863 Phila, Dark Chocolate Amber, Double Collar, Qt.................................. 96
Seal, Raised Hand, T.C., Wine, Cylindrical, Deep Olive, Dip Mold, Double Collar, 10 1/4 In. 300
Seal, T.C. Pearsall, Wine, Onion, Olive Green, Double Collar, Magnum, 1800-20, 10 3/8 In. 840
Seal, W. Floyd 1790, Wine, Deep Olive Green, Cylindrical, Dip Mold, String Lip, 9 1/4 In. 4200
Snuff, Cobalt Blue, Red Stopper, Disc Shape, 2 3/4 In. 170
Snuff, Flora & Fauna, Silver Cap, Purple Stone Finial, Chinese, 3 In. 480
Snuff, Glass, Cricket, Enameled, Yellow Ground, Marked, Qianlong, Chinese, 3 x 2 In. 1100
Snuff, Glass, Painted, 2 Cats, 2 Panda Bears On Reverse, Signed, Liu Shouben, 1977, 2 1/2 In... 1342
Snuff, Glass, Warriors On Horseback, Painted, Black, Chinese Characters, 1900s, 2 5/8 x 2 In. ...*illus* 23
Snuff, Ivory, Carved, Figures On Balcony, Figures In Boat, Painted, 1800s, 3 1/4 In. ....*illus* 1750
Snuff, Porcelain, 2 Neck, Molded Scene, Gilt & Gold Ground, Chinese, 1750s, 3 In. ....*illus* 488
Snuff, Porcelain, Blue & Iron Red Paint, Courtyard Scene, Chinese, 3 1/2 In............................... 549
Snuff, Porcelain, Blue & White, Figures, Chinese, 1900s, 3 In. 50
Snuff, Porcelain, Blue, White Clouds, Dragon, Stopper, Round Wood Base, Chinese, 2 3/4 In..... 219
Snuff, Porcelain, Portraits Of 18 Legendary Figures, Coral Lid, Multicolor, 1700s, 3 In. 878
Snuff, Wood, Carved Fish, Dragonfly, Flowers, Silver Top, Cabochons, Early 1900s, 2 5/8 In....... 156
Soda, Boley & Co., Sac City Cal, Cobalt Blue, Glass, 8 1/2 x 2 3/4 In. 210
Soda, E.M. Gatchell & Co., Charleston, S.C., Blue Green, Sloping Collar, 7 3/4 In. 330
Soda, Fowler's Smash, Triangular, Label, Fluted Cap, c.1910, 13 1/2 x 4 In. 2160
Soda, S.C. Dennis & Co., Hilton Head, S.C., Blue Green, Blob Top, 1860-70, 7 3/4 In..................... 1140
Soda, Smith & Co. Premium, Charleston, Cobalt Blue, 8-Sided, Sloping Collar, 7 1/2 In............ 720
Soda, Smith & Co. Premium, Charleston, Green, 8-Sided, Pontil, Sloping Collar, 7 1/2 In......... 264
Storage, Barrel, Cobalt Blue, Applied Ring Mouth, France, 14 1/2 In... 216
Storage, Jar, Old Amber, Flared Out Lip, 1830-50, 7 5/8 x 5 In... 300
Storage, Yellow Amber, 4 Arched Sides, Dip Mold, Sloping Double Collar, c.1840, 8 In.............. 1080
Tonic, Dr. Bates National, Centennial 1876, Red Amber, Torpedo, Wire Pull Closure, 9 In. 228
Utility, Globular, Blue Green, Tapered Neck, Round Mouth, Pontil Mark, 1797-1830, 8 In. 164
Whiskey, C.C.G., Rochester, N.Y., Full Pint, Amber, Flask, Tooled Lip, Pt.................................... 96
Whiskey, Campus, Gossler Bros., Columbus Ave., N.Y., Amber, Miniature Jug, 3 3/8 In. 180
Whiskey, Chestnut, Amber, Free Blown, Ring Mouth, Handle, 1850-60, 8 1/2 In.......................... 48

Bottle, Snuff, Ivory, Carved, Figures On Balcony, Figures In Boat, Painted, 1800s, 3 1/4 In.
$1,750

Eldred's

Bottle, Snuff, Porcelain, 2 Neck, Molded Scene, Gilt & Gold Ground, Chinese, 1750s, 3 In.
$488

Nadeau's Auction Gallery

Bottle, Whiskey, Cranberry, White Leaves, Silver Stopper, Cork Plug, Pontil, 11 1/2 In., Pair
$210

Woody Auctions

Bottle, Whiskey, J.H. Cutter Old Bourbon, No. 1, Orange Amber, Sloping Collar, Fifth
$102

American Bottle Auctions

Bottle, Whiskey, Seagram's, Crown Royal, Blended Scotch, Purple Felt Bag, 1964, 5 ¾ x 7 In.
$35

Witherell's

Dual Purpose

Many older bottle openers have a small square hole called a "Prest-O-Lite Key." It was used to turn the valve on automobile gas headlights from about 1910 through the early 1930s, before electric headlights were used.

Whiskey, Cranberry, White Leaves, Silver Stopper, Cork Plug, Pontil, 11 ½ In., Pair ....*illus* 210
Whiskey, Diamond Pattern, Ray Cut Base, Stopper, Pitkin & Brooks, 13 In. 225
Whiskey, J.H. Cutter Old Bourbon, No. 1, Orange Amber, Sloping Collar, Fifth .... *illus* 102
Whiskey, Jesse Moore, Antlers, Medium Shaded To Light Amber, 1876-85 226
Whiskey, Old Maryland, G. Riesmeyer, Pottery, Blue Logo, K.T. & K., 7 ½ In. 352
Whiskey, Old Mountain Dew, Thos. Oates, Pottery, Distillery Scene, Shamrocks, 7 In. 1140
Whiskey, Paul Jones Pure Rye, Man Pouring Whiskey, Clear, Enamel, Pinched Neck, 6 In. 132
Whiskey, Pennsylvania Club Pure Rye, Pottery, Logo, Bulbous, 7 x 5 In. 461
Whiskey, Seagram's, Crown Royal, Blended Scotch, Purple Felt Bag, 1964, 5 ¾ x 7 In. ....*illus* 35
Whiskey, Spirits, Barrel, Cobalt Blue, Horizontal Ribs, Coggle Bands, 4 Applied Feet, 4 x 7 In.. 1320
Whiskey, Udolpho Wolfe's Aromatic Schnapps, Olive Amber, 9 ½ In. 330
Whiskey, Udolpho Wolfe's Aromatic Schnapps, Yellow Olive Amber, 9 ¾ In. 204
Wine, Dutch Onion, Shaded Olive Green, Applied String Lip, Pontil, 1740, 7 In. 132
Wine, Dutch, Olive Green, Dip Mold, Cylindrical, Elongated Neck, String Lip, c.1790, 11 In. 84
Wine, Kidney, Light Green, Outward Rolled Lip, Pontil, 1760-90, 4 ½ In. 262
Wine, Mallet, Deep Olive Amber, Applied String Lip, Pontil, 1735-45, 6 ⅝ In. 192
Wine, Onion, Shaded Emerald Green, Applied String Lip, Pontil, 1720-50, 7 ¼ In. 144
Wine, Onion, Yellow Olive, String Lip, 1730-35, 6 ½ In. 510
Zanesville, 10 Diamonds, Amber, Tooled Lip, Pontil, 5 ⅛ In. 84

BOTTLE CAP

Bottle caps for milk bottles are the printed cardboard caps used since the 1920s. Crown caps, used after 1892 on soda bottles, are also popular collectibles. Unusual mottoes, graphics, and caps from bottlers that are out of business bring the highest prices.

Crown, Blue Bird Grape Soda, Blue Lettering, Cork Lined, 1940s 3
Crown, Metz Beer, Green Lettering, Metal, Cork Lined, Omaha, Nebraska, 1930s 10
Crown, Nesbitt's Fruit Punch, Red, White, Cork Lined, 1960s, 10 Piece 9
Crown, Pfeiffer's Beer, Yellow, Red Lettering, Cork Lined, Detroit, Mich., 1940s 10
Crown, RC Cola With A Twist, Yellow, Red, White, Green, Plastic Lined 2
Crown, Sioux City Sarsaparilla, White, Brown Lettering, Plastic Lined 2
Crown, Tudor, White, Blue Lettering, Metal, Cork Lined, 1950s 6
Crown, Vernor's Ginger Ale, Yellow, Green Lettering, Cork Lined, 9 Piece 7
Dairi-Rich Chocolate Drink, Brown Lettering, 1 ⅜ In., 9 Piece 3
F.C. Engel & Sons, Brown, Green Lettering, 1940s, 4 Piece 12
Sign, Figural, Alligator, Wood, Bottle Caps, Louisiana Bayou, c.1910, 15 x 60 In. ....*illus* 2700

BOTTLE OPENER

Bottle openers are needed to open many bottles. As soon as the commercial bottle was invented, the opener to be used with the new types of closures became a necessity. Many types of bottle openers can be found, most dating from the twentieth century. Collectors prize advertising and comic openers.

Antler, Stainless Steel Opener, Silver Ferrule, John Hasselbring, 10 ½ In. 115
Circus Man's Face, 4 Blurry Eyes, Handlebar Moustache, Teeth Opener 11
Dog, Dachshund, Brass, 1960s, 4 ½ In. 30
Dog, Spaniel, Pointing, Grassy Base, Cast Iron, Scott, N.J. 15
Donkey's Head, Open Mouth, Textured Silvertone Metal, 3 ¾ In. 19
Duck Head, Brass, 1970s, 3 x 4 In. 16
Fish, Abalone Inlay, Mexico, 1960s, 5 In. 24
Horn Handle, Steer's, Brass Opener End, Marked, Denmark, 1960s 24
Land Rover, Logo, Brass, Aged Patina, Wall Mount, 3 ¼ In., Pair 33
Log Man, Wood, Black Forest Carved, Germany, c.1950, 7 ½ In. 15
Nude Woman, Brass, Art Deco, c.1940 17
Owl, Sterling Silver, Wide Eyes, Stainless Steel Opener, Marked, Gorham, 4 In. 46
Parrot, Chrome, Open Mouth, Tail Opens To Corkscrew, Art Deco Style 17
Pheasant, Cast Aluminum, 4 In. 29
Silver, Cactus Pattern, Georg Jensen, 1930s, 4 ¾ In. 145

Bottle Cap, Sign, Figural, Alligator, Wood, Bottle Caps, Louisiana Bayou, c.1910, 15 x 60 In.
$2,700

Morphy Auctions

Collector's Lament

Here's a quote that really speaks to us: A lifelong collector said he "gravitates toward four categories: broken, large, heavy, and useless."

Box, Ballot, Metal Drum, Handle, Stenciled, Geo. D. Barnard & Co., 13 x 15 x 12 ½ In.
$300

Rich Penn Auctions

Box, Bandbox, Wallpaper, White, Brown, Blue Ground, Erie Canal, c.1830, 12 ½ x 21 x 17 In.
$1,968

Skinner, Inc.

Box, Bentwood, Oval, Laced Seams, Spring Latch, Red, Marked BCD, Strand, 1880, 4 x 9 In.
$210

Garth's Auctioneers & Appraisers

Box, Bible, Lid, Chippendale, Walnut, Interior Till, Brass Escutcheon, Pa., 9 x 18 x 11 In.
$2,750

Conestoga Auction Company

Box, Bride's, Bentwood, Carved Handle, Painted, Flowers, Scandinavia, Early 1800s, 7 x 12 x 7 In.
$339

Soulis Auctions

Box, Candle, Mahogany, Lift Lid, Whale Ivory Knob, 14 ¾ x 6 x 11 In.
$344

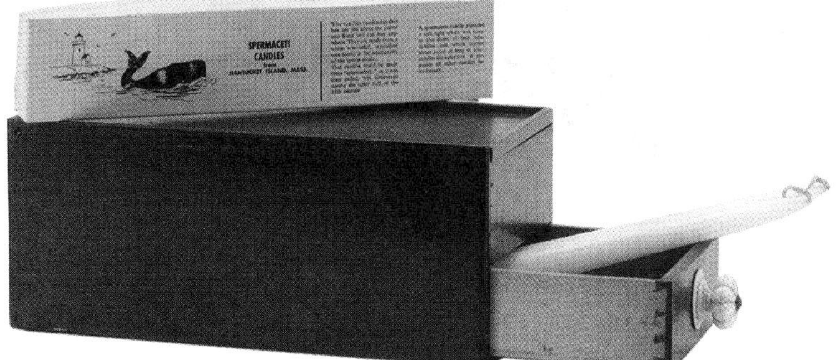

Eldred's

Box, Candle, Milk Paint, Wood, Hanging, 1800s, 10 x 17 In.
$403

Richard D. Hatch & Associates

Box, Candle, Slide Lid, Rectangular, Flat Handle, 3 ¾ x 15 x 6 ½ In.
$480

Soulis Auctions

Box, Candle, Slide Lid, Softwood, Sponge Swirl Paint, Fitted Interior, Pa., 1800s, 6 x 9 x 15 In.
$236

Conestoga Auction Company

TIP

Outdoor flea market displays of metal, glass, and pottery often get very hot. Do not use bubble wrap when packing items like this. The plastic may melt and stick to the antique. Wrap pieces in paper first, preferably white tissue paper, then wrap over the paper to protect against breakage.

Box, Cigarette, Silver, Gucci Monogram, Rectangular, Wood Interior, England, Mid 1900s
$375

Roland Auctioneers & Valuers

Box, Coal, Renaissance Revival, Repousse, Brass Panels, Pine, Late 1800s, 22 x 15 x 14 In.
$177

Leland Little Auctions

Box, Cricket, Hinged Lid, Openwork, Silver, Early 1900s, 3 ¾ In.
$86

Skinner, Inc.

Box, Cutlery, Hinged Lid, Tiger Maple, Turned Feet, Scroll Handle, 1830s, 11 x 14 x 10 In.
$2,223

Jeffrey S. Evans & Associates

Box, Cutlery, Whalebone, Wood, 2 Compartments, Carved Tooth Handle, 1800s, 5 x 13 x 8 In.
$492

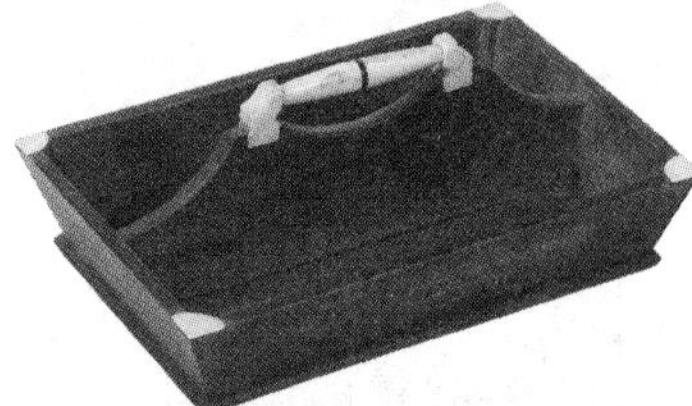

Skinner, Inc.

Box, Dome Lid, Basswood, Square Nail Construction, Red, Yellow, 1850s, 11 x 21 In.
$469

Garth's Auctioneers & Appraisers

Sterling Silver, Acorn Tip, Marked, Georg Jensen, Denmark, 4 ¾ In. 52
Toucan, Cast Iron, Painted Red & Yellow, Green Stand, c.1940 35

BOTTLE STOPPER

Bottle stoppers are made of glass, metal, plastic, and wood. Decorative and figural stoppers are used to replace the original cork stoppers and are collected today.

Porcelain, Cat, White, Yellow Eyes, Red Mouth, 4 ¾ In., 2 Piece 64
Silver Plate, King Francis Pattern, Reed & Barton, 3 ½ In. 54
Silver, Llama, Peru, 1930s, 3 ⅞ x 1 In. 175
Silver, Windmill, c.1900, 2 ¾ x 2 In. 204
Wood, Owl, Carved, Glass Eyes, Porcelain Base, 1960s, 3 ⅝ In. 9

BOX

Boxes of all kinds are collected. They were made of wood, metal, tortoiseshell, embroidery, or other material. Additional boxes may be listed in other sections, such as Advertising, Battersea, Ivory, Shaker, Tinware, and various Porcelain categories. Tea Caddies are listed in their own category.

Ballot, Metal Drum, Handle, Stenciled, Geo. D. Barnard & Co., 13 x 15 x 12 ½ In. .... *illus* 300
Bandbox, Lid, Bentwood, Block Printed Wallpaper, Gold Accent, 1830s, 7 ½ x 11 In. 240
Bandbox, Wallpaper, White, Brown, Blue Ground, Erie Canal, c.1830, 12 ½ x 21 x 17 In. *illus* 1968
Bentwood, Lid, Round, Yellow Milk Paint, Nail Construction, 1800s, 2 x 6 In. 226
Bentwood, Maple, Pine, Lapped & Tacked, Red Surface, 1850s, 6 ½ x 21 In. 600
Bentwood, Oval, Laced Seams, Spring Latch, Red, Marked BCD, Strand, 1880, 4 x 9 In. .*illus* 210
Bible, Hinged Lid, Oak, Heart, Wrought Iron Latch, Early 1800s 173
Bible, Lid, Chippendale, Walnut, Interior Till, Brass Escutcheon, Pa., 9 x 18 x 11 In. .... *illus* 2750
Bible, Lift Lid, Oak, Flowers, Carved, 1761, 7 ½ x 13 x 25 In. 305
Bible, Pine Lid, Oak Cleats, Carved Ends, Geometric Border, Bill McKeever, 9 x 24 x 13 In. 3198
Bride's, Bentwood, Carved Handle, Painted, Flowers, Scandinavia, Early 1800s, 7 x 12 x 7 In. *illus* 339
Bride's, Lid, Angular Ear, Painted, Scandinavia, 1800s, 8 ¾ In. 222
Bride's, Lid, Bentwood, Laced Seams, Roses, Couple, 1800s, 8 x 19 In. 300
Burl, Lid, Mahogany Geometric Inlay, Brass Lion's Paw Feet, 1800s, 4 x 10 x 7 ½ In. 360
Candle, Dome Lid, Tin, Punched Heart, Clover, 8 ½ x 4 x 4 ½ In. 118
Candle, Hinged Lid, Mahogany, Oval Inlaid Front Panel, 1800s, 20 x 8 x 7 In. 148
Candle, Mahogany, Carved, Inlaid, Cutout Top, 1800s, 19 x 8 ½ x 6 In. 295
Candle, Mahogany, Lift Lid, Whale Ivory Knob, 14 ¾ x 6 x 11 In. .... *illus* 344
Candle, Milk Paint, Wood, Hanging, 1800s, 10 x 17 In. .... *illus* 403
Candle, Oak, Heart Shape Cutout, Sliding Panel, Stamped Flower, Early 1800s, 15 ½ In. 138
Candle, Slide Lid, Cherry, Molded Edges, Dovetailed, Hanging Plate, 1800s, 15 x 5 x 4 In. 380
Candle, Slide Lid, Rectangular, Flat Handle, 3 ¾ x 15 x 6 ½ In. .... *illus* 480
Candle, Slide Lid, Rosewood, Dovetailed, c.1815, 6 x 12 ¾ x 4 In. 115
Candle, Slide Lid, Softwood, Sponge Swirl Paint, Fitted Interior, Pa., 1800s, 6 x 9 x 15 In. *illus* 236
Candle, Slide Lid, Walnut, Molded Top, Turned Knob, 1800s, 5 x 11 x 5 ⅝ In. 277
Candle, Spoon Rack, Lollipop Top, Wood, Brown Paint, 12 ½ In. 720
Candle, Wall, Tiger Maple, Pegged Hinges, Lollipop Back, 1900s, 9 ½ x 10 x 5 In. 300
Casket, Hinged Lid, Octagonal, Black, Red, Hardstone, Gioielleria Nardi Venezia, 5 ½ x 5 In... 313
Casket, Truncated Lid, Atop, Tufted Interior, 1700s, 9 ½ x 13 x 14 In. 3998
Chest, Walnut, 5 Drawers, Brass Handles, George II, 32 x 32 x 19 In. 1230
Cigarette, Austrian Bronze, Camel, Trees, Rectangular, Black Ground, c.1800s, 4 ½ In. 100
Cigarette, Lid, Enamel, Silver Plate, Black Ground, Wood Lined Interior, Los Castillo, Taxco .. 192
Cigarette, Parker Organ Shape, 2 Doors, Wood, Stepped Round Feet, c.1900, 9 x 5 x 6 In. 228
Cigarette, Silver, Gucci Monogram, Rectangular, Wood Interior, England, Mid 1900s ....*illus* 375
Coal, Renaissance Revival, Repousse, Brass Panels, Pine, Late 1800s, 22 x 15 x 14 In. .....*illus* 177
Cricket, Hinged Lid, Openwork, Silver, Early 1900s, 3 ¾ In. .... *illus* 86
Cutlery, Hinged Lid, Tiger Maple, Turned Feet, Scroll Handle, 1830s, 11 x 14 x 10 In. ......*illus* 2223
Cutlery, Sloping Sides, Rose, Leaf, Orange Ground, 3 x 13 x 5 In. 369
Cutlery, Tiger Maple, Turned Handle, Sloping Sides, 1800s, 5 x 14 x 10 In. 615

Box, Donation, Table Shape, Carved, Top Opens, Turned Legs, Early 1900s, 6 x 7 x 4 In.
$531

Leland Little Auctions

Box, Dresser, Gilt Metal, Enamel, Classical Scene, Scrolled Feet, Vienna, 3 ⅝ x 5 x 3 ¾ In.
$1,029

Fontaine's Auction Gallery

Boom!
Watch out for exploding antiques! Guns, shells, powder cans, nitrate movie film, and some chemicals left in old bottles or cans are dangerous. If you don't know about these items, contact your local police or fire department for help.

Box, Dresser, Lapis Lazuli, Hinged Lid, Tooled Bronze, Ball Feet, Continental, 2 x 3 ½ In.
$1,464

Neal Auction Company

Box, Dresser, Mixed Wood, Compass Star, American Flag, Shield Escutcheon, 1800s, 6 x 13 x 8 In.
$438

Cowan's Auctions

Box, Hat, Circular, Monogram, Brass Lock, Louis Vuitton
$531

Hindman Auctions

Box, Jewelry, Gilt Bronze, Tripod Base, Copper Portrait Of Woman, 1800s, 4 ¾ x 4 ¾ In.
$448

Cowan's Auctions

TIP

Look at your house from the outside and be sure valuable paintings, silver, or other belongings are not visible from the street, especially near doors and windows. It could be an invitation to a burglar.

Cutlery, Walnut, Canted Corners, Heart Handle, Dovetailed, 1800s, 15 ½ In. 1046
Cutlery, Whalebone, Wood, 2 Compartments, Carved Tooth Handle, 1800s, 5 x 13 x 8 In. *illus* 492
Document, Coromandel, Hinged Dome Lid, Silk Lined Interior, Early 1800s, 6 x 9 x 5 In. 384
Document, Dome Lid, Asphaltum Ground, Clasp & Bail Handle, 1810s, 7 x 10 x 7 In. 1404
Document, Dome Lid, Strap Hinges, Wrought Iron Handle, Carved, 1769, 11 x 18 x 10 In. 351
Document, Dome Lid, Walnut, Bridgeware Inlaid Bands, Lock, 6 x 12 x 9 In. 115
Document, Exotic Wood, Hand Painted, Brass Mounts, Colonial, Spain, 8 x 11 x 8 In. 1062
Document, Hardwood, Carved, Maps, Telescopes, Paw Feet, 1700s, 19 x 11 ½ x 11 ½ In. 2091
Document, Hinged Dome Lid, Tooled, Leather, 5 ½ x 8 x 3 ½ In. 250
Document, Hinged Lid, Molded 3 Sides, Brass, Mustard, Painted, 1800s, 9 x 18 x 11 In. 82
Document, Hinged Lid, Pine, Green, Signed James W. Webber Durham, 5 ½ x 12 x 6 In. 781
Document, Lift Lid, Wood, Black, Orange, Red Interior, Late 1800s, 4 ¾ x 12 x 8 In. 72
Document, Mixed Wood, Molding, Paneled Sides, Turned Feet, Late 1800s, 6 x 13 x 8 In. 138
Document, Oak, Carved, Stylized Flowers, Keyhole, English, 1700s, 9 x 27 In. 280
Document, Pine, Putty Painted, Lid, August Knapp, 1800s, 7 x 15 x 9 In. 308
Document, Pine, Sponge Painted, Blue Ground, Yellow Pinstripes, New England, 1800s, 6 x 14 In. .. 580
Document, Pine, Tacks, Hinged Metal Lid, Ring Handle, August Knapp, 1800s, 5 x 14 x 6 In. . 86
Document, Spanish Colonial, Walnut, Dovetailed, Bail Handles, 1700s, 10 x 23 x 15 In. 384
Dome Lid, Basswood, Square Nail Construction, Red, Yellow, 1850s, 11 x 21 In. ....*illus* 469
Dome Lid, Coffin Shape, Burl Inlay, Ebonized, Disk Feet, Handles, 12 x 16 ¾ In. 1790
Dome Lid, Continental, Painted Beech, Floral, Blue Ground, 1800s, 6 x 10 ½ In. 397
Dome Lid, Green Paint, Man, Woman, Child, Dog, Horse, Tree, 15 x 6 x 7 ½ In. 325
Dome Lid, Pine, Cylindrical, Putty Painted, 1800s, 13 x 28 x 14 ½ In. 185
Dome Lid, Pine, Paint Decorated, Lock, Scandinavia, 8 x 13 x 8 In. 338
Dome Lid, Pine, Yellow, Red, Black Striping, Embossed Brass On Lid, 1810s, 7 x 16 x 8 In. 870
Dome Lid, Red Ground, Black Spots, Heart Escutcheons, L. Hall, 1850s, 12 x 28 x 13 ½ In. 400
Dome Lid, Tin, Wrigglework Heart, Bail Handle, Rectangular, 1800s, 4 ½ x 8 ⅝ In. 1037
Donation, Table Shape, Carved, Top Opens, Turned Legs, Early 1900s, 6 x 7 x 4 In. ....*illus* 531
Dresser, Art Deco Style, Round, Orange Ground, Egyptian Woman Handle, 7 ½ x 4 ¾ In. 123
Dresser, Custard, Brass Mounts, 2 Children, Jumping Rope, Ball Feet, c.1900, 5 x 3 x 4 In. 351
Dresser, Flame Mahogany Top, Rectangular, Gilt Edging, Lock, Key, 4 x 9 ¾ x 7 In. 115
Dresser, Gilt Metal, Enamel, Classical Scene, Scrolled Feet, Vienna, 3 ⅝ x 5 x 3 ¾ In. ....*illus* 1029
Dresser, Hinged Lid, Lapis Veneer, Gilt Bronze Trim, Footed, 3 x 6 x 9 In. 726
Dresser, Hinged Lid, Silver, Isabel & Marjorie, Scroll Feet, 3 x 10 ½ x 5 In. 605
Dresser, Hinged Lid, Sterling Silver Collar, Round, Marked, C.F. Monroe, 3 ½ x 7 ½ In. 250
Dresser, Lapis Lazuli, Hinged Lid, Tooled Bronze, Ball Feet, Continental, 2 x 3 ½ In. ....*illus* 1464
Dresser, Milk Glass, Bronze, Painted, Paw Feet, Russia, 6 ½ x 6 ½ x 6 ½ In. 148
Dresser, Mixed Wood, Compass Star, American Flag, Shield Escutcheon, 1800s, 6 x 13 x 8 In. ..*illus* 438
Dresser, Pine, Black Calligraphy Style Scrolls, Yellow Ground, Smoked, 1800s, 3 x 8 In. 671
Dresser, Vineyard Scene, Capo-Di-Monte Style, Bronze Ormolu Mount, Porcelain, 4 x 5 In. 460
Dresser, Walnut, Veneer, Mother-Of-Pearl Inlay, Rectangular, Locked, 5 x 10 ¾ x 7 ¾ In. 120
Dresser, Wave Crest, Cream Tone, Enamel, Flower, Gilded, Claw Feet, Satin, 6 ½ x 7 x 7 In. 94
Friesian, Slide Lid, Oak, Geometric, Dovetailed, Heart Handle, 1700s, 3 ½ x 5 ¾ x 10 ½ In. 3690
Gambler, Chest, Wrought Iron, Card Design, Hinged Lid, Handles, Key, Padlock, 8 x 22 x 15 In. 3630
Hanging, Walnut, Inlaid Bird, Early 1800s, 5 ¾ x 16 In. 2196
Hat, Circular, Monogram, Brass Lock, Louis Vuitton ....*illus* 531
Hinged Lid, Hardstone, Brass, Mounted, Chinese, 4 x 8 x 5 ¾ In. 63
Honor, Tobacco, Brass, Ball Feet, Handle, Marked Rich's, Early 1800s, 7 x 9 x 4 ¾ In. 594
Humidor, Tiger Oak, Brass Trim, Hinged Doors, Interior Division, c.1900, 6 x 10 x 6 ½ In. 230
Iron, Hinged Lid, Openwork, Key, Lion, Footed, Signed, 1800s, 7 x 5 ½ x 4 ½ In. 147
Jewelry, Enamel Plaque, Classical Scene, Arched Top, Scrolled Gilt Metal Feet, 8 x 5 x 4 In. 3630
Jewelry, Gilt Bronze, Tripod Base, Copper Portrait Of Woman, 1800s, 4 ¾ x 4 ¾ In. ....*illus* 448
Jewelry, Hinged Lid, Hobstar Vesica, Flowers, Ray Base, 3 ½ x 5 ¾ In. 70
Jewelry, Hinged Lid, Walnut, Rectangular, Scrolled Legs, Dutch, 1700s, 20 x 15 x 9 In. 2214
Jewelry, Kingwood, Brass, Mother-Of-Pearl Medallion, Purple Satin Interior, c.1880, 13 x 5 In. 475
Jewelry, Mellow Finish, 3-D Grain, Dovetailed, Lift-Out Tray, c.1900, 5 x 13 x 9 In. 188
Jewelry, Puzzle, Carved, Landscape, Maple, Mahogany, Po Shun Leong, 6 x 6 ½ x 6 ½ In. 1003
Jewelry, Rosewood, Satinwood, Lift-Out Tray, Lock, Key, Victorian, 6 ½ x 8 ½ x 4 ½ In. 104
Jewelry, Sarcophagus Shape, Star, Banding & Herringbone, Brass Feet, c.1800, 7 x 13 x 9 In. *illus* 177
Keepsake, Burl & Brass, Sarcophagus Shape, Swing Handles, Paw Feet, 20 In. 1287

Box, Jewelry, Sarcophagus Shape, Star, Banding & Herringbone, Brass Feet, c.1800, 7 x 13 x 9 In.
$177

Leland Little Auctions

Box, Knife, Hinged Lid, Serpentine Shape, Conch Shell, George III, 14 ½ x 9 x 13 In.
$266

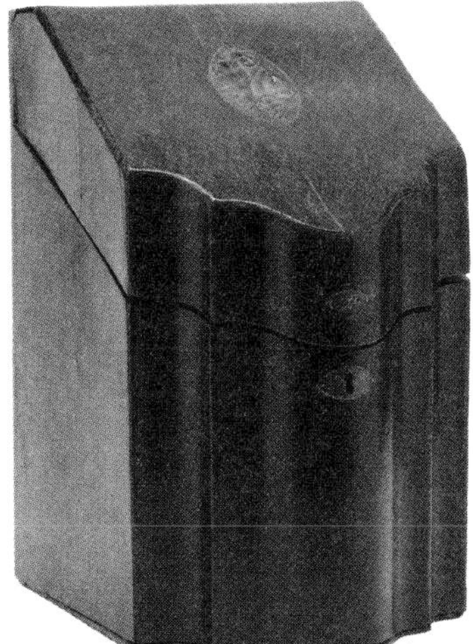

Leland Little Auctions

Box, Letter, Dome Lid, Mahogany, Engraved, Brassbound, Key, 4 x 6 x 3 In.
$226

Soulis Auctions

Box, Lift Lid, Walnut, Geometric Ivory Inlay, Dovetailed, Early 1900s, 5 x 15 ½ x 8 ¾ In.
$156

Eldred's

Box, Metal, Hinged Lid, Silvertone, Flowers, Vines, Carved Jade Oval, 3 ¾ x 6 x 4 In.
$3,250

Abington Auction Gallery

Box, Money, Hinged Lid, Rosewood, Bronze Mounts, 2 Handles, 9 ½ x 9 x 16 In.
$847

Fontaine's Auction Gallery

Box, Pantry, Lid, Bentwood, Round, Rosehead Nails, c.1800, 6 x 12 ½ In.
$240

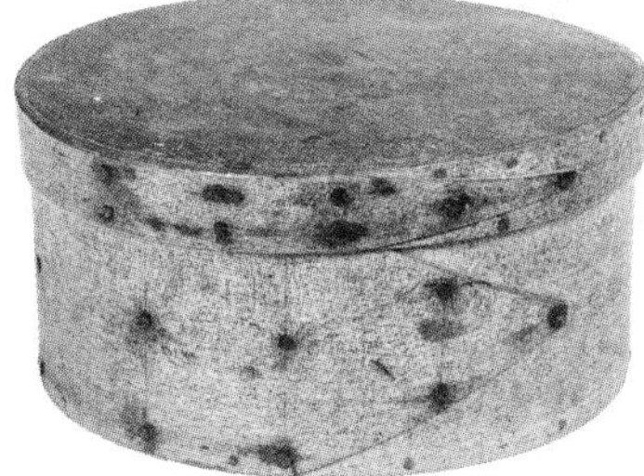

Garth's Auctioneers & Appraisers

TIP

Keep humidity levels between 45 and 55 percent. Over 65 is dangerous for your collectibles. It encourages mold, fungus, and mildew. An environment that is too dry encourages wood cracking, color change, flaking paint, yellowing of paper, and can cause fabric to deteriorate.

Box, Leather, Mother-Of-Pearl Inlay, Brass Hardware, Lock, c.1850, 3 ¾ x 12 ¾ x 9 In.
$532

Eldred's

Box, Pantry, Lid, Chrome, Yellow, Round, New England, 1800s, 2 ½ x 5 In.
$3,904

Pook & Pook

Box, Pantry, Oval, Finger Construction Pegs, Miniature, 1 ⅝ x 3 ¾ x 2 In.
$106

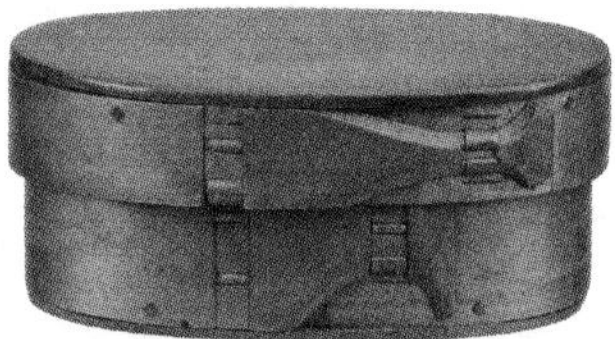

Bunch Auctions

TIP
Dust your antiques regularly but carefully. Dust leads to mold growth and attracts insects.

Box, Paper, Rectangles, Brown, Blue, Red, Beige, Weiner Werkstatte, c.1920, 3 x 6 x 6 In.
$308

Skinner, Inc.

Box, Picnic, Rosewood, 3 Tiers, Removable Trays, Chinese, 1900s, 11 x 7 x 13 ¾ In.
$263

Jeffrey S. Evans & Associates

Knife, 2 Lids, Heart Cutout Handle, H. William Koch, Pennsylvania, 16 ¾ In. 180
Knife, Hinged Lid, Serpentine Shape, Conch Shell, George III, 14 ½ x 9 x 13 In. ....*illus* 266
Knife, Hinged Lid, Silver Escutcheon, Ball Feet, c.1840, 15 x 8 ½ x 11 In., Pair 523
Knife, Lift Lid, Mahogany, Brass Hardware, Fitted Interior, Federal, Late 1700s, 14 x 9 In. 156
Knife, Painted, Wood, Shaped Handle, Fruits, Buff Background, 5 ¾ x 14 x 7 ¾ In. 103
Knife, Walnut, Scalloped Divider, Nailed Construction, 13 x 8 ½ In. 71
Lacquer, Hiramake-E, Bird Perched On Rock Overlooking Waves, Japan, 1 ½ x 2 x 3 In. 350
Leather, Mother-Of-Pearl Inlay, Brass Hardware, Lock, c.1850, 3 ¾ x 12 ¾ x 9 In. ....*illus* 532
Letter, Dome Lid, Mahogany, Engraved, Brassbound, Key, 4 x 6 x 3 In. ....*illus* 226
Letter, Napoleonic Crest Lid, Gilt Tooled Leather, Divided Interior, 1800s, 9 x 13 x 6 In. 250
Lid, Hoop Handle, Slide, Initialed H, Painted, 8 ½ x 10 ½ x 11 ½ In. 83
Lift Lid, Snipe Hinges, 2 Faux Drawers, Turned Bun Feet, Early 1700s, 15 x 20 x 14 In. 6765
Lift Lid, Walnut, Geometric Ivory Inlay, Dovetailed, Early 1900s, 5 x 15 ½ x 8 ¾ In. ....*illus* 156
Liquor, Hinged Lid, Pine, Painted, Charles Lee Pook Jr., c.1840, 12 ¾ x 15 x 11 ½ In. 293
Mahogany, Hinged Lid, Brass Swing Handle, Georgian, England, 1700s, 6 x 12 ¾ x 6 ½ In. 308
Mahogany, Lid, Inlaid, 4 Sliding Trays, Boy, Girl Knitting Tree, c.1900, 8 x 13 x 8 In. 168
Mail, Hinged Slant Lid, Oak, Brass Locks, Plaques & Hinges, c.1890, 13 x 10 ½ x 7 In. 339
Mail, Painted, Flame, Black & Orange, Padlock & Key, Jebco, 1981, 20 x 21 ½ x 49 ½ In. 300
Maple, Slide Lid, Carved, Heart Shape Handle, Whale Ivory Plaque, 1800s, 6 In. 369
Metal, Hinged Lid, Red, Painted, Richardson Mfg. Co., Worcester, Mass., 11 x 4 x 4 In. 51
Metal, Hinged Lid, Silvertone, Flowers, Vines, Carved Jade Oval, 3 ¾ x 6 x 4 In. ....*illus* 3250
Money, Hinged Lid, Rosewood, Bronze Mounts, 2 Handles, 9 ½ x 9 x 16 In. ....*illus* 847
Oak, Lid, Silver Mythical Creature On Lid, Arts & Crafts, Square, 3 x 5 x 7 In. 130
Painted, Chamfered Lid, Putty Color, Ring Handle, c.1850, 4 x 7 x 5 In. 431
Pantry, Lid, Bentwood, Bail Handle, Red, Yellow, Alum, c.1900, 6 ½ x 11 In. 176
Pantry, Lid, Bentwood, Round, Rosehead Nails, c.1800, 6 x 12 ½ In. ....*illus* 240
Pantry, Lid, Chrome, Yellow, Round, New England, 1800s, 2 ½ x 5 In. ....*illus* 3904
Pantry, Lid, Maple, Bentwood, Swing Bale Handle, Wood Grip, Pine, 1800s, 6 ½ x 11 In. 138
Pantry, Lid, Maple, Pine, Oval, Single Finger, Green, 1810s, 1 ¾ x 4 ¾ x 3 ½ In. 300
Pantry, Oval, 2 Finger, Spruce, Pine, Blue, 5 x 13 ½ x 9 ½ In. 413
Pantry, Oval, Birchbark, Stitched Joint, Flowers, Geometrics, 1800s, 9 x 13 x 9 ¾ In. 1353
Pantry, Oval, Finger Construction Pegs, Miniature, 1 ⅝ x 3 ¾ x 2 In. ....*illus* 106
Pantry, Round, Old Gray Paint, Maple, Pine, 5 In. 207
Paper, Dome Lid, Marbled, Red Edge, c.1850, 3 x 7 ¾ x 4 ½ In. 861
Paper, Rectangles, Brown, Blue, Red, Beige, Weiner Werkstatte, c.1920, 3 x 6 x 6 In. ....*illus* 308
Picnic, Rosewood, 3 Tiers, Removable Trays, Chinese, 1900s, 11 x 7 x 13 ¾ In. ....*illus* 263
Pigskin Covered, Hinged Lid, 2 Bail Handles, Black, Red, Chinese, 1900s, 8 x 20 x 12 In. 50
Pine, Slide Lid, Dovetailed Case, Vinegar Graining, 1850s, 9 x 18 x 10 In. 275
Pipe, Mahogany, Shaped Back, Brass Knob Finials, Drawer, c.1750, 19 ¾ x 4 ¾ x 4 ¾ In. 4613
Pipe, Shaped Lid, Tiger Maple, Lower Drawer, 1800s, 19 x 6 x 4 In. ....*illus* 1170
Poplar, Slide Lid, Painted, Double, White Knob, 1800s, 8 ¾ x 13 x 8 ½ In. 246
Postal, Pillar Shape, Mahogany, Hexagonal, Brass, Wood Beads, 21 ½ x 9 ¾ x 9 ¾ In. 1582
Ring, Enamel, Gilt Bronze, Cupid, Classical Figures, Red Velvet Interior, 6 In. 1029
Rosewood, Hinged Lid, Dragon, Applied Handles, Chinese, 1900s, 8 x 15 ¾ x 9 In. 322
Round, Turkey, Birds, Animals, Lacquerware, Footed, Russia, 8 ½ In. 345
Salt, Hinged Lid, Pine & Poplar, Wall, 2 Drawers, Red, Black Satin, 1800s, 15 x 12 In. ....*illus* 1586
Salt, Lid, Wall, Birds, Flower, Leather Strap, Painted, 1827, R.T., 12 x 6 x 8 In. ....*illus* 502
Salt, Wood, Carved On Front, Wall, 1800s, 15 ¾ x 8 x 9 ½ In. 266
Scroll, Camphor, Octagonal, Calligraphy Paper, Chinese, 1950s 101
Shoeshine, Shelf In Back, Sides Decor, Wood & Metal, 23 x 10 x 7 In. ....*illus* 51
Stenciled, Geometric, Flowers, Black Ground, Lined Interior, Caroline, 1800s, 5 x 9 x 6 In. 431
Storage, Basswood, Yellow Lettering, Green Ground, Ballard Vale Co., 1846, 12 x 25 ½ In. 336
Storage, Bentwood, Red Ground, Applied Lid Handle, 1800s, 19 ½ x 23 In. 854
Storage, Lid, Bentwood, Wood Pegs, Hickory Handle, Wood Pins, Pine Base, c.1850, 7 x 13 In. 184
Storage, Lid, Round, Stenciled, Wood, Flowers, 1800s, 6 ½ x 9 ¾ In. 70
Storage, Tile Lid, Wood, Painted, Rectangular, Jon Bok, 1990, 8 ¾ x 20 x 11 ¾ In. 120
Strong, Hinged Lid, Walnut, Side Handles, Rectangular, Spain, 1700s, 7 x 17 x 8 In. 944
Strong, Sheet Metal, Oak Slats, Iron Corners, Rosehead Nails, c.1870, 15 x 15 x 26 In. 678
Sugar, Lid, Bentwood, Swing Handle, Painted, New England, 1800s, 7 x 12 In. ....*illus* 2684
Sugar, Paneled Lid, Mixed Wood, Divided Interior, Painted, 1800s, 5 x 12 ¾ x 6 In. ....*illus* 313

Tantalus, Rosewood, Gilt, Brass Inlay, Mother-Of-Pearl Panels, Shaped Sides, Flattened Ball Feet 130
Tobacco, Brass, Engraved, Round, Dutch, 1700s, 5 ½ In. 185
Tobacco, Brass, Engraved, Scenes Of Neptune, Sailing Ships, Late 1700s, 5 ¾ In. 197
Tobacco, Hinged Lid, Oval, Brass & Copper, Late 1700s, 1 x 5 ½ x 1 ¾ In. 82
Tobacco, Lid, Mahogany, Sunburst Inlays, Hardwood, Tapered Columns, c.1820, 7 x 8 In. 196
Wall, 2 Tiers, Pine, Red Paint, Wood, c.1900, 11 ¾ x 5 x 16 ½ In. 1180
Wall, Cherry, 2 Tiers, Cutout Hearts, Square Nails, Ohio, c.1875, 28 x 14 In. *illus* 540
Wall, Pine, Nail Construction, Shaped Backboard, Mustard Brown, 1800s, 13 ¾ x 7 ¾ x 4 In. 211
Wall, Slant Lid, Grungy Red-Brown, Dovetailed Drawer, 1850s, 7 x 12 ½ x 5 In. 113
Wall, Slant Lid, Pine, Arched Crest, Leather Hinges, Rosehead, Early 1800s, 14 x 12 x 8 In. 923
Wall, Slide Lid, Oak, Dovetailed, Heart Handle, Hanger, Diamond Inlay, 1800s, 15 x 5 x 4 In. 277
Wall, Walnut, Alligatored Dark Finish, Scroll Crest, 1893, 8 x 13 ½ x 5 In. 281
Wallpaper, Dome Lid, Paper Board, Flowers, Yellow, Early 1800s, 20 x 10 x 10 In. 47
Wallpaper, Oval, Geometrics, 1813-14 Newspaper Lining, 3 x 8 ¾ x 4 ½ In. 325
Wood, Cylindrical, Folk Art, Black Bands, 7 ½ In. 92
Wood, Lift Lid, Tray, Brass Handle, Lock, Divided Bottom, Dovetailed, 7 ½ x 15 x 11 In. 102
Work, Baroque Style, Brass, Mounted, Porcelain Plaque, Calamander, 5 ½ x 11 ½ x 9 In. 308
Writing, Interior Compartments, Marked Lac Mahopac About 1871, Philippine, 13 x 9 x 6 In. 148
Writing, Lid, Mahogany, Brass, c.1860, 9 ⅞ x 21 x 11 In. 369

BOY SCOUT

Boy Scout collectibles include any material related to scouting, including patches, manuals, and uniforms. The Boy Scout movement in the United States started in 1910. The first Jamboree was held in 1937. Girl Scout items are listed under their own heading.

Bank, Mechanical, Camp Scene, J. & E. Stevens Co., c.1915 2250
Hat, Brown, Tan Band, Chin Strap, 12 x 13 x 5 In. 72
Poster, 2 Boys U.S.A. Bonds, Third Liberty Loan Campaign, 20 x 29 In 300
Toy, Cannon, Boy Scout Machine Gun, Kilgore, 8 x 17 x 5 ½ In. 253

BRADLEY & HUBBARD

Bradley & Hubbard is a name found on many metal objects. Walter Hubbard and his brother-in-law, Nathaniel Lyman Bradley, started making cast iron clocks, tables, frames, andirons, bookends, doorstops, lamps, chandeliers, sconces, and sewing birds in 1854 in Meriden, Connecticut. The company became Bradley & Hubbard Manufacturing Company in 1875. Charles Parker Company bought the firm in 1940. There is no mention of Bradley & Hubbard after the 1950s. Bradley & Hubbard items may be found in other sections that include metal.

Lamp, Electric, 2-Light, Palm Tree, Green, Circular Base, Early 1900s, 20 In. 201
Lamp, Frosted Glass Globe, Pink Filigree, Corinthian, Onyx Post, Square Base, 31 x 8 In. 484
Lampshade, Slag Glass, Caramel, 8 Panels, Berries, Leaves, 18 x 9 In. 117
Lighter, Cigar, Lamp, Cast Metal, Blue Opaline Glass, Woman, Urn, 2 Holders, c.1884, 18 x 6 In. *illus* 1404
Tray, Art Nouveau Style, Cherub Center, Cast Iron, 7 ½ x 4 In. 124

BRASS

Brass has been used for decorative pieces and useful tablewares since ancient times. It is an alloy of copper, zinc, and other metals. Additional brass items may be found under Bell, Candlestick, Tool, or Trivet.

Basin, Geometric Designs, Calligraphy, Cartouches, Tapering Neck, Persia, 1700s, 4 x 10 In. 585
Bed Warmer, Floral Lid, Pierced Pan, Turned Wood Handle, Early 1700s, 44 In. *illus* 738
Bed Warmer, Hinged Lid, Tooled Pan, Turned Wood Handle, 1800s, 41 In. 47
Bed Warmer, Iron, Holes, Metal Handle, Engraved, 33 In. *illus* 24
Bed Warmer, Pierced Lid, Engraved Seated Cat, Turned Wood Handle, Late 1700s, 45 In. 1046
Bed Warmer, Punched Goat, Turned Walnut Handle, Pierced Pan, 1800s, 45 In. 153
Bed Warmer, Turned Wood, Heart, Crown, Petal, Grapevine Border, Bird, 1800s, 49 In., 3 Piece 2031

Box, Pipe, Shaped Lid, Tiger Maple, Lower Drawer, 1800s, 19 x 6 x 4 In.
$1,170

Thomaston Place Auction Galleries

Box, Salt, Hinged Lid, Pine & Poplar, Wall, 2 Drawers, Red, Black Satin, 1800s, 15 x 12 In.
$1,586

Pook & Pook

Box, Salt, Lid, Wall, Birds, Flower, Leather Strap, Painted, 1827, R.T., 12 x 6 x 8 In.
$502

Copake Auctions

This is an edited listing of current prices. Visit **Kovels.com** to check thousands of prices from previous years and sign up for free information on trends, tips, reproductions, marks, and more.

Box, Shoeshine, Shelf In Back, Sides Decor, Wood & Metal, 23 x 10 x 7 In.
$51

Hartzell's Auction Gallery Inc.

Box, Sugar, Lid, Bentwood, Swing Handle, Painted, New England, 1800s, 7 x 12 In.
$2,684

Pook & Pook

Box, Sugar, Paneled Lid, Mixed Wood, Divided Interior, Painted, 1800s, 5 x 12 ¾ x 6 In.
$313

Cowan's Auctions

Box, Wall, Cherry, 2 Tiers, Cutout Hearts, Square Nails, Ohio, c.1875, 28 x 14 In.
$540

Garth's Auctioneers & Appraisers

Bradley & Hubbard, Lighter, Cigar, Lamp, Cast Metal, Blue Opaline Glass, Woman, Urn, 2 Holders, c.1884, 18 x 6 In.
$1,404

Jeffrey S. Evans & Associates

Brass, Bed Warmer, Floral Lid, Pierced Pan, Turned Wood Handle, Early 1700s, 44 In.
$738

Skinner, Inc.

Brass, Bed Warmer, Iron, Holes, Metal Handle, Engraved, 33 In.
$24

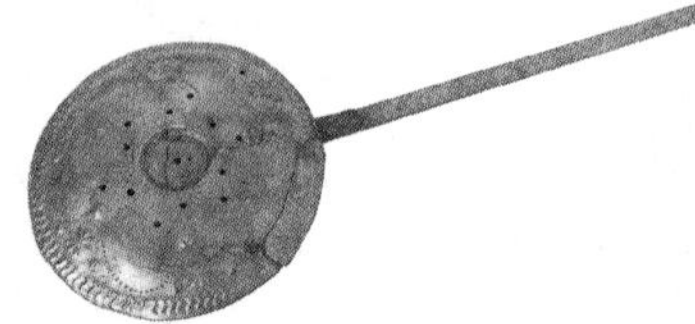

Copake Auctions

Brass, Bill Clip, Hand Shape, Fancy Ruffle, 5 x 2 ½ In.
$45

Hartzell's Auction Gallery Inc.

Brass, Cannonshell Ejector, Mahogany Carriage, Strong Mfg., Connecticut, 1800, 39 In.
$15,600

Bourgeault-Horan Antiquarians & Associates, LLC

Brass, Coffee Set, Coffeepot, Glass Mosaic Inlay, Salvador Teran, 8 ¾ In., 5 Piece
$750

Cowan's Auctions

Bill Clip, Hand Shape, Fancy Ruffle, 5 x 2 ½ In. ... *illus* 45
Bowl, Iron Handle & Feet, Hearth Pan, 23 In. ... 24
Bucket, Lid, Wreath Shape Handle, Lion's Paw Feet, 21 In. ... 72
Bucket, Swing Handle, Molded Rim, Round Base, Rivets, 1700s, 10 ½ In. ... 1722
Cannonshell Ejector, Mahogany Carriage, Strong Mfg., Connecticut, 1800, 39 In. ... *illus* 15600
Casket, Hinged Lid, Parquetry, Wood Interior, Footed, Persia, 1800s, 8 x 7 In. ... 546
Casket, Wagner's Siegfried, Rosewood, Quartz, Erhard & Sohne, c.1900, 8 x 12 x 8 ¾ In. ... 3250
Charger, Armorial, Multi-Beaded Rim, Engraved Crest, Early 1700s, 20 ⅜ In. ... 3998
Coffee Set, Coffeepot, Glass Mosaic Inlay, Salvador Teran, 8 ¾ In., 5 Piece ... *illus* 750
Dish, Alms, Baroque, Germany, 14 ¾ In. ... 1107
Eagle, Spread Wing, Perched Atop Globe, 24 x 21 ¾ In. ... 154
Easel, Aesthetic, Finialed Crest Rail, Adjustable Frame, Late 1800s, 60 x 25 x 24 In. ... 450
Figure, Steer, Walking, Longhorn, 20 In. ... 113
Girandole, Man, Woman, Mounted, Marble Base, 3 Arms, Dangling Prisms, c.1900, Pair ... 101
Ladle, Straining, Pierced, Impressed WR Boston, Late 1800s, 22 ½ In. ... 275
Ornament, Seahorse, Oval Base, Gondola Cavali, 1800s, 11 ¾ In. ... *illus* 720
Planter, Lid, Eagle & Ring Handles, Footed, Tin Liner, 15 x 13 In. ... 127
Plate, Box, Cartridge, Maryland State Seal, Iron Loop, c.1860, 2 x 3 In. ... *illus* 6150
Samovar, 2 Handles, Embossed Maker's Marks, Russia, 1800s, 22 x 14 x 15 In. ... *illus* 186
Sconce, 2-Light, Candle, Wall, Louis XV Style, Gilt, 1800s, 16 x 9 x 6 ½ In., Pair ... 234
Sconce, 5-Light, Leafy, Figural Supports, Continental, 17 x 10 ½ x 10 In., Pair ... 288
Sconce, Female, Nude, Standing, Candle Socket, 11 x 4 ½ x 5 In. ... 62
Sconce, Louis XV Style, Gilt, 5 Scrolling Leafy Arms, c.1970, 28 x 19 x 11 In., Pair ... 384
Scoop, Forest Scientific & Mechanical Specialties, 1800s, 16 ½ In. ... 96
Sculpture, Brooklyn Bridge, Wall Art, Attributed To C. Jere, 22 ½ x 58 In. ... 594
Tray, Engraved, Beauties & Landscape, Grapevine Rim, Chinese, 26 In. ... 92
Valet, Ball Style, Adjustable Arms, Hanging Rods, Round Stretcher, S-Style Feet, N.Y., 1950s ... 72
Vase, Enamel, Cabochons, Embossed, Brandt, Box, 5 ½ In. ... 800
Wall Plaque, Circular, Anchor & Rope, Engraved, Early 1900s, 19 In. ... 228
Wall Plaque, Eagle, Spread Wings, Gilt, Molded Sheet, c.1900, 13 x 25 ½ In. ... *illus* 512
Whistle, Steam, Wood Platform Base, Crosby, Boston, 15 ½ In. ... 177

BRASTOFF, *see Sascha Brastoff category.*

BREAD PLATE, *see various silver categories, porcelain factories, and pressed glass patterns.*

BRIDE'S BOWL OR BASKET

Bride's bowls or baskets were usually one-of-a-kind novelties made in American and European glass factories. They were especially popular about 1880 when the decorated basket was often given as a wedding gift. Cut glass baskets were popular after 1890. All bride's bowls lost favor about 1905. Bride's bowls and baskets may also be found in other glass sections. Check the index at the back of the book.

Blue Iridescent Glass Ruffled Bowl, Silver Plate Frame, Victorian, 13 x 11 x 11 In. ... 83
Cranberry Coin Spot Glass, Yellow & Pink Flowers, Silver Plate Frame, 15 x 9 In. ... 160
Cranberry Glass, Cased, Ruffled Silver Plate Frame, Forbes Silver Co., 12 x 10 In. ... 60
Mother-Of-Pearl Glass, Air Trap, Yellow Cased Pink, Wester Silver Plate, c.1900, 8 x 13 In. *illus* 497
Mother-Of-Pearl Glass, Apricot Satin, Diamond Quilted, Silver Plate Frame, 5 x 10 In. *illus* 210
Opaline Glass, Pink, Enamel, Beads, Silver Plate Frame, c.1880, 12 x 8 ¾ In. ... 147
Pink & White Cased, Ruffled Art Glass, Silver Plate Frame, Victorian, 11 x 10 ½ In. ... 70
Satin Glass, Blue, Silver Plate, Aurora, 10 In. ... 80

BRISTOL

Bristol glass was made in Bristol, England, after the 1700s. The Bristol glass most often seen today is a Victorian, lightweight opaque glass that is often blue. Some of the glass was decorated with enamels.

Tea Caddy, Hexagonal, George III, Blue Ovals, Mirror, 5 ¾ x 6 x 3 ⅝ In. ... 4800
Trinket Jar, Lid, Finial, Pink Roses, Round, 2 ½ In. ... 20

Brass, Ornament, Seahorse, Oval Base, Gondola Cavali, 1800s, 11 ¾ In.
$720

Eldred's

TIP
Brass tarnishes more quickly in direct sunlight.

Brass, Plate, Box, Cartridge, Maryland State Seal, Iron Loop, c.1860, 2 x 3 In.
$6,150

Skinner, Inc.

Brass, Samovar, 2 Handles, Embossed Maker's Marks, Russia, 1800s, 22 x 14 x 15 In.
$186

DuMouchelles

Brass, Wall Plaque, Eagle, Spread Wings, Gilt, Molded Sheet, c.1900, 13 x 25 ½ In.
$512

Cowan's Auctions

Bride's Basket, Mother-Of-Pearl Glass, Air Trap, Yellow Cased Pink, Wester Silver Plate, c.1900, 8 x 13 In.
$497

Jeffrey S. Evans & Associates

Bride's Basket, Mother-Of-Pearl Glass, Apricot Satin, Diamond Quilted, Silver Plate Frame, 5 x 10 In.
$210

Woody Auctions

TIP

Outdoor bronze sculptures need special care. Wash with soap, water, and a little ammonia to remove oil and dirt. Then rinse, dry, and rub with a cloth dipped in olive oil or boiled linseed oil. Rub with a dry cloth to remove extra oil. Outdoor bronzes should be oiled several times a year.

Vase, Blue, Hand Painted, Raised White Flowers, Orange Centers, Ruffled Top, 5 In. 38
Vase, Bulbous, Working In The Field, Tapered Stem, Flower, 14 ½ In., Pair 151
Vase, Cylindrical, Blue, Painted Flowers, Gilt Handles, 3-Footed, c.1890, 6 ½ In., Pair 130
Vase, Cylindrical, Footed, Flowers, Gold Paint, c.1900, 12 In., Pair 351
Vase, Cylindrical, Footed, Translucent, Gold Flowers, Green Leaves, 7 x 3 In., Pair 85
Vase, Frosted, Opaline, Hand Painted, Raised Gold & White Flowers, Gilt Trim, 7 x 3 In., Pair. 85
Wine, Emerald Green, Pontil Scars, c.1815, 4 ¾ In., 6 Piece 395

BRITANNIA, *see Pewter category.*

BRONZE

Bronze is an alloy of copper, tin, and other metals. It is used to make figurines, lamps, and other decorative objects. Bronze lamps are listed in the Lamp category. Pieces listed here date from the eighteenth, nineteenth, and twentieth centuries. Shown here are marks used by three well-known makers of bronzes.

Armor Bronze Corp.
c.1919–c.1926, 1934–1948

Bradley and Hubbard Mfg. Co.
1875–c.1940

POMPEIAN BRONZE COMPANY

Pompeian Bronze Co.
1920s

Beaker, Archaic Shape, Blossoms, Scroll Work, Dark Patina Ground, Chinese, 3 ¾ x 5 ⅝ In. .. 35
Bowl, Lid, Sorensen, Carl, Verdigris, Finial, Arts & Crafts, 7 ¾ x 7 ¾ x 7 In. 224
Bust, Carrier-Belleuse, Albert Ernest, Shakespeare, Marble Base, 22 In. 1062
Bust, Goodacre, Glenn, Kiolda Princess, Mounted, Black Square Base, 6 x 9 ½ In. 699
Bust, Goujon, Jean, Diane De Poitiers, Gilt, Patina, Square Base, 16 x 9 x 5 ½ In. ....*illus* 1063
Bust, Maiden, Wrap Around Her Shoulder, Art Nouveau, Bohemiene, Marble Base, 11 ½ In. 142
Bust, Nobleman, Patina, Stepped Round Marble Base, 6 ½ In. 228
Bust, Renda, Giuseppe, Woman, Blindfolded, Marble Base, 9 ½ x 3 In. 295
Bust, Woman, Flower, Black Dress, Hair, Footed, Hollow, 30 In. 156
Bust, Young Woman, Wreath, Green Patina, White Base, Art Nouveau, 17 ½ In. ....*illus* 584
Cannon, Wood Carriage, Mounted, 1900s, 40 In. 10800
Casket, Alabaster, Baroque Style, Lid Handle, Putti, Scroll Leaf Feet, 1800, 14 x 15 x 11 In. 1440
Censer, Bulbous, Dragon Shape Handles, Footed, 6-Character Mark, Chinese, Late 1800s, 4 In. 518
Censer, Handles, Tripod Feet, Xuande Mark, 1700s, 5 x 4 ¾ In. 29040
Censer, Openwork Lid, Foo Dog Finial, Bulbous Body, Dragon Handles, Seal, Japan, 7 ½ In. ... 369
Censer, Quatrefoil, Flared Rim, Footed, Chinese, c.1800, 2 ¾ x 8 ⅜ x 6 In. 497
Censer, Rectangular Handle, 4 Dragon Head Legs, Round Foot, Chinese, 8 x 7 x 5 ⅝ In. 201
Censer, Stylized Mythical Lion Handle, 9-Character Mark To Base, Chinese, 8 In. 649
Censer, Wood Lid, Jade Finial, 2 Handles, Stand, 6-Character Mark, Chinese, 7 ⅜ In. 510
Centerpiece, Fluted Burgundy Marble, Acanthus, Lion Busts, 9 x 9 In. 750
Compote, Rococo Style, Gilt, Patina, Figural Mount, 11 In. ....*illus* 346
Crucifix, Gothic Style, Silver Plated Figure Of Jesus, INRI, Hexagonal Base, 36 x 16 In. 726
Foot Warmer, Quatrefoil Lobed Medallion, Pierced Lid, Peacock, 6 ½ x 9 ½ x 7 ½ In. 50
Gong, Circular, Raised Center, Silver Star, Mallet, 1800s, 12 In. 48
Incense Burner, Dragon Shape Handle, 4-Character Mark To Base, Chinese. ....*illus* 216
Model, Leopard, Seated, Brown Patina, 1900s, 19 x 12 In. 3690
Plaque, 3 Owls, Huddled, Hammered Background, Dark Patina, 1900s, 8 x 9 ½ In. 151
Plaque, American Shield, Anchor, Outstretched Eagle Wings, c.1950s, 13 In. 72
Plaque, Caverly, C., George Washington, Bust, 1877, 21 x 17 In. 738
Plaque, Oval, 3 French Nymphs, Marble Backing, Gilt Wood Frame, Bertaux, 1889, 12 x 9 In.. 200
Plaque, Paul Revere Ride, Galloping Horse, Frame, 1900s, 11 x 22 In. 431
Sculpture, Mene, Pierre Jules, 2 Horses, Stepped Rectangular Base, 22 x 10 ½ x 15 In. ...*illus* 1180
Sculpture, 2 Mice, Brushed Finish, Hanko Marks, Japan, 4 ⅜ x 6 x 3 ½ In., Pair 1750
Sculpture, Antinous, Nude Man, Gladiator Shoes, Round Base, 1800s, 23 ¾ In. 826
Sculpture, Arneson, Old Bob Prone, Dog, Man's Face, Signed, 10 x 38 x 28 In. 37820

Bronze, Bust, Goujon, Jean, Diane De Poitiers, Gilt, Patina, Square Base, 16 x 9 x 5 ½ In.
$1,063

Abington Auction Gallery

Bronze, Bust, Young Woman, Wreath, Green Patina, White Base, Art Nouveau, 17 ½ In.
$584

Clars Auction Gallery

Bronze, Compote, Rococo Style, Gilt, Patina, Figural Mount, 11 In.
$346

Clars Auction Gallery

How a Bronze Is Made

Artists who create a bronze sculpture first sculpt the figure using clay or wax. Then the sculpture is taken to a foundry, where a rubber mold of the figure is made. Wax is poured in and sloshed around until a hollow wax model is made. A shell of ceramic coating is applied to the wax and the model is fired. The wax melts out. The ceramic shell that's left is filled with molten bronze. Then the shell is removed and the bronze sculpture is ground and polished.

Bronze, Incense Burner, Dragon Shape Handle, 4-Character Mark To Base, Chinese.
$216

Bunte Auction Services

Bronze, Sculpture, Mene, Pierre Jules, 2 Horses, Stepped Rectangular Base, 22 x 10 ½ x 15 In.
$1,180

Copake Auctions

Bronze, Sculpture, Barye, Antoine-Louis, Lion Qui Marche, Green To Black Patina, 9 x 15 In.
$1,845

Skinner, Inc.

Bronze, Sculpture, Berge, Edward Henry, Nymph Child, Standing, Flower Hat, 20 ½ x 6 In.
$1,815

Bruneau & Co. Auctioneers

Bronze, Sculpture, Bergmann, Franz, American Sailor, Vienna Cold Paint, 1900s, 6 ¾ In.
$1,200

Bourgeault-Horan Antiquarians & Associates, LLC

Bronze, Sculpture, Bergmann, Franz, Arab Man, Seated, Cold Paint, Marked NAM GREB, c.1900, 5 x 6 In.
$1,625

New Orleans Auction Galleries

Bronze, Sculpture, Bergmann, Franz, Arab Trader, Carrying Rifle, Cold Painted, 5 x 3 ½ x 6 In.
$681

Clars Auction Gallery

Bronze, Sculpture, Bergmann, Franz, Pheasant, Cold Painted, Foundry Mark, 13 In.
$354

Conestoga Auction Company

Bronze, Sculpture, Buswell, Blair, Driver, Man Leaning On Golf Club, Signed, 1993, 18 x 8 ½ In.
$2,125

New Orleans Auction Galleries

Bronze, Sculpture, Chiparus, Stalking Lioness, Rectangular Marble Base, 11 x 27 ½ In.
$1,778

Witherell's

Bronze, Sculpture, Deity, Empress Of Heaven, Holding Tablet, Phoenix Headdress, 1700s, 17 x 6 In.
$2,280

CRN Auctions

Bronze, Sculpture, Erte, Belle Du Bal, Painted, Elegant Woman, Signed, 17 ¾ In.
$1,250

Hudson Valley Auctions

Bronze, Sculpture, Fonderia Nelli Roma, Elder Furietti Centaur, Marble Base, c.1885, 17 x 9 In.
$2,250

New Orleans Auction Galleries

Bronze, Sculpture, Gori, Affortunato, Windy Day, Marble Face, Hands, Signed, Paris, 27 x 10 In.
$1,125

New Orleans Auction Galleries

Bronze, Sculpture, Hartmann, Jud, Sea Serpent, Patina, Marble Plinth, 1948, 27 x 17 x 15 In.
$3,335

Thomaston Place Auction Galleries

TIP
Don't use bleaching cleansing powders or disinfectant floor-washing products that contain chlorine in a room that has bronze figures on display. Chlorine harms bronzes.

Bronze, Sculpture, Knapp, Tom, Turtle, Incised Signature, 1987, 19 x 39 In.
$3,000

New Orleans Auction Galleries

Bronze, Sculpture, Lizard, Cold Painted, Franz Bergmann Style, Signed Geschutzt, Vienna, 2 In.
$173

Blackwell Auctions

Bronze, Sculpture, Lorenzl, Josef, Dancer, Headdress, Marble Base, Austria, 1892-1950, 15 x 3 ½ In.
$1,046

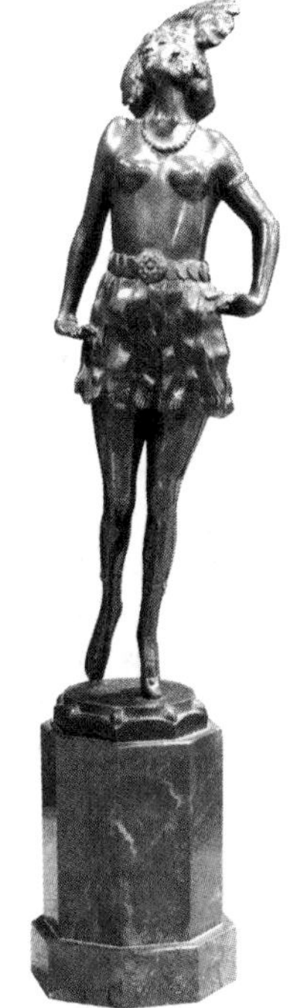

Clars Auction Gallery

Bronze, Sculpture, Parsons, Edith B., Every Dog Has Its Day, Standing, Rectangular Base, 6 x 7 In.
$492

Clars Auction Gallery

Bronze, Sculpture, Qilin, Mythical Horned Beast, Looking Back, Green, Chinese, 1800s, 5 x 10 x 6 In.
$344

Crescent City Auction Gallery

Bronze, Sculpture, Tucker, William, Ellipse Shape, Signed, c.1980, 12 x 14 x 3 ½ In.
$826

Ahlers & Ogletree Auction Gallery

Bronze, Vase, Woven Bamboo Body, Molded Ivy Leaves, Leaping Frog, Marked, Japan, 12 In.
$308

Clars Auction Gallery

Bronze, Water Dropper, Toad Shape, 3-Legged, Marked Underside, Chinese, 3 In.
$369

Clars Auction Gallery

Brush, Cookie Jar, Rag Doll, Red Hair, Patchwork Dress, 11 In.
$115

Belhorn Auction Services

Brush, Figurine, Frog, Sitting, Green, Ornamental, McCoy, 5 In.
$69

Belhorn Auction Services

Brush, Jardiniere, Pedestal, Greek Key, Green, Dome Base, McCoy, 16 ½ In.
$25

Skinner, Inc.

Sculpture, Barye, Antoine-Louis, Lion Qui Marche, Green To Black Patina, 9 x 15 In. ....*illus* 1845
Sculpture, Barye, Antoine-Louis, Stag, Le Cerf Bramant, Rocky Ground, c.1800, 9 ½ x 8 In.... 640
Sculpture, Bennett, Tom, Nude, Female Dancer, Autumn, Hand Signed, c.1980, 9 ½ x 18 In... 450
Sculpture, Berge, Edward Henry, Nymph Child, Standing, Flower Hat, 20 ½ x 6 In. ....*illus* 1815
Sculpture, Bergmann, Franz, American Sailor, Vienna Cold Paint, 1900s, 6 ¾ In. ....*illus* 1200
Sculpture, Bergmann, Franz, Arab Man, Seated, Cold Paint, Marked NAM GREB, c.1900, 5 x 6 In. *illus* 1625
Sculpture, Bergmann, Franz, Arab Trader, Carrying Rifle, Cold Painted, 5 x 3 ½ x 6 In. *illus* 681
Sculpture, Bergmann, Franz, Pheasant, Cold Painted, Foundry Mark, 13 In. ....*illus* 354
Sculpture, Bird, Grapevine Branch, Beetle, Oval Base, 5 x 4 ¾ In. 200
Sculpture, Buddha Sitting, Gilt, Stylized Lotus Base, Asian, 18 ½ In. 212
Sculpture, Buddha, Seated, Bodhisattva, 6 Arms, Avalokitesvara, Lotus, 12 x 8 x 5 ½ In. 372
Sculpture, Buhot, L.C.H., Hebe, Eagle Of Jupiter, Marble Base, Frolicking Cherubs, 20 ½ In.... 2420
Sculpture, Bunn, Kenneth, Fox In Chase, Oval Walnut Base, 6 x 11 In. 660
Sculpture, Buswell, Blair, Driver, Man Leaning On Golf Club, Signed, 1993, 18 x 8 ½ In. *illus* 2125
Sculpture, Chiparus, Stalking Lioness, Rectangular Marble Base, 11 x 27 ½ In. ....*illus* 1778
Sculpture, Deity, Empress Of Heaven, Holding Tablet, Phoenix Headdress, 1700s, 17 x 6 In. ... *illus* 2280
Sculpture, Eagle, Landing On Perch, Circular Base, 31 In. 480
Sculpture, Erte, Astra, Woman, Standing, Holding Star, Painted, Deco Style, Signed, 19 In..... 1125
Sculpture, Erte, Belle Du Bal, Painted, Elegant Woman, Signed, 17 ¾ In. ....*illus* 1250
Sculpture, Erte, La Danseuse, Woman Dancing Over Flame, Cold Painted, Signed, 1985, 13 In...... 847
Sculpture, Erte, Sirens, Crossing Iridescent Tails, Holding Fish, 12 x 16 In. 2300
Sculpture, Fonderia Nelli Roma, Elder Furietti Centaur, Marble Base, c.1885, 17 x 9 In. .*illus* 2250
Sculpture, Gori, Affortunato, Windy Day, Marble Face, Hands, Signed, Paris, 27 x 10 In. *illus* 1125
Sculpture, Hartmann, Jud, Sea Serpent, Patina, Marble Plinth, 1948, 27 x 17 x 15 In. ....*illus* 3335
Sculpture, Humphriss, Charles, Indian, Holding Sundial, Marble Plinth, 21 x 9 x 8 In. 438
Sculpture, Icart, Louis, Man, Woman Dancing Tango, Marble Base, c.1980, 20 x 12 ½ In. 295
Sculpture, Knapp, Tom, Turtle, Incised Signature, 1987, 19 x 39 In. ....*illus* 3000
Sculpture, Lanceray, Eugene, Man On Horse, Women In Cart, Retour Au Champs, 10 x 22 x 11 In.. 192
Sculpture, Little Girl, Standing On Stool, Black, 12 In. 81
Sculpture, Lizard, Cold Painted, Franz Bergmann Style, Signed Geschutzt, Vienna, 2 In. .*illus* 173
Sculpture, Lorenzl, Josef, Dancer, Headdress, Marble Base, Austria, 1892-1950, 15 x 3 ½ In. *illus* 1046
Sculpture, Moreau, Auguste, Young Lovers, Round Marble Base, France, 18 x 11 In. 394
Sculpture, Moreau, Auguste, Young Psyche, Stepped Round Base, Late 1800s-Early 1900s, 27 In... 1534
Sculpture, Parsons, Edith B., Every Dog Has Its Day, Standing, Rectangular Base, 6 x 7 In. *illus* 492
Sculpture, Parsons, Edith, Frog Baby, Holding 2 Frogs, Verdigris Patina, Gorham Co., 7 In..... 1080
Sculpture, Qilin, Mythical Horned Beast, Looking Back, Green, Chinese, 1800s, 5 x 10 x 6 In. *illus* 344
Sculpture, Railey, L., Hawk, Capsule Shape Pediment, Green Marble Base, France, c.1920, 12 In... 806
Sculpture, Romulus, Remus, She Wolf, La Lupa Capitolina, Bolted, c.1920, 5 ½ x 8 ½ In. 187
Sculpture, Clodion, Claude Michel, Satyr, Round Marble Base, France, 20 In........................... 978
Sculpture, Shaffer, Scott, Lobster, Standing, 2 Claws, Rotating Stand, 19 ¾ In. 1140
Sculpture, Tucker, William, Ellipse Shape, Signed, c.1980, 12 x 14 x 3 ½ In. ....*illus* 826
Sculpture, Ubando, Carlos Kunte, Mother, 2 Children, Green Patina, Black, Wood Base, 9 x 11 In. 238
Sculpture, Wolff, A.M., 2 Horses Tilling Field, Patina, 1903, 14 x 28 ½ In. 3933
Sculpture, Woman, Jeanne D'Arc, Standing, Rotating Base, Marble, 22 x 6 ½ In. 308
Sculpture, Woman, Nude, Standing, Butterfly On Arm, Circular Base, 4 In. 316
Sculpture, Woman, Sitting In Large Flower, Art Nouveau, 5 ½ x 9 ½ In. 469
Teapot, Berrocal, Miguel Ortiz, Paloma Jet, Bird Shape, Perched On Goblet, 6 ½ x 6 x 8 In. 2750
Umbrella Stand, Hexagonal, 2 Panels, Flowers, Molded Birds, Japan, 24 In. 427
Vase, Moreau, Auguste, Art Deco, Tapered, 8 Horses, France, 1900s, 10 x 8 ½ In. 885
Vase, Woven Bamboo Body, Molded Ivy Leaves, Leaping Frog, Marked, Japan, 12 In. ....*illus* 308
Water Dropper, Toad Shape, 3-Legged, Marked Underside, Chinese, 3 In. ....*illus* 369
Weight, Opium, Bird, Handle, Octagonal Base, Burmese, 8 ¾ In. 380

BROWNIES

Brownies were first drawn in 1883 by Palmer Cox (1840–1924). They are characterized by large round eyes, downturned mouths, and skinny legs. Toys, books, dinnerware, and other objects were made with the Brownies as part of the design.

Doll, Chinese Man, Felt, Painted, Blue Costume, Label, R. J. Wright, 2009, 8 ½ In. 288
Stein, Relief, Different International Costumes, Seated Brownie Finial, ½ Liter 200

BRUSH-MCCOY, *see Brush category and related pieces in McCoy category.*

BRUSH POTTERY

Brush Pottery was started in 1925. George Brush first worked in 1901 in Zanesville, Ohio. He started his own pottery in 1907, but it burned to the ground soon after. In 1909 he became manager of the J.W. McCoy Pottery. In 1911, Brush and J.W. McCoy formed the Brush-McCoy Pottery Co. After a series of name changes, the company became The Brush Pottery in 1925. It closed in 1982. Old Brush was marked with impressed letters or a palette-shaped mark. Reproduction pieces are being made. They are marked in raised letters or with a raised mark. Collectors favor the figural cookie jars made by this company. Because there was a company named Brush-McCoy, there is great confusion between Brush and Nelson McCoy pieces. Most collectors today refer to Brush pottery as Brush-McCoy. See McCoy category for more information.

MARK

Cookie Jar, Rag Doll, Red Hair, Patchwork Dress, 11 In. .... *illus* 115
Figurine, Frog, Sitting, Green, Ornamental, McCoy, 5 In. .... *illus* 69
Jardiniere, Pedestal, Greek Key, Green, Dome Base, McCoy, 16 ½ In. .... *illus* 25
Planter, Figural, Bull, Standing, Brown, Ferdinand, 9 In. 23

BUCK ROGERS

Buck Rogers was the first American science fiction comic strip. It started in 1929 and continued until 1967. Buck has also appeared in comic books, movies, and, in the 1980s, a television series. Any memorabilia connected with the character Buck Rogers is collectible.

Book, Strange Adventures In The Spider Ship, Pop-Up Pictures, Hard Cover, 1935 89
Toy, 25th Century Rocket Ship, Tin, Orange, Yellow, Graphics, Marx, Box, 12 In. 2040
Toy, Action Figure, Killer Kane, Buck Rogers, Metal, Britains 150
Toy, Atomic Pistol, Black, Daisy, Box, 10 In. 510
Toy, Atomic Ray Pistol, Daisy, 10 In. 252
Toy, Sonic Ray Gun, Top Secret Code Book, Commonwealth, Box 144

BUFFALO POTTERY

Buffalo Pottery was made in Buffalo, New York, beginning in 1901. The company was established by the Larkin Company, famous manufacturers of soap. The wares are marked with a picture of a buffalo and the date of manufacture. Deldare ware is the most famous pottery made at the factory. It has either a khaki-colored or green background with hand-painted transfer designs. The company reorganized in 1956 and was renamed Buffalo China before being bought by Oneida Silver Company.

Buffalo Pottery
1907

Deldare ware
1909

ABINO WARE
BUFFALO
POTTERY
1912

Emerald Deldare
1912

BUFFALO POTTERY

Pitcher, Abino Ware, Windmills, Boats, Ralph Stuart, c.1923, 12 In. 370
Pitcher, Roosevelt Bears, Cartoons & Text, Squared Rim, 8 In. 1000
Plate, Chesapeake & Ohio, George Washington, Gold Border, Stamped, 1930s, 10 ¾ In. ..*illus* 72

BUFFALO POTTERY DELDARE

Candlestick, Colonial Scene, Hand Painted, Hexagonal Base, c.1909, 8 ¾ In., Pair .... *illus* 142
Charger, Lost Sheep Huddled Together, Snow, Emerald, Signed, R. Stuart, 1911, 13 ½ In. *illus* 600

Buffalo Pottery, Plate, Chesapeake & Ohio, George Washington, Gold Border, Stamped, 1930s, 10 ¾ In.
$72

Garth's Auctioneers & Appraisers

TIP
Treat your antiques like your grandparents: Have proper respect for their age, but don't exaggerate their fragility.

Buffalo Pottery Deldare, Candlestick, Colonial Scene, Hand Painted, Hexagonal Base, c.1909, 8 ¾ In., Pair
$142

Bunch Auctions

Buffalo Pottery Deldare, Charger, Lost Sheep Huddled Together, Snow, Emerald, Signed, R. Stuart, 1911, 13 ½ In.
$600

Garth's Auctioneers & Appraisers

Buffalo Pottery Deldare, Pitcher, The Great Controversy, Straight-Sided, Handle, W. Foster, 1908, 12 ⅜ In.
$118

Bunch Auctions

Burmese Glass, Lamp, Fairy, Dog, Lying Down, Silver Plate Holder, Ball Feet, 11 In.
$413

Strawser Auction Group

Charger, The Fallowfield Hunt, Black Rim, 13 ½ In. 106
Pitcher, So Spare An Old Broken Soldier, Octagonal, Shaped Handle, c.1909, 7 ¾ In. 94
Pitcher, The Great Controversy, Straight-Sided, Handle, W. Foster, 1908, 12 ⅜ In. .... *illus* 118
Tray, Dancing Ye Minuet, Dancing Couples, Rectangular, 9 x 12 In. 106

BUNNYKINS, *see Royal Doulton category.*

BURMESE GLASS

Burmese glass was developed by Frederick Shirley at the Mt. Washington Glass Works in New Bedford, Massachusetts, in 1885. It is a two-toned glass, shading from peach to yellow. Some pieces have a pattern mold design. A few Burmese pieces were decorated with pictures or applied glass flowers of colored Burmese glass. Other factories made similar glass also called Burmese. Burmese glass was made by Mt. Washington until about 1895, by Gundersen until the 1950s, and by Webb until about 1900. Fenton made Burmese glass after 1970. Related items may be listed in the Fenton category and under Webb Burmese.

Lamp, Fairy, Dog, Lying Down, Silver Plate Holder, Ball Feet, 11 In. .... *illus* 413
Lamp, Leaves, Ball Shape, Pedestal Foot, Burner, Chimney, Korner & Co., c.1900, 8 x 3 In. .. *illus* 497
Pitcher, Pink & White, Ribbed Handle, Ruffled Crimped Top, c.1960, 9 In. 48
Toothpick Holder, Blue & White Daisies, Beaded Petals, Shaded Ground, 2 ½ In., Pair 281
Toothpick Holder, Embossed Scroll, Ribbed Mold, Enamel, Floral, Mt. Washington, 2 In. 250
Toothpick Holder, Fall Leaves, Blue Berries, Bulbous, Square Neck & Rim, 2 ¾ In. 281
Toothpick Holder, Fall Leaves, Blue Berries, Hat Form, Ruffled Rim, Mt. Washington, 2 ½ In. . 313
Toothpick Holder, Spider Mums, Round Base, Square Top, Mt. Washington, 2 ⅝ In. 250

BUSTER BROWN

Buster Brown, the comic strip, first appeared in color in 1902. Buster and his dog, Tige, remained a popular comic and soon became even more famous as the emblem for a shoe company, a textile firm, and other companies. The strip was discontinued in 1920. Buster Brown sponsored a radio show from 1943 to 1955 and a TV show from 1950 to 1956. The Buster Brown characters are still used by Brown Shoe Company, Buster Brown Apparel, Inc., and Gateway Hosiery.

Bank, Horse, Horseshoe, Black, Gold, Cast Iron, 4 ½ x 4 ¾ In. 68
Display, Buster Brown Shoes, Tin Lithograph, Countertop, 1950s, 15 In. .... *illus* 244
Pennant, Wool, Painted, Tige, Tug Of War, Hosiery Sock, c.1910, 11 ¾ x 29 ½ In. 203
Sign, Buster Winking, Tige With Big Eyes, Shoes Sold Here, Celluloid, 10 In. 1320

BUTTER CHIP

Butter chips, or butter pats, were small individual dishes for butter. They were the height of fashion from 1880 to 1910. Earlier as well as later examples are known. Many sell for under $15.

Flowers, Multicolor, Gold Trim, Scalloped Edge, 3 ¼ In., Pair 18
Malaysia Airlines, Kite Design, Noritake, 2 ⅞ In. 36
Morning Glory, Bird, Gold Trim, Transferware, Alfred Meakin, 1890s, 2 ⅞ In., Pair 30
Roses, Pink, Green Leaves, Scalloped Edge, Haviland, Limoges, 4 Piece 32
Transferware, Brown, Flowers, 3 In. 7

BUTTER MOLDS *are listed in the Kitchen category under Mold, Butter.*

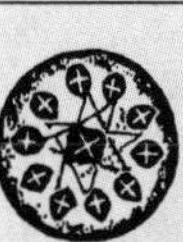

BUTTON

Button collecting has been popular since the nineteenth century. Buttons have been used on clothing throughout the centuries, and there are millions of styles. Gold, silver, or precious stones were used for the best

Burmese Glass, Lamp, Leaves, Ball Shape, Pedestal Foot, Burner, Chimney, Korner & Co., c.1900, 8 x 3 In.
$497

Jeffrey S. Evans & Associates

Buster Brown, Display, Buster Brown Shoes, Tin Lithograph, Countertop, 1950s, 15 In.
$244

Pook & Pook

Button Brass, Frog, Glass Cabochon, Paste Eyes, Greek Key Border, Leo Popper, 1890s
$8,750

Whitely's Auctioneers

TIP
If there is crossover interest between two different collector groups, prices go up, often over auction estimates.

Button, Coralene, Woman's Profile, Pastels, White Glass, Metal Mount
$438

Whitely's Auctioneers

Button, Enamel, Bleu-De-Roi, Cobalt Blue, Gilt Foil, Paste Border, 1700s
$500

Whitely's Auctioneers

Button, Gold, Fox's Head, Textured, Red Stone Eyes
$188

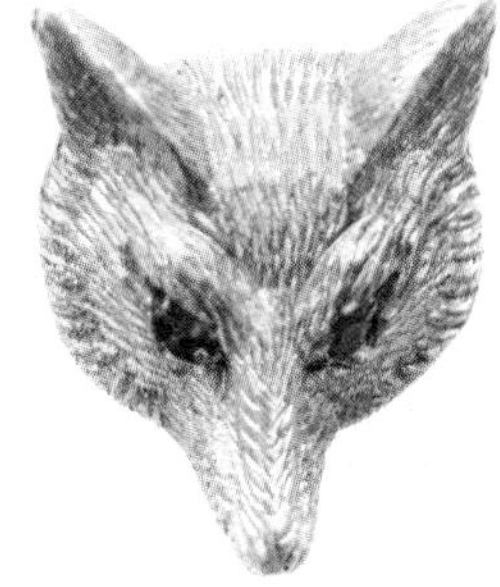

Whitely's Auctioneers

Button, Metal, Grapes & Leaves, Liquid Enamel Technique, Motiwala Studios, India, 1950s
$625

Whitely's Auctioneers

Button, Porcelain, Liverpool Transfer, Centurion's Head, Gilt Ground, Painted Border, Metal Mount
$38

Whitely's Auctioneers

Stolen Art & Antiques
It is said that art and antiques worth a total of $6 billion are stolen each year.

Button, Silver, Smuggler's, Gilt, Enamel, Garnet Tip, Unscrews, Hollow Cavity, 1600s
$250

Whitely's Auctioneers

Calendar, 1956, McCallum Motor Service, Victor Gaskets, Young Woman, Seated, Full Pad, 33 In.
$378

AntiqueAdvertising.com

Cameo Glass, Lamp, Boudoir, Le Verre Francais Style, Conical Shade, Metal Base, 6 In.
$738

Skinner, Inc.

buttons, but most were made of natural materials, like bone or shell, or from inexpensive metals. Only a few types favored by collectors are listed for comparison. Political buttons may also be listed in Political.

Brass, Frog, Glass Cabochon, Paste Eyes, Greek Key Border, Leo Popper, 1890s .... *illus* 8750
Coralene, Woman's Profile, Pastels, White Glass, Metal Mount .... *illus* 438
Enamel, Bleu-De-Roi, Cobalt Blue, Gilt Foil, Paste Border, 1700s .... *illus* 500
Gold, Fox's Head, Textured, Red Stone Eyes .... *illus* 188
Jupiter, Portrait, Brass On Carved Shell, ⅞ In. 24
Metal, Grapes & Leaves, Liquid Enamel Technique, Motiwala Studios, India, 1950s .... *illus* 625
Plique-A-Jour, Pierced Silvered Brass, Enamel, Arts & Crafts Style, Extra Large 375
Porcelain, Liverpool Transfer, Centurion's Head, Gilt Ground, Painted Border, Metal Mount *illus* 38
Shakudo, Scholar, Scroll, Metal, Inlaid Copper, Blue Purple Patina, Medium 175
Silver, Smuggler's, Gilt, Enamel, Garnet Tip, Unscrews, Hollow Cavity, 1600s .... *illus* 250

BUTTONHOOK

Buttonhooks have been a popular collectible in England for many years and are now gaining the attention of a few American collectors. The buttonhooks were made to help fasten the many buttons of the old-fashioned high-button shoes and other items of apparel.

Agate Handle, Brown, Orange, White, Silver Hook, 1902, 2 ½ In. 132
Brass, Bullet Casing, 5 In. 14
File, Silver, Repousse, Folding, Chatelaine, 2 ¾ In. 50
Silver, c.1906, 8 In. 34
Silver, Figural, Salmon, Folding, Penknife, Sheffield, 1894, 2 In. 275
Sterling Silver, Double Hearts, 2 ½ In. 100

CALENDAR

Calendars made to hang on the wall or to be displayed on a desk top have been popular since the last quarter of the nineteenth century. Many were printed with advertising as part of the artwork and were given away as premiums. Calendars illustrated by famous artists or with guns, gunpowder, or Coca-Cola advertising are most prized.

1892, Pad, Children, Color, 4 ¼ x 9 ½ In., 12 pages 35
1901, Bright Eyes Calendar Girls, Fan Shape, Full Pad, 13 x 8 In. 30
1906, Gibson Girl, Black & White, 12 x 15 In., 13 Pages 115
1956, McCallum Motor Service, Victor Gaskets, Young Woman, Seated, Full Pad, 33 In. ..*illus* 378
Perpetual, Singer Sewing Machine, Tin Lithograph On Cardboard, 1930s, 19 x 13 In. 342

CALENDAR PLATE

Calendar plates were popular in the United States as advertising giveaways from 1906 to 1929. Since then, a few plates have been made every year. A calendar and the name of a store, a picture of flowers, a girl, or a scene were featured on the plate.

1909, Hott Bakery, Ashville, Ohio, 2 Apples in Center, 7 In. 19
1974, God Bless Our House, Months, Zodiac, Meakin, 9 In. 12
1985, Cats, Various Breeds, Wedgwood, 10 In. 21

CAMARK POTTERY

Camark Pottery started out as Camden Art Tile and Pottery Company in Camden, Arkansas. Jack Carnes founded the firm in 1926 in association with John Lessell, Stephen Sebaugh, and the Camden Chamber of Commerce. Many types of glazes and wares were made. The company was bought by Mary Daniel in 1965 and it became Camark Pottery Incorporated. Production ended in 1982.

Figurine, Dog, Lying Down, Black, White, Painted Collar, Impressed Mark, 16 ½ x 9 In. 311
Sign, Ivory, Black Lettering, Camark Pottery, Shape Of Arkansas, Open Base, 6 x 5 ¾ In. 184
Vase, Fan Shape, Green Over Pink Matte Glaze, Impressed Mark, 6 x 6 ⅜ In. 40

CAMBRIDGE GLASS COMPANY

Cambridge Glass Company was founded in 1901 in Cambridge, Ohio. The company closed in 1954, reopened briefly, and closed again in 1958. The firm made all types of glass. Its early wares included heavy pressed glass with the mark *Near Cut.* Later wares included Crown Tuscan, etched stemware, and clear and colored glass. The firm used a *C* in a triangle mark after 1920.

Cambridge Glass Co. c.1906–c.1920 | Cambridge Glass Co. c.1937 | Cambridge Glass Co. 1936–1954

Crown Tuscan, Cornucopia, 3 x 2 In. 18
Dolphin, Candlestick, 9 ½ In. 90
Figurine, Draped Woman, Light Emerald Green, Round Base, 8 In. 229
Figurine, Heron, 12 In. 89
Marjorie, Punch Bowl, Stand, Pointed Rim 130
Rose Point, Candy Dish, Lid, 3 Sections, 8 In. 43
Roxbury, Bonbon, Tab Handles, Footed, 6 ¾ In. 30
Tally Ho, Cup & Saucer 12
Thistle, Bowl, 3-Toed, Scalloped, 5 ½ In. 35

CAMBRIDGE POTTERY

Cambridge Pottery was made in Cambridge, Ohio, from about 1895 until World War I. The factory made brown-glazed decorated artwares with a variety of marks, including an acorn, the name *Cambridge,* the name *Oakwood,* and the name *Terrhea.*

Vase, High Glaze, Shades Of Brown, Flowers, No. 220, Signed, 11 In. 120
Vase, Open Mum Design, Glaze, Marked, Cap, No. 226, 15 In. 207

CAMEO GLASS

Cameo glass was made in much the same manner as a cameo in jewelry. Parts of the top layer of glass were cut away to reveal a different colored glass beneath. The most famous cameo glass was made during the nineteenth century. Signed cameo glass pieces by famous makers are listed under the glasswork's name, such as Daum, Galle, Legras, Mt. Joye, Webb, and more. Others, signed or unsigned, are listed here. These marks were used by three lesser-known cameo glass manufacturers.

Albert Dammouse 1892+ | Ernest–Baptiste Lèveillé c.1869–c.1900 | François–Eugène Rousseau 1855–1885

Lamp, Boudoir, Le Verre Francais Style, Conical Shade, Metal Base, 6 In. .... *illus* 738
Plaque, Helios Chariot, Stars, 14K Gold Filigree Frame, Signed, 2 ⅞ x 2 ⅜ In. 230
Vase, Acid Etched, Cranberry Interior, Floral, Fish Scale, c.1915, 15 ⅝ x 3 ½ In. 351

Cameo Glass, Vase, Cotton Blossoms, Leaves, Green Matte, Signed, Nonconnah, 6 ¾ In.
$1,680

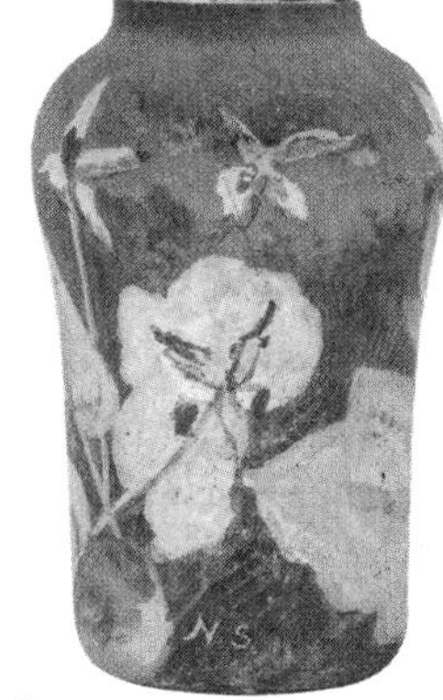

Case Antiques

Cameo Glass, Vase, Dark Purple Leaves, White Matte Ground, Flared Rim, Richard, 14 x 4 ¾ In.
$480

Soulis Auctions

Cameo Glass, Vase, Entwined Ribbons, Orange, Yellow, Marked Honesdale, Early 1900s, 14 In.
$461

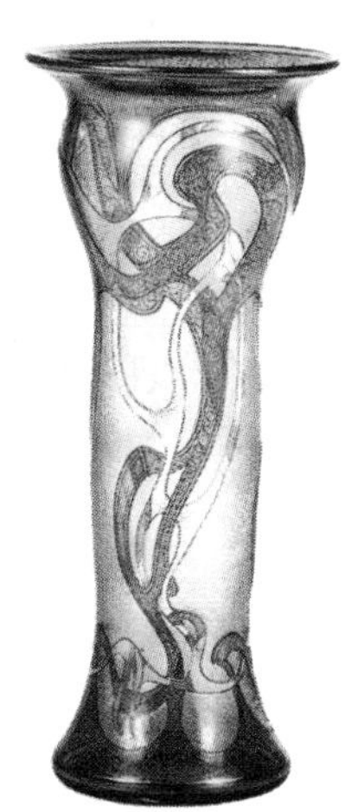

Skinner, Inc.

Candelabrum, 2-Light, Bronze, Egyptian Revival, Gilt, Figural Pharaoh, 1800s, 18 In., Pair
$3,200

Neal Auction Company

Candelabrum, 3-Light, Bronze, Nest, Bird, Rat, Dark Brown Patina, Cain, Late 1800s, 20 x 6 In., Pair
$2,750

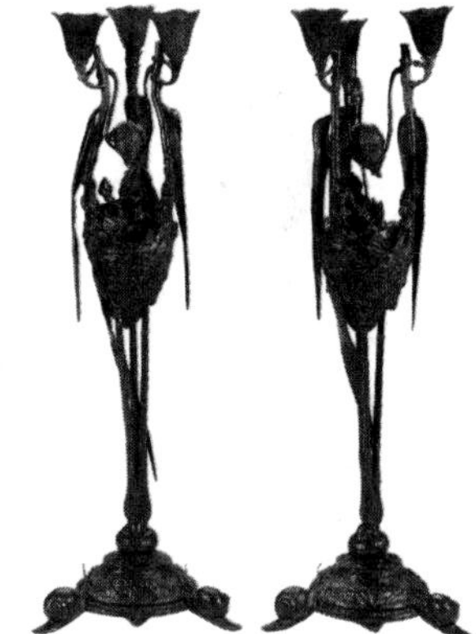

Freeman's Auctioneers & Appraisers

Candelabrum, 3-Light, Gilt Bronze, Neoclassical Style, Classical Maiden, Torch Finial, 27 In., Pair
$1,152

Neal Auction Company

Vase, Cotton Blossoms, Leaves, Green Matte, Signed, Nonconnah, 6 ¾ In. .... *illus* 1680
Vase, Dark Purple Leaves, White Matte Ground, Flared Rim, Richard, 14 x 4 ¾ In. .... *illus* 480
Vase, Entwined Ribbons, Orange, Yellow, Marked Honesdale, Early 1900s, 14 In. .... *illus* 461
Vase, Golden Ducks In Flight, Textured, Smoky Quartz Field, 6 In. 230
Vase, Hyacinth, Cobalt Blue, Frosted, Flower Sprays, Michael Nourot, 1998, 6 ½ x 8 In. 236

CAMPAIGN *memorabilia are listed in the Political category.*

CAMPBELL KIDS

Campbell Kids were first used as part of an advertisement for the Campbell Soup Company in 1904. The kids were created by Grace Drayton, a popular illustrator of the day. The kids were used in magazine and newspaper ads until about 1951. They were presented again in 1966; and in 1983, they were redesigned with a slimmer, more contemporary appearance.

Bank, Cast Iron, Boy & Girl, Gold Finish, c.1915, 4 x 3 ½ In. 149
Cookie Jar, Lid With Kids, Soup Can Shape, Red & White, 12 ½ In. 42
Doorstop, Girl, Boy, Dog, Painted, Red, Beige, Green, c.1940, 5 x 4 In. 65
Ornament, Chef, Joy On Spoon In Soup, 1993, 3 x 1 ¾ In. 25
Salt & Pepper, Red, Yellow, Plastic, c.1950, 4 In. 18
Sign, Tin, M'M Good, Kid Holding Soup Can, 1950s, 25 x 12 In. 495

CANDELABRUM

Candelabrum refers to a candleholder with more than one arm to hold many candles; a candlestick is designed to hold one candle. The eccentricity of the English language makes the plural of candelabrum into candelabra.

2-Light, Bronze, Egyptian Revival, Gilt, Figural Pharaoh, 1800s, 18 In., Pair .... *illus* 3200
2-Light, Gilt Bronze, Figural, Paw Feet, Signed, Carriere-Belleuse, 1800s, 9 x 10 ½ In., Pair.... 1250
2-Light, Gilt Bronze, Panther Head Terminal, Marble Base, 1810s, 18 x 8 x 4 In., Pair 2500
3-Light, Brass, Rococo Style, Gilt, 18 In., Pair 160
3-Light, Bronze, Flower Shape Nozzles, Art Nouveau Style, Leafy Base, c.1900, 12 In., Pair 215
3-Light, Bronze, Marble, Gilt, Flower Arms, 3-Legged Base, 1800s, 17 x 10 In. 1295
3-Light, Bronze, Nest, Bird, Rat, Dark Brown Patina, Cain, Late 1800s, 20 x 6 In., Pair ..*illus* 2750
3-Light, Gilt Bronze, Louis XVI Style, Acanthus Leaf, Adjustable Metal Shade, 1800s, 32 In., Pair.. 1800
3-Light, Gilt Bronze, Neoclassical Style, Classical Maiden, Torch Finial, 27 In., Pair ....*illus* 1152
3-Light, Sheffield Plate, Georgian, Gadroon Border, Hinged Candle Arms, c.1800, 20 In., Pair 400
3-Light, Silver Plate, Removable Arms, Stepped Round Base, 14 ¾ x 15 ½ In., Pair 188
3-Light, Silver, 2 Scroll Arms, Weighted Base, International, 14 In., Pair 389
3-Light, Silver, Scroll Arms, Fisher Silversmiths, N.J., 1900s, 10 ⅝ In., Pair 110
3-Light, Silver, Scrolling Branches, Drip Trays, Threaded Border, Mexico, 1950s, 14 In., Pair.. 1500
4-Light, Bronze, Gilt, Acanthus Leaves Cups, Ram's Heads, Black Marble Base, 26 x 12 In., Pair 480
4-Light, Bronze, Neoclassical, Round Base, Sweden, 25 x 12 ½ In., Pair 500
4-Light, Iron, Central Cup, Bobeche, Ocher Paint, 40 ½ x 17 In. 94
4-Light, Silver, Bamboo, Dragons, Birds, Scholars & Houses, Chinese, c.1850, 14 x 13 In. 923
4-Light, Silver, Beading, Acanthus Leaf, Central Bobeche, Circular Base, France, 15 In., Pair.. 351
5-Light, Bronze, Rococo Style, Cherub, Brown Patina, Gilt Plinth Base, Louis XV, 20 x 11 In. .. 226
5-Light, Cut Glass, Molded, Prisms, Swirl, Scalloped Base, 23 ½ In., Pair 861
5-Light, Gilt Bronze, Figural, Square Base, France, 1800s, 24 x 8 In., Pair 2832
5-Light, Gilt Bronze, Neo-Grec, 3 Graces, Pierced, Flora Figures, c.1850, 26 In., Pair ....*illus* 1250
5-Light, Gilt, Bronze, Renaissance, Removable Finial, 1800s, 19 ½ x 6 x 5 ¾ In. 200
5-Light, Glass, Hanging, Cut Prisms, Base, 27 In., Pair 1150
5-Light, Parcel Gilt, Baroque Style, Carved, Painted, 1800s, 20 ½ In., Pair 813
5-Light, Puffy Garland Shades, Glass Prisms, c.1915, 25 x 19 In. 1375
5-Light, Silver, Scroll Arms, Dome Base, 14 In., Pair 484
5-Light, Wood, Metal, Applied Flowers, Continental, 19 ½ x 35 In., Pair 266
6-Light, Bronze, Louis XVI Style, Gilt, Tripod Base, Scroll Feet, 1800s, 32 ½ In., Pair 819
6-Light, Bronze, Marble, Restauration Style, Flame Finial, Triangular Base, 28 x 10 In., Pair. 550
6-Light, Bronze, Woman, Cherub, Gilt, Marble Base, M. Moreau, c.1900, 33 x 13 In., Pair *illus* 800

6-Light, Giltwood, Carved, Scroll Arms, Plinth, Baroque Style, France, 1800s, 41 x 32 x 9 In. 767
6-Light, Silver, Bending Arms, Anton Michelsen, Denmark, 1900s, 6 ½ x 11 x 10 In. ......*illus* 531
7-Light, Bronze, Empire Style, Palmettes, Acanthus, Scrolls, 1800s, 28 x 10 In., Pair ......*illus* 500
7-Light, Silver, Wiener Werkstatte Style, Shell Base, Vienna, 1922, 11 ¾ x 13 ½ In. 3750
8-Light, Wood Beads On Wire, Gold Bells, Erzgebirge, 18 In. 660
10-Light, Brass, Grapes, Leaves, Tripod Feet, Victorian, Late 1800s, 65 In. 188
13-Light, Iron, Gilt Vase, Tree Shape, Early 1900s, 64 x 23 x 7 In., Pair 1599
Bronze, Victorian, Flowers, Leaves, Gilt, Carved, Tripod Base, Late 1800s, 23 In., Pair ....*illus* 313
Girandole, Brass, Bear & Beehive Figural Standard, Marble Base, 1800s, 15 In., 3 Piece .*illus* 295
Girandole, Ruffled Rim, Gilt, Crystal, Dome Base, Late 1800s, 17 In., Pair 125
Silver, Grape Leaf Border, Triangular Base, Robinson, Edkins & Aston, 1834, 12 In. 2500

CANDLESTICK

Candlesticks were made of brass, pewter, glass, sterling silver, plated silver, and all types of pottery and porcelain. The earliest candlesticks, dating from the sixteenth century, held the candle on a pricket (sharp pointed spike). These lost favor because in times of strife the large church candlesticks with prickets became formidable weapons, so the socket was mandated. Candlesticks changed in style through the centuries, and designs range from Classical to Rococo to Art Nouveau to Art Deco.

Brass, Baluster Stem, Stepped Base, Hexagonal Foot, Continental, 1700s, 26 In., Pair 585
Brass, Barley Twist Stem, Octagonal Base, 8 x 8 x 9 In. ....*illus* 118
Brass, Candleholder, Gothic Style, Incised Phila., Howard Keyser, 1947, 4 In. 250
Brass, Colonial Williamsburg, Virginia Metalcrafters Restoration, Marked CW 16-5, 1900s, 7 In., Pair. 35
Brass, Mid Drip, Scalloped Edges, Footed, 1700s, 8 ½ In. 610
Brass, Nude Female Figures, Valsuani Foundry, Signed Martin Borgord, 1925, 8 ¾ In. ....*illus* 660
Brass, Octagonal Base, Engraved Stems, William & Mary, c.1700, 8 ½ In., Pair 1920
Brass, Photophores, Glass, Louis XIV Style, 19 ¾ x 7 In., Pair 2583
Brass, Queen Anne, Petal Base, Baluster Turned Stems, 1700s, 8 ½ In. 71
Brass, Ringed, Tapering Column, Round Tray Base, Netherlands, 11 ½ x 8 ¼ In. 90
Brass, Square Base, Shaped Stem, Footed, 1700s, 6 x 6 x 8 ½ In. ....*illus* 148
Bronze, Dragon, Tripod Base, Paw Feet, Grand Tour, 2 ¾ In., Pair 185
Bronze, Female, Bust, Art Nouveau, Continental, Early 1900s, 15 x 8 ½ x 5 ½ In., Pair 375
Bronze, Gilt, Patinated Napoleon III, Fluted Shaft, Paw Foot Base, Late 1800s, 26 In., Pair...... 900
Bronze, Men, Robed, Holds Candle Cup, Green Marble Stand, Swags, 1800s, 13 ¾ In., Pair 510
Bronze, Patinated, Gothic, Charles X, c.1825, 10 ⅝ In., Pair 1180
Chamber, Silver, George II, Engraved Coat Of Arms On Base, Paul De Lamerie, 1741, 2 ½ x 6 In. 594
Copper, Twisting Base, Curving Top, Forming 5 Feet, Early 1900s, 12 x 7 In., Pair 135
Cut Glass, Hanging Prisms, Waterford, 10 x 5 In., Pair 152
Garniture, Rouge Marble, Dore Bronze, Converts To Candleholder, 10 ½ x 4 In., Pair ....*illus* 678
Gilt Bronze, Figural, Ebonized, Entwined, Dolphin Shape Base, Ball Feet, 1800s, 8 In., Pair... 469
Giltwood, Continental, Leaves, 3-Part Base, 1800s, 47 x 10 ½ In., Pair 650
Giltwood, Leaves, 3-Part Base, Mounted As Lamp, 1800s, 31 In., Pair 600
Giltwood, Pricket, Carved, White Shade, Mounted As Lamp, 1800s, 39 ¾ In., Pair 750
Giltwood, Pricket, Neoclassical, Carved, Mounted, 1900s, 33 In. 25
Glass, Acid Etched, Circular Base, Marc Jacobs, Waterford, 4 ¾ In., Pair 38
Glass, Clear, Columnar, Hurricane Shade, Etched Stars, American Eagles, 1900s, 15 In., Pair . 200
Iron, Hog Scraper, Gray, Green Banding, Flower, Vine, Round Base, 1800s, 6 ½ In. ....*illus* 369
Iron, Standing, 4 Scrolling Feet, Push-Up, c.1750, 35 In. 277
Metal, Woman, Half Nude, Standing, Art Deco, Circular Base, 10 ½ In., Pair ....*illus* 158
Pewter, Pricket, Wide Drip Catcher, Turned Stem, Round Base, 1728, 15 In. 369
Pricket, Circular Support, Spiral Shape Body, 43 x 10 ½ In., Pair 866
Rock Crystal, Gilt Bronze, Leaves, Reeded, Louis XVI Style, c.1875, 7 In., Pair ....*illus* 1625
Rock Crystal, Tapered, Discs, Hexagon Base, Gilt Metal Ball Feet, 12 In., Pair 1220
Silver Plate, Altar, Gothic Style, Hexagonal Collars, 3-Part Base, 1800s, 21 In., Pair 480
Silver Plate, Column Body, Electro, Embossed, Garland, Square Base, c.1910, 8 ¾ In., Pair *illus* 90
Silver Plate, George III Style, Stepped Base, 1800s, 13 In., Pair 344
Silver Plate, Snuffer, Shell, Heart Shape, Scroll Arms, 1800s, 2 ½ x 5 ½ In. 325

Candelabrum, 5-Light, Gilt Bronze, Neo-Grec, 3 Graces, Pierced, Flora Figures, c.1850, 26 In., Pair
$1,250

New Orleans Auction Galleries

Candelabrum, 6-Light, Bronze, Woman, Cherub, Gilt, Marble Base, M. Moreau, c.1900, 33 x 13 In., Pair
$800

Woody Auctions

TIP
You can remove stickers from most things by spraying them with a lubricant.

Candelabrum, 6-Light, Silver, Bending Arms, Anton Michelsen, Denmark, 1900s, 6 ½ x 11 x 10 In.
$531

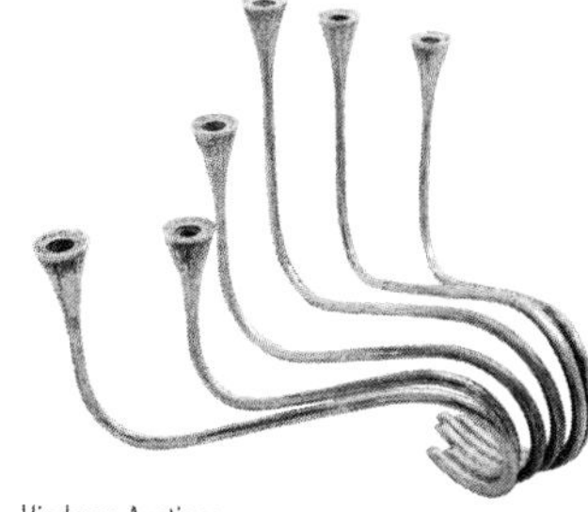

Hindman Auctions

Candelabrum, 7-Light, Bronze, Empire Style, Palmettes, Acanthus, Scrolls, 1800s, 28 x 10 In., Pair
$500

Neal Auction Company

Candelabrum, Bronze, Victorian, Flowers, Leaves, Gilt, Carved, Tripod Base, Late 1800s, 23 In., Pair
$313

Hindman Auctions

Candelabrum, Girandole, Brass, Bear & Beehive Figural Standard, Marble Base, 1800s, 15 In., 3 Piece
$295

Conestoga Auction Company

Candlestick, Brass, Barley Twist Stem, Octagonal Base, 8 x 8 x 9 In.
$118

Copake Auctions

Candlestick, Brass, Nude Female Figures, Valsuani Foundry, Signed Martin Borgord, 1925, 8 ¾ In.
$660

Eldred's

Candlestick, Brass, Square Base, Shaped Stem, Footed, 1700s, 6 x 6 x 8 ½ In.
$148

Copake Auctions

Candlestick, Garniture, Rouge Marble, Dore Bronze, Converts To Candleholder, 10 ½ x 4 In., Pair
$678

Soulis Auctions

Candlestick, Iron, Hog Scraper, Gray, Green Banding, Flower, Vine, Round Base, 1800s, 6 ½ In.
$369

Skinner, Inc.

Candlestick, Metal, Woman, Half Nude, Standing, Art Deco, Circular Base, 10 ½ In., Pair
$158

Hartzell's Auction Gallery Inc.

Silver, Baluster Shape, Weighted, 1900s, 10 In., 4 Piece 110
Silver, Bobeches, Scalloped Base, Schlau, Germany, 1700s, 6 1/2 In., Pair 1046
Silver, Embossed, Castle, Removable Bobeche, Marked, Loring Andrews Co., 1800s, 10 1/2 In., Pair.... 938
Silver, Fluted Stem, Footed, Engraved Armorial, George III, England, 1766-68, 13 In., 2 Pair.. 2460
Silver, George III, Rococo Shell, Removable Bobeches, Ebenezer Coker, 1760, 10 3/8 In. 4250
Silver, Gorham Column, Fluted, Beaded, Filigree, Marked, 10 x 4 3/4 In., Pair 182
Silver, Openwork, Cream, Hexagon Base, 11 In. 93
Silver, Round Base, Fluted, Crichton Bros., Weighted, 11 1/2 In., 4 Piece Set 976
Silver, Zolotnik, Flat Chased Flowers, Kamenetz-Podolsk, Russian 84, 1873, 14 3/8 In., Pair...... 700
Snuffer, Brass, Square Base Stand, Canted Corners, England, 1750s, 4 1/2 In. .... *illus* 861
Taperstick, Brass, Knopped Stem, Round Base, 1700s, 4 In., Pair .... *illus* 738
Wood, Oak, Barley Twist Shape, c.1890, 15 1/2 In., Pair 195
Wood, Pricket, Gesso, Carved, Fluted Column, Triangular Base, Ball Feet, 1700s, 23 In. 246
Wrought Iron, Socket, Mounted, Turned Base, Cylindrical Stem, 1800s, 8 1/2 In. 861

CANDLEWICK GLASS *items may be listed in the Imperial Glass and Pressed Glass categories.*

CANDY CONTAINER

Candy containers have been popular since the late Victorian era. Collectors have long favored the glass containers, but now all types, including tin and papier-mache, are collected. Probably the earliest glass container sold commercially was the Liberty Bell made in 1876 for sale at the Centennial Exposition. Thousands of designs were made until the cost became too high in the 1960s. By the late 1970s, reproductions were being made and sold without the candy. Containers listed here are glass unless otherwise described. A Belsnickle is a nineteenth-century figure of Father Christmas. Some candy containers may be listed in Toy or in other categories.

Airplane, Liberty Motor, Glass, Tin, West Glass Co., c.1920, 4 1/2 x 6 1/4 In. 1200
Cat, Winking, Glass, Painted, Metal Cap, Victory Glass Co., c.1925, 5 In. .... *illus* 4800
Chick, Driving Car, Figural, Glass, Painted, 2 3/8 x 4 1/2 In. .... *illus* 531
Dolly's Bathtub, Glass, Shell Feet, Victory Glass Co., 1920s, 4 3/4 In. 2040
Easter Bunny, Fuzzy, Glass Eyes, Standing, Chicks In Basket, Germany, 9 1/2 In. 510
Easter Bunny, Glass Eyes, Standing, Platform, Egg & Chick In Basket, Germany, 9 In. 840
Father Christmas, Felt Suit, Wood, Carved & Painted, Wood, 11 In. .... *illus* 523
Jonah & The Whale, Composition, Green Glass Eyes, Jonah Pops Out, 12 In. 3600
Rabbit, Mohair, Glass Eyes, Fur Tail Tuft, Card Stock Ears, c.1920, 7 1/2 x 6 x 2 In. 961
Refrigerator, G.E. Monitor Top, Glass, Victory Glass Co., c.1920, 4 In. .... *illus* 2400
Santa Claus, Woodcutter, Composition, Rabbit Fur Beard, Feather Tree, Germany, 11 In. *illus* 900
Sideboard, Flossie Fisher's Funnies, Tin, Helene Nyce, 1920s, 3 1/2 In. .... *illus* 510
Submarine, Glass, Tin Lithograph Sail & Flag, George Borgfeldt Co., c.1915, 2 x 5 In. 461
Taxi, Glass, Tin Wheels, Westmoreland, 2 x 4 In. 310
Village 5 & 10 Cent Store, Tin, 3 x 2 3/4 In. .... *illus* 461

CANE

Canes and walking sticks were used by every well-dressed man in the nineteenth century, but by World War I the style had changed. Today canes are used by few but the infirm. Collectors prize old canes made with special features, like hidden swords, whiskey flasks, or risqué pictures seen through peepholes. Examples with solid gold heads or made from exotic materials are among the higher-priced canes. See also Scrimshaw.

Antler, Silver Band, Wood Shaft, Monogram, England, 36 In. 115
Baton, Rosewood, Monkey Head Top, Silver Ferrule, Tip, 19 In. 35
Bird Beak Handle, Silver Relief, Vertebra Shaft, Ferrule, c.1920, 22 3/4 In. 523
Crook Handle, Wood, Carved, Glass-Eyed Frogs, Carved, Blackthorn-Type Shaft, 1800s, 37 In.. 452
Doctor's, Bone & Metal Handle, Rosewood, Syringe In Fitted Wood & Fabric Sleeve, 35 In........ 1573
Ebony Handle, Horn Tip, Shark Vertebrae, 35 1/2 In. .... *illus* 189
Folk Art, Lady's Leg Handle, Rustic Wood Shaft, 1800s, 34 In. 424

Candlestick, Rock Crystal, Gilt Bronze, Leaves, Reeded, Louis XVI Style, c.1875, 7 In., Pair
$1,625

New Orleans Auction Galleries

Candlestick, Silver Plate, Column Body, Electro, Embossed, Garland, Square Base, c.1910, 8 3/4 In., Pair
$90

Woody Auctions

Candlestick, Snuffer, Brass, Square Base Stand, Canted Corners, England, 1750s, 4 1/2 In.
$861

Skinner, Inc.

Candlestick, Taperstick, Brass, Knopped Stem, Round Base, 1700s, 4 In., Pair
$738

Skinner, Inc.

Candy Container, Cat, Winking, Glass, Painted, Metal Cap, Victory Glass Co., c.1925, 5 In.
$4,800

Morphy Auctions

Candy Container, Chick, Driving Car, Figural, Glass, Painted, 2 3/8 x 4 1/2 In.
$531

AntiqueAdvertising.com

Candy Container, Father Christmas, Felt Suit, Wood, Carved & Painted, Wood, 11 In.
$523

Skinner, Inc.

Candy Container, Refrigerator, G.E. Monitor Top, Glass, Victory Glass Co., c.1920, 4 In.
$2,400

Morphy Auctions

Candy Container, Santa Claus, Woodcutter, Composition, Rabbit Fur Beard, Feather Tree, Germany, 11 In.
$900

Bertoia Auctions

Candy Container, Sideboard, Flossie Fisher's Funnies, Tin, Helene Nyce, 1920s, 3 1/2 In.
$510

Morphy Auctions

Candy Container, Village 5 & 10 Cent Store, Tin, 3 x 2 3/4 In.
$461

Morphy Auctions

Cane, Ebony Handle, Horn Tip, Shark Vertebrae, 35 1/2 In.
$189

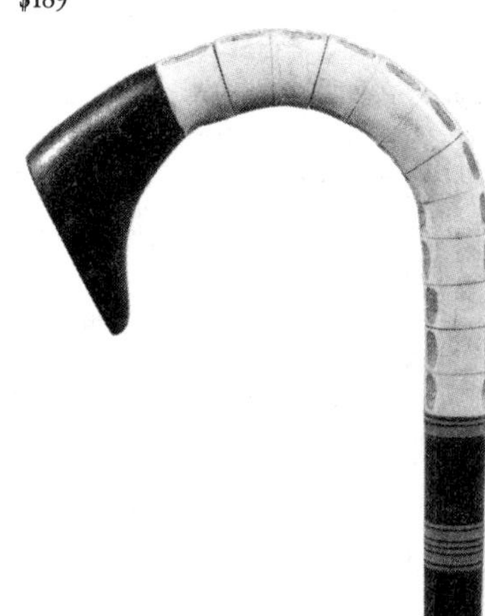

Conestoga Auction Company

Folk Art, Wood, Carved, Boot Handle, Silver Band, 35 ½ In. 763
Folk Art, Wood, Ebonized, Carved, Eagles & Flags, Metal Tip, 34 ½ In. 1107
Horn Handle, Bone Shaft, Wood, Carved, Yellow, 34 ½ In. 170
Hunting, Wood, Patriotic Scenes, Carved, Signed, Ed Seltzer, 1933, 38 ½ In. 62
Ivory Handle, Carved, Floral, Dancing Putti, Thin Metal Collar, Wood Shaft, 1800s, 33 ½ In. 213
Parade, Lantern, Figural, Man, Top Hat, c.1890s, 40 x 5 In. *illus* 6600
Silver Handle, Shaving Kit, Shaving Brush, Razor, Wood Shaft, c.1900, 35 ¾ In. 367
Silver, Monkeys, Climbing, Tree Branch, Wood, 35 x 4 In. 625
Silver, S-Curve Handle, Wood Shaft, Metal Heel, Germany, France, c.1890, 35 ¾ In. 108
Sword, Bamboo, Carved, 4 Warriors, Dagger Interior, 36 ½ In. 904
Walking Stick, Bone Cue Ball Handle, Tapering Wood Shaft, Mappin & Webb, c.1900, 32 ½ In. 439
Walking Stick, Bone Handle, Carved, Jovial Hunter, Ferrule Cap, Bolster, c.1917, 34 In. 199
Walking Stick, Bone Handle, Horn Tip, Wood Shaft, 38 ½ In. 369
Walking Stick, Bone Top, Wood Insert, Coconut Wood Palm Shaft, Bone Ferrule, c.1850, 33 In. 113
Walking Stick, Brass Handle, Profile Of Beauty, Marked Bridges, Black, 36 In. 216
Walking Stick, Brass, Silvered, English Coat Of Arms, Concealed Compass, Telescope, 38 In. 1063
Walking Stick, Brass, Wood, Steamship, Tube Vials, Southern Comfort, 36 In. 72
Walking Stick, Cherry, Carved Snakes Twist Down Shaft, Wood, Carved, 37 In., Pair 150
Walking Stick, Gold Filled Knob, Flowers, Malacca Shaft, Engraved, 14K, H.H. Inedeker, 37 In. *illus* 527
Walking Stick, Gold Handle, Ebony Shaft, White Metal Ferrule, Engraved, 37 In. 848
Walking Stick, Gold Plated Knob, Engraved, Ebony, c.1878, 36 In. 80
Walking Stick, Gold, Donkey's Head, Paste Eyes, Rose Gold Collar, Ebony Shaft, c.1907, 36 In. 3750
Walking Stick, Horn Handle, Bamboo, Silver Band, Metal Base Tip, 34 ⅝ In. 94
Walking Stick, Iroquois Maple, Carved, Spiraling Serpent, Adam & Eve, Mid 1800s, 36 ½ In. 1053
Walking Stick, Ivory Handle, Malacca, Knotted Serpent, Silver Ring, 1800s, 35 ½ In. 380
Walking Stick, Silver Top, Rosewood, 3 Small Panels, Lt. Henry Robinson, 1814, 34 In. 1755
Walking Stick, Silver, Crook Handle, Leafy, Cherry, Wood Shaft, 1905, 35 ½ In. 480
Walking Stick, Walnut, Carved, Rope Twist, Snake Around Tree Branch, c.1890, 36 In. 228
Walking Stick, Whalebone, Black, Red, Green Floral, Geometric, Ball Shape Handle, c.1920, 36 ½ In. 492
Walking Stick, Whalebone, Hexagonal, Carved Knob, Turned Finial, c.1850, 35 ⅜ In. 316
Walking Stick, Wood, Bust Of Woman, Snake, Spiral Flower Vine, Carved, Painted, 1900s, 36 In. 915
Walking Stick, Wood, Carved Eagle Head Handle, Wood Case, Mexico, 35 In. 173
Walking Stick, Wood, Carved, Frog, Alligator, Inlaid Eyes, Sailor's Knots, Top Knob, 34 ¾ In. 848
Walking Stick, Wood, Dog's Head Handle, Alligator, Rattlesnake Shaft, c.1900, 34 In. *illus* 293
Walking Stick, Wood, Dog's Head, Inlaid Eyes, Squared Crook, Cherry Wood Shaft, 35 In. 424
Walking Stick, Wood, Figural Man Grip, Snake Intertwined, Carved, Painted, 1936, 37 ¾ In. 2684
Whale Ivory, Faceted Handle, 2 Raised Bands, Baleen Dots, Whalebone Shaft, 1800s, 38 In. 313
Whalebone, Fist, Baton, Tapering Shaft, 34 In. 1062
Wood, Carved, Hare Handle, Long Ears, Red Glass Eyes, Stained Shaft, Gold Band, 1800s, 34 In. 593
Wood, Carved, Names, Dates & Places, Silver Tip, Thomas Jefferson Craddock, 34 In. 1107
Wood, Horse, Head, Neck, Saddle, Brass Ferrule, Carved, 1800s, 34 In. 138
Wood, Snake, Spiraling Around Shaft, Lizard, Frog, Carved, Painted, c.1900, 38 ⅜ In. 4613
Wood, Square Crook, Brass Ferrule, Spiral Shaft, Twisted, Intertwined, 34 In. 136

CANTON CHINA

Canton china is blue-and-white ware made near the city of Canton, in China, from about 1795 to the early 1900s. It is hand decorated with a landscape, building, bridge, and trees. There is never a person on the bridge. The "rain and cloud" border was used. It is similar to Nanking ware, which is listed in this book in its own category.

Basket, Chestnut, Underplate, Reticulated, White Ground, Blue Border & Handles, 11 In. *illus* 554
Platter, Octagonal, Landscape, Blue, White Ground, 17 In. *illus* 172

CAPO-DI-MONTE

Capo-di-Monte porcelain was first made in Naples, Italy, from 1743 to 1759. The factory moved near Madrid, Spain, and operated there from 1771 until 1821. The Ginori factory of Doccia, Italy, acquired the molds and began using

Cane, Parade, Lantern, Figural, Man, Top Hat, c.1890s, 40 x 5 In.
$6,600

Morphy Auctions

Cane, Walking Stick, Gold Filled Knob, Flowers, Malacca Shaft, Engraved, 14K, H.H. Inedeker, 37 In.
$527

Cordier Auctions

Cane, Walking Stick, Wood, Dog's Head Handle, Alligator, Rattlesnake Shaft, c.1900, 34 In.
$293

Jeffrey S. Evans & Associates

Canton, Basket, Chestnut, Underplate, Reticulated, White Ground, Blue Border & Handles, 11 In.
$554

Stair Galleries

Canton, Platter, Octagonal, Landscape, Blue, White Ground, 17 In.
$172

Skinner, Inc.

How Was Carnival Glass Made?

An iridescent finish is added to molded glass to make carnival glass. The glass, usually colored, is pressed in the mold, then removed. Additional shaping may be done by hand. Then the piece is sprayed with a coating of liquid metallic salts to create the iridescent finish.

Carnival Glass, Fruits & Flowers, Bowl, Amethyst, Piecrust Edge, Basketweave Exterior, Northwood, 9 ¾ In.
$40

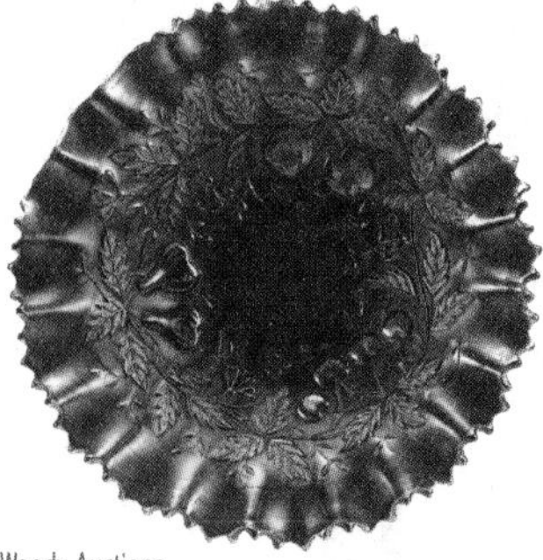

Woody Auctions

the crown and *N* mark. In 1896 the Doccia factory combined with Societa Ceramica Richard of Milan. It eventually became the modern-day firm known as Richard Ginori, often referred to as Ginori or Capo-di-Monte. This company also used the crown and *N* mark. Richard Ginori was purchased by Gucci in 2013. The Capo-di-Monte mark is still being used. "Capodimonte-style" porcelain is being made today by several manufacturers in Italy, sometimes with a factory name or mark. The Capo-di-Monte mark and name are also used on cheaper porcelain made in the style of Capo-di-Monte.

Ewer, Gilt Accents, Applied Flowers, 48 In., Pair 215
Group, Nativity Scene, Greek Columns, Urns, Arches, Vines, Flowers, 18 In. 700

CAPTAIN MARVEL

Captain Marvel was introduced in February 1940 in Whiz comic books. An orphan named Billy Batson met the wizard, Shazam, and whenever he said the magic word he was transformed into a superhero. A movie serial was released in 1940. The comic was discontinued in 1954. A second Captain Marvel appeared in 1966, a third in 1967. Only the original was transformed by shouting "Shazam."

Figure, Wood Composition, Red, Multi Products, 5 In. 435
Hat, Beanie, Felt, Shazam, Fawcett, 1945, 7 In. 130
Patch, Felt, Yellow, Lightning Bolt, Flying, 3 ½ x 5 In. 307
Wristwatch, Chromed, Green Vinyl Band, Box, Illustrated Lid, Fawcett, 1948, 1 In. 318

CAPTAIN MIDNIGHT

Captain Midnight began as a network radio show in September 1940. The first comic book appeared in July 1941. Captain Midnight was really the aviator Captain Albright, who was to defeat the Nazis. A movie serial was made in 1942 and a comic strip was published for a short time. The comic book version of Captain Midnight ended his career in 1948. Radio premiums are the prized collector memorabilia today.

Badge, Decoder, Patina, 1942, 2 x 2 In. 95
Premium Set, Badge, Mug, Ring, Code Book, 1957 118
Ring, Mystic Sun God, Red, Ovaltine Premium, Envelope, Folder, 1946 130
Ring, Secret Compartment Ring, 1942 119
Spinner Coin, Token, Skelly Oil, Chuck Ramsay, Propeller Blades, 1940 44

CARAMEL SLAG, *see Imperial Glass category.*

CARD

Cards listed here include advertising cards (often called trade cards), baseball cards, playing cards, and others. Color photographs were rare in the nineteenth century, so companies gave away colorful cards with pictures of children, flowers, products, or related scenes that promoted the company name. These were often collected and stored in albums. Baseball cards also date from the nineteenth century, when they were used by tobacco companies as giveaways. Gum cards were started in 1933, but it was not until after World War II that the bubble gum cards favored today were produced. Today over 1,000 cards are issued each year by the gum companies. Related items may be found in the Christmas, Halloween, Movie, Paper, and Postcard categories.

Advertising, Standard Screw & Fastened Boots & Shoes, Hot Air Balloons 5
Baseball, Joe Morgan, 2nd Base, Houston Astros, Topps, No. 195, 1966 105
Baseball, Luis Aparicio, Shortstop, Baltimore Orioles, Holding Bat, Topps, No. 410, 1956 42
Baseball, Mickey Lolich, Pitcher, Detroit Tigers, Portrait, 1965 35

Baseball, Ty Cobb, Hassan Cigarettes, T205, Gold Border, 1911 1638
Baseball, Whitey Ford, Pitcher, New York Yankees, No. 5, 1967 56
Baseball, Willie Stargell, Pittsburgh Pirates, Topps, No. 377 49
Football, Les Richter, Los Angeles Rams, Bowman, No. 82, 1955 34
Football, Nick Buoniconti, Linebacker, Boston Pirates, Portrait, Topps, No. 3, 1965 42
Football, O.J. Simpson, Rookie, Portrait, Topps, No. 90, 1970 25
Playing, Flags Of The World, Topps, 1956 395
Playing, Island Of Hokkaido, Nintendo, 52 Cards, c.1960 25
Playing, Pan American, Logo, White, Blue, Box, 3 ½ x 2 ½ In. 18
Playing, Panda, Bamboo Tree, 3 ½ x 2 ¼ In. 35
Playing, Secret Agent, Pepys, 39 Cards, c.1957 75
Tarot, Gypsy Fortune Telling, Piatnik, Instructions, Box, 36 Cards, 1986 23
Tarot, Karma, Phantasmagoric, Birgit Boline Erfurt, Box, 78 Cards, 1983 30
Trading, John F. Kennedy, Rosan Printing, 64 Cards, 1963, 2 ½ x 3 ½ In. 95

CARDER, *see Steuben category.*

CARLTON WARE

Carlton ware was made at the Carlton Works of Stoke-on-Trent, England, beginning about 1890. The firm traded as Wiltshaw & Robinson until 1957. It was renamed Carlton Ware Ltd. in 1958. The company was bought and sold several times. Production stopped in 1992. Frank Salmon bought the trademark, molds, and pattern books in 1997. Production was outsourced to other potteries. Carlton Ware production ceased by 2016.

Biscuit Jar, Lid, Day Oak, Acorn Finial, Wicker Handle, Marked, 1930s, 7 ½ x 7 In. 25
Biscuit Jar, Lid, Swing Handle, Flowers, Gilt, Silver, Marked, 10 ½ x 5 ½ In. 275
Condiment Set, Moderne, Blue, Tray, Mustard, Salt & Pepper, Art Deco, 4 ⅜ In. 68
Salt & Pepper, Blue Mary Jane Shoes, Luster, 4 ¾ x 1 ¾ In. 75
Vase, Pitcher, Night Oak, Blue, Orange Leaves, Handle, Marked, 1930s, 14 x 9 In. 32

CARNIVAL GLASS

Carnival glass was an inexpensive, iridescent pressed glass made from about 1907 to about 1925. More than 1,000 different patterns are known. Carnival glass is currently being reproduced. Here are three marks used by companies that have made 20th-century carnival glass.

Imperial
1910–1924

Northwood Glass Co.
1910–1918

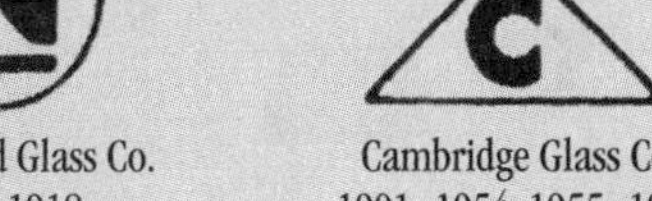

Cambridge Glass Co.
1901–1954, 1955–1958

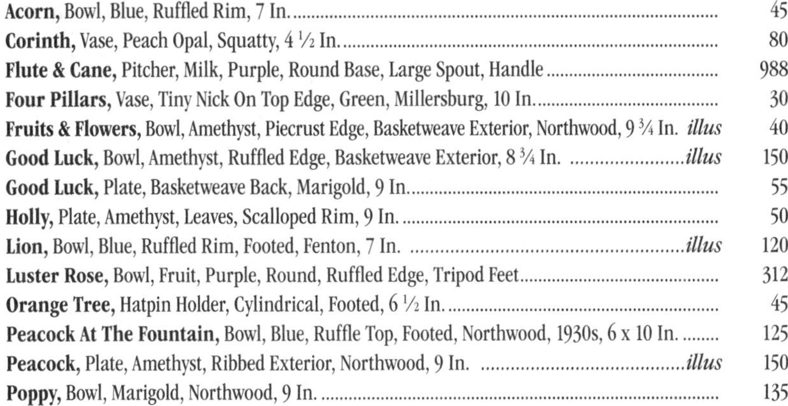

Acorn, Bowl, Blue, Ruffled Rim, 7 In. 45
Corinth, Vase, Peach Opal, Squatty, 4 ½ In. 80
Flute & Cane, Pitcher, Milk, Purple, Round Base, Large Spout, Handle 988
Four Pillars, Vase, Tiny Nick On Top Edge, Green, Millersburg, 10 In. 30
Fruits & Flowers, Bowl, Amethyst, Piecrust Edge, Basketweave Exterior, Northwood, 9 ¾ In. *illus* 40
Good Luck, Bowl, Amethyst, Ruffled Edge, Basketweave Exterior, 8 ¾ In. .... *illus* 150
Good Luck, Plate, Basketweave Back, Marigold, 9 In. 55
Holly, Plate, Amethyst, Leaves, Scalloped Rim, 9 In. 50
Lion, Bowl, Blue, Ruffled Rim, Footed, Fenton, 7 In. .... *illus* 120
Luster Rose, Bowl, Fruit, Purple, Round, Ruffled Edge, Tripod Feet 312
Orange Tree, Hatpin Holder, Cylindrical, Footed, 6 ½ In. 45
Peacock At The Fountain, Bowl, Blue, Ruffle Top, Footed, Northwood, 1930s, 6 x 10 In. 125
Peacock, Plate, Amethyst, Ribbed Exterior, Northwood, 9 In. .... *illus* 150
Poppy, Bowl, Marigold, Northwood, 9 In. 135

C

TIP
Always dust shelves from the top down. The dust falls.

Carnival Glass, Good Luck, Bowl, Amethyst, Ruffled Edge, Basketweave Exterior, 8 ¾ In.
$150

Woody Auctions

Carnival Glass, Lion, Bowl, Blue, Ruffled Rim, Footed, Fenton, 7 In.
$120

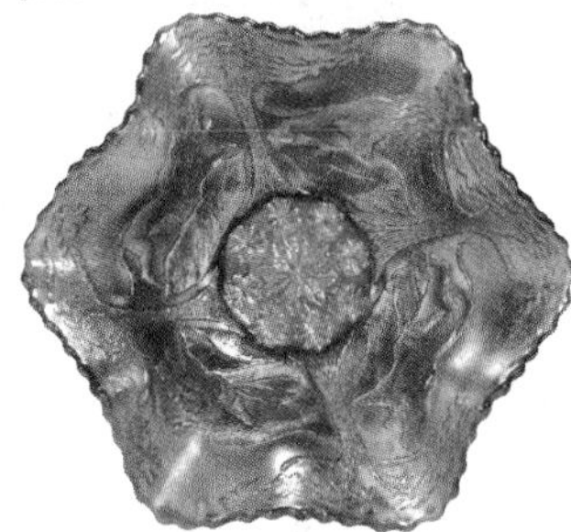

Woody Auctions

Carnival Glass, Peacock, Plate, Amethyst, Ribbed Exterior, Northwood, 9 In.
$150

Woody Auctions

This is an edited listing of current prices. Visit **Kovels.com** to check thousands of prices from previous years and sign up for free information on trends, tips, reproductions, marks, and more.

Carnival Glass, Rose Garden, Vase, Marigold, Letter Style, Ruffled Edge, 5 ¼ In.
$312

Seeck Auctions

Carnival Glass, Rose Show, Plate, Ice Green, Scalloped Rim, 9 In.
$700

Seeck Auctions

Carnival Glass, Ten Mums, Pitcher, Blue Handle & Base, Scalloped Rim, Fenton, 11 In.
$150

Woody Auctions

Carousel, Camel, Glass Eyes, Starburst Jewels, Plaster Mounts, Multicolor, Looff, c.1895, 54 x 66 In.
$12,300

Skinner, Inc.

TIP

Old, authentic carousel figures almost always have glass eyes or eyes shaped like those of a real horse. Reproductions have human-shaped eyes, either Asian or Caucasian.

Carousel, Deer, Prancer, Painted, Pole Stand, Heyn, Germany, 39 In.
$1,416

Bunch Auctions

Carousel, Horse, Jumper, Outside Row, Tucked Head, Armored, Jeweled Headstall, Looff, 57 In.
$6,490

Bunch Auctions

Carousel, Horse, Stander, Outside Row, Painted, E. J. Morris, c.1904, 65 x 61 In.
$5,310

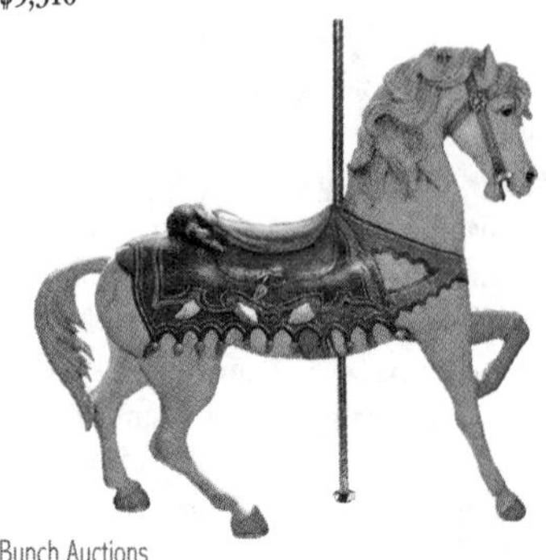

Bunch Auctions

Carousel, Panel, Flowers, Red, Yellow, Leaves, Wood, Carved, Painted, 17 x 16 ½ In., Pair
$59

Bunch Auctions

Carousel, Rounding Board, Jester Head, Plaster, 11 Light Sockets, Dentzel, 52 ½ x 27 ½ In.
$354

Bunch Auctions

Pulled Loop, Vase, Aqua, Rare Color, Circular Base, 10 ½ In. 85
Rose Garden, Vase, Marigold, Letter Style, Ruffled Edge, 5 ¼ In. .... *illus* 312
Rose Show, Plate, Ice Green, Scalloped Rim, 9 In. .... *illus* 700
Rustic, Vase, Green, Cylindrical Body, 16 ½ In. 45
Ten Mums, Pitcher, Blue Handle & Base, Scalloped Rim, Fenton, 11 In. .... *illus* 150
Three Fruits, Bowl, Cherries, Orange, Green, Iridescent, Ribbed, Northwood, 9 In. 290
Wild Strawberry, Bowl, Purple, Basketweave Back, 10 In. 60

CAROUSEL

Carousel or merry-go-round figures were first carved in the United States in 1867 by Gustav Dentzel. Collectors discovered the charm of the hand-carved figures in the 1970s, and they were soon classed as folk art. Most desirable are the figures other than horses, such as pigs, camels, lions, or dogs. A stander has all four feet on the carousel platform; a prancer has both front feet in the air and both back feet on the platform; a jumper has all four feet in the air and usually moves up and down. Both old and new animals are collected.

Camel, Glass Eyes, Starburst Jewels, Plaster Mounts, Multicolor, Looff, c.1895, 54 x 66 In. *illus* 12300
Centaur, Jumper, General White, Boer War, Multicolor, 69 In. 3540
Deer, Prancer, Painted, Pole Stand, Heyn, Germany, 39 In. .... *illus* 1416
Deer, Stander, Painted, Gilt, Carved Saddle, E.J. Morris, c.1900, 60 In. 4720
Goat, Prancer, Jewel, Painted, Looff, c.1900, 61 x 72 In. 2124
Horse Head, Wood, Carved, White, Rectangular Base, Parker, 9 ¾ x 9 ½ In. 35
Horse, Jumper, 2-Tone Brown, Yellow Saddle, Blue Blanket, Glass Eyes, 33 x 59 x 10 In. 605
Horse, Jumper, Brown Body, Flowing Mane, Iron Stirrups, c.1900, 37 ½ In. 6225
Horse, Jumper, Outside Row, Tucked Head, Armored, Jeweled Headstall, Looff, 57 In. .....*illus* 6490
Horse, Jumper, Saddle, Cast Metal, Stand, c.1920-30, 36 x 24 x 50 ½ In. 295
Horse, Jumper, Tucked Head, Ears Back, White, Blue Parcel Gilt Breast Strap, Brass Pole, 64 x 46 In. 2770
Horse, Stander, Outside Row, Jewel, White, Charles Carmel, c.1910, 59 x 57 In. 5015
Horse, Stander, Outside Row, Painted, E. J. Morris, c.1904, 65 x 61 In. .... *illus* 5310
Horse, Stander, White, Horsehair Tail, Painted Saddle, Mounted On Board, 36 x 36 In. 311
Lights, Zigzag Embossed, Metal, Half Moon Cups, Multicolor, 37 x 18 In., Pair 437
Panel, Flowers, Red, Yellow, Leaves, Wood, Carved, Painted, 17 x 16 ½ In., Pair .... *illus* 59
Rounding Board, Jester Head, Plaster, 11 Light Sockets, Dentzel, 52 ½ x 27 ½ In. ....*illus* 354
Shield, Viking Head, Carved, Painted, Wood, Plaque, Herschell-Spillman, c.1900, 21 x 16 In... 118

CARRIAGE

Carriage means several things, so this category lists baby carriages, buggies for adults, horse-drawn sleighs, and even strollers. Doll-sized carriages are listed in the Toy category.

Baby, Wicker, Victorian, Steel Wheel, Suspension, Red, 1800s, 38 x 52 x 22 In. 250
Cart, Pine, Spoke Wheels, Wood Body, Handles, Yellow, Red Trim, Early 1900s, 28 x 27 x 67 In. . 480
Pull Cart, Wood, Donkey, Painted, Blue, Brown, White, Green, Germany, c.1900, 33 In. 148
Push Cart, Child, Green, Red Leather, White Horse, Rubber Tires, 1880s, 33 x 44 x 14 In...*illus* 270
Sleigh, Push Handle, Green Seat, Cast Iron Runners, Gooseneck End, c.1900, 34 x 48 In....*illus* 390
Sleigh, Wood, Painted, Scrolled Iron Supports & Runners, 33 x 36 In., Child's .... *illus* 212
Stroller, Elm Wood, Brass Wheels, Handle, Chinese, Baby's, 23 x 13 x 23 In. .... *illus* 83

CASH REGISTER

Cash registers were invented in 1883 because an eye on the cash was a necessity in stores of the nineteenth century, too. John and James Ritty invented a large model that resembled a clock and kept a record of the dollars and cents exchanged in the store. John Patterson improved the cash register with a paper roll to record the money. By the early 1900s, elaborate brass registers were made. More modern types were made after 1920. Cash registers made by National Cash Register Company are most the most popular with collectors.

TIP
Going away for the weekend? If you have a car at home, park it in the driveway and lock it. It makes it look as if someone is home and it blocks easy access to a back door.

Carriage, Push Cart, Child, Green, Red Leather, White Horse, Rubber Tires, 1880s, 33 x 44 x 14 In.
$270

Garth's Auctioneers & Appraisers

Carriage, Sleigh, Push Handle, Green Seat, Cast Iron Runners, Gooseneck End, c.1900, 34 x 48 In.
$390

Garth's Auctioneers & Appraisers

Carriage, Sleigh, Wood, Painted, Scrolled Iron Supports & Runners, 33 x 36 In., Child's
$212

Conestoga Auction Company

Carriage, Stroller, Elm Wood, Brass Wheels, Handle, Chinese, Baby's, 23 x 13 x 23 In.
$83

Charleston Estate Auctions

Cash Register, Chicago, Candy Store, 9 Keys, 5 Cents To 1 Dollar, Nickel Plated, c.1895, 9 x 14 x 17 In.
$693

Auction Team Breker

Cash Register, National, Candy Store, Brass, Drawer, Wood Base, 17 x 16 In.
$400

Richard Opfer Auctioneering, Inc.

Chicago, Candy Store, 9 Keys, 5 Cents To 1 Dollar, Nickel Plated, c.1895, 9 x 14 x 17 In. ..*illus* 693
National, Brass, Paper Tape Dispenser, 23 In. 259
National, Candy Store, Brass, Drawer, Wood Base, 17 x 16 In. *illus* 400
National, Embossed Brass, Marble Sill, Wood Stepped Base, Drawer, 17 x 17 In. 923
National, Model 47, Nickel Plated, Cast Iron, Wood Base, Geo Eberhart, 21 ½ x 17 In. *illus* 600
National, Model 250, Cast Brass, c.1907, 20 ¾ x 10 In. 704
National, Model 313, Brass, Drawer, Scrolls, Banners, c.1920, 17 In. 357
National, Model 313, Brass, Marble Shelf, Candy Size, 21 x 16 x 10 In. 570
National, Model 317, Brass, Side Receipt Cage, Oak Base, c.1915, 17 x 12 x 16 In. *illus* 594
National, Model 337, Brass, Embossed, Drawer, Wood Shelf, 15 x 19 In. *illus* 420
National, Silver, Paisley & Festoon, 16 x 16 x 18 In. 590
Receipt Box, National, Cast Frame Lid, 2 Glass Panes, 1910s, 6 ½ x 6 ¾ In. *illus* 250

CASTOR JAR

Castor jars for pickles are glass jars about six inches in height, held in special metal holders. They became a popular dinner table accessory about 1890. Each jar had a top that was usually silver or silver plate. The frame, also of a silver metal, had a handle that arched above the jar and a hook that held a pair of tongs. The glass jar was often painted. By 1900, the pickle castor was out of fashion. Many examples found today have reproduced glass jars in old holders. Additional pickle castors may be found in the various Glass categories.

Pickle, Light Blue Glass Jar, Gilt, Silver Plate Stand, Tongs, Victorian, 10 ½ In. *illus* 120
Pickle, Satin Glass, Flower, Quadruple Plate, Pelton Bros. & Co., St. Louis, 13 x 7 In. 242
Pickle, Server, Blue Daisy & Button, Boat, Butterfly On Handle, 10 x 8 ½ In. 295
Pickle, Spatter Glass, Opal, Orange, Flower, James W. Tufts, c.1900, 12 x 5 In. *illus* 211

CASTOR SET

Castor sets holding just salt and pepper castors were used in the seventeenth century. The sugar castor, mustard pot, spice dredger (shaker), bottles for vinegar and oil, and other spice holders became popular by the eighteenth century. These sets were usually made of sterling silver with glass bottles. The American Victorian castor set, the type most collected today, was made of silver plated Britannia metal. Colored glass bottles were introduced after the Civil War. The sets were out of fashion by World War I. Be careful when buying sets with colored bottles; many are reproductions. Other castor sets may be listed in various porcelain and glass categories in this book.

Cut Glass, Silver Plate Holder, Center Handle, Footed, 6 Bottles, England, 1800s 144
Etched Glass, Silver Plate Stand, 6 Bottles, Victorian, 16 ½ In. 60
Ruby Flash, Clear Pressed Glass Stand, 4 Bottles, 10 In. 108

CATALOGS *are listed in the Paper category.*

CAULDON

CAULDON ENGLAND

Cauldon Limited worked in Staffordshire, Great Britain, and went through many name changes. John Ridgway made porcelain at Cauldon Place, Hanley, until 1855. The firm of John Ridgway, Bates and Co. of Cauldon Place worked from 1856 to 1859. It became Bates, Brown-Westhead, Moore and Co. from 1859 to 1862. Brown-Westhead, Moore and Co. worked from 1862 to 1904. About 1890, this firm started using the words *Cauldon* or *Cauldon Ware* as part of the mark. Cauldon Ltd. worked from 1905 to 1920, Cauldon Potteries from 1920 to 1962. Related items may be found in the Indian Tree category.

Platter, Turkey, Tall Grass, Flow Blue, Ironstone, c.1915, 16 ¾ x 14 In. *illus* 380
Tureen, Lid, 2 Handles, Undertray, Gilt Border, Retailer's Mark, Tureen 7 ½ x 12 ½ In. 154

CELADON

Celadon is the name of a velvet-textured green-gray glaze used by Chinese, Japanese, Korean, and other factories. This section includes pieces covered with celadon glaze with or without added decoration.

Bowl, Ceramic, Piecrust Rim, Glazed, Footed, Chinese, 7 ¾ In. 590
Bowl, Mallow, Glazed Terra-Cotta, Footed, Raised Decorations, Chinese, 1900s, 1 ½ x 5 ¾ In. 293
Bowl, Porcelain, Brass Rim, Fishing Boats, Mountains, Pagoda Temples, Chinese, 4 x 9 In. 177
Bowl, Shallow, Footed, Ruffled Rim, Leaves, Green, Chinese, 16 In. .... *illus* 118
Bowl, Strapped Edges, 4 Triple-Petal Feet, Blue Underglaze, 1700s, 2 x 6 ¾ In. 878
Figurine, Duck, Longquan Style, Incised Feathers, Blue Glaze, 6 x 9 In. 3360
Jar, Lid, Glazed, Molded Dragon On Neck, Chinese, 20 In. 366
Lamp Base, Electric, 2-Light, Lily, Brown, Glazed, Mounted, Wood Base, Chinese, 18 In. 554
Lamp, Trapezoidal White Shade, Bronze Mount Base, Chinese, 28 In. 767
Plaque, Deer, Leaves, Cut Back & Carved, c.1930, 2 x 15 ¾ In. 147
Teapot, Cadogan, Peach Shape, Flowering Vine, Chinese, 6 x 8 In. 295
Umbrella Stand, Gilt, Dragons Chasing Pearl, Bird, Porcelain, 1800s, 24 x 9 In. .... *illus* 1029
Vase, 2 Gourd Shape, Bulbous Body, Imperial, Paper Sticker, Chinese, 6 x 6 x 11 ½ In. 224
Vase, Crackle, Glazed, Flared Rim, Ribbed Neck, Raised Bands, 7 In. .... *illus* 461
Vase, Elephantine Handles, Garlic Shape Mouth, Soft Seafoam Green, 1800s, 12 In. 10370
Vase, Pear Shape, Long Neck, Flared Mouth, Peony Flower, Leaves, Chinese, 14 In. 1076
Vase, Square, Rippled, Bold Crackle Glaze, Qing Style, Chinese, 1800s, 10 ⅝ In. .... *illus* 222
Vase, Stick Neck, Crackle Glaze, Ribbed, Raised Bands, 7 In. 480

CELLULOID

Celluloid is a trademark for a plastic developed in 1868 by John W. Hyatt. Celluloid Manufacturing Company, the Celluloid Novelty Company, Celluloid Fancy Goods Company, and American Xylonite Company all used celluloid to make jewelry, games, sewing equipment, false teeth, and piano keys. The name *celluloid* was often used to identify any similar plastic. Celluloid toys are listed under Toy.

Album, Photo, Mother & Child, Sailboat, Palm Trees, Cream Ground, Victorian, 10 x 12 In. 30
Box, Hinged Lid, 2 Cherubs, Blue Ground, Scrolls, Filigree Metal Clasp, 3 x 8 x 8 In. 60
Box, Neckties, Victorian Woman, Brown Leafy Ground, Hinged Lid, 3 x 12 ¾ In. 30
Button, Cat's Head, Bow Tie, Green Tint, Faux Tortoiseshell Ground, Round 100
Button, Insect, Lacy, Ivory Color, Pierced 113
Button, Sergeant Preston Of The Yukon, Dog, Yukon King, 1956, 1 ¼ In. 288
Comb, Mantilla, Bright Green, Red Sphinx Medallion, Beaded Trim, Wavy Form 40
Comb, Tortoiseshell Color, Ornate Openwork, 5 Prongs 23
Rattle, Baby's Head, Flowers At Neck, Loop Handle 26

CELS *are listed in this book in the Animation Art category.*

CERAMIC ART COMPANY

Ceramic Art Company of Trenton, New Jersey, was established in 1889 by Jonathan Coxon and Walter Scott and was an early producer of American belleek porcelain. It became Lenox, Inc. in 1906. Do not confuse this ware with the pottery made by the Ceramic Arts Studio of Madison, Wisconsin.

Bowl, Blue, Tree Silhouette, White Interior, 1906-24, 3 x 8 In. 399
Tankard, Draped Woman, Pitcher, Purple, Yellow, Green, 1889-1906, 14 ½ In. 62
Tankard, Red & Purple Grapes, c.1900, 14 ½ x 6 ½ In. 895
Vase, Bulbous, Flowers, Bird In Flight, Gilt Handles, 1899-1906, 8 ½ x 8 In. 400

CERAMIC ARTS STUDIO

Ceramic Arts Studio was founded about 1940 in Madison, Wisconsin, by Lawrence Rabbitt and Ruben Sand. Their most popular prod-

Cash Register, National, Model 47, Nickel Plated, Cast Iron, Wood Base, Geo Eberhart, 21 ½ x 17 In.
$600

Rich Penn Auctions

Cash Register, National, Model 317, Brass, Side Receipt Cage, Oak Base, c.1915, 17 x 12 x 16 In.
$594

Cowan's Auctions

Cash Register, National, Model 337, Brass, Embossed, Drawer, Wood Shelf, 15 x 19 In.
$420

Rich Penn Auctions

Cash Register, Receipt Box, National, Cast Frame Lid, 2 Glass Panes, 1910s, 6 ½ x 6 ¾ In.
$250

Garth's Auctioneers & Appraisers

Castor, Pickle, Light Blue Glass Jar, Gilt, Silver Plate Stand, Tongs, Victorian, 10 ½ In.
$120

Bunte Auction Services

Castor, Pickle, Spatter Glass, Opal, Orange, Flower, James W. Tufts, c.1900, 12 x 5 In.
$211

Jeffrey S. Evans & Associates

Cauldon, Platter, Turkey, Tall Grass, Flow Blue, Ironstone, c.1915, 16 ¾ x 14 In.
$380

Jeffrey S. Evans & Associates

Celadon, Bowl, Shallow, Footed, Ruffled Rim, Leaves, Green, Chinese, 16 In.
$118

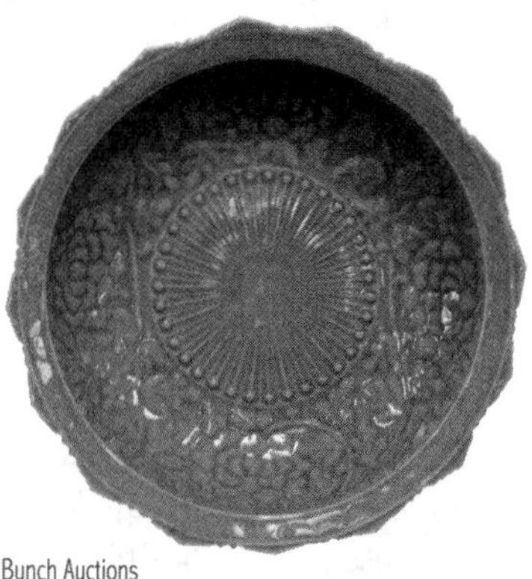

Bunch Auctions

Celadon, Umbrella Stand, Gilt, Dragons Chasing Pearl, Bird, Porcelain, 1800s, 24 x 9 In.
$1,029

Fontaine's Auction Gallery

Celadon, Vase, Crackle, Glazed, Flared Rim, Ribbed Neck, Raised Bands, 7 In.
$461

Clars Auction Gallery

Celadon, Vase, Square, Rippled, Bold Crackle Glaze, Qing Style, Chinese, 1800s, 10 ⅝ In.
$222

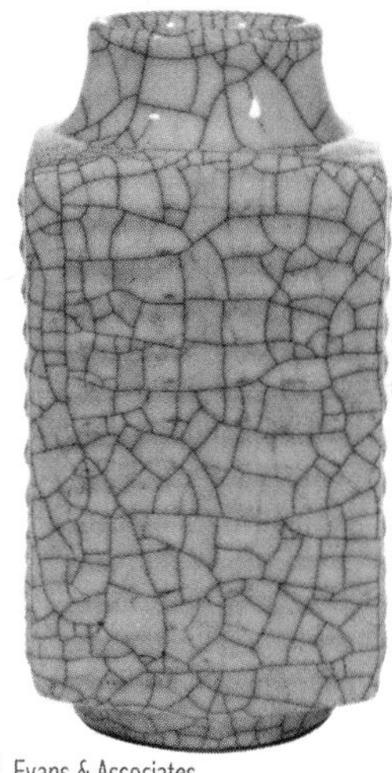

Jeffrey S. Evans & Associates

Chalkware, Figurine, Cat, Sitting, Cream Ground, Yellow Stripes, Mounted, 1800s, 7 In.
$2,440

Pook & Pook

ucts were molded figurines. The pottery closed in 1955. Do not confuse these products with those of the Ceramic Art Co. of Trenton, New Jersey.

Figurine, Cinderella & Prince, Green, White, Gilt, Marked, 6 ¾ In., Pair 20
Figurine, Girl, Head, Red Hair, Green Eyes, Blue Band Base, 9 ¾ In. 34
Figurine, Little Bo Peep, Yellow Skirt, Green Crook, c.1955, 5 ½ In. 25
Figurine, Turtle, Standing, Top Hat, Monocle, Cane, Marked, 3 In. 89
Salt & Pepper, Fighting Cocks, Green, Pink, Marked, 1940s, 4 In. 25
Salt & Pepper, Man & Woman, Chinese Dress, Yellow, Marked, 1947, 3 In. 30
Vase, Evolution, Woman, Signed, Norma Pineda, 1900s, 20 In. 85

CHALKWARE

Chalkware is really plaster of Paris decorated with watercolors. One type was molded from Staffordshire and other porcelain models and painted and sold as inexpensive decorations in the nineteenth century. This type is collected today. Figures of plaster, made from about 1910 to 1940 for use as prizes at carnivals, are also known as chalkware. Kewpie dolls made of chalkware will be found in the Kewpie category.

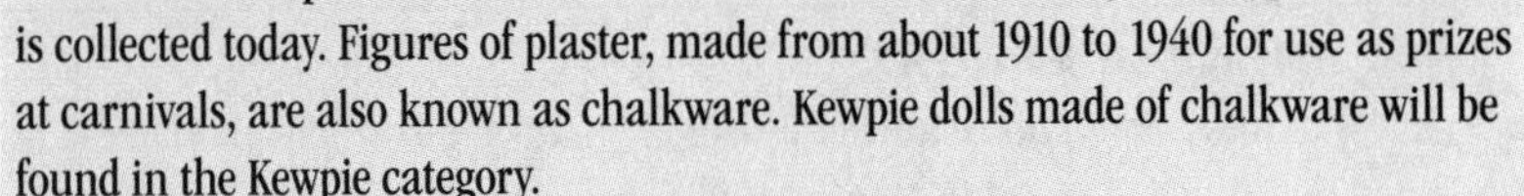

Bust, Native American, Bear, Painted, The Bailey Co., 1900, 17 ½ x 13 In. 480
Figurine, Cat, Sitting, Cream Ground, Yellow Stripes, Mounted, 1800s, 7 In. .... *illus* 2440
Figurine, Owl, Brown Body, Black Base, Yellow, Multicolor, 1800s, 13 ¾ In. 1586
Figurine, Ram, Sitting, White, Green Horns, Rectangular Platform Base, 4 x 4 In. 147
Garniture, Fruit, Leaves, Painted, Multicolor, Pennsylvania, 1800s, 9 ½ x 14 ½ In., Pair 1534

CHARLIE CHAPLIN

Charlie Chaplin, the famous comedian, actor, and filmmaker, lived from 1889 to 1977. He made his first movie in 1913. He did the movie *The Tramp* in 1915. The character of the Tramp has remained famous, and in the 1980s appeared in a series of television commercials for computers. Dolls, candy containers, and all sorts of memorabilia with the image of Charlie's Tramp are collected. Pieces are being made even today.

Candy Container, Ribbed Barrel, Glass, Painted, L.E. Smith Co., 4 In. .... *illus* 512
Mirror, Young Charlie Chaplin Portrait On Back, Rectangular, 1 ¾ In. 69
Purse, Mesh, Silver Plate, Portrait Of Charlie, Whiting & Davis, 6 x 4 In. 363
Toy, Black Hat, Cast Iron Feet, Tin Lithograph, Mechanical, Germany, 8 ½ In. 492
Toy, Charleston Dancer, On Drum, Tin, Crank, Marked, DRGM, 1930, 9 ½ In. 3879
Toy, Charlie Chaplin Walker, Tin, Windup, Germany, 8 In. 390
Toy, Charlie Chaplin, Spins Cane, Windup, Schuco, Box, 7 In. 1080
Toy, Push Pull, 2 Charlies Move, Strike 3 Bells, Cast Metal, Watrous, 9 ½ In. 410

CHARLIE McCARTHY

Charlie McCarthy was the ventriloquist's dummy used by Edgar Bergen from the 1930s. He was famous for his work in radio, movies, and television. The act was retired in the 1970s. Mortimer Snerd, another Bergen dummy, is also listed here.

Dummy, Ventriloquist, Composition, Cloth Checked Suit, Box, 28 In. 84
Dummy, Ventriloquist, Composition Head, Straw Body, Cloth Suit, Tie, 1930s, 34 In. .... *illus* 210
Photograph, Charlie & Edgar Bergen, Silver Print, Autograph, 1930s, 7 x 5 In. 156
Radio, Sitting On Edge Of Case, White Plastic, Majestic, 8 x 6 In. .... *illus* 400
Toy, Benzine Buggy, Charlie Driving, Tin, Black, Louis Marx, Box, 7 In. 813
Toy, Drummer Boy, Charlie, Drum, Strike Up The Band, Tin, Key, Marx, 9 In. 469
Toy, Private Car, Charlie & Mortimer Snerd, Tin, Windup, Marx, 16 In. 1375
Toy, Private Car, Charlie & Mortimer Snerd, Tin, Windup, Marx, Box, 16 In. 3438
Toy, Walker, Charlie, Tin, Key Wind, Louis Marx, Box, 8 ½ In. 469

Charlie Chaplin, Candy Container, Ribbed Barrel, Glass, Painted, L.E. Smith Co., 4 In.
$512

Morphy Auctions

Charlie McCarthy, Dummy, Ventriloquist, Composition Head, Straw Body, Cloth Suit, Tie, 1930s, 34 In.
$210

Rich Penn Auctions

Charlie McCarthy, Radio, Sitting On Edge Of Case, White Plastic, Majestic, 8 x 6 In.
$400

Richard Opfer Auctioneering, Inc.

Chelsea, Candlestick, Bird, Flowers, Iron Red, Painted, Anchor Mark, 10 ½ In., Pair
$369

Stair Galleries

Chelsea, Urn, Lid, Classical Style, Gilt, Pomegranate Finials, Square Plinth Base, 17 ½ In., Pair
$767

Leland Little Auctions

Chinese Export, Bowl, Classical Scenes, Judgment Of Paris, White Ground, Footed, 1700s, 4 x 9 In.
$390

CRN Auctions

C

CHELSEA

Chelsea porcelain was made in the Chelsea area of London from about 1745 to 1769. Some pieces made from 1770 to 1784 are called Chelsea Derby and may include the letter *D* for *Derby* in the mark. Ceramic designs were borrowed from the Meissen models of the day. Pieces were made of soft paste porcelain. The gold anchor was used as the mark, but it has been copied by many other factories. Recent copies of Chelsea have been made from the original molds. Do not confuse Chelsea porcelain with Chelsea Grape, a white pottery with luster grape decoration. Chelsea Keramic is listed in the Dedham category.

Candlestick, Bird, Flowers, Iron Red, Painted, Anchor Mark, 10 ½ In., Pair .... *illus* 369
Dish, Leaf Shape, Green Border, Scalloped Rim, Painted, 9 ¾ In. 1353
Urn, Lid, Classical Style, Gilt, Pomegranate Finials, Square Plinth Base, 17 ½ In., Pair ..*illus* 767
Vase, Turquoise Ground, Gilt Scrolled Handle, Flowers, 7 In., Pair................ 123

CHINESE EXPORT

Chinese export porcelain comprises the many kinds of porcelain made in China for export to America and Europe in the eighteenth, nineteenth, and twentieth centuries. Other pieces may be listed in this book under Canton, Celadon, Nanking, Rose Canton, Rose Mandarin, and Rose Medallion.

Bowl, Classical Scenes, Judgment Of Paris, White Ground, Footed, 1700s, 4 x 9 In. ....*illus* 390
Bowl, Equestrian Scene, Man, Horse, c.1780, 5 ¾ x 14 In. 4688
Bowl, Famille Rose, Birds, Butterflies, Floral, Leaves, 1800s, 5 ½ x 12 ¾ In. 580
Bowl, Famille Rose, Eggshell, Cockerels, Blue Border, Footed, 8 ⅝ In. 92
Bowl, Famille Rose, Figural Court Scenes, Flowers, Flared Sides, c.1875, 8 x 21 In. ....*illus* 6250
Bowl, Flower Bouquet, Scalloped Rim, Butterfly, Late 1800s, 10 In. 180
Bowl, Flower Form, Floral Panels, Multicolor, Late 1800s, 4 x 10 ½ In. 108
Bowl, Fruit, Lid, Scenic, Flowers, 2 Handles, Footed, Early 1800s, 11 ¾ In. ....*illus* 2196
Bowl, Gilt, Pomegranates, Rattray Of Scotland, Ex Hoc Victoria Signo, c.1755, 4 x 9 In. 1406
Bowl, Ming Style, Blue & White, Footed, c.1700, 6 x 15 In. ....*illus* 938
Bowl, Sacred Bird & Butterfly, Orange, White Ground, c.1815, 10 x 5 In. 201
Box, Game, Lacquer, 8 Chip Trays, 24 Counters, Fish, Flowers, 6 x 12 ½ x 5 In. 590
Cachepot, Figures, Panels, Landscapes, 1700s, 4 x 6 In. ....*illus* 312
Candleholder, Famille Rose, Figural, Court Woman, Gu-Form Candle Nozzles, 16 In., Pair..*illus* 2875
Charger, Central Flowers, Vignettes Of Birds, Pavilions Along Border, 1983, 13 ⅞ In. 840
Charger, Dragon & Phoenix, Green, Enameled, 16 In. 1680
Dish, Blue, Flowers, Lattice, White Ground, 1700s, 14 In. 492
Dish, Lid & Strap Handle, Blue & White, 1830s, 5 ½ x 12 x 9 ½ In. ....*illus* 120
Dish, Lozenge Shape, Blue & White, Landscape, 4 Shell Shape Feet, 1800s, 13 In. 330
Dish, Warming, 3 Parts, Bamboo Shape Handles, c.1850, 7 x 13 x 8 In. ....*illus* 111
Figurine, Famille Rose, Buddha, Holding Vase, Lotus, Character Mark, 27 x 12 In. 1003
Figurine, Famille Rose, Phoenix, Multicolor, Blue Base, 24 In., Pair................ 2460
Fishbowl, Famille Rose, Multicolor, Light Green Ground, People, 17 x 20 ½ In., Pair 246
Jar, Lid, Famille Rose, Flowers, Butterflies, Wood Base, 1900s, 14 x 9 In., Pair ....*illus* 150
Jar, Lid, Famille Rose, Flowers, Pomegranate Branches, Fruit Shape Finial, 8 ½ In................ 1020
Jar, Lid, Famille Rose, Ginger, Bats, 2 Coins, Peaches, Flowers, 6 ½ In. 413
Jug, Lid, Foo Dog Finial, Cask Shape, 2 Strap Handles, Blue & White, c.1850, 6 ¾ In................ 330
Lamp, Famille Rose, Hexagonal, Brass, White Ground, 1800s, 27 In. 500
Lamp, Mandarin, Baluster Shape, Flared Rim, 31 x 10 In. 600
Lantern, Wedding, Famille Verte, Reticulated, Octagonal, 2 Parts, 1800s, 11 x 7 ½ In. ...*illus* 510
Mug, Birds & Flowers, Interior Scene, Entwined Handle, Multicolor, Mid 1800s, 4 In................ 72
Pillow, Dragon, Blue & White, Bean Shape, Flaming Pearls, 4 x 9 ¾ x 6 In. 4500
Plate, 2 Scotsmen, White Ground, Birds & Landscapes Border, c.1800, 9 In., Pair ....*illus* 500
Plate, Armorial, Gilt Rim, Arms Of King Of Rockingham, c.1750, 9 In., Pair 800
Plate, Flowers, 1700s, 1 ⅗ x 8 In................ 288
Platter, Fitzhugh, Blue & White, Oval, 1900s, 17 In. ....*illus* 200
Platter, Octagonal, Blue & White, Landscape Scene, Floral Border, 1700s, 14 ¾ x 12 In........... 644
Platter, Octagonal, Central Blue, White Ground, Basket Weave Border, c.1790, 8 x 11 In........... 277

Chinese Export, Bowl, Famille Rose, Figural Court Scenes, Flowers, Flared Sides, c.1875, 8 x 21 In.
$6,250

New Orleans Auction Galleries

Chinese Export, Bowl, Fruit, Lid, Scenic, Flowers, 2 Handles, Footed, Early 1800s, 11 ¾ In.
$2,196

Pook & Pook

TIP
China can be washed in warm water with mild soapsuds. The addition of ammonia to the water will add that extra sparkle.

Chinese Export, Bowl, Ming Style, Blue & White, Footed, c.1700, 6 x 15 In.
$938

Hindman Auctions

Chinese Export, Cachepot, Figures, Panels, Landscapes, 1700s, 4 x 6 In.
$312

Neal Auction Company

Chinese Export, Candleholder, Famille Rose, Figural, Court Woman, Gu-Form Candle Nozzles, 16 In., Pair
$2,875

Neal Auction Company

Chinese Export, Dish, Lid & Strap Handle, Blue & White, 1830s, 5 ½ x 12 x 9 ½ In.
$120

Eldred's

Chinese Export, Dish, Warming, 3 Parts, Bamboo Shape Handles, c.1850, 7 x 13 x 8 In.
$111

Locati Auctions

Chinese Export, Jar, Lid, Famille Rose, Flowers, Butterflies, Wood Base, 1900s, 14 x 9 In., Pair
$150

Hindman Auctions

Chinese Export, Lantern, Wedding, Famille Verte, Reticulated, Octagonal, 2 Parts, 1800s, 11 x 7 ½ In.
$510

CRN Auctions

Chinese Export, Plate, 2 Scotsmen, White Ground, Birds & Landscapes Border, c.1800, 9 In., Pair
$500

Hindman Auctions

Chinese Export, Platter, Fitzhugh, Blue & White, Oval, 1900s, 17 In.
$200

Eldred's

TIP
All collectors seem to have clear memories of "the one that got away."

Chinese Export, Punch Bowl, Painted, 2 Figures, 12 ½ In.
$600

Bourgeault-Horan Antiquarians & Associates, LLC

Chinese Export, Serving Dish, Fitzhugh, Blue, 11 In.
$240

Bourgeault-Horan Antiquarians & Associates, LLC

Chinese Export, Tray, Leaf Shape, Flowers, Gilt Rim, Multicolor, 1800s, 8 ½ In.
$72

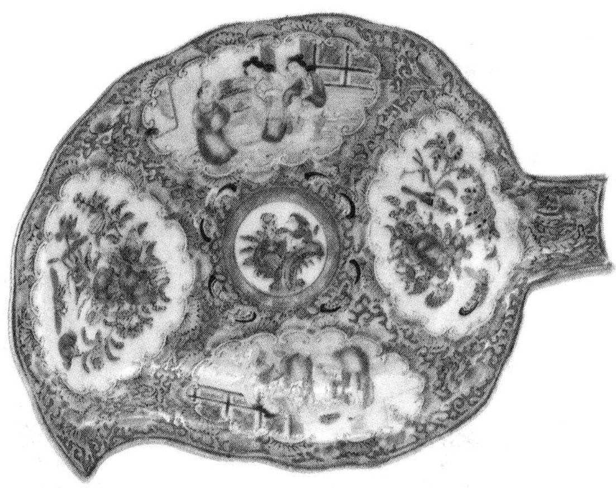

Eldred's

Chinese Export, Vase, Famille Rose, Gilt Dragons, Flowers, Green Ground, 9 ½ x 5 ¼ In.
$69

Blackwell Auctions

Platter, Oval, White Ground, Gold Line Border, Flowers, Early 1800s, 14 ½ In. 154
Punch Bowl, Birds On Branches, Landscape Scenes, Pavilions, Flower, 1700s, 6 ¾ x 15 ½ In. 2188
Punch Bowl, Enamel, Bird, Flowers, Footed, Late 1800s, 6 ½ x 15 ¾ In. 1112
Punch Bowl, Painted, 2 Figures, 12 ½ In. ....*illus* 600
Serving Dish, Armorial, Octagonal, Wreath Border, Early 1800s, 11 ¾ In., Pair 677
Serving Dish, Fitzhugh, Blue, 11 In. ....*illus* 240
Serving Dish, Lid, Enameled Figures, Landscape, Metal Handles, 6 ½ x 10 ¾ In. 1063
Tankard, Famille Rose, Garland, Cartouche, S-Scroll Handle, c.1790, 5 x 6 ½ In. 123
Tea Caddy, Lid, Famille Rose, Hand Painted, Insects, 5 In. 157
Teapot, Lid, White Ground, Iron Red, Late 1700s, 5 ½ In. 75
Tray, Leaf Shape, Flowers, Gilt Rim, Multicolor, 1800s, 8 ½ In. ....*illus* 72
Urn, Lid, Pistol Grip Handles, Sepia Western Scene, Blue, Coral Flowers, 1810s, 17 In. 2160
Vase, Famille Rose, Female Figure, Floral Ground, Phoenix Handles, 1900s, 25 In., Pair 900
Vase, Famille Rose, Gilt Dragons, Flowers, Green Ground, 9 ½ x 5 ¼ In. ....*illus* 69
Vase, Famille Rose, Palace, Gilt, 2 Handles, Multicolor, 1900s, 37 x 17 In., Pair 375
Vase, Famille Rose, Pierced & Gilt Handles, Late 1800s, 13 ¾ In. 156
Vase, Famille Rose, Script, Landscape, Floral Handles, Qianjiang, 18 ½ x 8 x 7 In. 1736
Vase, Famille Verte, Foo Dog, Seated, Yellow & Green, Rectangular Base, 9 ¾ In., Pair ....*illus* 177

CHINTZ

Chintz is the name of a group of china patterns featuring an overall design of flowers and leaves, similar to the design on chintz fabric. The design became popular with English makers about 1928. A few pieces are still being made. The best known are designs by Royal Winton, James Kent Ltd., Crown Ducal, and Shelley. Crown Ducal and Shelley are listed in their own sections.

Atlas China Co.
c.1934–1939

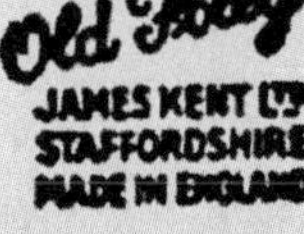

Old Foley/James Kent
c.1955

Royal Winton
c.1951+

Grosvenor, Cup & Saucer, Roses, Gold Trim, White Ground, Jackson & Gosling, 3 x 3 In. 35
Kew, Bowl, Multicolor, Gold Trim, Marked, Royal Winton, 5 In. 28

CHOCOLATE GLASS

Chocolate glass, sometimes mistakenly called caramel slag, was made by the Indiana Tumbler and Goblet Company of Greentown, Indiana, from 1900 to 1903. It was also made at other National Glass Company factories. Fenton Art Glass Co. made chocolate glass from about 1907 to 1915. More recent pieces have been made by Imperial and others.

Cactus, Compote, Shaped Rim, 5 ⅜ x 5 In. 72
Dewey, Creamer, Shaped Rim, Footed, Early 1900s, 4 x 5 In. 20
Leaf Bracket, Bowl, 3-Footed, c.1900, 2 x 4 ¾ In. 28
Leaf Bracket, Butter, Cover, Round, 1901, 5 x 7 In. 89

CHRISTMAS PLATES *that are limited edition are listed in the Collector Plate category or in the correct factory listing.*

CHRISTMAS

Christmas collectibles include not only Christmas trees and ornaments listed below, but also Santa Claus figures, special dishes, and even games and wrapping paper. A Belsnickle is a nineteenth-century figure of Father Christmas. A kugel is an early, heavy ornament made of thick blown glass, lined with zinc or lead, and often covered with colored wax. Christmas cards are listed in this

Chinese Export, Vase, Famille Verte, Foo Dog, Seated, Yellow & Green, Rectangular Base, 9 ¾ In., Pair
$177

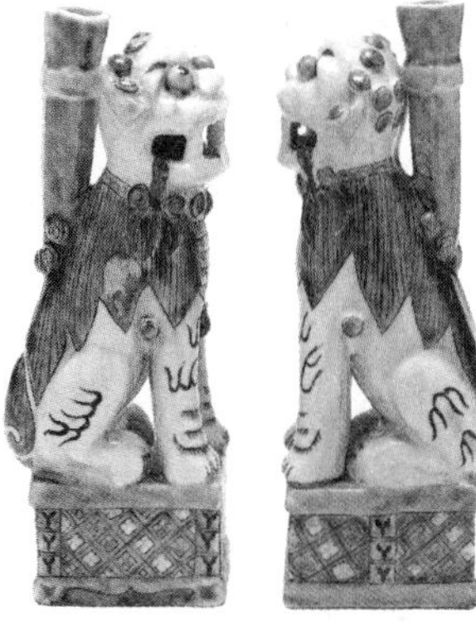
Leland Little Auctions

Christmas, Belsnickle, Holding Sack Of Toys, Redware, Painted, Pennsylvania, 11 In.
$15,600

Bertoia Auctions

Christmas, Display, Village, 3 Tiers, Candles, Spinner Top, Cardboard, Wood, 15 x 16 In.
$5,700

Bertoia Auctions

Christmas, Poster, Merry Christmas, 2 Gorillas, Ringling Bros. Circus, Frame, 1941, 46 In.
$540

Bertoia Auctions

Christmas, Santa Claus, Doll, Cloth Body, Felt Suit, Beard, Black Boots, 24 In.
$47

Bunch Auctions

Christmas, Santa Claus, Red & Black Robe, Long Beard, Holding Teddy Bear, Standing, 52 In.
$118

Copake Auctions

section under Greeting Card. Christmas collectibles may also be listed in the Candy Container category. Christmas trees are listed in the section that follows.

Belsnickle, Holding Sack Of Toys, Redware, Painted, Pennsylvania, 11 In. .... *illus* 15600
Candleholder, 2-Light, Coal Miner, Figural, Wood, Carved, Painted, Erzgebirge, 11 In. 480
Candleholder, Angel, Wood, White Robe, Gold Trim, Holds 6-Cup Arch, Germany, 20 In. 5100
Candy Containers are listed in the Candy Container category. ....
Decoration, Church, Octagon, Pressed Cardboard, Snow, Clock Tower, Erzgebirge, 17 In. 660
Display, Santa Claus Head, Composition, Wood, Blue Eyes, Dimples, Smile, Hangs, 43 In......... 1920
Display, Village, 3 Tiers, Candles, Spinner Top, Cardboard, Wood, 15 x 16 In. ....*illus* 5700
Nodder, Santa Claus, Celluloid, Rubber Band, Lantern, Green Sack, 7 In. 120
Nodder, Santa Claus, Papier-Mache, Sheepskin Hair & Beard, Key, Germany, 28 In. 2178
Poster, Merry Christmas, 2 Gorillas, Ringling Bros. Circus, Frame, 1941, 46 In. ....*illus* 540
Santa Claus In Auto, Red Robe, Fur Beard, Feather Tree, Toys In Loofah Decorated Car, 14 In. 2400
Santa Claus, Die Cut, Embossed, Glitter, Easel Back, Germany, c.1900, 15 x 7 In. 158
Santa Claus, Doll, Cloth Body, Felt Suit, Beard, Black Boots, 24 In. ....*illus* 47
Santa Claus, Lamp, Figural, Nutmeg Burner, Consolidated Lamp & Glass Co., c.1894, 9 In. 3240
Santa Claus, Letter Carrier, Composition, Cardboard, Wool Beard, Sack, Tree, Germany, 14 In. 1680
Santa Claus, Red & Black Robe, Long Beard, Holding Teddy Bear, Standing, 52 In. ....*illus* 118
Sign, Merry Christmas, Red Ground, White & Green Text, 2-Sided, 30 x 21 In.......................... 181
Sleigh, Santa, Reindeer, Painted, White, Cast Iron, Hubley, 6 ¾ x 15 x 3 ½ In. 360
Toy, Santa Claus On Elephant, Basket Of Toys On Back, Composition, Wheels, 11 ½ In............ 1680
Toy, Santa Claus Riding Reindeer, Skyhook, Balance, Hand Cut, Painted, 2 ½ In. 69
Toy, Santa Claus, Roly Poly, Marked, Schoenhut, 9 In.. 420

CHRISTMAS TREES

Christmas trees made of feathers and Christmas tree decorations of all types are popular with collectors. The first decorated Christmas tree in America is claimed by many states, including Pennsylvania (1747), Massachusetts (1832), Illinois (1833), Ohio (1838), and Iowa (1845). The first glass ornaments were imported from Germany about 1860. Paper and tinsel ornaments were made in Dresden, Germany, from about 1880 to 1940. Manufacturers in the United States were making ornaments in the early 1870s. Electric lights were first used on a Christmas tree in 1882. Character light bulbs became popular in the 1920s, bubble lights in the 1940s, twinkle bulbs in the 1950s, plastic bulbs by 1955. In this book a Christmas light is a holder for a candle used on the tree. Other forms of lighting include light bulbs. Other Christmas collectibles are listed in the preceding section.

Bottle Brush, Bushy, Snow-Tipped Branches, Red Glass Ball Tips, 48 In. 1920
Light Set, Visca, Green, 24 Matchless Star Lights, Electric Cord, 32 In. 2400
Light Set, Wonder Star, Multicolored, Display Box, Each 2 ¾ In., 10 Piece................................. 450
Ornament, Belsnickel, Yellow Coated, Gold Flecks, 8 In.. 708
Ornament, Kugel, Ball, Amber Glass, Baroque Cap, Germany, 2 ½ In. 207
Ornament, Kugel, Ball, Amethyst Glass, 5-Leaf Cap, Germany, 1 ¾ In. 354
Ornament, Kugel, Ball, Blue Glass, Painted Bands, Beehive Cap, Germany, 2 ¼ In.................. 118
Ornament, Kugel, Ball, Burgundy Glass, Fleur-De-Lis Cap, France, 1 ⅝ In.............................. 207
Ornament, Kugel, Ball, Burgundy, Art Deco Cap, France, 5 ¾ In. 207
Ornament, Kugel, Ball, Cobalt Blue, French Brass Cap, 7 ½ In. ....*illus* 100
Ornament, Kugel, Ball, Green Glass, Tree Cap, France, 6 In... 266
Ornament, Kugel, Ball, Light Violet Glass, Bunting Cap, Germany, 1 ¾ In. 561
Ornament, Kugel, Ball, Red Brown Glass, Germany, 1 ½ In. 59
Ornament, Kugel, Ball, Ribbed, Cobalt Blue Glass, Beehive Cap, Germany, 2 In....................... 325
Ornament, Kugel, Ball, Ribbed, Gold Glass, 10-Lobed Cap, Germany, 5 In.................................. 531
Ornament, Kugel, Ball, Silver Glass, Baroque Cap, Germany, 4 ¾ In. 106
Ornament, Kugel, Ball, Silver Glass, France, 3 ¾ In.. 295
Ornament, Kugel, Ball, Silver Glass, Painted Flower Band, Beehive Cap, 2 ½ In. 106
Ornament, Kugel, Berry Cluster, Amber Glass, Beehive Cap, Germany, 3 ¼ In. 944
Ornament, Kugel, Berry Shape, Glass, Green, Beehive Cap, Germany, 3 ½ In. ....*illus* 1062

Ornament, Kugel, Egg Shape, Black Amethyst Glass, Leaf Cap, Germany, 2 In. 325
Ornament, Kugel, Egg Shape, Cobalt Blue Glass, Beehive Cap, 3 In. 118
Ornament, Kugel, Egg Shape, Gold Glass, Ribbed Cap, France, 2 In. 94
Ornament, Kugel, Egg Shape, Green Glass, Baroque Cap, Germany, 2 ¾ In. 148
Ornament, Kugel, Egg Shape, Green Glass, Beehive Cap, 6 In. 82
Ornament, Kugel, Egg Shape, Red Glass, 5-Leaf Cap, Germany, 2 ¼ In. 236
Ornament, Kugel, Egg Shape, Vertical Ribs, Cobalt Blue, Beehive Cap, 3 In. 413
Ornament, Kugel, Grape Cluster, Amber Glass, Baroque Cap, Germany, 4 In. 266
Ornament, Kugel, Grape Cluster, Amber Glass, Baroque Cap, Germany, 6 In. 502
Ornament, Kugel, Grape Cluster, Amber Glass, Beehive Cap, 4 In. 118
Ornament, Kugel, Grape Cluster, Cobalt Blue Glass, Beehive Cap, Germany, 4 In. 295
Ornament, Kugel, Grape Cluster, Red Glass, 5-Leaf Cap, Germany, 5 In. 2360
Ornament, Kugel, Grape Cluster, Silver Glass, 5-Leaf Cap, Germany, 7 In. 413
Ornament, Kugel, Pear Shape, Amber, Glass, Tree Cap, Germany, 3 ¼ In. .... *illus* 1770
Ornament, Santa Claus, Cotton, Chromolithograph Face, 8 ¾ In. 177
Stand, Metal, Pinecone Holder, Music Box, Key Wind, Swiss, 8 In. 960

CHROME

Chrome items in the Art Deco style became popular in the 1930s. Collectors are most interested in high-style pieces made by the Connecticut firms of Chase Brass & Copper Co., Manning-Bowman & Co., and others.

Ashtray, Pelican Bird Cigarette Holder, Round, 5 ¾ In. 28
Bank, Barrel Shape, Still, Madison Square State Bank, Key, 2 ¾ x 2 In. 45
Cake Dome & Base, Black Handle, Everedy Co., 11 In. x 8 In. Diam. 17
Candleholder, 4-Light, Signed PM Italy, c.1950, 4 x 4 In., Pair 125
Cocktail, Shaker, Footed, Handle, 1950s, 12 In. 39
Flask, Radiator Grill Shape, Rolls-Royce, Ruddspeed Ltd., England, c.1960, 7 x 4 In. 895
Hood Ornament, Stallion, Rearing Up, 6 x 6 x 2 In. 68
Ice Bucket, Penguins, Ball Shape, Bakelite Knob & Handles, 10 x 8 In. 24
Knife Rest, Figural, Dog, Cat, Rabbit, Pig, Ram, Fox, Art Deco, 1930s, 3 ½ In., 6 Piece 125
Lamp, Orbiter, Adjustable, Arm, Ball Lamp Head, Robert Sonneman, 1960s, 65 x 19 x 38 In. 281
Magazine Rack, Loops, Expandable, Norman Bel Geddes, Revere Rome NY, 1930s, 18 x 12 In. *illus* 244
Sculpture, Deer, Art Deco, 14 In. 225
Seltzer Bottle, Taper, Art Deco, BOC, England, 12 ½ x 4 In. 45
Tea Infuser, Teakettle Shape, 1 ¼ In. 15
Teapot, Ball Shape, Midcentury, 10 x 6 In. 27
Tray, Simulated Horn Handles, Braided Rim, 19 x 13 In. 54

CIGAR STORE FIGURE

Cigar store figures of carved wood or cast iron were used as advertisements in front of the Victorian cigar store. The carved figures are now collected as folk art. They range in size from counter type, about three feet, to over eight feet tall.

Blackamoor, Carved, Painted, Mounted On Base, Countertop, 1800s, 26 In., Pair 2074
Bust, Indian, Chief Black Hawk, Painted Plaster, 18 x 12 In. 360
Indian Princess, Standing, Painted, Square Base, c.1900, 55 In. 2438
Indian, Standing, Painted, Round Base, 25 In. 1875

CINNABAR

Cinnabar is a vermilion or red lacquer. Pieces are made with tens to hundreds of thicknesses of the lacquer that is later carved. Most cinnabar was made in the Orient.

Box, 2 Peaches, Leaves, Flowers, Carved, Chinese, 2 x 6 x 4 ¾ In. .... *illus* 281
Box, Circular, Carved, Lotus Bloom, Camellia, Rose, Tree Peony, Chrysanthemum, 15 In. 960
Box, Peach Shape, Carved, Johan, Youth In Garden, 1800s, 5 x 9 ½ x 8 ½ In. 1169
Charger, Peony, Red, Round, Stand, 12 ½ In. 480
Dish, Figural Landscape, Flower Shape, Chinese, c.1900, 10 In. .... *illus* 144

Christmas Tree, Ornament, Kugel, Ball, Cobalt Blue, French Brass Cap, 7 ½ In.
$100

Bertoia Auctions

Christmas Tree, Ornament, Kugel, Berry Shape, Glass, Green, Beehive Cap, Germany, 3 ½ In.
$1,062

Conestoga Auction Company

Christmas Tree, Ornament, Kugel, Pear Shape, Amber, Glass, Tree Cap, Germany, 3 ¼ In.
$1,770

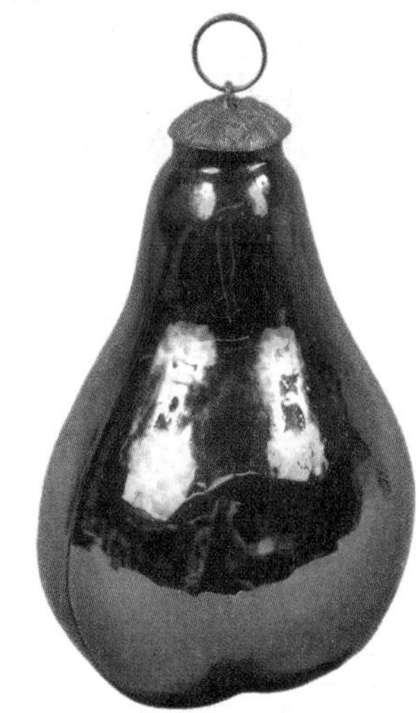

Conestoga Auction Company

Chrome, Magazine Rack, Loops, Expandable, Norman Bel Geddes, Revere Rome NY, 1930s, 18 x 12 In.
$244

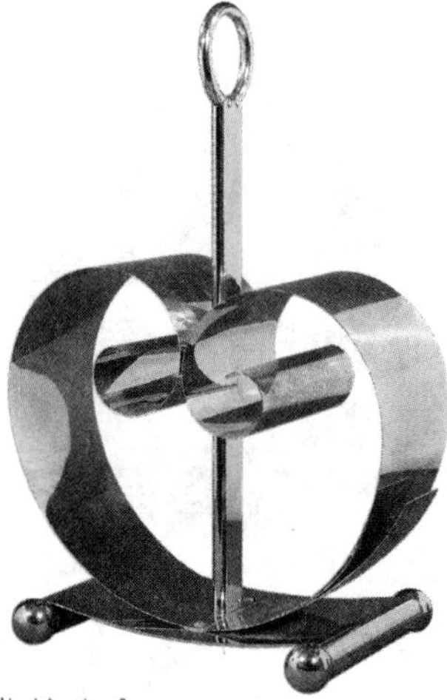

Neal Auction Company

TIP
Clarice Cliff pieces marked in black are worth two to three times as much as pieces marked in any other color.

Cinnabar, Box, 2 Peaches, Leaves, Flowers, Carved, Chinese, 2 x 6 x 4 ¾ In.
$281

Abington Auction Gallery

Cinnabar, Dish, Figural Landscape, Flower Shape, Chinese, c.1900, 10 In.
$144

Eldred's

Dish, Peony Blossoms, Leaves, Shallow Sides, Short Black Lacquer Foot, 12 In. 1000
Panel, Carved, Peaches, 8 Symbols Of The Immortals, Chinese, 13 x 13 In. 6490
Vase, Bulbous, Sung Shape, Red Lacquer, Carved, 6 ½ x 4 ¾ In. 3803

CIVIL WAR

Civil War mementos are important collectors' items. Most of the pieces are military items used from 1861 to 1865. Be sure to avoid any explosive munitions. Pictures are listed in this book in Photography.

Badge, Confederate, Fenner's Battery, Gold, Enamel, Cannon Wheel, Crescent, Star, 1 ¾ In. *illus* 2100
Badge, Corps, Brass Bastions, White Cloth Center, Pinback, c.1860, 1 ⅝ x 1 ⅝ In. 246
Belt Buckle, Brass, Virginian Sic Semper Tyrannis, 1 ⅞ x 3 ⅜ In. *illus* 3304
Belt, 1851 Pattern, Brass Eagle Wreath Plate, Buckle, Hanging Loop, c.1861, 2 x 3 In. 351
Bugle, Cavalry, Copper & Brass, Yellow Worsted Cords & Tassels, 15 ½ In. 861
Bugle, Nickel Plated, D.C. Hall Manufacturer, Boston, 20 In. 13570
Cartridge Box, Metal Breast Plate, Eagle, Arrows, Olive Branch, Strap, c.1860, 2 ½ In. 138
Chest, Poplar, Lid, Iron Handles, Marked Col. Rain's, Auguta, 19 x 21 x 33 In. *illus* 1968
Discharge Paper, Union Army Draft, 1864, 4 ½ x 8 ½ In. *illus* 81
Dog Tag, Major General Gab McClellan, Brass, A.M. Burns Co., 1861 1062
Dress Hat, Hardee, Black Felt, 1st Corps Badge, Brass Bugle, Leather, 5 ½ In. 3567
Drum, Bass, Painted, Rope Tensioners, Skin Heads, George Kilbourn, Label, 30 x 19 In. *illus* 640
Drum, Bentwood, Shell, Spread Wing Eagle, Union Shield, American Flag, 1860s, 4 x 16 In. 2106
Drum, Militia, Red Hoops, Painted, Plain Shell, Brass Tacks, Rope, c.1860, 15 x 17 In. *illus* 984
Fuse Box, Navy, Rectangular, Leather, Belt Loop, c.1860, 3 ½ x 4 ½ In. *illus* 154
Medal, G.A.R. Veteran, May 1887, V.D. Dubose, Star Shape, Gold & Silver, 1 ⅜ x 1 In. 3300
Pipe Bowl, Liberty Cap, Wood, Carved, Leaves, Flowers, Acorn, 3 In. 738
Pipe, Wood Bowl, Carved, Marked, c.1861-65, 3 In. 308
Pitcher, Washington Light Infantry, Charleston, Text, Confederate, Flag, Handle, 8 x 8 ½ In. *illus* 1250
Pocket Watch, Coin Silver, Hunter Case, Chain, Maj. Elial F. Carpenter, c.1862, 2 In. 3075
Powder Horn, Union, Woman Waving Flag, Scrimshaw, Signed Chantilly, Va., 1863, 13 In. *illus* 1200
Shaving Mirror, Wood Frame, George F. Maynard, c.1861-64, 6 x 3 In. 308
Spoon, Infantry, Silver, Engraved, George T. Matthews, c.1861, 7 In. 246
Surgeon's Set, Amputation Saw, Trephine, Detachable Handle, G. Tiemann, Box, 7 x 17 In. 3355
Surgical & Amputation Kit, W.F. Ford N.Y., Casewell, Hazard & Co., 16 In., 28 Piece *illus* 2750
Sword, Cavalry Saber, Sheath, Blade, Wrapped Grip, 39 In. 413
Sword, Cavalry Saber, Steel Blade, Leather Wrap, Brass Wire, Capt. Richard L. Myers, 42 In. 840
Sword, Confederate Field Officer, Brass Guard, Boyle & Gamble, Leather Scabbard, 30 In. 2050
Toy, Musket, 12 N.H. Vols, 1886 Reunion, Gold Paint, Cast Iron, 16 ¾ In. 124

CKAW, *see Dedham category.*

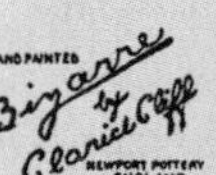

CLARICE CLIFF

Clarice Cliff was a designer who worked in several English factories, including A.J. Wilkinson Ltd., Wilkinson's Royal Staffordshire Pottery, Newport Pottery, and Foley Pottery after the 1920s. She is best known for her brightly colored Art Deco designs, including the Bizarre line. She died in 1972. Pieces of some of her early work have been made again by Wedgwood.

Biarritz, Plate, Cottage, Flowers, c.1933, 6 x 4 In. 97
Celtic Harvest, Bowl, Raised Flowers, Wheat, Handles, 1940s, 11 x 3 In. 325
Forest Glen, Honey Pot, Apple Shape, Twig Handle, c.1935, 3 ½ In. 400
Forest Glen, Plate, Multicolor, 1937, 9 In. 935
Honolulu, Cup & Saucer, Bizarre, 1930s, 5 In. 592
Lady Anne, Wall Pocket, Art Deco Woman, Trees, Newport Pottery, 1930s, 6 x 7 In. 187
Landscape, Bowl, Blue Sky, Pink & Purple Flowers, c.1935, 9 x 3 In. 145
Nasturtium, Lotus Jug, Flowers, Leaves, c.1932, 9 In. 750
Perth, Jug, Tankard, Stylized Blossoms, Orange, Blue Violet, 4 x 7 In. 375
Summerhouse Crown, Jug, Fantasque, Multicolor, 1931, 4 x 7 In. 327
Windbells, Toast Rack, c.1930, 5 In. 294

Civil War, Badge, Confederate, Fenner's Battery, Gold, Enamel, Cannon Wheel, Crescent, Star, 1 ¾ In.
$2,100

Neal Auction Company

Civil War, Belt Buckle, Brass, Virginian Sic Semper Tyrannis, 1 ⅞ x 3 ⅜ In.
$3,304

Cottone Auctions

Civil War, Chest, Poplar, Lid, Iron Handles, Marked Col. Rain's, Auguta, 19 x 21 x 33 In.
$1,968

Skinner, Inc.

Civil War, Discharge Paper, Union Army Draft, 1864, 4 ½ x 8 ½ In.
$81

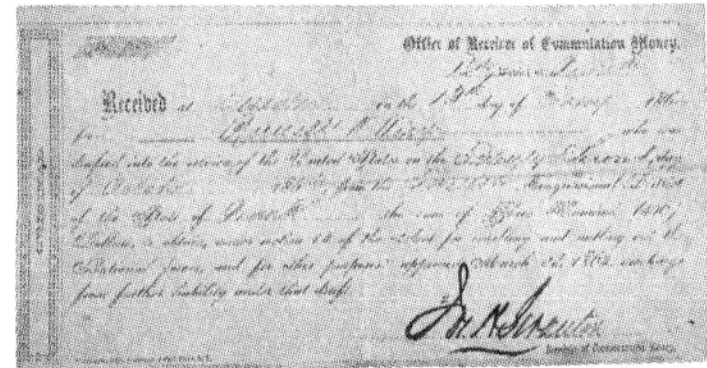

Office of Receiver of Commutation Money.

Received at

Blackwell Auctions

Civil War, Drum, Bass, Painted, Rope Tensioners, Skin Heads, George Kilbourn, Label, 30 x 19 In.
$640

Cowan's Auctions

Civil War, Drum, Militia, Red Hoops, Painted, Plain Shell, Brass Tacks, Rope, c.1860, 15 x 17 In.
$984

Skinner, Inc.

Civil War, Fuse Box, Navy, Rectangular, Leather, Belt Loop, c.1860, 3 ½ x 4 ½ In.
$154

Skinner, Inc.

Civil War, Pitcher, Washington Light Infantry, Charleston, Text, Confederate, Flag, Handle, 8 x 8 ½ In.
$1,250

Cowan's Auctions

Civil War, Powder Horn, Union, Woman Waving Flag, Scrimshaw, Signed Chantilly, Va., 1863, 13 In.
$1,200

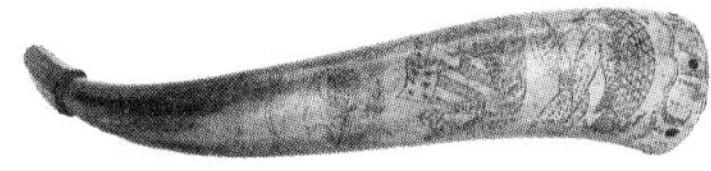

Case Antiques

Civil War, Surgical & Amputation Kit, W.F. Ford N.Y., Casewell, Hazard & Co., 16 In., 28 Piece
$2,750

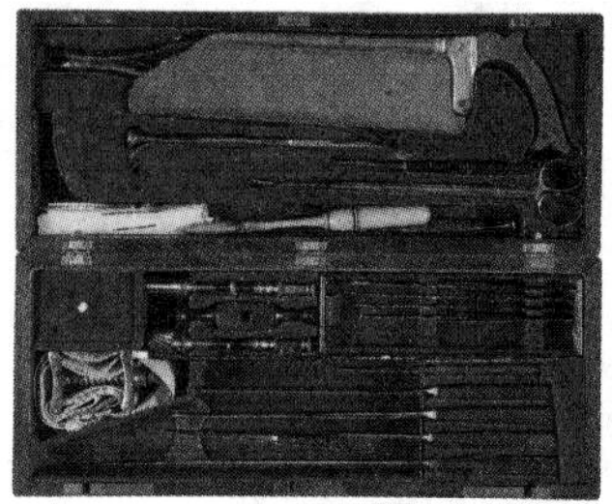

Cowan's Auctions

Clock, Advertising, Royal Crown Cola, Metal Face, Wood Case, Selected Devices Company, 15 ½ In.
$150

Rich Penn Auctions

Clock, Advertising, Sign, Pearl Beer, Plastic, Light-Up, Animated Waterfall, 16 x 17 In.
$264

Milestone Auctions

TIP
Clocks should be cleaned and lubricated every five years.

CLEWELL

Clewell was made in limited quantities by Charles Walter Clewell of Canton, Ohio, from 1902 to 1955. Pottery was covered with a thin coating of bronze, then treated to make the bronze turn different colors. Pieces covered with copper, brass, or silver were also made. Mr. Clewell's secret formula for blue patinated bronze was burned when he died in 1965.

Vase, Copper Clad, Bottle Shape, Charles Walter, 11 x 5 In., Pair 396
Vase, Copper Clad, Green Patina, Bulbous, Molded Rim, Footed, 1937, 6 In. 288
Vase, Green Matte, Verdigris Patina, Tapered, Flared Rim, 12 x 5 ½ In. 465

CLOCK

Clocks of all types have always been popular with collectors. The eighteenth-century tall case, or grandfather's, clock was designed to house a works with a long pendulum. The name on the clock is usually the maker but sometimes it is a merchant or other craftsman. In 1816, Eli Terry patented a new, smaller works for a clock, and the case became smaller. The clock could be kept on a shelf instead of on the floor. By 1840, coiled springs were used and even smaller clocks were made. Battery-powered electric clocks were made in the 1870s. A garniture set can include a clock and other objects displayed on a mantel.

Advertising, Calumet Baking Powder, Oak Case, Paper Face, Pendulum, Key, 1800s, 36 x 17 x 4 ½ In..... 319
Advertising, Gunther Beer, Wall, Light-Up, Reverse Glass, 15 In. 1046
Advertising, Jefferson Standard Insurance Co., Glass & Metal Case, 1963, 15 x 15 In. 41
Advertising, Monell's Teething Cordial, Children, Baird, Wood, Roman Numerals, 31 x 18 x 4 In.. 1725
Advertising, Royal Crown Cola, Metal Face, Wood Case, Selected Devices Company, 15 ½ In. *illus* 150
Advertising, Sign, Pearl Beer, Plastic, Light-Up, Animated Waterfall, 16 x 17 In. ....*illus* 264
Advertising, St. Charles Evaporated Cream, Cow, Standing, Base, 12 ½ x 8 ½ In. ....*illus* 170
Advertising, Walkden's Inks, Baird Block Company, Papier-Mache Case, Late 1800s, 31 x 18 In.. 1353
Advertising, White King Soap, Quick Dissolving, Longer Lasting Suds, Porcelain, 37 x 25 In. *illus* 2700
Alarm, Metal, Round, 2 Bells Strike, Raised Numbers, 4 Straight Feet, Germany, 9 ½ In.......... 35
Annular Dial, Frog, Snail, Aquamarine, Emeralds, 18K Gold, Rock Crystal Base, Zadora, Swiss, 5 In. 6563
Annular Dial, Mercury, Silver Plate, Gilt Bronze & Marble Base, Silver Chapter Ring, 9 In.... *illus* 1210
Ansonia, Colorado, Walnut, Nickel Trim, Arched Top, Scrolled Sides, Alarm, Label.......... 93
Ansonia, Regulator, Crystal, Beveled Glass & Brass Frame, Enamel Dial, 1880s, 12 x 7 In. 300
Ansonia, Regulator, Crystal, Marquis, Porcelain Dial, Faux Mercury Pendulum, 15 In. 295
Ansonia, Shelf, Rosalind, Cast Iron, Black Enamel, Diana Angels, 19 x 15 In. ....*illus* 303
Ansonia, Tambour, Mahogany, Scroll On Each Side, Porcelain Dial, 10 x 16 In.......... 70
Banjo, Federal, Mahogany, Inlaid, Pierced Brass Side Arms, c.1850, 29 x 10 In. 250
Banjo, Green Paint, Weight Driven, Pendulum, 33 In. 1410
Banjo, Mahogany, Gilt Acorn Finial, Turned Brass Bezel, Iron Dial, Roman Numerals, 37 In. . 1230
Banjo, Mahogany, Reverse Painted Tablet, Gilt Eagle Finial, 32 In. ....*illus* 173
Banjo, Waterbury, Mahogany, Glass Panels, Leaf Design, Red, Black, White, Gilt, 1900s, 41 x 10 In.. 293
Banjo, Willard, Giltwood, Naval Battle, Glass Door, Willard's Patent, 39 In. ....*illus* 360
Birge & Gilbert, 3-Decker, Gilt Eagle, Painted Wood Dial, Reverse Painted Glass, Pendulum, 38 In. 215
Black Forest, Cuckoo, House, Hunting Trophies, Horn, White Roman Numerals, 29 x 23 In.... *illus* 269
Black Forest, Cuckoo, Pheasants, Flowers, Mushroom, 3 Weights, 32 In. 2500
Blinking Eye, Bradley & Hubbard, Sambo, Cast Iron, Banjo Dial, 1850s, 16 x 7 In.......... 936
Boulle, Desk, Ormolu Mount, Roman Numerals, Outswept Feet, France, 12 x 6 ¼ In.......... 677
Carriage, Brass & Glass Case, White Dial, Arabic Numerals, 3 In. 154
Carriage, Brass, Enamel, Birds, French Movement, George Shreve & Co., c.1890, 5 ½ x 4 In. .. 1353
Carriage, Bronze, Cloisonne, Light Blue Ground, Chinoiserie, 8-Day, 8 x 4 In. 5100
Carriage, David Peterson, Brass, Beveled Glass, 13 Jewel, England, c.1900, 6 x 3 In. 99
Carriage, Gilt Brass, Porcelain Panel, Hour Repeater, Alarm Dial, Handle, c.1880, 7 In. .*illus* 1845
Carriage, Gilt Brass, Porcelain Panel, Hour Repeater, Handle, 6 ½ x 4 In.......... 4235
Carriage, Gilt Metal, Filigree, Silvered Dial, Alarm, 8-Day, France, 1800s ....*illus* 390
Carriage, Marti, Enameled Brass Case, Porcelain Dial, Finials, France, 11 ½ In. 620
Chelsea, Black Plastic Case, Plexiglas Cover, U.S. Navy Dial, 1900s, 6 ½ In. 360

Clock, Advertising, St. Charles Evaporated Cream, Cow, Standing, Base, 12 ½ x 8 ½ In.
$170

Hartzell's Auction Gallery Inc.

Clock, Advertising, White King Soap, Quick Dissolving, Longer Lasting Suds, Porcelain, 37 x 25 In.
$2,700

Morphy Auctions

Clock, Annular Dial, Mercury, Silver Plate, Gilt Bronze & Marble Base, Silver Chapter Ring, 9 In.
$1,210

Fontaine's Auction Gallery

Clock, Ansonia, Shelf, Rosalind, Cast Iron, Black Enamel, Diana Angels, 19 x 15 In.
$303

Fontaine's Auction Gallery

Clock, Banjo, Mahogany, Reverse Painted Tablet, Gilt Eagle Finial, 32 In.
$173

Apple Tree Auction Center

Clock, Banjo, Willard, Giltwood, Naval Battle, Glass Door, Willard's Patent, 39 In.
$360

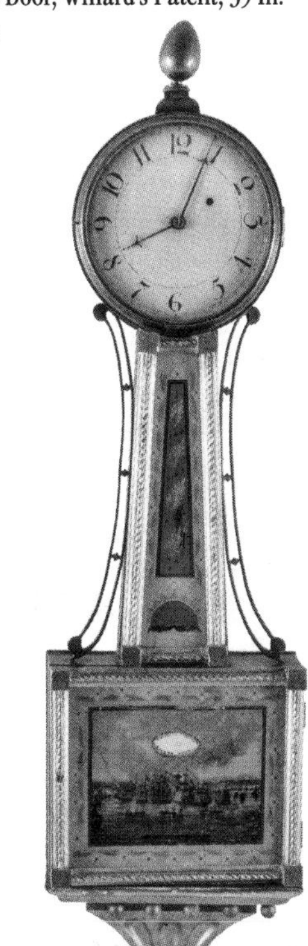

Eldred's

TIP
If you find a clock with a complete, original paper label, add 35 percent to the value.

Clock, Black Forest, Cuckoo, House, Hunting Trophies, Horn, White Roman Numerals, 29 x 23 In.
$269

Clars Auction Gallery

Clock, Carriage, Gilt Brass, Porcelain Panel, Hour Repeater, Alarm Dial, Handle, c.1880, 7 In.
$1,845

Skinner, Inc.

Clock, Carriage, Gilt Metal, Filigree, Silvered Dial, Alarm, 8-Day, France, 1800s
$390

Eldred's

Clock, Deluxe Clock Co., Bungalow, Painted, 12-Hour, 9 ¾ x 5 ½ In.
$48

Milestone Auctions

Clock, Ithaca Calendar Clock Co., Walnut, Metal Face, Roman Numerals, Pendulum, c.1880, 43 x 19 In.
$561

Leland Little Auctions

Clock, Lux, Saint Bernard, Brass, Minute Meter, Dial On Back, 30-Hour, 12 x 8 In.
$59

Bunch Auctions

Clock, Recording, International Time Co., Oak, Glass, Painted Metal Dial, Black, 48 x 17 In.
$345

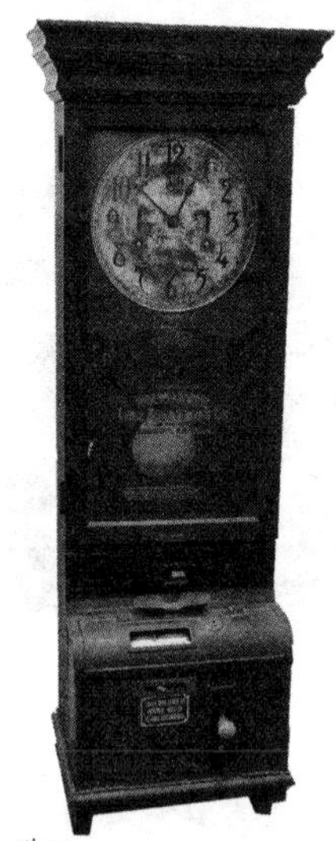

Blackwell Auctions

Clock, Shelf, Cloisonne, Columns, Beveled Glass, Urn Finial, Roman Numerals, 18 In.
$354

Clars Auction Gallery

Clock, Shelf, Empire, Bronze Dore, Monkeys, Dressed As Harlequin & Soldier, c.1800, 12 x 11 In.
$2,750

New Orleans Auction Galleries

Clock, Shelf, Empire, White Marble, Ormolu Mounts, Sunburst Pendulum, France, 15 x 9 x 3 In.
$210

CRN Auctions

Clock, Shelf, Louis XV Style, Bronze Patinated Spelter, Scrolls, A. Chapus, Paris, 13 In.
$354

Bunch Auctions

Clock, Shelf, Turning Ball, Dial Sphere, Crucifix, Landscape Base, Continental, 1900s, 9 x 4 In.
$671

Neal Auction Company

Clock, Shelf, Wadsworth, Lounsbury & Turners, Pillar & Scroll, Mahogany Case, Brass Urn, 31 x 16 In.
$427

Nadeau's Auction Gallery

Clock, Skeleton, B. Symons, Reticulated Silver Dial, Fusee, Marble Base, London, 1800s, 17 In.
$590

Cottone Auctions

Clock, Skeleton, Bunyan & Gardner, Salford, Brass, Glass Dome, Enamel Dial, England, c.1850, 11 In.
$3,600

CRN Auctions

Clock, Tall Case, Henry Harper, Burl, Marquetry, 8-Day, Time & Strike, Calendar, 1700s, 70 In.
$8,850

Cottone Auctions

Clock, Tall Case, Hepplewhite, Cherry, Inlay, Brass, Iron Face, Moon Phase, Pa., c.1810, 96 In.
$3,375

Garth's Auctioneers & Appraisers

Clock, Tall Case, Herschede, Mahogany, Putti, Garlands, Brass, Silvered Dial, Paw Feet, 106 x 25 In.
$9,225

Clars Auction Gallery

Clock, Tall Case, John Hamers, Regency, Marquetry, Vine Scrollwork, Gilt Cherubs, 84 x 25 In.
$9,360

Thomaston Place Auction Galleries

Clock, Tall Case, Walter Durfee, Mahogany, Brass Dial, 9 Tube, Moon Phase, 103 In.
$10,890

Fontaine's Auction Gallery

Chelsea, Shelf, Ship's Wheel, Bronze, 8-Day, Mahogany Base, c.1939, 17 x 12 x 5 In. 1140
Chelsea, Shelf, Slate, Enameled White Dial, Brass Works, Marked, 10 ¼ In. 78
Deluxe Clock Co., Bungalow, Painted, 12-Hour, 9 ¾ x 5 ½ In. *illus* 48
French, 2 Gilt Figures, Gilt Frame, Porcelain Dial, Alabaster Base, 12 In. 81
Ingraham, Regulator, Oak Case, Metal Face, Glass Panels, Late 1800s, 37 x 16 In. 236
Ithaca Calendar Clock Co., Walnut, Metal Face, Roman Numerals, Pendulum, c.1880, 43 x 19 In. *illus* 561
Japy Freres, Cartel, Ormolu, Brass Case, Enamel Dial, Roman Numerals, 19 x 11 In. 531
LeCoultre, Atmos, Brass & Glass Case, Revolving Pendulum, c.1950, 8 ¾ x 6 ½ In. 300
LeCoultre, Atmos, Brass Case, White Dial, Gilt Hands, Swiss, 9 x 7 ½ In. 512
LeCoultre, Atmos, Chinoiserie, Metal Dial, Gilt Hand, Brass Bezel, 9 x 7 x 5 In. 1680
LeCoultre, Atmos, Glass & Brass Case, Stick Indicators, 1900s 360
LeCoultre, Atmos, Perpetual Timepiece, Brass & Glass Case, 13 Jewel, Swiss, 9 x 7 In. 932
LeCoultre, Atmos, Perpetual, Applied Gilt Brass Markers, Pendulum, 9 x 7 x 5 ½ In. 484
LeCoultre, Atmos, Perpetual, Brass & Glass Case, Swiss, 1964, 9 x 8 x 6 ½ In. 531
LeCoultre, Atmos, Retirement Award, Gilt Hands, Brass & Glass Case, 1963, 10 x 8 x 6 In. 480
LeCoultre, Travel, Goldtone Metal, Black Enamel, Alarm, Fitted Box, c.1915, 5 x 3 In. 277
Lux, Saint Bernard, Brass, Minute Meter, Dial On Back, 30-Hour, 12 x 8 In. *illus* 59
Mappin & Webb, Carriage, Brass, Beveled Glass Panels, Roman Numerals, 5 In. 192
Pendant, Oval Brass Case, Woman Feeding Chickens, Roman Numerals, France, 6 x 4 In. 180
Pillar & Scroll, Stennes, Elmer, Mahogany, Brass Urn Form Finials, c.1950, 30 x 16 x 4 In. 360
Recording, Cincinnati Time Co., Oak, Painted Metal Dial, Week Indicator, 44 x 19 x 12 In. 156
Recording, International Time Co., Oak, Glass, Painted Metal Dial, Black, 48 x 17 In. *illus* 345
Regulator, Astronomical, Mahogany, Silvered Dial, Pendulum, c.1870, 96 In. 3690
Regulator, E. Ingraham & Co., Wall, Pendulum, Roman Numerals, c.1915, 36 x 19 In. 70
Regulator, Japy Freres, Brass Frame, Glass Panels, Enamel Face, 1880s, 10 x 4 ½ In. 120
Shelf, Black Slate, Marble, Enamel Dial, Roman Numerals, 13 x 11 ⅝ In. 60
Shelf, Black Wood, Gilt & Silvered, Red Marble, Bronze Dial, Chariot, Gallery, 21 x 14 In. 953
Shelf, Brass, Ornate, Painted Panel, Courting Scene, France, 1889, 14 x 7 In. 450
Shelf, Bronze, Gilt, Cupid & Psyche, Cherub Heads, Rectangular Base, 1800s, 20 In. 2337
Shelf, Cloisonne, Columns, Beveled Glass, Urn Finial, Roman Numerals, 18 In. *illus* 354
Shelf, Empire, Bronze Dore, Monkeys, Dressed As Harlequin & Soldier, c.1800, 12 x 11 In. *illus* 2750
Shelf, Empire, Ebonized Case, Roman Numerals, Spade Hands, Pendulum, France, 18 In. 194
Shelf, Empire, White Marble, Ormolu Mounts, Sunburst Pendulum, France, 15 x 9 x 3 In. *illus* 210
Shelf, French, Porcelain, Gilt Bronze Mount, Courting Couple, Cherub, 15 x 9 In. 615
Shelf, Gothic Revival, Bronze, Architectural Case, Roman Numerals, 1800s, 21 x 13 In. 545
Shelf, Herschede, Tambour, Mahogany, Quarter-Hour Strike, Metal Dial, c.1930, 10 x 20 In. 156
Shelf, Iron Front, Molded Flowers, Painted Buildings, Abalone Inlay, Time & Strike, 19 In. 139
Shelf, Louis XV Style, Bronze Patinated Spelter, Scrolls, A. Chapus, Paris, 13 In. *illus* 354
Shelf, Mahogany, Carved Half Columns, Painted Glass Tablet, Whiting, Riley, 33 In. 154
Shelf, Marquetry, Greek Columns, Reclining Man, Bench, Gallery, Red, 1700s, 25 x 16 ½ In. 1920
Shelf, Marshall & Adams, Empire, Mahogany, Brass Works, Roman Numerals, 35 In. 189
Shelf, Porcelain, Bronze, Gilt Scrollwork, Courting Couples, Love Birds, Rococo, 19 x 10 In. 1125
Shelf, Rococo Style, Gilt Metal Mounted, Marquetry, Inlaid Yew Wood, 22 ½ In. 104
Shelf, Seth Thomas, 8-Day, Roman Numerals, Painted Scene On Glass, 17 ½ In. 115
Shelf, Seth Thomas, Walnut Case, Painted Metal Face, Calendar Dial, Pendulum, 1876, 33 x 16 In. 944
Shelf, Turning Ball, Dial Sphere, Crucifix, Landscape Base, Continental, 1900s, 9 x 4 In. *illus* 671
Shelf, Wadsworth, Lounsbury & Turners, Pillar & Scroll, Mahogany Case, Brass Urn, 31 x 16 In. *illus* 427
Silver, Scrolls, Flowers, Monogram, Rectangular, Black, Starr & Frost, Early 1900s, 4 In. 123
Skeleton, B. Symons, Reticulated Silver Dial, Fusee, Marble Base, London, 1800s, 17 In. *illus* 590
Skeleton, Bunyan & Gardner, Salford, Brass, Glass Dome, Enamel Dial, England, c.1850, 11 In. *illus* 3600
Tall Case, Cherry, Fluted Columns, Moon Phase Dial, Landscape, Urn Finials, c.1800, 95 x 19 In. 738
Tall Case, Chippendale, Mahogany, Fluted Columns, Ogee Bracket Feet, 1900s, 60 x 12 In. 406
Tall Case, Gustavian Mora, Softwood, Painted, Shaped, Iron Dial, Sweden, 1838, 79 x 22 In. 327
Tall Case, Henry Harper, Burl, Marquetry, 8-Day, Time & Strike, Calendar, 1700s, 70 In. *illus* 8850
Tall Case, Hepplewhite, Cherry, Inlay, Brass, Iron Face, Moon Phase, Pa., c.1810, 96 In. *illus* 3375
Tall Case, Herschede, Mahogany, Putti, Garlands, Brass, Silvered Dial, Paw Feet, 106 x 25 In. *illus* 9225
Tall Case, John Hamers, Regency, Marquetry, Vine Scrollwork, Gilt Cherubs, 84 x 25 In. *illus* 9360
Tall Case, Jonat Beake, Mahogany, Spiral Columns, Eagle Finial, London, 1800s, 80 x 18 In. 930
Tall Case, Mahogany, Griffins, Acanthus, Chimes, 8 Bells, Germany, c.1900, 113 x 42 In. 12188
Tall Case, Mahogany, Square Painted Dial, Bird, Fluted Column, c.1825, 90 x 19 In. 443

Tall Case, Oak, Broken Arch Pediment, Carved Waist, Brass Face, 1810s, 86 x 21 In. 875
Tall Case, Oak, Mahogany Flame Veneer, Fluted Columns, Bonnet, Brass Face, c.1810, 85 In. 840
Tall Case, Pine, Tombstone Arch Bonnet, Crown, Floral Face, Cutout Feet, c.1800, 82 x 18 In. 360
Tall Case, Pine, Tombstone Hood Door, Gilt Eagle, Flowers, Roman Numerals, 80 in. 277
Tall Case, Provincial, Oak, Stepped Crown, Brass Face, Pendulum, 1800s, 98 x 16 x 8 ½ In. 688
Tall Case, Rd. Webster, Mahogany, Roman Numerals, Pendulum, England, 1800s, 84 x 17 In. 502
Tall Case, Shenandoah Co., Figured Walnut, Canted Reeded Corners, Turned Feet, c.1820, 99 In. 1872
Tall Case, Sligh, Mahogany, Roman Numerals, Aaron Willard Reproduction, 85 In. 885
Tall Case, Softwood, 30-Hour, Painted Steel Dial, Raised Panels, c.1800, 92 In. 295
Tall Case, Walter Durfee, Mahogany, Brass Dial, 9 Tube, Moon Phase, 103 In. *illus* 10890
Tall Case, Wood, Arched Top, 3 Sections, Metal Bezel, Roman Numerals, 87 In. 502

Tiffany clocks that are part of desk sets made by Louis Comfort Tiffany are listed in the Tiffany category. Clocks sold by the store Tiffany & Co. are listed here.

Tiffany & Co., Bronze Eagle, Crystal Ball, Roman Numerals, Green, Alabaster Base, 18 x 7 In. *illus* 2520
Tiffany & Co., Desk, Metal, Hygrometer, Barometer, Thermometer, P. Breguette, 4 In. 96
Tiffany & Co., Shelf, Steeple, Brass, Marble Panels, Square Tapered Legs, c.1890, 14 x 7 In. *illus* 492
Vincenti, Shelf, Marble, Gilt Bronze, Repousse Brass Dial, Roman Numerals, 33 x 22 x 9 In. 9680
Wag-On-Wall, Oak Case, Painted Dial, Lead-Filled Brass Weights, 1700s, 19 ½ In. 523
Wall, Becker, Gustav, Walnut, Carved Pilasters, Brass Movement, Signed, 53 In. 230
Wall, Wood Case, Time & Strike, Brass Face, Roman Numerals, Dutch, 24 In. 120
Wall, Wood, Black & Gilt Bands, Round, White Face, Roman Numbers, France, 1800s, 15 In. 295
Wall, Wood, Carved Columns, Crest, Embossed Brass Face, Flowers, Pendulum, Germany, 34 In. 104
Waterbury, Shelf, Brass, Walnut Case, Beveled Glass, Porcelain Face, 11 x 7 x 5 In. 132

CLOISONNE

Cloisonne enamel was developed during the tenth century. A glass enamel was applied between small ribbons of metal on a metal base. Most cloisonne is Chinese or Japanese. Pieces marked *China* were made after 1900.

Bowl, Cast Bronze, Scrolling Vines, 5 Lobed Blossoms, Angular Handles, Chinese, 3 x 9 In. *illus* 220
Bowl, Dragon, Flaming Pearl Of Wisdom, Gilt Rim, Green Waves, Chinese, c.1910, 5 ½ In. 47
Bowl, Gilt, Silver, Beading & Rope Twist Trim, Russia, c.1890, 3 In. *illus* 523
Box, Figural, Seated Elephant, Removable Head, Movable Ears, c.1920, 11 In. *illus* 374
Censer, Blue, Crane, Flowers, Bronze Rim & Handle, Tripod Feet, Chinese, 3 In. 615
Censer, Lid, 4 Elephant Heads, Gilt, Turquoise Ground, Scroll Feet, Foo Dog Finial, 1900s, 11 In. 944
Charger, Birds, Flowers, Plants, Multicolor, Blue Ground, Japan, 1900s, 18 In. 263
Charger, Butterfly, Dragon, Multicolor Ground, Scalloped Rim, c.1900, 12 In. 90
Charger, Phoenix, Rim Medallions, Multicolor, c.1900, 18 In. *illus* 281
Decanter, Silver, Flowers, Octagonal, Stopper, Russia, c.1900, 11 In. *illus* 5120
Ewer, Flowers, Gilt, Dragon Spout & Handle, Red Hardstone Finial, 10 ½ x 7 ½ In. *illus* 761
Figure, Foo Dog, Blue Ground, Brass, Jadeite Cap, 19 x 21 In. 460
Figure, Horse, Lift-Off Saddle, Opens To Box, Multicolor, 12 ½ x 8 ½ In. 288
Figure, Horse, Pulling Cart, Parasol, Monkey Faces, Birds, Chinese, 23 x 10 In. 1534
Figure, Man, Ivory Head, Hand, Hat, Mustache, Carved Base, Multicolor, Chinese, 10 ½ In. *illus* 115
Figure, Man, Multicolor, Ivory Head, Hands, Staff, Carved Base, Chinese, 15 In. 104
Jar, Lid, Goldstone, Flowers, Lotus Finial, 4-Footed, Japan, 1900s, 4 ½ In. 144
Jar, Turquoise Blue Ground, Flowers, Octagonal, Lion Masks, Footed, 1800s, 18 In. 384
Jardiniere, Bronze, Blue Ground, Lion Mask Handles, Hardwood Stand, Chinese, 15 x 23 In., Pair 1440
Kovsh, Silver, Shaded, Agates, Landscape, Swans, F. Ruckert, Russia, c.1900, 4 ½ In. 6875
Plate, Alternating Phoenix Bird & Dragon, 24 ½ In. 295
Plate, Cranes, Peonies, Leaves, Buds, Branches, Blue, 12 In. 215
Teapot, Cobalt Blue, Flowers, Vases, Teacups, 6-Sided, Bail Handle, 8 ½ In. 260
Umbrella Stand, Phoenix, Flowers, Archaic Style, Japan, 1800s, 24 In. 122
Vase, 3-Claw Dragon, Yellow Green Oval Body, Short Neck, Silver Rim, 7 ¼ In. 231
Vase, Baluster Shape, Scrolling Lotus Flowers, Turquoise Reserves, c.1900, 14 In. *illus* 344
Vase, Birds, Flowers, Pink Ground, Japan, 1800s, 12 In., Pair 336
Vase, Black Ground, Flowers, Japan, 1800s, 15 In. *illus* 458
Vase, Black, Yellow 5-Toed Dragon, Fireball, Wirework Cloud, Cylindrical, 10 In., Pair *illus* 219

Clock, Tiffany & Co., Bronze Eagle, Crystal Ball, Roman Numerals, Green, Alabaster Base, 18 x 7 In.
$2,520

CRN Auctions

Clock, Tiffany & Co., Shelf, Steeple, Brass, Marble Panels, Square Tapered Legs, c.1890, 14 x 7 In.
$492

Locati Auctions

Cloisonne, Bowl, Cast Bronze, Scrolling Vines, 5 Lobed Blossoms, Angular Handles, Chinese, 3 x 9 In.
$220

Witherell's

This is an edited listing of current prices. Visit **Kovels.com** to check thousands of prices from previous years and sign up for free information on trends, tips, reproductions, marks, and more.

Cloisonne, Bowl, Gilt, Silver, Beading & Rope Twist Trim, Russia, c.1890, 3 In.
$523

Skinner, Inc.

Cloisonne, Box, Figural, Seated Elephant, Removable Head, Movable Ears, c.1920, 11 In.
$374

Richard D. Hatch & Associates

Cloisonne, Charger, Phoenix, Rim Medallions, Multicolor, c.1900, 18 In.
$281

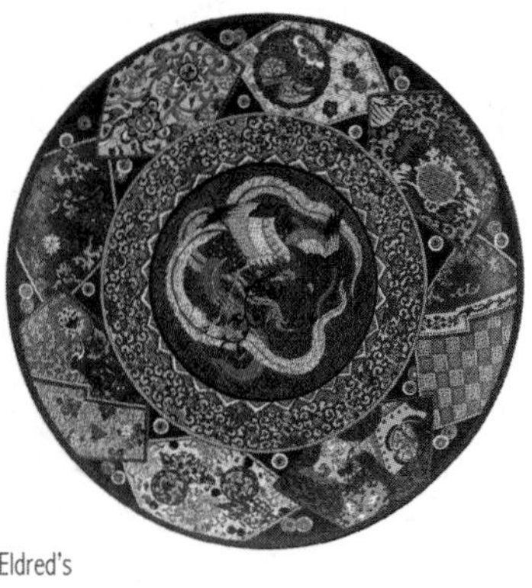

Eldred's

Cloisonne, Decanter, Silver, Flowers, Octagonal, Stopper, Russia, c.1900, 11 In.
$5,120

Cowan's Auctions

Cloisonne, Ewer, Flowers, Gilt, Dragon Spout & Handle, Red Hardstone Finial, 10 ½ x 7 ½ In.
$761

Cordier Auctions

Cloisonne, Figure, Man, Ivory Head, Hand, Hat, Mustache, Carved Base, Multicolor, Chinese, 10 ½ In.
$115

Apple Tree Auction Center

Cloisonne, Vase, Baluster Shape, Scrolling Lotus Flowers, Turquoise Reserves, c.1900, 14 In.
$344

Eldred's

Cloisonne, Vase, Black Ground, Flowers, Japan, 1800s, 15 In.
$458

Nadeau's Auction Gallery

Cloisonne, Vase, Black, Yellow 5-Toed Dragon, Fireball, Wirework Cloud, Cylindrical, 10 In., Pair
$219

Richard D. Hatch & Associates

Vase, Doves, Perched On Branch, Flower Heads Neck, Red Ground, Oval, c.1900, 12 In. 780
Vase, Dragons, Bulbous, Fluted Rim, 2 Part, Dragon Handles, 18 x 9 In. 460
Vase, Flower, Leaves, Dark Blue, Early 1900, 9 ¾ In. 480
Vase, Flowers, Birds, Black, Ground, c.1900, 34 In. 245
Vase, Flowers, Butterflies, Silver, Black Ground, Narrow Neck, M. Tomisaburo, 9 x 4 In., Pair 819
Vase, Flowers, Double Gourd Shape, Gold Trim, 2 Handles, 4-Character Mark, Chinese, 8 x 5 In. 173
Vase, Green & Blue Foo Dogs, Yellow Ground, Globular, Wood Stand, 1900s, 9 ½ x 9 In. 450
Vase, Koi, Multicolor, Blue & Pink Tinted Foil Water, Lobed, 1900s, 6 In. *illus* 780
Vase, Prunus, Flower, Gourd Shape, Gilt Mounts, Champleve, 16 ½ x 8 In., Pair 764
Vase, Totai, Carved Birds, Flowers, Textured Ground, Oval, Wide Mouth, 16 ½ In. 276
Vase, Turquoise, Goldfish, Bulbous, Short Neck, Gonda Hirosuke, Late 1800s, 7 In. 1599

CLOTHING

Clothing of all types is listed in this category. Dresses, hats, shoes, underwear, and more are found here. Other textiles are to be found in the Coverlet, Movie, Quilt, Textile, and World War I and II categories.

Christian Dior
1947–present

NORMAN NORELL
NEW YORK

Norman Norell
1958–1972

Scaasi

Arnold Scaasi
1956–2015

Blouse, Satin, Brown, Flowers & Insect Print, Full Sleeves, Low Waist, Gucci *illus* 344
Boots, Biker, Leather, Black, Quilted Shafts, Rubber Soles, Side Zippers, Chanel, 42 In. 750
Boots, Leather, Hobnails, Heel Plates, Toe Taps, Imperial Germany, Early 1900s, 7 ½ In. 246
Breastplate, Armor, Brass, Steel, 17 ½ x 13 ½ In. 177
Coat, Cashmere, Charcoal Gray, Removable Collar, Hermes, Size 38, 45 In. 1125
Coat, Fur, Lynx, Off-White Lining, Herbert's, San Francisco, c.1980, 22 ½ In. *illus* 660
Coat, Lamb's Wool, Black, Beads, Sequins, Embroidery, Leather Floss, Escada, Size 38 200
Coat, Leather, Fur Collar, Cuffs, Ear Muffs, Wood Toggle Buttons, Pollack Furs, 25 ½ x 18 In. 129
Coat, Mink, Chocolate Brown, Notched Collar, 5 Buttons, Man's, Size 48 1625
Coat, Mink, Driving, White, Henig Furs, 30 ½ x 18 In. *illus* 369
Coat, Mink, Tan, Collar, Satin Lining, Monogram, Embroidered, Gartenhaus Fs, 23 In. *illus* 176
Coat, Mink, White, Tie, Burkholder Furs, Ottawa, Canada, 41 In. *illus* 288
Coat, Silk, Cream, Marc Bohan Haute Couture, Christian Dior, 1961 1000
Coat, Velvet, Red, Sable Collar, Satin Lining, B. Foreman Co., c.1950, 43 In. 117
Dress & Jacket, Wool, Dark Gray, Sheath, Boat Neckline, Norman Norell, 1960s *illus* 281
Dress, Brocade, Gold, Multicolor Flowers, Long Sleeve, Inverted Pleat, Erdem, Size 8 132
Dress, Edwardian, Navy Blue, High Neck, Layered Sleeves, Gold Metal Tassels, c.1915, 56 In. 140
Dress, Sweater, Cashmere & Wool, Black, Stripes, Gold Thread, Chanel, 39 In. 344
Dress, Wool, Brown, Square Neckline, 2 Leather Buttons, Christian Dior Haute Couture, 1954 3750
Hat, Straw, Green, Brown, Gold Band, John B. Stetson Co., 1929, 13 In. 81
Jacket & Skirt, 2 Belts, Wool Boucle, Red, Marc Bohan, Christian Dior, 1965 4000
Jacket, Artillery, Blue Twill, Red Herringbone Tape, Cuffs & Collar, Brass Shoulder, Size 4 1845
Jacket, Bomber, Leather, Black, Removable Fur Collar, Zip Front, Pockets, Chanel, 2008, Size 36 *illus* 594
Jacket, Silk Mesh, Black, Cotton Lace, CC Logo Button, Chanel, Size 42, 36 x 22 In. 469
Jacket, Wool, Aqua, Front Snap Closure, Patch Pockets, Belt, Courreges, 1960-70, Size B 138
Jumpsuit, Safari Style, Belt, Button-Flap Pockets, Front Zip, Yves Saint Laurent, 1970-80s *illus* 438
Kimono, Furisode, Silk, 5 Crests, Flowers, Gold Couching, Japan, c.1870, 65 In. *illus* 938
Kimono, Juban, Painted Dragon, Clutching Pearl, Silk, Signed, 48 x 25 x 51 In. 500
Kimono, Silk Satin Damask, Embroidered Clouds, Flowers, c.1830, Japan, 65 In. *illus* 1375
Kimono, Silk, 5 Crests, Painted Flowers, Platinum Couching, Japan, c.1915, 66 In. *illus* 625
Kimono, Silk, Purple, Tie Dyed, Block Design, 53 x 23 x 48 ½ In. 1625
Kimono, Tomesode, Black Silk Crepe, Shibori Tie Dye, Gold Thread, c.1910, 64 In. *illus* 438
Kimono, Uchikake, Silk, 5 Crests, Landscape, Silver Embroidery, Japan, c.1890, 62 In. *illus* 625
Kimono, Uchikake, Silk, Damask, Flowers, Gold Embroidery, Japan, c.1840, 63 In. *illus* 1375
Poncho, Wool & Cashmere, Plaid, Pale Pink, Blue, Tan, Off-White, V Neck, Fringe, Burberry, 28 In. 200

Cloisonne, Vase, Koi, Multicolor, Blue & Pink Tinted Foil Water, Lobed, 1900s, 6 In.
$780

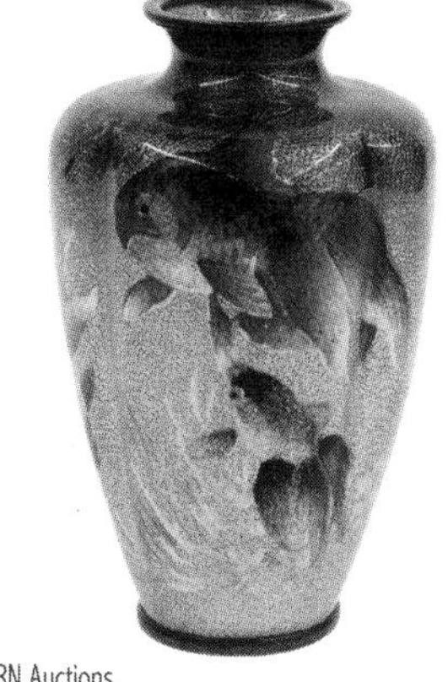

CRN Auctions

Clothing, Blouse, Satin, Brown, Flowers & Insect Print, Full Sleeves, Low Waist, Gucci
$344

Hindman Auctions

Clothing, Coat, Fur, Lynx, Off-White Lining, Herbert's, San Francisco, c.1980, 22 ½ In.
$660

Michaan's Auctions

Clothing, Coat, Mink, Driving, White, Henig Furs, 30 ½ x 18 In.
$369

Charlton Hall Auctions

Clothing, Coat, Mink, Tan, Collar, Satin Lining, Monogram, Embroidered, Gartenhaus Fs, 23 In.
$176

Cordier Auctions

Clothing, Coat, Mink, White, Tie, Burkholder Furs, Ottawa, Canada, 41 In.
$288

Blackwell Auctions

Clothing, Dress & Jacket, Wool, Dark Gray, Sheath, Boat Neckline, Norman Norell, 1960s
$281

Hindman Auctions

Clothing, Jacket, Bomber, Leather, Black, Removable Fur Collar, Zip Front, Pockets, Chanel, 2008, Size 36
$594

Abington Auction Gallery

Clothing, Jumpsuit, Safari Style, Belt, Button-Flap Pockets, Front Zip, Yves Saint Laurent, 1970-80s
$438

Hindman Auctions

Clothing, Kimono, Furisode, Silk, 5 Crests, Flowers, Gold Couching, Japan, c.1870, 65 In.
$938

Bruneau & Co. Auctioneers

Clothing, Kimono, Silk Satin Damask, Embroidered Clouds, Flowers, c.1830, Japan, 65 In.
$1,375

Bruneau & Co. Auctioneers

Clothing, Kimono, Silk, 5 Crests, Painted Flowers, Platinum Couching, Japan, c.1915, 66 In.
$625

Bruneau & Co. Auctioneers

Clothing, Kimono, Tomesode, Black Silk Crepe, Shibori Tie Dye, Gold Thread, c.1910, 64 In.
$438

Bruneau & Co. Auctioneers

Clothing, Kimono, Uchikake, Silk, 5 Crests, Landscape, Silver Embroidery, Japan, c.1890, 62 In.
$625

Bruneau & Co. Auctioneers

Clothing, Kimono, Uchikake, Silk, Damask, Flowers, Gold Embroidery, Japan, c.1840, 63 In.
$1,375

Bruneau & Co. Auctioneers

Clothing, Scarf, Silk, Black Ground, Gold Chain Link, Chanel, Paris, 34 x 33 In.
$281

Freeman's Auctioneers & Appraisers

Clothing, Scarf, Silk, Coaching Scenes, Figures, Hermes, France, Frame, 36 In., Square
$106

Selkirk Auctioneers & Appraisers

Clothing, Scarf, Silk, Soies Volantes, Chinese Kites, Neon, Cream Ground, Hermes, 1980s, 36 x 36 In.
$240

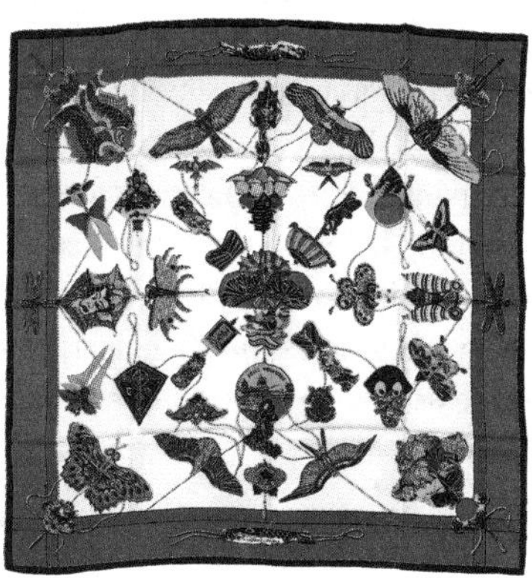

Eldred's

Clothing, Scarf, Silk, Vue De Carosse De La Galere Le Reale, Hugo Grygkar, Hermes, 35 x 35 In.
$144

Blackwell Auctions

Clothing, Shirt, Hawaiian, Elvis Presley Commemorative, Lavel, Reyn Spooner, Man's
$225

Clothing, Shirt, Hawaiian, Texas Theme, Man's
$255

CLOTHING

Clothing, Shoes, Suede, Woven Calf Hair, Bottega Veneta, Italy, c.1990, Man's
$64

Hindman Auctions

Clothing, Suit, Wool, Black, Jacket, Notched Lapel, Metal Buttons, Norman Norell, 1960s, Woman's
$125

Hindman Auctions

Clothing, Sweater, Cotton, Navy, Red & White, Gucci, 1980s, Size 52
$138

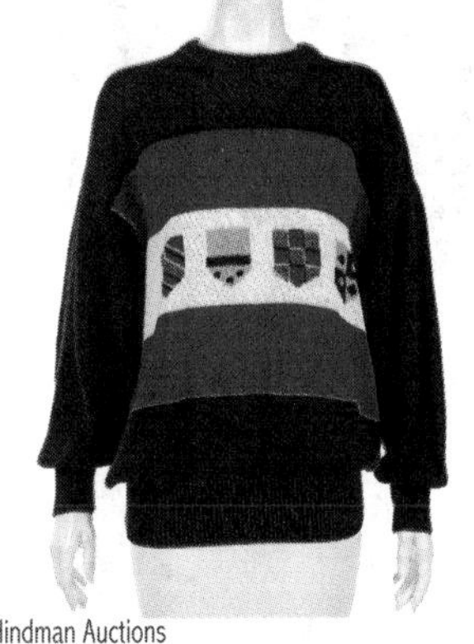

Hindman Auctions

C

Robe, Silk, Embroidered, 9 Dragon, Black Velvet Cap, Flaming Pearls, Chinese, 54 In. 1920
Scarf, Silk Brown & White, Tan Sable Fur Trim, Ex Libris, Hermes, Box, 36 x 36 In. 1750
Scarf, Silk, Black Ground, Gold Chain Link, Chanel, Paris, 34 x 33 In. .... *illus* 281
Scarf, Silk, Coaching Scenes, Figures, Hermes, France, Frame, 36 In., Square .... *illus* 106
Scarf, Silk, Serigraph, L, Leopard, Alphabet Series, Erte, Frame, 28 ½ x 27 ½ In. 144
Scarf, Silk, Soies Volantes, Chinese Kites, Neon, Cream Ground, Hermes, 1980s, 36 x 36 In. *illus* 240
Scarf, Silk, Vue De Carosse De La Galere Le Reale, Hugo Grygkar, Hermes, 35 x 35 In. .... *illus* 144
Shirt, Hawaiian, Elvis Presley Commemorative, Lavel, Reyn Spooner, Man's .... *illus* 225
Shirt, Hawaiian, Texas Theme, Man's .... *illus* 255
Shoes, Loafers, Beige Patent Leather, Gold Tone CC Logo, Chanel, Size 42 531
Shoes, Suede, Woven Calf Hair, Bottega Veneta, Italy, c.1990, Man's .... *illus* 64
Stole, Fur, Silver Fox, Variegated, Black Ends 163
Stole, Mink, Dyed, 2-Tone Purple, Mink Beads, Givenchy, 90 In. 168
Suit, Wool, Black, Fitted Jacket, Velvet Collar, Long Silk Skirt, c.1900 84
Suit, Wool, Black, Jacket, Notched Lapel, Metal Buttons, Norman Norell, 1960s, Woman's *illus* 125
Sweater, Cardigan, Cashmere, Black, Mink Collar, Rhinestone Buckle, B. Altman, 1950-60 200
Sweater, Cotton, Navy, Red & White, Gucci, 1980s, Size 52 .... *illus* 138
Wedding Dress, Lace & Tulle, Scalloped Neckline, Cap Sleeves, Buttons, c.1965, 30 x 24 In. 35
Wedding Gown, Silk Organza, Satin Tiers, Cotton Crocheted Petticoat, With 1918 Photo 108

CLUTHRA

Cluthra glass is a two-layered glass with small bubbles and powdered glass trapped between the layers. The Steuben Glass Works of Corning, New York, first made it in 1920. Victor Durand of Kimball Glass Company in Vineland, New Jersey, made a similar glass from about 1925. Durand's pieces are listed in the Durand category. Related items are listed in the Steuben category.

Bowl, Lavender, Oval, 4 Lobes, Signed, Steuben, c.1920, 4 ½ x 8 x 4 ¾ In. 550
Vase, Blue To White, 8 ¼ x 5 In. 250
Vase, Gourd Shape, Pink, Glazed, c.1920, 8 ½ x 7 ½ In. .... *illus* 350
Vase, Light Green, Bulbous, c.1930, 8 ½ x 7 ½ In. 2700

COALBROOKDALE

Coalbrookdale was made by the Coalport porcelain factory of England during the Victorian period. Pieces are decorated with floral encrustations.

Figurine, Duke Of Wellington, In Chair, Arms Folded, Parian, 10 x 10 In. 272
Vase, Lid, 2 Handles, Flower Encrusted, Multicolor, 14 ½ In. 158

COALPORT

Coalport ware was made by the Coalport Porcelain Works of England beginning about 1795. Early pieces were unmarked. About 1810–1825 the pieces were marked with the name *Coalport* in various forms. Later pieces also had the name *John Rose* in the mark. The crown mark was used with variations beginning in 1881. The date 1750 is printed in some marks, but it is not the date the factory started. Coalport was bought by Wedgwood in 1967. Coalport porcelain is no longer being produced. Some pieces are listed in this book under Indian Tree.

Coalport Porcelain Manufactory 1820

Coalport Porcelain Manufactory c.1881

Coalport Porcelain Manufactory 1960

Dish, Flowers, Wavy Rim, Blue Border, Shell Handle, c.1820, 9 x 8 ½ In., Pair .... *illus* 213

Fruit Cooler, Lid, Apple Green Ground, Flowers, Gilt Handles & Trim, c.1820, 11 In., Pair........ 1722
Plate, Dessert, Flower Bouquet Center, Gold Trim, c.1810, 8 ½ In. 88

COBALT BLUE

Cobalt blue glass was made using oxide of cobalt. The characteristic bright dark blue identifies it for the collector. Most cobalt glass found today was made after the Civil War. There was renewed interest in the dark blue glass in the late 1930s and glass dinnerware was made.

Compote, Folded Rim, Knop Stem, Stepped Base, 1800s, 4 ½ x 6 ½ In. 1230
Shaker, Nutmeg, Silver Lid, Rectangular, 4 ½ In. ....*illus* 354
Vase, Trumpet Shape, Bubble Weighted Base, 13 In., Pair 83

COCA-COLA

Coca-Cola was first served in 1886 in Atlanta, Georgia. It was advertised through signs, newspaper ads, coupons, bottles, trays, calendars, and even lamps and clocks. Collectors want anything with the word *Coca-Cola,* including a few rare products, like gum wrappers and cigar bands. The famous trademark was patented in 1893, the *Coke* mark in 1945. Many modern items and reproductions are being made.

Blotter, Drink Coca-Cola, Delicious, Ivory Paper, Shades Of Blue, 1904, 4 x 9 In. 256
Bookend, Bottle Shape, Bronze, c.1963, 7 ½ x 5 In. 180
Bookmark, Drink Coca-Cola, 5 Cents, Girl, Celluloid, Heart Shape, 1900, 2 In. 431
Bookmark, Drink Coca-Cola, 5 Cents, Girl, Purple, Flowers, 1903, 6 x 2 In. 431
Bookmark, Owl, Holding Book, What Shall We Drink?, Celluloid, 5 x 3 ¾ In. 431
Bottle Carrier, Drink Coca-Cola In Bottles, Wood, Yellow, Red, Stencil, 6-Pack, 1940s, 7 ½ In. ... *illus* 330
Bottle Rack, Wire, Round Metal Top Sign, 3 Tiers, c.1930s, 55 ½ x 12 x 19 ½ In. 270
Bottle, Drink Coca-Cola, Wreath, Applied Textured Color Label, 12 ½ In. 900
Bottle, Green, Coca-Cola, Tuskegee, Alabama Hutchinson, c.1903, 7 x 2 In. ....*illus* 2700
Bottle, Syrup, Coca-Cola, Fired Label, Cap, 1900-10, 12 ½ x 3 ½ In. ....*illus* 720
Bottle, Syrup, Drink Coca-Cola, White, Etched, Black Cap, 1920s, 12 In. ....*illus* 300
Bottle, Syrup, Wreath, Applied Color Label, c.1910, 12 ½ x 3 ½ In. ....*illus* 900
Bowl, Ice, Pottery, 6 Scallops Hold Bottles, Green, Embossed, Vernonware, 1930s, 10 In. 384
Button, Salesman's, Ask Me, Red Cooler, Bottle Carriers, Metal, Pinback, 2 ½ In. 677
Button, Sign, Drink Coca-Cola, Sign Of Good Taste, A.M. Sign Company, 16 In. 540
Calendar, 1917, Constance, Smiling Girl, White Dress, 12 Months, 31 ¾ x 13 In. ....*illus* 1875
Calendar, 1919, Girl Knitting, Airplanes, Soldiers, Full Pad, Frame, 44 In. 2700
Calendar, 1928, Druggist, Girl Holding Glass, White Fur, George C. Keene, January, 18 x 12 In.. 450
Calendar, 1928, Girl In Gold Gown, Fur Stole, Full Pad, Frame, 31 In. 523
Calendar, 1930, Girl In Bathing Suit, Rock, Tree, Water, Partial Pad, Frame, 32 In. 900
Calendar, 1935, January Page, Out Fishin', Norman Rockwell, Mat, Frame, 37 x 18 In. ...*illus* 148
Calendar, 1942, Bi-Monthly, Paper Lithograph, Metal Strip, 20 x 14 ½ In. ....*illus* 300
Cards, Playing, Deck, Silhouette, Girl Drinking, Yellow & Red Box, 1943, 3 ¾ x 2 ½ In. 270
Cash Register, Drink Coca-Cola, Brandt Automatic Cashier, Cast Aluminum, Iron, 10 x 16 In.. 480
Clicker, Chirp For Coca-Cola, Tin, Bottle Shape, Yellow, Red, 1930s, 2 ½ x ¾ In. ....*illus* 1200
Clock, Button With Silhouette Girl, Octagonal, Neon, 18 In. 840
Clock, Coca-Cola In Bottles, Ingraham, Regulator, Oak, Glass, c.1900, 39 x 16 ½ In. 367
Clock, Contessa, Logo On Face, Brass Base, Plastic Dome, Germany, 6 x 3 ½ In. 738
Clock, Drink Coca-Cola In Bottles, Button On Dial, Square, Wood Frame, 16 In. 473
Clock, Drink Coca-Cola In Bottles, Wall, White Face, Red, Wood Frame, Late 1930s, 16 x 16 In.. 450
Clock, Drink Coca-Cola, Wall, Bottle Shape Hands, Aluminum, Painted, Electric, 1950s, 18 In.. 142
Clock, Enjoy Coca-Cola, Curved Glass Face, Swihart Products Inc., Light-Up, 13 ½ x 16 In. 210
Clock, Things Go Better With Coke, Kirby Coggeshall Steinau Co., 1960, 17 x 17 In. 72
Cooler, Double Lift Lid, Tubular Legs, Metal, Red Ground, White Lettering, 35 x 38 In. 461
Cooler, Drink Coca-Cola, Embossed Logo, Bottle Opener, Drain Hole, 34 x 31 In. ....*illus* 168
Cooler, Drink Coca-Cola, Ice Cold, Metal, Enameled, Embossed, Lift Lid, 35 x 27 In. ....*illus* 923
Cooler, Drink Coca-Cola, Ice Cold, Red Metal, Bottle Opener, 1939, 34 ½ x 26 In. 660
Cooler, Drink Coca-Cola, Ice Cold, Red, Cap Catcher, Westinghouse, 34 x 25 In. ....*illus* 660
Cooler, Drink Coca-Cola, In Bottles, Red, Metal, Handle, 18 x 18 x 12 In. 180

Cluthra, Vase, Gourd Shape, Pink, Glazed, c.1920, 8 ½ x 7 ½ In.
$350

Woody Auctions

TIP
Most Coca-Cola trays had green or brown borders in the 1920s, red borders in the 1930s.

Coalport, Dish, Flowers, Wavy Rim, Blue Border, Shell Handle, c.1820, 9 x 8 ½ In., Pair
$213

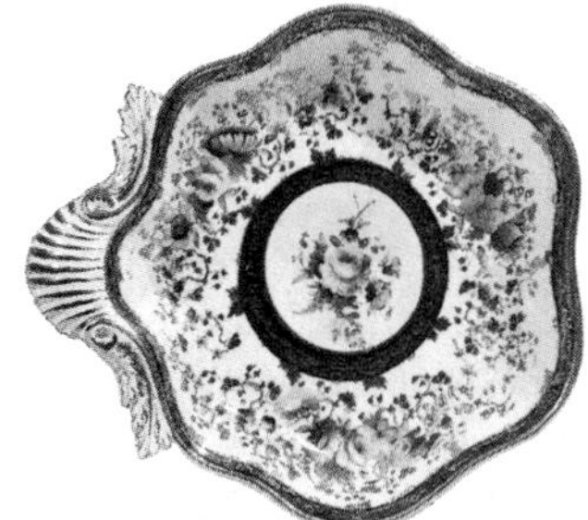

Freeman's Auctioneers & Appraisers

Cobalt Blue, Shaker, Nutmeg, Silver Lid, Rectangular, 4 ½ In.
$354

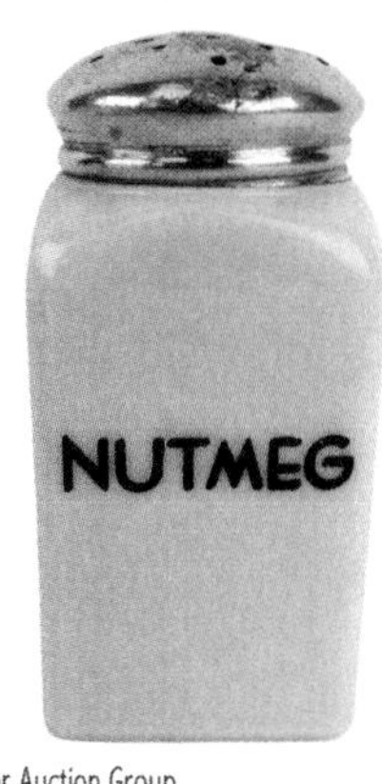

Strawser Auction Group

Coca-Cola, Bottle Carrier, Drink Coca-Cola In Bottles, Wood, Yellow, Red, Stencil, 6-Pack, 1940s, 7 ½ In.
$330

Morphy Auctions

Coca-Cola, Bottle, Green, Coca-Cola, Tuskegee, Alabama Hutchinson, c.1903, 7 x 2 In.
$2,700

Morphy Auctions

Coca-Cola, Bottle, Syrup, Coca-Cola, Fired Label, Cap, 1900-10, 12 ½ x 3 ½ In.
$720

Morphy Auctions

Cooler, Drink Coca-Cola, Red, White, Removable Lid, Bail Handle, Ice Pick, 1950s, 13 x 13 In. 480
Cooler, Drink Coca-Cola, Salesman's Sample, 2 Hinged Lids, 2 Wood Crates, 10 x 12 x 7 ⅜ In. 1560
Cooler, Ice Cold, Lift Lid, Door, Internal Racks, Red, Cylindrical, 50 x 26 In. 1920
Coupon, Coca-Cola, Free, This Card Entitles You, Paper, c.1908, 3 ½ x 2 In. 210
Dispenser, Counter, Mounted, Chrome Handle, Dole, 1950s, 22 x 20 In. 308
Dispenser, Have A Coke, Countertop, Plastic, Metal, Red & White, 1950s, 22 x 11 In. 300
Dispenser, Have A Coke, Plastic & Metal, Embossed, Dole Citation, c.1960, 16 x 18 In. 156
Display, Acrylic, Coke Cans, Detroit Tigers, World Champions, 1984, 26 x 16 In. *illus* 35
Display, Army Girl, In Uniform, Holding Bottle, Cutout, 1943, 17 ½ In. 608
Display, Drink Coca-Cola, Pause, Refresh, 2 Girls, Cloche Hats, Frame, 1928, 23 In. 16200
Display, Take Home A Carton, Girl Shopper, Blue Dress, Cardboard, 1937, 36 x 18 In. 1476
Door Pull, Tin, Bakelite, Black, 12 x 2 ¾ x 1 ¾ In. 720
Door Push, Come In, Have A Coca-Cola, Metal, Oval, 1939, 11 ½ x 3 ½ In. 554
Door Push, Drink Coca-Cola, Bottle, Tin, Embossed, Dasco, 1930, 14 x 4 ¾ In. *illus* 900
Door Push, Drink Coca-Cola, Pause, Refresh, Porcelain, Red, 33 x 3 In. *illus* 510
Festoon, Drink Coca-Cola, 3 Umbrella Girls, Flowers, Frame, 1918, 37 x 43 In. 4200
Jar, Pepsin Gum, Clear Glass, Square, Label, Shaped Stopper, 12 x 4 ¾ In. 308
Kit, Drink Coca-Cola, Salesman's Selling, Promotional Material, Record, 1955, 19 x 17 x 3 In. 148
Label, Pepsin Gum, 20 5-Ct. Pkgs., Tree, Coca-Cola Logo, c.1912, 12 x 7 In. 4305
Match Stand, Chromium Plated Bottle Stem, American Pullmatch, 1930s, 7 In. 900
Matchbook, Girl's Smiling Face, Holds Bottle, c.1912, 2 In. 540
Medal, Bottling Co. Annual Convention, Jan 1915, Metal, Cloisonne, Round, ¾ In. 1800
Menu, What Shall We Drink?, Girl Holding Flowers, Soda Menu, Frame, 16 In. 1080
Mirror, Coca-Cola In Oval, Girl In Black Bathing Costume, Beach, Oval, 1922, 3 In. 6600
Mirror, Coca-Cola Script, Bottles At Ends, Rectangular, Tab Handles, 1930s, 7 x 2 In. 900
Mirror, Drink Coca-Cola, Delicious Refreshing, Shaped Ends, 1930, 11 ¾ x 3 ½ In. 960
Mirror, Drink Coca-Cola, Girl With Curly Hair Holding Glass, Oval, 1907, 3 In. 338
Mirror, Drink Coca-Cola, Victorian Woman, Red Hat, Flowers, Oval, 1908, 3 In. 480
Mirror, Drink Delicious Coca-Cola, Girl, Wide-Brimmed Hat, 2 Roses, Oval, 1911, 3 In. 210
Plate, Bust, Draped Woman, Western Coca-Cola Bottling Co., Tin, Vienna Art, 1908, Frame, 14 In. 330
Plate, Drink Coca-Cola, Good With Food, Wellsville China, c.1950, 7 ½ In. 492
Playing Cards, 2 Ballet Dancers, Full Deck, Yellow Box, Sealed, 1943, 3 ¾ In. 277
Rack, 3-Pack, Take Home A Carton, 25 Cents, 50 x 16 ½ x 12 ½ In. 390
Rack, Enjoy Coca-Cola While We Check Your Tires, Wire, 31 x 27 x 7 In. 960
Sign, Be Refreshed, Bottle, Button, Cardboard, 2-Sided, Frame, McCandlish, 1951, 21 x 37 In. *illus* 452
Sign, Bottle Shape, Metal, Porcelain Enamel, Green, 1950s, 16 x 5 In. 283
Sign, Button, Arrow, Drink Coca-Cola, Red Ground, Tin, 1950s, 24 x 15 In. 1353
Sign, Button, Bottle, Logo, Red Ground, Tin, Round, 1948, 25 In. 1845
Sign, Button, Delicious, Refreshing, Boy & Girl, Holding Glasses, Cardboard, 1948, 15 In. 3000
Sign, Button, Drink Coca-Cola, Tin, Red Ground, White Lettering, 1950s, 36 In. 570
Sign, Button, Porcelain, Red Ground, White Lettering, 12 In. 367
Sign, Button, Red, White, Black, Enamel, Iron, Mounting Holes, 1950s, 24 In. 354
Sign, Chewing Gum, Baby, Netting, Blue Ribbon, Cardboard, Frame, 1903, 15 x 7 In. 10800
Sign, Coca-Cola Belongs, Navy Man & Woman, Cardboard, 1943, 25 x 41 In. 1920
Sign, Coke Belongs, Teenage Couple, Girl & Boy, Dark Green Ground, 1944, 27 x 56 ½ In. 79
Sign, Coke With Ice, Hanging, Neon Light, Black Grid, 20 x 20 In. 270
Sign, Curb Service, Coca-Cola Sold Here, Embossed Metal, 2-Sided, 32 x 20 In. *illus* 540
Sign, Delicious & Refreshing, Woman Aviator, Propeller, 1940, 26 x 42 In. 6000
Sign, Drink Coca-Cola, Girl At Ship's Wheel, Cardboard, Frame, 1936, 29 x 56 In. 7200
Sign, Drink Coca-Cola, Red, Green Border, Rectangular, 30 x 10 In. *illus* 330
Sign, Drink Coca-Cola, Tin, Red Ground, White Lettering, Frame, 11 ¾ x 23 ¾ In. 94
Sign, Dutch Advertising, Girl, Holding Glass, Cream Ground, Black Frame, 37 x 21 In. 630
Sign, Easy To Take Home, Girl On Bicycle, Carton In Rack, Cardboard, 1940, 20 x 43 In. 3075
Sign, For The Party, Woman & Army Man, Tandem Bike, Coke In Basket, 1945, 52 x 31 In. 3075
Sign, Have A Coke, Girl Offering Bottle, Cardboard, 1943, 27 x 16 In. 2000
Sign, Hospitality, Horizontal, Cardboard, Wood Frame, 1948, 27 x 41 In. *illus* 1046
Sign, Ice Cold Coca-Cola Sold Here, Bottle, Tin, Embossed, Red, Black, Frame, 1927, 20 x 28 In. 2400
Sign, Ice Cold Coca-Cola Sold Here, Tin, Embossed, Diamond Shape, 1932, 22 In. 3600
Sign, Ice Cold, Enjoy That Refreshing New Feeling, Tin, Painted, 1960s, 20 x 27 In. *illus* 271
Sign, It Cools You, Girl On Boat, Holds Bottle, Cardboard, A. Loomis, 1936, 38 x 21 In. 6150

Coca-Cola, Bottle, Syrup, Drink Coca-Cola, White, Etched, Black Cap, 1920s, 12 In.
$300

Morphy Auctions

Coca-Cola, Bottle, Syrup, Wreath, Applied Color Label, c.1910, 12 ½ x 3 ½ In.
$900

Morphy Auctions

Coca-Cola, Calendar, 1917, Constance, Smiling Girl, White Dress, 12 Months, 31 ¾ x 13 In.
$1,875

Cowan's Auctions

Coca-Cola, Calendar, 1935, January Page, Out Fishin', Norman Rockwell, Mat, Frame, 37 x 18 In.
$148

Richard Opfer Auctioneering, Inc.

Coca-Cola, Calendar, 1942, Bi-Monthly, Paper Lithograph, Metal Strip, 20 x 14 ½ In.
$300

Rich Penn Auctions

Coca-Cola, Clicker, Chirp For Coca-Cola, Tin, Bottle Shape, Yellow, Red, 1930s, 2 ½ x ¾ In.
$1,200

Morphy Auctions

Coca-Cola, Cooler, Drink Coca-Cola, Embossed Logo, Bottle Opener, Drain Hole, 34 x 31 In.
$168

Alderfer Auction Company

Coca-Cola, Cooler, Drink Coca-Cola, Ice Cold, Metal, Enameled, Embossed, Lift Lid, 35 x 27 In.
$923

Richard Opfer Auctioneering, Inc.

Coca-Cola, Cooler, Drink Coca-Cola, Ice Cold, Red, Cap Catcher, Westinghouse, 34 x 25 In.
$660

Morphy Auctions

Coca-Cola, Display, Acrylic, Coke Cans, Detroit Tigers, World Champions, 1984, 26 x 16 In.
$35

Copake Auctions

Coca-Cola, Door Push, Drink Coca-Cola, Bottle, Tin, Embossed, Dasco, 1930, 14 x 4 ¾ In.
$900

Morphy Auctions

Coca-Cola, Sign, Be Refreshed, Bottle, Button, Cardboard, 2-Sided, Frame, McCandlish, 1951, 21 x 37 In.
$452

Soulis Auctions

Coca-Cola, Sign, Curb Service, Coca-Cola Sold Here, Embossed Metal, 2-Sided, 32 x 20 In.
$540

Rich Penn Auctions

Coca-Cola, Sign, Drink Coca-Cola, Red, Green Border, Rectangular, 30 x 10 In.
$330

Morphy Auctions

Coca-Cola, Sign, Hospitality, Horizontal, Cardboard, Wood Frame, 1948, 27 x 41 In.
$1,046

Richard Opfer Auctioneering, Inc.

Coca-Cola, Sign, Ice Cold, Enjoy That Refreshing New Feeling, Tin, Painted, 1960s, 20 x 27 In.
$271

Leland Little Auctions

Coca-Cola, Sign, Lollipop, Drink, Refresh!, Porcelain, Embossed, Iron Base, 2-Sided, 1936, 64 x 30 In.
$780

Rich Penn Auctions

Coca-Cola, Door Push, Drink Coca-Cola, Pause, Refresh, Porcelain, Red, 33 x 3 In.
$510

Morphy Auctions

Sign, Jackie Cooper, It's So Good And Good For You, Cardboard, Frame, 1935, 34 x 62 In.......... 2700
Sign, Lollipop, Drink, Refresh!, Porcelain, Embossed, Iron Base, 2-Sided, 1936, 64 x 30 In. *illus* 780
Sign, Lunch Refreshed, Waitress, Tray, Sandwiches & Cokes, 1947, 32 x 25 In.......................... 3600
Sign, Pause That Refreshes, Girl In Moonlight, Water, Cardboard, 1939, 31 x 61 In. 11400
Sign, Pause That Refreshes, Military Boy & Girl, Talking, Holding Bottles, 1943, 50 x 30 In..... 1680
Sign, Play Refreshed, Tennis Girl, Sitting On Cooler, 1949, 32 x 21 In.................................... 1008
Sign, Refreshing, Girl, Large Hat, Holding Glass, Red Border, Frame, 1945, 30 x 47 ½ In.......... 3900
Sign, Sign Of Good Taste, Ice Cold, Coca Cola Bottle, Green Border, 1950-60, 18 x 54 In. .*illus* 443
Sign, Slow, School Zone, Policeman, Figural, Holding Sign, Coca-Cola On Reverse, 62 x 24 In. *illus* 2160
Sign, Take Some Home Today, Sprite Boy, 6-Pack, 1952, 36 x 20 In. 1140
Sign, The Drink They All Expect, Board, Gilt Wood & Metal Frame, c.1950, 33 x 22 In.............. 561
Sign, The Year Round Drink, Girl Holding Glass, Cardboard, Painted, Frame, 38 x 21 In.......... 660
Sign, Trolley, Man & Woman Toasting With Coke Glasses, Frame, 1927, 26 x 16 In. 1560
Stamp Holder, Compliments Of Coca-Cola Co., Girl, Obelisk, Celluloid, 1902, 3 In. 420
Thermometer, Bottle, Figural, Tin, Hanging Hook In Cap, 1958, 16 In....................................... 62
Thermometer, Bottle, Red Ground, Elongated Oval, 1923, 16 In. 148
Thermometer, Bottle, Tin Lithograph, Die Cut, Robertson, Made In U.S.A., 17 In. 113
Thermometer, Buve Coca-Cola, French, Silhouette, Girl Drinking, Porcelain, Red, Canada, 18 In.. 720
Thermometer, Drink Coca-Cola In Bottles, Refresh Yourself, Cigar Style, c.1950, 30 x 8 In. 240
Thermometer, Drink Coca-Cola, 2 Bottles, Shaped, Embossed, 1941, 15 ¾ x 7 In.................... 984
Tip Tray, 1914, Betty, Drink Coca-Cola, Delicious & Refreshing, Oval, 6 x 4 In.......................... 150
Toy, Truck, Coke Sign On Flat Bed, Metal, Louis Marx, Box, 1950s, 6 x 19 In............................. 1353
Toy, Truck, Delivery, Red, 10 Bottles, Every Bottle Sterilized, Metalcraft, c.1930 ....*illus* 144
Toy, Truck, Metal, Yellow, Red Stencil, Sign On Side, Marx, Box, 1950s, 6 x 19 x 7 In. ......*illus* 1320
Trade Card, Coca-Cola In Oval Frame, Girl In Feathered Hat, Ribbons, 1902, 7 x 5 In. 450
Trade Card, Girl In Bathtub, Folds Open, Waitress Serving 2 Men, c.1907, 6 x 3 ½ In............. 1476
Tray, 1903, Hilda Clark, Holding Glass & Paper, Refreshing, Delicious, Round, 9 ½ In. 4200
Tray, Drink Coca-Cola, Girl In White Bathing Suit, Striped Bench, 1939, 15 x 12 In.................. 210
Tray, Girl Fishing, Drinking Bottle Of Coca-Cola, Tin Color Lithograph, 1940, 13 In. 111
Tray, Thirst Knows No Season, Girl Holding Bottle, 13 ¼ x 10 ½ In.. 34
Tumbler, Bottle Coca-Cola, Acid Etched Glass, Flared, 1916, 3 ½ In... 720
Tumbler, Coca-Cola Script Logo, Stencil, Straight-Sided, 1900-04, 4 x 2 ½ In......................... 3900
Tumbler, Drink Coca-Cola, 5 Cents, Flared, 1913, 4 x 3 In.. 1920
Tumbler, Script Logo, Glass, Inverted Bell Form, 1941-46, 4 x 3 In... 96
Vending Machine, Cavalier 51, Ice Cold, 10 Cents, Thermometer, Key, Red, 66 x 25 In. 1200
Vending Machine, Vendo 44, Drink Coca-Cola, 10 Cents, Metal Racking, Key, 58 x 20 In........ 3300
Vending Machine, Vendo, Drink Coca-Cola In Bottles, 10 Cents, Red, 63 x 33 In...................... 960
Whistle, Bottle Shape, Cardboard, 1920s, 3 ¾ In. 500
Whistle, Drink Coca-Cola In A Bottle, Wood, Cylindrical, Flared Foot, 1920s............................. 492
Whistle, Drink Coca-Cola In Bottles, Wood, Yellow, Red Letters, 1920s, 1 ½ x ¾ In.................. 480

COFFEE MILLS

Coffee mills are also called coffee grinders, although there is a difference in the way each grinds the coffee. Large floor-standing or counter-model coffee mills were used in the nineteenth-century country store. Small home mills were first made about 1894. They lost favor by the 1930s. The renewed interest in fresh-ground coffee has produced many modern electric mills, hand mills, and grinders. Reproductions of the old styles are being made.

Enterprise, 2 Wheels, Cast Iron, Drawer, Oak, Philadelphia, 10 ½ x 9 x 13 In.......................... 374
Enterprise, 2 Wheels, Cast Iron, Painted, 1800s, 16 In. 461
Enterprise, Drawer, Porcelain Knob, Wood Base, Cast Iron, 11 ½ In. 85
Enterprise, No. 1, Cast Iron, Drawer, Porcelain Knob, Wood Base, c.1875, 12 ½ In. ....*illus* 215
Enterprise, No. 2, 2 Wheels, Cast Iron, Swivel Lid, Pa., c.1880, 12 ½ x 8 ¾ In. 702
Enterprise, No. 12, 2 Wheels, Cast Iron, Still, Eagle Handle, Red, Gold Highlights, 34 In. *illus* 390
Fairbanks Morse & Co., 2 Wheels, Hopper Lid, Iron Eagle Finial, 29 ½ x 15 ¾ x 20 In. 367
Fairbanks Morse & Co., Tin, Eagle Transfer, Painted, Cast Iron, 1887, 26 x 20 x 16 In............ 600
G. Minnick, Wood, Philadelphia Cherry, Drawer, Tin Hopper, 9 ½ In.. 171
J.C. Dell, Hopper, Catch Bin, Painted, 67 x 32 ¾ x 20 ½ In. ....*illus* 1920

Coca-Cola, Sign, Sign Of Good Taste, Ice Cold, Coca Cola Bottle, Green Border, 1950-60, 18 x 54 In.
$443

Copake Auctions

Coca-Cola, Sign, Slow, School Zone, Policeman, Figural, Holding Sign, Coca-Cola On Reverse, 62 x 24 In.
$2,160

Morphy Auctions

Coca-Cola, Toy, Truck, Delivery, Red, 10 Bottles, Every Bottle Sterilized, Metalcraft, c.1930
$144

Bunte Auction Services

Coca-Cola, Toy, Truck, Metal, Yellow, Red Stencil, Sign On Side, Marx, Box, 1950s, 6 x 19 x 7 In.
$1,320

Morphy Auctions

Coffee Mill, Enterprise, No. 1, Cast Iron, Drawer, Porcelain Knob, Wood Base, c.1875, 12 ½ In.
$215

Soulis Auctions

Coffee Mill, Enterprise, No. 12, 2 Wheels, Cast Iron, Still, Eagle Handle, Red, Gold Highlights, 34 In.
$390

Milestone Auctions

Landers, Frary & Clark, Red, Black, Eagle Finial, Wood Handle, 1850s, 14 In. ....*illus* 594
Wood Case, Dovetailed, Cast Iron, Knob Pull, Crank, 6 x 5 ¾ x 7 ½ In. 74

COIN-OPERATED MACHINE

Coin-operated machines of all types are collected. The vending machine is an ancient invention dating back to 200 B.C., when holy water was dispensed from a coin-operated vase. Smokers in seventeenth-century England could buy tobacco from a coin-operated box. It was not until after the Civil War that the technology made modern coin-operated games and vending machines plentiful. Slot machines, arcade games, and dispensers are all collected.

Arcade, 10th Inning, Baseball Game, 10 Cent, 25 Cent, Williams E.M.C., 71 x 66 In. ....*illus* 492
Arcade, Atlas Tilt Test, 5 Cents, Zigzag Playing Field, 18 In. 600
Arcade, Bally Skill Derby Horse Race, Electro Mechanical, 5 Cent, c.1960, 71 x 27 x 22 In. 1260
Arcade, Crane, Mahogany Case, Riverboat, Pier, Claw Arm, Borzini, France, 1935 7758
Arcade, Miniature Steam Shovel, Novelty Merchantman, 1934-42, 70 x 21 x 19 In. ....*illus* 4200
Arcade, Ms. Pac Man, Blue, Bally Midway, c.1980, 68 ½ x 24 ¾ x 34 In. 469
Dispenser, Diamond Matches, 1 Cent, Lithograph On Metal, Edwards Co., c.1920, 13 In. *illus* 531
Dispenser, Dixie, Cup, 1 Cent, Wall Mount Metal Base, Green, Key, Signed, 32 ½ x 4 x 5 In. 242
Fortune Teller, Madam X, 1 Cent, Answers Any Yes Or No Question, c.1950, 6 ½ x 7 In. 180
Gumball, 5 Cent, Novelties, Tokens, Marbles, 1950s, 14 x 7 ½ In. 367
Gumball, Bantam Model, 5 Cent, Aluminum Case, Atlas, c.1940, 10 ¾ x 7 ¾ x 7 In. 367
Mutoscope, Tabletop, Oak, Wood Case, Cast Iron Parts, Slot, 22 x 20 x 16 In. 720
Pinball, Aquarius, Electronic, Wood Case, Painted, 1970, 69 x 52 x 26 In. 791
Pinball, Sweet Hearts, 10 Cent, D. Gottliebs & Co., 69 x 51 In. 369
Pinball, Willy At The Bat, 3 Innings, 25 Cent Per Player, Electric, William, 30 x 22 x 9 In. 551
Pinball, Wow, 5 Cents, 10 Balls, 9 Pockets, Wood Case, 32 x 18 In. 225
Shooting Game, 10 Cent, U.S. Marshal Target Practice Shooter, 1950s, 53 x 29 x 15 In. ..*illus* 900
Skill, 4 Jacks, Pinball Style, Penny, Metal Front, Oak Case, 19 x 14 x 10 In. 489
Skill, Major Novelty, Marquee, Wood Case, Yellow, Red, 37 In. 420
Slot Machine Base, Oak, Ornate, 4 Pedestal Sides, Caster Feet, 38 x 16 x 16 In. 7200
Slot, 1 Cent, Gum Payout, Chrome, Lever, Caille Brothers, 18 x 14 x 9 In. 978
Slot, Bonanza Bank, 1 Cent, 5 Cent, 10 Cent, 25 Cent, 3-Reel, Atlantic City, 8 x 7 x 11 In. 136
Slot, Mills Castle, 5 Cent, 3 Rails, Cast Metal, Wood Slide, 26 In. 677
Slot, Mills Novelty Co., 1 Cent, Tabletop, Cast Metal Front, 26 x 16 x 16 In. ....*illus* 1452
Slot, Mills, 5 Cent, Cast Face, Keys, Oak Case, c.1920-30, 18 In. 708
Slot, Mills, 25 Cent, Castle Front, Shield, Red, Blue, Cobalt Blue, Wood Case 1200
Slot, Mills, Cherry Burst, 10 Cent, Wood, Multicolor, Red Cherries, 3-Reel, 1938, 20 x 15 x 15 In. *illus* 888
Strength Tester, Shake With Uncle Sam, 10 Traits, Oak Cabinet, 74 In., Copy ....*illus* 1610
Trade Stimulator, AJ 21 JA, 1 Cent, Drawer, White Knob, Wood Case, 22 In. 312
Trade Stimulator, Cent-A-Pack, Deco Style, Buckley Mfg. Co., c.1935, 12 ½ x 9 ½ In. 480
Trade Stimulator, Cigarette, Spinner, Countertop Style, Wood Case, 1939, 16 In. 337
Trade Stimulator, L.H. Buchanan, Pyramid, Cash Box, Wood, 1893, 23 x 12 x 8 ½ In. 4514
Trade Stimulator, Sparky, Playing Cards, 5 Cent, Wood Case, Star Amusements, 1952, 15 In. 240
Trade Stimulator, Whoopee Ball, 1 Cent, Flip Game, Aluminum, Wood Base, c.1930, 17 x 9 In. 226
Vending, Candy King, 5 Cent, Mirrored Face, Monterey Distributing Co., c.1930, 28 x 12 In. 480
Vending, Cigarette, O.D. Jennings & Co., 5 Cent, 10 Cent, Metal Top, Wood Case, 62 x 19 In. 3075
Vending, Dr Pepper, V-81, Green, Keys, 58 ½ x 28 x 22 In. 5400
Vending, Gum, Adams, Automatic, Silver, 1 Cent, Mills, 16 x 10 x 5 In. 324
Vending, Jumbo Size Ball Gum, 1 Cent, Painted Wood, Cast Iron Base, 46 In. 135
Vending, Nut, Dual, 1 Cent & 5 Cent, Cebco Electric, 18 In. ....*illus* 480
Vending, Peanut, Columbus A, Cast Iron, 2 Barrel Locks, Keys, c.1920, 17 In. ....*illus* 1200
Vending, Popcorn, 10 Cent, Thompson Gold Medal, Floor Model, 1950s, 60 In. 510
Vending, Popcorn, Gold Medal Anatomical, Model No. 100, 61 x 21 In. 277
Vending, Pulver Chewing Gum, Metal, Glass Front Panel, Yellow Kid, c.1920, 21 x 9 x 5 In. 826
Vending, Pulver, Porcelain Body, Red, White Receiver Plate, 20 ½ x 9 x 4 ½ In. 2400
Vending, Snacks, Lance, 25 Cent, Key, Red Cover, Aluminum, 25 x 13 x 59 In. 360
Vending, Stamp, 10 Cent, 15 Cent, Steiner Mfg. Co., 13 x 7 x 20 In. 156
Vending, Stamp, American Postmaster, White Paint, Dillon Mfg. Co., 1900s, 12 x 13 In. .*illus* 151

Coffee Mill, J.C. Dell, Hopper, Catch Bin, Painted, 67 x 32 ¾ x 20 ½ In.
$1,920

Morphy Auctions

Coffee Mill, Landers, Frary & Clark, Red, Black, Eagle Finial, Wood Handle, 1850s, 14 In.
$594

Garth's Auctioneers & Appraisers

Coin-Operated, Arcade, 10th Inning, Baseball Game, 10 Cent, 25 Cent, Williams E.M.C., 71 x 66 In.
$492

Richard Opfer Auctioneering, Inc.

Coin-Operated, Arcade, Miniature Steam Shovel, Novelty Merchantman, 1934-42, 70 x 21 x 19 In.
$4,200

Milestone Auctions

Coin-Operated, Dispenser, Diamond Matches, 1 Cent, Lithograph On Metal, Edwards Co., c.1920, 13 In.
$531

Conestoga Auction Company

Coin-Operated, Shooting Game, 10 Cent, U.S. Marshal Target Practice Shooter, 1950s, 53 x 29 x 15 In.
$900

Milestone Auctions

Coin-Operated, Slot, Mills Novelty Co., 1 Cent, Tabletop, Cast Metal Front, 26 x 16 x 16 In.
$1,452

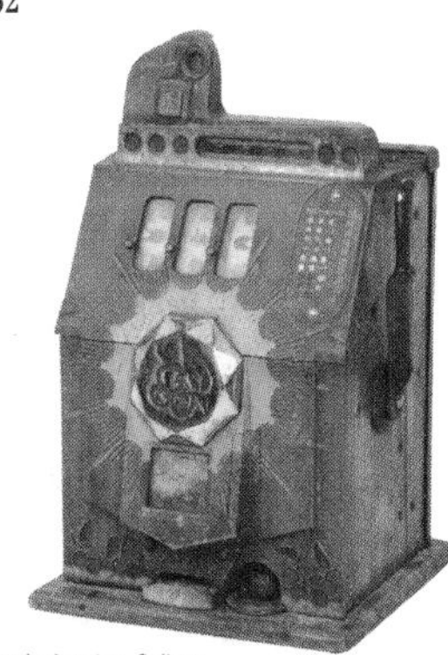

Fontaine's Auction Gallery

Coin-Operated, Slot, Mills, Cherry Burst, 10 Cent, Wood, Multicolor, Red Cherries, 3-Reel, 1938, 20 x 15 x 15 In.
$888

Cordier Auctions

Coin-Operated, Strength Tester, Shake With Uncle Sam, 10 Traits, Oak Cabinet, 74 In., Copy
$1,610

Rich Penn Auctions

Coin-Operated, Vending, Nut, Dual, 1 Cent & 5 Cent, Cebco Electric, 18 In.
$480

Milestone Auctions

Coin-Operated, Vending, Peanut, Columbus A, Cast Iron, 2 Barrel Locks, Keys, c.1920, 17 In.
$1,200

Rich Penn Auctions

Coin-Operated, Vending, Stamp, American Postmaster, White Paint, Dillon Mfg. Co., 1900s, 12 x 13 In.
$151

Bruneau & Co. Auctioneers

Commemorative, Dish, Royal Jubilee, George III, Order Of Garter, Ostrich Feathers, Wedgwood, 8 In.
$369

Stair Galleries

Commemorative, Jug, F. Burdett M.P., Yellow Glaze, Silver Luster Trim, Early 1800s, 4 ½ In.
$246

Skinner, Inc.

COLLECTOR PLATE

Collector plates are modern plates produced in limited editions. Some may be found listed under the factory name, such as Bing & Grondahl, Royal Copenhagen, Royal Doulton, and Wedgwood.

Danbury Mint, Uncle Ed, Dear Diary Series, Garfield The Cat, 1990, 8 ¼ In. 23
Franklin Mint, Mother & Child, Mother's Day, Silver, Etched, Box, 10 In. 69
Fukagawa, Beneath The Plum Branch, c.1977, 10 ½ In. 40
Perillo, Snowflake, Christmas Series, 1989, Bear & Baby, 9 In. 50
Reed & Barton, Twas The Night Before Christmas, Christmas, 1990, Children Dreaming, 10 In. 25

COMIC ART

Comic art, or cartoon art, includes original art for comic strips, magazine covers, book pages, and even printed strips. The first daily comic strip was printed in 1907. The paintings on celluloid used for movie cartoons are listed in this book under Animation Art.

Drawing, Black Panther & T'Challa, Pencil On Paper, Alan Davis, 2008, 11 x 7 ½ In. 432
Drawing, Jughead & Carnival Mirror, Jughead No. 195, Harry Lucey, 1971, 13 x 14 In. 1020
Drawing, Logan, Nick Fury, Wolverine No. 34, Marvel, Saltares, Texiera, 15 x 10 In. 168
Page, Ladies' Night Out, Babs Bunny, Fifi La Fume, Tiny Toons Adventures, 1990, 15 In. 35
Page, Mellow Drama, Archie, Laugh Comics No. 123, 1961, 17 ½ x 12 In. 480
Page, Sandman, Amazing Spider-Man No. 154, Buscema, Esposito, Hunt, 1976, 15 x 10 In. 2220
Page, The Captain & The Kids, Pen & Ink, Rudolf Dirks, Frame, 15 ½ x 22 ½ In. 313
Page, Timber Wolf, Super-Heroes, Superboy No. 197, Dave Cockrum, 1973, 15 x 10 In. 5760
Page, Tomb Of Dracula, Ink On Board, G. Colan, T. Palmer, 1977, 15 x 10 In. 840
Strip, Archie Jogging, Ink & Pencil On Board, 12 Panels, Dan DeCarlo, 1978, 14 x 21 In. 288
Strip, Breathless Mahoney, Dick Tracy, Chester Gould, October 10, 1945, 6 x 20 In. 720
Strip, Dagwood, Raids Refrigerator, Ink & Pencil On Board, J. Raymond, 1965, 5 x 17 In. 384
Strip, Garfield, Visits The Vet, Jim Davis, June 2006, 4 x 14 In. 840
Strip, Poor Loser, Mandrake The Magician, Phil Davis, November 1939, 4 ½ x 20 In. 156
Strip, Rusty Riley, Sunday Page, Frank Godwin, June 1953, 16 x 23 In. 690
Strip, Tales Of The Green Beret, Joe Kubert, May 6, 1966, 4 ½ x 15 In. 1440

COMMEMORATIVE

Commemorative items have been made to honor members of royalty and those of great national fame. World's Fairs and important historical events are also remembered with commemorative pieces. Related collectibles are listed in the Coronation and World's Fair categories.

Dish, Royal Jubilee, George III, Order Of Garter, Ostrich Feathers, Wedgwood, 8 In. ....*illus* 369
Jug, F. Burdett M.P., Yellow Glaze, Silver Luster Trim, Early 1800s, 4 ½ In. ....*illus* 246
Key, Old Home Week 05, Columbia Pa., Painted, Cast Iron, 10 In. 28
Lamp, George Washington, Gilt Metal, Marble, Etched Glass Shade, Drops, c.1900, 25 In. 500
Mug, Cylindrical, Lafayette & Washington, Portraits, Eagle, Yellow Glaze, c.1810, 2 ½ In. 400
Plate, Portrait, Pike, Pink Luster, Be Always Ready To Die, 1813-15, 10 In. ....*illus* 923

COMPACT

Compacts hold face powder. A woman did not powder her face in public until after World War I. By 1920, the beauty parlor, permanent waves, and cosmetics had become acceptable. A few companies sold cake face powder in a box with a mirror and a pad or puff. Soon the compact was designed by jewelers and made of gold, silver, and precious materials. Cosmetic companies began to sell powder in attractive compacts of less valuable metal or plastic. Collectors today search for Art Deco designs, famous brands, compacts from World's Fairs or political events, and unusual examples. Many were made with companion lipsticks and other fittings.

Commemorative, Plate, Portrait, Pike, Pink Luster, Be Always Ready To Die, 1813-15, 10 In.
$923

Skinner, Inc.

> **TIP**
> *Never put hot glass in cold water, or cold glass in hot water. The temperature change can crack the glass.*

Consolidated, Decanter, Ruba Rombic, Jungle Green, Solid Stopper, Pontil, c.1930, 9 In.
$344

Eldred's

Consolidated, Lampshade, Primrose, Ruby Satin, c.1902, 9 ¾ x 4 In.
$164

Jeffrey S. Evans & Associates

Consolidated, Vase, Ruba Rombic, Smoky Topaz, Reuben Haley, c.1930, 9 In.
$594

Eldred's

Copeland Spode, Figurine, Girl, Seated, Holding Dog, Go To Sleep, J. Durham, Copeland, 1862, 8 In.
$112

Strawser Auction Group

Copper, Boiler, Lid, Brass, Wooden Handles, c.1900, 17 x 27 x 14 In.
$72

Selkirk Auctioneers & Appraisers

C

Duval, Queen Of Hearts, Mirror & Powder, 1950s, 3 x 2 In. 95
Estee Lauder, Parrot, Gold, Yellow, Green, 1991, 2 ¾ x 1 ¼ In. 95
Flamingo, Brass, Applied Enamel Flowers, Red, Black, White, c.1955, 3 ½ In. 41
Guilloche, Sterling Silver, Enamel, Pink & Blue Flowers, Green, 2 x ⅜ In. 225
Tiffany & Co., Mirror, Circular, Hallmark, Sterling Silver, 3 In. 179
Volupte, Sterling Silver, Cloud Shape, 1940s, 3 x 2 In. 350

CONSOLIDATED LAMP AND GLASS COMPANY

Consolidated Lamp and Glass Company of Coraopolis, Pennsylvania, was founded in 1894. The company made lamps, tablewares, and art glass. Collectors are particularly interested in the wares made after 1925, including black satin glass, Cosmos (listed in its own category in this book), Martele (which resembled Lalique), Ruba Rombic (1928–1932 Art Deco line), and colored glasswares. Some Consolidated pieces are very similar to those made by the Phoenix Glass Company. The colors are sometimes different. Consolidated made Martele glass in blue, crystal, green, pink, white, or custard glass with added fired-on color or a satin finish. The company closed for the final time in 1967.

Decanter, Ruba Rombic, Jungle Green, Solid Stopper, Pontil, c.1930, 9 In. .... *illus* 344
Lampshade, Primrose, Ruby Satin, c.1902, 9 ¾ x 4 In. .... *illus* 164
Vase, Ruba Rombic, Smoky Topaz, Reuben Haley, c.1930, 9 In. .... *illus* 594

CONTEMPORARY GLASS, *see Glass-Contemporary.*

COOKBOOK

Cookbooks are collected for various reasons. Some are wanted for the recipes, some for investment, and some as examples of advertising. Cookbooks and recipe pamphlets are included in this category.

Better Homes & Gardens New Cookbook, Hardcover, Spiral Bound, 1962, 400 Pages 30
Fat Cat's Cookbook For Cooking & Coloring, 1971, 8 x 8 In., 39 Pages 95
Newman's Own Cookbook, Paul Newman, Signed, 1985, 6 x 9 In., 136 Pages 295
The Spice Cookbook, Watercolor Lithograph, 1964, 10 x 7 In., 623 Pages 32

COOKIE JAR

Cookie jars with brightly painted designs or amusing figural shapes became popular in the mid-1930s. They became very popular again when Andy Warhol's collection was auctioned after his death in 1987. Prices have gone down since then and are very low. Many companies made them and collectors search for cookie jars either by design or by maker's name. Listed here are examples by the less common makers. Major factories are listed under their own names in other categories of the book, such as Abingdon, Brush, Hull, McCoy, Metlox, Red Wing, and Shawnee. See also the Disneyana category. These are marks of three cookie jar manufacturers.

TWIN-WINTON ©

FITZ AND FLOYD, INC.
©MCMLXXX
FF

Brush Pottery Co. 1925–1982	Twin Winton Ceramics 1946–1977	Fitz and Floyd Enterprises LLC 1960–1980

Aunt Jemima, Googly-Eye, Red Polka Dot Bandanna, Bail Handle, Japan, 9 ½ In. 72
Baby Elephant, Eyes Closed, Trunk Turned Up, Blue Bib & Bonnet, c.1950, 12 In. 195
Black Lady, Stove, Pancake, Pond Scene, Rick Wisecarver, 1989, 12 x 9 ½ In. 219
Cinderella, White, Yellow, Turquoise, Brown, Marked, JC Napco, 1957, 9 ½ In. 69

Clown, Red Nose, Green Collar, Bulbous Body, Marked, Regal, 11 ½ In. 46
Gingerbread House, Board, Gable Ends, Side Molds, Carved, Early 1800s, 8 x 10 In. 1845
Goldilocks, Glaze, White, Red, Hood, Regal Art Pottery, c.1950, 12 ½ In. 50
Mrs. Rabbit, Detachable Head, Marked USA, American Bisque Co., 11 ⅝ In. 58
Peek-A-Boo, White, Red, Dotted, Regal China, Marked, Van Tellingen Copyright, 11 ½ In. 345
Sheriff, Lane, Red Hat, Bulbous Body, Black Shoes, Marked, 11 In. 150

COPELAND SPODE

COPELAND SPODE ENGLAND

Copeland Spode appears on some pieces of nineteenth-century English porcelain. Josiah Spode established a pottery at Stoke-on-Trent, England, in 1770. In 1833, the firm was purchased by William Copeland and Thomas Garrett and the mark was changed. In 1847, Copeland became the sole owner and the mark changed again. W.T. Copeland & Sons continued until a 1976 merger when it became Royal Worcester Spode. The company was bought by the Portmeirion Group in 2009. Pieces are listed in this book under the name that appears in the mark. Royal Worcester and Spode have separate listings.

Butter Chip, Reynolds Pattern, Fruit, Flowers, Marked, 3 ⅜ In. 9
Butter Pat, Indian Tree, Orange, Tan, Brown, Gold & Red Orange Borders, 3 ⅓ In. 15
Cheese Dish, Dome Lid, Finial, Raised Leaves, Gilt Trim, Copeland, 13 x 12 ½ In. 25
Cup & Saucer, Demitasse, Fairy Dell Pattern, Flowers, Marked, 2 ¼ x 4 ¾ In. 32
Figurine, Girl, Seated, Holding Dog, Go To Sleep, J. Durham, Copeland, 1862, 8 In. ....*illus* 112
Inkwell, Lid, Saucer, Cobalt Blue, Gilt, Fluted Edge, Marked, 3 ¼ x 6 ¾ In. 97
Plate, Dinner, Apple Green Border, Gilt, Enamel, Marked, c.1906, 10 In., Set Of 12 813
Plate, Dinner, Flower, Black, 10 ⅜ In., 6 Piece 497
Plate, Dinner, Wicker Lane Pattern, Flowers, Marked, 1933-69, 10 ½ In., 6 Piece 38
Platter, Primrose Pattern, Blue, Marked, Impressed, Copeland, c.1881, 17 x 13 ¾ In. 86
Platter, Spode's Tower Pattern, Bridge, Trees, Blue, Marked, 1895, 9 ¾ x 6 ¾ In. 45

COPPER

Copper has been used to make utilitarian items, such as teakettles and cooking pans, since the days of the early American colonists. Copper became a popular metal with the Arts & Crafts makers of the early 1900s, and decorative pieces, like desk sets, were made. Copper pieces may also be found in Arts & Crafts, Bradley & Hubbard, Kitchen, Roycroft, and other categories.

Chase Brass and Copper Co., Inc.
1930s

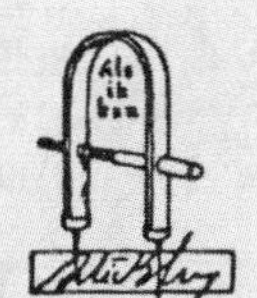

Craftsman Workshop
Mark of Gustav Stickley
c.1900–1915

POTTER STUDIO

Potter Studio
c.1900–1929

Alms Dish, 12 Enamel Appliques Mounted On Border, Gilt, c.1450, 15 In. 5310
Bed Warmer, Sphere, Brown, Pewter, 11 In. 51
Boiler, Lid, Brass, Wooden Handles, c.1900, 17 x 27 x 14 In. ....*illus* 72
Box, Lid, Hammered, Multicolor, Enamel, Peacock, Attributed To Frank Marshall, Early 1900s, 2 x 4 In. 3321
Chafing Dish, Lobster Shape Tripod Supports, Handle, Joseph Heinrichs, Early 1900s, 9 In. .*illus* 608
Chamberstick, Hammered Surface, Eta Shape, Benedict Studios, c.1910, 4 x 5 ¾ In. 47
Charger, Hammered, African Woman, Wearing Neck Rings, Continental, c.1930, 15 ½ In. 123
Figurine, Lobster, Jointed Limbs, Hammered Plates, Signed, Japan, 7 ½ In. 550
Fish Poacher, Rolled Rim, Dovetailed Seams, 2 Handles, Benham & Sons, 1800s, 8 x 24 x 16 In.. 263
Kettle On Stand, Embossed, Cast, Spirit Burner, Handle, Ebony, WMK Co., 13 x 7 In. 320
Kettle, Apple Butter, Dovetailed Construction, Rolled Rim, Bail Handle, c.1810, 28 x 17 In. 322
Kettle, Apple Butter, Dovetailed Seams, Rolled Rim, Iron Bail Handle, 1800s, 17 x 27 In. *illus* 688

Copper, Chafing Dish, Lobster Shape Tripod Supports, Handle, Joseph Heinrichs, Early 1900s, 9 In.
$608

Cowan's Auctions

Copper, Kettle, Apple Butter, Dovetailed Seams, Rolled Rim, Iron Bail Handle, 1800s, 17 x 27 In.
$688

Cowan's Auctions

Copper, Pail, Hammered, Iron Supports, Bail Handle, 7 ½ x 13 In.
$95

Conestoga Auction Company

TIP

Don't cook acid foods in copper pots unless they have a tin lining. The combination of acid and copper creates a poison.

Copper, Teakettle, Gooseneck Spout, Bail Handle, Sawtooth Border, H. Dehuff, Early 1800s, 12 In.
$523

Skinner, Inc.

Copper, Teakettle, Removable Lid, Loop Finial, Hinged Handle, H. Bonner, 1800s, 11 ½ In.
$813

Cowan's Auctions

Copper, Vase, Hammered, Waisted Cylinder, Flared Foot, Frederic J.R. Gyllenberg, c.1910, 8 In.
$369

Skinner, Inc.

Copper, Vase, Lacquered Dinanderie, Eggshell Inlay, Jean Dunand, France, 1920s, 7 x 9 In.
$43,750

Rago Arts and Auction Center

Coralene, Lamp, Fairy, White & Pink, Gilt Fern, 4 ½ In.
$201

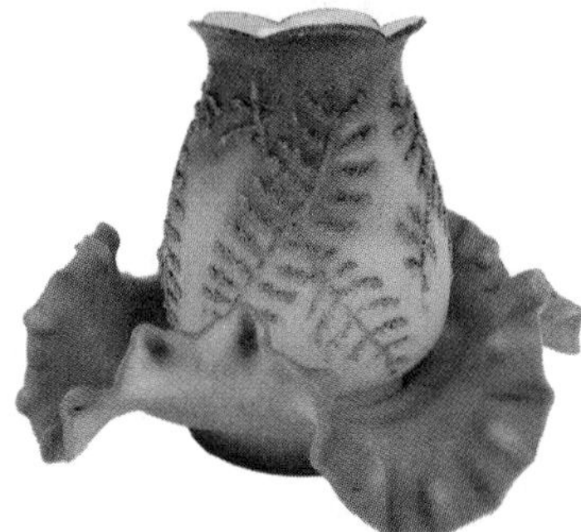

Strawser Auction Group

TIP
Coverlets made before the 1830s were done on a loom that was no more than 40 inches wide. Old coverlets are made of two panels joined at the center seam.

Corkscrew, Iron Shaft, Turned Wood Grip, Brush End, 5 x 5 ½ In.
$62

Hartzell's Auction Gallery Inc.

Coverlet, Jacquard, Center Medallion, Flower Borders, Multicolor, Wool, Cotton, 1850, 93 x 73 In.
$82

Jeffrey S. Evans & Associates

Coverlet, Jacquard, Eagle, Willow Border, Blue, White, Rose Medallions, 1847, 74 x 82 In.
$480

Garth's Auctioneers & Appraisers

Coverlet, Jacquard, Flowers, Stars, Blue, Gold, Red, Bird Border, Simon Riegel, 1869, 72 x 86 In.
$240

Garth's Auctioneers & Appraisers

Kettle, Apple Butter, Rolled Rim, Wrought Iron Bail Handle, c.1800, 20 ½ x 32 In. 413
Kettle, Apple Butter, Rolled Rim, Wrought Iron Handle, 13 ½ x 22 In. 189
Kettle, Dovetailed Construction, Gooseneck, Stamped J. Resor Cincinnati, 1850s, 13 In. 450
Molds are listed in the Kitchen category.
Pail, Hammered, Iron Supports, Bail Handle, 7 ½ x 13 In. *illus* 95
Planter, Floor, Petal Shape Bowl, Domed Foot, Flowers, India, c.1900, 55 In. 625
Teakettle, Gooseneck Spout, Bail Handle, Sawtooth Border, H. Dehuff, Early 1800s, 12 In. *illus* 523
Teakettle, Removable Lid, Loop Finial, Hinged Handle, H. Bonner, 1800s, 11 ½ In. *illus* 813
Vase, 2 Wrought Iron Handles, Pouring Spout, 20 x 10 In. 124
Vase, Hammered, Waisted Cylinder, Flared Foot, Frederic J.R. Gyllenberg, c.1910, 8 In. *illus* 369
Vase, Lacquered Dinanderie, Eggshell Inlay, Jean Dunand, France, 1920s, 7 x 9 In. *illus* 43750

COPPER LUSTER *items are listed in the Luster category.*

CORALENE

Coralene glass was made by firing many small colored beads on the outside of glassware. It was made in many patterns in the United States and Europe in the 1880s. Reproductions are made today. Coralene-decorated Japanese pottery is listed in the Japanese Coralene category.

Lamp, Fairy, White & Pink, Gilt Fern, 4 ½ In. *illus* 201
Vase, Gold Highlights, Blue Flowers, Green Leaves, Orange Background, 1909, 5 In. 320

CORKSCREW

Corkscrews have been needed since the first bottle was sealed with a cork, probably in the seventeenth century. Today collectors search for the early, unusual patented examples or the figural corkscrews of recent years.

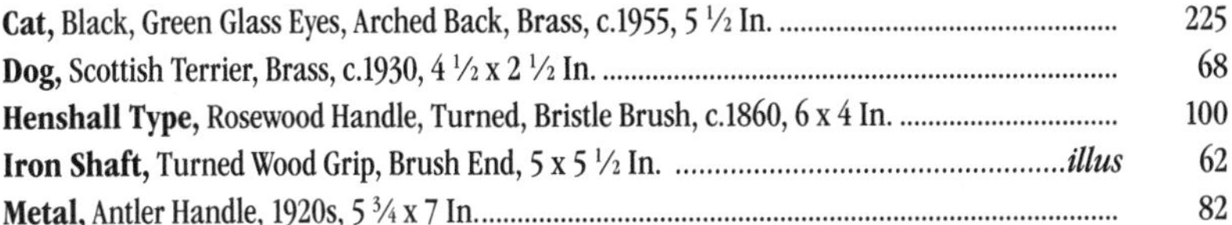

Cat, Black, Green Glass Eyes, Arched Back, Brass, c.1955, 5 ½ In. 225
Dog, Scottish Terrier, Brass, c.1930, 4 ½ x 2 ½ In. 68
Henshall Type, Rosewood Handle, Turned, Bristle Brush, c.1860, 6 x 4 In. 100
Iron Shaft, Turned Wood Grip, Brush End, 5 x 5 ½ In. *illus* 62
Metal, Antler Handle, 1920s, 5 ¾ x 7 In. 82

CORONATION

Coronation souvenirs have been made since the 1800s. Pottery, glass, tin, silver, and paper objects with a picture of the monarchs and date have been sold at many coronations. The pieces that mention King Edward VIII, the king who was never crowned, are not rare; collectors should be sure to check values before buying. Related pieces are found in the Commemorative category.

Beaker, King Edward VIII, Portrait, Crown, Acorns, 1937, 4 ⅜ In. 18
Beaker, Queen Elizabeth II, Bone China, England, 1953, 4 In. 38
Jug, King Edward VII, Queen Alexandra, Blue, Brown, Green, Handle, Silver Rim, 1902, 8 In. 125
Program, Souvenir, King George VI & Queen Elizabeth, May, 1937, 8 ½ x 11 In. 46

COVERLET

Coverlets were made of linen or wool during the nineteenth century. Most of the coverlets date from 1800 to the 1880s. There was a revival of hand weaving in the 1920s and new coverlets, especially geometric patterns, were made. The earliest coverlets were made on narrow looms, so two woven strips were joined together and a seam can be found. The weave structures of coverlets can include summer and winter, double weave, overshot, and others. Jacquard coverlets have elaborate pictorial patterns that are made on a special loom or with the use of a special attachment. Makers often wove a personal message in the corner. Quilts are listed in this book in their own category.

Coverlet, Jacquard, Tree Border, Lions, Blue, Natural, Jefferson Co., N.Y., 2 Panel, 1844, 82 x 89 In.
$1,298

Conestoga Auction Company

Coverlet, Overshot, 3 Colors, Geometric, 2 Panel, Mid 1800s, 74 x 86 In.
$177

Conestoga Auction Company

TIP

Be sure ladders, trash cans, sheds, and cars are not too close to the house. A burglar can use them to climb up to a second-story window.

Cowan, Bookends, Pelican's Head, Black, Silver & Copper Glaze, Jacobson, 5 ½ x 4 ¾ x 2 ⅝ In.
$2,214

Locati Auctions

Cowan, Charger, The Hunt, Fox Hunters, Dogs, Painted, Porcelain, Viktor Schreckengost, 11 In.
$344

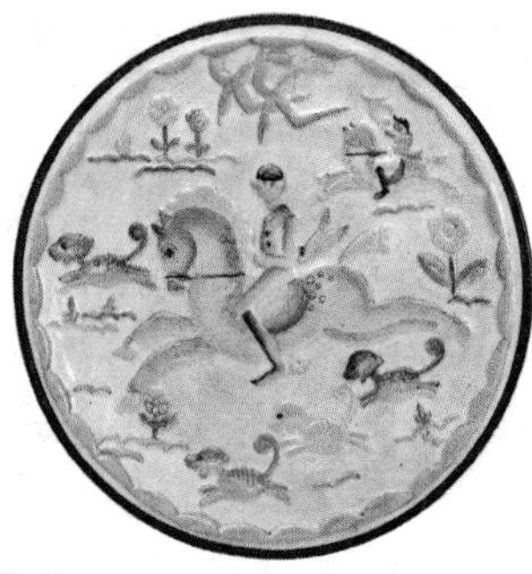

Treadway

Cowan, Figure, Head, Woman, Black Matte Glaze, Square Base, A. Dexter Jacobson, 10 x 3 ½ In.
$358

Treadway

Cracker Jack, Lunch Box, Metal, Aladdin, Thermos Bottle, c.1970, 8 x 7 x 3 ¾ In.
$97

Bruneau & Co. Auctioneers

John Henry Meily (1817–1884)
1842–1850s

Matthew Rattray (1796–1872)
1822–1872

Samuel Stinger (c.1801–1879)
1838–1879

Jacquard, Center Medallion, Flower Borders, Multicolor, Wool, Cotton, 1850, 93 x 73 In. *illus* 82
Jacquard, Eagle, Willow Border, Blue, White, Rose Medallions, 1847, 74 x 82 In. ....*illus* 480
Jacquard, Flowers & Leaves, Blue & Natural, Fringe, c.1850, 74 x 82 In. 147
Jacquard, Flowers, Birds, Navy Blue & Cream, Leah Garrabrant, 1833, N.J., 72 x 91 In............ 413
Jacquard, Flowers, Red, Blue, Green, Cream, J. Heilbronn, Ross Co., Ohio 1842, 72 x 88 In...... 472
Jacquard, Flowers, Stars, Blue, Gold, Red, Bird Border, Simon Riegel, 1869, 72 x 86 In. ..*illus* 240
Jacquard, Geometric, Flowers, Dark Blue, Pink Wool, 2 Panel, c.1890, 93 x 69 In...................... 117
Jacquard, Peace & Plenty 1845, 4 Colors, Fringed Sides, 76 x 89 In. 236
Jacquard, Red, Blue, Cream, Susannah Bayer 1838, Pennsylvania, 82 x 89 In. 531
Jacquard, Stars, Red, Blue, Green, Cream, John Brosey, Manheim, Penn., 1836, 84 x 96 In..... 325
Jacquard, Stars, Red, Peacock Corners, Blue, Green, Cream, Penn., 78 x 95 In.......................... 118
Jacquard, Tiled Sunburst, Flower Border, Blue White, Fringe, Seifert & Co., 89 x 96 In............ 330
Jacquard, Tree Border, Lions, Blue, Natural, Jefferson Co., N.Y., 2 Panel, 1844, 82 x 89 In.... *illus* 1298
Overshot, 3 Colors, Geometric, 2 Panel, Mid 1800s, 74 x 86 In. ....*illus* 177
Overshot, Blue, White, Grid Pattern, Cotton, Early 1800s, 82 x 73 In. 185
Summer & Winter, Blue, White, Birds, Flower Urns, Leaves, Wool, 2 Piece, 1850s, 84 x 88 In. 175
Wool, Blue, Flowers, Yellow Lining, Quilted, Cutout For Bedpost, 1700s, 96 x 92 In. 1476
Wool, Brown, Heart, Flower, Tan Lining, Quilted, 1700s, 88 x 102 In. 1353
Wool, Quilted, Heart, Floral Vine, Tan Lining, Raspberry Calamanco, 1700s, 96 x 86 In.......... 5228

COWAN POTTERY

Cowan Pottery made art pottery and wares for florists. Guy Cowan made pottery in Rocky River, Ohio, a suburb of Cleveland, from 1913 to 1931. A stylized mark with the word *Cowan* was used on most pieces. A commercial, mass-produced line was marked *Lakeware*. Collectors today search for the Art Deco pieces by Guy Cowan, Viktor Schreckengost, Waylande Gregory, Thelma Frazier Winter, and other artists.

Bookends, Pelican's Head, Black, Silver & Copper Glaze, Jacobson, 5 ½ x 4 ¾ x 2 ⅝ In. *.illus* 2214
Candlestick, Female, Nude, Art Nouveau Style, White, Glazed, 12 ¾ x 4 In., Pair..................... 215
Charger, The Hunt, Fox Hunters, Dogs, Painted, Porcelain, Viktor Schreckengost, 11 In. *illus* 344
Figure, Head, Woman, Black Matte Glaze, Square Base, A. Dexter Jacobson, 10 x 3 ½ In. *illus* 358

CRACKER JACK

Cracker Jack, the molasses-flavored popcorn mixture, was first made in 1896 in Chicago, Illinois. A prize was added to each box in 1912. Collectors search for the old boxes, toys, and advertising materials. Many of the toys are unmarked. New toys are usually paper, older toys are tin, paper, or plastic.

Book, Prizes, 1989.. 15
Doll, Dog, Original Box, Vogue, 16 In.. 84
Lunch Box, Metal, Aladdin, Thermos Bottle, c.1970, 8 x 7 x 3 ¾ In. ....*illus* 97

CRANBERRY GLASS

Cranberry glass is an almost transparent yellow-red glass. It resembles the color of cranberry juice. The glass has been made in Europe and America since the Civil War. It is still being made, and reproductions can fool the unwary. Related glass items may be listed in other categories, such as Rubina Verde.

Epergne, 3 Arms, Gold Leaf, Flower Tabs, Ruffled Edge, Italy, 1900s, 17 x 15 x 12 In. 236
Lamp, Banquet, Embossed, Floral Mounts, Brass, Footed, c.1900s, 29 In.................................... 151
Lamp, Diamond & Oval, Pinched Neck, Burner, Thiel & Bardenheuer, c.1900, 7 x 2 x 2 In.. *illus* 176
Lamp, Finger, Cut, Polished Flat Sides, Applied Glass Handle, 1800s, 11 ½ x 5 ¾ In. ....*illus* 113
Lamp, Hall, Swirl Shade, Opalescent, Smoke Bell, Embossed, Brass Frame, 28 x 7 ½ In.......... 151
Lamp, Hurricane, Daisy & Fern, Opalescent, Satin, Brass Base, Fenton, 22 In., Pair................. 384
Vase, Swirled, Ribbon Edge, Multicolor Decoration, Enamel, Footed, 11 x 9 In. ....*illus* 113

CREAMWARE

Creamware, or queensware, was developed by Josiah Wedgwood about 1765. It is a cream-colored earthenware that has been copied by many factories. Similar wares may be listed under Pearlware and Wedgwood.

Bowl, Black Print, Enamel Decorated, Ship, c.1785, 10 ½ In.. 840
Castor, Gourd, Green, Glaze, Circular Base, 4 In.. 83
Dish, Queen Shape, Pink Blossom, Ribbon Tied, Swag Border, c.1807, 13 x 8 ⅝ In.................. 263
Figurine, Monkey, Seated, Brown, Yellow Collar, Leash & Base, Late 1700s, 5 In. 615
Jug, American Ship, Flags, Inscriptions, Western & Eastern Staffs, Staffordshire, c.1807 .*illus* 5280
Jug, Bear, Muzzled, Dog Shape Spout, Translucent Brown Glaze, Staffordshire, c.1770, 9 In..... 1107
Pitcher, Woman, Seated Near Memorial, Flowers, John & Bettey Bennet, 1827, 8 In. ....*illus* 270
Plate, Scalloped, State Of The Nation, Printed In Liverpool, England, c.1778, 9 ¾ In. 2040
Platter, Central Overglaze, Tall Masted Ships, Green Enameling, c.1800, 15 x 12 In. ....*illus* 129
Stirrup Cup, Fox, Realistic Colors, Staffordshire, c.1790, 6 ¾ In. 570
Teapot, Lid, Globular Shape, Molded, Cauliflower Spout, Floral, Transfer, 1750s, 4 In. 211
Teapot, Lid, Globular, Crabstock Handle & Spout, Brown, Green, Blue, c.1765, 5 ½ In. ....*illus* 246
Teapot, Whieldon Type, Molded Lid, Bird Finial, 3 Paw Feet, Staffordshire, 1750s, 4 ½ In... *illus* 308
Tray, Rectangular, Lead Glazed, Loop Handles, Green, Brown, Gray, 1700s, 9 ½ In................. 923
Tureen, Bird Finial, Reticulated Rim & Lid, Footed, 7 ½ x 12 ½ In. ....*illus* 224

CROWN DERBY, *see Royal Crown Derby category.*

CROWN DUCAL

Crown Ducal is the name used on some pieces of porcelain made by A.G. Richardson and Co., Ltd., of Tunstall and Cobridge, England. The name has been used since 1916. Crown Ducal is a well-known maker of chintz pattern dishes. The company was bought by Wedgwood in 1974.

Bowl, Gainsborough, English Garden, Embossed Flowers, 1929, 9 In. 39
Canister, List, Golfers Series, Golfer & Caddie, 1920s, 7 x 6 In.. 288
Jardiniere, Victoria, Chintz, Crownware, 6 ¾ x 8 ⅞ In.. 55
Plate, Empress, Floral Center, Cobalt Blue Band, Gold Design Border, 8 In. 14

CROWN MILANO

Crown Milano glass was made by the Mt. Washington Glass Works about 1890. It was a plain biscuit color with a satin finish decorated with flowers and often had large gold scrolls. Not all pieces are marked.

Jar, Cushion Shape, Ruffled Silver Plate Mounts, Enamel, Flowers, Signed CM, 6 x 7 ½ In... *illus* 283
Perfume Bottle, Silver, Dome Lid, Gilt, Flowers, 2 ½ In. ....*illus* 325
Toothpick Holder, Opal Glass, Red Flowers, Sawtooth Trim, Ruffled Rim, 2 In. 219

CROWN TUSCAN *pattern is included in the Cambridge glass category.*

CRUET

Cruets of glass or porcelain were made to hold vinegar, oil, and other condiments. They were especially popular during Victorian times and have been made in a variety of styles since the eighteenth century. Additional cruets may be found in the Castor Set category and also in various glass categories.

Cranberry Glass, Lamp, Diamond & Oval, Pinched Neck, Burner, Thiel & Bardenheuer, c.1900, 7 x 2 x 2 In.
$176

Jeffrey S. Evans & Associates

Cranberry Glass, Lamp, Finger, Cut, Polished Flat Sides, Applied Glass Handle, 1800s, 11 ½ x 5 ¾ In.
$113

Soulis Auctions

Cranberry Glass, Vase, Swirled, Ribbon Edge, Multicolor Decoration, Enamel, Footed, 11 x 9 In.
$113

Soulis Auctions

Creamware, Jug, American Ship, Flags, Inscriptions, Western & Eastern Staffs, Staffordshire, c.1807
$5,280

Bourgeault-Horan Antiquarians & Associates, LLC

Creamware, Pitcher, Woman, Seated Near Memorial, Flowers, John & Bettey Bennet, 1827, 8 In.
$270

Eldred's

Creamware, Platter, Central Overglaze, Tall Masted Ships, Green Enameling, c.1800, 15 x 12 In.
$129

Jeffrey S. Evans & Associates

Creamware, Teapot, Lid, Globular, Crabstock Handle & Spout, Brown, Green, Blue, c.1765, 5 ½ In.
$246

Skinner, Inc.

Creamware, Teapot, Whieldon Type, Molded Lid, Bird Finial, 3 Paw Feet, Staffordshire, 1750s, 4 ½ In.
$308

Brunk Auctions

Creamware Tureen, Bird Finial, Reticulated Rim & Lid, Footed, 7 ½ x 12 ½ In.
$224

Strawser Auction Group

Crown Milano, Jar, Cushion Shape, Ruffled Silver Plate Mounts, Enamel, Flowers, Signed CM, 6 x 7 ½ In.
$283

Soulis Auctions

TIP
Use denture cleaning tablets to remove a stain from a ceramic teapot. Follow the directions for use with false teeth.

Crown Milano, Perfume Bottle, Silver, Dome Lid, Gilt, Flowers, 2 ½ In.
$325

Strawser Auction Group

Cobalt Blue Glass, Kings 500 Pattern, Stopper Plug, Clear Cabochon, 7 ½ In. 180
Cut Glass, Silver, Shell Foot, George John Richards & Edward Charles Brown, 1866, 7 In. 163
Vaseline Glass, Tricorner Spout, Opalescent, Frosted, Green Stripe, Stopper, 6 In. .... *illus* 240

CT GERMANY

CT Germany was first part of a mark used by a company in Altwasser, Germany (now part of Walbrzych, Poland), in 1845. The initials stand for C. Tielsch, a partner in the firm. The Hutschenreuther firm took over the company in 1918 and continued to use the *CT* until 1952.

Cake Plate, Pink Roses, Scalloped Edge, Cutout Handles, 10 In. 30
Mustache Cup, Saucer, Flowers, Leaves, Bows, White Ground, c.1880 35
Sugar & Creamer, Violets, White Ground, Gold Handles & Finial, Signed E.M.B. 131

CUP PLATE

Cup plates are small glass or china plates that held the cup while a diner of the mid-nineteenth century drank coffee or tea from the saucer. The most famous cup plates were made of glass at the Boston and Sandwich factory located in Sandwich, Massachusetts. There have been many new glass cup plates made in recent years for sale to gift shops or collectors of limited editions. These are similar to the old plates but can be recognized as new.

Opalescent, Even Scallop, Rose, New England, 1828-35, 3 In. 293
Redware, Slip Decorated, Coggled Rim, Pennsylvania, 3 In. 384

CURRIER & IVES

Currier & Ives made the famous American lithographs marked with their name from 1857 to 1907. The mark used on the print included the street address in New York City, and it is possible to date the year of the original issue from this information. Earlier prints were made by N. Currier and use that name from 1835 to 1847. Many reprints of the Currier or Currier & Ives prints have been made. Some collectors buy the insurance calendars that were based on the old prints. The words *large, small,* or *medium folio* refer to size. The original print sizes were very small (up to about 7 x 9 in.), small (8 ⅘ x 12 ⅘ in.), medium (9 x 14 in. to 14 x 20 in.), and large (larger than 14 x 20 in.). Other sizes are probably later copies. Copies of prints by Currier & Ives may be listed in Card, Advertising and in the Sheet Music category. Currier & Ives dinnerware patterns may be found in the Adams or Dinnerware categories.

Ethan Allen, Mate, Dexter, In Their Wonderful Race, 1867, 21 x 30 In. 1020
Four Seasons Of Life, Old Age, 1868, Frame, 15 ½ x 23 ¾ In. 375
Great Horse In A Great Race, Lithograph, Black Wood Frame, 27 ½ x 37 ½ In. .... *illus* 277
Looking Down The Yo-Semite, 12 x 16 In. 375
New York Bay, From Bay Ridge, L.I., 1860, Frame, 15 ¾ x 20 In. 413
On The Coast Of California, 1850s, Frame, 11 x 15 In. 405
Pacing For A Grand Purse, Horse Race, 1890, 20 ½ x 29 ½ In. 354
Queen Of The Turf, Maud S., Horse, Driver & Sulky, 1880, 25 x 33 In. 472
Tempting The Baby, Mother, Grandmother With Apple, 1866, 12 x 15 ½ In. 219
The Riverside, 2 People Fishing, 12 ¼ x 15 ¾ In. 156
View Of New York From Brooklyn Heights, 1849, 11 ½ x 17 In. 1063
Village Blacksmith, 1864, Giltwood Frame, 16 x 23 ⅜ In. 1250

CUSTARD GLASS

Custard glass is a slightly yellow opaque glass. It was made in England in the 1880s and was first made in the United States in the 1890s. It has been reproduced. Additional pieces may be found in the Cambridge, Fenton, and Heisey categories. Custard glass is called *Ivorina Verde* by Heisey and other companies.

Cruet, Vaseline Glass, Tricorner Spout, Opalescent, Frosted, Green Stripe, Stopper, 6 In.
$240

Woody Auctions

Currier & Ives, Great Horse In A Great Race, Lithograph, Black Wood Frame, 27 ½ x 37 ½ In.
$277

Skinner, Inc.

Cut Glass, Butter, Starburst, Diamond & Fan, Knob Handle, 7 ½ In.
$150

Richard D. Hatch & Associates

This is an edited listing of current prices. Visit **Kovels.com** to check thousands of prices from previous years and sign up for free information on trends, tips, reproductions, marks, and more.

C

Cut Glass, Compote, Neoclassical Style, Gilt Bronze Mount, Lion Drawn Chariot, 1800s, 9 x 9 5/8 In.
$600

Neal Auction Company

Cut Glass, Compote, Opaque White, Cranberry, Oval Cuts, Trumpet Stem, Bohemia, 1860s, 10 x 7 x 5 In.
$82

Jeffrey S. Evans & Associates

Cut Glass, Dresser Box, Sterling Silver Mount, Brilliant Period, 4 x 8 In.
$115

Blackwell Auctions

TIP
A signature adds 25 percent to the value of cut glass.

Lamp, Fall Leaves, Bell Shape Base, Krone Krystal Chimney, Korner & Co., c.1900, 7 In. 380
Maize is its own category in this book.

CUT GLASS

Cut glass has been made since ancient times, but the large majority of the pieces now for sale date from the American Brilliant period of glass design, 1875 to 1915. These pieces have elaborate geometric designs with a deep miter cut. Modern cut glass with a similar appearance is being made in England, Ireland, Poland, the Czech Republic, and Slovakia. Chips and scratches are often difficult to notice but lower the value dramatically. A signature on the glass, usually on the smooth inside of a bowl, adds significantly to the value. Other cut glass pieces are listed under factory names, like Hawkes, Libbey, Pairpoint, Sinclaire, and Stevens & Williams.

Basket, Bouquet, Double Thumbprint Handle, Sawtooth Rim, Circular Base, 13 x 10 x 5 In. ... 138
Biscuit Jar, Flute Pattern, Grapes & Leaves, Silver Plate Lid, 6 1/2 In. ... 84
Bowl, Amethyst To Clear, Saw Rim, Snowflakes Border, Pedestal Base, Irena, 10 1/2 x 11 In. ... 154
Bowl, Center, Oval, Clear, 4 x 14 In. ... 168
Bowl, Center, Scalloped Hobstar Foot, Faceted Knob Stem, c.1910, 9 x 12 In. ... 275
Bowl, Clear, Ruffled Rim, Pedestal Base, 7 x 14 In. ... 390
Bowl, Oval, Folded, Russian Pattern, Hobstar Center, Dorflinger, 3 x 10 x 8 In. ... 90
Bowl, Scalloped Rim, Fan, Flowers, 4 Panels, 10 x 3 In. ... 345
Bowl, Teardrops, Starburst, Trailing, Ruffled Rim, 8 In. ... 184
Butter, Starburst, Diamond & Fan, Knob Handle, 7 1/2 In. ... *illus* 150
Cachepot, Glass Bowl, Ormolu Rim, Paw Foot Base, Napoleon III, 1800s, 5 1/2 x 5 3/4 In., 2 Piece 325
Candlestick, Notched Prism, Strawberry Diamond Band, Hobstar, 8-Sided Foot, 14 In. ... 120
Carafe, Hobstar, Vesica, Cane, Strawberry Diamond, Prism, Star & Fan, 8 1/2 In. ... 240
Carafe, Nordica Pattern, Hobstar Base, Blackmer, 8 In. ... 400
Celery Tray, Gondola Shape, Persian, Scalloped Rim, 4 x 10 In. ... 72
Claret Jug, Hinged Lid, Hobnail, Floral Repousse Silver Mount, c.1900, 11 In. ... 800
Claret Jug, Star & Fan, Silver Mounted, 84 Zolotnik Mark, St. Petersburg, c.1908, 8 In. ... 700
Claret Jug, Sterling Silver, Mounted, Edward VII, Hukin & Heath Ltd., 1907-08, 8 1/2 In. ... 400
Compote, Neoclassical Style, Gilt Bronze Mount, Lion Drawn Chariot, 1800s, 9 x 9 5/8 In. *illus* 600
Compote, Opaque White, Cranberry, Oval Cuts, Trumpet Stem, Bohemia, 1860s, 10 x 7 x 5 In.... *illus* 82
Cordial, Clear, White Air Twist Stem, Engraved Stag, Scenic, Continental, 6 In. ... 150
Decanter, Bell Shape, Electra, 2 Notched Handles, Ray Base, Straus, 8 3/4 In. ... 175
Dish, Flower Shape, 8 Petals, Hobstar, 9 1/2 In. ... 518
Dish, Shell Shape, Prism Cut, 6 1/2 In. ... 150
Dresser Box, Intaglio, Floral Basket Lid, Geometric Highlights, 3 1/2 x 6 In. ... 70
Dresser Box, Sterling Silver Mount, Brilliant Period, 4 x 8 In. ... *illus* 115
Dresser Jar, Art Nouveau, Silver Lid, Woman's Face, Poppies, Unger Bros., 3 1/2 x 5 In. ... 400
Egg, Emerald Green, Gilt Metal Stand, Russia, 4 3/4 In. ... 1033
Epergne, Silver Plate Tree Trunk, Grapevines, Mappin & Webb, 34 x 16 In., 10 Piece ... 3540
Ewer, Cranberry, Cut Overlay, Opaque White, Footed, Handle, 1850s, 12 1/2 In. ... *illus* 351
Flask, Milk Glass, Enamel Decoration, Victorian Woman, Flowers, Fruit, Lid, c.1875, 8 In. *illus* 140
Inkwell, Carved Swirl, Sterling Silver Lid, Repousse, c.1900, 6 x 4 1/2 In. ... 489
Jug, Hobstar, Cane, Strawberry Diamond, Fan, Notched Handle, 4 3/4 In. ... 84
Knife Rest, Cased Cranberry, 4 In. ... 210
Ladle, Cranberry To Colorless, Montrose Handle, Dorflinger Glass Co., c.1900, 14 1/2 In. ... 3042
Lamp Base, Urn, Baluster Shape, Brass Handle & Base, Early 1900s, 38 1/2 In. ... 150
Lamp, Boudoir, Cambria, Prism, Dome Shade, Egginton, 15 x 7 1/2 In. ... 420
Lamp, Butterfly & Floral Shade, Crystal Prism, Electric, 12 x 6 1/2 In. ... 207
Lamp, Mushroom Shade, Hobstar Vesicas, Cane, Prism, Fan, 22 1/2 x 12 In., Pair ... 1100
Lamp, Strawberry Diamond, Convex Ribs, Pedestal Base, Clear, Everede & Co, c.1900, 11 x 4 In. 2223
Pitcher, Hobstar & Fan, Floral, Silver Rim, 3-Initial Monogram, Handle, 9 7/8 In. ... 142
Pitcher, Prism Body, Ray Base, Sterling Silver Spout, c.1910, 6 3/4 In. ... 50
Pitcher, Silver Plate Handle, Lid, Spout, 11 1/2 In. ... 48
Pitcher, Thistle, Thumbprint Handle, 6 x 9 x 4 1/2 In. ... 58

SELECTED CUT GLASS MARKS WITH DATES USED

J.D. Bergen & Co.
1885–1922
Meriden, Conn.

Tuthill Cut Glass Co.
1902–1923
Middletown, N.Y.

Pairpoint Corporation
1880–1938
New Bedford, Mass.

Libbey Glass Co.
1888–1925
Toledo, Ohio

C. Dorflinger & Sons
1852–1921
White Mills, Pa.

T.B. Clark and Co.
1884–1930
Honesdale, Pa.

Majestic Cut Glass Co.
1900–1916
Elmira, N.Y.

Wright Rich Cut Glass Co.
1904–1915
Anderson, Ind.

T.G. Hawkes & Co.
1880–1962
Corning, N.Y.

H.C. Fry Glass Co.
1901–1934
Rochester, Pa.

H.P. Sinclaire & Co.
1905–1929
Corning, N.Y.

House of Birks
c.1894–1907+
Montreal, Quebec, Canada

Laurel Cut Glass Co.
1903–1920
Jarmyn, Pa.

J. Hoare & Co.
1868–1921
Corning, N.Y.

L. Straus & Sons
c.1894–1917
New York, N.Y.

C

Cut Glass, Ewer, Cranberry, Cut Overlay, Opaque White, Footed, Handle, 1850s, 12 ½ In.
$351

Jeffrey S. Evans & Associates

Cut Glass, Flask, Milk Glass, Enamel Decoration, Victorian Woman, Flowers, Fruit, Lid, c.1875, 8 In.
$140

Jeffrey S. Evans & Associates

Cut Glass, Plate, Colorless, Scalloped Edge, Trellis, Acid Stamped, Egginton, 1810s, 7 In.
$644

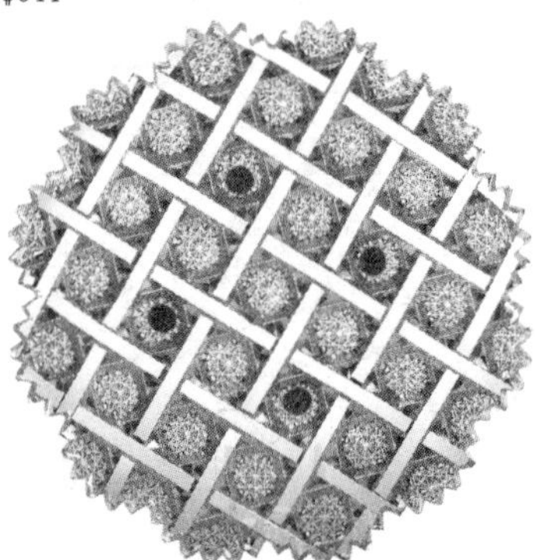

Jeffrey S. Evans & Associates

Cut Glass, Tray, Ruby To Colorless, Intaglio, Scalloped Edge, c.1900, 12 ½ In.
$2,457

Jeffrey S. Evans & Associates

Cut Glass, Vase, 5 Panels, Hobstar, Hobnail, Circular, Sawtooth Rim Base, 14 In.
$518

Stevens Auction Co.

Cut Glass, Wine, Hob Diamond, Cranberry To Clear, Faceted Knob, Ray Foot, 5 In., Pair
$800

Woody Auctions

Cybis, Figurine, Bull, Head Up, On Bended Knees, Bisque Porcelain, Wood Base, 11 x 16 x 7 In.
$188

Kamelot Auctions

Cybis, Figurine, Madonna Bust, Bird On Her Hand, 11 ½ x 7 ¾ In.
$90

Woody Auctions

Cybis, Sculpture, Eagle, Perched, 22 ½ x 10 In.
$156

Kamelot Auctions

Plate, Colorless, Scalloped Edge, Trellis, Acid Stamped, Egginton, 1810s, 7 In. ....*illus* 644
Plate, Heart Shape, Hobstar, Fan, Owl Face, 7 In. 60
Powder Jar, Silver Lid, Hobstar, Crosscut Diamond, Prism, Fan, Ray Cut Base, 3 ½ x 4 ½ In. . 72
Punch Bowl, Intaglio, Schooner Montauk Sailing, Sea Gulls Flying, c.1900, 9 x 15 ¾ In. 2691
Punch Bowl, Lid, Cut To Clear, White, Footed, Gilt, Bohemian, 15 x 9 ⅜ In. 150
Rose Bowl, Geometric Diamonds, Fan Design, Notched Rim, Hobstar Base, 5 x 7 In. 125
Tankard, Hobstar, Strawberry Diamond, Fan, Double Notched Handle, Ray Cut Base, 11 In. ... 60
Tray, Hobstar, Cane, Strawberry Diamond, Zipper & Fan, 12 In. 240
Tray, Ice Cream, Propeller, Marshall Field, Sawtooth Rim, 14 x 8 In. 295
Tray, Ruby To Colorless, Intaglio, Scalloped Edge, c.1900, 12 ½ In. ....*illus* 2457
Vase, 5 Panels, Hobstar, Hobnail, Circular, Sawtooth Rim Base, 14 In. ....*illus* 518
Vase, Amber, Cut To Clear, Engraved Stag, Forest, Scenic, Round Base, Bohemian, 9 In. 80
Vase, Black Amethyst, Clear, Footed, Bill Healy, 21 x 7 ⅞ In. 295
Vase, Cornucopia, Diamond Cut, Ornate Metal, Mythical Creatures, Birks, 1900s, 19 x 12 In. .. 556
Vase, Lead Crystal, Queen Elizabeth, Crown Shape Rim, Wood Base, 12 ⅜ In. 201
Vase, Lid, Yellow, Faceted Finial, Alternate Panel, Brunswick Stars, Footed, 1900s, 18 In. 472
Vase, Ruby To Clear, Sawtooth Rim, Fan, Buzz, Hobstar, 19 x 8 ½ In. 316
Vase, Square Shape, Harvard & Daisy Pattern, Flowers, Etched, 4 x 4 x 10 In. 83
Vase, Strawberry Diamond, Prism, Notched Fan, Hobstar Foot, 10 In. 420
Wine, Hob Diamond, Cranberry To Clear, Faceted Knob, Ray Foot, 5 In., Pair ....*illus* 800

CYBIS

CYBIS

Cybis porcelain is a twentieth-century product. Boleslaw Cybis came to the United States from Poland in 1939. He started making porcelains in Long Island, New York, in 1940. He moved to Trenton, New Jersey, in 1942 as one of the founders of Cordey China Co. and started his own company, Cybis Porcelains, about 1950. Boleslaw died in 1957. It appears Cybis made porcelains until the 1990s and old ones are still selling.

Figurine, Bull, Head Up, On Bended Knees, Bisque Porcelain, Wood Base, 11 x 16 x 7 In. *illus* 188
Figurine, Madonna Bust, Bird On Her Hand, 11 ½ x 7 ¾ In. ....*illus* 90
Sculpture, Eagle, Perched, 22 ½ x 10 In. ....*illus* 156

CZECHOSLOVAKIA

PEASANT ART INDUSTRY MADE IN CZECHOSLOVAKIA

Czechoslovakia is a popular term with collectors. The name, first used as a mark after the country was formed in 1918, appears on glass and porcelain and other decorative items. Although Czechoslovakia split into Slovakia and the Czech Republic on January 1, 1993, the name continues to be used in some trademarks.

CZECHOSLOVAKIA GLASS

Perfume Atomizer, Frosted, White Ground, Pink & Mauve Scene, Marked, 5 ½ In. 80
Perfume Bottle, Colorless, Vaseline, Figural Dabber, Art Deco, Hoffman, c.1925, 6 ½ x 5 In. *illus* 819
Vase, Trumpet, Lime Green, Cobalt Blue Rim, Round Base, 12 ⅜ x 8 In. ....*illus* 266

CZECHOSLOVAKIA POTTERY

Vase, Molded, Basket Shape, Lid, Child Side, Flowers, 10 ¾ x 6 x 6 In. 68
Vase, Portrait, 2 Women, Handles, Pearlized White Ground, Marked, Victoria, 11 ¾ In. ..*illus* 24

DANIEL BOONE

Daniel Boone, a pre–Revolutionary War folk hero, was a surveyor, trapper, and frontiersman. A television series, which ran from 1964 to 1970, was based on his life and starred Fess Parker. All types of Daniel Boone memorabilia are collected.

Book, Life & Times Of Col. Daniel Boone, Cecil Hartley, 1865, 7 x 5 In. 21
Doll, Cloth, Coonskin Hat, Jacket, c.1970, 26 In. 75
Match Safe, 29th Natl. Encpt, Louisville, Daniel Boone, Stamped, Brass, 1895, 3 In. 985

Czechoslovakia Glass, Perfume Bottle, Colorless, Vaseline, Figural Dabber, Art Deco, Hoffman, c.1925, 6 ½ x 5 In.
$819

Jeffrey S. Evans & Associates

Czechoslovakia Glass, Vase, Trumpet, Lime Green, Cobalt Blue Rim, Round Base, 12 ⅜ x 8 In.
$266

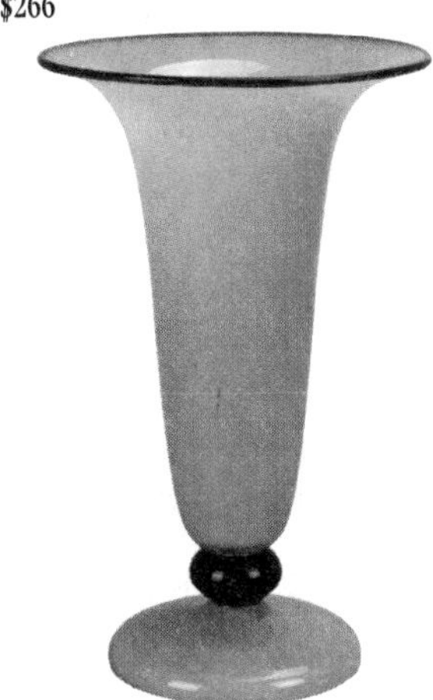

Bunch Auctions

Czechoslovakia Pottery, Vase, Portrait, 2 Women, Handles, Pearlized White Ground, Marked, Victoria, 11 ¾ In.
$24

Woody Auctions

D

Daum, Bowl, Clear, Pate-De-Verre, Green & Purple Iris Covered Base, Box, 4 x 10 ½ In.
$1,375

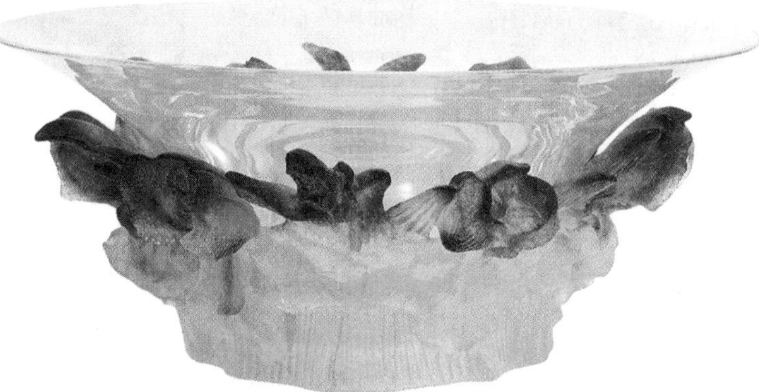

Abington Auction Gallery

Daum, Bowl, Dutch Waterscape, Grisaille, Multicolor, Flowers, 1895-1920, 6 x 10 x 8 In.
$2,952

Skinner, Inc.

Daum, Bowl, Pate-De-Verre, Crystal, Yellow & Purple Glass, Footed, Late 1900s, 4 ⅞ x 8 ½ In.
$374

Blackwell Auctions

Daum, Box, Lid, Fuchsia Blossoms, Leaves, Enameled, White To Violet, Cameo, Signed, 2 ½ x 3 In.
$819

Morphy Auctions

Daum, Figurine, Young Woman, Flowing Gown, Amber, Pate-De-Verre, 10 x 5 In.
$390

Morphy Auctions

Daum, Plate, Pate-De-Verre Royal Blue, Gilt, Salvador Dali, c.1950, 1 x 10 ½ In.
$154

Skinner, Inc.

Spoon, Old Kentucky Home, United We Stand, Mechanics Sterling, 5 In. 33
Spoon, Sterling Silver, Bust, State Seal, Gorham, 5 ½ In. 44

D'ARGENTAL

D'Argental is a mark used in France by the Compagnie des Cristalleries de St. Louis. The firm made multilayered, acid-cut cameo glass in the late nineteenth and twentieth centuries. Cameo glass was made with the D'Argental mark from 1919 to 1925. D'Argental is the French name for the city of Munzthal, home of the glassworks. Later the company made enameled etched glass.

Vase, Flowers, Leaves, Orange & Brown, Yellow Ground, 13 In. 1107

DAUM

Daum, a glassworks in Nancy, France, was started by Jean Daum in 1878. The company, now called *Cristalleries de Nancy,* is still working. The *Daum Nancy* mark has been used in many variations. The name of the city and the artist are usually both included. The term *martele* is used to describe applied decorations that are carved or etched in the cameo process.

Daum 1890 | Daum 1960–1971 | Daum 1960–1971

Bowl, Clear, Pate-De-Verre, Green & Purple Iris Covered Base, Box, 4 x 10 ½ In. ....*illus* 1375
Bowl, Dutch Waterscape, Grisaille, Multicolor, Flowers, 1895-1920, 6 x 10 x 8 In. ....*illus* 2952
Bowl, Frog On Lily Pad, Pate-De-Verre, Multicolor, Script Sign, 2 x 6 In. 354
Bowl, Pate-De-Verre, Crystal, Yellow & Purple Glass, Footed, Late 1900s, 4 ⅞ x 8 ½ In. ...*illus* 374
Box, Cut Edges, Riverscapes, Gilt, Flowers, 1895-1920, 3 x 5 x 4 ½ In. 1968
Box, Lid, Fuchsia Blossoms, Leaves, Enameled, White To Violet, Cameo, Signed, 2 ½ x 3 In. *illus* 819
Chandelier, Inverted Dome Shade, Mottled Green, Yellow, Floral, Cast Metal Arms, 31 x 14 In. 2160
Dish, Lid, Flowers, Orange, Cameo, 3 x 5 ½ In. 1250
Figurine, Bird, Clear Glass, Pate-De-Verre, Marked Underside, 6 ½ In. 151
Figurine, Chat Russe, Russian Cat, Blue Pate-De-Verre, Grand Modele, 6 x 2 ½ x 4 In. 283
Figurine, Proton, Abstract Face, Yellow, Pate-De-Verre, Paolo Santini, 12 In. 472
Figurine, Puffin, Clear Glass, Amber & Lavender Bill, c.1970, 8 ¾ In. 225
Figurine, Young Woman, Flowing Gown, Amber, Pate-De-Verre, 10 x 5 In. ....*illus* 390
Flask, Flower Sprays, Gilt, Enamel, Green Ground, Silver Cap, 6 In. 720
Hand Mirror, 2-Sided, Floral Bronze Surround, Foil Inclusion Handle, Sign, 12 ½ x 5 In. 708
Lamp, Electric, 2 Herons, Green, White Umbrella Shade, Pate-De-Verre, 20 x 8 In. 1375
Lamp, Electric, Floral Decorated Shade, Cameo, Signed, 15 In. 1574
Lamp, Wrought Iron, Patinated Metal, Engraved, Edgar Brandt, 1900s, 25 x 14 ½ In. 4688
Lamp, Wrought Iron, Wheel Carved, Signed, c.1920, 63 x 9 ¾ In. 4375
Perfume Bottle, Amethyst, Green, Yellow, Iris Pate-De-Verre Stopper, Frosted, 1950s, 8 In. 199
Perfume Bottle, Stopper, Amber To Turquoise, Clear Body, Pate-De-Verre, 11 ½ In. 400
Plate, Pate-De-Verre Royal Blue, Gilt, Salvador Dali, c.1950, 1 x 10 ½ In. ....*illus* 154
Rose Bowl, Pink, Gilt, Country Roads, Lake, Ducks, Trefoil Mouth, c.1900, 4 In. ....*illus* 1287
Sculpture, 2 Figures, Gilt Eye, Crown, Pate-De-Verre, Jose Aurelio, 15 x 13 In. 2519
Sculpture, Horse Head, Andalusian, Amber To Green, Pate-De-Verre, Marked, 9 x 9 In. ..*illus* 923
Sculpture, Peacock, Fanning Tail, Pate-De-Verre, Multicolor, Guy Petitfils, 14 x 12 In. 1260
Sculpture, Toucan, Pate-De-Verre, Amber Beak, Frosted Face, Clear Body, France, 9 ½ In. 431
Tray, Frog, Lily, Pate-De-Verre, Box, Signed, 6 x 5 ½ x 1 ¾ In. ....*illus* 176
Trinket Box, Fuchsia, Pink Cameo Glass, 3 ½ In. 266
Vase, Amaryllis, Blue To Green To Yellow, Trumpet Shape, Pate-De-Verre, 24 x 12 In. 7820
Vase, Aquarium, Etched, Fish, Reef Plants, Oval Shape, Green, 14 ¾ x 7 In. 2000
Vase, Bacchus Face, Grapes, Pate-De-Verre, Aquamarine To Amethyst, 14 x 8 In. 770

Daum, Rose Bowl, Pink, Gilt, Country Roads, Lake, Ducks, Trefoil Mouth, c.1900, 4 In.
$1,287

Jeffrey S. Evans & Associates

Daum, Sculpture, Horse Head, Andalusian, Amber To Green, Pate-De-Verre, Marked, 9 x 9 In.
$923

Clars Auction Gallery

Daum, Tray, Frog, Lily, Pate-De-Verre, Box, Signed, 6 x 5 ½ x 1 ¾ In.
$176

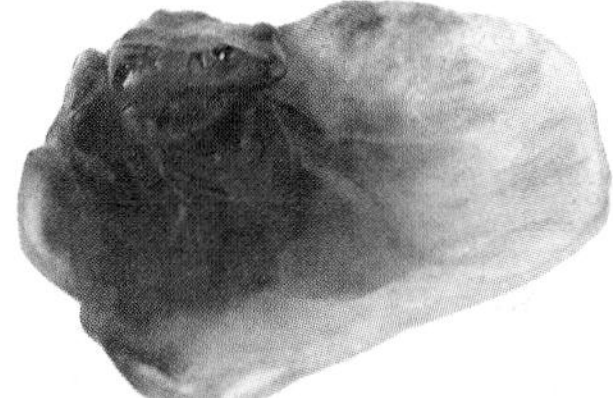

Cordier Auctions

TIP

Sunny windows are the enemy of antiques. Textiles and wood will fade; glass sometimes breaks from the heat.

TIP
In case of a major theft, keep careful records. You may be able to deduct part of the uninsured loss from your income tax.

D

Daum, Vase, Classical Style Figures, Black Cut To Orange, Cameo, Marked Underside, 6 In.
$512

Clars Auction Gallery

Daum, Vase, Pillow, Amber Ground, Brown, White, Winter, Cameo, c.1900, 5 x 2 ½ x 4 ¾ In.
$2,340

Jeffrey S. Evans & Associates

Decoy, Black Duck, Glass Eyes, Swimming Position, Marty Collins, 1900s, 20 ½ In.
$480

Eldred's

Vase, Blue, Iron, Mounted, Majorelle, 10 ½ x 9 In. 1230
Vase, Bud, Yellow To Brown, Flowers, Spider Webs, Leaves, Signed, c.1925, 6 ½ In. 1620
Vase, Classical Style Figures, Black Cut To Orange, Cameo, Marked Underside, 6 In. *illus* 512
Vase, Etched, 4 Vignettes, Riverscape, Cabochon, 1895-1920, 5 In. 4305
Vase, Flowers, Leaves, Brown, Orange, White, Enamel, c.1950, 24 x 7 In. 3500
Vase, Gorgonia, Yellow Green, Pate-De-Verre, Christian Ghion, 13 In. 1500
Vase, Leafless Trees, Snow, Orange Sky, Lobed Rim, Dimples, Enamel, 3 ¾ x 5 In. 2625
Vase, Metal Mounted, Iron, Engraved, Signed, L Majorelle, c.1900, 10 x 10 ½ In. 2125
Vase, Multicolor, Mounted, Silver Base, Cameo, 6 ¼ In. 1722
Vase, Orchid, Amethyst Rim, Purple, Blue, Foil Inclusions, Signed, 12 x 9 In. 3250
Vase, Oval, Cylindrical, Coral Bells, Cameo, 12 In. 1140
Vase, Pillow, Amber Ground, Brown, White, Winter, Cameo, c.1900, 5 x 2 ½ x 4 ¾ In. *illus* 2340
Vase, Scenic, Spring Landscape, Flowers, Trees, Enamel, Cylindrical, 4 x 2 In. 512
Vase, Tree, Field, Green, Yellow, Acid Etched, Enamel, France, c.1900, 13 ½ x 4 In. 6875
Vase, Trumpet, Square Base, Clear Amber Glass Ribs, Signed, 16 ½ x 12 x 12 In. 1800
Vase, Woodland Lake Scene, Brown, Green, Yellow Ground, Cameo, 7 ⅝ In. 726
Wine, Round Foot, Nose & Mouth Shaped Stem, Ruby Red, Salvador Dali, 10 ½ In., Pair 510

DAVENPORT

Davenport pottery and porcelain were made at the Davenport factory in Longport, Staffordshire, England, from 1793 to 1887. Earthenwares, creamwares, porcelains, ironstone, and other ceramics were made. Most of the pieces are marked with a form of the word *Davenport.*

Bowl, Gray & Gold Leaves, 9 ½ x 7 ½ In. 165
Bowl, Vegetable, Lid, Italian Veranda, Couple Courting, 6 x 12 ½ x 9 ½ In. 135
Compote, Dish, Rectangular, Gold Gilt, Grape Leaves, Flowers, c.1800, 11 x 8 In., Pair 400
Plate, Queen's Rose, Center Rose, Decorative Border, White Ground, 10 In. 250
Platter, Dragons, Red & Blue, Double Border, Blue & White Greek Keys, 9 x 7 In. 250
Soup, Dish, Stork, Chinoiserie, Flowers, Blue & Brown, c.1815, 9 ½ In. 145

DAVY CROCKETT

Davy Crockett, the American frontiersman, was born in 1786 and died in 1836. The historical character gained new fame in 1954 when the Walt Disney television show ran a series of episodes featuring Fess Parker as Davy Crockett. Coonskin caps and buckskins became popular and hundreds of different Davy Crockett items were made.

Booklet, Lyrics, Sheet Music, King Of The Wild Frontier, 1955, 9 x 12 In. 302
Game, Indian Target Set, Wood, Keystone 112
Plate, Souvenir, Fess Parker As Davy Crockett, Disneyland, c.1955, 10 in. 515

DE MORGAN

De Morgan art pottery was made in England by William De Morgan from the 1860s to 1907. He is best known for his luster-glazed Moorish-inspired pieces. The pottery used a variety of marks.

Tile, Flamingo, Pink Luster, Leafy Ground, c.1880, 6 In. 3762
Vase, Dome Lid, Peacocks, Legendary Dragons, Dolphins, Bands, 13 In. 12500

DE VEZ

De Vez was a signature used on cameo glass after 1910. E. S. Monot founded the glass company near Paris in 1851. The company changed names many times. Mt. Joye, another glass by this factory, is listed in its own category.

Bell, Daisies, Leaves, Shades Of Red, Etched, Bronze Attachment, c.1920, 10 x 7 In. 718
Vase, Bats Flying, Mountains, Lake, Rising Sun, Dark Red, Yellow, White Frost, 8 In. 938

DECORATED TUMBLERS *may be listed by maker or design or in Advertising, Coca-Cola, Pepsi-Cola, Sports, and other categories.*

DECOY

Decoys are carved or turned wooden copies of birds, fish, or animals. The decoy was placed in the water or propped on the shore to lure flying birds to the pond for hunters. Some decoys are handmade; some are commercial products. Today there is a group of artists making modern decoys for display, not for use in a pond. Many sell for high prices.

Black Duck, Carved, Driftwood Base, Wendell Gilley, Maine, 1900s, 4 ½ In. 900
Black Duck, Glass Eyes, Swimming Position, Marty Collins, 1900s, 20 ½ In. ....*illus* 480
Black Duck, Head Turned Right, Feather Details, Hollow, Glass Eyes, Marty Collins, 15 In. *illus* 594
Black Duck, Hollow, Glass Eyes, Head Turned Slightly Left, Ron Marino, 1900s, 16 In. 192
Black Duck, Painted, Wood, Lead Keel, Signed, R. Madison Mitchell, 1984, 8 x 18 In. 406
Bufflehead Drake, Preening, Marty Collins, 1900s, 10 In. ....*illus* 480
Canada Goose, Black & White, Painted, Mark Buck, 1988, 12 ½ In. 152
Canada Goose, Black Head, White Cheeks, Black Wings, Tan Breast, White Tail, 24 In. 445
Canada Goose, Carved, Painted, Black & White, James Gatreau, Lossier Settlement, c.1950, 26 ½ In. 246
Canada Goose, Feeding, Black Head, Tail, White Body, Early 1900s, 22 ½ In. 492
Canada Goose, Flying, Wood Body, Wire Frame, Black Metal Stand, Tuveson Mfg. Co., 24 x 15 In. 468
Canada Goose, Gunning, Carved Wood Body, Bulbous, Painted, Maryland, c.1940-50, 12 x 24 In. .. 375
Canada Goose, Painted, Carved, Wood, Gary Crossman, 29 ½ In. ....*illus* 325
Canada Goose, Stretched Canvas Body, Wood Carved, Painted, Early 1900s, 9 x 22 ½ In. 192
Canada Goose, Wood, Carved Feather, Glass Eyes, Stamped, Clare, 1960s, 23 In. 240
Canada Goose, Wood, Painted, Black, White & Brown, Early 1900s, 26 In. 293
Canvasback Drake, Carved, Painted, Ken Dahlka, 9 x 16 x 7 In. ....*illus* 351
Canvasback Drake, Hollow Carved, White Pine, Glass Eyes, Wildflower Company, 1900s, 15 In.. 200
Canvasback Drake, White & Black, Weight, Havre De Grace, 1948, 16 In. 177
Canvasback Drake, Wood, High Head Model, Painted, Otto Mish, c.1920, 17 ½ In. 236
Crow, Black, Painted, Heart Shape Stand, 9 ½ x 15 ½ x 6 In. 431
Curlew, Iron Bill, Carved, Painted Shorebird, Glass Eyes, Stand, 1910s-50s, 15 ½ x 15 In. *illus* 540
Dove, Painted, Carved White Cedar Body, Stick-Up Base, Stamped, Ken Kirby, 11 x 11 ½ In. 188
Duck Sink Box, Painted, Brown, Cast Iron, 1800s, 15 In. ....*illus* 452
Duck, Carved, Square Tail, Roswell Bliss, William Lattin, Early 1900s, 5 ¾ x 13 ½ In. ....*illus* 160
Duck, Eider, Carved, Painted, Horseshoe Weight Base, John Paxton, 10 ½ x 21 x 9 In. 702
Duck, Lower Bank, Carved, Painted, Wood, Metal Eyes, Inset Weight, Gene Hendrickson, 14 In. 413
Duck, Standing, Carved, Painted, Glass Eyes, Rock Base, Homer Lawrence, 12 ¾ x 13 x 6 In. .. 4095
Duck, Wood, Painted, Glass Eyes, Wildflower Decoys, Old Say, Conn, 19 x 18 ¾ In., Pair.......... 113
Eider Drake, Tucked Head, Black & White, Painted, Gus Wilson, 8 x 14 x 8 In. ....*illus* 3803
Golden Eye Drake, Carved Eyes, Head Turned Left, Marty Collins, 16 In. 150
Goose, Wood, Black, White, Tacks For Eyes, 11 ½ x 9 In. 125
Heron, White, Standing, Painted, Carved, Wood Base, 32 In. 83
Herring Gull, Standing, Rocky Base, Signed, Lewis Robichaud, 1900s, 11 ½ x 15 In. 228
Loon, Carved Tail Feathers, Red Glass Eyes, Lewis & Holland, Late 1900s, 4 x 12 In. 204
Mallard Drake, Glass Eyes, Carved, A.E. Crowell Style, Roger Mitchell, 1900s, 14 ½ In. 438
Mallard Drake, Multicolor, Wood, Carved, Inscribed, Hank Walters, 1939, 16 In. 123
Mallard Drake, Painted, Cast Iron, 6 ½ x 3 ½ In. ....*illus* 102
Mallard Drake, Yellow Bill, Glass Eyes, Carved & Painted, Bob White, 14 In. 590
Mallard Hen, Carved, Painted, Glass Eyes, Mason Factory, Stamped Leo, c.1925, 7 ½ x 12 In.. 70
Mallard, Hen, Glass Eyes, Detailed Feathers, Mark Whipple, 1900s, 15 ½ In. 313
Merganser, Preening, Carved, Painted Feather Details, 1900s, 16 In. 523
Merganser, Wood, Carved, Painted Feather Details, Early 1900s, 27 ½ In. 1107
Owl, 2-Sided, Carved Wood, Painted, Crusty White, Early 1900s, 22 x 7 ½ x 6 ½ In. 1170
Owl, Carved Body, Painted Face, Glass Eyes, Birch Base, Early 1900s, 15 ½ In. ....*illus* 2337
Owl, Great Horned, Mounted, Carved Wooden Rockery Base, Mike Borrett, 1900s, 25 In. 900
Partridge, Running, Carved, Glass Eyes, Rectangular Base, Homer Lawrence, 8 x 15 x 6 In. 3744
Pigeon Hawk, Carved, Painted, Glass Eyes, Perched, Wood, 10 x 20 In. 57

Decoy, Black Duck, Head Turned Right, Feather Details, Hollow, Glass Eyes, Marty Collins, 15 In.
$594

Eldred's

Decoy, Bufflehead Drake, Preening, Marty Collins, 1900s, 10 In.
$480

Eldred's

TIP
Wooden boxes, toys, or decoys should not be kept on the fireplace mantel or nearby floor areas when the fire is burning. The heat dries the wood and the paint. Unprotected wooden items on warm TV sets and stereos may also be damaged.

Decoy, Canada Goose, Painted, Carved, Wood, Gary Crossman, 29 ½ In.
$325

Bunch Auctions

TIP
Door hinges should never be on the outside of an entrance door. The pins can easily be removed.

Decoy, Canvasback Drake, Carved, Painted, Ken Dahlka, 9 x 16 x 7 In.
$351

Thomaston Place Auction Galleries

Decoy, Curlew, Iron Bill, Carved, Painted Shorebird, Glass Eyes, Stand, 1910s-50s, 15 ½ x 15 In.
$540

Brunk Auctions

Decoy, Duck Sink Box, Painted, Brown, Cast Iron, 1800s, 15 In.
$452

Hartzell's Auction Gallery Inc.

Decoy, Duck, Carved, Square Tail, Roswell Bliss, William Lattin, Early 1900s, 5 ¾ x 13 ½ In.
$160

Cowan's Auctions

TIP

Go to antiques shows early; there may be plenty of antiques left at the end of the show, but the dealers are tired and not as eager to talk to customers.

Decoy, Eider Drake, Tucked Head, Black & White, Painted, Gus Wilson, 8 x 14 x 8 In.
$3,803

Thomaston Place Auction Galleries

Decoy, Mallard Drake, Painted, Cast Iron, 6 ½ x 3 ½ In.
$102

Hartzell's Auction Gallery Inc.

Decoy, Owl, Carved Body, Painted Face, Glass Eyes, Birch Base, Early 1900s, 15 ½ In.
$2,337

Skinner, Inc.

Decoy, Pigeon, Animated Wings, Pull String, Glass Eyes, Carved, Painted, Late 1800s, 15 ½ In.
$976

Pook & Pook

Decoy, Puffin, Carved Wood, Painted, Dowel Leg, Pine Stand, Egg Island, 16 In.
$644

Thomaston Place Auction Galleries

Decoy, Snipe, Flying, Glass Eyes, Carved Wings, Rockery Backboard, Daniel Bruffee, 11 x 13 In.
$540

Eldred's

Decoy, Swan, Wood, Carved, White Body, Black Beak, 22 x 33 In.
$461

Skinner, Inc.

Decoy, Swan, Wood, Painted White, 34 x 55 In.
$354

Copake Auctions

Dedham, Horse Chestnut, Plate, Blue & White, c.1910, 8 ½ In.
$108

Eldred's

Dedham, Jardiniere, Chestnuts, Leaves, Hugh Robertson, c.1880, 4 x 9 In.
$1,000

Rago Arts and Auction Center

Dedham, Moth, Plate, Blue, White, Marked, Rabbit Head, 1920s, 6 In.
$150

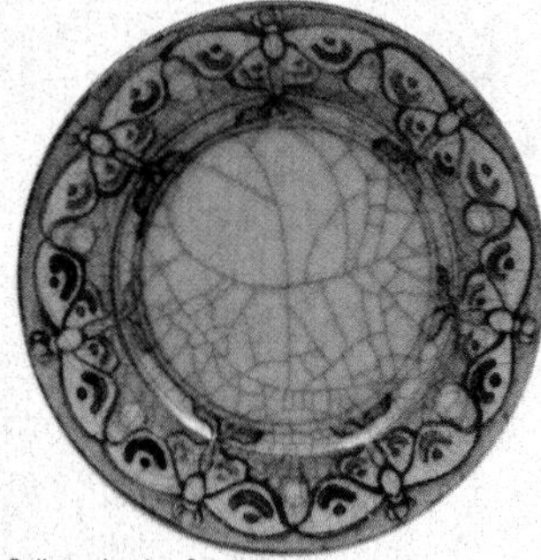

Belhorn Auction Servicesa

Unglazed Antique Delft Isn't White

Delft isn't always marked. Any marks should be underglaze rather than painted on the surface. Many makers signed their pieces with their initials, not a company name. Unglazed areas of old Dutch Delft are an earthy brown or sandy color, not white like porcelain.

Pigeon, Animated Wings, Pull String, Glass Eyes, Carved, Painted, Late 1800s, 15 ½ In. *.illus* 976
Pintail Drake, Painted, Wood, Signed, Dated, Harry Jobes 1960, 12 x 17 In. 125
Pintail Drake, Ward Brothers Style, Carved, Painted, Glass Eyes, Wood, 17 ½ In. 443
Plover, Crowell Style, Black Bellied, Glass Eyes, Daniel Bruffee, 12 In. 300
Puffin, Carved Wood, Painted, Dowel Leg, Pine Stand, Egg Island, 16 In. *illus* 644
Red-Breasted Merganser Drake, Carved Eyes, Dan Bruffee, 18 In. 330
Red-Breasted Merganser Drake, Head Turned Right, Leather Crest, Marty Collins, 1988, 19 In. 570
Redhead Drake, Carved, Painted, Wood, Glass Eyes, Ward Bros., Crisfield, Maryland, 1967, 15 In.. 2242
Sea Gull, Carved, Painted, White & Black, Weighted Plate, New Jersey, c.1950, 18 In. 325
Shorebird, Wooden, Carved, Brown, Folk Art, 15 x 7 x 14 In. 325
Shorebird, Yellowlegs, Carved, On Driftwood Base, Signed F Adamo, 1900s, 5 ½ x 5 ½ In. 406
Shorebird, Yellowlegs, Painted Eyes, Head Is Dovetailed Into The Body, Northshore, c.1890, 9 In.. 1800
Snipe, Flying, Glass Eyes, Carved Wings, Rockery Backboard, Daniel Bruffee, 11 x 13 In. *illus* 540
Swan, Laminated Body, Painted Detail, Carved, Preening, Conn River, 1975, 10 ½ x 32 In. 677
Swan, Wood, Carved, White Body, Black Beak, 22 x 33 In. *illus* 461
Swan, Wood, Long Neck, Carved, Black Beak, White Body, Oval Base, 18 x 30 In. 325
Swan, Wood, Painted White, 34 x 55 In. *illus* 354
Widgeon Drake, Brown Wings, Green Highlights, Metal Eyes, c.1940, 7 ¾ x 13 ¾ In. 530
Widgeon Drake, Carved, Painted, Signed, A. Elmer Crowell, East Harwich, Mass., 2 ½ x 4 In. 703
Widgeon Drake, Painted, Carved Wood, Lead Keel, Signed, R. Madison Mitchell, 1983, 8 x 14 In.. 406

DEDHAM POTTERY

Dedham Pottery was started in 1895. Chelsea Keramic Art Works was established in 1872 in Chelsea, Massachusetts, by members of the Robertson family. The factory closed in 1889 and was reorganized as the Chelsea Pottery U.S. in 1891. The firm used the marks *CKAW* and *CPUS*. It became the Dedham Pottery of Dedham, Massachusetts, in 1896. The factory closed in 1943. It was famous for its crackleware dishes, which picture blue outlines of animals, flowers, and other natural motifs. Pottery by Chelsea Keramic Art Works and Dedham Pottery is listed here.

Day & Night, Pitcher, Rooster, Crackle Glaze, Blue, White, Marked Underside, 5 In. 750
Horse Chestnut, Plate, Blue & White, c.1910, 8 ½ In. *illus* 108
Jardiniere, Chestnuts, Leaves, Hugh Robertson, c.1880, 4 x 9 In. *illus* 1000
Moth, Plate, Blue, White, Marked, Rabbit Head, 1920s, 6 In. *illus* 150
Polar Bear, Plate, Crackle White Ground, Marked, 1900s, 8 ½ In. *illus* 531
Rabbit, Cup & Saucer, Cream Ground, Blue, 2 ⅜ x 6 In. 81
Turkey, Plate, Blue & White, c.1910, 8 ½ In. *illus* 168
Urn, Loop Handles, Round Base, Marked CKAW, 1900s, 9 In. *illus* 330
Vase, Teardrop, Raised Chrysanthemum, Olive Green Ground, Marked CKAW, c.1910, 12 In. *.illus* 780

DELATTE

Delatte glass is a French cameo glass made by Andre Delatte. It was first made in Nancy, France, in 1921. Lighting fixtures and opaque glassware in imitation of Bohemian opaline were made.

Vase, Frosted, White, Lavender Ground, Carved, Flowers, Signed, c.1920, 15 ½ x 7 In. *illus* 650

DELDARE, *see Buffalo Pottery Deldare.*

DELFT

Delft is a special type of tin-glazed pottery. Early delft was made in Holland and England during the seventeenth century. It was usually decorated with blue on a white surface, but some was multicolor, decorated with green, yellow, and other colors. Most delftware pieces were dishes needed for everyday living. Figures were made from about 1750 to 1800 and are rare. Although the soft tin-glazed pottery was well-known, it was not named delft until after 1840, when it was named for the city in Holland where much of it was made. Porcelain became more popular because it was more durable, and Holland gradually stopped making the old delft. In 1876 De Porceleyne Fles factory in Delft introduced a porcelain ware that was decorated with blue and white scenes of Holland that reminded many of old delft. It became popular with the Dutch and tourists. By 1990 all of the blue and white porcelain with Dutch scenes was made in Asia, although it was marked *Delft*. Only one Dutch company remains that makes the traditional old-style delft with blue on white or with colored decorations. Most of the pieces sold today were made after 1891, and the name *Holland* usually appears with the Delft factory marks. The word *Delft* appears alone on some inexpensive twentieth- and twenty-first-century pottery from Asia and Germany that is also listed here.

Bowl, Blue, Man Flying Kite, Central Flower Image, Demi-Flower Head Border, 1760s, 10 In.... 468
Charger, Blue & White, Chinoiserie Style, 8 Sections, Flower, Figural Panels, 1700s, 16 ½ In.. 767
Charger, Blue, White, Woman In Landscape, Rim Edge, 13 ½ In. 420
Charger, Multicolor, Urn Of Flowers, Birds, Monogram, AK, 1700s, 16 ¾ In. 960
Charger, Parrot, On Stylized Tree, Marked GBS, 1750s, 16 ⅝ In. ....*illus* 556
Charger, William & Mary, Crowns, Curtain, Banner, Vine & Flower Rim, 13 ½ In. 2560
Dish, Blue & White, 4 Flower Patches, Gilt Rim, 1700s, 14 In., Pair.... 431
Figurine, Multicolor Dress, Tricorn Hat, Mop Cap, Bag, Circular Base, 1750s, 5 ¾ In.... 117
Jar, Blue & White, Gold Lid, Squat, T. D'Espagne, 13 In. 236
Lamp, Brass Burner, Jar Mounted, Cherubs, Flowers, White Ground, 1700s, 7 In. 192
Lamp, Opaque White, Nautical Scene, Umbrella Shape, Plume & Atwood, c.1900, 8 x 3 In.... 439
Plaque, Canal Scene, Hanging, Oval Shape, Blue, 1800s, 15 ½ x 13 In.... 150
Plate, Blue, Hand Painted, Winged Cupid, Holding Arrow, Dash Border, 1710s, 8 In. 644
Plate, Floral, White Ground, Multicolor, Holland, Late 1700s, 8 ⅞ In. 492
Plate, Flowers, Leaves, Birds, White Ground, Orange, Blue, PAK Monogram, 8 ⅝ In.... 185
Plate, White Ground, Blue, Urn Of Flowers, 1700s, 9 In. 160
Platter, Mimosa, Blue & White, Gilt Rim, 1700s, 13 ½ In. 266
Tile, Flowers, Birdcage, Wood Frame, 1800s, 17 x 17 In. 384
Tile, Woman, Lace Cap, Fancy Dress, Manganese, Frame, Holland, 1700s, 15 x 10 In., 6 Piece.. 984
Urn, Lid, Octagonal, Buddhist Lion, Bird, Flower Vignettes, Marked, 19 In., Pair.... 1180
Watch Holder, Tall Case Clock Shape, Blue, White, Couple, Tree, On Pendulum Doors, 12 In.. 380

DENTAL

Dental cabinets, chairs, equipment, and other related items are listed here. Other objects may be found in the Medical category.

Air Compressor, Robot Shape, Iron, Round Base, Ritter Dental Mfg., 36 In.... 160
Cabinet, Metal Case, Black Bakelite Trim, Drawers, Art Deco, 51 x 39 ½ x 15 In.... 360
Cabinet, Mixed Wood, 22 Drawers, 3 Doors, White Knobs, 63 x 41 In. 937
Cabinet, Walnut, Glass Door, 20 Drawers, Glass Knobs, 1900s, 60 x 36 x 12 ¾ In. 1080
Chair, Chrome, Green, Enamel, Leather Seat & Back, 39 x 34 In. 136
Sign, Tooth, Carved, Painted, Applied Cast Iron Ring, 1900s, 10 ½ In.... 1755

DENVER

Denver is part of the mark on an American art pottery. William Long of Steubenville, Ohio, founded the Lonhuda Pottery Company in 1892. In 1900 he moved to Denver, Colorado, and organized the Denver China and Pottery Company. This pottery, which used the mark *Denver*, worked until 1905, when Long moved to New Jersey and founded the Clifton Pottery. Long also worked for Weller Pottery, Roseville Pottery, and American Encaustic Tiling Company. Do not confuse this pottery with the Denver White Pottery, which worked from 1894 to 1955 in Denver.

Vase, Denaura, Green, Mistletoe, Glazed, Earthenware, c.1903, 7 x 3 In., Pair.... 1687
Vase, Denaura, Tulip, Green Matte, 4 ¾ x 8 In. 1725
Vase, Light Blue, White Banded Decor, 5 x 4 In.... 60

Dedham, Polar Bear, Plate, Crackle White Ground, Marked, 1900s, 8 ½ In.
$531

Eldred's

Dedham, Turkey, Plate, Blue & White, c.1910, 8 ½ In.
$168

Eldred's

Dedham, Urn, Loop Handles, Round Base, Marked CKAW, 1900s, 9 In.
$330

Eldred's

Dedham, Vase, Teardrop, Raised Chrysanthemum, Olive Green Ground, Marked CKAW, c.1910, 12 In.
$780

Eldred's

Delatte, Vase, Frosted, White, Lavender Ground, Carved, Flowers, Signed, c.1920, 15 ½ x 7 In.
$650

Woody Auctions

Delft, Charger, Parrot, On Stylized Tree, Marked GBS, 1750s, 16 ⅝ In.
$556

Jeffrey S. Evans & Associates

DEPRESSION GLASS

Depression glass is an inexpensive glass that was manufactured in large quantities during the 1920s and early 1930s. It was made in many colors and patterns by dozens of factories in the United States. Most patterns were also made in clear glass, which the factories called *crystal.* If no color is listed here, it is clear. The name *Depression glass* is a modern one and also refers to machine-made glass of the 1940s through 1970s. Sets missing a few pieces can be completed through the help of a matching service.

Adam, Coaster, Green, Square Shape, Jeannette, 4 In.	11
American Sweetheart, Serving Plate, Monax, Macbeth Evans, 10 ¾ In.	10
Aunt Polly, Candy Dish, Blue, Footed, Handles, 2 ½ x 7 ½ In.	30 to 39
Bubble, Goblet, Green, Anchor Hocking, 5 ⅝ x 3 ⅛ In.	16
Cameo, Tumbler, Green, Hocking, 5 In., Pair	26
Cherry Blossom, Cake Plate, Pink, 2 Handles, 10 In.	20
Cherry Blossom, Plate, Delphite, Jeannette, 9 ⅛ In.	32
Cloverleaf, Sugar & Creamer, Black, Hazel Atlas, 3 ⅝ x 3 ⅛ & 4 ½ In.	25
Colonial, Sherbet, Pink, Hocking, 3 ⅜ x 4 In.	6
Criss Cross, Butter, Green, Hazel Atlas, 6 ¾ x 3 In.	18
Diana, Cup & Saucer, Yellow, Federal Glass, 3 x 5 ⅞ In., Pair	10
Doric & Pansy, Cup & Saucer, Ultramarine, Children's, Jeannette, 1 ½ x 4 In.	21
Doric, Salt & Pepper, Pink, Domed Metal Top, Jeannette, 3 x 2 In.	35
Hermitage, Pitcher, Green, Ice Lip, Fostoria, 7 In.	194
Homespun, Tumbler, Pink, Flat, Jeannette, 4 ⅜ x 2 ⅞ In.	26
Horseshoe, Serving Dish, 3 Sections, Green, Indiana Glass, 8 ⅜ In.	32
Iris, Wine, Iridescent, Jeannette, 4 In.	14
Jane-Ray, Plate, Jade-Ite, Anchor Hocking, 7 ¾ In.	17
Lorain, Bowl, Fruit, Yellow, Square, Indiana Glass, 8 In.	140
Madrid, Plate, Blue, Indiana Glass, 10 ⅜ In.	10
Manhattan, Saucer, Clear, Anchor Hocking, 6 ⅛ In.	10
Mayfair Open Rose, Pitcher, Water, Blue, Hocking, 8 ½ In.	275
Miss America, Plate, Pink, Hocking, 10 In., Pair	28 to 35
Moderntone, Whiskey, Cobalt, Hazel Atlas, 2 ¼ In.	40 to 50
Moondrops, Creamer, Red, Footed, New Martinsville, 3 x 2 ½ In.	10
Newport, Bowl, Cereal, Amethyst, Hazel Atlas, 5 ½ In.	12 to 30
Oyster & Pearl, Relish, Divided, Pink, Handles, Anchor Hocking, 8 ½ x 12 In.	10 to 16
Parrot, Platter, Green, Oval Shape, Federal Glass, 11 ⅜ In.	46
Patrician, Plate, Yellow, Federal Glass, 11 In.	20
Patrician, Sugar & Creamer, Yellow, Federal Glass, 3 ½ x 3 ½ In.	10
Rock Crystal, Candlestick, Clear, McKee, 8 ½ In.	26
Royal Lace, Bowl, Pink, Hazel Atlas, 10 In.	30
Royal Ruby, Wine, Red, Anchor Hocking, 3 ⅜ x 2 ¼ In.	10
Sandwich, Ashtray, Amber, Club Shape, Indiana Glass, 3 ¾ In.	3
Swirl, Sugar, Blue Green, Footed, Jeannette, 3 ¼ In.	14
Thistle, Cake Plate, Green, Macbeth-Evans, 13 In.	85
Twisted Optic, Tidbit, Green, Center Handle, Imperial Glass, 4 ¾ x 10 In.	55

DERBY, *see Royal Crown Derby category.*

DICK TRACY

Dick Tracy, the comic strip, started in 1931. Tracy was also the hero of movies from 1937 to 1947 and again in 1990, and starred in a radio series in the 1940s and a television series in the 1950s. Memorabilia from all these activities are collected.

Badge, Secret Service Patrol, Captain, Leaf Border, Portrait, 1938, 2 In.	115
Badge, Shield, Nickel, Clip Back, Cereal Prize, 1960s, 1 ½ x 1 ¼ In.	23
Book, Better Little, Dick Tracy & The Bicycle Gang, No. 1424, c.1948, 3 x 4 In.	22

Book, Big-Little, On The Trail Of Larceny Lu, No. 1170, c.1931 12
Camera, Bakelite, Black, Seymour Sales, 1940s 18
Pin, Dick Tracy Detective, Celluloid, 1930s, 1 1/4 In. 10
Pin, Junior Tracy, Tin Lithograph, Pinback, Kellogg's, 1940s, 3/4 In. 11
Pin, Vitamin Flintheart, Tin Lithograph, Pinback, Kellogg's, 1940s, 3/4 In. 8
Ring, Secret Compartment, Brass, Adjustable, Portrait, Sunburst, Crescent Moon, 1938 30
Toy, Gun, Cap Pistol, Metal, Hubley, 1950s, 4 In. 35
Toy, Pistol, Police, Siren, Steel, Red, Not Working, Marx, 1935, 8 x 4 1/2 In. 50
Toy, Puppet, Composition, Movable Jaw, Pull String, 1940s, 13 In. 424
Wristwatch, Battery Operated, Leather Band, 8 1/2 In. 55

DICKENS WARE *pieces are listed in the Royal Doulton and Weller categories.*

DINNERWARE

Dinnerware used in the United States from the 1930s through the 1950s is listed here. Most was made in potteries in southern Ohio, West Virginia, and California. A few patterns were made in Japan, England, and other countries. Dishes were sold in gift shops and department stores, or were given away as premiums. Many of these patterns are listed in this book in their own categories, such as Autumn Leaf, Azalea, Coors, Fiesta, Franciscan, Hall, Harker, Harlequin, Red Wing, Riviera, Russel Wright, Vernon Kilns, Watt, and Willow. For more prices, go to kovels.com. Sets missing a few pieces can be completed through the help of a matching service. Three examples of dated dinnerware marks are shown here.

W.S. George Pottery Co.
Late 1930s–1940

Royal China Co.
1950s+

Salem China Co.
1940s–1960

Americana Wheat, Soup, Dish, Homer Laughlin, 8 In. 6
Betsy Rose, Plate, Luncheon, Harmony House, 9 1/4 In. 8
Blue Ridge, Pitcher, Pink Flowers, Green Leaves, Hand Painted, 8 1/2 In. 40
Bluebells, Sugar, Lid, Edwin Knowles, 3 1/8 In. 20
Calico Fruit, Platter, Oval, Universal Potteries, 13 5/8 x 10 1/2 In. 26
Chrysanthemum, Plate, Dessert, Blue Ridge, 6 1/8 In., 4 Piece 32
Contempo, Plate, Castleton, 6 In., 2 Piece 19
Currier & Ives, Plate, Old Grist Mill, Blue & White, Cabin, Royal China, 10 In. 10
Dogtooth Violet, Salt & Pepper, Brown Top, Flowers, Blue Ridge, 5 x 2 In. 35
Flamingo, Plate, Dinner, Iva Lure, Crooksville, 9 7/8 In. 6
Forsythia, Salt & Pepper, Flowers, Leaves, Gold Trim, Edwin Knowles, 2 1/4 In. 42
Friendly Village, Teapot, Lid, Johnson Brothers, 4 5/8 In. 130
His Majesty, Platter, Oval, Johnson Brothers, 20 1/4 In. 360
Luray Pastels, Tumbler, Blue, Taylor Smith & Taylor, 3 3/8 In. 46
Mardi Gras, Gravy Boat, Abstract Design, Salem China, 1963, 8 x 3 In. 49
Mexicana, Casserole, Lid, Rectangular, Handle Finial, Homer Laughlin 236
Mexicana, Jar, Lid, Oven Serve, Kitchen Kraft, Homer Laughlin .... *illus* 177
Patio, Platter, Vases, Flowers, Transferware, Paden City Pottery, 1940s, 12 x 8 In. 75
Pink Moss Rose, Plate, Salad, Paden City, 7 1/2 In. 10
Platinum Garland, Plate, Dinner, Harmony House, 10 In. 18
Regency, Plate, Salad, Square, Johnson Brothers, 7 5/8 In. 20
Rosebud, Creamer, Harmony House, 3 In. 20
Santa Fe, Casserole, Lid, Mikasa, 9 1/2 In. 32
Shell Pink, Cup & Saucer, Footed, Castleton, 2 1/2 In. 12
Spring Bouquet, Sauce Bowl, Rim, Edwin Knowles, 5 1/2 In. 8
Tongue Twister, Cup, 2 Green Turtles, Homer Laughlin, 3 In. .... *illus* 443

Recent Marks
Modern inventions have made new marks needed on dishes. "Cooking ware" was first used around 1923, "ovenproof" in 1934, "dishwasher proof" after 1955, "craze proof" around 1960, "freezer-oven-table" in the 1960s, "microwave safe" after 1970, and "oven-to-table" in 1978.

Dinnerware, Mexicana, Jar, Lid, Oven Serve, Kitchen Kraft, Homer Laughlin, $177

Strawser Auction Group

Dinnerware, Tongue Twister, Cup, 2 Green Turtles, Homer Laughlin, 3 In. $443

Strawser Auction Group

Dinnerware, Tongue Twister, Plate, Ox Center, Homer Laughlin, c.1941, 8 1/4 In. $384

Strawser Auction Group

Dirk Van Erp, Lamp, 3-Light, Copper, Hammered, Mica Shade, Rolled Rim, Conical Body, 19 x 18 In.
$7,995

Skinner, Inc.

Dirk Van Erp, Vase, Copper, Hammered, Tapered, Marked, c.1914, 7 ¾ In.
$896

Neal Auction Company

Disneyana, Comic Book, Donald Duck, No. 178, 4 Color, December, Dell Publishing, 1947, 13 x 8 In.
$393

Bruneau & Co. Auctioneers

Tongue Twister, Plate, Ox Center, Homer Laughlin, c.1941, 8 ¼ In. .... *illus* 384
Tongue Twister, Tumbler, 3 Gray Geese, Homer Laughlin, c.1941 443
Wembley, Bowl, Vegetable, Oval, Harmony House, 10 ⅞ In. 36
Whole Wheat, Plate, Dinner, Mikasa, 10 ¾ In. 20
Yorktowne, Cup & Saucer, Flat, Pfaltzgraff, 2 ½ x 4 In. 6

DIONNE QUINTUPLETS

Dionne quintuplets were born in Canada on May 28, 1934. The publicity about their birth and their special status as wards of the Canadian government made them famous throughout the world. Visitors could watch the girls play; reporters interviewed the girls and the staff. Thousands of special dolls and souvenirs were made picturing the quints at different ages. Emilie died in 1954, Marie in 1970, Yvonne in 2001. Annette and Cecile still live in Canada.

Bowl, Cereal, Porcelain, Marie, Highchair, c.1935, 5 ½ x 2 In. 40
Bowl, Tin, Inscribed Names, Embossed Faces, c.1935, 6 In. 20
Calendar, Majestic Bottling Works, 1937, 11 x 7 In. 40
Doll, Dr. Dafoe, Composition, Wide Smile, White Smock, 1937, 14 In. 460
Doll, Madame Alexander, Composition, Side-Glancing Eyes, 1936, 8 In., 5 Piece 460
Doll, Molded Hair, Clothing, Quintmobile, M. Alexander, 1930s, 5 ½ x 17 ½ In. 330
Ornament, Die Cut, Color, Hats & Coats, 4 In., 5 Piece 14
Plate, Girls, Highchairs, Tab Handles, Red Line Border, Pottery, 12 In. 104
Playing Cards, Blue Gingham Box, Girls' Faces, 1940s, 3 ¾ x 2 ½ In. 39

DIRK VAN ERP

Dirk Van Erp was born in 1860 and died in 1933. He opened his own studio in 1908 in Oakland, California. He moved his studio to San Francisco in 1909 and the studio remained under the direction of his son until 1977. Van Erp made hammered copper accessories, including vases, desk sets, bookends, candlesticks, jardinieres, and trays, but he is best known for his lamps. The hammered copper lamps often had shades with mica panels.

Basket, Hammered Copper Mounted, 4 Shaped Feet, Late 1800s, 5 x 7 In. 908
Box, Humidor, Copper, Hammered, Patina, 3 ½ x 6 ½ In. 4750
Jardiniere, Copper, Hammered, 14 ½ x 9 ¾ In. 12650
Lamp, 3-Light, Copper, Hammered, Mica Shade, Rolled Rim, Conical Body, 19 x 18 In. ..*illus* 7995
Lamp, Bean Pot, Copper, Hammered, Mica Shade, Marked, 13 In. 4600
Vase, Copper, Hammered, Tapered, Marked, c.1914, 7 ¾ In. .... *illus* 896

DISNEYANA

Disneyana is a collectors' term. Walt Disney and his company introduced many comic characters to the world. Mickey Mouse first appeared in the short film *Steamboat Willie* in 1928. Collectors search for examples of the work of the Disney Studios and the many commercial products modeled after his characters, including Mickey Mouse and Donald Duck, and well-known films, like *Beauty and the Beast, The Little Mermaid,* the *Toy Story* series, and *Frozen.*

Baby Rattle, Mickey Mouse, Pie Eyed, Celluloid, Red, c.1920, 6 x 3 In. 155
Bookends, Snow White, Figural, Plaster, Lamode, 7 In., Pair 195
Cel, see Animation Art category.
Clock, Mickey Mouse, Arms Are Hands, Cream Celluloid, Arched, Alarm, 4 ½ In. 44
Comic Book, Donald Duck, No. 178, 4 Color, December, Dell Publishing, 1947, 13 x 8 In. *illus* 393
Cookie Jar, Mickey Mouse, Leather Ears, Marked Walt Disney Productions, 9 ⅝ In. 46
Doll, Mickey Mouse, Fabric, Knickerbocker, 1935, 16 ¼ In. 714
Doll, Pinocchio, Composition, Swivel Head, Cloth Pants, Knickerbocker, 13 In. 120
Map, Souvenir, Disneyland, Color Offset, 1989, 29 x 42 In. 100
Pail, 3 Caballeros, Gold Exterior, Red Interior, Jose Carioca & Panchito, Shovel, 4 In. .....*illus* 510

Pail, Donald Duck, Blue, Red Interior, Loop Handle, Shovel, Ohio Art, 3 ½ In. ....*illus* 72
Pail, Mickey Mouse, Minnie Mouse, Happynak, 3 ½ In.. 1238
Painting, Mickey Mouse, Canvas, Signed, Trevor Carlton, Frame, 30 ½ In. ....*illus* 345
Pin, Mickey Mouse, Master Of Ceremonies, c.1928, 2 ¼ In. 4322
Pin, Mickey Mouse, Song Leader, c.1928, 2 ¼ In.. 999
Playset, Snow White & Seven Dwarfs, Britain's, Box, 8 Piece 1800
Poster, Travel, Mickey Mouse, Fly Eastern, Walt Disney World, 1983, 40 x 30 In. 250
Print, Pinocchio, Holding Jiminy Cricket's Coattails, Serigraph, 10 ¾ x 14 In.......................... 40
Rocker, Mickey Mouse, Wood, Painted, Early 1900s, 23 ½ x 35 ½ x 10 ½ In. ....*illus* 154
Sparkler, Mickey Mouse, Black & White, Nifty, 6 In. ....*illus* 240
Sweeper, Mickey Mouse, Mickey Playing Piano, Minnie Cleaning, Red Handle, Tin, Wide, 23 In. 276
Toy, Goofy, Cyclist, High Wheel Bike, Tin, Windup, Linemar, Box, 7 In. ....*illus* 1200
Toy, Mickey Mouse, Jazz Drummer, Jointed Arms, Nifty Toy Co., Germany, 7 In.......................... 845
Toy, Mickey Mouse, Roly Poly, Black & Red, Celluloid, Passco, Box, 4 In.................................. 72
Toy, Mickey Mouse, Tin, Windup, Circling Train, Airplane, Multicolor, 6 x 9 In. ....*illus* 311
Toy, Mickey Mouse, Unicycle, Windup, Tin, Painted, Linemar, 5 ½ In. ....*illus* 288
Toy, Pinocchio, Standing, Black Base, Windup, Tin, Marx, 1939, 8 In. ....*illus* 390

DOCTOR, *see Dental and Medical categories.*

DOLL

Doll entries are listed by marks printed or incised on the doll, if possible. If there are no marks, the doll is listed by the name of the subject or country or maker. Notice that Barbie is listed under Mattel. G.I. Joe figures are listed in the Toy section. Eskimo dolls are listed in the Eskimo section and Indian dolls are listed in the Indian section. Doll clothes and accessories are listed at the end of this section. The twentieth-century clothes listed here are in mint condition.

A.M., 253, Bisque Head, Dimples, Googly Eyes, Composition Toddler Body, c.1918, 11 In. .*illus* 690
A.M., 323, Jester, Bisque Socket Head, Googly Glass Eyes, Composition Toddler Body, 10 In. 575
A.M., Bisque Head, Cloth Body, Composition Hands, Sleep Eyes, 16 In. 100
A.M., Princess, Bisque, Composition, Sleep Eyes, Open Mouth, Germany, 22 In......................... 150
Acme, Annette, Composition Shoulder Head, Blue Tin Sleep Eyes, Human Hair, c.1930, 27 In. . 84
Alexander dolls are listed in this category under Madame Alexander. ....
American Character, Betsy McCall, Hard Plastic, Auburn Hair, Birthday Party Dress, 8 In. ... 46
American Character, Sweet Sue, Plastic, Vinyl, Blue Sleep Eyes, Blond Wig, Gown, 1953, 31 In. 180
Annette Himstedt, Panchita, Native American Girl, Vinyl, Costume, 26 In.................................. 104
Armand Marseille dolls are listed in this category under A.M. ....
Arranbee, Girl, Composition, Sleep Eyes, Human Hair Wig, Dress, Rabbit Fur Jacket, 18 In. 144
Automaton, Ballerina Pirouetting, Bisque, Wood, Roullet Et Decamps, France, c.1890, 19 In. ..*illus* 4313
Automaton, Bird On Perch, Round Gilt Brass Cage, Windup, France, 1910s, 11 x 6 ½ In......... 380
Automaton, Cat, Robin Hood Dress, L'Arbre A Pain, Music, France, 1880s, 18 x 7 x 8 In. 625
Automaton, Clown, Papier-Mache, Clockwork, Head & Arms Move, Wood Base, c.1890, 25 In. 1560
Automaton, Girl With Singing Bird, Stool, Velvet Cover, H. Vichy, Lioret, France, 26 In............ 9775
Automaton, Musical, Dome, Water Scene, Buildings, Windmill, Ship, 16 x 15 x 7 In................ 1210
Automaton, Whistler, Man Leaning On Lamppost, Wood, Key Wind, Movable Head, 19 In. *illus* 210
Averill, Uncle Wiggily, Cloth, Printed, Black Plastic Eyes, Flannel Suit, 19 In............................ 192
Barbie dolls are listed in this category under Mattel, Barbie.
Bergmann dolls are also in this category under S & H and Simon & Halbig. ....
Bergmann, Bisque Head, Blue Sleep Eyes, Wood Jointed Limbs, Hat, Purse, c.1916, 30 ½ In.... 222
Bild Lilli, Plastic, Blond Hair, Green Checked Dress, White Apron, Marked PRYM, 7 ½ In. 748
Bisque, Girl, Painted Eyes, Black & White Dress, France, 12 In.. 79
Bisque, Shoulder Head, Painted Features, Cloth Body, Leather Arms & Boots, Red Dress, 19 In.. 132
Black dolls are also included in the Black category.
Bru Jne, Leon Casimir, Bebe Brevete, Bisque Head, Human Hair, Gusset-Jointed Kid, 16 In...... 14900
Bye-Lo, Baby, Bisque, Painted, Brown Eyes, Cloth Body, Celluloid Hands, Gown, Grace Putnam, 15 In. 60
Chatty Cathy, Plastic, Brown Complexion, Sleep Eyes, Black Hair, Red Coat, Dress, 19 ½ In. .. 360
China Head, Porcelain, Red Cheeks, Black Hair, Brown Dress, Victorian, 27 ½ In. ....*illus* 276

Disneyana, Pail, 3 Caballeros, Gold Exterior, Red Interior, Jose Carioca & Panchito, Shovel, 4 In.
$510

Milestone Auctions

Disneyana, Pail, Donald Duck, Blue, Red Interior, Loop Handle, Shovel, Ohio Art, 3 ½ In.
$72

Milestone Auctions

Disneyana, Painting, Mickey Mouse, Canvas, Signed, Trevor Carlton, Frame, 30 ½ In.
$345

Blackwell Auctions

This is an edited listing of current prices. Visit **Kovels.com** to check thousands of prices from previous years and sign up for free information on trends, tips, reproductions, marks, and more.

Disneyana, Rocker, Mickey Mouse, Wood, Painted, Early 1900s, 23 ½ x 35 ½ x 10 ½ In.
$154

Charlton Hall Auctions

Disneyana, Sparkler, Mickey Mouse, Black & White, Nifty, 6 In.
$240

Milestone Auctions

Disneyana, Toy, Goofy, Cyclist, High Wheel Bike, Tin, Windup, Linemar, Box, 7 In.
$1,200

Milestone Auctions

Disneyana, Toy, Mickey Mouse, Tin, Windup, Circling Train, Airplane, Multicolor, 6 x 9 In.
$311

Soulis Auctions

Disneyana, Toy, Mickey Mouse, Unicycle, Windup, Tin, Painted, Linemar, 5 ½ In.
$288

Blackwell Auctions

Disneyana, Toy, Pinocchio, Standing, Black Base, Windup, Tin, Marx, 1939, 8 In.
$390

Milestone Auctions

Doll, A.M., 253, Bisque Head, Dimples, Googly Eyes, Composition Toddler Body, c.1918, 11 In.
$690

Theriault's

Doll, Automaton, Ballerina Pirouetting, Bisque, Wood, Roullet Et Decamps, France, c.1890, 19 In.
$4,313

Theriault's

Cloth, Christine Adams, Eric, Pressed & Painted Felt, Blond Human Hair, Toddler, 1980s, 16 In. 660
Cloth, Julia Beecher, Stockinet, Blue Painted Eyes, Gown, Leather Shoes, c.1900, 21 In. ..*illus* 938
Dressel, Bathing Beauty, Porcelain, Nude Woman, Reclining, Red Satin Daybed, c.1910, 4 In.. 1380
Effanbee, Anne Shirley, American Child, Composition, Painted Eyes, 20 In. 690
Effanbee, Boy, American Child, Painted Eyes, Human Hair, Suit, Tie, Shoes, 17 In. 690
Effanbee, Dy-Dee Baby, Hard Rubber Head, Sleep Eyes, Molded Hair, Romper, Box, 12 In. 450
Effanbee, Mary Lee, Composition, Green Sleep Eyes, Caracul Wig, Dress, Bonnet, 16 In. 69
Effanbee, Patsy, Composition, Painted Eyes, Polka Dot Dress, Shoes, 13 In. 104
Elisabeth Pongratz, Wood, Painted Features, Human Hair Braids, Knit Dress, 14 In. 1320
Frozen Charlie, China, Pink Tint, Molded & Painted Features & Hair, Germany, 15 In. 161
G.I. Joe figures are listed in the Toy category.
Gaultier, Bisque Swivel Head, Blue Glass Eyes, Blond Mohair, Kid Body, 22 In. *illus* 7188
Gebruder Heubach dolls may also be listed in this category under Heubach.
Gebruder Heubach, 7647, Boy, Bisque Socket Head, Laughing, Composition & Wood, 28 In.. 3910
Gebruder Heubach, 7845, Boy, Bisque Shoulder Head, Pouty Face, Muslin Body, 1912, 8 In.. 460
German, Bisque Head, Sculpted Cap, Googly Living Eyes, Muslin Body, H. Steiner, 11 In. 1035
German, Bisque Shoulder Head, Painted Eyes, Braided Coronet, Kid Body, c.1880, 14 In. 1610
German, Bisque Socket Head, Googly Eyes, Sculpted Golden Hair, 5-Piece Body, Dress, 7 In.... 805
German, Bisque, Papier-Mache, Ball-Jointed Body, Boy 17 In. 1185
German, Gibson Girl, Bisque, Sleep Eyes, Brown Mohair, Leather Pin-Jointed Body, 19 In. 480
German, Munich Art, Boy, Composition, Papier-Mache, Jointed, M. Kaulitz, c.1909, 18 In. 4500
German, Munich Art, Girl, Composition, Papier-Mache, Rosy Cheeks, M. Kaulitz, 17 In. 3900
German, Papier-Mache Head, Man, Holding Cigar, Leather Shoes, Hat, Wood Stand, 9 In. *illus* 118
German, Porcelain, Bathing Beauty, Green Swimsuit, Leg Bent, Painted, c.1920, 5 ½ In. 144
German, Porcelain, Bathing Beauty, Kneeling, Holding Fan, c.1915, 4 In. 201
German, Wax Over Papier-Mache, Painted, Molded Hat, Mohair Braids, Cloth Body, 15 In. 720
Greiner, Papier-Mache Head, Cloth Body, Kid Arms, c.1870, 21 In. *illus* 366
Half-Dolls are listed in the Pincushion Doll category.
Handwerck, Child, Bisque Socket Head, Brown Glass Sleep Eyes, 4 Upper Teeth, Shoes, 27 In. *illus* 106
Hasbro, Little Miss No Name, Vinyl, Plastic, Big Eyes, Teardrop, Clothes, 1965, 15 In. 133
Helen Jensen, Gladdie, Ceramic Head, Sleep Eyes, Smile, Cloth Body, Composition Limbs, 18 In.. 420
Heubach, see also Gebruder Heubach.
Heubach, 262, Boy, Bisque Socket Head, Painted, Side-Glancing Googly Eyes, Dimples, 10 In. 920
Heubach, 7603, Laughing Boy, Bisque Head, Molded Hair, Blue Intaglio Eyes, Jointed, Suit, 9 In.... 156
Heubach, 8192, Bisque Head, Blue Glass Eyes, Human Wig, Jointed Composition, Lawn Dress, 15 In. 554
Indian dolls are listed in the Indian category.
J.D.K., Baby Jean, Bisque Dome Head, Painted, Sleep Eyes, Bent Limb Baby, Gown, 22 In. 420
J.D.K. dolls are also listed in this category under Kestner.
Jan McLean, Lily II, Vinyl, Red Hair, Tiered Dress, Purple Socks, Holding Lollipop Doll, 14 In. 259
Japanese, Beautiful Lady, Gofun Finish, Enamel, Elaborate Hair, Silk Robe, Obi, 18 In. 978
Japanese, Ichimatsu, Child, Gofun Finish, Enamel Eyes, Black Human Hair, Kimono, 1930, 17 In.. 2990
Japanese, Ichimatsu, Child, Gofun Finish, Enamel, Human Hair, Silk Kimono, c.1930, 15 In. *illus* 2645
Jumeau, Bisque Swivel Head, Enamel Eyes, Blond Mohair, Kid Body, Jointed, Gown, 17 In. 3335
Jumeau, Bisque Swivel Head, Paperweight Eyes, Waist-Length Mohair, Kid Body, 15 In. 2645
Jumeau, Bisque, Brown Eyes, Eyelashes, Blond Hair, Earrings, Dress, Straw Hat, c.1880, 18 In. *illus* 6000
Just Me, Composition, Side-Glancing Sleep Eyes, Mohair Curls, Dress, Shoes, Germany, 13 In. 1440
K * R, 62, Bisque Head, Composition, White Dress, Germany, 23 In. *illus* 83
K * R, 107, Karl, Bisque Socket Head, Blond Mohair, Jointed Composition & Wood, 12 In. 8050
K * R, 115/A, Boy, Bisque Head, Sleep Eyes, Mohair Wig, Jointed Toddler Body, Suit, 13 In. 660
K * R, 126, Baby, Bisque Head, Human Hair Braids, Bent-Limb Baby Body, 10 In. 228
K * R, Elise, Bisque Socket Head, Painted Eyes, Mohair, Jointed Composition & Wood, 18 In.... 9775
K * R, Max & Moritz, Bisque, Papier-Mache, Jointed, Lederhosen, Alpine Hats, 16 In., Pair 1200
Kathe Kruse, Boy, Celluloid, Swivel Head, Blue Eyes, Human Hair, Lederhosen, Box, 16 In. 108
Kathe Kruse, Boy, Cloth, Pressed & Painted, Pouty Face, Stitch-Jointed, c.1915, 17 In. 2185
Kathe Kruse, Cloth, Painted, Stitch-Jointed, Folk Costume, c.1915, 17 In. 1495
Kathe Kruse, Cloth, Pressed & Painted, Dirndl Costume, Cap, Box, 1940s, 14 In. *illus* 2185
Kathe Kruse, Hampelchen, Cloth, Pressed & Painted Features, Human Hair, 1930s, 13 In. 748
Kathe Kruse, Robbi, Plastic, Pigtails, Red Pants, Checked Shirt, Hang Tag, Box, 14 ½ In. 58
Kenner, Blythe, Plastic, 4 Eye Colors, Blond Hair, Mod Outfit, 1972, 11 In. 780

Doll, Automaton, Whistler, Man Leaning On Lamppost, Wood, Key Wind, Movable Head, 19 In.
$210

Rich Penn Auctions

Doll, China Head, Porcelain, Red Cheeks, Black Hair, Brown Dress, Victorian, 27 ½ In.
$276

Clars Auction Gallery

Doll, Cloth, Julia Beecher, Stockinet, Blue Painted Eyes, Gown, Leather Shoes, c.1900, 21 In.
$938

Eldred's

Doll, Gaultier, Bisque Swivel Head, Blue Glass Eyes, Blond Mohair, Kid Body, 22 In.
$7,188

Theriault's

Doll, German, Papier-Mache Head, Man, Holding Cigar, Leather Shoes, Hat, Wood Stand, 9 In.
$118

Charleston Estate Auctions

Doll, Greiner, Papier-Mache Head, Cloth Body, Kid Arms, c.1870, 21 In.
$366

Charleston Estate Auctions

Kestner dolls are also in this category under J.D.K.

Kestner, 128, Socket Head, Fixed Eyes, Composition, Jointed, Nurse Outfit, 16 In. 875
Kestner, 151, Bisque, Blue Sleep Eyes, Human Hair, Loop-Jointed, Painted Yellow Boots, 5 In. 633
Kestner, 172, Gibson Girl, Bisque Head, Auburn Mohair, Kid, Pin-Jointed, 1910, 20 In. *illus* 978
Kestner, 184, Boy, Bisque Socket Head, Blue Sleep Eyes, Blond Mohair, Tyrolean Costume, 11 In. *illus* 2070
Kestner, 192, Bisque Head, Brown Glass Eyes, Jointed Composition, Dress, Muff, 1910, 22 In. 3464
Kestner, 221, Bisque Head, Googly Sleep Eyes, Pug Nose, Jointed Composition & Wood, 11 In. 5980
Kestner, 260, Bisque, Brown, Sleep Eyes, Fleecy Wig, Composition Toddler Body, 7 In. *illus* 690
Kestner, Bisque Head, Blue Sleep Eyes, Blond Mohair, Jointed Papier-Mache Toddler, 13 In. 390

Kewpie dolls are listed in the Kewpie category.

Kish & Co., Meredith, Sunday Best, Vinyl, Red Hair, Ivory Coat, Hat, Shoes, Box, 1996 90
Kish & Co., Pierrot, Famous Painters, Harlequin Costume, Box, 1997, 12 In. 54
Lenci, Schoolboy, Felt, Painted, Pouty Face, Mohair, Original Costume, c.1930, 17 In. *illus* 1725
Madame Alexander, Amy, Little Women, Blond Floss Loop Curls, Floral Gown, 1948, 14 In. 403
Madame Alexander, Babs Skating, Plastic, Mohair Curls, Satin & Marabou Costume, 18 In. 2185
Madame Alexander, Ballerina, Alexander-Kins, Plastic, Rosy Cheeks, Red Hair, 1953, 8 In. 230
Madame Alexander, Ballerina, Nina, Plastic, Blond Floss Hair, Rosebuds, Tutu, 1951, 21 In. 863
Madame Alexander, Cissy, Auburn Hair, Blue Floral Dress, Strappy High Heels, 1958, 20 In. 1380
Madame Alexander, Cissy, Plastic, Brunette, Ball Gown, Pink Camellias, Stole, 20 In. 1955
Madame Alexander, Cissy, Queen Elizabeth, Plastic, Brocade Gown, Jewel Crown, 1955, 20 In. 863
Madame Alexander, Godey Lady, Blond Chignon, Taffeta & Lace Gown, 1949, 14 In. 1150
Madame Alexander, Ice Capades Skater, Plastic, Jacqueline Face, Beaded Costume, 21 In. 1093
Madame Alexander, Little Butch, Composition, Cloth, Chubby Cheeks, Romper, 1942, 11 In. 115
Madame Alexander, Little Genius, Vinyl, Lamb's Wool Wig, Organdy Petticoat, 1958, 8 In. 345
Madame Alexander, Renoir, Composition, Sleep Eyes, Brunette Mohair, Gown, 1946, 20 In. 8625
Madame Alexander, Ring Bearer, Plastic, Blond Mohair Bob, Satin Suit, Pillow, 1950, 12 In. 230
Madame Alexander, Scarlet O'Hara, Composition, Black Human Hair, 1938, 11 In. 374
Madame Alexander, Southern Belle, Sleep Eyes, Blond Curls, Gown, Hat, Box, 1956, 8 In. 510
Madame Alexander, Wendy, Bride, Plastic, Sleep Eyes, Satin Gown, Tulle Veil, 1952, 18 In. 345
Madame Alexander, Wendy, So Grown Up, Tosca Wig, Bent-Knee Walker, Coat, 1957, 8 In. 805
Maggie Bessie, Cloth, Flat Face, Oil Painted Features, Stitch-Jointed, Chambray Dress, 21 In. 7800
Maggie Iacono, Rebecca, Felt, Pressed, Painted, Red Braids, Jointed Body, Dress, Label, 16 In. 120
Maggie Made, Alice, Pressed Felt, Painted Features, Blond Hair, Blue Dress, 1996, 16 In. 480
Maggie Made, Melinda, Pressed Felt, Painted, Jointed, Brown Hair, Green Print Dress, 16 In. 300
Marseille, Bisque Socket Head, Blue Eyes, Rose Dress, Bonnet, Socks, Shoes, Early 1900s, 37 In. 322
Mary Hoyer, Gigi, Plastic, Blue Sleep Eyes, Brown Wig, Clothing, 1950s, 18 In. 540
Mary Hoyer, Hard Plastic, Sleep Eyes, Mohair Wig, Knit Dress From Hoyer Pattern, 14 In. 84
Mattel, Barbie, Alfred Hitchcock's The Birds, Dressed As Tippi Hedren, Box, Birds 115
Mattel, Barbie, American Girl, Blond Bob, Saturday Matinee Ensemble, No. 1615 518
Mattel, Barbie, American Girl, Blond Pageboy, Holiday Dance Ensemble, No. 1639 431
Mattel, Barbie, American Girl, Brunette Bob, Swimsuit, Stripes, Turquoise Bottom, No. 1070 316
Mattel, Barbie, Bubble Cut, Titian, Country Fair Ensemble, No. 1603 161
Mattel, Barbie, Bubble Cut, Titian, Senior Prom Ensemble, Aqua Gown, No. 951 115
Mattel, Barbie, Bubble Cut, White Ginger, Striped Swimsuit 259
Mattel, Barbie, Color Magic, Ruby Red Hair, Swimsuit, Turquoise Shoes, Headband 575
Mattel, Barbie, Display, Barbie Beauty Secrets, Doll In Plastic Bubble, Easel Back, 20 x 20 x 8 In. 316
Mattel, Barbie, Growin' Pretty Hair, Blond, Pink Dress, Box, First Issue 316
Mattel, Barbie, Hair Happenin', Red Hair, Fuchsia & White Dress, Belt, No. 1174, 1971 431
Mattel, Barbie, Learns To Cook, Brunette Hair, Dress, Utensils, Box 121
Mattel, Barbie, No. 1, Blond Ponytail, Striped Swimsuit, Holes In Feet 5463
Mattel, Barbie, No. 3, Blond Ponytail, Blue Eyes, Curly Bangs, Stand 633
Mattel, Barbie, No. 4, Blond Ponytail, Let's Dance Ensemble, No. 978 173
Mattel, Barbie, No. 5, Blond Ponytail, Cotton Casual Ensemble, Accessories, No. 912 161
Mattel, Barbie, No. 7, Brunette Ponytail, Career Girl Ensemble, Black & White Suit, No. 954 138
Mattel, Barbie, No. 7, Titian Ponytail, Red Swimsuit & Shoes, Box, Booklet, Stand 196
Mattel, Barbie, Quick Curl, Blond, Turquoise Dress, Box, No. 9217 138
Mattel, Barbie, Rhapsody In Paris, Blond, Blue Gown, Ruffled, Limited Edition, 2006, Box 259
Mattel, Barbie, Silkstone, Fashion Model Collection, Soiree, Blond, Pink & Silver Gown, Box 460
Mattel, Barbie, Silkstone, Fashion Model Collection, Verushka, Box 288

Doll, Handwerck, Child, Bisque Socket Head, Brown Glass Sleep Eyes, 4 Upper Teeth, Shoes, 27 In.
$106

Bunch Auctions

Doll, Japanese, Ichimatsu, Child, Gofun Finish, Enamel, Human Hair, Silk Kimono, c.1930, 15 In.
$2,645

Theriault's

Doll, Jumeau, Bisque, Brown Eyes, Eyelashes, Blond Hair, Earrings, Dress, Straw Hat, c.1880, 18 In.
$6,000

Michaan's Auctions

TIP
If you buy an old cloth doll, put it in a closed box with an insect strip for 48 hours to be sure there are no insects. Be sure the strip does not touch the doll.

Doll, K * R, 62, Bisque Head, Composition, White Dress, Germany, 23 In.
$83

Bunch Auctions

Doll, Kathe Kruse, Cloth, Pressed & Painted, Dirndl Costume, Cap, Box, 1940s, 14 In.
$2,185

Theriault's

Doll, Kestner, 172, Gibson Girl, Bisque Head, Auburn Mohair, Kid, Pin-Jointed, 1910, 20 In.
$978

Theriault's

TIP
Never scrub porcelain dolls.

Doll, Kestner, 184, Boy, Bisque Socket Head, Blue Sleep Eyes, Blond Mohair, Tyrolean Costume, 11 In.
$2,070

Theriault's

Doll, Kestner, 260, Bisque, Brown, Sleep Eyes, Fleecy Wig, Composition Toddler Body, 7 In.
$690

Theriault's

Doll, Lenci, Schoolboy, Felt, Painted, Pouty Face, Mohair, Original Costume, c.1930, 17 In.
$1,725

Theriault's

Mattel, Barbie, Silkstone, Styled As Elizabeth Taylor, White Diamonds, Hankie Chic 92
Mattel, Barbie, Talking, Perfectly Plaid Gift Set, Brunette, Jumpsuit, Hat, No. 1193 230
Mattel, Barbie, Voyage In Vintage, Blond, Orange Dress, Hatbox, Box, 2009 219
Mattel, Francie, Quick Curl, Brunette, No. 4222, Box, 1972 196
Mattel, Julia, Twist 'N Turn, Brown Hair, Candlelight Capers Ensemble, No. 1753, 1969 115
Mattel, Ken, Brunette, Flocked Hair, Red Swimsuit, Jacket, Sandals, Box 104
Mattel, Ken, Walk Lively, Blue Shirt, Plaid Pants, Box, No. 1184, 1971 230
Milliner's Model, Papier-Mache, Woman, Wooden, Painted, 15 x 6 In. 1080
Moravian, Cloth, Ink, Hand Painted Details, Organdy Pinafore, Wool Bonnet, 1960s, 8 In. 216
Moravian, Polly Heckewelder, Cloth, Ink & Painted Features, Pink Check Dress, 1930s, 18 In. 228
Nancy Ann Storybook, East Side West Side, Plastic, Jointed, Red Dress, Hat, Box, 5 In. 259
Orsini, Vivi, Bisque, Sleep Eyes, Mohair Wig, Cotton Dress, 1919, 5 In. 720
Paper dolls are listed in their own category.
Parian, Emma Clear, Blue Scarf Lady, Shoulder Head, Painted, Blue Silk Gown, 1940s, 16 In. 120
Parian, Emma Clear, Jenny Lind, Pink Shoulder Head, Painted, Ivory Satin Gown, 1947, 18 In. 228
Parian, Emma Clear, Painted, Pierced Ears, Sculpted Bodice, Velvet Gown, 1949, 18 In. 270
Pincushion dolls are listed in their own category.
R. John Wright, Benjamin Bunny, Beatrix Potter Collection, Box, 2001, 12 In. 900
R. John Wright, White Rabbit, Alice In Wonderland Series, Plush, Cloth, 2004, 13 In. 570
Robert Tonner, Little Orphan Annie, Porcelain, Red Curly Mohair, Red Dress, 1995, 14 In. 54
S & H dolls are also listed here as Bergmann and Simon & Halbig.
S.F.B.J., 301, Bebe, Bisque, Glass Eyes, Porcelain Teeth, Human Hair, Walking Mechanism, 17 In... 1035
Sasha, Girl, Vinyl, Brown Skin, Brunette Wig, Checked Dress, Red Beret, Germany, 1960s, 16 In..... 390
Schmidt, 500, Asian Child, Bisque, Amber Tone, Glass Eyes, Mohair, Silk Costume, c.1900, 14 In... 3910
Schoenhut, 14/308, Girl, Wood, Brown Intaglio Eyes, Brown Mohair Wig, 14 In. 720
Schoenhut, Girl, Wood Socket Head, Painted, Carved Braids, Spring-Jointed, Dress, 1911, 19 In..... 1265
Schoenhut, Girl, Wood, Black Eyes, Bent Limb, Round Stand, c.1911, 15 In. 425
Sherman Smith, Hitty, Wood, Jointed, Mitt Hands, Gray Cloth Dress, Painted Slippers, 6 In. .. 204
Sherman Smith, Jackie Kennedy, Porcelain Head, Painted, Jointed Wood Body, 1963, 9 In. 120
Shirley Temple dolls are included in the Shirley Temple category.
Shmoo, White Plush Body, Blue Hat & Bowtie, Gund, 12 In. .... *illus* 275
Simon & Halbig dolls are also listed here under Bergmann and S & H.
Simon & Halbig, 151, Bisque Socket Head, Mohair, Jointed Composition & Wood, 18 In. *illus* 7188
Simon & Halbig, 1448, Girl, Bisque Head, Sleep Eyes, Braids, Composition & Wood, 16 In....... 12650
Simon & Halbig, 1469, Flapper, Bisque, Heart Shape Face, Brunette Mohair, Jointed, 14 In..... 4600
Simon & Halbig, 1489, Erika, Bisque Socket Head, Glass Sleep Eyes, Ball-Jointed, 26 In. 3163
Simon & Halbig, Bisque, Socket Head, Glass Sleep Eyes, 6 Upper Teeth, Lace Dress, 34 In. *illus* 236
Sonneberg, Bisque Head, Paperweight Eyes, Brown Human Hair Wig, Ball-Jointed, 20 In. 920
Steiff, Man, Cloth, Painted, Swivel Head, Shoebutton Eyes, Blue Uniform, Ear Button, 11 In. .. 1140
Steiff, Professor, Felt, Pressed, Painted, Mohair, Elongated, Leather Shoes, c.1915, 17 In. *illus* 2990
Steiner, Bisque Socket Head, Sleep Eyes With Lever, Auburn Hair, Jointed Composition, 38 In. 9200
Terri Lee, Bride, Plastic, Blond Curls, Gown, Veil, Garter, Tagged, Marked, 15 in 150
Tootsie, Composition, Molded Socket Head, 5-Piece Body, Dress, Sears Roebuck, 1929, 13 In... 84
Vogue, Ginny, Plastic, Blond Braids, Blue Sleep Eyes, Pink Bloomers, Socks, Box, 1956, 8 In.... 104
Vogue, Ginny, Wee Imp, Plastic, Orange Hair, Freckles, Green Sleep Eyes, Dress, c.1958, 8 In.. 84
Vogue, WAAC-Ette, Composition, Sleep Eyes, Army Uniform, U.S.A. Shoulderbag, 13 In. 270
Vogue, WAVE-Ette, Composition, Sleep Eyes, Navy Uniform, U.S.A. Shoulderbag, 1940s, 13 In.. 330
Wax Shoulder Head, Child, Glass Eyes, Tendrils, Cloth, Wax Limbs, England, c.1860, 29 In... 1035
Wax Shoulder Head, Rose Complexion, Glass Eyes, Muslin Body, Wax Limbs, 1865, 22 In...... 748
Wood, Jointed, Painted Eyes, Wispy Hair, Yellow Tuck Comb, Gown, 1860s, 8 In. 3600
Yellow Kid, Composition Head, Hands & Feet, Yellow Cotton Dress, 12 ½ In. .... *illus* 1400
Zook, Kaitlyn, Vinyl Head & Limbs, Cloth Body, Brown Hair, Flowered Dress, 1991, 21 In. 18

DOLL CLOTHES

Barbie, Beautiful Bride, Missing Garter, No. 1698 184
Barbie, Easter Parade, Dress, Coat, Hat, Gloves, No. 971 431
Barbie, Pan American Airways Stewardess, All Accessories, No. 1678 633
Barbie, Pretty Wild, Color Magic, Dress, Hat, Tote, No. 1777 196
Barbie, Red Flame, Red Velvet Coat, Original Box, No. 939 127
Barbie, Roman Holiday, No. 968, Sheath, Coat, Accessories 495

SELECTED DOLL MARKS WITH DATES USED

Effanbee Doll Co.
1922+
New York, N.Y.

Lenci
1922+
Turin, Italy

Hertwig & Co.
1864–c.1940
Katzhütte, Thuringia, Germany

Kämmer & Rheinhardt
1886–1932
Waltershausen, Thüringia, Germany

J.D. Kestner Jr.
1805–1938
Waltershausen, Thuringia, Germany

Ideal Novelty & Toy Co.
1955–1984
New York, N.Y.

L.A. & S.

Louis Amberg & Son
1909–1930
Cincinnati, Ohio; New York, N.Y.

BRU. J^NE R
11

Bru Jne. & Cie
c.1879–1899
Paris, France

Armand Marseille
c.1920
Köppelsdorf, Thüringia, Germany

DÉPOSE
TÊTE JUMEAU
6

Maison Jumeau
1886–1899
Paris, France

Bähr & Pröschild
1871–1930s
Ohrdruf, Thüringia, Germany

DÉPOSE
S.F.B.J.

S.F.B.J. (Société Française de Fabrication de Bébés & Jouets)
1905–1950+
Paris and Montreuil-sous-Bois, France

ALBEGO
10
Made in Germany

Alt. Beck & Gottschalck
1930–1940
Nauendorf, Thuringia, Germany

Schoenau & Hoffmeister
1901–c.1953
Sonneberg, Thuringia, Germany

Gebruder Heubach
1840–1938
Lichte, Thuringia, Germany

Doll, Shmoo, White Plush Body, Blue Hat & Bowtie, Gund, 12 In.
$275

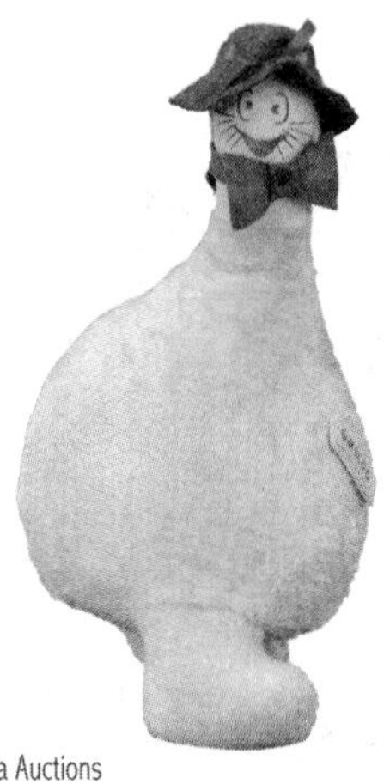

Bertoia Auctions

Doll, Simon & Halbig, 151, Bisque Socket Head, Mohair, Jointed Composition & Wood, 18 In.
$7,188

Theriault's

Doll, Simon & Halbig, Bisque, Socket Head, Glass Sleep Eyes, 6 Upper Teeth, Lace Dress, 34 In.
$236

Bunch Auctions

DONALD DUCK *items are included in the Disneyana category.*

DOORSTOPS

Doorstops have been made in all types of designs. The vast majority of the doorstops sold today are cast iron and were made from about 1890 to 1930. Most of them are shaped like people, animals, flowers, or ships. Reproductions and newly designed examples are sold in gift shops. These are three marks used by vintage doorstop makers.

Bradley & Hubbard Manufacturing Co. 1854–1940

HUBLEY

Hubley Manufacturing Co. 1894–1965

WILTON PRODUCTS INC WRIGHTSVILLE PA.

Wilton Products, Inc. c.1935–1989

Bird, Heron, Perched, Multicolor, Cast Iron, Albany Foundry, c.1926, 8 x 5 x 3 In. .... *illus* 311
Boston Terrier, Standing, Facing Right, Cast Iron, Hubley, c.1920, 10 x 9 In. .... *illus* 175
Castle On Hill, Winding Path, Leaves, Cast Iron, Painted, Albany Foundry, 8 In. 420
Cat, Lying Down, Cast Iron, 1900s, 9 In. 984
Cat, Red, Art Deco, Cast Iron, Hubley, c.1925, 5 ¼ x 4 ½ In. 375
Cat, Resting, Gray, White, Black Eyes, Yellow Iris, Cast Iron, Marked, Hubley, 6 x 10 ½ In. 275
Cat, Sitting, Trapezoid Base, Cast Iron, Painted, 12 ½ In. 424
Cat, Sleeping, Black Paint, Cast Iron, 1900s, 13 ½ In. 431
Cat, Standing, Tail Up, Green Eyes, Orange Brown, Cast Iron, Hubley, 11 x 8 In. 509
Cat, White, Green Eyes, Hollow Body, Cast Iron, Marked, Hubley, 6 x 6 ½ x 4 ½ In. 147
Clown, Full Figure, Blue Hat, Red Dress, Rectangular Base, Cast Iron, c.1940, 12 x 11 In. *illus* 236
Cockatoo, On Branch, Multicolor, Cast Iron, Albany Foundry, c.1920, 14 ½ In. 325
Dog, Boston Terrier, Full Figure, Cast Iron, 2-Piece Construction, 10 x 9 In. 102
Dog, German Shepherd, Standing, Cast Iron, Hubley, 10 ½ x 14 In. 225
Dog, Pekinese, Brown, Cast Iron, Hubley, 13 ½ x 5 ½ x 9 In. 1080
Dog, Scottie, Molded Fur, Body Details, Painted, Cast Iron, 1900s, 11 In. 246
Dog, Scottie, Standing, Tail Raised, Cast Iron, Painted Black, 11 x 8 ½ In. 92
Dog, Standing, Cast Iron, Stepped Base, c.1850, 6 x 7 In. .... *illus* 277
Dog, Terrier, Standing, Black & White, Base, Cast Iron, Bradley & Hubbard, c.1920, 11 x 10 In. *illus* 590
Duck, Painted, Cast Iron, Hollow, 13 In. 160
Figurine, Mexican, Guitar, Yellow Hat, Pants, Cast Iron, Art Deco, 6 x 2 x 11 ¾ In. .... *illus* 2700
Fish, Mermaid, Cast Iron, Copper, c.1930, 9 In. .... *illus* 1180
Flower Vase, Cast Iron, Signed, Bradley & Hubbard, 12 x 6 x 3 ¾ In. 254
Galleon, Sails, Painted, Red & Gold, Dragon Figurehead, Cast Iron, 1930, 11 ½ In. 148
Giraffe, Detailed Body, Yellow, Black Spots, Cast Iron, Early 1900s, 12 ½ In. .... *illus* 984
Golfer, A Difficult Lie, Overhead Swing, Cast Iron, Hubley, 8 ½ x 7 In. .... *illus* 480
Honey Bear, Black, Standing, Holding Pot, Licking Lips, Cast Iron, 5 ¾ x 5 x 15 In. .... *illus* 2400
Hunter & Dog, Standing, Oblong Base, Cast Iron, c.1920, 15 x 9 x 2 ½ In. 62
Lion, Lying Down, Black, Painted, Cast Iron, 14 x 28 ½ x 4 ½ In. 492
Lobster, Red, Painted, Cast Iron, Early 1900s, 13 In. 1080
Mary Quite Contrary, Watering Flowers, Yellow Dress, Cast Iron, Littco, 12 ½ In. 180
Monkey, Sitting, Eyes Open, Cast Iron, 9 In. .... *illus* 259
Nasturtiums, Striped Flowerpot, Cast Iron, Painted, Hubley, 7 ½ In. 300
Nude Child, Reaching, Checkered Book Base, Cast Iron, Ella Rood Studios, 17 In. 540
Owl, Cast Iron, Statue, Bradley & Hubbard, Marked, 8 In. .... *illus* 944
Parrot, Perched On Branch, Green & Yellow, Cast Iron, 9 ½ x 3 x 9 ¾ In. 1200
Parrot, Rectangular Base, Cast Iron, Bradley & Hubbard, 1910s, 8 x 6 ¾ In. 192
Peacock, Open Fan, Blue Shaded To Green, Yellow, Cast Iron, c.1920, 6 ½ x 6 ½ In. 738
Penguin, Looking Up, Painted, Red, Yellow & Black, Taylor Cook, 1930, 5 x 2 x 9 ½ In. 1680
Penguin, Standing, Copper, Painted, Black & White, c.1890, 14 In. .... *illus* 1074
Penguin, Standing, Top Hat, Black, White, Yellow Feet, Hubley, 1930s, 10 ½ In. 590

Doll, Steiff, Professor, Felt, Pressed, Painted, Mohair, Elongated, Leather Shoes, c.1915, 17 In.
$2,990

Theriault's

Doll, Yellow Kid, Composition Head, Hands & Feet, Yellow Cotton Dress, 12 ½ In.
$1,400

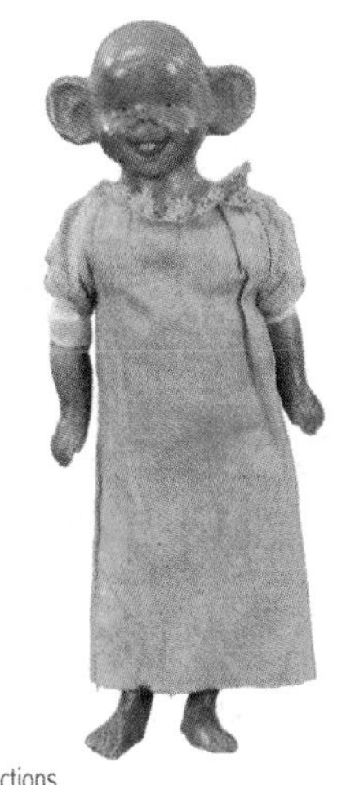

Bertoia Auctions

Doorstop, Bird, Heron, Perched, Multicolor, Cast Iron, Albany Foundry, c.1926, 8 x 5 x 3 In.
$311

Soulis Auctions

Doorstop, Boston Terrier, Standing, Facing Right, Cast Iron, Hubley, c.1920, 10 x 9 In.
$175

Eldred's

Doorstop, Clown, Full Figure, Blue Hat, Red Dress, Rectangular Base, Cast Iron, c.1940, 12 x 11 In.
$236

Copake Auctions

Doorstop, Dog, Standing, Cast Iron, Stepped Base, c.1850, 6 x 7 In.
$277

Skinner, Inc.

Doorstop, Dog, Terrier, Standing, Black & White, Base, Cast Iron, Bradley & Hubbard, c.1920, 11 x 10 In.
$590

Copake Auctions

Doorstop, Figurine, Mexican, Guitar, Yellow Hat, Pants, Cast Iron, Art Deco, 6 x 2 x 11 ¾ In.
$2,700

Morphy Auctions

D

D

Doorstop, Fish, Mermaid, Cast Iron, Copper, c.1930, 9 In.
$1,180

Copake Auctions

Doorstop, Honey Bear, Black, Standing, Holding Pot, Licking Lips, Cast Iron, 5 ¾ x 5 x 15 In.
$2,400

Morphy Auctions

Doorstop, Penguin, Standing, Copper, Painted, Black & White, c.1890, 14 In.
$1,074

Hartzell's Auction Gallery Inc.

Doorstop, Giraffe, Detailed Body, Yellow, Black Spots, Cast Iron, Early 1900s, 12 ½ In.
$984

Skinner, Inc.

Doorstop, Monkey, Sitting, Eyes Open, Cast Iron, 9 In.
$259

Apple Tree Auction Center

Doorstop, Pheasant, Head Turned, Cast Iron, Multicolor, Hubley, c.1930, 7 ½ x 8 ½ In.
$738

Copake Auctions

Doorstop, Golfer, A Difficult Lie, Overhead Swing, Cast Iron, Hubley, 8 ½ x 7 In.
$480

Morphy Auctions

Doorstop, Owl, Cast Iron, Statue, Bradley & Hubbard, Marked, 8 In.
$944

Copake Auctions

Doorstop, Squirrel, Sitting, Holding Nut, Painted, Red Nose & Ears, Hubley, 1900s, 9 In.
$509

Hartzell's Auction Gallery Inc.

Pheasant, Head Turned, Cast Iron, Multicolor, Hubley, c.1930, 7 ½ x 8 ½ In. .... *illus* 738
Punch, Dog Toby, Painted Black, Cast Iron, c.1880, 12 x 9 In. 84
Rabbit, Wearing Hat, Standing, Cast Iron, Early 1900s, 9 ½ In. 570
Skunk, Painted, Black & White, Glazed, Cast Iron, Early 1900s, 7 x 8 ½ In. 367
Snowman, Top Hat, Carrot Nose, Holding Broom, Cast Iron, Early 1900s, 8 In. 360
Soldier, Holding Gun, Painted, Square Base, Cast Iron, c.1940, 7 ½ In. 148
Squirrel, Sitting, Holding Nut, Painted, Red Nose & Ears, Hubley, 1900s, 9 In. .... *illus* 509
Troubadour, Man, Guitar, Singing, Standing, Painted, Cast Iron, 11 In. 443
Turkey, Cast Iron, Multicolor, Open Tail, Bradley & Hubbard, 10 x 3 x 12 In. .... *illus* 2750
Turtle, Cast Iron, c.1920, 8 In. 207
Whale, Tail Up, Aluminum, Black, Painted, Late 1800s, 7 x 13 In. 254
Windmill, Green Roof, Yellow Wheel, Cast Iron, National Foundry, c.1920, 6 ¾ x 7 In. .... *illus* 148

DOULTON

Doulton was founded about 1858 in Lambeth, England. A second factory was opened in Burslem, England, by 1871. The name *Royal Doulton* appeared on the company's wares after 1902 and is listed in the Royal Doulton category in this book. Other Doulton ware is listed here. Doulton's Lambeth factory closed about 1956.

Doulton and Co.
1869–1877

Doulton and Co.
1880–1912, 1923

Doulton and Co.
1885–1902

Vase, Blue Children, Cobalt Trim, Looking In Tree Hole, Burslem, c.1900, 13 ½ In., Pair 350
Vase, White Flowers, Leaves, Brown, J. Harding & J. Durtnall, Lambeth, c.1890, 9 ¼ In. 310

DRESDEN

Dresden and Meissen porcelain are often confused. Porcelains were made in the town of Meissen, Germany, beginning about 1706. The town of Dresden, Germany, has been home to many decorating studios since the early 1700s. Blanks were obtained from Meissen and other porcelain factories. Some say porcelain was also made in Dresden in the early years. Decorations on Dresden are often similar to Meissen, and marks were copied. Some of the earliest books on marks confused Dresden and Meissen, and that has remained a problem ever since. The Meissen "AR" mark and crossed swords mark are among the most forged marks on porcelain. Meissen pieces are listed in this book under Meissen. German porcelain marked "Dresden" is listed here. Irish Dresden and Dresden made in East Liverpool, Ohio, are not included in this section. These three marks say "Dresden" although none were used by a factory called Dresden.

Karl Richard Klemm
c.1891–1914

Ambrosius Lamm
c.1887+

Carl Thieme / Saxon Porcelain Manufactory
c.1903

Compote, Flowers, Scalloped, 3 Putti, Legs Crossed, Plinth Base, 15 x 11 In. .... *illus* 545
Figurine, Man Playing Violin, Woman On Sofa, Sitzendorf, 7 ⅝ x 9 x 6 In. 460
Figurine, Pug, Seated, White & Brown, Bell Collar, 1900s, 8 ½ x 8 ¾ x 5 ¾ In. 176
Group, Courting Scene, Gold Trim, Lace, Unterweissbach, Germany, 12 x 9 ⅝ In. .... *illus* 403
Urn, Gilt Bronze, Mounted, Ram's Head Handles, Cherubs Finial, 1800s, 23 ½ In. 316
Vase, Double Courting Scenes, Maroon Border, Gold Highlights, 2 Handles, 8 In. 290

Check the Screws

Boston Terrier iron doorstops are so popular they have been reproduced. Look at the heads of the screws that join the two halves of the body. If they are Phillips-head screws, it is a modern copy.

Doorstop, Turkey, Cast Iron, Multicolor, Open Tail, Bradley & Hubbard, 10 x 3 x 12 In.
$2,750

Morphy Auctions

Doorstop, Windmill, Green Roof, Yellow Wheel, Cast Iron, National Foundry, c.1920, 6 ¾ x 7 In.
$148

Copake Auctions

TIP

Be sure to put a dead bolt on each exterior door. Try to put it where it can't be reached from a nearby window. Use long screws.

TIP
To clean wax from glass candlesticks, scrape with a wooden stick, then wash off the remaining wax with rubbing alcohol.

Dresden, Compote, Flowers, Scalloped, 3 Putti, Legs Crossed, Plinth Base, 15 x 11 In.
$545

Fontaine's Auction Gallery

Dresden, Group, Courting Scene, Gold Trim, Lace, Unterweissbach, Germany, 12 x 9 5/8 In.
$403

Blackwell Auctions

Durand, Bowl, Pulled Feather, Red, Clear, Flared Rim, c.1920, 4 x 12 In.
$140

Jeffrey S. Evans & Associates

Durand, Candlestick, King Tut Design, Gold, Silver Iridescent Trim, c.1920, 10 In., Pair,
$1,100

Woody Auctions

Durand, Plate, Bridgeton Rose, Engraved, Green, White, Footed, 7 3/4 In.
$142

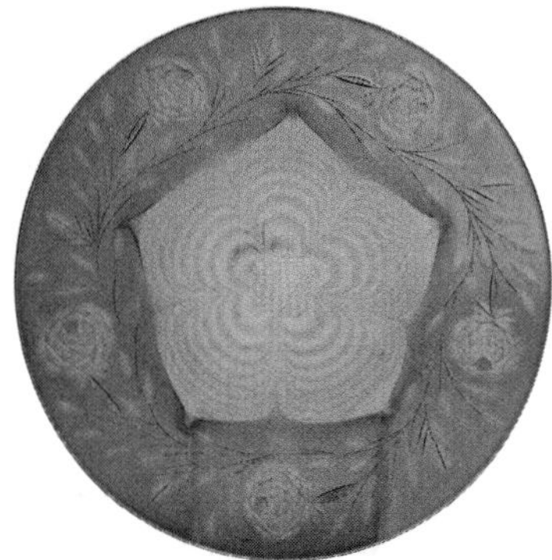

Bunch Auctions

Durand, Sherbet, Red, White, Feather, Tall Stem, Ruffled Rim, Round Base, 4 1/2 In.
$118

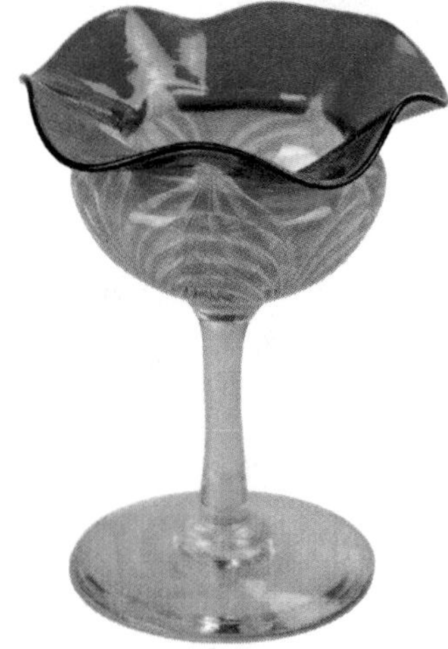

Bunch Auctions

Durand, Vase, Blue Iridescent Body, White Heart & Vine Design, 9 3/8 In.
$500

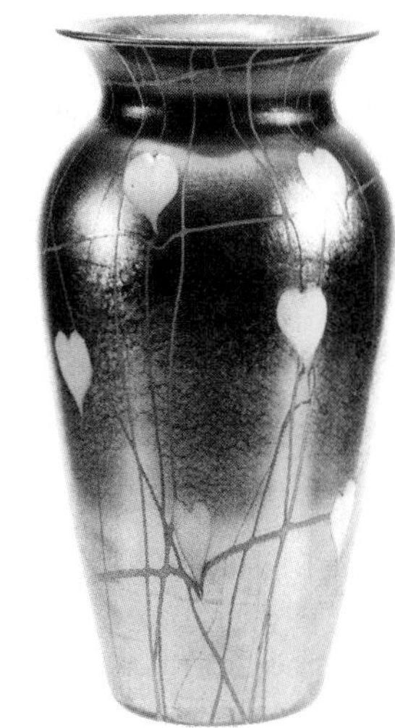

Woody Auctions

Durand, Vase, Gold Wave Pattern, Pink Iridescent Ground, Round Base, Signed, 7 In.
$2,124

Bunch Auctions

Enamel, Bowl, Juggler, Mottled Lime Green Ground, Karl Drerup, U.S.A., 3/4 x 4 1/2 In.
$228

Clars Auction Gallery

DUNCAN & MILLER

Duncan & Miller is a term used by collectors when referring to glass made by the George A. Duncan and Sons Company or the Duncan and Miller Glass Company. These companies worked from 1893 to 1955, when the use of the name *Duncan* was discontinued and the firm became part of the United States Glass Company. Early patterns may be listed under Pressed Glass.

Compote, Amberette, Open, Amber Stain, Footed, Ruffled Rim, 1885, 7 x 11 x 5 3/8 In. 234
Dish, Swan, Red Head & Neck, White Body, c.1950, 5 3/8 x 4 In. 75
Vase, Cornucopia, Yellow & White, Vaseline Glass, 13 In., Pair 47

DURAND

Durand art glass was made from 1924 to 1931. The Vineland Flint Glass Works was established by Victor Durand and Victor Durand Jr. in 1897. In 1924 Martin Bach Jr. and other artisans from the Quezal glassworks joined them at the Vineland, New Jersey, plant to make Durand art glass. They called their gold iridescent glass Gold Luster.

Bowl, Pulled Feather, Red, Clear, Flared Rim, c.1920, 4 x 12 In. ....*illus* 140
Candlestick, King Tut Design, Gold, Silver Iridescent Trim, c.1920, 10 In., Pair ....*illus* 1100
Ginger Jar, Blue Iridescent, Heart & Vine, c.1920, 8 3/4 x 7 1/2 In. 1060
Lamp Base, 2-Light, Blue Iridescent, Threaded, Gilt, 25 x 5 1/2 In. 212
Plate, Bridgeton Rose, Engraved, Green, White, Footed, 7 3/4 In. ....*illus* 142
Plate, Pulled Feather, Red, Clear, Waffle Cut, c.1925, 7 3/4 In. 211
Sherbet, Red, White, Feather, Tall Stem, Ruffled Rim, Round Base, 4 1/2 In. ....*illus* 118
Vase, Blue Iridescent Body, White Heart & Vine Design, 9 3/8 In. ....*illus* 500
Vase, Dark To Light Blue Iridescent, High Shoulders Taper Down To Base, Signed, 8 In. 580
Vase, Gold Iridescent, Mazarine Blue Finish, Graduating Neck, c.1900, 11 x 7 1/2 In. 496
Vase, Gold Wave Pattern, Pink Iridescent Ground, Round Base, Signed, 7 In. ....*illus* 2124
Vase, King Tut, Gold Iridescent, Urn Shape, Flaring Mouth, 6 5/8 x 3 1/2 x 3 In. 1872

ELVIS PRESLEY

Elvis Presley, the well-known singer, lived from 1935 to 1977. He became famous by 1956. Elvis appeared on television, starred in 27 movies, and performed in Las Vegas. Memorabilia from any of the Presley shows, his records, and even memorials made after his death are collected.

Doll, Plastic, Black Shirt, Pink Checked Jacket, Guitar, Box, 1993, 12 In. 12
Magazine, World Of Elvis Memorial, 1977 41
Necktie, Many Portraits, Silk, Blue Ground, RM Style, 1994 24
Photo, Corniche, Lithograph, Candymaster, c.1955, 27 x 19 In. 850
Photograph, Getting Physical In Army, Type 1, 1958 250
Plate, Looking At Legend, Studio Session, Delphi, 1990, 8 In. 15
Stickpin, Young Portrait, Goldtone, c.1955, 2 3/4 In. 42
Trading Cards, Boxcar Enterprises, 66 Cards, Display Box, 1978 25

ENAMEL

Enamels listed here are made of glass particles and other materials heated and fused to metal. In the eighteenth and nineteenth centuries, workmen from Russia, France, England, and other countries made small boxes and table pieces of enamel on metal. One form of English enamel is called *Battersea* and is listed under that name. There was a revival of interest in artist-made enameling in the 1930s and a new style evolved. There is a recently renewed interest in the artistic enameled plaques, vases, ashtrays, and jewelry. Enamels made since the 1930s are usually on copper or steel, although silver was often used for jewelry. Graniteware, the factory-made household pieces made of tin or iron, is a separate category in this book. Enameled metal

Enamel, Dish, Oval, Garlands & Symbols, France, 1800s, 1 x 5 x 3 3/4 In.
$154

Charlton Hall Auctions

Enamel, Kovsh, Silver, Flowers, Turquoise, Russia, 1 x 6 3/4 x 2 In.
$738

Charlton Hall Auctions

Enamel, Plaque, Oval, Chinoiserie, Children Playing, Brass Frame, 1700s, 5 1/2 x 6 1/2 In.
$4,973

Thomaston Place Auction Galleries

TIP

If you use a roller to paint your walls, watch out for tiny droplets that spot furniture and collectibles nearby. The first few days you may be able to get rid of the drops by rubbing them with a cloth dampened with soap and water. Later you may have to use solvents or try to pop the drop off with a fingernail or razor blade.

ES Germany, Jug, Iridescent, Green Ground, Woman Portrait, Floral Wreath, 7 ½ In.
$30

Woody Auctions

Faience, Wall Pocket, Basket Weave Shape, Multicolor, Leaves, Flowers, France, 10 ½ In.
$92

Stair Galleries

Fairing, Trinket Box, Lift Lid, Mahogany, 2 Drawers, Inlaid, Federal Style, c.1900s, 10 x 8 x 7 In.
$554

Skinner, Inc.

kitchen pieces may be included in the Kitchen category. Cloisonne is a special type of enamel using wire dividers and is listed in its own category. Descriptions of antique glass and ceramics often use the term *enamel* to describe paint, not the glass-based enamels listed here. Marks used by three important enamelists are shown here.

Kenneth F Bates

Lilyan Bachrach 1955–2015

Kenneth Bates 1920s–1994

Edward Winter 1932–1976

Bowl, Footed, Scroll Handles, Anthropomorphic Frieze, Splayed Foot, 1800s, 4 x 6 x 4 In. 300
Bowl, Juggler, Mottled Lime Green Ground, Karl Drerup, U.S.A., ¾ x 4 ½ In. ....*illus* 228
Dish, Oval, Garlands & Symbols, France, 1800s, 1 x 5 x 3 ¾ In. ....*illus* 154
Jewelry Box, Gilt Bronze, Green & Black, Beaded Handles, 4-Footed Base, 8 x 9 In. 360
Kovsh, Silver, Flowers, Turquoise, Russia, 1 x 6 ¾ x 2 In. ....*illus* 738
Plaque, Harlequins, Instruments, Dancing, Green, Blue, White, E. Winter, 27 x 33 In.............. 4840
Plaque, Oval, Chinoiserie, Children Playing, Brass Frame, 1700s, 5 ½ x 6 ½ In. ....*illus* 4973
Plate, Blue, Fish Scale, Gilt Rim, 8 ½ In.. 84

ERPHILA

Erphila is a mark found on Czechoslovakian and other pottery and porcelain made after 1920. This mark was used on items imported by Ebeling & Reuss, Philadelphia, a giftware firm that was founded in 1866 and out of business sometime after 2002. The mark is a combination of the letters *E* and *R* (Ebeling & Reuss) and the first letters of the city, Phila(delphia). Many whimsical figural pitchers and creamers, figurines, platters, and other giftwares carry this mark.

Figurine, Cat, Lying Down, Black & White Stripes, 6 x 6 x 3 In. 50
Pitcher, Abstract, Art Deco, 8 ¾ In.. 59
Teapot, Pig, Sitting Up, Head Is Lid, White, Black Trim, 7 ½ In... 46

ES GERMANY

ES Germany porcelain was made at the factory of Erdmann Schlegelmilch from 1861 to 1937 in Suhl, Germany. The porcelain, marked *ES Germany* or *ES Suhl*, was sold decorated or undecorated. Other pieces were made at a factory in Saxony, Prussia, and are marked *ES Prussia.* Reinhold Schlegelmilch also made porcelain. There is no connection between the two factories. Porcelain made by Reinhold Schlegelmilch is listed in this book under RS Germany, RS Poland, RS Prussia, RS Silesia, RS Suhl, and RS Tillowitz.

Jug, Iridescent, Green Ground, Woman Portrait, Floral Wreath, 7 ½ In. ....*illus* 30
Urn, Bolted, Gold Trim, Green & Maroon Ground, Erdmann Schlegelmilch, 19 x 7 ¾ x 8 In.... 124
Urn, Lid, 2 Handles, Blue Ground, Woman & Cherub Medallion Scene, 11 x 9 In. 48

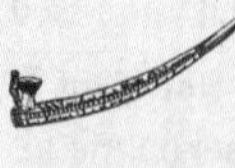

ESKIMO

Eskimo artifacts of all types are collected. Carvings of whale or walrus teeth are listed under Scrimshaw. Baskets are in the Basket category. All other types of Eskimo art are listed here. In Canada and some other areas, the term *Inuit* is used instead of Eskimo. It is illegal to sell some whale parts that are used to made decorative items. The law has changed several times, so check the legality before you buy or sell.

Armor Plate, Bone Panels, Pierced, Engraved Crosshatch Design, 1800s, 9 In. 390
Basket, Lid, Woven, Baleen, Carved Walrus Ivory Finial, John Omnik, 1991, 4 x 3 In. 330

Figure, Hooded, Holding Seal, Carved Soapstone, Marked, c.1979, 5 ¾ In. 156
Sculpture, Polar Bear, Elongated Neck, Carved Walrus Ivory, 4 In. 156

FABERGE

ФАБЕРЖЕ
КФ

Faberge was a firm of jewelers and goldsmiths founded in St. Petersburg, Russia, in 1842, by Gustav Faberge. Peter Carl Faberge, his son, was jeweler to the Russian Imperial Court from about 1870 to 1917. The rare Imperial Easter eggs, jewelry, and decorative items are very expensive today. The name *Faberge* is also used for art made of precious metals and jewels by Peter Carl Faberge's grandson. Theo Faberge launched a collection of artistic things made of expensive materials in 1985. He made jeweled eggs in several sizes. The collection is sold in several museums.

Bowl, Russian Silver Mounted, Cut Glass, 2 Handles, 1 x 7 ¾ In. 1830
Cigarette Case, Powder Blue, Silver Swags, Gold Mounts, Henrik Wigstrom, 3 x 2 x 1 In. 8400
Dish, Caviar, Cobalt Blue, Clear Glass, Footed, Box, 5 In. 220

FAIENCE

Faience refers to tin-glazed earthenware, especially the wares made in France, Germany, and Scandinavia. It is also correct to say that faience is the same as majolica or Delft, although usually the term refers only to the tin-glazed pottery of the three regions mentioned.

Jug, Hinged Lid, Blue Birds & Flowers, Mounted, Pewter, 9 ½ In. 738
Lamp Base, Electric, Flower Garlands, 3 Graces, Pink Dress, Early 1900s, 32 In. 113
Wall Pocket, Basket Weave Shape, Multicolor, Leaves, Flowers, France, 10 ½ In. *illus* 92

FAIRING

Fairings are small souvenir boxes and figurines that were sold at country fairs during the nineteenth century. Most were made in Germany. Reproductions of fairings are being made, especially of the famous *Twelve Months after Marriage* series.

Figurine, Couple In Bed, Stop Yer Ticklin Jock, c.1900, 3 x 3 In. 29
Figurine, Dog, Dalmation, Tree Sculpture, Germany, c.1880, 4 In. 110
Inkwell, Seated Woman, Victorian, Porcelain, Glazed, 7 In. 395
Trinket Box, Dome Top, Mother-Of-Pearl, Brass Stud, Moorish, 1800s, 4 x 7 ½ x 5 In. 120
Trinket Box, Girl & Cat, Dresser, Conta & Boehm 95
Trinket Box, Hinged Lid, Wood, Dovetailed, Rectangular, 8 x 5 x 4 ½ In. 325
Trinket Box, Lid, Woman, Sitting, Cherub, Holding Mirror, Enamel, 1800s, 5 In. 225
Trinket Box, Lift Lid, Mahogany, 2 Drawers, Inlaid, Federal Style, c.1900s, 10 x 8 x 7 In. *illus* 554
Trinket Box, Pitcher, Bowl, Washstand, Skirted Base, Victorian, Germany, 3 ¾ In. 49
Trinket Box, Split Hinged Lid, Whalebone, Oval, Iron Strap, Scrimshaw, Floral, 2 x 7 x 4 In. 1404
Trinket Box, Woman, Horse, Greyhound Dog, Victorian, White, Gold Accents, 1800s, 4 x 3 In. 125

FAIRYLAND LUSTER *pieces are included in the Wedgwood category.*

FAMILLE ROSE, *see Chinese Export category.*

FAN

Fans have been used for cooling since the days of the ancients. By the eighteenth century, the fan was an accessory for the lady of fashion and very elaborate and expensive fans were made. Sticks were made of ivory or wood, set with jewels or carved. The fans were made of painted silk or paper. Inexpensive paper fans printed with advertising were giveaways in the late nineteenth and early twentieth centuries. Electric fans were introduced in 1882. There are collectors of electric fans who like to buy damaged ones to repair.

Fan, Electric, 6 Brass Blades & Cage, Painted, Cast Iron, GE, 1901, 18 ½ In.
$583

Hartzell's Auction Gallery Inc.

Fan, Lace, Mother-Of-Pearl, Painted, Shadowbox Frame, 31 ¾ x 21 In.
$125

Hudson Valley Auctions

TIP

Smoking is bad for the health of your antiques! Smoke causes discoloration and weakens textiles. Another reason to stop smoking!

Fenton, Cookie Jar, Big Cookies, Jade Green, Wicker Handle, c.1933, 7 ¼ In.
$152

Jeffrey S. Evans & Associates

FAN

Fenton, Epergne, Blue Opalescent, Trumpet Vase, 3 Jack-In-The-Pulpits, Ruffled Rim, 1950s, 17 x 12 In.
$105

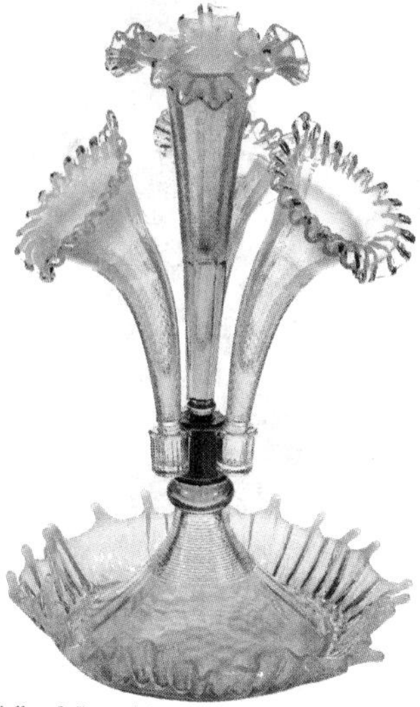

Jeffrey S. Evans & Associates

> **TIP**
> *If you have an alarm system, set it each time you leave the house, not just at night. Most home burglaries take place during the day or early evening.*

Fenton, Lamp, Cranberry Opalescent, Hobnail, Brass, 17 ½ x 8 In.
$150

Woody Auctions

Electric, 6 Brass Blades & Cage, Painted, Cast Iron, GE, 1901, 18 ½ In. .... *illus* 583
Electric, Ceiling, Art Deco, Aluminum, Brass, 2 Sets Of 3 Tapered Blades, c.1930, 26 x 14 In.... 7204
Lace, Mother-Of-Pearl, Cream, Handwoven, Velvet-Lined Gilt Frame, 16 x 22 ½ In. 89
Lace, Mother-Of-Pearl, Painted, Shadowbox Frame, 31 ¾ x 21 In. .... *illus* 125
Paper, Folding, Painted, Children Outside City Walls Flying Kite, A.J. Ramon, 9 x 10 In........... 130
Silver, Folding, Black Lacquer, Figures, Royal Household, Decoupage, 9 x 16 In. 600

FAST FOOD COLLECTIBLES *may be included in several categories, such as Advertising, Coca-Cola, Toy, etc.*

FEDERZEICHNUNG, *see Loetz category.*

FENTON

Fenton Art Glass Company was founded in 1905 in Martins Ferry, Ohio, by Frank L. Fenton and his brother, John W. Fenton. They painted decorations on glass blanks made by other manufacturers. In 1907 they opened a factory in Williamstown, West Virginia, and began making glass. The company stopped making art glass in 2011 and assets were sold. A new division of the company makes handcrafted glass beads and other jewelry. Copies are being made from leased original Fenton molds by an unrelated company, Fenton's Collectibles. The copies are marked with the Fenton mark and Fenton's Collectibles mark. Fenton is noted for early carnival glass produced between 1907 and 1920. Some of these pieces are listed in the Carnival Glass category. Many other types of glass were also made. Spanish Lace in this section refers to the pattern made by Fenton.

Fenton Art Glass Co.
1970–1975

Fenton Art Glass Co.
1980s

Fenton Art Glass Co.
1983+

Cookie Jar, Big Cookies, Jade Green, Wicker Handle, c.1933, 7 ¼ In. .... *illus* 152
Epergne, 3 Trumpet Vases, Light Blue, Iridescent Opalescent, Ruffled Rim, 11 In.................... 165
Epergne, Blue Opalescent, Trumpet Vase, 3 Jack-In-The-Pulpits, Ruffled Rim, 1950s, 17 x 12 In. *illus* 105
Epergne, Light Blue, Hanging Basket, 4 Ruffled Trumpet Vases, Crimped Dish, 22 In............. 204
Fine Rib, Vase, Red, Scalloped Rim, 9 In. 70
Free-Form, Bowl, Multicolor, Ruffled Rim, Signed, 14 x 8 In. 58
Heart, Optic, Basket, Clear Crest, Cranberry... 325
Hobnail, Syrup, Milk Glass, Burmese Overlay, Clear Handle, c.1961 85
Jefferson, Compote, Yellow, Lid, Eagle 410
Lamp, Cranberry Opalescent, Hobnail, Brass, 17 ½ x 8 In. .... *illus* 150
Lamp, Hurricane, Cranberry Opalescent, Swirl, Ruffled Rim, Brass, Marble Base, 16 In. .*illus* 154
Peach Blow, Bowl, Shell Shape, Silver Crest Edge, 1953, 10 x 3 In. 140
Plum Opalescent, Banana Stand, Ruffled Rim, Hobnail, Clear Dome Base, 6 x 12 ½ In. *illus* 413
Silver Crest, Pitcher, Bulbous, Handle, Ruffled Rim, White Ground, 9 In. .... *illus* 23
Vase, Black Amethyst, White Flowers, 11 In. 41
Vase, Red Karnac, Iridescent, Cobalt Blue Hearts & Vines, Handles, 1925, 9 x 6 In. 10325

FIESTA

Fiesta, the colorful dinnerware, was introduced in 1936 by the Homer Laughlin China Co., redesigned in 1969, and withdrawn in 1973. It was reissued again in 1986 in different colors and is still being made. New colors, including some that are similar to old colors, have been introduced. One new color is introduced in March every year. The simple design was characterized by a band of concentric circles beginning at the rim. Cups had full-circle handles until 1969, when partial-circle handles were made. Harlequin and Riviera were related wares. For more prices, go to kovels.com.

Fiesta
1936–1970

Fiesta Kitchen Kraft
1939–c.1943

Fiesta Casual
1962–c.1968

Chartreuse, Chop Plate, 15 In. 71
Cobalt Blue, Relish Tray, Circle Center, Cobalt Blue & Orange, Marked, c.1940, 11 In. 150
Cobalt Blue, Vase, Woman, Standing, Nude, 6 ⅞ In. .... *illus* 153
Forest Green, Eggcup, Footed, 3 In. 129
Gray, Bowl, Fruit, 6 ¼ In. 31
Gray, Coffeepot, Lid, Handle, Footed, 8 In., 5 Cup 559
Ivory, Candleholder, Bulb Shape, Square Base, 3 ¾ In. 30
Ivory, Mug, Round Handle, Tom & Jerry, 3 x 3 In. 80
Ivory, Tumbler, Rings At Top, 8 Oz., 4 ½ In. 43
Medium Green, Platter, Oval, 11 ⅝ In. .... *illus* 41
Multicolor, Stack Set, Red Lid, Cobalt, Green, Yellow, Kitchen Kraft, 4 Piece .... *illus* 130
Red, Candleholder, Tripod, Stepped Base, 3 ½ In. 53
Red, Shaker, Range, Globe, Footed, Kitchen Kraft, Pair 24
Turf Green, Pepper Shaker, 7 Holes, Round 60
Turf Green, Plate, Dinner, 10 In. 45
Turquoise, Bowl, Fruit, 11 ¾ In. 59
Turquoise, Relish, Maroon, Red, Yellow, Mauve Blue Inserts 502
Turquoise, Soup, Dish, Onion, Lid, 2 Handles, Footed, 4 ½ x 6 In. 3835
Yellow, Carafe, Lid, Handle, Glazed, Footed, c.1940, 9 ¾ In. .... *illus* 70
Yellow, Casserole, Lid, Handle, 8 ½ In. 65
Yellow, Creamer, Stick Handle, Footed, 3 In. 59
Yellow, Jar, Lid, Footed, Kitchen Kraft 106
Yellow, Jar, Mustard, Footed 119
Yellow, Mixing Bowl, No. 7, Molded Rim, 7 x 11 In. 165
Yellow, Spoon Rest, Leaf Shape, Rhythm 71
Yellow, Teapot, Lid, Round Handle, 7 x 9 In. 31
Yellow, Teapot, Lid, Spout & Handle, Footed .... *illus* 130
Yellow, Vase, Scalloped Rim, 12 In. 531

FINCH, *see Kay Finch category.*

FINDLAY ONYX AND FLORADINE

Findlay onyx and Floradine are two similar types of glass made by Dalzell, Gilmore and Leighton Co. of Findlay, Ohio, about 1889. Onyx is a patented yellowish white opaque glass with raised silver daisy decorations. A few rare pieces were made of rose, amber, orange, or purple glass. Floradine is made of cranberry-colored glass with an opalescent white raised floral pattern and a satin finish. The same molds were used for both types of glass.

Berry Bowl, Floradine, Ruby, White Opalescent Flowers, Satin Finish, c.1889, 1 ⅞ x 5 ¾ In. 560
Sugar, Lid, Ivory, Platinum Flowers, c.1889, 6 In. 311
Syrup, Blue Handle, Silver Lid, 6 ¾ In. .... *illus* 180

FIREFIGHTING

Firefighting equipment of all types is collected, from fire marks to uniforms to toy fire trucks. It is said that every little boy wanted to be a fireman or a train engineer 75 years ago and the collectors today reflect this interest.

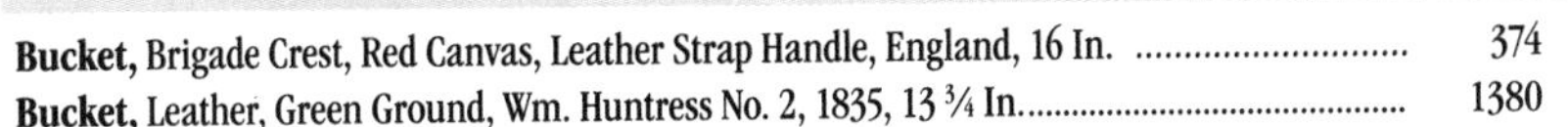

Bucket, Brigade Crest, Red Canvas, Leather Strap Handle, England, 16 In. 374
Bucket, Leather, Green Ground, Wm. Huntress No. 2, 1835, 13 ¾ In. 1380

Fenton, Lamp, Hurricane, Cranberry Opalescent, Swirl, Ruffled Rim, Brass, Marble Base, 16 In.
$154

Strawser Auction Group

Fenton, Plum Opalescent, Banana Stand, Ruffled Rim, Hobnail, Clear Dome Base, 6 x 12 ½ In.
$413

Strawser Auction Group

Fenton, Silver Crest, Pitcher, Bulbous, Handle, Ruffled Rim, White Ground, 9 In.
$23

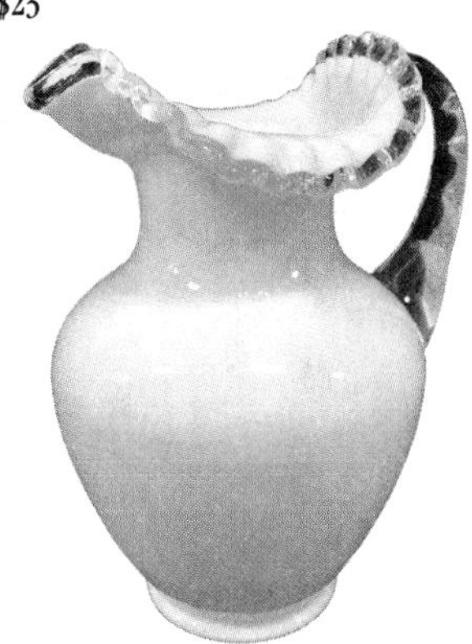

Apple Tree Auction Center

Fiesta, Cobalt Blue, Vase, Woman, Standing, Nude, 6 ⅞ In.
$153

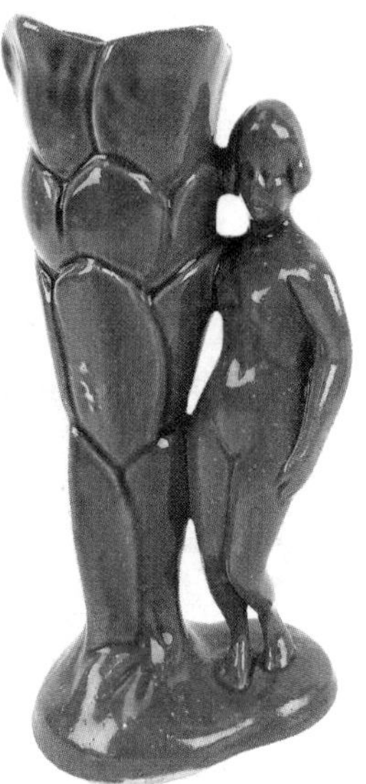

Strawser Auction Group

New Fiesta
Fiesta pottery has been reissued since 1986. Collectors call it New Fiesta or Post 86 Fiesta.

Fiesta, Medium Green, Platter, Oval, 11 ⅝ In.
$41

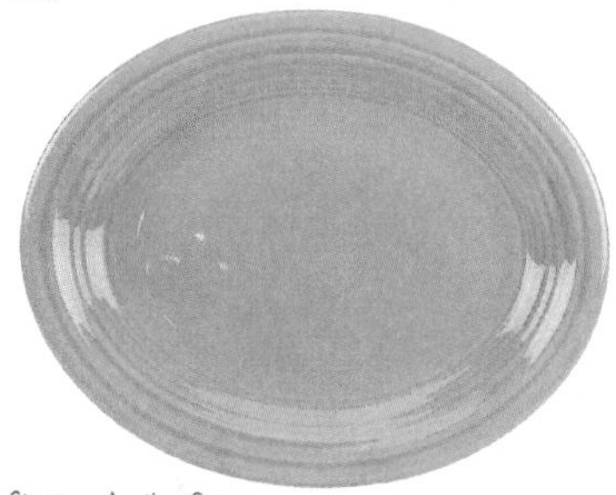

Strawser Auction Group

Fiesta, Multicolor, Stack Set, Red Lid, Cobalt, Green, Yellow, Kitchen Kraft, 4 Piece
$130

Strawser Auction Group

Fiesta, Yellow, Carafe, Lid, Handle, Glazed, Footed, c.1940, 9 ¾ In.
$70

Woody Auctions

Fiesta, Yellow, Teapot, Lid, Spout & Handle, Footed
$130

Strawser Auction Group

Findlay Onyx, Syrup, Blue Handle, Silver Lid, 6 ¾ In.
$180

Woody Auctions

Firefighting, Bucket, Leather, Green, Handle, Groton Fire Club, 19 In.
$960

Bourgeault-Horan Antiquarians & Associates, LLC

Firefighting, Bucket, Leather, Painted, Portrait, John Stanhope Damrell, Gilt Trim, 1800s, 12 x 8 ½ In.
$2,340

Thomaston Place Auction Galleries

Firefighting, Bucket, Leather, Swing Handle, Letter N, Horse, Lion, 16 In.
$148

Copake Auctions

Bucket, Leather, Green, Handle, Groton Fire Club, 19 In. .... *illus* 960
Bucket, Leather, Handle, W.H. Treadwell, Federal Fire Society, 1789, Pair....... 4500
Bucket, Leather, Painted, Portrait, John Stanhope Damrell, Gilt Trim, 1800s, 12 x 8 ½ In. *illus* 2340
Bucket, Leather, Red, Franklin Fire Society, Foster & Barton, Charlestown, Mass., 1830, 17 In. 2031
Bucket, Leather, Swing Handle, Letter N, Horse, Lion, 16 In. .... *illus* 148
Bucket, Leather, T. Peirce No. 2, Gold Lettering, Red & Black, Painted, 1900s, 18 In....... 132
Extinguisher, Fyr-Fyter, Model A, Brass, Black Text, 14 In. .... *illus* 132
Extinguisher, Minimax Refill, Lithographed Front Panel, Brown, Unused, 14 x 4 x 2 In....... 270
Extinguisher, Quick Aid Fire Guard, Copper, Brass Nozzle, 1930s-40s, 24 x 9 x 8 In. ......*illus* 210
Fire Mark, Baltimore Equitable Society, Iron, Painted, Gold, Red, Black, 1794, 9 x 10 In. *illus* 124
Fire Mark, Iron, Circular, Double Deck End Stroke Engine, Philadelphia Style, 1850s, 13 In. *illus* 117
Hat, Fire Chief, Speaker, Battery Operated, Plastic, Brown & Bigelow, Texaco, 9 ¾ In....... 228
Helmet, Leather, Eagle Head, Shield, William H. Wilson, 1866, 9 x 11 x 14 In. .... *illus* 3328
Helmet, Overlay Shield, Leather, New York, Cairns & Brother, c.1900, 6 ½ x 12 ¾ In. ......*illus* 187
Horn, Presentation, Silver Plate, C.G. Gunther P Club, 1864, 20 ¾ In....... 936
Hydrant, Bonnet Rim, Painted, Silver & Red, Kennedy Valve Mfg. Co., 36 In. .... *illus* 216
Nozzle, Solid Brass, Adjustable Lever, Leather Hand Straps, 3 Hose, Camden, 21 In. 293
Parade Hat, Sealskin, Stovepipe, Black Rosette, Bigelow Hatter, 1800s, 8 x 12 x 13 In. ....*illus* 936
Sign, Gould Island Fire Alarm Boxes, 7 Removable Painted Wood Slides, 1950s, 44 x 33 In. 330
Trumpet, Parade, Nickel Plate, Polished Pewter, Cloth Lanyard, 19 In....... 123

FIREPLACE

Fireplaces were used to cook food and to heat the American home in past centuries. Many types of tools and equipment were used. A pair of andirons held the logs in place, firebacks reflected the heat into the room, and tongs were used to move either fuel or food. Many types of spits and roasting jacks were made and may be listed in the Kitchen category.

Andirons, Bell Metal, Belted Ball Top, Steeple Finial, Arch-Spurred Legs, 1780s, 18 x 20 In. 144
Andirons, Brass & Iron, Belted Ball Top, 1800s, 19 x 9 ½ x 14 ½ In. .... *illus* 62
Andirons, Brass, Ball Feet, 21 x 10 x 23 In....... 185
Andirons, Brass, Ball Finial & Feet, George III, 19 x 13 x 23 In....... 246
Andirons, Brass, Claw Foot, Georgian Style, 28 ½ x 21 ½ In....... 83
Andirons, Brass, Empire Style, Ball Foot, 1900s, 19 ½ x 16 ½ In....... 148
Andirons, Brass, Lemon Top, Turned Log Stops, c.1810, 22 In. .... *illus* 488
Andirons, Brass, Spanish Style, Urn Shape Finials, Scrolled Iron Legs, c.1920, 17 x 25 x 11 In. 236
Andirons, Brass, Urn Top, Spurred Cabriole Legs, Claw Feet, Chippendale, 23 In. 1320
Andirons, Brass, Urn Top, Turned Shafts, Ball & Claw Feet, 25 ⅜ In. 488
Andirons, Bronze, Rococo Filigree, Iron Rear Bracket, 20 ½ x 12 x 24 In. 151
Andirons, Cast Iron, Colonial Man, Standing, 14 ½ In....... 123
Andirons, Cast Iron, Dachshund, Painted, Attached Chains, Early 1900s, 10 x 28 x 6 In....... 354
Andirons, Cast Iron, Goose Head, 21 ½ In., Pair 384
Andirons, Chromed Metal, Iron, Abstract, Donald Deskey, 13 x 18 x 8 In. .... *illus* 688
Andirons, Figural, Hessian Soldier, Cast Iron, Painted, c.1875, 20 In. .... *illus* 192
Andirons, George Washington, Black, Painted, Draped Plinth, Early 1900s, 20 x 9 x 17 In. 295
Andirons, Iron, Spiral Twist, Painted, Cannonball Finial, Scrolled Feet, Early 1900s, 23 x 12 x 23 In. 502
Andirons, Molded Brass, Spur Knee & Ball Feet, Chippendale, c.1800, 20 x 11 x 19 In. 266
Andirons, Silver Plate, Scrolled Legs, Bell Shape Feet, Georgian Style, England, Early 1900s, 27 In... 531
Andirons, Wrought Iron, Argente, Neoclassical Style, 25 ½ In....... 550
Andirons, Wrought Iron, Brass Panels & Finial, Knife Blade, Early 1800s, 21 ½ In. 216
Bellows, Red Ground, Floral, Brass Nozzle, Label, Henry Porter, 1800s, 20 In. .... *illus* 1220
Chenets, Andirons, Brass, Lion Heads, Urns & Balusters, 1800s, 12 x 40 In., 3 Piece ....*illus* 350
Coal Scuttle, Black Tole, Flowers, Paw Feet, 12 x 10 ½ x 23 In. .... *illus* 71
Coal Scuttle, Hinged Lid, Copper, Embossed Urn, Removable Insert, 16 x 10 x 15 In....... 79
Coal Scuttle, Mahogany, Brass, Handle, 2 Mechanical Doors, c.1900, 17 x 16 x 13 In. .....*illus* 59
Ember Tongs, Wrought Iron, Spring Loaded, Penny Pincers, Pick, Pipe Tamp, 1700s, 28 In.... 2460
Fender, Brass, Central Depiction Of Poseidon, Engraved, Georgia, 7 x 49 In....... 427
Fender, Brass, Chain Dogs Mounted, Rectangular Pedestal, Scrolled Feet, Late 1800s, 42 In.... 780
Fender, Brass, Claw Foot, Curved End, 49 x 10 x 8 ½ In....... 83
Fender, Brass, Federal, Reticulated, Paw Feet, 1810s, 11 x 42 ½ In. 240

Firefighting, Extinguisher, Fyr-Fyter, Model A, Brass, Black Text, 14 In.
$132

Alderfer Auction Company

Firefighting, Extinguisher, Quick Aid Fire Guard, Copper, Brass Nozzle, 1930s-40s, 24 x 9 x 8 In.
$210

Morphy Auctions

Firefighting, Fire Mark, Baltimore Equitable Society, Iron, Painted, Gold, Red, Black, 1794, 9 x 10 In.
$124

Soulis Auctions

F

Firefighting, Fire Mark, Iron, Circular, Double Deck End Stroke Engine, Philadelphia Style, 1850s, 13 In.
$117

Jeffrey S. Evans & Associates

Firefighting, Helmet, Leather, Eagle Head, Shield, William H. Wilson, 1866, 9 x 11 x 14 In.
$3,328

Fontaine's Auction Gallery

Firefighting, Helmet, Overlay Shield, Leather, New York, Cairns & Brother, c.1900, 6 ½ x 12 ¾ In.
$187

Jeffrey S. Evans & Associates

TIP
An old cotton sock is a good polishing cloth. So is an old cloth diaper.

Firefighting, Hydrant, Bonnet Rim, Painted, Silver & Red, Kennedy Valve Mfg. Co., 36 In.
$216

Alderfer Auction Company

Firefighting, Parade Hat, Sealskin, Stovepipe, Black Rosette, Bigelow Hatter, 1800s, 8 x 12 x 13 In.
$936

Thomaston Place Auction Galleries

Fireplace, Andirons, Brass & Iron, Belted Ball Top, 1800s, 19 x 9 ½ x 14 ½ In.
$62

Skinner, Inc.

Fireplace, Andirons, Brass, Lemon Top, Turned Log Stops, c.1810, 22 In.
$488

Pook & Pook

TIP
Andirons get tarnished and covered with resin from the smoke so they should be cleaned with liquid metal polish and 0000-grade steel wool.

Fireplace, Andirons, Chromed Metal, Iron, Abstract, Donald Deskey, 13 x 18 x 8 In.
$688

Palm Beach Modern Auctions

Fireplace, Andirons, Figural, Hessian Soldier, Cast Iron, Painted, c.1875, 20 In.
$192

Garth's Auctioneers & Appraisers

Fender, Brass, Leather Upholstery, Openwork, Stepped Base, 23 x 61 x 19 In. 431
Fender, Brass, Openwork, Screen, Footed, 1800s, 46 x 48 In. 346
Fender, Brass, Vertical Wire, Swags, Scrolls, 1810s, 12 x 55 ½ x 12 In. 125
Fender, Brass, Wire, D Shape, Scroll Design, Late 1700s-Early 1800s, 10 x 46 x 14 In. 351
Fender, Brass, Wirework, Ball Feet, Finial, 12 x 32 x 15 In. 461
Fender, Cast Steel, Openwork, Pineapple Finial, Neoclassical, c.1920, 40 In. 113
Fender, Patinated Steel, Argente, Brass Mounted, Urn Foliate, 1800s, 8 x 44 x 19 In. 300
Fire Dogs, Cast Iron, Flame Logo, Donald Deskey, 14 ¾ In. 123
Fireback, Cast Iron, Arched Top, Grapevine Surround, Man, Woman, 1800s, 22 x 17 In. 60
Fireback, Cast Iron, Freemason's Arms, Leafy Border, Joseph Webb, 1760s, 25 x 26 ½ In. 3321
Fireback, Cast Iron, Locomotive, Trees, 17 ½ x 21 In. 123
Fireback, Tombstone Arches, Henrich Weihelm, Elizabeth Furnace, Late 1700s, 23 x 25 In. 1260
Fireboard, Pine, Block Printed Wallpaper, Women, Shepherd, Blue Ground, 1810s, 35 x 46 In. . 281
Footman, Brass, Pierced, Black Steel Base, Wood Handle, 12 ½ x 14 x 6 ½ In. 154
Footman, Brass, Turned Handles, Cabriole Front Legs, 1800s, 10 ½ x 11 x 16 In. ....*illus* 123
Footman, Iron, Pierced Heart, Pinwheel, Scalloped Skirt, Late 1700s, 12 x 18 x 14 In. ....*illus* 369
Grate, Cast Iron, Vent, Circular, 10 In., Pair 107
Mantel is listed in the Architectural category. ....
Screen, Adjustable, Carved, Needlepoint Panel, Urn Finial, Tripod Base, c.1890, 66 In. 50
Screen, Brass, Flower, Mirror, Handle, 2 Legs, 1950s, 29 ½ x 19 ½ In. ....*illus* 101
Screen, Brass, Repousse, Continental, Pub Scene, Iron Frame, 1800s, 29 x 37 In. 150
Screen, Bronze, Medieval Style, 2 Shields, Mythical Heads, Sword, 37 x 36 x 10 In. 1331
Screen, Embroidery Panel, Silk, Mahogany, Shield Shape, Adjustable, 1800s, 56 x 14 x 10 In. . 89
Screen, George III, Mahogany, Pole, Needlework Panel, c.1760, 65 In. ....*illus* 1708
Screen, Gilt Bronze, Ornate, Rococo, Acanthus Leaf, Putti, 36 x 30 In. 354
Screen, Inlaid Satinwood, Urn Finial, Saber Legs, 1810s, 41 ½ x 28 x 15 ¾ In. 250
Screen, Needlepoint, Red, Walnut, Carved, Shield Shape, 1900s, 31 x 30 x 12 ½ In. ....*illus* 170
Screen, Oak, Sunburst Panel, Carved, Painted, Arts & Crafts Style, Iron Stand, 25 x 19 x 14 In.. 234
Screen, Pole, Mahogany, Embroidered Panel, Cabriole Legs, Chippendale, c.1760, 49 In. 2928
Screen, Pole, Mahogany, Floral Panel, Tripod Base, Embroidered, Georgia, 53 ½ In. 246
Screen, Pole, Mahogany, Needlework, Urn Final, Floral, George III, c.1800, 60 x 18 x 18 In. 90
Screen, Pole, Needlework, Cherry, Tripod Cabriole Legs, Frame, 1700s, 59 x 21 x 19 In. 1107
Screen, Pole, Walnut, Acorn Finial, Needlework, Tripod Base, Cabriole Legs, 1700s, 56 In. 615
Screen, Wood, 2 Geese, Standing In Tall Grass, Painted, 35 x 25 In. ....*illus* 94
Screen, Walnut, Bronze Mounted, Trestle Base, Early 1900s, 34 x 22 ¾ x 12 In. 150
Screen, Wood, Leather, Hand Painted, Peacock, Scenic, 37 x 37 In. 150
Screen, Wood, Painted Figures, Arts & Crafts, 1900s, 77 ½ In. ....*illus* 250
Screens are also listed in the Furniture category. ....
Surround, 15 Tiles, Greenish-Brown, Embossed, Butterflies, Vines, Birds, Urns, c.1900, 6 In... 300
Surround, Carrera Marble, Cupid Carved Frieze, Maidens, Neoclassical, Late 1800s, 54 x 83 In. 9000
Tinder Box, Iron, Cylindrical, Rotating Wheel, Door, 3 Compartments, Ives, 1800s, 5 ½ In. ... 351
Trammel, Wrought Iron, Sawtooth, Adjustable, 1828, 41 In. 1250

FISCHER

MF

Fischer porcelain was made in Herend, Hungary. The wares are sometimes referred to as Herend porcelain. The pottery was originally founded in Herend in 1826 and was bought by Moritz Fischer in 1839. Fischer made replacement pieces for German and Far Eastern dinnerware and later began making its own dinnerware patterns. Figurines were made beginning in the 1870s. The company was nationalized in 1948. Martin's Herend Imports, Inc., began importing Herend china into the United States in 1957. The company was privatized in 1993 and is now in business as Herend.

Basket, Rothschild Bird, Centerpiece, Openwork, Herend, 3 ½ x 9 ½ In. ....*illus* 144
Box, Lift Lid, Flowers, Strawberry Shape Finial, Herend, 1900s, 6 In. ....*illus* 210
Figurine, 2 Ducks, Blue Fish Scale, Green Wings, Gold Beak, Herend, 8 ½ x 15 x 10 In. ..*illus* 572
Figurine, 2 Rabbits, 1 Sitting, 1 Lying Down, Blue, White, Base, 5 ½ In. 150
Figurine, 2 Rabbits, Bunny Love, Hand Painted, Blue Fishnet, Herend, 7 x 5 ½ x 5 In. 897
Figurine, 2 Seahorses, Fishnet, Coral, Blue & Green, Herend, 7 In. ....*illus* 351
Figurine, Bird, Bald Eagle, Spread Wings, Painted, White, Brown, Herend, 7 In. 378

Fireplace, Bellows, Red Ground, Floral, Brass Nozzle, Label, Henry Porter, 1800s, 20 In.
$1,220

Pook & Pook

Fireplace, Chenets, Andirons, Brass, Lion Heads, Urns & Balusters, 1800s, 12 x 40 In., 3 Piece
$350

Woody Auctions

Fireplace, Coal Scuttle, Black Tole, Flowers, Paw Feet, 12 x 10 ½ x 23 In.
$71

Copake Auctions

Fireplace, Coal Scuttle, Mahogany, Brass, Handle, 2 Mechanical Doors, c.1900, 17 x 16 x 13 In.
$59

Cordier Auctions

Fireplace, Footman, Brass, Turned Handles, Cabriole Front Legs, 1800s, 10 ½ x 11 x 16 In.
$123

Skinner, Inc.

Fireplace, Footman, Iron, Pierced Heart, Pinwheel, Scalloped Skirt, Late 1700s, 12 x 18 x 14 In.
$369

Skinner, Inc.

TIP
Check stored items once a year to be sure there is no deterioration or bugs.

Fireplace, Screen, Brass, Flower, Mirror, Handle, 2 Legs, 1950s, 29 ½ x 19 ½ In.
$101

Selkirk Auctioneers & Appraisers

Fireplace, Screen, George III, Mahogany, Pole, Needlework Panel, c.1760, 65 In.
$1,708

Pook & Pook

Fireplace, Screen, Needlepoint, Red, Walnut, Carved, Shield Shape, 1900s, 31 x 30 x 12 ½ In.
$170

Soulis Auctions

TIP
Keep mousetraps, rat poison, and bug poison in the attic if you store antique furniture or textiles there.

Fireplace, Screen, Wood, 2 Geese, Standing In Tall Grass, Painted, 35 x 25 In.
$94

Copake Auctions

Fireplace, Screen, Wood, Painted Figures, Arts & Crafts, 1900s, 77 ½ In.
$250

Freeman's Auctioneers & Appraisers

Fischer, Basket, Rothschild Bird, Centerpiece, Openwork, Herend, 3 ½ x 9 ½ In.
$144

Blackwell Auctions

Fischer, Box, Lift Lid, Flowers, Strawberry Shape Finial, Herend, 1900s, 6 In.
$210

Eldred's

TIP
Glue broken china with an invisible mending cement that is waterproof.

Fischer, Figurine, 2 Ducks, Blue Fish Scale, Green Wings, Gold Beak, Herend, 8 ½ x 15 x 10 In.
$572

Charleston Estate Auctions

Fischer, Figurine, 2 Seahorses, Fishnet, Coral, Blue & Green, Herend, 7 In.
$351

Thomaston Place Auction Galleries

Fischer, Figurine, Boxer, Fighting Pose, Blanc De Chine, Impressed Mark, Herend, 12 In.
$748

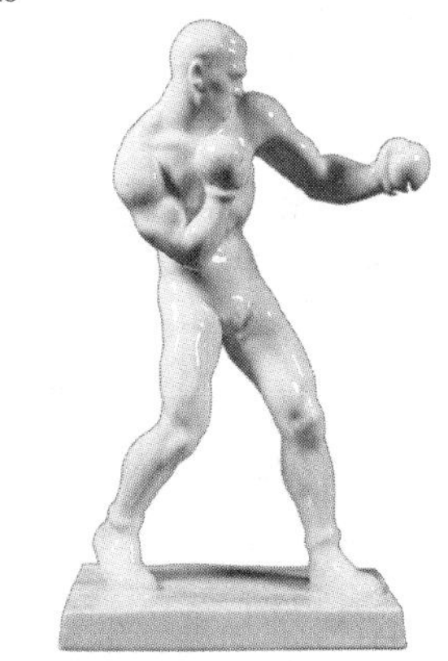

Blackwell Auctions

Fischer, Figurine, Rabbit, White Plinth, Swirl Motif, Blue Fish Scale, 11 ½ x 7 ½ x 4 ½ In.
$1,074

Charleston Estate Auctions

Fishing, Creel, Emile Robichaud, Wood, Carved, Painted, Sloped Lid, 7 ¾ x 14 ¾ x 6 In.
$1,989

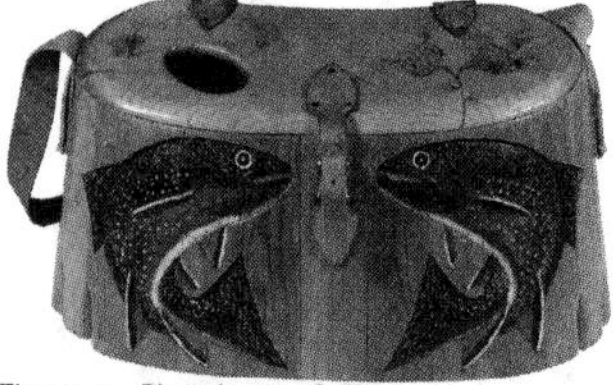
Thomaston Place Auction Galleries

Appraising Lures
There are sites online that will appraise antique fishing lures from a posted picture.

Fishing, Sign, Striped Bass Season Is Now Open, Painted, Blue Ground, Wood Frame, 1900s, 26 x 17 In.
$570

Eldred's

Flow Blue, Tureen, Ladle, 2 Handles, Hexagon Lid & Base, 1800s, 11 In.
$94

Thomaston Place Auction Galleries

Figurine, Bird, Kingfisher, Fish In Beak, Herend, c.1950, 7 x 5 In. 450
Figurine, Boxer, Fighting Pose, Blanc De Chine, Impressed Mark, Herend, 12 In. .... *illus* 748
Figurine, Duck, Golden Egg, Porcelain, Orange Fishnet, Herend, 7 ¾ In. 155
Figurine, Elephant, Walking, Blue, Fishnet, Gold Tusk & Nails, Herend, 10 x 16 In. 1652
Figurine, Frog, Red Fishnet, Gilt Feet, Signed, 1 ¾ x 2 x 3 In. 158
Figurine, Goose, Golden Egg, Fishnet, White & Blue, Herend, 7 ½ In. 443
Figurine, Pheasant, Porcelain, Orange Fishnet, White Round Base, Herend, 6 x 13 In. 310
Figurine, Rabbit, White Plinth, Swirl Motif, Blue Fish Scale, 11 ½ x 7 ½ x 4 ½ In. .... *illus* 1074
Figurine, School Of Fish, Black Fishnet, Gold Highlights, Painted, Marked, 3 ¼ In. 413
Morning Glory, 2 Flowers, 2 Butterflies, Painted, Blue, Pink Rim, Marked, Herend, 5 In., Pair. 224
Tureen, Lid, Putto Finial, 2 Handles, Multicolor, Birds, Butterflies, 10 x 11 ¾ In., Pair 484
Tureen, Rothschild Bird, Hand Painted, Butterfly, Flowers, Leafy Handle, 10 ½ In. 431
Turtle, Crawling, Painted, Green, Black, Gold Glaze, Herend, 4 ¼ In., 3 Piece 307
Vase, Ram's Head Handles, Chinese Bouquet, White Ground, Gilt, 12 In. 92

FISHING

Fishing reels of brass or nickel were made in the United States by 1810. Bamboo fly rods were sold by 1860, often marked with the maker's name. Lures made of metal, or metal and wood, were made in the nineteenth century. Plastic lures were made by the 1930s. All fishing material is collected today and even equipment of the past 30 years is of interest if in good condition with original box.

Creel, Emile Robichaud, Wood, Carved, Painted, Sloped Lid, 7 ¾ x 14 ¾ x 6 In. .... *illus* 1989
Lure, Cowrie Snail Shell, Volcanic Stone, 2 Hooks, Polynesian Island, 9 ½ In. 669
Scene, Wood, Carved, Dog, Man & Boy, Baiting Hook, Painted, Early 1900s, 10 ½ x 9 ⅝ In. 431
Sign, Fishing Supplies, Wood, Painted, Hanging Loops, 2-Sided, c.1950, 19 x 42 ¾ In. 585
Sign, Gig Fishing 50 Cents, Sturgeon Shape, Wood, Late 1900s, 12 x 64 In. 144
Sign, H.W. Fry Sporting Goods, Fish Shape, Scale Details, 2-Sided, Shultz, c.1930, 53 In. 4305
Sign, Live Bait & Fishing Tackle, Wood, Carved, Red Letters, Blue Scrolls, 11 x 47 ½ In. 118
Sign, Striped Bass Season Is Now Open, Painted, Blue Ground, Wood Frame, 1900s, 26 x 17 In. . *illus* 570
Sign, Winchester Lures Sold Here, Walleye Pike, Die Cut, 20 x 14 In. 678
Trout, Lawrence C. Irvine, Wood, Carved, Mounted On Map Of Maine, Plywood, 15 x 29 x 18 In. 1755

FLAGS *are included in the Textile category.*

FLASH GORDON

Flash Gordon appeared in the Sunday comics in 1934. The daily strip started in 1940. The hero was also in comic books from 1930 to 1970, in books from 1936, in movies from 1938, on the radio in the 1930s and 1940s, and on television from 1953 to 1954. All sorts of memorabilia are collected, but the ray guns and rocket ships are the most popular.

Book, Pop-Up, Tournament Of Death, 1935 264
Doll, Cloth Clothing, Red, Blue, Yellow, Mego, 1976 100
Toy, Rocket Fighter, Red & Yellow, Original Box, 12 In. 1937

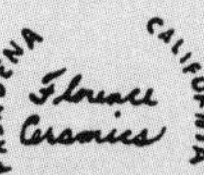

FLORENCE CERAMICS

Florence Ceramics were made in Pasadena, California, from the 1940s to 1977. Florence Ward created many colorful figurines, boxes, candleholders, and other items for the gift shop trade. Each piece was marked with an ink stamp that included the name *Florence Ceramics Co.* The company was sold in 1964 and although the name remained the same, the products were very different. Mugs, cups, and trays were made.

Figurine, Stephen, Man, Top Hat, Ivory, Gold Trim, Cane, 9 In. 69
Figurine, Victoria, Woman Sitting, Purple Couch, 7 ½ x 8 In. 61
Figurine, Woman, Rose Marie, Curtsy, c.1950, 7 In. 65

FLOW BLUE

Flow blue ceramics were made in England and other countries about 1830 to 1900. The dishes were printed with designs using a cobalt blue coloring. The color flowed from the design to the white body so that the finished piece has a smeared blue design. The dishes were usually made of ironstone china. More Flow Blue may be found under the name of the manufacturer. These three marks are used on flow blue dishes.

W.H. Grindley & Co. (Ltd.)
c.1880–1891

Johnson Brothers
c.1913+

Wood & Son(s) (Ltd.)
1891–1907

Planter, Carnation, White Enamel On Flowers, Gold Trim, Ironstone, 8 x 9 In. 92
Tray, Round, Messina Pattern, Scalloped Rim, c.1900, 16 3/4 In. 40
Tray, Willow, Allerton's, c.1926, 15 1/2 x 12 1/2 In. 48
Tureen, Ladle, 2 Handles, Hexagon Lid & Base, 1800s, 11 In. .... *illus* 94

FLYING PHOENIX, *see Phoenix Bird category.*

FOLK ART

Folk art is also listed in many categories of this book under the actual name of the object. See categories such as Box, Cigar Store Figure, Paper, Weather Vane, Wooden, etc.

Aardvark, Wood, Nailed, Flowers & Nut Eyes, Clyde Jones, 1992, 19 1/2 x 16 1/2 In. 378
Airplane, Brass, Cartridge Case, 7 In., Pair 7204
Airplane, Spirit Of St. Louis-Type, Copper, Zinc, Patina, c.1910, 19 x 37 In. .... *illus* 1920
Arrow, Weather Vane, Cast Iron, Painted, Mounted On Wood Base, 31 In. 192
Bandwagon, Circus, Painted Safari Scene, Star, American Flags, c.1890, 18 In. .... *illus* 234
Barn Door, Horses, Pony, Hinges, 48 x 34 In. 75
Bird, Carved, Wood, Multicolor, Painted, D & D Strawser, Chester Co., Pa., 8 1/2 In. 94
Bird, Standing, Painted, Wood & Metal, Base, Thomas Kloss, Late 1900s, 35 In. 118
Birdhouse, Church, Mixed Wood, 31 x 19 x 40 In. 177
Birdhouse, Sam, Dot Man, McMillan, Multicolor, Painted, Cutout, Wood, 36 x 11 1/2 In. 319
Book Box, Carved, Wood, Heart, Cross, 5 3/4 x 2 x 7 1/2 In. .... *illus* 472
Book, Carved Wood, Bible Carved On Spine, Painted, Miniature, 2 1/2 In. .... *illus* 106
Bottle, Whimsy, Clear, Rectangular, Paper Label, Stopper, Late 1800s-1930s, 10 1/2 In. 105
Bust, Sailor, Carved, Slouch Hat, Kerchief, Pill On Tongue, Apothecary Shop, 18 In. .... *illus* 2160
Bust, Train Conductor, Hat, Leather Brim, Tin Badge, Carved Log, GS, c.1910, 16 In. .... *illus* 510
Cat, Striped, Seated, Wood, Carved, 16 In. 738
Deer Head, Wood, Real Antlers, Yellow Paint, Incised Eyes, Nostrils, Lips, 19 In. .... *illus* 236
Desk, Roll Top, Chip Carved, Made Of Cigar Boxes, Wood, 13 x 7 x 10 In. .... *illus* 819
Diorama, Wax Figures, Print On Canvas Back, Franicisco Vargas, 34 1/2 x 9 x 24 In. 443
Dog & Cat Figure, Carved Walnut, Wrought Copper, 23 1/2 In. 277
Dresser, Mirror, Chip Carved, Leaves, 3 Drawers, 9 x 5 3/4 x 19 1/2 In. .... *illus* 311
Eaglet, Wood, Carved, Multicolor, Wilhelm Schimmel, 4 In. .... *illus* 8540
Figure, Black Man, Standing, Wood, Carved, 18 In. 59
Fish, Wood, Full Body, Carved, Mop Eye, Oval Pine Board, New England, Early 1900s, 9 x 19 In. 259
Frame, Adirondack Type, Cross, Heart, Cutout Felt Horse, Star Panel, Late 1800s, 22 x 17 In. .. 281
Head, Wood, Carved, Flattened Nose, No Hair, 21 In. 118
Jewelry Box, Cherry, Walnut, Oak, Mahogany, Carved, Heart, Flowers, 1900, 7 x 4 x 4 1/2 In. ... 69
Jug, Devil's Face, Ceramic Teeth, Alkaline Glaze, H.F. Reinhardt, Vale, N.C., 6 3/4 In. .... *illus* 5040
Jug, Face, Green Alkaline Glaze, Porcelain Eyes, Teeth, Ear Handle, L. Meaders, 1900s, 9 In. *illus* 900
Jug, Lid, Memory, Beads, Shells, Metals, 1900s, 18 1/2 x 11 1/2 In. .... *illus* 121
Lion, Carved, Front Paws, Penholder, Rectangular Base, Painted, 7 1/2 x 2 x 5 1/2 In. 431

Folk Art, Airplane, Spirit Of St. Louis-Type, Copper, Zinc, Patina, c.1910, 19 x 37 In.
$1,920

Garth's Auctioneers & Appraisers

Folk Art, Bandwagon, Circus, Painted Safari Scene, Star, American Flags, c.1890, 18 In.
$234

Richard Opfer Auctioneering, Inc.

Folk Art, Book Box, Carved, Wood, Heart, Cross, 5 3/4 x 2 x 7 1/2 In.
$472

Copake Auctions

This is an edited listing of current prices. Visit **Kovels.com** to check thousands of prices from previous years and sign up for free information on trends, tips, reproductions, marks, and more.

F

Folk Art, Book, Carved Wood, Bible Carved On Spine, Painted, Miniature, 2 ½ In.
$106

Conestoga Auction Company

Folk Art, Bust, Sailor, Carved, Slouch Hat, Kerchief, Pill On Tongue, Apothecary Shop, 18 In.
$2,160

Morphy Auctions

Folk Art, Bust, Train Conductor, Hat, Leather Brim, Tin Badge, Carved Log, GS, c.1910, 16 In.
$510

Garth's Auctioneers & Appraisers

Folk Art, Deer Head, Wood, Real Antlers, Yellow Paint, Incised Eyes, Nostrils, Lips, 19 In.
$236

Copake Auctions

Folk Art, Desk, Roll Top, Chip Carved, Made Of Cigar Boxes, Wood, 13 x 7 x 10 In.
$819

Hartzell's Auction Gallery Inc.

Folk Art, Dresser, Mirror, Chip Carved, Leaves, 3 Drawers, 9 x 5 ¾ x 19 ½ In.
$311

Hartzell's Auction Gallery Inc.

Folk Art is Younger
Folk art is still a hot collectible, but folk art can be "younger" items made into the early 1900s.

Folk Art, Eaglet, Wood, Carved, Multicolor, Wilhelm Schimmel, 4 In.
$8,540

Pook & Pook

Folk Art, Jug, Devil's Face, Ceramic Teeth, Alkaline Glaze, H.F. Reinhardt, Vale, N.C., 6 ¾ In.
$5,040

Case Antiques

Folk Art, Jug, Face, Green Alkaline Glaze, Porcelain Eyes, Teeth, Ear Handle, L. Meaders, 1900s, 9 In.
$900

Case Antiques

Folk Art, Jug, Lid, Memory, Beads, Shells, Metals, 1900s, 18 ½ x 11 ½ In.
$121

Bruneau & Co. Auctioneers

Folk Art, Man Wearing Baseball Cap, Made From Car Muffler, Mixed Metal, 1960s, 49 In.
$219

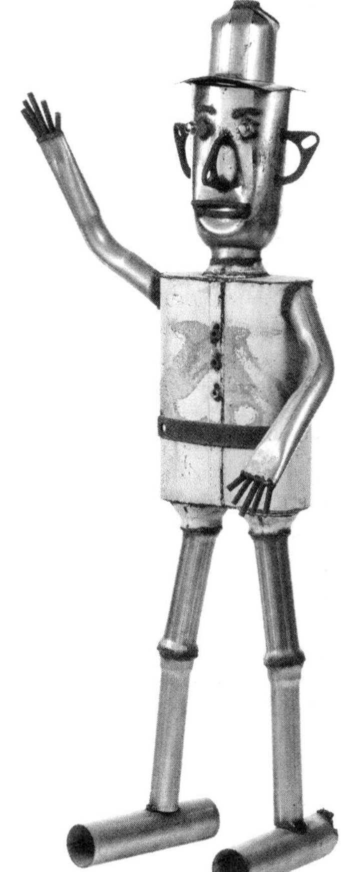

Garth's Auctioneers & Appraisers

TIP
If you are moving, be sure to get special insurance coverage for damage to your antiques. You may want valuable pieces covered by your insurance, not by the mover's policy.

Folk Art, Paddlewheeler, Signed, K. Will Kautz, 29 x 48 x 14 In.
$1,020

Eldred's

Folk Art, Polecat, Wood, Yellow, Brown, Black, Signed, M. And Greg Adkins, 1985, 14 x 58 x 4 In.
$540

Case Antiques

Folk Art, Mermaid, Holding Shell, Wood, Carved, Hand Painted, c.1910, 24 In.
$104

Blackwell Auctions

Hang a Horseshoe for Good Luck
When you hang a horseshoe today for good luck, you hang it so the opening faces the ceiling. In earlier days, you wanted the horseshoe opening to face the floor. During the Depression of the 1930s, the superstition changed and the idea was to hold the luck in, not let it run to the floor.

Folk Art, Sand Bottle, American Flag, Eagle, Fisherman, Andrew Clemens, c.1875, 5 ½ In.
$1,750

Garth's Auctioneers & Appraisers

Folk Art, Sculpture, Cubist, Sandstone, 2 Faces, Signed LH, 1983, 13 x 16 x 12 In.
$570

Case Antiques

Folk Art, Turtle, Pine, Carved, Painted, Copper Feet, Brass Tack Eyes, Engraved Shell, 7 x 40 x 21 In.
$497

Thomaston Place Auction Galleries

Lion, Seated, Welded, Salvage Steel, Whimsical, 27 In. 187
Man Wearing Baseball Cap, Made From Car Muffler, Mixed Metal, 1960s, 49 In. ....*illus* 219
Mermaid, Holding Shell, Wood, Carved, Hand Painted, c.1910, 24 In. ....*illus* 104
Noah's Ark, 23 Animals, Figures, Carved, Wood, Painted, 24 In. 734
Paddlewheeler, Signed, K. Will Kautz, 29 x 48 x 14 In. ....*illus* 1020
Parakeet, Carved, Painted, Green, Red Beak, Wood Stand, c.1850, 6 ¾ In. 523
Parakeet, Wood, Carved, Painted, Wood Stand, 7 x 2 ½ x 7 ½ In. 106
Parrot, Perched, Carved, Painted, Wood, Black Stand, 40 ½ x 16 ¾ x 8 In. 1053
Plaque, Dove On Cloud, Crossed Torches, Oak Branch, Multicolor, 1810s, 18 x 8 In. 995
Polecat, Wood, Yellow, Brown, Black, Signed, M. And Greg Adkins, 1985, 14 x 58 x 4 In. ..*illus* 540
Portrait, Young Girl, Blue Dress, Ink, Cut Paper, Gold Frame, c.1840, 8 ½ x 6 ½ In. 94
Rabbit, Seated, Grass, Tree Stump, Carved, Red Pincushion, Multicolor, 1800s, 6 x 2 x 5 In. ... 173
Sand Bottle, American Flag, Eagle, Fisherman, Andrew Clemens, c.1875, 5 ½ In. ....*illus* 1750
Sculpture, Cubist, Sandstone, 2 Faces, Signed LH, 1983, 13 x 16 x 12 In. ....*illus* 570
Shelf, Silhouette Of Hunter With Gun, Dog, Wood, 7 ½ x 12 ½ In. 45
Snake, Smiling, Pine, Sinuous, Red, Yellow, Black, Santa Fe, Jimbo Davila, 20 x 2 x ¾ In. 71
Swan, Wood, Carved, Glass Eyes, Dirty White, Black Beak, 1960s, 14 ½ x 28 ½ In. 240
Toy, Model, Mack AC Firetruck, Handmade, Wood, Metal, 1920, 10 x 19 ½ x 7 In. 1287
Turtle, Pine, Carved, Painted, Copper Feet, Brass Tack Eyes, Engraved Shell, 7 x 40 x 21 In. *illus* 497
Uncle Sam Figure, Cutout Wood, Movable Arms, Early 1900s, 67 ½ In. 180
Uncle Sam, Holding American Flag, Seal, Carved, Painted Wood, 69 ½ In. ....*illus* 492
Watch Holder, Deer Head, Inlaid, Wood, Marked, Loom, 8 x 4 ½ In. ....*illus* 57
Whirligig, Drummer, American Flag, Stars, 4-Blade Propeller, Removable Base, 18 x 10 In. *illus* 410
Whirligig, Horse & Buggy, Rider, Wood, Painted, Aqua Base, Octagonal Stand, 24 In. 410
Whirligig, Indian Chief, Yellow Shirt, Green Pants, Tomahawk Paddles, Trapezoidal Base, 15 In. . *illus* 4305
Whirligig, Man, Sawing, Beard, Hat, Carved, Painted, Wood, 18 In. ....*illus* 68
Whirligig, Man, Wearing Cap, Carved, Painted, Sawbuck Support, 23 x 15 x 12 ½ In. 246
Whirligig, Men, Sawing, Carved Wood, Sheet Iron, Stand, 70 x 32 In. 369
Whirligig, Mixed Media, PVC Pipe, Siding, Aluminum, 1900s, 59 ½ In. 122
Whirligig, Sailor, Wood, Painted, Paddles On Arms, 15 ¾ In. ....*illus* 165

FOOT WARMER

Foot warmers solved the problem of cold feet in past generations. Some warmers held charcoal, others held hot water. Pottery, tin, and soapstone were the favored materials to conduct the heat. The warmer was kept under the feet, then the legs and feet were tucked into a blanket, providing welcome warmth in a cold carriage or church.

Oak, Carved, Painted, Tin Lining, Handle, Marked, Eeg Tje Dekker, c.1800, 8 x 10 In. .....*illus* 406
Stoneware, Cream, Doulton's Improved Foot Warmer, Screw Top, 1881, 10 In. 144
Tin & Wood, Box, Red, Whale Oil Burner, Handle, 1800s, 8 x 5 In. 295
Walnut, Dovetailed, Pierced, Bail Handle, 1700s, 6 x 8 ¾ x 9 ¾ In. ....*illus* 201
Wood & Sheet Metal, Wire Bail Handle, Bridle Joints, 1800s, 9 x 6 In. 275
Wood, Carved, 6-Point Stars, Circle, Pierced Top, Red, c.1760, 7 ½ x 9 ⅞ x 7 ¾ In. ....*illus* 2829

FOOTBALL *collectibles may be found in the Card and the Sports categories.*

FOSTORIA

Fostoria glass was made in Fostoria, Ohio, from 1887 to 1891. The factory was moved to Moundsville, West Virginia, and most of the glass seen in shops today is a twentieth-century product. The company was sold to Lancaster Colony Corporation in 1983 and closed in 1986. Additional Fostoria items may be listed in the Milk Glass category. Original Fostoria Coin pattern was made in amber, blue, crystal, green, olive green, and red. Reproduction colors include crystal, dark green, pale blue, and red. All coins on original Fostoria are frosted or gold decorated. The coins on new Lancaster Colony pieces are not frosted. Some of these unfrosted coins are being frosted—with either acid or sandblasting—after they are purchased.

Folk Art, Uncle Sam, Holding American Flag, Seal, Carved, Painted Wood, 69 ½ In.
$492

Skinner, Inc.

Folk Art, Watch Holder, Deer Head, Inlaid, Wood, Marked, Loom, 8 x 4 ½ In.
$57

Hartzell's Auction Gallery Inc.

Folk Art, Whirligig, Drummer, American Flag, Stars, 4-Blade Propeller, Removable Base, 18 x 10 In.
$410

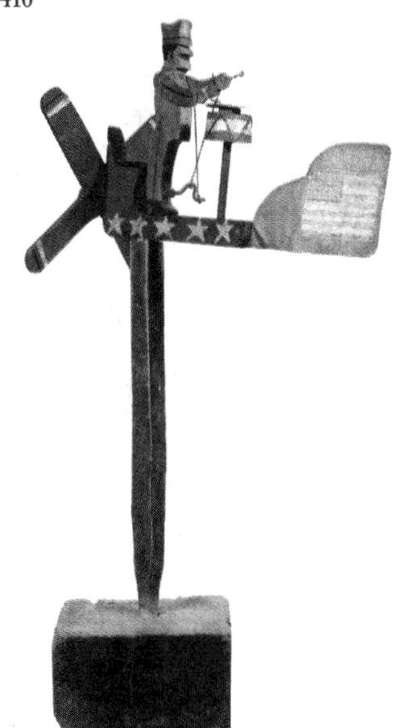

Thomaston Place Auction Galleries

Folk Art, Whirligig, Indian Chief, Yellow Shirt, Green Pants, Tomahawk Paddles, Trapezoidal Base, 15 In.
$4,305

Skinner, Inc.

Folk Art, Whirligig, Man, Sawing, Beard, Hat, Carved, Painted, Wood, 18 In.
$68

Hartzell's Auction Gallery Inc.

Folk Art, Whirligig, Sailor, Wood, Painted, Paddles On Arms, 15 ¾ In.
$165

Conestoga Auction Company

Foot Warmer, Oak, Carved, Painted, Tin Lining, Handle, Marked, Eeg Tje Dekker, c.1800, 8 x 10 In.
$406

Garth's Auctioneers & Appraisers

Foot Warmer, Walnut, Dovetailed, Pierced, Bail Handle, 1700s, 6 x 8 ¾ x 9 ¾ In.
$201

Bunch Auctions

Foot Warmer, Wood, Carved, 6-Point Stars, Circle, Pierced Top, Red, c.1760, 7 ½ x 9 ⅞ x 7 ¾ In.
$2,829

Skinner, Inc.

Fostoria, Lorraine, Cruet, Flat Diamond Box, Ruby Stain, Ribbed Stopper, c.1893, 7 In.
$105

Jeffrey S. Evans & Associates

Frankart, Cigarette Stand, Nude Woman, Holding Up Copper Cigarette Tray, Square Base, 23 ¾ x 7 In.
$590

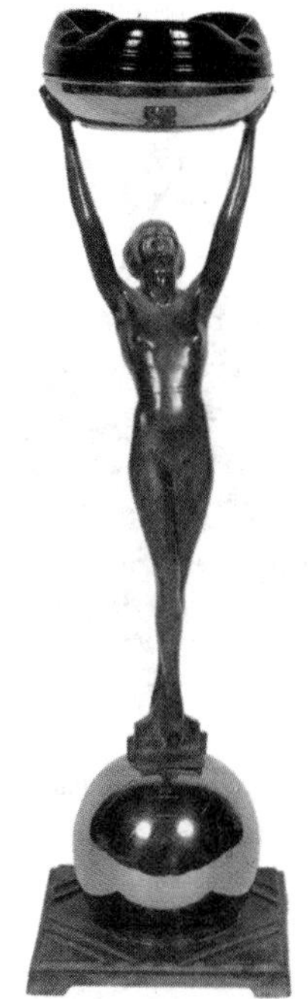

Ahlers & Ogletree Auction Gallery

Frankart, Lamp, Figural, 2 Female Nudes, Kneeling, Green Glass Globe, Signed, 8 x 14 x 5 In.
$840

Ripley Auctions

Lamp, Desk, Electric, White, Iridescent Glass, 16 x 7 In., Pair 3375
Lorraine, Cruet, Flat Diamond Box, Ruby Stain, Ribbed Stopper, c.1893, 7 In. .... *illus* 105
Versailles, Goblet, Azure Blue, Clear Stem & Base, 8 In., 13 Piece 420
Versailles, Plate, Azure Blue, Dodecagon Sides, 10 ½ In., 14 Piece 330

FOVAL, *see Fry category.*

FRAMES *are included in the Furniture category under Frame.*

FRANCISCAN

Franciscan is a trademark that appears on pottery. Gladding, McBean and Company started in 1875. The company grew and acquired other potteries. It made sewer pipes, floor tiles, dinnerware, and art pottery with a variety of trademarks. It began using the trade name *Franciscan* in 1934. In 1936, dinnerware and art pottery were sold under the name *Franciscan Ware.* The company made china and cream-colored, decorated earthenware. Desert Rose, Apple, El Patio, and Coronado were best sellers. The company became Interpace Corporation and in 1979 was purchased by Josiah Wedgwood & Sons. The plant closed in 1984, but production of a few patterns shifted to China and Thailand. For more prices, go to kovels.com.

Gladding, McBean & Co.
1934–1963

Gladding, McBean & Co.
c.1940

International Pipe and Ceramics
1963+

Apple, Platter, Round, 12 ½ In. 24
Desert Rose, Butter, 1940s, 7 ⅝ In. 15
Desert Rose, Napkin Holder, Upright, 6 ¾ x 2 ¾ x 5 In. 39
Ivy, Bowl, Compote, Footed, 4 x 8 In. 128
Starburst, Plate, Jam, Handle, c.1950, 8 x 6 In. 65
Tulip Time, Platter, Blue, Light Green, 1960s, 13 ¾ x 11 In. 15

FRANKART

Frankart Inc., New York, New York, mass-produced nude "dancing lady" lamps, ashtrays, and other decorative Art Deco items in the 1920s and 1930s. They were made of white lead composition and spray painted. *Frankart Inc.* and the patent number and year were stamped on the base.

Bookends, Spelter, Bronze, 2 Horse Heads, Square Base, 5 x 4 ⅞ x 5 In. 180
Cigarette Stand, Nude Woman, Holding Up Copper Cigarette Tray, Square Base, 23 ¾ x 7 In. . *illus* 590
Lamp, Black Gunmetal, Hand Blown, Durand Glass Shade, c.1928, 18 ½ x 7 ½ x 5 In. 1652
Lamp, Figural, 2 Female Nudes, Kneeling, Green Glass Globe, Signed, 8 x 14 x 5 In. .... *illus* 840
Lamp, Figural, Nude Female, Holding Frosted Glass Disc, Bronze, c.1930, 10 ½ In. .... *illus* 615

FRANKOMA POTTERY

Frankoma Pottery was originally known as The Frank Potteries when John F. Frank opened shop in 1933. The name "Frankoma," a combination of his last name and the last three letters of Oklahoma, was used beginning in 1934. The factory moved to Sapulpa, Oklahoma, in 1938. Early wares were made from a light cream-colored clay from Ada, Oklahoma, but in 1956 the company switched to a red clay from Sapulpa. The firm made dinnerware, utilitarian and decorative kitchenwares, figurines, flowerpots, and limited edition and commemorative pieces. John Frank died in 1973 and his daughter, Joniece, inherited the business. Frankoma went bankrupt in 1990. The pottery operated under various owners for a few years and was bought by Joe Ragosta in 2008. It closed in 2010. The buildings, assets, name, and molds were sold at an auction in 2011.

Bookends, Dogs, Red Irish Setter, Black, c.1943, 7 x 4 ½ x 6 In. 300
Bowl, Cornucopia, Brown, 12 x 5 x 6 In. 35
Vase, Bud, Prairie Green, Black Base, 1950s, 16 In. 130

FRATERNAL

Fraternal objects that are related to the many different fraternal organizations in the United States are listed in this category. The Elks, Masons, Odd Fellows, and others are included. Also included are service organizations, like the American Legion, Kiwanis, and Lions Club. Furniture is listed in the Furniture category. Shaving mugs decorated with fraternal crests are included in the Shaving Mug category.

Eastern Star, Gavel, Carved, Areme Chapter No. 192, Names, Initials, Wood, 1918, 9 ½ In. 176
Elks, Whiskey Bottle, Central Medallion, Enamel, Multicolor, 11 ½ x 9 ¼ In. 590
Masonic, Apron, Armorial Shield, 2 Figures, Lady Justice, Frame, 1860s, 22 x 23 ½ In. ..*illus* 270
Masonic, Bookmark, Silver, Enamel, Square & Compass, Art Deco, 1930s, 3 ⅜ In. 57
Masonic, Cane, Orb Handle, Masonic Symbols, Silver Plate, Ebonized Shaft, 35 ¾ In. 1750
Masonic, Cuff Links, Insignia, Goldtone, Anson Co., 1940s 20
Masonic, Hat, 32nd Degree, Scottish Rite, Black, Yellow, 7 In. 55
Masonic, Jug, Symbols, Melon Shape, Creamware, Handle, Liverpool, Early 1800s, 10 In. *illus* 420
Masonic, Needlework, Symbols, Glory Be To God On High, Frame, 6 ¾ x 7 ¾ In. ....*illus* 224
Masonic, Pendant, Globe, Compass, Star, 9K Gold, 1 ½ In. 723
Masonic, Pin, Lapel, Square & Compass, 14K White Gold, Screwback 80
Masonic, Pitcher, Coin Silver, Emblems, Footed, Wide Spout, Jones, Ball & Poor, 1850s, 10 In. 793
Masonic, Ring, Insignia, Plumb & Trowel, Red Glass, 10K Gold 665
Masonic, Trinket Box, Sterling Silver, Round, 4 Legs, Blue Fabric Lining, 1928, 1 ¾ In. 350
Masonic, Watch, Cretets, Embossed Case, Symbols, Signed, Sirom Swiss, Pocket ....*illus* 354
Masonic, Watch, Triangular Case, Symbols, Silver, Swiss Movement, Sheffield, Pocket ...*illus* 443
Odd Fellows, 2 Tablets, Ten Commandments, Gilt Letters, Gray Ground, 1880s, 22 x 7 ½ In. .. 223
Odd Fellows, Ceremonial Ax, 2-Sided, Black, Green Ground, c.1900, 49 ½ In. ....*illus* 468
Odd Fellows, Ceremonial Staff, Golden Hand, Red Heart, Black Pole, Carved, c.1900, 61 In. *illus* 3042
Odd Fellows, Gorget, Ceremonial, Motto, Symbols, Silver, 1800s, 3 x 4 In. 554

FRY GLASS

Fry glass was made by the H.C. Fry Glass Company of Rochester, Pennsylvania. The company, founded in 1901, first made cut glass and other types of glasswares. In 1922 it patented a heat-resistant glass called Pearl Ovenglass. For two years, 1926–1927, the company made Fry Foval, an opal ware decorated with colored trim. Reproductions of this glass have been made. Depression glass patterns made by Fry may be listed in the Depression Glass category. Some pieces of cut glass may also be included in the Cut Glass category.

FRY

Cocktail Shaker, Green Reeded Glass, Footed, Handle, Art Deco, 1930s 388
Compote, Footed, Ruffled Top, Baluster, Blue Top, Opalescent, 3 ½ x 6 In. 175
Reamer, Glass, Clear, 1920s, 2 ½ x 6 In. 23
Serving Dish, Lid, Silver Plate Handles, Etched, Oven Glass, Opalescent, 6 x 9 x 6 In. 106
Tray, Duquesne, Round, Ruffled Rim, 14 In. ....*illus* 800
Vase, Art Glass, Gold Threading, Trumpet Shape, 7 ¾ x 6 In. 495
Vase, Bud, Light Blue, Opalescent, 9 In. 84

FRY FOVAL

Candlestick, Footed, Opalescent, Blue Spiral, Signed, 10 ½ In., Pair 750
Coffeepot, Lid, Clear, Handle, 10 x 7 In. 306

Frankart, Lamp, Figural, Nude Female, Holding Frosted Glass Disc, Bronze, c.1930, 10 ½ In.
$615

Skinner, Inc.

Fraternal, Masonic, Apron, Armorial Shield, 2 Figures, Lady Justice, Frame, 1860s, 22 x 23 ½ In.
$270

Garth's Auctioneers & Appraisers

Fraternal, Masonic, Jug, Symbols, Melon Shape, Creamware, Handle, Liverpool, Early 1800s, 10 In.
$420

Case Antiques

Fraternal, Masonic, Needlework, Symbols, Glory Be To God On High, Frame, 6 ¾ x 7 ¾ In.
$224

Bunch Auctions

Fraternal, Masonic, Watch, Cretets, Embossed Case, Symbols, Signed, Sirom Swiss, Pocket
$354

Conestoga Auction Company

Fraternal, Masonic, Watch, Triangular Case, Symbols, Silver, Swiss Movement, Sheffield, Pocket
$443

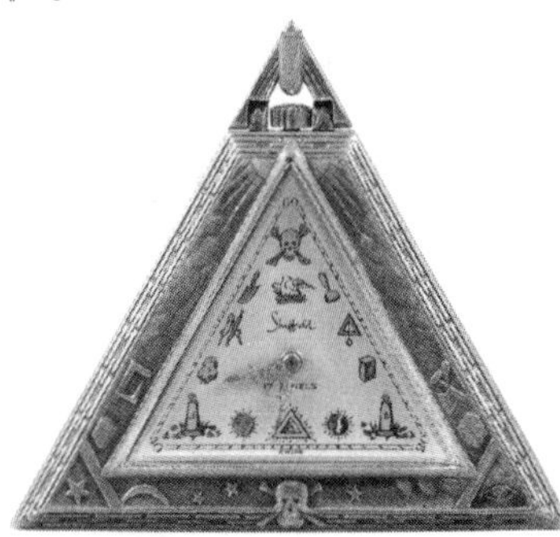
Conestoga Auction Company

Fraternal, Odd Fellows, Ceremonial Ax, 2-Sided, Black, Green Ground, c.1900, 49 ½ In.
$468

Jeffrey S. Evans & Associates

Fraternal, Odd Fellows, Ceremonial Staff, Golden Hand, Red Heart, Black Pole, Carved, c.1900, 61 In.
$3,042

Jeffrey S. Evans & Associates

Fry Glass, Tray, Duquesne, Round, Ruffled Rim, 14 In.
$800

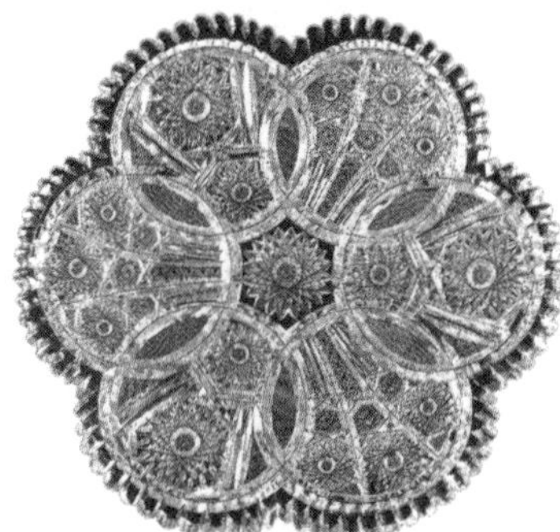
Woody Auctions

Fulper, Compote, Effigy, Shallow Bowl, Yellow Ground, 3 Squatting Men, Early 1900s, 7 In.
$984

Skinner, Inc.

Fulper, Figurine, Dog, Seated, Pink Glaze, Early 1900s, 7 ¾ In.
$148

Skinner, Inc.

Fulper, Vase, Bell Pepper, Green, Coppery Crystalline Glaze, Flemington, c.1910, 4 In.
$1,080

Case Antiques

Soup, Dish, Opalescent, Wide Rim, 8 ⅝ In.	29
Sugar & Creamer, Concave Shape, Green Handles, 3 In.	50
Vase, Opalescent, White & Blue, Applied Delft Rim & Foot, Polished Pontil, c.1950, 9 x 4 In.	468

FULPER

Fulper Pottery Company was incorporated in 1899 in Flemington, New Jersey. It made art pottery from 1909 to 1929. The firm had been making bottles, jugs, and housewares since 1805. Vasekraft is a line of art pottery with glazes similar to Chinese art pottery that was introduced in 1909. Doll heads were made about 1928. The firm became Stangl Pottery in 1929. Stangl Pottery is listed in its own category in this book.

FULPER

Basket, Twisted Rope Handle, Ruffled Rim, Flower, Blue, Vertical Ink Mark, 12 x 6 ½ In.	184
Compote, Effigy, Shallow Bowl, Yellow Ground, 3 Squatting Men, Early 1900s, 7 In. *illus*	984
Figurine, Dog, Seated, Pink Glaze, Early 1900s, 7 ¾ In. *illus*	148
Lamp, Electric, Trophy Shape, Scroll Handles, Brass Socket, Square Base, Pink, Green, 11 In.	219
Powder Box, Woman, Sitting, Dress, Orange, Blue, 7 ⅝ In.	173
Teapot, Lid, Hexagonal Body, Shaped Handle & Spout, 7 In.	177
Urn, Blue, Ivory, Flambe Glaze, 2 Handles, 14 ½ x 9 In.	750
Urn, Green & Brown, Mottled Gloss Glaze, Blue Tinge, Plum Red, Matte, 10 In.	311
Vase, Bell Pepper, Green, Coppery Crystalline Glaze, Flemington, c.1910, 4 In. *illus*	1080
Vase, Brown, Green, Flambe Glaze, Handles, Footed, Marked, 3 x 4 In.	58
Vase, Buttress Handle, Black Over Tan, High Glaze, Vertical Ink Mark, 6 x 8 In.	299
Vase, Crystalline Glaze, Green, Brown Drip, 2 Handles, Ribbed, 17 ½ In.	156
Vase, Cucumber Green, Oval, Narrow Mouth, Bulbous Body, Paper Label, 9 x 6 ½ In. *illus*	165
Vase, Mirror Black, Blue Sky, Flambe Glaze, c.1915, 34 x 10 In. *illus*	10000
Vase, Straight Neck, Green Glaze, Dark Brown Interior, Handles, 1915-25, 12 x 11 In.	825
Vase, Streak Light Blue Glaze, Vertical Ink Mark, 1910s, 15 ¾ In. *illus*	163

FURNITURE

Furniture of all types is listed in this category. Examples dating from the seventeenth century to 2010 are included. Prices for furniture vary in different parts of the country. Oak furniture is most expensive in the West; large pieces over eight feet high are sold for the most money in the South, where high ceilings are found in the old homes. Modern is popular in New York, California, and Chicago. Condition is very important when determining prices. These are NOT average prices but rather reports of unique sales. If the description includes the word *style,* the piece resembles the old furniture style but was made at a later time. It is not a period piece. Small chests that sat on a table or dresser are also included here. Garden furniture is listed in the Garden Furnishings category. Related items may be found in the Architectural, Brass, and Store categories.

Armchairs are listed under Chair in this category.	
Armoire, Louis XV Style, Mahogany, Carved, Mirror Doors, Cabriole Legs, c.1910, 101 x 57 In.	438
Armoire, Louis XV, Carved Medallion, Paneled Doors, Cabriole Legs, c.1750, 100 x 54 x 25 In.	523
Barstool, Shell Seat, Aluminum, 5-Leg Base, Ring Footrest, Pepe Cortez, 1994, 28 x 18 In., 6 Piece	1053
Bed, Federal Style, Molded Crest, Carleton, Drexel, 86 x 83 x 86 In.	277
Bed, Half-Tester, W.T. Davis, Mahogany, Rococo, Acanthus, Drapery, c.1860, 63 x 71 In.	6000
Bed, Ralph Lauren, Polo, Mahogany, Side Rail, Curved Crest, Spiral Column, 1900s, 78 x 85 x 80 In.	1416
Bed, Rococo Revival, Rosewood, Carved, Paneled, Turned Finials, c.1850, 95 x 74 In.	1280
Bed, Rosewood, Bronze Headboard, c.1950, 36 ½ x 65 x 80 In. *illus*	775
Bed, Shaker, Brother's, Pine, Maple, Turned Posts, Wheels, Rope, 31 x 72 In. *illus*	800
Bed, Wedding, Multi-Tier Valance, Gilt Plaques, Carved Legs, Chinese, 96 x 88 x 67 In.	735
Bench, Ali Baba, Roycroft, Oak, Ash, Carved, Orb & Cross Mark, c.1905, 19 x 42 In. *illus*	6875
Bench, Bucket, Pine, Open Shelves, Square Nails, Cutout Sides, c.1825, 48 x 37 In. *illus*	600
Bench, Bucket, Pine, Shallow Seat, Shaped Sides, Brown, 1800s, 50 ½ x 48 x 15 In.	204
Bench, Bucket, Red Paint, Bootjack Ends, 45 x 31 ½ x 11 ½ In.	840

Fulper, Vase, Cucumber Green, Oval, Narrow Mouth, Bulbous Body, Paper Label, 9 x 6 ½ In.
$165

Witherell's

Fulper, Vase, Streak Light Blue Glaze, Vertical Ink Mark, 1910s, 15 ¾ In.
$163

Rago Arts and Auction Center

Fulper, Vase, Mirror Black, Blue Sky, Flambe Glaze, c.1915, 34 x 10 In.
$10,000

Eldred's

F

Furniture, Bed, Rosewood, Bronze Headboard, c.1950, 36 ½ x 65 x 80 In.
$775

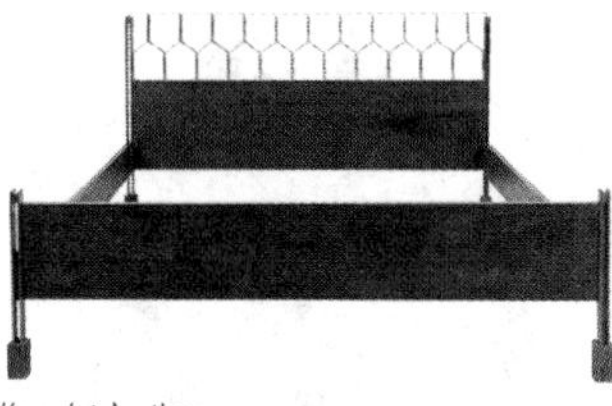

Kamelot Auctions

Furniture, Bed, Shaker, Brother's, Pine, Maple, Turned Posts, Wheels, Rope, 31 x 72 In.
$800

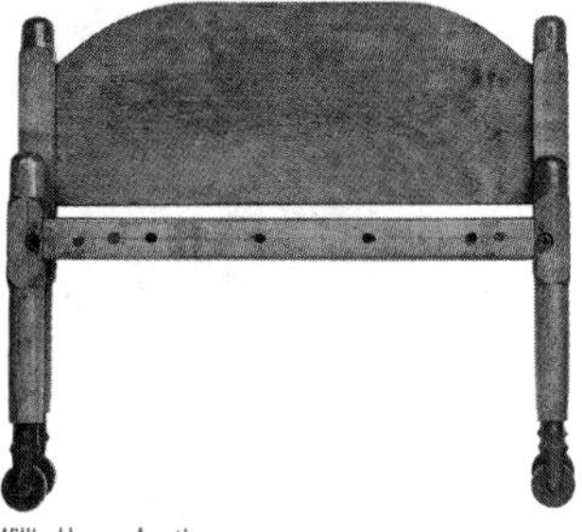

Willis Henry Auctions

Furniture, Bench, Ali Baba, Roycroft, Oak, Ash, Carved, Through Tenon, Orb & Cross Mark, c.1905, 19 x 42 In.
$6,875

Rago Arts and Auction Center

Borax

Borax is the slang name for very cheap furniture. It originally referred to cheap, poorly made but flashy furniture made for the bottom of the market during the Depression. It was often made of inexpensive gum or poplar wood with a printed veneer pattern. The term is still used today.

Bench, Carved Medallion, Warrior, Lion, Base Molding, Continental, c.1860, 55 x 59 x 20 In... 554
Bench, Crock, Pine, Mortised, Square Nails, Cutout Feet, Blue, 1850s, 48 x 42 x 12 In.............. 2280
Bench, Hall, R.J. Horner, Oak, Lift Seat, Scenic Carved Panels, Maiden Crest, 59 x 57 x 21 In. *illus* 2723
Bench, Mackenzie-Childs, Porcelain, Wood, Painted, Faux Marble, Gold Leaf, 21 x 28 In. *illus* 4375
Bench, Mahogany, Acanthus, Ball Feet, Cabriole Legs, Chippendale Style, England, 1800s, 17 x 25 In. 413
Bench, Teak, Carved, Dragon, Lotus, Chinese, c.1900, 52 x 52 x 21 In.. 350
Bench, Telephone, Mahogany, Eagle, Upholstered, Cabriole Legs, Victorian Style, 56 x 23 x 44 In. .*illus* 363
Bench, Wainscot, Oak, 4-Panel Back, Scroll Arms, Upholstered Cushion, 1700s, 42 x 72 x 26 In.. 472
Bench, Wormley, Long John, Drawer, Upholstered Section, Dunbar Plaque, 12 x 84 In. ...*illus* 1375
Bookcase, Danish Modern, Teak, Sliding Doors, Drop Down Surface, 1950s, 44 x 79 In. .*illus* 885
Bookcase, Ettore Sottsass, Carlton, Laminate On Wood, Memphis, 1981, 78 x 75 In. ....*illus* 15000
Bookcase, G. Stickley, Oak, 12-Pane Glass Doors, Iron Hardware, c.1910, 56 ½ x 60 x 13 In.... 2574
Bookcase, Grand Rapid, Wide Shelves, Lift Front Door, Oak Mullion, Waterfall Top, 75 x 14 x 51 In. 1356
Bookcase, L & J.G. Stickley, 3 Doors, Glass Panes, Escutcheons, Handles, c.1910, 55 x 72 In..... 5310
Bookcase, Mahogany, 2 Glass Doors, Column Front, Claw Feet, 54 x 50 x 16 In......................... 748
Bookcase, Mahogany, 4 Sections, Glass Door, Globe Wernicke Stack, 34 x 61 ½ In.................. 340
Bookcase, Mahogany, Glass Doors, 3 Shelves, 4 Drawers, George III, 88 x 21 ½ x 45 ½ In....... 1230
Bookcase, Mahogany, Green Paint, 2 Shelves, 3 Drawers, Bracket Feet, c.1800, 67 x 23 x 20 In. *illus* 590
Bookcase, Mahogany, Marble Top, 2 Drawers, 2 Doors, Fruit & Leaf Mounts, 48 x 55 x 17 In... 390
Bookcase, Oak, 2 Sections, Glass Door, File Drawers, Shaped Base, 1910s, 35 x 34 x 14 In........ 438
Bookcase, Oak, Sliding Glass Doors, Tapering Legs, c.1960, 53 x 51 x 10 In.............................. 750
Bookcase, Poul Hundevad, Rosewood, Adjustable Shelves, Tubular Steel Legs, 38 x 54 x 12 In. .*illus* 461
Bookcase, Renaissance Revival, Walnut, 3 Sections, Burl, Ebonized Trim, Victorian, 102 x 17 In... 1652
Bookcase, Table, Metamorphic, Oak, Iron, Hinged, Industrial, c.1880, 39 ½ x 24 x 17 In. 413
Bookcase, Teak, Shelves, Doors, Tapered Legs, Cord Hole, Denmark, 1950s, 53 x 75 x 11 In..... 590
Bookcase, Walnut, Revolving, 4 Vertical Slats, 4 Shelves, c.1910, 32 x 17 x 18 In. ....*illus* 1695
Bookcase, William IV, Mahogany, 2 Tiers, Glass Doors, Turned Feet, 1800s, 84 x 54 x 16 In. ..*illus* 2125
Bookcase-Cabinet, Neoclassical Style, Mahogany, Cupboard Doors, Glass Panels, 85 x 99 x 25 In. 1107
Bookrack, Black Forest Style, Folding Ends, Cows, Trees, Sliding Base, c.1900, 7 ¾ x 17 x 7 In.. 120
Bookrack, Sheep, Francois-Xavier Lalanne Style, Wood, Faux Fur, 28 x 36 In. ....*illus* 1188
Buffet, Louis XV, Walnut, Fruit, Berries, Acanthus, 4 Doors, Mesh, c.1780, 101 x 50 In. 2820
Buffet, Louis XVI Style, Marble Top, Walnut Case, Ormolu Mount, Tapered Legs, c.1900, 37 x 69 x 26 In. 1476
Buffet, Teak, 4 Doors, 4 Drawers, R.S. Montreal Furniture, Co., 78 x 18 x 29 In........................ 161
Bureau, Chippendale Style, Walnut, 4 Drawers, Beaded Edge, Ogee Bracket Feet, 1900s, 33 x 32 In.. 325
Bureau, Continental Style, 7 Drawers, Brass Pulls, Bracket Base, Late 1900s, 54 x 33 x 18 In.. 166
Bureau, Georgian, Mahogany, Bowfront, Beaded Drawer, Flared Feet, 41 ⅜ x 30 ½ x 30 In. *illus* 266
Bureau, Louis XVI Style, Dark Brown, Leather Top, 3 Drawers, Bronze Mounting, 32 ½ x 60 x 34 In. 204
Bureau, Sheraton, Mahogany, Bird's-Eye Maple, Overhang, c.1820, 25 x 18 In., Child's ...*illus* 330
Butler, Walking, Holding Bowl, Wood Cutout, Painted, Octagonal Base, 33 In. ....*illus* 106
Butler, Wood Cutout, Standing, Derby Hat, Red Coat, Black Pants, Brown Shoes, c.1950, 36 In........ 207
Cabinet, Altar, Elm, Mortise, Tenon, 3 Drawers, 2 Doors, Chinese, 35 x 85 x 20 In.................... 472
Cabinet, Arts & Crafts Style, Oak, Glass Door, 2 Tiers, 3 Shelves, 26 x 16 x 72 In....................... 226
Cabinet, China, Arts & Crafts, L. & J.G. Stickley, Oak, c.1910, 53 x 34 x 15 In............................ 4918
Cabinet, Chippendale Style, Tiger Maple, Molded Bracket Base, 1991, 12 x 11 x 9 In................. 1046
Cabinet, Corner, 2 Doors, Central Drawer, Scroll Cut Base, 1800s, 80 x 43 ½ x 22 In................ 791
Cabinet, Corner, Mahogany, Bowfront, Curved Glass, Carved Crest, Hoof Feet, 89 x 26 x 24 In. 726
Cabinet, Demilune, Sphere, Brass Handle, Painted, France, 31 x 24 x 12 In............................. 213
Cabinet, Display, Beaver & Tapley, Sliding Glass Doors, Tapered Legs, 1950s, 40 x 60 x 10 In... 185
Cabinet, Display, Countertop, Oak Case, Sliding Door, Open Interior, c.1920, 8 x 21 x 19 In. 248
Cabinet, Display, Countertop, Walnut, Glass Bowfront, 2 Glass Shelves, Door, 28 x 17 In......... 150
Cabinet, Display, Henredon, Walnut, Hardwood Case, 2 Glass Doors, 1900s, 103 x 60 x 23 In.. 2006
Cabinet, Display, Slant, 4 Panels, Glass, Wheel Feet, 62 ½ x 24 x 24 In.................................. 720
Cabinet, Drawers, Walnut, Marble Top, Bracket Footing, c.1900, 37 x 41 ½ x 19 In. 106
Cabinet, Ettore Sottsass, Casablanca, Laminate, Memphis, Italy, 1981, 85 x 63 In. ....*illus* 10625
Cabinet, Galle, Walnut & Fruitwood, 3 Shelves, Landscapes, Vegetation, 61 x 28 x 18 In.......... 4305
Cabinet, George III, 2 Parts, 3 Shelves, 9 Drawers, Plinth Base, 72 x 8 x 48 In. 2460
Cabinet, Jewelry, Walnut, Maple, Lacewood, 11 Drawers, 47 ¾ x 16 ½ x 16 ½ In...................... 345
Cabinet, Lacquered, Carved, Multiple Doors, Inlaid Scenes, Signed, Japan, 82 x 50 In. .... *illus* 1003
Cabinet, Louis XV Style, Walnut, Carved, Panel Back, Door, Cabriole Legs, France, 79 x 25 x 12 In. 469
Cabinet, Louis XV, Walnut, 2 Doors, Marble Top, Interior Shelf, 32 x 32 x 17 In........................ 1107

Cabinet, Low, Mahogany, 3 Drawers, Brass Handles, c.1960, 16 x 74 ¾ x 19 In.	375
Cabinet, Napoleon III, Boulle Parlor, Ebonized, Door, Bowed Glass Doors, c.1865, 46 x 72 In. *illus*	1188
Cabinet, Oak, Carved, Molded Cornice, Claw Feet, Curved Glass, Chinese, c.1900, 71 x 43 x 17 In.	420
Cabinet, Oak, Glass Door & Side Panels, 3 Shelves, Wood Pull, Early 1900s, 59 x 33 x 14 In.	936
Cabinet, P. Evans, Patchwork, Wall Mounted, 2 Adjustable Shelves, c.1968, 26 x 22 x 12 In. *illus*	4688
Cabinet, Renaissance Revival, Walnut, Carved, 4 Doors, Base Molding, 1800s, 66 x 39 x 25 In.	738
Cabinet, Roycroft, Oak, Door, Leaded Glass, Shelves, Orb & Cross, c.1905, 40 x 32 In. *illus*	16250
Cabinet, Shaker, Seeds, Cherry, Walnut, 24 Cubbies, Drawer, Enfield, Conn., 21 In. *illus*	1599
Cabinet, Side, Walnut, Molded Edge Top, Doors, Shaped Feet, 36 x 67 x 18 ½ In.	461
Cabinet, Spice, Oak, 8 Drawers, Shaped Top, Sides, Base, Turned Feet, c.1900, 13 x 10 In.	192
Cabinet, Spice, Pine, Tabletop, Green Ground, 4 Banks, Drawers, 1800s, 16 x 22 ¾ In.	1159
Cabinet, Walnut, Hand Carved, Black Marble Top, Drawer, Door, Beveled Edge, Va., c.1880, 44 x 21 In.	186
Cabinet, Widdicomb, Nakashima, Walnut, 4 Drawers, 2 Shelves, 1950s, 32 x 84 x 22 In.	6600
Cabinet-On-Stand, Mirrored, Cut Glass Diamonds, 2 Doors, Shelves, Wood Legs, 72 x 44 ½ In.	95
Candlestand, Chestnut, Pine, 2 Sheet Iron Sockets, Cross Base, Adjustable Ratchet, 1700s, 24 In.	2091
Candlestand, Federal, 2-Board Top, Vinegar Graining, Black Paint, c.1815, 26 x 18 In. *illus*	1080
Candlestand, Federal, Mahogany, Tilt Top, Octagonal, 3 Spider Legs, Early 1800s, 28 x 16 In.	156
Candlestand, Federal, Tilt Top, Flowers, Black, Gilt Surround, 3-Footed, c.1810, 29 In.	125
Candlestand, Hepplewhite, Mahogany, Drawer, Turned Pedestal, 3 Splayed Legs, c.1800, 25 In.	225
Candlestand, Hepplewhite, Mahogany, String Inlay, Tripod Legs, c.1800, 29 x 21 x 15 In.	117
Candlestand, Oval, Cherry, Snake Feet, Connecticut, 1700s, 27 x 16 ½ x 24 In.	148
Candlestand, Queen Anne, Cherry, Pedestal, Square Top, Cabriole Legs, c.1750, 25 x 15 x 14 In.	280
Candlestand, Queen Anne, Cherry, Round Top, Baluster Shaft, 3 Arched Legs, c.1750, 25 x 17 In. *illus*	240
Candlestand, Tilt Top, Checkerboard, Oval, Painted, Tripod Base, 1800s, 27 ½ x 21 ½ x 14 ¾ In.	644
Candlestand, Tilt Top, Mahogany, Joseph Short, Massachusetts, 28 ½ x 23 ½ x 13 In.	300
Canterbury, George III, Mahogany & Pine, Dividers, Drawer, Casters, c.1800, 18 x 18 ½ x 14 In.	443
Canterbury, Mahogany, Ball Feet, 15 x 10 x 6 ½ In.	203
Canterbury, William IV, Rosewood, Carved, Shelves, Dividers, Drawer, 1800s, 41 x 22 In. *illus*	375
Cart, Brass, Flowers, Acrylic, Removable Tray & Basket, Casters, c.1950, 24 x 24 x 21 In.	281
Cart, Pierre Cardin, Chromed Metal, Glass Top & Shelf, Castors, France, 31 x 32 In. *illus*	2625
Cart, Serving, Triangular, 2 Parts, Laminate Top, Wicker Bottom, Wheels, c.1950, 28 x 19 x 19 In.	594
Cellarette, Mahogany, Hinged Lid, Brass, Partitioned Interior, c.1700, 15 x 25 x 15 In.	702
Cellarette, William IV, Burl Oak, Removable Dovetail Box, Casters, 1800s, 22 x 28 x 21 In. *illus*	1440
Chair Set, George III Style, Ebonized, Upholstered, 37 x 22 x 22 In., 12	7995
Chair Set, Yolk Style, Cushions, Hardwood, Serpentine Splats, Carved, Chinese, 37 x 16 x 20 In., 6	187
Chair, Adirondack, Black, Painted, Slant Back, Hudson Valley, 38 ½ x 39 x 40 In.	923
Chair, American Rococo, Rosewood, Elaborate Carvings, Attributed To Belter, Arms, c.1855, 44 In. *illus*	13568
Chair, Arne Jacobsen, Egg, Leather, Aluminum, Fritz Hansen, Denmark, 1958, 42 In. *illus*	5000
Chair, Bamboo Wood, Cane Sides, c.1960, 29 ¾ x 27 ¾ x 31 In. *illus*	875
Chair, Banister Back, Black, Painted, Rush Seat, 2 Stretchers, 1700s, 43 x 16 In.	197
Chair, Banister Back, Sausage Turned Stretchers, Shaped Arms, c.1800, 45 ½ In.	360
Chair, Banister Back, Scrolled Molded Crest, Sloping Arms, Turned Spindles, 1710s, 48 In.	4613
Chair, Biedermeier, Walnut, Upholstered, Arms, 1800s, 37 In., Pair	875
Chair, Bugatti, Walnut, Copper, Vellum Panels, Bone Inlay, Italy, 1902, 57 In. *illus*	15000
Chair, Campeche, Cherry, Molded Flat Top, Curule Base, Pad Feet, 1810s, 36 ¾ x 25 x 36 In.	995
Chair, Campeche, Oak, Rolled Crest, Black Leather, Brass Tacks, Curule Base, Child's, 22 x 17 x 13 In.	468
Chair, Carved, Mermaids, Lion's Head, Fruit Garland, 1800s, 44 x 17 ½ In.	350
Chair, Chinoiserie, Cane Seat, Center Splat, Curved Legs, Flowers, Arms, 42 ½ x 29 In.	438
Chair, Chippendale, Grain Painted, Rush Seat, New England, 24 In., Child's *illus*	2040
Chair, Club, Navy Blue, White Striped Upholstery, Wheel Feet, 1900s, 32 ½ x 15 In.	132
Chair, Club, Upholstered, Iron Legs, c.1950, 34 x 33 In.	1125
Chair, Cockfighting, Shield Shape Back, Round Seat, Turned Legs, Early 1900s, 24 x 26 In. *illus*	1476
Chair, Committee, Jeanneret, High Court Of Chandigarh, India, Teak, Hide, 35 In. *illus*	12500
Chair, Corner, Chippendale, Mahogany, 2 Pierced Splats, Arms, 32 In. *illus*	189
Chair, Corner, Slat Back, Shaped Arms, Rush Seat, 2 Stretcher Base, 1700s, 29 x 15 In. *illus*	369
Chair, Corner, Yew, Vase Shape Splats, Upholstered, X-Stretcher, George III, c.1800s *illus*	360
Chair, Daniel Meyer, Metro, Wood, Acrylic, Painted, Square Base, 1993, 39 In. *illus*	2000
Chair, Danish Modern, Teak, Green, Teal & Gold Upholstery, 1950s, 38 x 25 In. *illus*	325
Chair, Eames, LAR, Fiberglass, Steel, Upholstered, Herman Miller, 25 In., Pair *illus*	1500
Chair, Eames, Lounge, Ottoman, Brown Leather Upholstery, 32 ½ x 32 ¾ In. *illus*	3240

Furniture, Bench, Bucket, Pine, Open Shelves, Square Nails, Cutout Sides, c.1825, 48 x 37 In.
$600

Garth's Auctioneers & Appraisers

TIP
A brisk rubbing with olive oil will remove most alcohol stains from wood.

Furniture, Bench, Hall, R.J. Horner, Oak, Lift Seat, Scenic Carved Panels, Maiden Crest, 59 x 57 x 21 In.
$2,723

Fontaine's Auction Gallery

Furniture, Bench, Mackenzie-Childs, Porcelain, Wood, Painted, Faux Marble, Gold Leaf, 21 x 28 In.
$4,375

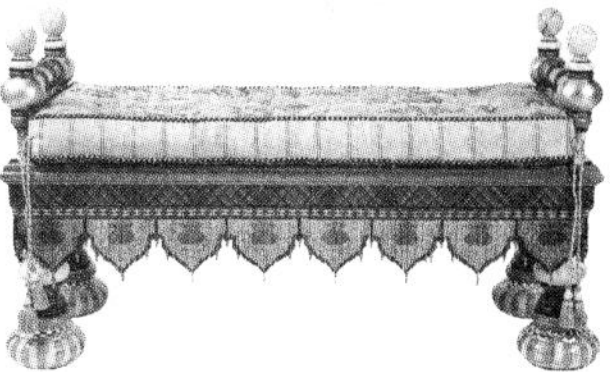

Abington Auction Gallery

Scalloped and Peg

One type of joint often found on drawers in Victorian furniture is called the "scalloped and peg" type. It was invented in 1867 by Charles Knapp, who made a machine that could cut the semicircular holes and other parts. He eventually sold his patented machine to a group of inventors.

Furniture, Bench, Telephone, Mahogany, Eagle, Upholstered, Cabriole Legs, Victorian Style, 56 x 23 x 44 In.
$363

Bruneau & Co. Auctioneers

Furniture, Bookcase, Ettore Sottsass, Carlton, Laminate On Wood, Memphis, 1981, 78 x 75 In.
$15,000

Wright

Furniture, Bench, Wormley, Long John, Drawer, Upholstered Section, Dunbar Plaque, 12 x 84 In.
$1,375

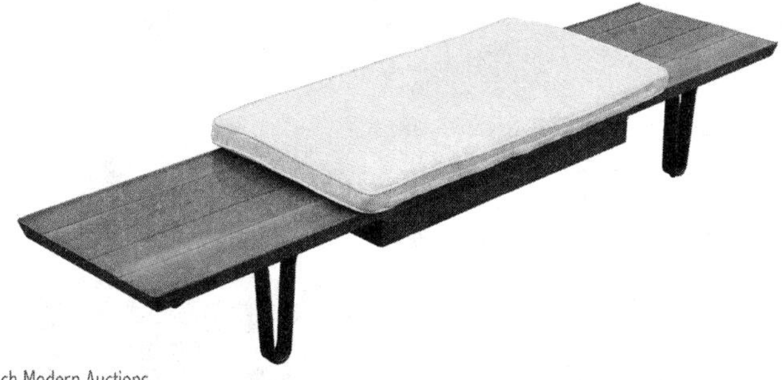

Palm Beach Modern Auctions

Furniture, Bookcase, Danish Modern, Teak, Sliding Doors, Drop Down Surface, 1950s, 44 x 79 In.
$885

Austin Auction Gallery

Furniture, Bookcase, Mahogany, Green Paint, 2 Shelves, 3 Drawers, Bracket Feet, c.1800, 67 x 23 x 20 In.
$590

Leland Little Auctions

Furniture, Bookcase, Poul Hundevad, Rosewood, Adjustable Shelves, Tubular Steel Legs, 38 x 54 x 12 In.
$461

Clars Auction Gallery

Furniture, Bookcase, Walnut, Revolving, 4 Vertical Slats, 4 Shelves, c.1910, 32 x 17 x 18 In.
$1,695

Soulis Auctions

Furniture, Bookcase, William IV, Mahogany, 2 Tiers, Glass Doors, Turned Feet, 1800s, 84 x 54 x 16 In.
$2,125

Hindman Auctions

Furniture, Bookrack, Sheep, Francois-Xavier Lalanne Style, Wood, Faux Fur, 28 x 36 In.
$1,188

Palm Beach Modern Auctions

Furniture, Bureau, Georgian, Mahogany, Bowfront, Beaded Drawer, Flared Feet, 41 3/8 x 30 1/2 x 30 In.
$266

Bunch Auctions

Furniture, Bureau, Sheraton, Mahogany, Bird's-Eye Maple, Overhang, c.1820, 25 x 18 In., Childs
$330

Eldred's

Furniture, Butler, Walking, Holding Bowl, Wood Cutout, Painted, Octagonal Base, 33 In.
$106

Copake Auctions

Furniture, Cabinet, Ettore Sottsass, Casablanca, Laminate, Memphis, Italy, 1981, 85 x 63 In.
$10,625

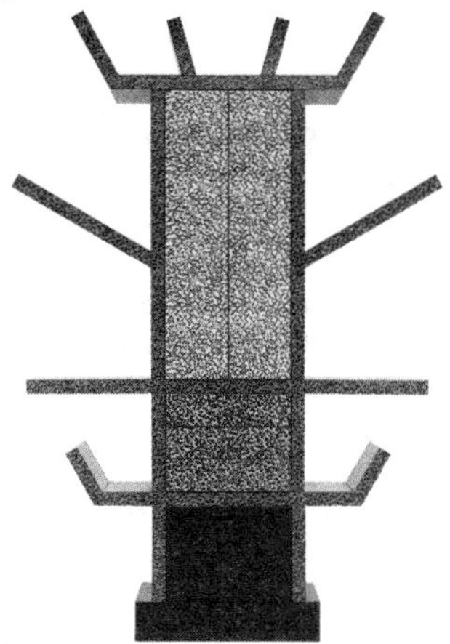

Wright

Furniture, Cabinet, Lacquered, Carved, Multiple Doors, Inlaid Scenes, Signed, Japan, 82 x 50 In.
$1,003

Cottone Auctions

Furniture, Cabinet, Napoleon III, Boulle Parlor, Ebonized, Door, Bowed Glass Doors, c.1865, 46 x 72 In.
$1,188

New Orleans Auction Galleries

Furniture, Cabinet, P. Evans, Patchwork, Wall Mounted, 2 Adjustable Shelves, c.1968, 26 x 22 x 12 In.
$4,688

Freeman's Auctioneers & Appraisers

F

Furniture, Cabinet, Roycroft, Oak, Door, Leaded Glass, Shelves, Orb & Cross, c.1905, 40 x 32 In.
$16,250

Rago Arts and Auction Center

Furniture, Cabinet, Shaker, Seeds, Cherry, Walnut, 24 Cubbies, Drawer, Enfield, Conn., 21 In.
$1,599

Willis Henry Auctions

Furniture, Candlestand, Federal, 2-Board Top, Vinegar Graining, Black Paint, c.1815, 26 x 18 In.
$1,080

Garth's Auctioneers & Appraisers

Chair, Eileen Gray, Bibendum, Red Leather, Chrome, Aram Designs, 29 x 38 In., Pair ....*illus* 10000
Chair, Fauteuil, Louis XIII, Upholstered, Flat Back, Carved Arms & Legs, 1800s, 44 x 24 x 25 In. 330
Chair, Fauteuil, Louis XV Style, Walnut, Flat Back, Damask Upholstery, France, c.1900, 34 In., Pair..... 900
Chair, Federal, Cherry, Yoke Crest Rail, Urn Splat, Cabriole Legs, Arms, 38 x 29 x 19 In........... 800
Chair, Federal, Mahogany, Drop Seat, Silk Upholstery, 32 ½ x 18 ½ x 19 In., Pair..................... 615
Chair, Finn Juhl, Chieftain, Walnut, Leather, Label, Baker Furniture, Denmark, 1949, 37 In. .*illus* 7187
Chair, Finn Juhl, Desk, Aluminum, Leather, Plastic, Mobelfabrik, Denmark, 1965, 39 In. *illus* 1000
Chair, Finn Juhl, Dining, Teak, Plywood, Marked, Bovirke, Denmark, 1953, 28 In., Pair .*illus* 2000
Chair, Flemish Baroque, Walnut, Upholstered, Barley Twist, Arms, c.1900, 53 In., Pair ...*illus* 1000
Chair, Folding, Wegner Style, Woven Fabric Seat & Back, 30 x 24 x 28 In., Pair......................... 625
Chair, Frank Lloyd Wright, Enameled Steel, Upholstered, Laminate, Maple, 34 x 21 x 24 In., Pair.. 5000
Chair, G. Stickley, Oak, Original Oilcloth, Brass Tacks, Arms, Signed, Red Mark, c.1910, 37 In., Pair *illus* 708
Chair, George II Style, Oak, Trapezoidal Back, Cabriole Legs, Upholstered, 1800s, 37 x 27 x 27 In..... 615
Chair, Hand Shape, Palm, Plastic, Orange, Plinth-Like Base, 34 ½ x 27 x 26 In. 283
Chair, Hand, Foot, Mahogany, Gilt, Carved, Signed, Pedro Friedeberg, 6 x 3 ½ x 5 In. 563
Chair, Hardwood, Dragon Mask, Plank Seat, Cabriole Legs, Arms, Chinese, c.1950, 33 x 25 x 19 In... 148
Chair, Herman Miller, Ash Plywood, Aniline Dyed, Decal Label, c.1950, 29 x 19 x 22 In. 585
Chair, Jacobean Style, Leather Upholstery, Steel Finials, Reclining Arm, 1900s, 43 x 40 x 37 In. 875
Chair, Kofod Larsen, Teak, Leather Upholstery, Arms, 1956, 28 x 31 In., Pair ....*illus* 23040
Chair, Levantine, Carved, Shaped Crest, Mother-Of-Pearl Inlay, X-Shape Legs, Syria, 42 x 25 In. *illus* 551
Chair, Lolling, Serpentine Crest Rail, Upholstered, Tapering Front Legs, Late 1700s, 46 x 17 In. 523
Chair, Louis XV Style, Beech, Upholstered, Arms, Early 1900s, 35 ½ x 25 x 11 ½ In., Pair......... 523
Chair, Louis XV, Walnut, Carved, Upholstered, Cabriole Legs, Arms, 1700s, 36 In. ....*illus* 215
Chair, M. Minale, Lego, Aluminum Frame, Droog, Dutch, 2004, 33 In. ....*illus* 13750
Chair, Marc Newson, Lounge, Ash, Beech, Steamed, Double Curve, Cappellini, 1988, 27 In. *illus* 5312
Chair, Metamorphic, Regency, Mahogany, Cane Seat, Arms, c.1810, 57 In. ....*illus* 3000
Chair, Michele Oka Doner, Sculptural, Bronze, 3 Legs, Stylized Spiral Back, 1900s, 34 In. *illus* 13750
Chair, Mies Van Der Rohe, Barcelona, Stainless Steel, Leather, Griffith, 30 In. ....*illus* 6875
Chair, Napoleon III, Upholstered, Red, Turned Legs, c.1860, 38 x 33 x 31 In............................. 1125
Chair, Neoclassical, Mahogany, Upholstered, Tufted Back, Padded Arms, 1800s, 41 In. ...*illus* 688
Chair, Queen Anne, Rush Seat, Arms, Ball Feet, 1700s, 44 ½ In.. 1416
Chair, Queen Anne, Rush Seat, Vase Shape Splats, Ring Turnings, Pad Feet, c.1750, 43 In. 4920
Chair, Queen Anne, S-Curve Arms, Mahogany, Upholstered, H-Stretcher, Arms, 41 x 19 In....... 84
Chair, Rattan, Iron Base, Janine Abraham, c.1950, 37 x 37 x 29 In. ....*illus* 2250
Chair, Reclining, Upholstered, Brass Frame, Arms, c.1950, 34 ½ x 24 x 31 In.......................... 313
Chair, Renaissance Revival, Walnut, Burl Veneer, Square Legs, 1800s, 49 x 20 x 21 In., Pair.... 338
Chair, Robsjohn-Gibbings Klismos, Walnut, Leather Rope Seat, 1961, 35 x 20 x 38 In. ....*illus* 2204
Chair, Rococo Revival, Upholstered Seat & Back, Padded Arms, Italy, c.1800, 37 In., Pair *illus* 366
Chair, Rohlfs, Mahogany, Upholstered Seat & Back, 1902, 35 ½ In., Pair ....*illus* 4130
Chair, Rohlfs, Oak, Signed, Buffalo, 47 ½ x 19 ½ x 18 ½ In. ....*illus* 1875
Chair, Rosewood, Upholstered, Scrolled Crest Rail, Cabriole Legs, Rococo, Arms, 1850s, 42 In., Pair 1708
Chair, Rust Color, Vegan Leather Upholstery, Arms, Georgia, 1800s, 45 x 19 In. ....*illus* 976
Chair, Salterini, Radar Bouncer, Spring, Green Paint ....*illus* 150
Chair, Shaker, Maple, Ladder Back, Shawl Bar, Splint Seat, 1880, Child's ....*illus* 554
Chair, Spindle Back, Woven Seat, Thai Silk Cushion, Chinese, Arms, 37 x 19 x 22 ½ In........... 117
Chair, Throne, Robert Whitley, Maple, Walnut, Ebony, Bucks County, Pa., 34 x 36 In. .....*illus* 6875
Chair, Upholstered, Fluted Legs, Reeded Arms, France, 37 In. ....*illus* 94
Chair, Walnut, Concave Upholstered Back, Square Tapered Legs, Marlboro Feet, 33 x 25 x 28 In..... 338
Chair, Walnut, Scroll Arms, Shaped Skirt, Slip Seat, Casters, c.1800, 43 x 26 x 23 ½ In. 819
Chair, Wegner, No. JH 502, Executive Swivel, Wood, Wheels, 1955, 29 In. ....*illus* 15000
Chair, Wegner, Peacock Back, Teak Arms, Papercord Seat, 1947, 41 x 31 x 29 In...................... 2950
Chair, Wegner, Peacock, Spindle Back, Splayed Legs, Denmark, c.1950s, 43 In. 1500
Chair, Wegner, Teak, Round, Rope Seat, Arms, 1950, 30 x 25 In., Pair ....*illus* 8190
Chair, Windsor, Fanback, Brown, Shaped Crest, 1800s, 35 ½ In.. 118
Chair, Windsor, Writing Arm, Bamboo Turnings, New England... 360
Chair, Rocker, is listed under Rocker in this category.
Chair-Table, Pine, Circular Top, Box Base, New England, 29 x 47 In. 2280
Chaise Longue, Wire Frame, White, Cushion, Richard Shultz, Knoll, 1960s.............................. 4550
Chest, Baroque, Walnut, 4 Drawers, Turned Knob, Bracket Feet, Italy, c.1720, 42 x 58 In. *illus* 4920
Chest, Blanket, 19th Century Style, Lift Top, Compartment, Brass, 1900s, 36 ½ x 38 x 24 In.... 144

Furniture, Candlestand, Queen Anne, Cherry, Round Top, Baluster Shaft, 3 Arched Legs, c.1750, 25 x 17 In.
$240

Eldred's

Furniture, Canterbury, William IV, Rosewood, Carved, Shelves, Dividers, Drawer, 1800s, 41 x 22 In.
$375

Neal Auction Company

Furniture, Cart, Pierre Cardin, Chromed Metal, Glass Top & Shelf, Casters, France, 31 x 32 In.
$2,625

Palm Beach Modern Auctions

Furniture, Cellarette, William IV, Burl Oak, Removable Dovetail Box, Casters, 1800s, 22 x 28 x 21 In.
$1,440

Brunk Auctions

Furniture, Chair, American Rococo, Rosewood, Elaborate Carvings, Attributed To Belter, Arms, c.1855, 44 In.
$13,568

Neal Auction Company

Furniture, Chair, Arne Jacobsen, Egg, Leather, Aluminum, Fritz Hansen, Denmark, 1958, 42 In.
$5,000

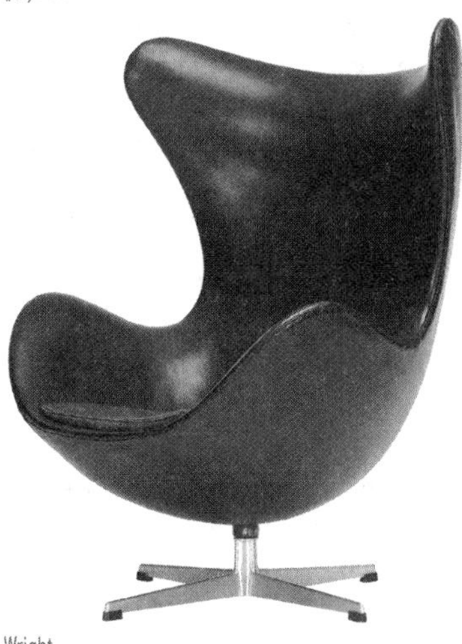

Wright

Furniture, Chair, Bamboo Wood, Cane Sides, c.1960, 29 ¾ x 27 ¾ x 31 In.
$875

Kamelot Auctions

Furniture, Chair, Bugatti, Walnut, Copper, Vellum Panels, Bone Inlay, Italy, 1902, 57 In.
$15,000

Wright

Furniture, Chair, Chippendale, Grain Painted, Rush Seat, New England, 24 In., Child's
$2,040

Bourgeault-Horan Antiquarians & Associates, LLC

Furniture, Chair, Cockfighting, Shield Shape Back, Round Seat, Turned Legs, Early 1900s, 24 x 26 In.
$1,476

Skinner, Inc.

Furniture, Chair, Committee, Jeanneret, High Court Of Chandigarh, India, Teak, Hide, 35 In.
$12,500

Wright

Furniture, Chair, Corner, Chippendale, Mahogany, 2 Pierced Splats, Arms, 32 In.
$189

Conestoga Auction Company

Chest, Blanket, Chippendale, Walnut, Hinged Lift Top, 3 Drawers, 1700s, 36 x 51 x 23 In. 2375
Chest, Blanket, Lift Top, Beaded Case, 2 Drawers, Bracket Base, Red, 49 x 36 x 18 In. 2829
Chest, Blanket, Pine, Dovetailed Case, Turned Feet, Moldings, Red, c.1830, 8 x 14 x 7 In. 720
Chest, Blanket, Pine, Lift Top, Drawers, Nantucket, c.1810, 43 x 45 In. ....*illus* 4500
Chest, Blanket, Poplar, Henry E. Martin, Star & Heart, Lancaster County, 1800s, 25 x 48 In. ... 3416
Chest, Blanket, Yellow Pine, Hinged 2-Board Rectangular Top, 1800s, 23 ½ x 45 x 21 In.......... 439
Chest, Bowfront, Mahogany & Oak, Drawers, Bracket Feet, Early 1800s, 40 x 41 x 21 In. 1121
Chest, Bowfront, Mahogany, Board Top, 4 Drawers, Bracket Feet, 1810s, 33 x 41 x 17 In. 322
Chest, Campaign, 2 Parts, Mahogany, Brass, 5 Drawers, Bracket Base, c.1850, 40 x 36 x 19 In. 4095
Chest, Campaign, Mahogany, 2 Parts, Brass Bound, Drawers, Bun Feet, 1800s, 41 x 36 In. .*illus* 2520
Chest, Campaign, Mahogany, Drop Front, Drawer, Ball Feet, Early 1800s, 45 x 45 x 20 In. *illus* 1872
Chest, Carved, Molded Cornice, 4 Doors, Floral Scrolls, Shoe Feet, 1815, 45 x 66 x 26 In. 492
Chest, Chippendale, 3 Drawers, Fluted Corner, Ogee Bracket Feet, Late 1700s, 32 x 33 x 18 In.. 750
Chest, Chippendale, 7 Drawers, Batwing, Bracket Feet, 59 x 39 ½ x 17 ½ In. 936
Chest, Chippendale, Cherry, 3 Over 2 Short Drawers, Ogee Feet, Oval Brass, 1700s, 62 x 45 x 22 In. 826
Chest, Chippendale, Mahogany, Molded Edge Top, Drawers, Brass Pulls, c.1780, 32 x 37 x 21 In...... 420
Chest, Chippendale, Maple, Serpentine Top, 4 Drawers, Bracket Base, 1700s, 36 x 39 x 20 In. .. 1770
Chest, Dowry Box, Hand Painted, Angel, Star, Fan, Footed, 11 ½ x 7 ¾ x 8 ¾ In....................... 230
Chest, Ebonized, 6 Drawers, White Marble Top, Louis XVI Style, c.1940, 52 x 32 x 17 In. 1375
Chest, Empire, Tiger Maple, 6 Drawers, Paneled Ends, Ogee Feet, 1860s, 54 x 34 x 20 In. 406
Chest, Federal, Cherry, Bowfront, 4 Drawers, Carved Skirt, 1800s, 37 x 42 x 25 In. 492
Chest, Federal, Mahogany & Burl, Brass Pulls, Drawers, Bracket Feet, c.1840, 44 x 43 x 20 In.. 558
Chest, Federal, Mahogany, White Pine, Board Top, Bracket Feet, Serpentine, c.1800, 37 x 40 x 22 In. 5100
Chest, Federal, Poplar, 4 Drawers, Paneled Back, Spiral Turned Feet, Early 1800s, 21 x 15 ½ x 11 In. 840
Chest, Federal, Softwood, Flame Grain Painted, Dovetailed, 4 Drawers, 42 x 41 ½ In. .....*illus* 265
Chest, French Provincial, Marquetry, Walnut Burl, 2 Drawers, Doors, c.1770, 43 x 42 x 14 In. . *illus* 615
Chest, Hepplewhite, 4 Drawers, Brass Knobs, Flared French Feet, c.1820, 37 x 39 x 17 In. *illus* 2760
Chest, Hepplewhite, Cherry, French Foot, 4 Drawers, Skirt, Lock, Handle, 36 ½ x 20 x 42 ½ In.. 196
Chest, Hepplewhite, Walnut, 5 Drawers, Inlay, Pa., 42 x 40 In. ....*illus* 450
Chest, Jacobean, Oak, Lift Top, Iron Hinges, Leaves, Geometrics, Late 1700s, 26 x 50 x 20 In. .. 168
Chest, Lift Top, Molded Edge, 2 Drawers, Turned Ball Feet, Red, Early 1700s, 39 x 38 x 17 In. .. 1968
Chest, Lingerie, Bombay Style, Marble Top, 5 Drawers, 1900s, 39 x 17 x 11 ½ In....................... 504
Chest, Military, Campaign, Leather Strap, Gen. Benjamin Lincoln's, c.1770, 18 x 42 x 21 In..... 2091
Chest, Molded Edge Top, Drawers, Bracket Feet, c.1800, 32 ¾ x 35 ½ x 19 In............................ 923
Chest, Oak, Hinged Lid, Carved, Flowers, Continental, 1800s, 26 x 48 ½ x 21 In........................ 406
Chest, Peter Hunt, 3 Drawers, Figural, Floral Panels, Heart, Swag, Cream Ground, 44 x 19 In. 480
Chest, Pine, 3 Drawers, Green Paint, Red & White Trim, 1900s, 29 x 29 ¾ x 16 ½ In. .....*illus* 510
Chest, Queen Anne, Cherry, 11 Drawers, Cabriole Legs, Pad Feet, Conn., 1700s, 70 x 20 x 38 In. *illus* 4688
Chest, Queen Anne, Cherry, Scroll Top, Drawers, Cabriole Legs, Brass Pull, 1700s, 85 x 40 ½ x 22 In. 1476
Chest, Rectangular Top, 4 Drawers, Brass Knobs, Ball Feet, 1830, 18 x 13 x 11 In. 384
Chest, Renaissance Revival, Pine, Strap Hinges, Carved, Flowers, Leaves, 1900s, 34 x 44 x 18 ½ In. . 369
Chest, Renaissance Revival, Walnut, Carved, Flowers, Iron Strap, Claw Feet, Italy, 1800s, 26 x 55 x 23 In. 338
Chest, Stand, Mahogany, Monogram, Silver Handles, Tapered Legs, 1900s, 20 ½ x 21 x 17 In.. 369
Chest, Stand, Oval, Gilt, Black, Lacquer, Tapered Legs, Chinese, 1900s, 27 x 20 x 15 In............ 138
Chest, Sugar, Painted, Folk Art, Soldier Portrait, Flowers, Signed, Peter Ompir, 26 x 20 In. *illus* 266
Chest, Tansu, Crane & Tortoise Escutcheons, Iron Handles, Japan, 53 x 45 x 17 In.................. 406
Chest, Walnut, Rectangular, 4 Drawers, Turned Feet, Paneled Ends, c.1830, 43 x 18 x 39 In..... 497
Chest, William & Mary, 7 Drawers, Stretcher Base, Ball Feet, 20 x 59 In.................................. 1000
Coat Rack, Victorian, Walnut, Carved Deer Head, Central Shelf, 5 Hooks, 29 x 38 x 11 In. 671
Coffer, Oak, Carved, England, c.1700, 22 x 15 x 49 ½ In. 1406
Coffer, Oak, Hinged Lid, 3 Panels, Carved, Leaves, 23 x 41 ½ x 19 In.. 192
Commode, Art Deco, 2 Doors, 2 Shelves, Mirrored, Brass Trim, 39 x 60 In. 130
Commode, Art Deco, Walnut Burl, 4 Drawers, 2 Doors, France, 1930s, 52 x 116 x 76 In. 2530
Commode, Baroque, Oak, Serpentine Top, Drawers, Recessed Spade Legs, c.1770, 32 x 46 x 25 In.. 643
Commode, Burl, Carved Trim, Sunburst Style Inlay, Drawers, Side Doors, Italy, 36 x 57 x 23 In. 546
Commode, Chinoiserie, Bombe Case, Drawers, Painted Scene, Gilt, 1800s, 36 x 42 In. ....*illus* 5250
Commode, Chinoiserie, Gilt, Marble Top, Floral Sprays, Drawers, Tapered Legs, 36 x 51 x 23 In. *illus* 1023
Commode, Fruitwood, Marble, Shaped Top, 4 Drawers, Brass Handles, 32 x 29 ½ x 18 ½ In. .. 461
Commode, George II, Mahogany, 2 Drawers, Brass Handles, c.1800, 30 ½ x 21 ½ x 19 In. 277
Commode, Italian Inlaid Walnut, Serpentine Bombe, Drawers, 1800s, 32 x 43 x 20 In. ..*illus* 688

Furniture, Chair, Corner, Slat Back, Shaped Arms, Rush Seat, 2 Stretcher Base, 1700s, 29 x 15 In.
$369

Skinner, Inc.

Furniture, Chair, Corner, Yew, Vase Shape Splats, Upholstered, X-Stretcher, George III, c.1800s
$360

Eldred's

Furniture, Chair, Daniel Meyer, Metro, Wood, Acrylic, Painted, Square Base, 1993, 39 In.
$2,000

Palm Beach Modern Auctions

Furniture, Chair, Danish Modern, Teak, Green, Teal & Gold Upholstery, 1950s, 38 x 25 In.
$325

Austin Auction Gallery

Furniture, Chair, Eames, LAR, Fiberglass, Steel, Upholstered, Herman Miller, 25 In., Pair
$1,500

Wright

Furniture, Chair, Eames, Lounge, Ottoman, Brown Leather Upholstery, 32 ½ x 32 ¾ In.
$3,240

Eldred's

Furniture, Chair, Eileen Gray, Bibendum, Red Leather, Chrome, Aram Designs, 29 x 38 In., Pair
$10,000

Los Angeles Modern Auctions

Furniture, Chair, Finn Juhl, Chieftain, Walnut, Leather, Label, Baker Furniture, Denmark, 1949, 37 In.
$7,187

Wright

Furniture, Chair, Finn Juhl, Desk, Aluminum, Leather, Plastic, Mobelfabrik, Denmark, 1965, 39 In.
$1,000

Wright

Furniture, Chair, Finn Juhl, Dining, Teak, Plywood, Marked, Bovirke, Denmark, 1953, 28 In., Pair
$2,000

Wright

Furniture, Chair, Flemish Baroque, Walnut, Upholstered, Barley Twist, Arms, c.1900, 53 In., Pair
$1,000

New Orleans Auction Galleries

Furniture, Chair, G. Stickley, Oak, Original Oilcloth, Brass Tacks, Arms, Signed, Red Mark, c.1910, 37 In., Pair
$708

Cottone Auctions

Furniture, Chair, Kofod Larsen, Teak, Leather Upholstery, Arms, 1956, 28 x 31 In., Pair
$23,040

Neal Auction Company

Furniture, Chair, Levantine, Carved, Shaped Crest, Mother-Of-Pearl Inlay, X-Shape Legs, Syria, 42 x 25 In.
$551

Clars Auction Gallery

Furniture, Chair, Louis XV, Walnut, Carved, Upholstered, Cabriole Legs, Arms, 1700s, 36 In.
$215

Clars Auction Gallery

Furniture, Chair, M. Minale, Lego, Aluminum Frame, Droog, Dutch, 2004, 33 In.
$13,750

Wright

TIP
Watch out for armchairs that have been made by adding arms to side chairs.

Furniture, Chair, Marc Newson, Lounge, Ash, Beech, Steamed, Double Curve, Cappellini, 1988, 27 In.
$5,312

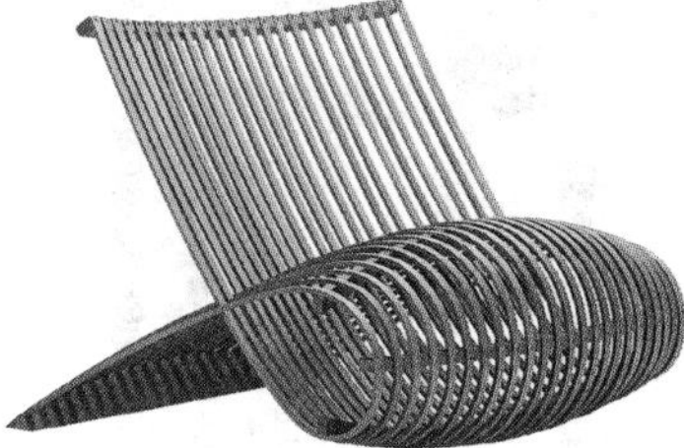

Rago Arts and Auction Center

Furniture, Chair, Metamorphic, Regency, Mahogany, Cane Seat, Arms, c.1810, 57 In.
$3,000

New Orleans Auction Galleries

Furniture, Chair, Michele Oka Doner, Sculptural, Bronze, 3 Legs, Stylized Spiral Back, 1900s, 34 In.
$13,750

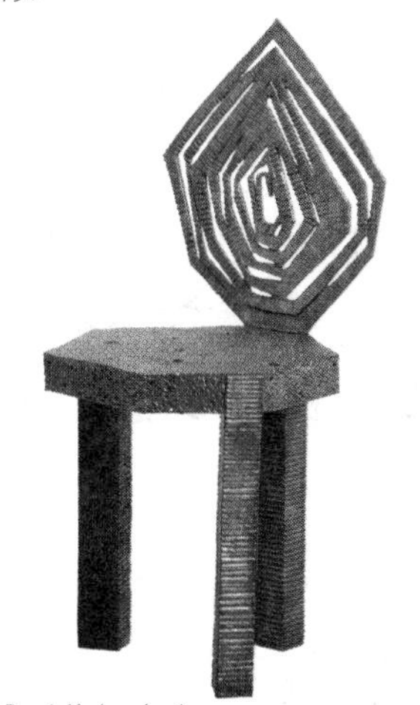

Palm Beach Modern Auctions

Furniture, Chair, Mies Van Der Rohe, Barcelona, Stainless Steel, Leather, Griffith, 30 In.
$6,875

Wright

Furniture, Chair, Neoclassical, Mahogany, Upholstered, Tufted Back, Padded Arms, 1800s, 41 In.
$688

Neal Auction Company

Furniture, Chair, Rattan, Iron Base, Janine Abraham, c.1950, 37 x 37 x 29 In.
$2,250

Kamelot Auctions

Furniture, Chair, Robsjohn-Gibbings Klismos, Walnut, Leather Rope Seat, 1961, 35 x 20 x 38 In.
$2,204

Clars Auction Gallery

Furniture, Chair, Rococo Revival, Upholstered Seat & Back, Padded Arms, Italy, c.1800, 37 In., Pair
$366

Neal Auction Company

Furniture, Chair, Rohlfs, Mahogany, Upholstered Seat & Back, 1902, 35 ½ In., Pair
$4,130

Cottone Auctions

Furniture, Chair, Rohlfs, Oak, Signed, Buffalo, 47 ½ x 19 ½ x 18 ½ In.
$1,875

Treadway

Furniture, Chair, Rust Color, Vegan Leather Upholstery, Arms, Georgia, 1800s, 45 x 19 In.
$976

Eldred's

Furniture, Chair, Salterini, Radar Bouncer, Spring, Green Paint
$150

Hudson Valley Auctions

Furniture, Chair, Shaker, Maple, Ladder Back, Shawl Bar, Splint Seat, 1880, Child's
$554

Willis Henry Auctions

Furniture, Chair, Throne, Robert Whitley, Maple, Walnut, Ebony, Bucks County, Pa., 34 x 36 In.
$6,875

Rago Arts and Auction Center

Furniture, Chair, Upholstered, Fluted Legs, Reeded Arms, France, 37 In.
$94

Copake Auctions

Furniture, Chair, Wegner, No. JH 502, Executive Swivel, Wood, Wheels, 1955, 29 In.
$15,000

Los Angeles Modern Auctions

Furniture, Chair, Wegner, Teak, Round, Rope Seat, Arms, 1950, 30 x 25 In., Pair
$8,190

Thomaston Place Auction Galleries

Furniture, Chest, Baroque, Walnut, 4 Drawers, Turned Knob, Bracket Feet, Italy, c.1720, 42 x 58 In.
$4,920

Clars Auction Gallery

TIP

Try to rearrange your furniture once a year to avoid noticeable sun fading.

Furniture, Chest, Blanket, Pine, Lift Top, Drawers, Nantucket, c.1810, 43 x 45 In.
$4,500

Eldred's

Furniture, Chest, Campaign, Mahogany, 2 Parts, Brass Bound, Drawers, Bun Feet, 1800s, 41 x 36 In.
$2,520

Eldred's

Commode, Louis XV, Tulipwood, Kingwood, Gilt Bronze Mounts, Marble Top, c.1735, 35 x 53 x 26 In. 3000
Commode, Louis XV, Walnut, Bronze Mounts, Curved Legs, Antoine Gosselin, 1700s, 31 x 42 x 21 In. 1121
Commode, Louis XVI Style, Mahogany, Brass Mounts, Marble Top, Top Shape Feet, 37 x 48 x 23 In. *illus* 3321
Commode, Louis XVI Style, Marble Top, Bronze Mounts, 3 Drawers, Cabriole Legs, 37 x 45 x 21 In... *illus* 338
Commode, Neoclassical Style, Multicolor, White Marble, 2 Drawers, Tapered Legs, 34 x 47 x 26 In... *illus* 2160
Commode, Pine, Faux Bamboo Banding, Turreted Corners, Drawers, France, c.1890, 32 x 39 In....*illus* 4000
Commode, Sacristy, Walnut, Pine, Rectangular Top, Strapwork, Spain, 1500s, 38 x 48 x 26 In....... 10620
Commode, Victorian, Bird's-Eye Maple, Paneled Cupboard, 4 Drawers, Late 1800s, 32 x 32 x 20 In... 120
Cradle, Pine, Hooded Shape, Rockers, Dovetailed Case, Late 1800s, 29 x 42 x 26 In. 89
Credenza, Ebonized, Parchment, Black & White, 4 Doors, Brass Hardware, 29 x 80 x 17 In..... 1625
Credenza, Florence Knoll, Brazilian Rosewood, Carrara Marble Top, 26 x 75 x 18 In. 7316
Credenza, Reach Line Design, Rectangular Top, Pullout Central Drawer, 2 Doors, 28 x 65 x 20 In. 923
Credenza, Walnut, 8 Drawers, Checkerboard Front, Sculptural Legs, Midcentury, 37 x 81 x 20 In.. 1750
Cupboard, 2 Sections, Cherry, Stepped Molded Cornice, Bracket Base, 88 x 40 x 20 In. 644
Cupboard, Chippendale, Cherry, Molded Cornice, Ogee Bracket Feet, 1700s, 66 x 42 x 33 In.... 1063
Cupboard, Corner, Architectural, Maple, Arched Glass Doors Over Doors, c.1825, 81 x 60 In.... *illus* 840
Cupboard, Corner, Federal, Maple, Cherry, 2 Doors, 8-Pane, Drawers, 2 Doors, c.1820, 86 In... *illus* 1920
Cupboard, Corner, Pine, Glass Door, 9-Pane, Cutout Apron, 2 Sections, Late 1800s, 78 x 34 x 20 In. *illus* 240
Cupboard, Corner, Pine, Architectural, 2 Sections, Blue, Green, Late 1700s, 100 x 52 ½ In. 2318
Cupboard, Corner, Pine, Compartment, Glass Doors, Painted, 1850, 86 x 51 In........................ 504
Cupboard, Corner, Pine, Glass Pane Top Door, 3 Shelves, Pullout Desk, 1700s, 92 In............... 1287
Cupboard, Court, Revival, Mixed Wood, 3 Sections, Drawers, Panel Doors, c.1910, 89 x 59 x 21 In......... 600
Cupboard, Danish Modern, Teak, Drawer Over Sliding Doors, 1950s, 31 x 35 In. ....*illus* 295
Cupboard, Federal, Panel Doors, Candle Drawers, Bracket Feet, Pennsylvania, 58 x 17 In. 840
Cupboard, Hanging, Dovetailed, Dentil, Molded Cornice, Shaped Shelves, Red, Brown, 26 x 25 x 15 In.. 7380
Cupboard, Hanging, Maple, Panel Door, 5 Drawers, Knob, Late 1800-1915, 21 x 20 x 9 In........ 351
Cupboard, Hanging, Rectangular Case, Shelf, Door, Escutcheon, 30 x 24 x 11 In...................... 263
Cupboard, Open Top, 2 Shelves, Doors, Hudson Valley, 1800s, 76 x 58 x 18 In. ....*illus* 944
Cupboard, Pine, Green, 4 Doors, 49 ½ x 25 ½ x 66 In.. 118
Cupboard, Pine, Open Top, Scalloped Edge, Square Nail Construction, 69 x 39 x 16 In........... 1440
Cupboard, Poplar, 4 Doors, 4 Shelves, Cornice, 1800s, 73 x 36 x 13 ½ In. 325
Cupboard, Shaker, Hanging, Pine, Pegged, 2-Panel Door, 4 Shelves, 40 x 28 In. ....*illus* 6765
Cupboard, Shaker, Pine, Stain, Plank Door, 5 Drawers, Harvard, Mass., 65 x 24 In. ....*illus* 3198
Cupboard, Shelves, Carved Sides, Doors, Barrel Back, 1800s, 92 x 43 x 27 In............................ 177
Cupboard, Sliding Doors, Tapered Legs, Denmark, 1950s, 29 ¾ x 31 ½ x 16 In........................ 325
Cupboard, Step Back, Pine, 2 Drawers, 4 Doors, Interior Shelves, 1800s, 84 x 50 ¾ x 18 In. 861
Cupboard, Step Back, Pine, 3 Shelves, 2 Hinged Doors, Molded Top, 76 x 50 x 20 In. 677
Cupboard, Step Back, Poplar, Flame Grained Surface, 4 Doors, Molding, c.1840, 79 x 42 In.... 2074
Cupboard, Walnut, Carved, Pitched Roof, Turned Stiles, Scroll Feet, France, 1800s, 39 x 31 x 15 In. 523
Cupboard, Zoar, Walnut, 4 Blind Doors, Inside Shelves, Painted, Ohio, c.1850, 70 x 60 In. *illus* 1560
Daybed, Provincial, Walnut, Carved, Varnished, c.1850, 36 x 38 ⅜ In.. 250
Daybed, Rosewood, 3-Panel Chamfered, Molded Back, Floral, Square Legs, Chinese, 41 x 78 x 22 In.... 1320
Desk, Campaign, Mahogany, Folding Sawhorse Legs, Drawers, Flush Mount Pulls, 30 x 50 x 27 In... 2106
Desk, Chippendale Style, Cherry, Ball & Claw Feet, Cabriole Legs, Drawers, 32 x 46 x 22 In...... 259
Desk, Chippendale, Mahogany, Slant Front, Apron, Ball & Claw Feet, 1700s, 44 x 46 x 21 In...*illus* 1298
Desk, Chippendale, Slant Front, Cherry, 4 Fitted Drawers, Brass Pulls, 1700s, 43 x 36 x 19 In. .. *illus* 1408
Desk, Chippendale, Slant Front, Mahogany, 4 Drawers, Brass Pulls, Late 1700s, 42 x 36 x 20 In. *illus* 480
Desk, Chippendale, Slant Front, Walnut, 4 Drawers, Brass Pulls, 1700s, 43 x 40 x 21 In........... 554
Desk, Chippendale, Slant Front, Walnut, French Feet, Pennsylvania, 47 x 42 x 20 In................ 300
Desk, Davenport, Burl Walnut, Shaped Leather Top, 4 Side Drawers, 35 x 21 In. 570
Desk, Davenport, Slant Front, Burl Walnut, Side Door, Turned Columns, 1800s, 37 x 24 In. *illus* 590
Desk, Empire Revival, Slant Front, Mahogany, Dovetail Drawers, c.1900, 43 x 36 x 31 In......... 125
Desk, Faux Bamboo, Hinged Slant, 3 Side Drawers, Chinese Export, 42 ½ x 24 x 21 In............ 431
Desk, Federal, Slant Front, 4 Drawers, Cock-Beaded Edge, Turned Feet, c.1830, 43 x 42 x 20 In. 322
Desk, G. Nelson, Home Office, Mahogany, Chrome Plated, 1946, 40 x 54 x 28 In. ....*illus* 4720
Desk, Gabriella Crespi Style, Z Shape, Brass, Rectangular Top, Drawer, 30 x 59 x 31 In. ..*illus* 1000
Desk, George III, Mahogany, Embossed Leather Top, 6 Drawers, Tapered Legs, 30 x 56 x 37 In. 923
Desk, Georgian, Slant Front, 4 Drawers, Bracket Feet, England, 43 x 40 x 21 In. 187
Desk, Kingwood, Tulipwood, 2 Drawers, Flowers, Cabriole Legs, 58 x 30 In. 1780
Desk, Lady's, Napoleon III, Palissandre, Brass, Mirror, Fluted Legs, c.1865, 50 x 33 In. ....*illus* 3000

Furniture, Chest, Campaign, Mahogany, Drop Front, Drawer, Ball Feet, Early 1800s, 45 x 45 x 20 In.
$1,872

Thomaston Place Auction Galleries

Furniture, Chest, Federal, Softwood, Flame Grain Painted, Dovetailed, 4 Drawers, 42 x 41 ½ In.
$265

Conestoga Auction Company

TIP
When repairing furniture, it is best to reglue before you refinish.

Furniture, Chest, French Provincial, Marquetry, Walnut Burl, 2 Drawers, Doors, c.1770, 43 x 42 x 14 In.
$615

Clars Auction Gallery

This is an edited listing of current prices. Visit **Kovels.com** to check thousands of prices from previous years and sign up for free information on trends, tips, reproductions, marks, and more.

Furniture, Chest, Hepplewhite, 4 Drawers, Brass Knobs, Flared French Feet, c.1820, 37 x 39 x 17 In.
$2,760

CRN Auctions

Furniture, Chest, Hepplewhite, Walnut, 5 Drawers, Inlay, Pa., 42 x 40 In.
$450

Conestoga Auction Company

Furniture, Chest, Pine, 3 Drawers, Green Paint, Red & White Trim, 1900s, 29 x 29 ¾ x 16 ½ In.
$510

Eldred's

Furniture, Chest, Queen Anne, Cherry, Carved, 11 Drawers, Cabriole Legs, Pad Feet, Conn., 1700s, 70 x 20 x 38 In.
$4,688

Freeman's Auctioneers & Appraisers

Furniture, Chest, Sugar, Painted, Folk Art, Soldier Portrait, Flowers, Signed, Peter Ompir, 26 x 20 In.
$266

Conestoga Auction Company

Furniture, Commode, Chinoiserie, Bombe Case, Drawers, Painted Scene, Gilt, 1800s, 36 x 42 In.
$5,250

New Orleans Auction Galleries

Names Are the Same
Craftsman, Arts & Crafts, Roycroft, and finally Crafts-style are all alternative names for Mission style furniture first popular from 1900 to 1920, then revived in the 1980s.

Furniture, Commode, Chinoiserie, Gilt, Marble Top, Floral Sprays, Drawers, Tapered Legs, 36 x 51 x 23 In.
$1,023

Clars Auction Gallery

Furniture, Commode, Italian Inlaid Walnut, Serpentine Bombe, Drawers, 1800s, 32 x 43 x 20 In.
$688

Hindman Auctions

Furniture, Commode, Louis XVI Style, Mahogany, Brass Mounts, Marble Top, Top Shape Feet, 37 x 48 x 23 In.
$3,321

Stair Galleries

Furniture, Commode, Louis XVI Style, Marble Top, Bronze Mounts, 3 Drawers, Cabriole Legs, 37 x 45 x 21 In.
$338

Clars Auction Gallery

Furniture, Commode, Neoclassical Style, Multicolor, White Marble, 2 Drawers, Tapered Legs, 34 x 47 x 26 In.
$2,160

Michaan's Auctions

Furniture, Commode, Pine, Faux Bamboo Banding, Turreted Corners, Drawers, France, c.1890, 32 x 39 In.
$4,000

New Orleans Auction Galleries

TIP
If the drawer on your antique-looking furniture is held together with new screws, nails, or staples, it is not an antique.

Furniture, Cupboard, Corner, Architectural, Maple, Arched Glass Doors Over Doors, c.1825, 81 x 60 In.
$840

Garth's Auctioneers & Appraisers

TIP
Ice cubes can be left in the indentations in the carpet made by the legs of furniture. They will encourage the fibers to fill in the dent.

Furniture, Cupboard, Corner, Federal, Maple, Cherry, 2 Doors, 8-Pane, Drawers, 2 Doors, c.1820, 86 In.
$1,920

Garth's Auctioneers & Appraisers

Furniture, Cupboard, Corner, Pine, Glass Door, 9-Pane, Cutout Apron, 2 Sections, Late 1800s, 78 x 34 x 20 In.
$240

Garth's Auctioneers & Appraisers

Furniture, Cupboard, Danish Modern, Teak, Drawer Over Sliding Doors, 1950s, 31 x 35 In.
$295

Austin Auction Gallery

Furniture, Cupboard, Open Top, 2 Shelves, Doors, Hudson Valley, 1800s, 76 x 58 x 18 In.
$944

Copake Auctions

Furniture, Cupboard, Shaker, Hanging, Pine, Pegged, 2-Panel Door, 4 Shelves, 40 x 28 In.
$6,765

Willis Henry Auctions

Furniture, Cupboard, Shaker, Pine, Stain, Plank Door, 5 Drawers, Harvard, Mass., 65 x 24 In.
$3,198

Willis Henry Auctions

Furniture, Cupboard, Zoar, Walnut, 4 Blind Doors, Inside Shelves, Painted, Ohio, c.1850, 70 x 60 In.
$1,560

Garth's Auctioneers & Appraisers

TIP
Look at the hinge on a tilt top table. The wear should show on both the top and the base if it is old.

Furniture, Desk, Chippendale, Mahogany, Slant Front, Apron, Ball & Claw Feet, 1700s, 44 x 46 x 21 In.
$1,298

Copake Auctions

Furniture, Desk, Chippendale, Slant Front, Cherry, 4 Fitted Drawers, Brass Pulls, 1700s, 43 x 36 x 19 In.
$1,408

Cowan's Auctions

Furniture, Desk, Chippendale, Slant Front, Mahogany, 4 Drawers, Brass Pulls, Late 1700s, 42 x 36 x 20 In.
$480

Soulis Auctions

Furniture, Desk, Davenport, Slant Front, Burl Walnut, Side Door, Turned Columns, 1800s, 37 x 24 In.
$590

Cottone Auctions

Furniture, Desk, G. Nelson, Home Office, Mahogany, Chrome Plated, 1946, 40 x 54 x 28 In.
$4,720

Cottone Auctions

Furniture, Desk, Gabriella Crespi Style, Z Shape, Brass, Rectangular Top, Drawer, 30 x 59 x 31 In.
$1,000

Clars Auction Gallery

Furniture, Desk, Lady's, Napoleon III, Palissandre, Brass, Mirror, Fluted Legs, c.1865, 50 x 33 In.
$3,000

New Orleans Auction Galleries

Furniture, Desk, Modern, Mahogany, Shaped Leather Top, Gloss Metal, Black Drawer, 30 x 35 ½ x 68 In.
$388

Nadeau's Auction Gallery

Furniture, Desk, Partners, George III Style, Mahogany, Leather, 6 Drawers, Trestle, 122 x 52 In.
$1,220

Neal Auction Company

TIP
When moving furniture, always tie drawers and doors in place. Use soft cloth tape.

Furniture, Desk, Queen Anne, Slant Front, Maple, Carved, 4 Drawers, Brass Pulls, 1700s, 43 x 36 x 18 In.
$523

Skinner, Inc.

TIP
After cleaning the brasses on a piece of furniture, wax the metal to help retard tarnish.

Furniture, Desk, School, Peter Hunt, Hand Painted, Roses, Hearts, School Supplies, 34 x 33 x 21 In.
$330

Eldred's

Furniture, Desk, Shaker, Kneehole, Pine, Porcelain Pulls, Elder A. Stewart, 1883, 45 In.
$1,230

Willis Henry Auctions

Furniture, Desk, Slant Front, Maple, Fitted Interior, 4 Drawers, Bracket Feet, c.1890, 41 x 36 In.
$360

Eldred's

Furniture, Desk, Wooton, Rotary, Walnut, Roll Top, Fitted Interior, 2 Pedestals, c.1875, 51 x 59 In.
$2,750

New Orleans Auction Galleries

Furniture, Dog Bed, Wicker, Gingham Upholstered, 18 ½ x 24 ½ x 16 ½ In.
$185

Stair Galleries

F

Furniture, Dry Sink, Hooded, Poplar, Grain Painted, Drawers Over Doors, c.1870, 48 x 43 In.
$384

Garth's Auctioneers & Appraisers

Furniture, Dry Sink, Poplar, 2 Parts, 4 Doors, Bracket Foot Base, c.1830, 76 x 54 x 25 In.
$308

Locati Auctions

Furniture, Etagere, Cylinder, Chrome, Glass Shelves, Contemporary, 66 ½ x 25 In.
$261

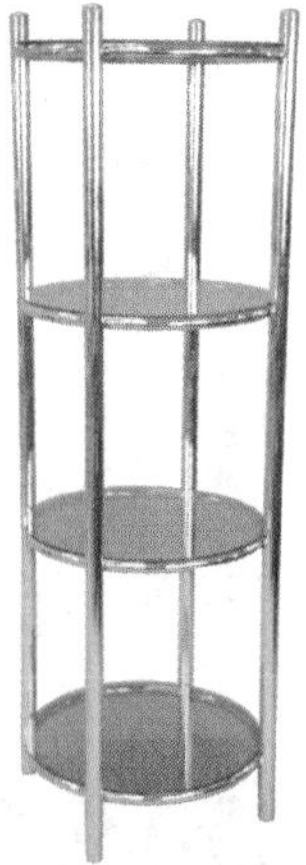

Nadeau's Auction Gallery

Desk, Louis XV Style, Parquetry, Gilt Metal Mounted, Leather Inset, 1800s, 30 x 41 ½ x 23 In.. 469
Desk, Mahogany, Mirror, Fitted Interior, Turned Legs, Early 1900s, 48 x 26 x 17 In.................. 216
Desk, Modern, Mahogany, Shaped Leather Top, Gloss Metal, Black Drawer, 30 x 35 ½ x 68 In. *illus* 388
Desk, Oak, 2 Drawers, Turned Legs, H-Stretcher, 1800s, 30 x 62 x 27 In.................................... 531
Desk, Oak, Drawer, Barley Twist Legs, Maple & Co., England... 212
Desk, Partners, Chippendale Style, Walnut, 3 Drawers, Cabriole Legs, 30 x 72 x 36 In.............. 1538
Desk, Partners, George III Style, Mahogany, Leather, 6 Drawers, Trestle, 122 x 52 In. ......*illus* 1220
Desk, Partners, R.J. Horner, Mahogany, Griffins, Spread Wings, Drawer, 29 x 57 x 28 In.......... 4538
Desk, Patent Cabinet, Compartments, Drawers, Postal Drawers, 59 x 58 In. 13860
Desk, Queen Anne, Slant Front, Maple, Carved, 4 Drawers, Brass Pulls, 1700s, 43 x 36 x 18 In. *illus* 523
Desk, Roll Top, Side Panels, Drawers, Wood Pulls, Divided Interior, 50 x 48 x 29 In. 226
Desk, School, Peter Hunt, Hand Painted, Roses, Hearts, School Supplies, 34 x 33 x 21 In. *illus* 330
Desk, Shaker, Kneehole, Pine, Porcelain Pulls, Elder A. Stewart, 1883, 45 In. ....*illus* 1230
Desk, Slant Front, Interior Drawers, Compartments, Turned Legs, c.1715, 38 x 25 x 15 In......... 3690
Desk, Slant Front, Mahogany, Pine, 4 Drawers, Brass Pulls, Bracket Base, 1900s, 34 x 24 x 15 In.... 300
Desk, Slant Front, Maple, Fitted Interior, 4 Drawers, Bracket Feet, c.1890, 41 x 36 In. ......*illus* 360
Desk, Stickley, Arts & Crafts Style, Oak, 3 Drawers, Inlay, Stamped, Label, 30 x 41 x 24 In........ 1725
Desk, Wooton, Oak, Molded Top, Drawers, Rotating Compartments, Label, c.1890, 32 x 54 In. 1920
Desk, Wooton, Rotary, Walnut, Roll Top, Fitted Interior, 2 Pedestals, c.1875, 51 x 59 In. ..*illus* 2750
Dog Bed, Wicker, Gingham Upholstered, 18 ½ x 24 ½ x 16 ½ In. ....*illus* 185
Dresser, Eastlake Style, Walnut, Tiered, Beveled Mirror, Marble Top, Drawers, 81 x 60 x 22 In. 475
Dresser, Hepplewhite, 4 Drawers, Plank Top, Mushroom Knob, French Feet, Yellow, 35 x 38 x 19 In.. 1112
Dresser, Venetian Style, Mirrored, 3 Drawers, Brass Trim Legs, c.1940, 29 x 32 x 18 In............ 281
Dry Sink, 2 Doors, Brass Handles, Red Paint, 42 ½ x 19 x 34 In.. 115
Dry Sink, Hooded, Poplar, Grain Painted, Drawers Over Doors, c.1870, 48 x 43 In. ....*illus* 384
Dry Sink, Pine, 2 Doors, Drawer, Block Foot, 1800s, 42 x 19 ½ x 35 ½ In.................................... 83
Dry Sink, Pine, 2 Doors, Rectangular Top, Shaped Crest, 1800s, 34 x 29 ½ x 17 ½ In............. 677
Dry Sink, Pine, 4 Doors, 2 Tiers, 5 Shelves, Knob Pulls, 44 x 20 ½ x 79 ½ In. 226
Dry Sink, Pine, Hutch Back, Nailed Drawers, Round Pulls, Paneled Door, 1850s, 49 x 41 x 19 In.... 420
Dry Sink, Poplar, 2 Parts, 4 Doors, Bracket Foot Base, c.1830, 76 x 54 x 25 In. ....*illus* 308
Easel, Mahogany, Burl, Openwork, Adjustable, Gilt, Late 1800s, 84 x 39 In. 4305
Etagere, Aesthetic Revival, Bamboo, Root Ball Finials, Oak Shelves, 55 x 23 In......................... 263
Etagere, Cylinder, Chrome, Glass Shelves, Contemporary, 66 ½ x 25 In. ....*illus* 261
Etagere, Mahogany, 3 Open Shelves, Turned Post, Drawers, 1800s, 45 x 22 x 14 In. 780
Etagere, Rosewood, Marble Top, Carved Crest, 4 Curved Shelves, Mirror, Drawer, 92 x 63 In.... 1210
Footstool, Cylindrical, Pig Face Ends, Gold Paint, Turned Legs, Late 1800s, 11 x 20 x 10 In...*illus* 338
Footstool, Oak, Leather Upholstery, Bow Shape Sides, Curved Stretchers, Square Legs, 15 x 11 In. *illus* 75
Footstool, Scalamandre, Upholstered, Leopard Print, Square Feet, 16 x 23 x 23 In. 349
Footstool, Victorian, Walnut, Needlepoint Cushion, Floral, Round, Feet, 11 x 19 In. ....*illus* 150
Footstool, Walnut, Painted Squirrel Top, 6 ¾ x 13 x 6 ¾ In. ....*illus* 200
Frame, Black Forest, Walnut, Bunch of Grapes, Vine, Oval, 1800s, 17 In...................................... 161
Frame, Iron, 2 Oval Apertures, Eagle, Flag, Union Shield, 1862, 19 ½ x 11 ¾ In. 420
Frame, Pierced Metal, African Animals, Enameled, Jeweled, Jay Strongwater, 9 ¾ x 11 In........ 1000
Frame, Silver Plate, Patinated Metal, Flowers, Embossed, Art Nouveau, Italy, 12 ½ x 10 ½ In. 98
Frame, Venetian, Giltwood, Gilt, Carved, Acanthus, 1800s, 39 x 34 In. ....*illus* 454
Hall Rack, Oak, Mirror, Brass Hangers, Side Holder, Seat, 81 x 50 x 16 In................................. 147
Hall Tree, Black Forest, Lindenwood, Carved, Mother Bear & Cub, Germany, 1800s, 76 In. *illus* 3422
Hall Tree, Oak, Scrolled Tendril Fleur-De-Lis, 6 Coat Hooks, 1800s, 93 x 45 x 10 In................. 273
Hamper, Lid, Rattan, Woven, Brown Leather Straps, Buckles, Glass Tops, 24 x 24 x 24 In., Pair . *illus* 1404
Highboy, Continental, 2 Sections, Walnut, Shape Cornice, 8 Drawers, Ball & Claw Feet, 71 ½ In.... 180
Highboy, Henkel-Harris, Chippendale Style, Bonnet, Drawers, Cabriole Legs, Brass Pulls, 88 ½ In. 489
Highboy, Queen Anne, Cherry, Flat Top, Molded Cornice, Cabriole Legs, Pad Feet, c.1760, 75 In. 960
Highboy, Queen Anne, Mahogany, 11 Drawers, Molded Top, Pad Feet, 1700s, 60 x 37 x 18 In. .. 2223
Highchair, Maple, Ash, Turned Finials, Shaped Slats, Plank Seat, Early 1700s, 35 ½ In.......... 1353
Humidor, Neoclassical Style, Mahogany, Hunter Inlaid Figure, Claw Feet, 41 x 26 x 20 ½ In... 363
Hutch, Colonial Revival, 2 Parts, Hardwood & Oak, Bracket Base, 1700s, 78 x 59 ½ x 22 In..... 1170
Kneeler, Prie-Dieu, Walnut, Carved, Lifts, Beveled, Lion's Head, Bun Feet, 1800s, 39 x 30 x 27 In. .. 369
Lap Desk, Oak, Hinged Slant Front, Fitted Interior, Base Molding, 1700s, 12 x 27 x 16 In. 187
Lap Desk, Wood, Brass Trim, Plaque, Bramah Lock, Inkwells, Compartments, Keys, 20 x 11 x 7 In. 410
Lectern, Country, Pine, Cross Base, Adjustable Book Holder, Tin Can Holder, 1850s, 53 In. 2280

Furniture, Footstool, Cylindrical, Pig Face Ends, Gold Paint, Turned Legs, Late 1800s, 11 x 20 x 10 In.
$338

Skinner, Inc.

Furniture, Footstool, Oak, Leather Upholstery, Bow Shape Sides, Curved Stretchers, Square Legs, 15 x 11 In.
$75

Witherell's

Furniture, Footstool, Victorian, Walnut, Needlepoint Cushion, Floral, Round, Feet, 11 x 19 In.
$150

Woody Auctions

TIP

Cover scratches on dark cherry or mahogany by rubbing them with a bit of cotton dipped in iodine. Scratches on lighter woods can be covered by rubbing with a solution of equal parts iodine and alcohol.

Furniture, Footstool, Walnut, Painted Squirrel Top, 6 ¾ x 13 x 6 ¾ In.
$200

Conestoga Auction Company

Furniture, Frame, Venetian, Giltwood, Gilt, Carved, Acanthus, 1800s, 39 x 34 In.
$454

Clars Auction Gallery

Furniture, Hall Tree, Black Forest, Lindenwood, Carved, Mother Bear & Cub, Germany, 1800s, 76 In.
$3,422

Conestoga Auction Company

Furniture, Hamper, Lid, Rattan, Woven, Brown Leather Straps, Buckles, Glass Tops, 24 x 24 x 24 In., Pair
$1,404

Thomaston Place Auction Galleries

Furniture, Library Steps, Spiraling, Brass Ball, 4-Step Ladder, Leather, England, Early 1900s, 66 In.
$504

Selkirk Auctioneers & Appraisers

Furniture, Mirror, Dieppe, Applied Bone Carvings, Legend, Sgotorum, c.1800, 32 x 20 In.
$826

Cottone Auctions

Furniture, Mirror, Federal, Giltwood, Reverse Painted, Carved, Eagle, Urns, Columns, c.1810, 35 x 15 In.
$2,928

Neal Auction Company

TIP
Gilt frames can be cleaned with beer.

Furniture, Mirror, Fornasetti, Bull's-Eye, Flower Border, Company Ink Stamp, 19 In.
$875

Freeman's Auctioneers & Appraisers

Furniture, Mirror, Giltwood, Carved, Silver, Italy, c.1900, 48 x 29 ½ In.
$923

Charlton Hall Auctions

TIP
Scratches can be rubbed off the glass in a mirror by using a piece of felt and polishing rouge from a paint store.

Furniture, Mirror, Modern Shape, Maple, Varnish, 71 x 17 In.
$308

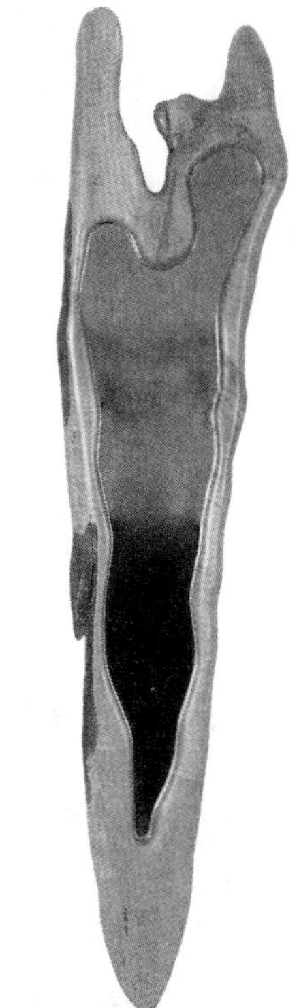

Locati Auctions

Furniture, Mirror, Queen Anne, Etched Glass, Frame, c.1740-60, 49 x 21 ½ In.
$620

Copake Auctions

Library Ladder, William & Mary Style, Oak, 5 Steps, Carved, 78 x 22 x 19 ½ In. 438
Library Steps, Spiraling, Brass Ball, 4-Step Ladder, Leather, England, Early 1900s, 66 In. *illus* 504
Love Seat, Mahogany, Sleigh Shape, Carved, Upholstered, c.1900, 50 x 52 x 21 In. 200
Lowboy, Queen Anne Style, Ollie Armentrout Jr., Maple, Cabriole Legs, 1985, 32 x 18 x 30 In. 150
Mirror, Arch, Giltwood, Flowers, Italy, 1800s, 63 x 40 In. 313
Mirror, Atomic Style, Multicolor Glass, Brass Border, 19 x 16 In. 594
Mirror, Bull's-Eye, Giltwood, Gesso, Circular Frame, Convex, Liner, Late 1800s, 24 In. 344
Mirror, Chippendale, Eagle Crest, Line Inlay, Beveled Glass, 1800s, 44 x 23 In. 384
Mirror, Chippendale, Flowering Basket Crest, Carved, Giltwood, England, c.1800, 53 x 33 In. 500
Mirror, Classic Wood Frame, Gold Leaf, Bevel, Round, 37 x 37 x 2 In. 277
Mirror, Colonial Revival, Giltwood, Cornucopia, Carved, Eagle Finial, 34 x 34 In. 369
Mirror, Convex, Ebonized Eagle Crest, Giltwood, Leaves, Carved, 1800s, 37 x 28 In. 1098
Mirror, Convex, Gold Leaves, Black Border, Signed, Walter J. Mazzanti, 1900s, 33 In. 413
Mirror, Convex, Round, Giltwood, Goat, Sunflowers, Grapes, Leaves, 43 ½ x 33 ½ In. 2700
Mirror, Dieppe, Applied Bone Carvings, Legend, Sgotorum, c.1800, 32 x 20 In. *illus* 826
Mirror, Dresser, Mahogany, Oval, Reverse Painted, 3 Drawers, 3 Ivory Fittings 3360
Mirror, Dresser, Shaped Plate, 2 Color Iron Brackets, Black Base, Art Deco, 26 x 27 x 6 In. 192
Mirror, Easel Shape, Scroll Leaf, Back Support, Bronze, Impressed, France, c.1900, 15 ¾ x 11 ½ In. 186
Mirror, Federal, Giltwood, Reverse Painted, Carved, Eagle, Urns, Columns, c.1810, 35 x 15 In. *illus* 2928
Mirror, Federal, Mahogany, Parcel Giltwood, Urn Shape Finial 554
Mirror, Federal, Maple, Reverse Painted, Country House, Molded Cornice, c.1820, 19 x 11 In. 263
Mirror, Fornasetti, Bull's-Eye, Flower Border, Company Ink Stamp, 19 In. *illus* 875
Mirror, Geometric Shape, 5 Panels, Black Base, Art Deco, c.1925, 27 x 55 In. 98
Mirror, Giltwood, Carved, Putto's Head Crest, Flowers, 1900s, 61 x 33 In. 1046
Mirror, Giltwood, Carved, Silver, Italy, c.1900, 48 x 29 ½ In. *illus* 923
Mirror, Giltwood, Rococo Style, Oval, Leafy Crest, Scrolling Leaves, 69 x 39 In. 500
Mirror, Girandole, Pembroke, Giltwood, Convex, Reeded Slip, Early 1800s, 32 ¾ x 20 In. 1440
Mirror, Gold, Giltwood, Carved, Mantel, c.1860, 64 x 59 In. 920
Mirror, Modern Shape, Maple, Varnish, 71 x 17 In. *illus* 308
Mirror, Ornate, Carved, Shell, Flower, Butterfly, Scrollwork, 17 x 17 In. 180
Mirror, Oval, Carved, Flowers, Gilt Frame, Continental, 1800s, 33 x 28 In. 750
Mirror, Pier, Eastlake, Walnut, Incised, Giltwood, Beveled Edge, Marble Top, 102 x 27 x 12 In. 826
Mirror, Pier, Eastlake, Walnut, Overhanging Crest, Teardrop Finial, 118 x 54 x 12 In. 2662
Mirror, Pier, Gilt, Carved Shield, Scroll Crest, Columnar Base, Stand, 1800s, 16 x 35 x 13 In. 625
Mirror, Pier, Giltwood, Molded Crown, Carved, Grapevine, Shell Panels, Half Column, 80 x 46 In. 1722
Mirror, Pier, Gothic Revival, Giltwood, Gesso, Breakfront Top, Trefoils, 1900s, 67 x 32 In. 625
Mirror, Plateau, Beveled Edge, Silver Plate Base, Footed, 11 x 14 ¾ In. 69
Mirror, Queen Anne, Etched Glass, Frame, c.1740-60, 49 x 21 ½ In. *illus* 620
Mirror, Queen Anne, Pine Frame, Molded Edge, Inset Plates, Black, 1700s, 8 x 6 In. 3998
Mirror, Regency Style, Giltwood, Flowers, Scrolls, Pierced, France, c.1885, 94 In. *illus* 2750
Mirror, Regency, Bull's-Eye, Spread Wing Eagle, Ebonized Surround, Early 1800s, 34 x 22 In. 2040
Mirror, Ria & Yiouri Augousti, Brass, Shagreen Finish, Metal Tag, 39 x 24 In. *illus* 2375
Mirror, Romain De Tirtoff, Scheherazade, Multicolor, Bronze Frame, 29 ½ x 15 ½ In. 1464
Mirror, Roycroft, Bark Frame, 40 x 51 In. *illus* 472
Mirror, Ruffled Blade Coral, Frame, Marked, Philippines, 48 x 38 x 7 In. 140
Mirror, Shadowbox Frame, Giltwood, Gesso & Wood, Shelf, Ornate, 1900s, 19 x 23 x 8 In. 330
Mirror, Silver Plate, Plateau, 3 Sections, Balusters, Pineapple Finials, Christofle, c.1900, 52 ½ In. 2250
Mirror, Silver Plate, Victorian Era, Flowers, Mahogany Base, Round, Wilkinson & Co., 1800s, 2 x 15 In. 266
Mirror, Sunburst, Bronze, Giltwood, 40 In. 3250
Mirror, Tabernacle, Sheraton, Giltwood, Reverse Painted, Mt. Vernon, c.1810, 31 x 19 In. *illus* 156
Mirror, Vanity, Brass, Bevel, Blue Painted Border, 14 x 12 In. 50
Mirror, Venetian Glass, Floral, Acanthus Leaf Panel, Scalloped Crest, 44 x 28 In. *illus* 266
Mirror, Victorian, Giltwood, Shield Shape Crest, Rocaille, 95 x 45 In. *illus* 523
Mirror, Wood, Carved, Gilt, Baroque Style, Quatrefoil Shape, 1900s, 35 ½ x 45 In. 354
Overmantel Mirror, see Architectural category.
Pedestal, Bronze Dore, Winged Griffin, Claw Feet, Green Striated Marble Top, 21 x 25 In. 9075
Pedestal, Bugatti, Walnut, Copper, 8 Spindles, 2 Shelves, c.1900, 47 x 12 In. *illus* 20000
Pedestal, Column, Wood, Burl, c.1915, 48 x 13 In., Pair 1353
Pedestal, Corkscrew Shape, Wood, Mounted, Metal Bands, 48 x 15 ¾ In. 984
Pedestal, Iron, Black Marble Top, Low Shelf, c.1925, 42 ¾ x 8 x 8 In. 1968

Furniture, Mirror, Regency Style, Giltwood, Flowers, Scrolls, Pierced, France, c.1885, 94 In.
$2,750

New Orleans Auction Galleries

Furniture, Mirror, Ria & Yiouri Augousti, Brass, Shagreen Finish, Metal Tag, 39 x 24 In.
$2,375

Abington Auction Gallery

Furniture, Mirror, Roycroft, Bark Frame, 40 x 51 In.
$472

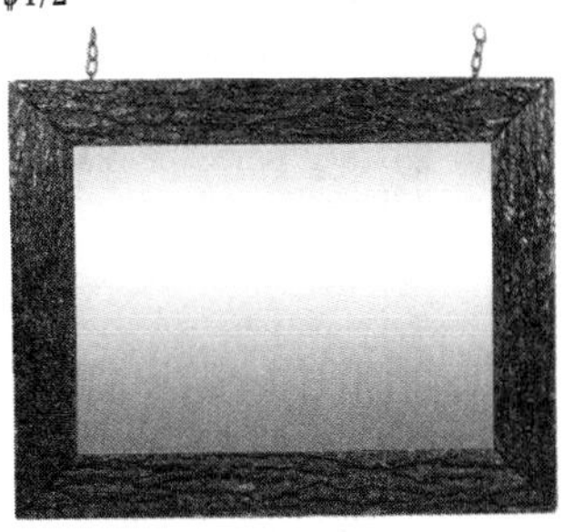
Cottone Auctions

Furniture, Mirror, Tabernacle, Sheraton, Giltwood, Reverse Painted, Mt. Vernon, c.1810, 31 x 19 In.
$156

Eldred's

Furniture, Mirror, Venetian Glass, Floral, Acanthus Leaf Panel, Scalloped Crest, 44 x 28 In.
$266

Bunch Auctions

Furniture, Mirror, Victorian, Giltwood, Shield Shape Crest, Rocaille, 95 x 45 In.
$523

Clars Auction Gallery

Furniture, Pedestal, Bugatti, Walnut, Copper, 8 Spindles, 2 Shelves, c.1900, 47 x 12 In.
$20,000

Rago Arts and Auction Center

Furniture, Pedestal, Marble, Shaped Top, On 3 Columns, 35 In.
$192

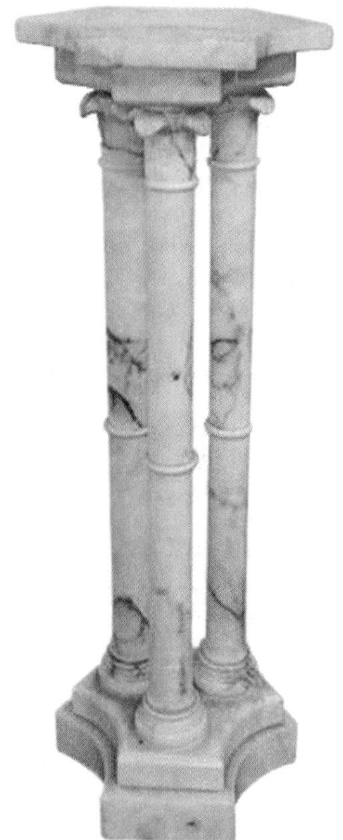
Bunte Auction Services

Furniture, Pie Safe, Walnut, Punched Tin Panel, Molded Edge, 2 Drawers, Turned Feet, 1800s, 49 x 46 x 19 In.
$878

Jeffrey S. Evans & Associates

TIP
Brown shoe polish is good to cover scuffs and slight damage on furniture.

Furniture, Planter, Adirondack, Varnished Twigs, Lower Shelf, 2 Sections, c.1835, 32 x 29 In.
$780

Garth's Auctioneers & Appraisers

Furniture, Rocker, Mammy Bench, Windsor, Black Paint, Baby Guard Rail, 48 x 28 x 29 In.
$104

Apple Tree Auction Center

Pedestal, Marble, Green, Bronze Mounts, Acanthus, Column, Bronze Feet, 42 x 11 x 11 In....... 215
Pedestal, Marble, Shaped Top, On 3 Columns, 35 In. ....*illus* 192
Pedestal, Modern, Scrolling, Leaves, Marble Top, 40 x 18 In. 113
Pedestal, Neoclassical, Marble, Gilt Bronze Mount, Female Masks, 41 3/8 x 13 x 13 3/4 In........... 360
Pedestal, Vernis Martin, Bombe, Marble Top, Scenic, 46 1/2 x 16 x 16 In. 469
Pedestal, Walnut, Panels, Green Marble Inserts, Square Base, 48 In. 104
Pedestal, Wood, Faux Painted, Columnar, Square Base, 43 3/4 x 13 1/2 In., Pair........ 861
Pie Safe, Pine, Punched Tin, 12 Geometric Panels, Tapered Legs, Painted, 1800s, 58 x 37 In... 1830
Pie Safe, Pine, Square Nails, Full Panel, Punched Tin, Stars, Man, Gray, 1850s, 31 x 27 In...... 900
Pie Safe, Walnut, Punched Tin Panel, Molded Edge, 2 Drawers, Turned Feet, 1800s, 49 x 46 x 19 In. *illus* 878
Planter, Adirondack, Varnished Twigs, Lower Shelf, 2 Sections, c.1835, 32 x 29 In. ....*illus* 780
Press, Mahogany, Vines, Berries, 4 Sunburst Panel Doors, 77 x 50 In. 3075
Rack, Drying, Shoe, Green Paint, 4 Shelves, Raised On Casters, 1910s, 56 x 33 x 15 In. 250
Rack, Wall, Wood, Ebonized, Embroidered Flowers, Silk Panel, 15 1/2 x 14 3/4 In. 83
Rocker, Arts & Crafts, Oak, Curved, Slat Back, Tenon Arms, Early 1900s, 34 x 27 x 28 In. 225
Rocker, Mammy Bench, Windsor, Black Paint, Baby Guard Rail, 48 x 28 x 29 In. ....*illus* 104
Rocker, Stickley & Brandt Co., Straight Arms, Side Slats Under Seat, 41 x 30 In. ....*illus* 780
Screen, 3-Panel, Hardwood, Carved, India, 60 x 77 In. 148
Screen, 3-Panel, Neoclassical Style, Landscapes, Folding, Continental, c.1900, 74 x 71 In. 211
Screen, 4-Panel, Louis XV, Country Scenes, Serpentine Top, 83 1/2 x 90 In. 580
Screen, 4-Panel, Mahogany, Geometric, Black Border, 82 x 120 In. ....*illus* 344
Screen, 6-Panel, Folding, Painted Birds, Leaves, Brass Capped Feet, Chinese, 72 x 16 In. 602
Screen, 8-Panel, Chinese Export, Wallpaper, Multicolor, Landscape, Village, Birds, 1800s, 97 In.... 8260
Screen, Table, Panel Under Glass, Embroidered Silk, Chinese, c.1920, 24 1/2 x 13 x 18 In. *illus* 345
Screens are also listed in the Fireplace category.
Secretary, 2 Tiers, Rosewood, Mirrored Doors, Shelves, Arched Top, Victorian, 96 x 21 In........ 4313
Secretary, Broken Pediment, 2 Doors, 3 Drawers, Parcel Gilt, Green, 83 x 47 In. 770
Secretary, Drop Front, Walnut Panel, Drawer, Compartment, 65 x 36 x 22 In. 847
Secretary, Federal Style, Mahogany, Molded Crown, c.1840, 85 x 44 x 21 In. 861
Secretary, Federal, Mahogany, Drawers, Bracket Feet, 1800s, 54 x 43 x 19 1/2 In. 960
Secretary, George III, Mahogany, Molded Cornice, Glazed Doors, 3 Drawers, 82 x 42 x 21 In... 369
Secretary, Oak, 2 Small Cabinets, Drawer, William J. Heney, San Francisco, c.1900, 97 x 60 In. 570
Secretary, Mahogany, Federal Style, Pullout Writing Surface, 3 Drawers, 71 x 39 In. 366
Secretary, Walnut, Bookcase, Compartment, 4 Drawers, Baker Furniture, Persia, 88 x 36 x 18 In. 682
Secretary, Walnut, Cornice Top, Glass Doors, 4 Drawers, c.1900, 89 x 44 x 20 In. 316
Secretary, William & Mary Style, Walnut, 2 Doors, 3 Drawers, 92 x 47 In. 1200
Semainier, Louis XVI Style, Fruitwood, Marble Top, 7 Banded Drawers, c.1890, 60 x 28 In. ..*illus* 1188
Semainier, Louis XVI Style, Walnut, 7 Drawers, Brass Mounted, Turned Legs, 53 x 27 x 13 In. 769
Server, Continental Style, Oak, 3 Drawers, Turned Legs, Stretcher, Bun Feet, 1900s, 32 x 60 x 17 In.. 300
Server, Oak, Marble Top, Carved, 2 Inlaid Doors, c.1920, Michel Dufet, 39 x 40 x 19 In. ..*illus* 2000
Settee, Longhorn, Horn Back & Legs, Crushed Velour, 1800s, 46 x 60 In. ....*illus* 2124
Settee, Louis XV Style, Painted, Leaf Carved Frame, Loose Cushions, c.1900, 40 x 52 x 33 In.... 750
Settee, Mahogany, Scroll Arms, Reeded Supports, Brass Tacking, 1800-10, 36 1/2 x 39 1/2 x 23 In..... 7800
Settee, Salem, Federal, Mahogany, Straight Back, Scroll Arms, Upholstered, 36 x 58 x 26 In. *illus* 1920
Settee, Upholstered, Rounded Ends, Bronze Feet, c.1950, 30 x 77 x 27 In. 1125
Settle, L. & J.G. Stickley, Even Arms, Padded Seat, 33 x 72 x 24 In. ....*illus* 2520
Settle, Windsor, Mixed Wood, Bamboo Turnings, Plank Seat, 1880s, 33 x 17 In. 510
Settle, Windsor, Spindle Back, Turned Legs, Black Stain, Pinstripe, 1800s, 33 x 18 x 68 In....... 424
Shelf, Corner, Hanging, Pine, 5 Tiers, Triangular Shape, 46 x 36 In. 840
Shelf, Corner, Hanging, Poplar, Spanish Brown Surface, Late 1700s, 44 x 27 1/2 In. 830
Shelf, Hanging, Burl, 2 Tiers, Scalloped Shelves, 20 x 25 1/2 x 7 In. 300
Shelf, Wall, Pine, Shaped End, Green Paint, 19 x 15 1/2 In. 461
Sideboard, Arne Vodder, Rosewood, Sliding Door, c.1960s, 32 1/2 x 18 1/2 x 80 In. 5313
Sideboard, Chippendale, Walnut, 2-Board, Molded Edge Top, 2 Drawers, 37 x 10 In. 10580
Sideboard, Empire, Mahogany, 4 Doors, 3 Drawers, Brass Pulls, Claw Feet, 46 x 67 x 23 In. 1495
Sideboard, Federal, Mahogany, Breakfront Top, 3 Drawers, Doors, Bellflower, 38 x 66 x 28 In. 1599
Sideboard, George III, Inlaid Mahogany, Drawers Flanked by Doors, c.1820, 37 x 91 x 27 In... 4484
Sideboard, George III, Mahogany, Satinwood, Inlay, Bow Front, 6 Drawers, 2 Doors, 35 x 107 In... 3000
Sideboard, Georgian Style, Door Over 2 Drawers, Pullout Shelf, Paw Feet, 38 x 51 x 22 In....... 330
Sideboard, Hepplewhite Style, Mahogany, Serpentine Front, Bellflower, 36 x 78 x 24 In. .*illus* 189

Furniture, Rocker, Stickley & Brandt Co., Straight Arms, Side Slats Under Seat, 41 x 30 In.
$780

California Historical Design

Furniture, Screen, 4-Panel, Mahogany, Geometric, Black Border, 82 x 120 In.
$344

Kamelot Auctions

Furniture, Screen, Table, Panel Under Glass, Embroidered Silk, Chinese, c.1920, 24 1/2 x 13 x 18 In.
$345

Richard D. Hatch & Associates

F

Furniture, Semainier, Louis XVI Style, Fruitwood, Marble Top, 7 Banded Drawers, c.1890, 60 x 28 In.
$1,188

New Orleans Auction Galleries

TIP
If the drawer in a cabinet sticks, buy some silicone spray at a craft store. Spray only the runners and the sides of the drawer. Do not let any spray get on the front finish of the cabinet.

Furniture, Server, Oak, Marble Top, Carved, 2 Inlaid Doors, c.1920, Michel Dufet, 39 x 40 x 19 In.
$2,000

Kamelot Auctions

Sideboard, Louis XVI Style, Cherry, Carved, Rectangular Top, France, 1900s, 39 x 61 x 21 In.. 500
Sideboard, Louis XVI Style, Mahogany, Ormolu, Marble Top, Drawers, 1900s, 41 x 105 x 21 In. *.illus* 1250
Sideboard, Macassar, Bronze Trim, Glass Door, Painted, Peacock, Flowers, c.1940, 40 x 77 x 20 In. 2500
Sideboard, Mahogany, Demilune Shape, Banded Inlay, Center Drawer, 36 x 72 x 25 In........... 489
Sideboard, Mahogany, Marble Top, Mirror, Cabriole Legs, Paw Foot, 1850s, 59 x 62 x 22 In..... 454
Sideboard, Mahogany, Tapered Legs, Spade Feet, Lion Mask Pulls, c.1810, 36 x 60 x 22 In....... 556
Sideboard, Marble Top, Mirror, Brass Pulls, 6 Drawers, 2 Doors, Caster Feet, 60 x 96 x 24 In.. 565
Sideboard, Parzinger, Charak Modern, 4 Doors, Green Marble, 1900s, 33 x 64 x 16 In............ 5310
Sideboard, Queen Anne, Oak, Rectangular Top, Cabriole Front Legs, 1700s, 31 x 84 x 19 In.... 2460
Sideboard, Renaissance Revival Style, Walnut, Mirror, Turned Finial, Molding Crest, 132 x 101 In. 6958
Sideboard, Renaissance Revival, Carved Griffins, Medallion, 2 Doors, Bun Feet, 102 x 66 x 22 In. *. illus* 861
Sideboard, Rosewood, 4 Doors, Parquetry, c.1955, 37 x 86 ½ x 19 In.. 2000
Sideboard, Scott Co., Safe, Walnut, Punched Tin Panel, 3 Drawers, 1850s, 45 x 64 x 16 In....... 9360
Sideboard, Sheraton Style, Mahogany, 2 Doors, 3 Drawers, Grain Finish, 45 x 44 x 20 In. 113
Sofa, Belter, Rosalie With Grapes, Rosewood, Serpentine Back, Cabriole Legs, 1800s, 72 ½ In. 635
Sofa, Belter, Rosewood, Henry Clay Pattern, Satin Upholstery, 40 x 88 x 37 In. ....*illus* 2760
Sofa, Berkeley Mills, Prairie, Cantilevered Armrests, Block Feet, 27 ½ x 90 In........................... 960
Sofa, Biedermeier, Carved Leg Ends, Rolled Armrest, Upholstered, Vienna, 26 In....................... 395
Sofa, Blue Woven, Upholstered, Bronze Metal Legs, Dunbar, 1950, 29 x 83 x 29 In.................... 3510
Sofa, Camelback, Kindel, Mahogany, Upholstered, 4 Chinese Chippendale Style Front Legs, 77 In.. 558
Sofa, Conversation Pit, M. Umeda, Tawaraya, Boxing Ring, Memphis, 1981, 110 In. ....*illus* 22500
Sofa, Eames, Compact, Chromed Metal, Enameled, Upholstered, Herman Miller, 36 x 72 In. *.illus* 375
Sofa, Empire, Mahogany Over Pine, Flame Grain, Scroll Arms, 1830s, 33 x 84 In. ....*illus* 240
Sofa, Frank Lloyd Wright, Art Deco Style, Cassina, 1980s, 25 x 95 In. ....*illus* 560
Sofa, Georgian, Hepplewhite, Rounded Top, Square Tapered Legs, Splayed Foot, 40 x 80 In..... 384
Sofa, Hepplewhite, Mahogany, Bellflower Inlay, Gold Damask Upholstery, c.1790, 38 x 74 In. .. 1200
Sofa, Mahogany, Upholstered, Paw Feet, Early 1800s, 33 ½ x 86 x 25 In. 615
Sofa, McCobb, Sectional, Upholstered, Geometric, Tapered Legs, 2 Piece, c.1950, 128 In. 1889
Sofa, Memphis Style, Bolt, Metal, Upholstered, 38 x 84 In. ....*illus* 750
Sofa, Needlepoint, Mahogany, Carved, Bouquets, Leaves, Flowers, Berries, 33 x 90 In. 540
Sofa, Neoclassical, Mahogany, Upholstered, Brass Pulls, Casters, Early 1800s, 76 In. 2040
Sofa, P. Shire, Big Sur, Laminate, Upholstered, Memphis, 1986, 36 x 83 In. ....*illus* 11250
Sofa, Prairie, Arts & Crafts Style, Upholstered Cushions, Square Block Feet, 27 x 90 x 46 In. *.illus* 923
Sofa, Provincial, Walnut, Carved, Upholstered, Cabriole Feet, 1700s, 19 x 102 x 27 In. 2583
Sofa, Walnut, Red Velour, Carved Fruit, Leaf Crest, Wheel Feet, Victorian, 41 x 65 In. 350
Stand, Artist's, George II, Mahogany, Adjustable, Candle Slides, England, 30 x 20 x 15 In. *illus* 1080
Stand, Burl, Octagonal Top, Painted Flowers, Stretcher Base, Continental, 28 x 14 x 14 In...... 270
Stand, Carved Mahogany, Chippendale Style, 3-Footed, 61 x 10 In. 173
Stand, Circular Top, Cross Base, Ring-Turned Post, Black, 1700s, 26 x 14 In............................ 554
Stand, Country, Sheraton, Cherry, Turned Legs, Dovetailed Drawer, 1830s, 28 x 20 x 18 In..... 210
Stand, Dictionary, Wendell Castle, Walnut, Sculpted, Tripod Base, 1968, 37 x 26 In. ....*illus* 25000
Stand, Federal, Curly Maple, 2 Drawers, Bottom Shelf, Casters, 30 x 20 x 17 In........................ 1298
Stand, Georgian, Dressing, Mahogany, 2 Section Flip Top, Pull-Up Mirror, 22 x 34 x 20 In. 118
Stand, Hardwood, Carved, Inset Marble Top, Shelf, Chinese, 1800s, 32 x 22 In. 660
Stand, Hepplewhite, Cherry, Inlay, Dovetailed Drawer, Brass Pulls, 1800s, 26 x 22 x 21 In. 896
Stand, Hepplewhite, Yellow Pine, Splayed Leg, Early 1800s, 27 x 18 x 20 In. 354
Stand, Magazine, L. & J.G. Stickley, Oak, Bears Decal, 4 Shelves, 41 ¾ x 21 x 12 In. 1143
Stand, Music, Brass, Lyre Shape Sheet Music Support, 43 In... 118
Stand, Music, Brass, Mahogany Veneer, Adjustable, Neoclassical Style, c.1900, 60 In................. 369
Stand, Music, Bronze Mounted, Inlaid Mahogany, Lyre Shape, Lobed Finial, 1800s, 62 x 21 x 19 In. 800
Stand, Oak, Marble Top, Brass Handles, Cabriole Legs, 1800s, 15 ¾ x 15 ¾ x 34 In., Pair 212
Stand, Ornate, 2 Drawers, Craftmaster, 1950s, 28 ½ x 16 x 24 In., Pair 210
Stand, Painted Top, 2 Women Having Tea, Anno Domini '46, Peter Hunt, 14 x 17 x 14 In. *illus* 468
Stand, Plant Pine, 3 Shelves, Legs, Supports, Chamfered Edges, 1850s, 39 x 42 x 25 In. 216
Stand, Plant, Arts & Crafts Style, Oak, Square Top, Trestle Legs, Plank Shelf, 37 x 10 In.......... 118
Stand, Plant, Bird Shape, Tripod Feet, Swirl Waist, Wrought Iron, 33 ¾ In................................ 277
Stand, Plant, Victorian, Walnut, 3 Legs, Round, Brown Marble Top, 28 x 12 In. 350
Stand, Plant, Wrought Iron, Brass, Round Marble Top, 16 x 35 In. 138
Stand, Reading, Pine, Slant Front, Round Base, Footed, Red, 37 ½ In. 369
Stand, Red Marble, Inverted Gothic Arches, Dolphin Corbels, Deer, 16 ½ x 12 In. 1035

Furniture, Settee, Longhorn, Horn Back & Legs, Crushed Velour, 1800s, 46 x 60 In.
$2,124

Cottone Auctions

Furniture, Settee, Salem, Federal, Mahogany, Straight Back, Scroll Arms, Upholstered, 36 x 58 x 26 In.
$1,920

CRN Auctions

Furniture, Settle, L. & J.G. Stickley, Even Arms, Padded Seat, 33 x 72 x 24 In.
$2,520

California Historical Design

TIP
Do not use soap on the bottom of sticking drawers. Eventually it will become sticky. Use paraffin wax.

Furniture, Sideboard, Hepplewhite Style, Mahogany, Serpentine Front, Bellflower, 36 x 78 x 24 In.
$189

Bunch Auctions

Furniture, Sideboard, Louis XVI Style, Mahogany, Ormolu, Marble Top, Drawers, 1900s, 41 x 105 x 21 In.
$1,250

Crescent City Auction Gallery

Furniture, Sideboard, Renaissance Revival, Carved Griffins, Medallion, 2 Doors, Bun Feet, 102 x 66 x 22 In.
$861

Clars Auction Gallery

Furniture, Sofa, Belter, Rosewood, Henry Clay Pattern, Satin Upholstery, 40 x 88 x 37 In.
$2,760

Stevens Auction Co.

Furniture, Sofa, Conversation Pit, M. Umeda, Tawaraya, Boxing Ring, Memphis, 1981, 110 In.
$22,500

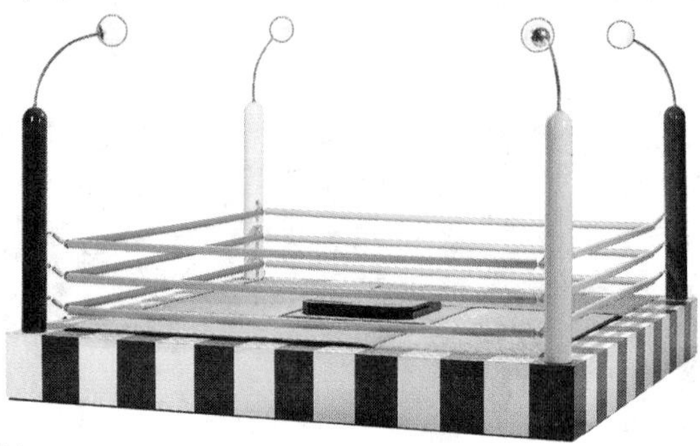

Wright

Furniture, Sofa, Eames, Compact, Chromed Metal, Enameled, Upholstered, Herman Miller, 36 x 72 In.
$375

Palm Beach Modern Auctions

Furniture, Sofa, Empire, Mahogany Over Pine, Flame Grain, Scroll Arms, 1830s, 33 x 84 In.
$240

Garth's Auctioneers & Appraisers

Furniture, Sofa, Frank Lloyd Wright, Art Deco Style, Cassina, 1980s, 25 x 95 In.
$560

Conestoga Auction Company

Furniture, Sofa, Memphis Style, Bolt, Metal, Upholstered, 38 x 84 In.
$750

Palm Beach Modern Auctions

Furniture, Sofa, P. Shire, Big Sur, Laminate, Upholstered, Memphis, 1986, 36 x 83 In.
$11,250

Wright

Furniture, Sofa, Prairie, Arts & Crafts Style, Upholstered Cushions, Square Block Feet, 27 x 90 x 46 In.
$923

Clars Auction Gallery

Furniture, Stand, Artist's, George II, Mahogany, Adjustable, Candle Slides, England, 30 x 20 x 15 In.
$1,080

CRN Auctions

TIP
A fresh ink stain on wood can be removed by washing with water and then applying lemon juice.

Furniture, Stand, Dictionary, Wendell Castle, Walnut, Sculpted, Tripod Base, 1968, 37 x 26 In.
$25,000

Rago Arts and Auction Center

TIP
For a pollution-free furniture cleaner, use a mixture of 1 cup olive or vegetable oil and ½ cup lemon juice.

Furniture, Stand, Painted Top, 2 Women Having Tea, Anno Domini '46, Peter Hunt, 14 x 17 x 14 In.
$468

Thomaston Place Auction Galleries

Furniture, Stool, McCobb, Brass, X-Stretcher, Upholstered Top, 15 x 20 ½ In., Pair
$1,625

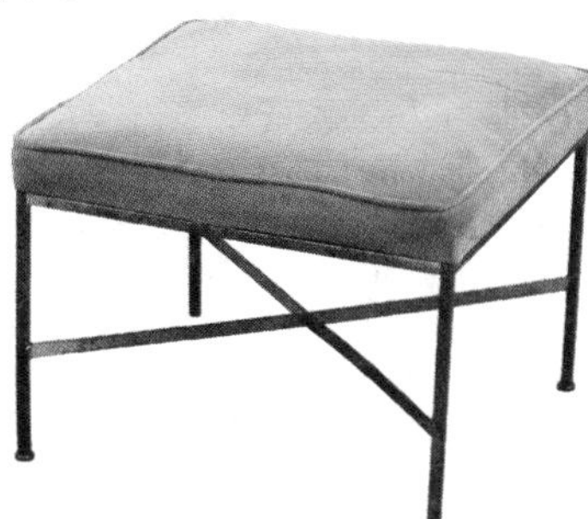

Palm Beach Modern Auctions

Furniture, Stool, Queen Anne, Walnut, Cabriole Legs, Shaped Stretchers, Pad Feet, c.1760, 18 x 22 In.
$3,904

Pook & Pook

Furniture, Stool, Step, Shaker, Walnut, Original Varnish, Arched, 2 Steps, 25 x 17 x 18 In.
$1,476

Willis Henry Auctions

Furniture, Table, Aesthetic Revival, Brass, Copper, Mirrored Top, Gilt, c.1900, 29 x 19 x 13 In.
$300

Michaan's Auctions

Furniture, Table, Altar, Elmwood, 2-Board Top, 4 Side-By-Side Drawers, c.1900, 35 x 68 In.
$360

Eldred's

Furniture, Table, Center, Verdigris, Parcel Gilt, Marble Top, Urn Stretcher, 1800s, 30 x 37 In.
$1,750

Neal Auction Company

Furniture, Table, Coffee, Chrome & Glass, Oval Base & Top, Circular Supports, 19 x 36 x 20 In.
$62

Locati Auctions

Cocktail or Coffee

When Prohibition ended in 1933, furniture makers started to sell low "cocktail tables" to be used in front of sofas to serve the newly legal mixed drinks. The public objected to the name, so it was renamed a "coffee table."

Stand, Sheraton Style, Drop Leaf, Tiger Maple, Turned Legs, 28 x 18 x 16 ¾ In., Pair 2925
Stand, Sheraton, Bird's-Eye Maple, Drawers, Turned Wood Knobs, Square Block Legs, c.1815, 29 In. 270
Stand, Sheraton, Flame Birch, Pine, Drop Leaf, Turned Legs, c.1820, 28 x 17 x 8 In. 270
Stand, Telescopic, Mahogany, Turned Circular Stem & Base, 1800s, Closed 8 ⅝ In., Pair 738
Stand, Walnut & Cherry, Dish Top, Cove Frame, Splayed Legs, 1800s, 26 x 17 x 18 In. 904
Stand, Walnut, 2 Drawers, Tapered Legs, c.1960, 20 ½ x 22 ½ In., Pair 344
Stand, Walnut, Splayed Legs, Pad Feet, Pennsylvania, Late 1700s, 28 ½ x 20 In. 7930
Stool, Chrome, X Shape, Upholstered Seat, 15 ½ x 36 x 15 In., Pair 615
Stool, Cloisonne, Carved Wood, Birds, Flower, Blue Field, Footed, Chinese, 13 x 12 x 16 In., Pair 230
Stool, Ifugao, Round Seat, 4 Carved Figural Supports, Philippines, 12 ½ x 10 In. 551
Stool, McCobb, Brass, X-Stretcher, Upholstered Top, 15 x 20 ½ In., Pair .... *illus* 1625
Stool, Mushroom Shape, Upholstered, Tripod Oak Downswept Legs, 20 x 16 In., Pair 625
Stool, Oak, Rectangular Top, Carved Apron, Turned Legs, 1900s, 20 x 25 x 11 ½ In. 330
Stool, Old Red Wash, Splayed Base, 1800s, 13 x 9 ½ x 20 In. 148
Stool, Piano, Adjustable, Tiger Maple, Upholstered Seat, Turned Legs, c.1850, 21 x 12 In. 185
Stool, Queen Anne, Walnut, Cabriole Legs, Shaped Stretchers, Pad Feet, c.1760, 18 x 22 In. *illus* 3904
Stool, Shaker, Step, Walnut, Original Varnish, Arched, 2 Steps, 25 x 17 x 18 In. .... *illus* 1476
Table, 2 Drawers, Inlay, Bronze Mounted, 34 ¾ x 19 x 29 In. 250
Table, Aesthetic Revival, Brass, Copper, Mirrored Top, Gilt, c.1900, 29 x 19 x 13 In. .... *illus* 300
Table, Altar, Elmwood, 2-Board Top, 4 Side-By-Side Drawers, c.1900, 35 x 68 In. .... *illus* 360
Table, Altar, Tibetan, Dragons, Brass, Bronze, Carved, 16 x 24 x 13 In. 390
Table, Art Nouveau, Walnut, Woman, Standing, Robed, Scalloped Inlaid Rosewood Top, 31 x 19 In. . 484
Table, Belter, Rosewood, Marble Top, Cabriole Legs, Acanthus Feet, 28 x 41 x 33 In. 2118
Table, Bouillotte, Slate Inset, Round Top, Painted Feet, Mid 1900s, 26 ½ x 16 ½ In. 563
Table, Card, Chippendale, Mahogany, Turret Corner Top, Cabriole Legs, c.1770, 29 x 32 In. 12200
Table, Card, Federal, Mahogany, Inlay, Drawer, Early 1800s, 29 ¾ x 36 x 17 ½ In. 185
Table, Center, French Provincial, Walnut, Circular Top, Tapered Legs, c.1770, 30 x 40 In. 1154
Table, Center, Oval, Walnut, 3 Legs, Wheel Feet, Victorian, 29 x 34 x 25 In. 100
Table, Center, Regence Style, Marble Top, Gilt, Mask, Scalloped Shell, 1850s, France, 32 x 30 In. 5015
Table, Center, Verdigris, Parcel Gilt, Marble Top, Urn Stretcher, 1800s, 30 x 37 In. .... *illus* 1750
Table, Center, Walnut, Leafy Carved Apron, Cabriole Legs, X-Stretcher, 1800s, 39 x 26 x 29 In. 121
Table, Coffee, Chrome & Glass, Oval Base & Top, Circular Supports, 19 x 36 x 20 In. .... *illus* 62
Table, Coffee, Contemporary, Onyx, 8-Sided, 1900s, 14 x 36 In. .... *illus* 1220
Table, Coffee, French Style, Black Glass Top, Bronze, c.1950, 17 ¾ x 21 x 16 In. 2000
Table, Coffee, Hugo Franca, Pequi Wood, Casters, Brazil, 2005, 21 x 51 x 49 In. .... *illus* 8125
Table, Coffee, Jeffrey Greene, Palette, 3 Angular Legs, Carved, Doylestown, 17 x 43 x 29 In. *illus* 1680
Table, Coffee, Mahogany, Frame Glass Top, Wood Rim, Boat Model, Base Molding, 19 x 51 x 22 In. 1404
Table, Coffee, Marge Carson, Regency, Glass Top, Oval, Ram's-Head Support, 23 x 60 x 41 In. 354
Table, Coffee, P. Evans, Stalagmite, Steel, Bronzed Resin, Glass Top, 17 x 42 x 30 In. .... *illus* 1625
Table, Console, Bernhard Rohne, Acid-Etched Mixed Metals, Black, Mastercraft, 26 x 60 In. ... 1410
Table, Console, Carved Demilune, Painted, Dolphin Base, Early 1900s, 32 x 26 x 13 In. ..*illus* 813
Table, Console, Demilune, Glass Top, Openwork, Gilt Metal, 26 x 19 In. 275
Table, Console, Jansen Type, Mahogany, Gray Marble Top, Brass Accents, 1900s, 31 x 36 x 17 In..... 554
Table, Console, Louis XV Style, Gilt, Carved, Early 1900s, 29 x 35 x 12 In., Pair 900
Table, Console, Mahogany, Drawer, Scroll Legs, Paw Feet, Marble Top, c.1820, 49 ¾ x 25 x 36 In. ... 2360
Table, Console, Marble, Acanthus, Animals, Scrolls, Lions, Fruits, Shells, 36 ¾ x 18 In. 8250
Table, Console, Pierced, Faux Marble Top, Figural Pilasters, Lions, Doors, 49 x 48 x 14 In........ 1023
Table, Console, Regency, Mahogany, Marble Top, Scroll Supports, c.1810, 36 x 38 In. ......*illus* 610
Table, Demilune, Animal Print, 2 Drawers, 2 Doors, Maitland Smith, 34 x 17 In. .... *illus* 750
Table, Dining, Alain Chervet, Glass Top, Bronze Ibex Head Legs, 19 ½ x 90 In. 2500
Table, Dining, Arne Jacobsen, 6 Star Series, Rosewood, Round, Label, c.1960, 28 x 57 In. 1625
Table, Dining, Drop Leaf, Walnut, Rectangular Top, c.1830, 30 x 16 x 48 In. 105
Table, Dining, Embossed Top, Lucite Base, Karl Springer, 60 In. .... *illus* 281
Table, Dining, Finn Juhl, Rosewood, Lacquered Oak, Baker Furniture, Denmark, 28 x 53 In. .*illus* 5312
Table, Dining, Hohnert Design, Teak, Draw Leaf, Tapered Legs, Label, c.1950, 30 x 84 x 31 In. 502
Table, Dining, Louis XVI Style, Walnut, Carved, Inlay, Cabriole Legs, 1900s, 60 x 100 x 44 In. . 531
Table, Dining, Rectangular Top, 2 Leaves, Chamfered Legs, 1900s, 30 x 42 x 70 In. 216
Table, Dining, Renaissance Revival, Rosewood, Pedestal, Leaves, c.1890, 184 x 60 In. .....*illus* 3125
Table, Dining, Stickley Bros., Quaint, Round, Squared Legs, X Base, 30 x 45 In. .... *illus* 2160
Table, Dressing, Federal, Mahogany, Lyre Shape Legs, Claw Feet, c.1800, 37 x 36 In. 225

Furniture, Table, Coffee, Contemporary, Onyx, 8-Sided, 1900s, 14 x 36 In.
$1,220

Neal Auction Company

Furniture, Table, Coffee, Hugo Franca, Pequi Wood, Casters, Brazil, 2005, 21 x 51 x 49 In.
$8,125

Rago Arts and Auction Center

Furniture, Table, Coffee, Jeffrey Greene, Palette, 3 Angular Legs, Carved, Doylestown, 17 x 43 x 29 In.
$1,680

Alderfer Auction Company

Furniture, Table, Console, Carved Demilune, Painted, Dolphin Base, Early 1900s, 32 x 26 x 13 In.
$813

Hindman Auctions

Furniture, Table, Console, Regency, Mahogany, Marble Top, Scroll Supports, c.1810, 36 x 38 In.
$610

Neal Auction Company

Furniture, Table, Coffee, P. Evans, Stalagmite, Steel, Bronzed Resin, Glass Top, 17 x 42 x 30 In.
$1,625

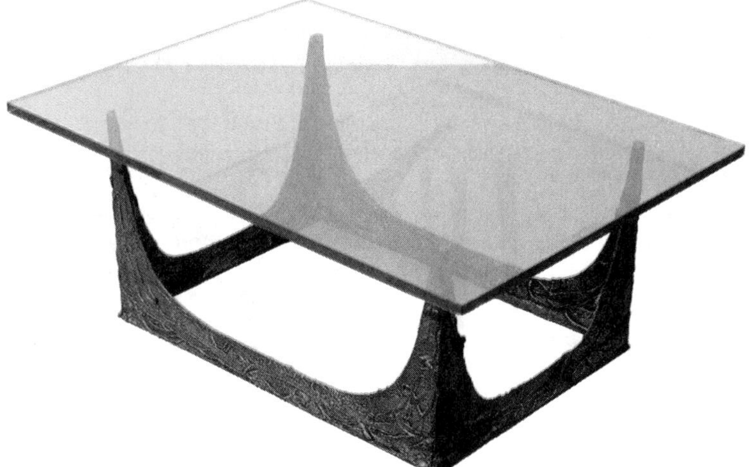

Palm Beach Modern Auctions

Furniture, Table, Demilune, Animal Print, 2 Drawers, 2 Doors, Maitland Smith, 34 x 17 In.
$750

Kamelot Auctions

Gateleg Table
The gateleg table was a seventeenth-century form. Usually the more legs on a gateleg table, the more expensive the table.

Furniture, Table, Dining, Embossed Top, Lucite Base, Karl Springer, 60 In.
$281

Hudson Valley Auctions

Furniture, Table, Dining, Finn Juhl, Rosewood, Lacquered Oak, Baker Furniture, Denmark, 28 x 53 In.
$5,312

Wright

F

Furniture, Table, Dining, Renaissance Revival, Rosewood, Pedestal, Leaves, c.1890, 184 x 60 In.
$3,125

Neal Auction Company

Furniture, Table, Dining, Stickley Bros., Quaint, Round, Squared Legs, X Base, 30 x 45 In.
$2,160

California Historical Design

TIP
Outdoor lights help prevent crimes, but install them high enough so they are difficult to unscrew.

Furniture, Table, Dressing, Mirror, Mahogany, 5 Drawers, Fitted, Fluted Legs, France, 31 x 33 x 18 In.
$390

Eldred's

Furniture, Table, Drop Leaf, Sunderland, Rosewood, Carved, Trestle Base, c.1845, Open 29 x 32 In.
$512

Neal Auction Company

Furniture, Table, Galle, Art Nouveau, 2 Tiers, Quatrefoil Top, Carved Legs, 29 x 29 x 29 In.
$2,375

Abington Auction Gallery

Furniture, Table, Galle, Art Nouveau, Inlay, 2 Tiers, Cats, Signed, Splayed Legs, 29 x 30 x 19 In.
$1,353

Stair Galleries

Furniture, Table, Game, Chessboard, Painted, Gilt, 4 Drawers, Cabriole Legs, 1900s, 26 x 21 x 21 In.
$431

Skinner, Inc.

Furniture, Table, Hepplewhite, Mahogany, Drawer, Oval, Inlay, Bellflower, Glass Top, 1930, 30 x 34 x 28 In.
$1,416

Bunch Auctions

Furniture, Table, Italian Baroque, Pietra Dura, Wrought Iron, Scroll Legs, 26 x 48 x 48 In.
$2,500

New Orleans Auction Galleries

Table, Dressing, Maple, Walnut, 4 Drawers, Pad Foot, 39 x 20 x 35 In. 207
Table, Dressing, Mirror, Mahogany, 5 Drawers, Fitted, Fluted Legs, France, 31 x 33 x 18 In. *illus* 390
Table, Dressing, Pine, Red Grained, Gilt Leaves Stencil, Drawer, Maine, c.1830, 35 x 34 In. 793
Table, Drop Leaf, Board Top, Mahogany, Drawer, Paw Feet, c.1825, 28 x 26 ½ x 39 In. 750
Table, Drop Leaf, Duncan Phyfe, Mahogany, Brass Paw Feet, 29 x 42 x 47 ½ In. 305
Table, Drop Leaf, Hepplewhite, Tiger Maple, Square Tapered Legs, c.1810, 28 x 16 x 47 In. 390
Table, Drop Leaf, Irish Wake Style, Mahogany, 29 In. 325
Table, Drop Leaf, Mahogany, Reeded Legs & Feet, 29 x 33 x 19 In. 185
Table, Drop Leaf, Queen Anne, Tiger Maple, Oval Top, Turned Legs, 1750s, 28 x 17 x 45 In. 390
Table, Drop Leaf, Queen Anne, Walnut, Trifid Foot, 1700s, 27 ½ x 20 x 46 ½ In. 400
Table, Drop Leaf, Rosewood, 2 Drawers, Wheel Feet, 35 x 37 x 27 ½ In. 88
Table, Drop Leaf, Sheraton, Maple, Swing Leg Supports, 1800s, 28 x 41 x 19 In. 3750
Table, Drop Leaf, Sunderland, Rosewood, Carved, Trestle Base, c.1845, Open 29 x 32 In. .*illus* 512
Table, Elm, Oval Top, Turned Legs, H-Stretcher, Ball Feet, 1800s, 25 x 39 x 31 In. 132
Table, Flip Top, Walnut, Inlay, Fruitwood, Saber Legs, 1700s, 32 ½ x 59 x 30 ½ In. 660
Table, Francesco Rigozzi, Pietra Dura, Octagonal Top, Mounted, Iron Base, 1900s, 60 In. 2250
Table, Galle, Art Nouveau, 2 Tiers, Quatrefoil Top, Carved Legs, 29 x 29 x 29 In. ....*illus* 2375
Table, Galle, Art Nouveau, Inlay, 2 Tiers, Cats, Signed, Splayed Legs, 29 x 30 x 19 In. ......*illus* 1353
Table, Galle, Mahogany, Circular Top, Floral Carved Rim, Apron, 1897, 29 ½ x 26 In. 600
Table, Game, Chessboard, Painted, Gilt, 4 Drawers, Cabriole Legs, 1900s, 26 x 21 x 21 In. *illus* 431
Table, Game, Convertible, Burl Walnut Checkerboard Top, Backgammon, Lucite Legs, 29 x 46 In. . 1660
Table, Game, Louis XV, Flip Top, Bronze Trim, X Shape Base, Signed, Blany, 26 x 16 x 31 In. ... 3450
Table, Harvest, Jacobean Style, Rounded Corners, 6-Legged Base, Bun Feet, 31 x 42 x 96 In. 648
Table, Hepplewhite, Mahogany, Drawer, Oval, Inlay, Bellflower, Glass Top, 1930, 30 x 34 x 28 In. ....*illus* 1416
Table, Italian Baroque, Pietra Dura, Wrought Iron, Scroll Legs, 26 x 48 x 48 In. ....*illus* 2500
Table, Library, Carved, Drawers, Rosette, Trestle, Keyed Stretcher, 1700s Style, c.1900s, 30 x 60 x 30 In. . 738
Table, Library, George IV, Burl Elm, 2 Drawers, Trestle, Caster Feet, 30 x 48 x 26 In., Pair 4305
Table, Library, Renaissance Revival Style, Walnut Top, 3 Drawers, Figural Carving, 31 x 79 In. . 2500
Table, Library, Spanish Revival, Wood, 5 Drawers, Rosette Reserves, Trestle Base, 30 x 60 In. .. 770
Table, Library, Stickley, Brown Oak, Rectangular Top, Brass Mount, 2 Drawers, 39 x 29 ½ x 30 In. 500
Table, Library, Stickley, Oak, Plank Top, Block Legs, Center Stretcher, 29 x 29 In. 520
Table, Library, Victorian, Oak, Leather Surface, 3 Drawers, Twist Legs, H-Stretcher, 30 x 60 x 33 In. 800
Table, Limbert, Oval, Oak, Cutout Sides, Signed, 29 ½ x 29 ½ x 45 In. 845
Table, Louis XVI, Fruitwood, Marble, Tapered Legs, Urn Stretcher, c.1790, 34 x 43 In. ....*illus* 2500
Table, Mahogany, Carved, Shelf, Hoof Feet, Round Top, Monogram, EG, 1897, 29 x 26 In. *illus* 600
Table, Mahogany, Leather Top, Drawers, Splayed Legs, 29 ½ x 44 In. 293
Table, Mahogany, Round, Pedestal Base, Flowers, Ball Feet, 29 x 37 ½ In. 311
Table, Marble, Granite, Brass & Iron, Inlay, Steel Base, Brass, Round, c.1890, 19 x 24 In. *illus* 4000
Table, Mies Van Der Rohe, Stainless Steel, Smoked Glass, Knoll, 20 x 27 In. ....*illus* 562
Table, Mint Julip, Gothic Style, Gold Marble Top, 41 x 41 x 19 In. 3450
Table, Neoclassical, Gilt, Marble, Frieze, Urn Medallion, X-Stretcher, 1800s, 56 x 24 In. ..*illus* 2375
Table, Neoclassical, Mahogany, Tilt Top, Sunburst, Pedestal, Round, c.1825, 29 x 42 In. .*illus* 2125
Table, Neoclassical, Round, Marble Top, Mahogany, Giltwood Paw Feet, Casters, 1900s, 28 x 31 In. 615
Table, Nesting, Black Lacquer, Chinoiserie, Continental, Largest 24 In., 4 Piece ....*illus* 375
Table, Nesting, Danish Modern, Teak, Trestle Legs, Largest 20 x 22 In., 3 Piece ....*illus* 177
Table, Oak, Breadboard Ends, Stretcher Base, England, 1700s, 125 x 37 x 31 In. ....*illus* 690
Table, Oak, Carved, Pyrography, Painted, Splayed Base, 29 x 18 x 18 In. ....*illus* 275
Table, Octagonal Top, Scalloped Skirt, Drop Finials, Turned Legs, c.1900, 26 x 32 x 32 In. . *illus* 791
Table, Octagonal, Mahogany, Leather Top, Reeded & Splayed, England, 1800s, 29 x 31 In. 2006
Table, P. Evans, Cityscape, Mixed Metal, Wood, Doors, Adjustable Shelf, 27 x 32 In. ....*illus* 3625
Table, P. Shire, Brazil, Lacquered Wood, Memphis, Italy, 1981, 28 x 79 ¾ In. ....*illus* 4062
Table, Pembroke, George III, Mahogany, Tea Caddy Drawers, Caster Feet, 27 x 30 x 20 In. 1534
Table, Pembroke, Hepplewhite, Cherry, X-Stretcher, c.1785, 28 x 19 x 36 In. ....*illus* 1800
Table, Pembroke, Mahogany, Board Top, Drawer, Tapered Legs, 1810s, 29 x 42 x 25 In. 468
Table, Rococo Revival, Carved, Walnut & Marquetry, 2 Tiers, 1900s, 28 In., Pair 344
Table, Rococo Revival, Inlaid Heart, Diamond, Eagle, Stars, Shield, Round, c.1876, 27 x 26 In. ..*illus* 380
Table, Sawbuck, Pine, X Trestle Base, Blue Paint, 1800s, 29 ½ x 67 ½ x 22 ¾ In. 1755
Table, Serving, Neoclassical, Mahogany, Brass, Marble, 2 Tiers, France, Early 1800s, 40 x 38 In. 308
Table, Sewing, Drawer, Brass Knob, Federal, 1800s, 29 ½ x 19 ¾ In. 245
Table, Sewing, Drop Leaf, Sheraton, Mahogany, 3 Drawers, Twist Turned Legs, c.1830, 18 x 37 In. . 183
Table, Sewing, Hepplewhite, Oak, 2-Board Top, Drawer, Tapered Legs, 1810s, 28 x 50 x 31 In. . 390

Furniture, Table, Louis XVI, Fruitwood, Marble, Tapered Legs, Urn Stretcher, c.1790, 34 x 43 In.
$2,500

New Orleans Auction Galleries

Furniture, Table, Mahogany, Carved, Shelf, Hoof Feet, Round Top, Monogram, EG, 1897, 29 x 26 In.
$600

Eldred's

Furniture, Table, Marble, Granite, Brass & Iron, Inlay, Steel Base, Brass, Round, c.1890, 19 x 24 In.
$4,000

New Orleans Auction Galleries

This is an edited listing of current prices. Visit **Kovels.com** to check thousands of prices from previous years and sign up for free information on trends, tips, reproductions, marks, and more.

F

Garage Sale Aftermath
We just heard of an after "garage sale" sale. If it is impossible to give the leftovers to charity, list the "after sale" on Craigslist or other free ad sources. Offer everything free. The "buyers" will cart off your unwanted items and your front lawn will be empty. We visited a ski resort where the town has a drop-off site for anything usable and unwanted. Just take what you need.

Furniture, Table, Mies Van Der Rohe, Stainless Steel, Smoked Glass, Knoll, 20 x 27 In.
$562

Wright

Furniture, Table, Neoclassical, Gilt, Marble, Frieze, Urn Medallion, X-Stretcher, 1800s, 56 x 24 In.
$2,375

New Orleans Auction Galleries

Furniture, Table, Neoclassical, Mahogany, Tilt Top, Sunburst, Pedestal, Round, c.1825, 29 x 42 In.
$2,125

New Orleans Auction Galleries

Furniture, Table, Nesting, Black Lacquer, Chinoiserie, Continental, Largest 24 In., 4 Piece
$375

Neal Auction Company

Furniture
George Nakashima learned traditional joinery skills from a Japanese carpenter in a U.S. internment camp in Idaho during World War II.

Furniture, Table, Nesting, Danish Modern, Teak, Trestle Legs, Largest 20 x 22 In., 3 Piece
$177

Austin Auction Gallery

Furniture, Table, Oak, Breadboard Ends, Stretcher Base, England, 1700s, 125 x 37 x 31 In.
$690

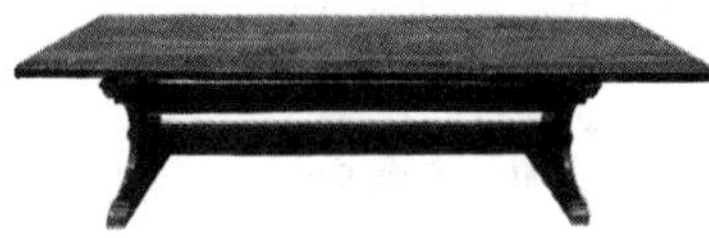

Apple Tree Auction Center

Furniture, Table, Oak, Carved, Pyrography, Painted, Splayed Base, 29 x 18 x 18 In.
$275

Thomaston Place Auction Galleries

Furniture, Table, Octagonal Top, Scalloped Skirt, Drop Finials, Turned Legs, c.1900, 26 x 32 x 32 In.
$791

Soulis Auctions

Furniture, Table, P. Evans, Cityscape, Mixed Metal, Wood, Doors, Adjustable Shelf, 27 x 32 In.
$3,625

Palm Beach Modern Auctions

Furniture, Table, P. Shire, Brazil, Lacquered Wood, Memphis, Italy, 1981, 28 x 79 ¾ In.
$4,062

Wright

Furniture, Table, Pembroke, Hepplewhite, Cherry, X-Stretcher, c.1785, 28 x 19 x 36 In.
$1,800

Eldred's

TIP
Pembroke tables with square legs sell for higher prices than Pembroke tables with turned or reeded legs.

Furniture, Table, Rococo Revival, Inlaid Heart, Diamond, Eagle, Stars, Shield, Round, c.1876, 27 x 26 In.
$380

Cordier Auctions

Furniture, Table, Sewing, Mixed Wood, Fitted Interior, Spool Turned Legs, 1800s, 31 x 22 In.
$142

Conestoga Auction Company

Furniture, Table, Sewing, Satinwood, Doves, Square Tapered Legs, 30 ½ x 22 ½ x 16 In.
$366

Nadeau's Auction Gallery

Furniture, Table, Side, Sheraton, 2 Drawers, Round Pulls, Tapered Legs, 30 x 26 x 17 In.
$142

Bunch Auctions

Furniture, Table, Tavern, Oval Top, Molded Apron, Splayed Tapered Legs, Button Feet, 26 x 34 x 25 In.
$3,936

Skinner, Inc.

Furniture, Table, Tavern, William & Mary, Stretcher Base, Center Finial, Drawer, 1700s, 29 x 38 x 24 In.
$590

Copake Auctions

Furniture, Table, Thevenin, Biomorphic, Bronze, Etched Base, 2 Glass Tiers, 1971, 24 x 35 In.
$4,375

Rago Arts and Auction Center

TIP
Old pantyhose are good to use to apply an oil finish to furniture. Remove all elastic first. The material does not leave lint.

F

Furniture, Table, Tilt Top, Mahogany, Walnut, Inlay, Diamond Design, Fluted Stand, c.1890, 29 x 26 In.
$1,000

New Orleans Auction Galleries

Furniture, Table, Tray, Tole, Caribbean Island Scenes, Faux Bamboo Stand, 1800s, 18 x 35 ½ In.
$610

Neal Auction Company

Furniture, Table, Victorian, Marble Top, Skirt, Rope Twist Carving, Central Post, 29 ½ x 32 x 22 In.
$480

Soulis Auctions

Furniture, Table, W. Platner Style, Steel, Glass Top, Gilt Paint, Round, 1900s, 29 x 42 In.
$397

Neal Auction Company

Furniture, Tantalus, Hinged Lid, Walnut, Glass Panels, Decanters, Cordials, Late 1800s, 12 x 15 x 14 In.
$295

Leland Little Auctions

TIP
If your wicker furniture becomes mildewed, wash it with a disinfectant cleaner.

Furniture, Tea Cart, Wicker, White, Painted, 2 Handles, Glass Tray, Wood Wheels, c.1920, 35 In.
$293

Thomaston Place Auction Galleries

Furniture, Teapoy, Regency, Rosewood, Sarcophagus Shape, Fitted Interior, Early 1800s, 33 x 15 x 9 In.
$480

Eldred's

Furniture, Umbrella Stand, Cast Iron, Figural, Jack Tar, Cannons, Anchors, c.1890, 28 In.
$1,800

Eldred's

Furniture, Vanity, J. Hoffmann, Stained Beech, Mirror, Drawer, Label, c.1906, 53 x 23 x 18 In.
$625

Rago Arts and Auction Center

Table, Sewing, Hinged Top, Fitted Interior, Drawer, Cabriole Legs, 1800s, 30 x 23 x 17 In. 330
Table, Sewing, Louis XV Style, Kingwood, Parquetry, Bronze Mounted, Mirror, c.1900, 28 x 24 x 16 In..... 308
Table, Sewing, Mixed Wood, Fitted Interior, Spool Turned Legs, 1800s, 31 x 22 In. ....*illus* 142
Table, Sewing, Satinwood, Doves, Square Tapered Legs, 30 ½ x 22 ½ x 16 In. ....*illus* 366
Table, Sewing, Sheraton, Mahogany & Satinwood, Drawers, Tapered & Turned Legs, 28 x 19 x 13 ½ In.. 854
Table, Sewing, Sheraton, Mahogany, Cookie Corner, 2 Drawers, 1800s, 29 x 19 x 18 In............ 266
Table, Sewing, Thomas Seymour, Mahogany, Interior Desk Flap, Mirror, 1815, 16 x 28 x 19 In. 826
Table, Sewing, Walnut, Rectangular Top, Drawer, Tapered Legs, c.1820-40, 28 x 15 ¾ x 20 In........ 246
Table, Side, Drop Leaf, Louis XV Style, Gilt, Bronze, Mounted, Early 1900s, 27 ½ x 26 In......... 200
Table, Side, Fruitwood, Shaped Skirt, Cabriole Legs, Dovetailed Drawer, Round Pull, 31 x 21 In. 120
Table, Side, MacKenzie, Checkerboard Top, Drawer, Painted, 31 ½ x 20 x 16 In., Pair.............. 500
Table, Side, Mahogany, Reticulated Edge, Rope Molding, Ball & Claw Feet, 32 x 21 In.............. 75
Table, Side, Mixed Wood, Carved, Hand Crafted, Harp II, Stand, 25 x 13 ½ x 10 ½ In............. 216
Table, Side, Red Inset Marble, Carved Animals, Flowers, Beaded Trim, 19 x 17 x 22 In............. 316
Table, Side, Sheraton, 2 Drawers, Round Pulls, Tapered Legs, 30 x 26 x 17 In. ....*illus* 142
Table, Side, Victorian Style, Gilt Metal, Square Marble Top, Cabriole Legs, 30 x 16 In. 113
Table, Side, Walnut, Marble Top, Carved Base, Casters, 32 x 23 x 30 In....................................... 181
Table, Starbay Co., Marine, Oval, Red Grandis Wood, Canted Legs, Folding Leaf, 29 x 39 x 59 In..... 1638
Table, Tabouret, Rosewood, Carved Skirt, Marble Top, Paw Feet, 16 x 19 In............................. 177
Table, Tavern, Oval Top, Molded Apron, Splayed Tapered Legs, Button Feet, 26 x 34 x 25 In. *illus* 3936
Table, Tavern, William & Mary, Stretcher Base, Center Finial, Drawer, 1700s, 29 x 38 x 24 In. ... *illus* 590
Table, Tea, Chippendale, Tilt Top, Walnut, Birdcage, Ball & Claw Feet, 1700s, 30 x 33 In......... 3600
Table, Tea, Mahogany, Block Legs, Chamfered Back, George III, Late 1700s, 25 x 33 x 21 In..... 108
Table, Tea, Mahogany, Tilt Top, Birdcage, Cabriole Legs, 1700s, 28 ½ x 29 In. 130
Table, Tea, Queen Anne, Drop Leaf, Birch, Oval, Cabriole Legs, Pad Feet, Portsmouth.............. 5100
Table, Tea, Tiger Maple, Pad Foot, J.L. Tachorn, Ohio, 26 x 18 x 26 In. 593
Table, Tea, Tilt Top, Mahogany, Birdcage, Snake Feet, 1700s, 28 In. 413
Table, Tea, Tilt Top, Mahogany, Round, Cabriole Legs, Birdcage, 1700s, 28 ½ x 30 ½ In......... 266
Table, Thevenin, Biomorphic, Bronze, Etched Base, 2 Glass Tiers, 1971, 24 x 35 In. ....*illus* 4375
Table, Tilt Top, Japanned & Parcel Gilt, Tripod Feet, Continental, 28 x 27 ¾ In........................ 738
Table, Tilt Top, KPM Porcelain Top, Birds, Nest, Brass Stand, Paw Feet, Germany, c. 1880, 30 x 16 In. 1665
Table, Tilt Top, Mahogany, Walnut, Inlay, Diamond Design, Fluted Stand, c.1890, 29 x 26 In. ..*illus* 1000
Table, Tray Top, Papier-Mache, Black, Bouquet, Faux Bamboo, England, 1800s, 19 x 26 In..... 216
Table, Tray, Tole, Caribbean Island Scenes, Faux Bamboo Stand, 1800s, 18 x 35 ½ In. ...*illus* 610
Table, Victorian, Marble Top, Skirt, Rope Twist Carving, Central Post, 29 ½ x 32 x 22 In. *illus* 480
Table, W. Platner Style, Steel, Glass Top, Gilt Paint, Round, 1900s, 29 x 42 In. ....*illus* 397
Table, Walnut, Marble Top, Urn Base, Caster Feet, Victorian, 30 x 29 ½ x 23 ½ In................... 124
Table, Walnut, Octagonal, Turned Legs, Square Base Stretchers, c.1800, 31 x 45 ½ x 46 In...... 923
Table, Wicker, Demilune Top, Woven, Butterfly, Scalloped, Beaded, Tripod Base, 28 x 24 x 12 ½ In. 199
Tabouret, Empire Style, Curule Shape, Upholstered, Ebonized, Gilt Parcel, 1800s, 20 In......... 1625
Tantalus, Hinged Lid, Walnut, Glass Panels, Decanters, Cordials, Late 1800s, 12 x 15 x 14 In. ..*illus* 295
Tea Cart, Wicker, White, Painted, 2 Handles, Glass Tray, Wood Wheels, c.1920, 35 In. .....*illus* 293
Teapoy, Regency, Rosewood, Sarcophagus Shape, Fitted Interior, Early 1800s, 33 x 15 x 9 In. .*illus* 480
Umbrella Stand, 13 Stag Horn Antlers, Wood Base, Metal Liner, 33 x 16 In............................. 290
Umbrella Stand, Cast Iron, Figural, Jack Tar, Cannons, Anchors, c.1890, 28 In. ....*illus* 1800
Umbrella Stand, Iron, Openwork, Painted, Flowers, c.1930, 24 ¾ x 12 ¾ In. 375
Vanity, Georgian Style, Shaped Top, 4 Drawers, Apron Legs, Ball & Talon Feet, 30 ½ x 38 x 15 In. .. 360
Vanity, J. Hoffmann, Stained Beech, Mirror, Drawer, Label, c.1906, 53 x 23 x 18 In. ....*illus* 625
Vanity, Mirror, Drawer, Inlay, Bronze Mounts, Candelabra Sconces, Curved, 63 x 46 In. 1375
Vitrine, Gilt, Bronze Mounts, Tabletop, Shell Veneer, Cabriole Legs, 11 x 14 ½ In. 1560
Vitrine, Marquetry, Bronze Mounts, Curved Glass Sides, Cabriole Legs, Claw Feet, c.1890, 44 x 58 x 14 In. 254
Wardrobe, Quartersawn Oak, Molded Crest, Hinged Door, c.1912, 84 x 42 ½ x 17 In. 1440
Wardrobe, Scandinavian, Pine, Door, Drawer, Rectangular Top, Round Pulls, 71 x 38 x 20 In. *illus* 554
Wardrobe, Walnut, 2 Doors, Compartments, England, 60 ½ x 72 x 21 In................................... 144
Washstand, Federal, Inlaid Mahogany, Drawer, Brass Pulls, Early 1800s, 41 x 24 x 17 In. 461
Washstand, Mahogany, Round, Scroll Flat Legs, Concave Base, Bun Feet, Continental, 36 ½ x 16 In...... 117
Washstand, Pine, Drawer, Turned Legs, 32 x 31 x 16 In.. 85
Washstand, Sheraton, Pine, Basswood, White, Red Top, Flowers, New England, c.1820, 36 x 15 In. *illus* 3172
Washstand, Tiger Maple, Cherry, 2 Tiers, Scrolled, Scalloped Gallery, c.1830, 37 x 15 x 19 In.*illus* 185
Washstand, Walnut, Marble Top, Lion's Head Pulls, Drawer, 2 Doors, c.1900............................ 113
Washstand, Walnut, Rectangular, Drawer, Turned Legs, Stretcher, c.1830, 31 x 18 x 29 In. 234

Furniture, Wardrobe, Scandinavian, Pine, Door, Drawer, Rectangular Top, Round Pulls, 71 x 38 x 20 In.
$554

Skinner, Inc.

Furniture, Washstand, Sheraton, Pine, Basswood, White, Red Top, Flowers, New England, c.1820, 36 x 15 In.
$3,172

Pook & Pook

Furniture, Washstand, Tiger Maple, Cherry, 2 Tiers, Scrolled, Scalloped Gallery, c.1830, 37 x 15 x 19 In.
$185

Locati Auctions

Furniture, Work Counter, Shaker, Pine, Butternut, Old Red Stain, 6 Drawers, 33 x 57 x 28 In.
$7,688

Willis Henry Auctions

TIP
New security idea: Have one of the neighbors park a second car in your driveway. Your house will look occupied and the car will be seen coming and going.

G. Argy-Rousseau, Bowl, Leaves, Pate-De-Verre, Amethyst, Green, 3-Leaf Cluster, c.1914, 1 ⅝ x 3 ½ In.
$2,106

Jeffrey S. Evans & Associates

G. Argy-Rousseau, Vase, Frosted, Molded, Flowers & Leaves, Pate-De-Verre, Early 1900s, 4 In.
$923

Skinner, Inc.

Window Seat, Regency Style, Ebonized, Padded Seat & Armrest, Fluted Legs, 23 x 48 In. 1750
Wine Cooler, Georgian, Mahogany, Hexagonal, Brass Banding, c.1780, 26 x 14 x 19 ½ In. 660
Wine Cooler, Neoclassical, Mahogany, Carved, Octagonal Top, Casters, Early 1800s, 36 x 19 x 19 In. 2640
Work Counter, Shaker, Pine, Butternut, Old Red Stain, 6 Drawers, 33 x 57 x 28 In. ....*illus* 7688

G. ARGY-ROUSSEAU

G. Argy-Rousseau is the impressed mark used on a variety of glass objects in the Art Deco style. Gabriel Argy-Rousseau, born in 1885, was a French glass artist. In 1921, he formed a partnership that made pate-de-verre and other glass. The partnership ended in 1931 and he opened his own studio. He worked until 1952 and died in 1953.

Bowl, Leaves, Pate-De-Verre, Amethyst, Green, 3-Leaf Cluster, c.1914, 1 ⅝ x 3 ½ In. ....*illus* 2106
Night-Light, La Coupe Fleurie, Orange Flowers, Pate-De-Verre, Wrought Iron, Signed, 5 ½ x 4 In.. 4063
Vase, Frosted, Molded, Flowers & Leaves, Pate-De-Verre, Early 1900s, 4 In. ....*illus* 923
Vase, Sousis, Red & Purple Flowers, Embossed, Pate-De-Verre, Signed, 6 x 4 In. 3750

GALLE

Galle was a designer who made glass, pottery, furniture, and other Art Nouveau items. Emile Galle founded his factory in France in 1874. After Galle's death in 1904, the firm continued to make glass and furniture until 1931. The *Galle* signature was used as a mark, but it was often hidden in the design of the object. Galle cameo and other types of glass are listed here. Pottery is in the next section. His furniture is listed in the Furniture category.

Bowl, Orange & Frosted, Green Maple Leaf, Seed, 3 ½ x 11 x 6 ¾ In. ....*illus* 420
Jar, Egg Shape, Rooster, Leaves On Lid, Translucent White Ground, Cameo, Signed, 6 In. 2904
Jar, Lid, Dragonfly, Blue, Brown, Overlay, Acid Etched, Signed, c.1900, 9 ⅞ x 5 In. 4063
Lamp, Butterflies, Brown, Green, Cream, Overlay, Acid Etched, Signed, c.1900, 14 x 7 In. 3750
Perfume Bottle, Flowers, Blue, Spider Web, Overlay, Acid Etched, Signed, c.1900 875
Scent Bottle, Red Flowers, Embossed, Stopper, Frosted, Signed, c.1900, 4 x 4 x 2 In. 1375
Scent Bottle, Red Flowers, Stopper, Overlay, Acid Etched, Signed, 9 x 4 In. 1500
Vase, Bulbous, Flower, Pink, White, Green, Gilt, Acid Etched, Signed, c.1890, 9 ¾ x 3 In. 2500
Vase, Bulbous, Flower, Red, Yellow, Cameo, Signed, 5 ½ x 3 ½ In. 715
Vase, Bulbous, Green Leaves, Pink Matte, Lavender Base, Cameo, Signed, 7 x 3 x 2 In. 254
Vase, Bulbous, Pink, Citron Flower, Leaves, Cameo, 1900-10, 17 In. 1130
Vase, Cream Ground, Ferns, Olive Green, Cameo, 5 ¾ In. 148
Vase, Crocosmia Orchid, Scalloped Rim, Silver Base, France, c.1925, 13 ¼ In. 875
Vase, Fire Polished, Maroon Leaves, Opaque White Ground, Cameo, 2 ½ x 5 In. ....*illus* 1200
Vase, Flowers, Multicolor, Cameo, Bulbous Body, Footed, Signed, 6 ⅜ In. 375
Vase, Frosted Amber, Pink Tones, Carved Flowers, Cameo, 5 ½ In. 350
Vase, Green Spiny Pods, Matte Ground, Cameo Glass, 8 ½ In. 396
Vase, Organic Shape, Soft Red, Burgundy, Leaf, Berry, Cameo, Signed, 8 ½ x 3 ½ In. 833
Vase, Pink & White Background, Green Leafy Overlay, Cameo, Signed, 7 ¾ In. 830
Vase, Pink Flowers, Brown Stems, Leaves, Waisted Neck, Cameo, 15 In. 810
Vase, Purple Hydrangeas, Green Leaves, Glass, Cameo, 17 ½ In. 1150
Vase, Ruffled Edge Rim, Pale Orange, Tree, Landscape, Cameo, 7 ½ In. ....*illus* 840
Vase, Scenic Landscape, Eye-Cut Top, Overlay, Signed, c.1900, 5 ¾ x 4 ¾ x 2 ½ In. 1000
Vase, Stick Neck, Shaped Body, Brown Floral, Grasshopper, Art Nouveau, 9 In. 896
Vase, White Flowers, Leaves, Cameo, Dark Base, Flared Rim, 11 In. 1230
Vase, Wisteria, Blue, Cream, Cameo, 9 ¾ x 3 In. 2500
Vase, Yellow Ground, Lavender, Green & Pink, Flowers, Cameo, Signed, 12 In. ....*illus* 72

GALLE POTTERY

Galle pottery was made by Emile Galle, the famous French designer, after 1874. The pieces were marked with the initials *E. G.* impressed, *Em. Galle Faiencerie de Nancy,* or a version of his signature. Galle is best known for his glass, listed above.

Galle, Bowl, Orange & Frosted, Green Maple Leaf, Seed, 3 ½ x 11 x 6 ¾ In.
$420

Woody Auctions

Galle, Vase, Fire Polished, Maroon Leaves, Opaque White Ground, Cameo, 2 ½ x 5 In.
$1,200

Morphy Auctions

Galle, Vase, Ruffled Edge Rim, Pale Orange, Tree, Landscape, Cameo, 7 ½ In.
$840

CRN Auctions

Galle, Vase, Yellow Ground, Lavender, Green & Pink, Flowers, Cameo, Signed, 12 In.
$72

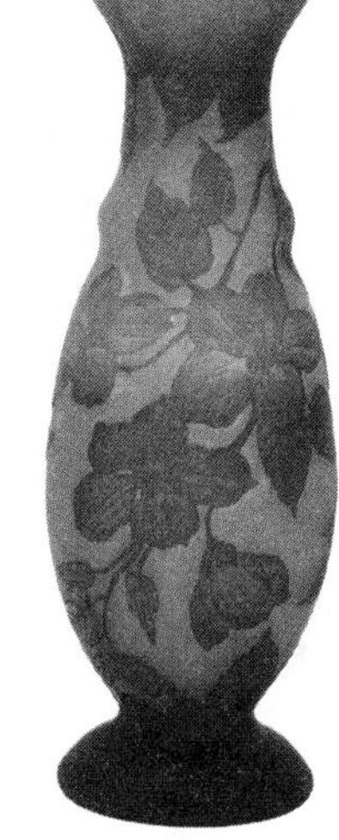

Woody Auctions

Galle Pottery, Ewer, Brown, Blue Rim, Moth, Flower, Lion's Head Handle, Mark, c.1880, 7 ½ In.
$575

Woody Auctions

Galle Pottery, Figurine, Cat, Seated, Yellow, Blue & White Dots & Hearts, Faience, Signed, 13 x 7 In.
$20,400

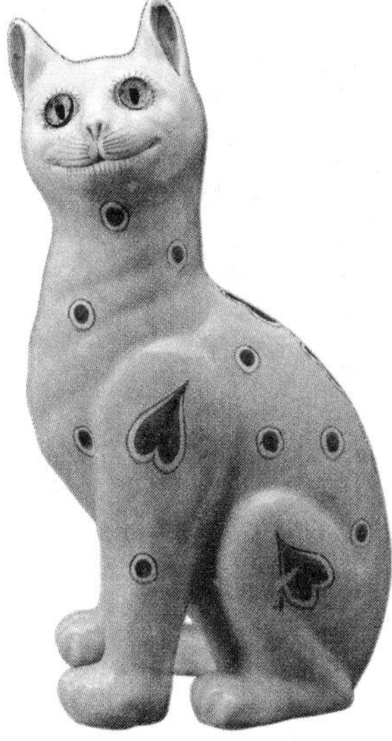

Morphy Auctions

G

Galle Pottery, Vase, Dark Blue, Mottled Gold, Enamel Flowers, Dragonfly, Signed, 5 ½ x 5 In.
$1,500

Woody Auctions

Game, Ball Toss, Multicolor, Wood, Winning Scores, Pierced, 60 x 18 In.
$1,476

Skinner, Inc.

TIP

If you want to keep your collections free from harm, always clean and dust them yourself.

Ewer, Brown, Blue Rim, Moth, Flower, Lion's Head Handle, Mark, c.1880, 7 ½ In. .... *illus* 575
Figurine, Cat, Seated, Yellow, Blue & White Dots & Hearts, Faience, Signed, 13 x 7 In. ....*illus* 20400
Plate, Reticulated, White, Butterfly, Snail, Signed, 9 In. 375
Vase, Dark Blue, Mottled Gold, Enamel Flowers, Dragonfly, Signed, 5 ½ x 5 In. ....*illus* 1500

GAME

Game collectors like all types of games. Of special interest are any board games or card games. Transogram and other company names are included in the description when known. Other games may be found listed under Card, Toy, or the name of the character or celebrity featured in the game. Gameboards without the game pieces are listed in the Gameboard category.

Bagatelle, Folding, Mahogany, Table On Stand, Brass Lock, 18 ¾ x 48 x 24 ¾ In. 410
Ball Toss, Multicolor, Wood, Winning Scores, Pierced, 60 x 18 In. ....*illus* 1476
Bingo, Box, Numbered Balls, Painted, Early 1900s, 15 x 15 x 2 ½ In. 148
Box, Bone, Dome Lid, Sliding Lid, Cribbage, Dominoes, France, England, c.1810, 2 x 6 In. *illus* 1080
Box, Puzzle, Hinged Lid, Wood, Mosaic On Top, Diamond Shapes, 4 x 6 x 2 ½ In. 58
Box, Rosewood, S-Scrolls, Flip Top Compartments, Escutcheon, Hinges, 7 x 17 In. 240
Chess Set, White & Black, Aluminum, Austin Enterprises 1962, Board, 18 x 18 In. ....*illus* 1375
Dart Board, Bull's-Eye, Red, Yellow & Blue Paint, Cork, Iron Banded, Chain, Early 1900s, 17 ½ In. *illus* 177
Dice, Chuck-A-Luck, Hourglass Shape Cage, Mounted, Square Base, Steel, 10 In. 144
Fox & Chickens, Green & Red Paint, Circular, Assortment Of Marbles, Board, 12 In. 420
Going To The Klondike, Paper On Wood, Board, Spinner, Box, McLoughlin Bros., 1898, 20 In. 570
Horse Race, Gambling, Cast Iron Spiral, Black & White, Numbered Sections, 14 x 6 ½ In. *illus* 600
Jeu De Course, Car Race, Painted Metal, Spring-Loaded Wood Box, J.L., 10 x 10 In. ....*illus* 338
Le Chemin De Fer, Railroad, Board, 6 Spelter Locomotives, Playing Pieces, Box, 15 In. 240
Penny Toss, Carnival, Painted Plywood, Black Ground, c.1940, 39 x 39 In. 366
Punch & Judy Tenpins, Lithographed Paper On Wood, Box, McLoughlin, 1902, 22 In. 3900
Rough Riders, Teddy Roosevelt, Board, Spinner, Parker Bros. Adventure Series, 21 In. 1560
Scoreboard, Collapsible, Painted Oak, Hinged Rear Leg, c.1950, 30 x 17 x 21 In. 165
Visit Of Santa Claus, Board, Spinner, Cards, Box, McLoughlin Bros., 20 x 10 In. 3300
Wheel Of Chance, Red Line Dividers, St. Paul, Minn. Dailey Mfg. Co., c.1910, 29 In. ......*illus* 900
Wheel, Gambling, Carnival, Numbers, Spokes, White, Red, Blue, Multicolor, c.1920, 36 In. *illus* 1003
Wheel, Gambling, Numbers, Metal Spokes, Painted, 29 In. 236
Wheel, Gambling, Wood, Metal Pins, Wall Mounted, Numbers, Dailey Mfg. Co., St. Paul, 14 In. .....*illus* 1200
World To World Airship Race, Board On Box, Spinner, Chicago Game Co., 21 In. 1560

GAME PLATE

Game plates are plates of any make decorated with pictures of birds, animals, or fish. The game plates usually came in sets consisting of 12 dishes and a serving platter. These sets were most popular during the 1880s.

Bird, Blue Jay Flying Over Water, Gold Trim, 10 ¼ In. 400
Birds, Quail, Browns, Grays, Mauve Background, c.1898, 11 In. 267
Deer, Family, Pine Trees, Snow, Mountain, Gold Trim, Limoges, 9 In. 156

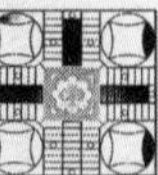

GAMEBOARD

Gameboard collectors look for just the board without the game pieces. The boards are collected as folk art or decorations. Gameboards that are part of a complete game are listed in the Game category.

Backgammon & Checkers, Multicolor, Painted, 2-Sided, 31 ½ x 14 ½ In. 221
Brown & Black, Painted, Marbleized Slate, Beveled Edge, 22 x 22 In. 339
Checkers & Backgammon, Red & Black, Painted, Pine, Brass, Late 1800s, 14 x 12 In. 185
Checkers & Parcheesi, Pine, Barn Red, Yellow, New England, 1800s, 28 ½ x 21 In. 176
Checkers, Black Box, Red Ground, Monogram, Wood, 21 ½ x 15 In. ....*illus* 1599
Checkers, Black, White, Patina, Folk Art, Late 1800s, 10 x 18 ½ In. 138

Game, Box, Bone, Dome Lid, Sliding Lid, Cribbage, Dominoes, France, England, c.1810, 2 x 6 In. $1,080

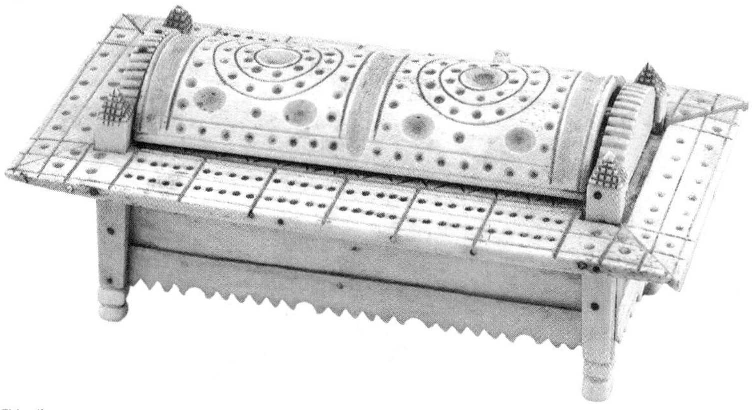

Eldred's

Game, Chess Set, White & Black, Aluminum, Austin Enterprises 1962, Board, 18 x 18 In. $1,375

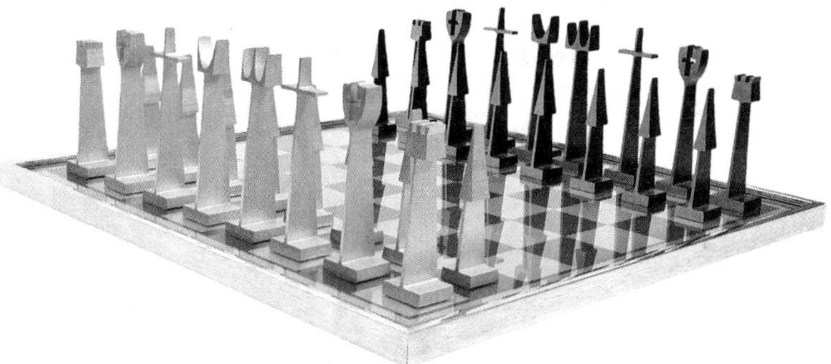

Abington Auction Gallery

Ford Charcoal
Henry Ford invented charcoal briquettes. They were made from leftover scraps of wood from Model T car manufacturing.

Game, Dart Board, Bull's-Eye, Red, Yellow & Blue Paint, Cork, Iron Banded, Chain, Early 1900s, 17 ½ In.
$177

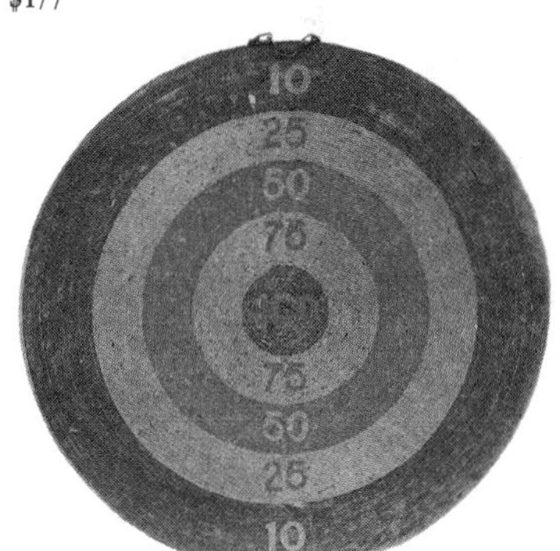

Copake Auctions

Game, Horse Race, Gambling, Cast Iron Spiral, Black & White, Numbered Sections, 14 x 6 ½ In.
$600

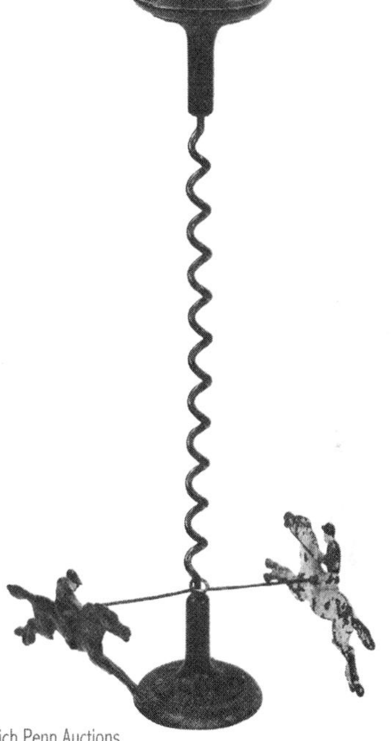

Rich Penn Auctions

Game, Jeu De Course, Car Race, Painted Metal, Spring-Loaded Wood Box, J.L., 10 x 10 In.
$338

Richard Opfer Auctioneering, Inc.

Game, Wheel Of Chance, Red Line Dividers, St. Paul, Minn. Dailey Mfg Co., c.1910, 29 In.
$900

Eldred's

Game, Wheel, Gambling, Carnival, Numbers, Spokes, White, Red, Blue, Multicolor, c.1920, 36 In.
$1,003

Copake Auctions

Game, Wheel, Gambling, Wood, Metal Pins, Wall Mounted, Numbers, Dailey Mfg. Co., St. Paul, 14 In.
$1,200

Rich Penn Auctions

Gameboard, Checkers, Nine Men's Morris, Gallery Edge, Red & Black Paint, c.1900, 15 x 21 In.
$2,640

Garth's Auctioneers & Appraisers

Gameboard, Checkers, Black Box, Red Ground, Monogram, Wood, 21 ½ x 15 In.
$1,599

Stair Galleries

Gameboard, Checkers, Slate, Painted, Marbleized, Square, 22 In.
$47

Conestoga Auction Company

Gameboard, Checkers, Marbleized Slate, Geometric Designs, Frame, 22 x 22 In.
$400

Bertoia Auctions

Garden, Bench, Cast Stone, Openwork Supports, Lovebirds, 13 x 33 x 14 In., Pair
$1,750

Kamelot Auctions

Checkers, Flourish Edge, Green Ground, Red, Cream, Frame, 1880s, 18 x 19 ½ In. 4680
Checkers, Marbleized Slate, Geometric Designs, Frame, 22 x 22 In. .... *illus* 400
Checkers, Marbleized, Square, Flowers, Painted, Decals, 20 x 20 In. 283
Checkers, Nine Men's Morris, Gallery Edge, Red & Black Paint, c.1900, 15 x 21 In. .... *illus* 2640
Checkers, Orange, Blue, 2-Sided, Yellow Border, Edge Molding, Late 1800s, 25 x 17 ½ In. 677
Checkers, Painted, Green Square, F. Jones, Dated '97, 20 x 14 ¾ x 1 ½ In. 236
Checkers, Parcheesi, Red, Yellow, Green Faux-Marble Painted Ground, c.1850, 20 x 20 In. 2020
Checkers, Red Ground, Black Squares, Pine, Rectangular, 29 ½ x 16 In. 98
Checkers, Red, Black, Pine, Painted, Border, 1800s, 16 x 16 In. 369
Checkers, Red, Black, White, Wood, Glass, Green Trim, Folk Art, Late 1800s, 15 In. 127
Checkers, Slate, Painted, Marbleized, Square, 22 In. .... *illus* 47
Checkers, Yellow & Black, Flower Corners, Edge Molding, Late 1800s, 15 x 14 ¾ In. 1722
Chess, Ash Wood, Mahogany Frame, Brass Corner, Bird's-Eye Maple, c.1910, 18 x 23 In. 136
Folk Art, Red Ground, White Stars, Square Shape, 36 x 36 In. 24
Parcheesi, Beveled Edge, 5-Point Star Corner, Red, Yellow, Late 1800s, 17 ½ x 17 ¾ In. 1722
Parcheesi, Wood, Light Brown Ground, Circle Corners, Multicolor, 25 x 25 In. 738

GARDEN

Garden furnishings have been popular for centuries. The stone or metal statues, urns and fountains, sundials, small figurines, and wire, iron, or rustic furniture are included in this category. Many of the metal pieces have been made continuously for years.

Armillary Sphere, Green, Painted, Aluminum & Copper, Mounted, Stone Base, c.1950, 51 In. 502
Armillary Sphere, Patinated Metal, Square Base, Directional, 23 x 16 In. 384
Armillary Sphere, Rotating Globe, 12-Gore Sun, Moon, Stepped Base, 1900s, 48 x 3 In. 2706
Armillary, Atlas Holding Globe Aloft, Cast Metal, Stone Pedestal Base, France, 1900s, 63 In. ... 767
Bench, 2 Tree Trunk Pedestal, Cast Cement, 54 x 16 ½ In. 461
Bench, Cast Concrete, Paneled Pedestal, Egg & Dart Border, 1910s, 18 x 49 x 14 In., 3 Piece..... 263
Bench, Cast Iron, Pierced Quatrefoil Seat Back, Trestle Base, 1800s, 33 x 55 x 20 In. 2000
Bench, Cast Stone, Openwork Supports, Lovebirds, 13 x 33 x 14 In., Pair .... *illus* 1750
Bench, Cedar, Natural Shape, Log Legs, 54 x 34 x 21 In. 995
Bench, False Wood, Grape Clusters, Openwork, Cast Iron, Verdigris, 31 x 50 In. .... *illus* 1375
Bench, Fern Back, Cast Iron, Painted, 34 x 55 x 19 In. 787
Bench, Limestone, Tree Trunk Form Supports, c.1880, 30 x 52 In. .... *illus* 2500
Bench, Oak Leaves & Pinecones, Openwork, Cast Iron, 39 x 68 In., Pair .... *illus* 18750
Bench, Regency Style, Triple Back, 8 Straight Legs, Aluminum, c.1915, 29 x 53 x 16 In., Pair... 2478
Bench, Victorian Style, Iron, Flowers, Tendril Back, Scroll Seat, Late 1900s, 50 x 75 x 25 In..... 813
Bench, Wood Slats, Griffin Supports, Black Paint, Cast Iron, 28 x 43 In. .... *illus* 1375
Birdbath, Circular Bowl, Stepped Pedestal Base, Cast Stone, 33 x 27 In. .... *illus* 63
Chair, Blue, Floral, 4-Season, Arms, Paw Feet, Cast Iron, 37 x 24 x 27 In. 2700
Chair, Bronze, Square Ears, Trellis, Scroll Arms, Legs, Continental, c.1900, 38 x 18 x 14 In....*illus* 1180
Figure, Blue Heron, Painted, Hollow Body, Aluminum, Late 1900s, 37 In. 502
Figure, Boy, Sailor Outfit, Seated, Marble Block, Bronze, Late 1900s, 33 x 20 x 12 In. 439
Figure, Rooster, Standing, Round Base, Red, 22 ½ In. 500
Figure, Victory, Pedestal Stand, Cast Iron, 61 x 91 ½ x 19 ½ In. .... *illus* 1300
Figure, Whippets, Octagonal Bases, Cast Stone, England, 1900s, 16 ½ x 26 x 10 ½ In., Pair.... 826
Finial, Pineapple, Black, Leaves, Stepped Bases, Iron, c.1900, 23 x 7 In., Pair.......... 450
Fountain, 2 Figural Fish, One On Top Of The Other, Cast Stone, 25 x 12 x 14 In. 125
Fountain, 3 Tiers, Flower Top, 2 Birds Surrounding, Cement, 55 In. .... *illus* 130
Fountain, 3 Tiers, Molded Cranes, Reeded Pans, Egg & Dart Edges, Sunflower, Iron, 19 x 45 In...... 3250
Fountain, Crane, Green, Round Base, Patinated Bronze, 42 ½ x 15 x 12 In. 875
Fountain, Cupid, Shell Bowl On Head, Dolphin Bracket, Bronze, 60 x 25 In., 2 Piece ......*illus* 1521
Fountain, Putti, Seated, Fish Holding Nozzle, c.1900, 34 In. .... *illus* 720
Fountain, Table, 2 Tiers, Putti, Flower Swags, Arcade Age, Continental, 15 x 18 In. 1000
Fountain, Wall, Lion Mask, Cast Iron, 46 x 27 x 16 In. 344
Hitching Post Top, Tether, Horse Head, Iron, Black, Painted, Marked, Carmody, 14 In. 283
Hitching Post, Animal Mask Finial, Iron, T.R. Pullis, c.1880, 60 In. 1350
Hitching Post, Horse Head, Hexagonal Base, Cast Iron, Late 1800s, 53 ½ In. 671

Garden, Bench, False Wood, Grape Clusters, Openwork, Cast Iron, Verdigris, 31 x 50 In.
$1,375

Kamelot Auctions

Garden, Bench, Limestone, Tree Trunk Form Supports, c.1880, 30 x 52 In.
$2,500

Kamelot Auctions

TIP

You can keep your antique birdbath clear of algae if you put a few pre-1982 pennies in the water. The copper discourages algae. Friends will probably toss in more money thinking you have a wishing well. They do it in every mall.

Garden, Bench, Oak Leaves & Pinecones, Openwork, Cast Iron, 39 x 68 In., Pair
$18,750

Kamelot Auctions

GARDEN

Garden, Bench, Wood Slats, Griffin Supports, Black Paint, Cast Iron, 28 x 43 In.
$1,375

Kamelot Auctions

Garden, Birdbath, Circular Bowl, Stepped Pedestal Base, Cast Stone, 33 x 27 In.
$63

Kamelot Auctions

Garden, Chair, Bronze, Square Ears, Trellis, Scroll Arms, Legs, Continental, c.1900, 38 x 18 x 14 In.
$1,180

Ahlers & Ogletree Auction Gallery

Hitching Post, Horse Head, Removable, Ring, Black, Octagonal Base, Iron, 1800s, 19 In. 203
Hitching Post, Horse Head, Twisted & Leafy Post, Octagonal Base, Iron, 67 ½ In. ....*illus* 767
Hitching Post, Horse Head, Welded, Cast Iron, 16 In., 2 Piece.......... 86
Hitching Post, Jockey, Holding Ball, Standing, Red, White, Black, Square Base, Iron, 46 ½ In....... 944
Hitching Post, Jockey, Racing Silks, Yellow, Black, Old Paint, Iron, c.1900, 46 In. ....*illus* 900
Hitching Post, Jockey, Square Plinth Base, Cast Iron, 1800s, 46 x 22 x 20 In. ....*illus* 1200
Hitching Post, Stylized Crowned Lion Head Base, White, Cast Iron, Early 1900s, 47 In., Pair.. 960
Hitching Post, Victorian, Ornamental Fence, Stove Top, Red, Cast Iron, 1900, 104 In. 120
Jardiniere, Secessionist, Copper, Art Nouveau Style Brass Handles, Stretcher, 37 x 17 In......... 1150
Jardiniere, Wood, White, Painted, Carved, Rectangular, c.1800, 34 In. 343
Light, Electric, Man, Holding Torch, Square Bronze Pedestal, 92 x 20 x 16 In. 1625
Obelisk, Stone, Concave Waist, Beveled Plinth, Iron Base, 1900s, 84 In., Pair.......... 1180
Plant Stand, see also Furniture, Stand, Plant
Planter, 3 Tiers, 3 Upper & 2 Side Planters, Faux Bois, Cement, 79 x 66 x 33 In. 625
Planter, Neoclassical, Lotus Molded Rim, Acanthus Leaf Sides, Fluted Base, Stone, 24 x 37 In. 1000
Planter, Scrolled Handles, Plinth Base, Cast Iron, Victorian, 15 x 29 In., Pair.......... 374
Seat, Barrel, Dragons, Birds, Flowers, Porcelain, Chinese Export, 19 In., Pair.......... 420
Seat, Green, Barrel Shape, Flowers, Embossed, Porcelain, 18 ½ In. 148
Seat, Orange Ground, Floral, Landscape, Famille Jaune, Porcelain, Chinese, 1900s, 19 x 12 In.. 228
Sprinkler, Alligator, Cast Iron, Painted, c.1920s, 10 ½ x 8 ½ In. ....*illus* 148
Sprinkler, Alligator, Iron & Brass, Hose Fitting, 1920s, 9 x 11 x 6 In. 354
Sprinkler, Black Boy, Standing, Wood & Metal Construction, 42 In. 264
Sprinkler, Mallard Duck, Feather Details, Cast Iron, Painted, 13 In. 523
Sundial, Golfer, Bronze, Stamped Gorham Foundry, E.E. Codman, 18 x 12 ½ In. ....*illus* 4320
Sundial, Metal, Mounted, Carved, Octagonal, Stone Base, 39 x 15 ½ x 15 ½ In. ....*illus* 492
Sundial, Sphere Shape, Atlas, Copper Floral, Faux Verdigris Finish, Iron, 28 x 16 In. ......*illus* 367
Table, Potting, Cast Iron, Molded Top, Phoenix Support, Trestle Base, 27 ½ x 41 x 21 In......... 900
Table, Rectangular Glass Top, Scrolling Concrete Bases, Iron Mounts, 80 x 46 In.......... 124
Urn, 2 Handles, Putti, Circular Fluted Foot, Cast Lead, Continental, 1800s, 19 x 23 In. 1888
Urn, 2 Handles, Traces Of Green Paint, Iron, 18 ¾ x 26 ½ x 15 ¾ In. ....*illus* 338
Urn, 2 Scrolled Handles, Flared Rim, Mounted, Base, Iron, 30 x 29 In., Pair ....*illus* 489
Urn, Classical Style, Black, Painted, Scroll Panel Socles, Aluminum, Late 1900s, 47 x 17 x 17 In., Pair.... 944
Urn, Continental, Egg & Dart Rim, Lobed, Plinth Base, Iron, 1800s, 47 ½ x 43 ½ In. .....*illus* 4750
Urn, Continental, Patinated, Bronze, Entwined Serpent Handles, 1900s, 34 x 32 x 23 In. 1000
Urn, Egg & Dart Rim, Lion's Head Handles, Anthemia, Leaves, Marked, J.W. Fiske, c.1875, 65 In. ....*illus* 4000
Urn, Greek Revival Style, Ram's Head Lug, Removable Lid, White Stone, 38 In., Pair.......... 702
Urn, Leafy Scrolled Handles, Lobed Body, Cast Iron, 1800s, 21 x 31 x 22 In., Pair 900
Urn, Lion Masks, Square Base, Gold Painted, Cast Iron, 41 ½ x 39 ½ In. ....*illus* 688
Urn, Marble, Cream, Gourd, Square Base, 12 x 8 ½ In. 615

GAUDY DUTCH

Gaudy Dutch pottery was made in England for the American market from about 1810 to 1820. It is a white earthenware with Imari-style decorations of red, blue, green, yellow, and black. Only sixteen patterns of Gaudy Dutch were made: Butterfly, Carnation, Dahlia, Double Rose, Dove, Grape, Leaf, Oyster, Primrose, Single Rose, Strawflower, Sunflower, Urn, War Bonnet, Zinnia, and No Name. Other similar wares are called Gaudy Ironstone and Gaudy Welsh.

Grape pattern
1810–1820

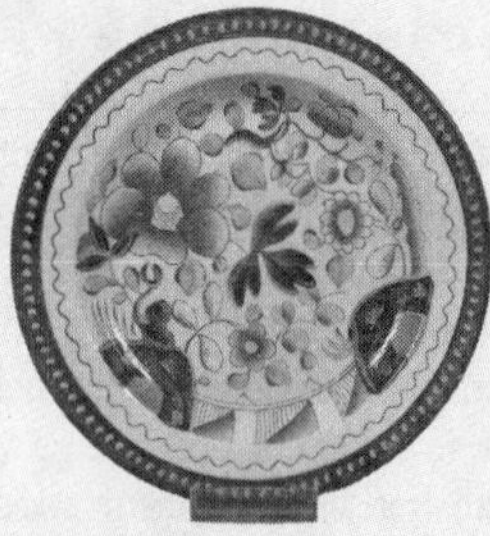

Single Rose pattern
1810–1820

War Bonnet pattern
1810–1820

Garden, Figure, Victory, Pedestal Stand, Cast Iron, 61 x 91 ½ x 19 ½ In.
$1,300

Neal Auction Company

Garden, Fountain, 3 Tiers, Flower Top, 2 Birds Surrounding, Cement, 55 In.
$130

Bunch Auctions

Garden, Fountain, Cupid, Shell Bowl On Head, Dolphin Bracket, Bronze, 60 x 25 In., 2 Piece
$1,521

Thomaston Place Auction Galleries

Garden, Fountain, Putti, Seated, Fish Holding Nozzle, c.1900, 34 In.
$720

Garth's Auctioneers & Appraisers

Garden, Hitching Post, Horse Head, Twisted & Leafy Post, Octagonal Base, Iron, 67 ½ In.
$767

Copake Auctions

Garden, Hitching Post, Jockey, Racing Silks, Yellow, Black, Old Paint, Iron, c.1900, 46 In.
$900

Garth's Auctioneers & Appraisers

Garden, Hitching Post, Jockey, Square Plinth Base, Cast Iron, 1800s, 46 x 22 x 20 In.
$1,200

Neal Auction Company

Garden, Sprinkler, Alligator, Cast Iron, Painted, c.1920s, 10 ½ x 8 ½ In.
$148

Copake Auctions

G

Garden, Sundial, Golfer, Bronze, Stamped Gorham Foundry, E.E. Codman, 18 x 12 ½ In.
$4,320

CRN Auctions

Garden, Sundial, Metal, Mounted, Carved, Octagonal, Stone Base, 39 x 15 ½ x 15 ½ In.
$492

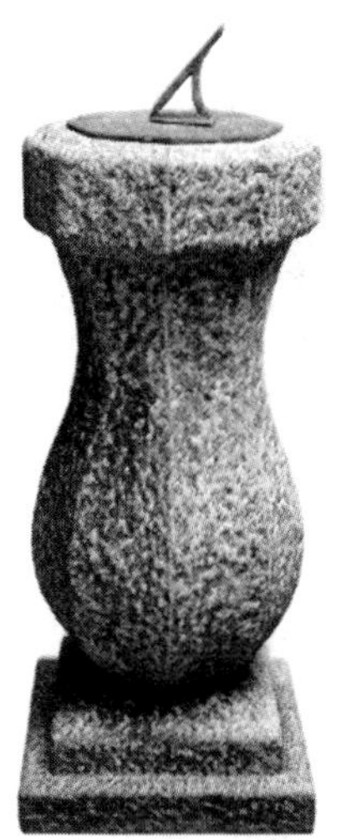

Stair Galleries

Garden, Sundial, Sphere Shape, Atlas, Copper Floral, Faux Verdigris Finish, Iron, 28 x 16 In.
$367

Thomaston Place Auction Galleries

Garden, Urn, 2 Handles, Traces Of Green Paint, Iron, 18 ¾ x 26 ½ x 15 ¾ In.
$338

Skinner, Inc.

TIP

Some types of stone and metal remain free of organic stains if they're left in partial sunlight and heat, but not if in deep shade.

Garden, Urn, 2 Scrolled Handles, Flared Rim, Mounted, Base, Iron, 30 x 29 In., Pair
$489

Stevens Auction Co.

Garden, Urn, Continental, Egg & Dart Rim, Lobed, Plinth Base, Iron, 1800s, 47 ½ x 43 ½ In.
$4,750

Neal Auction Company

Garden, Urn, Egg & Dart Rim, Lion's Head Handles, Anthemia, Leaves, Marked, J.W. Fiske, c.1875, 65 In.
$4,000

New Orleans Auction Galleries

Garden, Urn, Lion Masks, Square Base, Gold Painted, Cast Iron, 41 ½ x 39 ½ In.
$688

Kamelot Auctions

Gaudy Dutch, Cup & Saucer, Single Rose, Green & Yellow Leaves, Saucer 5 ½ In.
$106

Conestoga Auction Company

Bowl, Double Rose, Multicolor, Flowers, Hand Painted, 1810s, 6 In. 129
Coffeepot, Lid, Single Rose, Green & Yellow Leaves, 12 In. 767
Cup & Saucer, Single Rose, Green & Yellow Leaves, Saucer 5 ½ In. .... *illus* 106
Plate, Carnation, Red, Blue, Green & Yellow Leaves, 8 ⅜ In. 325
Plate, Double Rose, Soft Paste, 8 In. .... *illus* 59
Plate, Dove, Green & Yellow Leaves, 8 ⅜ In. .... *illus* 266
Plate, Primrose, Blue & Green Leaves, Impressed Riley, 8 ⅜ In. 325
Plate, Single Rose, Green & Yellow Leaves, Impressed Riley, 10 In. .... *illus* 236
Plate, Soup, Carnation, Red, White, Blue, 10 In. .... *illus* 708
Plate, Strawflower, Multicolor, Hand Painted, Floral, John & Richard Riley, 1810s, 10 In. *illus* 410
Plate, Sunflower, Green & Yellow Leaves, 8 ¼ In. .... *illus* 325
Plate, War Bonnet, Orange Flowers, Blue Leaves, Flat Rim, 9 ¾ In. .... *illus* 472
Teapot, Carnation, War Bonnet, Squat, Curved Handle, 7 x 11 x 6 ½ In. 2160

GAUDY IRONSTONE

Gaudy ironstone is the collector's name for the ironstone wares with the bright patterns similar to Gaudy Dutch. It was made in England for the American market after 1850. There may be other examples found in the listing for Ironstone or under the name of the ceramic factory.

Bowl, Chrysanthemum, Copper Luster & Flow Blue, Copper Luster Band, 7 ⅝ In. 55
Platter, Meat, Flowers, Butterfly, Blue, Red, Gold Flashing, 16 ½ In. 100
Tureen, Sauce, Lid, Flower Shape Finial, Flowers, Undertray, c.1840, 6 ¼ In. .... *illus* 120

GAUDY WELSH

Gaudy Welsh is an Imari-decorated earthenware with red, blue, green, and gold decorations. Most Gaudy Welsh was made in England for the American market. It was made from 1820 to about 1860.

Cup & Saucer, Flower Basket Pattern 85
Plate, Oyster, Blue, Orange, Brown, White Background, Allertons, 10 In. 204

GEISHA GIRL

Geisha girl porcelain was made for export in the late nineteenth century in Japan. It was an inexpensive porcelain often sold in dime stores or used as free premiums. Pieces are sometimes marked with the name of a store. Japanese ladies in kimonos are pictured on the dishes. There are over 125 recorded patterns. Borders of red, blue, green, gold, brown, or several of these colors were used. Modern reproductions are being made.

Bowl, 2 Geisha In Garden, Footed, Scalloped Edge, 8 x 4 In. 15
Bowl, 4 Geisha, Dancing, Flute, Cobalt Blue Border, Handle, 7 x 2 In. 25
Hatpin Holder, 3 Geisha, Fan, Rust Border, Gold Trim, 4 x 2 ½ In. 19
Mirror, Hand, Geisha Lying In Garden, Green, Faux Jade Handle, 5 In. 40
Vase, 2 Geisha In Flower Garden, Brown Trim Top & Bottom, 3 x 2 In. 14

GENE AUTRY

Gene Autry was born in 1907. He began his career as the "Singing Cowboy" in 1928. His first movie appearance was in 1934, his last in 1958. His likeness and that of the Wonder Horse, Champion, were used on toys, books, lunch boxes, and advertisements.

Book, Gene Autry & Ghost Riders, Whitman Publishing, Hardcover, 282 Pages, 1955, 7 x 5 In. 27
Comic Book, Dell Comics, Vol. 1 No. 14, 1948 300
Photograph, Gene, Waving Hat, Sepia, Signed, Porter Studio, 5 ¾ x 3 In. 195
Songbook, Country Songs & Mountain Ballads, 96 Pages, 1938, 12 x 9 In. 15

Gaudy Dutch, Plate, Double Rose, Soft Paste, 8 In.
$59

Conestoga Auction Company

Gaudy Dutch, Plate, Dove, Green & Yellow Leaves, 8 ⅜ In.
$266

Conestoga Auction Company

Gaudy Dutch, Plate, Single Rose, Green & Yellow Leaves, Impressed Riley, 10 In.
$236

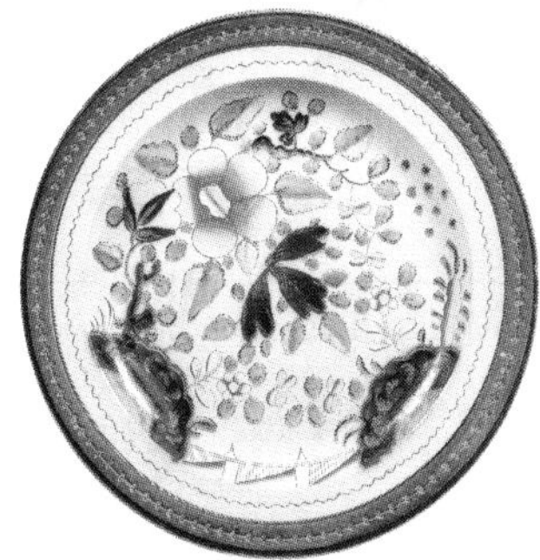

Conestoga Auction Company

TIP

If garage windows are painted, burglars won't be able to tell if cars are home or not. Use translucent paint to get light in the closed garage.

G

Gaudy Dutch, Plate, Soup, Carnation, Red, White, Blue, 10 In.
$708

Conestoga Auction Company

Gaudy Dutch, Plate, Strawflower, Multicolor, Hand Painted, Floral, John & Richard Riley, 1810s, 10 In.
$410

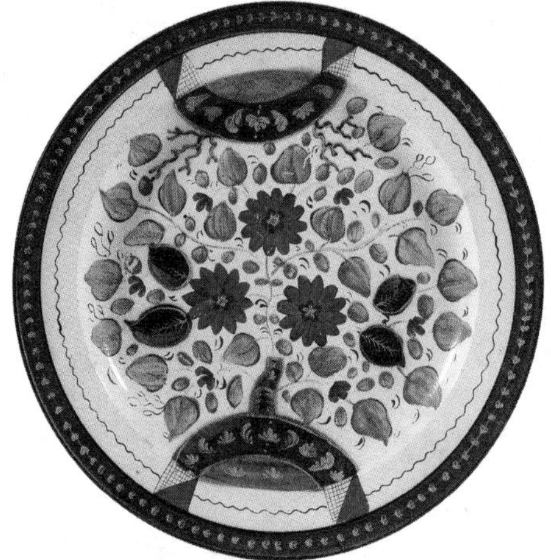

Jeffrey S. Evans & Associates

Gaudy Dutch, Plate, Sunflower, Green & Yellow Leaves, 8 ¼ In.
$325

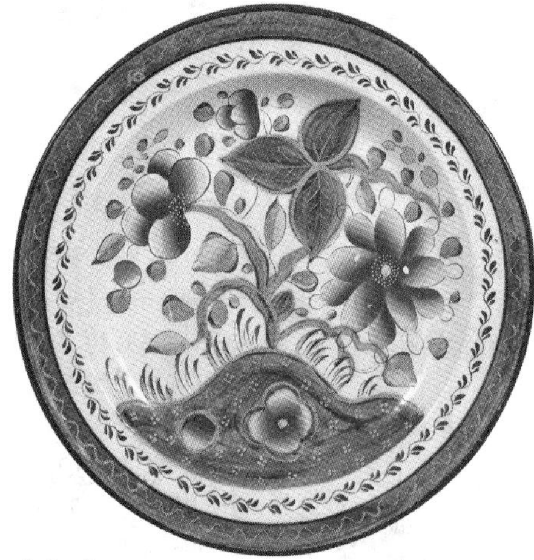

Conestoga Auction Company

Gaudy Dutch, Plate, War Bonnet, Orange Flowers, Blue Leaves, Flat Rim, 9 ¾ In.
$472

Conestoga Auction Company

Prevent Chipping

Use paper plates between your china plates to help prevent chipping.

Gaudy Ironstone, Tureen, Sauce, Lid, Flower Shape Finial, Flowers, Undertray, c.1840, 6 ¼ In.
$120

Eldred's

Glass-Art, Dresser Box, Hinged Lid, Swirled Mold, Flowers, Gold Trim, Victorian, 4 x 7 In.
$158

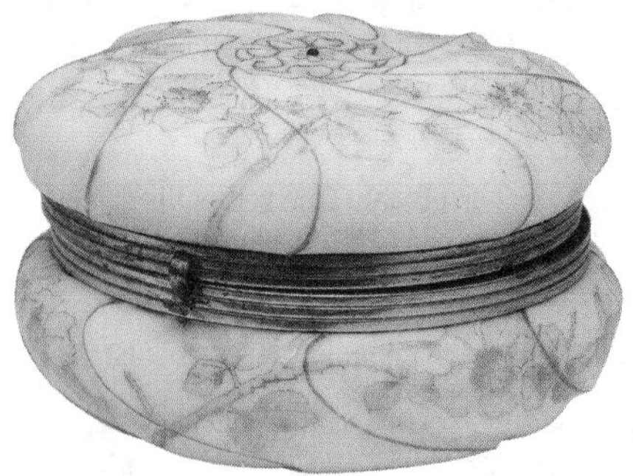

Soulis Auctions

Toy, Repeating Cap Pistol, Jr. Model, Box, 6 ½ In. 208
Wristwatch, Six-Shooter, Fires 120 Shots A Minute, Photo, Box, 1948, 6 ½ In. 130

GIBSON GIRL

Gibson Girl black-and-blue decorated plates were made in the early 1900s. Twenty-four different 10 ½-inch plates were made by the Royal Doulton pottery at Lambeth, England. These pictured scenes from the book *A Widow and Her Friends* by Charles Dana Gibson. Another set of twelve 9-inch plates featuring pictures of the heads of Gibson Girls had all-blue decoration. Many other items also pictured the famous Gibson Girl.

Box, Burnt Wood, Profile, Red Scarf In Hair, Cherries, 6 ½ x 6 ½ x 2 In. 100
Box, Dresser, Portrait, Pink Flowers, Blue & Cream, Sea Foam Mold, Nakara, 8 In. 10800
Cake Plate, Portrait, Peach & White, Iridescent Leaves, Marked, R.S. Prussia, 10 In. 575
Pin, Bust, Flowers On Her Shoulders, Shell Cameo, Silver, 1 ⅞ In. 195
Plate, She Is Disturbed By A Vision Which Appears, c.1901, 10 ½ In. 33
Plate, She Looks For Relief Among Some Of The Old Ones, c.1902, 10 ½ In. 43
Plate, They Take A Morning Run, Blue & Black Border, c.1904, 10 ½ In. 25
Tin, Gibson Girl Cigarettes, Girl, Blue Evening Dress, Lithographed, 4 x 3 x 1 In. 42

GIRL SCOUT

Girl Scout collectors search for anything pertaining to the Girl Scouts, including uniforms, publications, and old cookie boxes. The Girl Scout movement started in 1912, two years after the Boy Scouts. It began under Juliette Gordon Low of Savannah, Georgia. The first Girl Scout cookies were sold in 1928.

Booklet, Uniforms, Girl, Flags, Insignia, Handbooks, c.1955, 15 Pages 60
Doll, Green Uniform, Platinum Blond Hair, Green Hat, Terri Lee, c.1951, 16 In. 230
Flashlight, Orange & Green, G S In Clover, 1970s, 6 In. 20
Hat, Dark Green, Badge, 1950s, Size 22 30
Utensil Kit, Fork, Knife, Spoon, Camping, Green Case, 1953, 8 x 3 In. 57

GLASS-ART

Art glass means any of the many forms of glassware made during the late nineteenth or early twentieth century. These wares were expensive when they were first made and production was limited. Art glass is not the typical commercial glass that was made in large quantities, and most of the art glass was produced by hand methods. Later twentieth-century glass is listed under Glass-Contemporary, Glass-Midcentury, or Glass-Venetian. Even more art glass may be found in categories such as Burmese, Cameo Glass, Tiffany, and other factory names.

Bowl, Graduated Green Body, Footed, 4 x 12 In. 228
Centerpiece, Amber, Silver & Gold Enamel, Acorns, 4 Gilt Feet, 6 ½ x 10 x 4 In. 254
Compote, Rolled-Over Rim, Twisted Stem, Gold Iridescent, 1900s, 5 x 5 x 3 In. 82
Creamer, White Opalescent, Flowers, Pedestal Base, 4 In. 70
Decanter, Internal Cranberry, Clear Exterior, Art Deco Shape, Stopper, 10 In. 92
Dish, Quatrefoil, Acid Etched, Frosted, Floral, Brass Base, 1910s, 3 ⅝ x 8 x 12 In. 129
Dresser Box, Hinged Lid, Swirled Mold, Flowers, Gold Trim, Victorian, 4 x 7 In. *illus* 158
Epergne, 4 Lilies, Green Opalescent, Applied Rigaree, Victorian, 22 x 10 In. 150
Epergne, 4 Trumpet Shape Vases, Scalloped Rim, Silver Plate Base, 12 x 9 In. *illus* 240
Epergne, 7 Lilies, Cranberry, Vaseline, Opalescent, 23 In. 600
Epergne, Cranberry, 2 Candy Cane Hooks, 2 Hanging Baskets, 15 x 9 In. *illus* 150
Jug, Claret, Parrot, Blue, Yellow, Gilt Metal, Hinged Lid, Stopper, Continental, 9 In. *illus* 375
Lamp, Modern Style, Classic Shape Shade, Italy, 22 ½ x 12 In. 288
Sculpture, Female Head, Windblown Hair, Yellow, Mounted, Square Base, 7 x 6 In. 142
Sculpture, Large Blue Mask, Signed, Mats Jonasson, 12 x 10 In. *illus* 640
Tankard, Amethyst, Enamel, Flowers, Frosted Bulbous Base, 12 ½ In. 24

Glass-Art, Epergne, 4 Trumpet Shape Vases, Scalloped Rim, Silver Plate Base, 12 x 9 In.
$240

Woody Auctions

Glass-Art, Epergne, Cranberry, 2 Candy Cane Hooks, 2 Hanging Baskets, 15 x 9 In.
$150

Woody Auctions

Glass-Art, Jug, Claret, Parrot, Blue, Yellow, Gilt Metal, Hinged Lid, Stopper, Continental, 9 In.
$375

Neal Auction Company

Glass-Art, Sculpture, Large Blue Mask, Signed, Mats Jonasson, 12 x 10 In.
$640

Neal Auction Company

Glass-Art, Vase, Art Nouveau, Oval, Mottled Orange, Iridescent, Franz Hofstotter, c.1905, 4 ½ In.
$1,102

Clars Auction Gallery

Glass-Art, Vase, Topaz, Iridescent, Silver, Iris, Early 1900s, 10 In.
$1,020

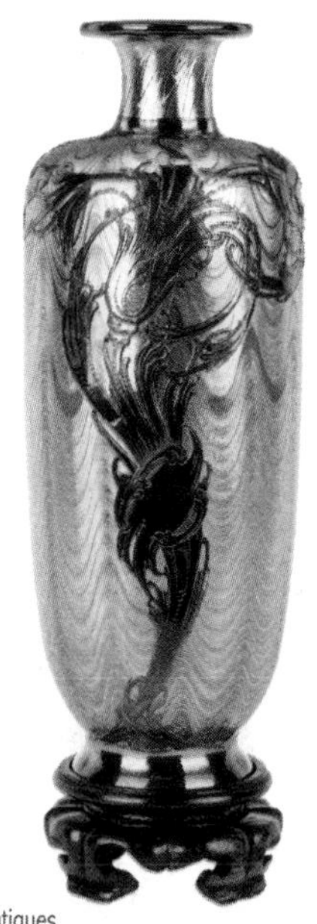

Case Antiques

Vase, Art Nouveau, Oval, Mottled Orange, Iridescent, Franz Hofstotter, c.1905, 4 ½ In. ....*illus* 1102
Vase, Brown, Iridescent, Pinched Neck, Flutter Rim, Footed, Dugan, 8 In. 71
Vase, Claritas, Black, White, Controlled Bubble, Timo Sarpaneva, 7 ¾ x 4 ½ In., Pair 510
Vase, Cylindrical, White Opaque, Cherub, Painted, c.1910, 12 ¾ In., Pair 150
Vase, Green Pulled Feather, Sunset Color Field, Ribbed, 8 ½ In. 230
Vase, Loetz Style, Green, Silver Plate Collar Rim, 6 In., Pair 240
Vase, Orange, Iridescent, Red Background, Oil Spots, Loetz Style, 10 In. 3000
Vase, Pink, Green, White, Mottled Exterior, White Interior, Mica, Scalloped Rim, 14 ½ In. 60
Vase, Red Orange, Bulbous, Iridescent, Ruffled Rim, Dark Blue, Pinched Base, 12 ¾ x 6 In. 242
Vase, Ruby Ground, Translucent, Silver Overlay, Flower, Leaves, 3 ½ In. 115
Vase, Squat, Red, Purple, White, Amber, Footed, Thick Walled, c.1925, 8 x 11 ½ In. 158
Vase, Topaz, Iridescent, Silver, Iris, Early 1900s, 10 In. ....*illus* 1020

GLASS-BLOWN

Blown glass was formed by forcing air through a rod into molten glass. Early glass and some forms of art glass were hand blown. Other types of glass were molded or pressed.

Epergne, Trumpet Shape, Flared Rim, Etched, Flowers, Footed Bowl, Late 1800s, 2 Parts, 15 In. 74
Flask, Bulbous Body, Short Neck, Molded Rim, Light Aqua, 10 In. 277
Goblet, Clear, Hand Engraved, Whaling Scene, Long Stem, Saucer Shape Foot, 1800s, 15 x 6 In. 1112
Jar, Cylindrical, Blue Bands, Lid & Finial, 1800s, 9 In. 492
Jug, Claret, Art Nouveau, Silver Mounted, Handle, Pontil, Heath & Middleton, England, 1899, 5 x 9 In. 106
Leech Jar, Yellow Topaz, Bulbous, Flared Lip, Pontil, 1850-70, 2 ⅜ In. 108
Pan, Amber, Folded Rim, Blown Pontil, 1810s, 2 x 8 In. 500
Sugar, Dome Lid, Cobalt Blue, Footed, Flame Finial, Penn., c.1785, 6 ½ In. 360
Vase, Nick Del Matto, Pulled Feather, Blue Green, Iridescent, 5 ¾ x 3 ¾ In. 59
Vase, This Garden, Floral, Signed, Chris Heilman, 7 ⅝ In. 489
Whimsy, Balloon Shape, Glass, Pontil, Stopper, Folded Rim, Flared Foot, 8 x 4 In., 2 Piece 150

GLASS-BOHEMIAN

Bohemian glass is an ornate overlay or flashed glass made during the Victorian era. It has been reproduced in Bohemia, which is now a part of the Czech Republic. Glass made from 1875 to 1900 is preferred by collectors.

Adolf Beckert
c.1914–1920s

Gräflich Schaffgotsch'sche
Josephinenhutte
c.1890

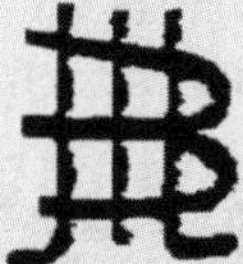

J. & L. Lobmeyr
1860+

Chalice, Green, Portrait Medallions, Flower, Globular, Crenellated Rim, 12 In. 381
Decanter, Cranberry, Gilt, Cone Shape Stopper, Persian Style, 18 In. 1375
Decanter, Flowers, Engraved, Silver Overlay, Square, Collar, Stopper, 1885, 7 x 5 ¾ In. 117
Decanter, Gourd, White Overlay, Enamel, Flowers, Stoppers, 9 ½ In., Pair ....*illus* 108
Goblet, Etched, Hand Blown, Green, 4 Yellow Panels, Wildlife Scene, 7 x 3 ¾ In. 124
Jar, Lid, Amber Panel, Engraved, Flowers, 13 In. ....*illus* 84
Pitcher, Water, Enamel & Gilt, Flower, Cylindrical Neck, Handle, c.1900, 11 ½ In. 129
Pokal, Lid, Ruby Flashed, Engraved, Deer, Castle & Scroll, 17 In., Pair ....*illus* 350
Tumbler, Cranberry Medallions, Frosted, Clear Base, Gold Enamel Highlights, 5 ½ In. ..*illus* 100
Vase, 6 Alternating Facet-Cut Panels, Scalloped Rim, Floral, Green, White, 15 In., Pair ...*illus* 832
Vase, Amber Flashed, Engraved Deer, Castle, Scroll & Lattice, 15 x 8 In., Pair 175
Vase, Cranberry Overlay, Arched Panels, Gold Stencil, c.1900, 10 ¾ In. ....*illus* 250
Vase, Elongated Urn, Woman's Portrait, Gilt Handles, Step Foot, 1860s, 16 In. ....*illus* 164
Vase, Gilt, Cranberry Glass, White Overlay, Portrait, Handles, Moser Style, 8 x 6 In, Pair 600
Vase, Gilt, Enameled, Faceted Shape, Flowers, 20 x 4 In., Pair 250
Wine, Roemer Shape, Dark Green, Conical Feet, Early 1800s, 4 ¾ In., 5 Piece ....*illus* 644

Glass-Bohemian, Decanter, Gourd, White Overlay, Enamel, Flowers, Stoppers, 9 ½ In., Pair
$108

Woody Auctions

Glass-Bohemian, Jar, Lid, Amber Panel, Engraved, Flowers, 13 In.
$84

Woody Auctions

Glass-Bohemian, Pokal, Lid, Ruby Flashed, Engraved, Deer, Castle & Scroll, 17 In., Pair
$350

Woody Auctions

Glass-Bohemian, Tumbler, Cranberry Medallions, Frosted, Clear Base, Gold Enamel Highlights, 5 ½ In.
$100

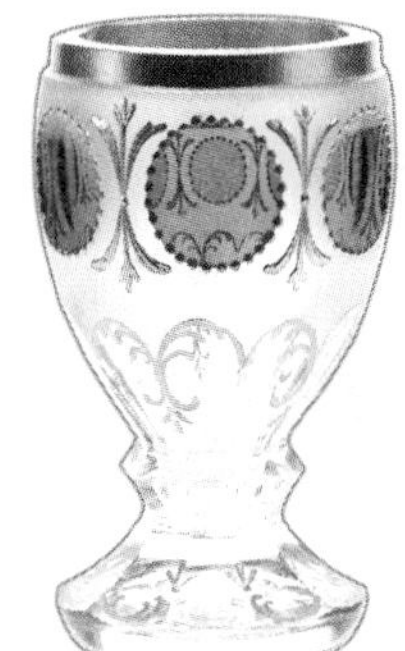

Woody Auctions

Glass-Bohemian, Vase, 6 Alternating Facet-Cut Panels, Scalloped Rim, Floral, Green, White, 15 In., Pair
$832

Cowan's Auctions

Glass-Bohemian, Vase, Cranberry Overlay, Arched Panels, Gold Stencil, c.1900, 10 ¾ In.
$250

Woody Auctions

Glass-Bohemian, Vase, Elongated Urn, Woman's Portrait, Gilt Handles, Step Foot, 1860s, 16 In.
$164

Jeffrey S. Evans & Associates

Glass-Bohemian, Wine, Roemer Shape, Dark Green, Conical Feet, Early 1800s, 4 ¾ In., 5 Piece
$644

Thomaston Place Auction Galleries

Glass-Contemporary, Bowl, Stacked, Persian, Blue, Carmine Edges, Dale Chihuly, 12 x 21 In., 9 Piece Set
$20,000

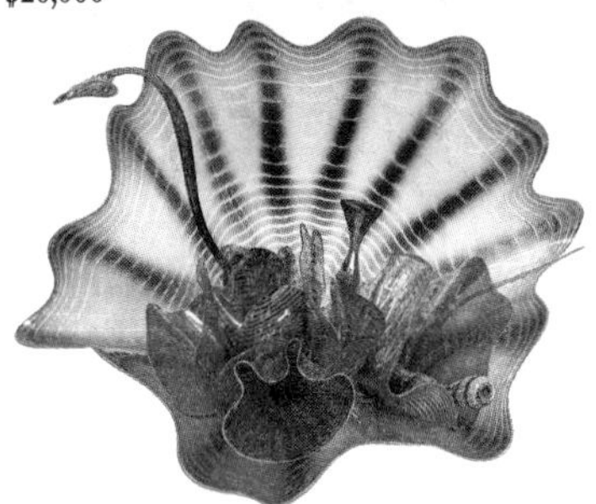

New Orleans Auction Galleries

Glass-Contemporary, Sculpture, Blue Brimstone, Blown, Fused, Pedestal Top, Caleb Nichols, 2009, 17 x 19 x 6 In.
$2,106

Thomaston Place Auction Galleries

Glass-Contemporary, Sculpture, Emergence, Cut & Polished, D. Labino, 1984, 8 ¼ In.
$2,500

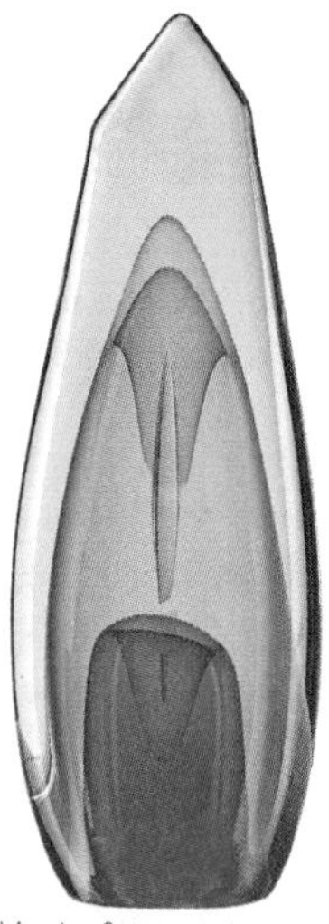

Rago Arts and Auction Center

Glass-Contemporary, Sculpture, Multicolor Mermaid, Gilt Turtle, Frosted Seabed, Robert Wyland, 8 ½ x 15 In.
$1,417

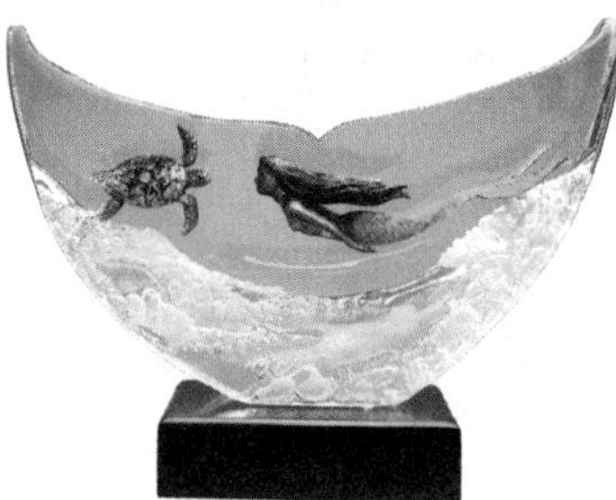

Clars Auction Gallery

Glass-Contemporary, Sculpture, Organic Shape, Ruffled, Multicolor, Dale Chihuly, 1983, 15 x 21 In.
$3,690

Clars Auction Gallery

Glass-Contemporary, Sculpture, Standing Stone, Blown, William Morris, 1985, 34 x 15 In.
$7,500

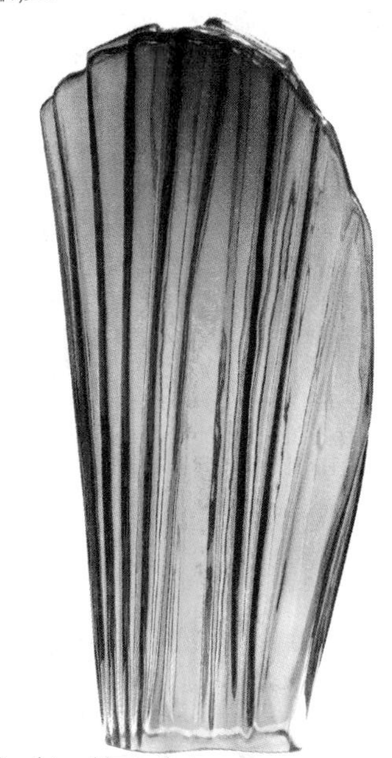

Rago Arts and Auction Center

Glass-Contemporary, Vase, Blue, Iridescent, Lotton, 5 ½ In.
$185

Skinner, Inc.

Glass-Contemporary, Vase, Bulbous Body, Long Neck, Blown, Yellow, Gold, Amber, Mexico, 10 x 10 x 21 In.
$30

Charleston Estate Auctions

Glass-Contemporary, Vase, Bulbous Body, Short Neck, Holmegaard, Michael Bang, c.1970, 7 In.
$100

Freeman's Auctioneers & Appraisers

Glass-Contemporary, Vase, Dichroic, Signed, Peter Vanderlaan, 8 x 5 ½ In.
$115

Blackwell Auctions

GLASS-CONTEMPORARY

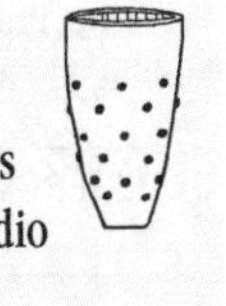

Glass-Contemporary includes pieces by glass artists working after 1970. Many of these pieces are free-form, one-of-a-kind sculptures. Paperweights by contemporary artists are listed in the Paperweight category. Earlier studio glass may be found listed under Glass-Midcentury or Glass-Venetian.

Bowl, Center, Clear & Frosted Red, Botanical Design, Tommie Rush, 8 ¾ x 21 x 17 ½ In. 380
Bowl, Fluted Rim, Round Base, Red, Yellow, Cohn-Stone Studios, 20 ¼ In. 201
Bowl, Stacked, Persian, Blue, Carmine Edges, Dale Chihuly, 12 x 21 In., 9 Piece Set ....*illus* 20000
Sculpture, Blue Brimstone, Blown, Fused, Pedestal Top, Caleb Nichols, 2009, 17 x 19 x 6 In. *illus* 2106
Sculpture, Blue, Triangular Top, Faceted, Ed Nesteruk, 5 ½ In. 172
Sculpture, Crimson, Seaform, Black Lip, Dale Chihuly, 1982, 7 x 12 In. 4305
Sculpture, Emergence, Cut & Polished, D. Labino, 1984, 8 ¼ In. ....*illus* 2500
Sculpture, Female, Crouching, Black, Base, Signed, L. Rosin, Late 1900s, 17 x 9 x 6 In. 390
Sculpture, Multicolor Mermaid, Gilt Turtle, Frosted Seabed, Robert Wyland, 8 ½ x 15 In. *illus* 1417
Sculpture, Nautilus Shell, Internal Anemone Canes, Cased, 2000, 5 In. 168
Sculpture, Organic Shape, Ruffled, Multicolor, Dale Chihuly, 1983, 15 x 21 In. ....*illus* 3690
Sculpture, Oval, Concave, Deep Red Glass, Pedestal, Louis Von Koelnau, 21 ½ x 26 In. 660
Sculpture, Pyramid, Electrified, Signed, Ray Howlett, 1988, 26 x 13 ½ In. 3245
Sculpture, Sea Anemone, 3 Parts, Hand Blown, Acid Etched, Robert Mickelsen, 2000, 13 x 6 In. 403
Sculpture, Standing Stone, Blown, William Morris, 1985, 34 x 15 In. ....*illus* 7500
Vase, Blue, Iridescent, Lotton, 5 ½ In. ....*illus* 185
Vase, Bulbous Body, Long Neck, Blown, Yellow, Gold, Amber, Mexico, 10 x 10 x 21 In. ......*illus* 30
Vase, Bulbous Body, Short Neck, Holmegaard, Michael Bang, c.1970, 7 In. ....*illus* 100
Vase, Bulbous, Coral, Flared Blue Rim, Thread Swirled, Daniel Lotton, 1990, 7 ¾ x 7 ½ In. 311
Vase, Bulbous, Lid, Chartreuse Matte, Iridescent Base, Edward Fields, 2003, 11 ½ In. 83
Vase, Butterscotch Ground, Pulled Feather Design, Orient & Flume, 8 ½ In. 192
Vase, Dichroic, Signed, Peter Vanderlaan, 8 x 5 ½ In. ....*illus* 115
Vase, Floral, Hanging Wisteria, Twisting Branches, Signed, Chris Heilman, 1996, 4 ½ x 5 In. . *illus* 345
Vase, Flower, Cylindrical, Orient & Flume, Signed, B. Sillars, 11 In. 194
Vase, Fluted, Ruffled Rim, Multicolor, Signed, James Nowak, 18 x 16 ½ In. ....*illus* 4313
Vase, Gold Ruby, Dogwood Flowers, Silver Blue Leaves, Daniel Lotton, 7 ½ In. ....*illus* 726
Vase, Lid, Applied Elements, Pulled Cane Handles, Round Base, Wes Hunting, 21 ½ In. 374
Vase, Mandarin Red, Expanded Rim, Tapering Body, Charles Lotton, 1990, 3 ½ x 4 ½ In. *illus* 102
Vase, Mottled Pink, Dark Purple Ground, Millefiori Canes, Monart, 5 ½ x 5 ¾ In. 270
Vase, Multicolor, Rolled Rim, Bulbous, Blown, William Morris, 1984, 14 In. ....*illus* 2952
Vase, Opalescent, Swirl, Bulbous, Mark Peiser, 1972, 4 In. 96
Vase, Oval, Purple Iridescent Rim, Gold Pulls, Signed, Charles Lotton, 1974, 8 ¾ In. ....*illus* 390
Vase, Petroglyph, Woman, Aventurine, William Morris, 1988, 18 In. .... *illus* 16250
Vase, Pink Pulled Feathers, Blue Iridescent, Molded Rim, Daniel Lotton, 1999, 4 x 7 ½ In. *illus* 311
Vase, Pulled Leaf Design, Gold Iridescent Interior, Ribbed Exterior, 13 In. 250
Vase, Rose Bowl Shape, Green, Interior Air Bubbles, Air Trap, 1969, 4 ½ x 3 ¾ In. 293
Vase, Square Ascension, Blown, Copper, Michael Glancy, 1982, 6 ¾ x 4 ½ In. ....*illus* 9375
Vase, Stromboli, Carved, Polished, Lino Tagliapietra, 2006, 19 In. ....*illus* 10000
Vase, Titan, Carved, Purple, Yellow Donut Shapes, Ethan Stern, 2004, 11 x 8 In. ....*illus* 2560
Vessel, Starlight Macchia Seaform, Blown, Dale Chihuly, 2004, 10 In. ....*illus* 3750

GLASS-CUT, *see Cut Glass category.*

GLASS-DEPRESSION, *see Depression Glass category.*

GLASS-MIDCENTURY

Glass-Midcentury refers to art glass made from the 1940s to the early 1970s. Some glass factories, such as Baccarat or Orrefors, are listed under their own categories. Earlier glass may be listed in the Glass-Art and Glass-Contemporary categories. Italian glass may be found in Glass-Venetian.

Bowl, Pezzati, Cased Glass, Multicolor Platelets, Anzolo Fuga, c.1960, 6 ¾ In. 1464

Glass-Contemporary, Vase, Floral, Hanging Wisteria, Twisting Branches, Signed, Chris Heilman, 1996, 4 ½ x 5 In.
$345

Blackwell Auctions

Glass-Contemporary, Vase, Fluted, Ruffled Rim, Multicolor, Signed, James Nowak, 18 x 16 ½ In.
$4,313

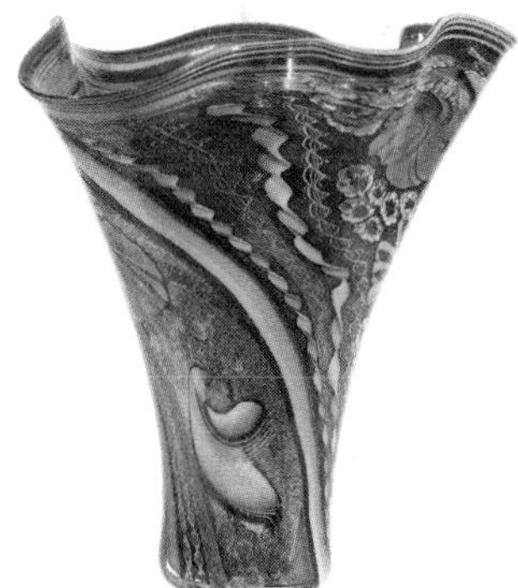

Blackwell Auctions

Glass-Contemporary, Vase, Gold Ruby, Dogwood Flowers, Silver Blue Leaves, Daniel Lotton, 7 ½ In.
$726

Humler & Nolan

This is an edited listing of current prices. Visit **Kovels.com** to check thousands of prices from previous years and sign up for free information on trends, tips, reproductions, marks, and more.

Glass-Contemporary, Vase, Mandarin Red, Expanded Rim, Tapering Body, Charles Lotton, 1990, 3 ½ x 4 ½ In.
$102

Soulis Auctions

Glass-Contemporary, Vase, Multicolor, Rolled Rim, Bulbous, Blown, William Morris, 1984, 14 In.
$2,952

Brunk Auctions

Glass-Contemporary, Vase, Oval, Purple Iridescent Rim, Gold Pulls, Signed, Charles Lotton, 1974, 8 ¾ In.
$390

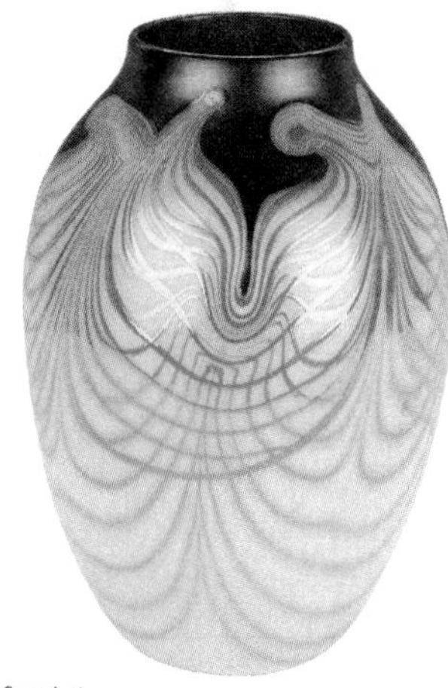

Case Antiques

Figurine, Praying Child, Mottled Green, Signed, Edris Eckhardt, 6 ½ In. 363
Mobile, 34 Fused Glass Panels, Copper, Higgins, c.1950, 46 x 22 x 19 In. 2600

GLASS-PRESSED, *see Pressed Glass category.*

GLASS-VENETIAN

Venetian glass has been made near Venice, Italy, since the thirteenth century. Thin, colored glass with applied decoration is favored, although many other types have been made. Collectors have recently become interested in the Art Deco, 1950s, and contemporary designs. Glass was made on the Venetian island of Murano from 1291. The output dwindled in the late seventeenth century but began to flourish again in the 1850s. Some of the old techniques of glassmaking were revived, and firms today make traditional designs and original modern glass. Since 1981, the name *Murano* may be used only on glass made on Murano Island. Other pieces of Italian glass may be found in the Glass-Contemporary and Glass-Midcentury categories of this book.

Bowl, Black, Center Decoration, Yalos Casa, 16 x 9 ½ x 5 ½ In. 38
Bowl, Pearl & Teal, Iridescent, Label, Murano, 19 x 19 x 4 In. 201
Bowl, Seashell, Ribbed, Multicolor, Murano, Late 1900s, 3 x 7 x 4 In. .... *illus* 136
Candlestick, Tree Shape, Sphere, Cylindrical Nozzle, Lobed Foot, Archimede Seguso, 18 In. 308
Chandelier, 6-Light, Blue, Clear Glass, Floral Cups, Daffodil, 32 x 28 In. 177
Chandelier, Leaf Fixture, Clear, Brass Chain, Camer Murano, 24 x 19 In. .... *illus* 594
Charger, Aquarium, Tropical Fish, Sky Blue, Stefano Toso, 16 In. 1338
Charger, Incalmo, 3 Way, Mottled Gold, Pink, Clear Glass, Striped Rim, Tapio Wirkkala, 17 In. 540
Compote, Swan Form Handles, Yellow, Circular Base, Murano, 9 ¼ In. 98
Cookie Jar, Cockatiel, Ruby Art Glass, Silvered Brass Head, Murano, Italy, 12 x 7 In. 540
Ewer, Wide Spout, Curved Handle, 1900s, 10 In., Pair 250
Figurine, Bird, Cenedese Style, Green Tones, 6 ½ x 4 In. .... *illus* 313
Figurine, Fisherman, Green, Gilt, Seguso, Flavio Puli, 1936, 10 x 6 ½ In. .... *illus* 960
Figurine, Pulcino, Bird, Ribbed Blue Body, Millefiori Eyes, Vistosi Murano, 6 ¾ x 4 x 3 In. *illus* 7200
Goblet, Green, Cabochon, Circular Base, 5 ⅝ In., 10 Piece 563
Mirror, Octagonal, Twisted, Flowers, Etched Accent, Double Frame, 1900s, 40 x 30 In. 767
Paperweight, Millefiori, Sphere, Murano, c.1950, 2 ½ x 2 ¾ In. 431
Platter, Venini Murano, Green, Laura Diaz De Santillana, 1996, 15 x 17 ½ x 13 In. 775
Sconce, 8-Light, Wall, Sputnik Style, Murano, 29 x 29 x 10 In., Pair 938
Sculpture, 2 Acrobats, Balance On The Back Of Other, Oval Base, Clear, 30 In. 433
Sculpture, Bird, Orange, Textured, Bronze Legs, Vistosi Murano, 8 ¾ In. .... *illus* 4160
Sculpture, Duck, Pink Opaline Head, Clear Body, Pino Signoretto, Murano, 6 x 4 ½ x 13 ½ In. 375
Sculpture, Flamingo, Glass, Gilt Legs, Signed, Licio Zanetti, 1956, 33 In., Pair 762
Sculpture, Torso, Adonis, Nude, Black Glass Base, Murano, Dino Rosin, c.1950, 12 x 7 x 4 In. .. *illus* 615
Vase, Abstract Design, Blue, Green Grid Pattern, Seguso Viro, Murano, 14 x 6 In. .... *illus* 345
Vase, Alterno, Patchwork, Murrine, Glass, Ercole Barovier, 10 x 6 ½ In. .... *illus* 1950
Vase, Bulbous, Seguso, Sommerso, Maurizio Albarelli, 1998, 6 ½ In. .... *illus* 250
Vase, Cobalt Blue, Frosted, Millefiori, Signed, Rons Murano, 11 ¾ x 7 ½ In. 490
Vase, Green, Snake, Circular Base, Pulegoso, Napoleone Martinuzzi, c.1930, 16 x 9 In. 750
Vase, Oval, 3 Layers, Blue, Pale Green, Dark Green, Murano, Cesare Sent, 9 x 6 x 2 ½ In. 82
Vase, Oval, Green, Ribbed, Gold Flecks, Barovier & Toso, Murano, 11 ½ x 7 x 6 In. 406
Vase, Purple, Frosted, Murano, Alfredo Barbini, 13 x 11 ½ In. 688
Vase, Ritagli, Amethyst, Pearly Iridescent, Flower, Fulvio Bianconi, Venini, 11 x 9 ½ In. 2125
Vase, Spuma Di Mare, Metallic Inclusions, Ercole Barovier, c.1940, 10 x 5 In. 9000
Vase, Twin Spout, Multicolor, Dino Martens, c.1950, 15 ½ x 6 ½ x 6 In. .... *illus* 2000
Vase, White Bands, Blue Knop & Rim, Barovier & Toso, Murano, Italy, 1950s, 12 In. ....*illus* 600
Wedding Cup, Amethyst Glass, Gilt, Classical Scene, Murano, 1900s, 5 x 4 ⅞ x 2 ½ In. ..*illus* 199

GLASSES

Glasses for the eyes, or spectacles, were mentioned in a manuscript in 1289 and have been used ever since. The first eyeglasses with rigid side pieces were made in

Glass-Contemporary, Vase, Petroglyph, Woman, Aventurine, William Morris, 1988, 18 In.
$16,250

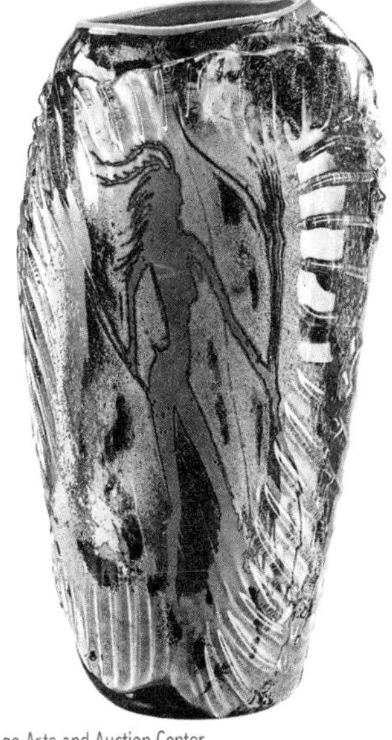

Rago Arts and Auction Center

Glass-Contemporary, Vase, Pink Pulled Feathers, Blue Iridescent, Molded Rim, Daniel Lotton, 1999, 4 x 7 ½ In.
$311

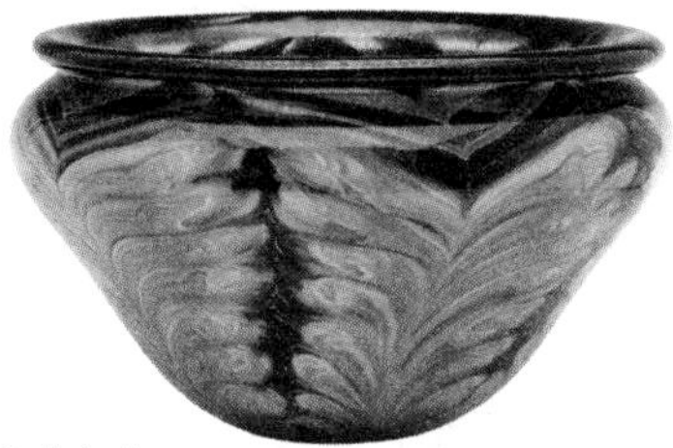

Soulis Auctions

Glass-Contemporary, Vase, Square Ascension, Blown, Copper, Michael Glancy, 1982, 6 ¾ x 4 ½ In.
$9,375

Rago Arts and Auction Center

Glass-Contemporary, Vase, Stromboli, Carved, Polished, Lino Tagliapietra, 2006, 19 In.
$10,000

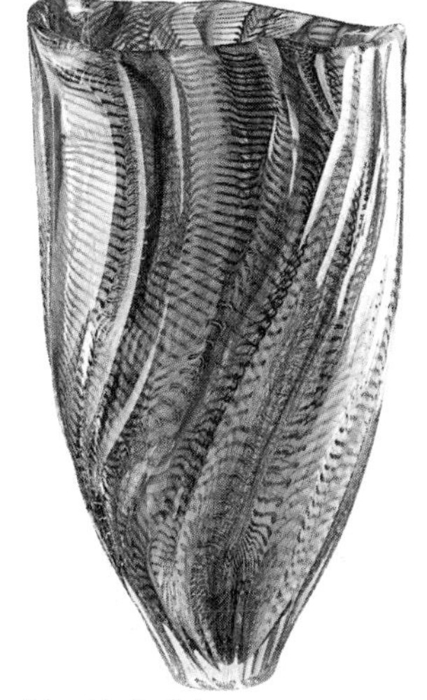

Rago Arts and Auction Center

Glass-Contemporary, Vase, Titan, Carved, Purple, Yellow Donut Shapes, Ethan Stern, 2004, 11 x 8 In.
$2,560

Rago Arts and Auction Center

Glass-Contemporary, Vessel, Starlight Macchia Seaform, Blown, Dale Chihuly, 2004, 10 In.
$3,750

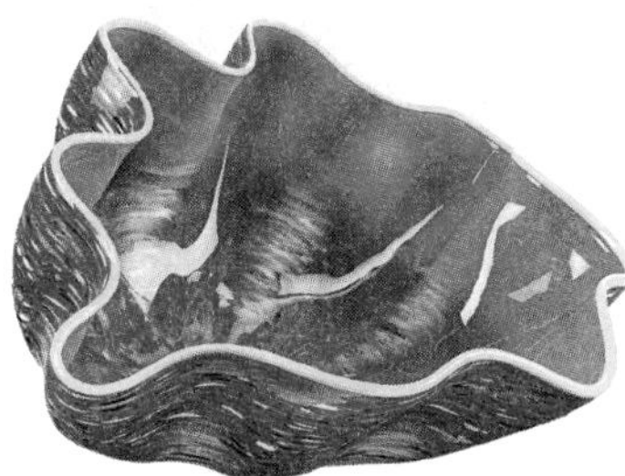

Rago Arts and Auction Center

Glass-Venetian, Bowl, Seashell, Ribbed, Multicolor, Murano, Late 1900s, 3 x 7 x 4 In.
$136

Soulis Auctions

Glass-Venetian, Chandelier, Leaf Fixture, Clear, Brass Chain, Camer Murano, 24 x 19 In.
$594

Hudson Valley Auctions

Ultraviolet

To tell where your old European glass was made, use an ultraviolet (black) light. The short explanation is that under the light, Bohemian glass is yellow, yellow-green, green, or orange; Venetian glass is pale yellow to yellow-green; and lead crystal is white-yellow to white.

Glass-Venetian, Figurine, Bird, Cenedese Style, Green Tones, 6 ½ x 4 In.
$313

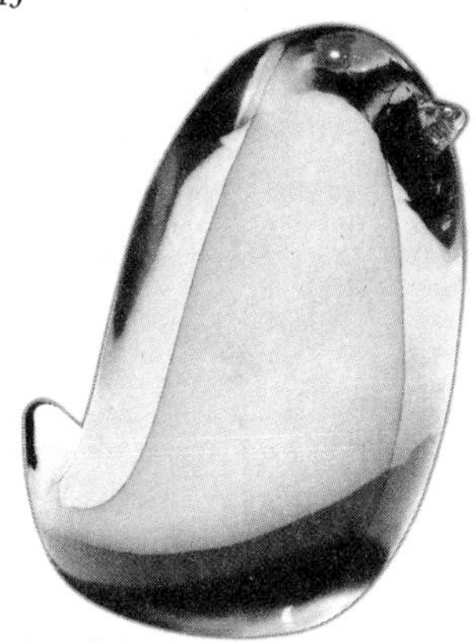

Palm Beach Modern Auctions

Glass-Venetian, Figurine, Fisherman, Green, Gilt, Seguso, Flavio Puli, 1936, 10 x 6 ½ In.
$960

Ripley Auctions

Glass-Venetian, Figurine, Pulcino, Bird, Ribbed Blue Body, Millefiori Eyes, Vistosi Murano, 6 ¾ x 4 x 3 In.
$7,200

Morphy Auctions

Glass-Venetian, Sculpture, Bird, Orange, Textured, Bronze Legs, Vistosi Murano, 8 ¾ In.
$4,160

Morphy Auctions

Glass-Venetian, Sculpture, Torso, Adonis, Nude, Black Glass Base, Murano, Dino Rosin, c.1950, 12 x 7 x 4 In.
$615

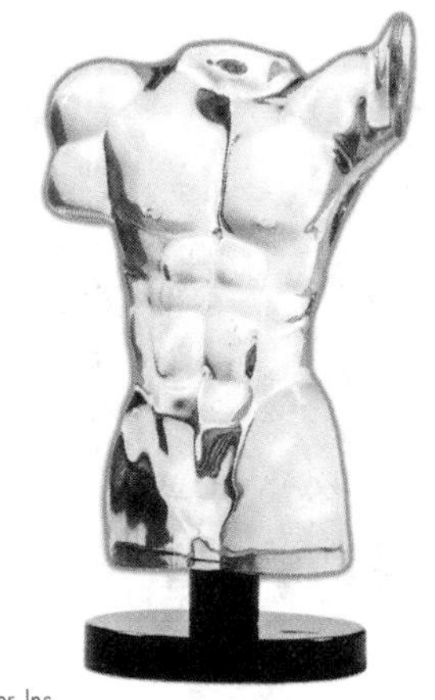

Skinner, Inc.

Glass-Venetian, Vase, Abstract Design, Blue, Green Grid Pattern, Seguso Viro, Murano, 14 x 6 In.
$345

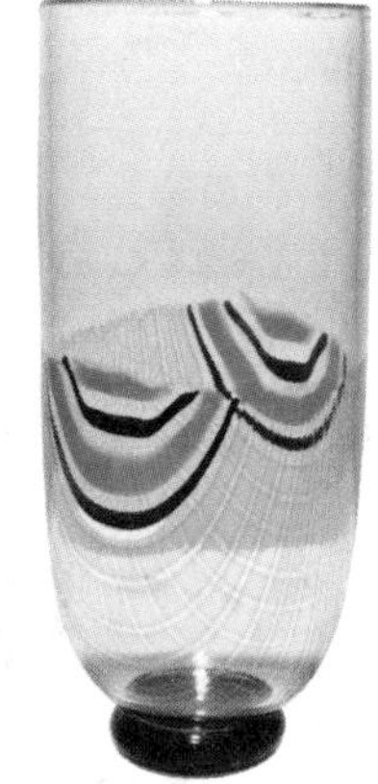

Palm Beach Modern Auctions

Glass-Venetian, Vase, Alterno, Patchwork, Murrine, Glass, Ercole Barovier, 10 x 6 ½ In.
$1,950

Treadway

Glass-Venetian, Vase, Bulbous, Seguso, Sommerso, Maurizio Albarelli, 1998, 6 ½ In.
$250

Freeman's Auctioneers & Appraisers

Glass-Venetian, Vase, Twin Spout, Multicolor, Dino Martens, c.1950, 15 ½ x 6 ½ x 6 In.
$2,000

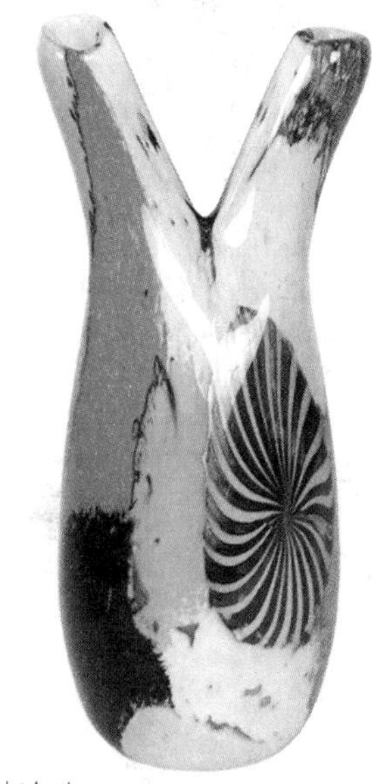

Kamelot Auctions

Glass-Venetian, Vase, White Bands, Blue Knop & Rim, Barovier & Toso, Murano, Italy, 1950s, 12 In.
$600

Eldred's

London in 1727. Bifocals were invented by Benjamin Franklin in 1785. Lorgnettes were popular in late Victorian times. Opera Glasses are listed in the Binoculars category.

Lorgnette, Gold Plate, Blue & White Enamel, Pendant, 1890s, 6 x 4 In. 165
Metal, Gold, Ful-Vue, Flex Wrap Temples, Shuron Optical, 1930s, 4 ½ In. 150
Octagonal Lenses, Rose Gold, Dr. Frank W. Limberg, Original Case, 1920s 96
Plastic, Black, Rounded Rectangle, Glass Lenses, 1950s, 4 ½ In. 20
Round, Yellow Lenses, Wire Frames, Case, J. Berris, Consulting Optician, MI 30
Sun, Cat's-Eye, Wraparound, Bifocal, Green Lenses, Gray Frames, Rhinestones, 1950s, 5 In. 62
Sun, Oval, Black Acrylic, Gray Lenses, Multicolor Chanel On Arms 779

GOEBEL

Goebel is the mark used by W. Goebel Porzellanfabrik of Oeslau, Germany, now Rodental, Germany. The company was founded by Franz Detleff Goebel and his son, William Goebel, in 1871. It was known as F&W Goebel. Slates, slate pencils, and marbles were made. Soon the company began making porcelain tableware and figurines. Hummel figurines were first made by Goebel in 1935. Since 2009 they have been made by another company. Goebel is still in business. Old pieces marked *Goebel Hummel* are listed under Hummel in this book.

Cookie Jar, Friar Tuck, Monk, Toes, Black Sandals, Robin Hood, 1960s, 7 x 9 In. 175
Creamer, Dutch Girl, Side-Glancing Eyes, Bulbous, Spout In Cap, 5 ¾ In. 13
Figurine, Dog, Boxer, Standing, Painted, Brown & White, Marked, 7 x 6 In. 25
Figurine, Gypsy Dancer, On Classical Sofa, Painted, 1930s, 6 ½ x 7 In. 224
Figurine, Nude Woman, Kneeling, White Glaze with Blond Hair, 13 In. 125
Figurine, Pelican, Label, L. Misic, 1984, 9 x 19 In. 35
Figurine, Pig's Head, Pink Glaze, Marked, 13 In. 266
Figurine, Westward Bound, Covered Wagon, Oxen, White Bisque, c.1970, 11 x 21 In. 138
Lamp, Perfume, Owl, On 2 Books, Glass Eyes, Electric, Marked, c.1930, 7 In. 25
Vase, Dog, Geometric, Brown & White, Art Deco Style, Marked, 1930s, 4 x 1 ½ In. 24

GOLDSCHEIDER

Goldscheider was founded by Friedrich Goldscheider in Vienna in 1885. The family left Vienna in 1938 and the factory was taken over by the Germans. Goldscheider started factories in England and in Trenton, New Jersey. They made figurines and other ceramics. The New Jersey factory started in 1940 as Goldscheider-U.S.A. In 1941 it became Goldscheider-Everlast Corporation. From 1947 to 1953 it was Goldcrest Ceramics Corporation. In 1950 the Vienna plant was returned to Mr. Goldscheider, but it closed in 1953. The Trenton, New Jersey, business, called Goldscheider of Vienna, is a wholesale importer.

Bust, Female, Curly Orange Hair, Green Shirt, Flower, c.1930, 8 In. .... *illus* 1169
Figurine, Girl Playing With Dog, Green Checked Dress, Bonnet, Art Deco, 8 In. 446
Figurine, Woman Dancing, Butterfly Costume, Red, Black, Blue, 8 In. 235
Sculpture, Woman, Dancer, Butterfly Girl, Wing-Like Sleeves, Lorenzl, c.1920, 18 In. .... *illus* 2091
Wall Plaque, Dachshund, Black, Burnt Orange Ground, Square, c.1915, 4 In. 125

GOLF, *see Sports category.*

GOOFUS GLASS

Goofus glass was made from about 1900 to 1930 by many American factories. It was originally painted gold, red, green, bronze, pink, purple, or other bright colors. Colors were cold painted or sprayed on, not fired on, and were not permanent. Many pieces are found today with flaking paint, and this lowers the value. Both goofus glass and carnival glass were sold at carnivals, but carnival glass colors are fired on and don't flake off.

Bowl, Fruit, Stemmed Roses, Red, Gold Ground, Edwardian, 1900s, 9 ¾ x 3 In. 23

Glass-Venetian, Wedding Cup, Amethyst Glass, Gilt, Classical Scene, Murano, 1900s, 5 x 4 ⅞ x 2 ½ In.
$199

Jeffrey S. Evans & Associates

Goldscheider, Bust, Female, Curly Orange Hair, Green Shirt, Flower, c.1930, 8 In.
$1,169

Skinner, Inc.

Goldscheider, Sculpture, Woman, Dancer, Butterfly Girl, Wing-Like Sleeves, Joseph Lorenzl, c.1920, 18 In.
$2,091

Skinner, Inc.

Gouda, Vase, Carved Serpent, Footed, Goedewaagen Distel, 7 ½ In.
$480

Soulis Auctions

Greentown, Herringbone, Cake Stand, Green Glass, Dome Base, 6 ½ x 10 In.
$767

Strawser Auction Group

TIP

A Grueby vase can be cleaned with a nylon scouring pad and a mild abrasive such as Soft Scrub. After it dries, rub a little petroleum jelly or mineral oil on the surface, then wipe it off. This system works for any matte-glazed pottery.

Grueby, Paperweight, Scarab, Beetle, Blue Gray, Curdled Glaze, Lotus Flower, 1 ½ x 3 ¼ In.
$748

Clars Auction Gallery

Bowl, Ruffled Rim, Opalescent, Blue, White, Red, Gold, c.1912, 8 x 2 In. 55
Pin, Basket, Roses Topiary, Carved Glass, C Clasp, c.1900, 1 ¼ In. 48

GOUDA

Gouda, Holland, has been a pottery center since the seventeenth century. Two firms, the Zenith pottery, established in 1749, and the Zuid-Hollandsche pottery, made the colorful art pottery marked *Gouda* from 1898 to about 1964. Other factories that made "Gouda" style pottery include Regina (1898–1979), Schoonhoven (1920–present), Ivora (1630–1965), Goedewaagen (1610–1779), Dirk Goedewaagen (1779–1982), and Royal Goedewaagen (1983–present). Many pieces featured Art Nouveau or Art Deco designs. Pattern names in Dutch are often included in the mark.

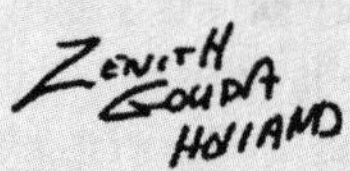

Gouda / Plateelbakkerij Zenith
1915

Gouda / Kon. Hollandsche Pijpen–en Aardewekfabriek Goedewaagen
1923–1928

Gouda / Zuid–Holland Platteelbakkerij
1926+

Vase, Carved Serpent, Footed, Goedewaagen Distel, 7 ½ In. .... *illus* 480
Vase, Yellow, Green & Peach, White Dots, Blue Ground, 13 ½ x 5 ½ In. 190
Wall Pocket, Black Ground, Multicolor, Signed, Regina Rosario Gouda Holland, 7 x 7 x 4 In. .. 51

GRANITEWARE

Graniteware is enameled tin or iron used to make kitchenware since the 1870s. Earlier graniteware was green or turquoise blue, with white spatters. The later ware was gray with white spatters. Reproductions are being made in all colors.

Geuder, Paeschke & Frey Co.
1905–c.1972

Iron Clad Manufacturing Co.
1888–1913

Lalance & Grosjean Manufacturing Co.
1877–1955

Bowl, Mottled Gray, 5 In. 28
Coffeepot, Mottled Blue & White, Hinged Lid, Wood Handle, c.1910, 10 In. 35
Funnel, Robin's-Egg Blue, Speckled, Handle, 3 ¾ In. 10
Jar, Drink Ma Ho Coffee, Mahoney & Co., Blue & White Bands, 5 ¾ In. 70
Lunch Pail, Tray, Water Reservoir, Cup, Mottled Gray, Bail Handle, 10 x 7 x 11 In. 75
Match Holder, Striker, 2 Compartments, Gray, Wall Mount, 5 x 4 ¾ In. 75
Pan, Handle, Red & White, c.1900, 10 x 6 x 2 ¾ In. 40
Pan, Lid, Green & White Swirl, Black Trim, Strap Handles, 4 x 8 In. 28
Roaster, Lid, Cobalt Blue, Swirl, White Insert, 19 x 11 x 7 In. 95
Teapot, Cream, Red Trim, 6 In. 30

GREENTOWN

Greentown glass was made by the Indiana Tumbler and Goblet Company of Greentown, Indiana, from 1894 to 1903. In 1899, the factory became part of National Glass Company. A variety of pressed glass was made. Additional pieces may be found in other categories, such as Chocolate Glass, Holly Amber, Milk Glass, and Pressed Glass.

Cat On Hamper, Dish, Lid, Clear, Yellow, Green, 1980s, 5 x 3 ½ In. 115
Connecticut, Skillet, Clear, 1900s, 3 x 3 In. 85
Feather, Pitcher, Handle, Footed, Chocolate Glass, 1896-1901, 8 In. 622
Herringbone Buttress, Bowl, Clear, Scalloped Feet, 1899, 7 In. 79
Herringbone, Cake Stand, Green Glass, Dome Base, 6 ½ x 10 In. ....*illus* 767
Rabbit, Dish, Lid, Blue, Diamond & Basketweave Base, c.1901, 4 x 5 ½ In. 265

GRUEBY

Grueby Faience Company of Boston, Massachusetts, was founded in 1894 by William H. Grueby. Grueby Pottery Company was incorporated in 1907. In 1909, Grueby Faience went bankrupt. Then William Grueby founded the Grueby Faience and Tile Company. Grueby Pottery closed about 1911. The tile company worked until 1920. Garden statuary, art pottery, and architectural tiles were made until 1920. The company developed a green matte glaze that was so popular it was copied by many other factories making a less expensive type of pottery. This eventually led to the financial problems of the pottery. Cuerda seca (dry cord) decoration uses a greasy pigment to separate different glaze colors during firing. Cuenca (raised line) decorations are impressed, leaving ridges that separate the glaze colors. The company name was often used as the mark, and slight changes in the form help date a piece.

GRUEBY FAIENCE CO. BOSTON. U.S.A.

Jardiniere, Leaves, Green, c.1905, 4 ¾ x 7 ½ In. 2500
Paperweight, Scarab, Beetle, Blue Gray, Curdled Glaze, Lotus Flower, 1 ½ x 3 ¼ In. ......*illus* 748
Tile, Water Lilies, Raised Outline, Glazed, Oak Frame, Marked, c.1915, 6 x 6 In. ....*illus* 1500
Tile, Yellow Tulip, Green Glaze, Boston, Frame, 7 In. ....*illus* 1125
Vase, Green Matte Glaze, Leaves, Carved, Lobed Rim, Boston, 8 x 4 ½ In. 1500
Vase, Leaves, Buds, Yellow Matte Glaze, c.1900, 7 x 4 In. 2375
Vase, Lobed, Leaves, Buds, Green, c.1905, 7 ¾ x 4 In. 1625

GUN. *Only toy guns are listed in this book. See Toy category.*

GUNDERSEN *Glass is listed in Pairpoint.*

GUSTAVSBERG

Gustavsberg ceramics factory was founded in 1827 near Stockholm, Sweden. It is best known to collectors for its twentieth-century artwares, especially Argenta, a green stoneware with metallic silver inlay. The company broke up and was sold in the 1990s but the name is still being used.

Gustavsberg 1839–1860

Gustavsberg 1940–1970

Gustavsberg 1970–1990s

Bowl, Sea Dragon, Silver Overlay, Argenta, W. Kage, 5 x 10 In. ....*illus* 1188
Charger, Twin Tail Mermaid, Silver Inlay, C.G. Lindblon, 1943, 15 In. 750
Jar, Lid, Mermaid, Silver Overlay, Argenta, W. Kage, 11 In. ....*illus* 1375
Tobacco Jar, Stepped Lid, Silver Overlay Art Deco Figures & Trim, Wilhem Kage, 1934, 9 x 8 In. 1188
Vase, Silver Swans, Nude, Gourd Shape, Wilhelm Kage, 1935, 7 ½ x 5 ½ In. 688
Vase, Twin Tail Mermaid, Waves, Globular, Stand-Up Rim, Silver Overlay, Kage, 1934, 8 x 7 In. 2125

HAEGER

Haeger Potteries, Inc., Dundee, Illinois, started making commercial artwares in 1914. Early pieces were marked with the name *Haeger* written over an *H*. About 1938, the mark *Royal Haeger* was used in honor of Royal Hickman, a designer at the factory. The firm closed in 2016. See also the Royal Hickman category.

Haeger

Grueby, Tile, Water Lilies, Raised Outline, Glazed, Oak Frame, Marked, c.1915, 6 x 6 In.
$1,500

Rago Arts and Auction Center

Grueby, Tile, Yellow Tulip, Green Glaze, Boston, Frame, 7 In.
$1,125

Treadway

TIP
Almost all Grueby pottery is expensive today, but some pieces have rare features that add to the price. Applied handles or added tendrils add value. So does extra color added to the floral design on a vase.

Gustavsberg, Bowl, Sea Dragon, Silver Overlay, Argenta, W. Kage, 5 x 10 In.
$1,188

Rago Arts and Auction Center

Gustavsberg, Jar, Lid, Mermaid, Silver Overlay, Argenta, W. Kage, 11 In.
$1,375

Rago Arts and Auction Center

Halloween, Candy Container, Witch, Composition, Corn Silk Hair, Germany, 1920s, 6 In.
$270

Bertoia Auctions

Halloween, Costume, Skeleton, Cloth, Papier-Mache Skull, Jaw Moves, Adult Size
$390

Bertoia Auctions

Halloween, Dancing Couple, Pressed Cardboard, Cloth Sailor Suits, Wheels, Germany, 9 In.
$1,920

Bertoia Auctions

Halloween, Jack-O'-Lantern, Cat, Pulp, Painted, Paper Insert Features, 7 In.
$540

Bertoia Auctions

Halloween, Jack-O'-Lantern, Sparkler, Tin Lithograph, Orange & Black, 4 ¾ x 2 ½ x 1 In.
$113

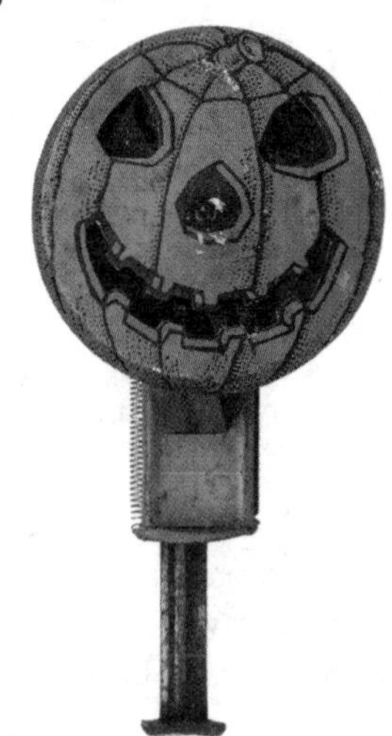

Soulis Auctions

Halloween, Lantern, Black Cat, Pressed Paper, Painted, Handle, 1940s, 7 ½ x 6 x 5 In.
$201

Charleston Estate Auctions

Halloween, Lantern, Trash Can Shape, Painted Metal, Cutout Ghost On Horse, 13 In.
$43

Richard Opfer Auctioneering, Inc.

Halloween, Nodder, Pumpkin Man, Smiling, Green Hat, Bobbing Head, 6 In.
$120

Bertoia Auctions

Figurine, Angry Red Bull, Glazed, 1960s, 18 In.	87
Figurine, Cat, Black Glaze, Arched Back, 1950s, 7 x 6 In.	177
TV Lamp, Gazelle, Rectangular Base, Glazed, Majolica, Marked Royal Haeger, 1950s, 14 x 19 x 6 In.	177
Vase, Gazelle, Long Legs & Horns, White, c.1940, 12 In.	60
Vase, Sailfish, Yellow & Black, 1940s, 9 x 12 In.	177
Wall Pocket, Swan, Blue, c.1950, 6 x 6 In.	61

HALF-DOLL, *see Pincushion Doll category.*

HALL CHINA

Hall China Company started in East Liverpool, Ohio, in 1903. The firm made many types of wares. Collectors search for the Hall teapots made from the 1920s to the 1950s. The dinnerware of the same period, especially Autumn Leaf pattern, is popular. The Hall China Company merged with Homer Laughlin China Company in 2010. Autumn Leaf pattern dishes are listed in their own category in this book.

Boston, Teapot, Cobalt Blue, 1920s, 4 x 7 In., 2 Cup	42
Crocus, Drip Bowl, Finial, c.1935, 5 In.	45
French Daisy, Teapot, 1950s, 2 Cup	50
Poppy, Reamer, 7 In.	100
Red Poppy, Casserole, Lid, 1 ½ Qt.	20
Rose White, Salt & Pepper, Art Deco, Handles, 1940s	47
Teapot, Teal, Gold Stars, Footed, c.1940, 6 In., 6 Cup	30
Wildfire, Custard Cup, 3 ½ In.	30

HALLOWEEN

Halloween is an ancient holiday that has changed in the last 200 years. The jack-o'-lantern, witches on broomsticks, and orange decorations seem to be twentieth-century creations. Collectors started to become serious about collecting Halloween-related items in the late 1970s. Old costumes and papier-mache decorations, now replaced by plastic, are in demand.

Candy Container, Witch, Composition, Corn Silk Hair, Germany, 1920s, 6 In.	*illus*	270
Candy Pail, Frankenstein, Orange, Vinyl, Carrying Handle, 7 ½ In.		389
Cat, Bobble-Eyes, Black, Curved Tin Base, Orange Bow, 7 In.		240
Costume, Morticia, The Addams Family, Box, 8 x 11 In.		118
Costume, Skeleton, Cloth, Papier-Mache Skull, Jaw Moves, Adult Size	*illus*	390
Dancing Couple, Pressed Cardboard, Cloth Sailor Suits, Wheels, Germany, 9 In.	*illus*	1920
Horn, Cardboard, Tin Lithograph, Black Graphics, Orange Ground, Wood Handle, Japan, 3 ¾ In.		40
Jack-O'-Lantern, Cat, Pulp, Painted, Paper Insert Features, 7 In.	*illus*	540
Jack-O'-Lantern, Hanging, Tin, Yellow Paint, 7 In.		3600
Jack-O'-Lantern, Sparkler, Tin Lithograph, Orange & Black, 4 ¾ x 2 ½ x 1 In.	*illus*	113
Jack-O'-Lantern, Witch's Head, Composition, Crepe Paper Collar, Candleholder Base, 10 In.		4500
Lantern, Black Cat, Pressed Paper, Painted, Handle, 1940s, 7 ½ x 6 x 5 In.	*illus*	201
Lantern, Devil Face, Horns, Cardboard, 8 In.		120
Lantern, Trash Can Shape, Painted Metal, Cutout Ghost On Horse, 13 In.	*illus*	43
Nodder, Pumpkin Man, Smiling, Green Hat, Bobbing Head, 6 In.	*illus*	120
Noisemaker, Whistle, Tin Lithograph, Hand Crank, 1916, 3 x 1 ¾ In.		181
Parade Torch, Jack-O'-Lantern, Metal, Orange & Green, Painted, 1900s, 8 In.	*illus*	360
Toy, Tambourine, Black Cat, Tin, Painted, 6 In.	*illus*	79
Toy, Witch Riding Motorcycle, Jack-O'-Lantern On Back, Wheels Turn, Plastic, 5 x 7 In.	*illus*	342

HAMPSHIRE

Hampshire pottery was made in Keene, New Hampshire, between 1871 and 1923. Hampshire developed a line of colored-glaze wares as early as 1883, including a Royal Worcester–type pink, olive green, blue, and

Halloween, Parade Torch, Jack-O'-Lantern, Metal, Orange & Green, Painted, 1900s, 8 In.
$360

Eldred's

Halloween, Toy, Tambourine, Black Cat, Tin, Painted, 6 In.
$79

Hartzell's Auction Gallery Inc.

Halloween, Toy, Witch Riding Motorcycle, Jack-O'-Lantern On Back, Wheels Turn, Plastic, 5 x 7 In.
$342

AntiqueAdvertising.com

TIP

Old papier-mache jack-o'-lanterns originally had a thin piece of paper in the eyes. The light from the candle showed through the paper. You can make a replacement with tracing paper and watercolor paint.

Handel, Lamp Base, 3-Light, Mermaid Rising Shape, Clamshell, Fleur-De-Lis Cap, 22 ½ x 9 x 7 In.
$1,200

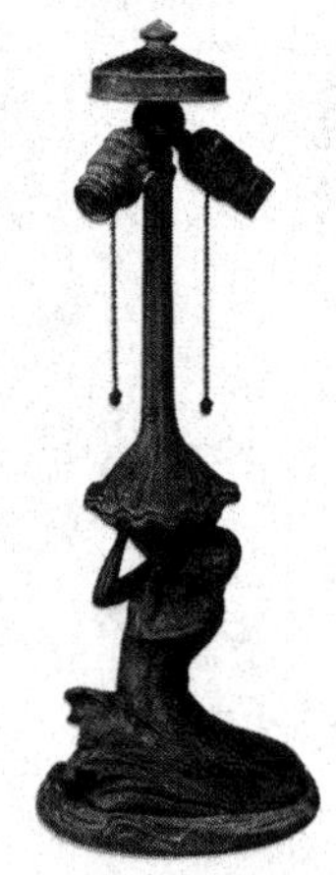

Morphy Auctions

Handel, Lamp, Boudoir, Reverse Painted Shade, Mushroom Form, Reeded Base, 13 ½ In.
$492

Locati Auctions

Handel, Lamp, 3-Light, Cattail, 8 Panels, Caramel Slag Glass, Joanne C. Grant, 1978, 23 In.
$4,914

Cordier Auctions

Handel, Lamp, Desk, Red Sunset, Tropical Palm Overlay, Slag Glass, Metal Harp Base, c.1915, 19 In.
$1,950

Rago Arts and Auction Center

Handel, Lamp, Birds Of Paradise Shade, Fuchsia, Purple, Citrine Yellow, Metal Tripod Base, 24 In.
$5,445

Fontaine's Auction Gallery

Handel, Lamp, Hall, Hanging Frame, Globe, Chipped Ice Shade, Sunset Fall, Trees, Birds, 26 In.
$1,100

Woody Auctions

mahogany. Pieces are marked with the printed mark or the impressed name *Hampshire Pottery* or *J.S.T. & Co., Keene, N.H.* (James Scollay Taft). Many pieces were marked with city names and sold as souvenirs.

Inkwell, Lid, Green Matte Glaze, White Insert, 4 In. 189
Lamp, Green Matte, Leaded Glass Shade, Embossed Letter, Signed, 21 x 15 ¾ In. 735

HANDBAG, *see Purse category.*

HANDEL

Handel glass was made by Philip Handel working in Meriden, Connecticut, from 1885 and in New York City from 1893 to 1933. The firm made art glass and other types of lamps. Handel shades were made not only of leaded glass in a style reminiscent of Tiffany but also of reverse painted glass. Handel also made vases and other glass objects.

Lamp Base, 3-Light, Mermaid Rising Shape, Clamshell, Fleur-De-Lis Cap, 22 ½ x 9 x 7 In. *illus* 1200
Lamp Base, 3-Light, Urn Style, Vent Cap, Finial, 24 In. 312
Lamp Base, Tripod, Splayed Legs, Teardrop Finial, Adjustable Arm, 60 x 14 ½ x 23 ½ In. 424
Lamp, 2-Light, Slag Glass, Stylized Flower Overlay, Metal, 21 x 16 ½ In. 1125
Lamp, 3-Light, Cattail, 8 Panels, Caramel Slag Glass, Joanne C. Grant, 1978, 23 In. *illus* 4914
Lamp, 3-Light, Leaded Glass Shade, Caramel Slag, Flower, Bronze Base, 18 x 27 In. 1755
Lamp, 3-Light, Reverse Painted Glass Shade, Trees, Orange Ground, Pull Chain, 23 ½ x 18 In. 2280
Lamp, 5-Light, Leaded Glass, Patinated Bronze, Flowering Lotus Bulb Shape, 30 ½ In. 7565
Lamp, Birds Of Paradise Shade, Fuchsia, Purple, Citrine Yellow, Metal Tripod Base, 24 In. *illus* 5445
Lamp, Boudoir, Reverse Painted Shade, Mushroom Form, Reeded Base, 13 ½ In. *illus* 492
Lamp, Boudoir, Sunset, Palm Tree, Scalloped Shade, Signed, 14 x 7 x 7 In. 1029
Lamp, Bronze, Harp Shape, Teroma Glass Shade, Yellow Enamel Ground, 17 ½ In. 565
Lamp, Desk, Adjustable, Slag Glass, Bronzed Metal, Signed, 10 x 15 In. 553
Lamp, Desk, Red Sunset, Tropical Palm Overlay, Slag Glass, Metal Harp Base, c.1915, 19 In. *illus* 1950
Lamp, Flowers, Stained, Leaded Glass Shade, Bronze Base, Sign, 57 x 10 In. 1800
Lamp, Hall, Hanging Frame, Globe, Chipped Ice Shade, Sunset Fall, Trees, Birds, 26 In. *illus* 1100
Lamp, Leaded Glass, Bell Shape Shade, Geometric, Flower Reserve, 24 x 16 ½ In. 2118
Lamp, Mosserine Shade, Green, Molded, Metal Top Ring, Early 1900s, 20 x 14 In. *illus* 1872
Lamp, Reverse Painted Shade, 1-Light, Mountains, Goldenrod, 14 ¾ x 6 ¾ In. 2000
Lamp, Reverse Painted Shade, Flowers, Butterflies, Light Blue Ground, Signed, 24 x 17 In. 5100
Lamp, Reverse Painted Shade, Jungle Bird, Oriental Urn Base, Signed, 24 x 18 In. 6490
Lamp, Reverse Painted Shade, Venetian Harbor, Boats, Patinated Metal, c.1915, 13 ½ x 6 ½ In. 2250
Lamp, Reverse Painted Shade, Winter Branches, Snow, Yellow, Orange, Tree Trunk Base, Metal, 14 x 7 In. 1875
Lantern, Hanging, Palm Tree Design, Bronzed Metal, Slag Glass, Meriden, 20 x 14 In. 2875
Vase, Dome Lid, Teroma, Landscape, Cylindrical, Bronze Dore Rim, Early 1900s, 10 In. 615

HARDWARE, *see Architectural category.*

HARKER

Harker Pottery Company was incorporated in 1890 in East Liverpool, Ohio. The Harker family had been making pottery in the area since 1840. The company made many types of pottery but by the Civil War was making quantities of yellowware from native clays. It also made Rockingham-type brown-glazed pottery and whiteware. The plant was moved to Chester, West Virginia, in 1931. Dinnerware was made and sold nationally. In 1971 the company was sold to Jeannette Glass Company, and all operations ceased in 1972. For more prices, go to kovels.com.

Amy, Rolling Pin, Flowers, White Ground, c.1935, 15 In. 32
Brown, Gravy Ladle, Footed, c.1970, 6 In. 40
Cameoware, Desert Server, Pink, Cream, 1950s, 9 In. 30
Chesterton, Teapot, Gray & White, c.1941 54
Dainty Flower, Serving Bowl, Blue, White Flowers, 1940s, 9 In. 18

Handel, Lamp, Mosserine Shade, Green, Molded, Metal Top Ring, Early 1900s, 20 x 14 In.
$1,872

Thomaston Place Auction Galleries

TIP
When you move, remember that there is no insurance coverage for breakage if the items are not packed by the shipper.

Harlequin, Red, Figurine, Cat, Seated
$502

Strawser Auction Group

Haviland, Charger, Hand Painted, Rose, Gold Trim, Limoges, Signed, Jennings, 12 ½ In.
$150

Woody Auctions

Haviland, Soup, Dish, Seashore, Crab, Rutherford B. Hayes, White Horseshoe, Theo. R. Davis, 9 In.
$2,124

Cottone Auctions

Broken Dishes
The French term for a mosaic made from broken dishes is "pique assiette." The term is also used by English-speaking artists.

Haviland Pottery, Vase, Duck, Natural Environment, Handles, Limoges, Barbotine, 8 x 12 In.
$375

Palm Beach Modern Auctions

Haviland Pottery, Vase, Flowers, Black Ground, Barbotine, Molded Handles, Edouard Girardo, 3 In.
$615

Stair Galleries

Ivy, Teapot, Lid, Royal Gadroon, 3 3/8 In., 4 Cup 139
Petit Point Rose, Jar, Lid, Grease, Drips, Skyscraper, 1930s, 5 x 4 1/2 In. 36
Petit Point Rose, Plate, Multicolor Flowers, Gold Trim, c.1940, 9 In. 30
Red Apple II, Mixing Bowl, Apple & Pear, Red Trim, Ivory Ground, 1940s, 9 In. 15

HARLEQUIN

Harlequin dinnerware was produced by the Homer Laughlin Company from 1938 to 1964, and sold without trademark by the F. W. Woolworth Co. It has a concentric ring design like Fiesta, but the rings are separated from the rim by a plain margin. Cup handles are triangular in shape. Seven different novelty animal figurines were introduced in 1939. For more prices, go to kovels.com.

Forest Green, Plate, Luncheon, c.1965, 9 In. 17
Gray, Bowl, Sugar, 2 Handles, Lid, Footed, c.1955, 9 In. 55
Red, Bowl, Vegetable, 8 3/4 In. 25
Red, Figurine, Cat, Seated .... *illus* 502
Rose, Cup & Saucer, Flat After Dinner, 2 x 2 3/4 In. 69
Rose, Salt & Pepper, Footed 29
Spruce Green, Candleholder, Glaze, Circular Base, 1 3/4 x 4 In., Pair 384
Yellow, Marmalade, Lid, Triangle Finial, Glaze, Molded Base, 4 In. 130

HATPIN

Hatpin collectors search for pins popular from 1860 to 1920. The long pin, often over four inches, was used to hold the hat in place on the hair. The tops of the pins were made of all materials, from solid gold and real gemstones to ceramics and glass. Be careful to buy original hatpins and not recent pieces made by altering old buttons.

Cameo, Gold Colored Filigree, 8 3/4 In. 75
Celluloid, Tulip Shape, Pink & Red Painted Flowers, 7 1/4 In. 25
Glass, Faceted, Purple, Paste Edge, 4 In. 48
Gold, Etched Sparrow, On Branch, 14K Rose Gold, 9 In. 225
Lucite, Faceted, Painted Red Flowers, 8 3/4 In. 75
Metal, Bell Shape, Diamante Stones, Victorian, 10 In. 75
Rhinestone, Red Glass Center, 9 In. 55
Silver Plate, Indian Chief, Feathered War Bonnet, c.1925, 8 In. 85
Silver, Winged Dragon, 6 In. 50

HATPIN HOLDER

Hatpin holders were needed when hatpins were fashionable from 1860 to 1920. The large, heavy hat required special long-shanked pins to hold it in place. The hatpin holder resembles a large saltshaker, but it often has no opening at the bottom as a shaker does. Hatpin holders were made of all types of ceramics and metal. Look for other pieces under the names of specific manufacturers.

Brass, Rooster, Red Stone Eyes, 4 x 3 In. 145
Porcelain, Figural, Pink Clover, Green Leaves, Bayreuth, 4 1/2 In. 660
Porcelain, Flower, Leaf, White, Marked, RS Germany, 4 1/2 In. 75
Porcelain, Forget-Me-Nots, Art Nouveau, Blue, Green, Bavaria, c.1900, 4 1/2 In. 55
Porcelain, Geisha, Red, Blue, Gilt, Japan, 4 x 2 1/2 In. 19
Porcelain, Hexagon, Violets, Gilt, Blue, Green, Purple, 5 In. 75
Porcelain, Paris, Sheep, White Glaze, Rectangular Plinth, 19th Century, 2 x 2 x 2 In. 525
Porcelain, Pig, Pink Ears & Nose, Japan, 4 x 2 In. 37
Porcelain, Raised Gold Flower & Leaf Design, Attached Ring Holder, Nippon, 4 x 4 In. 95
Porcelain, Twisted Swirl, Roses, Gilt, Scalloped Base, Z.S. & Co., Bavaria, c.1900, 5 x 2 In. 35
Silver Plate, Openwork, Scrolled Top, c.1895, 6 1/2 In. 75

HAVILAND

Haviland china has been made in Limoges, France, since 1842. David Haviland had a shop in New York City and opened a porcelain company in Limoges, France. Haviland was the first company to both manufacture and decorate porcelain. Pieces are marked *H & Co., Haviland & Co.*, or *Theodore Haviland.* It is possible to match existing sets of dishes through dealers who specialize in Haviland china. Other factories worked in the town of Limoges making a similar chinaware. Those porcelains are listed in this book under Limoges.

Haviland and Co.
1876–1878; 1889–1931

Théo Haviland
Limoges
FRANCE

Theodore Haviland
1893–early 1900s

Haviland
France

Haviland and Co.
c.1894–1931

Charger, Hand Painted, Rose, Gold Trim, Limoges, Signed, Jennings, 12 ½ In. .... *illus* 150
Plate, Pink Apple Blossoms, Gilt Rim, 1900s, 9 ¾ In., 6 Piece 30
Soup, Dish, Seashore, Crab, Rutherford B. Hayes, White Horseshoe, Theo. R. Davis, 9 In. *illus* 2124

HAVILAND POTTERY

Haviland Pottery began in 1872, when Charles Haviland decided to make art pottery. He worked with the famous artists of the day and made pottery with slip glazed decorations. Production stopped in 1885. Haviland Pottery is marked with the letters *H & Co.* The Haviland name is better known today for its porcelain.

HAVILAND & Co
Limoges

Haviland and Co.
1875–1882

H & Co
L

Haviland and Co.
1875–1882

CFH
GDM
FRANCE

Charles Field Haviland
1891+

Vase, Duck, Natural Environment, Handles, Limoges, Barbotine, 8 x 12 In. .... *illus* 375
Vase, Flattened, Handles, Footed, Duck On Grass, Barbotine, 8 x 12 x 4 In. 507
Vase, Flowers, Black Ground, Barbotine, Molded Handles, Edouard Girardo, 3 In. .... *illus* 615

HAWKES

Hawkes cut glass was made by T. G. Hawkes & Company of Corning, New York, founded in 1880. The firm cut glass blanks made at other glassworks until 1962. Many pieces are marked with the trademark, a trefoil ring enclosing a fleur-de-lis and two hawks. Cut glass by other manufacturers is listed under either the factory name or in the general Cut Glass category.

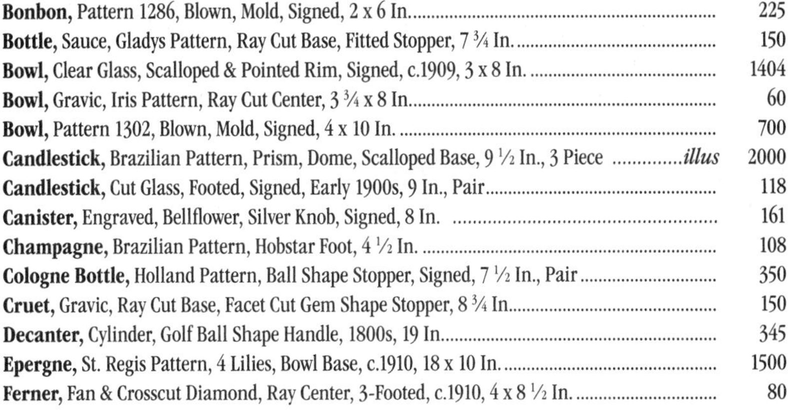

Bonbon, Pattern 1286, Blown, Mold, Signed, 2 x 6 In. 225
Bottle, Sauce, Gladys Pattern, Ray Cut Base, Fitted Stopper, 7 ¾ In. 150
Bowl, Clear Glass, Scalloped & Pointed Rim, Signed, c.1909, 3 x 8 In. 1404
Bowl, Gravic, Iris Pattern, Ray Cut Center, 3 ¾ x 8 In. 60
Bowl, Pattern 1302, Blown, Mold, Signed, 4 x 10 In. 700
Candlestick, Brazilian Pattern, Prism, Dome, Scalloped Base, 9 ½ In., 3 Piece .... *illus* 2000
Candlestick, Cut Glass, Footed, Signed, Early 1900s, 9 In., Pair 118
Canister, Engraved, Bellflower, Silver Knob, Signed, 8 In. 161
Champagne, Brazilian Pattern, Hobstar Foot, 4 ½ In. 108
Cologne Bottle, Holland Pattern, Ball Shape Stopper, Signed, 7 ½ In., Pair 350
Cruet, Gravic, Ray Cut Base, Facet Cut Gem Shape Stopper, 8 ¾ In. 150
Decanter, Cylinder, Golf Ball Shape Handle, 1800s, 19 In. 345
Epergne, St. Regis Pattern, 4 Lilies, Bowl Base, c.1910, 18 x 10 In. 1500
Ferner, Fan & Crosscut Diamond, Ray Center, 3-Footed, c.1910, 4 x 8 ½ In. 80

Hawkes, Candlestick, Brazilian Pattern, Prism, Dome, Scalloped Base, 9 ½ In., 3 Piece
$2,000

Woody Auctions

Hawkes, Pitcher, Squat, Clear Lead Glass, Applied Cut Faceted Handle, 1910s, 6 x 5 In.
$234

Jeffrey S. Evans & Associates

Hawkes, Plate, Clear Lead Glass, Scalloped Rim, Lattice, Rosettes, Acid Stamped, c.1911, 8 In.
$936

Jeffrey S. Evans & Associates

H

Hawkes, Tray, Round, North Star, Ruffled Rim, Clear, Signed, 10 In.
$300

Woody Auctions

Heintz Art, Vase, Iris, Sterling On Bronze, Mixed Metals, Ladies Golf Trophy, c.1928, 12 In.
$390

Case Antiques

Heisey, Crescent, Plate, Salad, Moongleam, 8 In.
$40

Apple Tree Auction Center

Humidor, Hobstar, Vertical Notched Columns & Fan, Ray Base & Lid, Signed, 7 ½ x 5 ½ In. 225
Pitcher, Queens Pattern, Hobstar Base, Triple Notched Handle, 8 ½ In. 330
Pitcher, Squat, Clear Lead Glass, Applied Cut Faceted Handle, 1910s, 6 x 5 In. .... *illus* 234
Plate, Clear Lead Glass, Scalloped Rim, Lattice, Rosettes, Acid Stamped, c.1911, 8 In. .... *illus* 936
Plate, Gravic, Strawberry, Hobstar Center, Signed, 7 In. 60
Tray, Holland, Ruffled Rim, Cut Glass, Signed, 9 ½ In. 173
Tray, Round, North Star, Ruffled Rim, Clear, Signed, 10 In. .... *illus* 300
Vase, Cylinder, Queens Pattern, Hobstar Base, Signed, 12 x 3 ¾ In. 950
Whisky Decanter, Glass, Intaglio, Horse Head, Flowers, Silver Stopper, 8 In. 840

HEAD VASE

Head vases, generally showing a woman from the shoulders up, were used by florists primarily in the 1950s and 1960s. Made in a variety of sizes and often decorated with imitation jewelry and other lifelike accessories, the vases were manufactured in Japan and the U.S.A. Less elaborate examples were made as early as the 1930s. Religious themes, babies, and animals are also common subjects. Other head vases are listed under manufacturers' names and can be located through the index in the back of this book. Collecting head vases was a fad in the 1960s–1970s and prices rose. There is less interest now and only a few are high priced.

Baby Girl, Blond Hair, Blue Eyes, Pink & White Blanket On Head, Enesco, c.1960, 3 ½ In. 38
Baby Girl, Bonnet, Ruffled Collar, Gold Bow, Blue Eyes, Pink Cheeks, Napco, 5 ¾ In. 75
Jackie Kennedy, In Mourning, Gloved Hand, Red Lips, Inarco, 6 In. 225
Kitten, Blue Floppy Bonnet, Wide Blue Eyes, Embossed Necklace, Hull, c.1955, 6 In. 86
Woman, Fringed Hat, Upraised Hand, Bracelet, Red Lips, Napco, c.1956, 5 ½ In. 62
Woman, Green Floppy Hat, Scarf, Pearl Earrings & Necklace, Napcoware, 1950s, 6 In. 75
Woman, Green, Art Deco, Lindsey B, 1980s, 12 x 7 In. 98
Woman, Orange High Collar Coat & Hat, Dangling Pearl Earrings, Blond, Relpo, Japan, 6 In.. 65
Woman, Rhinestone Bow, Fringed Hat, Gold Eyelashes & Eyebrows, 3 x 2 In. 45

Hedi Schoop
S

HEDI SCHOOP

Hedi Schoop emigrated from Germany in 1933 and started Hedi Schoop Art Creations, North Hollywood, California, in 1940. Schoop made ceramic figurines, lamps, planters, and tablewares. The business burned down in 1958. Some of the molds were sold and Schoop began designing for other companies. She died in 1995.

Figurine, Young China, Dancer & Musician, 3-Tiered Base, Green & Black Tops, 10 In. 125
Plaque, Cat, Face, Gray, Black, White, 7 x 7 In. 69
Plate, Cat, Sitting, No. 21, Stripes, 7 x 7 In. 60
Plate, Cat's Face, No. 20, Gray, Blue Eyes, 7 x 7 In. 69

HEINTZ

Heintz Art Metal Shop used the letters *HAMS* in a diamond as a mark. In 1902, Otto Heintz designed and manufactured copper items with colored enamel decorations under the name Art Crafts Shop. He took over the Arts & Crafts Company in Buffalo, New York, in 1903. By 1906 it had become the Heintz Art Metal Shop. It remained in business until 1930. The company made ashtrays, bookends, boxes, bowls, desk sets, vases, trophies, and smoking sets. The best-known pieces are made of copper, brass, and bronze with silver overlay. Similar pieces were made by Smith Metal Arts and were marked *Silver Crest*. Some pieces by both companies are unmarked.

Lamp, Boudoir, Poppies, Silver On Bronze Base, Art Deco, c.1925, 10 In. 288
Vase, Iris, Sterling On Bronze, Mixed Metals, Ladies Golf Trophy, c.1928, 12 In. .... *illus* 390

HEISEY

Heisey glass was made from 1896 to 1957 in Newark, Ohio, by A. H. Heisey and Co., Inc. The Imperial Glass Company of Bellaire, Ohio, bought some of the molds and the rights to the trademark. Some Heisey patterns have been made by Imperial since 1960. After 1968, they stopped using the *H* trademark. Heisey used romantic names for colors, such as Sahara. Do not confuse color and pattern names. The Custard Glass and Ruby Glass categories may also include some Heisey pieces.

Heisey
1900–1957

Heisey
Paper label

Heisey
Paper label

Aristocrat, Candlestick, 9 In., Pair 50
Ashtray, Oval, Whimsy, Flamingo, 4 ½ In. 52
Athena, Torte Plate, 14 In. 25
Bamboo, Bud Vase, Round Base, Moongleam, 6 In. 374
Basket, Bonnet Shape, Round Base, Ruffled Rim, Handle, Flamingo, 7 ½ In. 104
Beaded Panel & Sunburst, Compote, Footed, Round Base, Ruffled Rim, 8 In. 12
Charter Oak, Compote, High Footed, Round Base, Flamingo, 7 In. 29
Cobel, Cocktail Shaker, One For The Road, Silver Overlay, 2 Qt. 316
Crescent, Plate, Salad, Moongleam, 8 In. .... *illus* 40
Daisy & Leaves, Vase, Flowers, Frosted, 9 In. 400
Double Rib & Panel, Salver, Footed, Round Base, Octagonal Top, 11 ½ In. 345
Empress, Mustard, Lid 75
Empress, Plate, Dinner, Ruffled Edge, Square, Moongleam, 10 ½ In. 23
Empress, Plate, Salad, Ruffled Edge, Tangerine, 7 In. .... *illus* 58
Fancy Loop, Mustard, Lid 85
Fandango, Nappy, Oval, 11 In. 35
Fern, Tidbit, Handle, Zircon, 6 In. 52
Gallagher, Jug, Renaissance Etch, Bulbous Body, Handle, 73 Oz. 35
Greek Key, Bowl, Footed, 9 In. 115
Greek Key, Plate, Applied Copper Rim, 8 In. 52
Heron, Vase, Mermaid Etch, Ball Shape, Transparent, 7 In. 518
Hexagon, Basket, Plain, Flower Cutting, Handle, 8 In. 23
Ipswich, Plate, Salad, Square, Footed, Flamingo, 7 In. .... *illus* 40
Kohinoor, Bowl, Floral, Elaborate Cutting, Rectangular, 14 In. 58
Laverne, Bowl, Low Footed, Wavy Rim, Round Base, Flamingo, 11 In. 23
Lodestar, Celery Dish, Dawn, 10 In. 52
Narrow Flute, Tray, Japanese Garden, Round, 10 In. 58
No. 4224, Cocktail, Steeplechase, Clear Base, Sahara Bowl 150
Octagon, Basket, Handle, Transparent, Flamingo, 5 In. 92
Octagon, Tray, Lily Carving, Sections, 2 Handles, 12 In. .... *illus* 288
Old Queen Anne, Plate, 10 In. 20
Orchid Etch, Cocktail Shaker, Art Deco Style, Monogram On Stopper, Spout Insert, 12 In. 230
Peerless, Vase, Orchid, Bulbous Body, Ruffled Rim, 5 In. 40
Peerless, Vase, Swung, Elongated, Ruffled Edge, 14 ¾ In. 29
Pinwheel & Fan, Bowl, Ruffled Rim, Flamingo, 8 ½ In. 259
Pinwheel & Fan, Nappy, Ruffled Edge, Vaseline, 4 ¾ In. 150
Plaid, Vase, Elongated Body, Round Base, Ruffled Edge, 17 In. 173
Plantation, Relish, Round, 4 Sections 60
Pleat & Panel, Pitcher, Footed, Wide Spout, Handle, Moongleam, 3 Pt. 69
Pleat & Panel, Vase, Flared, Round Base, Cylindrical, Flamingo, 7 ½ In. 52
Prince Of Wales, Celery, Plumes, Oval, 10 In. 50
Punty & Diamond, Jelly, Footed 30

Heisey, Empress, Plate, Salad, Ruffled Edge, Tangerine, 7 In.
$58

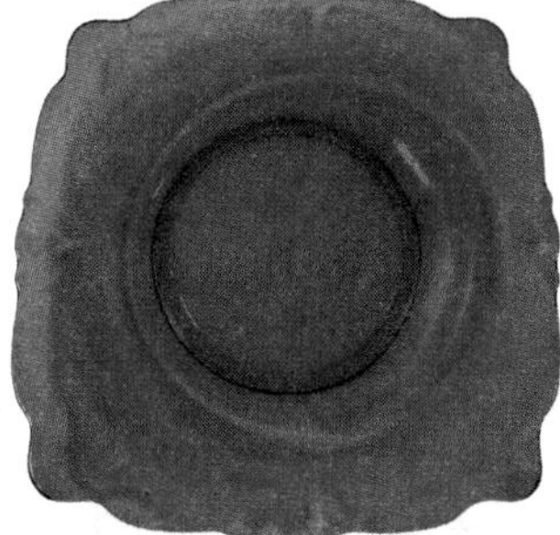

Apple Tree Auction Center

H in a Diamond

Heisey's mark is an "*H* in a diamond" designed by the son of company founder, Augusta H. Heisey, in 1901. After 1901, all Heisey glass left the factory with a molded mark or a paper label. The molded mark is sometimes hard to find. The company purposely put it in an inconspicuous place or hid it within the pressed design.

Heisey, Ipswich, Plate, Salad, Square, Footed, Flamingo, 7 In.
$40

Apple Tree Auction Center

Heisey, Octagon, Tray, Lily Carving, Sections, 2 Handles, 12 In.
$288

Apple Tree Auction Center

TIP
Have an inventory of your collections and adequate insurance.

Heisey, Ridgeleigh, Vase, Candle, Round Base, Zircon, 4 ½ In.
$40

Apple Tree Auction Center

Heisey, Tudor, Dish, Preserve, Finial On Lid, Round Base, Moongleam, 5 In.
$40

Apple Tree Auction Center

Heisey, Warwick, Vase, Horn Shape, Cornucopia, Cobalt Blue, 7 In.
$35

Apple Tree Auction Center

Ridgeleigh, Vase, Candle, Round Base, Zircon, 4 ½ In. .... *illus* 40
Ridgeleigh, Vase, Cylindrical, Scalloped Edge, Sahara, 8 In. 115
Saturn, Tidbit, Zircon, 6 In. 58
Sunflower, Relish, 3 Sections 30
Tudor, Dish, Preserve, Finial On Lid, Round Base, Moongleam, 5 In. .... *illus* 40
Tudor, Pitcher, Qt. 30
Warwick, Vase, Horn Shape, Cornucopia, Cobalt Blue, 7 In. .... *illus* 35
Waverly, Bowl, Salad, Ruffled Rim, Amber, 10 In. 138
Waverly, Compote, Footed, Round Base, Ruffled Rim, Honey Amber, 6 In. 161
Whaley, Beer Mug, Fox Chase Etch, C-Handle, Bulbous, 16 Oz. 91
Yeoman, Puff Box, Lid, Glass Insert, Finial, No. 1186, Flamingo 58
Yeoman, Soup, Dish, Shallow, Vaseline, 9 ½ In. 104
Zodiac, Sugar & Creamer 30

HEREND, *see Fischer category.*

HEUBACH

Heubach is the collector's name for Gebruder Heubach, a firm working in Lichten, Germany, from 1840 to 1925. It is best known for bisque dolls and doll heads, the principal products. The company also manufactured bisque figurines, including piano babies, beginning in the 1880s, and glazed figurines in the 1900s. Piano Babies are listed in their own category. Dolls are included in the Doll category under Gebruder Heubach and Heubach. Another factory, Ernst Heubach, working in Koppelsdorf, Germany, also made porcelain and dolls. These will also be found in the Doll category under Heubach Koppelsdorf.

Candy Container, Boy, Holding Snowball, Sitting On Large Snowball, c.1910 265
Candy Container, Boy, Skier, Cloth Vest, Cotton Snow, On Box, c.1910, 5 In. 365
Figurine, Young Girl Curtsying, Ballet Collection, 16 ½ In. 72

HISTORIC BLUE, *see factory names, such as Adams, Ridgway, and Staffordshire.*

HOBNAIL

Hobnail glass is a style of glass with bumps all over. Dozens of hobnail patterns and variants have been made. Clear, colored, and opalescent hobnail have been made and are being reproduced. Other pieces of hobnail may also be listed in the Duncan & Miller and Fenton categories.

Bowl, Cranberry, Opalescent, J.H. Hobbs, Brockunier & Co., c.1890, 3 ½ x 3 In. 95
Pitcher, Embossed Bubble, Handle, Black Glaze, 8 ½ In. 50
Vase, Bud, Clear, E.O. Brody Co., 7 ½ x 3 ½ In. 8

HOLT-HOWARD

Holt-Howard was an importer that started working in New York City in 1949 and moved to Stamford, Connecticut, in 1955. The company sold many types of table accessories, such as condiment jars, decanters, spoon holders, and saltshakers. Its figural pieces have a cartoon-like quality. The company was bought out by General Housewares Corporation in 1968. Holt-Howard pieces are often marked with the name and the year or *HH* and the year stamped in black. The *HH* mark was used until 1974. The company also used a black and silver paper label. Holt-Howard production ceased in 1990 and the remainder of the company was sold to Kay Dee Designs. In 2002, Grant Holt and John Howard started Grant-Howard Associates and made retro pixie cookie jars marked *GHA* that sold from a mail-order catalog. Other GHA retro pixie pieces were made until 2006.

Holt-Howard, Cookie Jar, Candy, Santa Claus, White, Red, Marked HH Japan, Gold Labels, 8 In.
$35

Belhorn Auction Services

Hopalong Cassidy, Radio, Arvin, Red Metal Case, c.1950, 5 x 8 In.
$210

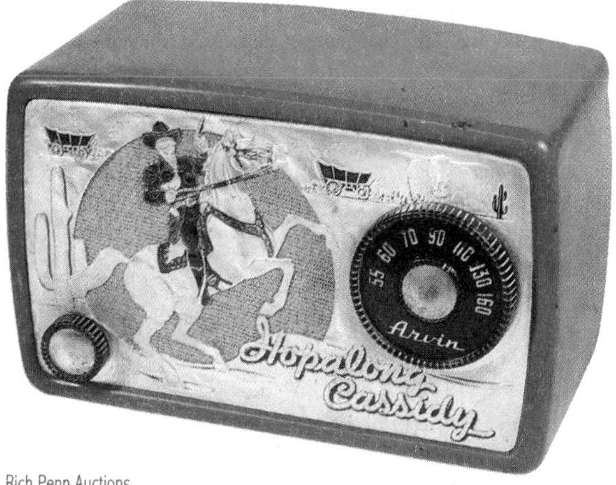

Rich Penn Auctions

Horn, Cup, Libation, Deep Red, Leaves & Figures, Buffalo, Chinese, 3 ⅞ In.
$115

Blackwell Auctions

Hull, Calla Lily, Vase, Light Green, Cream, 2 Handles, 6 x 5 In.
$115

Belhorn Auction Services

Hull, Four Seasons, Clock, Deep Blue Edge, 4 Small Scenes, Multicolor, 7 x 2 In.
$288

Belhorn Auction Services

Hull, Gingerbread Man, Cookie Jar, Brown Drip Glaze, 12 In.
$120

Woody Auctions

Hull, Little Red Riding Hood, Wall Pocket, Gold Trim, Floral, Marked, 9 ½ In.
$115

Belhorn Auction Services

Hutschenreuther, Figurine, Lion, Walking Pose, White Glaze, 1814, 14 x 22 x 5 In.
$363

Fontaine's Auction Gallery

TIP
Dust the backs of your framed pictures once a year.

Icon, Christ Pantocrator, Brass Oklad, Russia, 12 x 10 In.
$308

Clars Auction Gallery

Ashtray, Li'l Old Lace, Granny, Glasses, Lavender, Blue, Signed, 1958 56
Candelabrum, 3 Snowmen, Spaghetti Earmuffs, c.1955, 7 ¾ x 2 In. 95
Cookie Jar, Candy, Santa Claus, White, Red, Marked HH Japan, Gold Labels, 8 In. .... *illus* 35
Eggcup, Double, Coq Rouge, Red Rooster, 3 ¾ In. 16
Figure, Japanese Girl, Blue Dress, 1959, 5 ½ x 3 ½ In. 64
Jar, Ketchup, Spoon, 1958, 5 ¾ x 4 ½ In. 58
Mug, Novelty, For This I Went To College, Woman Scrubbing Floor, 1972, 3 In. 8
Pepper Shaker, Moo Cow, Red Lips, Yellow Tie, Sticker, 1958, 3 In. 12
Salt & Pepper, Coq Rouge, Roosters, Red, Tan, 4 ¾ In. 16
Sundae Topping Set, 2 Lids, Chocolate, Nuts, Berries, Butterscotch, 1959, 4 ½ x 3 In. 129
Tureen, Tomato Shape, Red, Green Stem, c.1962, 8 x 6 ½ In. 15

HOPALONG CASSIDY

Hopalong Cassidy was a character in a series of 28 books written by Clarence E. Mulford, first published in 1907. Movies and television shows were made based on the character. The best-known actor playing Hopalong Cassidy was William Lawrence Boyd. His first movie appearance was in 1919, but the first Hopalong Cassidy film was not made until 1934. Sixty-six films were made. In 1948, William Boyd purchased the television rights to the movies, then later made 52 new programs. In the 1950s, Hopalong Cassidy and his horse, named Topper, were seen in comics, records, toys, and other products. Boyd died in 1972.

Binoculars, Metal, Plastic, Decals, Sport Glass Chicago, 1950s, 5 ½ In. 95
Book, Hopalong Cassidy Takes Cards, Clarence Mulford, 186 Pages, c.1935 10
Figure, Vinyl Head, Hands, Boots, Stuffed Body, 1950s, 23 In. 279
Glass, Milk, Lasso, Wagon, Black, 5 In., Pair 79
Invitation, Howdy Pards, Kids In Western Wear, 3 x 4 In. 15
Lunch Box, Metal, Wagon, Cassidy In Mountains, Blue, c.1950, 8 x 7 x 3 In. 165
Movie Poster, Six Shooter Justice, c.1950, 27 x 41 In. 45
Mug, Hopalong On Horse, Holding Gun, Signature, Milk Glass, Hazel Atlas, 1950s, 3 In. 20
Plate, Dinner, Hoppy On Horse, Black Outfit, Signed, 9 In. 85
Radio, Arvin, Red Metal Case, c.1950, 5 x 8 In. .... *illus* 210
Thermos, Aladdin, Cassidy & Horse, William Boyd, c.1950, 6 x 3 In. 75
Wristwatch, Saddle Display, Box, Ingersoll, 1950, 4 In. 118

HORN

Horn was used to make many types of boxes, furniture inlays, jewelry, and whimsies. The Endangered Species Act makes it illegal to sell many of these pieces. See also Powder Horn.

Cup, Libation, Deep Red, Leaves & Figures, Buffalo, Chinese, 3 ⅞ In. .... *illus* 115

HOWARD PIERCE

Howard Pierce began working in Southern California in 1936. In 1945, he opened a pottery in Claremont. He moved to Joshua Tree in 1968 and continued making pottery until 1991. He made contemporary-looking figurines. Though most pieces are marked with his name, smaller items from his sets often were not marked.

Figurine, Cat, Stylized, Raised Ears, Short Tail, White, Brown, Signed, 1950s 95

HOWDY DOODY

Howdy Doody and Buffalo Bob were the main characters in a children's series televised from 1947 to 1960. Howdy was a redheaded puppet. The series became popular with college students in the late 1970s when Buffalo Bob began to lecture on campuses.

Lamp, Night-Light, Cosmic Scout, Wood Base, 6 In., Pair 62
Periscope, Wonderbread, Collapsible Cardboard, 2 x 29 In. 118

HULL

Hull pottery was made in Crooksville, Ohio, from 1905. Addis E. Hull bought the Acme Pottery Company and started making ceramic wares. In 1917, A. E. Hull Pottery began making art pottery as well as the commercial wares. For a short time, 1921 to 1929, the firm also sold pottery imported from Europe. The dinnerware of the 1940s (including the Little Red Riding Hood line), the matte wares of the 1940s, and the high gloss artwares of the 1950s are all popular with collectors. The firm officially closed in March 1986.

Hull Pottery
c.1915

Hull Pottery
1930s

Hull Pottery
c.1950

Barefoot Boy, Cookie Jar, Red Hat, Blue Pants, Louise Bauer, 12 ½ In. 69
Blushing Apple, Cookie Jar, Lid, Green Steam, Red, Yellow, 1940s, 12 x 12 In. 49
Bow Knot, Wall Pocket, Whisk Broom, Blue, Green, 2 Flowers, Marked, 8 x 5 ¾ In. 127
Calla Lily, Vase, Light Green, Cream, 2 Handles, 6 x 5 In. .... *illus* 115
Corky Pig, Bank, Pink, Blue, Cork, Handle, Marked, 1957, 7 x 4 ¾ In. 92
Ebb Tide, Basket, Seashell Shape, Fish Handle, 16 ⅜ x 10 In. 115
Four Seasons, Clock, Deep Blue Edge, 4 Small Scenes, Multicolor, 7 x 2 In. .... *illus* 288
Gingerbread Man, Cookie Jar, Brown Drip Glaze, 12 In. .... *illus* 120
Green Drip, Vase, Glaze, Footed, 1960s, 4 ¾ x 4 ¾ In. 42
Little Red Riding Hood, Canister, Lid, Flour, Marked, 9 ½ In. 230
Little Red Riding Hood, Cookie Jar, Holding Basket, Cape, Flowers, Gold Stencil, c.1943, 13 In. 75 to 100
Little Red Riding Hood, Wall Pocket, Gold Trim, Floral, Marked, 9 ½ In. .... *illus* 115
Open Rose, Vase, Pink, Blue, Oil Lamp Shape, Marked, 10 ⅝ In. 92
Sand Gingerbread, Cookie Jar, Tan Glaze, 1940s 465
Sunglow, Wall Pocket, Pink, Butterfly, Pansies, 1940s, 9 x 6 In. 42
Woodland, Teapot, Lid, Pink Flower, 1950s, 11 x 4 In. 84

HUMMEL

Hummel figurines, based on the drawings of the nun M.I. Hummel (Berta Hummel), were made by the W. Goebel Porzellanfabrik of Oeslau, Germany, now Rodental, Germany. They were first made in 1935. The *Crown* mark was used from 1935 to 1949. The company added the *bee* marks in 1950. The *full bee* with variations, was used from 1950 to 1959; *stylized bee*, 1957 to 1972; *three line mark*, 1964 to 1972; *last bee*, sometimes called *vee over gee*, 1972 to 1979. In 1979 the V bee symbol was removed from the mark. *U.S. Zone* was part of the mark from 1946 to 1948; *W. Germany* was part of the mark from 1960 to 1990. The Goebel *W. Germany* mark, called the *missing bee* mark, was used from 1979 to 1990; *Goebel, Germany*, with the crown and *WG*, originally called the *new mark*, was used from 1991 through part of 1999. A new version of the bee mark with the word *Goebel* was used from 1999 to 2008. A special *Year 2000* backstamp was also introduced. Porcelain figures inspired by Berta Hummel's drawings were introduced in 1997. These are marked *BH* followed by a number. They were made in the Far East, not Germany. Goebel discontinued making Hummel figurines in 2008 and Manufaktur Rodental took over the factory in Germany and began making new Hummel figurines. Hummel figurines made by Rodental are marked with a yellow and black bee on the edge of an oval line surrounding

Icon, Christ Pantocrator, Holding Bible, Gilt Silver, Oklad Cover, Russia, 1800s, 9 x 7 In.
$250

Hindman Auctions

Icon, Mother Of God, Silver Oklad, Wood Frame, Russia, 8 x 7 In.
$394

Clars Auction Gallery

Icon, Santos, Figure, Arm Outstretched, Carved Wood, Plinth Base, 1700s, 13 ½ In.
$530

Clars Auction Gallery

Icon, St. Francis, Wood, Standing, Painted, Hooded Robe, Glass Eyes, 1700s, 20 ½ In.
$878

Thomaston Place Auction Galleries

Icon, St. George, Dragon, 2 Horizontal Black Slats, Multicolor, Russia, c.1900, 14 x 12 In.
$2,250

Cowan's Auctions

Imari, Bowl, Flower Shape, Sho Chiku Bai, Stylized Lotus, c.1900, 10 In.
$120

Eldred's

the words *Original M.I. Hummel Germany*. The words *Manufaktur Rodental* are printed beneath the oval. Manufaktur Rodental was sold in 2013 and new owners, Hummel Manufaktur GmbH, took over. It was sold again in 2017, but figurines continue to be made in the factory in Rodental. Other decorative items and plates that feature Hummel drawings were made by Schmid Brothers, Inc. beginning in 1971. Schmid Brothers closed in 1995.

Hummel
1935–1949

Hummel
1950–1959

Hummel
2009–present

Ashtray, No. 34, Singing Lessons, Boy, Black Bird, 4 x 7 x 6 In. 48
Bell, Annual, Seated Girl, Bird On Flower, 1981, 6 In. 65
Collector Plate, Singing Lessons, Boy & Bird, Goebel, 1979, 7 ½ In. 18
Figurine, No. 6/0, Sensitive Hunter, 4 ¾ In. 60
Figurine, No. 21/1, Heavenly Angel, 7 In. 91
Figurine, No. 81 2/0, School Girl, 4 ½ In. 54
Holy Water Font, No. 521, Heavenly Angel, 1949, 4 ¾ In. 45
Ornament, No. 296, Flying High, 1991, 4 In. 35
Plaque, No. TM2, Madonna, Child 75
Plate, No. 406, Valentine Gift, 6 In. 25
Plate, No. 684, Umbrella Girl, 1982, 7 ½ In. 75

HUTSCHENREUTHER

Hutschenreuther Porcelain Factory was founded by Carolus Magnus in Hohenburg, Bavaria, in 1814. A second factory was established in Selb, Germany, in 1857. The company made fine quality porcelain dinnerware and figurines. The mark changed through the years, but the name and the lion insignia appear in most versions. Hutschenreuther became part of the Rosenthal division of the Waterford Wedgwood Group in 2000. Rosenthal became part of the Arcturus Group in 2009.

Figurine, Lion, Walking Pose, White Glaze, 1814, 14 x 22 x 5 In. .... *illus* 363
Group, Roebuck & Doe, Lying Down, Glazed, Max Hermann Fritz, 4 x 9 ½ In. 68
Plate, Dinner, Band Gilt Rim, Marked, Royal Bavarian, c.1950, 11 In., 12 Piece 708
Plate, Flower Spray, Ivory Ground, Green Border, Crown & Lion Backstamp, 10 ¾ In., 12 Piece. 102

ICON

Icons, special, revered pictures of Jesus, Mary, or a saint, are usually Russian or Byzantine. The small icons collected today are made of wood and tin or precious metals. Many modern copies have been made in the old style and are being sold to tourists in Russia and Europe and at shops in the United States. Rare, old icons have sold for over $50,000. The riza is the metal cover protecting the icon. It is often made of silver or gold.

Christ Pantocrator, Brass Oklad, Russia, 12 x 10 In. .... *illus* 308
Christ Pantocrator, Brass Oklad, Wood Frame, Russia, 9 x 7 In. 269
Christ Pantocrator, Holding Bible, Gilt Silver, Oklad Cover, Russia, 1800s, 9 x 7 In. ...... *illus* 250
Hodigitria Mother Of God, Tempera On Wood Panel, Painted, Kovcheg, Russia, 11 x 6 In. 144
Holy Trinity, Father & Son, Orb, Multicolor, Enamel, Gold, 1800s, 20 ½ In. 984
Madonna & Child, Angels, Florentine, Gold Gilt Triptych, Italy, 5 x 9 x 1 In. 153
Madonna & Child, Hand Painted, Oklad, Saints, Frame, Russia, 1842, 6 x 5 In. 930

Mother Of God, Panagia, Silver, Russia, 3 ½ In. 551
Mother Of God, Silver Oklad, Wood Frame, Russia, 8 x 7 In. *illus* 394
Mother Of God, Silver, Oil On Panel, Oklad, Russia, Late 1800s, 9 x 7 In. 819
Plaque, St. Nicholas, Engraved Silver Riza, Gilt, Oklad, Russia, 1700s, 7 x 5 In. 6600
Saint, Holding 2-Headed Cane, Partial Gilt, Painted, Russia, 10 ½ x 8 ½ In. 236
Saints, St. Cosmas & St. Damien, Silver Oklad, Ivan Konstantinev, 1875, 11 ½ x 10 x 2 In. 1755
Santos, Figure, Arm Outstretched, Carved Wood, Plinth Base, 1700s, 13 ½ In. *illus* 530
Silver, Mary In Red Robe, Holding Jesus, Halos, High Relief Borders, 7 ½ x 6 In. 225
St. Francis, Wood, Standing, Painted, Hooded Robe, Glass Eyes, 1700s, 20 ½ In. *illus* 878
St. George, Dragon, 2 Horizontal Black Slats, Multicolor, Russia, c.1900, 14 x 12 In. *illus* 2250
St. Nicholas, Gilt Sgraffito, Oil On Panel, Russia, Late 1800s, 12 x 10 ½ In. 1112
St. Nicholas, Holding Book, Silver Oklad, Wood Frame, Russia, 11 ½ x 9 ½ In. 630
Traveling, Triptych, Passing Of Mary, Saints, Red, Blue, Green, Enamel, Silver, Russia, 1 x 2 ½ In. 250
Triptych, Virgin Mary & Child, Silver, Saint, Wood Frame, c.1900, 8 ½ x 6 ¾ In. 341
Virgin Of Tikhvin, Child, Silver Filigree, Enamel, Flowers, Leaves, Russia, c. 1896, 9 x 7 In. 1280

IMARI

Imari porcelain was made in Japan and China beginning in the seventeenth century. In the eighteenth century and later, it was copied by porcelain factories in Germany, France, England, and the United States. It was especially popular in the nineteenth century and is still being made. Imari is characteristically decorated with stylized bamboo, floral, and geometric designs in orange, red, green, and blue. The name comes from the Japanese port of Imari, which exported the ware made nearby in a factory at Arita. Imari is now a general term for any pattern of this type.

Bowl, Flower Shape, Sho Chiku Bai, Stylized Lotus, c.1900, 10 In. *illus* 120
Bowl, Lotus, Cranes, Landscape Roundel, Enameled, Footed, Japan, 4 x 9 ¾ In. 89
Bowl, Scalloped Edge, Gilt, Flower Crests, Phoenix, Cobalt Blue, Iron Red, 4 x 8 ½ In. 410
Bowl, Scalloped Rim, Gilt, Multicolor, Alternating Panels, Central Medallion, 4 ½ x 15 ¾ In. 413
Charger, Gilt, Phoenix, Flowers, Tapering Rim, Japan, c.1800, 4 x 18 In. 761
Jar, Dome Lid, Foo Dog Finial, Blue, Red, Flowers, Carved, Wood Stand, Late 1800s, 21 In. 266
Lamp, Painted, Glazed, Cobalt Blue, Iron Red, Mounted, Wood Stand, Late 1900s, 30 ½ In. 177
Plate, Scalloped & Gilded Rim, Multicolor, Gilt Accents, Flowers, 9 ½ In., 12 Piece *illus* 400
Temple Jar, Lid, Melon Shape, Flowers, Birds, Round Finial, Japan, 33 ½ In. 2242
Umbrella Stand, Cylindrical, Flowers, Iron Red, Blue, Underglaze, 24 x 9 In. 489
Vase, Maple Tree Garden, Allover Leaf, Red, White, 13 In. 144

IMPERIAL

Imperial Glass Corporation was founded in Bellaire, Ohio, in 1901. It became a subsidiary of Lenox, Inc., in 1973 and was sold to Arthur R. Lorch in 1981. It was sold again in 1982, and went bankrupt in 1984. In 1985, the molds and some assets were sold. The Imperial glass preferred by the collector is freehand art glass, carnival glass, slag glass, stretch glass, and other top-quality tablewares. Tablewares and animals are listed here. The others may be found in the appropriate sections.

Imperial Glass
1911–1932

Imperial Glass
1913–1920s

Imperial Glass
1973–1981

Candlestick, Cobalt Blue, Iridescent, Polished Pontils, Early 1900s, 10 ¾ In., Pair 677
Candlewick, Tray, Round, Beaded Rim, 13 ½ In. 130
Vase, Free Hand, Heart & Vine, Green Iridescent, Maroon, Cobalt Blue Rim, c.1925, 7 x 3 In. *illus* 1053
Vase, Gold, Iridescent, Red Threading, Circular Base, Early 1900s, 10 In. 1230

Imari, Plate, Scalloped & Gilded Rim, Multicolor, Gilt Accents, Flowers, 9 ½ In., 12 Piece
$400

Locati Auctions

Imperial, Vase, Free Hand, Heart & Vine, Green Iridescent, Maroon, Cobalt Blue Rim, c.1925, 7 x 3 In.
$1,053

Jeffrey S. Evans & Associates

Indian, Bag, Prairie, Black Wool, Beaded, Multicolor Flowers, Fabric Handle, c.1935, 15 In.
$813

Cowan's Auctions

This is an edited listing of current prices. Visit **Kovels.com** to check thousands of prices from previous years and sign up for free information on trends, tips, reproductions, marks, and more.

Indian, Bag, Sioux, Blue Cloth, Beaded, Tinklers, Signed, Doug Fast Horse, Late 1900s, 22 x 8 In.
$339

Soulis Auctions

Indian, Bandolier, Ojibwe, Beaded, Multicolor, Fringe, Wide Strap, c.1900, 44 x 13 In.
$1,625

Cowan's Auctions

Indian, Basket, Apache, Bowl, Coiled, Monochrome, 3 x 14 In.
$1,664

Clars Auction Gallery

Indian, Bolo, Hopi, Turquoise, Silver, Leather Necklace, 5 x 4 ½ In.
$805

Blackwell Auctions

Indian, Bolo, Navajo, Silver, Gold Overlay, Turquoise & Coral Settings, Braided Cord
$53

Conestoga Auction Company

INDIAN

Indian art from North and South America has attracted the collector for many years. Each tribe has its own distinctive designs and techniques. Baskets, jewelry, pottery, and leatherwork are of greatest collector interest. Eskimo art is listed under Eskimo in this book.

Bag, Nez Perce, Cornhusk, Pinwheel, Rawhide String Handle, c.1890, 9 x 8 In. 263
Bag, Prairie, Black Wool, Beaded, Multicolor Flowers, Fabric Handle, c.1935, 15 In. ....*illus* 813
Bag, Sioux, Blue Cloth, Beaded, Tinklers, Signed, Doug Fast Horse, Late 1900s, 22 x 8 In. *illus* 339
Bandolier, Ojibwa, Beaded, Multicolor, Fringe, Wide Strap, c.1900, 44 x 13 In. ....*illus* 1625
Basket, Apache, Bowl, Coiled, Monochrome, 3 x 14 In. ....*illus* 1664
Basket, Apache, Coiled, Stepped Geometric Pattern, Central Circle, 15 In. 640
Basket, Cahuilla, Coil, Woven, Mission, Circular, Multicolor, c.1900, 3 x 10 In. 4110
Basket, Cherokee, River Cane, Tapered, Circular Neck, Geometric Band, Square Base.......... 443
Basket, Cherokee, Storage, River Cane, Rectangular, Walnut Dyed, 1800s, 4 x 9 ½ x 10 In. 578
Basket, Pima, Woven Coil, Interior Pincushion, Greek Key, 1910s, 1 x 2 ⅜ In. 199
Basket, Yurok, Hat, Geometric, Brown, Black, Tan, c.1940, 7 In. 270
Belt, Navajo, Turquoise Cabochon, Buckle, Flowers, Butterflies, Black Leather, 52 ½ In. 622
Bolo, Hopi, Turquoise, Silver, Leather Necklace, 5 x 4 ½ In. ....*illus* 805
Bolo, Navajo, Silver, Gold Overlay, Turquoise & Coral Settings, Braided Cord ....*illus* 53
Bowl, Hopi, Squat, Pottery, Bands Of Geometrics, Signed, Fannie Nampeyo, 1950s, 3 x 6 In. 772
Bowl, San Ildefonso, Feather, Geometric, Crucita Gonzalez Calabaza, 1930s, 6 In. 826
Bowl, San Ildefonso, Squat, Redware, Knife Wing, Signed, Juanita, Early 1900s, 2 ½ x 6 In. 1056
Bowl, Yokuts, Coiled Basket, Multicolor, Hourglass, Early 1900s, 6 ¼ x 14 In. ....*illus* 1440
Bowl, Zuni, Geometric, Multicolor, Museum Accession, c.1890-1910, 3 ¾ x 8 In. 1265
Box, Sioux, Lid, Painted Exterior, Great Plains, 4 In. 276
Box, Sioux, Parfleche, Multicolor Paint, Red Wool Corners, c.1890, 9 ½ x 16 x 10 In. ......*illus* 1875
Bracelet, Hopi, Cuff, Spider, Web, Turquoise Cabochons, Silver, P. Monongye, 1 ½ In. Wide ..*illus* 10625
Bracelet, Navajo, Cluster, Bird's-Eye Turquoise, Signed, Kirk Smith, 6 In. 735
Bracelet, Navajo, Cuff, Red, White, Blue, Silver Bezels, Navajo Tears, Hogan Drops, Kirk Smith, 7 ½ In... 452
Bracelet, Navajo, Cuff, Silver, Channel Inlay, Signed, Lorraine Long, 2 In. Wide ....*illus* 173
Bracelet, Navajo, Cuff, Turquoise Cabochons, Rope Bezels, c.1925, 6 In. ....*illus* 1000
Bracelet, Navajo, Silver, Yei, Eagle, Coral, Opal, Lapis, E.P. Tsosie, 1900s, 2 ½ In. Wide ....*illus* 1484
Buckle, Navajo, Silver, Inlaid Turquoise Mosaic, Tommy Singer, c.1970, 3 x 2 x 1 ⅜ In. ..*illus* 230
Charger, San Ildefonso Pueblo, Redware, Geometric Slip, Crucita Calabaza, Late 1900s, 9 ½ In. *illus* 452
Club, Northwest Coast, Seal, Wood, Bear & Killer Whale, 18 In. 123
Doll, Seminole, Faint Ink, Velvet Jacket, Yarn Hair, Silver Pin, Early 1900s, 17 In. 138
Doll, Skookum, Wood, Leather & Cotton Clothing, Moccasins, c.1890, 34 In. ....*illus* 270
Dress, Sioux, Buckskin, Beaded, Fringe Trim & Drops, Charles Fast Horse, 49 ½ In. 2260
Figure, Owl, Acoma, White, Corrugated, S Shutiva, 6 ½ In. ....*illus* 106
Headdress, Sioux, Bonnet, Quills, Beads, Feathers, Buckskin, Tinklers, 50 In. 2486
Jar, Acoma, Leaves, Squat, Cream Ground, 9 ½ In. 374
Jar, Jemez, Geometric, Multicolor, Squat, Signed, Mary Small, 7 x 7 In. ....*illus* 164
Jar, Mata Ortiz, Black, Snake On Body & Rim, c.1970, 10 x 11 In. 100
Jar, Mata Ortiz, Lizard & Geometric, Multicolor, c.1970, 9 ½ x 10 ½ In. 70
Jar, San Ildefonso, Blackware, Carved, Turquoise Eye, Shoulder Band, Dora Tse-Pe, 1977, 6 x 8 ½ In. 1074
Jar, San Ildefonso, Seed, Ladybugs, Spider & Web, Blackware, Barbara Gonzales, 2 x 3 ¾ In.... 203
Jar, Santa Clara, Carved, Feathers, Red, Anna Archuleta, 1900s, 9 In. ....*illus* 230
Jar, Zuni, Geometric, Multicolor, Museum Accession, c.1890-1910, 6 ½ x 7 ½ In. 374
Katsina, Hopi, Deer Dancer, Wood, Carved, Painted, 1950s, 14 ½ In. ....*illus* 1563
Katsina, Hopi, Heheya, Signed, Walter Howato, c.1925, 20 ½ In. ....*illus* 750
Knife, Ojibwa, Floral, Rawhide Back, Wood Handle, Sheath, J. Russel & Co., Late 1800s, 19 In. .*illus* 1020
Ladle, Northwest Coast, Sheep Horn, 1900s, 12 In. ....*illus* 120
Ladle, Woodlands, Maple, Carved, Rooster Head Hook Handle, 1800s, 10 ½ In. ....*illus* 236
Mask, Northwest Coast, Carved, Wood, Painted, Raised Eyebrows, Early 1900s, 9 x 7 x 3 In. .*illus* 1404
Mask, Northwest Coast, Painted, Smiling, Wood, Multicolor, 20 ½ x 12 In. ....*illus* 531
Mirror Bag, Plateau, Hide, Wool Strap, Beaded, Multicolor, Fringe, c.1885, 25 x 7 In. .....*illus* 8750
Moccasins, Arapaho, Sky Blue, Orange, Red & Blue Beads, Parfleche Bottoms, 3 x 9 x 3 In. ... *illus* 283

Indian, Bowl, Yokuts, Coiled Basket, Multicolor, Hourglass, Early 1900s, 6 ¼ x 14 In.
$1,440

Brunk Auctions

TIP
Nineteenth-century Indian blankets are generally not restored by museums. They stabilize them, mount them on a backing fabric to avoid further damage, and hang or frame them. There is some thought that even the dirt may be wanted in its original state in the future.

Indian, Box, Sioux, Parfleche, Multicolor Paint, Red Wool Corners, c.1890, 9 ½ x 16 x 10 In.
$1,875

Cowan's Auctions

Indian, Bracelet, Hopi, Cuff, Spider, Web, Turquoise Cabochons, Silver, P. Monongye, 1 ½ In. Wide
$10,625

Cowan's Auctions

Indian, Bracelet, Navajo, Cuff, Silver, Channel Inlay, Signed, Lorraine Long, 2 In. Wide
$173

Blackwell Auctions

Indian, Bracelet, Navajo, Cuff, Turquoise Cabochons, Rope Bezels, c.1925, 6 In.
$1,000

Cowan's Auctions

Indian, Bracelet, Navajo, Silver, Yei, Eagle, Coral, Opal, Lapis, E.P. Tsosie, 1900s, 2 ½ In. Wide
$1,484

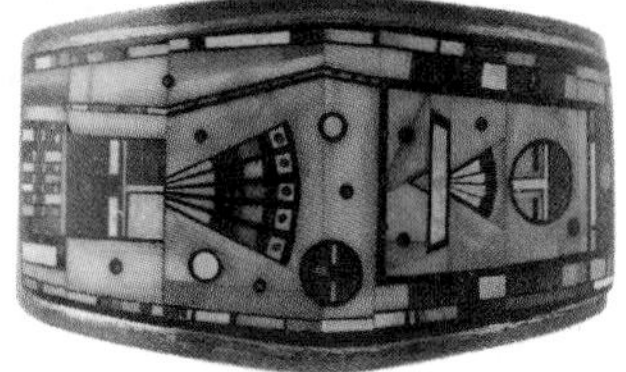

Freeman's Auctioneers & Appraisers

Indian, Buckle, Navajo, Silver, Inlaid Turquoise Mosaic, Tommy Singer, c.1970, 3 x 2 x 1 ⅜ In.
$230

Blackwell Auctions

Indian, Charger, San Ildefonso Pueblo, Redware, Geometric Slip, Crucita Calabaza, Late 1900s, 9 ½ In.
$452

Soulis Auctions

Indian, Doll, Skookum, Wood, Leather & Cotton Clothing, Moccasins, c.1890, 34 In.
$270

Rich Penn Auctions

Indian, Figure, Owl, Acoma, White, Corrugated, S Shutiva, 6 ½ In.
$106

Bunch Auctions

Indian, Jar, Jemez, Geometric, Multicolor, Squat, Signed, Mary Small, 7 x 7 In.
$164

Cordier Auctions

Indian, Jar, Santa Clara, Carved, Feathers, Red, Anna Archuleta, 1900s, 9 In.
$230

Blackwell Auctions

Skookum

Skookum Indian dolls can be dated by the material used for the parts. The earliest dolls from the mid to late 1910s had apple heads, no feet, and a block of wood for a body. In the early 1920s, some apple-head dolls had composition shoes. In the 1930s, the feet were leather-over-wood moccasins. From the 1910s to the 1940s, dolls had composition masks, some marked "Germany." In the 1940s, plastic masks were used.

Indian, Katsina, Hopi, Deer Dancer, Wood, Carved, Painted, 1950s, 14 ½ In.
$1,563

Freeman's Auctioneers & Appraisers

Indian, Katsina, Hopi, Heheya, Signed, Walter Howato, c.1925, 20 ½ In.
$750

Cowan's Auctions

Indian, Knife, Ojibwa, Floral, Rawhide Back, Wood Handle, Sheath, J. Russel & Co., Late 1800s, 19 In.
$1,020

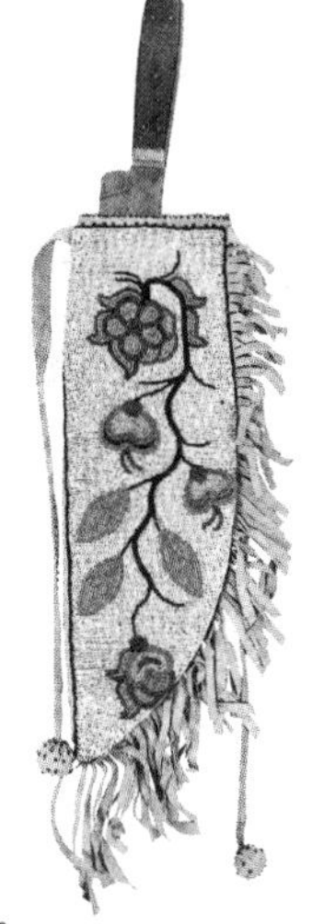

Brunk Auctions

Indian, Ladle, Northwest Coast, Sheep Horn, 1900s, 12 In.
$120

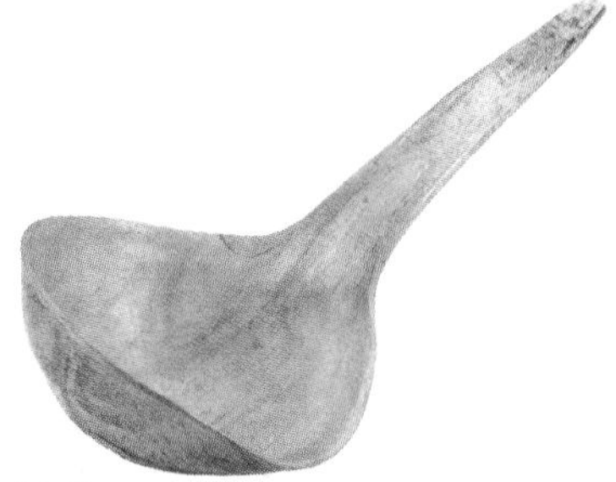

Eldred's

Indian, Ladle, Woodlands, Maple, Carved, Rooster Head Hook Handle, 1800s, 10 ½ In.
$236

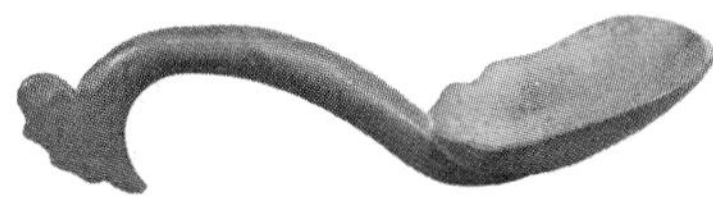

Conestoga Auction Company

TIP
Look in your hardware store for the new glues that can fix almost anything. Buy the proper one to fix transparent glass, porous pottery, or nonporous metals. There will be one that will work.

Indian, Mask, Northwest Coast, Carved, Wood, Painted, Raised Eyebrows, Early 1900s, 9 x 7 x 3 In.
$1,404

Thomaston Place Auction Galleries

Indian, Mask, Northwest Coast, Painted, Smiling, Wood, Multicolor, 20 ½ x 12 In.
$531

Copake Auctions

Indian, Mirror Bag, Plateau, Hide, Wool Strap, Beaded, Multicolor, Fringe, c.1885, 25 x 7 In.
$8,750

Cowan's Auctions

Indian, Moccasins, Arapaho, Sky Blue, Orange, Red & Blue Beads, Parfleche Bottoms, 3 x 9 x 3 In.
$283

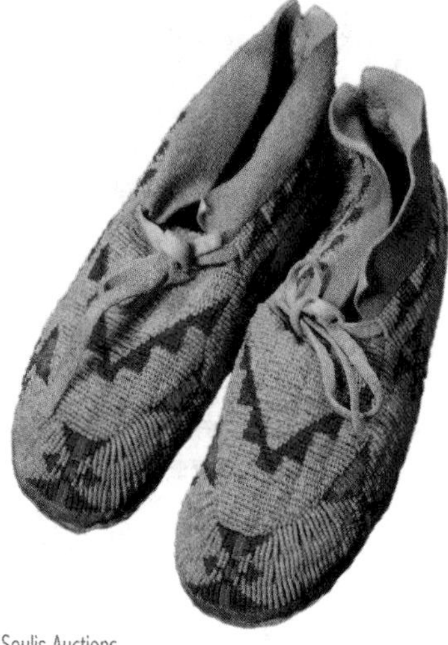

Soulis Auctions

Indian, Moccasins, Eastern Woodlands, Wool, Embroidered
$98

Skinner, Inc.

Indian, Moccasins, Sioux, Hide, Beaded, Quilled, c.1910, 10 ¾ In.
$938

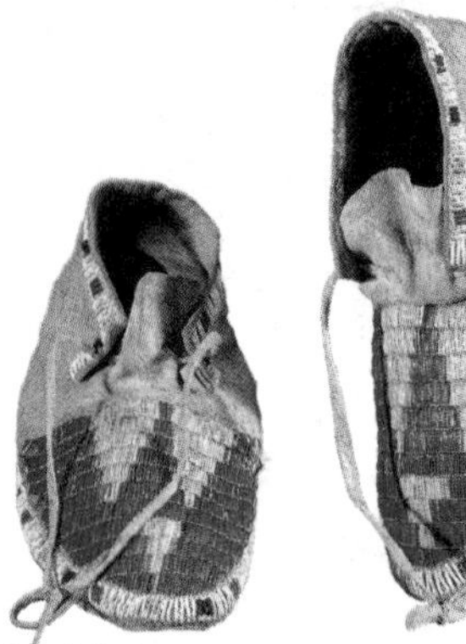

Cowan's Auctions

Indian, Necklace, Acoma, 5 Graduated Strands, Coral, c.1965, 24 In.
$1,625

Cowan's Auctions

Indian, Plaque, Blackware, 3 Carved Bear Paws, Turquoise Cabochons, Signed, Virginia Ebelacker, 11 In.
$2,000

Cowan's Auctions

Indian, Pot, Acoma, White, Black, Geometric, Brown Interior, D. Brown, 9 x 8 In.
$94

Copake Auctions

Indian, Pot, Zuni, Band Of Long-Tailed Birds, Geometric Shapes, Scrolls, 10 x 14 In.
$4,688

Palm Beach Modern Auctions

Indian, Rug, Navajo, Diamonds, Woven, Central Field, Black Border, c.1940, 70 ½ x 37 ½ In.
$1,074

Soulis Auctions

Indian, Scoop, Woodlands, Burl, Round Bowl, Flat Bottom, Arched Handle, c.1800, 15 x 6 ¾ In.
$677

Skinner, Inc.

Moccasins, Eastern Woodlands, Wool, Embroidered .... *illus*	98
Moccasins, Plateau, Beaded, Diamonds, Hide, Sawtooth Edging, c.1910, 9 In.	650
Moccasins, Sioux, Hide, Beaded, Quilled, c.1910, 10 ¾ In. .... *illus*	938
Necklace, Acoma, 5 Graduated Strands, Coral, c.1965, 24 In. .... *illus*	1625
Olla, Acoma, Black, Sienna, White Ground, Signed CC, 1900s, 9 ½ x 8 ½ In.	100
Olla, Acoma, Redware, Brown & White Geometric Slip, Signed, Loretta Joe, 13 ½ x 14 In.	452
Olla, Zuni, Geometric, Red, Brown, White, Elongated Neck, Late 1800s, 9 x 11 ¾ In.	2040
Pipe Bowl, Blackfoot, Stone, Black, Square Base, 1920s, 2 ⅞ In.	369
Pipe, Plains, Horse, Running, Catlinite, Lead Circles, Patina, c.1870, 6 x 1 x 4 ¾ In.	805
Pitcher, Cochiti, Bird Head Spout, Stylized Feathers, I. Packard, Early 1900s, 8 In.	1320
Plaque, Blackware, 3 Carved Bear Paws, Turquoise Cabochons, Signed, Virginia Ebelacker, 11 In. *illus*	2000
Plate, San Ildefonso, Geometric, Blackware, Maria & Popovi, 6 In.	787
Pot, Acoma, White, Black, Geometric, Brown Interior, D. Brown, 9 x 8 In. .... *illus*	94
Pot, Zuni, Band Of Long-Tailed Birds, Geometric Shapes, Scrolls, 10 x 14 In. .... *illus*	4688
Pouch, Plains, Figural, Cowhide, Calf's Head, Beaded Facial, Lazy Stitch, c.1900, 12 ½ In.	1200
Rug, Navajo, Diamonds, Woven, Central Field, Black Border, c.1940, 70 ½ x 37 ½ In. ......*illus*	1074
Rug, Navajo, Eyedazzler, Woven, 4-Ply, Germantown, Pennsylvania Mills, c.1890, 57 x 88 In...	4388
Rug, Navajo, Landscape, Mountains, Cars, Cows, Birds, Houses, Airplanes, Desert, 73 x 88 In..	1020
Rug, Navajo, Red & Black Stripes, Geometric, Ivory, 29 x 55 In.	96
Rug, Navajo, Wool, Geometric, Flowers, Red Accent, 1910s, 41 x 69 In.	570
Rug, Navajo, Yeibichai Dancers, 3 Cornstalks, Rainbow Guardian, Wool, 1950s, 60 x 32 In.	234
Scoop, Woodlands, Burl, Round Bowl, Flat Bottom, Arched Handle, c.1800, 15 x 6 ¾ In. .*illus*	677
Sculpture, Massasoit, Brave, Standing, Rectangular Base, Bronze, Cyrus Dallin, 11 x 3 x 4 In. ...... *illus*	1599
Seed Jar, Hopi, Geometric, Squat, Faint Pencil Inscription On Base, 2 x 6 ½ In.	540
Seed Jar, Santa Clara, Sgraffito, Geometric, Signed, Kevin Naranjo, Late 1900s, 3 In.	391
Shirt, Sioux, Hide, Blue & Yellow Pigment, Thread & Sinew, Beaded, c.1885, 33 x 42 In. .*illus*	17920
Snowshoes, Athabaskan, Wood, Woven Sinew Webbing, c.1900, 55 ½ In. .... *illus*	500
Totem Pole, Northwest Coast, Walrus Tusk, Carved, Mounted, Wood Base, 1900s, 10 ½ In.	338
Tray, Pima, Coil Basket, Willow, Devil's Grass, Linear Fret, Early 1900s, 11 ¾ x 3 ½ In.	293
Vase, Acoma, Ball Shape, Deer, White & Black, Signed, Rose Chino-Garcia, 5 x 5 In.	283
Vase, Hopi, Cylindrical, Feather Motif, Red & Black, 1900s, 8 ⅜ In.	410
Vase, Sioux, Geometric, Painted, Footed, Signed, Red Starr, 3 ½ In.	177
Vase, Wedding, Acoma, Clay, Painted, Black, White, Terra-Cotta, R. Keene, New Mexico, 6 x 5 x 8 In.	94
Vest, Santee Sioux, Hide, Quilled, Cotton Lining, Flowers, American Flags, c.1890, 24 x 37 In. *illus*	4375
Vest, Woodlands, Flower Beadwork, Heart, Leather Front, Early 1900s, Child's, 16 x 15 In.	1500
War Club, Penobscot, Carved, Warrior Face, 2 Handles, Birch Root Ball, Early 1900s, 34 In.	1170
Water Jar, Acoma, Bird, Geometric Multicolor, Bulbous, W. Garcia, c.1965, 15 x 6 In. ......*illus*	439
Weaving, Navajo, Wool, Red, Earth Tones, Geometrics, Crosses, J.B. Moore, c.1910, 81 x 52 In. *illus*	1664
Yoke, Nez Perce, Canvas, Thread Sewn, Multicolor Flowers, Beaded Hide Thongs, c.1900, 36 In. *illus*	3000

INDIAN TREE

Indian Tree is a china pattern that was popular during the last half of the nineteenth century. It was copied from earlier Indian textile patterns that were very similar. The pattern includes the crooked branch of a tree and a partial landscape with exotic flowers and leaves. Green, blue, pink, and orange were the favored colors used in the design. Coalport, Spode, Johnson Brothers, and other firms made this pottery. Don't be confused by a pattern called India Tree made by Copeland.

Pitcher, Gold Ground, Hand Painted, Staffordshire, Early 1900s, 9 In.	108
Plate, Orange Rust, Red Trim, Scalloped Edge, 10 ⅜ In.	60
Plate, Salad, Multicolor, 8 In.	20
Tea Set, Teapot, Sugar, Creamer, Miniature, Teapot 2 In., Sugar 1 ¾ In., Creamer 1 ½ In.	65
Teapot, Swirl, Gold Trim, Sadler, 5 In.	65

Indian, Sculpture, Massasoit, Brave, Standing, Rectangular Base, Bronze, Cyrus Dallin, 11 x 3 x 4 In.
$1,599

Clars Auction Gallery

Indian, Shirt, Sioux, Hide, Blue & Yellow Pigment, Thread & Sinew, Beaded, c.1885, 33 x 42 In.
$17,920

Cowan's Auctions

Indian, Snowshoes, Athabaskan, Wood, Woven Sinew Webbing, c.1900, 55 ½ In.
$500

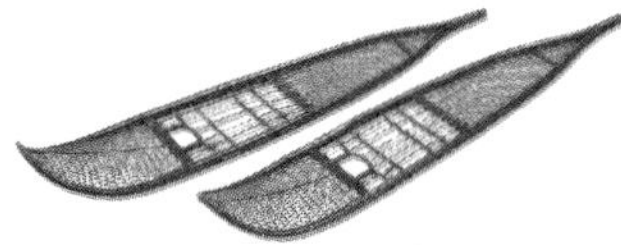

Cowan's Auctions

Indian, Vest, Santee Sioux, Hide, Quilled, Cotton Lining, Flowers, American Flags, c.1890, 24 x 37 In.
$4,375

Cowan's Auctions

Indian, Water Jar, Acoma, Bird, Geometric Multicolor, Bulbous, W. Garcia, c.1965, 15 x 6 In.
$439

Cordier Auctions

Indian, Yoke, Nez Perce, Canvas, Thread Sewn, Multicolor Flowers, Beaded Hide Thongs, c.1900, 36 In.
$3,000

Cowan's Auctions

Inkstand, Bronze, Stag, White Painted, 6 ½ x 9 In.
$160

Skinner, Inc.

TIP
Small collectibles can be hung as window shade pulls.

Indian, Weaving, Navajo, Wool, Red, Earth Tones, Geometrics, Crosses, J.B. Moore, c.1910, 81 x 52 In.
$1,664

Cowan's Auctions

Inkwell, Bronze, Cat, Fish Basket, Hinged Lid, Signed, I. Bonheur, c.1875, 3 ¾ In.
$472

Conestoga Auction Company

TIP
Do not display glass inkwells in a window or sunny location. The glass may turn slightly purple.

Inkwell, Bronze, Enamel, Footed, Art Crafts Shop, Buffalo, 3 x 5 In.
$188

Treadway

Inkwell, Cast Iron, Man In Barrel, Figural, Hinged Lid, Painted, 3 ½ In.
$431

Richard Opfer Auctioneering, Inc.

INKSTAND

Inkstands were made to be placed on a desk. They held some type of container for ink, and possibly a sander, a pen tray, a pen, a holder for pounce, and even a candle to melt the sealing wax. Inkstands date to the eighteenth century and have been made of silver, copper, ceramics, and glass. Additional inkstands may be found in these and other related categories.

2 Wells, Lids, Penholders, Stag & Hounds, Gilt, Brass Stand, Signed, Bradley & Hubbard, 5 x 9 x 5 In. 170
Brass, Acorn, Marble Base, 2 Wells, Signed, E. Famin, c.1900, 2 x 11 In. 105
Bronze, Bust, Green Marble, Wreath, Flowers, 2 Wells, Empire Style, 10 ½ x 18 In. 380
Bronze, Parrot, Cold Painted, Austria, 3 ½ x 10 In. 374
Bronze, Stag, White Painted, 6 ½ x 9 In. *illus* 160
Milk Glass, 2 Snail Fonts, Revolves On Brass Stand, 3 Penholders, 4 x 7 In. 192
Milk Glass, Bulldog's Head Font, Revolves On Metal Scrolling Stand, 4 ½ In. 450
Mother-Of-Pearl, Bronze, Chinese Man, Parasol, Cut Glass Ink Pots, Winged Feet, 11 In. 7813
Oak, Glass, Nickel Silver Trim, Footed, Center Handle, 2 Wells, England, 6 ½ x 12 In. 219
Porcelain, Snail Font, White, Blue Stripe, Metal Scroll Stand, Porcelain Dish, 3 x 5 In. 180
Silver, Neoclassical Style, 2 Wells, Oil Lamp, Walter & John Barnard, 8 x 14 x 10 In. 1063

INKWELL

Inkwells, of course, held ink. Ready-made ink was first made about 1836 and was sold in bottles. The desk inkwell had a narrow hole so the pen would not slip inside. Inkwells were made of many materials, such as pottery, glass, pewter, and silver.

Art Glass, Green, Threaded Crystal, Hinged Brass, Mushroom Lid, 2 x 4 In. 113
Brass, Hinged Lid, Koi Fish In Relief, Stylized Waves, Bulbous, Early 1900s, 4 ½ x 7 ½ In. 416
Bronze, Cat, Fish Basket, Hinged Lid, Signed, I. Bonheur, c.1875, 3 ¾ In. *illus* 472
Bronze, Enamel, Footed, Art Crafts Shop, Buffalo, 3 x 5 In. *illus* 188
Bronze, Flip Lid, Figural, Elk Head, Clear Glass Well, 5 ½ x 6 ½ In. 350
Bronze, Gilt, Leaves Finial, Footed, Signed, Maison Millet, Late 1800s, 5 In. 215
Bronze, Hinged Lid, Cat, Mouth Open, Patina, Ribbon, 4 In. 338
Bronze, Hunting Dog, Flower Caps, Putti Face, Feather, 12 x 12 In. 360
Cast Iron, Man In Barrel, Figural, Hinged Lid, Painted, 3 ½ In. *illus* 431
Cut Glass, Hinged Silver Lid, Hobnail Base, 3 ½ x 3 ¾ x 2 ¾ In. 219
Glass, Enamel, Octagonal Cut, Electric Blue, Floral, White, Brass Mounts, c.1900, 3 In. 70
Glass, Silver, Black, Starr & Frost, Cherub Finial, Beveled Edges, Signed, 7 x 3 x 3 In. 242
Hat Shape, Rigi-Kulm, Switzerland, Black Forest, Carved, 4 x 2 In. 66
Loetz Type, Cranberry, Circular Shape, Swirled Feather, 1910s, 1 ¾ x 5 In. 380
Metal, Pear, Leaves, Stem, Green, Yellow, 8 ½ In. 207
Porcelain, Art Nouveau Style, Blue Body, Gilt, Leaves, Stems, Bronze Base, Louchet, 5 x 17 In. 605
Porcelain, Ball Shape Lid, Square, Figures, Insert, Satsuma, Japan, 3 ⅞ x 3 ⅞ x 6 ½ In. *illus* 163
Silver, Christopher Dresser Style, Spherical, Circular Handles, Drip Plate, 3 x 3 ⅞ In. *illus* 236
Silver, Urn Shape, Mounted, Tray, Claw Feet, Alexandre Vaguer, France, c.1800, 5 ½ In. 185
Spelter, Figural, Parrot, Green, Standing, 4 ½ In. 236
Wood, Blackamoor Head, Glass Eyes, Porcelain Inkpot, Depose, Late 1800s, 6 x 4 ½ In. 625
Wood, Carved, Young Woman, Blown Glass Eyes, Painted, 1800s, 4 ½ In. *illus* 207

INSULATOR

Insulators of glass or pottery have been made for use on telegraph or telephone poles since 1844. Thousands of styles of insulators have been made. Most common are those of clear or aqua glass; most desirable are the threadless types made from 1850 to 1870. CD numbers are Consolidated Design numbers used by collectors to indicate shape. Lists of CD numbers and other identifying marks can be found online.

Glass, Canadian Pacific Ry Co., Purple, 3 ¾ In. 40
Hemingray, No. 42, Aqua Green, Embossed, 3 ¾ x 4 In. 35
Porcelain, Brown Glaze, 1920s, 3 ½ In. 12

Inkwell, Porcelain, Ball Shape Lid, Square, Figures, Insert, Satsuma, Japan, 3 ⅞ x 3 ⅞ x 6 ½ In.
$163

Hudson Valley Auctions

Inkwell, Silver, Christopher Dresser Style, Spherical, Circular Handles, Drip Plate, 3 x 3 ⅞ In.
$236

Leland Little Auctions

Inkwell, Wood, Carved, Young Woman, Blown Glass Eyes, Painted, 1800s, 4 ½ In.
$207

Cottone Auctions

Iron, Boot Scraper, Cat, Black, Yellow Eyes, Oval Base, 15 ½ x 9 In.
$236

Copake Auctions

Iron, Boot Scraper, Duck, Patina, 15 In.
$102

Hartzell's Auction Gallery Inc.

TIP

Remove the rust from iron by soaking the piece in kerosene for 24 hours, or use any one of several commercial preparations made for the removal of rust. Wash, dry, and coat the piece with a light oil to protect it.

Iron, Bootjack, Naughty Nellie, Painted, Black & White, 1800s, 9 ¾ In.
$226

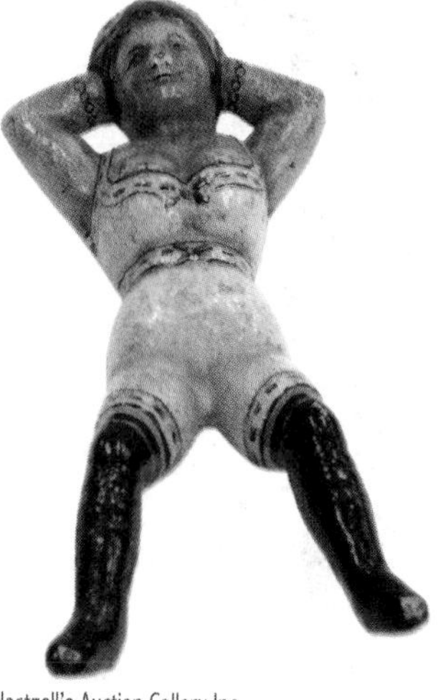

Hartzell's Auction Gallery Inc.

IRISH BELLEEK, *see Belleek category.*

IRON

Iron is a metal that has been used by man since prehistoric times. It is a popular metal for tools and decorative items like doorstops that need as much weight as possible. Items are listed here or under other appropriate headings, such as Bookends, Doorstop, Kitchen, Match Holder, or Tool. The tool that is used for ironing clothes, an iron, is listed in the Kitchen category under Iron and Sadiron.

Boot Scraper, Cat, Black, Yellow Eyes, Oval Base, 15 ½ x 9 In. .... *illus* 236
Boot Scraper, Duck, Patina, 15 In. .... *illus* 102
Boot Scraper, H Shape, Curl Post Finial, Limestone Block, 1800s, 7 x 15 x 8 In. 819
Bootjack, Naughty Nellie, Painted, Black & White, 1800s, 9 ¾ In. .... *illus* 226
Candleholder, Candle Socket, Round Drip Catcher, Threaded Post, 1700s, 7 ½ In., Pair 1046
Candleholder, Puss & Boots, Standing, 1800s, 3 ¾ In. 68
Cannon, Signal, Gold Painted Barrel, Black, Orange Carriage, Model, 1800s, 15 In. 240
Card Holder, 2 Dogs, Standing, Legs On Base, Painted, 11 ½ x 6 In. .... *illus* 158
Cuspidor, Top Hat, Porcelain Interior, Cast, Pat. Appl. For On Bottom, 7 In. 246
Figure, Bell, Bird, Mounted, 13 ½ In. 620
Figure, Bull, Flattened, Separate Horns, Mounted On Flat Bar, Late 1800s, 10 x 18 ¾ In. *illus* 3075
Figure, Deer, Buck, Painted, Attributed To J.W. Fiske, c.1890, 60 x 48 In. .... *illus* 2640
Figure, Dog, Lying Down, Painted, Black, 3 x 1 ¾ x 6 In. 46
Figure, Eagle, Cast, Perched On Spear, Spread Wings, Gold Paint, Late 1800s, 14 In. 210
Figure, Eagle, Full Body, Raised Base, Black Paint, Plaque, Crown, 1910s, 13 x 17 x 6 In. *illus* 438
Figure, Eagle, Spread Wings, Gold Paint, Wood Base, c.1900, 13 x 30 In. 188
Figure, Lion, Full-Bodied, Hair, Tail, Details, Early 1900s, 13 ½ x 23 x 3 In. 60
Hat Rack, Horseshoe Center, 6 Hooks, Leaves, Hanging, 28 x 14 ½ In. 561
Holder, Skewer, Heart, Skewers, 11 In. .... *illus* 177
Mailbox, Blue, La Levee De Est Faite, Hinged Door, France, Early 1900s, 26 x 13 x 9 In. 492
Patent Model, Sadiron, Flat Iron, No. 37118, J. Webster, 1862, 6 In. 1695
Patent Model, Sadiron, Fluter, Original Tag, No. 224323, C.A. Babcock, Feby 10, 1880, 3 In. ... 311
Penholder, Figural, Cat, Katz Drug Store, Painted, 7 In. 400
Pin Tray, Woman, Green, Enamel, Marked, Pemco, Victorian, 7 x 6 In. .... *illus* 57
Plaque, UF Steam Engine, Mounted, Wood, 15 x 12 In. 132
Post, Memorial Garland Cross, Scrollwork, Painted Medallion, Bobby, Late 1800s, 29 In. 240
Sculpture, Brutalism, Rusted Patina, Matsumoto, 24 x 18 x 20 In. 531
Sculpture, Flat Floating Disc, Offset Orb, Cylindrical Base, Arlie Regier, 39 x 24 x 8 In. ..*illus* 1130
Sculpture, Globe, Convex Parallel Rod Central Sphere, Flat Beaded Ring, c.1900, 84 In. 584
Sculpture, Mobile, Fish Shape, Painted, Black, 1950s, 39 x 56 In. 187
Seat, Tractor, Cast Iron, American Harrow Co., c.1880, 14 x 15 ½ In. 145
Shield, Embossed, Mythological Battle, Dark Brown Patina, 1800s, 28 ¾ In. 1845
Sign, 2 Eskimos, Dog Sled Race, Arrow, Grenfell Style, Sheet Iron, 1900s, 18 x 48 x 5 In. 1680
Sign, Horseshoe, Surrounded By 13 Horseshoes, Horse & 2 Shoes In Center, 30 x 27 In. ..*illus* 325
Target, Shooting Gallery, Bird, Yellow, Painted, Round Base, 3 x 2 ¾ In. 90
Target, Shooting Gallery, Duck, Wood Base, 6 x 6 ½ In. 71
Target, Shooting Gallery, Indian Chief, Mounted, Red & White, Painted, 6 In. 215
Target, Shooting Gallery, Man, Rifle, Wood Base, 13 x 8 In. .... *illus* 83
Target, Shooting Gallery, Old Woman, Green Dress, Painted, c.1920, 69 ½ In. 923
Target, Shooting Gallery, Pig, Standing, Painted White, 22 x 15 In. .... *illus* 118
Target, Shooting Gallery, Rooster, Wood Base, 5 x 4 ½ In. 94
Weight, Horse, Black, Painted, Lewis Stable, 1800s, 6 ½ In. 226
Weight, Tassel Shape, Painted, Pulley Top, 1800s, 8 In., Pair 338
Windmill Weight, Bull, Mounted, Fairbury Windmill Co., c.1920, 17 ¾ x 24 In. 439
Windmill Weight, Bull, Rectangular Base, Fairbury Nebr., Early 1900s, 19 x 24 In. 1920
Windmill Weight, Horse, Bobtail, Brown, Black Base, Dempster, c.1900, 18 x 19 In. .... *illus* 609
Windmill Weight, Horse, Bobtail, Brown, Standing, 17 x 17 In. .... *illus* 207
Windmill Weight, Moon, Eclipse, Rectangular Base, 10 In. .... *illus* 369
Windmill Weight, Rooster, 4 Feathers, Mounted, Wood Base, Hummer, 10 x 7 ½ In. 295
Windmill Weight, Rooster, Mounted, Rectangular Base, Late 1800s, 15 ½ In. .... *illus* 336

Iron, Card Holder, 2 Dogs, Standing, Legs On Base, Painted, 11 ½ x 6 In.
$158

Hartzell's Auction Gallery Inc.

Iron, Figure, Bull, Flattened, Separate Horns, Mounted On Flat Bar, Late 1800s, 10 x 18 ¾ In.
$3,075

Skinner, Inc.

TIP
If the hinge that holds the lid on a stein or other metal object is balky, try lubricating it.

Iron, Figure, Deer, Buck, Painted, Attributed To J.W. Fiske, c.1890, 60 x 48 In.
$2,640

Garth's Auctioneers & Appraisers

Iron, Figure, Eagle, Full Body, Raised Base, Black Paint, Plaque, Crown, 1910s, 13 x 17 x 6 In.
$438

Garth's Auctioneers & Appraisers

Iron, Holder, Skewer, Heart, Skewers, 11 In.
$177

Copake Auctions

Iron, Pin Tray, Woman, Green, Enamel, Marked, Pemco, Victorian, 7 x 6 In.
$57

Hartzell's Auction Gallery Inc.

Iron, Sculpture, Flat Floating Disc, Offset Orb, Cylindrical Base, Arlie Regier, 39 x 24 x 8 In.
$1,130

Soulis Auctions

Iron, Sign, Horseshoe, Surrounded By 13 Horseshoes, Horse & 2 Shoes In Center, 30 x 27 In.
$325

Copake Auctions

Iron, Target, Shooting Gallery, Man, Rifle, Wood Base, 13 x 8 In.
$83

Bunch Auctions

TIP
Ivory will darken if kept in the dark. Keep a piano open so the keys will be in natural light. Keep figurines, chess sets, and other ivory in the open.

Iron, Target, Shooting Gallery, Pig, Standing, Painted White, 22 x 15 In.
$118

Copake Auctions

Iron, Windmill Weight, Horse, Bobtail, Brown, Black Base, Dempster, c.1900, 18 x 19 In.
$609

Freeman's Auctioneers & Appraisers

Iron, Windmill Weight, Horse, Bobtail, Brown, Standing, 17 x 17 In.
$207

Copake Auctions

Iron, Windmill Weight, Moon, Eclipse, Rectangular Base, 10 In.
$369

Richard Opfer Auctioneering, Inc.

Iron, Windmill Weight, Rooster, Mounted, Rectangular Base, Late 1800s, 15 ½ In.
$336

Pook & Pook

Iron, Windmill Weight, Rooster, Yellow, Red, Elgin Wind Power & Pump, c.1880, 18 x 17 In.
$923

Skinner, Inc.

Iron, Windmill Weight, Star, Mounting Hole, 10 ½ x 10 In.
$2,185

Forsythes' Auctions

TIP
Changes in temperature may cause old ivory to crack.

Ivory, Cane Handle, Fist Clenching Snake, Whale, c.1850, 4 ½ In.
$2,750

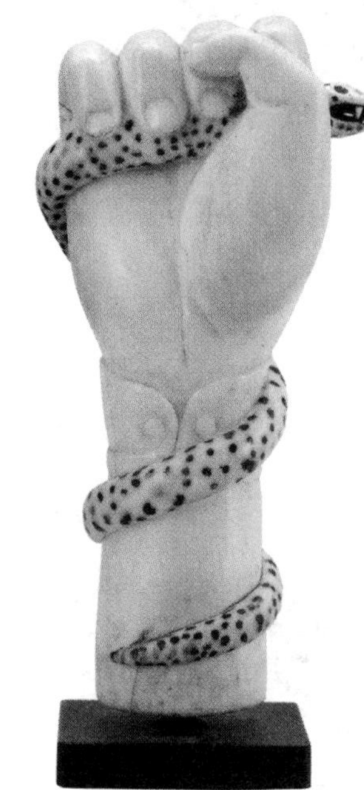

Eldred's

TIP
Washing your hands is good for your health and that of your collections. Grease and dirt can stain pieces and permanently lower the value. You can't always wash your hands in the middle of a flea market, but you can take wipes along to use.

Windmill Weight, Rooster, Red & White, Elgin Wind Power & Pump Co., 1930, 16 x 16 In. 468
Windmill Weight, Rooster, White, Red, c.1900, 17 x 22 In. 4160
Windmill Weight, Rooster, Yellow, Red, Elgin Wind Power & Pump, c.1880, 18 x 17 In. ..*illus* 923
Windmill Weight, Star, Mounted, Square Stand, 14 ½ x 14 ½ In. 561
Windmill Weight, Star, Mounting Hole, 10 ½ x 10 In. .....*illus* 2185

IRONSTONE

Ironstone china was first made in 1813. It gained its greatest popularity during the mid-nineteenth century. The heavy, durable, off-white pottery was made in white or was decorated with any of hundreds of patterns. Much flow blue pottery was made of ironstone. Some of the decorations were raised. Many pieces of ironstone are unmarked, but some English and American factories included the word *Ironstone* in their marks. Additional pieces may be listed in other categories, such as Chelsea Grape, Chelsea Sprig, Flow Blue, Gaudy Ironstone, Mason's Ironstone, Moss Rose, Staffordshire, and Tea Leaf Ironstone. These three marks were used by companies that made ironstone.

TJ & J Mayer's
1842–1855

W. Baker & Co. (Ltd.)
1893+

Wood & Son(s) (Ltd.)
1910+

Platter, Blue & White, Boaters, Punts On Lake, Church, Flower Border, 1840s, 12 x 15 ½ In. .. 92
Tureen, Platter, Lid Finial, 2 Handles, White Ground, Flowers, Transfer, 12 x 15 In. 123
Tureen, Soup, Fruit Basket, Blue, White, Footed, 2 Handles, 13 x 9 x 10 In. 307

IVORY

Ivory from the tusk of an elephant is thought by many to be the only true ivory. To most collectors, the term *ivory* also includes such natural materials as walrus, hippopotamus, or whale teeth or tusks, and some of the vegetable materials that are of similar texture and density. Other ivory items may be found in the Scrimshaw and Netsuke categories. Collectors should be aware of the recent laws limiting the buying and selling of elephant ivory and scrimshaw.

Cane Handle, Fist Clenching Snake, Whale, c.1850, 4 ½ In. .....*illus* 2750
Crucifix, Christ, INRI Placket, Carved, Ebony Cross, Continental, 1800s, 18 x 9 In. 702
Figurine, Apostle, Standing, Holding Bible, Wood Plug, Hollow Tusk, Late 1700s, 19 In. ..*illus* 3510
Figurine, Fisherman, Standing, Hat, Net On Shoulder, Fish, Stand, Late 1900s, 10 ½ In. *illus* 1260
Group, Man Carrying 2 Children, Basket Of Fruit, Signed, Hideyuki, Japan, c.1890, 10 ½ In. ...*illus* 563
Pie Crimper, Carved, Openwork Heart, Star, Lady's Leg In Boot, Fluted Wheel, c.1850, 8 In. ... *illus* 2880
Pincushion, Elephant, Carved, Acanthus, Tabletop, Clamp, Chinese, c.1850, 6 ¾ In. ......*illus* 300
Seam Rubber, Whale, Turk's Head Knot Handle, Metal Stand, c.1850, 5 In. .....*illus* 1140
Spinning Top, Whale, Engraved, Ink Numbers, 1 Through 8, 1800s, 8 In. .....*illus* 510

JACK-IN-THE-PULPIT

Jack-in-the-pulpit vases, shaped like trumpets, resemble the wildflower named jack-in-the-pulpit. The design originated in the late Victorian years. Vases in the jack-in-the-pulpit shape were made of ceramic or glass.

Bride's Bowl, Enamel, Flowers, Gilt Frame, Woman, Mirror, Ruffled Rim, Hobnail, 10 In. 384
Vase, Vaseline Opalescent, Ruffled Rim, Applied Petal Feet, 7 In. 72

JACOB PETIT

Jacob Petit (1796–1868) was a porcelain painter who worked for the Sevres factory in France. He opened his own shop near Paris sometime after 1830

Ivory, Figurine, Apostle, Standing, Holding Bible, Wood Plug, Hollow Tusk, Late 1700s, 19 In.
$3,510

Thomaston Place Auction Galleries

Ivory, Figurine, Fisherman, Standing, Hat, Net On Shoulder, Fish, Stand, Late 1900s, 10 ½ In.
$1,260

Morphy Auctions

Ivory, Group, Man Carrying 2 Children, Basket Of Fruit, Signed, Hideyuki, Japan, c.1890, 10 ½ In.
$563

Eldred's

Ivory, Pie Crimper, Carved, Openwork Heart, Star, Lady's Leg In Boot, Fluted Wheel, c.1850, 8 In.
$2,880

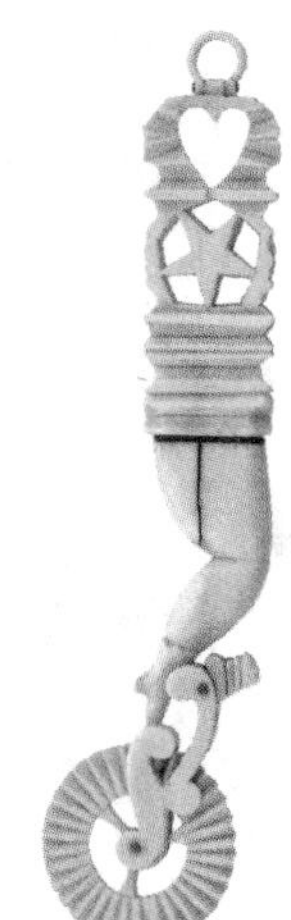

Eldred's

Ivory, Pincushion, Elephant, Carved, Acanthus, Tabletop, Clamp, Chinese, c.1850, 6 ¾ In.
$300

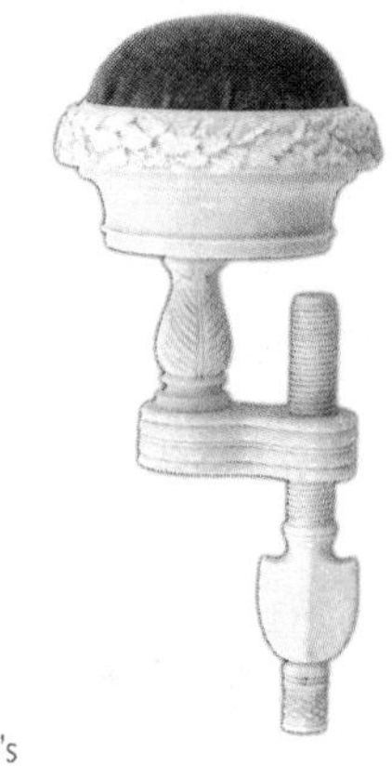

Eldred's

Ivory, Seam Rubber, Whale, Turk's Head Knot Handle, Metal Stand, c.1850, 5 In.
$1,140

Eldred's

and took over a nearby factory in about 1834. The factory made ornamental vases, statues, clocks, inkwells, and perfume bottles. A specialty were figural veilleuses shaped like sultans or fortune tellers. These were meant for use in the bedroom. He used the cobalt blue initials *J.P.* as his mark, but many of his pieces were not marked. His customers wanted "antique" style china, so he made copies of Sevres vases, Meissen figurines, many patterns of English dinnerware, Chinese export porcelain and more. Petit sold his factory to one of his employees in 1862, but he continued to work in Paris until 1866.

Compote, Bird & Flower Reserve, Gilt Base, Marked, c.1850, 11 x 9 In. ....*illus* 313
Figurine, Sultan, Sultana, Marked JP, 5 In., Pair ....*illus* 427
Jug, Wine & Water, 2 Spouts, Man's Head & Eagle, Vent, Grapes, c.1850, 10 In., Pair ....*illus* 1125
Vase, Gilt, Rhyton, Flower Sprays, Green Ground, 1800s, 8 x 6 x 3 In., Pair............................ 450

JADE

Jade is the name for two different minerals, nephrite and jadeite. Nephrite is the mineral used for most early Oriental carvings. Jade is a very tough stone that is found in many colors from dark green to pale lavender. Jade carvings are still being made in the old styles, so collectors must be careful not to be fooled by recent pieces. Jade jewelry is found in this book under Jewelry.

Belt Buckle, Carved Russet, Gray, Fitted Wood Stand, 2 Piece, Chinese, 1 ⅜ x 4 In. 1180
Belt Hook, Carved Mythical Beast, Chinese, 3 ½ In.............................. 720
Belt Hook, Dragon, Pale Celadon, Carved, Wood Stand, 1900s, 4 ½ In. 878
Boulder, White, Carved, Nature, Scholars, Seated, Mountain Grotto, Wood Stand, 9 x 14 In. .. *illus* 2583
Bowl, Dragons, Geometrics, Emerald Green, Silver Mounted, 2 ½ x 4 ½ In............................ 176
Bowl, Lotus Style, Scalloped Rim, Carved, Chinese, 1 ¾ x 10 ½ In. 861
Censer, Carved, Foo Dogs, Rings In Mouth, Handles, 4-Footed, 7 x 7 ½ In. ....*illus* 1200
Cigarette Case, Gold, Mounted, Eagle Head Mark, 3 ⅜ In. 1230
Citron, Buddha's Hand, Leafy Branch, Carved, Chinese, 2 ½ In. 1920
Cup, Lobes, Plum Blossom Branches Handle, Relief Bamboo Leaves, Raised Base, 2 x 4 In....... 1080
Figurine, 2 Fish, Carved, Lotus Pod, Chinese, 7 ½ x 4 ½ In. 323
Figurine, Buddha, Seated, Carved, Light Green, Wood Base, 2 x 4 ½ In............................. 58
Figurine, Buddha, Seated, Carved, Lotus, Mandorla, Wood Base, Chinese, 10 x 6 x 2 ½ In. ...*illus* 800
Figurine, Cabbage, Grasshoppers, Carved, Soapstone Base, 10 x 8 x 4 In. ....*illus* 113
Figurine, Carved Spinach, Standing, Holding Fan, Biwa, 8 ½ In., Pair............................ 720
Figurine, Cat & Kitten, Facing Each Other, Wood Stand, Footed, Chinese, 2 ½ In. ....*illus* 960
Figurine, Deer, Green, Small Deer At Top, Carved, Footed, Chinese, 3 ¾ x 5 In., c.1900 ...*illus* 900
Figurine, Dog, Lying Down, Carved, Wood Stand, Chinese, 3 In. ....*illus* 3355
Figurine, Elephant, Boy, Carrying Lingzhi, Gray, White, Carved, Chinese, 4 x 5 ½ In. ....*illus* 800
Figurine, God Of Longevity, Mutton Fat, Peach, Chinese, 2 In............................. 59
Figurine, Horse, Bucking, Mounted, Carved Wood Base, Green, Chinese, 10 x 13 x 3 In........... 279
Figurine, Horse, Lying Down, Carved, Wood Stand, 7 x 4 x 3 ⅞ In. ....*illus* 92
Figurine, Horse, Lying Down, Legs Tucked, Russet Speckles, Eastern Han Dynasty, 3 x 2 ½ In.. 360
Figurine, Water Buffalo, Celadon, Oval Pad, Paper Label Remnant, Chinese, 1800s, 2 ⅝ In.... 1112
Pendant, Bats, Carved, Coins, Russet Highlights, Chinese, 1 ¾ In............................. 35
Pendant, Slab Shape, White, Scenic, Archaic Bracket, Chinese, 1800s, 2 ⅜ x 1 ½ x 1 In.......... 585
Scepter, Phoenix, Immortal, Wilderness, Deer, Dragon, Crouching, Cicada, 15 In. 6500
Table Screen, Carved Hardstone, Gilt Metal Accents, Stand, Green, 9 ¾ x 4 x ½ In. 480
Table Screen, Rectangular, Phoenix & Dragon, Hand Carved, Wood Stand, 7 ½ x 5 In. 81
Urn, Lid, Double Dragon Handles, Reticulated, Puzzle Ball, Rings, 14 x 13 ½ In. 320
Vase, High Shoulder, Allover Scales, Ribbed Top & Bottom, Chinese, 1900s, 9 x 5 In................. 1872
Vase, Lid, White, Carved, Handles, Chinese, 9 x 3 In. 1845
Vase, Light Green, Carved, Wood Stand, Bird Handle, Chinese, 1 ⅜ x 3 ½ In............................ 978
Vase, Mughal, Incised Body, Xi Medallion, 2 Handles, Chinese, 8 ½ In. 1102

JAPANESE WOODBLOCK PRINTS *are listed in this book in the Print category under Japanese.*

Ivory, Spinning Top, Whale, Engraved, Ink Numbers, 1 Through 8, 1800s, 8 In.
$510

Eldred's

Jacob Petit, Compote, Bird & Flower Reserve, Gilt Base, Marked, c.1850, 11 x 9 In.
$313

Neal Auction Company

Jacob Petit, Jug, Wine & Water, 2 Spouts, Man's Head & Eagle, Vent, Grapes, c.1850, 10 In., Pair
$1,125

New Orleans Auction Galleries

Jade, Boulder, White, Carved, Nature, Scholars, Seated, Mountain Grotto, Wood Stand, 9 x 14 In.
$2,583

Charlton Hall Auctions

Jacob Petit, Figurine, Sultan, Sultana, Marked JP, 5 In., Pair
$427

Neal Auction Company

Jade, Censer, Carved, Foo Dogs, Rings In Mouth, Handles, 4-Footed, 7 x 7 ½ In.
$1,200

Milestone Auctions

Jade, Figurine, Buddha, Seated, Carved, Lotus, Mandorla, Wood Base, Chinese, 10 x 6 x 2 ½ In.
$800

Charlton Hall Auctions

Jade, Figurine, Cabbage, Grasshoppers, Carved, Soapstone Base, 10 x 8 x 4 In.
$113

Hudson Valley Auctions

Jade, Figurine, Cat & Kitten, Facing Each Other, Wood Stand, Footed, Chinese, 2 ½ In.
$960

Brunk Auctions

Jade, Figurine, Deer, Green, Small Deer At Top, Carved, Footed, Chinese, 3 ¾ x 5 In., c.1900
$900

Case Antiques

Jade, Figurine, Dog, Lying Down, Carved, Wood Stand, Chinese, 3 In.
$3,355

Nadeau's Auction Gallery

Jade
The most valuable jade is known as "Imperial Jade." It is a clear, dark green. Jade is one of two minerals, nephrite or jadeite. Both are usually a pale to dark green, but they occur in nature in other colors, including black, red, pink, violet, and white. Jade is a hard, compact stone that can be carved only by abrasives, not cutting tools.

JASPERWARE

Jasperware can be made in different ways. Some pieces are made from a solid-colored clay with applied raised designs of a contrasting colored clay. Other pieces are made entirely of one color clay with raised decorations that are glazed with a contrasting color. Additional pieces of jasperware may also be listed in the Wedgwood category or under various art potteries.

Urn, Dancing Hours, Black & White, Acorn Shape, Pedestal Base, 9 ½ In. 720
Urn, Lid, Festoons, Hoof Legs, Triangular Base, Flower Finial, c.1780, 8 ½ In., Pair ....*illus* 1968
Vase, Phrygian Cap, White Relief, Black Ground, 1800s, 10 ½ In. 800

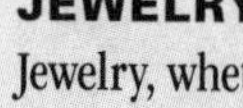

JEWELRY

Jewelry, whether made from gold and precious gems or plastic and colored glass, is popular with collectors. Values are determined by the intrinsic value of the stones and metal and by the skill and fame of the craftsmen and designers. Although costume jewelry has been made since the 17th century, it became fashionable in the 1920s. Victorian and older jewelry has been collected since the 1950s. Edwardian and Art Deco jewelry were copied in the first half of the 1900s, then Modernist jewelry designs appeared. Bakelite jewelry was a fad from the 1930s to the 1990s. Copies of almost all styles are being made. American Indian jewelry is listed in the Indian category in this book. Tiffany jewelry is listed here.

Bracelet, Bakelite, Philadelphia, Red Clamper, Multicolor Fins, 2 ⅜ In. 960
Bracelet, Bangle, Doughnut, 18K Gold, Elsa Peretti, Tiffany & Co., 1980s, 7 In. 7188
Bracelet, Bangle, Doughnut, Sterling Silver, Elsa Peretti, Tiffany & Co., 1980s, 7 In., Pair 1125
Bracelet, Bangle, Love, Screws, 18K Gold, Cartier, Box, Man's, 7 ½ In. 3500
Bracelet, Belt, Silver, Heavy Curved Links, Buckle Ends, Hermes, 8 In. 1750
Bracelet, Charm, Faceted Plastic Beads, Goldtone, Napier, 1960s, 7 In. ....*illus* 96
Bracelet, Cuff, Hinged, Alternating Bands, Silver, Gold, Rhodium, A. Soldier, 2010 2200
Bracelet, Link, Nautical, 18K Gold, Victorian, 1880s 7850
Cigarette Case, Gemstone Cabochon Clasp, 14K Gold, 3 ¼ x 3 In. 3068
Clip, Bird In Hand, Figural, Goldtone, Enamel, Pave Rhinestones, Reja, 1940s, 2 In. 330
Clip, Diamonds, Elliptical, Overlapping Ends, 1940s, 1 x 1 ¾ In., Pair 2583
Clip, Duette, Bow, Clear & Aqua Faceted Stones, Pearls, Vermeil, Coro, 1950s, 3 ¾ In. .....*illus* 216
Clip, Fruit Basket, Jelly Belly, Enamel, Pave & Ruby Crystals, A. Katz, Coro, 1940s, 2 ½ In. 600
Clip, Mandarin Dancers, Yellow Enamel, Diamante, Coro, 2 In., Pair 330
Clip, Shield Form, Diamonds, Emeralds, Rubies, Platinum, Beaded, Art Deco, 1 ⅜ In. 3998
Cuff Links, Button, Lapis Lazuli, 14K Gold Crossed Thread Detail, Tiffany & Co., ¾ In. 1188
Cuff Links, Lips, Gold, Michael Kanners, c.2000 3950
Cuff Links, Playing Cards, King Of Diamonds, Queen Of Spades, Enamel, Gold, S. Fox, 2010 .. 4940
Dress Set, Man's, Acorns, Malachite, 18K Gold, Tiffany & Co., Box 2500
Dress Set, Man's, Bulldog Heads, Silver, Sapphire Eyes, Deakin & Francis, 6 Piece ....*illus* 1250
Earrings, Hoop, Apricot, Plastic, Rhinestone Studs, Sharra Pagano, Italy, 3 In. 192
Earrings, Hoop, Navy Blue Enamel, Gold Stripes, Bulgari, 1970s 9500
Earrings, Knot Shape, White Coral, Ribbed 18K Gold, Van Cleef & Arpels, ⅞ In. 5000
Earrings, Modernist, Dangle, Lock & Key, Diamonds, Silver, 3 In. ....*illus* 938
Earrings, Modernist, Dangle, Starburst, 24 Rays, Gold, 6 With Diamonds, Umrao, 3 In. 6150
Earrings, Modernist, Stylized Feather, Diamond Fronds, 18K White Gold, Umrao, 3 ¼ In. 5658
Hatpins are listed in this book in the Hatpin category. ....
Necklace & Bracelet, Dos Pesos, 22 Mexican Coins, 14K Gold, c.1945, 33 In. & 7 In. ......*illus* 2250
Necklace & Earrings, Blue Acrylic, Faux Pearls, Glass Cabochons, Trifari, 17 In. ....*illus* 240
Necklace, 18K White Gold, Platinum, Diamonds, Rock Crystal Lorgnette, 32 In. ....*illus* 2000
Necklace, 2 Tassels, 14K Gold, Green, Rose & White Gold Leaves, c.1885, 26 In. 1250
Necklace, Bakelite, Oranges, Leaves, Pink Celluloid Chain, 1940s, 17 In. 432
Necklace, Collar, French Glass Beads, Gilt Filigree, W. DeLillo, 1980s, 15 In. ....*illus* 720
Necklace, Collar, Half & Half, Brass, Abstract Form, Marked, Art Smith, c.1949, 14 In. 7380
Pendant, 10 Wasps, Green Molded Glass, Lalique, Early 1900s, 2 ⅜ In. ....*illus* 800
Pendant, Cameo, Hardstone, Jupiter, Oak & Laurel Frame, Diamonds, Pearl Drop, c.1890, 3 In. 2091

Jade, Figurine, Elephant, Boy, Carrying Lingzhi, Gray, White, Carved, Chinese, 4 x 5 ½ In.
$800

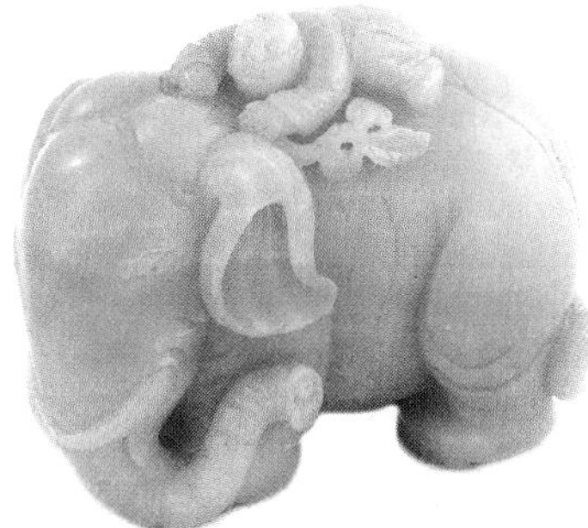
Charlton Hall Auctions

Jade, Figurine, Horse, Lying Down, Carved, Wood Stand, 7 x 4 x 3 ⅞ In.
$92

Blackwell Auctions

Jasperware, Urn, Lid, Festoons, Hoof Legs, Triangular Base, Flower Finial, c.1780, 8 ½ In., Pair
$1,968

Skinner, Inc.

Jewelry, Bracelet, Charm, Faceted Plastic Beads, Goldtone, Napier, 1960s, 7 In.
$96

Ripley Auctions

TIP

Gemstones are colder to the touch than glass. Colored gems like emeralds, rubies, and sapphires should not appear scratched. If there are scratches, the "stone" is probably colored glass.

Jewelry, Clip, Duette, Bow, Clear & Aqua Faceted Stones, Pearls, Vermeil, Coro, 1950s, 3 ¾ In.
$216

Ripley Auctions

Jewelry, Dress Set, Man's, Bulldog Heads, Silver, Sapphire Eyes, Deakin & Francis, 6 Piece
$1,250

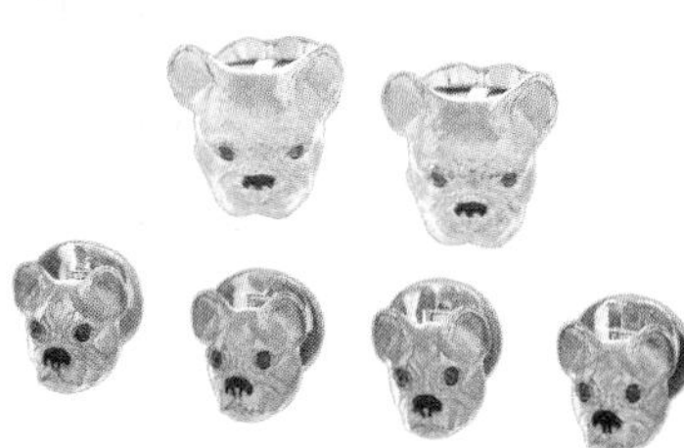
New Orleans Auction Galleries

Jewelry, Earrings, Modernist, Dangle, Lock & Key, Diamonds, Silver, 3 In.
$938

New Orleans Auction Galleries

Jewelry, Necklace & Bracelet, Dos Pesos, 22 Mexican Coins, 14K Gold, c.1945, 33 In. & 7 In.
$2,250

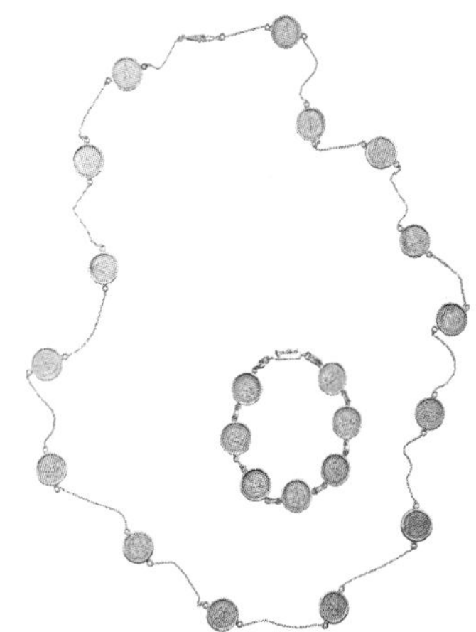
New Orleans Auction Galleries

Jewelry, Necklace & Earrings, Blue Acrylic, Faux Pearls, Glass Cabochons, Trifari, 17 In.
$240

Ripley Auctions

Jewelry, Necklace, 18K White Gold, Platinum, Diamonds, Rock Crystal Lorgnette, 32 In.
$2,000

Freeman's Auctioneers & Appraisers

Jewelry, Necklace, Collar, French Glass Beads, Gilt Filigree, W. DeLillo, 1980s, 15 In.
$720

Ripley Auctions

Jewelry, Pendant, 10 Wasps, Green Molded Glass, Lalique, Early 1900s, 2 3/8 In.
$800

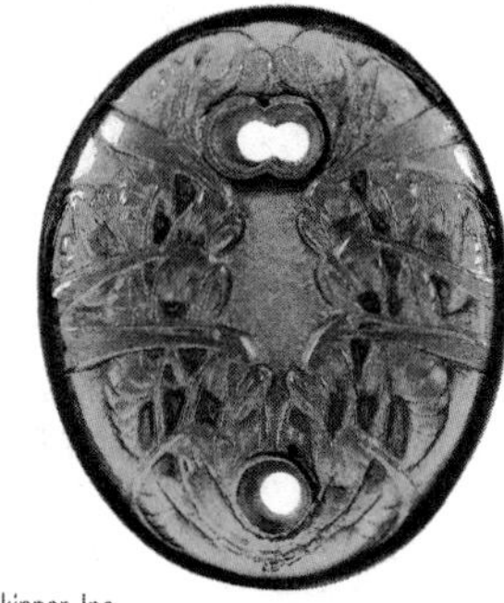

Skinner, Inc.

Pendant, Cigar Cutter, 10K Gold, Engraved Flower, Fob Ring, 1 3/4 x 1/2 In. .... *illus* 124
Pendant, Dog, Rottweiler, Glass, Painted, 18K Gold Stirrup Mount, Chain, J.P. Miller, 2 In. 5143
Pendant, Heart, Amethyst, Diamond Frame & Chain, Belle Epoque, c.1900, 2 1/2 In. 3444
Pendant, Modernist, Concave, Textured 18K Gold, Diamond, Opal, W. Schluep, Canada, 2 In. *illus* 2500
Pin & Earrings, Faceted Green Stones, Diamante Leaves, Sarah Coventry, c.1970, Pin 2 In. ..*illus* 96
Pin & Earrings, Heart, Goldtone, Basket Weave, Diamante, Trifari, 1940s, Pin 1 1/2 In. 144
Pin, 2 Acorns, 2 Leaves, Signed, Georg Jensen, 2 In. ....*illus* 150
Pin, 2 Cherries On Branch, Marbleized Red Enamel, Goldtone Leaves, HAR, 1950s, 2 In. 72
Pin, 2 Flamenco Dancers, Figural, 18K Gold, Sapphires, Diamonds, Retro, 2 1/2 In. 1968
Pin, 3 Fife & Drummers, Revolutionary War, Flag, Enamel, Coro, c.1940, 2 1/2 In. 144
Pin, 4 Maple Leaves, 18K Gold, Diamond Dew Drops, Buccellati, 1850s 9850
Pin, 5 Flowers, Turquoise, Diamond Centers, 18K Gold, Van Cleef & Arpels, 2 5/8 In. 4613
Pin, Agave Basket, Black & Yellow Enamel, Jewel-Tone Stones, Gold, Eisenberg, 1940, 3 In. 780
Pin, Amethyst, 18K Granulated Gold Mount, Arthur King, 2 x 1 In. ....*illus* 1105
Pin, Bakelite, Baseball Player, Ball, Bat, Red, Yellow, Articulated Limbs, Shultz, 3 1/2 In. 144
Pin, Bakelite, Deer, Butterscotch, Spots, Leather Ears, Martha Sleeper, c.1940, 3 In. 216
Pin, Bakelite, Hat, Wide Brim, Carved Flowers, Cherry Juice, 1940s, 3 In. 648
Pin, Bakelite, Sailor, Wood, Navy Blue, Brown, Articulated Limbs, 3 1/2 In. 144
Pin, Ballet Dancer, Goldtone, Turquoise Cabochon Tutu, Rhinestones, Trifari, 1940s, 2 In. 96
Pin, Bee, Figural, Gold, Diamond Eyes, Chaumet, 1970s 4500
Pin, Big Fly, Jelly Belly, Gold Over Silver, Jeweled Accents, Trifari, 1945, 1 In. 120
Pin, Blackamoor, Goldtone, Clear & Green Rhinestone Collar, Reja, 1940s, 3 In. 300
Pin, Blackamoor, Pink & Clear Rhinestones, Faux Pearl Dangles, Hattie Carnegie, 1960s, 1 In.. 192
Pin, Bow, Diamonds, Platinum Over Gold, Pearl Drop Ends, Edwardian, 2 3/4 In. 2706
Pin, Bow, Full Cut Diamonds, Tiffany & Co., 1 7/8 In. 2829
Pin, Crown, Diamonds, Platinum Over Gold Mount, Edwardian, 1 3/4 In. 2337
Pin, Dog, Nodding Head, Enamel, Pave Rhinestones, 1950, 2 1/2 In. 72
Pin, Duette, Jeweled Dolphins, 2 Leaping, Jelly Belly Open Mouths, Coro, 1944, 2 In. 780
Pin, Dutch Boy, Nylon, Celluloid, Lucite, Articulated, Pigtails, Coro, 1940s, 3 In. 144
Pin, Elephant's Head, Trunk Up, Gray Enamel, Gold Tusks, Blue Crystal Eye, Vendome, 1960s, 3 In. 84
Pin, Faux Coral, Malachite Glass Cabochons, William De Lillo, c.1969, 3 In. ....*illus* 240
Pin, Frog, Jelly Belly, Black Enamel, Faceted Jewel Eye, Valentino, c.1970, 3 In. 84
Pin, Frog, Leaping, Jelly Belly, Green Cabochon Eyes, Pave Rhinestones, Coro, 1940s, 2 In. 360
Pin, Gazelle, Leaping, Gold, Enamel, Green Cabochon Saddle, Hattie Carnegie, 1960s, 2 1/2 In. 300
Pin, Harlequin, Musician, Silver, Crosshatching, Yellow Rhinestones, 1940, 3 In. 144
Pin, Lion's Head, Goldtone, Marbled Blue Cabochons, Kenneth J. Lane, 1960s, 3 In. 240
Pin, Mallard Duck, Flying, Jelly Belly, Pave Rhinestone Accents, Coro, 1944, 2 In. 96
Pin, Man, Woman, Arms & Legs Move, Gold, Red Enamel, Diamante Bellies, Reja, 1940s, 2 In., Pair 240
Pin, Modernist, Opal, 14K Gold, Ronald Pearson, Maine, 2 x 1 1/4 In. ....*illus* 343
Pin, Penguin, Jelly Belly, Silver, Rhinestones, Cabochon Eye, A. Philippe, Trifari, 1943 330
Pin, Plaque, Modernist, Blue Enamel, Sterling Silver, Adda Husted Andersen, 1960s, 1 3/4 In. .*illus* 1062
Pin, Plaque, Silver, Oxidized, Blue & Green Glass, Modernist, Frances Boothby, 1960s, 2 In. ..*illus* 260
Pin, Ribbon, Rhinestones, Chanel, 1960-70, 3 In. ....*illus* 288
Pin, Stylized Flower, Diamond Center, Coiled 18K Gold Mount, D. Webb, 1960s, 2 In. 7380
Pin, Stylized Ribbon, 14K Rose & White Gold, Sapphires, Diamonds, 1950s ....*illus* 1708
Pin, Surreal Eye, Taxidermy Eye, Sterling Silver, Sam Kramer, c.1960, 3 x 1 In. ....*illus* 2860
Pin, Sweetheart, Chatelaine, Sailboat, Anchor, Silver, Diamante, 1940s, 2 1/2 In. 72
Pin, Thewa Work, Gold Foil Fused Onto Green Glass, Beaded Rim, India, 1 1/2 In. ....*illus* 424
Ring, Jadeite, Navette, Ruby & Diamond Border, Filigree, Art Deco, Size 4 1/2 7380
Ring, Rolex President Mount, 7 Round Diamonds, 18K Gold, Man's, Size 10 1/4 1250
Tie Bar, Caddis Worm, 18K Textured Gold, Segmented, John Paul Miller, 1964, 1 3/8 In. 4538
Watches are listed in their own category.
Wristwatches are listed in their own category.

JOHN ROGERS

John Rogers statues were made from 1859 to 1892. The originals were bronze, but the thousands of copies made by the Rogers factory were of painted plaster. Eighty different figures were created. Similar painted plaster figures were produced by some other factories. Rights to the figures were sold

Jewelry, Pendant, Cigar Cutter, 10K Gold, Engraved Flower, Fob Ring, 1 ¾ x ½ In.
$124

Hartzell's Auction Gallery Inc.

Jewelry, Pendant, Modernist, Concave, Textured 18K Gold, Diamond, Opal, W. Schluep, Canada, 2 In.
$2,500

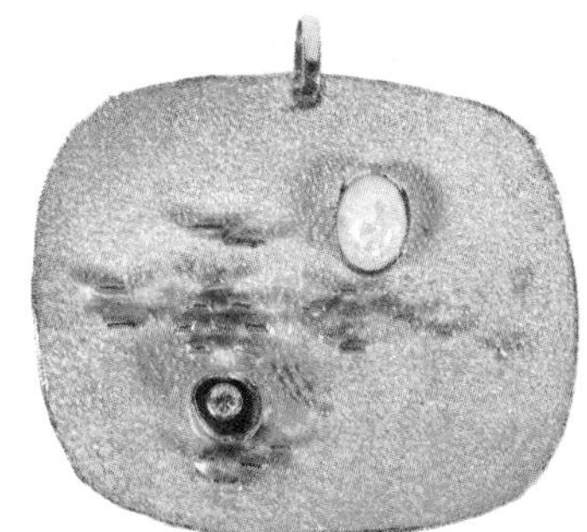

Abington Auction Gallery

Jewelry, Pin & Earrings, Faceted Green Stones, Diamante Leaves, Sarah Coventry, c.1970, Pin 2 In.
$96

Ripley Auctions

Newark, Home of Gold Jewelry
Most of the gold jewelry made in the United States before the 1930s was made in Newark, New Jersey. The name of the retailer, not the maker, was often used as the mark.

Jewelry, Pin, 2 Acorns, 2 Leaves, Signed, Georg Jensen, 2 In.
$150

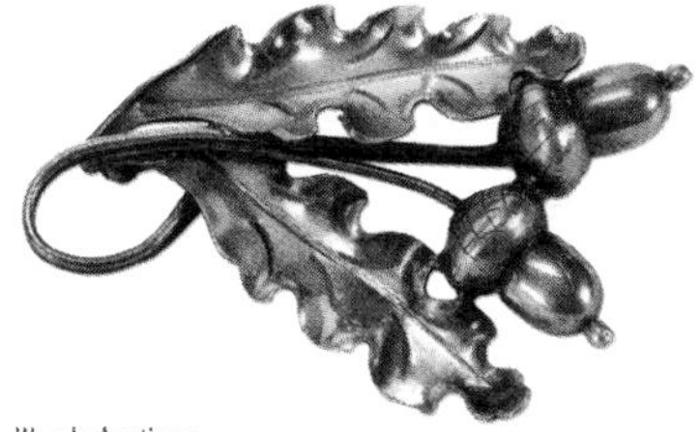

Woody Auctions

Jewelry, Pin, Amethyst, 18K Granulated Gold Mount, Arthur King, 2 x 1 In.
$1,105

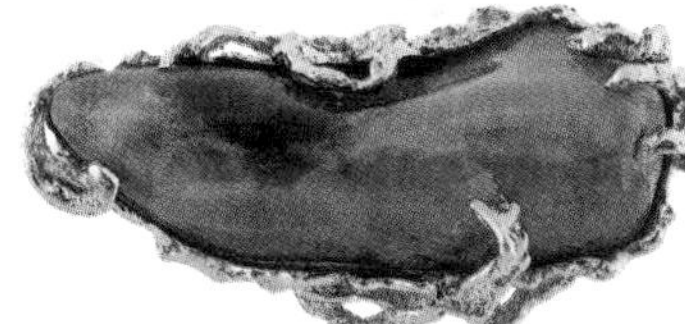

Toomey & Co. Auctioneers

TIP
If one link in your antique gold chain breaks, be very careful. There are probably other worn links that will soon break.

Jewelry, Pin, Faux Coral, Malachite Glass Cabochons, William De Lillo, c.1969, 3 In.
$240

Ripley Auctions

Jewelry, Pin, Modernist, Opal, 14K Gold, Ronald Pearson, Maine, 2 x 1 ¼ In.
$343

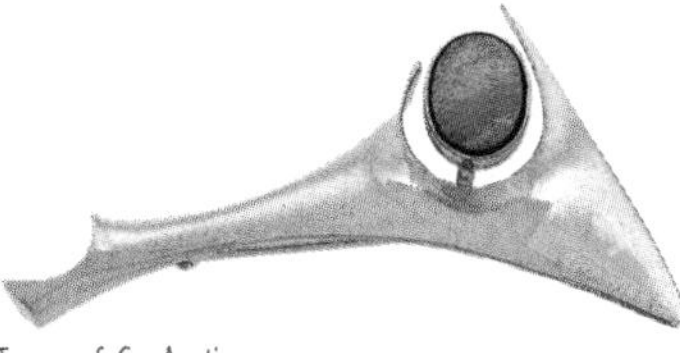

Toomey & Co. Auctioneers

Jewelry, Pin, Plaque, Modernist, Blue Enamel, Sterling Silver, Adda Husted Andersen, 1960s, 1 ¾ In.
$1,062

Toomey & Co. Auctioneers

Jewelry, Pin, Plaque, Silver, Oxidized, Blue & Green Glass, Modernist, Frances Boothby, 1960s, 2 In.
$260

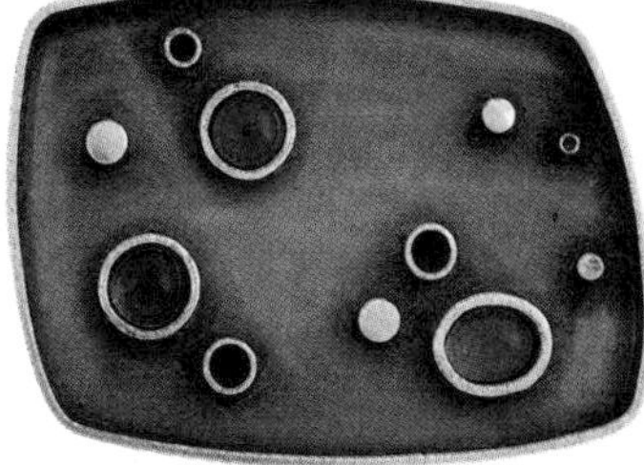

Toomey & Co. Auctioneers

Platinum
Platinum jewelry is marked Platinum, Plat, Pt 900, or Pt 950. If it is less than 900 parts pure platinum, it will say 850 or 800 or another number.

Jewelry, Pin, Ribbon, Rhinestones, Chanel, 1960-70, 3 In.
$288

Blackwell Auctions

Jewelry, Pin, Stylized Ribbon, 14K Rose & White Gold, Sapphires, Diamonds, 1950s
$1,708

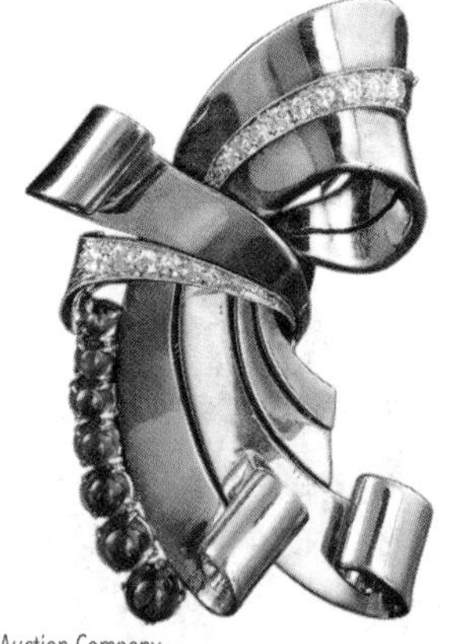

Neal Auction Company

Jewelry, Pin, Surreal Eye, Taxidermy Eye, Sterling Silver, Sam Kramer, c.1960, 3 x 1 In.
$2,860

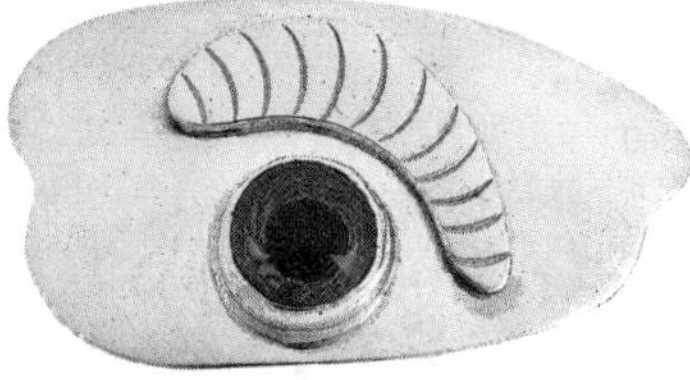

Toomey & Co. Auctioneers

Jewelry, Pin, Thewa Work, Gold Foil Fused Onto Green Glass, Beaded Rim, India, 1 ½ In.
$424

Soulis Auctions

Judaica, Etrog Container, Hinged, Silver, Gilt Interior, Flower Finial, Claw Feet, 1900s, 5 ½ x 7 In.
$406

Kamelot Auctions

Judaica, Menorah, Hanukkah, 8 Candle Holders, Silver, Claw Feet, Pitcher, 7 x 2 ½ In.
$420

Morphy Auctions

Judaica, Menorah, Silver, Oil Ewer, Embossed, Crown Finial, Lions, 10 Commandments, 11 x 8 In.
$900

Alderfer Auction Company

Judaica, Spice Box, Besamim, Pear Shape, Engraved Crest, 3-Legged Base, Dutch, 4 In.
$125

Susanin's Auctioneers & Appraisers

TIP

Store all jewelry so it doesn't touch other pieces and scratch them. Put jewelry in compartments in trays or flannel or plastic zip bags. (Pearls can't be put in plastic.) Silver jewelry should be kept in tarnish-proof bags.

Jugtown, Vase, Chinese Glaze, Runny Mottled Blue & Red, Low Shoulder, c.1930, 6 x 7 In.
$420

Brunk Auctions

in 1893, and the figures were manufactured until about 1895 by the Rogers Statuette Co. Never repaint a Rogers figure because this lowers the value to collectors.

Figure, Bust Of A Gentleman, Bushy Sideburns, Marble, Inscribed Rome, 30 In. 3383
Group, Council Of War, Lincoln, Grant, Stanton, Patent Date 1868, 24 x 14 In. 1888
Group, Traveling Magician, Pulling Rabbit Out Of Hat, 1877, 22 x 14 In. 3068

JOSEF ORIGINALS

Josef Originals ceramics were designed by Muriel Joseph George. The first pieces were made in California from 1945 to 1962. They were then manufactured in Japan. The company was sold to George Good in 1982 and he continued to make Josef Originals until 1985. The company was sold two more times. The last owner went bankrupt in 2011.

Figurine, Bird, Road Runner, Paper Label, 7 x 4 In. 40
Figurine, Birthday Mushroom Girl, March, Foil Sticker, 3 ½ In. 28
Figurine, Cat, Big Eyes, Bell Collar, 4 x 3 ½ In. 24
Figurine, Girl, Blond, Birthday Series, April, 4 In. 20
Figurine, Girl, Musical, December, Layered Dress, Hat, Bouquet, 6 ¼ In. 42
Figurine, Girl, Yellow Dress, International Series, Portugal, 4 In. 30
Music Box, Boy & Girl, Sitting In Meadow, Red Bird, Shadow Of Your Smile, 5 x 4 In. 34
Night-Light, Owl, Brown, Red & Black Glass Eyes, 4 ¾ In. 44
Ornament, Siamese Cat On Bell, 1970s, 2 ¾ x 2 ⅞ In. 16
Pie Vent, Canary, Yellow, 3 In. 38
Planter, Hen, Hat, Foil Sticker, 3 x 1 ¾ In. 12
Salt & Pepper, Santa & Mrs. Claus Waving, 1950s, 4 ½ In. 35

JUDAICA

Judaica is any memorabilia that refers to the Jews or the Jewish religion. Interests range from newspaper clippings that mention eighteenth- and nineteenth-century Jewish Americans to religious objects, such as menorahs or spice boxes. Age, condition, and the intrinsic value of the material, as well as the historic and artistic importance, determine the value.

Bible, Silver Plate Cover, Engraved Border, 4 ½ x 5 ½ x 2 ½ In. 106
Etrog Container, Hinged, Silver, Gilt Interior, Flower Finial, Claw Feet, 1900s, 5 ½ x 7 In. *illus* 406
Etrog, Jugendstil Style, Engraved, Lid, Paw Feet, Marked FR Silver, Early 1900s, 5 In. 584
Menorah, 8-Light, Silver, Detachable Oil Ewer, Wilhelm Weinranck, Hanau, 11 x 12 In. 2750
Menorah, Hanukkah, 8 Candle Holders, Silver, Claw Feet, Pitcher, 7 x 2 ½ In. *illus* 420
Menorah, Iron, Tapered Triangle Prism Candle Cups, Cross Bars, c.1935, 26 ½ In. 300
Menorah, Silver, Crescents Support Candle Cups, 7 x 8 ½ In. 220
Menorah, Silver, Oil Ewer, Embossed, Crown Finial, Lions, 10 Commandments, 11 x 8 In. *illus* 900
Spice Box, Besamim, Pear Shape, Engraved Crest, 3-Legged Base, Dutch, 4 In. *illus* 125
Spice Box, Silver, Twisted Stem, Openwork Cage, Bird Finial, Round Base, Russia, 5 ¾ In. 438

JUGTOWN POTTERY

Jugtown Pottery refers to many pottery pieces made in North Carolina as far back as the 1750s. In 1915, Juliana and Jacques Busbee set up a training and sales organization for what they named Jugtown Pottery. In 1921, they built a shop at Jugtown, North Carolina, and in 1923 hired Ben Owen as a potter. The Busbees moved the village store where the pottery was sold to New York City. Juliana Busbee sold the New York store in 1926 and moved into a log cabin near the Jugtown Pottery. The pottery closed in 1959. It reopened in 1960 and is still working near Seagrove, North Carolina.

Bowl, Mottled Green, Albany Slip Inside, Thumbprint Band, Footed, 5 x 7 In. 59
Bowl, Speckled Green High Glaze, Dimpled Band, Footed, 3 x 6 In. 73

Senior Shooter
Annie Oakley, the famous star of Buffalo Bill's Wild West Show, kept performing her amazing sharpshooting act until she was in her 60s. She quit because of injuries from a car accident.

Jukebox, Rock-Ola, Model 1458, 25 Cent, 120 Songs, 60 Records, 53 x 31 x 27 In.
$1,521

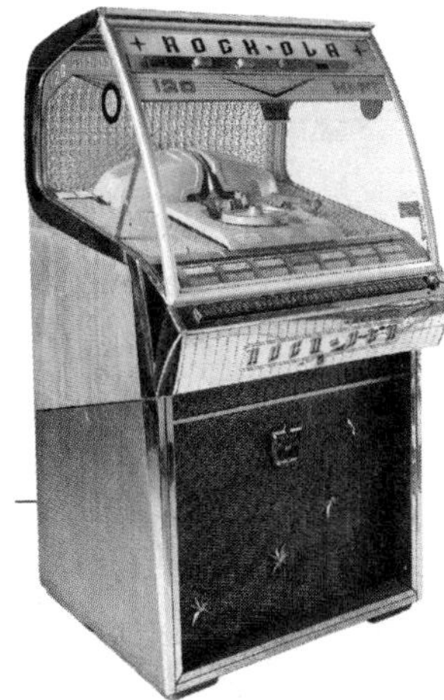

Cordier Auctions

Jukebox, Seeburg, Symphanola, Wood, Chrome, Plastic, Light-Up, 58 x 33 In.
$1,353

Richard Opfer Auctioneering, Inc.

This is an edited listing of current prices. Visit **Kovels.com** to check thousands of prices from previous years and sign up for free information on trends, tips, reproductions, marks, and more.

Jar, Blue, Green & Red Glaze, Meandering Rope, 4 Applied Strap Handles, 1930s, 13 ¾ In. 7800
Jar, Lid, Orange Speckled Glaze, Ball Shape, Horizontal Ribs, Marked, c.1930, 6 ½ In. 51
Pie Dish, Dove, Painted Blue, Green Glaze, Deep Dish, Scalloped Edge, 10 ½ In. 12
Planter, Incised Face, Green Glaze, Painted Features, Moustache, V. Owens 123
Vase, Chinese Blue Glaze, Bulbous, Dogwood Knop Handles, 2000, 7 x 6 In. 266
Vase, Chinese Glaze, Runny Mottled Blue & Red, Low Shoulder, c.1930, 6 x 7 In. ....*illus* 420
Vase, Frog, Raised Details, Hands On Belly, Green Speckled Glaze, 11 ¾ x 6 In. 163
Vase, Frogskin Glaze, Globular, Marked, Ben Owen, 6 x 5 In. 38
Vase, Tan Salt Glaze, Chinese Blue & Red Drip Top, Shaped Sides, 7 x 4 In. 120
Vase, White Glaze, Speckled, Undulating Sides, Double Gourd, Stamped, 6 ¾ In. 177

JUKEBOX

Jukeboxes play records. The first coin-operated phonograph was demonstrated in 1889. In 1906 the Automatic Entertainer appeared, the first coin-operated phonograph to offer several different selections of music. The first electrically powered jukebox was introduced in 1927. Collectors search for jukeboxes of all ages, especially those with flashing lights and unusual design and graphics.

Rock-Ola, Model 1458, 25 Cent, 120 Songs, 60 Records, 53 x 31 x 27 In. ....*illus* 1521
Seeburg, Symphanola, Wood, Chrome, Plastic, Light-Up, 58 x 33 In. ....*illus* 1353
Speaker, Seeburg, Model RSI-8, Teardrop, Faux Marble, Chrome, Wall, 17 x 11 In., Pair......... 424
Speaker, Wurlitzer, Domed, Glass Panels, Neon Lights, 38 ½ In. 1102
Wurlitzer, Model 2900, Multi Selector, Chrome, 50 x 34 In. 677
Wurlitzer, Wall Box, 5, 10 & 25 Cent, Chrome, Bakelite Switch, 13 x 12 In. 360

KATE GREENAWAY

Kate Greenaway (1846–1901), who was a famous illustrator of children's books, drew pictures of children in high-waisted Empire dresses. Her designs appear on china, glass, napkin rings, and other pieces as well as prints and storybooks.

Box, Women, Chatting, Seated, Blue Glass, Brass Mount, C.F, Monroe, 4 x 6 In. 420
Napkin Ring, Silver Plate, Girl Holding Rifle On Shoulder, 3 In. 180
Napkin Ring, Silver Plate, Girl Holding Umbrella, Frightened Dog, 4 x 4 In. 270

Kay Finch
CALIFORNIA

KAY FINCH CERAMICS

Kay Finch Ceramics were made in Corona del Mar, California, from 1935 to 1963. The hand-decorated pieces often depicted whimsical animals and people. Pastel colors were used.

Figurine, Asian Woman, White, Blue & Turquoise Kimono & Dress, 10 ½ In. 45
Figurine, Bear, On Back, Smiling, Brown Speckled Glaze, Marked, 4 ½ In. 29
Figurine, Cat, Mehitabel, Luster Glaze, Purple Ears & Paws, Flowers, 8 ½ x 7 In. 33
Figurine, Dog, Cocker Spaniel, Gold Wash, Incised Mark, F. McFarlin, 8 ½ In. 125
Figurine, Dog, Skye Terrier, Gold Wash, Incised Mark, F. McFarlin, 11 In. 85
Figurine, Elephant, Trunk Up, Flowers On Ears, Pink, Purple, Yellow, 8 ½ x 6 ½ In. 29
Figurine, Pig, Pink, Yellow Flowers, Green Leaves, White Tail, 6 ½ x 8 In. 20
Figurine, Rooster, Cream, Burgundy Comb & Wattle, Blue Feathers, Stamped, 10 ½ In. 32
Figurine, Stylized Fish, Pink, Silver Details, Marked, 4 ½ x 8 In. 47
Mug, Missouri Mule, Southern Comfort, White, Gilt Mane, Red Bridle, 1949, 4 ½ In. 64

KAYSERZINN, *see Pewter category.*

KELVA

KELVA

Kelva glassware was made by the C. F. Monroe Company of Meriden, Connecticut, about 1904. It is a pale, pastel-painted glass decorated with flowers, designs, or scenes. Kelva resembles Nakara and Wave Crest, two other glasswares made by the same company.

Kelva, Jewelry Box, White Flowers, Beaded Tapestry, Mottled Lavender Brown Ground, 3 x 6 In.
$400

Woody Auctions

Kew Blas, Vase, Iridescent White, Urn Shape, Ribbed Column, Union Glass Co., 1890-1924, 6 x 3 In.
$761

Jeffrey S. Evans & Associates

Kewpie, Bisque, Side-Glancing Eyes, Marked, Heart Label, Rose O'Neill, 12 In.
$225

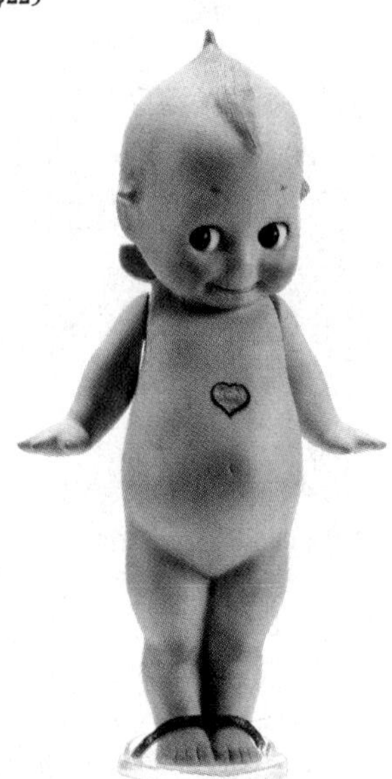

Woody Auctions

Bonbon, Pink Flowers, Mottled Blue Ground, Gilt Metal Rim & Handle, 2 x 6 In. 125
Box, Lid, Blown Out Rose, Mottled Pink Ground, 6-Sided, Metal Mount, 3 x 4 In. 500
Box, Lid, Hinged, Mottled Pink & White, Blue Flowers, Round, Metal Mount, 3 x 4 ½ In. 300
Box, Lid, Hinged, Pink & Yellow Flowers, Mottled Blue Ground, Square, 3 x 4 In. 350
Humidor, Lid, Cigars, Peach Flowers, Marbled Blue Ground, Cylindrical, 5 In. 450
Humidor, Lid, Cigars, Pink Flowers, Marbled Blue Ground, Bulbous, 6 In. 650
Jardiniere, Pink Poppies, Mottled Green Ground, Branches, Beaded Rim, Squat, 7 ¾ x 10 In. 300
Jewelry Box, White Flowers, Beaded Tapestry, Mottled Lavender Brown Ground, 3 x 6 In. *illus* 400
Match Holder, White Flowers, Mottled Pink Ground, 6-Sided, Silver Scroll Handles, 3 In. 150
Vase, Pink & Purple Flowers, Mottled Green Ground, Metal Openwork Fittings, 14 ½ In. 300
Vase, Stick, Pink Flowers, Mottled Green Ground, Gilt Metal Feet, Squat Bottom, 9 In. 350

KENTON HILLS

Kenton Hills Pottery in Erlanger, Kentucky, made artwares, including vases and figurines that resembled Rookwood, probably because so many of the original artists and workmen had worked at the Rookwood plant. Kenton Hills opened in 1939 and closed during World War II.

Bowl, Pink Roses, Cream Ground, Glazed, Marked, R. Dickman, 2 ⅝ x 8 In. 162
Figurine, Woman With Hand Up, Evening Star, Jungle Black Glaze, David Seyler, 9 In. 500
Vase, Spanish Red Glaze, Harold Bopp Design, 5 ½ In. 137

KEW BLAS

KEW-BLAS

Kew Blas is a name used by the Union Glass Company of Somerville, Massachusetts. The name refers to an iridescent golden glass made from the 1890s to 1924. The iridescent glass was reminiscent of the Tiffany glass of the period.

Vase, Iridescent White, Urn Shape, Ribbed Column, Union Glass Co., 1890-1924, 6 x 3 In. *illus* 761

KEWPIES

Kewpies, designed by Rose O'Neill (1874–1944), were first pictured in the *Ladies' Home Journal*. The figures, which are similar to pixies, were a success, and Kewpie dolls and figurines started appearing in 1911. Kewpie pictures and other items soon followed. Collectors search for all items that picture the little winged people. They are still popular with collectors.

Bisque, Side-Glancing Eyes, Marked, Heart Label, Rose O'Neill, 12 In. .... *illus* 225
Composition, Black, Heart On Chest, Red Wings On Back, Cameo, 1940s, 11 In. 195
Composition, Red & White Jumper, Original Box, c.1930, 12 In. 325
Cup & Saucer, Kewpies Playing, Green Leaves, Gold Trim, Child's, c.1915, 2 x 5 In. 84
Paper Doll, Sailor Suit, Blue & White, Ragsy & Ritzy, Whitman Publishing Co., 1932, 10 In. 22
Paper, Gift Wrapping, Birthday Scenes, American Greetings, Cameo, 1973, 8 Sq. Ft. 14
Tray, Mid-West Ice Cream, Kewpies Eating Ice Cream, Sundae, 13 x 13 In. .... *illus* 210

KING'S ROSE, *see Soft Paste category.*

KITCHEN

Kitchen utensils of all types, from eggbeaters to bowls, are collected today. Handmade wooden and metal items, like ladles and apple peelers, were made in the early nineteenth century. Mass-produced pieces, like iron apple peelers and graniteware, were made in the nineteenth century. Also included in this category are utensils used for other household chores, such as laundry and cleaning. Other kitchen wares are listed under manufacturers' names or under Advertising, Iron, Tool, or Wooden.

Board, Cutting, Wood, Lollipop Handle, 1800s, 16 x 20 ½ In. 183
Board, Dough, Slate, Black, Round, Hanging Hole, 19 In. 57

Kewpie, Tray, Mid-West Ice Cream, Kewpies Eating Ice Cream, Sundae, 13 x 13 In.
$210

Morphy Auctions

TIP
If you don't have a pie bird, you can use macaroni to vent a pie. Make decorative holes in the top crust and insert about five pieces of macaroni. These "mini" chimneys" allow steam to escape and keep the pie juices from boiling over.

Kitchen, Board, Dough, Slate, Round, Angular End, Hanging Hole, 18 In.
$91

Hartzell's Auction Gallery Inc.

Kitchen, Bowl, Dough, Wood, Rim, Sloping Walls, Ringed Footing, 1800s, 8 x 22 x 23 In.
$173

Selkirk Auctioneers & Appraisers

Kitchen, Box, Pantry, Wood, Oval, Freyes Measure Mill, 4 x 1 ½ to 8 x 4 In., 5 Piece Set
$158

Hartzell's Auction Gallery Inc.

Kitchen, Broiler, Wrought Iron, Scrolling Trefoils, Hanging Loop, Shenandoah Co., c.1800, 9 x 25 In.
$644

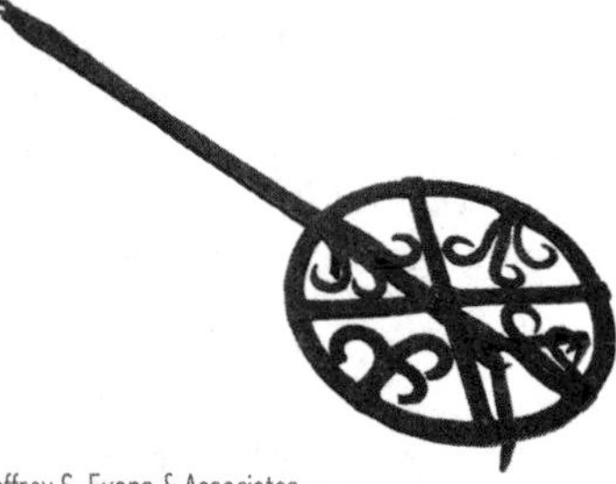

Jeffrey S. Evans & Associates

Kitchen, Butcher Block, Table, Wooden, Square, Turned Wood Legs, 31 x 27 x 34 In.
$325

Copake Auctions

Kitchen, Butter Stamp, Tulip, Rosettes, Treen, Carved, Round, 1850s, 4 In.
$234

Jeffrey S. Evans & Associates

Kitchen, Cabinet, Wilson, 2 Door, Drop Front, Swing Out Dispenser, 3 Drawers, 71 x 43 x 25 In.
$311

Soulis Auctions

Kitchen, Cake Board, Hearts, Birds, Wood, Carved, France, 1790, 9 In.
$438

Garth's Auctioneers & Appraisers

Kitchen, Cake Board, Man On Horseback, Stars, Couple On Reverse, Walnut, Carved, 1800s, 15 x 13 In.
$1,708

Pook & Pook

Kitchen, Churn, Glass, Metal & Wood Crank, Dazey, No. 80, 15 x 7 ½ In.
$102

Hartzell's Auction Gallery Inc.

Kitchen, Churn, Wood, Turned Body, Painted, Red, Yellow Bands, Late 1800s, 5 In.
$1,353

Skinner, Inc.

Board, Dough, Slate, Round, Angular End, Hanging Hole, 18 In. ....*illus* 91
Bowl, Dough, Wood, Rim, Sloping Walls, Ringed Footing, 1800s, 8 x 22 x 23 In. ....*illus* 173
Box, Pantry, Bentwood, 1-Finger, Tacked, Oval, Lid, 1800s, 2 x 5 ½ x 4 In. 154
Box, Pantry, Wood, Oval, Freyes Measure Mill, 4 x 1 ½ to 8 x 4 In., 5 Piece Set ....*illus* 158
Box, Utensil, Wood, Painted, Center Handle, Divided, 11 x 13 ½ In. 173
Broiler, Wrought Iron, Scrolling Trefoils, Hanging Loop, Shenandoah Co., c.1800, 9 x 25 In. *illus* 644
Butcher Block, Table, Wooden, Square, Turned Wood Legs, 31 x 27 x 34 In. ....*illus* 325
Butcher Block, Turned Wood Legs, American Stores Co., 18 x 18 x 32 In. 215
Butter Mold, look under Mold, Butter in this category.
Butter Stamp, Pineapple, Treen, Carved, Lollipop Shape, Handle, 1850s, 6 ½ x 2 ¾ In. 263
Butter Stamp, Pinwheel, Serrated Edge, Maple, Carved, Paddle, Scotland, 1850s, 11 In. 396
Butter Stamp, Tulip, Rosettes, Treen, Carved, Round, 1850s, 4 In. ....*illus* 234
Cabinet, Wilson, 2 Door, Drop Front, Swing Out Dispenser, 3 Drawers, 71 x 43 x 25 In. ...*illus* 311
Cake Board, Hearts, Birds, Wood, Carved, France, 1790, 9 In. ....*illus* 438
Cake Board, Man On Horseback, Stars, Couple On Reverse, Walnut, Carved, 1800s, 15 x 13 In. *illus* 1708
Cheese Strainer, Tin, Pierced, Round, 3 Simple Feet, 1860s, 2 ½ x 6 In. 117
Churn, Barrel, Stave Construction, Square Top, Bracket Feet, Hall Brothers, 14 x 11 In. 181
Churn, Glass, Embossed, Cast Iron Top, Wood Handle, Dazey Churn & Mfg. Co., 11 x 3 ½ In. 518
Churn, Glass, Metal & Wood Crank, Dazey, No. 80, 15 x 7 ½ In. ....*illus* 102
Churn, Wood, Turned Body, Painted, Red, Yellow Bands, Late 1800s, 5 In. ....*illus* 1353
Clothespin, Man's Shape, Bone, Hand Carved, 6 In. ....*illus* 181
Coffee Grinders are listed in the Coffee Mill category.
Coffee Mills are listed in their own category.
Cookie Board, Wood, Chip Carved, Man Drinking, Rectangular, 31 x 10 In. ....*illus* 68
Cookie Board, Wood, Heart Cutout, Tapered Handle, 1799, 15 ½ x 8 In. 3075
Dipper, Coconut Shell, Whale Ivory, Wood Handle, Ring In Hand End, 1800s, 15 In. ....*illus* 390
Dipper, Coconut Shell, Whalebone, Scroll Handle, 1800, 9 ½ In. ....*illus* 1800
Dipper, Coconut, Cherry Handle, Carved, Pewter Socket & Banding, 1800s, 17 In. 123
Dipper, Copper, Wrought Iron, Brass Inlay, Vine & Berry, Heart End, 1800s, 20 In. ....*illus* 369
Dough Box, Softwood, Rectangular Board Top, Splayed Legs, Round Feet, 44 ½ x 23 x 29 In. *illus* 118
Dough Box, Stand, Burl Wood, Carved, Women, Holding Hands, Shaped Apron, 35 x 39 In. 390
Dough Box, Wood, Gray Blue Paint, Canted Sides, Lid, Cutout Handle, c.1810, 30 In. ....*illus* 270
Dough Scraper, Punched Rosettes, Initials M.H., Wrought Iron, 1800s, 3 x 3 ¾ In. 256
Dough Scraper, Wrought Iron, Curved Handle, Shenandoah Co., c.1825, 2 x 4 ½ In. ....*illus* 176
Food Chopper, Heart, Iron, Wooden Handle, 12 ½ x 6 In. 226
Grater, Walnut, Cutout Heart, Pennsylvania, 24 In. ....*illus* 120
Grinder, Wood, Painted, Blue, Tulips, Tin Sieve, Steel Paddles, Crank, 1800s, 10 x 8 In. .*illus* 338
Heater, Sadiron, Cast Iron, Holds 4 Irons, Cone Shape Base, 9 In. 170
Hoosier Cabinet, Glass Doors, Flour, Sugar Sifters, Drawer, c.1930, 71 ½ In. ....*illus* 288
Hoosier Cabinet, Oak, 5 Doors, Blue Slag Glass Panels, Porcelain Top, 41 x 24 x 70 In. 259
Icebox, 2 Doors, Carved Scroll, Footed, Mascot, Early 1900s, 46 x 40 x 22 ½ In. 330
Icebox, Oak, 2 Doors, Brass Handles, Aluminum Interior, 23 ½ x 19 x 53 ½ In. 115
Iron, Alcohol, 2 Faces, Chrome, Rotates, Wood Handle, 3 x 6 x 11 In. 633
Iron, Electric, Silver Streak, Blue Glass, Saunders, 8 ½ In. ....*illus* 791
Iron, Flat, Embossed, Snake, Flower Border, Flattened Handle, 7 ½ In. 181
Iron, Fluter, Painted, Multicolor, Round Base, Manville, 5 In. ....*illus* 452
Iron, Fluter, Rocker Type, Horseshoe, Good Luck, L.L. Brill & D.C. Place, 5 ¾ In. 45
Iron, Gas, Hat, Rotary, Black Handle, 9 ½ In. 45
Iron, Pan, Bone Handle, Chinese Characters, 4 In. 124
Iron, Slug, Bonnet, Removable Top, Dome Base, 12 In. 509
Iron, Slug, Brass, Wood Handle, 2 x 3 ½ In. 104
Iron, Travel, Sterno, Porcelain Handle, Bugolette, 5 ½ In. 28
Kettle, Copper, 2 Handles, Spigot, Marked, Galliard Paris, 18 x 26 In. ....*illus* 240
Kettle, Sugar, Flared Rim, Cast Iron, 1800s, 16 x 36 In. 1200
Lard Tin, Lid, Handles, Green Paint, 12 x 10 ¾ In. ....*illus* 71
Mangle Board, 2 Horse Head Handle, Carved, Painted, 1832, 24 ½ In. 367
Mangle Board, Horse Handle, Carved, Geometric, Painted, 29 In. ....*illus* 339
Match Holders can be found in their own category.
Match Safes can be found in their own category.
Molds may also be found in the Pewter and Tinware categories.
Mold, Cookie, Animals & Fruit, 12 Images, Cast Iron, 1800s, 9 x 6 In. 147

Kitchen, Clothespin, Man's Shape, Bone, Hand Carved, 6 In.
$181

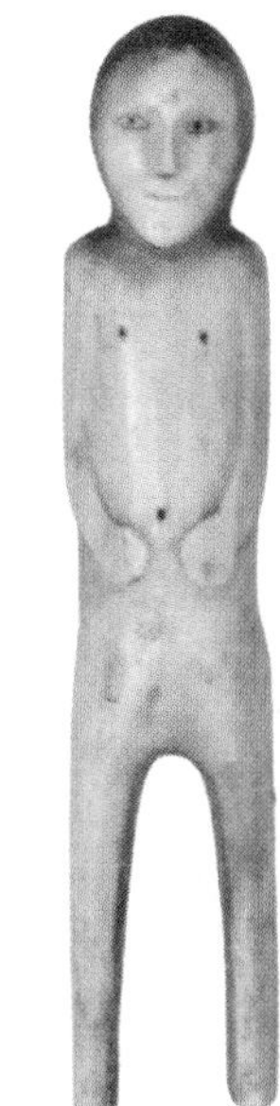

Hartzell's Auction Gallery Inc.

Kitchen, Cookie Board, Wood, Chip Carved, Man Drinking, Rectangular, 31 x 10 In.
$68

Hartzell's Auction Gallery Inc.

K

Kitchen, Dipper, Coconut Shell, Whale Ivory, Wood Handle, Ring In Hand End, 1800s, 15 In.
$390

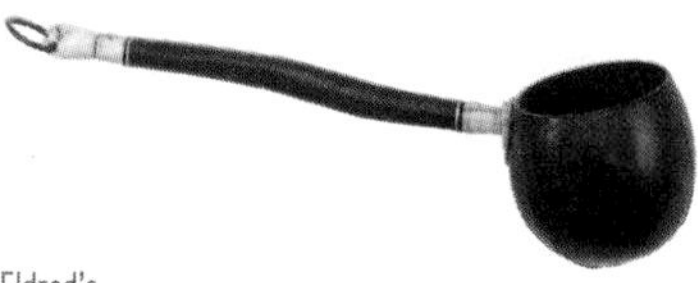

Eldred's

Kitchen, Dipper, Coconut Shell, Whalebone, Scroll Handle, 1800, 9 ½ In.
$1,800

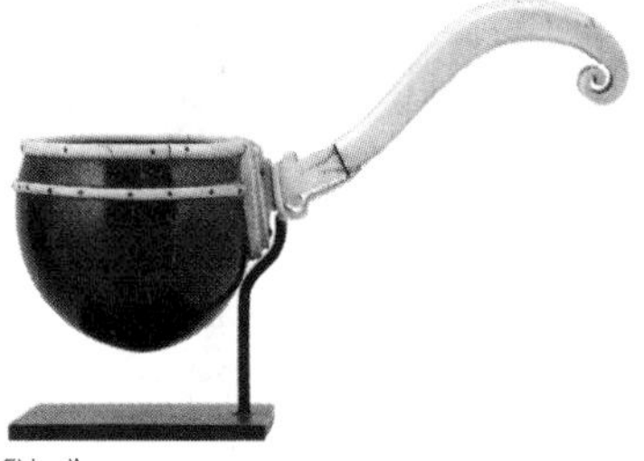

Eldred's

Kitchen, Dipper, Copper, Wrought Iron, Brass Inlay, Vine & Berry, Heart End, 1800s, 20 In.
$369

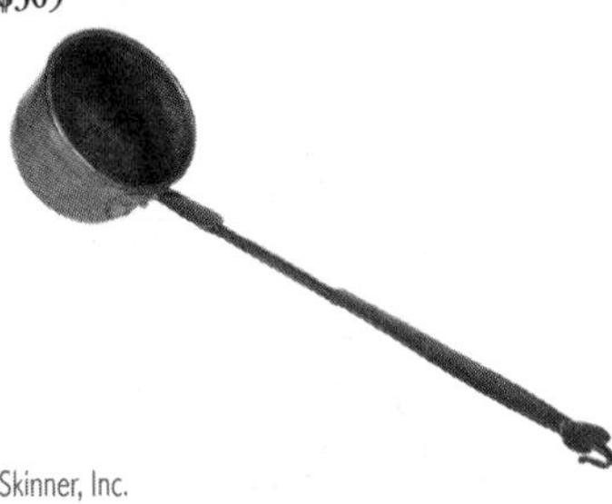

Skinner, Inc.

Kitchen, Dough Box, Wood, Gray Blue Paint, Canted Sides, Lid, Cutout Handle, c.1810, 30 In.
$270

Eldred's

Kitchen, Dough Scraper, Wrought Iron, Curved Handle, Shenandoah Co., c.1825, 2 x 4 ½ In.
$176

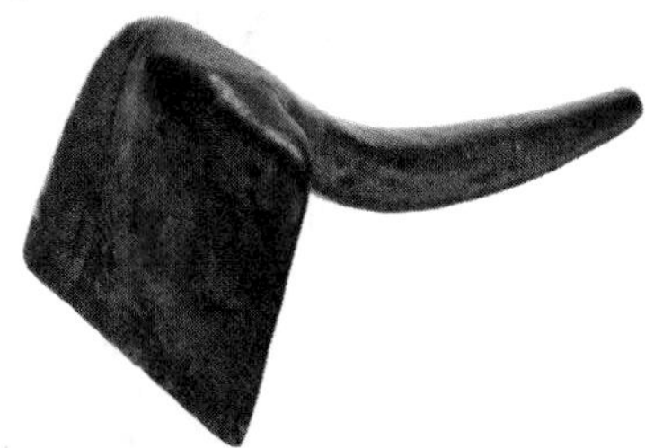

Jeffrey S. Evans & Associates

TIP
Oil your butcher-block table to keep it from splitting. Use mineral oil. You must oil it at least once a month.

Kitchen, Dough Box, Softwood, Rectangular Board Top, Splayed Legs, Round Feet, 44 ½ x 23 x 29 In.
$118

Bunch Auctions

Kitchen, Grater, Walnut, Cutout Heart, Pennsylvania, 24 In.
$120

Bourgeault-Horan Antiquarians & Associates, LLC

Kitchen, Grinder, Wood, Painted, Blue, Tulips, Tin Sieve, Steel Paddles, Crank, 1800s, 10 x 8 In.
$338

Skinner, Inc.

TIP
If you wash an iron pot with soap or detergent, it will remove the seasoning.

Kitchen, Hoosier Cabinet, Glass Doors, Flour, Sugar Sifters, Drawer, c.1930, 71 ½ In.
$288

Selkirk Auctioneers & Appraisers

Kitchen, Iron, Electric, Silver Streak, Blue Glass, Saunders, 8 ½ In.
$791

Hartzell's Auction Gallery Inc.

Kitchen, Iron, Fluter, Painted, Multicolor, Round Base, Manville, 5 In.
$452

Hartzell's Auction Gallery Inc.

Kitchen, Kettle, Copper, 2 Handles, Spigot, Marked, Galliard Paris, 18 x 26 In.
$240

Bunte Auction Services

Kitchen, Lard Tin, Lid, Handles, Green Paint, 12 x 10 ¾ In.
$71

Conestoga Auction Company

Kitchen, Roaster, Round, Serpentine Grill, Lollipop Handle, Wrought Iron, c.1800, 28 ¾ In.
$277

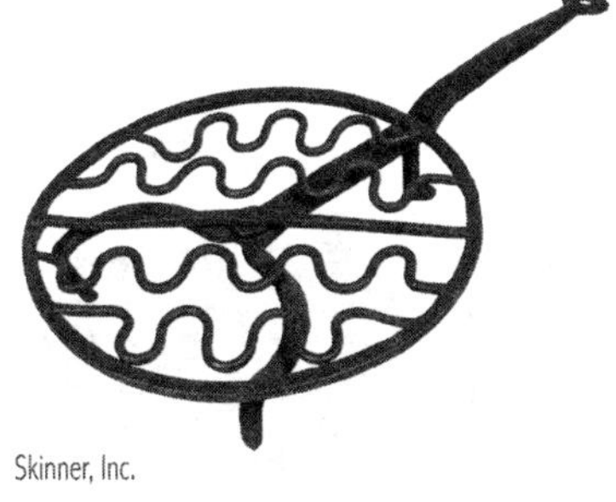

Skinner, Inc.

Kitchen, Scoop, Ice Cream Sandwich, Ice Cream Pie, United Products, Plated Brass, c.1930, 8 In.
$106

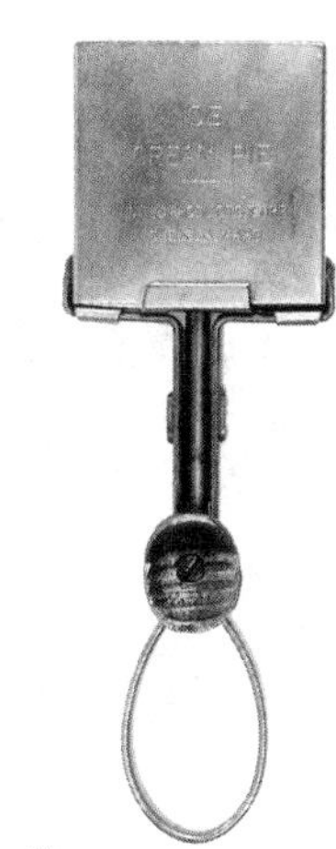

AntiqueAdvertising.com

Two-in-One Appliances

Some odd combination appliances were invented during the twentieth century. The Perc-O-Toaster, introduced by Armstrong in 1918, made coffee while it also toasted bread or waffles. In the 1930s, Merit-Made used the same idea to make a "moderne" coffeemaker-toaster. Ronson introduced a Cook 'n Stir in 1965 that blended and cooked simultaneously.

Kitchen, Mangle Board, Horse Handle, Carved, Geometric, Painted, 29 In.
$339

Hartzell's Auction Gallery Inc.

Kitchen, Skimmer, Ash, Oval Bowl, Short Handle, Carved Flower, 1800s, 5 In.
$984

Skinner, Inc.

Kitchen, Spice Box, Step Back, Pine, 4 Tiered Rows Of Drawers, New England, 1800s, 18 x 18 In.
$671

Pook & Pook

Kitchen, Spit Jack, Scrolled Brass Front Plate, Steel Mechanism, Flywheel, England, 1700s, 10 In.
$5,843

Skinner, Inc.

Kitchen, Spoon Rack, Hanging, Carved Oak, Shaped Ends, Scalloped Sides, 2 Shelves, 25 x 15 In.
$554

Skinner, Inc.

Kitchen, Strawholder, Glass, Metal Lid, c.1915, 12 x 4 ½ x 4 ½ In.
$270

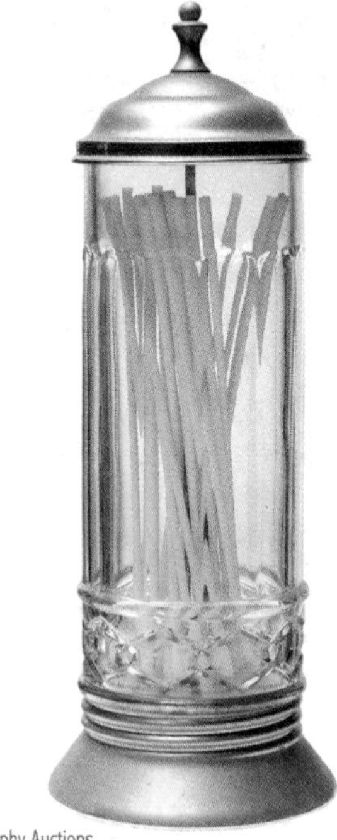

Morphy Auctions

Kitchen, Toaster, Wrought Iron, Tripod Base, 1700s, 27 ¾ In.
$189

Bunch Auctions

Kitchen, Waffle Iron, Griswold, American, No. 0, Cast Iron, Salesman's Sample, 1908, 5 In.
$780

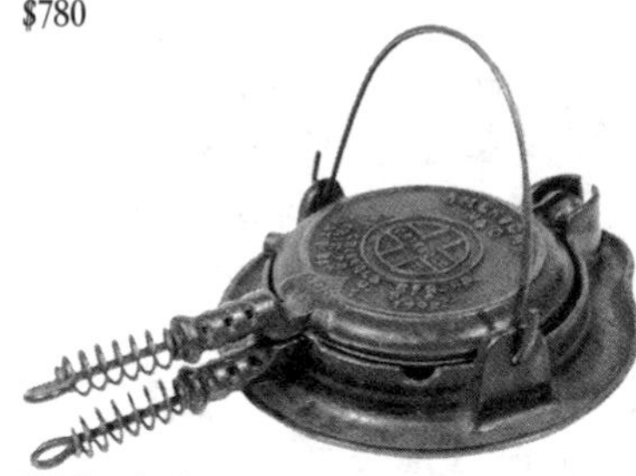

Rich Penn Auctions

Knife, Bowie, Folding, Etched Verse, Scrolls, Oval Escutcheon, R.C. Congreve, c.1830, 18 In.
$9,600

Morphy Auctions

K

Mold, Candle, see Tinware category.
Mold, Ice Cream, see also Pewter category.
Pestle, Blown Glass, Clear, Internal White Looping, Tooled, Wooden End, c.1850, 9 In. ... 84
Pot, Posnet, Cast Iron, Straight Handle, 3-Footed, Savery & Co., 1800s, 18 ½ In. ... 71
Reamers are listed in their own category.
Roaster, Round, Serpentine Grill, Lollipop Handle, Wrought Iron, c.1800, 28 ¾ In. ...*illus* 277
Rolling Pin, Blown Glass, Dark Olive Amber, Pontil Ends, 12 ½ In. ... 84
Rolling Pin, Blown Glass, Fiery Opalescent Milk Glass, 3 Painted Ships, 13 In. ... 144
Rolling Pin, Blown Glass, Pink Amethyst, Painted, From A Friend, Flowers, 13 ¾ In. ... 108
Rolling Pin, Turned Ash, Whalebone Handle, Custom Stand, 1800s, 15 In. ... 1046
Salt & Pepper Shakers are listed in their own category.
Scoop, Ice Cream Sandwich, Ice Cream Pie, United Products, Plated Brass, c.1930, 8 In. .*illus* 106
Skillet, Cast Iron, Share & Rider, Baltimore, Md., c.1830, 20 In. ... 3438
Skillet, Ye Wager Of Sin Is Death, Inscribed Handle, 3-Footed, 1700s, 16 ½ In. ... 1722
Skimmer, Ash, Oval Bowl, Short Handle, Carved Flower, 1800s, 5 In. ...*illus* 984
Skimmer, Flat Handle, Hanging Ring, Wrought Iron, 1844, 20 ½ In. ... 59
Skimmer, Pierced Pinwheel Bowl, Wrought Iron, 1810s, 20 ½ In. ... 360
Spice Box, Pine, Wallpaper, 4 Compartments, Lids, 1810s, 2 x 6 ¾ x 4 In. ... 204
Spice Box, Poplar Case, Shaped Back, 6 Drawers, Porcelain Pulls, Red, 1800s, 12 x 8 x 4 ⅝ In.. 3321
Spice Box, Sloped Sides, 14 Graduated Drawers, Wood, 13 x 11 ½ x 10 ½ In. ... 900
Spice Box, Step Back, Pine, 4 Tiered Rows Of Drawers, New England, 1800s, 18 x 18 In. .*illus* 671
Spit Jack, Scrolled Brass Front Plate, Steel Mechanism, Flywheel, England, 1700s, 10 In. *illus* 5843
Spoon Rack, Hanging, Carved Oak, Shaped Ends, Scalloped Sides, 2 Shelves, 25 x 15 In. *illus* 554
Spoon Rack, Walnut, Carved, Square Nails, Drawer, Lift Lid, Pa., 1810s, 17 x 12 x 6 In. ... 690
Strainer, Wrought Iron, Brass, Shaped Handle, Brass Inlay, JK 1848, 18 In. ... 397
Strawholder, Glass, Metal Lid, c.1915, 12 x 4 ½ x 4 ½ In. ...*illus* 270
Sugar Nippers, Steel, Moon, Stars, Compass, Patina, Early 1800s, 9 In. ... 92
Timer, Kodak, Orange Metal, 2 Hands, Round, Shaped Rectangular Swivel Base ... 35
Toaster, Wrought Iron, Hearth, Swiveling, 2 Arched Sides, c.1750, 16 x 13 In. ... 111
Toaster, Wrought Iron, Rotating, Swiveling Holder, 3-Footed, c.1800, 5 ¾ x 27 In. ... 117
Toaster, Wrought Iron, Tripod Base, 1700s, 27 ¾ In. ...*illus* 189
Tray, Cutlery, Walnut, Heart Cutout Handle, 1800s, 17 ½ x 14 x 10 In. ... 266
Tray, Herb Drying, Gouge, Wood, Carved, 1800s, 3 x 3 In. ... 147
Tray, Utensil, 2 Sections, Tiger Maple, Center Handle, 1800s, 4 ½ x 13 x 8 In. ... 1159
Trencher, Bird's-Eye Maple, Carved, 1850s, 22 x 15 In. ... 420
Trencher, Bowl, Wood, Red Paint, Rectangular, 28 ½ x 12 ½ x 4 In. ... 443
Trencher, Oblong, Wood, Carved, Patina, Early 1800s, 18 ½ x 10 ¾ x 4 In. ... 150
Trencher, Wood, Oval, Lined, Cut Handles, Patina, 25 x 13 x 5 In. ... 161
Trencher, Wood, Rectangular, Painted Exterior, Green, 1800s, 4 ½ x 19 x 10 In. ... 677
Trivet, see Trivet category.
Waffle Iron, Griswold, American, No. 0, Cast Iron, Salesman's Sample, 1908, 5 In. ...*illus* 780
Washing Machine, Columbia Washer, Wood, Crank, Salesman's Sample, 1895, 20 x 12 In. ... 413
Washing Machine, Manual, Wood, Painted, Stencil, Improved Favorite, Muncie, Ind., 35 x 29 In. 320

KNIFE

Knife collectors usually specialize in a single type. In the 1960s, the United States government passed a law that required knife manufacturers to mark their knives with the country of origin. This seemed to encourage the collectors, and knife collecting became an interest of a large group of people. All types of knives are collected, from top quality twentieth-century examples to old bone- or pearl-handled knives in excellent condition.

Bone Handle, Silver Pommel, Counterguard, Carved, Steel Blade, Wood Box, c.1780, 13 In. ... 1046
Bowie, Blade, Wood Handle, 7 ½ x 30 ½ x 2 In. ... 480
Bowie, Copper Pommel, Leather, Wood, Iron Guard, c.1900, 19 ½ In. ... 369
Bowie, Folding, Etched Verse, Scrolls, Oval Escutcheon, R.C. Congreve, c.1830, 18 In. ...*illus* 9600
Bowie, Ruana, Model 35B, Brass Back, Stainless Blade, Horn Grip, 15 In. ... 960
Bowie, Sweeping Blade, Clip Point, Lion Pommel, Stamped, Samuel Robinson, Sheffield, 15 In. 3300
Bowie, Wood Handle, Leather Scabbard, Edge Mark, Solingen, Germany, 15 ½ In. ... 71

Kosta, Vase, Glass Art, Birds, Acid Etched, Brown, Ove Sandeberg, c.1960, 8 ¾ x 6 In.
$200

Freeman's Auctioneers & Appraisers

Kosta, Vase, Rio Face, Multicolor, Orange Neck, Boda, Kjell Engman, 14 x 9 x 5 In.
$250

Kamelot Auctions

Kosta, Vase, White Ground, Black Stripes Line, Marked On Bottom, 13 ½ In.
$60

Bunte Auction Services

K

KPM, Lamp Base, Multicolor, Green & Blue Ground, Late 1800s, 20 In., Pair
$246

Skinner, Inc.

KPM, Vase, Portrait, King Frederick II, Cobalt Blue, Gilt, Handles, c.1900, 20 x 11 In.
$610

Neal Auction Company

Lacquer, Box, Coffer Shape, Black, Brass Corners, Lock, Family Crests, Japan, 3 x 5 ¾ In.
$923

Clars Auction Gallery

Dagger, Brass Tang & Cap, Carved Stag Horn Handle, Eagle, Damascene Blade, c.1990, 13 In. 192
Dagger, Quillon, Left Hand, 4-Sided Blade, Fluted Gilt Ricasso & Pommel, Finger Ring, 18 ½ In. . 4500
Dagger, Tanto, Gold Metal Mounts, Curved Blade, Ornate Orange Scabbard, Japan, 1800s, 9 ½ In. . 660
Pike, Boarding, U.S. Navy, Model 1797, Wrought Blade, Oak Haft, Ball Butt, 1797, 97 In. 984
Pocket, Steel, Tapered & Curved Brass Grip, Engraved Leaves, 1793, 4 ½ In. 420
Stiletto, Quadrangular Blade, Writhen Quillon, Turban Pommel, Wire Wrapped Grip, 25 In. 2400
Trench, L.F.&C., Brass Handle, Pointed Knuckle, Leather Scabbard, 1918, 12 ½ In. 590

KNOWLES, *Taylor & Knowles items may be found in the KTK and Lotus Ware categories.*

KOSTA

KOSTA

Kosta, the oldest Swedish glass factory, was founded in 1742. During the 1920s through the 1950s, many pieces of original design were made at the factory. Kosta and Boda merged with Afors in 1964 and created the Afors Group in 1971. In 1976, the name Kosta Boda was adopted. The company merged with Orrefors in 1990 and is still working.

Sculpture, Horse, Well, Oval Wood Base, Multicolor, Boda, Kjell Engman, 9 In. 142
Vase, Glass Art, Birds, Acid Etched, Brown, Ove Sandeberg, c.1960, 8 ¾ x 6 In. *illus* 200
Vase, Rio Face, Multicolor, Orange Neck, Boda, Kjell Engman, 14 x 9 x 5 In. *illus* 250
Vase, Trumpet Shape, Orange, White, Brown, Swirl, Kjell Engman, 14 ½ x 6 ½ In. 91
Vase, White Ground, Black Stripes Line, Marked On Bottom, 13 ½ In. *illus* 60

K.P.M

KPM

KPM refers to Berlin porcelain, but the same initials were used alone and in combination with other symbols by several German porcelain makers. They include the Konigliche Porzellan Manufaktur of Berlin, initials used in mark, 1823–1847; Meissen, 1723–1724 only; Krister Porzellan Manufaktur in Waldenburg, after 1831; Kranichfelder Porzellan Manufaktur in Kranichfeld, after 1903; and the Krister Porzellan Manufaktur in Scheibe, after 1838.

Compote, Floral Central Reserve, Raised Gilt, Shaped Handle, Tapered, Footed, 8 x 11 In. 846
Figurine, Lion, Lying Down, Faux Marble Base, Biscuit, 6 ½ In. 1353
Lamp Base, Multicolor, Green & Blue Ground, Late 1800s, 20 In., Pair *illus* 246
Lithophane, see also Lithophane category.
Plaque, Prussian Royalty, Jeweled Crown, Gold Dress, Lace, Fur Cape, Porcelain, 8 x 7 In. 310
Plate, Basket Weave, Reticulated Rims, Gilt Monogram & Highlights, c.1900, 8 ½ In., Pair 118
Punch Bowl, Lid, Bacchus Finial, Multicolor, Enamel, Painted, 1800s, 12 In., Pair 800
Urn, Blanc-De-Chine, Shaped Handle, Plinth Base, Marked, 1800s, 13 In., Pair 469
Vase, Portrait, King Frederick II, Cobalt Blue, Gilt, Handles, c.1900, 20 x 11 In. *illus* 610

K.T.&K.
CHINA

KTK

KTK are the initials of the Knowles, Taylor & Knowles Company of East Liverpool, Ohio, founded by Isaac W. Knowles in 1853. The company made many types of utilitarian wares, hotel china, and dinnerware. It made belleek and the fine bone china known as Lotus Ware from 1891 to 1896. The company merged with American Ceramic Corporation in 1928. It closed in 1934. Lotus Ware is listed in its own category in this book.

Vase, Blue Ground Glaze, Black, Orange, Yellow, Green, c.1900, 9 x 5 In. 129

KUTANI

Kutani porcelain was made in Japan after the mid-seventeenth century. Most of the pieces found today are nineteenth century. Collectors often use the term *Kutani* to refer to just the later, colorful pieces decorated with red, gold, and black pictures of warriors, animals, and birds.

Bowl, Men Sitting, River, Staff, Incense, Book, Mountains, Black, Red, 5 ½ x 15 In. 280
Figurine, Jurojin, Seated, Holding Scroll, Blue, White, Porcelain, Marked, 1900s, 11 ½ In. 120

L.G. WRIGHT

L.G. Wright Glass Company of New Martinsville, West Virginia, started selling glassware in 1937. Founder "Si" Wright contracted with Ohio and West Virginia glass factories to reproduce popular pressed glass patterns like Rose & Snow, Baltimore Pear, and Three Face, and opalescent patterns like Daisy & Fern and Swirl. Collectors can tell the difference between the original glasswares and L.G. Wright reproductions because of colors and differences in production techniques. Some L.G. Wright items are marked with an underlined *W* in a circle. Items that were made from old Northwood molds have an altered Northwood mark—an angled line was added to the *N* to make it look like a *W*. Collectors refer to this mark as "the wobbly W." The L.G. Wright factory was closed and the existing molds sold in 1999. Some of the molds are still being used.

Candy Dish, Lid, Iron Shape, Amethyst Glass, Handle, 8 ½ x 4 ½ In. 49
Sugar Shaker, 3 Faces, Frosted, Metal Top, Clear Foot, 1930s, 4 ⅞ In. 35
Syrup, Cranberry Opalescent, Globular Shaped, Applied Clear Reeded Handle, 1950s, 6 ½ In. 125

LACQUER

Lacquer is a type of varnish. Collectors are most interested in the Chinese and Japanese lacquer wares made from the Japanese varnish tree. Lacquer wares are made from wood with many coats of lacquer. Sometimes the piece is carved or decorated with ivory or metal inlay.

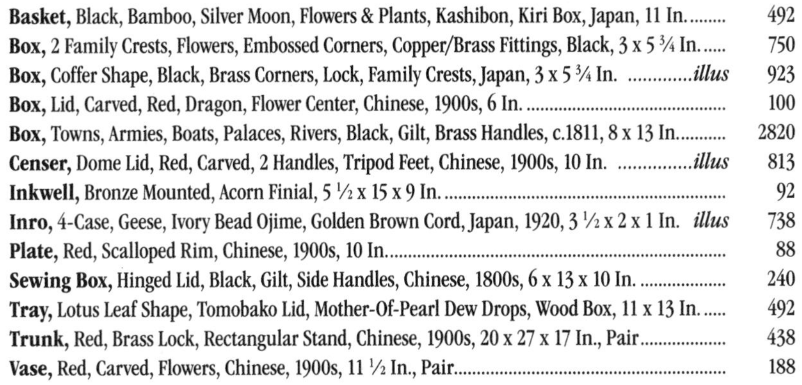

Basket, Black, Bamboo, Silver Moon, Flowers & Plants, Kashibon, Kiri Box, Japan, 11 In. 492
Box, 2 Family Crests, Flowers, Embossed Corners, Copper/Brass Fittings, Black, 3 x 5 ¾ In. 750
Box, Coffer Shape, Black, Brass Corners, Lock, Family Crests, Japan, 3 x 5 ¾ In. *illus* 923
Box, Lid, Carved, Red, Dragon, Flower Center, Chinese, 1900s, 6 In. 100
Box, Towns, Armies, Boats, Palaces, Rivers, Black, Gilt, Brass Handles, c.1811, 8 x 13 In. 2820
Censer, Dome Lid, Red, Carved, 2 Handles, Tripod Feet, Chinese, 1900s, 10 In. *illus* 813
Inkwell, Bronze Mounted, Acorn Finial, 5 ½ x 15 x 9 In. 92
Inro, 4-Case, Geese, Ivory Bead Ojime, Golden Brown Cord, Japan, 1920, 3 ½ x 2 x 1 In. *illus* 738
Plate, Red, Scalloped Rim, Chinese, 1900s, 10 In. 88
Sewing Box, Hinged Lid, Black, Gilt, Side Handles, Chinese, 1800s, 6 x 13 x 10 In. 240
Tray, Lotus Leaf Shape, Tomobako Lid, Mother-Of-Pearl Dew Drops, Wood Box, 11 x 13 In. 492
Trunk, Red, Brass Lock, Rectangular Stand, Chinese, 1900s, 20 x 27 x 17 In., Pair 438
Vase, Red, Carved, Flowers, Chinese, 1900s, 11 ½ In., Pair 188

LADY HEAD VASE, *see Head Vase.*

LALIQUE

Lalique glass and jewelry were made by Rene Lalique (1860–1945) in Paris, France, between the 1890s and his death in 1945. Beginning in 1921 he had a manufacturing plant in Alsace. The glass was molded, pressed, and engraved in Art Nouveau and Art Deco styles. Most pieces were marked with the signature *R. Lalique.* Lalique glass is still being made. Most pieces made after 1945 bear the mark *Lalique.* After 1978 the registry mark was added and the mark became *Lalique ® France.* In the prices listed here, this is indicated by Lalique (R) France. Some pieces that are advertised as ring dishes or pin dishes were listed as ashtrays in the Lalique factory catalog and are listed as ashtrays here. Names of pieces are given here in French and in English. The Lalique brand was bought by Art & Fragrance, a Swiss company, in 2008. Lalique and Art & Fragrance both became part of the Lalique Group in 2016. Lalique is still being made. Jewelry made by Rene Lalique is listed in the Jewelry category.

Lacquer, Censer, Dome Lid, Red, Carved, 2 Handles, Tripod Feet, Chinese, 1900s, 10 In.
$813

Hindman Auctions

Lacquer, Inro, 4-Case, Geese, Ivory Bead Ojime, Golden Brown Cord, Japan, 1920, 3 ½ x 2 x 1 In.
$738

Charlton Hall Auctions

TIP

Small lacquered pieces should be displayed in a cabinet near a small open dish of water to keep the humidity level at 55 percent.

Lalique, Bowl, Nemours, Flower Heads, Clear & Frosted, Mark, 4 x 10 In.
$250

Hindman Auctions

Lalique, Champagne Bucket, Ganyemeade, Nude Dancers, Leaves, Frosted, Engraved Lalique, 9 x 7 In.
$984

Clars Auction Gallery

Lalique, Hood Ornament, Tete D'Aigle, Eagle Head, Clear, Frosted, 4 In.
$116

Nadeau's Auction Gallery

TIP

To find a small crack in porcelain or glass, try this. Put the piece on a table. Tap it with your fingernail. A cracked piece gives off a dull thud, a perfect piece will "ring." Learn to recognize the sound by practicing on some pieces you know are broken.

Lalique, Figurine, Cygne, Tete Haute, Swan, Head Up, Frosted, Marked, Post 1978, 9 ½ x 10 ½ In.
$1,125

New Orleans Auction Galleries

Lalique, Figurine, Dove, Frosted, Molded, Acid Etched Lalique, 11 ½ In.
$125

Hindman Auctions

Lalique, Lamp, Ariane, 2 Doves, Frosted, Silk Drum Shade, Engraved Lalique, 16 In
$1,338

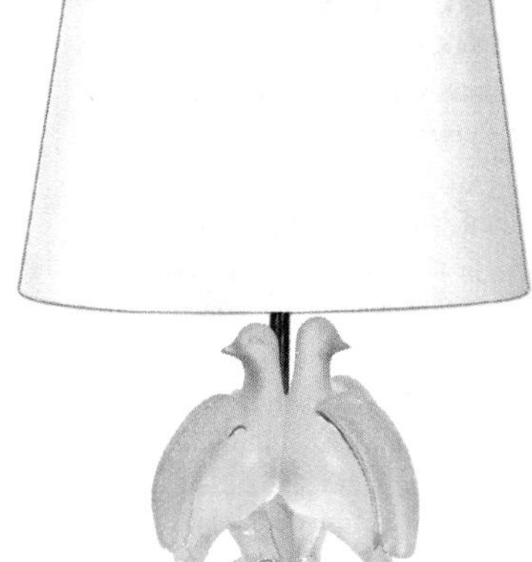

Clars Auction Gallery

Lalique, Table, Cactus, Molded, Frosted, Demilune, Engraved Lalique, 32 x 51 x 30 In.
$19,375

Abington Auction Gallery

Lalique, Vase, Aigrettes, Egrets, Reeds, Frosted, Gray Patina, Molded R. Lalique, 9 ¾ x 8 In.
$7,150

Treadway

Lalique, Vase, Jaguar, Jungle Leaves, Clear & Frosted, Angular, Engraved Lalique, 10 x 10 In.
$813

Abington Auction Gallery

Lalique, Vase, Sauterelles, Grasshoppers, Blue Patina, Engraved R. Lalique, 11 In.
$4,200

Bunte Auction Services

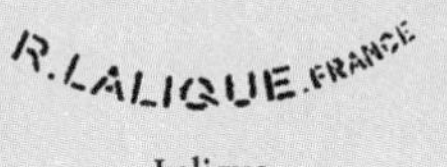	LALIQUE FRANCE	Lalique ® France
Lalique c.1925–1930s	Lalique 1945–1960	Lalique 1978+

Bowl, 2 Sparrows, Perched, Frosted, Wide Rim, Engraved Lalique, 15 ½ In. 240
Bowl, 4 Leopards, Frosted, Etched Ferns, Flared Rim, Engraved Lalique, 4 x 9 ¾ In. 563
Bowl, Amber Mood, Fan Panels, Raised Swirls, Engraved Lalique, 3 x 12 ¾ In. 512
Bowl, Bamako, Clear, Applied Green Salamanders, Engraved Lalique, 3 x 9 In. 630
Bowl, Champs Elysees, Maple Leaves, Acid Etched, Oval, Flared, Engraved Lalique, 18 x 10 In. 1815
Bowl, Gui, Mistletoe, Clear, Green Patina, Molded Lalique, 4 x 9 In. 200
Bowl, Marguerites, Daisies, Frosted, Engraved Lalique, 13 In. 374
Bowl, Nemours, Flower Heads, Clear & Frosted, Mark, 4 x 10 In. ....*illus* 250
Bowl, Nemours, Flower Heads, Frosted, Black Centers, 4 x 10 In. 413
Bowl, Ondines, Water Nymphs, Opalescent, R. Lalique, 1910s, 3 x 7 ¾ In. 780
Bowl, Pinsons, Finches, Frosted, Clear, Engraved Lalique, 9 x 3 ¾ In. 363
Bowl, Serpents, Clear, 2 Applied Amber Snakes, Engraved Lalique, 3 x 9 In. 708
Bowl, Yeso, 2 Stylized Fish, Opalescent Green, Clear, Engraved Lalique, 4 x 9 In. 570
Box, Dresser, Lid, Coppelia, Roses In Relief, Frosted, Engraved Lalique, c.1990, 3 x 7 x 5 ½ In. 177
Candlestick, Paquerettes, Daisies, Stamped Squares, Sepia, Clear, 9 x 3 In. 1000
Champagne Bucket, Ganyemeade, Nude Dancers, Leaves, Frosted, Engraved Lalique, 9 x 7 In. *illus* 984
Champagne, Anges, Angel's Head, Molded Stem, Etched Bowl, Lalique, 8 In., 14 Piece 510
Chandelier, 6-Light, Champs Elysees, Maple Leaves, Clear & Frosted, 4 Chrome Rods, 29 x 21 In. . 5650
Chandelier, 6-Light, Chene, Oak Leaves, Frosted, Clear Edges, Engraved Lalique, 23 x 11 In. .. 4068
Chandelier, Soleil, Sunbursts, Flowers, Gray Patina, 4 Silk Cords, R. Lalique, 9 x 12 In. 2700
Compote, Clear Bowl, Frosted Flower Stem, Circular Foot, Engraved Lalique, 8 ½ In. 461
Compote, Nogent, Frosted, 4 Birds, Clear Bowl, Engraved Lalique, 3 In., Pair 170
Dish, Lid, Honfleur, Geranium Leaf, Handles, Frosted, Marked, Lalique, 8 In. 180
Figurine, Ariane, 2 Doves, Frosted, 8 ½ x 6 In. 260
Figurine, Caroline, Turtle, Clear, Amber, Marked, Lalique, 1900s, 2 x 3 ½ x 6 In. 117
Figurine, Chat Assis, Cat, Seated, Frosted, Engraved Lalique, 8 In. 413
Figurine, Chrysis, Nude Woman, Kneeling, Clear, Frosted, Engraved Lalique, 1960, 5 x 2 ¾ x 6 ½ In. 155
Figurine, Cygne, Tete Haute, Swan, Head Up, Frosted, Marked, Post 1978, 9 ½ x 10 ½ In. *illus* 1125
Figurine, Deux Poissons, 2 Koi Fish, Intertwined, Art Deco Style, Marked, Lalique, 11 x 10 In. 1180
Figurine, Dog, Yorkshire Terrier, Standing, Frosted, Engraved Lalique, 3 ½ In. 277
Figurine, Dove, Frosted, Molded, Acid Etched Lalique, 11 ½ In. ....*illus* 125
Figurine, Leda & The Swan, Nude Woman, Frosted, Engraved Lalique, 4 ½ x 2 In. 186
Figurine, Madonna & Child, Molded, Black Glass Base, Engraved Lalique, 14 In. 369
Figurine, Sparrow, Wings Out, Frosted, Engraved Lalique, 5 x 3 ¾ In. 59
Figurine, Turtle, Mottled Amber, Frosted, Marked, 2 x 3 ½ x 5 ½ In. 96
Hood Ornament, Coq Nain, Rooster, Molded, Frosted, Late 1900s, France, 8 ½ In. 236
Hood Ornament, Tete D'Aigle, Eagle Head, Clear, Frosted, 4 In. ....*illus* 116
Lamp, Ariane, 2 Doves, Frosted, Silk Drum Shade, Engraved Lalique, 16 In ....*illus* 1338
Perfume Bottle, 3 Graces, Clear & Frosted, Art Deco, Engraved Lalique, Late 1900s, 8 In. 207
Perfume Bottle, Grande Pomme, Apple, Frosted, Leaves Stopper, Engraved Lalique, 5 ½ In. .. 230
Perfume Bottle, Samurai, Japanese Warrior, Marked, Box, 2005, 7 In. 266
Plaque, Masque De Femme, Woman's Face, Frosted, Chrome Frame, Lalique, 13 x 13 In. 3835
Plate, Algues, Seaweed, Black, Round, Engraved Lalique, 7 ¾ In. 83
Plate, Ondes, Waves, Opalescent, Blue, Stenciled R. Lalique, 11 In. 176
Platter, Piriac, Fish & Waves, Frosted, Clear, Oval, Engraved Lalique, 11 x 9 In. 187
Statue, Nude Woman Dancer, Frosted, Round Base, 9 x 4 ½ In. 230
Table, Cactus, Molded, Frosted, Demilune, Engraved Lalique, 32 x 51 x 30 In. ....*illus* 19375
Vase, Aigrettes, Egrets, Reeds, Frosted, Gray Patina, Molded R. Lalique, 9 ¾ x 8 In. ....*illus* 7150
Vase, Avallon, Birds, Berries, Frosted, Engraved R. Lalique, 5 ¾ x 6 ⅜ In. 439
Vase, Baccantes, Nudes, Frosted, Tapered, Stenciled R. Lalique, 9 ½ x 7 ½ In. 2834
Vase, Bagatelle, Birds Nesting, Frosted, Clear, Engraved Lalique, 6 ¾ In. 204
Vase, Flowers, Lavender, Frosted, Flared Rim, Engraved Lalique, 11 ¾ x 7 ½ In. 812
Vase, Formose, Swirling Carp, Blue Patina, Frosted, Engraved R. Lalique, 6 ¾ x 6 ½ In. 1560
Vase, Gui, Mistletoe, Leaves, Frosted, Etched R. Lalique, 6 ⅝ In. 540

Lalique, Vase, Tourbillons, Whirlwind, Clear, Black Enamel, Engraved Lalique, 8 In.
$1,664

Neal Auction Company

Lalique, Vase, Vibration, Raised Waves, Frosted & Clear, Globular, Engraved Lalique, 11 x 10 In.
$1,875

Abington Auction Gallery

Lamp, Aladdin, G-163, Double Nudes, Tinted & Opaque Glass, Metal Base, Art Deco, 23 In.
$2,000

Woody Auctions

L

Lamp, Argand, 2-Light, Cut Glass, Prisms, Bobeche, Brass, Clark & Coit, 1800s, 19 x 17 In.
$148

Leland Little Auctions

Lamp, Betty, Copper, Oval Font, Hinged Lid, Chain, Hook, 1800s, 4 ¾ x 3 ½ x 5 In.
$105

Jeffrey S. Evans & Associates

Lamp, Butler, Holding Tray, Ashtray, Match Holder, Cast Iron, Steel, 59 x 9 x 7 ¾ In.
$450

Morphy Auctions

Lamp, Candle, Church Shape, Painted Glass Windows, Chalkware, c.1890, 17 x 9 In.
$63

Garth's Auctioneers & Appraisers

Lamp, Candle, Hanging, Qajar Brass, Accordion, 1800s, 22 ½ In.
$225

Hindman Auctions

Lamp, Chandelier, 3-Light, Glass Globes, Enameled, Lightolier, G. Sarfatti, Italy, 1950s, 11 In.
$1,875

Rago Arts and Auction Center

Lamp, Chandelier, 4-Light, Brass, Spiral Stem, Blue Opalescent Shade, 32 x 21 In.
$180

Woody Auctions

Lamp, Chandelier, 8-Light, Candle Shape Lights, Bronze, Giacometti, c.1980, 33 x 20 x 20 In.
$375

Kamelot Auctions

Lamp, Chandelier, 10-Light, 2 Tiers, Metal, Glass, Barovier & Toso, 1950-60, 22 x 24 In.
$2,375

Palm Beach Modern Auctions

Vase, Ingrid, Clear & Frosted, 10 ½ In. 819
Vase, Jaguar, Jungle Leaves, Clear & Frosted, Angular, Engraved Lalique, 10 x 10 In. ....*illus* 813
Vase, Macao, 2 Cockatoos, Frosted Jade, Head Handles, Box, 1999, 13 x 10 In. 4161
Vase, Malesherbes, Loquat Leaves, Frosted, Teardrop Shape, R. Lalique, c.1927, 9 In. 1093
Vase, Martinets, Birds, Swirling, Clear, Engraved Lalique, 9 ⅝ In. 649
Vase, Ondines, Nude Water Nymphs, Frosted, Engraved Lalique, 9 x 7 ½ In. 620
Vase, Orchidee, Orchids, Opalescent, 6 ½ x 8 In. 650
Vase, Perruches, Parakeets, Butterscotch, Tree Limbs, Flowers, Engraved R. Lalique, 10 In. 8610
Vase, Rosine, 2 Birds, In Flight, Frosted, Tapered, Footed, Engraved Lalique, 5 x 3 ½ In. 197
Vase, Sauterelles, Grasshoppers, Blue Patina, Engraved R. Lalique, 11 In. ....*illus* 4200
Vase, Sylvie, 2 Lovebirds, Clear & Frosted, Flower Frog Insert, Engraved Lalique, 8 ¼ In. 189
Vase, Tourbillons, Whirlwind, Clear, Black Enamel, Engraved Lalique, 8 In. ....*illus* 1664
Vase, Vibration, Raised Waves, Frosted & Clear, Globular, Engraved Lalique, 11 x 10 In. ....*illus* 1875

LAMP

Lamps of every type, from the early oil-burning Betty and Phoebe lamps to the recent electric lamps with glass or beaded shades, interest collectors. Fuels used in lamps changed through the years; whale oil (1800–1840), camphene (1828), Argand (1830), lard (1833–1863), solar (1843–1860s), turpentine and alcohol (1840s), gas (1850–1879), kerosene (1860), and electricity (1879) are the most common. Early solar or astral lamps burned fat. Modern solar lamps are powered by the sun. Other lamps are listed by manufacturer or type of material.

Aladdin, B-70, Solitaire, White Moonstone, Lox-On Chimney, 1938, 25 x 7 In. 2486
Aladdin, G-163, Double Nudes, Tinted & Opaque Glass, Metal Base, Art Deco, 23 In. ....*illus* 2000
Aladdin, G-375, Alacite, Ivory, Urn, Dancing Women, Brass, c.1942, 9 ⅝ x 5 In. 585
Aladdin, Nu-Type, Model B, Red, Chicago, Oil, 15 ¾ x 12 ⅝ In. 288
Alcohol, Pressed Glass, Cobalt Blue, Jar Shape Base, Fuel Vial, Vapor Burner, 1910s, 9 x 3 In. 293
Argand, 2-Light, Brass, Bell Shape Font, Pineapple Finial, Stepped Base, B. Gardiner, 21 x 17 In., Pair . 1815
Argand, 2-Light, Cut Glass, Prisms, Bobeche, Brass, Clark & Coit, 1800s, 19 x 17 In. ....*illus* 148
Argand, 2-Light, Gilt Bronze, Griffin Support, Frosted Shades, c.1830, 17 x 17 In., Pair 1500
Argand, Gilt Bronze, Spread Wing Eagle, Octagonal Base, Messenger & Sons, c.1835, 19 x 10 In., Pair 3000
Art Deco, Cast Metal, Resin, Twisted Cobra, Tassel, Round Base, 1900, 55 ½ In., Pair 1770
Art Deco, Egyptian Style, Mica Shades, Bronze Base, 17 x 10 In., Pair 374
Art Deco, Spelter, Robed Woman, Jeweled & Leaded Glass Shade, Brown Patina, 14 In. 605
Art Nouveau, Bronze, Frog Holding Lily Pad, Elongated Arms, Beadwork, Jugendstil, 14 x 10 In. 9440
Banquet, Art Nouveau, Brass Font, Pottery Base, Milk Glass Shade, Flowers, c.1890, 39 In. 300
Banquet, Brass, Marble Shelf, Paw Feet, Painted Globe, Flowers, 68 x 15 In. 300
Banquet, Wood, Carved, White Globe, Brass Font, Medallions, Claw Feet, c.1890, 40 x 12 In. 450
Betty, Copper, Oval Font, Hinged Lid, Chain, Hook, 1800s, 4 ¾ x 3 ½ x 5 In. ....*illus* 105
Bouillotte, 3-Light, Gilt Bronze, Flame Finial, Hoof Feet, Electrified, France, 1800s, 22 x 10 In. 944
Bouillotte, 5-Light, Neoclassical Style, Argente Brass, Paw Feet, Silvered Tole Shade, 22 x 15 In. 450
Bradley & Hubbard lamps are included in the Bradley & Hubbard category.
Brass, Lighthouse Shape, Mahogany Turned Wooden Base, 1900s, 13 ½ In. 420
Brass, Ring Handles, Chilong, Stylized Masks, Shade, Wood Base, Chinese, c.1950, 36 In. 148
Butler, Holding Tray, Ashtray, Match Holder, Cast Iron, Steel, 59 x 9 x 7 ¾ In. ....*illus* 450
Candle, Church Shape, Painted Glass Windows, Chalkware, c.1890, 17 x 9 In. ....*illus* 63
Candle, Electric, 2-Light, Brass, Adjustable Arm, Saucer Base, Black Shade, 1850s, 21 ½ In. 288
Candle, Georgian Style, Mahogany, Glass Shades, Carved, Felt Base, 31 In., Pair 293
Candle, Hanging, Qajar Brass, Accordion, 1800s, 22 ½ In. ....*illus* 225
Chalice, Lid, Bronze, Glass, Mosaics, Beaded Rim, Multicolor, Griffins, 24 x 8 In. 3750
Chandelier, 3-Light, Brass, Hydrangea, 2 Arms, Glass Shade, Early 1900s, 30 x 36 In. 182
Chandelier, 3-Light, Glass Globes, Enameled, Lightolier, G. Sarfatti, Italy, 1950s, 11 In. .*illus* 1875
Chandelier, 3-Light, Lantern Shape, Bronze Pendant, 1900s, 20 In. 300
Chandelier, 3-Light, Rams' Heads, Torch, Bacchus Medallions, 1900s, 37 x 24 In. 1350
Chandelier, 4-Light, Brass, Spiral Stem, Blue Opalescent Shade, 32 x 21 In. ....*illus* 180
Chandelier, 4-Light, French Glass, Beaded, Flower Form, Multicolor, 1900s, 23 x 15 In. 313
Chandelier, 4-Light, Glass Shell Shades, Rope Form Supports, Gilt Metal, 1950s, 36 x 24 In. 936
Chandelier, 4-Light, Medieval Style, Wrought Iron, Ram's Head, Ivy, Early 1900s, 34 x 30 In. 354

Lamp, Chandelier, 10-Light, Bronze, Glass Leaf Shape, c.1950, 34 x 20 x 20 In.
$500

Kamelot Auctions

Lamp, Chandelier, Brass, Stained Glass, Green Panels, Prisms, Jugenstil, c.1910, 35 x 8 In.
$338

Clars Auction Gallery

Lamp, Chandelier, Cloud, Molded Plastic, Remo Saraceni, 30 x 33 x 12 In.
$1,062

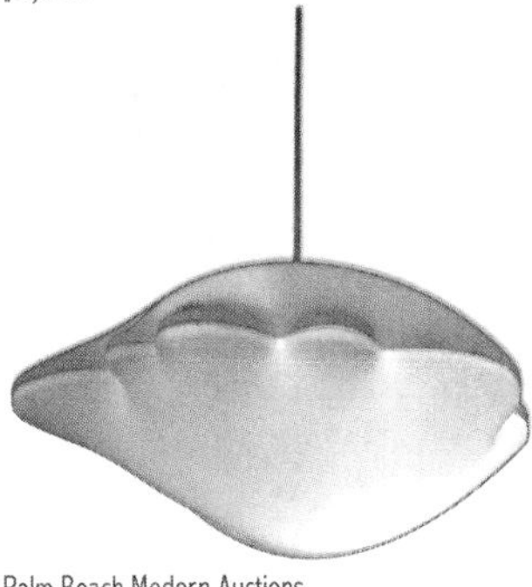

Palm Beach Modern Auctions

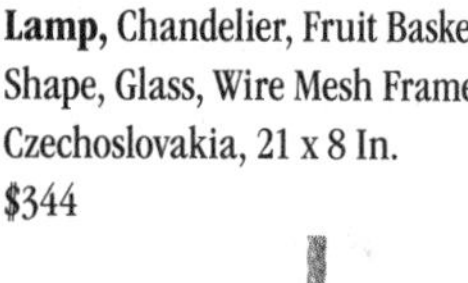

Lamp, Chandelier, Fruit Basket Shape, Glass, Wire Mesh Frame, Czechoslovakia, 21 x 8 In.
$344

Kamelot Auctions

Lamp, Chandelier, Poul Henningsen, Artichoke, Enameled Aluminum, Steel, Chromed, 1900s, 30 In.
$3,750

Palm Beach Modern Auctions

Lamp, Electric, 1-Light, Chrome, 2-Gourd Stem, Cream Fabric Shade, France, c.1970, 18 In.
$156

Kamelot Auctions

Chandelier, 5-Light, 4 Brass Arms, Opaline Glass Shade, Art Deco, 1920, 62 x 28 In. 217
Chandelier, 5-Light, Brass, Vase Shape, Scroll Arms, Hanging Prism, 1800s, 26 x 28 In. 800
Chandelier, 5-Light, Candle Shape Sockets, Wheat, Leaves, Bronze, 18 In. 118
Chandelier, 5-Light, Rococo Style, Gilt Bronze, Leaves, 1800s, 30 In. 1920
Chandelier, 6-Light, 3 Tiers, Baroque Style, Rock Crystal Stem, Ball Finial, 48 x 34 In. 3198
Chandelier, 6-Light, Air Balloon Shape, Flower Ribbon, France, 32 x 18 In. 1107
Chandelier, 6-Light, Baluster Shaft, Scrolling Branches, Continental, 1800s, 24 x 26 In. 800
Chandelier, 6-Light, Empire Style, Brass, 31 x 32 In. 118
Chandelier, 6-Light, Gas & Electric, Bronze, Etched Glass Shade, 40 x 25 In. 363
Chandelier, 6-Light, Louis XV Style, Curved Brass Frame, Glass Prisms, 1900s, 42 x 29 In. 1003
Chandelier, 6-Light, Louis XV Style, Painted Metal, Porcelain Flowers, Early 1900s, 33 In. 438
Chandelier, 6-Light, Maple, Iron, Red Paint, 1700s, 22 x 13 ½ In. 1180
Chandelier, 6-Light, Scrolled Arms, Brass Pins, Dutch, 1800s, 18 x 19 In. 120
Chandelier, 6-Light, Tin, Hanging, 18 In. 83
Chandelier, 7-Light, Italian Opalescent Art Glass Discs, Chrome, White, 20 x 19 In. 340
Chandelier, 7-Light, Scrolled Arm, Wrought Iron, 36 x 35 In. 71
Chandelier, 8-Light, Candle Shape Lights, Bronze, Giacometti, c.1980, 33 x 20 x 20 In. ..*illus* 375
Chandelier, 8-Light, Classical Style, Brass Frame, Molded Glass Beads, 1900s, 55 x 38 In. 360
Chandelier, 8-Light, Crystal, Bent Arm, Glass Beads, c.1910, 28 x 26 In. 240
Chandelier, 8-Light, Flame Shade, Anthemion, Black, Bronze, Empire Style, France, 1950s, 36 x 24 In. 885
Chandelier, 8-Light, Louis XV Style, Bronze & Glass, c.1800, 34 x 27 In. 625
Chandelier, 8-Light, Louis XV Style, Curved Glass Arms, Prism Chains, 1900s, 18 x 22 In. 375
Chandelier, 8-Light, Renaissance Style, Bow Shape Canopy, Flower Shades, c.1920, 34 x 27 In. 577
Chandelier, 9-Light, Degue, Wrought Iron, Frosted Glass, Basket Weave, Flowers, c.1930, 48 x 28 In. 1968
Chandelier, 9-Light, Iron, Hanging, Colonial Style, 23 x 31 In. 620
Chandelier, 10-Light, 2 Tiers, Metal, Glass, Barovier & Toso, 1950-60, 22 x 24 In. ....*illus* 2375
Chandelier, 10-Light, Bronze, Glass Leaf Shape, c.1950, 34 x 20 x 20 In. ....*illus* 500
Chandelier, 14-Light, 3 Tiers, Discs, Stars, Serpentine Branch, 1800s, 28 x 22 In. 7380
Chandelier, 14-Light, Candle Sockets, Chrome Fixture, Lightolier, 26 x 20 In. 88
Chandelier, Alabaster, White Shade, Bronze Chain, Continental, 9 ½ x 16 In. 469
Chandelier, Brass Scroll, Ruby Red, Vase Shape, c.1910, 27 x 10 ½ x 10 ½ In. 281
Chandelier, Brass, Stained Glass, Green Panels, Prisms, Jugenstil, c.1910, 35 x 8 In. ....*illus* 338
Chandelier, Cloud, Molded Plastic, Remo Saraceni, 30 x 33 x 12 In. ....*illus* 1062
Chandelier, Fruit Basket Shape, Glass, Wire Mesh Frame, Czechoslovakia, 21 x 8 In. ......*illus* 344
Chandelier, Poul Henningsen, Artichoke, Enameled Aluminum, Steel, Chromed, 1900s, 30 In. *illus* 3750
Electric, 1-Light, Chrome, 2-Gourd Stem, Cream Fabric Shade, France, c.1970, 18 In. ....*illus* 156
Electric, 1-Light, Empire Style, Brass, Black Shade, Bouillotte, 22 In. 406
Electric, 1-Light, Steel, Black Shade, Columnar, Brass, c.1970, 26 x 18 ½ In. 219
Electric, 2 Putti, Marble, Mounted On Circular Sienna Base, Italy, 36 x 9 In. 570
Electric, 2-Light, Adjustable, Tole, Black, Painted, Jeanne Reed's Ltd., 24 In., Pair 176
Electric, 2-Light, Art Deco, Brass, Tapered Segments, Stepped Base, c.1925, 60 In. 400
Electric, 2-Light, Hexagonal Shade, Triangular Base, Bakelite, Art Deco, 23 ½ x 15 In. 390
Electric, 2-Light, Painted, Glass Shade, Lakeside Scene, Urn Shape Base, Early 1900s, 23 In. .. 322
Electric, 2-Light, Peacock, Leaves, Stems, Bronze, Oval Satin Glass, Scenic Panel, 18 ½ x 15 ½ In. 2057
Electric, 2-Light, Reverse Painted Shade, Flowers, Cast Metal Base, 8 x 18 ½ In. 840
Electric, 2-Light, Reverse Painted Shade, Mums, Yellow, Moe Bridges, 23 x 17 ¾ In. ....*illus* 3300
Electric, 2-Light, Reverse Painted Shade, Sunset, Field, Trees, Gilt Metal Base, 21 x 16 In. 350
Electric, 2-Light, Soapstone, Cloth Shade, Birds, Wood Base, 1900s, 26 In. 100
Electric, 2-Light, Sphinx Figures, Dome Fringed Shade, Tripod Feet, Art Deco, 61 ½ In. 140
Electric, 2-Light, Urn Shape, Mounted, Pistol Handles, Silver Plate, 25 ½ In., Pair 1722
Electric, 3-Light, Brass & Wood, Marble Base, Adjustable, 60 In. 124
Electric, 3-Light, Bronze, Lily Shape Glass Shade, Buffalo Metal Works, 12 x 11 In. ....*illus* 396
Electric, 3-Light, Bronze, Woman, Tree, Brown Patina, Newell, 32 x 11 In. 1150
Electric, 3-Light, Goffredo Reggiani, Chromed Metal, Adjustable, Floor ....*illus* 188
Electric, 3-Light, Handel Style, Reverse Painted Domed Glass Shade, c.1930, 24 ½ x 18 In. 1080
Electric, 3-Light, Pole, Brass, White Enamel, Smoked Glass, Teak, Denmark, c.1960, 95 In. 338
Electric, 3-Light, Stiffel, Tole Style, Brass, Black Shade, 30 In. 60
Electric, 3-Light, Water Lily, Brown, Slag Glass, Duffner & Kimberley, c.1905, 25 x 22 In. 3300
Electric, 4-Light, Figural, Eros Holding Torch, Leafy Branches, Newell, 26 x 15 x 16 In. 484

L

Lamp, Electric, 2-Light, Reverse Painted Shade, Mums, Yellow, Moe Bridges, 23 x 17 ¾ In.
$3,300

Morphy Auctions

Lamp, Electric, 3-Light, Bronze, Lily Shape Glass Shade, Buffalo Metal Works, 12 x 11 In.
$396

Soulis Auctions

Lamp, Electric, 3-Light, Goffredo Reggiani, Chromed Metal, Adjustable, Floor
$188

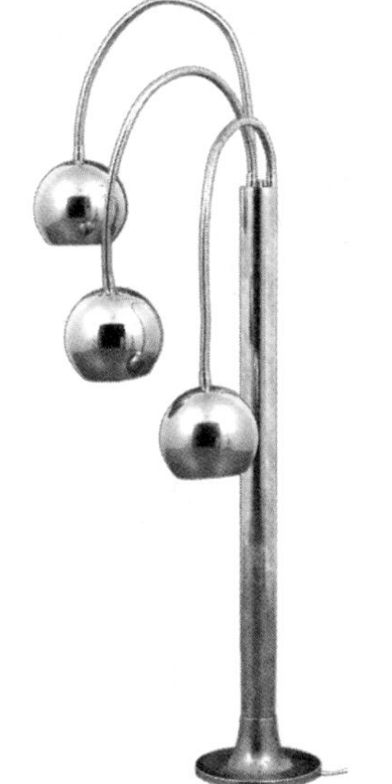

Palm Beach Modern Auctions

Lamp, Electric, 4-Light, Mica Shade, 5 Panels, Copper Base, Arts & Crafts, 16 x 18 In.
$1,140

Milestone Auctions

Lamp, Electric, Brass & Lucite Column, Square Base, Black Shade, c.1970, 27 x 6 ¾ In.
$375

Kamelot Auctions

Lamp, Electric, Ceiling, Artichoke, Copper, Steel, Aluminum, Brass, Poul Henningsen, 1957, 34 In.
$5,937

Rago Arts and Auction Center

The Lamp Shade Is Important

The prices of lamps with painted, blown out, or stained glass shades are based primarily on the shade. A substitute base of the expected quality does not lower the value by much.

Lamp, Electric, Ceiling, Max Ingrand, Glass, Brass, Steel, Fontana Arte, Italy, c.1965, 23 In.
$17,500

Phillips

Lamp, Electric, Child's, Shade, Multicolor, Wood Base, Mackenzie, 40 In.
$1,373

Nadeau's Auction Gallery

L

Lamp, Electric, Chrome, Molecular, Mirrored Bulbs, Torino, 1960, 55 In.
$531

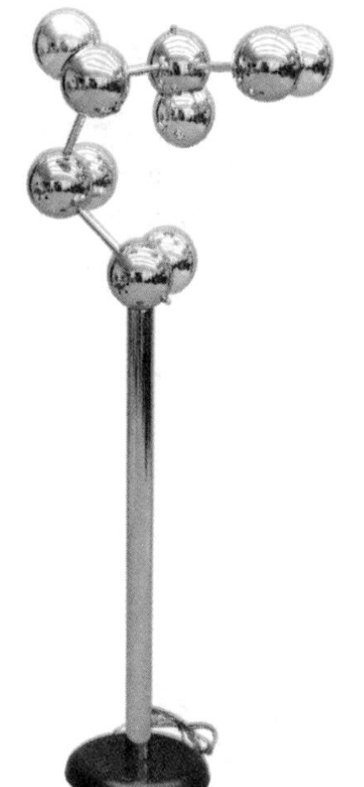

Copake Auctions

Lamp, Electric, Duffner & Kimberly, Whaley, Leaded Glass, Thistles, Green, Brown, Blue, 25 In.
$5,228

Morphy Auctions

Lamp, Electric, Desk, Emeralite, Roll Top, Adjustable Swing Arm, 1900s, 11 x 7 x 7 In.
$406

Cowan's Auctions

Lamp, Electric, Hanging, Snowball, Aluminum, Poul Henningsen, Denmark, 14 x 18 In.
$1,888

Cottone Auctions

Lamp, Electric, Lighthouse Shape, Rocky Outcrop, Candle Bulb Socket, Bronze, 12 ½ x 6 ¾ In.
$176

Thomaston Place Auction Galleries

Lamp, Electric, Desk, Nude, Patinated Bronze, Art Nouveau, Tulip Shade, Gustav Gurschner, 15 In.
$400

Clars Auction Gallery

Lamp, Electric, Light, Clear Cut Glass, Button, Round Base, Russia, 25 x 12 In.
$450

Woody Auctions

Lamp, Electric, Parrot, Tiffin Glass, Wood Base, 14 In.
$225

Woody Auctions

Electric, 4-Light, Mica Shade, 5 Panels, Copper Base, Arts & Crafts, 16 x 18 In. ....*illus* 1140
Electric, 4-Light, Opalescent Jewels, Filigree, Art Nouveau Style Woman, Flower, 30 x 18 In..... 6050
Electric, 6-Light, Torchiere, Black, White, Marble Disc Shape Base, 65 ½ In. 298
Electric, Airplane, Blue, Glass Body, Silver Lines, Art Deco, Chromed Metal Frame, 7 x 13 x 13 In.. 424
Electric, Arts & Crafts Style, Domed Shade, Panel, Round Base, Early 1900s, 24 x 19 In. 189
Electric, Bell Shape Shade, Woodland Path Scene, Jefferson, 21 ½ x 15 ¾ In. 650
Electric, Blown Glass, Peacock, Pulled Feather Base, Charles Lotton, 22 x 17 In. 1955
Electric, Boudoir, Acid Cut, Glass Shade, Switch Marked, Leviton, 5 In. 94
Electric, Brass & Lucite Column, Square Base, Black Shade, c.1970, 27 x 6 ¾ In. ....*illus* 375
Electric, Brass, Bamboo, Reed, Black Metal Tapered Shade, 52 ¾ In. 94
Electric, Brass, Dragon, Snake, Green, Patina, Stephen Hills, c.1897, 24 x 15 x 9 In. 567
Electric, Brass, Moroccan Style, White Alabaster Mounts, Reticulated Shade, c.1910, 62 In. 384
Electric, Brass, Mushroom Shade, Flowers, Hanging Prisms, Round Base, 21 In. 288
Electric, Bronze Tone Spelter, Greco Roman, Green Marble, France, c.1900, 31 In., Pair 1298
Electric, Bronze, Female, Nude, Conical Amber Glass Shade, Robert Thew, c.1930, 19 In. 160
Electric, Bronze, Glass, Pheasants, Tree Base, Teardrop Shade, Art Nouveau, Austria, 20 x 9 In. 7800
Electric, Candlestick Style, Silver Plate, Black Shade, 31 In., Pair 185
Electric, Caramel, Painted White Base, Slag Glass Shade, 22 x 17 In. 72
Electric, Carved Mahogany, Leaded Glass, Dragonfly Shade, Cabochon, c.1915, 64 x 22 In. 424
Electric, Ceiling, Artichoke, Copper, Steel, Aluminum, Brass, Poul Henningsen, 1957, 34 In. .*illus* 5937
Electric, Ceiling, Max Ingrand, Glass, Brass, Steel, Fontana Arte, Italy, c.1965, 23 In. .....*illus* 17500
Electric, Child's, Shade, Multicolor, Wood Base, Mackenzie, 40 In. ....*illus* 1373
Electric, Chrome, Molecular, Mirrored Bulbs, Torino, 1960, 55 In. ....*illus* 531
Electric, Crystal Ball, Chrome Base, White Shade, Italy, 66 In. 384
Electric, Cylindrical Jar, Sweet Pea, Ball Finial, Black Base, 9 In. 96
Electric, Dancer, Seminude, Holding Glass Globe, Iron Base, Art Deco, c.1940, 13 x 13 ¾ x 4 ¾ In. 537
Electric, Desk, Emeralite, Roll Top, Adjustable Swing Arm, 1900s, 11 x 7 x 7 In. ....*illus* 406
Electric, Desk, Nude, Patinated Bronze, Art Nouveau, Tulip Shade, Gustav Gurschner, 15 In. *illus* 400
Electric, Domed Shade, Lakeside Landscape, Cameo Glass Stem, Iron Base, Early 1900s, 18 x 8 In.. 424
Electric, Domed Shade, Reverse Painted, Sheep, Bronze Water Lily Base, c.1922, 22 x 14 In. 585
Electric, Duffner & Kimberly, Whaley, Leaded Glass, Thistles, Green, Brown, Blue, 25 In. *illus* 5228
Electric, Exotic Bird, Reverse Painted, Urn Shape, Claw Feet, Moe Bridges, 24 x 18 In. 2480
Electric, Feather Blown, Pink, Green, Blue Iridescent Glass, Daniel Lotton, 22 In. 633
Electric, Frankart Style, Patina, 2 Female Nudes, Stepped Glass Shade, 1900s, 19 In. 431
Electric, Glass Ball, Dancing, Marble Base, Art Deco, Pixie & Millefiori, 8 ½ x 7 ½ x 3 In. 363
Electric, Glass Dome, Blue Tinted Mirror, Aluminum Pedestal Base, c.1950, 56 x 19 ¾ In. 234
Electric, Glass, White Overlay, Green, Gilt, Brass Base, Bohemia, 38 In., Pair 531
Electric, Gone With Wind, Fruit & Flowers, Art Nouveau, 19 In. 59
Electric, Green To Blue Domed Shade, Iridescent, Signed, Lundberg Studios, 1986, 16 In. 1102
Electric, Hanging, Leaded Glass Shade, Flowers, Unique Art & Metal Co., c.1920, 25 x 25 x 18 In. 3000
Electric, Hanging, Snowball, Aluminum, Poul Henningsen, Denmark, 14 x 18 In. ....*illus* 1888
Electric, Hexagon Umbrella Shade, Mottled Cranberry, White Glass, Bronze Trim, 20 In. 230
Electric, Iridescent, Glass, Feather Design, Mushroom Shade, Lundberg Studios, 1900s, 21 In. 492
Electric, Leaded Glass Shade, Flowers, Scalloped Rim, Duffner & Kimberly, 66 x 24 In. 7800
Electric, Leaded Glass Shade, Geometric, Bud Finial, Brass, Early 1900s, 21 x 16 In. 2034
Electric, Leaded Glass, Bronze Base, Green Shade, Flowers, 20 In. 2400
Electric, Light, Clear Cut Glass, Button, Round Base, Russia, 25 x 12 In. ....*illus* 450
Electric, Lighthouse Shape, Gilt Bronze, Weather Vane, H.F. Bodmer, San Francisco, 15 In. 833
Electric, Lighthouse Shape, Rocky Outcrop, Candle Bulb Socket, Bronze, 12 ½ x 6 ¾ In. *illus* 176
Electric, Lucite, Tapered Shape, Gold Ball, Round Plinth Base, Modernist, 34 ½ In. 24
Electric, Monkey, Bronze, Patina, Book Shape Base, Maitland-Smith, 1900s, 23 x 12 In. 944
Electric, Opaline Shade, Bird, Silvered Bronze Mount, Flowers, France, 1900s, 17 x 13 x 7 In.. 7080
Electric, Paperweight, Flowers, Wood Pedestal Base, John Lotton, 1994, 10 x 7 In. 1984
Electric, Parrot, Tiffin Glass, Wood Base, 14 In. ....*illus* 225
Electric, Patinated White Metal Base, Painted 6-Pane Shade, Classical, 1910s, 22 x 19 In. *illus* 150
Electric, Pink Opalescent, Hobnail Shade, Brass Base, c.1910, 18 ½ x 8 In. 150
Electric, Poppy Flowers & Buds, Yellow Orange Ground, Shade Ring, Signed, Jefferson, 22 In.. 1513
Electric, Pulled Green To Lavender Shade, Ribbed Base, Lundberg Studios, 1999, 15 In. 1103
Electric, Red Vase, White Shade, Brass, Wood Base, 1900s, 31 ½ In. 384

Lamp, Electric, Patinated White Metal Base, Painted 6-Pane Shade, Classical, 1910s, 22 x 19 In.
$150

Garth's Auctioneers & Appraisers

Lamp, Electric, Tiffany Style, Acorn Shade, Bronze Base, Turtleback Tiles, 26 In.
$1,230

Locati Auctions

Lamp, Electric, Tommi Parzinger Style, 9-Light, Plus 3-Light Under Shade, Brass, Stiffel, 50 In.
$188

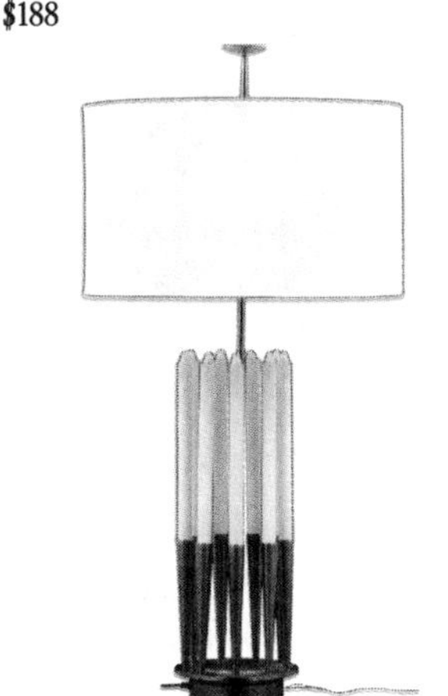

Palm Beach Modern Auctions

L

Lamp, Electric, Wood, Trapezoidal Shade, Painted Screen Panel, Folk Art, 19 x 19 x 14 In.
$866

Clars Auction Gallery

Lamp, Fluid, Ruby Frosted Glass Ball, Hanging, 10 In.
$189

Conestoga Auction Company

Lamp, Hanging, 6-Light, Empire Style, Parcel Gilt Fixture, Bronze, Composite Frame, 25 x 24 In.
$480

Brunk Auctions

Lamp, Hanging, Hall Light, Cranberry, Art Glass Shade, Bronze, 11 In.
$150

Woody Auctions

TIP
Reverse-painted lampshades should never be washed. Just dust them.

Lamp, Kerosene, Butterfly Shade, Slag, Wire Overlay, Bent Glass Novelty Company, 27 x 9 ½ In.
$3,630

Fontaine's Auction Gallery

Lamp, Kerosene, Coral Reef, Blue Opalescent, Hobbs, Brockunier, Beaumont Glass, c.1900, 2 x 3 In.
$263

Jeffrey S. Evans & Associates

Lamp, Kerosene, Reeded Body, Gilt Brass Mounts, Emerald Green, c.1850, 5 ⅜ In.
$923

Skinner, Inc.

Lamp, Lard, Argand, Tole, Wick Pick, Handle, Tray Bottom, Pa., c.1850, 8 In.
$59

Conestoga Auction Company

Lamp, Mission Style, 4-Panel Shade, Slag Glass, Lily Pad, Square Base, 13 x 13 x 23 In.
$367

Hartzell's Auction Gallery Inc.

Lamp, Oil, Bronze, Frosted, Cut Glass, Flower, Embossed, Foo Dog Handles, 13 x 7 x 24 In.
$117

Cordier Auctions

Lamp, Oil, Green Slag Glass, 4 Panels, Metal Base, Flared Feet, Marked, Success, Electrified, 22 In.
$70

Cordier Auctions

Lamp, Oil, Nude Man, Standing, Leaf Handle, 2 Spouts, Silver & Bronze, Late 1800s, 11 In.
$300

Eldred's

Lamp, Oil, Student, Harvard, Green Shade, Chimney, Kosmos Burner, Wild & Wessel, 21 x 7 In.
$1,180

Cottone Auctions

Lamp, Sconce, Bacchus, Cornucopia, Iridescent Teardrop Shades, Caldwell, 16 x 6 In., Pair
$5,700

Morphy Auctions

Lamp, Sinumbra, Cut Glass Shade, Brass Standard, Leaves, Electrified, 29 In.
$1,000

Neal Auction Company

Lamp, Sconce, 2-Light, Chippendale Style, Carved Limewood, 1800s, 48 x 29 x 10 In., Pair
$4,250

Neal Auction Company

Lamp, Solar, Brass, Bronze, Ball Shade, Triangular Base, Dietz, c.1850, 23 x 14 x 7 In.
$936

Jeffrey S. Evans & Associates

Lamp, Student, Brass, 2 Arms, Acorn Shape, Adjustable, Green Glass Shades, Chimneys, 22 x 27 In.
$234

Cordier Auctions

Lamp, Whale Oil, Flint Glass, Amethyst, Purple, Pewter Rim, Late 1800s, 17 x 9 3/8 In.
$115

Blackwell Auctions

Lamp Base, Pottery, Multicolor, Brass Socket, Marked, Makoto Yabe, Late 1900s, 28 x 18 In.
$209

Skinner, Inc.

Lampshade, Hurricane, Green Glass, 21 In., Pair
$1,599

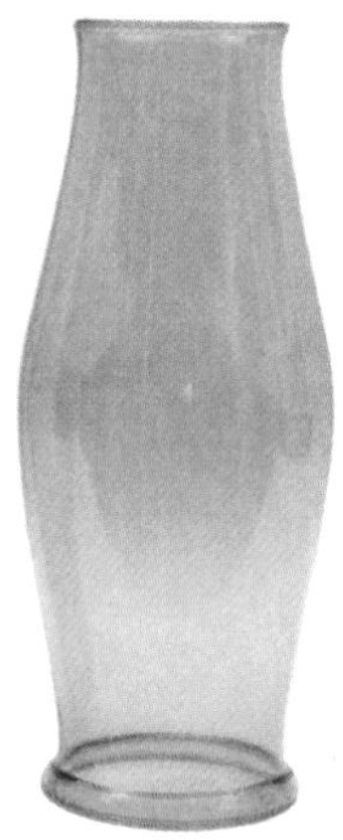

Stair Galleries

Lampshade, Leaded Glass, Hanging, Dome Shape, Brass, Leaves, Grapes, Cream Ground, 14 x 23 In.
$185

Clars Auction Gallery

Electric, Reverse Painted, Daisies Encircling, Green Leaves, Moe Bridges, 23 ½ x 18 In.	1440
Electric, Slag Glass Shade, Black Patina, Footed, Cast Metal, 26 In.	127
Electric, Slag Glass, Leaded Shade, Green Patina Base, 27 x 20 In.	1000
Electric, Tiffany Style Shade, Round Base, Cast Metal, Multicolor, 22 In.	431
Electric, Tiffany Style, Acorn Shade, Bronze Base, Turtleback Tiles, 26 In. *illus*	1230
Electric, Tiffany Style, Bronze, Turtle Shell Shade, 80 In.	944
Electric, Tommi Parzinger Style, 9-Light, Plus 3-Light Under Shade, Brass, Stiffel, 50 In. *illus*	188
Electric, Wheatsheaf, Copper, Bronze, Patina, Hollywood Regency, 26 ½ In.	500
Electric, Woman Sitting, Flower, Cast Metal, Vanity, Marble Base, 13 ½ In.	173
Electric, Wood, Trapezoidal Shade, Painted Screen Panel, Folk Art, 19 x 19 x 14 In. *illus*	866
Electric, Wooden, Pineapple Finial, Art Deco, 25 ½ In.	177
Equilibrium, Cantilever, Chrome, Round Base, Ralph Lauren, 58 In.	144
Fairy, 2-Light, Candelabrum, Silver Plate Stand, Stepped Base, Clarke, c.1900, 18 x 14 In.	250
Figural, Cherubs, Bronze, Gilt, Swirled Opalescent Shade, Marble Base, 21 x 6 ½ x 5 In.	303
Finger, Panel Optic, Cranberry, Glass, Ribbed, Prince & Simmons Lion Lamp Works, c.1900, 7 x 3 In.	2808
Fluid, Cut Glass Shade, Prisms, Brass, Marble Base, 1800s, 26 x 10 In.	147
Fluid, Peacock, Pressed Glass, Sandwich, Faceted Font, Square Base, c.185, 10 ½ In.	2214
Fluid, Ruby Frosted Glass Ball, Hanging, 10 In. *illus*	189
Gasolier, 6-Light, Descending Tiers, Spear Point Prisms, Bellflower Drops, Brass, 43 x 23 In.	1750
Gone With The Wind, Column & Drape Design, Ice Green Satin Glass, 21 ½ In.	900
Hall, Ruby Glass, Enamel, Jeweled, Embossed, Birds, Flowers, Brass Frame, 17 x 7 x 7 In.	424
Handel Lamps are included in the Handel category.	
Hanging, 6-Light, Empire Style, Parcel Gilt Fixture, Bronze, Composite Frame, 25 x 24 In. *illus*	480
Hanging, Caramel Slag Glass, Dome Shape, Gilt Metal Frame, Early 1900s, 13 x 21 In.	293
Hanging, Hall Light, Cranberry, Art Glass Shade, Bronze, 11 In. *illus*	150
Hanging, Leaded Glass Shade, Geometric, Greek Key Border, c.1920, 14 x 23 In.	279
Hanging, Pewter, 3 Atlantes, Loop Handles, Continental, 1700s, 16 In.	369
Hanging, Wall Light, Etched Glass Globe, Cast Iron, 1800s, 34 In.	136
Hanging, White, Umbrella Shape, Brass Frame, Amber Prisms, Acorn Burner, c.1900, 14 In.	995
Kerosene, Brass Font, Angle, Wall, Clear Globe, White Opaque Chimney, 13 x 15 In.	150
Kerosene, Butterfly Shade, Slag, Wire Overlay, Bent Glass Novelty Company, 27 x 9 ½ In. *illus*	3630
Kerosene, Clear Glass, Opalescent, Flower Font, Matched Base, 12 In.	150
Kerosene, Coral Reef, Blue Opalescent, Hobbs, Brockunier, Beaumont Glass, c.1900, 2 x 3 In. *illus*	263
Kerosene, Cranberry Opal, Sheldon Swirl, Brass, c.1880, 9 In.	150
Kerosene, Glass Globe, Brass & Cast Iron, Perkins & House Safety, 1871, 16 ¾ In.	45
Kerosene, Gone With The Wind, Opaque Glass, Pink & Yellow Roses, 31 In.	141
Kerosene, Pale Yellow, White Opalescent, Swirl, 5 ½ In.	96
Kerosene, Reeded Body, Gilt Brass Mounts, Emerald Green, c.1850, 5 ⅜ In. *illus*	923
Kerosene, Swan, Embossed, Clear Glass, Blue Opaque, 6-Sided Base, 11 In.	400
Lard, Argand, Tole, Wick Pick, Handle, Tray Bottom, Pa., c.1850, 8 In. *illus*	59
Leaded Glass, Geometric, Grapes, Leaves, Vines, Socket, Spelter Base, 11 ½ x 7 In.	424
Mission Style, 4-Panel Shade, Slag Glass, Lily Pad, Square Base, 13 x 13 x 23 In. *illus*	367
Nude Woman, Holding Torch, 4-Footed, Base, 2-Sided, 6 ¾ x 6 ¾ x 20 In.	720
Oil, Blue Glass, Swirl, Square Base, Hinks & Sons Patent, England, 1800s, 25 In.	300
Oil, Brass Plate, Lamp A Moderateur, Hurricane Shade, France, 1800s, 5 ¾ x 5 ¾ x 11 In.	30
Oil, Brass, Blue Glass, Flowers, Square Base, Hink & Son's, 32 x 5 ¾ x 5 ¾ In., Pair	92
Oil, Bronze, Frosted, Cut Glass, Flower, Embossed, Foo Dog Handles, 13 x 7 x 24 In. *illus*	117
Oil, Famille Rose, Vase, Gagneau Gilt Metal Rococo Style Mounts, c.1900, 17 ¾ In., Pair	1536
Oil, Green Slag Glass, 4 Panels, Metal Base, Flared Feet, Marked, Success, Electrified, 22 In. *illus*	70
Oil, Hanging, Koftgari Inlay, Steel, Calligraphy, Tendrils, 1800s, 4 ¾ x 9 In.	514
Oil, Nude Man, Standing, Leaf Handle, 2 Spouts, Silver & Bronze, Late 1800s, 11 In. *illus*	300
Oil, Student, Harvard, Green Shade, Chimney, Kosmos Burner, Wild & Wessel, 21 x 7 In. *illus*	1180
Organ, Brass Frame, Alabaster Shelf, Painted Ball Shade, Red, Orange, Green, 1880s, 64 In.	120
Pairpoint Lamps are in the Pairpoint category.	
Parlor, Turquoise Glass, 3 Columns, Enamel, Flowers, Bird, Brass, c.1900, 30 ¾ In.	277
Sconce, 1-Light, Applique, Carnival Figures, Murano Glass, Wood, Mirrors, 24 x 18 In., Pair	7813
Sconce, 2 Candlearms, Federal, Giltwood, Eagle Crest, Brass Holder, c.1800, 14 ½ x 14 In.	3660
Sconce, 2-Light, Candle, Drum, Cannon, Horn, Flags, Painted, Tin, c.1950, 32 x 14 x 8 In., Pair	527
Sconce, 2-Light, Chippendale Style, Carved Limewood, 1800s, 48 x 29 x 10 In., Pair *illus*	4250

Lampshade, Slag Glass, Hanging, Dome, Swan Panel, Leaded, Filigree, Red Flowers, 14 x 24 In.
$363

Fontaine's Auction Gallery

Lantern, Candle, Punched Tin, Hinged Door, Multicolor, 17 In.
$148

Copake Auctions

Lantern, Carriage, Brass, Beveled Glass Plates, Urn Shape Finial, 45 x 8 ½ x 10 ½ In., Pair
$984

Stair Galleries

This is an edited listing of current prices. Visit **Kovels.com** to check thousands of prices from previous years and sign up for free information on trends, tips, reproductions, marks, and more.

L

Lantern, Glass, Pillar, Molded Globe, Iron Wire Cage, Pierced Tin Vent, 1850s, 14 x 11 In.
$2,214

Skinner, Inc.

Lantern, Glass, Yellow, Neoclassical, Gilt Metal, Ring Handle, Beads, Early 1900s, 26 In.
$439

Hindman Auctions

Lantern, Tin, Pierced, Round, Cone Shape Top, Lafayette, c.1824, 13 ½ In.
$6,150

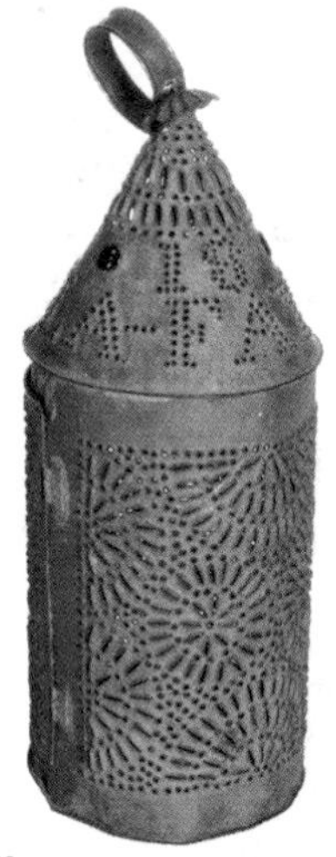

Skinner, Inc.

Sconce, 2-Light, Napoleon III Style, Silver Plate & Cut Glass, 20 ½ In., Pair 1722
Sconce, 2-Light, Regency Style, Tassel Carved Shape, Eagle, c.1900, 19 x 16 x 9 In. 1800
Sconce, 2-Light, Urn Shape, Gilt, Ebonized, Eagle Bracket, c.1900, 35 x 18 x 10 In., Pair 900
Sconce, 4-Socket, Nickel Plated Steel, Glass Panels, Wood Back, c.1930, 50 In., Pair 492
Sconce, Bacchus, Cornucopia, Iridescent Teardrop Shades, Caldwell, 16 x 6 In., Pair .....*illus* 5700
Sconce, Chromed Metal, Frosted Glass, Art Deco, c.1930, 20 ½ In., Pair 369
Sconce, Eagle, Wood, Gilt, Tapestry Pulls, Tassels, Metal Candleholders, 26 In., Pair 300
Sconce, Molded, Frosted Glass, Geometric, Chromed Steel, c.1925, 17 x 8 ¾ x 5 In., 4 Piece 2091
Sconce, Tin, Crimped Oval Reflector, Scalloped Drip Pan, 1800s, 16 ½ x 10 In., Pair 1599
Sconce, Winged Mythical Mermaid, Bronze, Gasolier, France, 1800s, 13 x 4 ½ x 8 ½ In., Pair 875
Sinumbra, Brass, Fluted, Cut Glass Shade, Stepped Marble Base, 1800s, 30 In. 610
Sinumbra, Cut Glass Shade, Brass Standard, Leaves, Electrified, 29 In. ....*illus* 1000
Sinumbra, Hand Cut, Bulbous Body Shade, Stand, Square Base, 1800s, 30 ½ x 13 In. 2065
Skater, Sapphire Blue, Oil, Swing Bail Handle, Tin, 3 x 5 ½ In. 184
Solar, Brass, Bronze, Ball Shade, Triangular Base, Dietz, c.1850, 23 x 14 x 7 In. ....*illus* 936
Student, 2-Light, Green Shades, Chains, Brass Base, Emeralite, 18 ½ x 13 x 8 ½ In. 787
Student, Brass, 2 Arms, Acorn Shape, Adjustable, Green Glass Shades, Chimneys, 22 x 27 In. *illus* 234
Student, Brass, Cylindrical Chimney, Adjustable, 20 ½ In. 72
Tiffany Lamps are listed in the Tiffany category.
Wall Light, Dome Shape, Neon, Argon Tubes, Dante Leonelli, c.1970 3500
Whale Oil, Brass, 2 Burners, Bulbous, Circular Stepped Base, Early 1800s, 9 x 3 ¾ In., Pair ... 351
Whale Oil, Flint Glass, Amethyst, Purple, Pewter Rim, Late 1800s, 17 x 9 ⅜ In. ....*illus* 115
Whale Oil, Fluid Stand, 2 Tubes, Drop-In Burner, c.1835, 8 ¾ x 3 In. 140
Wood Base, Green, Multicolor Slag Glass Inserts, Arts & Crafts, 20 x 13 In. 630

LAMP BASE

Electric, 2-Light, Gilt Bronze, Inset Quartz Stones, Tassel Pulls, 37 ½ x 8 In., Pair 1020
Electric, 2-Light, Neoclassical, Green Marble, Ormolu, Square Base, Early 1900s, 31 In., Pair. 1140
Electric, Nude Woman, Sitting, Art Deco, Nuart Creation, New York, 8 ½ x 4 ½ x 8 In. 148
Electric, Octagonal, Blue, Crackle Glaze, Stiffel, c.1955, 45 ½ x 38 ½ In. 83
Electric, Ormeaux, Leaves, Frosted, Bulbous, c.1926, 6 ½ In. 240
Pottery, Multicolor, Brass Socket, Marked, Makoto Yabe, Late 1900s, 28 x 18 In. ....*illus* 209

LAMPSHADE

Glass, Umbrella Shape, Green, Fitter Rim, Gilt Thistle, 11 ¾ In. 94
Hanging, Dome Shape, Blue Glass Panels, Brass, Chain & Canopy, 48 x 23 In. 303
Hanging, Leaded, Caramel Slag Dome, Multicolor, Flower Border, 1900s, 13 x 24 In. 60
Hurricane, Green Glass, 21 In., Pair ....*illus* 1599
Leaded Glass, Dome Shape, Bell Shape Finial, Hanging, Flowers, Multicolor, 27 In. 300
Leaded Glass, Dome Shape, Flower, Brick Pattern, Geometric, Irregular Edge, 11 x 18 In. 545
Leaded Glass, Hanging, Dome Shape, Brass, Leaves, Grapes, Cream Ground, 14 x 23 In. *illus* 185
Peachblow, Hobnail, Dome Shape, Open Top, Pink Glass Shading, New England, 10 In. 182
Slag Glass, 4 Panels, Multicolor Diamonds, Oak Frame, 17 x 22 ½ In. 800
Slag Glass, 6 Panels, Rose Motif, Cream Ground, 10 x 18 ½ In. 79
Slag Glass, Hanging, Dome, Swan Panel, Leaded, Filigree, Red Flowers, 14 x 24 In. ....*illus* 363

LANTERN

Lanterns are a special type of lighting device. They have a light source, usually a candle, totally hidden inside the walls of the lantern. Light is seen through holes or glass sections.

Bear, Cast Iron, Pierced Stomach, Holding Sake Jar, Hat, Japan, Early 1900s, 24 x 12 In. 660
Bronze, Dome Top, Octagonal, Rosette Medallions, Graduated Base, 69 x 30 In. 830
Candle, Pine, Smoke Cap, Ring Handle, Candle Socket, Glass, c.1800-20, 8 x 15 ¾ In. 374
Candle, Punched Tin, Hinged Door, Multicolor, 17 In. ....*illus* 148
Candle, Punched Tin, Sliding Glass, Ring Handle, Early 1800s, 4 ¾ x 5 x 13 ½ In. 196
Candle, Tin, 4 Sockets, Painted, Side Handle, Carry, 9 ¾ In. 366
Carriage, Brass, Beveled Glass Plates, Urn Shape Finial, 45 x 8 ½ x 10 ½ In., Pair ....*illus* 984
Glass, Pillar, Molded Globe, Iron Wire Cage, Pierced Tin Vent, 1850s, 14 x 11 In. ....*illus* 2214
Glass, Yellow, Neoclassical, Gilt Metal, Ring Handle, Beads, Early 1900s, 26 In. ....*illus* 439

Le Verre Francais, Bowl, Cameo Glass, Red Ground, Signed In Etch, 10 x 11 In.
$1,599

Stair Galleries

Le Verre Francais, Ewer, Cobalt Blue, Mottled Ground, Flowers, Footed, c.1925, 11 ½ In.
$923

Skinner, Inc.

Le Verre Francais, Lamp, Boudoir, Vase Shape Shade, Candelabra Socket, Metal Base, c.1925, 8 In.
$523

Skinner, Inc.

Le Verre Francais, Vase, Flower Stem, Blossom Shading, Mottled Yellow Ground, Signed, 17 x 5 x 5 In.
$1,680

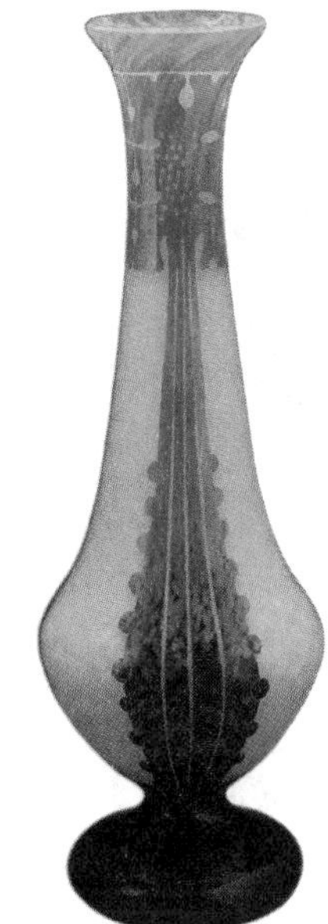

Morphy Auctions

Leather, Case, Cartridge, Oval Brass Patch On Front, C. Schreiber, 8 x 7 In.
$62

Hartzell's Auction Gallery Inc.

Leather, Donkey, Standing, Ottoman, Dimitri Omersa, c.1960, 21 ½ x 6 In.
$527

Thomaston Place Auction Galleries

L

Leather, Figure, Elephant, Liberty Of London, Abercrombie & Fitch, 23 x 29 In.

$960

Alderfer Auction Company

TIP
Castor oil is good for dried-out leather. Clean the leather with saddle soap and water, dry, then rub in castor oil with a soft cloth. It leaves a shiny finish. Neat's-foot oil is also good, but it leaves a dull appearance.

Legras, Vase, Barren Trees, Enameled, Blue & Green Ground, Cameo, Signed, 6 x 2 ⅜ In.
$1,169

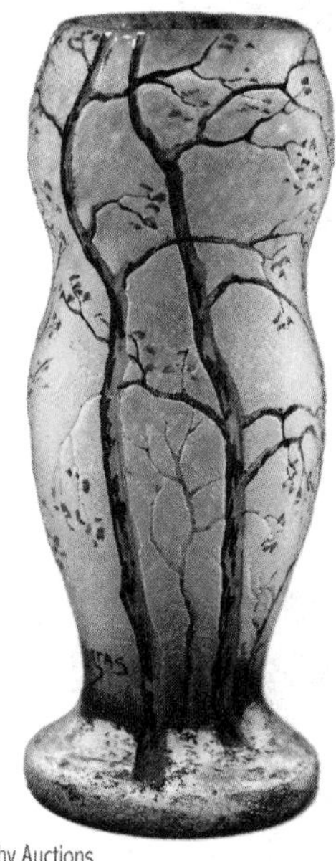

Morphy Auctions

Globe, Sheet Iron, Bull's-Eye, Clear, Strap Ring Handle, Drop-In Burner, 1900s, 14 x 5 In. 410
Hall, Brass, Etched Glass, Globe, Tall Ships, Teardrop Finial, England, 26 x 9 In. 1500
Hall, Bronze, Leaded Glass, Hexagonal, Portrait Bust, Figure, Griffin, c.1920, 27 x 13 In. 500
Hall, Candle Socket, Patinated, Metal, Leafy Mounts, Tapered Glass Shade, 1810s, 26 x 9 In. 800
Hall, Neo-Gothic, Glass Panes, Etched, Patinated Metal Frame, England, 1850s, 21 x 9 In. 384
Hall, Oil Font, Brass Pull Down, Burner Thumbwheel, Edward Miller & Co., 27 x 8 x 7 In. 121
Hall, Venetian Style, Bronze Crown Shape, 4 Tapered Glass Pendants, c.1900, 32 In. 960
Hanging, 3-Light, Swan, Brass & Etched Glass, c.1880, 34 x 9 In. 625
Hanging, 4-Light, Brass Hardware, Glass Inserts, Ribbon Garland, 27 x 12 In. 341
Hanging, Hexagonal, Openwork, Bronze, Blue & Red Glass Panels, Victorian, 52 x 20 x 20 In. 615
Iron, Gas, Outdoor, Swirl Finial, Scroll Base, New York, 1800s, 64 In. 236
Metal, Chrome, Swing Handle, Glass Side Panel, Hinged Door, 44 ½ In., Pair 152
Millwatcher's, Brass, Glass Globe, Handle, F.O. Dewey Co. Makers, Boston, 11 In. 212
Oil, Black, Domed Foot, Cylindrical Top, Swing Handle, Steel, Brass, 2 Spouts, 13 x 5 ½ In. 138
Oil, Hanging, Pierced, Tin & Glass, 1800s, 10 In. 277
Onion, Brass, Red Globe, Marked, Perkins, Early 1900s, 17 ½ In. 300
Skater's, Brass, Amethyst Glass Globe, Cap, Bail Handle, c.1900, 11 x 3 In. 263
Tin, Oil, Burner, Round, Clear Glass, Wire Frame, Swing Bail Handle, 7 x 9 ½ In. 127
Tin, Pierced, Round, Cone Shape Top, Lafayette, c.1824, 13 ½ In. *illus* 6150
Tin, Round, Pierced, Painted, Red, Yellow, Green, Ring Handle, 1800s, 13 In. 431

LE VERRE FRANCAIS

Le Verre Francais is one of the many types of cameo glass made by the Schneider Glassworks in France. The glass was made by the C. Schneider factory in Epinay-sur-Seine from 1918 to 1933. It is a mottled glass, usually decorated with floral designs, and bears the incised signature *Le Verre Francais.*

Bowl, Cameo Glass, Red Ground, Signed In Etch, 10 x 11 In. *illus* 1599
Ewer, Cobalt Blue, Mottled Ground, Flowers, Footed, c.1925, 11 ½ In. *illus* 923
Lamp, Boudoir, Vase Shape Shade, Candelabra Socket, Metal Base, c.1925, 8 In. *illus* 523
Lamp, Electric, Boudoir, Digitalis, Flowers, Violet To Orange, 3-Arm Holder, 13 x 6 x 6 In. 2400
Vase, Abstract Flowers, Violet, Orange, Flared Base, c.1925, 19 In. 1353
Vase, Flower Stem, Blossom Shading, Mottled Yellow Ground, Signed, 17 x 5 x 5 In. *illus* 1680
Vase, Fuchsia, Leaves, Pinched Neck, 9 x 10 In. 649

LEATHER

Leather is tanned animal hide and has been used to make decorative and useful objects for centuries. Leather objects must be carefully preserved with proper humidity and oiling or the leather will deteriorate and crack. This damage cannot be repaired.

Bag, Traveling, Red, Hermes, Padlock, Fob, Handles, 23 x 23 x 11 In. 6000
Basket, Tooled, Key, Handle, Oval, Virginia, 1850s, 6 ½ x 5 ⅞ In. 3438
Case, Cartridge, Oval Brass Patch On Front, C. Schreiber, 8 x 7 In. *illus* 62
Donkey, Standing, Ottoman, Dimitri Omersa, c.1960, 21 ½ x 6 In. *illus* 527
Figure, Elephant, Liberty Of London, Abercrombie & Fitch, 23 x 29 In. *illus* 960
Powder Flask, Deer, Buck, Trees, Animals Scene, Embossed Brass Nozzle, 3 ½ x 10 x 1 In. 104

LEEDS

LEEDS POTTERY

Leeds pottery was made at Leeds, Yorkshire, England, from 1774 to 1878. Most Leeds ware was not marked. Early Leeds pieces had distinctive twisted handles with a greenish glaze on part of the creamy ware. Later ware often had blue borders on the creamy pottery. A Chicago company named Leeds made many Disney-inspired figurines. They are listed in the Disneyana category.

Coffeepot, Dome Lid, Baluster, Oriental Figures In Garden, 10 ½ In. 219
Platter, Well & Tree, Classical Temple By River, Blue Transfer, 18 ½ x 13 ¾ In. 50
Tea Bowl, Pearlware, Soft Paste, 1 ¾ x 2 ¾ In. 65

COLLECTING TRENDS:

ICONIC DESIGNERS OF TWENTIETH-CENTURY LIGHTING

By Al Eiber

As a collector of 20th-century furniture, I have long been fascinated with lighting fixtures designed during this period and the innovative industrial designers who were designing them.

It was always my feeling that the lights of this period were an "everyman's" collection of sculptures that also served the function of adding light to a space.

The early 20th century was the beginning of modernism, with lamps and lighting that had minimal ornamentation. In the 1940s and later, designers were eager to push the boundaries of the stark modern style by using new lighting technologies and plastics that allowed greater experimentation with form and less expensive production. In the 1960s, Italy became one of the innovative manufacturing centers utilizing the new materials and methods. Young designers flocked there and created lighting in sharp contrast to the severity of international modernism.

Important 20th-century lighting is collected based on the design and the designer. Light fixtures required technical and manufacturing capabilities, so few designers produced their own products. Some designers worked exclusively with one manufacturer and others worked for multiple manufacturers. Many important designers worked for three manufacturers: Arredoluce and Arteluce of Italy and Louis Poulsen of Denmark. Other important manufacturers were Flos, Superstudio, Alchimia, Artemide, Ingo Maurer, and the design company Droog.

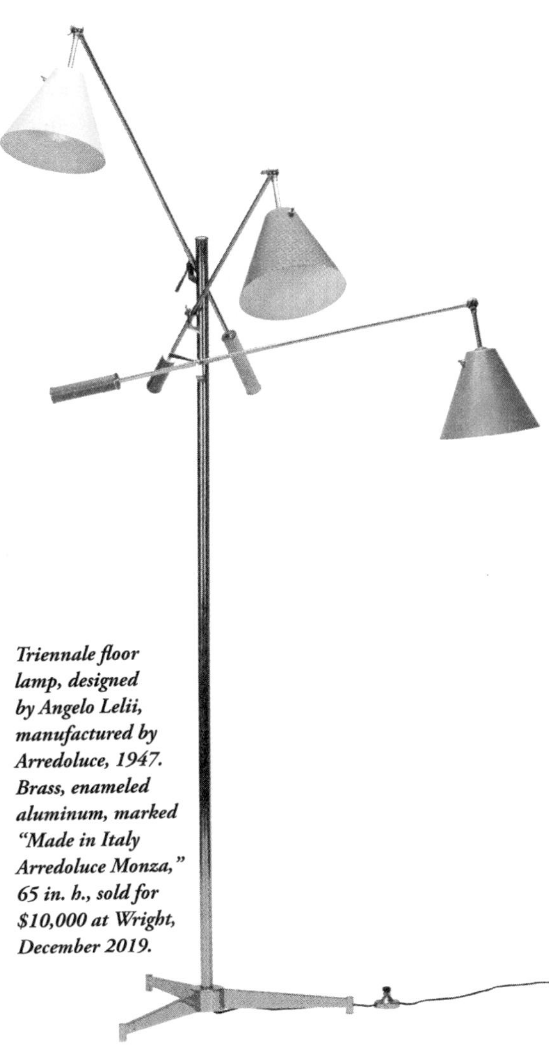

Triennale floor lamp, designed by Angelo Lelii, manufactured by Arredoluce, 1947. Brass, enameled aluminum, marked "Made in Italy Arredoluce Monza," 65 in. h., sold for $10,000 at Wright, December 2019.

A note about value

Price is determined by the designer, rarity, condition, and the date of manufacture. If the lighting was manufactured after a designer's death but by the same manufacturer, some consider this less valuable. If a different manufacturer makes the piece, it is considered a knockoff, with no collectible value.

Arredoluce was founded in 1943 in Monza, Italy, by Angelo Lelii, an entrepreneur and designer passionate about American culture. His curiosity about international trends in design innovation, love of traditional materials

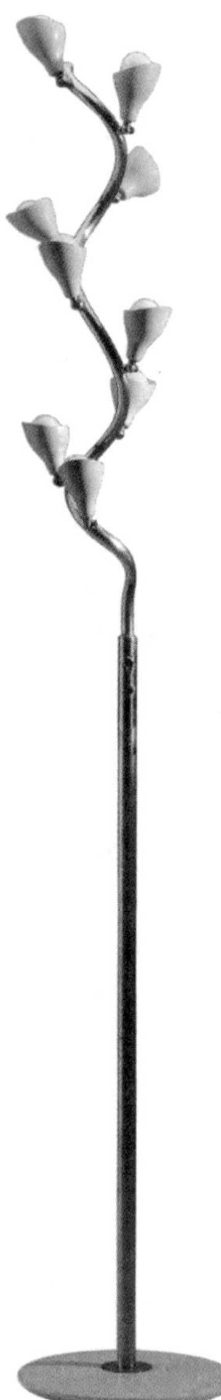

Model 1034 floor lamp, designed by Gino Sarfatti, manufactured by Arteluce, 1946–51. Brass, enameled aluminum, marble, 81 in. h., sold for $18,750 at Wright, March 2019.

(particularly glass), and great attention to detail all influenced and characterized the products of the company over the years. Today many of Arredoluce's lamps, defined by their visual weightlessness, are heralded as paragons of mid-century design, and are extremely collectible.

Arteluce, established in 1939, is a premier lighting company founded by Gino Sarfatti (1912–1985). Born in Venice, Sarfatti moved to Genoa in 1930 and studied aeronautical engineering. During the 1930s, the political situation in Italy caused a downturn in his family's economic situation. These hardships forced Gino Sarfatti to abandon his engineering career, and he decided instead to focus on designing Modernist lamps. Sarfatti's entrepreneurial instincts, design talent, and drive rewarded him with success. In 1939, Sarfatti founded lighting studio Arteluce and moved his manufacturing facility to Milan. There he opened a new retail shop on Corso Matteotti.

It's estimated that Sarfatti designed between 400 and 700 lighting pieces in his career. This may explain why Arteluce lamps are found in a wide variety of settings, including stylish homes and apartments, stores, and even the Teatro Regio in Turin.

In 1950, Gino Sarfatti took a long, important trip to the United States. During his absence, he assigned the artistic directorship of Arteluce to his friend Vittoriano Viganò. While in this position, Viganò made some important design contributions. Some of his most successful designs were light fixtures with large cone-shaped reflectors and articulated arms, such as his Model 2062 ceiling light.

Model 1063, floor lamp, designed by Gino Sarfatti, manufactured by Arteluce, 1954. Enameled steel with tubular florescent bulb, decal: "AL Milano Arteluce," 85 in. h., sold for $25,000 at Wright, June 2017.

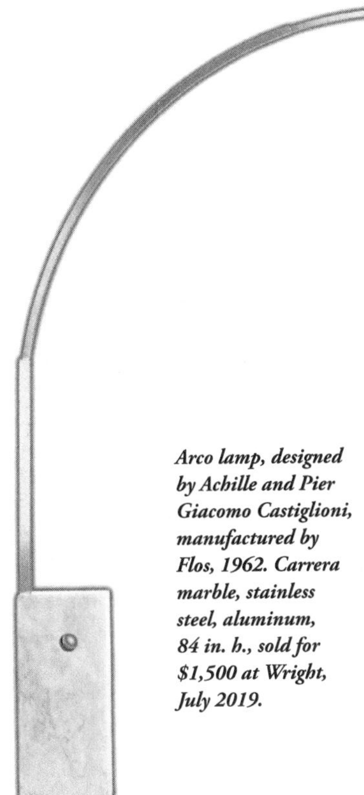

Arco lamp, designed by Achille and Pier Giacomo Castiglioni, manufactured by Flos, 1962. Carrera marble, stainless steel, aluminum, 84 in. h., sold for $1,500 at Wright, July 2019.

Gino Sarfatti understood the importance of the Arteluce shop in Milan, and in 1953, he invited the prominent Italian designer Marco Zanuso to redesign the shop. The following year, Arteluce was awarded the Grand Prix at the Triennale di Milano (Milan Triennial) for the rollout of the innovative and minimalist floor lamp, Model 1063, with a design centered on a visible fluorescent tubular bulb, which remains popular to this day. During the late 1950s and 1960s, Arteluce collaborated with important Italian designers of the time including Franco Albini, Franca Helg, Ico Parisi, Vittoriano Viganò, and Massimo Vignelli.

By the late 1960s, the complexity of Arteluce's business had grown and required a larger managerial workforce. Sarfatti's sons and other family members joined the company. In 1973, at the peak of Arteluce's sales and profits, Gino Sarfatti decided to sell his company to Flos, another lighting manufacturer.

Flos continues to manufacture some Arteluce designs, which are sold under the Flos brand worldwide.

Louis Poulsen, a Danish lighting manufacturer in the Scandinavian design tradition, was founded in 1874. The function and design of the company's products were tailored to reflect and support the effect of natural light. Every detail in the design had a purpose.

Poul Henningsen (1894–1967) began to design for Louis Poulsen in the 1920s. Henningsen's childhood was illuminated by the glow of gas lamps. When electricity arrived in his small Danish hometown and left his neighbors' windows ablaze with the glare of electric light bulbs, Henningsen began to grapple with a design quandary that defined his entire career. He was determined to calm the harsh, powerful light bulb. In 1925, Poul Henningsen created his influential Paris lamp for Louis Poulsen. This lamp was revolutionary because of how the design enhanced the light and made it part of its design.

Paris ceiling light, designed by Poul Henningsen for Louis Poulsen, 1925. Brass, painted brass, tubular brass, 23⅝ in. dia., sold for $113,750 at Phillips, September 2016.

Henningsen's design became even more elaborate with the Artichoke lamp. He combined simple planar shapes to form a sculptural, modern design. The lamp's 72 copper "leaves" are staggered to form a layered artichoke-like exterior that conceals its central bulb from every angle.

Louis Poulsen partnered with designers, architects, and other talents like Arne Jacobsen, Verner Panton, Øivind Slaatto, Alfred Homann, Oki Sato, and Louise Campbell. The company emphasized expert craftsmanship and produced quality lighting that is functional and pleasing to the eye.

Artichoke lamp, designed by Poul Henningsen, manufactured by Louis Poulsen, 1957. Copper, enameled steel, enameled aluminum, chrome-plated brass, chrome-plated steel, and steel wire, 34 in. dia., sold for $5,937 at Rago Arts and Auction Center, January 2020

Serge Mouille (1922–1988) was a French industrial designer and goldsmith. He is best known for his lighting designs. His three-arm standard floor lamp is his most famous fixture and is considered one of the most collectible floor lamps of the 1950s. It was designed as a skeleton with three thin arms ending in lacquered aluminum shades with shapely forms styled after a woman's breast and nipple (by many accounts, those of his wife).

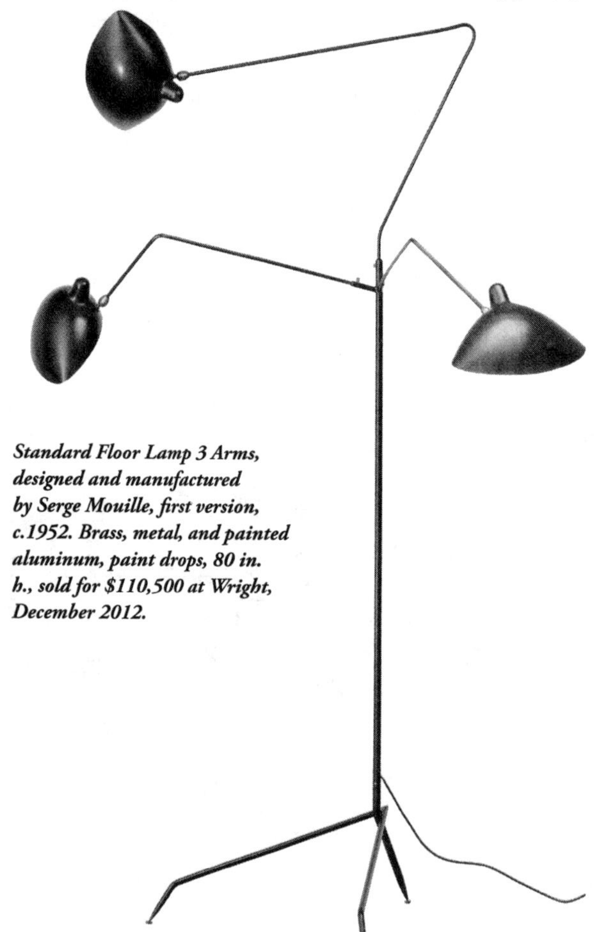

Standard Floor Lamp 3 Arms, designed and manufactured by Serge Mouille, first version, c.1952. Brass, metal, and painted aluminum, paint drops, 80 in. h., sold for $110,500 at Wright, December 2012.

Ingo Maurer (1932–2019) was a German industrial designer who specialized in the design of lamps and light installations. His nickname was the "poet of light." Maurer's lamps featured shattered crockery, scribbled memos, holograms, and even incandescent bulbs with feathered wings.

Bulb table lamp, designed and manufactured by Ingo Maurer, 1966. Chrome-plated brass and glass, 11½ in. h. by 7½ in. w., sold for $875 at Wright, August 2016.

Porca Miseria chandelier, designed and manufactured by Ingo Maurer, 1994. Porcelain and metal, 47½ by 39⅜ in. dia., sold for $156,770 at Christie's, 2017.

One of Maurer's most important lighting fixtures, Porca Miseria, was designed for the Villa Wacker on Lake Constance in Germany. The interiors of the 19th-century villa were being redesigned by German architect and designer Bruno Paul, one of the founders of Jugendstil. The kitchen called for something dynamic. Maurer initially titled the work Zabriskie Point because he was reminded of an explosive slow-motion scene in Michelangelo Antonioni's film of the same name. When the work was exhibited at the Milan showroom of Spazio Krizia, an Italian gentleman proclaimed *"Porca Miseria!* (What a disaster!) Che fantastic, Ingo! Tu sei pazzo, geniale! (You are crazy, brilliant!)." And the final title of the work was born.

Svincolo floor lamp, designed by Ettore Sottsass, manufactured by Studio Alchimia, 1979. Laminate, chrome-plated steel, colored fluorescent tubes, 99 in. h. by 24½ in. w., sold for $15,000 at Phillips, June 2008.

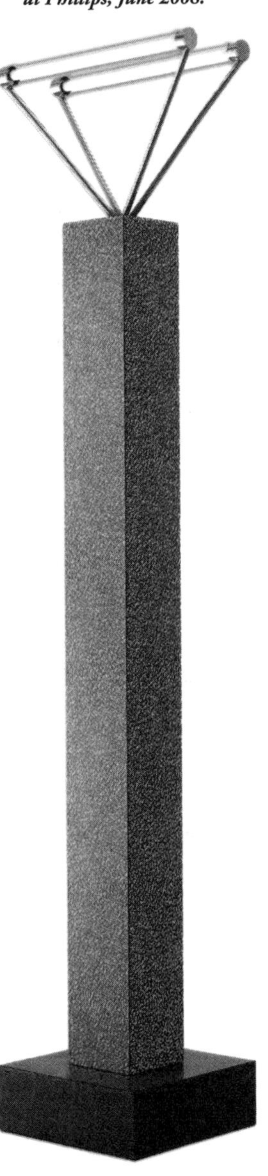

The construction of the hanging fixture is a combination of controlled disorder and free composition, a characteristic seen in many of Maurer's designs. "Chance rules our life, much more than intention," he said. Time-consuming and requiring great consideration, each piece of porcelain was broken and smoothed by hand before all of the rods were soldered. Each lamp took several workers a week of intense effort to complete, so only a limited number were made each year.

Paramount table lamp, designed by Lapo Binazzi, manufactured by Studio Alchimia, 1970 / 1975. Glazed earthenware, nylon, chrome-plated steel, 31 in. h. by 24 in. dia., sold for $7,500 at Wright, October 2014.

Studio Alchimia was founded in 1976 by Alessandro and Adriana Guerriero and Bruno and Giorgio Gregori, whose aim was to design and manufacture exhibition pieces using historical references. The furniture and lighting they designed had lots of color and decoration, a major departure from the minimal modernist furniture of the time. They considered their designs radical and anti-establishment. Important designers who worked with them include Alessandro Mendini, Ettore Sottsass, Andrea Branzi, and Lapo Binazzi.

Poltronova was founded in the 1960s in the Tuscany region of Italy by Sergio Camilli and Ettore Sottsass as the artistic director. Designers who worked for them included renowned architectural groups experimenting with new materials such as Superstudio and Archizoom. Poltronova was also part of the radical design movement in Italy at this time.

Gherpe lamp, designed by Superstudio, manufactured by Poltronova, 1967. Acrylic, chrome-plated steel, 16 in. h. by 11½ in. w. by 24 in. d., sold for $2,812 at Los Angeles Modern Auctions, November 2018.

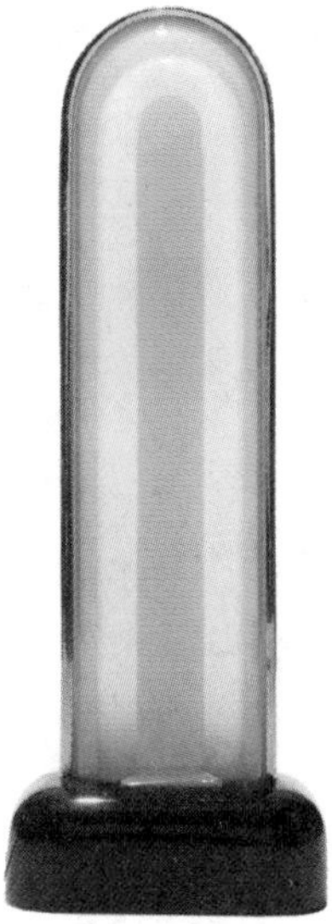

Asteroid table lamp, designed by Etttore Sottsass, manufactured by Poltronova, 1968, sold for $7,500 at Wright, March 2011.

Artemide, founded in 1960 by Ernesto Gismondi, created many lamps that are considered icons of contemporary design and have been exhibited in most design museums around the world. Important designers who worked for Artemide include Richard Sapper, Gae Aulenti, and architectural groups Herzog & de Meuron and BIG.

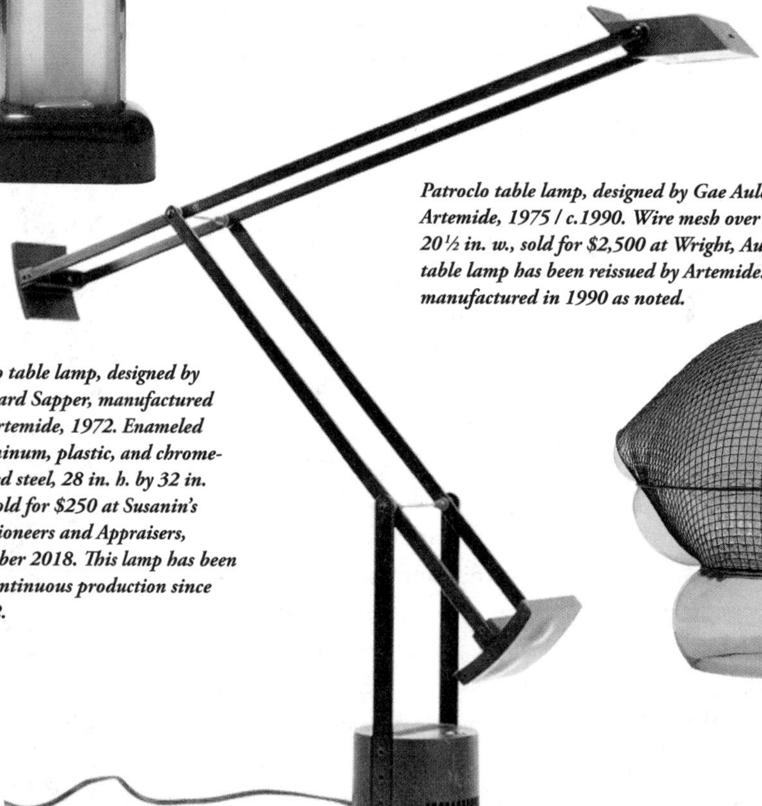

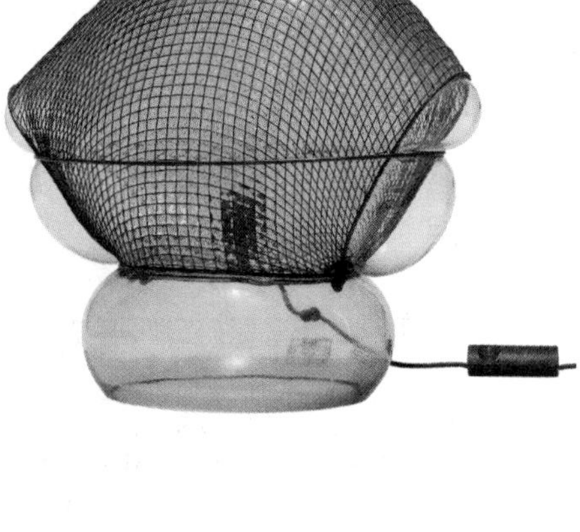

Patroclo table lamp, designed by Gae Aulenti, manufactured by Artemide, 1975 / c.1990. Wire mesh over glass, 17½ in. h. by 20½ in. w., sold for $2,500 at Wright, August 2016. The Patroclo table lamp has been reissued by Artemide. This example was manufactured in 1990 as noted.

Tizio table lamp, designed by Richard Sapper, manufactured by Artemide, 1972. Enameled aluminum, plastic, and chrome-plated steel, 28 in. h. by 32 in. w., sold for $250 at Susanin's Auctioneers and Appraisers, October 2018. This lamp has been in continuous production since 1972.

Droog was founded in 1993 by product designer Gijs Bakker and design historian Renny Ramakers. The pair hand selected and produced designs reflecting the spirit of their times. Their concept was anti-luxury, anti-formal, and anti-product as seen by the "85 Bulb" or "85 Lamps" chandelier and the "Milk Bottle" lamp.

11. Milk Bottle lamp, DMD 04, designed by Tejo Remy, sold by Droog, 1991. Stainless steel, 12 milk bottle shades, 12 in. by 14 in. by 10 in., sold for $1,375 at Heritage Auctions, April 2014.

85 Lamps chandelier, designed by Rody Graumans, sold by Droog, 1993. Plastic-coated wire, light bulbs, 35 in. h. by 24 in. dia., sold for $1,875 at Hindman Auctions, May 2017. This lamp was redesigned for LED bulbs and is still in production.

There are other iconic designers of 20th-century lighting whose work appeals to collectors. Some favorites are George Nelson, Isamu Noguchi, and Casati and Ponzio.

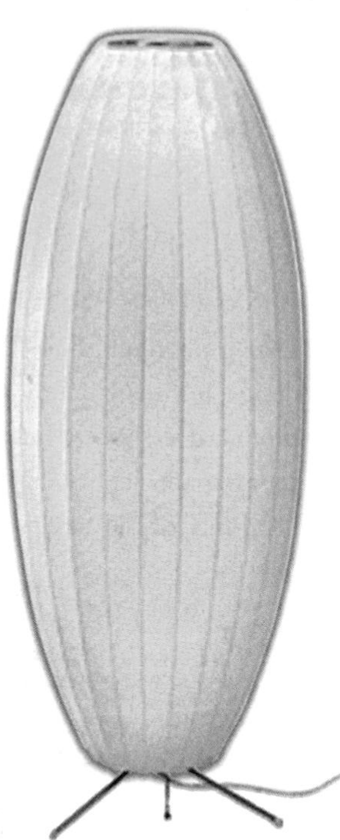

Bubble lamp, designed by George Nelson, manufactured by Herman Miller Clock Co., 1952. Sprayed fiberglass over metal frame, steel, sold for $1,560 at Wright, October 2004. Nelson was one of the most prominent post–World War II American industrial designers and was the design director for Herman Miller Co.

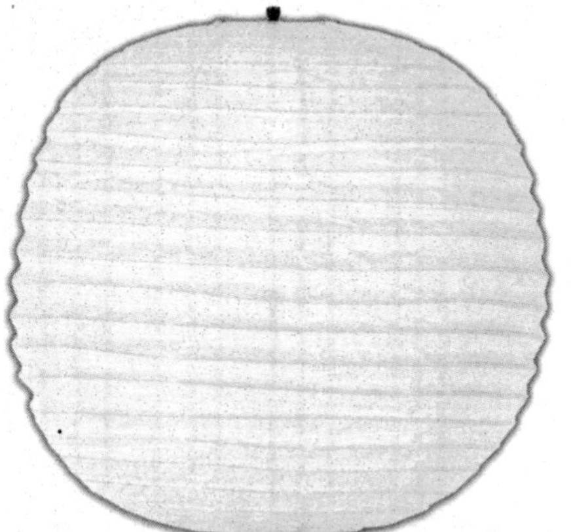

Akari floor lamp, designed by Isamu Noguchi, manufactured by Ozeki & Co., 1951. Bamboo, washi paper, and cast iron, signed "I. Noguchi" on shade with manufacturer's mark, 70 in. h. by 22½ in. dia., sold for $3,500 at Wright, February 2020. Noguchi was best known for his sculpture and landscape architecture. He also designed furniture and a limited number of lamps, which are sold around the world.

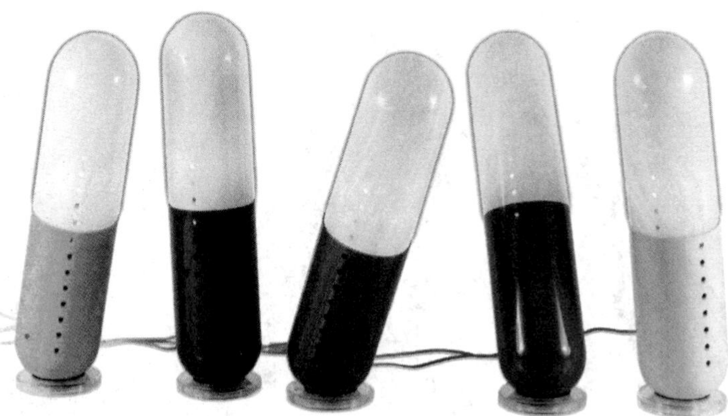

Set of 5 Pillola lamps, designed by Cesare Casati and Emanuele Ponzio for Ponteur, 1968. Plastic, 21 ½ in. h. by 5 ¼ in. dia., sold for $10,000 at Quittenbaum Kunstauktionen GmbH auction, March 2015. Pillola lamps are representative of Italy's anti-design movement of the 1960s and 1970s. Challenging notions of "good design," the anti-design movement took its cues from Pop Art's use of bright colors and banal subject matter.

LEFTON

Lefton is a mark found on pottery, porcelain, glass, and other wares imported by the Geo. Zoltan Lefton Company. The company started in 1941. George Lefton died in 1996 and members of the family continued to run the company. Lefton was sold to OMT Enterprises of Gardena, California, in 2005 and is now a division of that company. The name "Lefton" is still used. The company mark has changed through the years and a mark is usually used for a long period of time.

Lefton China
1948–1953

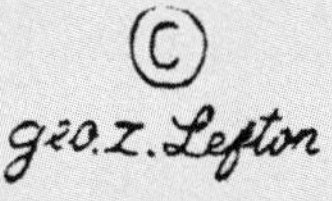

Lefton China
1950–1955

Lefton China
1949–2001

Bookends, Persian Cat, White, Long Hair, Sitting On Book, Gold Label, 6 x 5 x 3 In. 48
Compote, Crimped Rim, Pink Roses, Hand At Base, Rose & Leaves On Wrist, 6 x 5 In. 37
Creamer, Scroll Handle, 3-Footed, Pink Roses, 4 In. 12
Figurine, Dog, German Shepherd, Standing By Fence, Foil Label, 5 x 4 x 2 In. 28
Hand, Ring, Pink Nails, Rose On Wrist, 4 In. 25
Head Vase, Blond, Green Scarf, Hat, Black Gloves, Feather, Pearl Earrings, 6 In. 125
Head Vase, Woman, Barrel Curls, Blond, Rhinestone Tiara, Downcast Eyes, 6 In. 42
Planter, Baby Stork, Hat, Matte Glaze, 8 In. 12
Planter, Figural, Woman With Umbrella, Burgundy Flowers, Hat, Cap Sleeves, 8 In. 75
Puppy, Beagle, Sad Eyes, Tan & Brown, Seated, Paper Sticker, 3 ¾ In. 18
Salt & Pepper, Grape Bunches, Purple, 3 x 2 In. 18
Sugar & Creamer, To A Wild Rose Pattern, c.1950s 49
Teabag Holder, Sleeping Pig, Foil Label, 5 ½ In. 7
Trinket Box, White, Gold Roses, 4 x 3 ½ x 2 In. 15
Wall Plaque, Mother Goose, Riding Goose, 6 ½ x 7 ½ In. 98
Wall Pocket, Bashful Girl, Curly Hair, Fan, Flowers, Paper Label, 7 x 4 In., Pair 125

LEGRAS

Legras was founded in 1864 by Auguste Legras at St. Denis, France. It is best known for cameo glass and enamel-decorated glass with Art Nouveau designs. Legras merged with Pantin in 1920 and became the Verreries et Cristalleries de St. Denis et de Pantin Reunies.

Bowl, Enamel, Rectangular, Waterscape, Early 1900s, 3 ½ In. 185
Bowl, Sunset Snow Scene, Trees, Brush, Birds, Pinched Rim, Signed, 2 ¾ x 4 x 4 In. 272
Lamp, Sailboats, Enameled, Acid Etched, Patinated Metal, Signed, 18 x 7 In. 1875
Vase, Barren Trees, Enameled, Blue & Green Ground, Cameo, Signed, 6 x 2 ⅜ In. .... *illus* 1169
Vase, Maple Leaves, Cranberry Cut To Frosted, Cameo, Signed, 16 ½ In. 420
Vase, Onion Shape, Thin Inverted Teardrop Stem, Trumpet Rim, Bulbous Base, 12 ½ In. 605
Vase, Oval, Triangular Rim, Forest Scene, Sunset In Autumn, Frosted, Cameo, 1910s, 5 ½ In.. 140
Vase, Red Fruits & Leaves, White Ground, Footed, Cameo, 8 In. 215

LENOX

Lenox porcelain is well-known in the United States. Walter Scott Lenox and Jonathan Coxon founded the Ceramic Art Company in Trenton, New Jersey, in 1889. In 1896 Lenox bought out Coxon's interest, and in 1906 the company was renamed Lenox, Inc. The company makes porcelain that is similar to Irish Belleek. In 2009, after a series of mergers, Lenox became part of Clarion Capital Partners. The marks used by the firm have changed through the years, so collectors can date the ceramics. Related pieces may also be listed in the Ceramic Art Co. category.

Lenox, Figurine, Woman, Standing, White Gown, Glaze, Gold Stencil, 1900s, 8 ¾ In.
$30

Woody Auctions

Lenox, Platter, Oval, Ivory, Gold Trim Handle, Footed, Marked Side, 16 x 11 In.
$71

Charleston Estate Auctions

TIP

Mayonnaise can be used to remove old masking tape, stickers, or labels from glass or china.

Libbey, Bowl, Rose, Stratford Pattern, Cut, Ball Shape, 5 ½ x 7 In.
$250

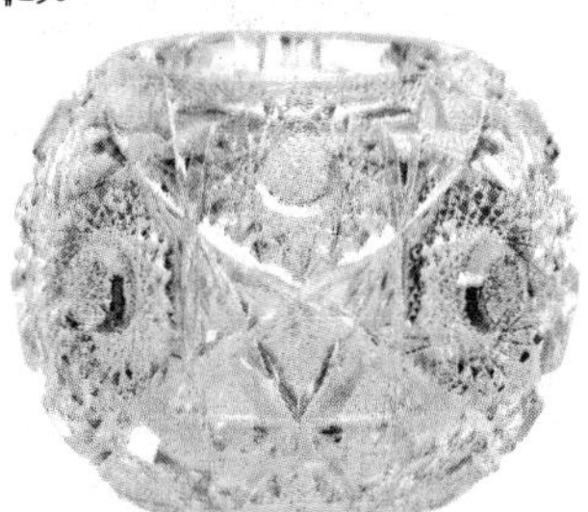

Woody Auctions

Libbey, Tray, Ice Cream, Senora, Sawtooth Rim, Signed, 17 ½ x 10 In.
$1,000

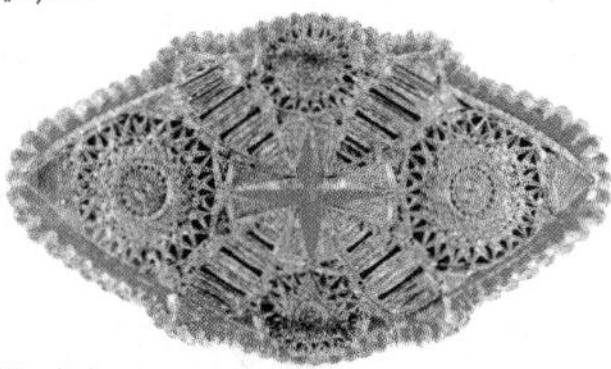

Woody Auctions

Lighter, Advertising, Lillian Russell Cigars, Miniature Lamp, Brunhoff Mfg. Co., Early 1900s, 16 In.
$2,223

Jeffrey S. Evans & Associates

Lighter, Cigar, Hunter, Shotgun, Spelter, Countertop, Gas, c.1870, 14 In.
$738

Copake Auctions

Figurine, Woman, Standing, White Gown, Glaze, Gold Stencil, 1900s, 8 ¾ In. ....*illus* 30
Plate, Dinner, Westchester Pattern, Gilt Rim, Chinese, 10 In., 8 Piece 152
Plate, Gilt Rim, Painted, Enamel Fish Center, Tiffany & Co., 1900s, 9 ⅛ In., 12 Piece 369
Platter, Oval, Ivory, Gold Trim Handle, Footed, Marked Side, 16 x 11 In. ....*illus* 71

LETTER OPENER

Letter openers have been used since the eighteenth century. Ivory and silver were favored by the well-to-do. In the late nineteenth century, the letter opener was popular as an advertising giveaway and many were made of metal or celluloid. Brass openers with figural handles were also popular.

Alligator, Iron, Independent Stove Co., 5 ½ In. 65
Belt Shape, Silver, Engraved, Ralph Lauren, London, 2004, 9 ½ In. 219
Bird Handle, Bronze, 1900s, 9 ⅝ In. 125
Wood, Carved Handle, Pencil Case, 9 ½ In. 52

LIBBEY

Libbey Glass Company has made many types of glass since 1888, including the cut glass and tablewares that are collected today. The stemwares of the 1930s and 1940s are once again in style. The Toledo, Ohio, firm was purchased by Owens-Illinois in 1935 and is still working under the name Libbey Inc. Maize is listed in its own category.

Basket, Easter, Triple Notched Handles, Ray Base, Signed, 12 ¾ In. 300
Bowl, Flared Rim, Senora, Signed, 4 x 9 In. 175
Bowl, Rose, Stratford Pattern, Cut, Ball Shape, 5 ½ x 7 In. ....*illus* 250
Compote, Somerset Pattern, Notched Stem, Scalloped Hobstar Foot, Signed, 10 x 8 ¾ In. 225
Tray, Ice Cream, Senora, Sawtooth Rim, Signed, 17 ½ x 10 In. ....*illus* 1000
Vase, Senora, Cut Flared Rim, Ray Base, Signed, 6 ½ In. 225

LIGHTER

Lighters for cigarettes and cigars are collectible. Cigarettes became popular in the late nineteenth century, and with the cigarette came matches and cigarette lighters. All types of lighters are collected, from solid gold to the first disposable lighters. Most examples found were made after 1940. Some lighters may be found in the Jewelry category in this book.

Advertising, Lighter, Lillian Russell Cigars, Miniature Lamp, Brunhoff Mfg. Co., Early 1900s, 16 In. *illus* 2223
Cigar, Chrysanthemum, Silver, Marked Gorham, Shiebler Trademark, 4 In. 1000
Cigar, Dunhill, Stainless Steel Cutter, Wave, Yellow Gold, Fold-Out Style, 1 ½ x 1 ½ In. 288
Cigar, Hunter, Dog, Spelter, Metal, Countertop, c.1870, 16 In. 384
Cigar, Hunter, Shotgun, Spelter, Countertop, Gas, c.1870, 14 In. ....*illus* 738
Cigar, Lamp Form, Brass, Cloisonne, Medallions, Ball Handle, Glass Shade, c.1900, 9 In. 439
Dupont, Gold, Black Enamel Case, 2 x 1 ½ In. 150
Figural, Cherub, Lid, Head Opens, Holding Torch, Bronze, Continental, c.1900, 7 ¾ In. ..*illus* 122
Figural, Microphone Shape, World Globe Base, Electric, Glass Dome, 12 In. 240
Figural, Party Girl, Standing, Vase, Flowers, Copper, Spelter, Patina, 1900s, 8 x 4 In. 121
Ronson, Hound Dog, Seated, Metal, Bronze Finish, Stamped Art Metal Works, 1935, 4 x 4 In. . *illus* 61
Tinder, Flintlock Mechanism, Brass, Handle, Iron Feet, Engraved Dog, 1750s, 6 ½ In. 1107
Woman's Head, Copper, Switch On Bottom, c.1920, 7 ½ In. 70

LIGHTNING ROD AND LIGHTNING ROD BALL

Lightning rods and lightning rod balls are collected. The glass balls were at the center of the rod that was attached to the roof of a house or barn to avoid lightning damage. The balls were made in many colors and many patterns. Collectors prefer examples made before 1940.

LIGHTNING ROD

Copper Rod, Sheet Metal Duck Flying, Milk Glass Ball, 55 x 19 In. 313
Copper Rod, Twisted, Sunburst Finial, White Glass Ball, 46 In. 281
Copper, Balls, Barbs, Circles, Verdigris, 112 x 20 In. 280
Copper, Rust, Diamond Quilted Milk Glass Ball, 24 In. 288
Globe, Iron, Copper, Milk Glass, Stars, Swags, 3-Legged, Late 1800s, 32 ½ In. 104

LIGHTNING ROD BALL

Amber Glass, Swollen Medial Band, W.C. Shinn, Lincoln, Neb., 4 In. 60
Cobalt Blue Glass, Quilt Flat Pattern, George E. Thompson Co. 110
Electra, Lightning Bolts, Embossed, Honey Amber, 5 In. 73
Milk Glass, 10-Sided, D & S 20
Milk Glass, Smooth Finish, 5 In. 19
Milk Glass, Spiral Ribs, Mast 45
Opaque Green Milk Glass, 4 ½ In. 172
Opaque Powder Blue Glass, 3 Rows Of Bull's-Eyes, Ribbed, 5 In., Pair 134
Ruby Glass, 3 Rows Of Bull's-Eyes, Ribbed Ends, 5 ½ In. 25
Silver Mercury Glass, Swollen Medial Band, Shinn 150
Sun Colored Amethyst Glass, Swollen Medial Band, Shinn, 5 ½ In. 53

LIMOGES

Limoges porcelain has been made in Limoges, France, since the mid-nineteenth century. Fine porcelains were made by many factories, including Haviland, Ahrenfeldt, Guerin, Pouyat, Elite, and others. Modern porcelains are being made at Limoges. The word *Limoges* as part of the mark is not an indication of age. Porcelain called "Limoges" was also made by Sebring China in Sebring, Ohio, in the early 1900s. The company changed its name to American Limoges China Company after the Limoges Company in France threatened to sue. American Limoges China Company went out of business in 1955. Haviland, one of the Limoges factories, is listed as a separate category in this book. These three marks are for factories in Limoges, France.

A. Klingenberg
c.1880s–1890s

D & Co.
c.1881–1893

M. Redon
c.1882–1896

Bonbonniere, Fennec Fox, Lid, White Ground, Edouard Marcel Sandoz, 1900s, 5 ½ In. 360
Bowl, Red Berries, Pink Flowers, Footed, Shaped Rim, Early 1900s, 6 x 14 In. ....*illus* 322
Centerpiece, Tazza, Gilt, Cast Floral Center Lug, Bronze Mounts, 1900s, 5 x 12 ¾ In. 91
Charger, Hand Painted, Yellow Rose, Leaves, Stem, Signed EAZ, 18 In. ....*illus* 400
Compote, White Ground, Yellow Tones, Painted, Lavender, Flowers, Gold Trim, 9 x 6 In. 72
Dresser Box, Hinged Lid, Painted, Flower Cluster Center, Gilt Borders, 3 x 6 ½ In. 236
Egg, Faberge Style, Gilt Metal, Tripod Base, Oval Medallions, 5 ¾ In. 826
Jardiniere, Flowers, Gold Trim, Painted, T & V, France, 7 ½ x 5 ¾ In. 45
Lamp, White Bisque, Triangular, Draped Woman, Candelabra Socket, c.1930, 14 In., Pair 215
Pen Tray, Chrysanthemum, White & Pink Ground, Gold Trim, 9 x 4 ¾ In. 30
Plaque, 2 Game Birds, Scalloped Gilt Rim, A. Broussillon, 1910s, 15 ½ In. 152
Plaque, Hunting Dog In Landscape, Enamel On Copper, Frame, c.1950, 12 x 14 In. 510
Plate, Fish, Hand Painted, Mounted, Gilt Composite Frame, 1896-1905, 16 x 13 x 2 In. 71
Plate, Flowers, Gilt Trim Border, Signed, Wm Guerin & Co., 10 ⅞ In., 12 Piece 350
Plate, Indian Portrait Center, Bisque, M. Redon, C. Schwartz, c.1901, 9 ½ In. ....*illus* 400
Plate, Sailboat Center, Cobalt Blue Border, Gold Stencil, c.1910, 9 ½ In. 90
Punch Bowl, Hand Painted, Grapes, Vines, Gilt Trim, Scalloped Edge, France, 6 x 14 In. *illus* 156
Punch Bowl, Stand, Painted, Grapevines, Leaves, Marked, T & V, 8 ½ x 13 In. 156
Tankard, White Ground, Flowers, Gold Trim Highlights, 15 In. 50
Tray, Serving, Painted, Berry, Branch & Blossom, Edith Smith, 13 ½ x 12 In. ....*illus* 420

Lighter, Figural, Cherub, Lid, Head Opens, Holding Torch, Bronze, Continental, c.1900, 7 ¾ In.
$122

Neal Auction Company

Lighter, Ronson, Hound Dog, Seated, Metal, Bronze Finish, Stamped Art Metal Works, 1935, 4 x 4 In.
$61

Bruneau & Co. Auctioneers

Limoges, Bowl, Red Berries, Pink Flowers, Footed, Shaped Rim, Early 1900s, 6 x 14 In.
$322

Jeffrey S. Evans & Associates

Limoges, Charger, Hand Painted, Yellow Rose, Leaves, Stem, Signed EAZ, 18 In.
$400

Woody Auctions

Limoges, Plate, Indian Portrait Center, Bisque, M. Redon, C. Schwartz, c.1901, 9 ½ In.
$400

Woody Auctions

Limoges, Punch Bowl, Hand Painted, Grapes, Vines, Gilt Trim, Scalloped Edge, France, 6 x 14 In.
$156

Milestone Auctions

TIP
Don't stop your mail and newspapers when you go away if you can get a friend to pick them up. A stop-order may alert a burglar.

Vase, Cream & Pink Ground, Lavender Flowers, 2 Handles, Gilt Rim, 14 ½ In. ....*illus* 270
Vase, Painted, Gilt Edge, Birds, Perched, Flowers, Branches, Late 1800s, 14 In. ....*illus* 708
Vase, Textured Enamel On Brass, Shades Of Blue, Flowers, Camille Faure, 8 x 6 ½ In. 4130

LINDBERGH

Lindbergh was a national hero. In 1927, Charles Lindbergh, the aviator, became the first man to make a nonstop solo flight across the Atlantic Ocean. In 1932, his son was kidnapped and murdered, and Lindbergh was again the center of public interest. He died in 1974. All types of Lindbergh memorabilia are collected.

Bank, Still, You Can Bank On Lindy, Metal, Copper Finish, c.1930, 6 In. 205
Bookends, Propeller, Engine, Lindbergh Wearing Helmet, Bronze Over Metal, 8 x 4 In. 306
Bookends, The Aviator, Metal, Felt Base, c. 1929, 5 ½ x 5 In. 80
Bust, Helmet, Bronze, Wood Base, Don Wiegand, 16 In. 5800
Button, Portrait, Our Hero, Capt. C.A. Lindbergh, Spirit Of St. Louis, 1927, 1 ¼ In.................... 40
Handkerchief, Sketch, Lindy, Signature, Lace Edges, 11 x 11 In. 45
Postcard, Portrait, Published By German Ross, 3 x 5 In. 36

LITHOPHANE

Lithophanes are porcelain pictures made by casting clay in layers of various thicknesses. When a piece is held to the light, a picture of light and shadow is seen through it. Most lithophanes date from the 1825–1875 period. A few are still being made. Many lithophanes sold today were originally panels for lampshades.

Candle Shield, Castle, River, Eagle, Tripod Base, Hennebergsche Porzellan, c.1900, 8 x 4 x 3 In. *illus* 468
Oil Lamp Shade, Porcelain, White, Gold Trim, 4 ⅜ In. 113

LIVERPOOL

Liverpool, England, has been the site of many pottery and porcelain factories since the eighteenth century. Color-decorated porcelains, transfer-printed earthenware, stoneware, basalt, figurines, and other wares were made. Sadler and Green made print-decorated wares starting in 1756. Many of the pieces were made for the American market and feature patriotic emblems, such as eagles and flags. Liverpool pitchers are called Liverpool jugs by collectors.

Bowl, Classical Vignettes Exterior, Ship Interior, Transfer, 5 x 12 In. 308
Bowl, White Ground, Imari Pattern, Blue & Orange Border, Footed, 6 In. 92
Jug, Commemorative, George Washington, Oval Panel, Black Transfer, 1800-05, 10 In............ 944
Jug, Curved Handle, Scenic, Cream Ground, James Millns, Transfer, 1792, 10 In. ....*illus* 111
Jug, Sailing Ship, Creamware, Transfer, 10 In. 492
Jug, Ship, Flag, Melon Shape, Curving Lip, Strap Handle, Creamware, Early 1800s, 9 ⅝ In. *illus* 1440
Jug, Ships, Maritime, Woman, Sitting, Multicolor, Creamware, England, c.1800, 11 In. ...*illus* 1172
Jug, Watermans Arms, Firemen, Ship Herculaneum, Thomas Paul Langport, 1816, 10 ⅝ In. *illus* 1342
Jug, Werter Going To Shoot Himself, Black Text, White Ground, Late 1700s, 6 ¾ In. ....*illus* 369
Punch Bowl, Warships, 13 Colonies, Flower Swags, Creamware, England, c.1800, 5 ½ x 12 In.. 1172

LLADRO

LLADRÓ

Lladro is a Spanish porcelain. Brothers Juan, Jose, and Vicente Lladro opened a ceramics workshop in Almacera in 1951. They soon began making figurines in a distinctive, elongated style. In 1958 the factory moved to Tabernes Blanques, Spain. The company makes stoneware and porcelain figurines and vases in limited and unlimited editions. Dates given are first and last years of production. Marks since 1977 have the added word *Daisa,* the acronym for the company that holds the intellectual property rights to Lladro figurines.

Figurine, Garden Song, Round Base, No. 7618, 1992, 8 ¾ In. 106

Limoges, Tray, Serving, Painted, Berry, Branch & Blossom, Edith Smith, 13 ½ x 12 In.
$420

Woody Auctions

Limoges, Vase, Cream & Pink Ground, Lavender Flowers, 2 Handles, Gilt Rim, 14 ½ In.
$270

Woody Auctions

Limoges, Vase, Painted, Gilt Edge, Birds, Perched, Flowers, Branches, Late 1800s, 14 In.
$708

Leland Little Auctions

Lithophane, Candle Shield, Castle, River, Eagle, Tripod Base, Hennebergsche Porzellan, c.1900, 8 x 4 x 3 In.
$468

Jeffrey S. Evans & Associates

Liverpool, Jug, Curved Handle, Scenic, Cream Ground, James Millns, Transfer, 1792, 10 In.
$111

Skinner, Inc.

Liverpool, Jug, Ship, Flag, Melon Shape, Curving Lip, Strap Handle, Creamware, Early 1800s, 9 ⅝ In.
$1,440

Case Antiques

Liverpool, Jug, Ships, Maritime, Woman, Sitting, Multicolor, Creamware, England, c.1800, 11 In.
$1,172

Freeman's Auctioneers & Appraisers

Liverpool, Jug, Watermans Arms, Firemen, Ship Herculaneum, Thomas Paul Langport, 1816, 10 ⅝ In.
$1,342

Pook & Pook

Liverpool, Jug, Werter Going To Shoot Himself, Black Text, White Ground, Late 1700s, 6 ¾ In.
$369

Skinner, Inc.

L

LLADRO

Lladro, Figurine, Marketing Day, Woman, Basket, Pack On Head, No. 4502, 1969-85, 13 ¾ In.
$51

Hartzell's Auction Gallery Inc.

Lladro, Group, Lovers From Verona, Romeo & Juliet, Glaze, No. 1250, 1974-90, 15 ½ x 8 x 6 In.
$246

Locati Auctions

Loetz, Bowl, Flared & Crimped Rim, Gold Trim, Green Iridescent, Signed, 2 x 6 In.
$170

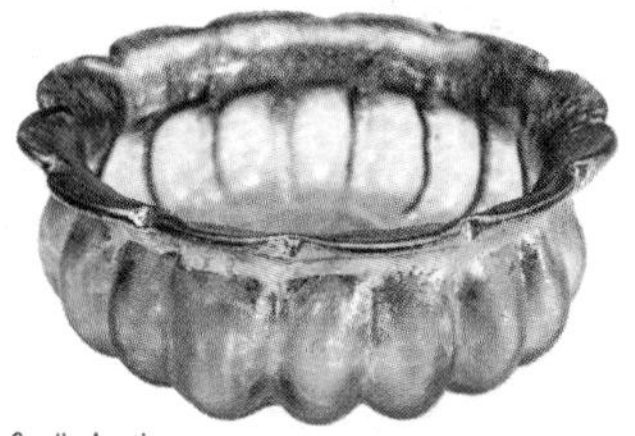

Soulis Auctions

Figurine, Lyric Muse, Woman, Holding Harp, Signed, Antonio Ruiz, No. 2031, 1971-86, 35 x 19 x 10 In. .. 780
Figurine, Marketing Day, Woman, Basket, Pack On Head, No. 4502, 1969-85, 13 ¾ In. ...*illus* 51
Figurine, Over The Clouds, Boy, Airplane, Goggles, Blue, No. 5697, 1990-2005, Box, 5 In. 80
Figurine, Pensive Clown, Chin On His Hands, Wood Stand, No. 5130, 1982-2001, 10 In. 104
Figurine, Say Cheese, Photographer, Camera, No. 5195, 1984-89, 13 ¾ x 5 ½ x 5 In. 279
Figurine, Swinging, Victorian Girl On Swing, Dog, No. 1297, 1974-90, 13 x 8 x 15 ½ In........... 585
Figurine, Two Elephants, Elephant, Calf, Oval Base, Painted, No. 1151, 1971-99, 12 In............ 157
Group, Antique Car, Family, Jumping Dog, Wood Base, No. 1146, 1971-86, 13 x 22 In............... 830
Group, Lovers From Verona, Romeo & Juliet, Glaze, No. 1250, 1974-90, 15 ½ x 8 x 6 In. ..*illus* 246
Group, Masquerade Ball, Couple Dancing, No. 5452, 1988-93, 8 ¾ In. 70

LOETZ

Loetz glass was made in many varieties. Johann Loetz bought a glassworks in Klostermuhle, Bohemia (now Klastersky Mlyn, Czech Republic), in 1840. He died in 1848 and his widow ran the company; then in 1879, his grandson took over. Most collectors recognize the iridescent gold glass similar to Tiffany, but many other types were made. The firm closed during World War II.

Bowl, Flared & Crimped Rim, Gold Trim, Green Iridescent, Signed, 2 x 6 In. ....*illus* 170
Decanter, Green Iridescent, Pinched, Tooled Rim, Floral, 1910s, 11 ½ In. ....*illus* 410
Lamp, Art Nouveau, Bronze, Gimbal Mechanism, Oil Spot Shades, 11 x 7 x 6 In., Pair............. 6600
Lampshade, Blue Feather, Iridized Translucent Ground, 2 x 4 ½ In.. 295
Lampshade, Gold, Green, Blue Iridescent, Ruffled Edge, 4 ½ x 4 ½ In...................................... 358
Vase, Black Amethyst, Iridescent, Oil Spot Design, Brass Base, 13 ½ In., Pair ....*illus* 1020
Vase, Dragged Loop, Metallic Green, Pink, Bronze Frame, Leaves, Wreath, 14 x 6 In. 512
Vase, Formosa, Butterscotch, Aqua Iridescent, Polished Pontil, c.1902, 4 x 7 In. ....*illus* 3000
Vase, Green, Metal Fitted Top & Holder, 9 In. 106
Vase, Lava Type, Cobalt Blue, Angled Legs, Acid Stamp, Czecho-Slovakia, 3 x 7 In. ....*illus* 272
Vase, Malachite, White, Enamel, Red Jewel, c.1893, 7 ½ x 4 In. ....*illus* 500
Vase, Metallin, Pink, Silver Overlay, Flowers & Ribbons, c.1908, 6 ½ In. ....*illus* 800
Vase, Papillon, Lily Pads, Silver Overlay, Blue Iridescent, c.1900, 8 ½ In.................................. 1250
Vase, Titania, Green Waves, Light Blue Swirls, Pinched Sides, Floral, 7 x 4 x 4 In. ....*illus* 1560
Vase, Titania, Silver Overlay, Asian Motif, 10 x 3 In. ....*illus* 4063
Vase, Trumpet, Tulip Rim, Blue, Green, Violet, Iridescent, Cushioned Foot, 9 ½ In. ....*illus* 454
Vase, Tulip Shape, Silver Overlay, Leaf, Blue, Iridescent, 11 In... 633

LONE RANGER

Lone Ranger, a fictional character, was introduced on the radio in 1932. Over three thousand shows were produced before the series ended in 1954. In 1938, the first Lone Ranger movie was made. The latest movie was made in 2013. Television shows were started in 1949 and are still seen on some stations. The Lone Ranger appears on many products and was even the name of a restaurant chain from 1971 to 1973 that gave out silver bullets and other souvenirs.

Animation Cel, Lone Ranger, Tonto, Filmation Studios, c.1981, 6 x 3 In. 425
Board Game, Lone Ranger & Tonto, Warren Paper Products, 1978, 17 x 9 ½ In......................... 28
Book, The Lone Ranger, Little Golden Book, Simon & Schuster, 1956, 6 ½ x 8 In. 20
Charm, Lone Ranger On Rearing Horse, Red Shirt, Sterling Silver.. 35
Doll, Composition Head, Tag, Hat, Guns, 15 ½ In... 314
Figure, Composition, Jointed, Mask, Hat, Gabriel Ind., 1973, 10 In. 38

LONGWY WORKSHOP

Longwy Workshop of Longwy, France, first made ceramic wares in 1798. The workshop is still in business. Most of the ceramic pieces found today are glazed with many colors to resemble cloisonne or other enameled metal. Many pieces were made with stylized figures and Art Deco designs. The factory used a variety of marks.

Loetz, Decanter, Green Iridescent, Pinched, Tooled Rim, Floral, 1910s, 11 ½ In.
$410

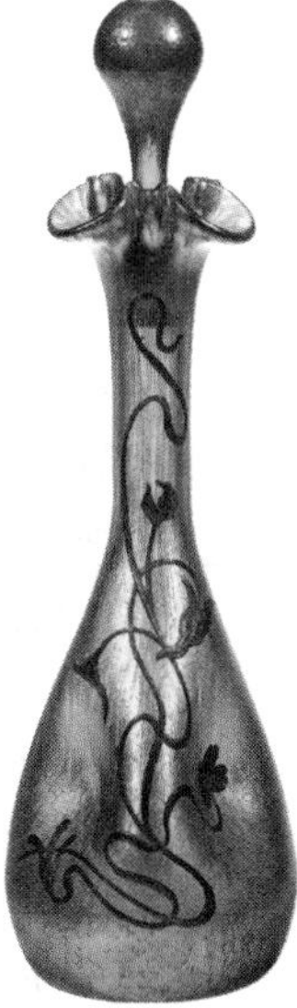

Jeffrey S. Evans & Associates

Loetz, Vase, Black Amethyst, Iridescent, Oil Spot Design, Brass Base, 13 ½ In., Pair
$1,020

Woody Auctions

Loetz, Vase, Formosa, Butterscotch, Aqua Iridescent, Polished Pontil, c.1902, 4 x 7 In.
$3,000

Woody Auctions

Loetz, Vase, Lava Type, Cobalt Blue, Angled Legs, Acid Stamp, Czecho-Slovakia, 3 x 7 In.
$272

Humler & Nolan

Loetz, Vase, Malachite, White, Enamel, Red Jewel, c.1893, 7 ½ x 4 In.
$500

Woody Auctions

Loetz, Vase, Metallin, Pink, Silver Overlay, Flowers & Ribbons, c.1908, 6 ½ In.
$800

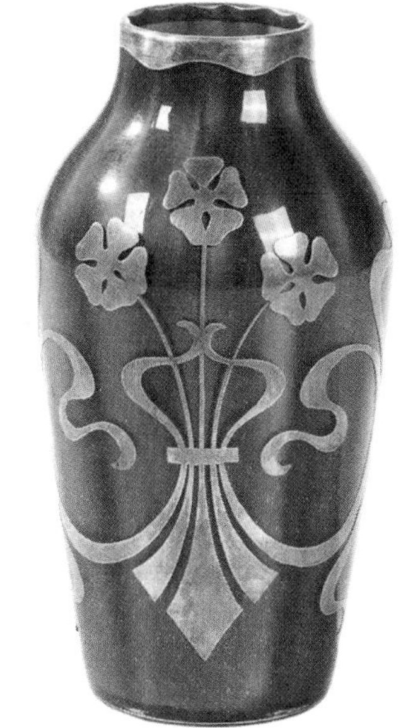

Skinner, Inc.

L

Loetz, Vase, Titania, Green Waves, Light Blue Swirls, Pinched Sides, Floral, 7 x 4 x 4 In.
$1,560

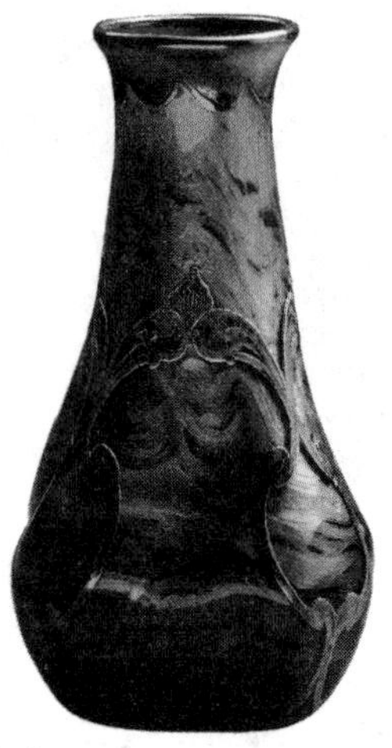

Morphy Auctions

Loetz, Vase, Titania, Silver Overlay, Asian Motif, 10 x 3 In.
$4,063

Abington Auction Gallery

Longwy, Charger, Medallion, 2 Female Nudes, Gazelle, Atelier Primavera, c.1925, 15 In.
$800

Skinner, Inc.

Longwy, Lamp, Brass Oil Canister, Filigree Borders, Yellow Glass Shade, Bulbous, 6 x 10 In.
$182

Fontaine's Auction Gallery

Longwy, Vase, Spherical, Floral, Yellow, Red, Pink, Brown, Light Blue Ground, Footed, Signed, 15 In.
$600

Morphy Auctions

Lotus Ware, Pitcher, Lid, Molded, Gilt, Chicks, Cricket, Handle, Pink Bottom, Early 1900s, 9 x 6 In.
$514

Bruneau & Co. Auctioneers

Loetz, Vase, Trumpet, Tulip Rim, Blue, Green, Violet, Iridescent, Cushioned Foot, 9 ½ In.
$454

Clars Auction Gallery

Lotus Ware, Vase, Cylindrical, White, Painted, Birds, Butterfly, Flowers, 3-Footed, c.1890, 8 In.
$200

Woody Auctions

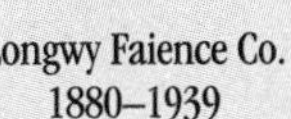
Longwy Faience Co.
1880–1939

Longwy Faience Co.
1890–1948

Longwy Faience Co.
1951–1962

Chamberstick, 2 Panels, Girl, Gilt Brass, Ceramic Saucer, Central Candle Nozzle, c.1900, 7 In. 129
Charger, Medallion, 2 Female Nudes, Gazelle, Atelier Primavera, c.1925, 15 In. ....*illus* 800
Lamp, Brass Oil Canister, Filigree Borders, Yellow Glass Shade, Bulbous, 6 x 10 In. ....*illus* 182
Vase, Central Medallion, Nude White Female, Dancing, Veil, c.1925, 10 ¾ In. 738
Vase, Spherical, Floral, Yellow, Red, Pink, Brown, Light Blue Ground, Footed, Signed, 15 In. *illus* 600

LOTUS WARE

Lotus Ware was made by the Knowles, Taylor & Knowles Company of East Liverpool, Ohio, from 1890 to 1900. Lotus Ware, a thin porcelain that resembles Belleek, was sometimes decorated outside the factory. Other types of ceramics that were made by the Knowles, Taylor & Knowles Company are listed under KTK.

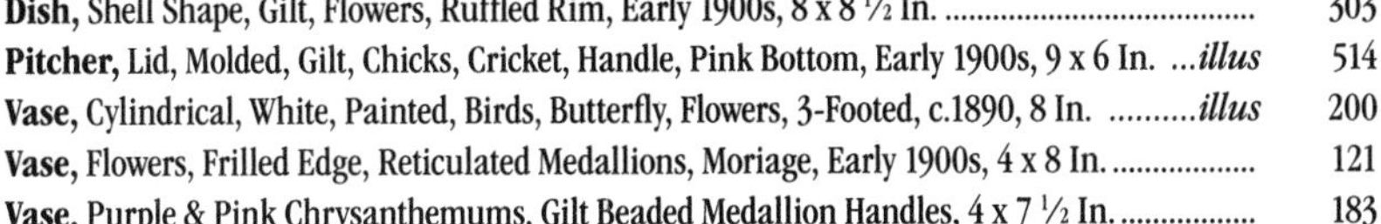
Dish, Shell Shape, Gilt, Flowers, Ruffled Rim, Early 1900s, 8 x 8 ½ In. 303
Pitcher, Lid, Molded, Gilt, Chicks, Cricket, Handle, Pink Bottom, Early 1900s, 9 x 6 In. ...*illus* 514
Vase, Cylindrical, White, Painted, Birds, Butterfly, Flowers, 3-Footed, c.1890, 8 In. ....*illus* 200
Vase, Flowers, Frilled Edge, Reticulated Medallions, Moriage, Early 1900s, 4 x 8 In. 121
Vase, Purple & Pink Chrysanthemums, Gilt Beaded Medallion Handles, 4 x 7 ½ In. 183

LOW

J.&J.G.LOW

Low art tiles were made by the J. and J. G. Low Art Tile Works of Chelsea, Massachusetts, from 1877 to 1902. A variety of art and other tiles were made. Some of the tiles were made by a process called "natural," some were hand-modeled, and some were made mechanically.

Tile, Portrait, Profile, Green High Glaze, Impressed Marks, 6-In. Square Tile, Oak Frame........ 162

LOY-NEL-ART, *see McCoy category.*

LUNCH BOX

Lunch boxes and lunch pails have been used to carry lunches to school or work since the nineteenth century. Today, most collectors want either early tin tobacco advertising boxes or children's lunch boxes made since the 1930s. These boxes are made of metal or plastic. Vinyl lunch boxes were made from 1959 to 1982. Injection molded plastic lunch boxes were made beginning in 1972. Legend says metal lunch boxes were banned in Florida in 1972 after a group of mothers claimed children were hitting each other with them and getting injured. This is not true. Metal lunch boxes stopped being made in the 1980s because they were more expensive to make than plastic lunch boxes. Boxes listed here include the original Thermos bottle inside the box unless otherwise indicated. Movie, television, and cartoon characters may be found in their own categories. Tobacco tin pails and lunch boxes are listed in the Advertising category.

Bullwinkle, Hot Air Balloon, Rocky, Top Hat, Yellow Ground, Metal, 1963 336
Monkees, Band Members, Red & White, Vinyl, Thermos, 1967 660
Mork & Mindy, Metal, Thermos, King Seeley, 1979.. 97
The Partridge Family, Bus, Singing, Metal, Thermos, 1971 276

LUNEVILLE

Luneville, a French faience factory, was established about 1730 by

Luster, Copper, Charger, Hispano-Moresque, Convex Center, Geometric, 1900s, 19 In.
$540

Eldred's

Lunch Boxes

About 650 different children's metal lunch box designs have been made in the United States. The first, a Hopalong Cassidy lunch box, was made in 1951, and the last, a Rambo box, dates from 1985. Now children's lunch boxes are plastic.

Luster, Copper, Creamer, Lafayette, Cornwallis Resigning His Sword at York Town, 4 In.
$175

Conestoga Auction Company

Luster, Copper, Mug, Birth, David Linton Born 21st June 1862, Open Ear Handle, 4 x 3 ½ In.
$49

Locati Auctions

L

Luster, Pink Splash, Figurine, Cat, England, 6 ⅝ In.
$677

Skinner, Inc.

Luster, Pink, Jug, Cartouche, E.G., Clasped Hands, Peace & Unity, England, 1838, 7 ½ In.
$246

Skinner, Inc.

Luster, Silver, Bust, Maiden, Mounted, Waisted, Circular Socle, c.1810, 13 ½ In.
$369

Skinner, Inc.

Jacques Chambrette. It is best known for its fine bisque figures and groups and for large faience dogs and lions. The early pieces were unmarked. The firm was acquired by Keller and Guerin and is still working.

Plate, Dinner, Old Strasbourg Faience, Flowers, Multicolor, 10 In., 4 Piece 126
Wall Pocket, Curved, Multicolor Flowers, 15 In., Pair 200

LUSTER

Luster glaze was meant to resemble copper, silver, or gold. The term *luster* includes any piece with some luster trim. It has been used since the sixteenth century. Some of the luster found today was made during the nineteenth century. The metallic glazes are applied on pottery. The finished color depends on the combination of the clay color and the glaze. Blue, orange, gold, and pearlized luster decorations were used by Japanese and German firms in the early 1900s. Fairyland Luster was made by Wedgwood in the 1900s. Copies made by modern methods started appearing in 1990. Tea Leaf pieces have their own category.

Copper, Charger, Hispano-Moresque, Convex Center, Geometric, 1900s, 19 In. *illus* 540
Copper, Creamer, Lafayette, Cornwallis Resigning His Sword at York Town, 4 In. *illus* 175
Copper, Mug, Birth, David Linton Born 21st June 1862, Open Ear Handle, 4 x 3 ½ In. *illus* 49
Copper, Pitcher, Yellow Ground, Brown Transfer, Lafayette, c.1825, 5 ⅝ In. 222
Fairyland Luster is included in the Wedgwood category.
Gold Iridescent, Light Fixture Shade, White & Green Wavy, c.1920, 5 In., Pair 150
Pink Splash, Figurine, Cat, England, 6 ⅝ In. *illus* 677
Pink, Jug, Cartouche, E.G., Clasped Hands, Peace & Unity, England, 1838, 7 ½ In. *illus* 246
Silver, Bust, Maiden, Mounted, Waisted, Circular Socle, c.1810, 13 ½ In. *illus* 369
Silver, Jug, Great Seal Of U.S., Yellow Glaze, Staffordshire, c.1825, 4 ¾ In. *illus* 1476
Silver, Jug, Napoleon, Satirical Cartoons, Transfer Prints, Staffordshire, 5 ½ In. *illus* 492
Silver, Jug, Puzzle, Pierced Rim, Central Chamber, Leeds, Early 1900s, 12 In. 308

SUNDERLAND *Luster pieces are in the Sunderland category.*

LUSTRES

Lustres are mantel decorations or pedestal vases with many hanging glass prisms. The name really refers to the prisms, and it is proper to refer to a single glass prism as a lustre. Either spelling, luster or lustre, is correct.

Candlestick, Bronze, Gilt, Marble Base, Drop Prisms, 17 ¾ In., Pair 246
Candlestick, Hurricane Shades, Cut Scallop Rims, Blue Prisms, 1800s, 24 In., Pair *illus* 1582
Cranberry Glass, White Cased, Enamel, Gilt, Cut Glass, Mantel, Late 1800s, 12 In., Pair *illus* 720
Deep Blue Cut To Clear, White Case, Crystal Teardrop Prisms, Late 1800s, 12 In., Pair 345
Emerald Cathedral Panel, Long Cut Glass Prisms, Mantel, Moser, 11 In. 403
Green, Reverse Taper, Flowers, Clear Glass Prisms, 11 In., Pair 704
Vase, Ruby, Ruffled Rim, Hanging Prisms, Gold, Painted, Dome Base, 14 x 7 In., Pair *illus* 230

MACINTYRE, *see Moorcroft category.*

MAJOLICA

Majolica is a general term for any pottery glazed with an opaque tin enamel that conceals the color of the clay body. It has been made since the fourteenth century. Today's collector is most likely to find Victorian majolica. The heavy, colorful ware is rarely marked. Some famous makers include George Jones & Sons, Ltd.; Griffen, Smith and Hill; Joseph Holdcroft; and Minton. Majolica made by Wedgwood is listed in the Wedgwood category. These three marks can be found on majolica items.

Luster, Silver, Jug, Great Seal Of U.S., Yellow Glaze, Staffordshire, c.1825, 4 ¾ In.
$1,476

Skinner, Inc.

Luster, Silver, Jug, Napoleon, Satirical Cartoons, Transfer Prints, Staffordshire, 5 ½ In.
$492

Skinner, Inc.

Lustres, Cranberry Glass, White Cased, Enamel, Gilt, Cut Glass, Mantel, Late 1800s, 12 In., Pair
$720

Case Antiques

TIP
Never use bleach on luster-decorated pottery. It will destroy the luster effect.

Lustres, Vase, Ruby, Ruffled Rim, Hanging Prisms, Gold, Painted, Dome Base, 14 x 7 In., Pair
$230

Stevens Auction Co.

Lustres, Candlestick, Hurricane Shades, Cut Scallop Rims, Blue Prisms, 1800s, 24 In., Pair
$1,582

Soulis Auctions

Majolica, Basket, Holly, Berry Rustic, Branch Handle, Turquoise, 7 ½ x 10 In.
$118

Strawser Auction Group

M

Majolica, Bowl, Center, Lion, Elephant Handles, Footed, 7 ½ x 12 ½ In.
$106

Strawser Auction Group

Majolica, Candy Dish, Young Girl, Pushing Sleigh, 6 x 6 In.
$60

Woody Auctions

Majolica, Centerpiece, Shell Shape, Turquoise Exterior, Pink Interior, Mottled Base, c.1880, 8 In.
$390

Eldred's

TIP
An old majolica pitcher has a small hole inside where the handle meets the body. A new pitcher will not have this hole but will often have a large hole in the base.

Majolica, Cachepot, Cobalt Blue, Square, Cattail Corners, Leaves, 8 In., Pair
$1,534

Strawser Auction Group

Majolica, Bowl, Cobalt Blue, Acanthus Leaves, Yellow Rope Trim, Footed, George Jones, 5 x 10 In.
$201

Strawser Auction Group

Majolica, Box, Turtle, Shell Is Lid, Green, Eichwald, 9 ½ In.
$112

Strawser Auction Group

Majolica, Cake Stand, Shell, Seaweed, Multicolor, Etruscan, 5 x 9 ½ In.
$212

Strawser Auction Group

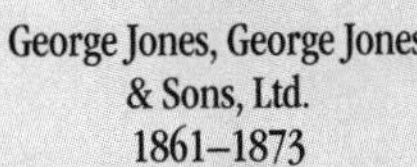
George Jones, George Jones & Sons, Ltd. 1861–1873

Griffen, Smith and Hill c.1879–1889

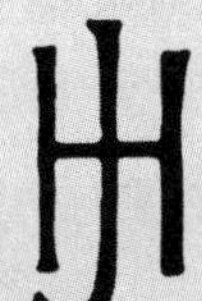
Joseph Holdcroft, Sutherland Pottery 1865–1906

Basket, Holly, Berry Rustic, Branch Handle, Turquoise, 7 ½ x 10 In. ... *illus* 118
Basket, Strawberry, 4 Parts, Vine Handle & Feet, Flowers, Leaves, George Jones, 11 ½ In. ... 212
Birdbath, Ormolu, Scrolling Leaves, Young Girl, Standing, Ornate Base, 25 In. ... 570
Bowl, Center, Lion, Elephant Handles, Footed, 7 ½ x 12 ½ In. ... *illus* 106
Bowl, Cobalt Blue, Acanthus Leaves, Yellow Rope Trim, Footed, George Jones, 5 x 10 In. ... *illus* 201
Bowl, Leaves, Flowers, Turquoise, Strap Footed, 12 ½ In. ... 89
Box, Lid, Shell & Coral Covered, Dolphin Corners, 5 x 5 ½ In. ... 389
Box, Turtle, Shell Is Lid, Green, Eichwald, 9 ½ In. ... *illus* 112
Bust, Woman, Blond Hair, Ruffled Sleeves, Necklace, Square Base, 18 ½ In. ... 266
Butter, Cobalt Blue, Butterfly Finial, George Jones, 5 ¾ In. ... 384
Cachepot, Birds, Cobalt Blue, Red Interior, Leaves, Footed, France, 9 x 8 In., Pair ... 502
Cachepot, Cobalt Blue, Square, Cattail Corners, Leaves, 8 In., Pair ... *illus* 1534
Cake Stand, Cobalt Blue, Flowers, Leaves, Yellow Rim, George Jones, 3 x 9 In. ... 153
Cake Stand, Shell, Seaweed, Multicolor, Etruscan, 5 x 9 ½ In. ... *illus* 212
Candy Dish, Young Girl, Pushing Sleigh, 6 x 6 In. ... *illus* 60
Centerpiece, Shell Shape, Turquoise Exterior, Pink Interior, Mottled Base, c.1880, 8 In. *illus* 390
Cheese Keeper, Leaves, Fern, Underplate, Green, Yellow, 7 ½ x 10 ½ In. ... 118
Compote, 3 Intertwined Dolphins, Lily Bowl, Triangular Platform Base, Holdcroft, 9 ½ In. ... *illus* 212
Compote, Chestnut, Leaves, White, Yellow Rim, 5 ½ x 9 In. ... 153
Compote, Shell, Wedge, Brown Glaze, 7 In. ... *illus* 266
Creamer, Bird, Handle, Green, 4 ½ In. ... 53
Dish, Game, Cobalt Blue, Lattice, Ribbon, Quail On Lid, Rope Trim, 13 ½ In. ... *illus* 384
Dish, Oval, 3 Central Fish, Crab, Beetle, Pseudo Crest, Avisseau, Palissy, 1869, 10 In. ... 1476
Dish, Quatrefoil, Turquoise Ground, Faux Bois Handles & Feet, George Jones, c.1880, 11 In. ... *illus* 120
Dish, Rabbit & Cabbage, Mother, 3 Kittens Peeking, Leaves On Lid, Pink Insert, c.1885, 5 In. ... *illus* 761
Dish, Spider Crab, Red, Palissy Style Spider, Stamped, Portugal, c.1900, 2 ½ x 7 x 7 In. ... 313
Figurine, Bird, Perched, Stump, Leaves, Painted, c.1800s, Italy, 11 In., Pair ... 176
Figurine, Frog, Pulling Conch Shell, Flower, Multicolor, 4 ½ x 3 In. ... 177
Figurine, Parrot, Chain, Hanging, Life Size, Delphin Massier, 24 ½ x 14 x 8 In. ... 4375
Garden Seat, Bulbous, Calla Lily, Turquoise, George Jones, 18 In. ... 2242
Humidor, 2 Monkeys, Footed, Painted, 14 In. ... 325
Humidor, Alligator, Smoking, Tobacco, Green, Standing, 6 ½ In. ... *illus* 561
Humidor, Elephant, Red Jacket, Smoking Pipe, 8 In. ... *illus* 354
Humidor, Frog, Red Jacket, Smoking Pipe, 6 ½ In. ... 708
Humidor, Hippo, Tobacco, Seated, Green, 5 In. ... 201
Humidor, Owl, Standing, Wood, Tobacco, Brown, White, 7 In. ... *illus* 325
Inkstand, Lion, Standing, Blue & White, Shield, 1800s, 4 ½ x 9 ½ In. ... *illus* 500
Jardiniere, 3 Dolphins, Turquoise, Gold Rim, Green Foot, Holdcroft, 13 ½ x 10 ½ In. ... 189
Jardiniere, Grasshopper, Figural, Glazed, Oval Base, Signed, D.M., Late 1800s, 6 ¾ x 13 In. ... 3750
Jardiniere, Pedestal Stand, Green, Blue, Brown, 32 x 16 x 19 In. ... 270
Jardiniere, Pedestal, Blue Glaze, Lion's Heads, Paws, 47 In. ... 295
Jardiniere, Pedestal, Cobalt Blue, Pink Flower, 35 In. ... 266
Jardiniere, Pink Brown Glaze, Raised Leaves, Stand, Early 1900s, 16 x 10 In., 2 Piece ... 200
Jardiniere, Swan, Handles, Signed, Delphin, Massier, 10 x 13 In. ... 1063
Jug, Hunt Scene, Fox, Rabbit, Dog, Quail, Cobalt Blue, George Jones, 12 In. ... *illus* 502
Match Striker, Boat Tied On Shore, Coil Of Rope, Brown, George Jones, 4 ¾ x 2 In. ... 885
Match Striker, Figural, Frog, Playing Mandolin, Red Coat, Hat, Continental, 8 ½ In. ... 118
Match Striker, Figural, Frog, Swords, Auto, Driving, Multicolor, Continental, 9 In. ... *illus* 295
Match Striker, Figural, Stork, Standing, Multicolor, 10 ½ In. ... *illus* 472

Majolica, Compote, 3 Intertwined Dolphins, Lily Bowl, Triangular Platform Base, Holdcroft, 9 ½ In.
$212

Strawser Auction Group

Majolica, Compote, Shell, Wedge, Brown Glaze, 7 In.
$266

Strawser Auction Group

Majolica, Dish, Game, Cobalt Blue, Lattice, Ribbon, Quail On Lid, Rope Trim, 13 ½ In.
$384

Strawser Auction Group

Majolica Mark

The word *majolica* was never used on any French majolica except Sarreguemines pieces. The Sarreguemines mark includes the company's name and the word *majolica*.

M

Majolica, Dish, Quatrefoil, Turquoise Ground, Faux Bois Handles & Feet, George Jones, c.1880, 11 In.
$120

Eldred's

Majolica, Dish, Rabbit & Cabbage, Mother, 3 Kittens Peeking, Leaves On Lid, Pink Insert, c.1885, 5 In.
$761

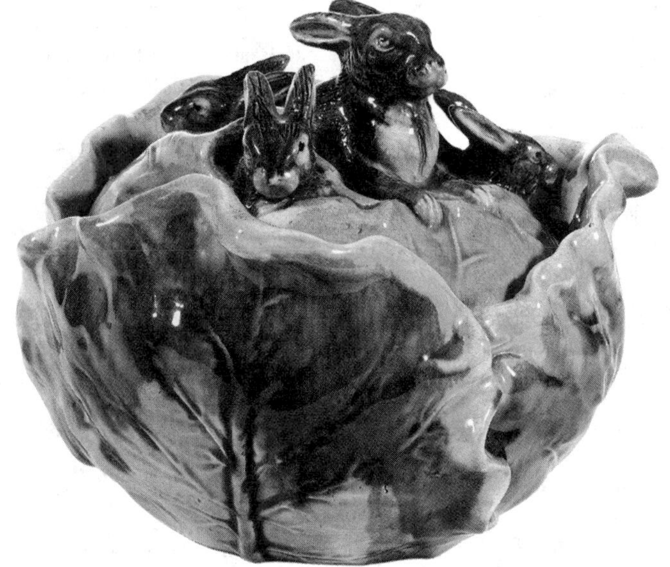

Jeffrey S. Evans & Associates

Majolica, Humidor, Alligator, Smoking, Tobacco, Green, Standing, 6 ½ In.
$561

Strawser Auction Group

Majolica, Humidor, Elephant, Red Jacket, Smoking Pipe, 8 In.
$354

Strawser Auction Group

Majolica, Humidor, Owl, Standing, Wood, Tobacco, Brown, White, 7 In.
$325

Strawser Auction Group

TIP
Put ceramic saucers or glass or plastic plant holders under vases of flowers or potted plants. There are inexpensive throwaway plastic dishes that have a rim and are exactly the right size and shape for a plant.

Majolica, Inkstand, Lion, Standing, Blue & White, Shield, 1800s, 4 ½ x 9 ½ In.
$500

Hindman Auctions

TIP
Unglazed earthenware, terra-cotta, creamware, and other unglazed ceramics should not be washed. Never put them in the dishwasher. The heat will harm the clay body.

Majolica, Jug, Hunt Scene, Fox, Rabbit, Dog, Quail, Cobalt Blue, George Jones, 12 In.
$502

Strawser Auction Group

Majolica, Match Striker, Figural, Frog, Swords, Auto, Driving, Multicolor, Continental, 9 In.
$295

Strawser Auction Group

Majolica, Match Striker, Figural, Stork, Standing, Multicolor, 10 ½ In.
$472

Strawser Auction Group

Majolica, Pitcher, Cat, Paw On Mouse, Green, Minton, 10 In.
$236

Strawser Auction Group

Majolica, Pitcher, Figural, Duck, Winged Handle, Multicolor, 15 In.
$165

Strawser Auction Group

Majolica, Pitcher, Water, Shell, Seaweed, Pink, Green, Brown, Etruscan, 6 ¾ In.
$100

Strawser Auction Group

Majolica, Plaque, Fish, Snake, Frog, Shell, Crab, Leaves, Round, Barbizet, Palissy Ware, 9 ½ In.
$826

Strawser Auction Group

M

Majolica, Plate, Lobster, Bocage, Mussel Shell, Hanging, Caldas Da Rainha, Palissy Ware, 1835, 12 In.
$120

Eldred's

TIP
Store paintings under the bed. It's dark, has good air circulation, and the paintings can be kept horizontal.

Majolica, Platter, Asparagus, Sunflower, Leaves, Glazed, Footed, Continental, c.1800, 3 ¼ In.
$140

Thomaston Place Auction Galleries

Majolica, Platter, Shell, Seaweed, Yellow Center, Etruscan, 13 ½ In.
$236

Strawser Auction Group

Majolica, Sauceboat, Asparagus, Undertray, Multicolor, 9 ½ In.
$103

Strawser Auction Group

Majolica, Server, 3 Parts, Vine Handle, Blue, Minton, 11 In.
$224

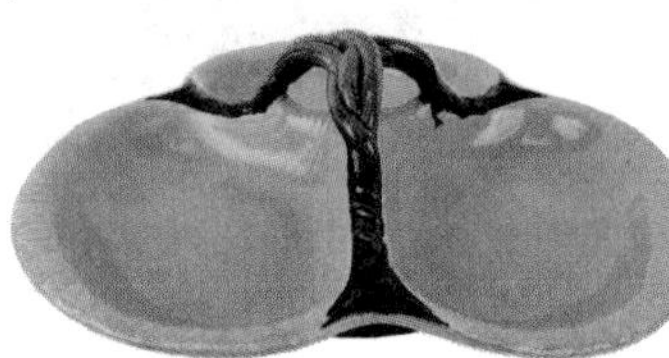

Strawser Auction Group

Majolica, Sardine Box, Figural Fish, Lavender Ground, Lift-Off Lid, George Jones & Sons, 4 x 8 x 7 In.
$367

Soulis Auctions

Majolica, Sardine Box, Pineapple, Leaves, 3 Fish On Lid, Attached Underplate, 8 In.
$130

Strawser Auction Group

Majolica, Teapot, Figural, Isle Of Man, Seated, Blue Suit, Hat, Tree Stump, Branch Handle, 9 ½ In.
$118

Strawser Auction Group

Majolica, Teapot, Fish, Swallowing Fish, Spout, Handle, Green Glaze, 11 In.
$189

Strawser Auction Group

Majolica, Toothpick Holder, Butterfly, Square, Blue, T.S. Palissy Ware, 2 ½ In.
$153

Strawser Auction Group

Pedestal, Model, Griffin, Shaped Plinths, Round Tops, Late 1800s, 40 x 12 x 24 In., Pair 800
Pitcher, Bear, Holding Spoon, Brown, 9 In. 100
Pitcher, Cat, Paw On Mouse, Green, Minton, 10 In. *illus* 236
Pitcher, Figural, Duck, Winged Handle, Multicolor, 15 In. *illus* 165
Pitcher, Flowers, Ferns, Acanthus Leaves, Rope Handle & Trim, Multicolor, 10 ½ x 7 In. 81
Pitcher, Hunt, Hanging Game, Fox Handle, Footed, Multicolor, 9 In. 69
Pitcher, Water, Shell, Seaweed, Pink, Green, Brown, Etruscan, 6 ¾ In. *illus* 100
Plant Stand, Pedestal, 2 Storks, Lily Flowers, Green Glaze, 27 ½ In. 142
Planter, Monkey Base, Green, Holding Tan Basket, Grapes, 13 ¾ In., Pair 325
Planter, Poseidon Head, Mermaid Busts, Seaweed, Turquoise, Lonitz, c.1870, 8 x 15 In. 830
Plaque, Fish, Snake, Frog, Shell, Crab, Leaves, Round, Barbizet, Palissy Ware, 9 ½ In. *illus* 826
Plate, Cherubs In Central Panel, Shaded Enamel, Brown, Footed, 1800s, 12 ¾ In. 72
Plate, Leaves, Fern, Turquoise, Yellow Rim, Round, 8 ½ In. 94
Plate, Lily, Green, White, George Jones, 8 ½ In. 177
Plate, Lobster Center, Green Rim, Wedgwood, 8 ½ In. 177
Plate, Lobster, Bocage, Mussel Shell, Hanging, Caldas Da Rainha, Palissy Ware, 1835, 12 In. *illus* 120
Platter, Asparagus, Sunflower, Leaves, Glazed, Footed, Continental, c.1800, 3 ¼ In. *illus* 140
Platter, Corn, Oval, Yellow, Green, 13 ½ In. 165
Platter, Napkin, Woven, Cobalt Blue Ground, Bamboo Handles, Wedgwood, 12 ½ In. 224
Platter, Seafood, Mermaid, Fish, Crab, Shell Corners, Birds, France, 21 x 12 In. 413
Platter, Shell, Seaweed, Yellow Center, Etruscan, 13 ½ In. *illus* 236
Salt, Figural, Dog, Hat, Black, Brown, Purple, Holdcroft, 5 In. 201
Salt, Figural, Frog, Pond, Lily On His Back, Green, Red, 2 ½ In. 142
Sardine Box, Cobalt Blue, Bird Finial, Rectangular, Underplate, 8 In. 177
Sardine Box, Figural Fish, Lavender Ground, Lift-Off Lid, George Jones & Sons, 4 x 8 x 7 In. *illus* 367
Sardine Box, Pineapple, Leaves, 3 Fish On Lid, Attached Underplate, 8 In. *illus* 130
Sauceboat, Asparagus, Undertray, Multicolor, 9 ½ In. *illus* 103
Server, 3 Parts, Vine Handle, Blue, Minton, 11 In. *illus* 224
Server, Cobalt Blue, White Flowers, Leaves, Orange Center Bowl, George Jones, 11 ½ In. 266
Strawberry Server, Flower, Leaves, 2 Attached Cups, Cream, Yellow, Etruscan, 10 ½ In. 130
Teakettle, Twig Spout, Twist Handle, Mottled Green & Brown Glaze, Wedgwood, 7 In. 212
Teapot, Figural, Isle Of Man, Seated, Blue Suit, Hat, Tree Stump, Branch Handle, 9 ½ In. *illus* 118
Teapot, Fish, Swallowing Fish, Spout, Handle, Green Glaze, 11 In. *illus* 189
Teapot, Shells, Coral, Fish Handle, Pewter Lid, 9 In. 384
Tile, Lily Of The Valley, Turquoise, Square, George Jones, 8 In. 354
Toothpick Holder, Butterfly, Square, Blue, T.S. Palissy Ware, 2 ½ In. *illus* 153
Toothpick Holder, Mouse, Corn, Green, Yellow, 3 ½ x 4 In. *illus* 212
Tray, Cobalt Blue, Butterfly, Bee, Wheat, Wicker Border, 12 In. 649
Tray, Leaves, Flower, Green, Majolica, George Jones, Minton, 12 ½ In. 189
Tray, Squirrel, Eating Nut, Cobalt Blue, Leaves, 10 In. 77
Tray, Turquoise, Butterfly, Bee, Dragonfly, Wheat, Wicker Border, 13 In. 885
Tureen, Lid, Asparagus, White, Footed, 8 x 11 In. 266
Tureen, Lid, Rooster, Hen Finial, Woven, Continental, 10 x 7 ½ In. 472
Umbrella Stand, Stork, Turquoise, Landscape Aqua, Standing, Holdcroft, 21 In. 325
Urn, Classical Figure Scene, Winged Cherubs, Serpent Handles, Lion's Heads, 26 ½ In. 545
Urn, Lid, Yellow Brown, White Swirled Faux, Head Handles, Finial, 1700s, 21 ½ In. *illus* 513
Vase, 3 Dolphins, Supporting Shell, Multicolor, Palissy Ware, Thomas Sergent, 9 ½ In. 325
Vase, Albarello, Center Medallion, Cobalt Blue Ground, 11 ½ x 6 In. 424
Vase, Brown, Yellow, Green Glaze, Iris, Leaves, Marked, Choisy-Le-Roi, 8 ½ In. 100
Vase, Bulldog, Seated, Trunk, Brown & Green Glaze, 4 In., Pair 295
Vase, Monkey, Holding Pineapple, Yellow, Black, Green, 7 In. *illus* 153
Vase, Shell, 2 Dolphins, Supporting Shell, Green, Yellow, Brown, 9 ½ In. 153
Vase, Slip, Incised, Art Nouveau Flowers, Earth Tones, Thomas Forester & Sons, 11 In. 216
Vase, Spill, Pheasant, Multicolor, Glaze, Naturalistic Base, Jerome Massier, 8 In. 1200
Vase, Venetian, Portrait, Globular, Multicolor, Enamel, Scrolled Leaves, 1700s, 11 ¾ In. *illus* 1230
Wall Pocket, Celadon, Green, White Flowers, George Jones, 11 In. 154
Wall Pocket, Duck, Flying, Painted, 9 x 7 ½ In., Pair 53
Wall Pocket, Hummingbird, Flower, Leaves & Ferns, Marked, George Jones, c.1880, 13 In. 960

Majolica, Toothpick Holder, Mouse, Corn, Green, Yellow, 3 ½ x 4 In.
$212

Strawser Auction Group

Majolica, Urn, Lid, Yellow Brown, White Swirled Faux, Head Handles, Finial, 1700s, 21 ½ In.
$513

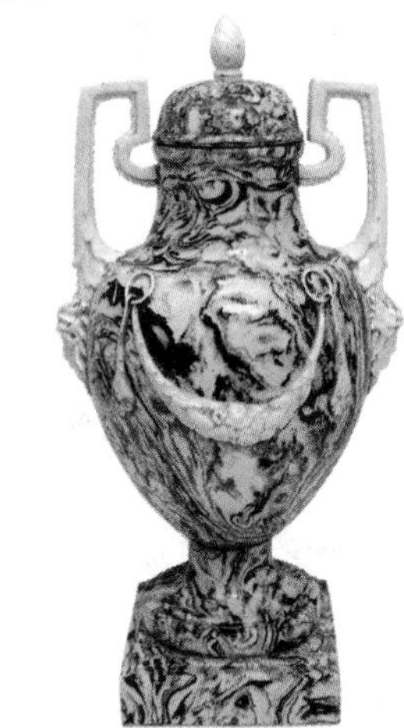

Charleston Estate Auctions

Majolica, Vase, Monkey, Holding Pineapple, Yellow, Black, Green, 7 In.
$153

Strawser Auction Group

This is an edited listing of current prices. Visit **Kovels.com** to check thousands of prices from previous years and sign up for free information on trends, tips, reproductions, marks, and more.

M

Majolica, Vase, Venetian, Portrait, Globular, Multicolor, Enamel, Scrolled Leaves, 1700s, 11 ¾ In.
$1,230

Skinner, Inc.

Malachite, Basket, Gilt, Brass, Mounted, Loop Handle, 8 x 6 ¾ x 9 In.
$861

Stair Galleries

Malachite, Box, Green Stone, Lift-Off Lid, Rectangular, 2 x 4 x 5 ¾ In.
$219

Richard D. Hatch & Associates

TIP
Do not mount old maps, prints, etc. on cardboard. The acid in the cardboard causes stains. Use an all rag board. An art store can help.

MALACHITE

Malachite is a green stone with unusual layers or rings of darker green shades. It is often polished and used for decorative objects. Most malachite comes from Siberia or Australia. Copies are made of molded glass.

Basket, Gilt, Brass, Mounted, Loop Handle, 8 x 6 ¾ x 9 In. .... *illus* 861
Box, Green Stone, Lift-Off Lid, Rectangular, 2 x 4 x 5 ¾ In. .... *illus* 219
Vase, 6 Women, Nude, Standing, Molded Glass, Reproduction, 5 In. .... *illus* 96
Vase, Birds, Aquatic Animals, Ocean Waves, Flat Foot, Molded Glass, Reproduction, 7 x 4 In., Pair.... *illus* 79
Vase, Black & White Cameo Jewels, Hexagonal, Tapers, Stepped Base, Pair, 22 x 8 ½ In. 2820

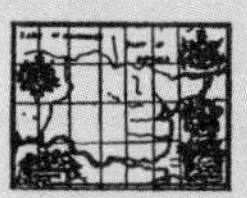

MAP

Maps of all types have been collected for centuries. The earliest known printed maps were made in 1478. The first printed street map showed London in 1559. The first road maps for use by drivers of automobiles were made in 1901. Collectors buy maps that were pages of old books, as well as the multifolded road maps popular in this century. Terrestrial globes are spherical maps of the earth. Celestial globes show the position of the stars and constellations in the sky.

Alaska, U.S. Geological Survey, Principal Previous Routes Of Exploration, 1898, 32 x 24 In. *illus* 250
Cape Cod, Major Roads, Vignettes Borders, Red Rope Outline, Frame, 1945, 24 x 35 In. ..*illus* 420
Chart, Navigation, Block Island Off Rhode Island, George Eldridge, Early 1900s, 14 x 19 In..... 150
England, Title Cartouche, Shield, Acanthus, Multicolor, Robert Morden, 1695, 14 ½ x 16 ¾ In.. 140
Europe, Europae Discripto Anno 1500, Coat Of Arms, Reproduction, Print, Frame, 19 x 23 In. . *illus* 24
Florida, Folding, Hand Colored, J.H. Colton, 1856, 5 x 3 ½ In........ 288
Globe, Celestial, Mahogany, Turned Stand, Wilson's, C. Lancaster, 1837, 18 In. ....*illus* 780
Globe, Celestial, Rand McNally & Co., Pasteboard, Cast Iron Base, Art Nouveau Style, 8 In. *illus* 115
Globe, Terrestrial, Calibrated Meridian, Mahogany Base, Rand McNally, 1930s, 17 In. ....*illus* 154
Globe, Terrestrial, Carved Wood Stand, Baroque Style, Signed, W. & A.K. Johnston, 18 In. *illus* 1140
Globe, Terrestrial, Electrified, Brass Stand, 15 In........ 207
Globe, Terrestrial, Engraved Gores, Rosewood Stand, Wm. Bardin, 1782, 29 ½ x 16 ½ In........ 2800
Globe, Terrestrial, Figural, Woman, Holding Stand & Globe, G. Barrere Et Thomas, 38 In........ 160
Globe, Terrestrial, Fruitwood, Turned, Recessed Meridians, France, c.1880, 5 ¾ In........ 183
Globe, Terrestrial, Gemstone, Gold Plated Meridian, Claw Foot Frame, 19 x 19 In. ....*illus* 367
Globe, Terrestrial, Heirloom, Lights Up By Tapping Globe, Wood Stand, Replogle, 31 x 20 In.... 144
Globe, Terrestrial, Joseph Schedler, Iron Meridian Ring, 4 Quadrant Scale, 1850s, 12 In........ 1353
Globe, Terrestrial, Maple Stand, Zodiac Figures, Turned Legs, Boston, 1859, 19 x 16 ¾ In....... 2040
Globe, Terrestrial, Metal, Nickel Plated, Tripod Base, Nims & Knight, N.Y., c.1935, 34 In. .*illus* 1188
Globe, Terrestrial, On Cast Iron Base, Joslin, Boston, 37 x 12 In. ....*illus* 1534
Globe, Terrestrial, Paper On Metal, Glass, Iron Mount, Green Patina, 1930, 14 x 9 x 9 In........ 537
Globe, Terrestrial, Pocket, Fish Skin Covered Case, Hemispheres Line, Nicholas Lane, 1776, 3 In. 3998
Globe, Terrestrial, Tabletop, Months On Circular Base, Cram's Deluxe, 23 In........ 354
Globe, Terrestrial, Tabletop, Starlight, Black Ground, White Metal Stand, Replogle, 12 In....... 77
Globe, Terrestrial, Wood Stand, Turned Legs, Gilman Joslin, Boston, 18 In........ 1098
Globe, Terrestrial, Zodiac Ring, Turned Wood Base, Kittinger Co., Late 1800s, 14 ½ In. ..*illus* 2214
Louisiana, Carte De La Louisiane Et Pays Voisins, Bellin, Paris, Frame, 8 ¾ x 12 In........ 300
Louisiana, Mississippi River, John Senex, London, Frame, 1721, 19 x 23 In........ 600
Mid-Atlantic & New England, Engraved, N. Visscher, Amsterdam, Frame, 1684, 23 x 27 In... 1920
New York City, Subway, Wall, Hand Colored, Frame, 41 x 26 In........ 472
New York State, Survey, Lithograph, 1796, 16 x 19 In........ 708
North America, 48 Segments Laid Down, Linen Backing, Eman Bowen, 1763, 40 x 46 ½ In... 3690
North America, School, Relief, Central School Supply House, Frame, 47 ¾ x 34 In........ 192
Rocky Mountains, Oregon & North California, J.C. Fremont, 1845, 33 x 54 ½ In........ 685
Southeastern Coast, Chesapeake Bay Southward To St., Frame, Johannes Cloppenburg, 14 x 16 ¼ In... 413
Texas & Indian Territory, Frank & O.W. Gray & Sons, Frame, 17 x 27 ½ In........ 192
United States, Schoolgirl, Ink, Batten & Roller, Olive Little Marshfield, Early 1800s, 29 x 38 In. 1638
Vermont, New Hampshire, Lewis Robinson, Part Of Massachusetts, 1840, 32 x 25 ¾ In........ 677
World, Needlework, Silk Threads, Elizabeth Willson, Pennsylvania, 1815, 26 ½ x 16 In. ..*illus* 2600

TIP
All types of light—sunlight, fluorescent lights, and electric lights—will eventually harm paper.

Malachite, Vase, 6 Women, Nude, Standing, Molded Glass, Reproduction, 5 In.
$96

Woody Auctions

Malachite, Vase, Birds, Aquatic Animals, Ocean Waves, Flat Foot, Molded Glass, Reproduction, 7 x 4 In., Pair
$79

Soulis Auctions

Map, Alaska, U.S. Geological Survey, Principal Previous Routes Of Exploration, 1898, 32 x 24 In.
$250

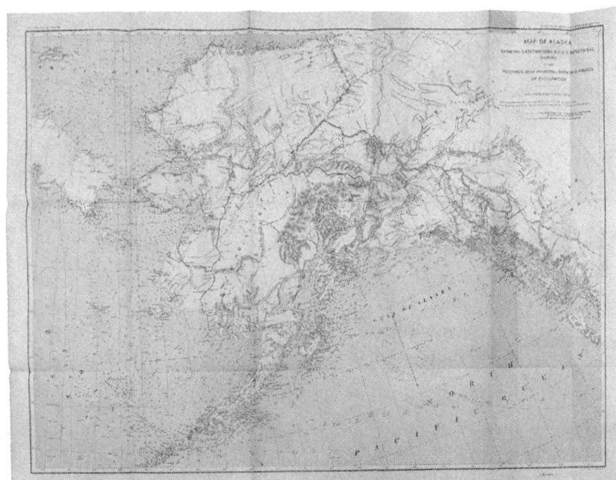

Eldred's

Map, Cape Cod, Major Roads, Vignettes Borders, Red Rope Outline, Frame, 1945, 24 x 35 In.
$420

Eldred's

Map, Europe, Europae Discripto Anno 1500, Coat Of Arms, Reproduction, Print, Frame, 19 x 23 In.
$24

Charleston Estate Auctions

M

Map, Globe, Celestial, Mahogany, Turned Stand, Wilson's, C. Lancaster, 1837, 18 In.
$780

CRN Auctions

Map, Globe, Celestial, Rand McNally & Co., Pasteboard, Cast Iron Base, Art Nouveau Style, 8 In.
$115

Apple Tree Auction Center

Map, Globe, Terrestrial, Calibrated Meridian, Mahogany Base, Rand McNally, 1930s, 17 In.
$154

Locati Auctions

Map, Globe, Terrestrial, Carved Wood Stand, Baroque Style, Signed, W. & A.K. Johnston, 18 In.
$1,140

Case Antiques

Map, Globe, Terrestrial, Gemstone, Gold Plated Meridian, Claw Foot Frame, 19 x 19 In.
$367

Soulis Auctions

Map, Globe, Terrestrial, Metal, Nickel Plated, Tripod Base, Nims & Knight, N.Y., c.1935, 34 In.
$1,188

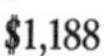

New Orleans Auction Galleries

Map, Globe, Terrestrial, On Cast Iron Base, Joslin, Boston, 37 x 12 In.
$1,534

Cottone Auctions

Map, Globe, Terrestrial, Zodiac Ring, Turned Wood Base, Kittinger Co., Late 1800s, 14 ½ In.
$2,214

Skinner, Inc.

Map, World, Needlework, Silk Threads, Elizabeth Willson, Pennsylvania, 1815, 26 ½ x 16 In.
$2,600

Freeman's Auctioneers & Appraisers

MARBLE

Marble collectors pay highest prices for glass and sulphide marbles. The game of marbles has been popular since the days of the ancient Romans. American children were able to buy marbles by the mid-eighteenth century. Dutch glazed clay marbles were least expensive. Glazed pottery marbles, attributed to the Bennington potteries in Vermont, were of a better quality. Marbles made of pink marble were also available by the 1830s. Glass marbles seem to have been made later. By 1880, Samuel C. Dyke of South Akron, Ohio, was making clay marbles and The National Onyx Marble Company was making marbles of onyx. The Navarre Glass Marble Company of Navarre, Ohio, and M. B. Mishler of Ravenna, Ohio, made the glass marbles. Ohio remained the center of the marble industry, and the Akron-made Akro Agate brand became nationally known. Other pieces made by Akro Agate are listed in this book in the Akro Agate category. Sulphides are glass marbles with frosted white figures in the center.

Clambroth, Teal Striping, ¾ In. 200
Gooseberry, Copper Puce, Burgundy & White Striations, 1 In. 200
Latticinio Core Swirl, Yellow & Orange Core, Blue & White Swirls, 1 ¼ In. 213
Latticinio Core Swirl, Yellow Core, Blue, White & Orange Swirls, Germany, 1 ⅛ In. 63
Latticinio Swirl, Blue, Red, Yellow, Black, Green, Oversized, c.1900, 2 ½ In. 800
Onionskin, 4 Panels, Gray, Pink, White, Teal 99
Onionskin, Blue, White, Pink, 1 ⅛ In. 313
Onionskin, Green & White Stripes, Gold Sparkles, ¾ In. 281
Onionskin, Rainbow Colors, Double Pontil, 1³⁄₁₆ In. 119
Ribbon Core, Green, Red, Orange & Blue Ribbon, Pontil, 1³⁄₁₆ In. 213
Ribbon Core, Salmon, Pink, White, Blue, Aqua, Yellow Swirls, Germany, 1 In. 150
Sulphide, Lucky 7, 1 ¹⁄₁₆ In. 475
Sulphide, Monkey, Sitting, Eating Fruit, 1860-80, 1 ½ In. 238

MARBLE CARVING

Marble carvings, such as large or small figurines, groups of people or animals, and architectural decorations, have been a special art form since the time of the ancient Greeks. Reproductions, especially of large Victorian groups, are being made of a mixture using marble dust. These are very difficult to detect and collectors should be careful. Other carvings are listed under Alabaster.

Birdbath, Classical Style, Draped Putto, Molded Clamshell Dish, c.1910, 42 x 15 In. ....*illus* 1750
Bowl, Scroll Shape, White, 15 ½ x 11 ½ x 3 In. 384
Bust, Actor, Wearing Comic Mask, Socle Base, Continental, 1900s, 14 In. 238
Bust, Ancient Greek Man, White, Carrara, c.1880, 20 ½ In. ....*illus* 1560
Bust, Bearded Man, Classical Attire, Scottish Nobleman, L. Macdonald, 1836, 22 ¾ In. 1521
Bust, Blackamoor, Pedestal, White, Gray Veins, 31 x 24 In. 885
Bust, Christ, White, Veined, Marble Pedestal, Square Base, 1800s, 44 In. 1476
Bust, Gentleman, Pedestal Base, Randolph John Rogers, 30 x 21 x 11 In. ....*illus* 3383
Bust, Gentleman, White, Classical Robe, Signed, R. Cauer, 1864, 28 x 20 x 12 In. ....*illus* 2160
Bust, Girl, Nude, Hat, Bow, Signed, P.L. Carrara, 19 x 11 In. 968
Bust, Woman, Flowers On Sides, Mounted, Round Base, Signed, G. Pugi, Italy, 23 ½ In. .*illus* 2000
Bust, Woman, Gilded Bronze, Collared Dress, G. Van Vaerenbergh, c.1900, 8 ½ x 8 In. 600
Bust, Woman, Wavy Hair, Lacy Chemise, Green Marble Base, 24 In. 570
Bust, Woman, Wearing Head Scarf, Square Neck Dress, 1910s, 10 In. ....*illus* 281
Bust, Woman, White, Lace Hat, Shawl, 27 x 20 In. 240
Bust, Young Beauty, Girl, Marked Cleo On Dress, Dirty White, 7 ½ In. 72
Bust, Young Beauty, Wearing Laurel Wreath, Gazing Downward, Pious Expression, 14 In. 539
Bust, Young Boy, Creamy, c.1900, 15 ½ x 10 In. ....*illus* 767
Bust, Young Girl, Smiling, Wearing Wrap, Beige, Early 1900s, 15 In. 396
Figure, Crouching Venus, Mounted, Florence, Signed P. Barranti, 1800s, 22 x 12 x 8 In. 4720
Figure, Dawn, Nude, Female, Nero Portoro Base, Dominique Alonzo, 32 ¾ In. 9225
Head, Medusa Rondanini, Curly Hair, Framed By Snakes, White, 18 ½ In. 7500

Marble Carving, Birdbath, Classical Style, Draped Putto, Molded Clamshell Dish, c.1910, 42 x 15 In.
$1,750

New Orleans Auction Galleries

Marble Carving, Bust, Ancient Greek Man, White, Carrara, c.1880, 20 ½ In.
$1,560

Eldred's

Marble Carving, Bust, Gentleman, Pedestal Base, Randolph John Rogers, 30 x 21 x 11 In.
$3,383

Clars Auction Gallery

M

MARBLE CARVING

Marble Carving, Bust, Gentleman, White, Classical Robe, Signed, R. Cauer, 1864, 28 x 20 x 12 In.
$2,160

Case Antiques

Marble Carving, Bust, Woman, Flowers On Sides, Mounted, Round Base, Signed, G. Pugi, Italy, 23 ½ In.
$2,000

Cowan's Auctions

Marble Carving, Bust, Woman, Wearing Head Scarf, Square Neck Dress, 1910s, 10 In.
$281

Garth's Auctioneers & Appraisers

Lion, Lying Down, Grand Tour, Dark Egyptian Marble Base, 1800s, 5 x 8 ½ x 3 In., Pair 1700
Model, Temple Of Castor & Pollux, Grand Tour Sienna, Onyx Base, 13 x 6 x 2 ½ In. 3100
Model, Temple Of Vespasian, Grand Tour Sienna, Slate Base, 11 x 5 In. ....*illus* 1344
Panel, Christ, Cross, Saints, Metal & Wood Base, Byzantine, 22 x 18 x 2 ¾ In. 3321
Pedestal, Brass Fittings, Octagonal Top, Dome Base, 45 In. 203
Pedestal, Classical Style, 3 Sections, Intertwined Dolphin, c.1900, 44 x 14 x 14 In. 540
Pedestal, Continental Style, Burl Walnut, Bronze Gilt, 48 x 14 x 14 In., Pair 625
Pedestal, Spiraling Column, Gadrooned Flare, Octagonal Base, c.1900 ....*illus* 259
Pedestal, Square Top, Cut Corners, Turned Column, Octagonal Base, White, Italy, 1910s, 36 In. 300
Pedestal, Verde Antico, Fluted Shaft, Octagonal Base, 42 x 11 ¾ In. 650
Plaque, Allegorical Figure, Iron Surround, Loop Hanger, Italy, 1900s, 31 ½ In., Pair 700
Statue, Faun, Kneeling, White, Pan Flute, Le Songe D'Une Nuit D'Ete, 40 x 15 x 13 In. 10313
Statue, Michelangelo, Sitting, Square Base, Italy, 1800s, 23 x 9 x 10 In. 1046
Statue, Woman, Nude, Goblet, Spilling Urn, Italy, 26 In. 600
Statue, Woman, Nude, Rough Hewn Base, c.1915, 22 ½ In. ....*illus* 590
Statue, Woman, Nude, Standing, Carrara, Columnar Pedestal, 1900s, 71 In. ....*illus* 3300
Statue, Woman, Nude, Standing, White, Circular Base, 46 In. ....*illus* 978
Statue, Woman, Nude, Taking Off Shirt, Oval Base, 45 ½ In. 679
Tazza, Mottled, White & Black, Plinth Base, c.1850, 10 x 11 ½ In. 1000
Urn, Black, Turnings, Shoulder & Stepped Socle, 1900s, 7 In., Pair 1599
Urn, Dark Gray, Gilt Bronze Goat Head Mount, Floral Swag, Pinecone Finial, 18 In. 130
Urn, Neoclassical Style, Bold Reeds, Molded Base, Italy, 1900s, 20 x 15 In., Pair ....*illus* 1125

MARBLEHEAD POTTERY

Marblehead Pottery was founded in 1904 by Dr. J. Hall as a rehabilitative program for the patients of a Marblehead, Massachusetts, sanitarium. Two years later it was separated from the sanitarium and it continued operations until 1936. Many of the pieces were decorated with marine motifs.

Bowl, Bronze, Green Matte Glaze, Tree Silhouettes, Sarah Tutt, Early 1900s, 3 ½ In. ....*illus* 1169
Tile, Ship, Blue, White Matte, Square, Marked, 4 ¾ In. ....*illus* 196
Vase, Flared, Blue Matte Exterior, Speckled Blue Interior, Marked, 6 ¾ x 5 In. ....*illus* 184
Vase, Oval, Stylized Trees, Fruits, Brown Glazed, Painted, 7 x 4 In. ....*illus* 1875
Vase, Stylized Trees, Incised, Gray, Blue, Glazed, 1908-20, 3 x 4 ½ In. ....*illus* 1750

MARDI GRAS

Mardi Gras, French for "Fat Tuesday," was first celebrated in seventeenth-century Europe. The first celebration in America was held in Mobile, Alabama, in 1703. The first krewe, a parading or social club, was founded in 1856. Dozens have been formed since. The Mardi Gras Act, which made Fat Tuesday a legal holiday, was passed in Louisiana in 1875. Mardi Gras balls, carnivals, parties, and parades are held from January 6 until the Tuesday before the beginning of Lent. The most famous carnival and parades take place in New Orleans. Parades feature floats, elaborate costumes, masks, and "throws" of strings of beads, cups, doubloons, or small toys. Purple, green, and gold are traditional Mardi Gras colors. Mardi Gras memorabilia ranges from cheap plastic beads to expensive souvenirs from early celebrations.

Beads, Plastic, Multicolor, Multi Shapes, 1970s, 42 In. 16
Doubloon, Old Reliable Pleasure Club Chief Choctaw, Bronze-Like Metal, 1968 14
Perfume Bottle, Krewe Of Mithras, Silver Plate, Reed & Barton, 1993, 2 x 1 In. 20
Pin, Mask, Pewter, Rollover Clasp, Signed, Maurice Milleur, 1 ¾ In. 20
Pin, Russian Cathedral, Silver Plated Brass, Carnival Krewe, Signed, T.M.C., 1991, 1 In. 50

MARTIN BROTHERS

Martin Brothers of Middlesex, England, made Martinware, a salt-glazed stoneware, between 1873 and 1915. Many figural jugs and vases were made by the four

Marble Carving, Bust, Young Boy, Creamy, c.1900, 15 ½ x 10 In.
$767

Ahlers & Ogletree Auction Gallery

Marble Carving, Model, Temple Of Vespasian, Grand Tour Sienna, Slate Base, 11 x 5 In.
$1,344

Neal Auction Company

Marble Carving, Pedestal, Spiraling Column, Gadrooned Flare, Octagonal Base, c.1900
$259

Selkirk Auctioneers & Appraisers

Marble Carving, Statue, Woman, Nude, Rough Hewn Base, c.1915, 22 ½ In.
$590

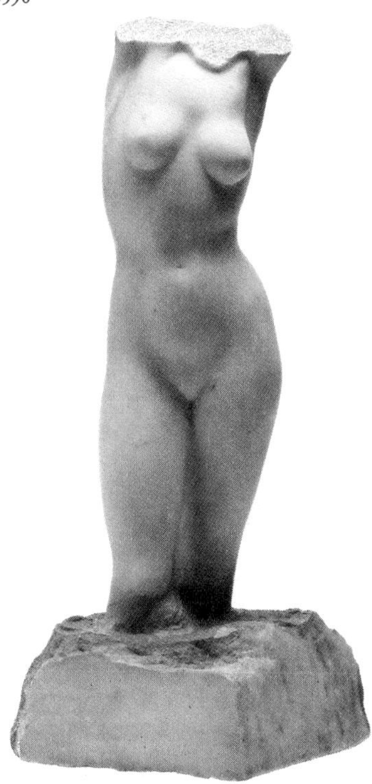

Leland Little Auctions

Marble Carving, Statue, Woman, Nude, Standing, Carrara, Columnar Pedestal, 1900s, 71 In.
$3,300

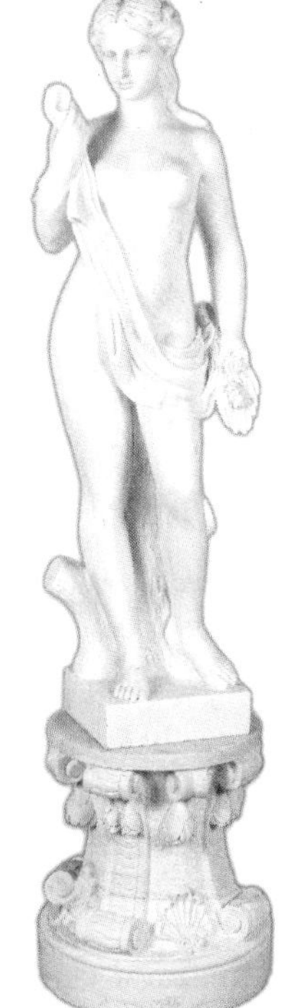

Selkirk Auctioneers & Appraisers

Marble Carving, Statue, Woman, Nude, Standing, White, Circular Base, 46 In.
$978

Stevens Auction Co.

Marble Carving, Urn, Neoclassical Style, Bold Reeds, Molded Base, Italy, 1900s, 20 x 15 In., Pair
$1,125

New Orleans Auction Galleries

TIP
When moving, stuff glasses and cups with crumpled paper, then wrap in bubble wrap.

Marblehead, Bowl, Bronze, Green Matte Glaze, Tree Silhouettes, Sarah Tutt, Early 1900s, 3 ½ In.
$1,169

Skinner, Inc.

Marblehead, Tile, Ship, Blue, White Matte, Square, Marked, 4 ¾ In.
$196

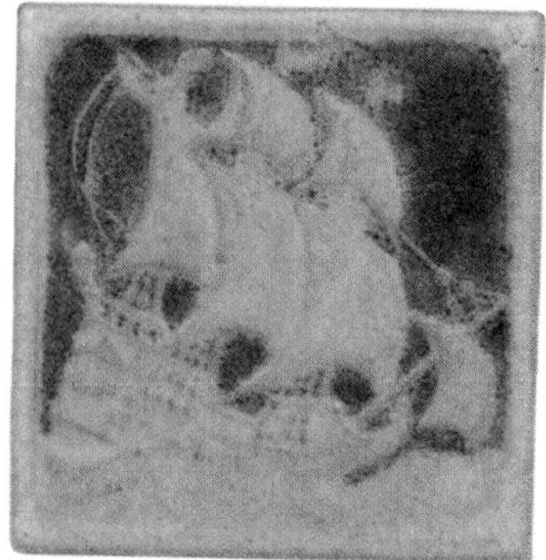

Belhorn Auction Services

Marblehead, Vase, Flared, Blue Matte Exterior, Speckled Blue Interior, Marked, 6 ¾ x 5 In.
$184

Belhorn Auction Services

Marblehead, Vase, Oval, Stylized Trees, Fruits, Brown Glazed, Painted, 7 x 4 In.
$1,875

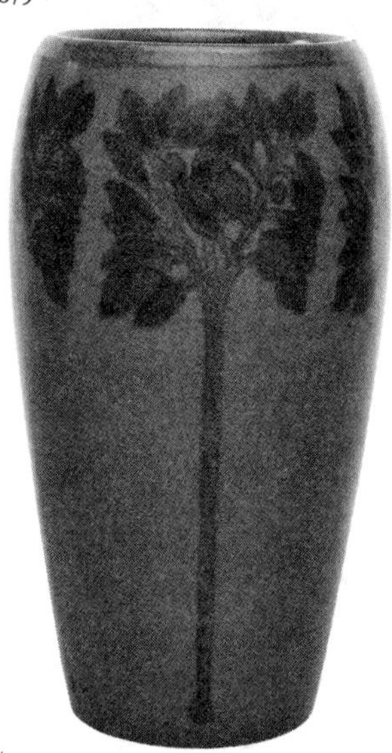

Treadway

Martin Brothers, Vase, Bulbous, Fish, Embossed, Carved, Painted, Signed, 2 ½ x 2 In.
$715

Treadway

Massier, Charger, Metallic Glazes, Landscape, Golfe-Juan, Clement, Late 1800s, 9 ¾ In.
$1,476

Skinner, Inc.

Marblehead, Vase, Stylized Trees, Incised, Gray, Blue, Glazed, 1908-20, 3 x 4 ½ In.
$1,750

Rago Arts and Auction Center

brothers. Of special interest are the fanciful birds, usually made with removable heads. Most pieces have the incised name of the artists plus other information on the bottom.

Tankard, Incised, Painted, Ducks, Pelicans, Grasses, Mosquito, 1894, 9 ½ In. 2394
Vase, Bulbous, Fish, Embossed, Carved, Painted, Signed, 2 ½ x 2 In. .... *illus* 715
Vase, Gourd, Round, Lobed, Inscribed Marks, Dated 5-1911, 4 x 3 ¾ In. 1569

MARY GREGORY

Mary Gregory is the name used for a type of glass that is easily identified. White figures were painted on clear or colored glass as the decoration. The figures chosen were usually children at play. The first glass known as Mary Gregory was made in about 1870. Similar glass is made even today. The traditional story has been that the glass was made at the Boston & Sandwich Glass Company in Sandwich, Massachusetts, by a woman named Mary Gregory. Recent research has shown that none was made at Sandwich. In fact, all early Mary Gregory glass was made in Bohemia. Beginning in 1957, the Westmoreland Glass Co. made the first Mary Gregory–type decorations on American glassware. These pieces had simpler designs, less enamel paint, and more modern shapes. France, Italy, Germany, Switzerland, and England, as well as Bohemia, made this glassware. Children standing, not playing, were not pictured until after the 1950s.

Bowl, Centerpiece, Blue, White, Girl, Watching, Geese, Circular Foot, c.1900, 10 x 11 In. 94
Box, Black, Coffin Shape, Children, Ivy Vine Swags, Gilt Brass, 5 x 5 ½ In. 260
Pitcher, Tankard, Blue, Cylindrical, Bulge Base, Handle, c.1900, 13 x 13 ½ In., Pair 94

MASONIC, *see Fraternal category.*

MASON'S IRONSTONE

MASON'S PATENT IRONSTONE CHINA

Mason's Ironstone was made by the English pottery of Charles J. Mason after 1813. Mason, of Lane Delph, was given a patent for this improved earthenware. He usually called it *Mason's Patent Ironstone China*. It resisted chipping and breaking, so it became popular for dinnerware and other table service dishes. Vases and other decorative pieces were also made. The ironstone was decorated with orange, blue, gold, and other colors, often in Japanese-inspired designs. The firm had financial difficulties but the molds and the name *Mason* were used by many owners through the years, including Francis Morley, Taylor Ashworth, George L. Ashworth, and John Shaw. Mason's joined the Wedgwood group in 1973 and the name was used for a few years and then dropped.

Bowl, Chinese Scenes, Scalloped Edge, Blue, Gold, 10 In. 103
Bowl, Vegetable, Red & White, Vista, Paneled Sides, Scalloped Rim, 9 In. 50
Cake Plate, Vista Pattern, Red & White, Handles, 11 x 11 In. 35
Chop Plate, Vista Pattern, Red & White, Scalloped, 14 In. 84
Compote, Indian Grasshopper Pattern, Molded Flower Edge, c.1813, 10 In. 295
Cup & Saucer, Brown & White, Vista, Transfer, c.1950 18
Eggcup, Blue & Pink Flowers, White Ground, 2 In. 10
Jug, Imari Pattern, Snake Handle, Paneled Sides, 6 ½ In. 95
Jug, Scalloped Round Edges, Entwined Strap Handle, Asian Flowers, c.1840, 8 ¾ In. 165
Pitcher, Chartreuse, Green, Gold Design On White Ground, Scalloped Mouth, 6 ¾ In. 45
Planter, Dolphin Shape Handles, White Ground, Flowers, 1800s, 9 x 18 x 13 In. 330
Plate, Flowers, Multicolor, Fluted & Scalloped Edge, c.1890, 10 In. 60
Plate, River, Swans, Couple, Dog, Alton Towers, Blue Transfer, c.1900, 9 In. 32
Platter, Imari Pattern, Tobacco Leaf Design, 13 x 10 ½ In. 90
Platter, Vase & Symbol Pattern, c.1940s, 16 x 12 In. 599
Spittoon, Multicolor Chinese Design, White Ground, 12 x 12 ½ In. 281
Sugar, Lid, Red Vista, Couple, Child, Dog, Cityscape, Handles, 6 x 4 x 5 In. 50

Massier, Jardiniere, Grasshopper, Figural, Green, 10 x 21 In.
$7,670

Strawser Auction Group

Massier, Vase, Young Woman Clinging, Iridescent Metallic, Iris, Signed, Delphin, 7 ½ In.
$1,320

Ripley Auctions

M

TIP
Old iron heating grates have a new use. Put them on the outdoor mat to be used as mud scrapers.

Match Holder, Ashtray, Flower Shape, Footed, Marked, Bradley & Hubbard, 1811, 2 ¾ x 5 x 4 In.
$124

Hartzell's Auction Gallery Inc.

Match Holder, Black Man, Breaking Through Tambourine, Painted, Cast Iron, 4 ½ In.
$226

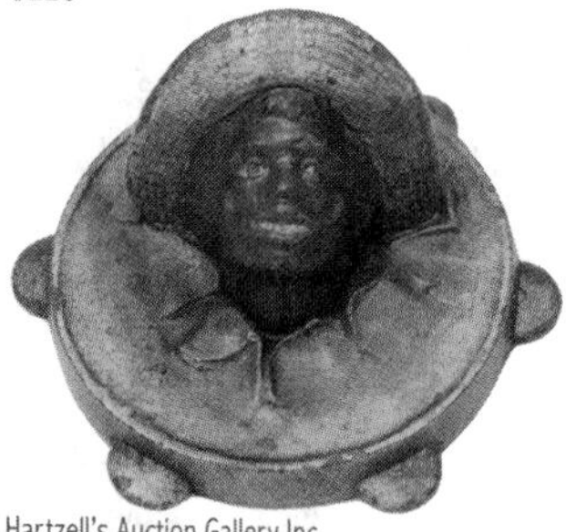

Hartzell's Auction Gallery Inc.

Match Holder, Yellow Kid, Icebox Holds Matches, Embossed, Metal, 6 ½ x 5 ¾ In.
$625

AntiqueAdvertising.com

Match Safe, House, Complete Match Safe, Roof Swivels, Cast Iron, Painted, 1883, 4 In.
$123

Richard Opfer Auctioneering, Inc.

Sugar, Red & White, Vista Pattern, Square Shape, 4 In. 35
Tray, Dessert, Lotus Pattern, Tab Handle, 9 x 8 In. 199
Tray, Vase & Rock Pattern, Blue, Gold, Orange, c.1825, 9 x 7 In. 149
Tureen, Soup, Lid, Imari Pattern, Square Shape, Flower Bud Finial, 10 ½ x 9 ½ In. 475

MASSIER

Massier, a French art pottery, was made by brothers Jerome, Delphin, and Clement Massier in Vallauris and Golfe-Juan, France, in the late nineteenth and early twentieth centuries. It has an iridescent metallic luster glaze that resembles the Weller Sicardo pottery glaze. Most pieces are marked *J. Massier.* Massier may also be listed in the Majolica category.

Charger, Metallic Glazes, Landscape, Golfe-Juan, Clement, Late 1800s, 9 ¾ In. *illus* 1476
Jardiniere, Grasshopper, Figural, Green, 10 x 21 In. *illus* 7670
Jardiniere, Swans, France, c.1960, 12 x 16 In. 470
Vase, Frog, Playing Mandolin, Posey, Open Mouth, Green, 3 ¾ In. 77
Vase, Young Woman Clinging, Iridescent Metallic, Iris, Signed, Delphin, 7 ½ In. *illus* 1320

MATCH HOLDER

Match holders were made to hold the large wooden matches that were used in the nineteenth and twentieth centuries for a variety of purposes. The kitchen stove and the fireplace or furnace had to be lit regularly. One type of match holder was made to hang on the wall, another was designed to be kept on a tabletop. Of special interest to collectors today are match holders that have advertisements as part of the design.

Ashtray, Flower Shape, Footed, Marked, Bradley & Hubbard, 1811, 2 ¾ x 5 x 4 In. *illus* 124
Black, Aunt Jemima, Hard Plastic, Blue, Marked, Made In USA, 6 x 3 In. 300
Black Man, Breaking Through Tambourine, Painted, Cast Iron, 4 ½ In. *illus* 226
Brass, Arts & Crafts, Indian Design, Mounted, Rectangular Base, 3 ¾ x 3 In. 68
Iron, Modern Molding Machine, Arcade Mfg. Co., 4 x 3 In. 136
Metal, Ax Shape, George Washington, Inaugurated, President Of The U.S., 1789, 9 In. 90
Old Man, Holding Umbrella & Tobacco, Standing, Hat, Cigar Holder, Square Base, 9 In. 24
Rooster, 2 Piece, Removable Top, Footed, Cast Iron, 3 x 3 In. 136
Tin, Painted, Black Ground, Red, Green & Yellow, Leaves, c.1850, 6 x 4 ½ In. 400
Woman, Basket & Fish, Painted, Pot Metal, 3 ¾ x 4 ½ x 2 ½ In. 57
Yellow Kid, Icebox Holds Matches, Embossed, Metal, 6 ½ x 5 ¾ In. *illus* 625

MATCH SAFE

Match safes were designed to be carried in the pocket or set on a table. Early matches were made with phosphorus and could ignite unexpectedly. The matches were safely stored in the tightly closed container. Match safes were made in sterling silver, plated silver, or other metals. The English call these "vesta boxes."

Cat, Mouse, Brass, Japan, 3 In. 200
Cottage, Striker Swings, Embossed, Cast Iron, c.1885, 4 x 4 ⅜ x 3 ⅞ In. 468
Devil, Glass Eyes, Horns, Pointy Nose, Red, Brass Plated Copper, 2 In. 280
Dog, Begging, Collar, Wood, 4 In. 93
Domino, Double Threes, Vulcanite, Celluloid, 2 In. 87
Flowers, Arcs, Circles, Blue, Green, Silver, Enamel, Russia, 1 ¾ x 2 In. 896
House, Complete Match Safe, Roof Swivels, Cast Iron, Painted, 1883, 4 In. *illus* 123
Judy & The Cat, Book Shape, Enameled Cover, Silver, England, c.1880, 1 ½ x 1 In. *illus* 813
Knight, Profile, Applied, Raised, Gilt, Black, 2 In. 200
Punch, Puppet, Hinged Lid, Painted, Cast Iron, Zimmerman, 5 In. 461
Scroll, Shell, Flower, 14K Gold, Monogram, Gorham, Late 1800s, 2 ½ x 1 ½ In. *illus* 960
Silver, Oval, Rococo Style, 2 Thumbgrips, Hinged Lid, Gold Washed Interior, c.1850, 2 ¾ In. 190
Silver, Red Guilloche, France, 1 ¾ x 1 In. 544

McCOY

McCoy pottery was made in Roseville, Ohio. Nelson McCoy and J.W. McCoy established the Nelson McCoy Sanitary and Stoneware Company in Roseville, Ohio, in 1910. The firm made art pottery after 1926. In 1933 it became the Nelson McCoy Pottery Company. Pieces marked *McCoy* were made by the Nelson McCoy Pottery Company. Cookie jars were made from about 1940 until December 1990, when the McCoy factory closed. Since 1991 pottery with the McCoy mark has been made by firms unrelated to the original company. Because there was a company named Brush-McCoy, there is great confusion between Brush and Nelson McCoy pieces. See Brush category for more information.

Bank, Billy Possum, Olive Green Gloss, Coin Slot, 5 ½ In. .... *illus* 207
Cookie Jar, Train, Pumpkin Orange Gloss, 8 x 11 ½ In. 374
Figurine, Frog, Lying Down, Amused Expression, Green, 1930s, 5 ½ x 10 ½ In. .... *illus* 38
Jardiniere, Pedestal, Butterfly, White Sand, Matte, Leaves, 21 In. .... *illus* 431
Jardiniere, Pedestal, White Matte, Quilted Leaf Garland, 21 In. .... *illus* 113
Jardiniere, Pedestal, Yellow Daffodils, Shaded Brown Ground, 31 x 13 ½ In. 235
Pitcher, Donkey, Yellow, Semigloss, Handle, Marked, 6 ⅝ In. 161
Planter, Figural, Duck, Umbrella, Cream Body, Orange, Green, 7 In. .... *illus* 138
Planter, Hunting Dog, Leaves, Cream Ground, Fence, Rectangular Base, 12 In. 65
Vase, 2 Tulips, Gold Trim, Glossy Finish, Marked, 6 In. .... *illus* 115
Vase, 3 Giraffes, Semimatte Glaze, Lavender, Brown, Marked, Sidney Cope, 9 ⅜ x 8 In. ... *illus* 4830
Vase, Strapwork, Aqua Green Glaze Body, Ribbed, Footed, 12 x 7 ½ In. .... *illus* 45
Wall Pocket, Apple, Gold Trimmed, Glossy Finish, 1950s, 7 ⅜ In. 58
Wall Pocket, White, Brown, Green Accent, Hanging, Marked, 7 ¾ In. 75

McKEE

McKee is a name associated with various glass enterprises in the United States since 1836, including J. & F. McKee (1850), Bryce, McKee & Co. (1850 to 1854), McKee and Brothers (1865), and National Glass Co. (1899). In 1903, the McKee Glass Company was formed in Jeannette, Pennsylvania. It became McKee Division of the Thatcher Glass Co. in 1951 and was bought out by the Jeannette Corporation in 1961. Pressed glass, kitchenwares, and tablewares were produced. Jeannette Corporation closed in the early 1980s. Additional pieces may be included in the Custard Glass and Depression Glass categories.

McKee Glass Co.
c.1870

PRESCUT

McKee Glass Co.
c.1904–1935

McKee Glass Co.
1935–1940

Compote, Leaf Pattern, Flared, Wafered Stem, Scalloped Edge, 1860s, 9 ½ x 12 In. 30
Dispenser, Lemonade, Pale Yellow, Horizontal Ribs, 5 Sections, Spigot, 19 ½ In. 175
Goblet, Water, Red, Swollen Top, Scrolls, Faceted Knop, 8-Sided Base, 5 ¾ In., 6 Piece 102
Lamp, Oil, Wild Rose & Bowknot, Chocolate Pedestal, Clear Font, Taplin Burner, 9 In. 213
Mixing Bowl Set, Jade, Flared, 2 With Pour Spout, Largest 9 In., 4 Piece 180
Mixing Bowl, Milk Glass, Black Sailboat, Fouled Anchor & Ship's Wheel, 9 ½ In. 30
Pitcher, Baby Face, Clear, Frosted Baby's Head & Foot, 10 ⅞ In. 144
Pitcher, Milk, Feather, Doric, Chocolate Glass, Footed, 1896-1901, 8 In. 600
Pitcher, Nortec, Pres Cut, Clear, Mold Blown, Squat, 7 In. 14
Pitcher, Water, Clear, Ruby Stained Band, Beading, Oval, Spread Foot, c.1910, 10 In. 108
Pitcher, Water, Ruby Stain, Colorless, Round Base, Handle, Spout, c.1910, 10 In. .... *illus* 105
Range Set, Shakers, Custard Glass, Black Letters, Sugar, Salt, Pepper, Flour, 5 In., 4 Piece 250
Reamer, Custard Glass, Footed, 1930s, 2 ½ x 5 x 7 In. 36
Reamer, Sunkist, Pink, Depression Glass 37
Sugar, Lid, Eugenie, Colorless, Dolphin Form Finial, c.1859, 9 ½ In. 48
Tumbler, Chrysanthemum Leaf, Chocolate Glass, c.1902, 3 ¾ In. 180

Match Safe, Judy & The Cat, Book Shape, Enameled Cover, Silver, England, c.1880, 1 ½ x 1 In.
$813

Cowan's Auctions

Match Safe, Scroll, Shell, Flower, 14K Gold, Monogram, Gorham, Late 1800s, 2 ½ x 1 ½ In.
$960

Brunk Auctions

McCoy, Bank, Billy Possum, Olive Green Gloss, Coin Slot, 5 ½ In.
$207

Belhorn Auction Services

M

McCoy, Figurine, Frog, Lying Down, Amused Expression, Green, 1930s, 5 ½ x 10 ½ In.
$38

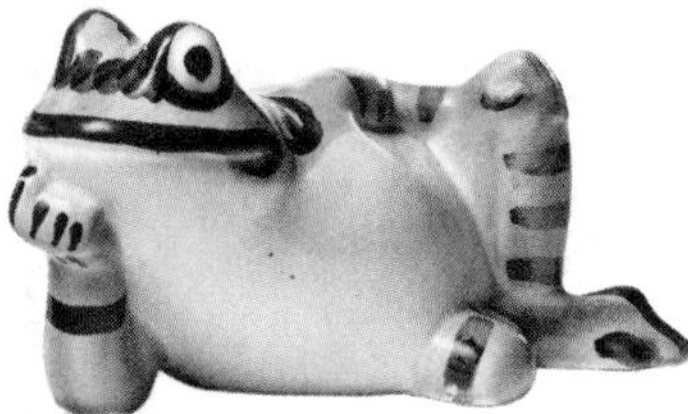

Garth's Auctioneers & Appraisers

McCoy, Jardiniere, Pedestal, Butterfly, White Sand, Matte, Leaves, 21 In.
$431

Belhorn Auction Services

McCoy, Jardiniere, Pedestal, White Matte, Quilted Leaf Garland, 21 In.
$113

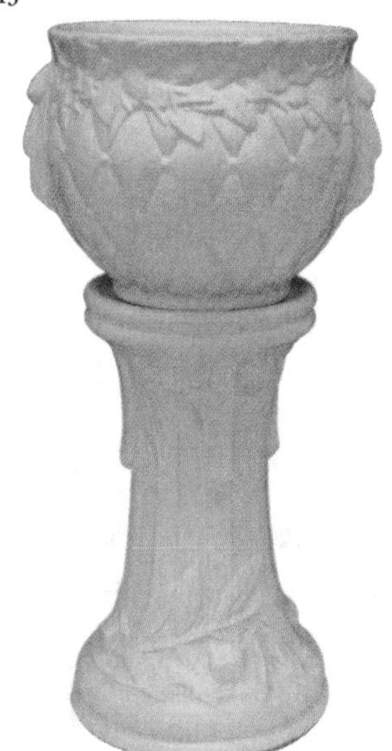

Hartzell's Auction Gallery Inc.

McCoy, Planter, Figural, Duck, Umbrella, Cream Body, Orange, Green, 7 In.
$138

Belhorn Auction Services

McCoy, Vase, 2 Tulips, Gold Trim, Glossy Finish, Marked, 6 In.
$115

Belhorn Auction Services

McCoy, Vase, 3 Giraffes, Semimatte Glaze, Lavender, Brown, Marked, Sidney Cope, 9 ⅜ x 8 In.
$4,830

Belhorn Auction Services

McCoy, Vase, Strapwork, Aqua Green Glaze Body, Ribbed, Footed, 12 x 7 ½ In.
$45

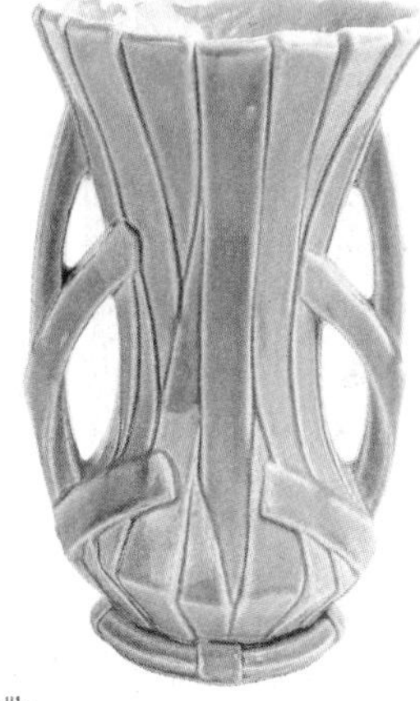

Witherell's

McKee, Pitcher, Water, Ruby Stain, Colorless, Round Base, Handle, Spout, c.1910, 10 In.
$105

Jeffrey S. Evans & Associates

Medical, Cabinet, Apothecary, 45 Dovetail Drawers, Paper Labels, Chinese, c.1900, 45 x 37 x 23 In.
$1,375

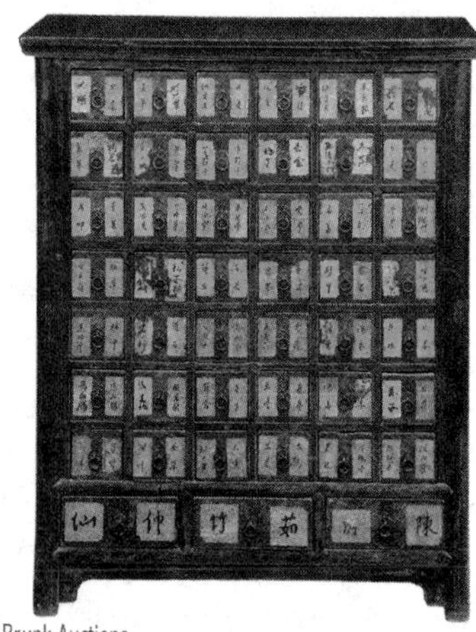

Brunk Auctions

MECHANICAL BANKS *are listed in the Bank category.*

MEDICAL

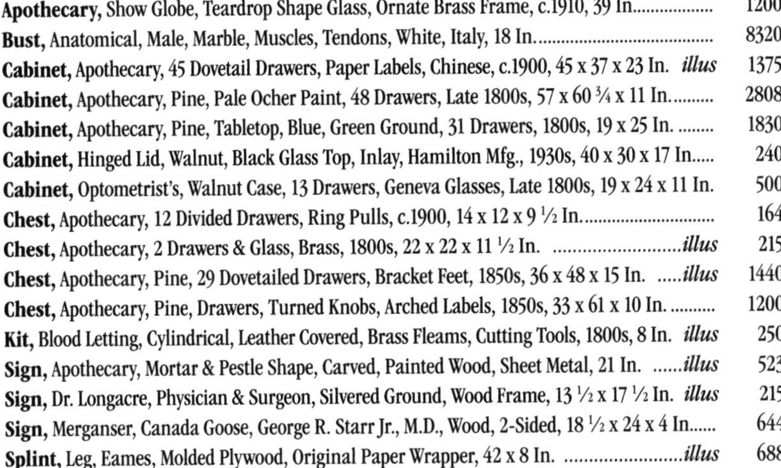

Medical office furniture, operating tools, microscopes, thermometers, and other paraphernalia used by doctors are included in this category. Veterinary collectibles are also included here. Medicine bottles are listed in the Bottle category. There are related collectibles listed under Dental.

Apothecary, Show Globe, Teardrop Shape Glass, Ornate Brass Frame, c.1910, 39 In.	1200
Bust, Anatomical, Male, Marble, Muscles, Tendons, White, Italy, 18 In.	8320
Cabinet, Apothecary, 45 Dovetail Drawers, Paper Labels, Chinese, c.1900, 45 x 37 x 23 In. *illus*	1375
Cabinet, Apothecary, Pine, Pale Ocher Paint, 48 Drawers, Late 1800s, 57 x 60 ¾ x 11 In.	2808
Cabinet, Apothecary, Pine, Tabletop, Blue, Green Ground, 31 Drawers, 1800s, 19 x 25 In.	1830
Cabinet, Hinged Lid, Walnut, Black Glass Top, Inlay, Hamilton Mfg., 1930s, 40 x 30 x 17 In.	240
Cabinet, Optometrist's, Walnut Case, 13 Drawers, Geneva Glasses, Late 1800s, 19 x 24 x 11 In.	500
Chest, Apothecary, 12 Divided Drawers, Ring Pulls, c.1900, 14 x 12 x 9 ½ In.	164
Chest, Apothecary, 2 Drawers & Glass, Brass, 1800s, 22 x 22 x 11 ½ In. *illus*	215
Chest, Apothecary, Pine, 29 Dovetailed Drawers, Bracket Feet, 1850s, 36 x 48 x 15 In. *illus*	1440
Chest, Apothecary, Pine, Drawers, Turned Knobs, Arched Labels, 1850s, 33 x 61 x 10 In.	1200
Kit, Blood Letting, Cylindrical, Leather Covered, Brass Fleams, Cutting Tools, 1800s, 8 In. *illus*	250
Sign, Apothecary, Mortar & Pestle Shape, Carved, Painted Wood, Sheet Metal, 21 In. *illus*	523
Sign, Dr. Longacre, Physician & Surgeon, Silvered Ground, Wood Frame, 13 ½ x 17 ½ In. *illus*	215
Sign, Merganser, Canada Goose, George R. Starr Jr., M.D., Wood, 2-Sided, 18 ½ x 24 x 4 In.	644
Splint, Leg, Eames, Molded Plywood, Original Paper Wrapper, 42 x 8 In. *illus*	688

MEISSEN

Meissen is a town in Germany where porcelain has been made since 1710. Any china made in the town can be called Meissen, although the famous Meissen factory made the finest porcelains of the area. The crossed swords mark of the great Meissen factory has been copied by many other firms in Germany and other parts of the world. Pieces of Meissen dinnerware in the Onion pattern are listed in their own category in this book.

Bowl, Basket Shape, Woven, Gilt, Floral Center, 1800s, 6 x 2 In. *illus*	173
Centerpiece, Man, Woman, Flowers, Pink, Scrolled Rim, 2 Handles, Rococo Style, c.1900, 19 In.	2520
Centerpiece, Putto, 4 Scroll Feet, Bird Knees, Rococo Style, 1800s, 25 x 13 ½ x 16 ¾ In.	7073
Clock, Shelf, Cupid, Floral Encrusted Garland, Lovebirds, Gilt Bezel, 11 x 9 x 5 In. *illus*	1338
Compote, Children, Eating, Flower, Leaves, Gilt, Footed Base, Germany, 21 x 15 In.	390
Compote, Gilt, Cobalt Blue, Leaves, Knopped Stem, Spreading Foot, Late 1800s, 10 ½ In.	180
Dish, Praline, 3 Tiers, Figural Top, Fruits, White Ground, 19 x 11 ¾ In.	313
Figurine, 2 Birds, Oriole Perched On Stump, Flowers, Painted, Early 1900s, 5 ½ In.	270
Figurine, Boy, Standing, Gilt, Glaze, Modeled, Ducks, Late 1800s, 4 ⅞ In.	369
Figurine, Girl, Feeding Chickens, Marked, 4 ¾ In. *illus*	90
Figurine, Man, Mustache, Fur Lined Cape, Mounted, c.1930, 8 ¾ In. *illus*	212
Figurine, The Reader, Woman, Reading Book, Rococo Style Base, Marked, 8 x 6 In.	472
Group, 2 Women, 1 Holding Flower Garland, 2 Putti, 1800s, 9 x 7 ½ In. *illus*	650
Group, Children, Seated, 2 Swans, Multicolor, Enamel, Gilt, Rococo Base, Late 1800s, 9 In.	2337
Group, Soldier Holding Severed Head, King, Putti Holding Ball, Marked, 12 x 11 In. *illus*	2875
Group, Venus & Cupid Embracing, Bisque, Crossed Swords Mark, 1910s, 23 ½ In.	650
Group, Winter, 7 Children, Grapes, Wine Glasses, Multicolor, Oval, 9 ½ x 7 ½ x 6 ½ In. *illus*	875
Platter, Hand Painted, Floral Bouquet, Gilded Rim, Crossed Swords Mark, Late 1800s, 23 In.	216
Potpourri, Urn Shape, Fruit Finial, Reticulated Lid, Crossed Swords Mark, 7 x 6 In.	227
Saucer, Hunting Scene, Orange Border, White Ground, 5 In., Pair	308
Sugar, Lid, Round, White Ground, Flowers, Bud Finial, 4 In.	185
Tureen, Underplate, Lid, Pink Rose Finial, Flower Bouquets, Insects, Latticework, 5 ½ x 9 In.	450
Urn, Cobalt Blue, Gilt Highlights, Scroll Handles, Blue Crossed Sword Mark, 1800s, 19 In.	390
Vase, Flower Encrusted, Tapering Body, Scenic Reserves, 2 Handles, Footed, 1800s, 20 x 9 In.	1889

Meissen Myth

The crossed sword mark was used only on German porcelain made by Meissen. NOT TRUE. The mark is the most copied mark found on porcelain and was used on English, French, and other wares as well as dishes made by other German companies.

Medical, Chest, Apothecary, 2 Drawers & Glass, Brass, 1800s, 22 x 22 x 11 ½ In.
$215

Locati Auctions

Medical, Chest, Apothecary, Pine, 29 Dovetailed Drawers, Bracket Feet, 1850s, 36 x 48 x 15 In.
$1,440

Garth's Auctioneers & Appraisers

Medical, Kit, Blood Letting, Cylindrical, Leather Covered, Brass Fleams, Cutting Tools, 1800s, 8 In.
$250

Freeman's Auctioneers & Appraisers

M

Medical, Sign, Apothecary, Mortar & Pestle Shape, Carved, Painted Wood, Sheet Metal, 21 In.
$523

Skinner, Inc.

TIP
Civil War re-enactors have been warned that some old medical instruments could still carry germs or viruses that are infectious. Be very careful when handling any old medical items. They should be carefully disinfected.

Medical, Sign, Dr. Longacre, Physician & Surgeon, Silvered Ground, Wood Frame, 13 ½ x 17 ½ In.
$215

Soulis Auctions

Medical, Splint, Leg, Eames, Molded Plywood, Original Paper Wrapper, 42 x 8 In.
$688

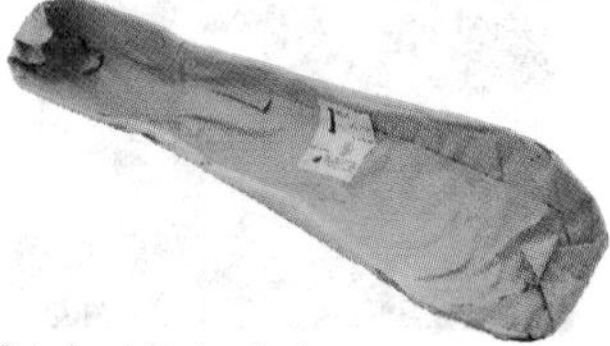

Palm Beach Modern Auctions

MERCURY GLASS

Mercury glass, or silvered glass, was first made in the 1850s. It lost favor for a while but became popular again about 1910. It looks like a piece of silver but it is a hollow glass piece with mercury coloring inside. It was copied again in 2017.

Ice Bucket, Cork, Brown, Cylindrical Lid, c.1950, 15 x 9 x 9 In. .... *illus* 113
Ornament, Grape Cluster, Kugel, Brass Cap, Germany, 4 ½ In. 350
Sphere On Pedestal, Hand Blown, c.1800, 10 In. 687
Vase, Tabletop, c.1990, 14 ½ x 6 ½ In. 12

METLOX POTTERIES

Metlox Potteries was founded in 1927 in Manhattan Beach, California. Dinnerware was made beginning in 1931. Evan K. Shaw purchased the company in 1946 and expanded the number of patterns. Poppytrail (1946–1989) and Vernonware (1958–1980) were divisions of Metlox under E.K. Shaw's direction. The factory closed in 1989.

Aztec California, Bowl, Vegetable, Divided Twin, 14 In. 230
California Contempora, Bowl, Free Form, 7 In. 40
California Ivy, Creamer, Footed 14
California Ivy, Platter, Round, 13 In. 25
California Ivy, Tumbler, 6 ½ In., 6 Piece 23
California Provincial, Bread Tray, Green Rooster, 9 x 6 In. 24
California Provincial, Plate, Dinner, 10 In. 20
Colorstax, Bowl, Apricot, 6 ½ In. 10
Della Robia, Cup & Saucer, 3 x 3 ⅜ In. 8
Homestead Provincial, Bread Tray, Blue, 9 x 6 In. 34
La Mancha, Plate, Salad, 8 In. 8
May Flower, Teapot, Footed, Poppytrail, Vernon, 5 Cup, 10 x 7 In. 130
Navaho, Platter, Turquoise, Brown, Round, 12 In. 35
Poppy Trail, Candlestick, White, Spiral, 4 ⅜ In., Pair 36
Purple Cow, Cookie Jar, Yellow Butterfly, Marked, 10 x 11 In. .... *illus* 69
Red Rooster, Canister, Flour, Sugar, Coffee, Tea, 4 Piece 125
Rose A Day, Cup & Saucer, Vernonware, c.1955 12
Sculptured Grape, Bowl, Vegetable, Divided, 9 ½ In. 25

METTLACH

Mettlach, Germany, is a city where the Villeroy and Boch factories worked. Steins from the firm are marked with the word *Mettlach* or the castle mark. They date from about 1842. *PUG* means painted under glaze. The steins can be dated from the marks on the bottom, which include a date-number code that can be found online. Other pieces may be listed in the Villeroy & Boch category.

Plaque, Dwarf, Book, Mushrooms, Multicolor, Etched, Signed Schlitt, 17 ½ In. 5750
Plaque, No. 1244/1044, 2 Girls & Dog, Shaded Green Ground, PUG, 17 In. 120
Plaque, No. 2899, Woman Carrying Sheaves Of Wheat In Field, Etched, 17 ¾ In. 840
Plaque, No. 2998, Woman Smelling Blossoms On Tree, Etched, 17 ¾ In. 900
Plaque, Sea Nymphs, Warrior, Mountains, Multicolor, 17 In. 1187
Pokal, Romanesque Women, Pan, Figural Boy Finial, Blue, Green, 27 In., Pair 13750
Stein, No. 228, Celebration Of Song, Relief, Inlaid Lid, ½ Liter 390
Stein, No. 952, Bicycling Scene, PUG, Inlaid Lid, ½ Liter 180
Stein, No. 1053, Gnomes, Etched, Inlaid Lid, C. Warth, 1 Liter 180
Stein, No. 1109, Soldiers Drinking Scene, Marked, Villeroy & Boch, 5 In. 270
Stein, No. 1154, Hunters, Etched, Inlaid Lid, 1 Liter 240
Stein, No. 1675, View Of Heidelberg, Etched, Pewter Mount, c.1911, ½ Liter 180
Stein, No. 1756, Student Drinking, Relief, Pewter Lid, C. Warth, 1 Liter 192

Meissen, Bowl, Basket Shape, Woven, Gilt, Floral Center, 1800s, 6 x 2 In.
$173

Blackwell Auctions

Meissen, Clock, Shelf, Cupid, Floral Encrusted Garland, Lovebirds, Gilt Bezel, 11 x 9 x 5 In.
$1,338

Clars Auction Gallery

Meissen, Figurine, Girl, Feeding Chickens, Marked, 4 ¾ In.
$90

Hartzell's Auction Gallery Inc.

Meissen, Figurine, Man, Mustache, Fur Lined Cape, Mounted, c.1930, 8 ¾ In.
$212

Bunch Auctions

Meissen, Group, 2 Women, 1 Holding Flower Garland, 2 Putti, 1800s, 9 x 7 ½ In.
$650

Hindman Auctions

Meissen, Group, Soldier Holding Severed Head, King, Putti Holding Ball, Marked, 12 x 11 In.
$2,875

Palm Beach Modern Auctions

Meissen, Group, Winter, 7 Children, Grapes, Wine Glasses, Multicolor, Oval, 9 ½ x 7 ½ x 6 ½ In.
$875

Abington Auction Gallery

Mercury Glass, Ice Bucket, Cork, Brown, Cylindrical Lid, c.1950, 15 x 9 x 9 In.
$113

Hindman Auctions

Metlox, Purple Cow, Cookie Jar, Yellow Butterfly, Marked, 10 x 11 In.
$69

Belhorn Auction Services

M

Mettlach, Stein, No. 2829, Rodenstein Castle, Village Scene, Ornate, 11 ½ In.
$750

Milestone Auctions

Mettlach, Stein, No. 2882, The Thirsty Knight, H. Schlitt, 9 ½ x 5 ½ In.
$254

Hartzell's Auction Gallery Inc.

Milk Glass, Globe, Hanging, Gilt Fitting, Art Deco Style, 22 ½ x 14 In.
$225

Hudson Valley Auctions

Millefiori, Epergne, 3 Trumpet Shape Vases, Ruffled Rim Bowl, Metal Mount, 15 ½ x 11 In.
$295

Strawser Auction Group

Millefiori, Paperweight, Whitefriars, Christmas, Angel, Blue, Yellow, Green, Pontil Mark, 1975, 3 In.
$105

Jeffrey S. Evans & Associates

Minton, Vase, Draped Classical Figures, Celadon Ground, White Pate-Sur-Pate Filigree, 15 ¾ In.
$3,328

Fontaine's Auction Gallery

Stein, No. 1757, Brewer, Relief, Pewter Lid, C. Warth, 1 Liter 216
Stein, No. 1758, Soldier Drinking, Relief, Pewter Lid, 1 Liter 510
Stein, No. 1759, Man Smoking Pipe, Relief, Inlaid Lid, 1 Liter 300
Stein, No. 1856, German Postal Eagle, Etched, Inlaid Lid, Otto Hupp, 1 Liter 1620
Stein, No. 1934, German Soldier Uniform Evolution, Etched, Inlaid Lid, ½ Liter 360
Stein, No. 1941, Saxony Coat Of Arms, Beer, Pewter Lid, 3 Liter, 14 ½ In. 7200
Stein, No. 1998, Trumpeter Of Sackingen, Etched, Relief, Inlaid Lid, ½ Liter 180
Stein, No. 2051, Student Banquet, Etched Sides, Inlaid Lid, 1890s-1910, ½ Liter, 8 ½ In. ..... 164 to 240
Stein, No. 2075, Railroad Symbols, Etched, Inlaid Lid, Otto Hupp, ½ Liter 870
Stein, No. 2098, Art Nouveau Flowers, Mosaic, Inlaid Lid, Swollen, 12 ¼ In. 240
Stein, No. 2122, Crusaders, Monks, Sun Face, Etched, Relief, C. Warth, 3 ¾ Liter, 19 In. 2400
Stein, No. 2210, Peasants Bowling, Cameo, Terra-Cotta, Blue Ground, Bulbous, 13 In. 240
Stein, No. 2285, Guitar Player, Couple, Etched, Inlaid Lid, ½ Liter 180
Stein, No. 2286, Drinker With The Owner Of Zur Linde, Etched, Inlaid Lid, 2 ½ Liter 240
Stein, No. 2382, Thirsty Knight, Etched, Inlaid Lid, H. Schlitt, ½ Liter, 9 In. 240
Stein, No. 2403, View Of Wartburg, Etched, Inlaid Lid, Pewter Mount, ½ Liter 120
Stein, No. 2480, King & Knights, Relief, Stahl, Gambrinus, Inlaid Lid, ½ Liter 180
Stein, No. 2580, Die Kannenburg, Knight, Castle, Etched, Inlaid Lid, Schlitt, ½ Liter 210
Stein, No. 2692, Drinker & Hostess, Etched, Inlaid Lid, 3 Liter, 17 In. 810
Stein, No. 2693, Drinker & Hostess, Etched, Inlaid Lid, ½ Liter 240
Stein, No. 2727, Printer, Etched, Inlaid Lid, ½ Liter 2281
Stein, No. 2766, Drinker, Etched, Inlaid Lid, ½ Liter 264
Stein, No. 2776, Cooper, Beer Cellar, Etched, Inlaid Lid, ½ Liter 300
Stein, No. 2778, Drinkers At Carnival, Etched, Inlaid Lid, 10 In. 420
Stein, No. 2780, Lovers, Etched, Inlaid, 1 Liter 300
Stein, No. 2823, Woman With Rifle, Etched, Pewter Lid, ½ Liter 120
Stein, No. 2829, Rodenstein Castle, Village Scene, Ornate, 11 ½ In. .... *illus* 750
Stein, No. 2869, Buildings In Munich, Bavarian Lion Inlaid Lid, 3 Liter, 19 In. 4080
Stein, No. 2871, Cornell University Graduate, Etched, Inlaid Lid, 1 Liter 240
Stein, No. 2882, The Thirsty Knight, H. Schlitt, 9 ½ x 5 ½ In. .... *illus* 254
Stein, No. 2921, Thieves' Campfire & Song, Etched, Inlaid Lid, 2 ¾ Liter, 15 ½ In. 300
Stein, No. 2956, Bowling, Etched, Inlaid Lid, 3 Liter, 16 ½ In. 300
Stein, No. 2966, Man Drinking On Barrel, Etched, Pewter Lid, ½ Liter 120
Stein, No. 3085, Bavarian Postman, Etched, Pewter Lid, 1 Liter 204
Stein, No. 3087, Tyrolean Woman, Etched, Pewter Lid, ½ Liter 252
Stein, No. 3282, Man With Children In Wreath, Bavaria, Inlaid Lid, ½ Liter 180
Stein, No. 5188, Dutch Drinker, Delft, Blue & White, Pewter Lid, ½ Liter 240
Vase, No. 2537, Spindly Flowers, Leaves, Elongated Oval, 12 In. 523

MILK GLASS

Milk glass was named for its milky white color. It was first made in England during the 1700s. The height of its popularity in the United States was from 1870 to 1880. It is now correct to refer to some colored glass as blue milk glass, black milk glass, etc. Reproductions of milk glass are being made and sold in many stores. Related pieces may be listed in the Cosmos, Vallerysthal, and Westmoreland categories.

Globe, Hanging, Gilt Fitting, Art Deco Style, 22 ½ x 14 In. .... *illus* 225
Jar, Barber, Lid, Gilded Flowers, Gold Trim, 3 ⅝ x 4 In. 25
Lamp, White, Mounted, Brass, Circular Base, 1900s, 20 In., Pair 225

MILLEFIORI

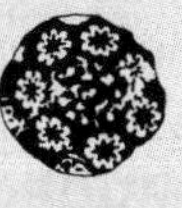

Millefiori means, literally, a thousand flowers. Many small pieces of glass resembling flowers are grouped together to form a design. It is a type of glasswork popular in paperweights and some are listed in that category.

Epergne, 3 Trumpet Shape Vases, Ruffled Rim Bowl, Metal Mount, 15 ½ x 11 In. .... *illus* 295
Lamp, Multicolor, Mushroom Shape Shade, Dome Base, 19 x 11 In. 649
Paperweight, Whitefriars, Christmas, Angel, Blue, Yellow, Green, Pontil Mark, 1975, 3 In. *illus* 105

Minton, Vase, Lid, Cupids, White Slip, Gilt, Grapevines, Pate-Sur-Pate, Albion Birks, 10 In.
$3,690

Stair Galleries

Mocha, Flask, Seaweed, Blue, Yellow, White Ground, 1829, 7 ½ In.
$3,540

Strawser Auction Group

Mocha, Mug, Red, White Bands, Handle, Footed, D.G. Carpenter, 5 ½ In.
$354

Copake Auctions

This is an edited listing of current prices. Visit **Kovels.com** to check thousands of prices from previous years and sign up for free information on trends, tips, reproductions, marks, and more.

M

Mocha, Mustard Pot, Seaweed, Salmon Field, Brown Line Border, Strap Handle, Early 1800s, 3 In.
$984

Skinner, Inc.

Mocha, Pepper Pot, Earthworm, Round Base, Pierced Lid, Yellow, White Ground, 1800s, 5 In.
$461

Skinner, Inc.

Mocha, Pepper Pot, Seaweed & Dot, Yellow Ground, Blue & Green Stripes, Footed, 1800s, 4 In.
$226

Hartzell's Auction Gallery Inc.

MINTON

Minton china was made in the Staffordshire region of England beginning in 1796. The firm became part of the Royal Doulton Tableware Group in 1968, but the wares continued to be marked *Minton*. In 2009 the brand was bought by KPS Capital Partners of New York and became part of WWRD Holdings. The company no longer makes Minton china. Many marks have been used. The word *England* was added in 1891. Minton majolica is listed in this book in the Majolica category.

Minton
c.1822–1836

Minton
c.1863–1872

Minton
1951–c.2009

Charger, Cherub, Carp, Stingray, Blue, Glazed Earthenware, William Coleman, c.1880, 10 ½ In.	1750
Plate, Cupid, Grasses, Pate-Sur-Pate Center, Reticulated Rim, Gilt, 9 In.	1625
Plate, Portrait Plate, Woman, Jewelry, Veil, Behold All My Treasures, Pink, 9 In.	160
Plate, White Slip, Maiden, Sweeping, Broom, Pate-Sur-Pate, Frame, 16 ½ x 13 ½ In.	3690
Platter, Oval, Marked Merrion Japan, Impressed New Stone, 1860s, 16 ¾ x 21 In.	82
Vase, Draped Classical Figures, Celadon Ground, White Pate-Sur-Pate Filigree, 15 ¾ In. *illus*	3328
Vase, Lid, Cupids, White Slip, Gilt, Grapevines, Pate-Sur-Pate, Albion Birks, 10 In. *illus*	3690

MIRRORS *are listed in the Furniture category under Mirror.*

MOCHA

Mocha pottery is an English-made product that was sold in America during the early 1800s. It is a heavy pottery with pale coffee-and-cream coloring. Designs of blue, brown, green, orange, black, or white were added to the pottery and given fanciful names, such as Tree, Snail Trail, or Moss. Mocha designs are sometimes found on pearlware. A few pieces of mocha ware were made in France, the United States, and other countries.

Bowl, Seaweed, Blue, White Ground, Footed, 5 In.	118
Coffeepot, Lid, Mocha, Molded Acorn Finial, Ribbed, Strap Handle, Gilt, Pearlware, c.1785, 9 ⅞ In.	878
Flask, Seaweed, Blue, Yellow, White Ground, 1829, 7 ½ In. *illus*	3540
Mug, Earthworm, Strap Handle, Yellowware, 1850s, 3 x 3 In.	819
Mug, Red, White Bands, Handle, Footed, D.G. Carpenter, 5 ½ In. *illus*	354
Mug, Seaweed, Brown Band, White Ground, Handle, 2 In., Pair	189
Mug, Seaweed, Tan Ground, Handle, Blue Wave, 1800s, 5 x 5 In.	396
Mustard Pot, Seaweed, Cylindrical, Bell Shape Lid, Orange Ground, c.1900, 4 ¾ In.	250
Mustard Pot, Seaweed, Salmon Field, Brown Line Border, Strap Handle, Early 1800s, 3 In. *illus*	984
Pepper Pot, Earthworm, Round Base, Pierced Lid, Yellow, White Ground, 1800s, 5 In. *illus*	461
Pepper Pot, Seaweed & Dot, Yellow Ground, Blue & Green Stripes, Footed, 1800s, 4 In. *illus*	226
Pitcher, Cat's-Eye, Blue Engine-Turned Bands, Handle, Early 1800s, 6 ¾ In. *illus*	1169
Pitcher, Cat's-Eye, Seaweed, Bands, Green, Blue, Orange, Handle, 6 ¾ x 8 ½ In.	1582
Pitcher, Earthworm, Cat's-Eye, Footed, Side Handle, 1800s, 5 ¾ In. *illus*	1952
Pitcher, Earthworm, Yellow Ground, White Bands, 4 ½ In. *illus*	1298
Salt, Earthworm, White, Brown Slip, Broad Blue Band, Pearlware, Footed, 1810s, 2 In. *illus*	644
Teapot, Agate Glaze, Blue, Machined Bands, Molded Acanthus Leaf Handle, c.1825, 8 In. *illus*	144

MONT JOYE, *see Mt. Joye category.*

MOORCROFT

Moorcroft pottery was first made in Burslem, England, in 1913. William Moorcroft had managed the art pottery department for James Macintyre & Company of England from 1898 to 1913. The Moorcroft pottery continues today, although William Moor-

Mocha, Pitcher, Cat's-Eye, Blue Engine-Turned Bands, Handle, Early 1800s, 6 ¾ In.
$1,169

Skinner, Inc.

Mocha, Pitcher, Earthworm, Cat's-Eye, Footed, Side Handle, 1800s, 5 ¾ In.
$1,952

Pook & Pook

Mocha, Salt, Earthworm, White, Brown Slip, Broad Blue Band, Pearlware, Footed, 1810s, 2 In.
$644

Jeffrey S. Evans & Associates

Mocha, Teapot, Agate Glaze, Blue, Machined Bands, Molded Acanthus Leaf Handle, c.1825, 8 In.
$144

Garth's Auctioneers & Appraisers

Mocha, Pitcher, Earthworm, Yellow Ground, White Bands, 4 ½ In.
$1,298

Strawser Auction Group

Moorcroft, Vase, Cobalt Blue Body, Round Rim, Floral, 1980, 12 ½ x 7 In.
$368

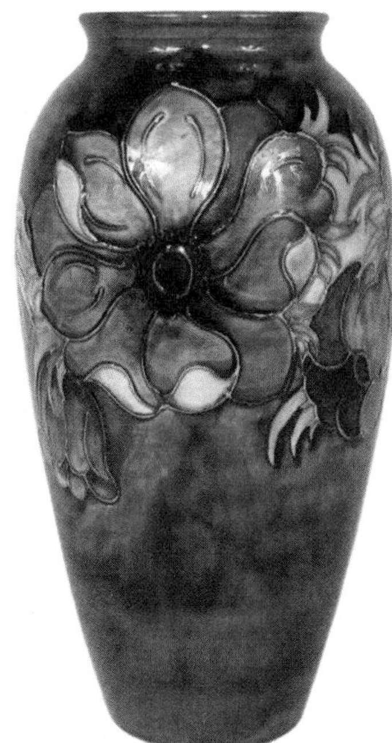

Belhorn Auction Servicese

Moorcroft, Vase, Penguins & Chicks, Gray Ground, Sally Tuffin, 1989, 10 In.
$308

Skinner, Inc.

Moorcroft, Vase, Purple, Fuchsia Flowers, Teal, Green Ground, 1953-78, 8 In.
$164

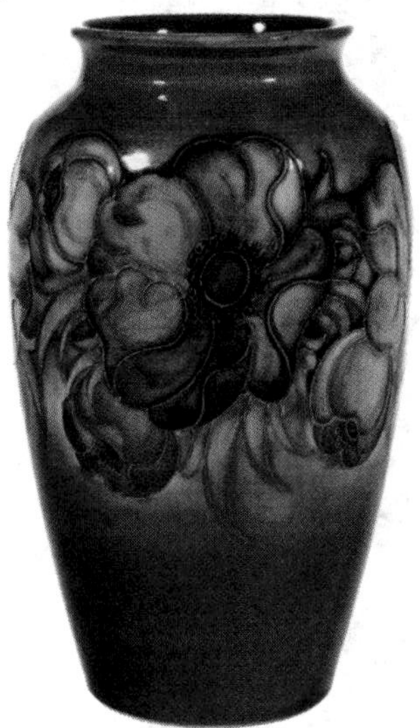

Jeffrey S. Evans & Associates

Mosaic Tile Co., Figurine, Bear, Black Glaze, Green Highlights, Impressed Logo, 5 ¾ In., Pair
$157

Humler & Nolan

Moser, Atomizer, 10-Sided, Panel Cut, Gold Scroll, Brass Lid, 8 ½ In.
$60

Woody Auctions

croft died in 1945. The earlier wares are similar to the modern ones, but color and marking will help indicate the age.

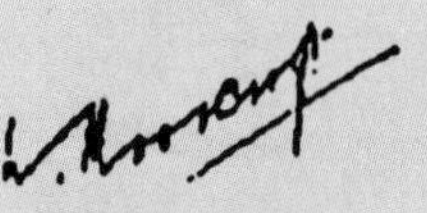

W. Moorcroft Ltd.
1898–c.1905

W. Moorcroft Ltd.
1898–1913

W. Moorcroft Ltd.
1928–1978

Ewer, Claremont, Silver Overlay, Squeezebag Decoration, Mushroom Body, c.1905, 16 x 5 ¾ In. 11531
Ice Bucket, Silver Overlay, Trees, Blue, Green, Handles, Signed, Moorcroft, Shreve Co., 8 x 12 In.... 2500
Lamp Base, Orchids, Baluster Shape, Swollen Base, White Ground, 23 ¾ x 8 ¾ In. 311
Vase, Cobalt Blue Body, Round Rim, Floral, 1980, 12 ½ x 7 In. ....*illus* 368
Vase, Lamia, Yellow Iris, Water Lilies, Cattails, Pinched Waist, Rachel Bishop, 1995, 10 x 4 ½ In..... 290
Vase, Penguins & Chicks, Gray Ground, Sally Tuffin, 1989, 10 In. ....*illus* 308
Vase, Purple, Fuchsia Flowers, Teal, Green Ground, 1953-78, 8 In. ....*illus* 164
Vase, Red Flowers, Leaves, Mottled Amber Green Ground, Signed, 17 x 11 In., Pair 4500

MORIAGE

Moriage is a special type of raised decoration used on some Japanese pottery. Sometimes pieces of clay were shaped by hand and applied to the item; sometimes the clay was squeezed from a tube the way we apply cake frosting. One type of moriage is called Dragonware by collectors.

Bowl, Lid, 3 Handles, Footed, Jeweled, Gold, Pink & Purple Roses, 7 x 7 ¾ In............................ 250
Figurine, Buddha, Red & Blue Paint, Gold Trim, 3 ½ In. 18
Humidor, Lid, Egyptian Scene, Pyramids, Palm Trees, Raised Leaves, Squat, 5 In.................... 171
Pitcher, Pink Roses, Green Ground, Beading, Raised Trim, Shaped Handle, 7 ½ In................. 207
Plate, Dragon, Flames, Raised, Mottled Gray Shaded To Green Ground, 9 ¾ In. 24
Vase, 2 Handles, Footed, Flowers, Pink, Cream, Lavender, 8 ½ x 4 ½ x 12 In............................ 181
Vase, Celadon, White Paste, Birds, Branches, Flowers, Oval, Flared Neck & Rim, 14 In............. 1000
Vase, Elongated, Yellow Ground, Flowers, Leaves, 16 ½ In.. 104
Vase, Flowers, Light Green Ground, Gold Trim, Shaped Handles, Footed, Japan, 16 In............... 24
Vase, Lamp, White Dragon, 4 Toes, Green Ground, Swirling Clouds, Wood Base, 35 ½ In. 93
Vase, Warriors, Painted, Raised Flowers, Beading, Bulbous, Flared Neck & Rim, 1800s, 16 In.. 75

MOSAIC TILE COMPANY

Mosaic Tile Company of Zanesville, Ohio, was started by Karl Langerbeck and Herman Mueller in 1894. Many types of plain and ornamental tiles were made until 1959. The company closed in 1967. The company also made some ashtrays, bookends, and related giftwares. Most pieces are marked with the entwined MTC monogram.

Figurine, Bear, Black Glaze, Green Highlights, Impressed Logo, 5 ¾ In., Pair ....*illus* 157
Figurine, Bear, White, Semigloss, Rectangular Base, MTC Logo, 9 ½ x 6 In.............................. 219

MOSER

Moser glass is made by a Bohemian glasshouse founded by Ludwig Moser in 1857. Art Nouveau–type glassware and iridescent glassware were made. The most famous Moser glass is decorated with heavy enameling in gold and bright colors. The firm, Moser Glassworks, is still working in Karlovy Vary, Czech Republic. Few pieces of Moser glass are marked.

Atomizer, 10-Sided, Panel Cut, Gold Scroll, Brass Lid, 8 ½ In. ....*illus* 60

Bell, Green, Gold Stencil Trim, Cabochon, c.1910, 5 In. 70
Bowl, Console, Faceted, Amethyst, Gilt Band, Footed, c.1925, 3 ½ x 8 In. 102
Decanter, Blue, Steeple Stopper, Gold Stencil, Cabochon, c.1910, 19 ½ In. 175
Dresser Box, Cranberry Glass, Ormolu Mount, Flowers, Leaves, Lobed, Hinged Lid, 4 ½ In. 1320
Goblet, Brandy, Amethyst, Gold Trim, Stencil, Scalloped Foot, Cabochon, c.1910, 5 In., 8 Piece 500
Goblet, Gilt, Green, Enamel, Flowers, Blown, 6 ½ In. 237
Goblet, Lid, Ruby, Ornate Gilt, Octagonal, Cabochon, Czech Republic, c.1900, 9 x 6 ¾ In. *illus* 117
Sherbet, Underplate, Cranberry Glass, Gold Flowers, Jagged Edge, 3 ½ x 5 In. 220
Tumbler, Green, Gold Trim & Stencil, Engraved Flowers, Cabochon, c.1910, 5 ½ In., Pair 125
Vase, Amethyst To Clear, Butterflies, Oak Leaves, Applied Acorns, Blown, 4 In. 275
Vase, Cranberry, Butterfly, Insects, Floral, Footed, 13 In., Pair 978
Vase, Cylindrical, Sapphire Blue, Amber Drip Rim, 7 In. 120
Vase, Peasant Couple, Cranberry Glass, Enameled, Gilt, Art Nouveau, c.1900, 10 ¾ x 5 In. *illus* 300
Vase, Trumpet Shape, Portrait, Young Woman, Green Glass, Gilt, Footed, 14 In. .... *illus* 189

MOSS ROSE

Moss Rose china was made by many firms from 1808 to 1900. It has a typical moss rose pictured as the design. The plant is not as popular now as it was in Victorian gardens, so the fuzz-covered bud is unfamiliar to most collectors. The dishes were usually decorated with pink and green flowers.

Candleholder, Cornucopia, 1950s, 3 x 4 In., Pair 16
Cup & Saucer, Swing Shape, Loop Handle, c.1941 10
Egg Cup, Scalloped, Gilt Rim, 2 ¼ In. 13
Platter, Oval, Gilt Rim, 1870s, 11 x 7 In. 53

MOTHER-OF-PEARL GLASS

Mother-of-pearl glass, or pearl satin glass, was first made in the 1850s in England and in Massachusetts. It was a special type of mold-blown satin glass with air bubbles in the glass, giving it a pearlized color. It has been reproduced. Mother-of-pearl shell objects are listed under Pearl.

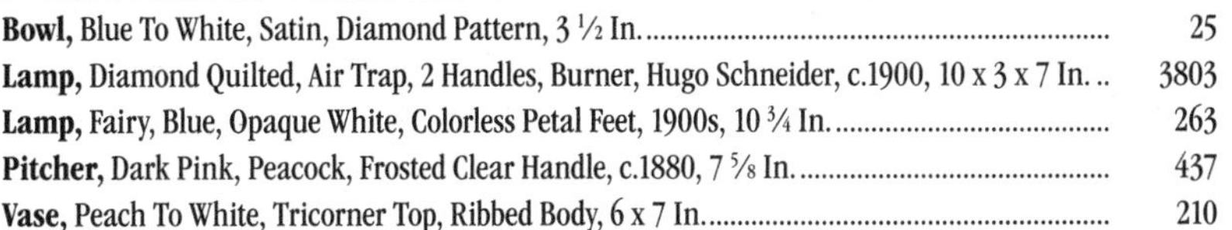

Bowl, Blue To White, Satin, Diamond Pattern, 3 ½ In. 25
Lamp, Diamond Quilted, Air Trap, 2 Handles, Burner, Hugo Schneider, c.1900, 10 x 3 x 7 In. .. 3803
Lamp, Fairy, Blue, Opaque White, Colorless Petal Feet, 1900s, 10 ¾ In. 263
Pitcher, Dark Pink, Peacock, Frosted Clear Handle, c.1880, 7 ⅝ In. 437
Vase, Peach To White, Tricorner Top, Ribbed Body, 6 x 7 In. 210

MOTORCYCLE

Motorcycles and motorcycle accessories of all types are being collected today. Examples can be found that date back to the early twentieth century. Toy motorcycles are listed in the Toy category.

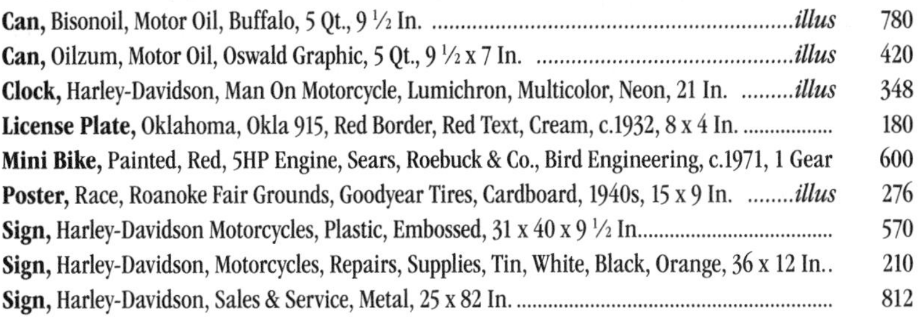

Can, Bisonoil, Motor Oil, Buffalo, 5 Qt., 9 ½ In. .... *illus* 780
Can, Oilzum, Motor Oil, Oswald Graphic, 5 Qt., 9 ½ x 7 In. .... *illus* 420
Clock, Harley-Davidson, Man On Motorcycle, Lumichron, Multicolor, Neon, 21 In. .... *illus* 348
License Plate, Oklahoma, Okla 915, Red Border, Red Text, Cream, c.1932, 8 x 4 In. 180
Mini Bike, Painted, Red, 5HP Engine, Sears, Roebuck & Co., Bird Engineering, c.1971, 1 Gear 600
Poster, Race, Roanoke Fair Grounds, Goodyear Tires, Cardboard, 1940s, 15 x 9 In. .... *illus* 276
Sign, Harley-Davidson Motorcycles, Plastic, Embossed, 31 x 40 x 9 ½ In. 570
Sign, Harley-Davidson, Motorcycles, Repairs, Supplies, Tin, White, Black, Orange, 36 x 12 In. .. 210
Sign, Harley-Davidson, Sales & Service, Metal, 25 x 82 In. 812

MOUNT WASHINGTON, *see Mt. Washington category.*

Moser, Goblet, Lid, Ruby, Ornate Gilt, Octagonal, Cabochon, Czech Republic, c.1900, 9 x 6 ¾ In.
$117

Jeffrey S. Evans & Associates

Moser, Vase, Peasant Couple, Cranberry Glass, Enameled, Gilt, Art Nouveau, c.1900, 10 ¾ x 5 In.
$300

Michaan's Auctions

Moser, Vase, Trumpet Shape, Portrait, Young Woman, Green Glass, Gilt, Footed, 14 In.
$189

Bunch Auctions

Motorcycle, Can, Bisonoil, Motor Oil, Buffalo, 5 Qt., 9 ½ In.
$780

Morphy Auctions

Motorcycle, Can, Oilzum, Motor Oil, Oswald Graphic, 5 Qt., 9 ½ x 7 In.
$420

Morphy Auctions

Motorcycle, Clock, Harley-Davidson, Man On Motorcycle, Lumichron, Multicolor, Neon, 21 In.
$348

Milestone Auctions

MOVIE

Movie memorabilia of all types are collected. Animation Art, Games, Sheet Music, Toys, and some celebrity items are listed in their own section. A lobby card is usually 11 by 14 inches, but other sizes were also made. A set of lobby cards includes seven scene cards and one title card. An American one sheet, the standard movie poster, is 27 by 41 inches. A three sheet is 40 by 81 inches. A half sheet is 22 by 28 inches. A window card, made of cardboard, is 14 by 22 inches. An insert is 14 by 36 inches. A herald is a promotional item handed out to patrons. Press books, sent to exhibitors to promote a movie, contain ads and lists of what is available for advertising, i.e., posters, lobby cards. Press kits, sent to the media, contain photos and details about the movie, i.e., stars' biographies and interviews.

Poster, Beast From Haunted Cave, Horror, Frame, 1959, 21 x 28 In. 325
Poster, King-Kong, Formidable!, French Promo, Marcel Bloch, 1942, 44 x 31 In. 18000
Poster, Led Zeppelin, Song Remains The Same, Black Ground, Frame, 43 x 29 In. 266
Poster, L'Odyssee De L'African Queen, Offset & Lithographic, 1965, 62 ½ x 47 In. ....*illus* 215
Poster, Passage To Marseille, Humphrey Bogart, Warner Bros., 1944, 41 x 27 In. 240
Poster, What'll You Do After You Graduate?, Dustin Hoffman, The Graduate, Vista, 1968 420
Sign, Hotel Waldron, Manhattan Murder Mystery, Black Ground, Woody Allen, c.1993, 25 x 13 In. 125

MT. JOYE

Mt. Joye is an enameled cameo glass made in the late nineteenth and twentieth centuries by Saint-Hilaire Touvier de Varraux and Co. of Pantin, France. This same company made De Vez glass. Pieces were usually decorated with enameling. Most pieces are not marked.

Vase, Amethyst To Clear, Wavy Top, Round, Raised Flowers, 7 In. 228
Vase, Cylindrical, Acid Etched Ground, Enamel, Gilt, Flowers, 13 ¾ x 5 ½ In., Pair 452
Vase, Green, Enamel Gold Flowers, Jack-In-The-Pulpit Shape, 12 In. 120
Vase, Lavender, Shading To Clear, Cylinder, Twist Shape, Flowers, 10 In. 240

MT. WASHINGTON

Mt. Washington Glass Works started in 1837 in South Boston, Massachusetts. In 1870 the company moved to New Bedford, Massachusetts. Many types of art glass were made there until 1894, when the company merged with Pairpoint Manufacturing Co. Amberina, Burmese, Crown Milano, Cut Glass, Peachblow, and Royal Flemish are each listed in their own category.

Biscuit Jar, Silver Lid & Handle, Melon Shape, Green, Flowers, 7 In. ....*illus* 153
Bride's Basket, Enamel Fruits, Gilt Leaves, Folded Rim, Silver Plate Stand, 8 ½ In. ....*illus* 678
Bride's Basket, Ruffled Rim, Flowers, Silver Plate Frame, Paw Feet, 8 ½ x 10 In. 60
Bride's Bowl, Amberina, Flowers, Butterflies & Leaves, Silver Plate Frame, 15 x 12 In. ....*illus* 1888
Bride's Bowl, Satin, Diamond Quilted, Flowers, Cherubs, Wilcox Silver Plate Base, 15 In. 2478
Cologne Bottle, Diamond & Star, Ball Shape Stopper, Hobstar Base, 5 ½ In. 125
Cologne Bottle, Stopper, Satin, Gold Floral, Enamel, Smith Bros., 5 In. 502
Cruet, Burmese, Opaque Handle, Stopper, Pontil Mark, c.1900, 6 ¾ In. ....*illus* 176
Pitcher, White Satin, Enamel, Thistle & Beetle, 8 ¾ In. 72
Rose Bowl, Burmese, Multicolor, Flower, Pontil Mark, c.1900, 5 x 5 ½ In. 105
Sugar Shaker, White Satin, Flowers, Copper Lid, 5 In. 72
Syrup, Opaque Glass, Multicolor, Egg Shape, Silver Plate Lid, Handle, c.1900, 5 In. ....*illus* 199
Toothpick Holder, Milk Glass, Square Rim, Flowers, c. 1880, 2 ½ In. 150
Vase, Napoli, Clear, Poppy Decor, Gilt Rim, 3 ½ x 6 ¾ In. ....*illus* 180
Vase, Pink Satin, Curved Neck, Footed, 11 ½ In., Pair 130

MULLER FRERES

Muller Freres, French for Muller Brothers, made cameo and other glass

Motorcycle, Poster, Race, Roanoke Fair Grounds, Goodyear Tires, Cardboard, 1940s, 15 x 9 In.
$276

Milestone Auctions

Movie, Poster, L'Odyssee De L'African Queen, Offset & Lithographic, 1965, 62 ½ x 47 In.
$215

Clars Auction Gallery

Mt. Washington, Biscuit Jar, Silver Lid & Handle, Melon Shape, Green, Flowers, 7 In.
$153

Strawser Auction Group

Mt. Washington,Bride's Basket, Enamel Fruits, Gilt Leaves, Folded Rim, Silver Plate Stand, 8 ½ In.
$678

Soulis Auctions

Mt. Washington, Bride's Bowl, Amberina, Flowers, Butterflies & Leaves, Silver Plate Frame, 15 x 12 In.
$1,888

Strawser Auction Group

Mt. Washington, Cruet, Burmese, Opaque Handle, Stopper, Pontil Mark, c.1900, 6 ¾ In.
$176

Jeffrey S. Evans & Associates

Mt. Washington, Syrup, Opaque Glass, Multicolor, Egg Shape, Silver Plate Lid, Handle, c.1900, 5 In.
$199

Jeffrey S. Evans & Associates

Mt. Washington, Vase, Napoli, Clear, Poppy Decor, Gilt Rim, 3 ½ x 6 ¾ In.
$180

Woody Auctions

Muller Freres, Vase, 2 Arab Men, Woman Seated, Landscape, Blue, Yellow, Cameo, Signed, 13 ½ In.
$11,192

Humler & Nolan

Muller Freres, Vase, Lily Pond, Frog, Bulbous Body, Light Red Shading, Cream Ground, Cameo, 17 ¾ In.
$900

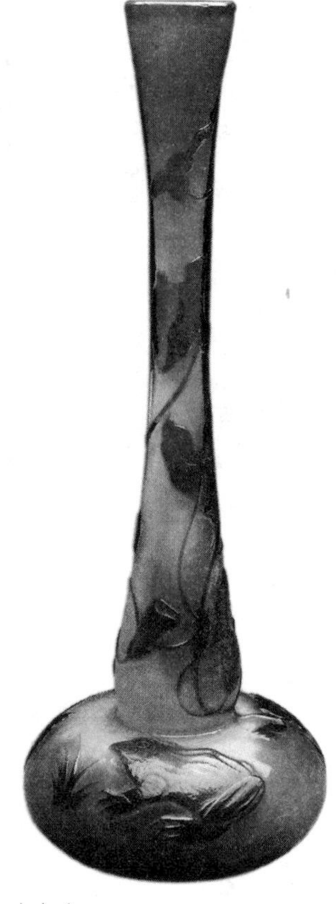

Morphy Auctions

Muncie, Vase, Aorta, Green Over Orange, Spanish Line, 6 In.
$83

Strawser Auction Group

Music, Accordion, Accordiana, Excelsior, Leather Strap, Case, 23 x 18 x 19 In.
$95

Copake Auctions

Music, Accordion, Giulietti, Black Plastic, Faux Mother-Of-Pearl Keys, Case, 20 x 22 x 10 In.
$1,169

Locati Auctions

Music, Box, B.A. Bremond, 3 Cylinders, Inlaid, Integral Base, Stand, Swiss, 1800s, 35 x 42 x 17 In.
$3,000

Neal Auction Company

TIP

The longer the cylinder on an old music box, the higher the price.

Music, Box, Etouffoirs En Acier, Cylinder, Inlay, 8 Tunes, 16 ¾ x 7 ¾ x 5 ½ In.
$295

Bunch Auctions

Music, Box, Olympia, Double Comb, Disc, Winter Scene, Carved Mahogany Case, 22 x 19 x 12 In.
$1,440

Milestone Auctions

Music, Box, Orchestral Style, 6 Bells, Drum, Walnut Case, Table Stand, B.A. Bremond, Swiss, c.1880
$5,412

Charlton Hall Auctions

from about 1895 to 1933. Their factory was first located in Luneville, then in nearby Croismare, France. Pieces were usually marked with the company name.

Chandelier, 3-Light, 4 Bulbs, Iron, Black & Orange Art Glass Shade, 1900s, 36 x 27 In. 182
Lamp, Bird, Standing, Iron, Red & Blue Glass, Marble Base, Chapelle Nancy, c.1925, 14 In....... 3198
Lamp, Pheasant, Openwork Bronze Body, Blue, Yellow, Orange, Marble Foot, 16 x 24 x 5 ¾ In. 3600
Vase, 2 Arab Men, Woman Seated, Landscape, Blue, Yellow, Cameo, Signed, 13 ½ In. .....*illus* 11192
Vase, Etched & Enameled, Silver & Gold, Signed, 6 ½ x 6 In. 861
Vase, Lily Pond, Frog, Bulbous Body, Light Red Shading, Cream Ground, Cameo, 17 ¾ In. *illus* 900

MUNCIE

Muncie Clay Products Company was established by Charles Benham in Muncie, Indiana, in 1918. The company made pottery for the florist and giftshop trade. Art pottery was made beginning in 1922. Rombic is pottery made by this company and Ruba Rombic is glass made by the Consolidated Glass Company. Both were designed by Reuben Haley. The company closed by 1939. Pieces are marked with the name *Muncie* or just with a system of numbers and letters, like *1A*.

Vase, Aorta, Green Over Orange, Spanish Line, 6 In. ....*illus* 83

MURANO, *see Glass-Venetian category.*

MUSIC

Music boxes and musical instruments are listed here. Phonograph records, jukeboxes, phonographs, and sheet music are listed in other categories in this book.

Accordion, Accordiana, Excelsior, Leather Strap, Case, 23 x 18 x 19 In. ....*illus* 95
Accordion, Giulietti, Black Plastic, Faux Mother-Of-Pearl Keys, Case, 20 x 22 x 10 In. ....*illus* 1169
Amplifier, Fender, Twin, 10 Band Equalizer, Handle, Foot Pedal, 52 ¾ x 26 x 10 ¾ In. 295
Box, B.A. Bremond, 3 Cylinders, Inlaid, Integral Base, Stand, Swiss, 1800s, 35 x 42 x 17 In.. *illus* 3000
Box, Cylinder, 6 Bells, Hinged Lid, Rosewood Case, 12 Tunes, c.1880, 13 x 25 x 14 ½ In. 1170
Box, Cylinder, Burl, Ebony Case, Hinged Lid, Swiss, 5 ½ x 18 x 8 ½ In. 450
Box, Cylinder, Figural Automaton Strikers, Bell, Organ, Swiss, 1903, 15 x 34 x 14 In. 10925
Box, Cylinder, Hinged Lid, Wood Case, Swiss, 4 ¾ x 15 x 7 ½ In. 600
Box, Cylinder, Satinwood, Floral Inlaid Top, Mandoline Tremolo, 8 Tunes, Swiss, 6 x 9 x 22 In.. 726
Box, Cylinder, Wood Case, 10 Tunes, Late 1800s, 20 In. 325
Box, Etouffoirs En Acier, Cylinder, Inlay, 8 Tunes, 16 ¾ x 7 ¾ x 5 ½ In. ....*illus* 295
Box, Kalliope, Disc, 10 Bells, Walnut Case, Comb Movement, 7 ½ x 16 x 15 In. 1513
Box, Langdorff, 4 Cylinders, 2-Spring Motor, Trumpet Turned Legs, Table, c.1890, 47 In. 3444
Box, Mermod Freres, Inlay, Musical Instruments, Flowers, Wood, Tune Card, 10 x 21 In. 900
Box, Olympia, Double Comb, Disc, Winter Scene, Carved Mahogany Case, 22 x 19 x 12 In. *illus* 1440
Box, Orchestral Style, 6 Bells, Drum, Walnut Case, Table Stand, B.A. Bremond, Swiss, c.1880 . *illus* 5412
Box, Organ Shape, Baroque Style, Clock Center, Walnut Inlaid Bottom, 1700s, 33 x 21 In. 469
Box, Paillard, Cylinder, Rosewood, 12 Tunes, Geneva, Swiss, c.1885, 22 x 8 ½ x 6 In. 1150
Box, Polyphon, Floral Inlaid Top, Single Comb Mechanism, 14 Discs, 15 ½ In. 338
Box, Regina, Disc Type, Mahogany Case, Raised Panels, Coin-Operated, c.1900, 75 ½ x 43 x 17 In... 5850
Box, Regina, Double Comb, Mahogany Case, 17 Discs, 11 x 17 In. ....*illus* 944
Box, Regina, Double Comb, Mahogany Case, Wood Stand, 1800s, 34 x 25 x 22 In. ....*illus* 2500
Box, Reginaphone Style, Crank, Morning Glory Horn, Mahogany Case, c.1900, 15 ½ x 17 In.... 1404
Box, Singing Bird, 2 Birds, Brass Cage, Hanging, Ornate Multicolor Stand, Key, 73 x 20 x 13 In. 2118
Box, Singing Bird, Automaton, Brass Cage, Karl Griesbaum, 11 ½ x 6 ½ In. 215
Box, Singing Bird, Brass Case, Wire Cage, Plumage, Clockwork Mechanism, 1900s, 11 In. 800
Box, Singing Bird, Coffin Shape, Silver Gilt, Bird Seller, Gem Set, Birdcages, Germany, c.1890, 8 In.. 9100
Box, Singing Bird, Enameled, Painted, 1800s, 1 ½ x 4 In. ....*illus* 2200
Box, Singing Bird, Gilt, Birdcage, Footed, Marked, 11 ½ x 6 In. ....*illus* 277
Case, Viola, Red Leather Exterior, Green Velvet Interior, W.E Hill & Sons, 15 ½ In. 400
Drum, Militia, Eagle & Shield, Handwritten Label, Nathan Darling, Groton, 17 x 17 In. 2760

Music, Box, Regina, Double Comb, Mahogany Case, 17 Discs, 11 x 17 In.
$944

Cottone Auctions

Music, Box, Regina, Double Comb, Mahogany Case, Wood Stand, 1800s, 34 x 25 x 22 In.
$2,500

Cowan's Auctions

Music, Box, Singing Bird, Enameled, Painted, 1800s, 1 ½ x 4 In.
$2,200

Hindman Auctions

Music, Box, Singing Bird, Gilt, Birdcage, Footed, Marked, 11 ½ x 6 In.
$277

Clars Auction Gallery

Music, Dulcimer, Wood, Orb Shape, Heart, Carved, 31 In.
$52

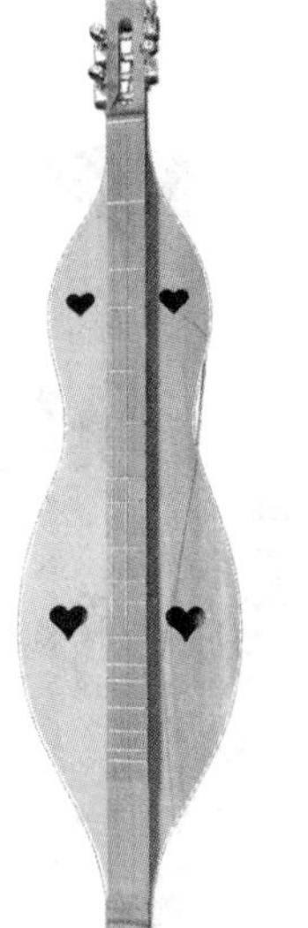

Apple Tree Auction Center

Music, Guitar, Ruan, Fretted Neck, Circular Body, 4 Strings, Chinese, 25 In.
$52

Apple Tree Auction Center

Music, Harp, Regency, Hardwood, Giltwood, Gilt Bronze, Christian Erard, c.1815, 67 x 30 In.
$2,125

New Orleans Auction Galleries

Music, Harp, Regency, Single Action, Pedal, Empire, Sebastian Erard, c.1818, 65 In.
$1,181

Clars Auction Gallery

Drum, Wood, Patches, Eagle, Carl Fischer, New York, 16 3/8 In. 147
Dulcimer, Wood, Orb Shape, Heart, Carved, 31 In. *illus* 52
Flute, No. 15 Piazza, Silver Rim, Rosewood, Leather Case, Rudall & Rosh, c.1840, 12 x 4 In. 3803
Flute, Silver, Case, Wm. S. Haynes Co., Boston, 1964, 28 In. 2214
Flute, Wood, Carved & Ebonized, Black Tip, 15 3/4 In. 62
Guitar, Flamenco, Cedar Top, Rosewood Back & Sides, Aaron Green, 1999, 26 In. 2583
Guitar, Gibson, Mahogany Flat Top, Tortoise Binding, Signed, c.1966, 19 x 14 x 40 In. 666
Guitar, Martin, Dreadnought, Acoustic, 6 Strings, V Shape Neck 1534
Guitar, Ruan, Fretted Neck, Circular Body, 4 Strings, Chinese, 25 In. *illus* 52
Harp, Regency, Hardwood, Giltwood, Gilt Bronze, Christian Erard, c.1815, 67 x 30 In. *illus* 2125
Harp, Regency, Single Action, Pedal, Empire, Sebastian Erard, c.1818, 65 In. *illus* 1181
Harp, Semi-Grand, 8 Pedals, Gilt, Filigree, Flowers, Paw Feet, J.F. Browne & Co., 69 x 44 In. 4800
Mandolin, Folk Art, 4 Strings, Carved Neck, Stylized Greenman Face, c.1900, 36 In. 270
Mandolin, Mahogany Neck, Ebony Bridge, Tiger Maple, Lyon & Healy, 25 x 10 In. 3075
Organ, Chautauqua Roller, Cherry Case, 12 1/2 x 18 x 15 In. 197
Organ, Hand Roller, Walnut Case, Filigree, Melodia, Gately & Co., 11 1/2 x 12 x 10 In. *illus* 182
Piano, Baby Grand, Marshall & Wendell, Mahogany, Multicolor Rosettes, 68 x 56 1/2 x 60 In. 1984
Piano, Baby Grand, Sojin, Ebony Finish, Bench, 3 Pedals, 57 1/2 x 68 1/2 x 40 In. 403
Piano, Baby Grand, Steinway & Sons, Ornamental, Tubular Metallic Action Frame 3050
Piano, Baby Grand, Steinway & Sons, Tubular Metallic Frame, 1920, 39 x 77 x 54 In. *illus* 4600
Piano, Baby Grand, Steinway & Sons, Walnut Case, Marlborough Feet, Casters, 38 x 66 In. 5904
Piano, Grand, Chickering, Rosewood, Open Fretwork, Fluted Legs, 1850s, 38 x 81 x 56 In. 875
Piano, Grand, Kawai, K Series, Ebonized, Brass Pedals, Casters, Bench, 72 x 57 1/2 x 72 In. 3300
Piano, Grand, Steinway & Sons, Mahogany Case, Casters Feet, 1924, 38 1/2 x 67 In. 9840
Piano, Grand, Steinway & Sons, Model M, Mahogany, Square Tapered Legs, 39 x 58 x 66 In. 2950
Saxophone, Gold, Engraved Flower, Leaves, Buffet Crampon Cie, Case, 24 x 11 In., Pair *illus* 468
Ukulele, Koa Wood, 4 Strings, Case, Hawaii, K. Kamaka, 26 1/2 In. 575
Violin, Guarneri Model, Red Brown Varnish, Case & Bow, Joseph H. Schellinger, 1892, 23 In. 1112
Violin, Kurt Lothar Meisel, Owatonna, 2001, 14 In. 2460
Violin, Matchstick, Linear, Geometric, Scroll, Tailpiece, Folk Art, Early 1900s, 24 1/2 In. 1107
Violin, Wood, Carved, Jerome Thibouville-Lamy, France, 24 x 8 In. 847
Violin, Wood, Carved, String Inlay, Case, 31 1/2 x 9 x 3 3/4 In. 363
Violoncello, Roderich Paesold, Red Varnish, Model No. 602, 29 1/2 In. 492

MUSTACHE CUP

Mustache cups were popular from 1850 to 1900 when the large, flowing mustache was in style. A ledge of china or silver held the hair out of the liquid in the cup. This kept the mustache tidy and also kept the mustache wax from melting. Old left-handed mustache cups are rare and have been reproduced since the 1960s.

Grass, Cream Ground, Black Mark, Saucer, Belleek, 3 1/4 x 3 5/8 In. 157
Rose, Pink, Flowers, RS Prussia, 3 1/2 x 3 1/2 In. 30
Tapestry, Castle Scene, Saucer, Royal Bayreuth, c.1900, 3 x 4 In. 169

MZ AUSTRIA

MZ Austria

MZ Austria is the wording on a mark used by Moritz Zdekauer on porcelains made at his works in Altrolau, Austria, from 1884 to 1909. The mark was changed to MZ *Altrolau* in 1909, when the firm was purchased by C.M. Hutschenreuther. The firm operated under the name Altrolau Porcelain Factories from 1909 to 1945. It was nationalized after World War II. The pieces were decorated with lavish floral patterns and overglaze gold decoration. Full sets of dishes were made as well as vases, toilet sets, and other wares.

Cake Plate, Pink Flowers, Gold Trim, 2 Gold Handles, 9 x 9 In. 25
Pitcher, Handle, Green & White, Daffodils, 7 5/8 In. 25
Tray, Pen, Bone Shape, Light Blue, Pink Roses, Gold Border, 9 x 3 1/2 In. 24

Music, Organ, Hand Roller, Walnut Case, Filigree, Melodia, Gately & Co., 11 1/2 x 12 x 10 In.
$182

Fontaine's Auction Gallery

Music, Piano, Baby Grand, Steinway & Sons, Tubular Metallic Frame, 1920, 39 x 77 x 54 In.
$4,600

Blackwell Auctions

Music, Saxophone, Gold, Engraved Flower, Leaves, Buffet Crampon Cie, Case, 24 x 11 In., Pair
$468

Cordier Auctions

Nanking, Tray, Blue & White, Flowers, Reticulated Edge, c.1850, 10 ¾ x 9 ½ In.
$150

Eldred's

Napkin Ring, Silver, Oval, Wreath, Ribbon, Greek Key, Monogram, Faberge, 1800s, 2 In.
$420

Brunk Auctions

Nautical, Bell, Yacht, Tanaquill, Bronze Clapper, Mast Mounting Bracket, Mid 1900s, 12 x 13 In.
$761

Thomaston Place Auction Galleries

NAILSEA

Nailsea glass was made in the Bristol district in England from 1788 to 1873. The name also applies to glass made by many different factories, not just the Nailsea Glass House. Many pieces were made with loopings of either white or colored glass as decoration.

Basket, Pink & White, Tricornered, Ruffled Rim, Clear Applied Handle, 7 In. 72
Fairy Lamp, Blue & Cranberry, Lamp Cup, Candle Cup, c.1900, 3 ⅛ In., Pair 702

NAKARA

NAKARA

Nakara is a trade name for a white glassware made about 1900 by the C. F. Monroe Company of Meriden, Connecticut. It was decorated in pastel colors. The glass was very similar to another glass, called Wave Crest, made by the company. The company closed in 1916. Boxes for use on a dressing table are the most commonly found Nakara pieces. The mark is not found on every piece.

Dresser Box, Collars & Cuffs, Hinged Lid, Green Ground, Pink & Red Flowers, c.1900, 8 x 6 In. 1200
Dresser Box, Diamond Shape, Daisies, Pink, 3 ½ x 3 ¼ In. 300
Napkin Ring, Blue Ground, Pink & Cream Shapes, White Enamel Beads, 2 ¼ In. 300

NANKING

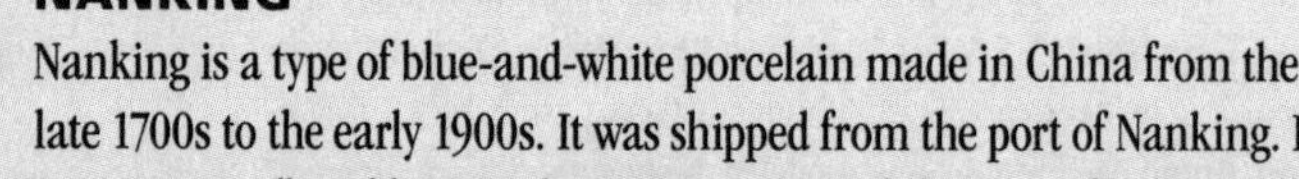

Nanking is a type of blue-and-white porcelain made in China from the late 1700s to the early 1900s. It was shipped from the port of Nanking. It is similar to Canton wares (listed here in the Canton category), but it is of better quality. The blue design was almost the same, a landscape, building, trees, and a bridge. But a person was sometimes on the bridge on a Nanking piece. The "spear and post" border was used, sometimes with gold added. Nanking sells for more than Canton.

Tray, Blue & White, Flowers, Reticulated Edge, c.1850, 10 ¾ x 9 ½ In. .... *illus* 150
Tureen, Lid, Scenic, Blue, White, 2 Handles, Footed, 1800s, 4 ¾ x 8 In. 154

NAPKIN RINGS

Napkin rings were in fashion from 1869 to about 1900. They were made of silver, porcelain, wood, and other materials. They are still being made today. Collectors pay the highest prices for the silver plated figural examples. Small, realistic figures were made to hold the ring. Good and poor reproductions of the more expensive rings have been made since the 1950s and collectors must be very careful.

Bakelite, Dog, Scottie, Black, Rodded Amber Color Eyes, 2 x 2 ¾ In. 50
Cut Glass, Middlesex, American Brilliant, 2 x 2 ½ In. 24
Cut Glass, Middlesex, Hawkes, 2 In. 24
Figural, Silver Plate, Chair, Applied Ring, Engraved Leaves, 4 ⅜ x 1 ¾ In. 65
Figural, Silver Plate, Fox, Oak Tree, Derby Silver, Footed, 3 In. 96
Figural, Silver Plate, Girl, Skater, Children At Play, Repro, Lance, 1979, 3 ½ In. 49
Figural, Silver Plate, Hunter, Dog, Rip Van Winkle, Simpson, Hall & Miller, Victorian, 5 ½ In. 800
Silver, Nursery Rhyme, Goosey Gander, Paye & Baker, c.1920, 2 x 2 In. 213
Silver, Oval, Wreath, Ribbon, Greek Key, Monogram, Faberge, 1800s, 2 In. .... *illus* 420

NATZLER

Natzler pottery was made by Gertrud Amon and Otto Natzler. They were born in Vienna, met in 1933, and established a studio in 1935. Gertrud threw thin-walled, simple, classical shapes on the wheel, while Otto developed glazes. A few months after Hitler's regime occupied Austria in 1938, they married and fled to the United States. The Natzlers set up a workshop in Los Angeles. After Gertrud's death in 1971, Otto continued creating pieces decorated with his distinctive glazes. Otto died in 2007.

Bowl, Mottled Red Over Black, Fluted Rim, Signed, 2 x 6 In. 2430
Bowl, Round, Light Blue, Beveled Rim, Round Foot, 4 x 5 In. 330

NAUTICAL

Nautical antiques are listed in this category. Any of the many objects that were made or used by the seafaring trade, including ship parts, models, and tools, are included. Other pieces may be found listed under Scrimshaw.

Bell, Yacht, Tanaquill, Bronze Clapper, Mast Mounting Bracket, Mid 1900s, 12 x 13 In. *illus* 761
Binnacle, Brass, Helmet Style, Compass, Mounted, Wood Base, 1800s, 11 x 11 In. *illus* 234
Binnacle, Brass, Iron, Mahogany, Compass, Adjustable Prism, H. Hughes & Son, 19 x 17 In. 1230
Binnacle, Copper, Compass, Tin Burner Lamp, Handle, E.S. Ritchie, 1800s, 9 x 8 In. 156
Binnacle, Yacht, Brass Case, Whale Oil Lamps, Gimbal Compass, 1800s, 14 x 10 x 9 In. 527
Boat Motor, Evinrude, Painted Wood Stand, Lightfour Start, 56 x 25 In. *illus* 360
Boat, Wood, Glass Case, E. Boston Co., 13 x 39 x 10 ½ In. 192
Chart Box, Pine, Flat, Graphite, Incised Sailing Ship, Flag, Shield, 1810s, 4 x 21 x 13 In. 344
Chart Box, Whaling Ship's, Bark Peri, NBF, Pine, Green, Hinged Lid, Iron Hasp, 11 x 36 In. 644
Chronometer, Brass Gimbals, Key Wind Chain, Wood Case, Thomas Mercer, 6 ¾ x 7 ¾ x 7 In. 904
Chronometer, Brass, Samuell Brothers & Co., Liverpool, Mahogany, Inscription, c.1875, 6 In. *illus* 875
Clock & Barometer, Brass, Silver Dial, 8-Day Chelsea Movement, John Bliss & Co., 5 ½ In. 1230
Clock, Naval, Brass Case, White Face, Mounting Hole, Cover, CCCP, Russia, 8 ⅜ x 7 In. 96
Clock, Ship's Bell, Brass Case, White Dial, Roman Numerals, Seth Thomas, 1900s, 6 In. 225
Clock, Ship's Bell, Chelsea Clock Co., Brass Case, Mahogany Base, 7 ¾ x 8 ½ x 4 ¾ In. 554
Clock, Ship's, Bell, Chelsea, Brass Case, Dial, Key, Numerals, 1901, 6 x 8 ½ In. 460
Clock, Ship's, Bell, Chelsea, Brass, Steel Dial, Crystal, Early 1900s, 5 ½ In. 480
Clock, Ship's, Bell, Chelsea, Mariner, Yacht Wheel, Silver Arabic Numerals, Mahogany Case, 14 In. *illus* 677
Compass, Brass Frame, Mahogany Case, Paper Label In Lid, Richard Patten, 15 x 8 In. 649
Compass, Ship's, Brass, Red, Wood Box, 9 x 9 x 14 In. 207
Compass, Ship's, Copper & Glass, Case, Swing Handle, Ritchie, 10 In. 277
Diorama, Sailing Ship, Painted, Mounted, Backboard, Carved, 12 x 14 x 3 In. 176
Ditty Box, Hinged Lid, Mahogany, Bone Label, Drawer, Civil War, 1800s, 6 x 14 In. *illus* 660
Diving Helmet, Brass & Copper, 14 x 18 In., On 43-In. Base *illus* 1800
Figurehead, Maiden, Carved Wood, Ocher, Crimson & Black Paint, 1900s, 38 x 15 In. *illus* 936
Foghorn, 3 Cylinder Brass Whistle, Bellows, Wood Top, E.A. Gill, 1800s, 13 x 16 x 5 In. 380
Foghorn, TyFon, Brass, Hand Operated, Malmo, Sweden, 24 In. *illus* 374
Half-Model, Dungeness, Iron Ship, Multicolor, 1900s, 11 ¾ x 57 ½ In. 352
Half-Model, Hull, Mahogany Board, Green, White, 1900s, 45 In. 1046
Half-Model, Mounted, 10 Lifts, Oak Backboard, 1800s, 8 ½ x 51 In. 900
Half-Model, Wooden Hull, Mahogany, Maple, Planked Construction, 3 x 15 x 21 In. 117
Hat, Royal Navy, Bicorn Cocked, Black Felt, Metal Case, Gieves, c.1920, 6 ½ x 16 In. 185
Lantern, Brass, Clear Glass Lens, Swing Handle, 1900s, 24 In. *illus* 330
Life Preserver, Blue, Yellow, Rope, Mounted, Metal Bracket, 28 In. 144
Light, Brass Case, Red Globe, Marked, Port Bow Light, 6 In. *illus* 68
Medical Chest, Tin, Stenciled SS Oceanic 1899 White Star Line, Opium, 9 x 13 x 9 ½ In. *illus* 1875
Model, Clipper Ship, Red Jacket, Oak & Glass Case, c.1900, 30 x 40 x 17 In. *illus* 439
Model, Dos Amigos, 2-Masted, Brown Stained Hull, Case, 1950s, 30 x 41 x 16 In. *illus* 1500
Model, Marine Steam Engine, Handmade, Plastic & Oak Case, c.1910, 9 x 12 ½ x 9 ½ In. *illus* 936
Model, Racing Yacht, Wood Hull, Rigged Cloth Sails, Deck Hardware, Cradle, 65 x 68 x 10 In. 293
Model, Sailboat, Schooner, Wood Sails, Lifeboats, Oak Base, c.1900, 28 x 31 In. *illus* 976
Model, Ship, 2-Masted, Fully Rigged, Flags, Painted Wood, Glass Case, 16 x 16 In. 308
Model, Ship, Ocean Liner, 2-Masted, 3-Stacked, Wood Hull, 1900s, 26 ½ x 35 In. 276
Model, Ship, Schooner, Glass & Wood Case, 1900s, 26 x 11 x 35 In. *illus* 1563
Model, Ship, White Sail, Green Base, Carved & Painted, Wood, 34 In. *illus* 923
Model, Ship, Wood, Carved, 5-Masted, 3 Lifeboats, Stand, Shelf, 1800s, 52 x 33 In. *illus* 189
Model, Steamboat, Paddle Wheel, Brass Boiler, Painted Wood, Tin, 42 In. 677
Model, Steamboat, Robert E. Lee, Miniature Passengers, Wood, Glass Case, 8 ½ x 24 In. 1910
Model, Steamship, Ironclad Ramship, Hardwood, Brass, Display Crew, Bristol, 29 ½ x 48 In. 1800
Model, Steamship, SS Bear, Painted, Rectangular Base, Early 1900s, 9 ½ x 20 In. 336
Model, Tugboat, Hand Carved, Wood Stand, Bumper, Metal Whistle, 10 x 27 ½ In. 293

Nautical, Binnacle, Brass, Helmet Style, Compass, Mounted, Wood Base, 1800s, 11 x 11 In.
$234

Thomaston Place Auction Galleries

Nautical, Boat Motor, Evinrude, Painted Wood Stand, Lightfour Start, 56 x 25 In.
$360

Rich Penn Auctions

Nautical, Chronometer, Brass, Samuell Brothers & Co., Liverpool, Mahogany, Inscription, c.1875, 6 In.
$875

Eldred's

N

Nautical, Clock, Ship's, Bell, Chelsea, Mariner, Yacht Wheel, Silver Arabic Numerals, Mahogany Case, 14 In.
$677

Skinner, Inc.

Nautical, Figurehead, Maiden, Carved Wood, Ocher, Crimson & Black Paint, 1900s, 38 x 15 In.
$936

Thomaston Place Auction Galleries

Nautical, Lantern, Brass, Clear Glass Lens, Swing Handle, 1900s, 24 In.
$330

Eldred's

TIP
Wear cotton gloves when cleaning any type of metal. Oils in the skin will leave a mark.

Nautical, Ditty Box, Hinged Lid, Mahogany, Bone Label, Drawer, Civil War, 1800s, 6 x 14 In.
$660

CRN Auctions

Nautical, Light, Brass Case, Red Globe, Marked, Port Bow Light, 6 In.
$68

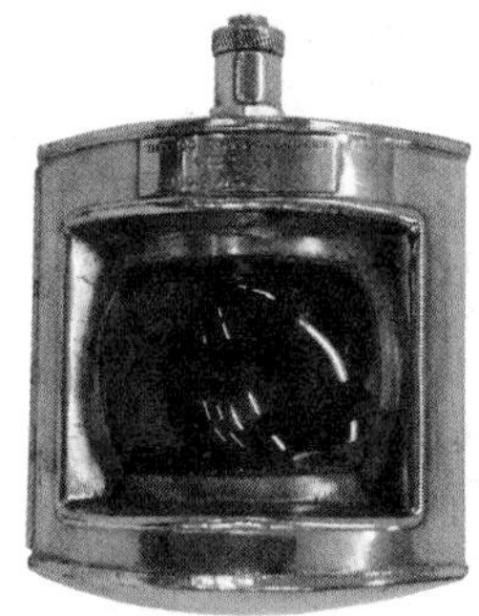

Hartzell's Auction Gallery Inc.

Nautical, Diving Helmet, Brass & Copper, 14 x 18 In., On 43-In. Base
$1,800

Wolfs Gallery

Nautical, Foghorn, TyFon, Brass, Hand Operated, Malmo, Sweden, 24 In.
$374

Apple Tree Auction Center

Nautical, Medical Chest, Tin, Stenciled SS Oceanic 1899 White Star Line, Opium, 9 x 13 x 9 ½ In.
$1,875

Eldred's

TIP
When cleaning or repairing antiques, remember less is more.

Nautical, Model, Clipper Ship, Red Jacket, Oak & Glass Case, c.1900, 30 x 40 x 17 In.
$439

Thomaston Place Auction Galleries

Nautical, Model, Dos Amigos, 2-Masted, Brown Stained Hull, Case, 1950s, 30 x 41 x 16 In.
$1,500

Eldred's

Nautical, Model, Marine Steam Engine, Handmade, Plastic & Oak Case, c.1910, 9 x 12 ½ x 9 ½ In.
$936

Thomaston Place Auction Galleries

Nautical, Model, Sailboat, Schooner, Wood Sails, Lifeboats, Oak Base, c.1900, 28 x 31 In.
$976

Pook & Pook

Nautical, Model, Ship, Schooner, Glass & Wood Case, 1900s, 26 x 11 x 35 In.
$1,563

Freeman's Auctioneers & Appraisers

Nautical, Model, Ship, White Sail, Green Base, Carved & Painted, Wood, 34 In.
$923

Skinner, Inc.

Nautical, Model, Ship, Wood, Carved, 5-Masted, 3 Lifeboats, Stand, Shelf, 1800s, 52 x 33 In.
$189

Bunch Auctions

Nautical, Model, USS Constitution, Painted, Wood Hull, Copper Bottom, 29 x 25 x 9 ¾ In.
$330

Eldred's

N

Nautical, Pond Boat, Wood, Cedar, Cloth Sails, Stand, Charles Gonday, 1932, 71 x 50 In.
$1,125

Cowan's Auctions

Nautical, Porthole, Brass, Single Hinge, Double Dog Latch, Mounting Flange, 1900s, 12 In., Pair
$212

Eldred's

Nautical, Sailor's Valentine, Forget Me Not, Hinged Octagonal Case, 1800s, 9 In.
$1,200

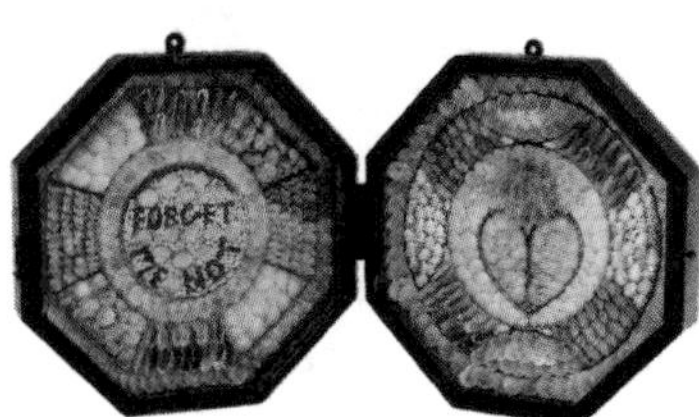

CRN Auctions

Nautical, Sailor's Valentine, Octagonal, Shellwork, Walnut Shadowbox Frame, Gilt Lip, 5 x 28 In.
$1,521

Thomaston Place Auction Galleries

Nautical, Sailor's Valentine, Shells, Crab, Heart, Concentric Rings, Mahogany Case, 1800s, 9 In.
$1,560

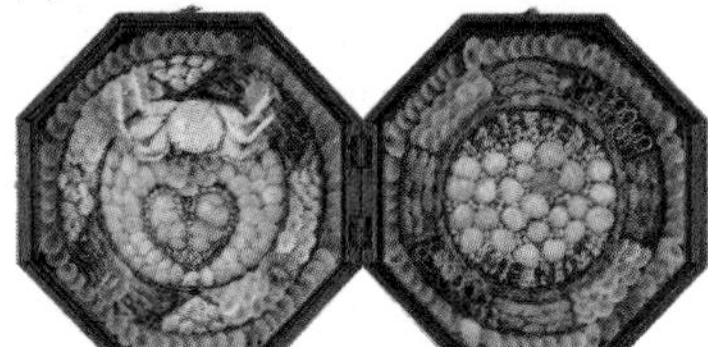

Eldred's

Nautical, Sailor's Valentine, Trinket Box, Wood, Glass Top, Octagonal, Sandi Blanda, 1900s, 3 x 10 x 10 In.
$410

Thomaston Place Auction Galleries

Nautical, Sextant, Brass, National Physical Laboratory Class A, Elliott, Case, 1902, 5 x 9 x 10 In.
$336

Nadeau's Auction Gallery

Nautical, Ship's Wheel, 8 Spokes, Brass, Circular, Turned Handles, 43 In.
$461

Richard Opfer Auctioneering, Inc.

Nautical, Stadimeter, Navigation, Gunnery, Brass, Wood Handle, Schick, c.1950, 8 x 8 x 4 In.
$117

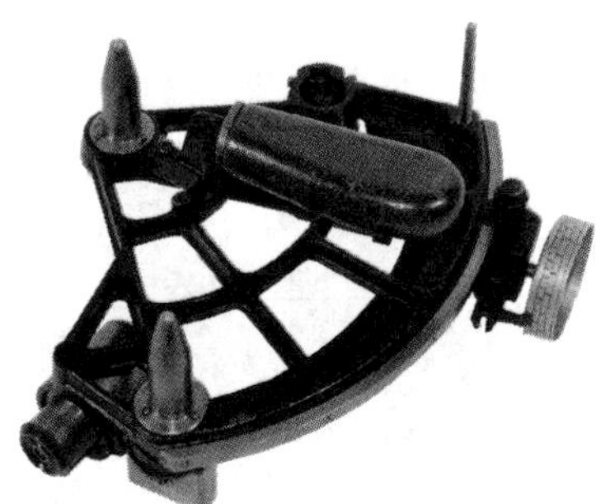

Thomaston Place Auction Galleries

N

Model, USS Constitution, Painted, Wood Hull, Copper Bottom, 29 x 25 x 9 ¾ In. ....*illus* 330

Octant, Brass, Inlaid Scale, Whyte Glasgow, Ebony Frame, 11 x 9 ¾ In. 280

Plaque, Half Hull, Great Lakes, Bland Fitch & Company, 1847, 8 x 44 ¾ In. 780

Pond Boat, Sailboat, Wood, Cloth Sails, Ropes, Stand, 48 x 63 In. 472

Pond Boat, Wood, Cedar, Cloth Sails, Stand, Charles Gonday, 1932, 71 x 50 In. ....*illus* 1125

Porthole, Brass, Single Hinge, Double Dog Latch, Mounting Flange, 1900s, 12 In., Pair ..*illus* 212

Porthole, Ship, Brass Mountings, Round, Glass, 1800-1900s, 18 In., Pair 313

Sailor's Valentine, Forget Me Not, Hinged Octagonal Case, 1800s, 9 In. ....*illus* 1200

Sailor's Valentine, Octagonal, Shellwork, Walnut Shadowbox Frame, Gilt Lip, 5 x 28 In. *illus* 1521

Sailor's Valentine, Shells, Crab, Heart, Concentric Rings, Mahogany Case, 1800s, 9 In. *illus* 1560

Sailor's Valentine, Shells, Flowers, Triangles, Oval, Walnut Shadowbox, 1900s, 16 x 19 In. 2640

Sailor's Valentine, Shells, Heart & Flower Center, Walnut Frame, 20 x 20 In. 976

Sailor's Valentine, Trinket Box, Wood, Glass Top, Octagonal, Sandi Blanda, 1900s, 3 x 10 x 10 In. *illus* 410

Sea Chest, Dark Green, Clipper Ship On Lid, Flag, Rope Handles, 1900s, 23 x 33 x 18 In. 375

Sextant, Brass, National Physical Laboratory Class A, Elliott, Case, 1902, 5 x 9 x 10 In. ..*illus* 336

Sextant, Ebony, Brass, Glass, Bone, Case, Marked, W. Basnett, c.1875, 5 ½ x 12 In. 310

Sextant, Ebony, Brass, Oak Case, Hinged Lid, Salem & Boston Labels, 1800s, 12 In. 216

Sextant, Oxidized Brass, 2 Telescopes, Mahogany Grip, L.A. Hurlimann, Paris, Case, c.1895 ... 290

Ship Model, see Nautical, Model.

Ship's Nameboard, George, Painted, Green, Carved, Scroll Ends, c.1880, 11 ½ x 127 ½ In. 1599

Ship's Wheel, 8 Spokes, Brass, Circular, Turned Handles, 43 In. ....*illus* 461

Ship's Wheel, 10 Spokes, Bronze Band, Wooden, Turned Handle, 64 In. 500

Ship's Wheel, 10 Spokes, Wood, Brass Hub, Turned Wood Handles, 48 In. 329

Ship's Wheel, Iron, Wood, 8 Cut-Down Spokes, A.P. Staddart, Gloucester, 1881, 39 In. 216

Ship's Wheel, Mahogany, 11 Turned Spokes, Copper Plaque, 1900s, 75 In. 439

Sign, 4 Sail, Yellow, Navy Blue, Green Border, Fiberboard, 7 x 24 In. 118

Sign, Nantucket, Quarterboard, Carved, Painted, Black, Shells, Gold Letters, 8 x 60 In. 660

Sign, Ship Chandlery, J.E. Grady, Prop., Nantucket, White Whale, 16 x 46 In. 2091

Sign, Texaco Sky Chief Marine Gasoline, Petrox, Porcelain, 1955, 22 x 12 In. 870

Sign, Trade, Ring For Boat Launch, Wood, Adirondack Style, 27 x 29 In. 354

Signal Cannon, Yacht, Bronze, Oak Firing Carriage, 1800s, 7 ½ x 20 x 5 ½ In. 1404

Stadimeter, Navigation, Gunnery, Brass, Wood Handle, Schick, c.1950, 8 x 8 x 4 In. ....*illus* 117

Sternboard, Boat, Essex, Ct., Oval, Lacquered Mahogany, Gold Edge, 35 ¾ x 6 In. 187

Table, Yacht Wheel, Hardwood, Walnut Pedestal, 3-Blade Propeller Base, 1900s, 22 x 38 In. 72

Telegraph, Bendix, Aviation Corps Marine Division, S.F.S.E. Transindicator, 1942, 49 In. *illus* 1046

Telegraph, Brass Case, Stand, Wood Handle, Swan, Hunter & Wigham Richardson, 1900s, 18 In. *illus* 250

Telegraph, Ship's, Brass, A. Robinson & Co., England, 41 ½ In. ....*illus* 413

Telegraph, Ship's, Engine Room, Stand, Robinson & Co., Liverpool & Glasgow, 37 In. 460

Telescope, Ship Captain's, Collapsible, Shagreen Ray Skin Trim, Late 1800s, 22 ½ In. 207

NETSUKE

Netsukes are small ivory, wood, metal, or porcelain pieces used as toggles on the end of the cord that held a Japanese money pouch or inro. The earliest date from the sixteenth century. Many are miniature carved works of art. This category also includes the ojime, the slide or string fastener that was used on the inro cord. There are legal restrictions on the sale of ivory. Check the laws in your state.

Bone, Animals, Carved, Meisu Okusa, 1800s, 1 ⅝ In. 1989

Inro, Shibayama, 2 Piece, Carved, Gilt, Japan, 2 ¼ x 1 ⅜ In. ....*illus* 173

Jade, Monkey, Peaches, Carved, Mottled Brown, ½ In. ....*illus* 570

Lacquer, Reddish Brown, Painted Moths, Ojime, Inro, 2 ½ x 2 ¾ In. ....*illus* 308

Wood, Boy Climbing On Reclining Ox, Japan, 1800s, 1 ½ In. 360

NEW HALL

New Hall

New Hall Porcelain Works was in business in Shelton, Hanley, Staffordshire, England, from 1781 to 1835. Simple decorated wares were made. Between 1810 and 1825, the factory made a glassy bone porcelain sometimes

Nautical, Telegraph, Bendix, Aviation Corps Marine Division, S.F.S.E. Transindicator, 1942, 49 In.
$1,046

Richard Opfer Auctioneering, Inc.

Nautical, Telegraph, Brass Case, Stand, Wood Handle, Swan, Hunter & Wigham Richardson, 1900s, 18 In.
$250

Eldred's

Nautical, Telegraph, Ship's, Brass, A. Robinson & Co., England, 41 ½ In.
$413

Conestoga Auction Company

N

Netsuke, Inro, Shibayama, 2 Piece, Carved, Gilt, Japan, 2 ¼ x 1 ⅜ In.
$173

Blackwell Auctions

Netsuke, Jade, Monkey, Peaches, Carved, Mottled Brown, ½ In.
$570

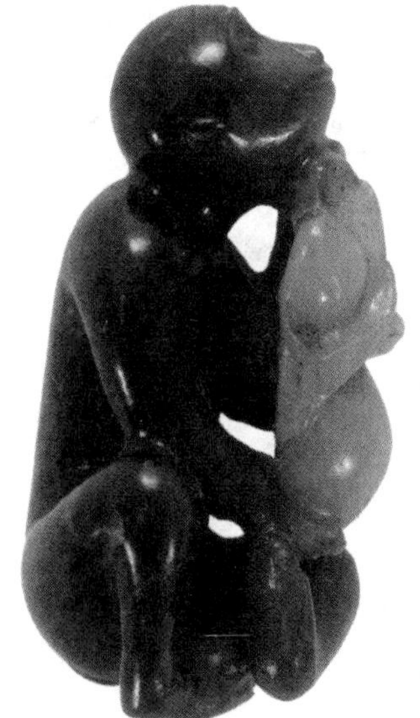

Alderfer Auction Company

Netsuke, Lacquer, Reddish Brown, Painted Moths, Ojime, Inro, 2 ½ x 2 ¾ In.
$308

Clars Auction Gallery

New Martinsville, Pitcher, Water, No. 724, Heart In Sand, Clear, Ruby Stain, 1914, 8 In.
$263

Jeffrey S. Evans & Associates

TIP

For removing ink marks and prices on matte-finished pottery, try paste silver polish. It is a little abrasive and contains some cleaning chemicals that may help.

Newcomb, Bowl, Hammered Copper, Flower Shape, May Ashbury Jones, c.1920, 3 x 9 ⅜ In.
$450

Neal Auction Company

Newcomb, Jar, Lid, Cherokee Roses, Matte Glaze, Blue, Green, Anna Frances Simpson, 1919, 7 In.
$7,250

Neal Auction Company

Newcomb, Pitcher, Trees, Stylized, Light Green, Handle, Sara Bloom Levy, 1898, 5 In.
$3,998

Skinner, Inc.

Newcomb, Pot, Leaves, Stylized, Blue, Green, Yellow, Sadie Irvine, 2 x 3 In.
$1,125

Neal Auction Company

Newcomb, Vase, Buds, Stylized, Yellow, Green Stems, Harriet Joor, 1904, 5 ½ x 4 ½ In.
$5,312

Rago Arts and Auction Center

marked with the factory name. Do not confuse New Hall porcelain with the pieces made by the New Hall Pottery Company, Ltd., a twentieth-century firm working from 1899 to 1956 at the New Hall Works.

Bowl, Pasta, Pink Lotus, Gold Rim, Footed, c.1780, 9 In. 300
Creamer, Blue & Red Flowers, Gilt Branches, Gold Trim, c.1805, 5 ½ In. 110
Cup, Coffee, Mother & Child, Gold Rim, Adam Buck, c.1815, 3 ⅜ x 2 ⅜ In. 165
Plate, Bird Eating Insect, Flowers, Multicolor, c.1805, 8 ½ In. 145
Sucrier, Lid, White Lotus, Blue, Gold Trim, c.1815, 4 x 8 In. 365

NEW MARTINSVILLE

New Martinsville Glass Manufacturing Company was established in 1901 in New Martinsville, West Virginia. It was bought and renamed the Viking Glass Company in 1944. In 1987 Kenneth Dalzell, former president of Fostoria Glass Company, purchased the factory and renamed it Dalzell-Viking. Production ceased in 1998.

Ashtray, Green, Art Deco, Footed, c.1925, 4 ⅜ In. 31
Bowl, Bride's, Yellow & Pink, Tri Form, Ruffled, Footed, c.1910 48
Cake Plate, Prelude Pattern, Footed, 11 x 4 ½ In. 69
Pitcher, Water, No. 724, Heart In Sand, Clear, Ruby Stain, 1914, 8 In. .... *illus* 263

NEWCOMB POTTERY

Newcomb Pottery was founded at Sophie Newcomb College, New Orleans, Louisiana, in 1895. The work continued through the 1940s. Pieces of this art pottery are marked with the printed letters *NC* and often have the incised initials of the artist and potter as well. A date letter code was printed on pieces made from 1901 to 1941. Most pieces have a matte glaze and incised decoration. From 1942 to 1952 the Newcomb mark was revived and put on pieces of pottery from the college. New names were used.

Bowl, Bulbous Body, Ribbed, Matte Glaze, Sadie Irvine, 1932, 3 ¾ x 6 In. 1088
Bowl, Daffodils, Relief Carved, Matte Glaze, Blue, Green, Marked, Sadie Irvine, 1924, 3 x 5 In. 900
Bowl, Hammered Copper, Flower Shape, May Ashbury Jones, c.1920, 3 x 9 ⅜ In. .... *illus* 450
Inkwell, Jasmine, Leaves, Relief Carved, Matte, Blue, Green, Yellow, Marked, 1928, 2 x 3 In. 900
Jar, Alibaba, 40 Thieves, Yellow, Glazed Rim, Marked, 3 ¾ x 3 In. 250
Jar, Lid, Cherokee Roses, Matte Glaze, Blue, Green, Anna Frances Simpson, 1919, 7 In. ... *illus* 7250
Pitcher, Trees, Stylized, Light Green, Handle, Sara Bloom Levy, 1898, 5 In. .... *illus* 3998
Pot, Leaves, Stylized, Blue, Green, Yellow, Sadie Irvine, 2 x 3 In. .... *illus* 1125
Vase, Buds, Stylized, Yellow, Green Stems, Harriet Joor, 1904, 5 ½ x 4 ½ In. .... *illus* 5312
Vase, Flowers, Blue Hi-Glaze, 5 ½ x 6 In. .... *illus* 3125
Vase, Flowers, Leaves, Blue Green, Ivory Inside, Cynthia Littlejohn, c.1913, 6 In. .... *illus* 761
Vase, Grape Clusters, Blue Shaded To Lavender, Sadie Irvine, c.1919, 8 In. 1680
Vase, Iris, High Glaze, Blue, Green, Yellow, Henrietta Bailey, 1904, 7 x 6 ½ In. 5750
Vase, Irises, Blue, Anna Frances Simpson, 1909, 10 x 5 In. .... *illus* 12500
Vase, Landscape, Moss Draped Oaks, Full Moon, Blue, Anna Frances Simpson, 1918, 6 In. 3444
Vase, Landscape, Trees, Blue, Anna Frances Simpson, 1916, 8 ¾ In. 5469
Vase, Leaves, Berries, Green, Pink, Blue Ground, Tapered, Marked NC, 83, HEH, 10 ⅝ In. 1840
Vase, Moon & Moss, Blue & Green Matte Glaze, Anna Frances Simpson, 1925, 10 ½ In. 4500
Vase, Moon, Moss, Blue, Anna Frances Simpson, c. 1922, 5 x 3 ½ In. 1920
Vase, Narcissus, Paperwhite, Green, Cream & Blue Matte, Anna Frances Simpson, 9 In. 1560
Vase, Pine Trees, Full Moon, Blue, Green, Sadie Irvine, 1917, 10 ¾ In. .... *illus* 393

NILOAK POTTERY

Niloak Pottery (*Kaolin* spelled backward) was made at the Hyten Brothers Pottery in Benton, Arkansas, between 1910 and 1947. Although the factory did make cast and molded wares, collectors are most interested in the marbleized art pottery line made

Newcomb, Vase, Flowers, Blue Hi-Glaze, 5 ½ x 6 In.
$3,125

Treadway

Newcomb, Vase, Flowers, Leaves, Blue Green, Ivory Inside, Cynthia Littlejohn, c.1913, 6 In.
$761

Jeffrey S. Evans & Associates

Newcomb, Vase, Irises, Blue, Anna Frances Simpson, 1909, 10 x 5 In.
$12,500

Rago Arts and Auction Center

Newcomb, Vase, Pine Trees, Full Moon, Blue, Green, Sadie Irvine, 1917, 10 ¾ In.
$393

Humler & Nolan

Niloak, Planter, Fox, Sitting, Ozark, Dawn Glaze, Marked, 7 In.
$52

Belhorn Auction Services

Niloak, Vase, Marbleized, Blue, Cream, Brown, Impressed, 10 In.
$242

Humler & Nolan

of colored swirls of clay. It was called Mission Ware. By 1931 the company made cast-ware, and many of these pieces were marked with the name *Hywood.*

NILOAK
Niloak
1910

Niloak
c.1910–1920s

NILOAK
Niloak
1930s–1947

Planter, Fox, Sitting, Ozark, Dawn Glaze, Marked, 7 In. ... *illus* 52
Vase, Marbleized, Blue, Cream, Brown, Impressed, 10 In. ... *illus* 242
Vase, Marbleized, Cylindrical, Multicolor, Marked, 8 In. ... *illus* 75

NIPPON

Nippon porcelain was made in Japan from 1891 to 1921. *Nippon* is the Japanese word for "Japan." The McKinley Tariff Act of 1891 mandated that goods imported to the United States had to be marked with the country of origin. A few firms continued to use the word *Nippon* on ceramics after 1921 as a part of the company name and not to identify things as made in Japan. More pieces marked *Nippon* will be found in the Dragonware, Moriage, and Noritake categories.

Nitto
1890–1921

Nippon
1894–1920

Morimura/Noritake
c.1911–1921

Biscuit Jar, Mill & Lake Scene, Gold Trim, Lid, 3-Footed, 8 In. ... 413
Box, Landscape, Lake & Trees, Gold Bands, Beading, 4 ½ In. ... 144
Candlestick, White Ground, Gilt, Flowers, Square Base, 9 ½ In. ... 209
Charger, Tapestry, Flowers, Gilt, Maple Leaf Backstamp, 12 In. ... 1540
Ewer, Landscape, Floral, Gilt Scroll Handle, Wide Spout, Footed, 1900s, 12 In. ... 138
Humidor, 2 Molded Owls, Lid, Wreath Backstamp, 6 ¾ In. ... 550
Humidor, Horses' Heads, Trees, Oval, Flattened Sides, Marked, 4 ¾ In. ... 144
Inkwell, Egyptian, Lid, Wreath Backstamp, 4 x 4 In. ... 154
Plaque, Iris, Gilt Border, Raised Outlines, Beading, Wreath Backstamp, 9 ¾ In. ... *illus* 168
Plaque, Lion's Face, Molded, Wreath Backstamp, 13 ½ In. ... 1700
Plate, Portrait, Madame Recamier, Gold Beadwork, Maple Leaf Backstamp, 10 In. ... 358
Plate, Portrait, Young Woman, Flower Border, Coralene, Kinran Mark, 9 ⅝ In. ... *illus* 1200
Urn, Swan Scene, Jewels, Brass Handles & Finial, Dome Base, Marked, 23 In. ... 5325
Vase, Flowers, 2 Handles, Paw Feet, Maple Leaf Backstamp, 8 ½ In. ... 413
Vase, Flowers, Gilt, Yellow Ground, Ruffled Rim, Marked, 12 In. ... 84
Vase, Poppies, Lavender, Shaded Gray & Brown Ground, Gold Trim, Ruffled Rim, 12 In. ... *illus* 240
Vase, Wisteria, Purple, Shaded Green Ground, Gold Trim, Jewelwork, 16 In. ... *illus* 1020

NODDER

Nodders, also called nodding figures or pagods, are figures with heads and hands that are attached to wires. Any slight movement causes the parts to move up and down. They were made in many countries during the eighteenth, nineteenth, and twentieth centuries. A few Art Deco designs are also known. Copies have been made. A more recent type of nodder is made of papier-mache or plastic. These often represent sports figures or comic characters. Sports nodders are listed in the Sports category.

Asian Man, Floral Robe, Moving Hands & Tongue, Meissen, 1800s, 10 ¾ In. ... *illus* 3250
Cat, Bell Collar, Papier-Mache, Painted, White Ground, 1800s, 7 In. ... 369

Donkey, Standing, Full-Bodied, Cast Iron, Painted, 11 In. 160
Salt & Pepper Shakers are listed in the Salt & Pepper category.

NORITAKE

Noritake porcelain was made in Japan after 1904 by Nippon Toki Kaisha. A maple leaf mark was used from 1891 to 1911. The best-known Noritake pieces are marked with the *M* in a wreath for the Morimura Brothers, a New York City distributing company. This mark was used primarily from 1911 to 1921 but was last used in the early 1950s. The *N* mark was used from 1940 to the 1960s, and *N Japan* from 1953 to 1964. Noritake made dinner sets with pattern names. Noritake Azalea is listed in the Azalea category in this book.

Berry Bowl, Rainbow, 5 In. 8
Bowl, Vegetable, Amenity, 10 x 7 In. 12
Bowl, Vegetable, Imperial, 10 ½ x 8 In. 22
Bowl, Vegetable, Lid, Imperial, Scrolling Handles, 10 ½ x 8 In. 35
Creamer, Nancy, Gold Trim 10
Creamer, White Palace, Gold, Footed, 4 In. 40
Cup & Saucer, Etienne 10
Cup & Saucer, Fairmont 15
Cup & Saucer, Moriage 22
Cup & Saucer, Trailing Ivy, Footed 12
Cup, Tea, 3 Arrows, Footed, 1947, 2 ½ In., Pair 8
Figurine, Koala & Baby, c.1976, 5 ½ In. 125
Figurine, Mother & Baby Crane, Toki Kaisha, 1960s, 6 ½ In. 275
Gravy Boat, Carolyn, Underplate 55
Gravy Boat, Imperial, Underplate 30
Gravy Boat, Olympia, Underplate 16
Humidor, Egyptian Style Decoration, Curved Ends, M In Wreath Mark, 7 ½ In. .... *illus* 144
Platter, Amenity, 13 x 10 In. 10
Platter, Blue Dawn, Oval, 12 In. 18
Platter, Cho San, 15 In. 30
Platter, Summerville, Oval, 13 In. 25
Platter, White Palace, Gold, 14 x 10 In. 95
Platter, Willowbrook, Oval, 14 In. 55
Serving Bowl, Arabella, 10 x 7 In. 18
Sugar & Creamer, Carolyn 50
Sugar & Creamer, Moonlight 45
Sugar & Creamer, Summerville 20
Sugar & Creamer, Timberlake 14
Sugar & Creamer, Willowbrook 65
Trinket Box, Barrymore, 5 ¼ x 3 ¾ x 2 In. 36

NORSE POTTERY

Norse Pottery Company started in Edgerton, Wisconsin, in 1903. In 1904 the company moved to Rockford, Illinois. The company made a black pottery, which resembled early bronze relics of the Scandinavian countries. The firm went out of business in 1913.

Candlestick, Handle, Black, Green Design, 5 x 3 ½ In. 214
Tray, Man, Beard, Open Mouth, Black & Green, 6 ½ x 2 ¾ In. 467
Vase, Cylinder, Walking Baby Ducks, Green, Black, Gold, Marked, 9 ½ In. 625

NORTH DAKOTA SCHOOL OF MINES

North Dakota School of Mines was established in 1898 at the University of North Dakota. A ceramics course was established in 1910. Students made pieces from the clays found in the region. Although very early pieces were marked *U.N.D.*, most

Niloak, Vase, Marbleized, Cylindrical, Multicolor, Marked, 8 In.
$75

Belhorn Auction Services

Nippon, Plaque, Iris, Gilt Border, Raised Outlines, Beading, Wreath Backstamp, 9 ¾ In.
$168

Eldred's

Nippon, Plate, Portrait, Young Woman, Flower Border, Coralene, Kinran Mark, 9 ⅝ In.
$1,200

Eldred's

N

Nippon, Vase, Poppies, Lavender, Shaded Gray & Brown Ground, Gold Trim, Ruffled Rim, 12 In.
$240

Woody Auctions

Nippon, Vase, Wisteria, Purple, Shaded Green Ground, Gold Trim, Jewelwork, 16 In.
$1,020

Eldred's

Nodder, Asian Man, Floral Robe, Moving Hands & Tongue, Meissen, 1800s, 10 ¾ In.
$3,250

Cowan's Auctions

Noritake, Humidor, Egyptian Style Decoration, Curved Ends, M In Wreath Mark, 7 ½ In.
$144

Eldred's

Who's Huck?
"Huck" is the mark used by Flora Cable Huckfield on North Dakota School of Mines pottery. She worked there from 1924 to 1949.

North Dakota, Bowl, Purple Ground, Blue Lines & Dots, Margaret Cable, 7 In.
$288

Belhorn Auction Services

North Dakota, Pitcher, Viking Ship, Waves, Sea Gull, Handle, Light Blue, Semigloss, Cable, 6 x 7 In.
$719

Belhorn Auction Services

North Dakota, Vase, Animals, Multicolor Drip Glaze, Julia Mattson, 7 ½ In.
$1,331

Humler & Nolan

North Dakota, Vase, Cylindrical, Lavender Matte, Bronze Green Overlay, Margaret Cable, 1912, 5 In.
$1,599

Skinner, Inc.

North Dakota, Vase, Squat, Flowers, Pink Matte Glaze, Grand Forks, 3 ¾ x 5 ½ In.
$813

Treadway

N

pieces were stamped with the full name of the university. After 1963 pieces were only marked with students' names.

U.N.D.

North Dakota School of Mines
1910–1963

North Dakota School of Mines
c.1913–1963

Bowl, Purple Ground, Blue Lines & Dots, Margaret Cable, 7 In. ....*illus* 288
Pitcher, Viking Ship, Waves, Sea Gull, Handle, Light Blue, Semigloss, Cable, 6 x 7 In. ....*illus* 719
Vase, Animals, Multicolor Drip Glaze, Julia Mattson, 7 ½ In. ....*illus* 1331
Vase, Cylindrical, Lavender Matte, Bronze Green Overlay, Margaret Cable, 1912, 5 In. ....*illus* 1599
Vase, Robin's-Egg Blue, High Glaze, 4 Panels, Incised Flower, Margaret Cable, 3 In. 150
Vase, Squat, Flowers, Pink Matte Glaze, Grand Forks, 3 ¾ x 5 ½ In. ....*illus* 813
Vase, Wheat, Stylized, Tan, Brown, Flora Huckfield, Margaret Cable, c.1932, 5 ½ In. 3125

NORTHWOOD

Northwood glass was made by one of the glassmaking companies operated by Harry C. Northwood. His first company, Northwood Glass Co., was founded in Martins Ferry, Ohio, in 1887 and moved to Ellwood City, Pennsylvania, in 1892. The company closed in 1896. Later that same year, Harry Northwood opened the Northwood Co. in Indiana, Pennsylvania. Some pieces made at the Northwood Co. are marked "Northwood" in script. The Northwood Co. became part of a consortium called the National Glass Co. in 1899. Harry left National in 1901 to found the H. Northwood Co. in Wheeling, West Virginia. At the Wheeling factory, Harry Northwood and his brother Carl manufactured pressed and blown tableware and novelties in many colors that are collected today as custard, opalescent, goofus, carnival, and stretch glass. Pieces made between 1905 and about 1915 may have an underlined *N* trademark. Harry Northwood died in 1919, and the plant closed in 1925.

Northwood Glass Co.
1905–c.1915

Northwood Glass Co.
1905–c.1915

Northwood Glass Co.
1905–c.1915

Cherries, Pitcher, Purple, Gold Leaves & Vines, c.1932, 8 ½ x 8 In. 67
Chrysanthemum Swirl, Vase, Cranberry, c.1890, 6 ½ x 4 ½ In. 640
Grape Frieze, Bowl, Emerald Green Ground, Sawtooth Rim, 3 Feet, 3 x 10 ¾ In. 180
Leaf Mold, Pitcher, Water, Cranberry & Opal Spatter, Handle, 1891, 7 ¾ In. ....*illus* 497
Southern Gardens, Bowl, Amethyst, Gold, Flowers, Leaves, 3 Feet, 3 x 10 In. ....*illus* 2110
Threaded Butterfly, Bowl, Green, Gold, 2 Handles, Ruffled Edge, c.1900, 7 ½ x 2 In. 498

NU-ART *see Imperial category.*

NUTCRACKER

Nutcrackers of many types have been used through the centuries. At first the nutcracker was probably strong teeth or a hammer. But by the nineteenth century, many elaborate and ingenious types were made. Levers, screws, and hammer adaptations were the most popular. Because nutcrackers are still useful, they are still being made, some in the old styles.

African Tribesman, Wood, 8 In. 375

Northwood, Leaf Mold, Pitcher, Water, Cranberry & Opal Spatter, Handle, 1891, 7 ¾ In.
$497

Jeffrey S. Evans & Associates

Northwood, Southern Gardens, Bowl, Amethyst, Gold, Flowers, Leaves, 3 Feet, 3 x 10 In.
$2,110

Woody Auctions

N

TIP

To get rid of smoke smell, try boiling an onion for an hour or two. Make sure there is enough water, so it stays covered while boiling.

Nutcracker, Dragon, Standing, Full-Bodied, Cast Iron, Painted, 14 In.
$554

Richard Opfer Auctioneering, Inc.

This is an edited listing of current prices. Visit **Kovels.com** to check thousands of prices from previous years and sign up for free information on trends, tips, reproductions, marks, and more.

Nutcracker, Lion's Head, Wood, Carved, Glass Eyes, 8 In.
$124

Hartzell's Auction Gallery Inc.

Nutcracker, Squirrel, Bronze, Tail Lever, Removable Tray, 1870-75, 13 ½ x 6 ½ In.
$200

Bertoia Auctions

Nutcracker, Squirrel, Cast Iron, Holding Nuts, Mounted, Wood Base, 10 x 4 x 10 In.
$354

Copake Auctions

Nutcracker, Squirrel, Cast Iron, Painted, Mounted On Wood Base, Patent Date On Feet, 10 In.
$234

Richard Opfer Auctioneering, Inc.

Office, Check Protector, Mechanical, Cast Iron, Brass, Defiance Machine Co., c.1904, 11 x 13 In.
$2,494

Auction Team Breker

Ohr, Bowl, Slumped, Folded, Blue, Black, Signed, 4 x 6 In.
$25,000

Palm Beach Modern Auctions

N

Barley Twist, Iron, Green Patina, 6 In. 58
Boar's Head, Metal, Glass Eyes, Victorian, 19th Century, 6 1/2 In. 450
Brass, Carved Wood Handles, Inlaid, Riveted, India, 1970s, 7 x 2 In. 23
Cherub, Holding Shield, 2-Sided, Brass, 19th Century, 6 In. 210
Chimney Sweep, Holding Ladder, Carved Wood, Painted, c.1980, 13 In. 65
Dog, Scottie, Folk Art, Carved, Black Forest, 7 x 5 In. 375
Dog, St. Bernard, Mechanical, Nickel Plated, Althoff Mfg. Co., c.1905, 6 x 10 In. 129
Dog's Head, Black Forest, Signed, Freiburg, 19th Century, 7 3/4 In. 595
Dog's Head, Glass Eyes, Carved, Wood, Swiss, c.1915, 7 x 3 In. 275
Dog's Head, Labrador, Black Forest, Carved, Germany, c.1900, 7 1/2 In. 275
Dragon, Standing, Full-Bodied, Cast Iron, Painted, 14 In. *illus* 554
Eagle's Head, Beaded Eyes, Black Forest, Germany, c.1890, 6 3/4 In. 198
Elephant, Wood, Metal Button Eyes, Art Deco, 1920s, 9 x 4 In. 395
Embracing Couple, Brass, England, 5 3/4 In. 78
German Man, Plume Hat, Hand Carved, Wood, Black Forest, c.1950, 13 In. 68
Gnome, Carved, Wood, Black Forest, 1940s, 7 1/2 In. 80
Hippo, Cast Iron, Mouth Open, Rono, 8 In. 277
Kangaroo, Nickel Plated, Cast Iron, Nestor, England, 5 1/2 In. 221
Lion's Head, Crown, Copper, 5 3/4 In. 100
Lion's Head, Wood, Carved, Glass Eyes, 8 In. *illus* 124
Man, Hat With Plume, Red Cheeks, Painted, Wood, Black Forest, Germany, 13 In. 58
Man, Smoking Pipe, Full Figure, Twist To Crack, Wood, c.1875, 7 3/8 In. 425
Man's Head, Bald, Mustache, Carved, Wood, Bavaria, c.1900, 8 In. 274
Mermaid, Brass, Germany, 6 In. 75
Older Couple, Embracing, Brass, 5 3/4 In. 78
Parrot, Brass, Arts & Crafts, 6 In. 38
Parrot, Brass, Feathered, Arts & Crafts, 2 Holding Areas, 6 In. 79
Parrot, Green, Feather Details, Tail, Rectangular Base, Cast Iron, 9 In. 197
Ram's Head, Glass Eyes, Carved, Wood, c.1880, 8 In. 155
Soldier, Wood, Painted, Rabbit Fur Beard & Hair, Erzgebirge, Germany, 18 In. 3600
Squirrel, Bronze, Tail Lever, Removable Tray, 1870-75, 13 1/2 x 6 1/2 In. *illus* 200
Squirrel, Cast Brass, Stretched Arms, Standing, 6 1/2 x 9 1/2 In. 125
Squirrel, Cast Iron, Holding Nuts, Mounted, Wood Base, 10 x 4 x 10 In. *illus* 354
Squirrel, Cast Iron, Painted, Mounted On Wood Base, Patent Date On Feet, 10 In. *illus* 234
Squirrel, Standing On Log, Outreached Arms, Brass, 6 1/2 x 9 In. 95
Sterling Silver, Cross Bar, Repousse, Webster Co., 6 3/4 In. 75

NYMPHENBURG, *see Royal Nymphenburg.*

OCCUPIED JAPAN

Occupied Japan was printed on pottery, porcelain, toys, and other goods made during the American occupation of Japan after World War II, from 1947 to 1952. Collectors now search for these pieces. The items were made for export. Ceramic items are listed here. Toys are listed in the Toy category in this book.

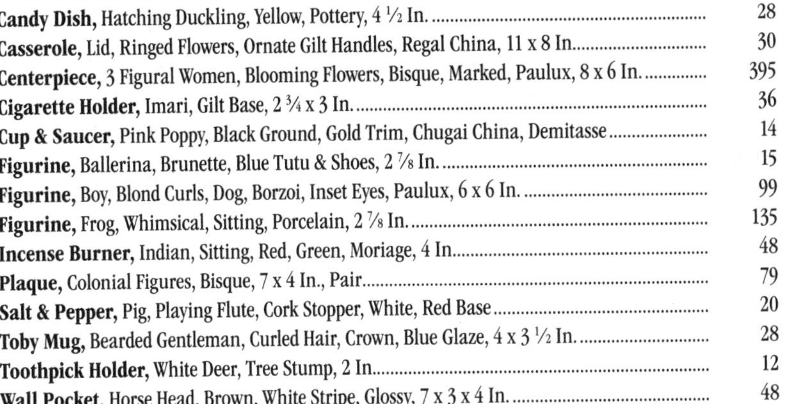

Candy Dish, Hatching Duckling, Yellow, Pottery, 4 1/2 In. 28
Casserole, Lid, Ringed Flowers, Ornate Gilt Handles, Regal China, 11 x 8 In. 30
Centerpiece, 3 Figural Women, Blooming Flowers, Bisque, Marked, Paulux, 8 x 6 In. 395
Cigarette Holder, Imari, Gilt Base, 2 3/4 x 3 In. 36
Cup & Saucer, Pink Poppy, Black Ground, Gold Trim, Chugai China, Demitasse 14
Figurine, Ballerina, Brunette, Blue Tutu & Shoes, 2 7/8 In. 15
Figurine, Boy, Blond Curls, Dog, Borzoi, Inset Eyes, Paulux, 6 x 6 In. 99
Figurine, Frog, Whimsical, Sitting, Porcelain, 2 7/8 In. 135
Incense Burner, Indian, Sitting, Red, Green, Moriage, 4 In. 48
Plaque, Colonial Figures, Bisque, 7 x 4 In., Pair 79
Salt & Pepper, Pig, Playing Flute, Cork Stopper, White, Red Base 20
Toby Mug, Bearded Gentleman, Curled Hair, Crown, Blue Glaze, 4 x 3 1/2 In. 28
Toothpick Holder, White Deer, Tree Stump, 2 In. 12
Wall Pocket, Horse Head, Brown, White Stripe, Glossy, 7 x 3 x 4 In. 48

Ohr Pottery Fakes

A well-known pottery dealer said that in the 1970s he spent $3,000 to buy Ohr pottery. Most of the research on the pottery had not yet been done. A while later he learned all of his pieces had been reglazed and would sell as virtual fakes. He lost a lot of money. Many Ohr pieces discovered in the 1970s were unglazed bisque and showed streaky colored clay. Someone glazed many pieces to get higher prices. Today unglazed pieces sell for thousands of dollars, while reglazed pieces sell for a few hundred dollars apiece.

Ohr, Mug, Chamber Pot Shape, Central Band, Dark Blue Splotches, Lead Glazed, c.1900, 2 x 3 In.
$585

Jeffrey S. Evans & Associates

Ohr, Vase, Dark Gunmetal Glaze, 6 x 5 In.
$2,875

Treadway

Ohr, Vase, Dimpled, In-Body Twist, Ocher & Gunmetal Glaze, Signed, 1895-96, 4 ¾ x 2 In.
$3,000

Rago Arts and Auction Center

TIP
Remove traces of gum, adhesive tape, and other sticky tape by rubbing the glue with lemon juice.

Ohr, Vase, In-Body Twist, Indigo Glaze, Signed, 1895-96, 2 x 2 ¾ In.
$5,312

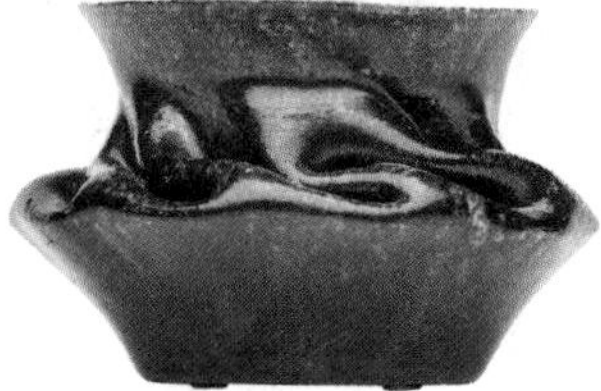

Rago Arts and Auction Center

Ohr, Vase, Pinched, Irregular Shape, Bisque, Signed, 1898-1910, 4 ½ x 6 ¾ In.
$20,000

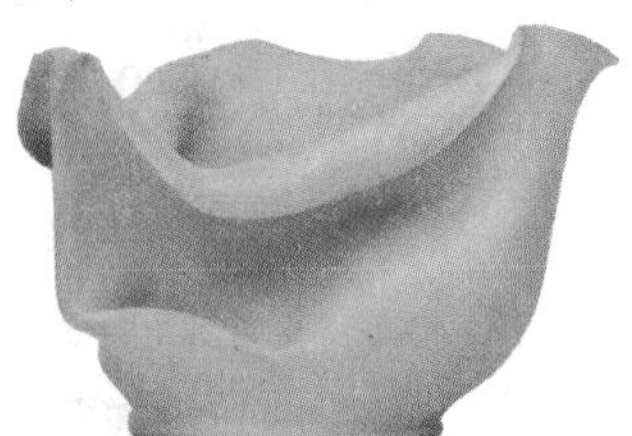

Rago Arts and Auction Center

OFFICE TECHNOLOGY

Office technology includes office equipment and related products, such as adding machines, calculators, and check-writing machines. Typewriters are in their own category in this book.

Adding Machine, Commonwealth Adding Machine Co., No. 320, 10-Key Adder, c.1915 1490
Adding Machine, Glass End Panels, Internal Gears, Burroughs, c.1910, 44 x 14 x 23 In. 96
Adding Machine, Triumph Adding Machine Co., No. 1067, Art Nouveau Decoration................ 377
Adding Machine, Wooden Base, Black Metal Cover, Rapid Calculator Co., 13 x 5 x 7 In. 151
Check Protector, Mechanical, Cast Iron, Brass, Defiance Machine Co., c.1904, 11 x 13 In. *illus* 2494
Stapler, Swingline No. 13, Steel, Gray, 7 x 4 ½ In. 30

OHR

Ohr pottery was made in Biloxi, Mississippi, from 1883 to 1906 by George E. Ohr, a true eccentric. The pottery was made of very thin clay that was twisted, folded, and dented into odd, graceful shapes. Some pieces were lifelike models of hats, animal heads, or even a potato. Others were decorated with folded clay "snakes." Reproductions and reworked pieces are appearing on the market. These have been reglazed, or snakes and other embellishments have been added.

Bowl, Slumped, Folded, Blue, Black, Signed, 4 x 6 In. ....*illus* 25000
Inkwell, Cabin, Olive Glaze, Overhanging Roof, Stamped G.E. Ohr Biloxi, 3 In........................ 1620
Mug, Chamber Pot Shape, Central Band, Dark Blue Splotches, Lead Glazed, c.1900, 2 x 3 In. .*illus* 585
Sculpture, Top Hat Shape, Green, Mottled, Stamped, c.1897, 3 x 3 In....................................... 2000
Vase, Dark Gunmetal Glaze, 6 x 5 In. ....*illus* 2875
Vase, Dimpled, In-Body Twist, Ocher & Gunmetal Glaze, Signed, 1895-96, 4 ¾ x 2 In. ....*illus* 3000
Vase, Dimpled, Ruffled Rim, Gunmetal, Indigo, Sponge Glaze, Stamped, 3 ¾ x 5 In. 3500
Vase, In-Body Twist, Indigo Glaze, Signed, 1895-96, 2 x 2 ¾ In. ....*illus* 5312
Vase, Pinched, Irregular Shape, Bisque, Signed, 1898-1910, 4 ½ x 6 ¾ In. ....*illus* 20000
Vase, Ruffled Rim, Gunmetal Blister Glaze, c.1897, 4 ½ x 3 In. 5312

OLD PARIS, *see Paris category.*

OLD SLEEPY EYE, *see Sleepy Eye category.*

OLYMPICS

Olympics memorabilia include commemorative pins, posters, programs, patches, mascots, and other items from the Olympics, even the torch carried before the games. The Olympics are thought to have started as a religious festival held in Olympia, Greece, in 776 BC. It included a foot race in the stadium. After that games were held every four years until 393 AD and more athletic events were added. The games were revived in 1896 when the first modern Olympics were held in Athens, Greece, with fourteen countries participating. The Olympics were held only in the summer until 1924 when the first Winter Olympics were held in Chamonix, France. The current schedule of an Olympics every two years, alternating between Summer and Winter Olympics, began in 1994. The Olympic flag was introduced in 1908; official Olympics posters were first commissioned in 1912; the Olympic torch first appeared in 1928; and the first relay to light the torch was held in 1936 at the Olympics in Berlin.

Pin, Los Angeles, 1932, Enamel, Red & Blue, 1 ½ In. 28
Playing Cards, Montreal, 1976, Double Deck, Plastic Box, 1976, 4 x 2 In................................. 25
Torch, Los Angeles, 1984, Summer, Fortius, 23 In... 2000

ONION PATTERN

Onion pattern, originally named bulb pattern, is a white ware decorated with cobalt blue or pink designs of a vine with buds that look like onions. Although it is commonly associated with Meissen, other companies made the pattern in the late nineteenth and the twentieth centuries. A rare type is called *red bud* because there are added red accents on the blue-and-white dishes.

Pitcher, Blue & White, Scrolled Handle, Scalloped Foot, Johnson Brothers, 1800s, 9 In. 69
Platter, Blue & White, Villeroy & Boch, c.1900, 15 ½ In. 261
Rolling Pin, Blue & White, Wood Handles, 1920s, 6 In. 120
Serving Dish, Divided, Meissen, 13 In. 325
Strainer, Blue & White, Handle, Funnel Shape, c.1890, 6 In. 65
Tray, Square, 2 Handles, Blue & White, Shell & Crest Border, Meissen, 1900s, 16 In. 144
Tureen, Lid, 2 Handles, Blue & White, Twisted Finial, Meissen, 1900s, 13 In. 120

OPALESCENT GLASS

Opalescent glass is translucent glass that has the tones of the opal gemstone. It originated in England in the 1870s and is often found in pressed glassware made in Victorian times. Opalescent glass was first made in America in 1897 at the Northwood glassworks in Indiana, Pennsylvania. Some dealers use the terms *opaline* and *opalescent* for any of these translucent wares. More opalescent pieces may be listed in Hobnail, Pressed Glass, and other glass categories.

Lighter, Cigar, Peg Lamp, Bell, Blue Glass, Brass, A & P Gaudard, c.1900, 18 x 6 In. ....*illus* 702
Pitcher, Swirl Body, Pink, Applied Green Ribbed Handle, Victorian, 8 ¾ In. ....*illus* 224

OPALINE

Opaline, or opal glass, was made in white, green, and other colors. The glass had a matte surface and a lack of transparency. It was often gilded or painted. It was a popular mid-nineteenth-century European glassware.

Lamp, 2-Light, Yellow, Brass Base, Mounted, Early 1900s, 38 In. 200
Vase, Blue, Gold Plated Caryatid Handles, Enamel, Acanthus Feet, 1900s, 11 x 6 In. ....*illus* 226
Vase, Gilt, White Ground, Etruscan Style, Sanguine Neoclassical Figures, 18 ½ In. 200
Vase, Multicolor Flowers, Gilt, Applied Mask Handles, 1800s, 19 In. 700

OPERA GLASSES, *see Binoculars category.*

ORPHAN ANNIE

Orphan Annie first appeared in the comics in 1924. The last strip ran in newspapers on June 13, 2010. The redheaded girl, her dog Sandy, and her friends were on the radio from 1930 to 1942. The first movie based on the strip was produced in 1932. A second movie was produced in 1938. A Broadway musical that opened in 1977, a movie based on the musical and produced in 1982, and a made-for-television movie based on the musical produced in 1999 made Annie popular again, and many toys, dishes, and other memorabilia have been made. An adaptation of the movie based on the musical opened in 2014.

Bandanna, Horseshoe Border, Sandy, Ginger, Joe Corntassel, Cotton, 1930s, 18 x 18 In. 30
Big Little Book, No. 716, Little Orphan Annie & Sandy, Harold Gray, 1933 15
Big Little Book, No. 1140, Little Orphan Annie & The Big Train Robbery, 1934 12
Decoder Badge, Brass, c.1937, 1 ⅞ x 1 $^{3}/_{16}$ In. 45
Diaper Stacker, Red Dress, White Collar, Zipper Closure, Applause, c.1982, 24 In. 34
Figure, Jointed Wood, Painted, 5 In. 115
Game, Path To Happiness, Board, Parker Brothers, 1981 29
Hat, Secret Guard, Insignia, Blue, 1941, 10 In. 236
Playing Cards, Annie & Sandy, Western Miniature, 1930s 15
Ring, Altascope, 10,000 Ft., Gold 1296
Wristwatch, Round Dial, Leather Band, Box, 1950, 6 ¾ In. 118

Opalescent, Lighter, Cigar, Peg Lamp, Bell, Blue Glass, Brass, A & P Gaudard, c.1900, 18 x 6 In.
$702

Jeffrey S. Evans & Associates

Opalescent, Pitcher, Swirl Body, Pink, Applied Green Ribbed Handle, Victorian, 8 ¾ In.
$224

Bunch Auctions

Opaline, Vase, Blue, Gold Plated Caryatid Handles, Enamel, Acanthus Feet, 1900s, 11 x 6 In.
$226

Soulis Auctions

Orrefors, Bowl, Ariel, Blue, Round, Fluted, Signed, Ingeborg Lundin, Sweden, 3 ½ x 9 In.
$406

Treadway

Orrefors, Vase, Ariel, Blue Gray & Clear, Bubbles, Swollen, Edvin Ohrstrom, 4 ½ In.
$219

Treadway

Orrefors, Vase, Cylindrical, Violet, Flared Rim, Etched Base, Ingeborg Lundin, c.1970, 7 In.
$1,968

Skinner, Inc.

ORREFORS

Orrefors

Orrefors Glassworks, located in the Swedish province of Smaaland, was established in 1898. The company is still making glass for use on the table or as decorations. There is renewed interest in the glass made in the modern styles of the 1940s and 1950s and after. In 1990, the company merged with Kosta Boda and is still working as Orrefors. Most vases and decorative pieces are signed with the etched name *Orrefors*.

Bowl, Ariel, Blue, Round, Fluted, Signed, Ingeborg Lundin, Sweden, 3 ½ x 9 In. ....*illus* 406
Vase, Ariel, Blue & Clear, Bulbous, Edvin Ohrstrom, 6 ½ In. 1063
Vase, Ariel, Blue Gray & Clear, Bubbles, Swollen, Edvin Ohrstrom, 4 ½ In. ....*illus* 219
Vase, Ariel, Blue, Ingeborg Lundin, Sweden, 4 x 6 In... 438
Vase, Cylindrical, Violet, Flared Rim, Etched Base, Ingeborg Lundin, c.1970, 7 In. ....*illus* 1968
Vase, Fish Swimming, Aquatic Plants, Clear, Graal, 5 x 5 ½ In.. 600
Vase, Fish, Aquatic Plants, Signed, Edvard Hald, 4 x 4 ¾ In. ....*illus* 512

OTT & BREWER

Ott & Brewer Company operated the Etruria Pottery at Trenton, New Jersey, from 1871 to 1892. It started making belleek in 1882. The firm used a variety of marks that incorporated the initials *O & B.*

Coffeepot, Brown, White, Gold, Painted Clouds, 9 In.. 34
Cup & Saucer, Blue Flowers, Gold Leaves & Trim, Ruffled, Belleek, c.1890, 3 x 4 In................. 137
Dish, Cream, Pink Cherry Blossoms, Gold Gilt Leaves, Ruffled Edge, 1900s, 8 x 8 ½ In............ 156

OVERBECK POTTERY

Overbeck Pottery was made by four sisters named Overbeck at a pottery in Cambridge City, Indiana. They started in 1911. They made all types of vases, each one of a kind. Small, hand-modeled figurines are the most popular pieces with today's collectors. The factory continued until 1955, when the last of the four sisters died.

Figurine, Victorian Woman, Going To Market, Marked, Logo, 4 ⅝ x 3 In. 424

OWENS POTTERY

Owens Pottery was made in Zanesville, Ohio, from 1891 to 1928. The first art pottery was made after 1896. Utopian Ware, Cyrano, Navarre, Feroza, and Henri Deux were made. Pieces were usually marked with a form of the name *Owens.* The company continued to make tiles but production of art pottery was discontinued about 1907 and the company was sold. The new owners went bankrupt in 1909. J.B. Owens started the J.B. Owens Floor & Wall Tile Company in 1909. It closed in 1928.

Owens Pottery
1896–1907

J. B. Owens

Owens Pottery
1896–1907

Owens Pottery
1905+

Tankard, Utopian, Iris Decor, Round Base, Small Spout, Handle, 11 ½ x 6 ½ In. ....*illus* 150
Vase, Green Matte, Bulbous Body, Footed, 4 In.. 138
Vase, Light Blue To Cream Ground, 2 Lotus Blossoms, Charles W. Chilcote, 16 ⅜ In................. 1553
Vase, Utopian, Fuchsia, Yellow Flower, Green Ground, Glaze, 12 In. ....*illus* 95
Vase, Utopian, Green, Pansy, Narrow Neck, Sea Green Glaze, Marked, 7 ¾ In. ....*illus* 253
Wall Pocket, Green, Swirl Body, Cone Shape, Marked, 11 In. 63

OYSTER PLATE

Oyster plates were popular from 1840 to 1900. Each course at dinner was served in a special dish. The oyster plate had indentations shaped like oysters. Usually six oysters were held on a plate. There is no greater value to a plate with more oysters, although that myth continues to haunt antiques dealers. There are other plates for shellfish, including cockle plates and whelk plates. The appropriately shaped indentations are part of the design of these dishes.

5 Wells, Majolica, Crescent Shape, Sky Blue Ground, Copeland, 9 In. ....*illus* 325
5 Wells, Ocean, Wedgwood, Wave Shape Ground, Multicolor, Glaze, 9 In. 384
5 Wells, Oriental, Yellow Ground, Gilt Flowers, Porcelain, 7 In. ....*illus* 561
6 Wells, Majolica, Pink, White Center, George Jones, 9 In. 413
Fish Head, Shell Center, Gray Scale Ground, Majolica, France, 9 In. 154
Pink, Majolica, Seashells, Brown Ground, Blue Center, Minton, 9 In. ....*illus* 502

PAINTINGS *may be listed in the Folk Art category. Watercolors on paper are listed in Picture.*

PAIRPOINT

Pairpoint Manufacturing Company was founded by Thomas J. Pairpoint in 1880 in New Bedford, Massachusetts. It soon joined with the glassworks nearby and made glass, silver-plated pieces, and lamps. Reverse-painted glass shades and molded shades known as "puffies" were part of the production until the 1930s. The company reorganized and changed its name several times. It became the Pairpoint Glass Company in 1957. The company moved to Sagamore, Massachusetts, in 1970 and now makes luxury glass items. Items listed here are glass or glass and metal. Silver-plated pieces are listed under Silver Plate. Three marks are shown here.

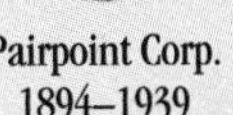

Pairpoint Corp.
1894–1939

Gunderson–Pairpoint Glass Works
1952–1957

Pairpoint Manufacturing Co.
1972–present

Basket, Fan Shape, Engraved, Flowers, Amethyst Handle & Base, 11 x 8 In. 60
Biscuit Jar, Black Lid & Handle, Gold Floral & Leaf, 5 ½ In. ....*illus* 118
Castor, Sugar, Cranberry, Enamel, Flowers, Silver Plate Frame, 10 ¾ In. ....*illus* 180
Centerpiece, Ruby Red Glass, Flowers, Leaves, Vines, Antelope, Signed, 10 x 8 ¾ x 8 ¾ In. 2178
Chandelier, Puffy, Papillon, Reverse Painted, Butterflies, Rose, White Ground, 25 x 15 In. 9680
Humidor, Nevada Pattern, Ray Cut Base & Lid, 7 ½ x 4 In. 275
Ladle, Hobstar, Vesica, Cane & Fan, Silver Plate Bowl, 14 In. 125
Lamp, 1-Light, Seville Shade, Macaw Parrots, Jungle, 22 x 14 In. 1500
Lamp, 2-Light, Reverse Painted, Garden Of Allah, Acorn Pulls, Bronze Base, 20 x 16 In. 3360
Lamp, 3-Light, Reverse Painted Shade, Egypt Scene, Wood Base, 7 ½ x 7 ¾ In. ....*illus* 1170
Lamp, Bronze Base, Verdigris Finish, Green Shade, Slag Glass, 1960s, 16 x 14 In. 300
Lamp, Mushroom Shade, White Enamel, Bronze Base, Early 1900s, 21 ½ x 16 In. 735
Lamp, Puffy, Balmoral Shade, Daisies, Butterflies, Tree Trunk Base, 12 x 6 In. .... 750 to 812
Lamp, Puffy, Papillon, Butterflies, Reverse Painted, Roses, Gilt Outlines, 21 ½ In. .... 2759 to 3630
Lamp, Puffy, Papillon, Creamy White Ground, Petal Shape Base, 14 ½ In. 1815
Lamp, Puffy, Rose Bouquet Shade, Roses, Green Leaf Ground, Cast Metal Base, 20 x 13 In. *illus* 9000
Lamp, Reverse Painted Shade, Ocean Scene, Ships, Brass Base, 16 x 19 In. 810
Lamp, Reverse Painted Shade, Trees, Brass, Early 1900s, 15 In. 563
Paperweight, Cranberry, Snake, Globe, White, Opalescent Foot, Sign, 1973, 5 x 3 In. 293
Urn, Lid, Amethyst, Engraved, Grapes & Leaves, 10 ¾ In. 84
Vase, Clear, Oval, Florentine, Applied Amethyst Handles, Rim, 1910s, 11 ¾ In. 117

PALMER COX, *Brownies, see Brownies category.*

Orrefors, Vase, Fish, Aquatic Plants, Signed, Edvard Hald, 4 x 4 ¾ In.
$512

Morphy Auctions

Owens, Tankard, Utopian, Iris Decor, Round Base, Small Spout, Handle, 11 ½ x 6 ½ In.
$150

Belhorn Auction Services

Owens, Vase, Utopian, Fuchsia, Yellow Flower, Green Ground, Glaze, 12 In.
$95

Strawser Auction Group

Owens, Vase, Utopian, Green, Pansy, Narrow Neck, Sea Green Glaze, Marked, 7 ¾ In.
$253

Belhorn Auction Services

Oyster Plate, 5 Wells, Majolica, Crescent Shape, Sky Blue Ground, Copeland, 9 In.
$325

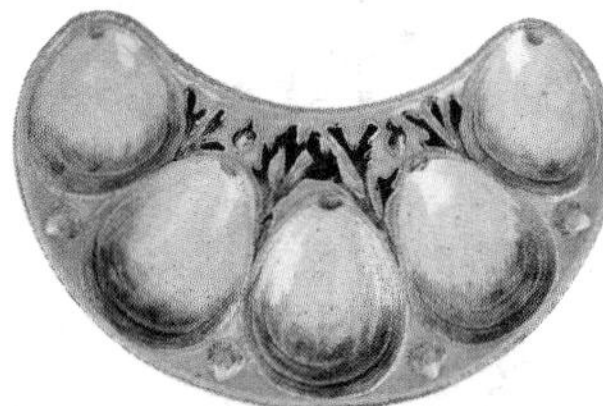
Strawser Auction Group

Oyster Plate, 5 Wells, Oriental, Yellow Ground, Gilt Flowers, Porcelain, 7 In.
$561

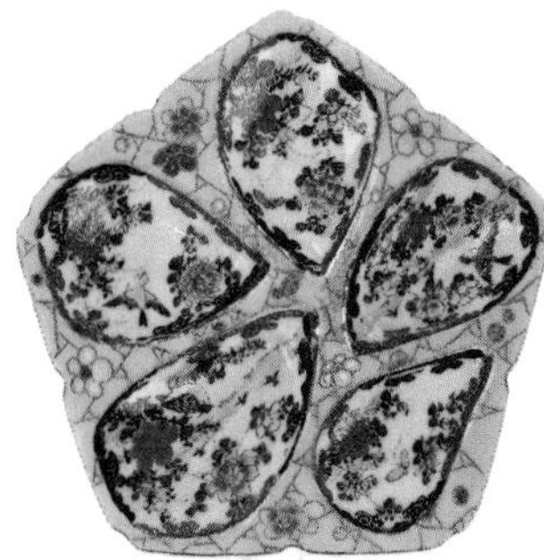
Strawser Auction Group

PAPER

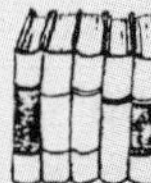

Paper collectibles, including almanacs, catalogs, children's books, some greeting cards, stock certificates, and other paper ephemera, are listed here. Paper calendars are listed separately in the Calendar category. Paper items may be found in many other sections, such as Christmas and Movie.

Cutwork, Scherenschnitte, Family Register, Vines, Flowers, Vase, Ohio, 1881, 25 x 30 In. *illus* 344
Cutwork, Scherenschnitte, Horse, Driver, 2-Wheel Cart, Dog, Pencil, Frame, 1800s, 8 x 10 In. *illus* 240
Family Record, Newell, 25 Members, Lithographed, Mahogany Frame, 12 x 16 In. 185
Fraktur, Birth, Baptism, Watercolor, Ink, Angel, Flowers, Frame, 1798, 15 x 18 In. *illus* 590
Fraktur, Distelfink Perched On Flowering Tulip, Watercolor, Frame, c.1830, 7 x 6 In. 1872
Fraktur, Heart, Ink On Paper, Frame, German Text, 1848, 10 ½ x 12 ½ In. 325
Fraktur, Susanna Schtegel, Birth Certificate, Ink, Watercolor, Blousy Angel, 12 x 15 In. 732
Fraktur, Tulip, Leaves, Flowers, Pink, Green, Frame, 10 ½ x 8 In. 147
Fraktur, Watercolor On Paper, Heart, Scrolling Vines, Flowers, 1794, 9 x 14 In. 1952
Fraktur, Watercolor, Ink On Paper, Vase, Flowers, 2 Birds, 1787, 9 ½ x 5 In. 427
Fraktur, Watercolor, Ink, Angels, Eagle, Birds, German Text, Birth Record, 1847, 20 x 13 In. *illus* 1860
Land Deed, On Vellum, Joseph Gill Of Ohio, Frame, 1824, 12 x 18 ½ In. 338
Panel, Manuscript, Arabic Calligraphy, Multicolor, Paint, Gilt, Wood Frame, 16 ⅝ x 11 In. 164
Panel, Wallpaper, Chinoiserie, Families In Garden, Gilt Frame, 36 In., Pair *illus* 1375
Panel, Wallpaper, Scenic Vista, El Dorado, Zuber, France, c.1937, 80 x 19 In., Pair *illus* 1375
Valentine, Pen & Ink, Paint, True Loves Knot, Cross, Painted Frame, Pa., c.1875, 12 x 11 In. *illus* 570

PAPER DOLL

Paper dolls were probably inspired by the pantins, or jumping jacks, made in eighteenth-century Europe. By the 1880s, sheets of printed paper dolls and clothes were being made. The first paper doll books were made in the 1920s. Collectors prefer uncut sheets or books or boxed sets of paper dolls. Prices are about half as much if the pages have been cut.

Tweedledum & Tweedledee, McCall's Magazine, Sept., 1917, 1 Sheet, Uncut 15
Victorian Woman, Doll, 7 Outfits, Embossed, Germany, c.1890, 2 Pages, Uncut 40

PAPERWEIGHT

Paperweights must have first appeared along with paper in ancient Egypt. Today's collectors search for every type, from the very expensive French weights of the nineteenth century to the modern artist weights or advertising pieces. The glass tops of the paperweights sometimes have been nicked or scratched, and this type of damage can be removed by polishing. Some serious collectors think this type of repair is an alteration and will not buy a repolished weight; others think it is an acceptable technique of restoration that does not change the value. Printie is the flat or concave surface formed when a paperweight is shaped on a grinding wheel. Baccarat paperweights are listed separately under Baccarat.

Abelman, Stuart, 2 Fish, Fish Tank, Spherical, Art Glass, 4 ½ In. 173
Ayotte, Rick, Clear, Red & Black Bird, Yellow Flowers, New Hampshire, 1988, 1 ¾ In. 263
Ayotte, Ronald, Kingfisher, Lady Slippers, Signed, 1988, 2 x 3 ¾ In. 804
Banford, Ray, Flowers, Green, Yellow, Leaves, Blue Ribbon, New Jersey, 1980s, 1 ¾ In. 164
Banford, Ray, Yellow Flower, White Fields, Signed, 2 x 3 In. 431
Boston & Sandwich, Poinsettia, Pink Flower, Squat Globular Shape, 1 ¾ x 2 ¾ In. 135
Bronze, Dog, Sleeping, Black Marble Base, Germany, 1945, 1 ¾ x 4 ¾ x 3 In. 254
Clichy, Pink & Green Rose, White Star, Red, Pastry Mold & Pink Floret Canes, 2 ⅝ In. *illus* 840
Dog, Lying Down, Cast Iron, Victorian, 2 ½ x 5 ½ In. 125
Eickholtz, Ball Shape Glass, Painted, Signed On Bottom, 1989, 4 In. 30
Hacker, Harold, Salamander, Terrarium Style, Signature, 2 ½ In. 228
Inkwell, Pink, Yellow, Lavender, Mushroom Stopper, Concave Base, Arculus, 6 x 4 In. *illus* 152
Iron, Cat, Painted, White & Black, 4 x 3 ½ In. *illus* 79

Oyster Plate, Pink, Majolica, Seashells, Brown Ground, Blue Center, Minton, 9 In.
$502

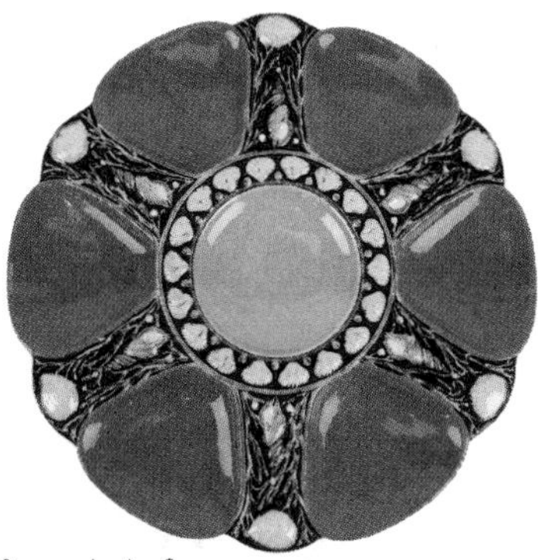

Strawser Auction Group

Pairpoint, Biscuit Jar, Black Lid & Handle, Gold Floral & Leaf, 5 ½ In.
$118

Strawser Auction Group

Pairpoint, Castor, Sugar, Cranberry, Enamel, Flowers, Silver Plate Frame, 10 ¾ In.
$180

Woody Auctions

Pairpoint, Lamp, 3-Light, Reverse Painted Shade, Egypt Scene, Wood Base, 7 ½ x 7 ¾ In.
$1,170

Milestone Auctions

Pairpoint, Lamp, Puffy, Rose Bouquet Shade, Roses, Green Leaf Ground, Cast Metal Base, 20 x 13 In.
$9,000

Morphy Auctions

Paper, Cutwork, Scherenschnitte, Family Register, Vines, Flowers, Vase, Ohio, 1881, 25 x 30 In.
$344

Garth's Auctioneers & Appraisers

Paper, Cutwork, Scherenschnitte, Horse, Driver, 2-Wheel Cart, Dog, Pencil, Frame, 1800s, 8 x 10 In.
$240

Garth's Auctioneers & Appraisers

Paper, Fraktur, Birth, Baptism, Watercolor, Ink, Angel, Flowers, Frame, 1798, 15 x 18 In.
$590

Conestoga Auction Company

Paper, Fraktur, Watercolor, Ink, Angels, Eagle, Birds, German Text, Birth Record, 1847, 20 x 13 In.
$1,860

Garth's Auctioneers & Appraisers

P

Paper, Panel, Wallpaper, Chinoiserie, Families In Garden, Gilt Frame, 36 In., Pair
$1,375

New Orleans Auction Galleries

Paper, Panel, Wallpaper, Scenic Vista, El Dorado, Zuber, France, c.1937, 80 x 19 In., Pair
$1,375

New Orleans Auction Galleries

Paper, Valentine, Pen & Ink, Paint, True Loves Knot, Cross, Painted Frame, Pa., c.1875, 12 x 11 In.
$570

Garth's Auctioneers & Appraisers

Iron, Dog, Setter, Lying Down, Head Up, Collar, c.1900, 6 In. ... 177
Iron, Owl, Winking, Deco Style, Painted, 2 ¾ In. ... 68
Kain, Lewis, Lampwork, White, Yellow, Blue, Flower, Leaves, Signed, 1980s, 2 In. ... 117
Ritter, Richard, Mountain, Children, Flower, Bird, Cameo, Glass, 1986, 3 ⅜ In. ... 129
Salazar, Daniel, Tidepool, Clear, Blue, Purple Fish, Sign, California, 1990, 2 ½ In. ... *illus* 211
Satava, Rick, Stone, Deer, Bull, Human Hand, Sign, California, 1991, 3 ½ x 3 In. ... 117
St. Louis, Ruby Dahlia, Clear, Faceted, Signature Cane, France, 1970, 3 In. ... *illus* 556
Stankard, Paul, Blue Forget-Me-Nots, Clear, Signature Cane, 1986, 2 x 3 In. ... 690
Stankard, Paul, Wild Carolina Roses, Pink, Green Stems, Signature Cane, 2 ¾ In. ... 660
Trabucco, Victor, Orchids, Blue Field, Signed, 1987, 3 x 4 In. ... *illus* 518
Ysart, Clear, 10-Petal Flower, Yellow, Green Stem, 3 Leaves, 1900s, 2 ⅝ In. ... 293

PAPIER-MACHE

Papier-mache is made from paper mixed with glue, chalk, and other ingredients, then molded and baked. It becomes very hard and can be painted. Boxes, trays, and furniture were made of papier-mache. Some of the nineteenth-century pieces were decorated with mother-of-pearl. Papier-mache is still being used to make small toys, figures, candy containers, boxes, and other giftwares. Furniture made of papier-mache is listed in the Furniture category.

Bust, Milliner's Model, Woman, Hand Painted, Kidskin Straps, France, Late 1800s, 15 In. *illus* 875
Bust, Milliner's Model, Woman, Painted, Blue Eyes, France, c.1875, 16 In. ... *illus* 1000
Elephant, Standing, Sergio Bustamante, Sermel, Tonala Mexico, c.1970, 31 In. ... 24
Jewelry Box, Victorian, Mother-Of-Pearl Inlay, Flowers, Black, 1850s, 13 x 12 x 10 In. ... 313
Sculpture, Lion, Standing, Sergio Bustamante, Sermel, 26 x 26 x 13 In. ... *illus* 313
Tray, Black, Moths, Trailing Vines, Paint, Gilt, Stand, 21 x 25 x 19 In. ... 192
Tray, Rectangular, Painted, 3 Puppies, White Ground, Late 1800s, 5 x 8 In. ... 123

PARASOL, *see Umbrella category.*

PARIAN

Parian is a fine-grained, hard-paste porcelain named for the marble it resembles. It was first made in England in 1846 and gained favor in the United States about 1860. Figures, tea sets, vases, and other items were made of Parian at many English and American factories.

Pitcher, George Washington, Military Figure Standing, Bamboo Molded Handle, 1850s, 10 In. 322

PARIS

Paris, Vieux Paris, or Old Paris, is porcelain ware that is known to have been made in Paris in the eighteenth or early nineteenth century. These porcelains often have no identifying mark but can be recognized by the whiteness of the porcelain and the lines and decorations. Gold decoration is often used.

Basket, Gilt & Blue De Roi, Oval, Rectangular Base, 10 ¾ x 13 x 7 In. ... *illus* 550
Bottle, Scent, Multicolor, Gilt, Marked, Rihouet, Rue De La Paix, 1880-1910, 5 In., Pair ..*illus* 244
Urn, Empire Style, Hunt Scene, 2 Sphinx Handles, Early 1800s, 8 ⅜ x 6 x 5 In. ... 531
Urn, Lid, Gilt, Multicolor, Incised Mark, Medallion, 1800s, 18 x 12 x 7 In. ... 800
Vase, Gilt & Blue Royal, Swan's Neck Handle, Square Plinth Base, 1800s, 9 ¾ In., Pair ... 450
Vase, Multicolor, Gilt, Looped Stem Handles, Floral, Magenta Grounds, 1800s, 16 In., Pair ... 700

PATENT MODEL

Patent models were required as part of a patent application for a United States patent until 1880. In 1926 the stored patent models were sold by the U.S. Patent Office. Some were given to the Smithsonian, some were returned to inventors' descendants, and the rest were sold as a group. As groups

Paperweight, Clichy, Pink & Green Rose, White Star, Red, Pastry Mold & Pink Floret Canes, 2 ⅝ In.
$840

Alderfer Auction Company

Paperweight, Inkwell, Pink, Yellow, Lavender, Mushroom Stopper, Concave Base, Arculus, 6 x 4 In.
$152

Thomaston Place Auction Galleries

Paperweight, Iron, Cat, Painted, White & Black, 4 x 3 ½ In.
$79

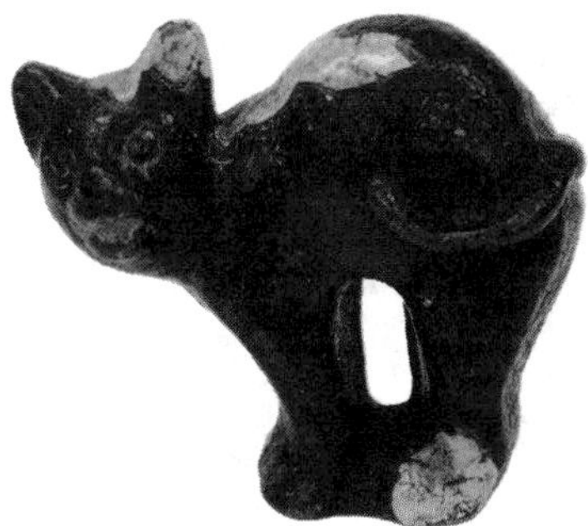

Hartzell's Auction Gallery Inc.

Paperweight, Salazar, Daniel, Tidepool, Clear, Blue, Purple Fish, Sign, California, 1990, 2 ½ In.
$211

Jeffrey S. Evans & Associates

Paperweight, St. Louis, Ruby Dahlia, Clear, Faceted, Signature Cane, France, 1970, 3 In.
$556

Jeffrey S. Evans & Associates

Paperweight, Trabucco, Victor, Orchids, Blue Field, Signed, 1987, 3 x 4 In.
$518

Richard D. Hatch & Associates

Papier-Mache, Bust, Milliner's Model, Woman, Hand Painted, Kidskin Straps, France, Late 1800s, 15 In.
$875

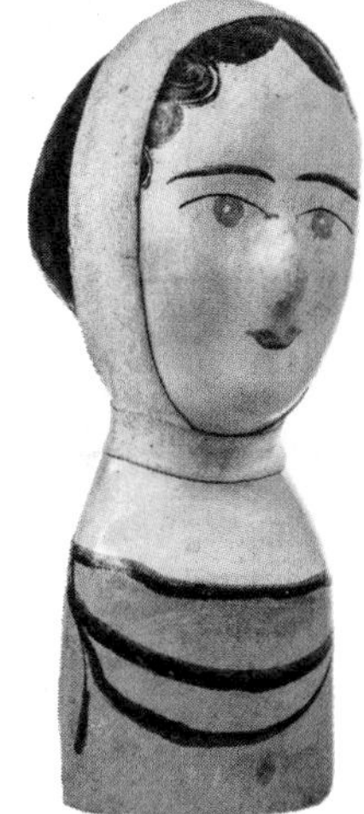

Garth's Auctioneers & Appraisers

Papier-Mache, Bust, Milliner's Model, Woman, Painted, Blue Eyes, France, c.1875, 16 In.
$1,000

Garth's Auctioneers & Appraisers

Papier-Mache, Sculpture, Lion, Standing, Sergio Bustamante, Sermel, 26 x 26 x 13 In.
$313

Kamelot Auctions

P

Paris, Basket, Gilt & Blue De Roi, Oval, Rectangular Base, 10 ¾ x 13 x 7 In.
$550

Neal Auction Company

Paris, Bottle, Scent, Multicolor, Gilt, Marked, Rihouet, Rue De La Paix, 1880-1910, 5 In., Pair
$244

Neal Auction Company

Pate-De-Verre, Compote, Floral Accents, Yellow, Round Base, 7 x 10 In.
$246

Clars Auction Gallery

TIP

If you have a lightweight vase that tips easily, fill it with sand.

Pate-De-Verre, Figurine, Dancing Couple, Amber, Rectangular Base, 9 In.
$369

Clars Auction Gallery

Pate-Sur-Pate, Dish, Green, Round, Water Scene, 2 Women, Frederick Schenk, 1880, 12 In.
$492

Stair Galleries

Pate-Sur-Pate, Vase, White Angel, Spread Wings, Blue Ground, Gilt Stars, Limoges, 7 ¾ x 3 In.
$1,560

Morphy Auctions

Peachblow, Fairy Lamp, Man, Glossy, Ruffled Edge, c.1900, 7 x 5 ½ In.
$152

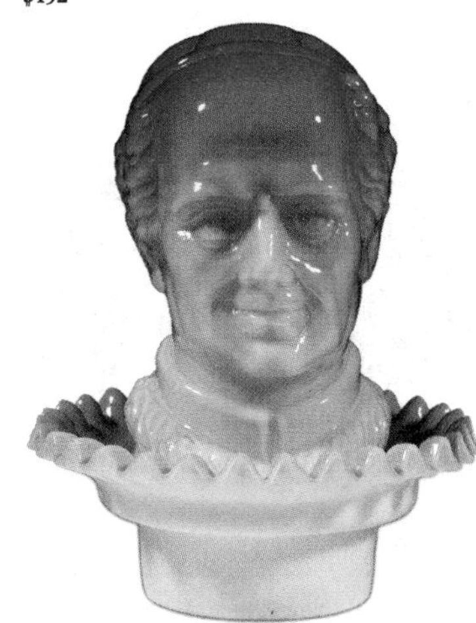

Jeffrey S. Evans & Associates

Peanuts, Comic Strip Panel, Snoopy, Marker On Paper, Signed, Charles Schulz, Frame, 22 In.
$1,560

Alderfer Auction Company

Peanuts, Lunch Box, Have Lunch With Snoopy, Dome Top, Metal, Thermos, King Seeley, 1968
$73

Bruneau & Co. Auctioneers

changed hands in later years in unsuccessful attempts to start a museum individual models started appearing in the marketplace. A model usually has an official tag.

Calculator, Exchange Rate, Brass, Pounds To Dollars, E.L. Bill, 1878, 4 x 2 In. 1304
Canning Jar, Stoneware, Wood Frame, May 16, 1865, 11 x 7 In. 236
Churn, Wood, Floor Model, O.R. Flyers, 1852 390
Clothes Wringer, Wood, Chain Drive, Judson W. Hall, 1876, 8 ½ x 9 ½ In. 774
Electric Railway Semiphore, No. 225633, J. Nesbitt, March 16, 1880, 9 x 9 In. 452
Fire Escape Ladder, Detmer, 1878, 15 x 5 In. 660
Folding Chair, Wood, Tapestry Back & Seat, Beny F. Little, February 8, 1876, 9 In. 420
Gas Pump Nozzle, Tokheim, Model 1063, Metal, 15 In. 66
Green Corn Cutter, Wood, Metal, Tobias Witmer, July 27, 1875, Original Tag, 12 In. 570
Huller, Rice & Buckwheat, No. 33040, C.B. Horton, Wood, August 13, 1861, Tag 1140
Locomotive Lamp, Tin, Tower Form, No. 13537, S. Bidwell, Sept. 4, 1855, 13 x 12 In. 3616
Railroad Directory, Walnut Case, Cloth Rollers, W.H.H. Day, 1800s, 12 x 9 In. 226
Tobacco Cutter, Cast Iron, No. 1512929, M. Himoff, Oct. 28, 1924, 11 x 7 In. 660
Washing Machine, No. 69609, O. Baldwin, Oct. 8, 1867, Wood, 6 ½ x 8 In. 1080
Washing Machine, Tag, No. 19299, E. Julier, Feby 9, 1858, 10 ½ In. 989

PATE-DE-VERRE

Pate-de-verre is an ancient technique in which glass is made by blending and refining powdered glass of different colors into molds. The process was revived by French glassmakers, especially Galle, around the end of the nineteenth century.

Bowl, Iris Sprays, Lavender, Soft Yellow, Tapering Shape, 7 x 10 ½ In. 866
Compote, Floral Accents, Yellow, Round Base, 7 x 10 In. .... *illus* 246
Figurine, Dancing Couple, Amber, Rectangular Base, 9 In. .... *illus* 369

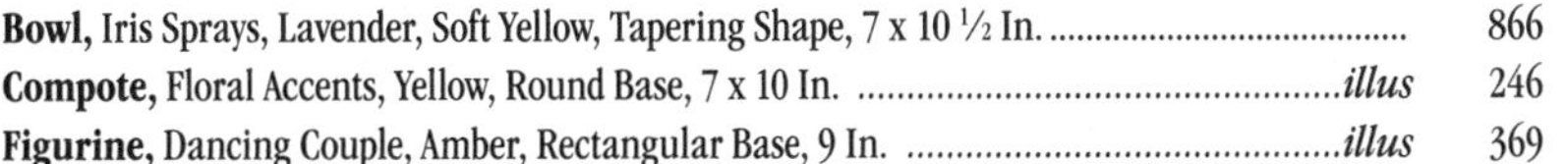

PATE-SUR-PATE

Pate-sur-pate means paste on paste. The design was made by painting layers of slip on the ceramic piece until a relief decoration was formed. The method was developed at the Sevres factory in France about 1850. It became even more famous at the English Minton factory about 1870. It has since been used by many potters to make both pottery and porcelain wares.

Dish, Green, Round, Water Scene, 2 Women, Frederick Schenk, 1880, 12 In. .... *illus* 492
Vase, Female, Nude, Branches, Leaves, Flowers, 1800s, 16 ¾ In. 420
Vase, Seated Muse, Cherubs, Smoking Brazier, Brown, White Slip, A. Birks, 12 In. 2300
Vase, White Angel, Spread Wings, Blue Ground, Gilt Stars, Limoges, 7 ¾ x 3 In. .... *illus* 1560

PAUL REVERE POTTERY

Paul Revere Pottery was made at several locations in and around Boston, Massachusetts, between 1906 and 1942. The pottery was operated as a settlement house program for teenage girls. Many pieces were signed *S.E.G.* for Saturday Evening Girls. The artists concentrated on children's dishes and tiles. Decorations were outlined in black and filled with color.

Hatpin Holder, Blue, Trees, Landscape Band, Marked, SEG, 3 ¼ x 5 ½ In. 2000
Trivet, Blue, Sailboat, Water, Saturday Evening Girls, 5 ½ In. 343
Vase, Brown, Gunmetal Glaze, Marked, 4 ⅝ x 4 In. 150

PEACHBLOW

Peachblow glass was made by several factories beginning in the 1880s. New England Peachblow is a one-layer glass shading from red to white. Mt. Washington Peachblow shades from pink to bluish-white. Hobbs, Brockunier and

The Signers
Fifty-six men signed the Declaration of Independence. Five were captured by the British, tortured and killed as traitors. Twelve had their homes burned down. Two had sons who were American soldiers that were captured, two had soldier sons who died. Nine died from wounds or other problems caused by the war.

Pearlware, Jug, Brown Slip, Dipped Fans, Green Glaze, Strap Handle, Leaf Ends, c.1810, 4 In.
$3,690

Skinner, Inc.

Pearlware, Jug, Chinoiserie, Blue, White Ground, Handle, c.1700, 9 In.
$554

Skinner, Inc.

TIP
Rinse food off plates as soon as possible after use to avoid stains.

P

Pearlware, Pepper Pot, Cylindrical, 3 Colored Slip Branches, Buff Ground, c.1810, 5 In.
$923

Skinner, Inc.

Pearlware, Pitcher, Farmers Arms, Country House, White Ground, Inscribed, William Dean, 1804, 9 In.
$793

Pook & Pook

TIP
For a pollution-free glass cleaner, use a mixture of white vinegar and water.

Peking Glass, Bowl, Ruby Red, Carved, Bird, Leaves, Flared Rim, Footed, 3 ¾ x 9 In.
$1,287

Thomaston Place Auction Galleries

Company of Wheeling, West Virginia, made Coral glass that it marketed as Peachblow. It shades from yellow to peach and is lined with white glass. Reproductions of all types of peachblow have been made. Related pieces may be listed under Webb Peachblow.

Fairy Lamp, Man, Glossy, Ruffled Edge, c.1900, 7 x 5 ½ In. .... *illus* 152
Salt & Pepper, Satin Glass, Black Lid, Wheeling, 3 ¾ In. 201
Vase, Bulbous, Quatrefoil Folded Top Rim, 3 ¾ x 4 In. 113
Vase, Glossy, Opaque White Foot, New England Glass Co., c.1900, 12 In., Pair 380

PEANUTS

Peanuts is the title of a comic strip created by cartoonist Charles M. Schulz (1922–2000). The strip, drawn by Schulz from 1950 to 2000, features a group of children, including Charlie Brown and his sister Sally, Lucy Van Pelt and her brother Linus, Peppermint Patty, and Pig Pen, and an imaginative and independent beagle named Snoopy. The Peanuts gang has also been featured in books, television shows, and a Broadway musical. The comic strip is being rerun in some newspapers.

Book, Pop-Up, The Peanut Philosophers, Hallmark, Hardcover, 1972, 9 x 7 In. 78
Comic Strip Panel, Snoopy, Marker On Paper, Signed, Charles Schulz, Frame, 22 In. ....*illus* 1560
Figurine, Snoopy, Turban, Gold Pitcher, Ceramic, 3 In. 155
Lunch Box, Have Lunch With Snoopy, Dome Top, Metal, Thermos, King Seeley, 1968 .....*illus* 73
Pillow, Snoopy Lying On Doghouse, It's Nice To Get Home To Your Own Bed, 1968, 16 In. 35

PEARL

Pearl items listed here are made of the natural mother-of-pearl from shells. Such natural pearl has been used to decorate furniture and small utilitarian objects for centuries. The glassware known as mother-of-pearl is listed by that name. Opera glasses made with natural pearl shell are listed in the Binoculars category.

Tray, Rosewood, Mother-Of-Pearl Inlay, 2 People, Landscape, Leaves, Flowers, 9 ½ x 6 ½ In. 138

Pearl

PEARLWARE

Pearlware is an earthenware made by Josiah Wedgwood in 1779. It was copied by other potters in England. Pearlware is only slightly different in color from creamware and for many years collectors have confused the terms. Wedgwood pieces are listed in the Wedgwood category in this book. Most pearlware with mocha designs is listed under Mocha.

Dish, Peafowl, Blue Shell Edge, M. Austin & Jill R. Fine, New York, 1987, c.1810 600
Figurine, Lion, Lying Down, Rectangular Base, Wood & Caldwell, 5 In., Pair 2706
Figurine, Shepherd, Lost Sheep Found, Pratt Type, Multicolor, 1780s, 9 ⅝ In. 199
Flask, Man Holding Dagger, Acanthus Leaves, Multicolor, c.1800, 5 ⅜ In. 94
Jug, Brown Slip, Dipped Fans, Green Glaze, Strap Handle, Leaf Ends, c.1810, 4 In. ....*illus* 3690
Jug, Chinoiserie, Blue, White Ground, Handle, c.1700, 9 In. ....*illus* 554
Mug, Brown & Black Dots, Blue Field, Coggled Bands, Strap Handle, c.1810, 4 ⅝ In. 1599
Pepper Pot, Cylindrical, 3 Colored Slip Branches, Buff Ground, c.1810, 5 In. ....*illus* 923
Pitcher, Fair Hebe, Molded, Tree Trunk Shape, Bold Colors, c.1788, 9 ¾ In. 234
Pitcher, Farmers Arms, Country House, White Ground, Inscribed, William Dean, 1804, 9 In. ..*illus* 793
Plate, Eagle, White Ground, Scalloped Rim, Feather Edge, c.1820, 6 In. 584
Platter, Blue Flowers & Band, Tassel Border, Scalloped Rim, England, c.1825, 15 x 12 In. 380
Platter, Chinese Landscape, Marked, Mandarino Opaque China, 8 x 14 ½ In. 173
Teapot, Lid, Flowers, Leaves, Multicolor, Blue Band, Footed, Early 1800s, 7 In. 861
Tureen, Pagodas, Boats, Blue Transfer, Oval, Fruit Basket Finial, 1810s, 16 x 11 In. 70

PEKING GLASS

Peking glass is a Chinese cameo glass first made popular in the eighteenth century. The Chinese have continued to make this layered glass in the old manner, and many new pieces are now available that could confuse the average buyer.

Bowl, Ruby Red, Carved, Bird, Leaves, Flared Rim, Footed, 3 ¾ x 9 In. ....*illus* 1287
Snuff Bottle, Orange, Koi Fish, Wave, Silver Dipper Stopper, c.1910, 2 ½ x 2 In. ....*illus* 156
Vase, Bulbous, Flared Rim, Ring Foot, 4 Character Mark, Chinese, 4 ¾ x 5 In. ....*illus* 1652
Vase, White, Ruby Red Overlay, Aquatic Scene, Cranes, Chinese, 11 x 6 In. ....*illus* 95

PEN

Pens replaced hand-cut quills as writing instruments in 1780, when the first steel pen point was made in England. But it was 100 years before the commercial pen was a common item. The fountain pen was invented in the 1830s but was not made in quantity until the 1880s. All types of old pens are collected, everything from quill pens to fountain pens. Float pens feature small objects floating in a liquid as part of the handle. Advertising pens are listed in the Advertising section of this book.

Fountain, 14K Gold Nib, Holder, Black Onyx Base, Tiger, c.1915, 4 ½ x 5 ½ In. 207
Fountain, Omas, Brown, Arco Celluloid, Piston Fill, 18K Gold, 1993, 5 ½ In. ....*illus* 863
Montblanc, Ballpoint, Imperial Dragon, Silver Dragon-Shaped Clip, Limited Edition ....*illus* 1375
Montblanc, Fountain, Meisterstuck, Black Resin Body, Nib, Case, 5 ½ In. 215
Montblanc, Fountain, Meisterstuck, No. 149, Case, 1900s, 5 ¾ In. 410
Montblanc, Fountain, Red, 14K Gold Trim & Nib, 1995, 5 ⅜ In. ....*illus* 230
Montblanc, Meisterstuck, Ballpoint, Silver, Rose Gold Plate, Diamond, Limited Edition .*illus* 2375
Parker, Fountain, Filigree Button, Black & 16K Gold, 4 ½ In. ....*illus* 259
Senna, Ballpoint, Montegrappa, Ayrton, Black Carbon Fiber, Twist Mechanism, 5 ½ In. *illus* 62
Sheaffer, Fountain, Connaisseur, 18K Gold, Electroplate, Medium Nib, Cap, Box, 1920, 5 ½ In. 316
Waterman, Fountain, Ideal, Gold Plated, Repousse Scroll, 1984, 5 ¼ In. 897

PEN & PENCIL

Parker 75, Fountain Pen, Mechanical Pencil, Sterling Silver, Gold Nib, Case, 5 In. 115
Sheaffer, Fountain Pen, Mechanical Pencil, Black & Gold Pattern, Box, 6 In. 84
Sheaffer, Pen With Lever Feed, Pencil Twist Action, Pearl Cap & Barrel, Box, 1935 84

PENCIL

Pencils were invented, so it is said, in 1565. The eraser was not added to the pencil until 1858. The automatic pencil was invented in 1863. Collectors today want advertising pencils or automatic pencils of unusual design. Boxes and sharpeners for pencils are also collected. Advertising pencils are listed in the Advertising category. Pencil boxes are listed in the Box category.

Eversharp, Calendar, Red, Black, White, Autopoint, Eraser, 1964, 5 ½ In. 25
Mechanical, 14K Gold, L Monogram, 6-Sided, c.1925, 4 In. 695
Mechanical, Tiffany & Co., Retractable Ruler, Sterling Silver, c.1900, 5 In. 500
Propelling, Rose Gold, Swirls, Flowers, Victorian, Bloodstone Seal, 3 In. 169
Propelling, Sterling Silver, Mordan & Riddle, 1825 250
Silver, Owl, Glass Eyes, Edwardian, 2 In. 275
Wahl, Eversharp, Mechanical, Gold Filled, Chevron Pattern, c.1920, 4 ½ In. 50

PENCIL SHARPENER

Boston 55 Ranger, Crank Handle, 6 Hole Sizes, 1950s, 3 x 4 In. 49
Cat, Bakelite, Butterscotch, 1 ½ In. 110
Dexter 3-A, Crank Handle, Nickel Plated Steel, c.1948 28
Fan, Die Cast Metal, Painted, Hong Kong, 3 ¼ x 2 In. 10
Fat Man In Lederhosen, Tin Litho, Pedestal Base, KUM, West Germany, 4 In. 60
Peerless Pencil Whittler No. A, Black, Metal, Wood, 5 x 6 In. ....*illus* 226
Violin, Metal, Germany, 1930s, 2 ½ In. 50

Peking Glass, Snuff Bottle, Orange, Koi Fish, Wave, Silver Dipper Stopper, c.1910, 2 ½ x 2 In.
$156

Crescent City Auction Gallery

Peking Glass, Vase, Bulbous, Flared Rim, Ring Foot, 4 Character Mark, Chinese, 4 ¾ x 5 In.
$1,652

Bunch Auctions

Peking Glass, Vase, White, Ruby Red Overlay, Aquatic Scene, Cranes, Chinese, 11 x 6 In.
$95

Witherell's

P

Pen, Fountain, Omas, Brown, Arco Celluloid, Piston Fill, 18K Gold, 1993, 5 ½ In.
$863

Blackwell Auctions

Pen, Parker, Fountain, Filigree Button, Black & 16K Gold, 4 ½ In.
$259

Blackwell Auctions

Presidential Pens
United States presidents since Gerald Ford traditionally have used Cross brand pens to sign legislation at publicized events. The Rhode Island company has been producing quality writing instruments since 1846.

Pen, Montblanc, Ballpoint, Imperial Dragon, Silver Dragon Shaped Clip, Limited Edition
$1,375

New Orleans Auction Galleries

Pen, Montblanc, Fountain, Red, 14K Gold Trim & Nib, 1995, 5 ⅜ In.
$230

Blackwell Auctions

Pen, Montblanc, Meisterstuck, Ballpoint, Silver, Rose Gold Plate, Diamond, Limited Edition
$2,375

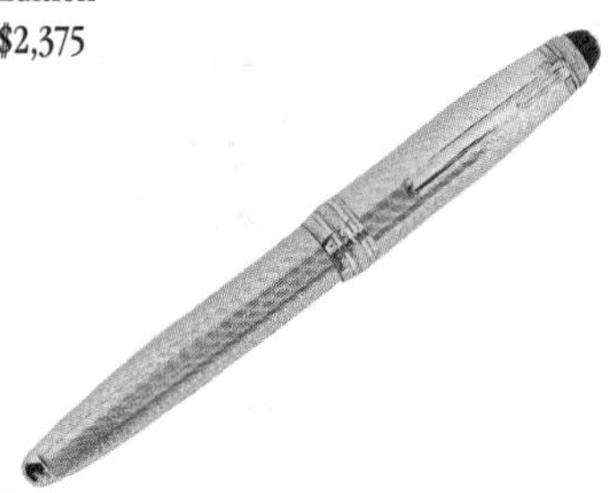

New Orleans Auction Galleries

Pen, Senna, Ballpoint, Montegrappa, Ayrton, Black Carbon Fiber, Twist Mechanism, 5 ½ In.
$62

Skinner, Inc.

TIP
If buying a vintage fountain pen, examine it carefully. Look for extra holes in the cap that indicate a missing clip, and signs of glue near the clip or trim. Run your fingernail around the cap lip to check for cracks or chips.

Pencil Sharpener, Peerless Pencil Whittler No. A, Black, Metal, Wood, 5 x 6 In.
$226

Hartzell's Auction Gallery Inc.

Pennsbury, Figurine, Western Tanager, Multicolor, No. 140, Initialed B.P., 6 In.
$276

Belhorn Auction Services

PENNSBURY POTTERY

Pennsbury Pottery worked in Morrisville, Pennsylvania, from 1950 to 1971. Full sets of dinnerware as well as many decorative items were made. Pieces are marked with the name of the factory.

Cake Plate, 2 Birds, Heart, Blue, Green, Burgundy, Footed, 1960s, 4 x 11 In. 40
Figurine, Western Tanager, Multicolor, No. 140, Initialed B.P., 6 In. .... *illus* 276
Plate, Angel Holding Holly, 2 Candles, Noel, 1970, 8 In. 20
Red Rooster, Chip & Dip Sever, c.1976, 12 x 2 ½ In. 45

PEPSI-COLA

Pepsi-Cola, the drink and the name, was invented in 1898 but was not trademarked until 1903. The logo was changed from an elaborate script to the modern block letters in 1963. Several different logos have been used. Until 1951, the words *Pepsi* and *Cola* were separated by two dashes. These bottles are called "double dash." In 1951 the modern logo with a single hyphen was introduced. All types of advertising memorabilia are collected, and reproductions are being made.

Pepsi-Cola
1903

Pepsi-Cola
1939–1951

Pepsi-Cola
1965

Calendar, March 1909, Woman Holding Up Glass Of Pepsi, Pad, Frame, 26 ½ x 17 In. ....*illus* 10200
Clock, Drink The Light Refreshment, Plastic, Light-Up, Dualite, 17 In. .... *illus* 720
Clock, Neon, Rocking Bottle Cap, Numerals, White Dial, Swihart Products, 20 In. 2400
Clock, Think Young, Say Pepsi Please, Back Lit, Double Bubble Light, Round, 15 In. 735
Clock, Think Young, Say Pepsi Please, Yellow Ground, Bottle Cap, Square, c.1960, 16 In. .*illus* 168
Clock, Twirling Dancer In Window, Metal, Plastic, Shaped, Germany, c.1950, 6 In. 677
Door Push, Say Pepsi Please, White, Red, Blue, Yellow, Black, Metal, Stout, 5 x 30 In. 204
Door Push, Thank You Call Again On Reverse, Porcelain, Enamel, 31 x 3 In. 203
Poster, Big Shot, Boy & Girl, Holding Bottle, White Ground, Cardboard, 11 x 28 In. 144
Sign, Brunette Beauty, Straw Hat, Self-Framed, Double-Dash, 1942, 34 x 24 In. 2400
Sign, Drink Pepsi-Cola, Red, White, Blue, Celluloid, Tin, Button, 9 In. 192
Sign, Have A Pepsi, Tin, Yellow Ground, Marked Made In USA M-239, 11 x 9 In. 96
Thermometer, Have A Pepsi, Embossed, Tin, Bottle Cap, 1950s, 27 In. .... *illus* 264
Thermometer, The Light Refreshment, Tin, Embossed Cap, Glass, 27 x 7 In. 204
Tip Tray, I Love Its Flavor, Woman Drinking Through Straw, Rim Border, Oval, 1910, 6 x 4 In.. 3600
Vending Machine, Blue, 10 Cents, Embossed, V-81, Keys, 59 x 28 x 23 In. 6000
Watch Fob, Delicious, Healthful, Blue, Copper, Brass Ground, c.1905-10, 1 ¾ x 1 ½ In. 240

PERFUME BOTTLE

Perfume bottles are made of cut glass, pressed glass, art glass, silver, metal, jade, enamel, and even plastic or porcelain. Although the small bottle to hold perfume was first made before the time of ancient Egypt, it is the nineteenth- and twentieth-century examples that interest today's collector. DeVilbiss Company has made atomizers of all types since 1888 but no longer makes the perfume bottle tops so popular with collectors. These were made from 1920 to 1968. The glass bottle may be by any of many manufacturers even if the atomizer is marked *DeVilbiss*. The word *factice*, which often appears in ads, refers to large store display bottles. Glass or porcelain examples may be found under the appropriate name such as Lalique, Czechoslovakia, Glass-Bohemian, etc.

Art Glass, Flowers, Ribbon, Teardrop Stopper, C. Lotton, 1992, 9 ½ x 3 ¾ In. 770
Atomizer, Glass, Frosted & Clear Panels, Red Stars, Art Deco, France, 7 ½ In. .... *illus* 201
Atomizer, Gold Aurene, Gilt, Etched, Black Cloth, Finial, Round Base, 10 In. .... *illus* 142

Pepsi-Cola, Calendar, March 1909, Woman Holding Up Glass Of Pepsi, Pad, Frame, 26 ½ x 17 In.
$10,200

Morphy Auctions

Pepsi-Cola, Clock, Drink The Light Refreshment, Plastic, Light-Up, Dualite, 17 In.
$720

Rich Penn Auctions

Pepsi-Cola, Clock, Think Young, Say Pepsi Please, Yellow Ground, Bottle Cap, Square, c.1960, 16 In.
$168

Alderfer Auction Company

P

Pepsi-Cola, Thermometer, Have A Pepsi, Embossed, Tin, Bottle Cap, 1950s, 27 In.
$264

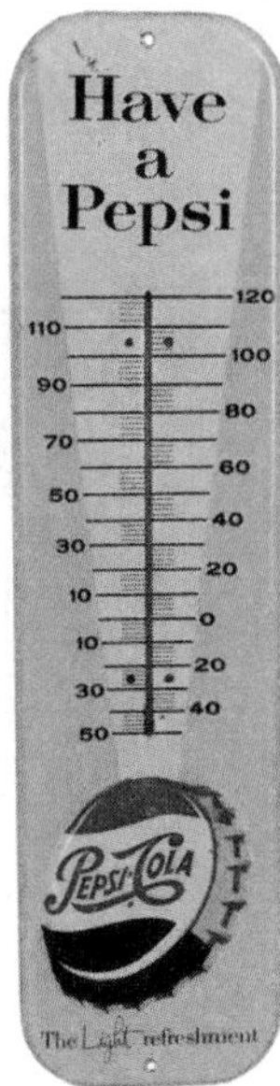

Milestone Auctions

Perfume Bottle, Atomizer, Glass, Frosted & Clear Panels, Red Stars, Art Deco, France, 7 ½ In.
$201

Blackwell Auctions

Perfume Bottle, Atomizer, Gold Aurene, Gilt, Etched, Black Cloth, Finial, Round Base, 10 In.
$142

Bunch Auctions

Perfume Bottle, Cut Glass, Ornate Repousse Screw-Off Top, Cane Style, Round Base, 4 ½ In.
$259

Richard D. Hatch & Associates

Perfume Bottle, Rock Crystal, Doughnut Shape, Hinged 18K Gold Top, Gemstones, c.1890, 3 In.
$1,375

Freeman's Auctioneers & Appraisers

Peters & Reed, Vase, Landsun, Horn Shape, Blue, Green, Brown & Orange Matte Glaze, 6 In.
$109

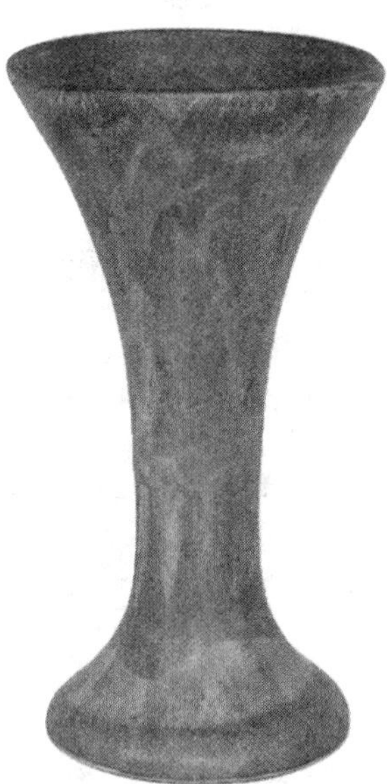

Belhorn Auction Services

Cut Glass, Ornate Repousse Screw-Off Top, Cane Style, Round Base, 4 ½ In. ....*illus*	259
Daisy & Button, Cylindrical, Repousse Silver Hinged Top, Inner Stopper, 3 ½ In.	173
Rock Crystal, Doughnut Shape, Hinged 18K Gold Top, Gemstones, c.1890, 3 In. ....*illus*	1375
Thousand Eye, Cobalt Cut-To-Clear, Repousse Silver Hinged Top, Inner Stopper, 5 In.	288

PETERS & REED

Peters & Reed Pottery Company of Zanesville, Ohio, was founded by John D. Peters and Adam Reed in 1897. Chromal, Landsun, Montene, Pereco, and Persian are some of the art lines that were made. The company, which became Zane Pottery in 1920 and Gonder Pottery in 1941, closed in 1957. Peters & Reed pottery was unmarked.

Medallion, Moss Aztec, Grand Lodge F. & A.M., Ohio Bethesda Hospital, 1915, 2 ¼ In.	184
Vase, Landsun, Horn Shape, Blue, Green, Brown & Orange Matte Glaze, 6 In. ....*illus*	109
Vase, Moss Aztec, Cylindrical, Brown, Green, Marked MZX RAE, 21 In. ....*illus*	316

PETRUS REGOUT, *see Maastricht category.*

PEWABIC POTTERY

Pewabic Pottery was founded by Mary Chase Perry Stratton in 1903 in Detroit, Michigan. The company made many types of art pottery, including pieces with matte green glaze and an iridescent crystalline glaze. The company continued working until the death of Mary Stratton in 1961. It was reactivated by Michigan State University in 1968.

Bowl, Iridescent Metallic Glaze, Oxidation, 2 Handles, I. & E. Peters, 3 x 5 In.	186
Rose Bowl, Ocher & Umber Matte Drip Glaze, Marked, 4 x 5 ½ In..	496
Rose Bowl, Turquoise Luster Glossy Glaze, Copper Tones, Lobed, Marked, 4 x 5 ½ In..............	682
Tile, American Indian, Hunting Bird, Relief, Iridescent Glaze, Oval, I. & E. Peters, 9 In.	124
Vase, Blue Iridescent Glaze, Lavender & Platinum Tones, Ball Shape, 12 x 10 In.......................	1116
Vase, Cobalt Blue Matte Drip Glaze, Squat, 3 ¼ x 4 ¾ In.	372
Vase, Luster Glaze, Lavender, Cobalt Blue & Brass Tones, Bulbous, Marked, 7 ½ x 4 In.	806
Vase, Metallic Luster Glaze, Lavender & Brass Tones, 3 Ribbed Strap Handles, 15 In.................	2108
Vase, Ocher Drip Glaze, Blue Inside, Swollen Shoulder, J. Frederick, 1999, 8 ½ In.....................	217
Vase, Oval, Multicolor Glaze, Detroit, 8 ½ x 6 ½ In. ....*illus*	1875
Vase, Oxblood Iridescent Glaze, Turquoise & Copper Tones, Squat, Peters, 3 x 4 In.	217
Vase, Turquoise Drip, Copper To Oxidized Ground, 1920-40, 7 x 6 ½ In....................................	1984

PEWTER

Pewter is a metal alloy of tin and lead. Some of the pewter made after 1840 has a slightly different composition and is called Britannia metal. This later type of pewter was worked by machine; the earlier pieces were made by hand. In the 1920s pewter came back into fashion and pieces were often marked *Genuine Pewter*. Eighteenth-, nineteenth-, and twentieth-century examples are listed here. Marks used by three pewter workshops are pictured.

Thomas Danforth
1727–1733

Timothy Boardman
1822–1825

William Will
1764–1798

Biscuit Jar, Castilian, Green Glass, Lotus, Dragonfly Handle, Footed, Poland, 9 x 7 ½ In. *illus*	212
Bowl, Portuguese De Campos, Stag Head Motif, 2 Handles, 15 ½ In.	74
Candelabrum, 3-Light Bat, Kayserzinn, Cologne, Germany, 1901-02, 12 x 11 In., Pair.............	2125
Coffeepot, Hinged Lid, Black Handle, Palethorp & Connell, Philadelphia, c.1840, 11 In.	118
Eagle, Spread Wings, Monarch Of The Sky, Victor Hayton, 1979, 10 ½ In..................................	45
Jug, Loop Handle, No. 4498, Kayserzinn, Germany, 1900-01, 8 x 4 x 7 In.	219
Lamp, Bull's-Eye, Whale Oil Burner, Patent On Hood, 1810s, 8 ½ In.	240

Peters & Reed, Vase, Moss Aztec, Cylindrical, Brown, Green, Marked MZX RAE, 21 In.
$316

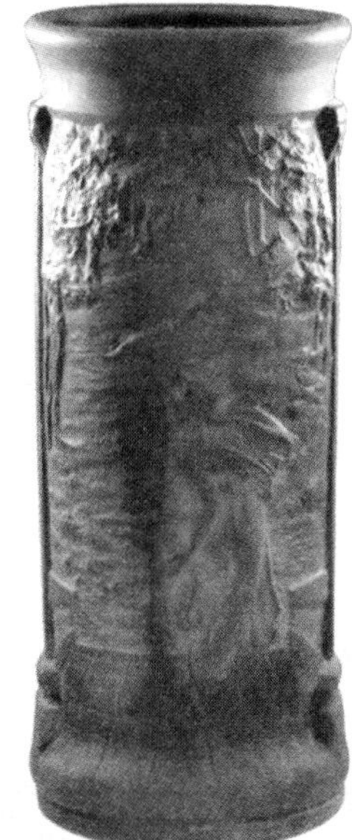

Belhorn Auction Services

TIP
Don't display pewter on a wooden shelf. Paint and wood give off gases that damage pewter.

Pewabic, Vase, Oval, Multicolor Glaze, Detroit, 8 ½ x 6 ½ In.
$1,875

Treadway

This is an edited listing of current prices. Visit **Kovels.com** to check thousands of prices from previous years and sign up for free information on trends, tips, reproductions, marks, and more.

P

The Monteith Bowl
Mr. Monteith was a Scotsman who wore a cloak with a scalloped hem. A large punch bowl with a similar scalloped edge is called a "Monteith bowl." It is usually at least 12 inches in diameter.

Pewter, Biscuit Jar, Castilian, Green Glass, Lotus, Dragonfly Handle, Footed, Poland, 9 x 7 ½ In.
$212

Bunch Auctions

Pewter, Tankard, Albert Schuder, Hinged Lid, Tapered Body, Handle, 1700s, 7 ¾ In.
$622

Hartzell's Auction Gallery Inc.

Lamp, Oil, Kayserzinn, Cologne, Germany, 1903-1904, 19 x 9 x 8 ⅜ In. 594
Monteith Bowl, Fluted Body, Shaped Rim, Handles, Beaded Foot, 1700s, 9 x 14 In. 6765
Punch Bowl, Frog, Snail, Glass Liner, Kayserzinn, Germany, c.1902, 13 x 13 In. 625
Rabbit Hunter, Curled Shoes, Wall Mount, Towel Hook, 14 x 5 In. 74
Sconce, Louis XVI Style, Angel, Shell, 2 Scroll Arms, 14 ½ In. 50
Spoon, Wavy End, Elongated Bowl, Marked, 1700s, 7 In., 12 Piece 221
Sundial, Roman Numerals, Gnomon, 1700s, 3 In. 277
Tankard, Albert Schuder, Hinged Lid, Tapered Body, Handle, 1700s, 7 ¾ In. ....*illus* 622
Tea Caddy, Scene, Lacquered, Hinged Lid, Chinese Export, 4 x 8 ½ x 5 ¾ In. 246
Teapot, Boardman & Hart, Engraved Thistle, Footed, Shaped Handle, c.1840, 7 ¾ In. ....*illus* 366
Tray, Flowers & Leaves, Fish, Oval, Kayserzinn, c.1894-1912, 24 x 11 In. 96
Wine Cooler, Crane, Funicular Railway, Lighthouse, Kayserzinn, Germany, c.1902, 9 In. 188

PHOENIX GLASS

Phoenix Glass Company was founded in 1880 in Pennsylvania. The firm made commercial products, such as lampshades, bottles, and glassware. Collectors today are interested in the "Sculptured Artware" made by the company from the 1930s until the mid-1950s. Some pieces of Phoenix glass are very similar to those made by the Consolidated Lamp and Glass Company. Phoenix made Reuben Blue, lavender, and yellow pieces. These colors were not used by Consolidated. In 1970 Phoenix became a division of Anchor Hocking, which was sold to the Newell Group in 1987. The factory is still working.

Cheese Dish, Dome Lid, Cranberry Opalescent, Craquelle, c.1885, 7 x 9 In. 263
Pitcher, Water, Flowers, White Threading, Bulbous, c.1900, 7 In. ....*illus* 82
Pitcher, Water, Spot Optic, Satin Mother-Of-Pearl, c.1900, 10 ½ In. ....*illus* 176

PHONOGRAPH

Phonographs, invented by Thomas Edison in 1877, have been made by many firms. This category also includes other items associated with the phonograph. Jukeboxes and Records are listed in their own categories.

Columbia, Grafonola, Oak, Floor Model, Record, Cabinet, 23 x 21 x 42 In. 81
Columbia, Graphophone, AH Disc, Oak Case, Horn, c.1904-05, 8 ½ x 12 x 12 In. 767
Columbia, Graphophone, Oak, Disc Player, Spear Tip Horn, 36 x 20 x 16 In. ....*illus* 3025
Columbia, Graphophone, Type C, Oak Dome Top Case, c.1900, 11 ½ x 6 x 9 In. 293
Edison, Diamond, Disc, Oak Mission Style Cabinet, Speed Control, Decal, 16 x 17 In. 242
Edison, Fireside, Model A, Combination Type, Black Horn, Oak Case, c.1909, 35 x 9 x 11 In. 3042
Edison, Horn, White Roses, Green Leaves, Burgundy, Oak Case, 13 x 9 ½ In. 220
Figurine, Dog, Nipper, Sitting, Painted, Chalkware, Base, 14 In. 124
Harmony Talking Machine, Blue & Gold Horn, Columbia Phonograph Co., c.1910, 23 x 17 x 17 In. 293
Lamp, Copper Base, Brass Claw Feet, Shade, Burns-Pullock Electric Mfg. Co., c.1915, 21 In. *illus* 995
Standard, Model A, Talking Machine, Oak Case, Blue Horn, c.1915, 22 x 11 In. 351
Talk-O-Phone, Oak Case, Stenciled Panel, Black, Brass Horn, 10 x 13 x 17 In. ....*illus* 726
Victor Victrola, Talking Machine, Model VV4-40, Mahogany Finish, c.1927, 37 x 36 In. 263
Victor Victrola, Talking Machine, Oak Case, Side Crank, 15 x 16 In. ....*illus* 250
Victor Victrola, Talking Machine, Oak Case, Stepped Base, Black Iron Arm, Horn, 22 In. 923
Victor, Talking Machine, Type R Disc, Square Oak Case, Bell Shape Horn, 14 x 9 In. 787
Victor, Type II, Talking Machine, Oak Case, c.1915, 21 x 11 ½ In. 761

PHONOGRAPH NEEDLE CASE

Phonograph needle cases of tin are collected today by music and phonograph enthusiasts and advertising addicts. The tins are very small, about 2 inches across, and often have attractive graphic designs lithographed on the top and sides.

Golden Pyramid, Embossed, Pyramid Shape, 200 Needles, Blue Shield, 2 ½ In. 125
Herold-Needles, Highly Refined, Phonograph, Hinged Lid, Blue, Yellow, 1 ⅝ x 2 In. 38

Pewter, Teapot, Boardman & Hart, Engraved Thistle, Footed, Shaped Handle, c.1840, 7 ¾ In.
$366

Pook & Pook

Phoenix Glass, Pitcher, Water, Flowers, White Threading, Bulbous, c.1900, 7 In.
$82

Jeffrey S. Evans & Associates

Phoenix Glass, Pitcher, Water, Spot Optic, Satin Mother-Of-Pearl, c.1900, 10 ½ In.
$176

Jeffrey S. Evans & Associates

Phonograph, Columbia, Graphophone, Oak, Disc Player, Spear Tip Horn, 36 x 20 x 16 In.
$3,025

Fontaine's Auction Gallery

Phonograph, Lamp, Copper Base, Brass Claw Feet, Shade, Burns-Pullock Electric Mfg. Co., c.1915, 21 In.
$995

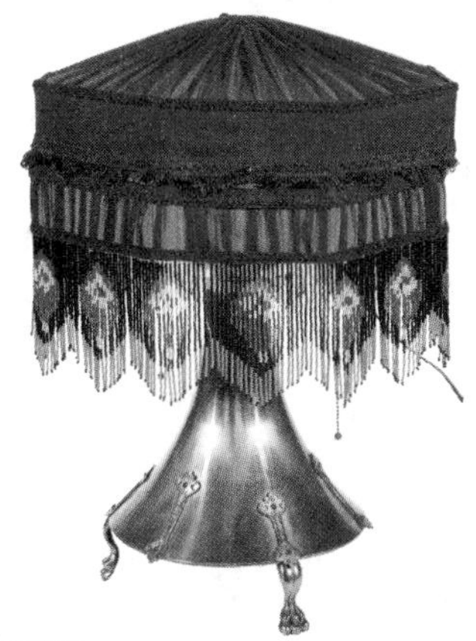

Jeffrey S. Evans & Associates

Phonograph, Talk-O-Phone, Oak Case, Stenciled Panel, Black, Brass Horn, 10 x 13 x 17 In.
$726

Fontaine's Auction Gallery

P

Phonograph, Victor Victrola, Talking Machine, Oak Case, Side Crank, 15 x 16 In.
$250

Bertoia Auctions

Photography, Albumen, First Lady Julia Dent Grant, Mat, Frame, 1860s, 13 x 15 In.
$375

Cowan's Auctions

Found Photographs

In the 1990s a few dealers and galleries "discovered" photographs by amateurs. They searched boxes of snapshots, pored over work by news and sports photographers, and looked for other sources of photographs of daily life. The best were matted, framed, and hung in galleries to be sold to collectors as art. These are known as "found photographs," and many show remarkable artistic talent and photographic skill.

Imperial, 200 Needles, Green, Red, Germany, 2 x 1 3/8 In. 30
Kosmos Extra, Cherub With Wreath, Germany, 2 x 1 In. 95
Natural Voice, Talking Machine Needles, Dogs, Red, White, Tin Lithograph, 1930s 49

PHOTOGRAPHY

Photography items are listed here. The first photograph was a view from a window in France taken in 1826. The commercially successful photograph started with the daguerreotype introduced in 1839. Today all sorts of photographs and photographic equipment are collected. Albums were popular in Victorian times. Cartes de visite, popular after 1854, were mounted on 2 ½-by-4-inch cardboard. Cabinet cards were introduced in 1866. These were mounted on 4 ¼-by-6 ½-inch cards. Stereo views are listed under Stereo Card. Stereoscopes are listed in their own section.

Albumen, First Lady Julia Dent Grant, Mat, Frame, 1860s, 13 x 15 In. .... *illus* 375
Cabinet Card, Buffalo Soldier, Wearing Buffalo Coat Over Uniform, Standing, c.1886 .... *illus* 16250
Camera, Daguerreotype, Brass, Cone Shape, Stand, Voigtlander, Replica Of 1840 Model 713
Camera, Hasselblad, 500CM, Chrome Trim, Lens Collar, 80 mm Zeiss Planar CF Lens 878
Camera, Hasselblad, 503CX, Zeiss Lenses, Branded Carrying Case, 10 x 13 In. 1970
Camera, Zeiss Ikon, Contaflex Twin Lens, 50 mm F1.5 Primary Lens, 1930s .... *illus* 805
Carte De Visite, Abraham Lincoln, By Alexander Gardner, August 9, 1863 .... *illus* 688
Daguerreotype, Girl, Toddler, Leather Case, 1/6 Plate .... *illus* 281
Daguerreotype, Young Woman, Black Dress, Holding Book, 1/6 Plate, c.1850 .... *illus* 3125
Photograph, Boy, Holding Rifle, Frame, c.1890, 7 5/8 x 5 5/8 In. 69
Photograph, Candy Sam, Black Man, Basket, Seated, George K. Warren, 1865, 9 x 11 In. *illus* 1625
Photograph, Spanish-American War, Frame, C.H. Anderson, New York, 1899, 19 ½ x 28 In. 94
Photograph, U.S. Cavalry Soldier, Horse, Winter Haven, Frame, c.1898, 6 x 8 In. 92
Tintype, 2 Men With Motorcycles, Barn, Box, 1900s, 3 x 4 In. 182

PIANO BABY

Piano baby is a collector's term. About 1880, the well-decorated home had a shawl on the piano. Bisque figures of babies were designed to help hold the shawl in place. They usually range in size from 6 to 18 inches. Most of the figures were made in Germany. Reproductions are being made. Other piano babies may be listed under manufacturers' names.

Boy, Crawling, Head Up, Blond Hair, Gebruder Heubach, 6 x 9 In. 215
Boy, Sitting, Smiling, Holding Toes, Victorian Gown, 8 ½ In. 60
Boy, Yellow Dress, Teeth, Laying On Stomach, Puppy On Back, 4 x 9 In. 125
Girl, Leaning On Elbow, Waving, Nightdress, Blue Bow, Gebruder Heubach, 5 x 2 In. 95

PICKARD

Pickard China Company was started in 1893 by Wilder Pickard. Hand-painted designs were used on china purchased from other sources. In the 1930s, the company began to make its own china wares in Chicago, Illinois. The company made a line of limited edition plates and bowls in the 1970s and 1980s. It now makes many types of porcelains.

Pickard/Edgerton Art Studio
1893–1894

Pickard/Pickard Studios, Inc.
1925–1930

Pickard, Inc.
1938–present

Cake Plate, Peacock, Gold Brocade Border, Bavaria Blank, c.1910, 12 In. .... *illus* 125
Charger, Pheasant Scene, Gold Brocade Border, Signed, Challinor, 12 In. .... *illus* 80
Vase, Peacock, Gold Brocade Bottom, Scalloped Rim, c.1910, 9 In. .... *illus* 400

Photography, Cabinet Card, Buffalo Soldier, Wearing Buffalo Coat Over Uniform, Standing, c.1886
$16,250

Cowan's Auctions

Photography, Camera, Zeiss Ikon, Contaflex Twin Lens, 50 mm F1.5 Primary Lens, 1930s
$805

Blackwell Auctions

Photography, Carte De Visite, Abraham Lincoln, By Alexander Gardner, August 9, 1863
$688

Cowan's Auctions

Photography, Daguerreotype, Girl, Toddler, Leather Case, 1/6 Plate
$281

Cowan's Auctions

Photography, Daguerreotype, Young Woman, Black Dress, Holding Book, 1/6 Plate, c.1850
$3,125

Cowan's Auctions

Photography, Photograph, Candy Sam, Black Man, Basket, Seated, George K. Warren, 1865, 9 x 11 In.
$1,625

Cowan's Auctions

Pickard, Cake Plate, Peacock, Gold Brocade Border, Bavaria Blank, c.1910, 12 In.
$125

Woody Auctions

Pickard, Charger, Pheasant Scene, Gold Brocade Border, Signed, Challinor, 12 In.
$80

Woody Auctions

Pickard, Vase, Peacock, Gold Brocade Bottom, Scalloped Rim, c.1910, 9 In.
$400

Woody Auctions

PICTURE

Picture, Lithograph, Pteroglossus Prasinus, Edward Lear, Frame, 21 x 14 In.
$384

Neal Auction Company

Picture, Needlework, Crewel, Flowers, Gilt Basket, Frame, c.1875, 31 x 23 In.
$120

Garth's Auctioneers & Appraisers

Picture, Needlework, Memorial, Bowman Family, Silk Embroidery, Frame, c.1800, 18 x 17 In.
$1,755

Jeffrey S. Evans & Associates

Picture, Needlework, Memorial, Silk, Watercolor On Paper, Sisters, Frame, c.1816, 28 x 28 In.
$600

Garth's Auctioneers & Appraisers

Picture, Needlework, Memorial, Silk, Woman, Child, Tombstone, Frame, c.1820, 23 x 26 In.
$570

Eldred's

Picture, Needlework, Portrait Of Lincoln, Wool & Silk, Gilt Frame, Stars, c.1890, 34 In.
$388

Garth's Auctioneers & Appraisers

Picture, Needlework, Silk, Embroidery, Mourning Scene, Martha Sharp, 1832, 16 x 13 In.
$861

Clars Auction Gallery

Picture, Needlework, Wool, Portrait, British Frigate, Wood Frame, England, 1800s, 18 x 23 In.
$461

Skinner, Inc.

Picture, Pencil, On Paper, Drypoint, House, Man & Woman, Tree, Alfred Hutty, 1929, 9 x 11 In.
$2,337

Charlton Hall Auctions

PICTURE

Pictures, silhouettes, and other small decorative objects framed to hang on the wall are listed here. Some other types of pictures are listed in the Print and Painting categories.

Lithograph, Pteroglossus Prasinus, Edward Lear, Frame, 21 x 14 In. ....*illus* 384
Miniature Portrait, Joseph Smith, Frame, England, c.1837, 2 ¾ In. x 2 In. 351
Needlework, Animals, Flag, Wool, Under Glass, Cove Molded Frame, Victorian, 26 x 23 In. 129
Needlework, Courting Scenes, Lacework, Blue Ground, England, c.1900, 12 x 15 In., 2 Piece .. 266
Needlework, Crewel, Flowers, Gilt Basket, Frame, c.1875, 31 x 23 In. ....*illus* 120
Needlework, Family Outdoors, Mary Ann Lotts Work Reading 1859, Mahogany Frame, 32 x 26 In. 118
Needlework, Family Register, Thomas Family, 26 x 21 In. 360
Needlework, Happy Easter, Wool On Linen, Flowers, Bird, Sarah Wurz, Frame, 1844, 18 x 17 In. ... 70
Needlework, Memorial, Bowman Family, Silk Embroidery, Frame, c.1800, 18 x 17 In. ..... *illus* 1755
Needlework, Memorial, In Memory Of William Dean, Willow Tree, c.1809, 11 x 12 In. 497
Needlework, Memorial, Silk, Watercolor On Paper, Sisters, Frame, c.1816, 28 x 28 In. ....*illus* 600
Needlework, Memorial, Silk, Woman, Child, Tombstone, Frame, c.1820, 23 x 26 In. ......*illus* 570
Needlework, Minnie Mouse, Woven Fabric, Black Frame, c.1930, 16 x 12 ⅝ In. 461
Needlework, Portrait Of Lincoln, Wool & Silk, Gilt Frame, Stars, c.1890, 34 In. ....*illus* 388
Needlework, Silk, Embroidery, Mourning Scene, Martha Sharp, 1832, 16 x 13 In. ....*illus* 861
Needlework, Silk, Painted, Garden Scene, 2 Women, Boy In Tree, Frame, 16 x 19 In. 840
Needlework, Wool, Peacock, Tree, Black Frame, Gilt Liner, Under Glass, c.1840, 15 x 14 In...... 410
Needlework, Wool, Portrait, British Frigate, Wood Frame, England, 1800s, 18 x 23 In. ...*illus* 461
Needlework, Wreath, Flowers, Multicolor, Frame, 20 x 26 In... 170
Pencil, On Paper, Drypoint, House, Man & Woman, Tree, Alfred Hutty, 1929, 9 x 11 In. ...*illus* 2337
Sandpaper, Landscape, Sailboats, Mountains, Signed, Julia Hamond, Frame, 1800s, 14 x 16 In. *illus* 148
Scherenschnitte, Memorial, Bust, Man, Flags, Shield, Geometric Border, c.1825, 13 x 13 In. . *illus* 384
Sculpture, Metal, Irregular Squares, Patina, Signed, Curtis Jere, 37 x 57 In. ....*illus* 406
Silhouette, Woman, Hollow Cut, Concave Corners, Painted, Gold Frame, 1800s, 3 ⅝ x 4 ⅜ In.. 554
Theorem, Eagle, Red, White, Blue, Banner, Liberty Justice Equality, 19 x 21 In. 413
Theorem, Watercolor, Basket of Fruit, Grain Painted Frame, 18 x 21 ¼ In. ....*illus* 2160
Wall Hanging, Oak Leaves, Mixed Metals, Signed, C. Jere, 1969, 29 x 59 In. 224
Watercolor, Family Record, Robinson, Tucker, White Border, Frame, 1700-1800s, 18 x 14 In.. 677
Watercolor, Folksy, Urn, Tulips, Lovebirds, Flowers, Frame, c.1850, 17 x 13 In. ....*illus* 300
Watercolor, Frame, Frinks Locks, Foot Of The Five, Pennsylvania, 17 x 20 In.......................... 180
Watercolor, Young Woman, Black Dress, Bird's-Eye Maple Frame, c.1830, 11 x 9 In................. 1320
Wreath, Flowers, Dyed, Cut Feather, Walnut Frame, Oval, 30 x 22 In.. 102

PICTURE FRAMES *are listed in this book in the Furniture category under Frame.*

PIERCE, *see Howard Pierce category.*

PILKINGTON

Pilkington Tile and Pottery Company was established in 1892 in England. The company made small pottery wares, like buttons and hatpins, but soon started decorating vases purchased from other potteries. By 1903, the company had discovered an opalescent glaze that became popular on the Lancastrian pottery line. The manufacture of pottery ended in 1937. Pilkington's is still making tiles.

Vase, Medieval Knight, On Horseback, Blue Green Ground, Royal Lancastrian, 9 x 4 In. .*illus* 1080

PILLIN

Pillin pottery was made by Polia (1909–1992) and William (1910–1985) Pillin, who set up a pottery in Los Angeles in 1948. William shaped, glazed, and fired the clay, and Polia painted the pieces, often with elongated figures of women, children, flowers, birds, fish, and other animals. The company closed in 2014. Pieces are marked with a stylized Pillin signature.

Picture, Sandpaper, Landscape, Sailboats, Mountains, Signed, Julia Hamond, Frame, 1800s, 14 x 16 In.
$148

Conestoga Auction Company

TIP
Attach hanging wire to a picture two-thirds of the way up the back of the picture. Be sure the wire does not show above the top of the frame when the picture is hung.

Picture, Scherenschnitte, Memorial, Bust, Man, Flags, Shield, Geometric Border, c.1825, 13 x 13 In.
$384

Garth's Auctioneers & Appraisers

Picture, Sculpture, Metal, Irregular Squares, Patina, Signed, Curtis Jere, 37 x 57 In.
$406

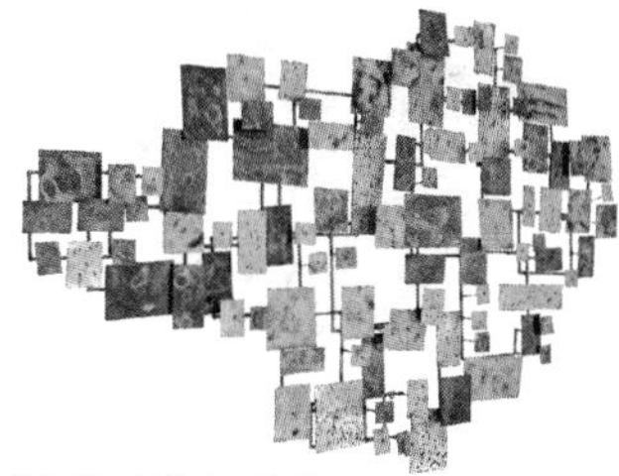

Palm Beach Modern Auctions

P

Picture, Theorem, Watercolor, Basket of Fruit, Grain Painted Frame, 18 x 21 ¼ In.
$2,160

Bourgeault-Horan Antiquarians & Associates, LLC

Picture, Watercolor, Folksy, Urn, Tulips, Lovebirds, Flowers, Frame, c.1850, 17 x 13 In.
$300

Garth's Auctioneers & Appraisers

Pilkington, Vase, Medieval Knight, On Horseback, Blue Green Ground, Royal Lancastrian, 9 x 4 In.
$1,080

Morphy Auctions

Bowl, Nude Woman, Seated, Blue Hair, Tree, Bluebird, Brown, Cream, 6 x 11 In. 1300
Charger, Irregular Shape, 4 People, Stylized Tree, Signed, 16 x 12 ¾ In. 910
Vase, Bud, Orb Shape, Stylized Roosters, Blue Ground, Signed, 4 In. 1250
Vase, Bulbous, Narrow Neck, Flared Mouth, Orange, Red, Yellow Glaze, Signed, 9 x 7 In. 125

PINCUSHION DOLL

Pincushion dolls are not really dolls and often were not even pincushions. Some collectors use the term "half-doll." The top half of each doll was made of porcelain. The edge of the half-doll was made with several small holes for thread, and the doll was stitched to a fabric body with a voluminous skirt. The finished figure was used to cover a hot pot of tea, powder box, pincushion, whiskbroom, or lamp. They were made in sizes from less than an inch to over 9 inches high. Most date from the early 1900s to the 1950s. Collectors often find just the porcelain doll without the fabric skirt.

Child, Arms Extended, Dresden Flowers & Feathers On Cap, c.1910, 4 In. .... *illus* 1035
Flapper, Black Hair, Red Hairband, Green Feather, Germany, c.1920, 4 ½ In. .... *illus* 115
Girl, Arms Extended, Holding Fruit Platter, Jeweled Coronet, 5 ½ In. .... *illus* 575
Tennis Player, Flapper, Holding Tennis Racquet, Germany, 4 In. .... *illus* 115
Woman, Arms Extended, Holding Dresden Rose, Germany, 7 In. .... *illus* 633

PINK SLAG *pieces are listed in this book in the Slag Glass category.*

PIPE

Pipes have been popular since tobacco was introduced to Europe. Carved wood, porcelain, ivory, and glass pipes and accessories may be listed here.

Burl, Carved, Eagle, Spread Wing, Shield, Silver Ferule, Early 1900s, 4 In. 523
Fruitwood, Root, Carved, Napoleon, Animals, Men, Mustaches, Female, 1811, 9 In. .... *illus* 584
Gourd, Sprawling Arch, Metal Mouthpiece, Bulbous, Africa, 1950s 36
Meerschaum, African Female, Feathered Hat, Etched Silver Decorative Band, 4 ½ In. 60
Meerschaum, Cavalier Shape, Carved, Leather Case, Carl Heiss, 1800s, 7 ½ In. .... *illus* 527
Meerschaum, Nude Woman, Cherubs, Tobacco Leaves, Carved, Leather Case, 8 In. 410
Meerschaum, Nude Woman, Winged Cherub, Carved, c.1900, Case, 6 ¾ In. 575
Opium, Silver, Wirework, Peacock, Southeast Asia, 1900s, 14 In., Pair 177
Wood, Carved, Lady's Leg, Stocking & Boot, Metal Stand, Early 1900s, 5 In. .... *illus* 228
Wood, Hunter's, Painted, Porcelain Bowl, Pewter Mounts, 40 In. 94

PIRKENHAMMER

Pirkenhammer Austria

Pirkenhammer is a porcelain manufactory started in 1803 by Friedrich Holke and J. G. List. It was located in Bohemia, now Brezova, Czech Republic. The company made tablewares usually decorated with views and flowers. Lithophanes were also made. It became Manufaktura Pirkenhammer I.S. Original Porcelan Fabrik Brezova s.r.o. in 2002. The mark of the crossed hammers is easy to remember as the Pirkenhammer symbol.

Figurine, Flapper, Walking Dog, Cream, 9 In. 500
Figurine, Owl, Speckled Chest, White Base, 1930s, 6 x 4 In. 105
Vase, Poppy Design, Rounded Shoulder, Gilt Rim, 5 ½ x 2 In. 145

PISGAH FOREST

Pisgah Forest Pottery was made in North Carolina beginning in 1926. The pottery was started by Walter B. Stephen, who had been making pottery in that location since 1914. The pottery continued in operation after his death in 1961. It closed in 2014. The most famous Pisgah Forest ware are the turquoise crackle glaze wares and the cameo type with designs made of raised glaze.

Pincushion Doll, Child, Arms Extended, Dresden Flowers & Feathers On Cap, c.1910, 4 In.
$1,035

Theriault's

Pincushion Doll, Flapper, Black Hair, Red Hairband, Green Feather, Germany, c.1920, 4 ½ In.
$115

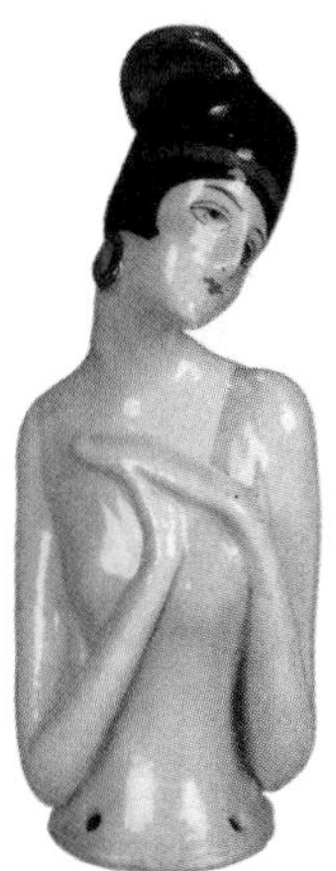

Theriault's

Pincushion Doll, Girl, Arms Extended, Holding Fruit Platter, Jeweled Coronet, 5 ½ In.
$575

Theriault's

Pincushion Doll, Tennis Player, Flapper, Holding Tennis Racquet, Germany, 4 In.
$115

Theriault's

Pincushion Doll, Woman, Arms Extended, Holding Dresden Rose, Germany, 7 In.
$633

Theriault's

Pipe, Fruitwood, Root, Carved, Napoleon, Animals, Men, Mustaches, Female, 1811, 9 In.
$584

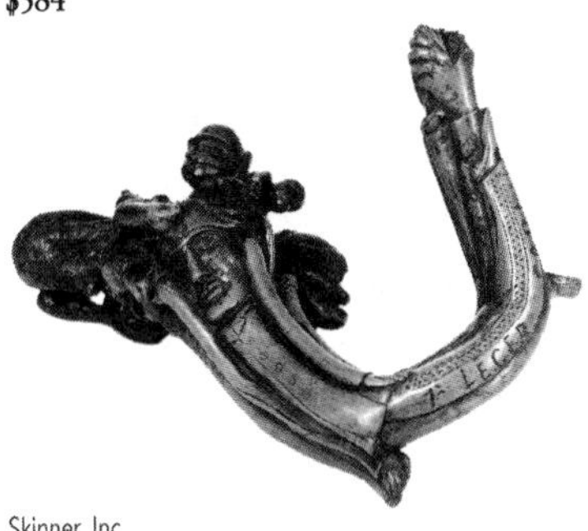

Skinner, Inc.

Pipe, Meerschaum, Cavalier Shape, Carved, Leather Case, Carl Heiss, 1800s, 7 ½ In.
$527

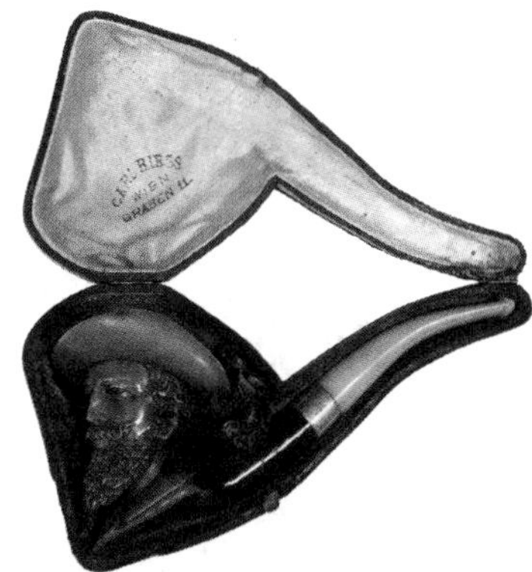

Thomaston Place Auction Galleries

Pipe, Wood, Carved, Lady's Leg, Stocking & Boot, Metal Stand, Early 1900s, 5 In.
$228

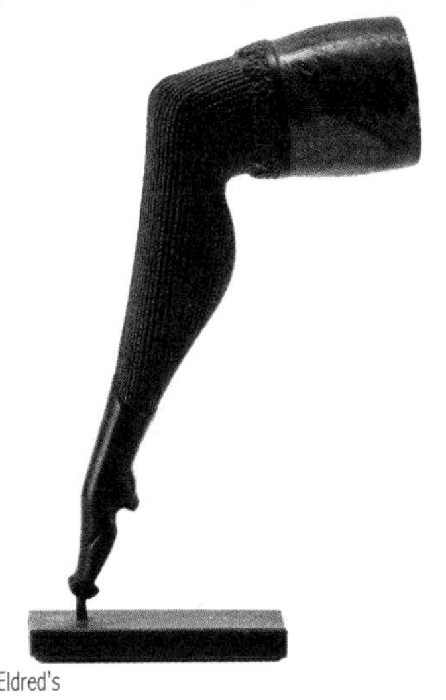

Eldred's

Pisgah Forest, Humidor, Lid, Round Finial, Green Glaze, Marked, 1953, 6 ⅞ In.
$75

Belhorn Auction Services

PISGAH FOREST

Pisgah Forest, Lamp Base, Buffalo Hunt, Teepee, Green Matte, Glossy Teal, W.B. Stephen, 11 In.
$600

Brunk Auctions

Planters Peanuts, Jar, Clear Glass, Lid, Finial, Yellow Label, 1936, 9 ½ x 8 In.
$83

Copake Auctions

Political, Ballot Box, Mahogany, Pediment Top, Brass Handle, 2 Drawers, 1800s, 13 x 11 In.
$554

Skinner, Inc.

Pisgah Forest Pottery
1926+

Pisgah Forest Pottery
Late 1940s

Pisgah Forest Pottery
1961+

Humidor, Lid, Round Finial, Green Glaze, Marked, 1953, 6 ⅞ In. ... *illus* 75
Lamp Base, Buffalo Hunt, Teepee, Green Matte, Glossy Teal, W.B. Stephen, 11 In. ... *illus* 600
Vase, Bulbous, Squat, Blue, Pink Inside, Round Rim, 1950, 3 ⅝ x 4 ⅜ In. ... 69

PLANTERS PEANUTS

Planters peanuts memorabilia are collected. Planters Nut and Chocolate Company was started in Wilkes-Barre, Pennsylvania, in 1906. The Mr. Peanut figure was adopted as a trademark in 1916. National advertising for Planters Peanuts started in 1918. The company was acquired by Standard Brands, Inc., in 1961. Standard Brands merged with Nabisco in 1981. Nabisco was bought by Kraft Foods in 2000. Kraft merged with H.J. Heinz Company in 2015. Planters brand is now owned by Kraft Heinz. Some of the Mr. Peanut jars and other memorabilia have been reproduced and, of course, new items are being made.

Canister, Lid, Peanut Finial, Glass, Clear, Figures Of Mr. Peanut, Hexagonal, 10 In. ... 57 to 108
Jar, Clear Glass, Lid, Finial, Yellow Label, 1936, 9 ½ x 8 In. ... *illus* 83
Jar, Display, Peanut Shape, Blown-Out, Lid, Footed, 14 In. ... 295
Jar, Lid, Planters Peanuts, Logo, Embossed, Peanut Handle, 13 In. ... 288

PLASTIC

Plastic objects of all types are being collected. Some pieces are listed in other categories; gutta-percha cases are listed in the Photography category. Celluloid is in its own category. Some bakelite may also be found in the Jewelry category.

Clock, Red, Bakelite, Domino Design On Side, Gold Dots, Metal Dial, Square, Art Deco, 3 ¼ In.. 216
Knife Set, Butterscotch, Bakelite, Black, Machine Age, Knives, Holder, 6 ⅝-In. Knife, 7 Piece. 216

PLATED AMBERINA

Plated amberina was patented June 15, 1886, by Joseph Locke and made by the New England Glass Company. It is similar in color to amberina, but is characterized by a cream colored or chartreuse lining (never white) and small ridges or ribs on the outside.

Bowl, Mahogany To Amber, Twisted Shape, Folded Edge, 8 In. ... 5400
Bowl, Rose & Mahogany To Custard, Oval, Ribbed, Inverted Rim, 4 ¾ In. ... 2400
Creamer, Red To Cream, Squat, Ribbed, Applied Handle, New England Glass Co., 5 In. ... 1800
Pitcher, Mahogany To Custard, Bulbous, Ribbed Neck, Applied Handle, 8 In. ... 19800
Salt & Pepper, Rose To Amber, Bulbous, Optic Spot, Footed, Metal Caps, 4 In., Pair ... 240
Saltshaker, Amber To Cream, Ribbed, Pinched Waist, Metal Cap, 3 ½ In. ... 2520
Spooner, Rose & Mahogany To Custard, Bulbous, Ribbed, Flared Rim, 4 In. ... 2520
Vase, Rose To Custard, Pinched Sides, Flared, Crimped Edge, 4 In. ... 960

PLIQUE-A-JOUR

Plique-a-jour is an enameling process. The enamel is laid between thin raised metal lines and heated. The finished piece has transparent enamel held between the thin metal wires. It is different from cloisonne because it is translucent.

Box, Gilt, Enamel, Ivory, 1800s, ¾ x 3 ⅝ In. ... 277

Kovsh, Gilt Silver, Flowers, Birds, Russia, 8 x 4 x 1 In. 1875

Pin, Dragon Fly, Diamonds, 18K Gold, Pink, Green, White, 2 x 3 In. 3000

Spoon, Leaf Shape, Silver, Green, Red Flower On Handle, c.1900, 4 ½ In. 74

POLITICAL

Political memorabilia of all types, from buttons to banners, are collected. Items related to presidential candidates are the most popular, but collectors also search for material related to state and local offices. Memorabilia related to social causes, minor political parties, and protest movements are also included here. Many reproductions have been made. A jugate is a button with photographs of both the presidential and vice presidential candidates. In this list a button is round, usually with a straight pin or metal tab to secure it to a shirt. A pin is brass, often figural, sometimes attached to a ribbon.

Ballot Box, Mahogany, Pediment Top, Brass Handle, 2 Drawers, 1800s, 13 x 11 In. .... *illus* 554

Bandanna, George Washington, Profile Bust, Seals, Red, White, 25 x 22 In. 4500

Bandanna, Memorial, George Washington, Eagle, Ships, Cotton, c.1806, 11 x 12 In. ...... *illus* 312

Bank, Dime, William Jennings Bryan, Shall The People Rule, Brass, Leather Cover, 4 In. 2125

Bank, Peaceful Bill, Smiling Jim, Taft, Sherman, Metal, Busts, J.M. Harper, 1908, 4 In. 625

Banner, Campaign, Harrison, Reid, Jugate, Ecce Homo, Eagle, Stars, Sailcloth, 57 x 68 In. 6250

Banner, McKinley, Safe, Supporters, Flags, Glazed Cotton, Honest Money, 35 x 24 In. 3875

Banner, Re-Elect President Franklin D. Roosevelt, Portrait, Oilcloth, 1936, 55 x 41 In. 625

Banner, Washington Patriae Pater, Bust, Shields, Laurel, Red, White, 1896, 22 x 25 In. 4500

Banner, Win With Willkie, Blue Cotton, Silkscreen Image, Grommets, 1940, 36 x 35 In. 313

Banner, Zachary Taylor, Flag, Brave Old Zach, Cotton, 1848, Frame, 21 x 26 In. .... *illus* 200000

Bunting, Dwight D. Eisenhower, Crossed Flags, Red, White, Blue, Yellow Fringe, 32 x 96 In. 177

Button, Abraham Lincoln, Hannibal Hamlin, Ferrotype, Brass, 1860, 1 In. .... *illus* 920

Button, Bryan, 16 To 1, Clock Face Portrait, 1 ¼ In. 359

Button, Cartoon, Roosevelt & Johnson, Bull Moose, Jugate, Moose On Map, 1912, 1 ¼ In. 7500

Button, Charles Evans Hughes, Our Next President, Portrait, 2 Shields, 1916, 1 ¼ In. ..... *illus* 17500

Button, Elect U.S. Senator John F. Kennedy Vice President, Portrait, 1956, 2 In. 450

Button, George Washington Inauguration, Long Live The President, Ringed Star, Brass 7500

Button, Kennedy, Boosters, Vote Democratic, 1960, 1 ¾ In. 454

Button, Roosevelt, Churchill, Stalin, Victory, For United Nations, Blue, Trigate, 1 In. 813

Button, Roosevelt, Fairbanks, Lady Liberty, Jugate, Celluloid, Whitehead & Hoag, 2 In. 1500

Button, Suffrage, Vote For Women Suffrage, November 1916, Oval, Bastian Bros., 1 In. 688

Button, Suffrage, Votes For New Jersey Women, Black, Gold, Sommer, ⅞ In. 938

Button, Suffrage, Woman Holding Banner, Forward, Denver, Metal, Pinback, ⅞ In. 1313

Button, Suffrage, Woman Trumpeter, Banner, 6 Stars, Sunrise, Votes For Women, Metal, 1 ¼ In. .. 1750

Button, Theodore Roosevelt, Our Greatest American, Portrait, Stars, Stripes, 1 ¼ In. ..... *illus* 750

Button, Theodore Roosevelt, Rough Rider, On Horse, Baltimore Badge, 1 ¼ In. 875

Cane, Handle, William McKinley, Figural Head, Black, c.1896, 3 ½ In. .... *illus* 72

Cane, U.S. Grant's Head Handle, Figural, Spelter, Wood Shaft, Metal Top, 34 In. 688

Cane, Walking Stick, Ulysses S. Grant, Cast Iron Bust, Wood Shaft, c.1868, 35 In. 819

Canteen, Bryan, Stevenson, Jugate, Glass Flask, Eagle, Capitol, Rope Handle, 4 ½ In. 1188

Cigar Case, Henry Clay, American Statesman, Portrait, Papier-Mache, Leather, 3 x 5 In. 1625

Clock, McKinley, Oak, Gingerbread, Pressed Portrait, Battleship On Glass, Ingraham, 23 In.... 688

Collar Box, Hayes, Wheeler, Jugate, Tin Litho, Orange, Yellow, Wire Handle, 1877, 5 In. 525

Doorknob, W.H. Harrison, Portrait, Bust, Sulphide, Bakewell, Page & Bakewell, 3 In. 3125

Figure, George Washington, Standing, Holding Document, Cast Iron, 47 ½ x 14 In. 9840

Figure, George Washington, Standing, Holding Sword, Slate Base, Late 1900s, 22 In. 192

Flask, Washington, Jackson, Presidential Election, Dark Green, Keene Glass Works, 1828, 7 In.. 780

Goblet, Franklin D. Roosevelt Inauguration, Acid Etched Silhouette, Vernay, 1933, 6 In. 425

Inkwell, Hard Cider, Tippecanoe Extract, W.H. Harrison, Glass, Barrel Shape, 2 In. 250

Inkwell, Harding, Coolidge, Jugate, Names, Metal, Chrome Plating, 1920, 3 x 5 In. 2000

Lamp, Franklin D. Roosevelt, Head Shape Shade, Frosted Glass, 9 In. 625

Lantern, Bryan, Sewall, Glass, Etched, Jugate, Flags, Silver On Shield, Wire Handle, 6 In. 525

Political, Bandanna, Memorial, George Washington, Eagle, Ships, Cotton, c.1806, 11 x 12 In.
$312

Cowan's Auctions

Political, Banner, Zachary Taylor, Flag, Brave Old Zach, Cotton, 1848, Frame, 21 x 26 In.
$200,000

Heritage Auctions

TIP
You should not regild, resilver, or repaint political buttons or badges. It lowers the value.

Political, Button, Abraham Lincoln, Hannibal Hamlin, Ferrotype, Brass, 1860, 1 In.
$920

Blackwell Auctions

Political, Button, Charles Evans Hughes, Our Next President, Portrait, 2 Shields, 1916, 1 ¼ In.
$17,500

Heritage Auctions

Political, Button, Theodore Roosevelt, Our Greatest American, Portrait, Stars, Stripes, 1 ¼ In.
$750

Heritage Auctions

Political, Cane, Handle, William McKinley, Figural Head, Black, c.1896, 3 ½ In.
$72

Rich Penn Auctions

Political, Picture, Needlework, Abraham Lincoln, Washington Bust, Frame, 1800s, 29 x 21 In.
$502

Conestoga Auction Company

Political, Plate, Benjamin Harrison, Cornstalks, Cobalt Blue Border, Gilt Rim, 1892, 9 ½ In.
$669

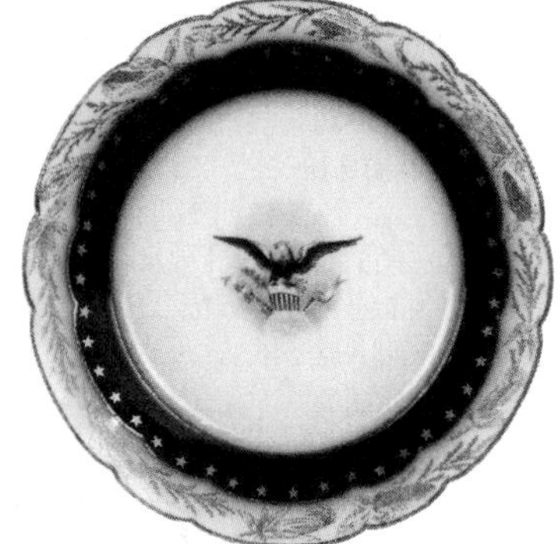
Clars Auction Gallery

Political, Textile, Teddy Roosevelt, Charles Fairbanks, Slogan, American Eagle, Frame, 1904, 25 x 21 In.
$438

Garth's Auctioneers & Appraisers

Political, Textile, Washington, America, Franklin, Lady Liberty, Toile, Frame, c.1790, 38 x 32 In.
$510

Garth's Auctioneers & Appraisers

Political, Toy, Scale, Balance Beam, Benjamin Harrison, Grover Cleveland, Bisque, 1888, 5 ½ in.
$750

Heritage Auctions

License Plate Attachment, Smith, For President, Brown Derby Hat, 4 x 8 ¾ In. 1558
Mask, Franklin Delano Roosevelt, Carved, Wire Glasses, Cigarette, Stand, c.1940, 12 In. 123
Match Safe, Cleveland, Harrison, Figural, 1888, 2 ½ In., Pair 325
Mug, Munroe, Portrait, Blue, White, Eagle, Stars, Ribbon, c.1825, 2 ½ In. 9375
Painting, Miniature, Zachary Taylor, Bust, Uniform, Enamel, 1 x 1 ¼ In. 2000
Paper, Appointment, Abraham Lincoln, Gold Frame, 1863, 12 ½ x 15 ½ In. 4095
Picture, Needlework, Abraham Lincoln, Washington Bust, Frame, 1800s, 29 x 21 In. .....*illus* 502
Pin, Cleveland, Portrait, Cardboard, Hanging, Eagle, 1 ½ In. 143
Pin, Cleveland, Thurman, Democratic Clubs, Jugate, Gilt Brass, Anchor, 1888, 6 In. 1625
Pin, Gold Bug, McKinley & Hobart, Mechanical, Gilt Metal, Jugate, 1896, 1 ½ In. 425
Pitcher, Garfield, Born 1831, President 1881, Transfers, Etruria, Wedgwood, 8 In. 375
Plate, Benjamin Harrison, Cornstalks, Cobalt Blue Border, Gilt Rim, 1892, 9 ½ In. ....*illus* 669
Plate, Elect Landon, Save America, Raised Portrait & Letters, Glass, Heisey, 1936, 8 In. 156
Plate, William McKinley, Portrait, Gold & Red Band, Porcelain, Royal Vienna, 9 ½ In. 938
Portrait, Thomas Jefferson, Clipped Autograph, Gold Frame, 13 x 11 ½ In. 1521
Poster, Adlai Stevenson, Which Will Be Safer For You, Portrait, Paper, 1952, 28 x 22 In. 1750
Poster, For Our Sake Vote No On Liquor, 2 Children, Cardboard, 22 x 14 In. 1250
Poster, For President, Eugene V. Debs, Half-Length Color Portrait, 1920, 24 x 18 In. 650
Poster, Kennedy For President, A Time For Greatness, J.F.K. Photo, 28 x 18 In. 781
Poster, R.F.K. Gala, Sat., June 1st, 1968, San Francisco, Portrait, Stars, 20 In. 400
Poster, Racism Chains Both, White & Black Fists, Communist Party, H. Gellert, 22 In. 513
Poster, Suffrage, Woman, 2 Soldiers, Will You Give Us The Vote?, WWI, 21 x 11 In. 3250
Poster, Wake Up, America, Sleeping Columbia, Stars & Stripes, J.M. Flagg, 1917, 41 In. 7800
Ribbon, Buchanan, Breckinridge, Keystone Club Dayton, Ohio, 1856, 7 In. 362
Ribbon, Grant, The People's Choice, Portrait, Red, White, Blue, 7 In. 221
Rug, Alton Parker, Henry Davis, American Flags, Eagle, Shield, 29 ½ x 54 ½ In. 720
Sign, Davis, Bryan, Jugate, Die Cut Teapot, Against Teapot Dome, 1924, 10 x 13 In. 1375
Snuffbox, Gen. Zachary Taylor, Portrait, Papier-Mache, Round, 1848, 3 ¼ In. 625
Snuffbox, George Washington, Portrait, Papier-Mache, Lacquer, Round, c.1832, 3 ½ In. 938
Snuffbox, James K. Polk, 10th President Of The U.S., Portrait, Papier-Mache, 3 ¼ In. 3000
Spare Tire Cover, Help Re-Elect Herbert Hoover, Portrait, Oilcloth, 1932, 28 In. 1063
Stickpin, Hand, Winfield Hancock, Brass, Rebus, Hand, Cock, Portrait On Cuff, 2 In. 5250
Stickpin, Teddy Roosevelt, Rough Rider, Bucking Horse, Sword, 1898, 1 ¾ x 1 In. 130
Teapot, W.H. Harrison, Log Cabin & Hard Cider Barrel Scenes, Red, White, Adams, 7 In. 500
Textile, Teddy Roosevelt, Charles Fairbanks, Slogan, American Eagle, Frame, 1904, 25 x 21 In. *illus* 438
Textile, Washington On Horse, Federal Shields, Stars, Frame, Centennial 4850
Textile, Washington, America, Franklin, Lady Liberty, Toile, Frame, c.1790, 38 x 32 In. ..*illus* 510
Toby Jug, Woodrow Wilson, Bi-Plane, Welcome Uncle Sam, Wilkinson, 1918, 10 In. 513
Toy, Scale, Balance Beam, Benjamin Harrison, Grover Cleveland, Bisque, 1888, 5 ½ in. .*illus* 750
Tray, McKinley, Roosevelt, Portrait, Tin Lithograph, Multicolor, Oval, 1900, 16 x 13 In. 3000
Tray, T. Roosevelt, Portrait, Tin Lithograph, Golden Seal Whiskey Ad, Oval, 18 In. 2750
Watch Fob, Warren Harding, Celluloid, Portrait, Mirror Reverse, Metal Loop, 1 ¾ In. 1500
Window, James A. Garfield, Strangulatus Pro Republica, Stained Glass, Frame, 27 x 26 In. 2375

POMONA

Pomona glass is a clear glass with a soft amber border decorated with pale blue or rose-colored flowers and leaves. The colors are very, very pale. The background of the glass is covered with a network of fine lines. It was made from 1885 to 1888 by the New England Glass Company. First grind was made from April 1885 to June 1886. It was made by cutting a wax surface on the glass, then dipping it in acid. Second grind was a less expensive method of acid etching that was developed later.

Candlestick, Green & Transparent, Mica Flecked, Applied Prunts, 12 x 5 In., Pair 281
Toothpick Holder, Polished Pontil Base, Trifold Top, New England Glass Co., 2 In. 96
Vase, Green, Urn Shape, Optic Ribs, Raised Circular Foot, 12 x 10 In. 184

PONTYPOOL, *see Tole category.*

TIP
Have an emergency plan for your collection. For storms with advance warning, arrange to move the collection or at least pack it and move it to the safest part of the house. Be sure to have packing materials available.

Popeye, Display, Popeye Flashlites, Cardboard, Character Images, Standup, c.1960, 15 x 10 In.
$590

AntiqueAdvertising.com

Popeye, Doorstop, Popeye, Standing, White Hat, Black Shirt & Shoes, Hubley, 4 x 2 x 9 In.
$1,560

Morphy Auctions

P

Popeye, Lunch Box, Metal, Thermos, King Seeley, 1964
$133

Bruneau & Co. Auctioneers

Popeye, Toy, Popeye & Olive Oyl Ball Toss, Tin Lithograph, Windup, Linemar, Box, 4 x 19 In.
$1,800

Rich Penn Auctions

Popeye, Toy, Popeye & Olive Oyl Juggling, Chair, Tin, Windup, Linemar, Box, Japan, 10 In.
$1,800

Bertoia Auctions

Popeye, Toy, Popeye, Driving Spinach Cart, Hubley, 6 In.
$1,700

Bertoia Auctions

Lunch Box Collecting

Lunch box collecting started in earnest after the publication in the 1960s of a book about lunch boxes and values by Bruce Scott.

Popeye, Toy, Popeye, Roller Skating, Holds Can of Spinach, Windup, Tin, Linemar, 6 ½ In.
$500

Milestone Auctions

Popeye, Toy, Popeye, Waddler, Standing, Orange Shoes, Windup, Tin, Chein, 6 In.
$300

Milestone Auctions

Porcelain, Bowl, Gilt Flowers, Scroll, Ruffled Rim, Continental, Victorian, 5 ½ x 10 ½ In.
$42

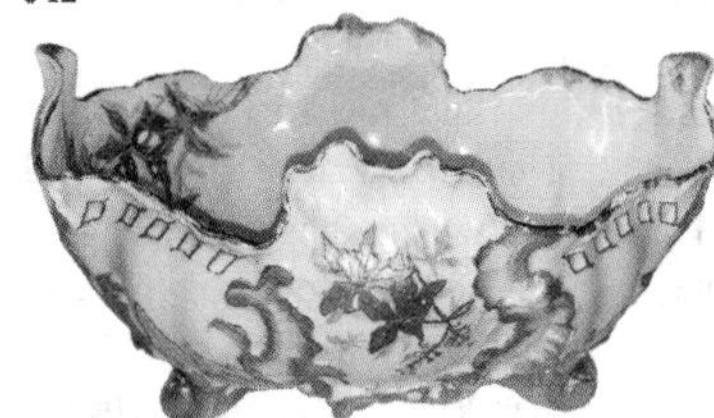

Bunte Auction Services

Porcelain, Chamber Pot, Dragon, Quail, Molded Mask, Du Paquier, Austria, c.1735, 4 x 9 In.
$9,688

New Orleans Auction Galleries

Porcelain, Charger, Farm Scene, 2 Bison, Painted, Gilt Rim, Bavaria, 12 In.
$300

Woody Auctions

Porcelain, Dish, Lid, Chicken, Nest, Feathers, White Speckles, Painted, Continental, c.1865, 8 In.
$152

Jeffrey S. Evans & Associates

POOLE POTTERY

Poole Pottery was founded by Jesse Carter in 1873 in Poole, England, and has operated under various names since then. The pottery operated as Carter & Co. for several years and established Carter, Stabler & Adams as a subsidiary in 1921. The company specialized in tiles, architectural ceramics, and garden ornaments. Tableware, bookends, candelabra, figures, vases, and other items have also been made. *Poole Pottery Ltd.* became the name in 1963. The company went bankrupt in 2003 but continued under new owners. Poole Pottery became part of Burgess & Leigh Ltd. in 2012. It is still in business, now making pottery in Middleport, Stoke-on-Trent.

Poole Pottery
1921–1924

Poole Pottery
1924–1950

Poole Pottery Ltd.
1990–1991

Cup, Volcano Lava Glaze, Orange, Red, Blue, Green, 3 ¾ In. 32
Figurine, Penguin, Black & White, Standing, 8 ½ In. 94
Vase, Lime Green, Textured Floral Panels, Orange & Yellow Drip Decoration, 8 In. 62
Vase, XE Pattern, Multicolor Flowers, White Ground, Oval, Ogee Neck, 12 ½ In. 587

POPEYE

Popeye was introduced to the Thimble Theatre comic strip in 1929. The character became a favorite of readers. In 1932, an animated cartoon featuring Popeye was made by Paramount Studios. The cartoon series continued and became even more popular when it was shown on television starting in the 1950s. The full-length movie with Robin Williams as Popeye was made in 1980. KFS stands for King Features Syndicate, the distributor of the comic strip.

Bank, Head Figure, Pipe, American Bisque, 7 ½ In. 316
Corkscrew, Figurine, Pewter, Gilt, Bulls, c.1937, 5 ½ In. 179
Display, Popeye Flashlites, Cardboard, Character Images, Standup, c.1960, 15 x 10 In. ...*illus* 590
Doorstop, Popeye, Cast Iron, Full-Figure, Hubley, No. 328, 1929, 9 In. 1800
Doorstop, Popeye, Standing, White Hat, Black Shirt & Shoes, Hubley, 4 x 2 x 9 In. ....*illus* 1560
Lunch Box, Metal, Thermos, King Seeley, 1964 ....*illus* 133
Target, Bubble, Graphics, Wood Frame, 26 x 17 In. 240
Thimble, Bernice The Whiffle Hen, Chrome Luster, 3 ½ In. 590
Toy, Popeye & Olive Oyl Ball Toss, Tin Lithograph, Windup, Linemar, Box, 4 x 19 In. ....*illus* 1800
Toy, Popeye & Olive Oyl Juggling, Chair, Tin, Windup, Linemar, Box, Japan, 10 In. ....*illus* 1800
Toy, Popeye, Driving Spinach Cart, Hubley, 6 In. ....*illus* 1700
Toy, Popeye, Roller Skating, Holds Can of Spinach, Windup, Tin, Linemar, 6 ½ In. ....*illus* 500
Toy, Popeye, Waddler, Standing, Orange Shoes, Windup, Tin, Chein, 6 In. ....*illus* 300
Toy, Turnover Tank, Silver, Windup, Tin, Linemar, 4 In. 276
Watch, Popeye, Multiple Character Faces, Arm Shape Hands, 1934, 2 In. 389

PORCELAIN

Porcelain factories that are well known are listed in this book under the factory name. This category lists pieces made by the less well-known factories. Additional pieces of porcelain are listed in this book in the categories Porcelain-Contemporary, Porcelain-Midcentury, and under the factory name.

Basket, Silver, Gilt Rim & Base, Woven Style, Buccellati, 1900s, 2 ½ x 5 ½ In. 150
Biscuit Jar, Carpet Bag Shape, Indian Tree Variation, Brass Mount, Handle, c.1885, 6 In. 300
Bowl, Gilt Flowers, Scroll, Ruffled Rim, Continental, Victorian, 5 ½ x 10 ½ In. ....*illus* 42

Porcelain, Eggcup, Coquetier Poule, Chicken Eggcup, Francois-Xavier Lalanne, 3 x 3 ½ In.
$2,500

Palm Beach Modern Auctions

Porcelain, Ewer, Painted, Shades Of Purple, Berry, Round Base, Wide Spout, France, 15 In.
$127

Apple Tree Auction Center

P

Porcelain, Figurine, Dog, Mastiff, Gilt, Red Collar, Bisque, Germany, c.1885, 12 x 15 In.
$187

Eldred's

Porcelain, Group, Bridal, Man, Women, Children, White, Flowers, Oblong Base, 11 ½ In.
$615

Stair Galleries

Porcelain, Group, Peasant Woman & Child, Seated, Round Base, Popov, Russia, 4 In.
$1,353

Stair Galleries

Porcelain, Pitcher, Flowers, Gilt, Monogram, Reeded Base, Tucker & Hemphill, Phila., 9 In.
$781

Freeman's Auctioneers & Appraisers

Porcelain, Plate, Order Of St. George, Interwoven Sash & Laurel, Russia, 1800s, 9 ½ In.
$2,432

Cowan's Auctions

Porcelain, Plate, Portrait, Queen Louisa, Scarf, Wide Pink Border, Bavaria, 9 ¾ In.
$40

Woody Auctions

Porcelain, Urn, Transfer Scenes, Cobalt Ground, Gold Enamel, Openwork Handles, 33 x 10 In.
$283

Soulis Auctions

Bowl, Glazed Faience, Blue, Enamel Flowers, France, 1920s, 3 x 10 In. 230
Bracket, Meissen Style, Nude Female, Couples, Flowers, c.1900, 17 x 16 In., Pair 1080
Butter Boat, Leaf Shape, White Glazed, Molded, Italy, 3 ½ In., Pair 154
Centerpiece, Winged Griffin, Women, Bronze Frame, Signed, Josef Steidl, 9 x 10 x 5 In. 212
Chamber Pot, Dragon, Quail, Molded Mask, Du Paquier, Austria, c.1735, 4 x 9 In. *illus* 9688
Charger, Blue & White, Peacock, Phoenix, Landscape, Geometric, Late 1800s, 3 x 21 In., Pair 439
Charger, Farm Scene, 2 Bison, Painted, Gilt Rim, Bavaria, 12 In. *illus* 300
Cider Jug, Figure On Bridge, Pagoda, Relief, Lowestoft, 1700s, 8 In. 576
Corbeille, Cupid Kneeling, Supporting Basket, Bleu De Roi, Bisque, Gilt, 1800s, 12 x 9 In. 450
Dish, Lid, Chicken, Nest, Feathers, White Speckles, Painted, Continental, c.1865, 8 In. *illus* 152
Dresser Box, Scrolls, Shells, Yellow, Woman In Pink Bathing Suit On Lid, Sitzendorf, 5 In. 115
Eggcup, Coquetier Poule, Chicken Eggcup, Francois-Xavier Lalanne, 3 x 3 ½ In. *illus* 2500
Ewer, Painted, Shades Of Purple, Berry, Round Base, Wide Spout, France, 15 In. *illus* 127
Figurine, Cat, Spaghetti, Seated, Black Ears, Green Eyes, Marked, Italy, 11 In. 91
Figurine, Dog, Cavalier, Glass Stand, Marked, Copenhagen, Denmark, 3 x 4 x 4 In. 35
Figurine, Dog, Mastiff, Gilt, Red Collar, Bisque, Germany, c.1885, 12 x 15 In. *illus* 187
Figurine, Man, Standing, Yellow Vest, Emblematic Of Fall, 10 In. 185
Figurine, Matador, Slim Male Figure, Salmon Shirt, Black Striped Pants, 1900s, 24 In. 150
Figurine, Rabbit, Cubist, Angular Body, Red Circles, Squares & Triangles, c.1925, 6 In., Pair 1476
Group, Bird, 2 Parrots, Perched, Multicolor, White Base, Continental, 10 In. 92
Group, Bridal, Man, Women, Children, White, Flowers, Oblong Base, 11 ½ In. *illus* 615
Group, Fortune Teller, 3 Women, Gilt Flowers, Marbled Blue, Green, Beehive Mark, 13 x 8 In. 2030
Group, Peasant Woman & Child, Seated, Round Base, Popov, Russia, 4 In. *illus* 1353
Group, Pianist, Dancers, Lace, Crinoline, Flowered Skirts, Germany. 11 ½ x 16 In. 384
Group, Spring, Man, Bagpipes, Woman, Seated, Basket, Flowers, Strausbourg, c. 1750, 9 In. 920
Group, Woman With Mandolin, Man With Cello, Dancers, Courting Couples, 15 x 22 In. 1540
Mug, Blue & White, Oriental Scenes, Diaperwork Border, Lowestoft, 5 In. 431
Pitcher, Flowers, Gilt, Monogram, Reeded Base, Tucker & Hemphill, Phila., 9 In. *illus* 781
Pitcher, Flowers, Multicolor, Gilt Handle & Rim, Enamel, England, 1800s, 6 In. 185
Plaque, Portrait, Artist, Standing, Brush In Hand, Gilt Frame, 33 x 23 In. 756
Plaque, Portrait, Women, Painted, Venetian Frame, 1800s, 11 x 8 ½ In. 283
Plate, Order Of St. George, Interwoven Sash & Laurel, Russia, 1800s, 9 ½ In. *illus* 2432
Porcelain, Plate, Portrait, Queen Louisa, Scarf, Wide Pink Border, Bavaria, 9 ¾ In. *illus* 40
Plate, White Ground, Printed, Blue Building & Boat Scene, Lowestoft, 2 ⅞ In. 215
Platter, 2 Dogs Center, Transfer Print, Yellow Border, Octagonal, Hermes, 19 In. 2583
Salt Bowl, Radish Shape, Spoon, Green, White, Schierholz 175
Sauceboat, Chinoiserie, Figures, Flowers, Painted, Footed, Lowestoft, 4 ½ In. 492
Sauceboat, White Glazed, Molded Prunus, Scalloped Rim, Footed, 8 In. 308
Tea Caddy, Woman, Flowers, Gilt, Lid, Albert Martine, 5 x 4 In. 454
Tray, Safety Pin, Life Preserver Shape, Magnetic, Label, Walter Starnes, 5 In. 51
Urn, Bisque, Molded Rim & Flowers, Square Base, Continental, 8 In., Pair 123
Urn, Champleve, Cobalt, Turquoise, Enamel, Romantic Cherub Scene, c.1900, 10 x 4 In. 185
Urn, Lid, Scenic, Women, Green Ground, Gilt Metal Mount, Vienna Style, 1900s, 12 In. 50
Urn, Pink, Couple, Cherubs, Gilt, Ormolu, Bronze Ram's Head Handles, Sevres Style, 23 x 11 In. 480
Urn, Transfer Scenes, Cobalt Ground, Gold Enamel, Openwork Handles, 33 x 10 In. *illus* 283
Vase, Birds, Cobalt Blue Ground, Gilt, 1910s, 11 ½ x 7 In. 180
Vase, Cartouches, Village On River, Birds, Flowers, Blue Ground, 21 ½ In. 1560
Vase, Celadon, Flowers, Rocaille, Spindle Shape, Gilt Rim, Art Nouveau, 22 In., Pair 5100
Vase, Cherubs, Putti, Capturing Goat, Reticulated Rim, Swags, Stellmacher, 15 x 5 ½ In. 60
Vase, Cherubs, Rose Pompadour Ground, Gilt, Sevres Style, Collot, 1800s, 30 In. 5000
Vase, Cobalt Blue, Gilt Handles, Painted Flower Sprays, 7 ½ In. 92
Vase, Double Gourd, White & Blue, Morning Glories, Hand Fans, Wood Stand, 1800s, 7 x 7 In. 234
Vase, Egyptian Design, Whimsical Handles, Graduated Roundels, France, 1850s, 11 ½ In. 96
Vase, Flowers, White Ground, Octagonal Rim, 2 Handles, Carl Thieme, c.1800s, 7 In. 63
Vase, Lid, Sevres Style, Bronze Mounted, Portrait, Pink Ground, Plinth, 1800s, 18 In. 2214
Vase, Woman In Garden, Dogs, Birds, Blue & Gold Enamel Beading, Prov Saxe, 4 In. 120

Porcelain-Asian includes pieces made in Japan, Korea, and other Asian countries. Asian porcelain is also listed in Canton, Chinese Export, Imari, Japanese Coralene,

Porcelain-Asian, Jardiniere, Blue & White, Flowers, Japan, 12 x 17 In.
$554

Stair Galleries

Porcelain-Asian, Planter, Bonsai, Bird, Foliage, White Ground, Footed, Japan, 5 x 9 x 13 In.
$104

Richard D. Hatch & Associates

TIP
When a house floods, special care is required. Save the things that are undamaged first, not the items that are soaked. Get metal legs off oriental rugs. Rust leaves a permanent stain.

Porcelain-Chinese, Bowl, Figures In Landscape, Flowers, 5 Goldfish Inside, 15 x 19 In.
$270

CRN Auctions

Porcelain-Chinese, Brush Coupe, Beehive Shape, Daoist Immortals, Blue & Red, 5 ½ In.
$923

Clars Auction Gallery

Porcelain-Chinese, Charger, Flowers, White Ground, Gilt Border, 15 In.
$354

Cottone Auctions

Porcelain-Chinese, Hat Stand, Cylindrical, Painted, Tree, Woman, Marked, c.1800, 11 In.
$148

Leland Little Auctions

TIP

Display groups of at least three of your collectibles to get decorating impact.

Moriage, Nanking, Occupied Japan, Porcelain-Chinese, Satsuma, Sumida, and other categories.

Charger, Painted, River, Buildings, Figures, Red, Yellow Rim, c.1800, 11 ¾ In. 67
Dish, Blue & White, Flowers on Center, Japan, 12 ½ In. 984
Jardiniere, Blue & White, Flowers, Japan, 12 x 17 In. .... *illus* 554
Planter, Bonsai, Bird, Foliage, White Ground, Footed, Japan, 5 x 9 x 13 In. .... *illus* 104
Vase, Red Flambe, White Ground, Faceted Seed Shape, Japan, 1950s, 8 ½ In. 108
Vase, Tapered Body, Straight Neck, Dragon Chasing Pearl, Joseon Dynasty, Korea, 20 ½ In. 2750
Vase, Tulipiere, Pyramid Shape, Bird, Blue & White, 23 In., Pair 468

Porcelain-Chinese is listed here. See also Canton, Chinese Export, Imari, Moriage, Nanking, and other categories.

Basin, Flared Rim, Blue Interior, Brown Glaze, Band Across, 15 ½ In. 369
Bowl, Aqua, Red Design, Cylindrical, Kangxi Mark Underside, 2 x 7 ⅜ In. 207
Bowl, Figures In Landscape, Flowers, 5 Goldfish Inside, 15 x 19 In. .... *illus* 270
Bowl, Flowers, Rosewood Stand, 1900s, 16 ½ x 16 ½ x 7 In. 661
Bowl, Footed, Bulbous, Round Rim, Olive Green Finish, 4 ½ x 6 In. 60
Bowl, Purple, Splash, Blue, Banded Rim, Jun Ware, 1800s, 1 ¾ x 5 ½ In. 576
Bowl, Thin, Milk, Vines, Lotus Blossoms, 6-Character Mark, Doucai, 3 x 5 ½ In. 576
Bowl, Urn Center, Diaper Border, Blue & White, Kangxi Period, 8 In., Pair 123
Box, Dragon, Multicolor Glaze, Marked, 4 ½ x 9 x 5 In. 248
Brush Coupe, Beehive Shape, Daoist Immortals, Blue & Red, 5 ½ In. .... *illus* 923
Brush Washer, Blue, Compressed Body, Chilong Relief On Rim, 10 ½ In. 800
Brushpot, Crayfish, Incised Border, Blue & White, Square Foot, 6 ½ x 4 In. 1680
Brushpot, Gilt Script, Blue Ground, Marked, 6 x 8 In. 674
Brushpot, Pale Celadon, Cylindrical, Turquoise, Hawk, Pine Tree, 5 ½ In. 1845
Candleholder, Buddhistic Lion, Glazed, Green & Yellow, 7 ½ In., Pair 123
Charger, Flowers, White Ground, Gilt Border, 15 In. .... *illus* 354
Charger, Wucai, Qing Style, Multicolor, Immortals, Fish, Dragon, 1662-1722, 16 In. 936
Cup, Flower Shape, Turned-Out Rim, Ge Type, Crackled Design, 2 In., Pair 2700
Cup, White Ground, Garden Scene, Footed, Blue, White, 6-Character Mark, 2 ½ In. 1320
Dish, Narcissus, Curved, Carved Wood Stand, Marked, Dayazhai, 3 x 10 In. 3162
Figurine, Blanc De Chine, Flowing Robes, Ruyi Scepter, Gourd Seal, 1900s, 19 In. 322
Figurine, Cai Shen, Holding Ruyi, Dragon Robe, Incised, Seal On Base, 26 x 9 In. 492
Figurine, Guanyin, Flowing Robes, Blanc De Chine, Bronze Base, 22 x 7 In. 527
Figurine, Guanyin, Lotus Petal Platform, Sea Waves, 2-Part, 1800s, 13 In. 1140
Fishbowl, Blue & White, Dragons, Flowers, Wood Stand, 18 x 20 In., Pair 2706
Ginger Jar, Lid, Wucai, Fish, Ming Style, Jiajing Character Mark, 14 x 13 In. 708
Hat Stand, Cylindrical, Painted, Tree, Woman, Marked, c.1800, 11 In. .... *illus* 148
Jar, Blue & White Glaze, Flowers, Molded Rim, 1900s, 11 ½ In., Pair .... *illus* 117
Jar, Lid, Dragon, Flowers, Wave, Blue & White, Round Finial, 1900s, 14 x 6 In. 250
Jar, Lid, Famille Verte, Warriors, Great Wall, Marked, 17 x 9 ½ In. 1376
Jar, Lid, Foo Dog Finial, Landscape, Blue & White, c.1700, 25 x 15 In. .... *illus* 1440
Jardiniere, 2 Dragons, Flaming Pearl, Hand Painted, Wood Stand, 5 x 6 ½ In. 185
Lamp, 2 Medallions, Flowers, Mint Green Ground, Square, 25 x 5 In., Pair 1375
Lamp, Barrel Shape, Multicolor, Tobacco Leaf, Brass, Wood Base, 1900s, 24 ½ In. 938
Lamp, Blue Ground, White Flowers, Crackle Ice & Prunus, 1800s, 14 In. 563
Lamp, Iron Red, Foo Dog, White Shade, Wood Base, 1800s, 34 In. 502
Planter, Powder Blue Ground, Gilt Edged Panels, Kangxi Mark, 7 x 5 ¾ In. 688
Plate, Blue & White, Stylized Lotus Scrolls, Apocryphal Xuande Mark, 7 In. 1046
Plate, Yellow, Waves, Mums, Sgraffito, Scalloped, 6-Character Mark, 7 ½ In. .... *illus* 720
Snuff Bottle, Blue & White, 6-Character Mark, Wood Base, 3 In. 123
Stand, Landscape, Calligraphy On Edge, White Ground, c.1915, 11 ½ In. 60
Teapot, Lid, Family Scene, Bulbous Body, Handle, 1800s, 5 In. 127
Teapot, Woman, Children, Swing Handle, Finial, Tongzhi Mark, 6 In. 215
Urn, Lid, Green, Bulbous, Footed, Finial, 36 In. 71
Vase, Arabic Inscription, Blue & White, Bottle Shape, 19 ¾ In. .... *illus* 8400
Vase, Blanc De Chine, An Hua Flowers, Flared, Republic Period, 13 x 10 In. 360
Vase, Blanc De Chine, Scholar, Students, Verse, Dragon Handles, Kangxi, 15 In. 780

Porcelain-Chinese, Jar, Blue & White Glaze, Flowers, Molded Rim, 1900s, 11 ½ In., Pair
$117

Thomaston Place Auction Galleries

Porcelain-Chinese, Jar, Lid, Foo Dog Finial, Landscape, Blue & White, c.1700, 25 x 15 In.
$1,440

CRN Auctions

Porcelain-Chinese, Plate, Yellow, Waves, Mums, Sgraffito, Scalloped, 6-Character Mark, 7 ½ In.
$720

Selkirk Auctioneers & Appraisers

TIP
If you have a small-neck decanter or bottle that doesn't seem to dry after it is washed, try putting a small amount of rubbing alcohol in the bottle. Shake, pour out, and wait for the remaining drops to evaporate.

Porcelain-Chinese, Vase, Arabic Inscription, Blue & White, Bottle Shape, 19 ¾ In.
$8,400

Michaan's Auctions

Porcelain-Chinese, Vase, Children Holding Buddhist Treasures, Oval, Marked, 1700s, 7 ¾ In.
$3,075

Clars Auction Gallery

Porcelain-Chinese, Vase, Flat Circular Body, Cylindrical Opening, Open Handles, Early 1900s, 13 In., Pair
$215

Locati Auctions

TIP
Crayons are wax, so crayon marks can be removed by melting the wax and blotting it away.

Porcelain-Chinese, Vase, Flower Medallion, Mythical Creatures, Wu Tsai, 1800s, 7 ¼ In.
$432

Selkirk Auctioneers & Appraisers

Porcelain-Contemporary, Figurine, Jesus Burger, Bun, Toppings, Frog, David Gilhooly, 2004, 9 In.
$2,125

New Orleans Auction Galleries

Porcelain-Contemporary, Figurine, Parrot, Gold Trim, Stand, Giulia Mangani, Oggetti, Italy, 14 In.
$531

Bunch Auctions

Porcelain-Midcentury, Cooler, Wine, Garlands, Blossoms, Pedestal Base, Mangani, c.1950, 7 In., Pair
$236

Leland Little Auctions

Postcard, Black Girl, School Books, American Flag, c.1918
$448

Cowan's Auctions

Poster, Circus, Ringling Bros. & Barnum & Bailey, The Great Alzanas, Frame, 1952, 33 x 30 In.
$270

Rich Penn Auctions

Poster, Kar-Mi, Swallows Loaded Gun Barrel, Sideshow, J. B. Hallworth, Frame, 1914, 34 x 47 In.
$420

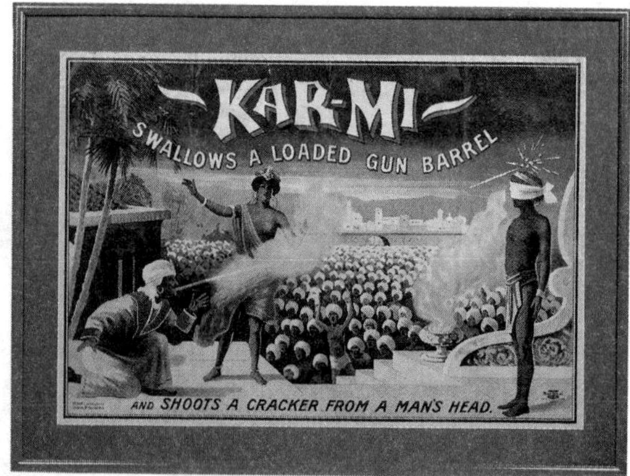

Rich Penn Auctions

Vase, Blue & White, Dragon, Bulbous, Xuande Style Mark, 12 x 11 ½ In. ... 236
Vase, Blue & White, Scrolling Lappet Band, 6-Character Mark, 1700s, 9 In. ... 5400
Vase, Blue Flowers, White Ground, Hexagonal, 10 ½ In. ... 1107
Vase, Bulbous Green Ground, 2-Circle Mark, 13 In. ... 2478
Vase, Celestial Sphere Shape, Blue Underglaze, Famille Verte, 17 In. ... 360
Vase, Children Holding Buddhist Treasures, Oval, Marked, 1700s, 7 ¾ In. ... *illus* 3075
Vase, Dark Blue Glaze, Flared Rim, Meiping, 1800s, 10 In. ... 2124
Vase, Double Gourd, Blue & White, Scenic, Bulbous, 13 x 7 In. ... 1180
Vase, Double Gourd, Shou Medallions, Blue, White Ground, 14 In. ... 584
Vase, Flat Circular Body, Cylindrical Opening, Open Handles, Early 1900s, 13 In., Pair ... *illus* 215
Vase, Flower Medallion, Mythical Creatures, Wu Tsai, 1800s, 7 ¼ In. ... *illus* 432
Vase, Footed, Bulbous Body, Long Neck, Blue Ground, 6-Character Mark, 10 ⅞ In. ... 192
Vase, Garlic Head, Chrysanthemums, Butterflies, Marked, 1700s, 12 x 7 In. ... 395
Vase, Long Neck, Garlic Mouth, Shallow Foot, Peach Bloom, 1700s, 6 x 3 In. ... 585
Vase, Meiping, Qing Style, Blue & White, 5-Claw Dragon, Waves, 1800s, 15 In. ... 263
Vase, Palace, Mandarin, Alternating Panels, Figures, Bird, Flower, 1800s, 25 In. ... 885
Vase, Pheasant Medallion, Gold Trim, 2 Handles, c.1910, 10 In. ... 225
Vase, Stick Neck, Blue, Bulbous Bottom, 9 ¾ In. ... 173
Vase, Tapered Neck, Sang De Boeuf Glaze, 4-Character Mark, 14 In. ... 480

Porcelain-Contemporary lists pieces made by artists working after 1975.

Figurine, Artichoke, White, Glazed, Pedestal Base, 13 In., 3 Piece ... 129
Figurine, Couple Dancing, Box, Signed, Giuseppe Armani, 1988, 13 x 7 x 21 In. ... 242
Figurine, Jesus Burger, Bun, Toppings, Frog, David Gilhooly, 2004, 9 In. ... *illus* 2125
Figurine, Lady On Horse, Wood Base, G. Armani, 1985, 10 x 12 ¾ In. ... 164
Figurine, Monkey, Seated, Holding Onion, Mottahedeh, 5 ½ In., Pair ... 50
Figurine, Parrot, Gold Trim, Stand, Giulia Mangani, Oggetti, Italy, 14 In. ... *illus* 531

Porcelain-Midcentury includes pieces made from the 1940s to about 1975.

Cooler, Wine, Garlands, Blossoms, Pedestal Base, Mangani, c.1950, 7 In., Pair ... *illus* 236

POSTCARD

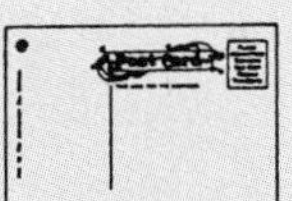

Postcards were first legally permitted in Austria on October 1, 1869. The United States passed postal regulations allowing the card in 1872. Most of the picture postcards collected today date after 1910. The amount of postage can help to date a card. The rates are: 1872 (1 cent), 1917 (2 cents), 1919 (1 cent), 1925 (2 cents), 1928 (1 cent), 1952 (2 cents), 1958 (3 cents), 1963 (4 cents), 1968 (5 cents), 1971 (6 cents), 1973 (8 cents), 1975 (7 cents), 1976 (9 cents), 1978 (10 cents), March 1981 (12 cents), November 1981 (13 cents), 1985 (14 cents), 1988 (15 cents), 1991 (19 cents), 1995 (20 cents), 2001 (21 cents), 2002 (23 cents), 2006 (24 cents), 2007 (26 cents), 2008 (27 cents), 2009 (28 cents), 2011 (29 cents), 2012 (32 cents), 2013 (33 cents), 2014 (34 cents), 2016 (35 cents beginning January 17 and back to 34 cents beginning April 10, 2016), 2018 (35 cents beginning January 21, 2018). Collectors search for early or unusual postmarks, picture postcards, or important handwritten messages (that includes celebrity autographs). While most postcards sell for low prices, a small number bring high prices. Some of these are listed here.

Black Girl, School Books, American Flag, c.1918 ... *illus* 448
Daniel Boone Grave Site ... 5
Easter, Chicks Climbing Into Blimp, Ladder, Flowers, Happy Easter On Back, 1911 ... 24
Halloween, Boy, Girl, Jack-O'-Lantern, A Merry Halloween, 1910 ... 24
Holy Land, New Synagogue, Tombs Of The Kings, Jerusalem, 1901 ... 125
New Year, Second Zionist Congress, Happy New Year, English, Hebrew, 1898 ... 312
New York World's Fair, Bridge Of Tomorrow, Orange Ground, 1939, 3 x 5 In. ... 12
Photograph, F.W. Conradi-Horster, German Magic Dealer, 1908 ... 343
Photograph, Harry Houdini, Handcuff, Full Body Manacles, 1900s, 5 ⅜ x 3 In. ... 2375
Photograph, The Last Of The Miamis, Kil-So-Quah & Son, Tepee, c.1910 ... 118

Poster, R. Lichtenstein, Sweet Dreams Baby, Lithograph, Signed, 22 x 18 In.
$600

Michaan's Auctions

Poster, Uncle Sam, Belles Of The Ballet, Patriotic Theme, Mounted, Harrie R. Pierce, 44 x 30 In.
$1,860

Milestone Auctions

Poster, United Front, TCB, Black Male, Female & Child, Broadside, c.1968, 15 x 20 In.
$625

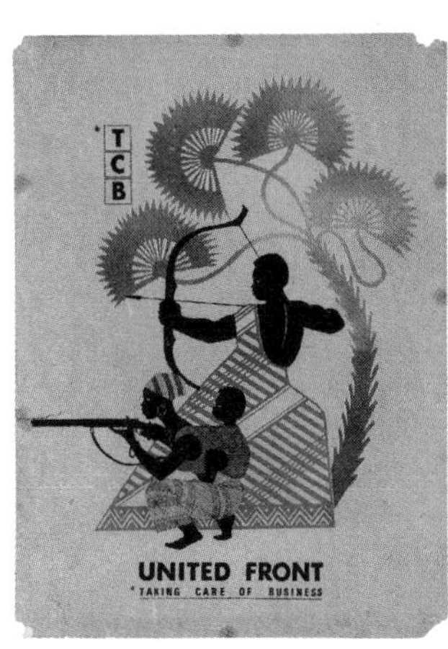

Cowan's Auctions

Portrait, Chung Ling Soo, Divided Back, 1908 343
Price's Hill Incline, Signed, Harry Kellar, Cincinnati, Ohio 468

POSTER

Posters have informed the public about news and entertainment events since ancient times. Nineteenth-century advertising and theatrical posters and twentieth-century movie and war posters are of special interest today. The price is determined by the artist, the condition, and the rarity. Other posters may be listed under Movie, Political, and World War I and II.

Alexander, Man Who Knows, Grayscale Portrait, Magician, c.1915, 108 x 80 In. 1560
Ballets Russes De Diaghilev, Ballet Dancer, Jean Cocteau, 1939, 60 x 32 In. 1680
Carrington, Le Formidable Magician, Plays With Supernatural, Portrait, 1925, 63 x 47 In. 219
Circus, Barnum & Bailey, Greatest Show On Earth, 2 Portraits, 1897, 40 x 30 In. 688
Circus, Cole Bros., 3 Railroad Trains, Erie Lithograph, 1930s, 28 x 41 In. 531
Circus, Ringling Bros. & Barnum & Bailey, The Great Alzanas, Frame, 1952, 33 x 30 In. *illus* 270
Concert, Phish, Pittsburgh Civic Arena, Frame, 1995, 23 x 11 ¾ In. 413
Concert, The Supremes, Lincoln Center Philharmonic Hall, October 15, 1965, 38 x 25 In. 510
Dubonnet, Fan Dancer, Red Dress, Holding Glass, Art Nouveau Style, G. Boano, 31 x 22 In. 1080
Folies Bergere, Caricature, Orange-Haired Dancer, L. Cappiello, 1900, 52 x 37 In. 3120
Jean Avril, Can-Can Dancer, Art Nouveau Style, Lithograph, M. Biais, 1895, 47 x 31 In. 3600
Kar-Mi, Swallows Loaded Gun Barrel, Sideshow, J. B. Hallworth, Frame, 1914, 34 x 47 In. *illus* 420
Marc Chagall, Four Seasons, Chicago, Lithograph, 1974, 37 x 25 In. 156
Martha's Vineyard Fair, West Tisbury, Young Girl, Chicken, c.1940, 21 x 13 In. 420
R. Lichtenstein, Sweet Dreams Baby, Lithograph, Signed, 22 x 18 In. ....*illus* 600
Travel, Alaska, Pan American, Inuit Child, Totem Pole, Aaron Amspoker, 1960s, 35 x 22 In. 570
Travel, Bogota, Colombia, Braniff International Airways, Church Door, Arch, 1950s, 26 x 20 In. 219
Travel, Boston, Fly TWA, Harbor Through Marina Window, W.W. Beecher, 1955, 40 x 25 In. 344
Travel, Cuba, Braniff International Airways, Man Playing Bongos, Lithograph, 1950s, 26 x 20 In. .. 840
Travel, Far East, Air France, Stylized Pagoda & Carp Streamer, G. Georget, 1956, 39 x 25 In. ... 240
Travel, Fly By BOAC, South Africa, Multicolor Landscape, X. Berkeley, 1952, 30 x 20 In. 720
Travel, Fly TWA, Las Vegas, Woman, Half Day & Night, D. Klein, 1950, 40 x 25 In. 960
Travel, France, Evian Les Bains, Lithographic, Louis Tauzin, 46 ½ x 34 ½ In. 677
Travel, Hawaii, American Airlines, Woman Under Palm Tree, Leis, J. Fernie, 1960s, 40 x 30 In. .. 510
Travel, Hong Kong, Swissair, Aerial View Of Junks, Color Offset, G. Gerster, 1971, 40 x 25 In. ... 188
Travel, India, Taj Mahal, Black & White Image, Lithograph, 1957, 39 x 25 In. 900
Travel, Ireland, By Cie, Tour Bus By Castle, Lithograph, Linen Back, 1950s, 39 x 25 In. 344
Travel, Italy, Air France, Stylized Mandolin Player, Guy Georget, 1962, 39 x 25 In. 180
Travel, Jet Your Way To Singapore, By BOAC, Harbor, Silkscreen, 1957, 30 x 20 In. 188
Travel, Middle East, Fly By BOAC, Mosque, Silkscreen, Linen Back, 1954, 30 x 20 In. 210
Travel, National Parks USA, Canyon De Chelly, Ansel Adams, Black & White, 1968, 41 x 28 In. 240
Travel, Palace Hotel, St. Moritz, Golfing At Picnic, Alpine Landscape, 1922, 49 x 35 In. 4320
Travel, Paris, Air France, Man & Woman, Artist, Cathedral, G. Lang, 1960s, 39 x 24 In. 156
Travel, Puerto Rico, Delta Air Lines, Woman, Head Scarf, Silkscreen, 1960s, J. Hardy, 28 x 22 In. 450
Travel, Pyrenees, French Countryside, Woman & Dog, Painted Image, P. Martial, 1951, 9 x 24 In... 150
Travel, Texas, American Airlines, 4 Stylized Longhorn Steer Heads, M. Glanzman, 1960s, 39 In. 688
Travel, Visit Japan, Bridge, Leaves, Mounted, Canvas, Japan Mail, 30 ½ x 21 In. 138
Travel, Visit Spain, Mounted, Canvas, Jara Diaz, 1929, 40 x 28 In. 163
Triple-Sec, Fournier, Black Inner Demons, Red Ground, L. Cappiello, 1907, 63 x 46 In. 9600
Uncle Sam, Belles Of The Ballet, Patriotic Theme, Mounted, Harrie R. Pierce, 44 x 30 In. *illus* 1860
United Front, TCB, Black Male, Female & Child, Broadside, c.1968, 15 x 20 In. ....*illus* 625
Warhol, Basquiat, Paintings, Exhibit, Lithograph, Yellow Ground, Signed, 1985, 19 x 12 In. 5843

POTLID

Potlids are just that, lids for pots. Transfer-printed potlids had their heyday from the 1840s to the early 1900s. The English Staffordshire potteries made ceramic containers with decorative lids for bear's grease, shrimp or meat paste, cold cream, and toothpaste. Printed advertising and

Potlid, Bazin's Ambrosial Shaving Cream, Eagle With Banner, Purple Transfer, 3 ½ In.
$240

Glass Works Auctions

Potlid, Bears Grease, Jules Hauel, Perfumer, Philadelphia, Bear, Black Transfer, 2 ⅞ In.
$570

Glass Works Auctions

Potlid, Genuine Beef Marrow, X. Bazin, Steer, Blue Transfer, Original Base, 2 ⅝ In.
$480

Glass Works Auctions

P

pictures of historical events, portraits of famous people, or scenic views were designed in black and white or color. Reproductions have been made.

Bazin's Ambrosial Shaving Cream, Eagle With Banner, Purple Transfer, 3 ½ In. ....*illus* 240
Bears Grease, Jules Hauel, Perfumer, Philadelphia, Bear, Black Transfer, 2 ⅞ In. ....*illus* 570
Genuine Beef Marrow, X. Bazin, Steer, Blue Transfer, Original Base, 2 ⅝ In. ....*illus* 480
Jules Hauel Saponaceous Shaving Compound, Purple Transfer, Base, 4 In. ....*illus* 264
Pine Wood Charcoal Tooth Paste, T.H. Peters, Black Transfer, 2 ¾ In. ....*illus* 252
Wright's Saponaceous Shaving Compound, Man Shaving, Black Transfer, 3 ½ In. ...*illus* 4500

POTTERY

Pottery and porcelain are different. Pottery is opaque; you can't see through it. Porcelain is translucent. If you hold a porcelain dish in front of a strong light, you will see the light through the dish. Porcelain is colder to the touch. Pottery is softer and easier to break and will stain more easily because it is porous. Porcelain is thinner, lighter, and more durable. Majolica, faience, and stoneware are all pottery. Additional pieces of pottery are listed in this book in the categories Pottery-Art, Pottery-Contemporary, Pottery-Midcentury, and under the factory name. For information about pottery makers and marks, see *Kovels' Dictionary of Marks—Pottery & Porcelain: 1650–1850* and *Kovels' New Dictionary of Marks—Pottery & Porcelain: 1850 to the Present.*

Bowl, Brown Drip Glaze, Stand Up Rim, 2 Small Handles, Chinese, 7 In. 3738
Bowl, Butterfly, Flowers, Leaves, White Ground, Footed, 1800s, 11 ½ In. ....*illus* 75
Bust, Inuit, Signed, Erica Deichmann, N.B., Canada, 1938, 9 In. ....*illus* 813
Bust, Louis XVI, Curly Hair, Black Marble Socle Base, Continental, 8 ½ In. ....*illus* 123
Charger, Woman, Irises, Leaves & Stems, Art Nouveau, Ernst Wahliss, Austria, 16 In. 182
Figurine, Cheetah, Sitting, Marked, 1900s, 22 x 15 In. ....*illus* 480
Figurine, Elephant, Sancai Glaze, Trunk Down, Chinese, 1800s, 9 x 9 x 4 In. 1404
Figurine, Spaniel, Freestanding Front Legs, Buff Clay, Brown, Molded Base, 1850s, 10 ½ In.... 120
Jar, Grapevine, Molded, Brown Drip Glaze, Earthenware, Lancaster County, c.1870, 8 In. *illus* 502
Jug, Face, Chocolate Matte Glaze, White Teeth, Strap Handle, Lanier Meaders, 1900s, 10 In. 585
Jug, Face, Salamander On Forehead, Teeth, Hooked Nose, Green Black, Handles, 9 ½ In. 130
Lamp, Embossed Pinecones, Crystalline Glaze, George Smyth, Late 1900s, 20 In. 367
Pitcher, Embossed Vineyard, Acorn, Mythological Spout, Earthenware, 8 In. ....*illus* 210
Pitcher, Green, Cylindrical, Curved Handle, 8 ½ In. 63
Planter, Flambe Glaze, Purple, Round Rim, Stand, 17 ½ In. 149
Planter, Flower, Fish, Deer, Yellow, Brown Ground, Bulbous, Molded Rim, 28 x 26 In. 148
Puzzle Jug, Pierced, Reticulated Neck, Molded Fish Head Spout, Bouquet, 1832, 7 ¾ In. .*illus* 211
Sculpture, Dog, Pug, Seated, Glass Eyes, Paint, 13 ½ In. 944
Tureen, Dome Lid, Mottled Glaze, Footed, France, 14 x 12 ½ In. 861
Vase, Blackware, Feather, Marie & Julian Martinez, Mexico, c.1930, 3 ½ x 5 In. ....*illus* 995
Vase, Double Fish Shape, Raised Scales, Brown Details, Cizhou, Chinese, c.1900, 8 In. ....*illus* 150
Vase, Flowers In Landscape, Dark Yellow, Carved Fretwork Border, Chinese, 13 x 8 In. 649
Vase, Textured Leaves, Orange & Green Matte Glaze, Incised, Markham, 6 ⅞ In. ....*illus* 2420
Vase, Turquoise, Painted, Birds, Prunus, Bretby, Late 1800s, 8 x 4 ½ In., Pair ....*illus* 136

Pottery-Art. Art pottery was first made in America in Cincinnati, Ohio, during the 1870s. The pieces were hand thrown and hand decorated. The art pottery tradition continued until studio potters began making the more artistic wares about 1930. American, English, and Continental art pottery by less well-known makers is listed here. Most makers listed in *Kovels' American Art Pottery*, such as Arequipa, Ohr, Rookwood, Roseville, and Weller, are listed in their own categories in this book. More recent pottery is listed under the name of the maker or in another pottery category.

Bank, Rabbit Shape, Golden Yellow, Glaze, Nicodemus, 4 ½ In. 92
Bowl, Dome Lid, Green, Cream Ground, Vivika Heino, 1900s, 3 ½ In., Pair 221

Potlid, Jules Hauel Saponaceous Shaving Compound, Purple Transfer, Base, 4 In.
$264

Glass Works Auctions

Potlid, Pine Wood Charcoal Tooth Paste, T.H. Peters, Black Transfer, 2 ¾ In.
$252

Glass Works Auctions

Potlid, Wright's Saponaceous Shaving Compound, Man Shaving, Black Transfer, 3 ½ In.
$4,500

Glass Works Auctions

This is an edited listing of current prices. Visit **Kovels.com** to check thousands of prices from previous years and sign up for free information on trends, tips, reproductions, marks, and more.

Pottery, Bowl, Butterfly, Flowers, Leaves, White Ground, Footed, 1800s, 11 ½ In.
$75

Hindman Auctions

Pottery, Bust, Inuit, Signed, Erica Deichmann, N.B., Canada, 1938, 9 In.
$813

Abington Auction Gallery

Pottery, Bust, Louis XVI, Curly Hair, Black Marble Socle Base, Continental, 8 ½ In.
$123

Stair Galleries

Pottery, Figurine, Cheetah, Sitting, Marked, 1900s, 22 x 15 In.
$480

Eldred's

Pottery, Jar, Grapevine, Molded, Brown Drip Glaze, Earthenware, Lancaster County, c.1870, 8 In.
$502

Bunch Auctions

Pottery, Pitcher, Embossed Vineyard, Acorn, Mythological Spout, Earthenware, 8 In.
$210

Woody Auctions

Pottery, Puzzle Jug, Pierced, Reticulated Neck, Molded Fish Head Spout, Bouquet, 1832, 7 ¾ In.
$211

Jeffrey S. Evans & Associates

Pottery, Vase, Blackware, Feather, Marie & Julian Martinez, Mexico, c.1930, 3 ½ x 5 In.
$995

Thomaston Place Auction Galleries

Pottery, Vase, Double Fish Shape, Raised Scales, Brown Details, Cizhou, Chinese, c.1900, 8 In.
$150

Eldred's

Bowl, Ivy, Green, Shallow Dish Style, Early 1900s, 2 x 10 In.	*illus*	12
Bowl, Mottled Celadon Glaze, Shallow Foot, Thomas Bezanson, 7 x 14 In.	*illus*	1053
Bowl, Raised Blue Flowers, Salt Glaze, Squat, Susan Frackelton, 1900, 4 x 9 In.	*illus*	2125
Charger, Flowers, Multicolor, Iznik Style, Theodore Deck, 1870, 19 ½ In.		3690
Compote, Multicolor, Angular Handles, Wiener Werkstatte, 1920s, 4 x 10 In.	*illus*	1936
Figurine, Dog, Pekingese, Pillow Base, White Accents, Nicodemus, 4 ½ In.	*illus*	196
Figurine, Elephant, Trunk Up, Glazed, Nicodemus, 1 ¾ In.	*illus*	259
Figurine, St. Francis, Holding Bowl, Birds, White, 14 In.	*illus*	374
Jardiniere, Stylized Flowers, Bulbous Body, Reticulated Rim, 9 x 12 In.		104
Jug, Wihoa Sands, Handle, Signed, J. Ault, 10 In.	*illus*	69
Lamp Base, Flame Painted, Molded Flowers, Theophilus Brouwer, c.1910, 12 x 7 In.	*illus*	8125
Pitcher, Grotesque, Brown, Vance Avon Faience Co., Late 1800s, 5 ½ x 6 ¾ In.	*illus*	104
Pitcher, Pussy Willow Glaze, Handle, Nicodemus, 3 ½ In.		23
Urn, Salt Glaze, Wood Fired, Frogskin Interior, Handles, D. Steumpfle, 17 x 14 In.		318
Vase, Art Deco Flowers, Bulbous, Stamped, Louis Lourioux, c.1925, 11 ½ In.	*illus*	960
Vase, Beetles, Crystalline Glaze, Handles, Footed, Pierrefonds, 1912-28, 7 In.		113
Vase, Bronze Green Matte Glaze, Molded Leaves, W.J. Walley, c.1910, 5 In.	*illus*	1968
Vase, Celadon & Blue Crystalline Glaze, Adelaide Robineau, 1915, 4 x 5 In.	*illus*	27500
Vase, Egg Shape, Tapered, Oribe Glaze, Small Mouth, Ben Owen III, 11 In.		331
Vase, Hibiscus Flowers, Brown, Pink, Green, John Bennett, 1881, 11 x 7 In.	*illus*	3000
Vase, Lion Handles, Black, Brown, Green & Blue Glaze, 9 ¾ x 5 In.		81
Vase, Oval, Gilt Bronze, Black Scrolling, Luc Lanel, c.1925, 8 ¾ In.		492
Vase, Oval, Green Glaze, Signed, Theophilus Brouwer, 7 x 4 In.	*illus*	813
Vase, Oxblood Drip Glaze, Green, Red, White, Pierre-Adrien Dalpayrat, 1900s, 5 ¾ In.		1625
Vase, Pasque Flower, White & Light Green Mottled Glaze, c.1930, 4 In.		250
Vase, Peacock, Frederick Hurten Rhead, For Jervis Pottery, c.1908, 10 ½ In.	*illus*	8125
Vase, Reclining Nudes, Leaves, Grapes, Glazed, Rene Buthaud, 1920s, 11 ½ x 8 In.		3000
Vase, Roses, Leaves, Limoges Style, Black, Cincinnati Art Pottery, c.1900, 14 In.	*illus*	182
Vase, Square, Swollen, Blue Green Glaze, Theodore Deck, 9 x 3 In., Pair		1320
Vase, Tenmoku Glaze, Bottle Shape, Flared Rim, Thomas Bezanson, 10 x 3 In.		1404
Vase, Urn, Lid, Portrait, Young Woman, Handles, Ernst Wahliss, Austria, 8 x 6 In.	*illus*	420

Pottery-Contemporary lists pieces made by artists working about 1975 and later.

Bust, Indian Chief, Feather, Bead, Braids, Rick Wisecarver, 1996, 21 x 14 In.	*illus*	805
Charger, Gouged, Incised, Cobalt Oxide, Peter Voulkos, 1980, 22 In.	*illus*	5312
Container, Lid, Stylized Face, Painted, Dolphin Finial, 28 In.	*illus*	112
Figurine, Angel, Eyes Closed, Georgia Blizzard, Virginia, c.1996, 8 In.		468
Figurine, Girl, Barefoot, Atlantic Mold, Rick Wisecarver, 1972, 14 ⅞ In.		207
Figurine, Lion, Sitting, Painted, Lisa Larson, 6 ½ x 5 ½ In.	*illus*	90
Figurine, Modest Lady, Teapot Head, M. Lucero, 1996, 37 x 10 In.		4160
Jar, Lid, Globular, Green, Gray, Rose, Loop Handle, Nerikomi, Makoto Yabe, 7 x 8 In.		234
Jar, Oval, Alkaline Glaze, 4 Loop Handles, Applied Snake, K. Ellington, 12 x 8 In.		260
Plaque, Decagon, Blue, Brown, Red, Iron Banded Edge, C. Counts, 36 x 38 In.	*illus*	660
Sculpture, Horse, Galloping, Raku Glaze, Stand, Louise W. King, 12 x 11 In.		94
Vase, 3 Navajo Women, Multicolor, Bulbous, Rudolph C. Gorman, 9 ½ In.		219
Vase, Aperture Opening, Mottled Earth Tones, Leonora Morrow, 21 In.		89
Vase, Blue Glaze, Vivika & Otto Heino, 3 ½ In.	*illus*	197
Vase, Cerros, Glaze Stoneware, Incised, Glass Liner, Claude Conover, c.1980, 11 x 19 In.	*illus*	5938
Vase, Cone Shape, Volcanic Glaze, Beatrice Wood, 1979, 32 x 9 In.	*illus*	3000
Vase, Hocah, Elongated, Brown Glaze, Stoneware, Claude Conover, c.1980, 19 x 8 In.		5200
Vase, Metallic Volcanic Glazed Tendrils, Paul Katrich, 12 ½ In.	*illus*	510
Vase, Multicolor Glaze, Pyramid Shape, Signed, D. Cornell, 20 In.		92
Vase, Nude Figures, Walking, Standing, Lying Down, E. Eberle, 12 ½ In.		2750
Vase, Salt Glaze, Painted, Multicolor, Whimsical, Jane Peiser, 8 In.		449

Pottery-Midcentury includes pieces made from the 1940s to about 1975.

Bean Pot, Lid, Grape Clusters, Leaves, Alkaline Glaze, Arie Meaders, 9 In.	*illus*	360
Bowl, Bird On Branch, White Clay, Stamped Underside, Pablo Picasso, 1 ⅝ x 6 In.	*illus*	2125
Bowl, Green Glazes, Round, Signed, Toshiko Takaezu, 3 x 11 ⅝ In.		666

Pottery, Vase, Textured Leaves, Orange & Green Matte Glaze, Incised, Markham, 6 ⅞ In.
$2,420

Humler & Nolan

Pottery, Vase, Turquoise, Painted, Birds, Prunus, Bretby, Late 1800s, 8 x 4 ½ In., Pair
$136

Soulis Auctions

Pottery-Art, Bowl, Ivy, Green, Shallow Dish Style, Early 1900s, 2 x 10 In.
$12

Charlton Hall Auctions

P

Pottery-Art, Bowl, Mottled Celadon Glaze, Shallow Foot, Thomas Bezanson, 7 x 14 In.
$1,053

Thomaston Place Auction Galleries

Pottery-Art, Bowl, Raised Blue Flowers, Salt Glaze, Squat, Susan Frackelton, 1900, 4 x 9 In.
$2,125

Rago Arts and Auction Center

Pottery-Art, Compote, Multicolor, Angular Handles, Wiener Werkstatte, 1920s, 4 x 10 In.
$1,936

Humler & Nolan

Pottery-Art, Figurine, Dog, Pekingese, Pillow Base, White Accents, Nicodemus, 4 ½ In.
$196

Apple Tree Auction Center

Pottery-Art, Figurine, Elephant, Trunk Up, Glazed, Nicodemus, 1 ¾ In.
$259

Apple Tree Auction Center

TIP

Having a garage (tag) or house sale? Use a fanny pack worn in front to keep your money. Be sure to have lots of change, bills and coins, for the sale.

Pottery-Art, Figurine, St. Francis, Holding Bowl, Birds, White, 14 In.
$374

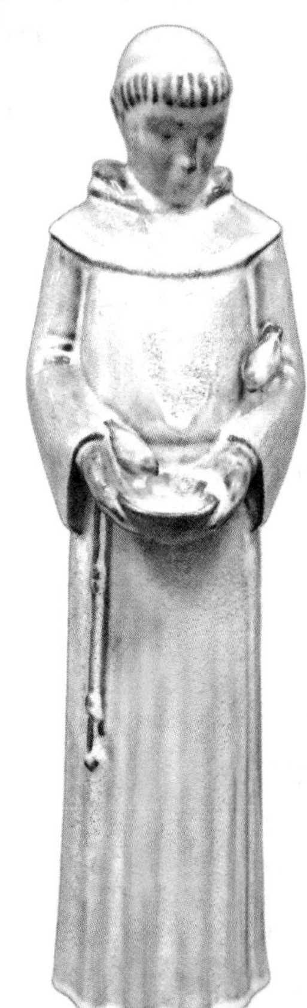

Apple Tree Auction Center

Pottery-Art, Jug, Wihoa Sands, Handle, Signed, J. Ault, 10 In.
$69

Belhorn Auction Services

Pottery-Art, Lamp Base, Flame Painted, Molded Flowers, Theophilus Brouwer, c.1910, 12 x 7 In.
$8,125

Rago Arts and Auction Center

Pottery-Art, Pitcher, Grotesque, Brown, Vance Avon Faience Co., Late 1800s, 5 ½ x 6 ¾ In.
$104

Belhorn Auction Services

Pottery-Art, Vase, Art Deco Flowers, Bulbous, Stamped, Louis Lourioux, c.1925, 11 ½ In.
$960

Ripley Auctions

Pottery-Art, Vase, Bronze Green Matte Glaze, Molded Leaves, W.J. Walley, c.1910, 5 In.
$1,968

Skinner, Inc.

TIP
Never leave the key under the doormat.

Pottery-Art, Vase, Celadon & Blue Crystalline Glaze, Adelaide Robineau, 1915, 4 x 5 In.
$27,500

Rago Arts and Auction Center

Pottery-Art, Vase, Hibiscus Flowers, Brown, Pink, Green, John Bennett, 1881, 11 x 7 In.
$3,000

Rago Arts and Auction Center

Pottery-Art, Vase, Oval, Green Glaze, Signed, Theophilus Brouwer, 7 x 4 In.
$813

Treadway

Pottery-Art, Vase, Peacock, Frederick Hurten Rhead, For Jervis Pottery, c.1908, 10 ½ In.
$8,125

Rago Arts and Auction Center

Pottery-Art, Vase, Roses, Leaves, Limoges Style, Black, Cincinnati Art Pottery, c.1900, 14 In.
$182

Humler & Nolan

Pottery-Art, Vase, Urn, Lid, Portrait, Young Woman, Handles, Ernst Wahliss, Austria, 8 x 6 In.
$420

Morphy Auctions

Pottery-Contemporary, Bust, Indian Chief, Feather, Bead, Braids, Rick Wisecarver, 1996, 21 x 14 In.
$805

Belhorn Auction Services

Pottery-Contemporary, Charger, Gouged, Incised, Cobalt Oxide, Peter Voulkos, 1980, 22 In.
$5,312

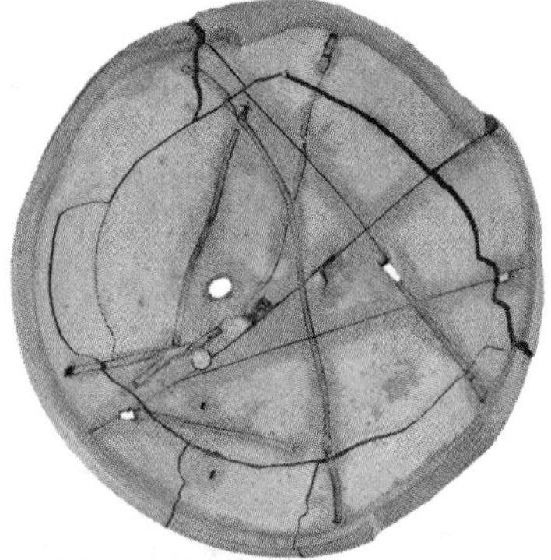

Rago Arts and Auction Center

Pottery-Contemporary, Container, Lid, Stylized Face, Painted, Dolphin Finial, 28 In.
$112

Nadeau's Auction Gallery

Pottery-Contemporary, Figurine, Lion, Sitting, Painted, Lisa Larson, 6 ½ x 5 ½ In.
$90

Hartzell's Auction Gallery Inc.

Pottery-Contemporary, Plaque, Decagon, Blue, Brown, Red, Iron Banded Edge, C. Counts, 36 x 38 In.
$660

Case Antiques

Pottery-Contemporary, Vase, Blue Glaze, Vivika & Otto Heino, 3 ½ In.
$197

Skinner, Inc.

TIP

Remove stains from old ceramic vases by scrubbing with salt.

Pottery-Contemporary, Vase, Cerros, Glaze Stoneware, Incised, Glass Liner, Claude Conover, c.1980, 11 x 19 In.
$5,938

Brunk Auctions

Pottery-Contemporary, Vase, Cone Shape, Volcanic Glaze, Beatrice Wood, 1979, 32 x 9 In.
$3,000

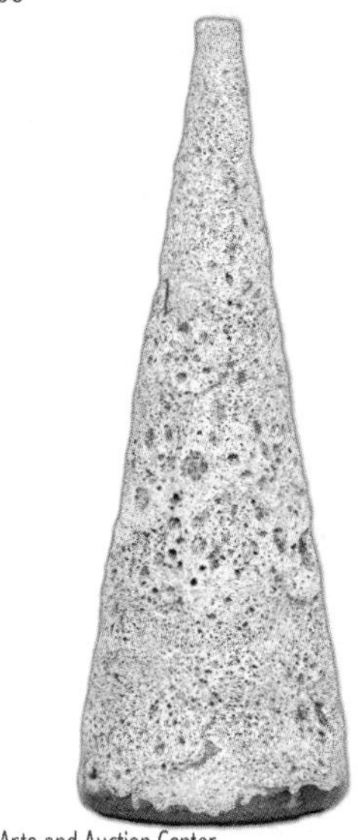

Rago Arts and Auction Center

Pottery-Contemporary, Vase, Metallic Volcanic Glazed Tendrils, Paul Katrich, 12 ½ In.
$510

Ripley Auctions

Pottery-Midcentury, Bean Pot, Lid, Grape Clusters, Leaves, Alkaline Glaze, Arie Meaders, 9 In.
$360

Case Antiques

Pottery-Midcentury, Bowl, Bird On Branch, White Clay, Stamped Underside, Pablo Picasso, 1 5/8 x 6 In.
$2,125

Abington Auction Gallery

Pottery-Midcentury, Bowl, Peacocks, Tan, Blue, K. & K. Sadowski, N.B., Canada, 2 x 4 In.
$125

Abington Auction Gallery

Pottery-Midcentury, Charger, Goat's Head Profile, Madoura, Pablo Picasso, 16 In.
$11,590

Pook & Pook

Pottery-Midcentury, Egghead, White Ground, Black Lines, Glazed, Lagardo Tackett, c.1959, 12 x 7 In.
$219

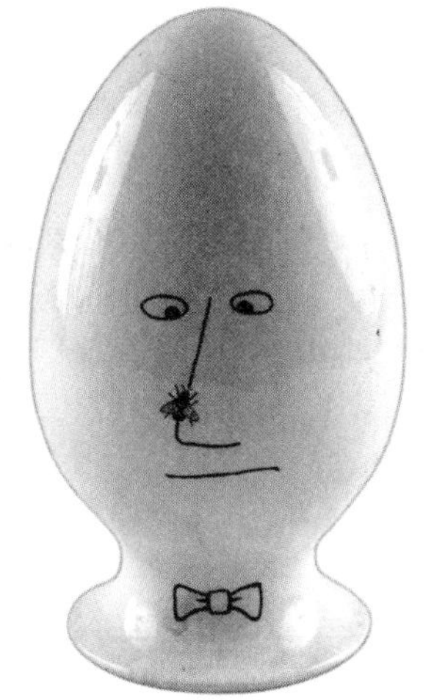

Kamelot Auctions

Pottery-Midcentury, Figurine, Bunny Rabbit, Cottontail, Semicircular Impressed, Nicodemus, 2 3/4 x 4 In.
$92

Belhorn Auction Services

Pottery-Midcentury, Figurine, Head, Woman, Blue Glaze, Stamped Amaco American Art Clay, 7 In.
$121

Humler & Nolan

Pottery-Midcentury, Figurine, Mushrooms, Amanita Citrina, E. & A. Lorenzen, Canada, 5 In.
$313

Abington Auction Gallery

Pottery-Midcentury, Jug, Hibou, Incised, Glazed, Handle, Pablo Picasso, 1955, 10 x 4 1/2 In.
$11,250

Rago Arts and Auction Center

P

Pottery-Midcentury, Planter, Earthenware, Glazed, Signed, Bjorn Wiinblad, 35 x 15 In.
$2, 006

Cottone Auctions

Pottery-Midcentury, Plate, Tete De Taureau, Bull's Head, Pablo Picasso, 17 In.
$28,750

Palm Beach Modern Auctions

Pottery-Midcentury, Vase, Brown Glaze, Wrapped Lizard, A. Hagen, Canada, 7 In.
$750

Abington Auction Gallery

Pottery-Midcentury, Vase, Feelie, Brown Matte Glaze, Signed, Rose Cabat, 3 x 3 In.
$358

Treadway

Pottery-Midcentury, Vase, Feelie, Forest Green, Brown, Signed, Rose Cabat, 2 ¾ In.
$207

Belhorn Auction Services

Pottery-Midcentury, Vase, Marbleized, Flared Rim, Ozark, Charles Stehm, 1950s, 6 In.
$144

Selkirk Auctioneers & Appraisers

Pottery-Midcentury, Vase, Round, 8 Holders, Brown, Tan, Bruno Gambone, Italy, 1960s, 37 x 25 In.
$3,200

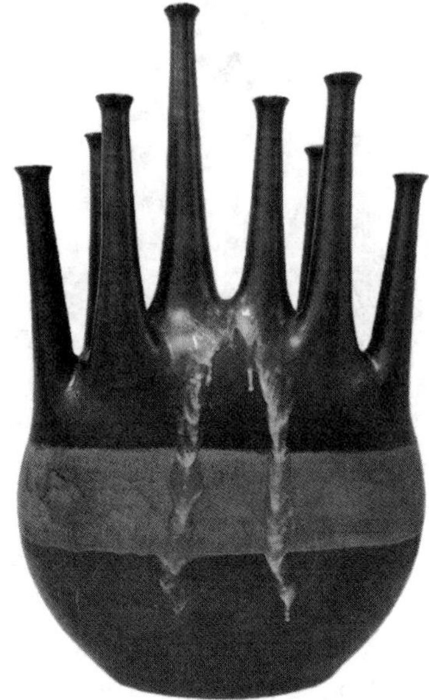

World Auction Gallery

TIP

Don't brag about the value of your collection to strangers. It might lead to extra interest by the local burglary groups.

Pottery-Midcentury, Vase, Stoneware, Spherical, Green, Vertical Lines, Harrison McIntosh, 7 In.
$2,091

Clars Auction Gallery

P

Bowl, Peacocks, Tan, Blue, K. & K. Sadowski, N.B., Canada, 2 x 4 In. *illus* 125

Charger, Goat's Head Profile, Madoura, Pablo Picasso, 16 In. *illus* 11590

Creamer, White, Brown Incised Design, Stoneware, Lucie Rie, c.1958, 6 In. 1300

Dough Bowl, Hand Coiled, Red & Buff, Irregular Opening, 8 x 12 In. 875

Egghead, White Ground, Black Lines, Glazed, Lagardo Tackett, c.1959, 12 x 7 In. *illus* 219

Figurine, Bunny Rabbit, Cottontail, Semicircular Impressed, Nicodemus, 2 ¾ x 4 In. *illus* 92

Figurine, Head, Woman, Blue Glaze, Stamped Amaco American Art Clay, 7 In. *illus* 121

Figurine, Mushrooms, Amanita Citrina, E. & A. Lorenzen, Canada, 5 In. *illus* 313

Figurine, Quail, Brown, White & Yellow, Signed, Thelma Winter, 1970s, 6 In., Pair 145

Figurine, Quail, Multicolor Glazes, Signed, Thelma Winter, 1970s, 4 In., Pair 303

Jug, Elixer, Art Deco Style, Chrome Red, Glaze, 1940s, 8 ½ x 7 In. 317

Jug, Hibou, Incised, Glazed, Handle, Pablo Picasso, 1955, 10 x 4 ½ In. *illus* 11250

Planter, Earthenware, Glazed, Signed, Bjorn Wiinblad, 35 x 15 In. *illus* 2006

Plate, Tete De Taureau, Bull's Head, Pablo Picasso, 17 In. *illus* 28750

Plate, White On White, Raised Stylized Nude, Madoura, Picasso, 10 ½ In. 5605

Vase, Aqua, Tapered, Angular Peek-A-Boo Handles, A.R. Cole, 1940s, 21 In. 201

Vase, Blue, Brown & Green Glaze, Peacock Eye, Einar Johansen, 1960, 4 ¾ In. 72

Vase, Brown Glaze, Wrapped Lizard, A. Hagen, Canada, 7 In. *illus* 750

Vase, Face, Handle In Back, Green, Blue, Signed, Bjorn Wiinblad, Denmark, 8 In. 96

Vase, Feelie, Brown Matte Glaze, Signed, Rose Cabat, 3 x 3 In. *illus* 358

Vase, Feelie, Forest Green, Brown, Signed, Rose Cabat, 2 ¾ In. *illus* 207

Vase, Feelie, Variegated Green, Rose Cabat, c.1980, 3 ¾ x 3 In. 487

Vase, Garlic Head Shape, Collared Mouth, Brown, Amber, Jack Troy, 19 In. 248

Vase, Lid, Turquoise Glaze, Edmond Lachenal, France, c.1950, 14 In. 500

Vase, Live Oaks, Earthenware, Lydia B. Angell, New Orleans, c.1945, 3 x 6 In. 1100

Vase, Marbleized, Flared Rim, Ozark, Charles Stehm, 1950s, 6 In. *illus* 144

Vase, Round, 8 Holders, Brown, Tan, Bruno Gambone, Italy, 1960s, 37 x 25 In. *illus* 3200

Vase, Semicircular, Red Rim, Impressed Mark, Chester Nicodemus, 6 ½ In. 46

Vase, Stoneware, Spherical, Green, Vertical Lines, Harrison McIntosh, 7 In. *illus* 2091

POWDER FLASK AND POWDER HORN

Powder flasks and powder horns were made to hold the gunpowder used in antique firearms. The early examples were made of horn or wood; later ones were of copper or brass.

POWDER FLASK

Brass, Colt Navy Revolver, Eagle, Flags, Cannon, Anchor, Tilted Spout, 7 In. 245

Brass, Eagle, Stars, 2 Hands Shaking, Civil War, 9 x 4 In. 60

Brass, Embossed, Silvered, Wood, Black, Scroll Accents, North Africa, 1850s, 14 In. 187

Brass, U.S. Military, Peace, Eagle, Shield, Model 1855, 9 x 4 In. *illus* 201

Wood, Iron Collar, Round Bone Medallion Mask, Brass Dots, 5 x 3 In. 2832

POWDER HORN

Carved, Brass Spout, Compass, Ships, Eagle, Flags, Tombstone, c.1800, 17 In. *illus* 2583

Carved, Fist, Holding Ring, Whale Ivory Mount, Dog Cap, 1800s, 15 ½ In. 400

Carved, Whale's Mouth, Wood Acorn Cap, Eagle, Shield, Banner, 1821, 13 In. 2640

Eagle, Shield, Fish, Trees, Dog, Thin Neck, James Smith, 1816, 10 In. 2000

Horn, Engraved, Britannia, 13 In. 264

Horn, Flat Wood Cap, Swirl Carved Throat, Shenandoah Valley, Va., 1810s, 12 In. 211

Map, New York, Lt. Francis List, Engraved, 1900, 12 ½ In. 360

Mexican Eagle Perched On Cactus, Snake In Beak, 14 In. 153

Revolutionary War, John Von Vlac, Dutchess County, New York, 1777, 9 In. 4320

Scrimshaw, Carved, Inscribed James Noyes, Octagonal Spout, c.1800, 10 In. 1180

Steer Horn, Eagle, Whale, c.1849, 14 In. 687

PRATT

PRATT
FENTON

Pratt ware means two different things. It was an early Staffordshire pottery, cream colored with colored decorations, made by Felix Pratt during the late eighteenth century. There was also Pratt ware made with transfer

Powder Flask, Brass, U.S. Military, Peace, Eagle, Shield, Model 1855, 9 x 4 In.
$201

Bunch Auctions

Powder Horn, Carved, Brass Spout, Compass, Ships, Eagle, Flags, Tombstone, c.1800, 17 In.
$2,583

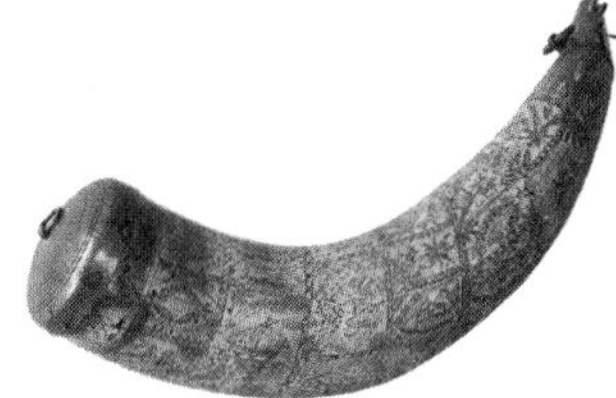

Skinner, Inc.

Pressed Glass, Broken Column, Biscuit Jar, Lid, Finial, c.1891, 9 ¾ In.
$702

Jeffrey S. Evans & Associates

Pressed Glass, Finecut & Block, Compote, Lid, Blue Stain, King, c.1880, 13 ½ x 9 In.
$176

Jeffrey S. Evans & Associates

Pressed Glass, Jumbo, Compote, Clear, Elephant Finial, Canton Glass, c.1881, 13 x 8 In.
$140

Jeffrey S. Evans & Associates

Pressed Glass, Lion, Powder Jar, Lid, Frosted, Gillinder & Sons, c.1876, 4 ½ x 3 In.
$1,638

Jeffrey S. Evans & Associates

designs during the mid-nineteenth century in Fenton, England. Reproductions of the transfer-printed Pratt are being made.

Jug, Heart Shape Cartouches, Children Playing, Sportive Innocence, Molded, c.1790, 7 In. 795
Plate, On Guard, Night Watchman & Dog Sleeping, With Base 350
Potlid, Garibaldi, England, 1865, 4 In. 120
Scent Bottle, Shield Shape, Blue Sponge, Flowers, Yellow Trim, c.1810, 3 In. 187
Syrup, Pewter Lid, 5 Putti, Grapevine, Multicolor, Pearlware Glaze, c.1860, 8 x 4 In. 293
Tea Canister, Relief Figures, Man & Servant, Woman & Servant, Blue, Ocher, c.1790, 5 In. 248

PRESSED GLASS

Pressed glass, or pattern glass, was first made in the United States in the 1820s after the invention of glass pressing machines. Hundreds of patterns of pressed glass were made in complete table settings. Although the Boston and Sandwich Works was the most famous of the pressed glass factories, there were about sixteen other factories making pressed glass from 1830 to 1850, and still more from 1850 to 1900, when pressed glass reached its greatest popularity. It is now being widely reproduced. The pattern names used in this listing are based on the information in the book *Pressed Glass in America* by John and Elizabeth Welker. There may be pieces of pressed glass listed in this book in other categories, such as Lamp, Ruby Glass, Sandwich Glass, and Souvenir.

Broken Column, Biscuit Jar, Lid, Finial, c.1891, 9 ¾ In. .... *illus* 702
Broken Column, Dish, Rectangular, c.1891, 6 ½ x 9 ½ In. 152
Cameo, Spooner, Beaded Rim & Base, 4 x 6 In. 58
Crystal Wedding, Pitcher, Stained, Applied Handle, Footed, 1891, 10 In. 129
Dolphin, Salt, Shell Shape, Block & Recess Base, France, c.1840, 2 ½ x 3 In. 293
Excelsior, Punch Bowl, Ruby Stain, Engraved Vine, Berry, Adams & Co., 1891, 9 x 12 In. 761
Finecut & Block, Compote, Lid, Blue Stain, King, c.1880, 13 ½ x 9 In. .... *illus* 176
Gonterman, Cake Stand, Amber Stain, Frosted, Geo. Duncan & Sons, 1887-90, 6 ½ x 10 In. 497
Jumbo, Compote, Clear, Elephant Finial, Canton Glass, c.1881, 13 x 8 In. .... *illus* 140
Lion, Powder Jar, Lid, Frosted, Gillinder & Sons, c.1876, 4 ½ x 3 In. .... *illus* 1638
Log Cabin, Pickle Jar, Amber, Textured, Central Glass, c.1884, 7 x 3 In. .... *illus* 995
Pavonia, Tumbler, Ruby Stain, Arlington Hotel, Hot Springs, Bohemian Style, 1893, 4 In. . *illus* 187
Peacock, Vase, Tulip Shape, Blue, Hexagonal Base, Sandwich, c.1850, 10 ½ In. 277
Roanoke, Pitcher, Ruby Stain, Applied Handle, Ripley & Co., 1888-1898, 10 In. 23
Shield & Anchor, Nappy, Clear, Lacy, Scalloped Rim, 1830-40, 8 In. 94
Snail, Cruet, Ruby Stain, Stopper, Handle, Clear Cut, Geo. Duncan & Sons, c.1890, 6 ¾ In. *illus* 176
Three Face, Compote, Clear & Frosted, Engraved Stars, Dots, Duncan, c.1880, 9 In. .... *illus* 878
Wellington, Water Pitcher, Ruby Stain, Clear Handle, Westmoreland, 1903, 6 ¾ In. .... *illus* 129
Westward Ho, Compote, Lid, Frosted Indian Finial, 16 x 9 In. .... *illus* 380

PRINT

Print, in this listing, means any of many printed images produced on paper by one of the more common methods, such as lithography. The prints listed here are of interest primarily to the antiques collector, not the fine arts collector. Many of these prints were originally part of books. Other prints will be found in the Advertising, Currier & Ives, Movie, and Poster categories.

J.W.Audubon **Audubon** bird prints were originally issued as part of books printed from 1826 to 1854. They were issued in two sheet sizes, 26 ½ inches by 39 ½ inches and 11 inches by 7 inches. The height of a picture is listed before the width. The quadrupeds were issued in 28-by-22-inch prints. Later editions of the Audubon books were done in many sizes, and reprints of the books in the original sizes were also made. The words *After John James Audubon* appear on all of the prints, including the

Pressed Glass, Log Cabin, Pickle Jar, Amber, Textured, Central Glass, c.1884, 7 x 3 In.
$995

Jeffrey S. Evans & Associates

Pressed Glass, Pavonia, Tumbler, Ruby Stain, Arlington Hotel, Hot Springs, Bohemian Style, 1893, 4 In.
$187

Jeffrey S. Evans & Associates

Pressed Glass, Snail, Cruet, Ruby Stain, Stopper, Handle, Clear Cut, Geo. Duncan & Sons, c.1890, 6 ¾ In.
$176

Jeffrey S. Evans & Associates

Pressed Glass, Three Face, Compote, Clear & Frosted, Engraved Stars, Dots, Duncan, c.1880, 9 In.
$878

Jeffrey S. Evans & Associates

Pressed Glass, Wellington, Water Pitcher, Ruby Stain, Clear Handle, Westmoreland, 1903, 6 ¾ In.
$129

Jeffrey S. Evans & Associates

Pressed Glass, Westward Ho, Compote, Lid, Frosted Indian Finial, 16 x 9 In.
$380

Jeffrey S. Evans & Associates

Print, Audubon, American White Pelican, Color Reproduction, 38 x 26 In.
$915

Neal Auction Company

Print, Audubon, Bachman's Finch, Hand Colored, Engraving, Aquatint, Frame, 45 x 37 In.
$240

Eldred's

Print, Audubon, Common Mouse, Male, Female & Young, Lithograph, Frame, 21 x 27 ½ In.
$4,000

Neal Auction Company

P

Print, Audubon, Red-Shouldered Hawk, Hand-Colored Aqua Tint, Engraving, Havell, 38 x 25 ½ In.
$8,500

Neal Auction Company

Print, Chicago, National Exposition Of Railway Appliances, May 24-June 23, 1883, Frame, 19 x 26 In.
$59

Cottone Auctions

Print, Icart, Woman, 2 Leopards, Oval, Gold, Green, Signed, Frame, 21 ⅝ x 26 ⅝ In.
$351

Cordier Auctions

Print, Jacoulet, Les Perles, The Pearls, Woodblock, 1950, 18 ¾ x 14 In.
$438

Eldred's

Print, Kurz & Allison, Battle Of New Orleans, Chromolithograph, Frame, 1890, 21 x 27 In.
$793

Neal Auction Company

Print, Warhol, Andy, Campbell's Soup Can, Shopping Bag, Handles, 16 x 9 ¾ In.
$1,440

Michaan's Auctions

originals, because the pictures were made as copies of Audubon's original oil paintings. The bird pictures have been so popular they have been copied in myriad sizes using both old and new printing methods. This list includes originals and later copies because Audubon prints of all ages are sold in antiques shops.

Audubon, American White Pelican, Color Reproduction, 38 x 26 In. ....*illus* 915
Audubon, Bachman's Finch, Hand Colored, Engraving, Aquatint, Frame, 45 x 37 In. ....*illus* 240
Audubon, Common Mouse, Male, Female & Young, Lithograph, Frame, 21 x 27 1/2 In. ....*illus* 4000
Audubon, Louisiana Hawk, Aquatint, Elephant Folio Paper, Watermarked J. Whatman, 25 1/2 x 38 In. .. 3250
Audubon, Red-Shouldered Hawk, Hand-Colored Aqua Tint, Engraving, Havell, 38 x 25 1/2 In. *illus* 8500
Audubon, Wild Turkey, Photolithograph, Frame, G. Shut & Zonen, 1971-72, 39 3/8 In. 800
Chicago, National Exposition Of Railway Appliances, May 24-June 23, 1883, Frame, 19 x 26 In. *illus* 59
Currier & Ives prints are listed in the Currier & Ives category.
Declaration Of Independence, Lithograph, Engraved William Woodruff, Frame, 1841, 22 x 30 In... 1265

Icart prints were made by Louis Icart, who worked in Paris from 1907 as an employee of a postcard company. He then started printing magazines and fashion brochures. About 1910 he created a series of etchings of fashionably dressed women, and he continued to make similar etchings until he died in 1950. He is well known as a printmaker, painter, and illustrator. Original etchings are much more expensive than the later photographic copies.

Icart, Woman, 2 Leopards, Oval, Gold, Green, Signed, Frame, 21 5/8 x 26 5/8 In. ....*illus* 351

Jacoulet prints were designed by Paul Jacoulet (1902–1960), a Frenchman who spent most of his life in Japan. He was a master of Japanese woodblock print technique. Subjects included life in Japan, the South Seas, Korea, and China. His prints were sold by subscription and issued in series. Each series had a distinctive seal, such as a sparrow or butterfly. Most Jacoulet prints are approximately 15 x 10 inches.

Jacoulet, Chagrins D'Amour, Kusaie, Est Carolines, Woman, Parrot, 1940, 15 1/2 x 11 In. 584
Jacoulet, Fumee De Santal Manchoukuo, Reclining Female, Gilt Frame, 15 1/2 x 13 In. 400
Jacoulet, Jeu Princier, Mongol, Sport Of Princes, Peony Stamp, Frame, 1956, 16 3/4 x 13 In. 1107
Jacoulet, Les Perles, The Pearls, Manchuria, Peach Stamp, Frame, 1950, 16 x 13 In. 615
Jacoulet, Les Perles, The Pearls, Woodblock, 1950, 18 3/4 x 14 In. ....*illus* 438
Jacoulet, Souvenirs D'Autrefois, Memories Of The Past, Old Woman, 1941, 18 1/2 x 14 In. 221

Japanese woodblock prints are listed as follows: Print, Japanese, name of artist, title or description, type, and size. Dealers use the following terms: *Tate-e* is a vertical composition. *Yoko-e* is a horizontal composition. The words *Aiban* (13 by 9 inches), *Chuban* (10 by 7 1/2 inches), *Hosoban* (13 by 6 inches), *Koban* (7 by 4 inches), *Nagaban* (20 by 9 inches), *Oban* (15 by 10 inches), *Shikishiban* (8 by 9 inches), and *Tanzaku* (15 by 5 inches) denote approximate size. Modern versions of some of these prints have been made. Other woodblock prints that are not Japanese are listed under Print, Woodblock.

Japanese, Chikanobu, Toyohara, Blooming Garden, 3 Women & Crane, Seal, 13 3/4 x 9 In. 277
Japanese, Hashimoto, Okiie, Girl & Irises, Signed, Seal, Frame, 1955, 16 x 22 1/2 In. 523
Japanese, Hasui, Kawase, Evening Snow At Terashima, 12 Scenes Of Tokyo, 15 3/8 x 10 1/2 In... 5843
Japanese, Hasui, Kawase, Kiyomizu Temple In Kyoto, Seal, 1933, Oban Tate-e, 15 x 10 In. 1107
Japanese, Hasui, Kawase, Morning Rain At Asakusa, Seal, 1930, Oban Tate-e, 15 1/2 x 10 In. ... 1169
Japanese, Hasui, Kawase, Mt. Fuji From Yuimachi At Suruga, Seal, 1934, 15 3/8 x 10 In. 554
Japanese, Hiroshige, Utagawa, Beautiful Woman, Moonlit Town In Background, 13 1/2 x 10 In. 221
Japanese, Hiroshige, Utagawa, Monkey Bridge In Winter, Ko-Tanzaku Tate-e, 13 x 2 3/4 In. 277
Japanese, Hiroshige, Utagawa, Odawara, Sakawa River, 53 Stations Of Tokaido Road, 8 x 13 In. ... 431
Japanese, Hiroshige, Utagawa, Shigetaka Asaji In Front Of Midori Chidori, Hundred Poets, 10 x 8 In..... 338
Japanese, Hokusai, Katsushika, Still Life, Lacquer Tray, Chopsticks, Okimono, Seal, 8 x 7 In.. 185

Print, Warhol, Andy, Marilyn, Screenprint, Pencil, Signed, 11 3/8 x 8 In.
$527

Cordier Auctions

TIP
Don't frame a good print in a clip frame. There should be air space between the paper and the glass.

Print, Wood, Grant, In The Spring, Lithograph, Mat, Frame, Signed, 9 x 11 3/4 In.
$1,652

Cottone Auctions

Print, Woodblock, Lazzell, Banche, Sailboat, Signed, 1931, 12 x 14 In.
$66,000

Eldred's

Purse, Bamboo, Backpack, Brown Suede, Calf Leather, Gucci, 12 x 10 ½ x 3 ¾ In.
$530

Clars Auction Gallery

Purse, Canvas, Wallet, Sarah, White Monogram, Multicolor, Coated, Louis Vuitton, 8 ½ x 10 x 2 In.
$315

Clars Auction Gallery

Purse, Crystals, Minaudiere, Domino, Onyx Push Closure, Square, Judith Leiber, 4 In.
$938

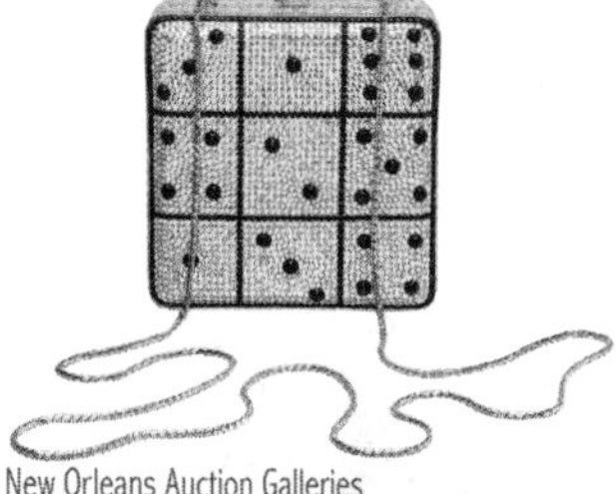

New Orleans Auction Galleries

TIP

Use a magnet to test the beads on vintage beaded bags. The best beads are steel, and steel sticks to a magnet. Do not soak a beaded bag in water to clean it. The knit threads will weaken and may break. Use a damp cloth and little pressure.

Japanese, Hoshi, Joichi, High Treetop, Red, Signed, Frame, 1976, 7 ¾ x 5 In. 400
Japanese, Kasamatsu, Shiro, Woman With Umbrella, Pagoda, Frame, 20 ¾ x 16 ¾ In. 151
Japanese, Koitsu, Tsuchiya, Aki Miyajima, Seal, 1936, O-Hosoban Tate-e, 16 x 7 ¾ In. 123
Japanese, Kunisada, Utagawa, Geisha, Red Kimono, River, Frame, 24 x 18 In. 212
Japanese, Kunisada, Utagawa, Woman, Standing In River, Kimono, Oban Tate-e, Frame, 24 x 18 In. 212
Japanese, Kuniyoshi, Utagawa, Battle Of Ishibashiyama In Rain, Triptych, 14 ½ x 19 In. 492
Japanese, Naoyoshi, Hashimoto, 3 Daimyo Figures In Room Setting, 13 ¾ x 8 ⅞ In. 123
Japanese, Sadahiro, Young Samurai & Fox, Oban Tate-E, Frame, 14 ½ x 9 ¾ In. 185
Japanese, Saito, Kiyoshi, Dog, Dachshund, Red, Black, Gray, Signed, c.1950, 9 x 6 ⅝ In. 369
Japanese, Shigemaru, Below Yatsuyama In Takanawa, Famous Places In Edo, 8 x 12 ½ In. 123
Japanese, Toyokuni, Utagawa, 5 Actors Posing On Bridge, Pentaptych, Oban Tate-e, 14 ⅜ x 10 In. . 492
Japanese, Toyokuni, Utagawa, Actor, Segawa Roko, Oban Tate-E, Frame, 15 ⅝ x 9 ⅝ In. 185
Japanese, Yoshida, Hiroshi, Tea House, Signed, Frame, 1956, 22 ½ x 14 ¾ In. 234
Japanese, Yoshitsuya, Utagawa, Enju Tosuke, 54 Battle Stories Of Hisago Army, 12 ⅝ x 8 ⅝ In. 185
Kent, Melanie Taylor, Michael Jordan, Autograph, Space Jam, Serigraph, Frame, 46 x 34 In. ... 908
Kurz & Allison, Battle Of New Orleans, Chromolithograph, Frame, 1890, 21 x 27 In. .....*illus* 793
Marilyn Monroe, Yankees Cap, Joe DiMaggio Uniform, No. 5, Photograph, Frame, 30 x 21 In. . 192

Nutting prints are popular with collectors. Wallace Nutting is known for his pictures, furniture, and books. Collectors call his pictures Nutting prints although they are actually hand-colored photographs issued from 1900 to 1941. There are over 10,000 different titles. Wallace Nutting furniture is listed in the Furniture category.

Nutting, 2 Women By A Hearth, Frame, 9 ½ x 11 In. 30
Nutting, A Canopied Road, Frame, 10 ½ x 13 In. 38
Nutting, By The Fireside, 4 ¾ x 6 In. 56
Nutting, Flowering Time, Frame, 12 x 19 In. 180
Nutting, Honeymoon Winds, Frame, 15 ¾ x 20 ½ In. 30
Nutting, Larkspur, Signed, Frame, 22 ¾ x 18 ¾ In. 44
Nutting, Where The Woodman Ceased, Frame, 1921, 12 ¾ x 10 ¾ In. 96
Nutting, Whitsunday, Frame, 4 x 9 ½ In. 108

Parrish prints are wanted by collectors. Maxfield Frederick Parrish was an illustrator who lived from 1870 to 1966. He is best known as a designer of magazine covers, posters, calendars, and advertisements. His prints have been copied in recent years. Some Maxfield Parrish items may be listed in Advertising.

Parrish, Arabian Nights, Complete Set Of 12 Prints, Portfolio Case, Each 11 ½ x 9 In. 625
Parrish, Daybreak, 1923, 17 ½ x 29 ½ In. 188
Parrish, Dusk, House On A Snowy Hill, 12 x 14 ½ In. 1680
Parrish, Garden Of Allah, 15 x 30 In. 300
Parrish, Reveries, Gilt Wood Frame, 1927, 27 x 20 ½ In. 150
Parrish, Romance, c.1922, 14 x 22 In. 510
Parrish, The Waterfall, Frame, 22 x 16 ½ In. 225
Warhol, Andy, Campbell's Soup Can, Shopping Bag, Handles, 16 x 9 ¾ In. ....*illus* 1440
Warhol, Andy, Marilyn, Screenprint, Pencil, Signed, 11 ⅜ x 8 In. ....*illus* 527
Wood, Grant, In The Spring, Lithograph, Mat, Frame, Signed, 9 x 11 ¾ In. ....*illus* 1652

Woodblock prints that are not in the Japanese tradition are listed here. Most were made in England and the United States during the Arts and Crafts period. Japanese woodblock prints are listed under Print, Japanese.

Woodblock, Baumann, Gustave, Autumnal Glory, Frame, 1917, 13 x 13 In. 6250
Woodblock, Canton, Shelly, Autumn, Old Craggy Woman, Black Robe, Tree, 1960, 18 x 12 In. 225
Woodblock, Gearhart, Frances, Canyon Landscape, Frame, c.1930, 13 x 10 In. 8750
Woodblock, Lazzell, Banche, Sailboat, Signed, 1931, 12 x 14 In. ....*illus* 66000
Woodblock, Rappaport, Fred, Jump Rope, Double Dutch, Mid-1900s, 5 ½ x 6 In. 295
Woodblock, Stein, Alex, Factory Workers, German Expressionist, 1932, 11 ½ x 7 ½ In. 225

PURINTON

Purinton Pottery Company was incorporated in Wellsville, Ohio, in 1936. The company moved to Shippenville, Pennsylvania, in 1941 and made a variety of hand-painted ceramic wares. By the 1950s Purinton was making dinnerware, souvenirs, cookie jars, and florist wares. The pottery closed in 1959.

Purinton Pottery

Apple, Sugar, Lid, 6 In. 25
Man & Woman, Salt & Pepper, Blue & White Stripes, 3 ¼ In. 74
Normandy Plaid, Jug, Kent, Handle 29
Normandy Plaid, Tray, Oblong, 11 x 7 x 1 In. 65
Pussy Willow, Vase, 6 ½ In. 15

PURSE

Purses have been recognizable since the eighteenth century, when leather and needlework purses were preferred. Beaded purses became popular in the nineteenth century, went out of style, but are again in use. Mesh purses date from the 1880s and are still being made. How to carry a handkerchief, lipstick, and cell phone is a problem today for every woman, including the Queen of England.

Bamboo, Backpack, Brown Suede, Calf Leather, Gucci, 12 x 10 ½ x 3 ¾ In. .... *illus* 530
Basket, Nantucket, Oval, Lightship, Swing Handle, Stanley M. Roop, 1971, 7 ½ x 8 ¾ In. 2691
Basket, Nantucket, Shoulder Bag, Lightship, Ivory Plaque, c.1960, 7 x 7 ½ In. 1638
Calf, Black, Tote, Suede Leather, Handle, Gucci, 14 ½ x 10 ½ x 5 ½ In. 577
Canvas, Handbag, Sac Plat, Brown Monogram, Coated, Louis Vuitton, 15 x 14 x 4 In. 738
Canvas, Wallet, Sarah, White Monogram, Multicolor, Coated, Louis Vuitton, 8 ½ x 10 x 2 In. *illus* 315
Clutch, Gold Flora, Edidi, Pastel Stones, Gold Mesh Ground, Wendy Lau, 3 x 8 In. 2750
Crocodile, Wallet, Black, Card Slots, Slip & Zipper Pocket, Hermes, France, 8 x 6 x ¾ In. 2125
Crystals, Minaudiere, Bird, Multicolor, Gold Hardware, Crystal Closure, Judith Leiber, 4 x 5 In. 2125
Crystals, Minaudiere, Butterfly, Multicolor, Lapis Lazuli Cabochon Closure, Judith Leiber, 3 x 6 In. . 4000
Crystals, Minaudiere, Domino, Onyx Push Closure, Square, Judith Leiber, 4 In. .... *illus* 938
Crystals, Minaudiere, Dragonfly, Silver Hardware, Chain, Judith Leiber, 3 x 6 In. .... *illus* 6000
Crystals, Minaudiere, Fish, Multicolor, Push Ball, Judith Leiber, 5 ½ In. .... *illus* 2125
Crystals, Minaudiere, Lucky Dice, Onyx Pips, Chain, K. Baumann, 4 x 4 x 4 In. 1000
Crystals, Minaudiere, Multicolor Violins, Judith Leiber, 6 ¼ x 4 ¾ In. 489
Crystals, Minaudiere, Satin, Gold Scrolls, Gray Pearls, Strap, Judith Leiber, 4 In. .... *illus* 2250
Hardwood, Handbag, Gancini, Incised Logo, Goldtone, Salvatore Ferragamo, 13 x 8 x 4 In. 350
Hide, Leather Handle & Sling, Reddish Brown, Silver Lock, 12 ½ In. 156
Jet Rhinestones, Minaudiere, Hardstone, Shaped Top, Clasp Set, Judith Leiber, 1970s-80s, 7 In. 563
Lambskin, Black, Gray Satin Lined, Bijou Chain, 2 Quilted Flaps, Chanel, 12 x 7 In. 1375
Lambskin, Black, Quilted, Leather Strap, Gold CC Turn Closure, Chanel, 1997, 5 x 10 In. 1625
Lambskin, Deep Olive Green, Woven Design, Knotted Strap, Bottega Veneta, 10 In. 216
Leather, Calfskin, Black, Tan Stitched, Magnetic Closure, Flat Straps, Chanel, 11 x 15 In. 1872
Leather, Orange Caviar, Quilted, Chain Detail, Gusseted Envelope Flap, Chanel, 10 x 13 In. 1625
Leather, Ruched, Gaufre Frame, Push Lock Closure, Red, Prada, 14 x 14 In. 1000
Leather, Shoulder Bag, Popincourt Haut, Monogram, Louis Vuitton, 10 ¾ x 9 In. 863
Leather, Tote, Negonda, Mosaic Toile, Rolled Handles, Hermes, France, 19 x 9 x 14 In. ...*illus* 1125
Leather, Travel Bag, 2 Handles, Gold Zipper, Red, Epi Keepall, Vuitton, 13 x 20 x 9 In. ....*illus* 677
Leather, Travel Bag, Epi, Keepall, Black Stitching, Louis Vuitton, 12 x 22 ½ x 10 In. 923
Leather, White, Leather & Chain Strap, Zip Pocket, Chanel, 14 ½ x 9 x 12 In. .... *illus* 1020
Mesh, 14K Gold, Engraved Frame, Flower Motifs, Chain Strap 3600
Minaudiere, Gold, Diamond Scrolls & CC Logo, 2 Hinged Lids, Oval, Cartier, 3 x 2 In. 7995
Minaudiere, Golf, Cabochons, Vanity Mirror, Drop Chain, Push Closure, Judith Leiber, 4 x 5 In. 2500
Patent Leather, Tote, Bellevue, Purple, Gold Metal Hardware, Louis Vuitton, 17 x 11 In. 1400
Persian Lamb, Leather, Black, Muse Bag, Gold Hardware, Padlock, Y. St. Laurent, 14 x 18 In. 750
Silk, Embroidery, Metallic Threads, Pheasants, 2 Jade Bangles, Chinese, 13 x 10 In. ....*illus* 2125
Silver, Black Velvet, Bag, Elaborately Pierced, c.1920, 11 ½ x 9 In. .... *illus* 154
Snakeskin, Hardstone Mount, Purple, 2 Pouches, Removable Strap, Judith Leiber, c.1985, 8 In. 526
Suede & Fur, Quilted, Black, Goldtone CC Logo, Clasp & Chain Handle, Chanel .... *illus* 469

Purse, Crystals, Minaudiere, Dragonfly, Silver Hardware, Chain, Judith Leiber, 3 x 6 In.
$6,000

New Orleans Auction Galleries

Purse, Crystals, Minaudiere, Fish, Multicolor, Push Ball, Judith Leiber, 5 ½ In.
$2,125

New Orleans Auction Galleries

TIP
Be careful when choosing a purse to use with a vintage gown. The fabric could be damaged by the rough surface of a beaded bag or a jeweled closure.

Purse, Crystals, Minaudiere, Satin, Gold Scrolls, Gray Pearls, Strap, Judith Leiber, 4 In.
$2,250

New Orleans Auction Galleries

Purse, Leather, Tote, Negonda, Mosaic Toile, Rolled Handles, Hermes, France, 19 x 9 x 14 In.
$1,125

Abington Auction Gallery

Buy a Magazine, Get a Purse
Mesh purses were given as gifts with fashion magazine subscriptions before 1917.

Purse, Leather, Travel Bag, 2 Handles, Gold Zipper, Red, Epi Keepall, Vuitton, 13 x 20 x 9 In.
$677

Clars Auction Gallery

Purse, Silk, Embroidery, Metallic Threads, Pheasants, 2 Jade Bangles, Chinese, 13 x 10 In.
$2,125

Neal Auction Company

TIP
Store vintage handbags on a shelf; never hang by the handle.

Purse, Silver, Black Velvet, Bag, Elaborately Pierced, c.1920, 11 ½ x 9 In.
$154

Locati Auctions

Purse, Leather, White, Leather & Chain Strap, Zip Pocket, Chanel, 14 ½ x 9 x 12 In.
$1,020

Case Antiques

P

Wallet, Coated Canvas, Compact Zip, Brown Monogram, Louis Vuitton, 4 ¼ x 4 In. 303
Wallet, Wool, Flame Stitch, Yellow, Red, Blue, Green, 2 Pockets, 1700s, 4 x 8 In. ....*illus* 2583
Wallet, Wool, Flowers, Needlework, Red Ground, Green, 1700s, 6 ½ In. 625
Wool, Boho Bag, Multicolor, Fabric Flowers, Etro Green 213

PYREX

Pyrex glass baking dishes were first made in 1915 by the Corning Glass Works. Pyrex dishes are made of a heat-resistant glass that can go from refrigerator or freezer to oven or microwave and are nice enough to put on the table. Clear glass dishes were made first. Pyrex Flameware, for use on a stovetop burner, was made from 1936 to 1979. A set of four mixing bowls, each in a dfferent color (blue, red, green, and yellow), was made beginning in 1947. The first pieces with decorative patterns were made in 1956. After Corning sold its Pyrex brand to World Kitchen LLC in 1998, changes were made to the formula for the glass.

Butter, Milk Glass, Old Town Blue, Lid, 1970s.......... 14
Cake Pan, Glass Insert, Silver Outer Liner With Handles, 9 ⅜ x 15 ½ In. 329
Carafe, Clear Glass, Cork Ball Stopper, Leather Strap, 5 x 5 x 10 In. 38
Mixing Bowl, Red, No. 402, 1 ½ Qt. 25
Mug, Snowflake, Blue Garland, White Ground, 3 ⅜ In. 7
Pitcher, Butterfly Gold, Yellow, Brown, c.1975, 9 ½ In. 49

QUEZAL

Quezal glass was made from 1901 to 1924 at the Queens, New York, company started by Martin Bach. Other glassware by other firms, such as Loetz, Steuben, and Tiffany, resembles this gold-colored iridescent glass. Martin Bach died in 1921. His son-in-law, Conrad Vahlsing Jr., went to work at the Lustre Art Company about 1920. Bach's son, Martin Bach Jr., worked at the Durand Art Glass division of the Vineland Flint Glass Works after 1924.

Bowl, Golden Iridescent, Flaring Foot, Signed, 1910s, 4 ⅝ x 8 x 4 ½ In. ....*illus* 176
Goblet, Pulled Feather, Gold Iridescent, Opal, Green, 5-Petal Flower, 1910s, 8 x 2 x 3 In. 1112
Lamp, 3-Light, Pulled Feather Shades, White Ribbed Ground, Bronze Base, 16 ½ x 12 In. 3900
Lamp, 5-Light, Tubular Stems, Leafy Fitters, Lily Shades, Ribbed, Bronze Base, 16 x 12 In. 3025
Lamp, Golden Aurene Vine Shade, Bronze Tree Trunk Base, Signed, 13 ½ x 7 In. ....*illus* 431
Lampshade, Blue Hook Feather, Cream White Ground, Iridescent, 2 x 5 In. ....*illus* 224
Lampshade, Domed, King Tut, Green Waves, Orange, Creamy Ground, 5 ¾ x 3 x 6 In. ...*illus* 1080
Lampshade, Gold Iridescent, Pulled Feather, Bell Shape, Signed, 6 ½ x 6 In., Pair 163
Lampshade, White Iridescent, Green Pulled Feather, 4 x 5 In. 70
Vase, Pulled Feather, Flare Top, 5 Sections, Bulbous Base, Gold Iridescent, 8 ⅞ In. 6655
Vase, Slag Glass, Silver Overlay, Flowers, Leaves, Multicolor, 6 In. 1140
Vase, Vertical Stripe, Opal Iridescent, Green, Bud Shape, 1910s, 7 ⅞ x 3 ½ x 3 In. 936

QUILT

Quilts have been made since the seventeenth century. Early textiles were very precious and every scrap was saved to be reused. A quilt is a combination of fabrics joined to a filler and a backing by small stitched designs known as quilting. An appliqued quilt has pieces stitched to the top of a large piece of backing fabric. A patchwork, or pieced, quilt is made of many small pieces stitched together. Embroidery can be added to either type.

Album, Appliqued, 36 Blocks, Flowers, Martha Mendenhall, c.1850, 89 x 89 ¾ In. ....*illus* 5850
Amish, Broken Dishes, 30 Blocks, Yellow, Green, Blue, Calico, 80 x 68 In. 367
Amish, Hand Stitched, Postage Stamp, Princess Feather, Lancaster County, 1810s, 77 x 77 In. 360
Amish, Patchwork, Trip Around The World, Rayon, 84 x 84 In. ....*illus* 153
Appliqued, Adam & Eve, Hand Stitched, Trapunto, Chintz, Sinclair Family, c.1840, 93 x 88 In. 7995

TIP
To remove gum, put an ice cube in a zip-up plastic bag, then set it on the gum. When the gum hardens, hit it with a hammer and it will break off.

Purse, Suede & Fur, Quilted, Black, Goldtone CC Logo, Clasp & Chain Handle, Chanel
$469

Hindman Auctions

Purse, Wallet, Wool, Flame Stitch, Yellow, Red, Blue, Green, 2 Pockets, 1700s, 4 x 8 In.
$2,583

Skinner, Inc.

Quezal, Bowl, Golden Iridescent, Flaring Foot, Signed, 1910s, 4 ⅝ x 8 x 4 ½ In.
$176

Jeffrey S. Evans & Associates

Quezal, Lamp, Golden Aurene Vine Shade, Bronze Tree Trunk Base, Signed, 13 ½ x 7 In.
$431

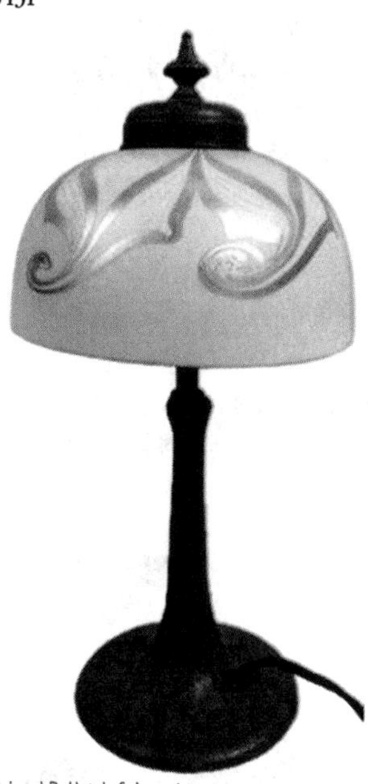

Richard D. Hatch & Associates

Quezal, Lampshade, Blue Hook Feather, Cream White Ground, Iridescent, 2 x 5 In.
$224

Bunch Auctions

Quezal, Lampshade, Domed, King Tut, Green Waves, Orange, Creamy Ground, 5 ¾ x 3 x 6 In.
$1,080

Morphy Auctions

Appliqued, Crossed Laurel Leaf Variation, Red Scalloped Border, Green Vine, c.1850, 110 x 114 In. 2860
Appliqued, Embroidered, Farm Animals, Birds, Flowers, Velvet, Satin, Silk, Wool, 1884, 61 x 46 In.. 311
Appliqued, Floral, White Ground, Red Diamonds, Green, 1850s-90s, 84 x 102 In. 610
Appliqued, Flower Basket, Sprays Of Coxcomb, Red, Green, Cotton, 86 ¾ x 84 ½ In., 1850s..... 660
Appliqued, Flowers, Red, Green, White, Red Border, Ohio, c.1860, 88 x 88 In. *illus* 1416
Appliqued, Grand Army, Military Symbols, Cross, U.S. Flag, Late 1800s, 60 x 74 In. 938
Appliqued, Hand Stitched, 9 Blocks, 4-Leaf Clover, Grapevine, 1852, 80 x 79 ½ In. *illus* 164
Appliqued, Princess Feather, Red, Green, White, Machine Sewn Binding, c.1890, 80 x 80 In. *illus* 300
Appliqued, Tulip & Circle, Handmade, Green, Red Line Border, 64 x 71 In. 161
Appliqued, Tulip, Green, Red, Feather, Diamond Quilting, c.1880, 75 x 76 ½ In. 259
Appliqued, Tulips, Flower Buds, Scalloped Border, Green & Yellow Borders, 63 x 73 In. 660
Barn Raising, 48 Squares, Blue Interior, Red Exterior Border, c.1900, 82 x 82 In. *illus* 519
Chintz, Flowers, Cutouts For Bedpost, 1800s, 102 x 102 In. *illus* 738
Crazy, Embroidered, Velvet, Satin, Silk, Cord Edges, Fringe, c.1890, 70 x 36 In. *illus* 960
Fleur-De-Lis, Red & White, Tulip & Vine Border, 64 x 80 In. 177
Flowers, Pink, Green Leaves, Stems, White Ground, Early 1900s, 92 x 88 In. 523
Lone Star, Crib, Basket Corners, Flowers, Multicolor, c.1900, 43 x 43 In. *illus* 580
Mennonite, Patchwork, Log Cabin, Squares & Diamonds, Penn., c.1890, 86 x 82 In. *illus* 480
Mennonite, Star Of Bethlehem, Multicolor, Label, Ida Moe Bradshaw, Cotton, 1983, 66 x 78 In...... 250
Patchwork & Appliqued, Alternating Squares, Stars, Elizabeth Jane Fryfogle, Cotton, 90 x 88 In. 741
Patchwork & Appliqued, Bear Paw, Red, White, Flower Stuffed, East Tennessee, c.1900, 79 x 68 In. 450
Patchwork, Blue & White, Hand Stitched, 9 Blocks, Star Motif, c.1900, 89 x 75 In. 176
Patchwork, Blue, White, Squares, Striped Border, Pennsylvania, 81 x 73 ½ In. *illus* 136
Patchwork, Cathedral Window, White, Sprigged Cotton Prints, 83 x 85 In. 311
Patchwork, Feedsack, Scalloped Fan Blocks, Yellow & Green, Yellow Border, 1930, 87 x 74 In. *illus* 203
Patchwork, Flying Geese, Satin, Line Border, Multicolor, c.1900, 81 x 64 In. 427
Patchwork, Jacob's Coat, Dated May 3, 1883, 82 x 84 In. *illus* 175
Patchwork, Lone Star, Multicolor, White Ground, Mitered Borders, Green Binding, 82 x 96 In.. 181
Patchwork, Monkey Wrench, Green, Orange, Cream, Brown, York County, Pa., 72 x 72 In. *illus* 130
Patchwork, Red, 6-Point Stars, White Squares, Frame, Early 1900s, 48 x 46 ½ In. 240
Patchwork, Star, Zigzag, Diamond Border, 1800s, 80 x 82 In. 1037
Patchwork, Star Pattern, Green Ground, Kaleidoscope, c.1820, 92 x 72 In. 420
Patchwork, Wagon Wheel, Green & Brown, Cotton, c.1880, 91 x 79 In. *illus* 352
Star Of Bethlehem, Hand Stitched, White Ground, Striped Border, Early 1900s, 76 x 76 In. *illus* 738
Star Of Virginia, 20 Blocks, Hand Stitched, 8-Point Stars, Red, White Ground, 89 x 74 In....... 187
Star, Red, White Points, Green Center, Yellow, Floral Print, c.1900, 84 x 78 In. 492

QUIMPER

HR Quimper

Quimper pottery has a long history. Tin-glazed, hand-painted pottery has been made in Quimper, France, since the late seventeenth century. The earliest firm was founded in 1708 by Pierre Bousquet. In 1782, Antoine de la Hubaudiere became the manager of the factory and the factory became known as the HB Factory (for Hubaudiere-Bousquet), de la Hubaudiere, or Grande Maison. Another firm, founded in 1772 by Francois Eloury, was known as Porquier. The third firm, founded by Guillaume Dumaine in 1778, was known as HR or Henriot Quimper. All three firms made similar pottery decorated with designs of Breton peasants and sea and flower motifs. The Eloury (Porquier) and Dumaine (Henriot) firms merged in 1913. Bousquet (HB) merged with the others in 1968. The group was sold to an American holding company in 1984. More changes followed, and in 2011 Jean-Pierre Le Goff became the owner and the name was changed to Henriot-Quimper.

Bowl, Cobalt Blue Scrollwork, Breton Couple, 2 Handles, Footed, Multicolor, 4 x 12 In. 84
Inkstand, Orange & Blue Flowers, Man In Folk Costume, Shaped, 2 Inserts, 4 x 7 In. 180
Oyster Plate, 24 Black Wells, Orange, Yellow & Pink Flowers, 16 ½ In. 120
Pitcher, Bird, Leaves, Branch, White, France, 11 In. 106
Planter, Cobalt Blue Scroll, Scenic, Flowers, 2 Handles, White Interior, 4 ¾ x 18 ½ In. 192
Platter, Flowers, Multicolor, Marked Underside, Round, 8 ½ In. 84
Tray, Man & Woman, Field, Flowering Bushes, Border, 9 x 12 In. 95

Quilt, Album, Appliqued, 36 Blocks, Flowers, Martha Mendenhall, c.1850, 89 x 89 ¾ In.
$5,850

Jeffrey S. Evans & Associates

Quilt, Amish, Patchwork, Trip Around The World, Rayon, 84 x 84 In.
$153

Conestoga Auction Company

Quilt, Appliqued, Flowers, Red, Green, White, Red Border, Ohio, c.1860, 88 x 88 In.
$1,416

Copake Auctions

Quilt, Appliqued, Hand Stitched, 9 Blocks, 4-Leaf Clover, Grapevine, 1852, 80 x 79 ½ In.
$164

Jeffrey S. Evans & Associates

Quilt, Appliqued, Princess Feather, Red, Green, White, Machine Sewn Binding, c.1890, 80 x 80 In.
$300

Garth's Auctioneers & Appraisers

Quilt, Barn Raising, 48 Squares, Blue Interior, Red Exterior Border, c.1900, 82 x 82 In.
$519

Pook & Pook

Quilt, Chintz, Flowers, Cutouts For Bedpost, 1800s, 102 x 102 In.
$738

Skinner, Inc.

Quilt, Crazy, Embroidered, Velvet, Satin, Silk, Cord Edges, Fringe, c.1890, 70 x 36 In.
$960

Cowan's Auctions

Quilt, Lone Star, Crib, Basket Corners, Flowers, Multicolor, c.1900, 43 x 43 In.
$580

Pook & Pook

Quilt, Mennonite, Patchwork, Log Cabin, Squares & Diamonds, Penn., c.1890, 86 x 82 In.
$480

Cowan's Auctions

Quilt, Patchwork, Blue, White, Squares, Striped Border, Pennsylvania, 81 x 73 ½ In.
$136

Hartzell's Auction Gallery Inc.

Quilt, Patchwork, Feedsack, Scalloped Fan Blocks, Yellow & Green, Yellow Border, 1930, 87 x 74 In.
$203

Soulis Auctions

Quilt, Patchwork, Jacob's Coat, Dated May 3, 1883, 82 x 84 In.
$175

Conestoga Auction Company

Quilt, Patchwork, Monkey Wrench, Green, Orange, Cream, Brown, York County, Pa., 72 x 72 In.
$130

Conestoga Auction Company

Quilt, Patchwork, Wagon Wheel, Green & Brown, Cotton, c.1880, 91 x 79 In.
$352

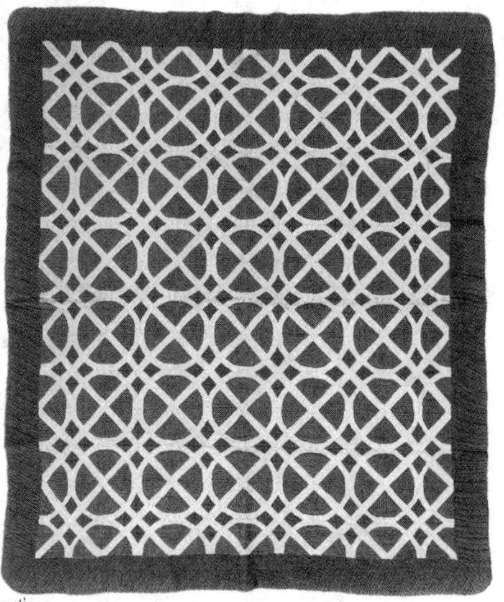

Cowan's Auctions

Vase, Pierced Handles, Flowers, Armorial, Figural, Early 1900s, 13 In., Pair ....*illus* 375
Wall Pocket, Cone Shape, Flowers, Scenic, Multicolor, Marked Underside, 8 ½ In.................... 84

RADIO

Radio broadcast receiving sets were first sold in New York City in 1910. They were used to pick up the experimental broadcasts of the day. The first commercial radios were made by Westinghouse Company for listeners of the experimental shows on KDKA Pittsburgh in 1920. Collectors today are interested in all early radios, especially those made of Bakelite plastic or decorated with blue mirrors. Figural advertising radios and transistor radios are also collected.

Fada, Bakelite, Orange, 2 Knobs, Electric, 11 x 7 In. ....*illus* 677
Fada, Cloud, Model 845XA, Onyx, Alabaster, Styrene Plastic, Green, 6 x 11 In. ....*illus* 1000
Fada, Model 790, Dark Brown, Red Turnings, Electric, 14 ½ x 7 x 8 In.................... 113
General Electric, Model HJ624, Light Brown, Stepped Top, 16 x 8 x 8 ½ In.................... 85
Microphone, Desk Stand, RCA Type, 74-B, 10 x 6 ½ x 4 ½ In. ....*illus* 484
Philips, Model 228B, 4 Tubes, Speaker, Canvas Covered Case, Rotating Base, 1939, 12 In......... 2611
RCA Victor, Model 8R71, AM, 4 Turnings, 14 x 8 x 9 In.................... 68
Sonora, Knobs, Orange, Applied Handle, Bakelite, 6 x 9 x 6 In. ....*illus* 1440
Sparton, Model 558-B, Blue Mirrored Glass, Chrome Trim, Art Deco, W.D. Teague, 1938 319
Zenith, Model H511, Racetrack, Oblong, Circular Dial, 13 ¾ x 6 x 7 In.................... 79

RAILROAD

Railroad enthusiasts collect any train memorabilia. Everything is wanted, from oilcans to whole train cars. The Chessie system has a store that sells many reproductions of its old dinnerware and uniforms.

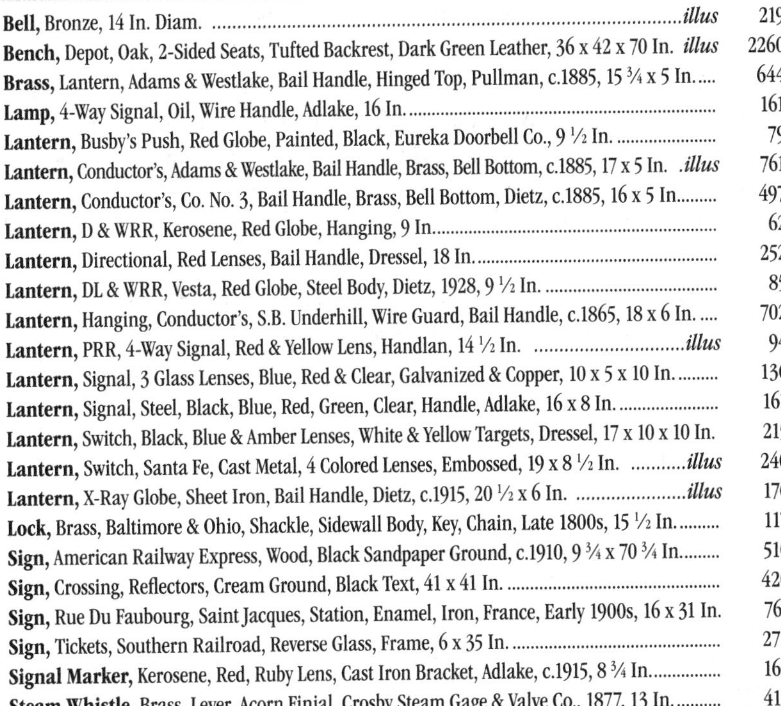

Bell, Bronze, 14 In. Diam. ....*illus* 219
Bench, Depot, Oak, 2-Sided Seats, Tufted Backrest, Dark Green Leather, 36 x 42 x 70 In. *illus* 2260
Brass, Lantern, Adams & Westlake, Bail Handle, Hinged Top, Pullman, c.1885, 15 ¾ x 5 In..... 644
Lamp, 4-Way Signal, Oil, Wire Handle, Adlake, 16 In.................... 161
Lantern, Busby's Push, Red Globe, Painted, Black, Eureka Doorbell Co., 9 ½ In.................... 79
Lantern, Conductor's, Adams & Westlake, Bail Handle, Brass, Bell Bottom, c.1885, 17 x 5 In. .*illus* 761
Lantern, Conductor's, Co. No. 3, Bail Handle, Brass, Bell Bottom, Dietz, c.1885, 16 x 5 In......... 497
Lantern, D & WRR, Kerosene, Red Globe, Hanging, 9 In.................... 62
Lantern, Directional, Red Lenses, Bail Handle, Dressel, 18 In.................... 252
Lantern, DL & WRR, Vesta, Red Globe, Steel Body, Dietz, 1928, 9 ½ In.................... 85
Lantern, Hanging, Conductor's, S.B. Underhill, Wire Guard, Bail Handle, c.1865, 18 x 6 In. 702
Lantern, PRR, 4-Way Signal, Red & Yellow Lens, Handlan, 14 ½ In. ....*illus* 94
Lantern, Signal, 3 Glass Lenses, Blue, Red & Clear, Galvanized & Copper, 10 x 5 x 10 In......... 136
Lantern, Signal, Steel, Black, Blue, Red, Green, Clear, Handle, Adlake, 16 x 8 In.................... 161
Lantern, Switch, Black, Blue & Amber Lenses, White & Yellow Targets, Dressel, 17 x 10 x 10 In. 215
Lantern, Switch, Santa Fe, Cast Metal, 4 Colored Lenses, Embossed, 19 x 8 ½ In. ....*illus* 240
Lantern, X-Ray Globe, Sheet Iron, Bail Handle, Dietz, c.1915, 20 ½ x 6 In. ....*illus* 176
Lock, Brass, Baltimore & Ohio, Shackle, Sidewall Body, Key, Chain, Late 1800s, 15 ½ In......... 117
Sign, American Railway Express, Wood, Black Sandpaper Ground, c.1910, 9 ¾ x 70 ¾ In......... 510
Sign, Crossing, Reflectors, Cream Ground, Black Text, 41 x 41 In.................... 420
Sign, Rue Du Faubourg, Saint Jacques, Station, Enamel, Iron, France, Early 1900s, 16 x 31 In. 767
Sign, Tickets, Southern Railroad, Reverse Glass, Frame, 6 x 35 In.................... 277
Signal Marker, Kerosene, Red, Ruby Lens, Cast Iron Bracket, Adlake, c.1915, 8 ¾ In.................... 164
Steam Whistle, Brass, Lever, Acorn Finial, Crosby Steam Gage & Valve Co., 1877, 13 In.......... 413

RAZOR

Razors were used in ancient Egypt and subsequently wherever shaving was in fashion. The metal razor used in America was made in Sheffield, England, until about 1870. After 1870, machine-made hollow-ground

Quilt, Star Of Bethlehem, Hand Stitched, White Ground, Striped Border, Early 1900s, 76 x 76 In.
$738

Skinner, Inc.

Quimper, Vase, Pierced Handles, Flowers, Armorial, Figural, Early 1900s, 13 In., Pair
$375

Cowan's Auctions

Radio, Fada, Bakelite, Orange, 2 Knobs, Electric, 11 x 7 In.
$677

Richard Opfer Auctioneering, Inc.

R

This is an edited listing of current prices. Visit **Kovels.com** to check thousands of prices from previous years and sign up for free information on trends, tips, reproductions, marks, and more.

razors were made in Germany or America. Plastic or bone handles were popular. The razor was often sold in a set of seven, one for each day of the week. The set was often kept by the barber who shaved the well-to-do man each day in the shop.

Celluloid Handle, Straight, Forged, Iron Blade, Faux Horn, Folk Art, c.1900, 19 In. 170
Dime Safety Razor, International Safety Razor Co., Wood Handle, Tin, 1907, 3 In. 125
Double Arrow, Barber Razor, Straight Edge, Case, 6 ½ In. 24
Hoffritz, Straight Edge, Case, Germany, 6 ½ In. 34
Maryolet, Safety, Gold Tone, Box 68
Straight, Bakelite Handle, D.H. Lory, N.Y. Solingen, Germany, 9 In. 225
Straight, Celluloid, Maiden, Long Hair, Art Nouveau, Union Razor Co., 6 In. 150

REAMERS

Reamers, or juice squeezers, have been known since 1767, although most of those collected today date from the twentieth century. Figural reamers are among the most prized.

Depression Glass, Clear, Thumb Handle, Hazel Atlas, c.1940, 1 ½ x 6 In. 18
Depression Glass, Green, Shallow Bowl, 4 x 6 In. 24
Glass, Clear, Footed, 3 ½ x 7 ½ x 6 In. 9
Glass, Clear, Hexagonal, No Handle, 2 ½ x 6 In. 16
Lustroware, Yellow, Original Packaging, Columbus Plastic Products 22
Silver Plate, Roberts & Dore, Sheffield, c.1930, 2 ½ x 4 ¾ In. 461

RECORD

Records have changed size and shape through the years. The cylinder-shaped phonograph record for use with the early Edison models was made about 1889. Disc records were first made by 1894, the double-sided disc by 1904. High-fidelity records were first issued in 1944, the first vinyl disc in 1946, the first stereo record in 1958. The 78 RPM became the standard in 1926 but was discontinued in 1957. In 1932, the first 33 ⅓ RPM was made but was not sold commercially until 1948. In 1949, the 45 RPM was introduced. Compact discs became available in the United States in 1982 and many companies began phasing out the production of phonograph records. Vinyl records are popular again. People claim the sound is better on a vinyl recording, and new recordings are being made. Some collectors want vinyl picture records. Vintage albums are collected for their cover art as well as for the fame of the artist and the music.

Abba, Dancing Queen, That's Me, 45 RPM, 7 In. 9
Beatles, Love Me Do, Parlophone, Promotional Copy, 45 RPM, 1962 .... *illus* 10473
Bill Haley & His Comets, Rudy's Rock, 45 RPM, 1956 15
Fats Domino, Here Comes Fats, Vol. 1, London Label, 1950s 18
Four Freshman, Greatest Hits, RCA Records, 33 ⅓ RPM, 1970s 27
Freddie Mercury, Love Kills, 45 RPM, 1984 15
Ray Price, Burning Memories, Autographed, Columbia Records, 1965 68
Rocky Movie Theme, Gonna Fly Now, Columbia Records, 1977, 45 RPM 14
Sex Pistols, God Save The Queen, A&M Records, 45 RPM, 1977 .... *illus* 16125

RED WING

Red Wing Pottery of Red Wing, Minnesota, was a firm started in 1877. The company first made utilitarian pottery, including stoneware jugs and canning jars. In 1906, three companies combined to make the Red Wing Union Stoneware Company and began producing flowerpots, vases, and dinnerware. Art pottery was introduced in 1926. The name of the company was changed to Red Wing Potteries in 1936. Many dinner sets and vases were made before the company closed in

TIP

A crack or chip in the plastic cover of a vintage radio cuts the price in half or more.

Radio, Fada, Cloud, Model 845XA, Onyx, Alabaster, Styrene Plastic, Green, 6 x 11 In.
$1,000

Palm Beach Modern Auctions

Radio, Microphone, Desk Stand, RCA Type, 74-B, 10 x 6 ½ x 4 ½ In.
$484

Fontaine's Auction Gallery

Radio, Sonora, Knobs, Orange, Applied Handle, Bakelite, 6 x 9 x 6 In.
$1,440

Morphy Auctions

Railroad, Bell, Bronze, 14 In. Diam.
$219

Apple Tree Auction Center

Railroad, Lantern, PRR, 4-Way Signal, Red & Yellow Lens, Handlan, 14 ½ In.
$94

Conestoga Auction Company

Railroad, Bench, Depot, Oak, 2-Sided Seats, Tufted Backrest, Dark Green Leather, 36 x 42 x 70 In.
$2,260

Soulis Auctions

Railroad, Lantern, Conductor's, Adams & Westlake, Bail Handle, Brass, Bell Bottom, c.1885, 17 x 5 In.
$761

Jeffrey S. Evans & Associates

Railroad, Lantern, Switch, Santa Fe, Cast Metal, 4 Colored Lenses, Embossed, 19 x 8 ½ In.
$240

Rich Penn Auctions

Railroad, Lantern, X-Ray Globe, Sheet Iron, Bail Handle, Dietz, c.1915, 20 ½ x 6 In.
$176

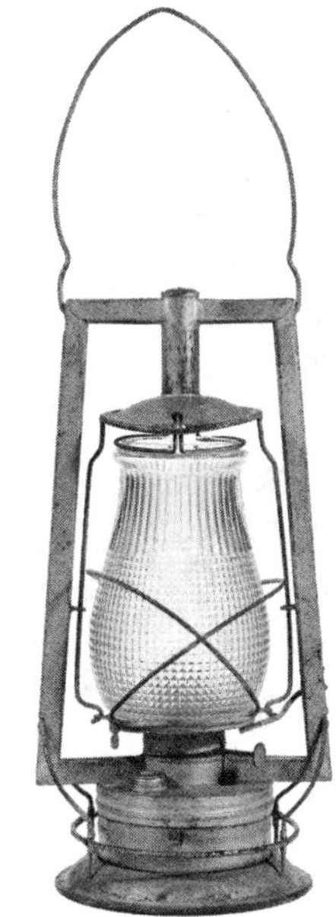

Jeffrey S. Evans & Associates

Record, Beatles, Love Me Do, Parlophone, Promotional Copy, 45 RPM, 1962
$10,473

Discogs.com

Record, Sex Pistols, God Save The Queen, A&M Records, 45 RPM, 1977
$16,125

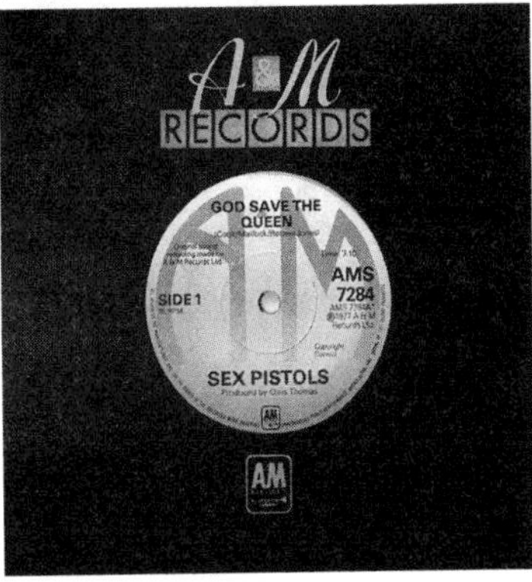

Discogs.com

Redware, Bank, Birth, 18 Applied Chickens, Chicken Finial, Jane Sorey, 1834, 7 In.
$189

Strawser Auction Group

Redware, Crock, Bulbous, Loop Handles, 9 ½ In.
$71

Copake Auctions

Redware, Figurine, Dog, Spaniel, Seated, Painted, John Bell, Waynesboro, 1800s, 10 In.
$2,196

Pook & Pook

Redware, Figurine, Goose, Slightly Turned Head, Impressed Eyes, Oval Base, c.1870, 2 ⅞ x 4 In.
$1,534

Bunch Auctions

Redware, Flask, Figural, Crayfish, Green Glaze, Fish Bottle, 5 ½ In.
$620

Copake Auctions

Redware, Jug, Embossed Floral Panels, Molded Rim, Impressed Henry Swope Pottery, 1800s, 10 ½ In.
$580

Pook & Pook

Redware, Loaf Pan, Coggled Rim, Yellow Slip Design, 1850s, 2 ½ x 14 ½ In.
$719

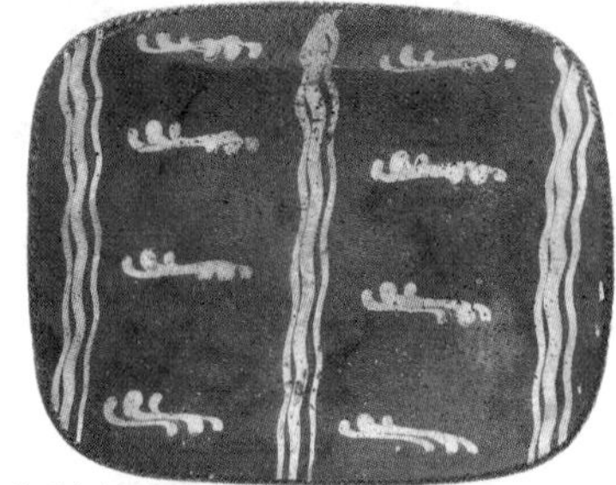
Garth's Auctioneers & Appraisers

Redware, Pie Plate, Green, Brown, Cream Slip, Floral, 1800s, 8 In.
$4,148

Pook & Pook

TIP

Re-key all locks when you move to a new house or apartment or if you lose a key.

Redware, Pitcher, Applied Fish, Salamander Handle, Glazed, 10 ½ In.
$118

Conestoga Auction Company

1967. R. Gillmer bought the company in 1967 and operated it as a retail business. The name was changed again, to Red Wing Pottery. The retail business closed in 2015. Red Wing Stoneware Company was founded in 1987. It was sold to new owners in 2013. They bought Red Wing Pottery and combined the two companies to become Red Wing Stoneware & Pottery. The company makes stoneware crocks, jugs, mugs, bowls, and other items with cobalt blue designs. Rumrill pottery made by the Red Wing Pottery for George Rumrill is listed in its own category. For more prices, go to kovels.com.

Cattail, Vase, Cylindrical, Brown, Green, Stamped, 9 ⅞ In. 109
Clock, Mammy, Lanshire Movement, Electric, 10 x 8 In. 96
Gray Line, Bowl, Console, Coral Interior, Scalloped Edge, 12 In. 24
Stoneware, Crock, Cobalt Blue, 8, Metal & Wood Handles, c.1915, 8 Gal., 15 ½ x 14 In. 289
Stoneware, Crock, Jug, Lid, c.1900, 14 x 17 In. 110
Vase, Red, Blue, Speckles, White Ground, Glaze, 9 ½ x 2 ¾ In. 32
Vase, Yellow, Speckles, Footed, Marked, 12 In. 50

REDWARE

Redware is a hard, red stoneware that has been made for centuries and continues to be made. The term is also used to describe any common clay pottery that is reddish in color. American redware was first made about 1625.

Baking Dish, Oval, Handles, 17 ½ In. 24
Bank, Birth, 18 Applied Chickens, Chicken Finial, Jane Sorey, 1834, 7 In. .... *illus* 189
Bank, Figural, Dog, Spaniel, Seated, Multicolor, Glazed, Marked 4, Pa., 1850s, 7 In. 500
Charger, Yellow, Green Slip, Singer, Bucks County, 1850s, 12 ½ In. 2684
Coffeepot, Dome Lid, Baluster, Molded Reeded Spout, Ribbed, c.1775, 10 ½ In. 878
Crock, Bulbous, Loop Handles, 9 ½ In. .... *illus* 71
Dish, Circle, Slip Decorated, Coggled Rim Edge, Glaze, Pennsylvania, 1950, 14 In. 420
Figurine, Dog, Spaniel, Seated, Painted, John Bell, Waynesboro, 1800s, 10 In. .... *illus* 2196
Figurine, Goose, Slightly Turned Head, Impressed Eyes, Oval Base, c.1870, 2 ⅞ x 4 In. ... *illus* 1534
Figurine, Lion, Lead Glaze, Tongue Extended, Billy Ray Hussey, Early 2000s, 7 x 4 ½ In. 468
Flask, Figural, Crayfish, Green Glaze, Fish Bottle, 5 ½ In. .... *illus* 620
Flowerpot, Flared Foot, Ruffled Rim, Manganese, Pennsylvania, 1800s, 7 ½ In. 519
Jar, Lid, Bulbous, Flowers, Tendril Bands, 4 ¾ In. 62
Jar, Oval, Lid, Yellow, Green, Orange Spots, Glaze, New England, 1810s, 8 In. 660
Jug, Bulbous, Glazed, Rolled Lip, Applied Strap Handle, c.1850, 2 ½ In. 197
Jug, Bulbous, Rolled Lip, Arm Shape Handles, Hands, 11 ½ In. 1003
Jug, Embossed Floral Panels, Molded Rim, Impressed Henry Swope Pottery, 1800s, 10 ½ In. . *illus* 580
Jug, Mottled Green Glaze, Molded Rim, Handle, 1800s, 9 In. 561
Jug, Oval, Green Glaze, Orange Spots, Ribbed Handle, Galena, 1850s, 9 In. 600
Jug, Oval, Manganese, Strap Handle, Footed, New England, 1810s, 8 ½ In. 469
Jug, Oval, Mottled Green, Orange Glaze, Flared Neck, Applied Strap Handle, Early 1800s, 6 ½ In. 461
Loaf Pan, Coggled Rim, Yellow Slip Design, 1850s, 2 ½ x 14 ½ In. .... *illus* 719
Loaf Pan, Yellow Slip, Semi Oval, Pennsylvania, 1800s, 14 x 20 ½ In. 2684
Mug, Mottled Orange, Green Glaze, Side Handle, Footed, 1800s, 3 x 4 ½ In. 244
Pie Plate, Green, Brown, Cream Slip, Floral, 1800s, 8 In. .... *illus* 4148
Pitcher, Applied Fish, Salamander Handle, Glazed, 10 ½ In. .... *illus* 118
Pitcher, Batter, Green, Yellow, Orange Glaze, Applied Handle, New England, 1810s, 6 ½ In. 564
Pitcher, Molded, Embossed, Lady Liberty, 13 Stars, 8 In. .... *illus* 440
Plate, Concave, Coggled Rim, Yellow Slip Line, Wave, Green Glaze, Early 1800s, 14 In. 1599
Plate, Green & Yellow Slip, Molded, 1810s, 9 ½ In. 420
Plate, Inscribed Deb, Wavy Yellow Slip, Early 1800s, 10 In. 492
Tub, Molded Rim, Rope Twist Handle, John Bell, Pennsylvania, 1800s, 5 ¾ x 8 ½ In. .... *illus* 366

REGOUT, *see Maastricht category.*

Redware, Pitcher, Molded, Embossed, Lady Liberty, 13 Stars, 8 In.
$440

Conestoga Auction Company

Redware, Tub, Molded Rim, Rope Twist Handle, John Bell, Pennsylvania, 1800s, 5 ¾ x 8 ½ In.
$366

Pook & Pook

Riviera, Red, Syrup, Lid, Handle, Footed
$100

Strawser Auction Group

R

TIP

Modern bleach can damage eighteenth-century and some nineteenth-century dishes. To clean old dishes, try hydrogen peroxide or bicarbonate of soda. Each removes a different type of stain.

Rockingham, Figurine, Dog, Spaniel, Seated, Glazed, Rectangular, Canted Base, 1800s, 10 x 8 x 6 In.
$62

Locati Auctions

Rookwood, Bookends, Ladybug On Yellow Sunflower, Painted, 1937, 4 In.
$908

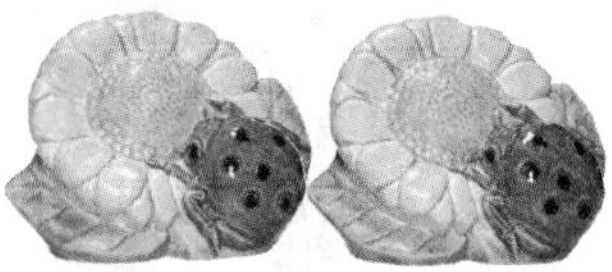

Humler & Nolan

Rookwood, Bowl, Maria Longworth Nichols, Limoges Style, Spider, Dragonfly, Foot, 1882, 16 In.
$1,150

Belhorn Auction Services

First Woman-Run Business

The Rookwood Pottery is said to be the first manufacturing company run by a woman in the United States. It was founded in 1880 by Maria Longwork Nichol Storer.

RICHARD

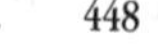

Richard was the mark used on acid-etched cameo glass vases, bowls, night-lights, and lamps made by the Austrian company Loetz after 1918. The pieces were very similar to the French cameo glasswares made by Daum, Galle, and others.

Vase, Purple, Lakeside Scene, Buildings, Bridge, Mountains, Cameo, Signed, 11 ½ In. 448

RIDGWAY

Ridgway pottery has been made in the Staffordshire district in England since 1792 by a series of companies with the name Ridgway. The company began making bone china in 1808. Ridgway became part of Royal Doulton in the 1960s. The transfer-design dinner sets are the most widely known product. Other pieces of Ridgway may be listed under Flow Blue.

Creamer, Windsor, Flowers, Birds, White & Green, 8 Oz. 20
Cup & Saucer, Royal Vistas Ware, Windmill, Sailboats, Gold To Brown, Earthenware 37
Plate, Dickens Characters, Sam Weller Astonishes Job Trotter, Blue & White, 10 In. 117
Platter, Cream Color, Red Flowers, Gray-Green Leaves, 18 x 13 ¾ In. 145
Platter, Warwick Castle, Baronial Castles Series, Purple Transferware, Ironstone, 14 x 11 In. . 95
Teapot, Coaching Days, Amber, Brown Transfer, 5 ¾ In. 79

RIFLES *that are firearms made after 1900 are not listed in this book.*

RIVIERA

Riviera dinnerware was made by the Homer Laughlin Co. of Newell, West Virginia, from 1938 to 1950. The pattern was similar in coloring to Fiesta and Harlequin. The Riviera plates and cup handles were square. For more prices, go to kovels.com.

Green, Butter, Undertray, ¼ Lb. 188
Mauve Blue, Pitcher, Juice, Disc Shape, Wide Spout 71
Red, Dish, Oval, Scalloped Rim, 9 x 7 x 2 In. 65
Red, Syrup, Lid, Handle, Footed .... *illus* 100
Yellow, Bowl, Square, 8 In., Pair 35

ROCKINGHAM

Rockingham, in the United States, is a pottery with a brown glaze that resembles tortoiseshell. It was made from 1840 to 1900 by many American potteries. Mottled brown Rockingham wares were first made in England at the Rockingham factory. Other types of ceramics were also made by the English firm. Related pieces may be listed in the Bennington category.

Figurine, Dog, Spaniel, Seated, Glazed, Rectangular, Canted Base, 1800s, 10 x 8 x 6 In. .*illus* 62
Pitcher, Yellowware, Hunting Scenes, Hound Handle, 8 ¾ In. 78
Plate, Brownware, Molded Border, Square, 8 ⅜ In. 44
Teapot, Lid, Bennington Glaze, Chinese Man, Smoking, Carrying Box, 8 ½ In. 89

ROGERS, *see John Rogers category.*

ROOKWOOD

Rookwood pottery was made in Cincinnati, Ohio, beginning in 1880. All of this art pottery is marked, most with the famous flame mark. The *R* is reversed and placed back to back with the letter *P*. Flames surround the letters. After 1900, a Roman numeral was added to the mark to indicate the year. The company went bankrupt in 1941. It was bought and sold several times after that. For several years various owners tried to revive the pottery, but by 1967 it was out of business. The name and some of the molds were bought by a collector in Michigan in 1982. A few items were made beginning in 1983. In 2004, a group of Cincinnati investors bought the company and 3,700 original molds, the name, and trademark. Pottery was made in Cincinnati again beginning in 2006. Today the company makes architectural tile, art pottery, and special commissions. New items and a few old items with slight redesigns are made. Contemporary pieces are being made to complement the dinnerware line designed by John D. Wareham in 1921. Pieces are marked with the RP mark and a Roman numeral for the four-digit year date. Mold numbers on pieces made since 2006 begin with 10000.

ROOKWOOD
1882

Rookwood
1882–1886

Rookwood
1886

Rookwood
1901

Bookends, Ladybug On Yellow Sunflower, Painted, 1937, 4 In. .... *illus* 908
Bowl, Console, Flower Frog, Ivory Matte, Green Interior, Marked, 1928, 10 ¾ In. 127
Bowl, Maria Longworth Nichols, Limoges Style, Spider, Dragonfly, Foot, 1882, 16 In. .... *illus* 1150
Compote, Elephants, Crystalline Green Matte Glaze, Shirayamadani, 1929, 6 x 11 In. .... *illus* 363
Ewer, Bird In Flight, Textured Field, Hand Painted, Gold Trim, Signed A.M.B., 8 ½ In. 288
Ewer, Black, Dark Red, Glazed, Flowers, Signed, Hattie Wilcox, 1888, 8 x 5 In. 215
Ewer, Brown Glaze, Flowers, Bulbous Body, Handle, Wide Spout, 1900, 5 In. 175
Ewer, Mums, Brown, Standard Glaze, Silver Overlay, Signed, William McDonald, 9 x 7 In. *illus* 2500
Ewer, Silver Overlay, Scrolling Acanthus Leaf, Flowers, c.1880, 6 ¾ In. 1000
Figurine, Dog, Boxer, Standing, Monogram, Oblong Base, 1944, 4 x 10 x 10 In. 263
Flower Holder, Ivory Matte, Leaves, Marked, 1926, 4 ½ x 7 ½ In. .... *illus* 184
Humidor, Lid, Indian Man, Portrait, Standard Glaze, Sadie Markland, 1898, 5 ⅝ In. .... *illus* 3146
Jar, Vellum Glaze, Pink Flower & Vine, Blue, Pink, Green, Signed E.D., 1930, 9 In. .... *illus* 660
Jardiniere, Magnolia, Yellow To Blue, Gold Incised Band, A. Valentien, 1886, 14 In. .... *illus* 5203
Jug, Claret, Cherry Blossom Prunus, Gold, Limoges Style, Laura Anne Fry, c.1883, 11 x 6 In. 424
Lamp Base, Flared Body, 3 Leaf Feet, Green To Reddish Brown Glaze, 1912, 22 ½ x 8 ½ In. 720
Lamp Base, Fuchsia, Green, Glaze, Molded Rim, 11 ½ In. 106
Lamp Base, Wheat, Glaze, Round Base, Electric, Margaret H. McDonald, 1892, 11 x 24 ½ In. . 489
Lamp, Banquet, Poppy, Gold, Brown & Green, Matthew A. Daly, 1894, 22 ½ x 9 ¾ In. 2712
Paperweight, Chick, Yellow Matte Glaze, Louise Abel, 1930, 3 ¾ In. .... *illus* 145
Paperweight, Frog, Mottled Green Matte Glaze, 1911, 3 In. .... *illus* 545
Paperweight, Monkey, Brown Over Tan Matte Glaze, Shirayamadani, 1930, 4 In. .... *illus* 145
Paperweight, Rook, Brown Matte Glaze, Speckled Blue, 1922, 2 ¾ In. .... *illus* 272
Paperweight, Seal, Nubian Black Glaze, Shirayamadani, 1928, 3 In. .... *illus* 424
Paperweight, Squirrel, Tan & Green Matte Glaze, S. Toohey, 1928, 4 ¼ In. .... *illus* 218
Pitcher, Ewer Shape, Leaf, Glaze, Handle, Anna M. Valentien, 1896, 7 ½ In. 288
Pitcher, Gray Glaze, Metal Mounted, Swing Handle, c.1886, 11 x 8 In. 185
Pitcher, Trefoil Rim, Painted, Branch, Grapes, Loop Handle, Lenore Asbury, 1900, 6 In. 185
Plaque, Enamel, Trees, Path, Grasses, Purple, Louise Abel, Frame, 1927, 8 x 4 In. 1540
Plaque, Landscape, Trees, Vellum Glaze, Signed, Fred Rothenbusch, Frame, 13 ½ x 19 In. 3125
Plaque, Sailboats, Fishermen, Vellum Glaze, E.T. Hurley, Logo, 1943, 9 ⅝ x 12 In. .... *illus* 5808
Plaque, Scenic, River, Tree, Vellum Glaze, Signed, Lorinda Epply, Frame, 13 x 8 ½ In. ... *illus* 1625
Plaque, Sunrise, Sunset, Vellum Pastels, Leonore Asbury, 1910s, 8 ⅜ x 4 ½ x 12 In. .... *illus* 1989
Sconce, Roses, Blue Glaze, 8 ½ x 4 ½ In. 325
Sign, Rookwood, Cincinnati, Scrollwork, Engraved, 13 ½ x 2 ½ x 4 ½ In. .... *illus* 325
Vase, 2 Handles, Flower, Drip Glaze, William E. Hentschel, Ohio, 3 ½ x 5 ½ In. 230
Vase, Blossoms, Leaves, Heavy Slip, Matte Finish, Albert Valentien, 1886, 13 ⅜ In. .... *illus* 2420
Vase, Blue Ground, Flowers, Bulbous, Vellum, Fred Rothenbusch, 1925, 5 ½ In. 189
Vase, Blue Ground, White Tones, Flowers, Bulbous, Fluted Rim, 1904, 3 ¾ x 3 ¾ In. 175
Vase, Blue, Multicolor Top, Shoulder, W.E. Hentschel, 1915, 5 ⅝ In. 403
Vase, Branches Of Berries, Dark Over Light Blue, Matte Glaze, Marked, 1934, 4 ⅝ In. .... *illus* 363

Rookwood, Compote, Elephants, Crystalline Green Matte Glaze, Shirayamadani, 1929, 6 x 11 In.
$363

Humler & Nolan

Rookwood, Ewer, Mums, Brown, Standard Glaze, Silver Overlay, Signed, William McDonald, 9 x 7 In.
$2,500

Treadway

TIP

Silver and gold trim will wash off dishes in time. Do not unload from the dishwasher any dishes with metallic trim until they have completely cooled.

Rookwood, Flower Holder, Ivory Matte, Leaves, Marked, 1926, 4 ½ x 7 ½ In.
$184

Belhorn Auction Services

R

Rookwood, Humidor, Lid, Indian Man, Portrait, Standard Glaze, Sadie Markland, 1898, 5 ⅝ In.
$3,146

Humler & Nolan

Rookwood, Jar, Vellum Glaze, Pink Flower & Vine, Blue, Pink, Green, Signed E.D., 1930, 9 In.
$660

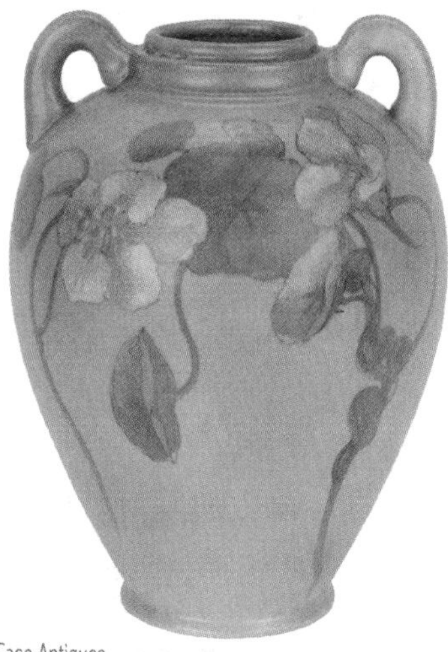

Case Antiques

Rookwood, Jardiniere, Magnolia, Yellow To Blue, Gold Incised Band, A. Valentien, 1886, 14 In.
$5,203

Humler & Nolan

Rookwood, Paperweight, Chick, Yellow Matte Glaze, Louise Abel, 1930, 3 ¾ In.
$145

Humler & Nolan

Rookwood, Paperweight, Frog, Mottled Green Matte Glaze, 1911, 3 In.
$545

Humler & Nolan

Rookwood, Paperweight, Monkey, Brown Over Tan Matte Glaze, Shirayamadani, 1930, 4 In.
$145

Humler & Nolan

Rookwood, Paperweight, Rook, Brown Matte Glaze, Speckled Blue, 1922, 2 ¾ In.
$272

Humler & Nolan

TIP
Take off your rings and bracelets before you start to wash figurines or dishes.

Rookwood, Paperweight, Seal, Nubian Black Glaze, Shirayamadani, 1928, 3 In.
$424

Humler & Nolan

Rookwood, Paperweight, Squirrel, Tan & Green Matte Glaze, S. Toohey, 1928, 4 ¼ In.
$218

Humler & Nolan

R

Rookwood, Plaque, Sailboats, Fishermen, Vellum Glaze, E.T. Hurley, Logo, 1943, 9 ⅝ x 12 In.
$5,808

Humler & Nolan

Rookwood, Plaque, Scenic, River, Tree, Vellum Glazed, Signed, Lorinda Epply, Frame, 13 x 8 ½ In.
$1,625

Treadway

Rookwood, Plaque, Sunrise, Sunset, Vellum Pastels, Leonore Asbury, 1910s, 8 ⅜ x 4 ½ x 12 In.
$1,989

Jeffrey S. Evans & Associates

Rookwood, Sign, Rookwood, Cincinnati, Scrollwork, Engraved, 13 ½ x 2 ½ x 4 ½ In.
$325

Copake Auctions

Rookwood, Vase, Blossoms, Leaves, Heavy Slip, Matte Finish, Albert Valentien, 1886, 13 ⅜ In.
$2,420

Humler & Nolan

Rookwood, Vase, Branches Of Berries, Dark Over Light Blue, Matte Glaze, Marked, 1934, 4 ⅝ In.
$363

Humler & Nolan

Rookwood, Vase, Flowering Vine, Pale Rose Ground, Vellum, Signed, 1929, 9 In.
$308

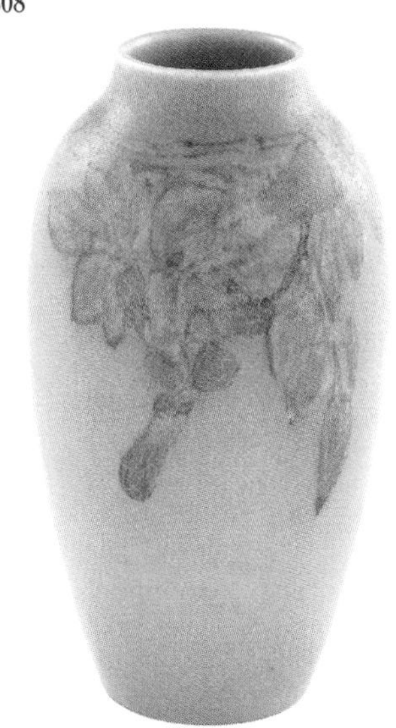

Charlton Hall Auctions

Rookwood, Vase, Iris Glaze, Clovers, Light Brown Ground, Olga Geneva Reed, 1903, 7 x 3 In.
$920

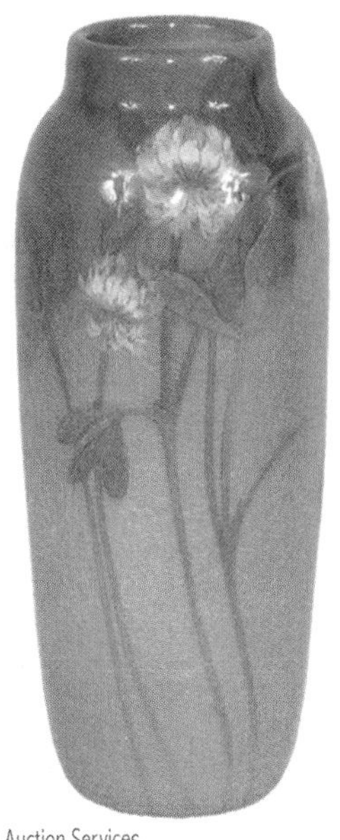

Belhorn Auction Services

R

Rookwood, Vase, Iris Glaze, Flowers, Red & Yellow, Green Stems & Leaves, 1903, 7 In.
$367

Soulis Auctions

Rookwood, Vase, Pale Plum Glaze, Mottled Surface, Trumpet Vines, Charles Todd, 12 x 5 ½ In.
$360

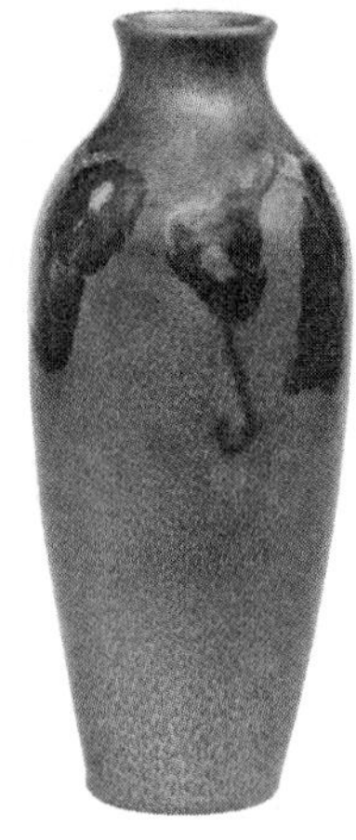

Witherell's

Rookwood, Vase, Scenic, Trees, Peach Colored Sky, Vellum, Ed Diers, 1920, 6 In.
$388

Charleston Estate Auctions

Rookwood, Vase, Sparrow, Branch, Cloud Shape Reserves, Rolled Rim, Footed, 1885, 5 In.
$236

Clars Auction Gallery

Rookwood, Vase, Wax Matte Glaze, Lily Pads, Signed, Carrie Steinle, 1931, 13 x 5 In.
$1,130

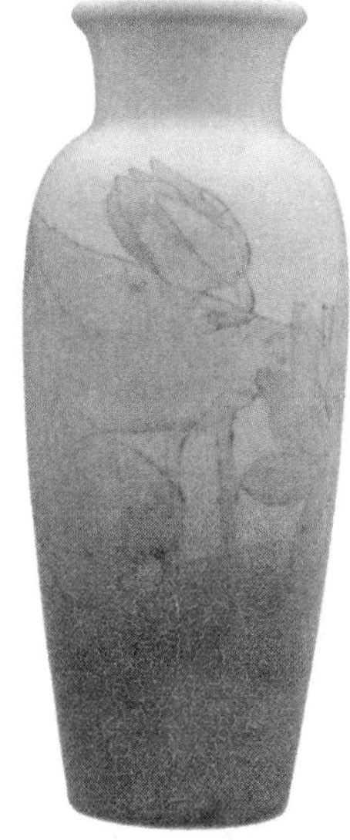

Soulis Auctions

Rookwood, Wall Pocket, Brown, Leaves, Marked 1389, XXI, Logo, 7 ¾ In.
$138

Belhorn Auction Services

Vase, Brown, Yellow Flowers, Signed, Elizabeth N. Lincoln, c.1900, 9 In. 366
Vase, Flowering Vine, Pale Rose Ground, Vellum, Signed, 1929, 9 In. .... *illus* 308
Vase, Flowers Along Shoulder, Vellum, Sara Sax, 1910, 7 ½ In. 750
Vase, Flowers, Orange To Black, Glazed, 7 In. 173
Vase, Fluted Rim, Brown, Green, Marked XII, Logo, 1909, 6 ¾ In. 173
Vase, Iris Glaze, Clovers, Light Brown Ground, Olga Geneva Reed, 1903, 7 x 3 In. .... *illus* 920
Vase, Iris Glaze, Flowers, Red & Yellow, Green Stems & Leaves, 1903, 7 In. .... *illus* 367
Vase, Molded Rim, Light Blue Matte, Marked, 1927, 6 ⅜ In. 127
Vase, Oval, Japonesque Bird, Flowers, Arthur Conant, 1921, 8 In. 677
Vase, Pale Plum Glaze, Mottled Surface, Trumpet Vines, Charles Todd, 12 x 5 ½ In. .... *illus* 360
Vase, Scenic, Trees, Peach Colored Sky, Vellum, Ed Diers, 1920, 6 In. .... *illus* 388
Vase, Slip, Multicolor, Pinched Base, Footed, Signed, Elizabeth Barrett, 1928, 7 ¾ In. 502
Vase, Sparrow, Branch, Cloud Shape Reserves, Rolled Rim, Footed, 1885, 5 In. .... *illus* 236
Vase, Squat, Yellow Vellum, Brown Glaze, Signed, Lenore Asbury, 6 x 5 In. 469
Vase, Wax Matte Glaze, Lily Pads, Signed, Carrie Steinle, 1931, 13 x 5 In. .... *illus* 1130
Vase, Wax Matte, Shaped Body, Decorated Neck, Blue, Green, Charles Todd, 1915, 8 x 4 In. 718
Vase, Yellow Ground, White Ducks, Molded Rim, Footed, 1937, 5 In., Pair 148
Wall Pocket, Brown, Leaves, Marked 1389, XXI, Logo, 7 ¾ In. .... *illus* 138
Water Jug, Bats, Branches, Yellow, Fired-On Gold, Maria Nichols, Impressed, 1882, 9 In. *illus* 2299

RORSTRAND

Rorstrand was established near Stockholm, Sweden, in 1726. By the nineteenth century Rorstrand was making English-style earthenware, bone china, porcelain, ironstone china, and majolica. The three-crown mark has been used since 1884. Rorstrand became part of the Hackman Group in 1991. Hackman was bought by Iittala Group in 2004. Fiskars Corporation bought Iittala in 2007 and Rorstrand is now a brand owned by Fiskars.

Bowl, Mottled Green Glaze, Textured Herringbone Foot, Harry Stalhane, 4 x 5 ½ In. 125
Vase, Apple Green Glaze, Bulbous, Tapered Neck, 1960s, 5 In. 213
Vase, Cream Glaze, Elongated Bottle Form, Flared Rim, Gunnar Nylund, 14 In. 688
Vase, Dragonfly, Leaves, Reticulated, White Ground, Oval, K. Lindstrom, c.1920, 8 In. 2250
Vase, Reclining Nudes, Blue Bands, Pottery, Ball Shape, Flared Rim, c.1900, 8 x 9 In. 438
Vase, Scenic, Trees, Lakes, Mountains, Pink Clouds, Oval, Signed NTE, 1930s, 12 x 5 In. 750
Vase, White, Bulbous, Pink & Green Petal Rim, M. Anderberg, c.1900, 5 x 6 In. 375

ROSALINE, *see Steuben category.*

ROSE BOWL

Rose bowls were popular during the 1880s. Rose petals were kept in the open bowl to add fragrance to a room, a popular idea in a time of limited personal hygiene. The glass bowls were made with crimped tops, which kept the petals inside. Many types of Victorian art glass were made into rose bowls.

Burmese Glass, Pale Pink, Hand Painted Flowers, Blue, Green, 3 ¾ x 4 ½ In. 28
Cut Glass, Pinwheel, 7 x 6 In. 25
Hobstar, Prism & Fan, Notched Rim, Cut Base, 8 ½ x 10 In. 225
Opalescent Glass, Spanish Lace, Canary Yellow, Northwood, 4 In. 48
Roses, Pale Green Ground, Gold Trim, Signed Betty Foster 1979, 5 ¾ x 3 ½ In. 24

ROSE CANTON

Rose Canton china is similar to Rose Mandarin and Rose Medallion, except that no people are pictured in the decoration. It was made in China during the nineteenth and twentieth centuries in greens, pinks, and other colors.

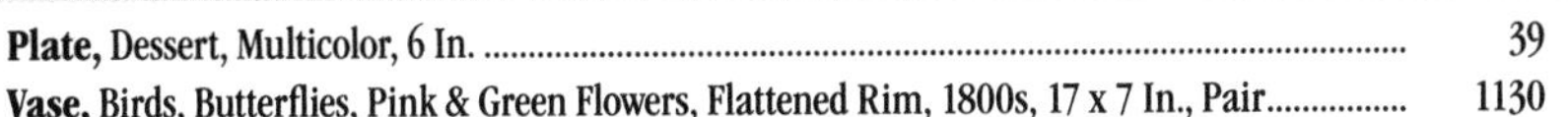

Plate, Dessert, Multicolor, 6 In. 39
Vase, Birds, Butterflies, Pink & Green Flowers, Flattened Rim, 1800s, 17 x 7 In., Pair 1130

Rookwood, Water Jug, Bats, Branches, Yellow, Fired-On Gold, Maria Nichols, Impressed, 1882, 9 In.
$2,299

Humler & Nolan

TIP

Don't stack cups. If you must do it, separate the two cups with a piece of paper or felt.

Rose Mandarin, Dish, Curry, Figures, Flower Border, Shaped Rim, Footed, c.1830, 14 In.
$330

Eldred's

Rose Mandarin, Dish, Shrimp, Figures, Flower & Bird Border, Salmon & Gilt Handle, c.1830, 10 In.
$312

Eldred's

Rose Medallion, Charger, Alternating Panels, Village & Family Scenes, 1800s, 15 In.
$219

Richard D. Hatch & Associates

Rose Medallion, Plate, Center Medallion, 6 Panels, Butterflies, Flowers, 1850s, 13 In.
$144

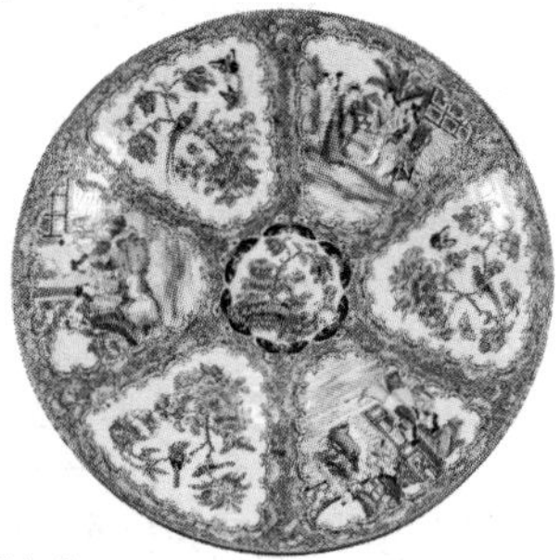

Eldred's

Dishwasher Damage
Be careful about putting antique china or glass in the dishwasher. Glass will sometimes crack from the heat. Porcelains with gold overglaze decoration often lose the gold. Damaged or crazed glaze will sometimes pop off the plates in large pieces.

Rose Medallion, Platter, Figures, Flowers, Birds, White Ground, Gilt, Oval, 1800s, 15 x 12 In.
$111

Locati Auctions

ROSE MANDARIN

Rose Mandarin china is similar to Rose Canton and Rose Medallion. If the design pictures people in scenes, often in a garden, and is framed with a border of flowers, birds, insects, fruit, or fish, it is Rose Mandarin.

Bowl, Women At Leisure, Square, Cut Corners, Shaped Rim, c.1830, 9 ½ In. 360
Cuspidor, Court Scene, Figures In Garden, White Ground, Stamp, 8 x 4 In. 367
Dish, Curry, Figures, Flower Border, Shaped Rim, Footed, c.1830, 14 In. *illus* 330
Dish, Shrimp, Figures, Flower & Bird Border, Salmon & Gilt Handle, c.1830, 10 In. *illus* 312
Plate, Figures Outside, Butterfly & Flower Border, Gold Trim, c.1830, 10 In. 120
Platter, Center Court Scene, Figures, Flower Border, Gilt, 6-Sided, c.1890, 14 In. 163
Tureen, Sauce, Lid, Figures, Gilt Entwined Handles Flower Finial, c.1830, 9 In. 270

ROSE MEDALLION

Rose Medallion china was made in China during the nineteenth and twentieth centuries. It is a distinctive design with four or more panels of decoration around a central medallion that includes a bird or a peony. The panels show combinations of birds, people, flowers, fish, fruit, or insects. The panels have border designs of tree peonies and leaves. Pieces are colored in greens, pinks, and other colors. It is similar to Rose Canton and Rose Mandarin.

Bowl, Enameled Figures, Flowers, Birds, Butterfly, Wood Stand, c.1880, 4 x 10 In. 144
Bowl, Figures Talking, Flowers, Shaped Rim, 1800s, 4 ½ x 10 In. 207
Bowl, Figures, Flowers, Birds, White Ground, Wood Base, c.1900, 5 ½ x 13 In. 565
Bowl, Fish, Enameled, Bird, Flowers, Fruit, Marked, 14 ½ x 19 In. 75
Charger, Alternating Panels, Village & Family Scenes, 1800s, 15 In. *illus* 219
Charger, Thousand Butterflies, Flowers, Leaves, 13 In. 154
Dish, Oval, Shaped Edge, Bird, Flowers, Late 1800s, 7 In. 72
Flask, Moon Form, European Figures, Symbols, Purple Bamboo Handles, c.1900, 6 In. 468
Jardiniere, Ducks, Flowers, Bats, Koi Inside, White Ground, 19 x 21 In. 115
Jug, Lid, Figures, Flowers, Butterflies, Gilt Foo Dog Finial, Twist Handle, 1800s, 10 In. 585
Plate, Center Medallion, 6 Panels, Butterflies, Flowers, 1850s, 13 In. *illus* 144
Plate, Figures, Birds, Butterfly, Flowers, Gold Trim, 1800s, 9 ½ In., Pair 313
Plate, Panels Of Figures & Flowers, Reticulated, Looping Border, Late 1800s, 9 In. 104
Platter, 5 Panels, Figural Scenes, Landscapes, Gilt, Oval, c.1880, 12 ½ In. 168
Platter, Figures, Flowers, Birds, White Ground, Gilt, Oval, 1800s, 15 x 12 In. *illus* 111
Punch Bowl, Court Scenes, Flowers, Flower Borders, c.1840, 6 x 14 In. 584
Punch Bowl, Painted Panels, Flowers, Courtyard Scenes, White Ground, Gilt, 15 In. 732
Punch Bowl, Panels, Figures, Courtyard, Birds, Flowers, 10 ¼ In. 400
Punch Bowl, Panels, Villagers, Butterflies, Flowers, 1800s, 5 ½ x 13 In. 403
Punch Bowl, Scenes Of Figures, Flower & Butterfly Borders, Gilt, 7 x 14 In. *illus* 787
Teapot, Lid, Wrapped Metal Handle, Spout, 6 x 7 In. 155
Vase, Alternating Panels, Court Scenes, Figures, Flowers, Birds, 1800s, 12 x 8 In. 354
Vase, Alternating Panels, Figures, Birds, Flowers, Gilt, 1800s, 25 In. 1003
Vase, Gu Form, Figures, Flowers & Bird Panels, Flared Rim, Late 1800s, 16 In. 270
Vase, Panels, Bird & Figures In Garden, White Ground, Swollen, 15 ½ In. 488
Vase, Warriors, Shaped Handle, 24 ½ In. 961

ROSE O'NEILL, *see Kewpie category.*

ROSE TAPESTRY

Rose Tapestry porcelain was made by the Royal Bayreuth factory of Tettau, Germany, during the late nineteenth century. The surface of the porcelain was pressed against a coarse fabric while it was still damp, and the impressions remained on the finished porcelain. It looks and feels like a textured cloth. Very skillful reproductions are being made that even include a variation of the Royal Bayreuth mark, so be careful when buying.

Nut Set, Master Bowl, 6 In., Footed, 6 Individual Bowls, 3 In. 120

ROSENTHAL

Rosenthal porcelain was made at the factory established in Selb, Bavaria, in 1891. The factory is still making fine-quality tablewares and figurines. A series of Christmas plates was made from 1910. Other limited edition plates have been made since 1971. Rosenthal became part of the Arcturus Group in 2009.

Rosenthal China
1891–1904

Rosenthal China
1928

Rosenthal China
1948

Figurine, Colt, Standing, Bisque, Oval Base, Alb., Hinrich Hussmann, 10 ½ In. ... *illus* 240
Figurine, Draped Woman On Horse, Multicolor, Gustav Oppel, Germany, c.1930, 15 In. .. *illus* 1046
Figurine, Nude, Female Athlete, Standing, Bisque, Max Hermann Fritz, 1900s, 22 x 8 In. ... 354
Fish Tray, Fish, Clams, Pond, Acanthus Leaves, Coral, Gold Trim, 14 x 9 In. ... 220

ROSEVILLE

Roseville Pottery Company was organized in Roseville, Ohio, in 1890. Another plant was opened in Zanesville, Ohio, in 1898. Many types of pottery were made until 1954. Early wares include Sgraffito, Olympic, and Rozane. Later lines were often made with molded decorations, especially flowers and fruit. Most pieces are marked *Roseville.* Many reproductions made in China have been offered for sale since the 1980s.

Roseville Pottery Company
1914–1930

Roseville Pottery Company
1935–1954

Roseville
U.S.A.

Roseville Pottery Company
1939–1953

Aztec, Vase, Obelisk Shape, Gray Glaze, Squeezebag, 1905, 10 ½ x 3 In. ... 311
Baneda, Jardiniere, Pink, Band Of Orange Blossoms, Handles, 4 In. ... *illus* 121
Baneda, Urn, Yellow Flowers, Orange Fruit, Green Leaves, 2 Handles, Footed, 9 x 8 In. ... 450
Bittersweet, Candlestick, Gray, Brown, Purple, 1940s, 3 x 3 In., Pair ... 153
Blackberry, Bowl, Green Interior, 2 Handles, Red Crayon Mark, Low, 7 ⅞ x 3 In. ... *illus* 242
Blackberry, Vase, Green Ground, 2 Handles, Leaves, Marked, 6 In. ... 242
Blackberry, Vase, Green, Leaves, 2 Handles, 6 In. ... 181
Carnelian I, Ewer, Cream Ground, Green, Round Base, Wide Spout, Handle, 10 ⅜ x 8 ½ In. .. 196
Carnelian II, Vase, Pink, Green, Bulbous, Footed, Marked 454 In Red Crayon, 16 In. ... 1955
Cherry Blossom, Vase, Brown, Foil Label, Marked 624 In Red Crayon, 8 In. ... *illus* 265
Clematis, Vase, Wall Pocket, Blue, 6 x 3 x 9 In. ... 115
Corinthian, Vase, Green, Yellow, Ribbed, Footed, 8 x 5 In. ... 109
Della Robbia, Teapot, Rooster & Owl, Frederick Hurten Rhead, 1906-07, 6 x 7 ½ In. ... *illus* 1152
Della Robbia, Vase, Courtier, Frederick Hurten Rhead, 1906-07, 18 In. ... *illus* 15000
Della Robbia, Vase, Storks, 3 Handles, Glazed, Frederick Rhead, 1906-07, 13 x 8 In. ... *illus* 6875
Donatello, Jardiniere, Cherubs, Pedestal, Salesman's Sample, 17 ½ x 7 ½ In. ... 182
Egypto, Vase, Bullet, Blossoms, Leaves, Matte Green Glaze, Splayed Legs, 8 ¾ x 3 ½ In. ... 155
Falline, Vase, Molded Peapods, Horizontal Ribbing, Handles, 9 x 8 In. ... 1410
Ferella, Basket, Blue Glaze, Oval, Reticulated Rim, Openwork Base, 5 ¾ x 12 ¾ x 7 ½ In. *illus* 254
Ferella, Bowl, Console, Brown Ground, Flower Frog, 9 ½ In. ... *illus* 154
Ferella, Candlestick, Brown Ground, Flowers, Dome Base, 4 ½ In., Pair ... 142
Foxglove, Vase, Pink, 2 Handles, 18 ½ In. ... *illus* 283
Foxglove, Vase, White Flowers, Soft Forest Green To Pink, 2 Handles, c.1942, 16 In. ... *illus* 240

Rose Medallion, Punch Bowl, Scenes Of Figures, Flower & Butterfly Borders, Gilt, 7 x 14 In.
$787

Fontaine's Auction Gallery

TIP

Try not to immerse figurines in water. Many have small holes in the bottom that will let water get inside. It is difficult to remove the water and it may drip out and stain a wooden table or the figurine.

Rosenthal, Figurine, Colt, Standing, Bisque, Oval Base, Alb., Hinrich Hussmann, 10 ½ In.
$240

Bunte Auction Services

Rosenthal, Figurine, Draped Woman On Horse, Multicolor, Gustav Oppel, Germany, c.1930, 15 In.
$1,046

Skinner, Inc.

Roseville, Baneda, Jardiniere, Pink, Band Of Orange Blossoms, Handles, 4 In.
$121

Humler & Nolan

Roseville, Blackberry, Bowl, Green Interior, 2 Handles, Red Crayon Mark, Low, 7 ⅞ x 3 In.
$242

Belhorn Auction Services

Roseville, Cherry Blossom, Vase, Brown, Foil Label, Marked 624 In Red Crayon, 8 In.
$265

Belhorn Auction Services

Roseville, Della Robbia, Teapot, Rooster & Owl, Frederick Hurten Rhead, 1906-07, 6 x 7 ½ In.
$1,152

Rago Arts and Auction Center

Roseville, Della Robbia, Vase, Courtier, Frederick Hurten Rhead, 1906-07, 18 In.
$15,000

Rago Arts and Auction Center

Roseville, Della Robbia, Vase, Storks, 3 Handles, Glazed, Frederick Rhead, 1906-07, 13 x 8 In.
$6,875

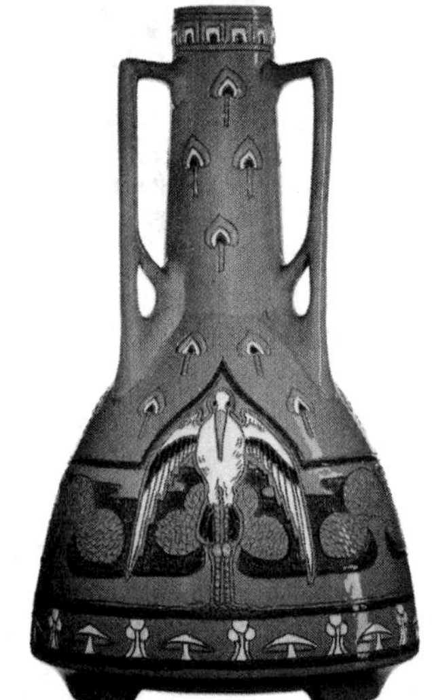

Rago Arts and Auction Center

Roseville, Ferella, Basket, Blue Glaze, Oval, Reticulated Rim, Openwork Base, 5 ¾ x 12 ¾ x 7 ½ In.
$254

Soulis Auctions

Roseville, Ferella, Bowl, Console, Brown Ground, Flower Frog, 9 ½ In.
$154

Strawser Auction Group

Roseville, Foxglove, Vase, Pink, 2 Handles, 18 ½ In.
$283

Soulis Auctions

Roseville, Foxglove, Vase, White Flowers, Soft Forest Green To Pink, 2 Handles, c.1942, 16 In.
$240

Morphy Auctions

R

Roseville, Fuschia, Ewer, Blue Ground, Handle, No. 902, 10 In.
$120

Woody Auctions

Roseville, Fuchsia, Jardiniere, Burnt Orange, Green, Red, Brown Matte, Round Base, 1930s, 32 In.
$300

Garth's Auctioneers & Appraisers

Roseville, Fuchsia, Jardiniere, Pedestal, Blue Ground, Leaves, 8 In.
$885

Strawser Auction Group

Roseville, Futura, Jardiniere, Brown, Blue, Green, Wide Body, 2 Handles, No. 616-6, 6 x 9 In.
$299

Belhorn Auction Services

Roseville, Futura, Vase, Tank, 2-Tier Base, Blue To Ivory Matte Glaze, Geometric, c.1934, 9 ½ In.
$10,455

Skinner, Inc.

Roseville, Futura, Wall Pocket, Brown Ground, Green, Yellow & Blue, 8 In.
$96

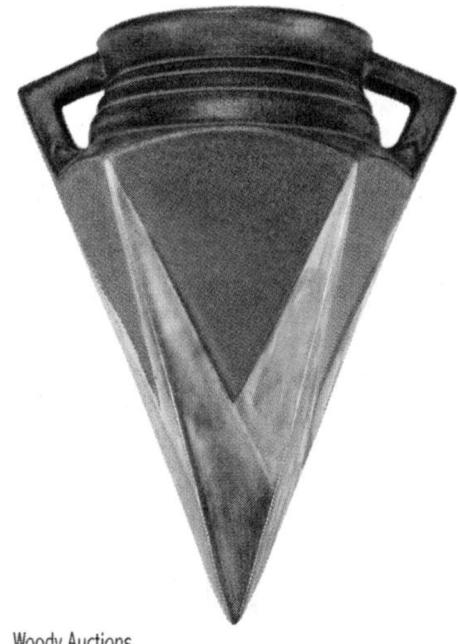

Woody Auctions

Roseville, Monticello, Vase, Southwestern Design, 2 Handles, Red Crayon On Base, 8 ½ In.
$123

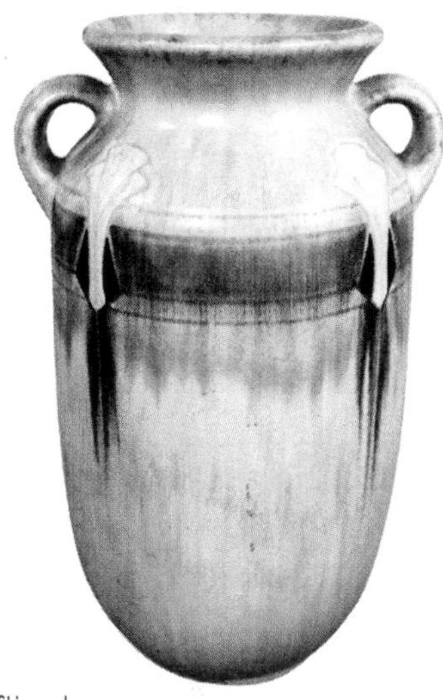

Skinner, Inc.

Roseville, Peony, Basket, Green, Floral, Footed, Handle, Marked, 11 ⅜ x 13 ⅜ In.
$127

Belhorn Auction Services

Roseville, Primrose, Jardiniere, Pedestal, White Flowers, Stems, Heart Shape Leaves, c.1936, 23 ½ In.
$129

Jeffrey S. Evans & Associates

Roseville, Snowberry, Vase, Pink, Round Base, 2 Small Handles, 12 In.
$69

Apple Tree Auction Center

Roseville, Sunflower, Jardiniere, Blue Ground, Oval, Swirling Stems, Pedestal Base, 27 ½ x 12 In.
$2,421

Clars Auction Gallery

Freesia, Bowl, Green, Flowers, 2 Handles, c.1905, 10 ½ x 3 In. 100
Fuschia, Ewer, Blue Ground, Handle, No. 902, 10 In. .... *illus* 120
Fuchsia, Jardiniere, Burnt Orange, Green, Red, Brown Matte, Round Base, 1930s, 32 In. *illus* 300
Fuchsia, Jardiniere, Pedestal, Blue Ground, Leaves, 8 In. .... *illus* 885
Fuchsia, Vase, Gourd, Blue Ground, 2 Handles, Footed, 6 In., Pair 142
Fujiyama, Vase, Gold, Blue, Enamel, 1906, 4 x 6 ½ In. 1980
Futura, Jardiniere, Brown, Blue, Green, Wide Body, 2 Handles, No. 616-6, 6 x 9 In. .... *illus* 299
Futura, Sailboat Bowl, Flower Frog, Blue, Beige, 12 ⅜ In. 196
Futura, Vase, Tank, 2-Tier Base, Blue To Ivory Matte Glaze, Geometric, c.1934, 9 ½ In. ..*illus* 10455
Futura, Wall Pocket, Brown Ground, Green, Yellow & Blue, 8 In. .... *illus* 96
Gardenia, Ewer, Green, Handle, Footed, 5 In. 135
Lamp, 2-Light, White, Green Ground, Electric, 10 ½ In. 219
Monticello, Vase, Southwestern Design, 2 Handles, Red Crayon On Base, 8 ½ In. .... *illus* 123
Panel, Vase, Fan, Nude, Green, Footed, 6 x 4 ½ In. 164
Peony, Basket, Green, Floral, Footed, Handle, Marked, 11 ⅜ x 13 ⅜ In. .... *illus* 127
Pine Cone, Bowl, Blue, Green Needles, Branch Shape Handles, 6 In. 258
Primrose, Jardiniere, Pedestal, White Flowers, Stems, Heart Shape Leaves, c.1936, 23 ½ In. *illus* 129
Rozane, Vase, Horse Portrait, Standard Glaze, Flared Rim, 14 In. 480
Snowberry, Vase, Pink, Round Base, 2 Small Handles, 12 In. .... *illus* 69
Sunflower, Jardiniere, Blue Ground, Oval, Swirling Stems, Pedestal Base, 27 ½ x 12 In. *illus* 2421
Sunflower, Vase, Handles, 6 In. .... *illus* 302
Tangerine Freesia, Cookie Jar, Orange, 2 Handles, 9 x 8 ½ In. 121
Wall Pocket, Brown Panel, Nude Woman, Black Ground, 7 In. .... *illus* 213
Water Lily, Ewer, Blue, Flowers, Footed, Handle, Marked, 15 ⅜ x 8 In. 173
Zephyr Lily, Ewer, Green, Bulbous Body, Wide Spout, Handle, Round Base, No. 24-15, 16 In. ... 115
Zephyr Lily, Vase, Brown, Dark Green, Fan Shape, 2 Handles, 1940s, 8 x 8 In. 154

ROWLAND & MARSELLUS

Rowland & Marsellus Company is part of a mark that appears on historical Staffordshire dating from the late nineteenth and early twentieth centuries. *Rowland & Marsellus* is the mark used by an American importing company in New York City. The company worked from 1893 to about 1937. Some of the pieces may have been made by the British Anchor Pottery Co. of Longton, England, for export to a New York firm. Many American views were made. Of special interest to collectors are the plates with rolled edges, usually blue and white.

Plate, Alaska-Yukon-Pacific Exposition, Seattle, 1909, 10 In. 50
Plate, Topeka Kansas, Vignettes Of Buildings, 10 In. 117
Pitcher, Independence Hall, Portraits, Signers, Multicolor, 7 In. 153

ROY ROGERS

Roy Rogers was born in 1911 in Cincinnati, Ohio. His birth name was Leonard Slye. In the 1930s, he made a living as a singer; in 1935, his group started work at a Los Angeles radio station. He appeared in his first movie in 1937. He began using the name Roy Rogers in 1938. From 1952 to 1957, he made 101 television shows. The other stars in the show were his wife, Dale Evans, his horse, Trigger, and his dog, Bullet. Rogers died in 1998. Roy Rogers memorabilia, including items from the Roy Rogers restaurants, are collected.

Belt Buckle, Brass Plated, 1960s, 2 In. 23
Book, Happy Trails, Dale Evans, Signed, 1979 100
Clock, Alarm, Trigger, Aqua Ground, 1950s, 4 ½ In. 71
Mug, Figural, Molded Plastic, 4 x 4 ¼ In. 20
Postcard, Black & White Photo, Roy Rogers, Dale Evans, 1952 22
Sheet Music, Dale Evans, Tim Spencer, 1944, 12 x 9 In. 20
Sheet Music, Dust, Johnny Marvin, 1938 7
Thermos, Metal, Plastic Cup, 1950s, 8 ⅜ In. 57
Toy, Fix It Stagecoach, Original Box, Ideal 50

Toy, Jeep, Nellybelle, Marx, 1950s ... 531
Toy, Roy Rogers & Trigger, Colored Plastic, Original Box, 1957, 10 x 9 In. ... 295

ROYAL BAYREUTH

Royal Bayreuth is the name of a factory that was founded in Tettau, Bavaria, in 1794. The factory closed in 2019. The marks have changed through the years. A stylized crest, the name Royal Bayreuth, and the word *Bavaria* appear in slightly different forms from 1870 to about 1919. Later dishes may include the words *U.S. Zone* (1945–1949), the year of the issue, or the word *Germany* instead of *Bavaria*. Related pieces may be found listed in the Rose Tapestry, Snow Babies, and Sunbonnet Babies categories.

Royal Bayreuth
1887–1902

Royal Bayreuth
c.1900+

Royal Bayreuth
1968+

Biscuit Jar, 2 Handles, Child & Frog Scene, Gold Trim, c.1900, 5 ½ x 7 ½ In. ... 125
Bowl, Peacock, Shell, Leaf Mold, Multicolor Central Image, 1910s, 10 ⅝ In. ... *illus* 439
Pitcher, Molded Image, Woman, Flowing Dress, White, Orange, Yellow, 1910s, 6 ½ In. ... 556
Sugar, Lid, Devil Finial, Cards, Hearts, Red, White, c.1900, 4 x 4 ½ In. ... *illus* 150
Tray, Dresser, Raised Art Nouveau Woman, Drapery, Shaded Pink, Yellow, Marked, c.1900, 10 x 7 In. 200
Vase, Polar Bears, Glazed, Marked, c.1900, 8 ½ x 5 In. ... *illus* 650
Wall Pocket, Farm Scene, Woman & Chicken, Marked, 8 ¾ In. ... *illus* 120

ROYAL BONN

Royal Bonn is the nineteenth- and twentieth-century trade name used by Franz Anton Mehlem, who had a pottery in Bonn, Germany, from 1836 to 1931. Porcelain and earthenware were made. Royal Bonn also made cases for Ansonia clocks. The factory was purchased by Villeroy & Boch in 1921 and closed in 1931. Many marks were used, most including the name *Bonn*, the initials *FAM*, and a crown.

Vase, Basket Shape, 2 Handles, Flowers, Gilt Rim, Paw Feet, Marked, 16 x 7 x 9 In. ... 403
Vase, Hand Painted, Roses, Floral, Gilt, Teal Ground, Bolted, c.1900, 39 In. ... *illus* 468

ROYAL COPENHAGEN

Royal Copenhagen porcelain and pottery have been made in Denmark since 1775. The Christmas plate series started in 1908. The figurines with pale blue and gray glazes have remained popular in this century and are still being made. Many other old and new style porcelains are made today. In 2001 Royal Copenhagen became part of the Royal Scandinavia Group owned by the Danish company Axcel. Axcel sold Royal Copenhagen to the Finnish company Fiskars in December 2012.

Royal Copenhagen
1892

Royal Copenhagen
1894–1900

Royal Copenhagen
1935–present

Basket, Fruit, Multicolor Flowers, Vine Handles, c.1900, 3 x 7 In. ... 1625
Bowl, Flora Danica, White Body, Clover Leaves, Blossoms, Gilded Rim, 8 x 2 In. ... 330
Dish, Flora Danica, Oval, Lavender, Green, Water Mint Flower, 1900s, 8 ¾ x 6 ¾ In. ... *illus* 322
Figurine, Foal, Lying Down, Glazed, Knud Kyhn, 7 x 7 ½ In. ... *illus* 136

Roseville, Sunflower, Vase, Handles, 6 In.
$302

Humler & Nolan

Roseville, Wall Pocket, Brown Panel, Nude Woman, Black Ground, 7 In.
$213

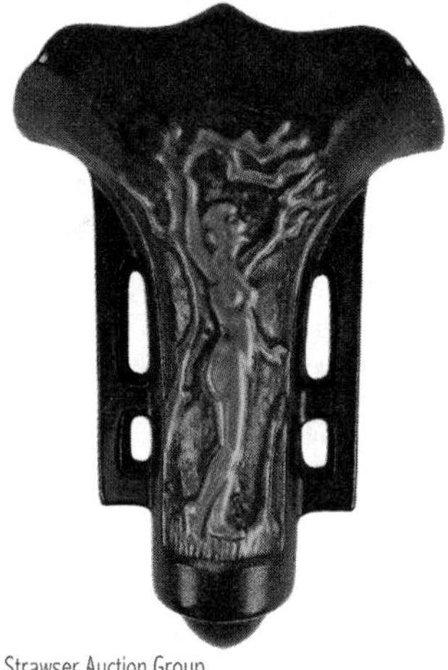
Strawser Auction Group

Royal Bayreuth, Bowl, Peacock, Shell, Leaf Mold, Multicolor Central Image, 1910s, 10 ⅝ In.
$439

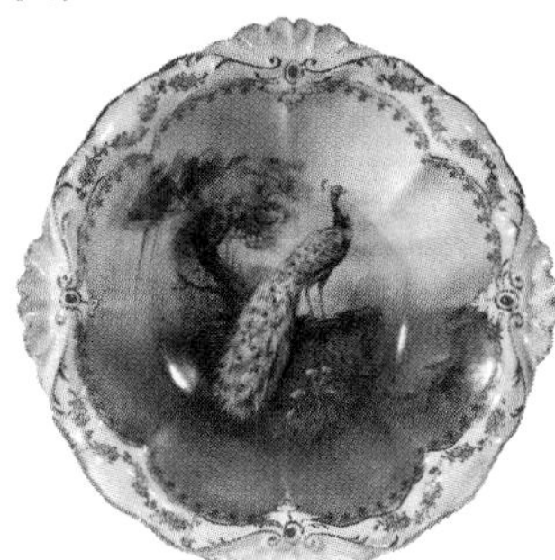
Jeffrey S. Evans & Associates

R

Royal Bayreuth, Sugar, Lid, Devil Finial, Cards, Hearts, Red, White, c.1900, 4 x 4 ½ In.
$150

Woody Auctions

Royal Bayreuth, Vase, Polar Bears, Glazed, Marked, c.1900, 8 ½ x 5 In.
$650

Woody Auctions

Royal Bayreuth, Wall Pocket, Farm Scene, Woman & Chicken, Marked, 8 ¾ In.
$120

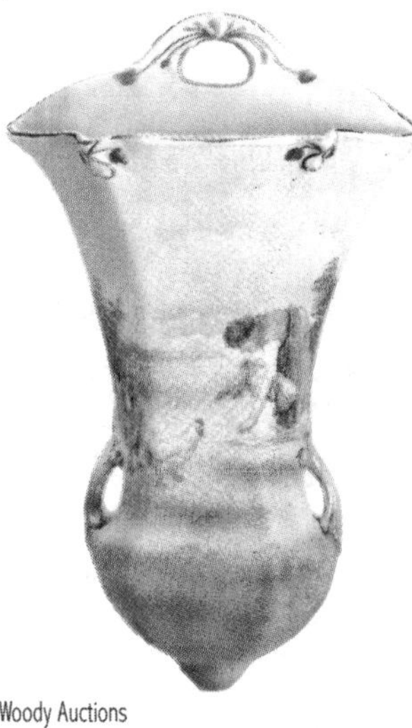

Woody Auctions

Flora Danica, Bowl, Gilt, Sawtooth Rim, Multicolor, 1900s, 9 In. 400
Plate, Dinner, Flora Danica, Botanical Specimen, Reticulated, Mark, 1985-91, 10 In., Pair 900
Platter, Flora Danica, Pierced, Yellow Flower, c.1880, 14 In. 1100
Tray, Lizard, Blue Waves, Flowers, c.1800, 2 x 8 In. .... *illus* 396
Tureen, Lid, Flora Danica, Branch Handle, Flowers, Gilt, 7 ½ x 15 In. 1540
Vase, Budding Fruits, Glazed, Axel Salto, 1951, 6 x 9 x 8 In. .... *illus* 10625
Vase, Warriors, Shields, Sandals, Robes, White Crackle Ground, Denmark, c.1950, 17 x 10 In. .. 1125

ROYAL COPLEY

Royal Copley china was made by the Spaulding China Company of Sebring, Ohio, from 1939 to 1960. The best known are the figural planters and the small figurines, especially those with Art Deco designs.

Head Vase, Blackamoor, Headdress, Creamy White, 8 x 5 In. 25
Head Vase, Horse, Brown Bay, Dark Brown Eyes, Black Mane, c.1950, 6 x 5 In. 49

ROYAL CROWN DERBY

Royal Crown Derby Company, Ltd., is a name used on porcelain beginning in 1890. There is a complex family tree that includes the Derby, Crown Derby, and Royal Crown Derby porcelains. *Derby* has been marked on porcelain and bone china made in the city of Derby, England, since about 1750 when Andrew Planche and William Duesbury established the first china factory in Derby. In 1775, King George III honored the company by granting them a patent to use the royal crown in their backstamp and the company became known as *Crown Derby.* Pieces are marked with a crown and the letter *D* or the word *Derby.* When the original Derby factory closed in 1848, some of its former workers opened a smaller factory on King Street, Derby, and used Crown Derby's original molds and patterns. About 1876 the present company was formed when another factory opened under the name Derby Crown Porcelain Co. (1876–1890). Queen Victoria granted Derby Crown Porcelain a royal warrant in 1890 and the name became Royal Crown Derby Porcelain Co. Finally, in 1935 Royal Crown Derby bought the King Street factory, which brought Derby china under one company again. The Royal Crown Derby mark includes the name and a crown. The words *Made in England* were used after 1921. The company became part of Allied English Potteries Group in 1964 then merged into Royal Doulton Tableware. Royal Crown Derby Co. Ltd. was acquired by Steelite International in 2013. Kevin Oakes bought Royal Crown Derby in 2016. It is still in business.

Royal Crown Derby
1877–1890

Royal Crown Derby
1890–1940

Royal Crown Derby
c.1976–2014

Bowl, Olde Avesbury, Gold, White Ground, Footed, 3 x 8 ½ In. 112
Candlestick, Upturned Cup, Canted Corners, Convex Sides, Dolphins, 10 ½ x 5 x 5 In., Pair *illus* 480
Figurine, Dog, Pug, Seated, Black & Gold Collar, Rectangular Green Base, 3 In., Pair .... *illus* 738
Figurine, Woman, Standing, Emblematic Of Love, Flowers, Gilt Base, 9 In. 431
Plate, Gilt Rim, Black Ground, Pink Flowers, Imari, Signed, 10 ¾ In., 12 Piece 735
Sauceboat, Duck Shape, White Ground, Orange Beak, Blue, Painted Marked, 4 In., 4 Piece 1845
Tray, Rectangular, Gilt Rim, Canted Corners, Shell Handles, 19 x 12 ½ In. .... *illus* 848
Vase, Gilt, Dunluce Castle, Ellis Clark, 1894, 6 ½ x 3 ½ In. 250

ROYAL DOULTON

Royal Doulton is the name used on Doulton and Company pottery made from 1902

Royal Bonn, Vase, Hand Painted, Roses, Floral, Gilt, Teal Ground, Bolted, c.1900, 39 In.
$468

Jeffrey S. Evans & Associates

Royal Copenhagen, Tray, Lizard, Blue Waves, Flowers, c.1800, 2 x 8 In.
$396

Soulis Auctions

Royal Copenhagen, Vase, Budding Fruits, Glazed, Axel Salto, 1951, 6 x 9 x 8 In.
$10,625

Rago Arts and Auction Center

Royal Crown Derby, Tray, Rectangular, Gilt Rim, Canted Corners, Shell Handles, 19 x 12 ½ In.
$848

Soulis Auctions

TIP

If a capital letter A is printed next to the usual Royal Doulton mark, it means the piece was made between about 1939 and 1955.

Royal Copenhagen, Dish, Flora Danica, Oval, Lavender, Green, Water Mint Flower, 1900s, 8 ¾ x 6 ¾ In.
$322

Jeffrey S. Evans & Associates

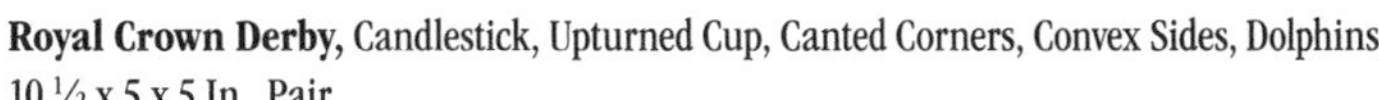

Royal Crown Derby, Candlestick, Upturned Cup, Canted Corners, Convex Sides, Dolphins, 10 ½ x 5 x 5 In.. Pair
$480

Soulis Auctions

Royal Copenhagen, Figurine, Foal, Lying Down, Glazed, Knud Kyhn, 7 x 7 ½ In.
$136

Soulis Auctions

Royal Crown Derby, Figurine, Dog, Pug, Seated, Black & Gold Collar, Rectangular Green Base, 3 In., Pair
$738

Stair Galleries

Royal Doulton, Bowl, Orange Brown, Painted, Landscape, Pedestal Foot, c.1910, 10 x 16 ½ In.
$396

Soulis Auctions

Royal Doulton, Figurine, Cockerel, Standing, Glazed, Flambe, 8 In.
$175

Woody Auctions

Royal Doulton, Figurine, Letter To Santa, Tree, Green, Red & Brown, Circular Base, 11 In.
$316

Apple Tree Auction Center

Royal Doulton, Jar, Red Cherry Blossoms, Shaded Blue Ground, Flambe, Sung, Stand, Marked, 10 ¾ x 8 In.
$960

Morphy Auctions

to the present. Doulton and Company of England was founded in 1853. Pieces made before 1902 are listed in this book under Doulton. Royal Doulton collectors pay high prices for the out-of-production figurines, character jugs, vases, and series wares. Some vases and animal figurines were made with a special red glaze called flambe. Sung and Chang glazed pieces are rare. The multicolored glaze is very thick and looks as if it were dropped on the clay. Bunnykins figurines were first made by Royal Doulton in 1939. In 2005 Royal Doulton was acquired by the Waterford Wedgwood Group. It was bought by KPS Capital Partners of New York in 2009 and became part of WWRD Holdings. WWRD was bought by Fiskars Group in 2015. Beatrix Potter bunny figurines were made by Beswick and are listed in that category.

Royal Doulton
1902–1922, 1927–1932

Royal Doulton
1922–1956

Royal Doulton
c.2000–present

Bowl, Orange Brown, Painted, Landscape, Pedestal Foot, c.1910, 10 x 16 ½ In. .... *illus* 396
Bowl, White Ground, Flowers, Monogram, Andrew Wyeth, 4 ½ x 12 ⅞ In. 129

Royal Doulton character jugs depict the head and shoulders of the subject. They are made in four sizes: large, 5 ¼ to 7 inches; small, 3 ¼ to 4 inches; miniature, 2 ¼ to 2 ½ inches; and tiny, 1 ¼ inches. Toby jugs portray a seated, full figure.

Character Jug, Captain Ahab, D 6500, 7 In. 24
Character Jug, Cardinal, D 5614, Scarlet Robes, Purple Handle, 1936-60, 6 ½ In. 62
Character Jug, Dick Turpin, D 6128, Pistol Handle, 2 In. 264
Figurine, Cockerel, Standing, Glazed, Flambe, 8 In. .... *illus* 175
Figurine, Letter To Santa, Tree, Green, Red & Brown, Circular Base, 11 In. .... *illus* 316
Figurine, St. George & The Dragon, Hand Painted, Fire Gloss, 7 ¾ In. 118
Jar, Red Cherry Blossoms, Shaded Blue Ground, Flambe, Sung, Stand, Marked, 10 ¾ x 8 In. *illus* 960
Plate, Tridecagon, Gilt Rim, White Ground, 10 ½ In., 11 Piece 313
Tobacco Jar, Green Ground, Painted, Fish, Metal Twist Top Handle, Stoneware Lid, 4 x 5 In... 29
Vase, Flambe, Sung, Peacock In Tree, Red, C. Noke, F. Moore, Marked, 7 ⅝ In. .... *illus* 1452
Vase, Flambe, Tapering, Peacock, Signed, A. Eaton, England, 1900s, 12 ½ In. .... *illus* 2160
Vase, Fuchsia, Gourd, Green Rim, Enamel, 6 In. 83

ROYAL DUX

Royal Dux is the more common name for the Duxer Porzellanmanufaktur, which was founded by E. Eichler in Dux, Bohemia (now Duchcov, Czech Republic), in 1860. By the turn of the twentieth century, the firm specialized in porcelain statuary and busts of Art Nouveau–style maidens, large porcelain figures, and ornate vases with three-dimensional figures climbing on the sides. The firm is still in business. It is now part of Czesky Porcelan (Czech Porcelain).

Centerpiece, Conch Shell, Lilies, Rocky Base, Semiclad Nude, Sitting, 14 x 13 x 6 In. .....*illus* 283
Centerpiece, Young Woman, Sitting On Bowls, 2 Birds, 2 Bowls, 12 ½ x 13 In. 175
Group, Camel, Rider & Foot Servant, Signed, 18 ¾ x 14 x 6 ¾ In. 113
Vase, Barefoot Woman, Molded Leaves, Stems, Flowers, Ginkgo Leaf Handles, c.1925, 16 In...... 125
Vase, Shell, Sinewy Tulip & Leaves, 2 Women, Red Robes, Art Nouveau, 16 ½ In. 181
Vase, Twig Handles, Green, White, Marbleized Ground, Embossed Iris, c.1920, 13 ¾ In. ..*illus* 275

ROYAL FLEMISH

Royal Flemish glass was made during the late 1880s in New Bedford, Massachusetts, by the Mt. Washington Glass Works. It is a colored satin glass decorated with dark colors and raised gold designs. The glass was patented in 1894. It was supposed to resemble stained glass windows.

Jar, Lid, Multicolor Flowers, Blue Pinwheels, Gold Scrolls On Lid, 2 Handles, 7 In. 1600
Rose Bowl, Pink Roses, Green Leaves, Blue, White, Pulled & Crimped Top, 5 ½ In. 2750
Vase, Round, Large Circles, Stars, Scrolls, Beading, Gold, Greens, Brown, 6 ½ In. 885

ROYAL HAEGER, *see Haeger category.*

ROYAL HICKMAN

Royal Hickman designed pottery, glass, silver, aluminum, furniture, lamps, and other items. From 1938 to 1944 and again from the 1950s to 1969, he worked for Haeger Potteries. Mr. Hickman operated his own pottery in Tampa, Florida, during the 1940s. He moved to California and worked for Vernon Potteries. During the last years of his life he lived in Guadalajara, Mexico, and continued designing for Royal Haeger. He died in 1969. Pieces made in his pottery listed here are marked *Royal Hickman* or *Hickman.*

Vase, Beehive, Purple-Blue, c.1940, 8 In. 125
Vase, Free-Form, Coral Reef, Gray, Petty Crystal, 1940s, 8 In. 45
Vase, Gladiola, Pierced, Brown, Chartreuse Glaze, c.1950, 11 In. 150
Vase, Swan, Green Agate, 10 In. 40

ROYAL NYMPHENBURG

Royal Nymphenburg is the modern name for the Nymphenburg porcelain factory, which was established at Neudeck ob der Au, Germany, in 1753 and moved to Nymphenburg in 1761. The company is still in existence. Marks include a checkered shield topped by a crown, a crowned *CT* with the year, and a contemporary shield mark on reproductions of eighteenth-century porcelain.

Figurine, Baroque Lion Of Bavaria, Shield, Base, Josef Wackerle, 1946, 5 x 4 ½ x 9 In. 153
Figurine, Capitano & Leda, Impressed Shield Mark, 7 ½ In., Pair .... *illus* 960
Figurine, Equestrian Models, Man & Woman, White Horse, 8 ½ In., Pair 185

ROYAL RUDOLSTADT, *see Rudolstadt category.*

ROYAL VIENNA, *see Beehive category.*

ROYAL WORCESTER

Royal Worcester is a name used by collectors. Worcester porcelains were made in Worcester, England, from about 1751. The firm went through many periods and name changes. It became the Worcester Royal Porcelain Company, Ltd., in 1862. Today collectors call the porcelains made after 1862 "Royal Worcester." In 1976, the firm merged with W.T. Copeland to become Royal Worcester Spode. The company was bought by the Portmeirion Group in 2009. Some early products of the factory are listed under Worcester. Related pieces may be listed under Copeland, Copeland Spode, and Spode.

Royal Worcester
1862–1875

Royal Worcester
1891

Royal Worcester
c.1959+

Creamer, Tusk Shape, Cream Ground, Butterfly, Flowers, Gilt Handle & Rim, 6 In. 120

Royal Doulton, Vase, Flambe, Sung, Peacock In Tree, Red, C. Noke, F. Moore, Marked, 7 ⅝ In.
$1,452

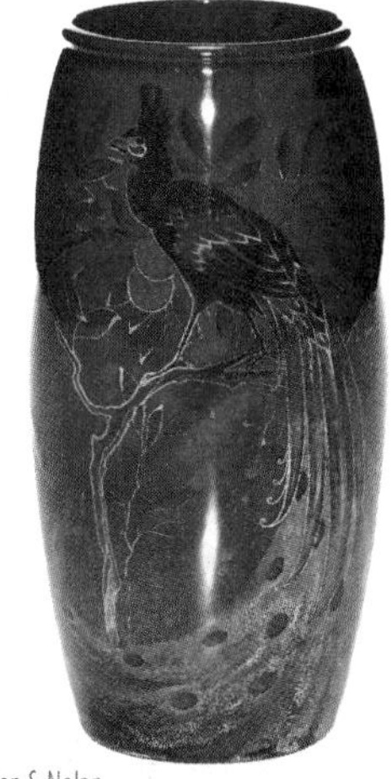
Humler & Nolan

Royal Doulton, Vase, Flambe, Tapering, Peacock, Signed, A. Eaton, England, 1900s, 12 ½ In.
$2,160

Brunk Auctions

Royal Dux, Centerpiece, Conch Shell, Lilies, Rocky Base, Semiclad Nude, Sitting, 14 x 13 x 6 In.
$283

Soulis Auctions

Royal Dux, Vase, Twig Handles, Green, White, Marbleized Ground, Embossed Iris, c.1920, 13 ¾ In.
$275

Woody Auctions

Royal Nymphenburg, Figurine, Capitano & Leda, Impressed Shield Mark, 7 ½ In., Pair
$960

Neal Auction Company

Royal Worcester, Ornament, Nautilus Shell Coral Branch Base, Multicolor, Majolica, c.1850, 7 In.
$390

Eldred's

Royal Worcester, Pitcher, Fish Handle, Pike Head, Open Mouth, Majolica, 12 In.
$2,714

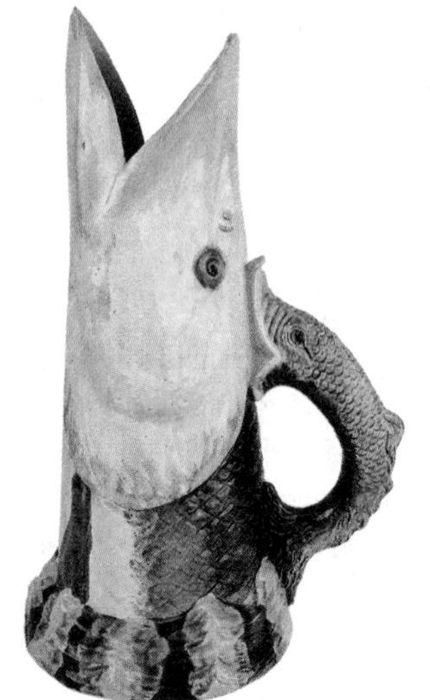
Strawser Auction Group

Royal Worcester, Planter, Art Nouveau, Lily Pad, Gold Accent, Scrolled Feet, 7 x 7 In.
$295

Bunch Auctions

Royal Worcester, Vase, Cream, Gilt, Bamboo Handle, Hummingbird, c.1900, 8 In.
$230

Selkirk Auctioneers & Appraisers

Royal Worcester, Vase, Ivory Ground, 2 Scrolled Handles, Gilt & Enamel, 1883, 11 In.
$540

Eldred's

Royal Worcester, Vase, Persianate Style, Painted, Nocturnal Theme, Birds, c.1887, 10 x 6 In.
$339

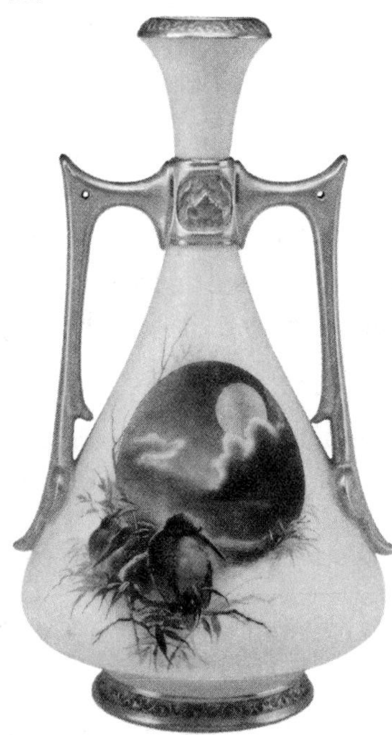
Soulis Auctions

R

Figurine, Hooded Warbler, Cherokee Rose, Dorothy Doughty, 1961, 12 In.	122
Ornament, Nautilus Shell Coral Branch Base, Multicolor, Majolica, c.1850, 7 In. *illus*	390
Pitcher, Fish Handle, Pike Head, Open Mouth, Majolica, 12 In. *illus*	2714
Planter, Art Nouveau, Lily Pad, Gold Accent, Scrolled Feet, 7 x 7 In. *illus*	295
Tea Set, Tray, Teapot, Waste Bowl, Creamer, 4 Cups & Saucers, Flowers, c.1880	1080
Toothpick Holder, Crate, Snail, Butterfly, Ivy, Brown, Majolica, 2 ½ In.	153
Tureen, Lid, Transfer, Blue Willow, Elephant Shape Handles, Underplate, 1879, 6 x 14 In.	325
Vase, Blue Flowers, Yellow Leaves, Reticulated Neck & Handles, 14 ½ In.	220
Vase, Cream, Gilt, Bamboo Handle, Hummingbird, c.1900, 8 In. *illus*	230
Vase, Ivory Ground, 2 Scrolled Handles, Gilt & Enamel, 1883, 11 In. *illus*	540
Vase, Nocturnal Scene, Birds In Moonlight, Flight Back, Handles, Gold Trim, 9 ½ In.	196
Vase, Persianate Style, Painted, Nocturnal Theme, Birds, c.1887, 10 x 6 In. *illus*	339

ROYCROFT

Roycroft products were made by the Roycrofter community of East Aurora, New York, from 1895 until 1938. The community was founded by Elbert Hubbard, famous philosopher, writer, and artist. The workshops owned by the community made furniture, metalware, leatherwork, embroidery, and jewelry. A printshop produced many signs, books, and the magazines that promoted the sayings of Elbert Hubbard. Furniture by the Roycroft community is listed in the Furniture category.

Bookends, Copper, Hammered, Triangular Shaped, 3 x 5 In., Pair	73
Candlestick, Copper, Hammered, Handle, 3 ¼ In. *illus*	83
Inkwell, Lid, Copper, Hammered, Dome Shape, Glass Liner, c.1920, 2 ½ x 2 ½ In.	50
Lamp, Desk, Copper, Hammered, 13 ½ In.	984
Tray, Oval, Copper, 2 Handles, Patina, Marked, 21 x 10 In.	375

ROZANE, *see Roseville category.*

RRP

RRP, or RRP Roseville, is the mark used by the firm of Robinson-Ransbottom. It is not a mark of the more famous Roseville Pottery. The Ransbottom brothers started a pottery in 1900 in Ironspot, Ohio. In 1920, they merged with the Robinson Clay Product Company of Akron, Ohio, to become Robinson-Ransbottom. The factory closed in 2005.

Cookie Jar, Dutch Girl, Gold Trim, Marked, 12 In. *illus*	104

RS GERMANY

RS Germany is part of the wording in marks used by the Tillowitz, Germany, factory of Reinhold Schlegelmilch from 1914 until about 1945. The porcelain was sold decorated and undecorated. The Schlegelmilch families made porcelains marked in many ways. See also ES Germany, RS Poland, RS Prussia, RS Silesia, RS Suhl, and RS Tillowitz.

Biscuit Jar, 2 Handles, Yellow, Green Tones, Rose, Gold Trip, Lid, 6 In.	70
Plaque, Dancing Girls, Trees, Gold Rim, 10 In.	540
Pot, 2 Handles, Lilies, White & Green Ground, Signed, Clarize Spencer, 1928, 10 In.	96

RS POLAND

RS Poland (German) is a mark used by the Reinhold Schlegelmilch factory at Tillowitz from about 1946 to 1956. After 1956, the factory made porcelain marked *PT Poland.* This is one of many of the RS marks used. See also ES Germany, RS Germany, RS Prussia, RS Silesia, RS Suhl, and RS Tillowitz.

Roycroft, Candlestick, Copper, Hammered, Handle, 3 ¼ In.
$83

Conestoga Auction Company

RRP, Cookie Jar, Dutch Girl, Gold Trim, Marked, 12 In.
$104

Belhorn Auction Services

RS Poland, Vase, Pedestal, 2 Gilt Handles, Yellow & Green Ground, White Flowers, 8 In.
$60

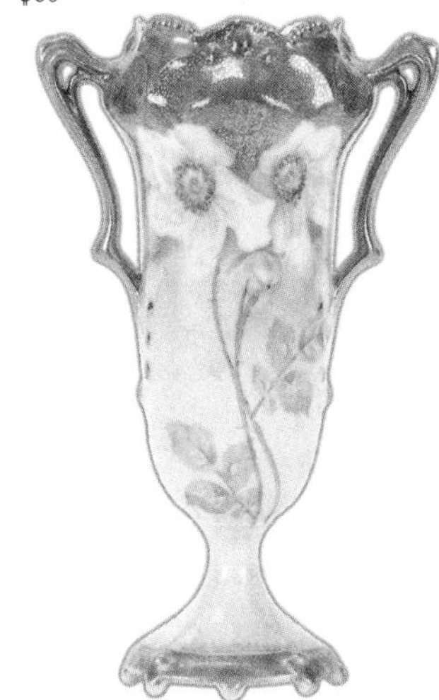

Woody Auctions

This is an edited listing of current prices. Visit **Kovels.com** to check thousands of prices from previous years and sign up for free information on trends, tips, reproductions, marks, and more.

RS Poland
c.1945–1956

PT Tulowice
After 1945–1956

Hatpin Holder, Chinese Pheasants, Grasses, Green Tones, Marked, 4 In. 210
Jar, Squat, Lid, Ostriches In Landscape, Trees, Green & Brown Tones, 2 ½ In. 330
Tea Strainer, White, Pink & Blue Flowers In Wavy Ovals Border, Tab Handle, 2 x 6 In. 48
Vase, 3 Classical Maidens & A Boy, Cobalt Blue & Gilt Ground, 2 Handles, 9 ½ In. 600
Vase, Black Swans, Tan Shaded To Cream Ground, Bulbous, Pinched Neck, 5 x 5 In. 1320
Vase, Hummingbirds, Brown Shaded To Yellow Ground, Bulbous, Pinched Neck, 5 In. 720
Vase, Oval, Black Swans, Grass, Cattails, Flared Rim, Marked, 8 ¾ In. 1440
Vase, Pedestal, 2 Gilt Handles, Yellow & Green Ground, White Flowers, 8 In. ....*illus* 60
Vase, Rural Cottage Scene, Man, Cows, Trees, Bulbous, Pedestal Base, 7 ¾ x 7 ¾ In. 330
Vase, White Flowers, Red & Gold Stencil Trim, Gilt Metal Lattice Flower Frog Lid, 6 In. 84

RS PRUSSIA

RS Prussia appears in several marks used on porcelain before 1917. Reinhold Schlegelmilch started his porcelain works in Suhl, Germany, in 1869. See also ES Germany, RS Germany, RS Poland, RS Silesia, RS Suhl, and RS Tillowitz.

RS Prussia
Late 1880s–1917

RS Prussia
c.1895–1917

Berry Set, Castle Scene, Dish, Green, Red, Orange, Yellow, 5 ½ In., Pair 80
Biscuit Jar, Lid, Brown Tones, Castle Scene, Gold Highlights, 7 In. ....*illus* 100
Biscuit Jar, Lid, LeBrun Portraits, Lily Mold, Blue, Yellow, Gold Border, Handles, 5 x 9 In. 450
Biscuit Jar, Lid, White, Green & Cream Ground, Flowers, 2 Handles, Footed, 5 x 9 In. 108
Biscuit Jar, Mill Scene, Castle On Lid, Brown Tones, 2 Shaped Handles, 4 ½ x 8 In. 240
Bowl, Carnation Mold, Cobalt Blue, Pink & Yellow Rose, Gold Stencil Highlights, 12 In. ..*illus* 450
Bowl, Carnation Mold, Flowers, Pink, White, Gold Stencil, 10 In. 180
Bowl, Dice Throwers, Cobalt Blue, Green, Gold, 8 ½ In. 990
Bowl, Portrait Center, Lily, Green Ground, Pink Domes, c.1910, 10 ½ In. ....*illus* 400
Bowl, Portrait, Madame LeBrun, Transfer, Iridescent, Tiffany Finish, c.1900, 10 In. 410
Bowl, Winter Season, Medallion Portraits, 10 ¾ In. 1320
Bowl, Yellow & White Center, Pink Rose Decor, Green Border, Lavender Iris, 9 In. ....*illus* 108
Box, Lid, 3 Swans On Water, Blue Tones, Gold Trim, Icicle Mold, Square, 3 x 4 In. 210
Cake Plate, 6 Lobes, Roses, Clover Mold, Opal Jewel Border, Open Handles, 11 In. 150
Cake Plate, Central Recamier Transfer Image, Iridescent, Gilt, 1910s, 10 In. ....*illus* 410
Cake Plate, Iris Mold, White Center, Flowers, Peacock Tiffany Border, 9 ½ In. 96
Cake Plate, Summer Season Portrait, Iris Mold, White, Lavender, Gold Trim, 2 Handles, 11 In. *illus* 750
Charger, Flower, Carnation Mold, Cobalt Blue, Scalloped Rim, 11 ¾ In. 175
Chocolate Pot, Pink Roses, Raised Details, Tapered Lid, Finial, 12 In. 75
Coffeepot, Lily Mold, LeBrun Portrait In Ribbon, Gold Border, Multicolor, 9 ½ In. 420
Coffeepot, Poppy, Rose, Pink, Yellow, Gold Trim, 9 In. 275
Ewer, Pedestal, Woman, Peacock, Iridescent White, Gold Stencil, 10 In. 225
Hair Receiver, Swag & Tassel Mold, Cottage, Bluebird, Green, Footed, 5 In. 100
Muffineer, Swan Scenic, Black, Green Tones, 6 ½ In. ....*illus* 100
Mug, Flower, Lavender, White Satin Finish, c.1910, 3 ½ In. 2000
Mustard Jar, Fleur-De-Lis Mold, Cream & Green, Pink Flowers, Gilt, 3 ¾ In. 96
Nappy, Flower, Pink, Cream, Blue, Pink, Figural Handles, 6 ½ x 5 In. 80

RS Prussia, Biscuit Jar, Lid, Brown Tones, Castle Scene, Gold Highlights, 7 In.
$100

Woody Auctions

RS Prussia, Bowl, Carnation Mold, Cobalt Blue, Pink & Yellow Rose, Gold Stencil Highlights, 12 In.
$450

Woody Auctions

RS Prussia, Bowl, Portrait Center, Lily, Green Ground, Pink Domes, c.1910, 10 ½ In.
$400

Woody Auctions

R

Pen Tray, Flower, Pink, Yellow, Lavender, Mold, Quill Pen, Cream, 9 x 4 In. 500
Pin Tray, Iris Mold, Winter Season, Woman, White & Green Satin, Gold Trim, 7 In. 200
Pitcher, Mold, Green & White Tones, Yellow Rose, Pansy Decor, 7 ¾ In. 100
Plate, Fleur-De-Lis Mold, Green & Yellow Ground, Pink Flowers, Gold, 10 ¾ In. 72
Plate, Flower, Raindrop Mold, Green, Yellow, Lavender Tones, Scalloped Rim, 8 ½ In. 30
Plate, Rosebud Mold, Cream, Lavender & Blue Ground, Marked, Steeple, 8 In. 84
Relish, Jewel Mold, Children, Dice Throwers, Ribbon, Gold, Opal, 9 ½ In. 275
Shaving Mug, Lily Mold, Potocka Medallion, Gold Background, Pink, 3 In. *illus* 650
Tankard, Carnation Mold, Green, White & Lavender Satin, Pink Flowers, 13 In. 240
Tankard, Flower, Orange, Yellow Carnation, Green, White, Cream, Magnolia Blossom, 14 In. 200
Teapot, Hidden Image Mold, Flowers, Green, White, Gold Stencil, 5 x 7 In. 250
Tray, Dresser, Lily Mold, Yellow, Blue, Lavender, Violet, Rectangular, 11 ½ In. 70
Tray, Iris Mold, Spring Season, Woman, 11 x 7 In. 1560
Urn, Lid, Tiffany, Woman, Peacock, Doves, 4 Panels, Gold Trim, Blue Enamel Beaded, 12 ½ In. 350
Vase, Gazelle Scene, Green, Jungle, 2 Handles, Urn Shape, 5 In. *illus* 2750
Vase, Woman, Sitting, Fan, Sheep, Flowers, Transfer, Gilt, 1910s, 13 ⅝ In. 263
Vase, Yellow Roses, Multicolor Ground, 2 Handles, Footed, 11 x 6 x 4 In. *illus* 113

RS SILESIA

RS Silesia appears on porcelain made at the Reinhold Schlegelmilch factory in Tillowitz, Germany, from the 1920s to the 1940s. The Schlegelmilch families made porcelains marked in many ways. See also ES Germany, RS Germany, RS Poland, RS Prussia, RS Suhl, and RS Tillowitz.

Coffeepot, Green & White Striped Body, White Handle, Spout, 8 ½ In. 24
Plate, Luncheon, Flowers, White Ground, Yellow Highlights, Gold Rim 22
Tray, Art Deco Design, Flowers, Leaves, Gilt Handles, 16 x 5 In. 151

RS SUHL

RS Suhl is a mark used by the Reinhold Schlegelmilch factory in Suhl, Germany, between 1900 and 1917. The Schlegelmilch families made porcelains in many places. See also ES Germany, RS Germany, RS Poland, RS Prussia, RS Silesia, and RS Tillowitz.

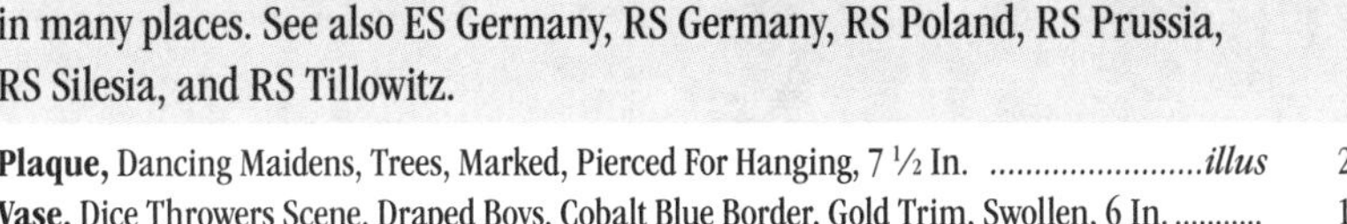

Plaque, Dancing Maidens, Trees, Marked, Pierced For Hanging, 7 ½ In. *illus* 225
Vase, Dice Throwers Scene, Draped Boys, Cobalt Blue Border, Gold Trim, Swollen, 6 In. 120
Vase, Napoleon Campaign Scene, Brown Tones, Oval, Flared Rim, 8 ¾ In. 150
Vase, Old Sheepherder Scene, 2 High Gilt Scrolled Handles, 6 In. 60
Vase, Violets, Light Shaded To Dark Green, Gold Trim, Curled Up Handles, 12 In. 47
Vase, Yellow Roses, Stems, Cream Shaded To Gray Ground, Curled Up Handles, 14 In. 270

RS TILLOWITZ

RS Tillowitz was marked on porcelain by the Reinhold Schlegelmilch factory at Tillowitz from the 1920s to the 1940s. Table services and ornamental pieces were made. See also ES Germany, RS Germany, RS Poland, RS Prussia, RS Silesia, and RS Suhl.

RS Tillowitz
1920s–1940s

RS Tillowitz
1932–1983

Berry Bowl, Women In Pastoral Scene, Cut Corners, Marked, 5 In., Pair 150
Box, Egg Shape, Pink Rose, White, Cream, Gray, Gold Trim, 6 ½ x 4 In. 100
Box, Lid, Pink Rose, Shaded Gray To Cream, Egg Shape, 3 Legs, Round Base, 6 ½ In. 120
Bread Tray, Snowbirds, Icy Lake, Snowy Trees, Oval, Open Handles, Marked, 12 In. 60
Figurine, Young Child, Kneeling, Praying, White, 5 In. *illus* 300

TIP
Gummed tags can be removed by heating the tag with a hair dryer, then loosening it with a flat knife.

RS Prussia, Bowl, Yellow & White Center, Pink Rose Decor, Green Border, Lavender Iris, 9 In.
$108

Woody Auctions

RS Prussia, Cake Plate, Central Recamier Transfer Image, Iridescent, Gilt, 1910s, 10 In.
$410

Jeffrey S. Evans & Associates

RS Prussia, Cake Plate, Summer Season Portrait, Iris Mold, White, Lavender, Gold Trim, 2 Handles, 11 In.
$750

Woody Auctions

RS Prussia, Muffineer, Swan Scenic, Black, Green Tones, 6 ½ In.
$100

Woody Auctions

RS Prussia, Shaving Mug, Lily Mold, Potocka Medallion, Gold Background, Pink, 3 In.
$650

Woody Auctions

RS Prussia, Vase, Gazelle Scene, Green, Jungle, 2 Handles, Urn Shape, 5 In.
$2,750

Woody Auctions

RS Prussia, Vase, Yellow Roses, Multicolor Ground, 2 Handles, Footed, 11 x 6 x 4 In.
$113

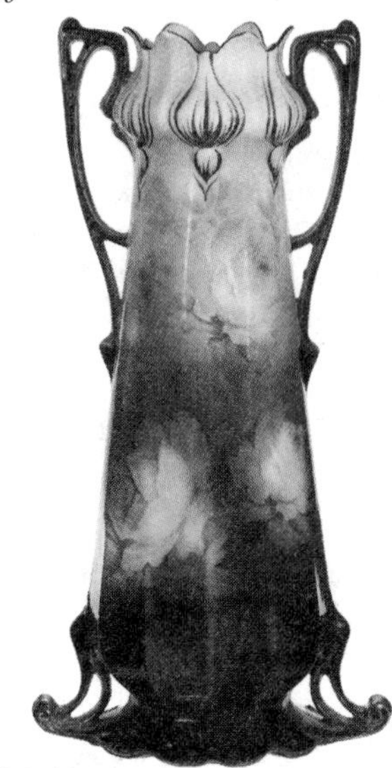

Soulis Auctions

RS Suhl, Plaque, Dancing Maidens, Trees, Marked, Pierced For Hanging, 7 ½ In.
$225

Woody Auctions

RS Tillowitz, Figurine, Young Child, Kneeling, Praying, White, 5 In.
$300

Woody Auctions

Rubina, Pitcher, Water, Polka Dot, Pontil Mark, Hobbs, Brockunier & Co., c.1884, 7 ¾ In.
$140

Jeffrey S. Evans & Associates

Rubina, Vase, Jack-In-The-Pulpit Shape, Petal Feet, 8 ½ In.
$60

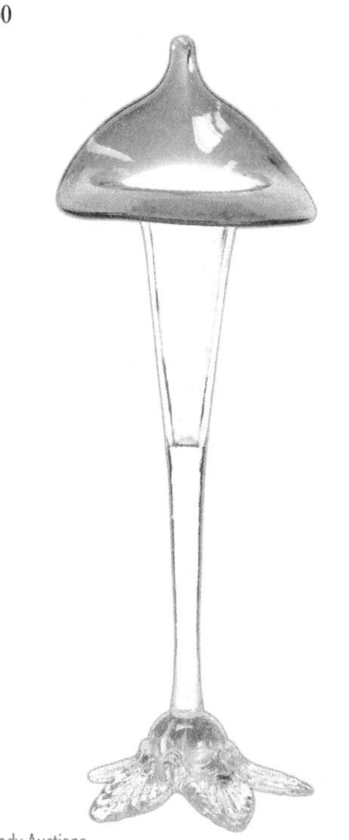

Woody Auctions

Ruby Glass, Punch Bowl, King's Crown, Ruby Stain, Clear, Engraved, 9 x 12 In.
$761

Jeffrey S. Evans & Associates

Relish, 2 Parrots, Perched On Branch, Blue Ground, Elliptical, 8 In. 36
Vase, Black Swans, Tapered, Gold Band At Rim, 4 ½ In. 420

RUBINA

Rubina is a glassware that shades from red to clear. It was first made by George Duncan and Sons of Pittsburgh, Pennsylvania, in about 1885. This coloring was used on many types of glassware.

Pitcher, Water, Polka Dot, Pontil Mark, Hobbs, Brockunier & Co., c.1884, 7 ¾ In. *illus* 140
Syrup, Hobnail Pattern, Silver Lid, 6 ½ In. 30
Vase, Jack-In-The-Pulpit Shape, Petal Feet, 8 ½ In. *illus* 60

RUBY GLASS

Ruby glass is the dark red color of a ruby, the precious gemstone. It was a popular Victorian color that never went completely out of style. The glass was shaped by many different processes to make many different types of ruby glass. There was a revival of interest in the 1940s when modern-shaped ruby table glassware became fashionable. Sometimes the red color is added to clear glass by a process called flashing or staining. Flashed glass is clear glass dipped in a colored glass, then pressed or cut. Stained glass has color painted on a clear glass. Then it is refired so the stain fuses with the glass. Pieces of glass colored in this way are indicated by the word *stained* in the description. Related items may be found in other categories, such as Cranberry Glass, Pressed Glass, and Souvenir.

Decanter, Overlay, Relief, Masks, Globe Stopper, 10 In. 200
Punch Bowl, King's Crown, Ruby Stain, Clear, Engraved, 9 x 12 In. *illus* 761
Scent Bottle, Screw-In Stopper, Silver Handle, Spout, Chain, 3 ¾ In. 480

RUDOLSTADT

Rudolstadt was a faience factory in the Thuringia region of Germany from 1720 to about 1791. In 1854, Ernst Bohne began working in the area. From about 1887 to 1918, the New York and Rudolstadt Pottery made decorated porcelain marked with the RW and crown familiar to collectors. This porcelain was imported by Lewis Straus and Sons of New York, which later became Nathan Straus and Sons. The word *Royal* was included in their import mark. Collectors often call it "Royal Rudolstadt." Most pieces found today were made in the late nineteenth or early twentieth century. Additional pieces may be listed in the Kewpie category.

Figurine, Piper, Seated, Red Coat, Yellow Cuffs, Green Pants, Hat, 8 ½ In. 129
Pitcher, White, Multicolor Daisies, Molded Scrolling Leafy Design Around Neck, 9 In. 105
Vase, White, Leaves, Flowers, Ornate Gilt Handles, Art Nouveau, 13 ½ In. 210

RUG

Rugs have been used in the American home since the seventeenth century. The oriental rug of that time was often used on a table, not on the floor. Rag rugs, hooked rugs, and braided rugs were made by housewives from scraps of material. American Indian rugs are listed in the Indian category.

Aubusson Style, Pink & Cream Ground, Paneled Design, Flower Sprays, France, 10 x 13 Ft. 704
Bakhtiari, Orange Field, Geometric Medallion, Ivory Border, 8 Ft. 9 In. x 11 Ft. 10 In. 560
Balouch, Red Diamonds, Blue, Cream, Fringe, 7 Ft. 6 In. x 2 Ft. 11 In. 125
Bergama, Terra-Cotta Lozenge Medallions, Flowers, Vine Border, Runner, 7 Ft. 5 In. x 2 Ft. 8 In. 124
Bibikabad, Black Ground, Potted Plant, Birds, Floral Border, Persia, 1900s, 6 Ft. 7 In. x 4 Ft. 4 In. 1440
Bidjar, Handmade, Flowers, Geometrics, 1 Ft. 9 In. x 14 Ft. 10 In. 288
Caucasian, Blue & Ivory Borders, Runner, Late 1900s, 2 Ft. 6 In. x 10 Ft. 360
Caucasian, Blue Field, Red, Pink, Blue, Gold Geometric Medallion, Vines, 3 Ft. 8 In. x 5 Ft. 2 In. 344

Rug, Heriz, 4 Geometric Medallions, Floral, Salmon Field, Handmade, Runner, 2 Ft. 8 In. x 1 Ft.
$288

Richard D. Hatch & Associates

Rug, Hooked, 4 Canada Geese, Flying, Grenfell, Canada, c.1910, 27 x 38 In.
$510

Eldred's

Rug Quality

Oriental rugs are graded for quality by dealers. In most cases the quality is determined by the knot count over a measured distance on the width of a rug. A 90 line count for a Chinese rug means if 1 foot of the width is marked off there will be 90 knots. Pakistani rugs have quality measured by counting knots on 1 inch of the width and 1 inch of the length, so it might be 16/18.

Rug, Hooked, 4 Sailboats, Icebergs, Black & White Border, Grenfell, Early 1900s, 26 x 39 ¾ In.
$3,360

Eldred's

TIP

Be sure your rug is clean before you store it. It is best to have some light in the room to discourage moths and be sure there is no excess humidity or no extreme heat or cold. Don't use the garage or attic. Roll or fold it, and put the roll flat on the shelf, not standing up or leaning. Do not stack rugs on top of each other. It is best to open the rug bundle once a year and put it flat in natural light for a few days.

Rug, Hooked, Pink Roses, Leaves & Buds, Scalloped Border, 32 x 62 In.
$300

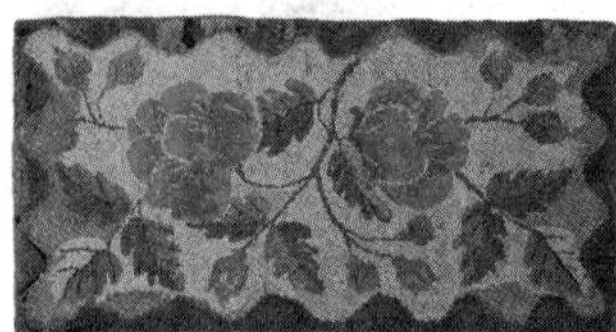

Bourgeault-Horan Antiquarians & Associates, LLC

Rug, Hooked, Welcome, Sculpted Leaf Border, Waldoboro, Stretcher, c.1875, 31 x 58 In.
$390

Garth's Auctioneers & Appraisers

Caucasian, Bright Red Field, Pale Yellow, Blue Stylized Element, 1980s, 3 Ft. 5 In. x 4 Ft. 6 In. 238
Hamadan, Red, Central Medallion, Navy Field, Red Guard Border, 4 Ft. 6 In. x 7 Ft. 144
Heriz, 4 Geometric Medallions, Floral, Salmon Field, Handmade, Runner, 2 Ft. 8 In. x 1 Ft. ... *illus* 288
Heriz, Central Medallion, Red Ground, Blue Border, White Spandrels, 8 Ft. x 11 Ft. 3 In. 2300
Heriz, Central Medallion, Red, Ivory Spandrels, Gold, Blue Brown Borders, 1950s, 7 Ft. x 10 Ft. 3 In. 138
Heriz, Flowers, Vines, Navy Field, Red Medallion, White, Blue Border, 10 Ft. 3 In. x 12 Ft. 9 In. 2829
Heriz, Red Ground, Triple Medallion, Flowers, 3 Ft. 9 In. x 5 Ft. 5 In. 500
Heriz, Rust & Blue Ground, Central Medallion, Serrated Spandrels, 10 Ft. x 13 Ft. 9 In. 3000
Hooked, 4 Canada Geese, Flying, Grenfell, Canada, c.1910, 27 x 38 In. *illus* 510
Hooked, 4 Sailboats, Icebergs, Black & White Border, Grenfell, Early 1900s, 26 x 39 ¾ In. *illus* 3360
Hooked, Dog Sled Team, Wool, Cotton, Grenfell, Newfoundland, 1900s, 42 x 32 In. 1800
Hooked, Horse & Man, Pictorial, Line Border, Mounted, c.1920, 18 x 34 In. 277
Hooked, Pink Roses, Leaves & Buds, Scalloped Border, 32 x 62 In. *illus* 300
Hooked, Red Central Star, Striated Ground, Mounted On Stretcher, c.1900, 32 x 43 In. 938
Hooked, Welcome, Sculpted Leaf Border, Waldoboro, Stretcher, c.1875, 31 x 58 In. *illus* 390
India, William Morris Style, Wool, Hand Woven, Burgundy, Yellow, 2000s, 12 x 9 Ft. *illus* 1280
Isfahan, Central Medallion, Cream, Blue, Red Ground, Vining Leaves, 9 Ft. 10 In. x 17 Ft. 7 In. *illus* 5100
Kazak, Geometric Medallion, Burgundy Field, Multiple Border, 1900s, 5 Ft. 4 In. x 8 Ft. 2 In. 270
Kazak, Geometric Medallions, Ivory, Red, Blue, Borders, Late 1900s, 4 Ft. 5 In. x 5 Ft. 9 In. *illus* 300
Kilim, Dark Red Field, Geometric Medallions, Blue Spandrels, 1910s, 5 Ft. 7 In. x 9 Ft. 3 In. 390
Kurdish, Central Stepped Medallions, Red, Geometric, Runner, Late 1900s, 11 Ft. x 4 Ft. 3 In. 600
Lillihan, Geometric, Flowers, Blue Border, Dark Blue Field, 5 x 7 Ft. 148
Mahal, Flowering Vine, Ivory Field, Multi-Border, Handmade, 9 x 12 Ft. *illus* 1725
Mexican, Geometric, Earth Tone, Checkerboard, 2-Sided, 1900s, 7 Ft. 2 In. x 6 Ft. 8 In. 61
Moghan, Cream, Blue Border, Flowers, Leaves, Geometric Patterns, 4 Ft. 10 In. x 10 Ft. 9 In. 3000
Oushak, Central Medallion, Geometric, Flowers, Turkey, 4 Ft. x 7 Ft. 2 In. 230
Persian, Blue Ground, Red Border, Flowers, 11 Ft. 11 In. x 20 Ft. 11 In. 9500
Persian, Blue Medallion, Honey Color Pendant, Vine, Orange Border, 4 Ft. x 5 Ft. 10 In. *illus* 225
Persian, Geometric Medallions, Red, Brown, Blue & Ivory, Late 1900s, 6 Ft. x 8 Ft. 6 In. *illus* 780
Serapi, Bright Red Field, Yellow, Blue, Pink, Ivory, Flowering Branch, 22 Ft. 9 In. x 2 Ft. 7 In. 840
Serapi, Red Ground, Central Medallion, Spandrels, Floral, 9 Ft. 3 In. x 14 Ft. 4000
Serapi, Red, Cream Ground, Central Medallion, Blue Border, Flowers, 10 Ft. 8 In. x 13 Ft. 6 In. 2100
Serapi, Repeating Geometric, Floral, Blue Field, Red Inner Border, 1900s, 4 Ft. 4 In. x 2 Ft. 10 In. 1875
Shag, Midcentury, Abstract, Geometric, Red Ground, 7 Ft. 9 In. x 5 Ft. 7 In. *illus* 246
Shirred, Central Flowers, Scroll Border, Mounted On Stretcher, 1800s, 2 Ft. 1 In. x 3 Ft. 9 In. 240
Sultanabad, Oriental, Cascading Columns, Verdigris Ground, Gold Borders, 9 Ft. 7 In. x 13 Ft. 9 In. 344
Tabriz, 8-Point Star, Red Center, Navy Border, Silk Inlay, Wool, Cotton, 9 Ft. 10 In. x 13 Ft. 4 In. 2700
Tabriz, Red Ground, Central Medallion, Stylized Leaves, 9 x 10 Ft. 2250
Tabriz, Silk, Wall Hanging, Flowering Vine, Ivory Field, Multi-Bordered, 3 Ft. 1 In. x 5 Ft. 2 In. 633
Talish, Blue Field, Yellow Spearpoint, Blossoms, Red Guard, Ivory Border, 3 Ft. 3 In. x 7 Ft. 3 In. 1320
Turkish, Geometric Shapes, Figures, Borders, Red, Tan, Black, Cream, 1800s, 5 Ft. 9 In. x 3 Ft. 8 In. *illus* 590
Turkish, Red Ground, Blue Border, Repeating Design, 8 Ft. 8 In. x 11 Ft. 2 In. 1600

RUMRILL POTTERY

RumRill

Rumrill Pottery was designed by George Rumrill of Little Rock, Arkansas. From 1933 to 1938, it was produced by the Red Wing Pottery of Red Wing, Minnesota. In January 1938, production was transferred to the Shawnee Pottery in Zanesville, Ohio. It was moved again in December of 1938 to Florence Pottery Company in Mt. Gilead, Ohio, where Rumrill ware continued to be manufactured until the pottery burned in 1941. It was then produced by Gonder Ceramic Arts in South Zanesville until early 1943.

Vase, Aqua Glaze, Raised Fruit & Leaves, Flared, Round Pedestal Base, 9 x 5 ¾ In. 135
Vase, Green Matte Glaze, Ring Handles, Molded Leaf Pattern Around Base, Red Wing, 7 In. 85
Vase, Oval Twist, White Matte Glaze, Blue Interior, Handles, Footed, No. 706, 4 x 8 x 4 In. 36

RUSKIN

Ruskin is a British art pottery of the twentieth century. The Ruskin Pottery was started by William Howson Taylor, and his name was used as the mark until about 1899. The factory, at West Smethwick, Birmingham, England,

Rug, India, William Morris Style, Wool, Hand Woven, Burgundy, Yellow, 2000s, 12 x 9 Ft.
$1,280

Rago Arts and Auction Center

Rug, Isfahan, Central Medallion, Cream, Blue, Red Ground, Vining Leaves, 9 Ft. 10 In. x 17 Ft. 7 In.
$5,100

Neal Auction Company

TIP
Do not store rugs with mothballs. They often affect the dyes.

Rug, Kazak, Geometric Medallions, Ivory, Red, Blue, Borders, Late 1900s, 4 Ft. 5 In. x 5 Ft. 9 In.
$300

Eldred's

Rug, Mahal, Flowering Vine, Ivory Field, Multi-Border, Handmade, 9 x 12 Ft.
$1,725

Richard D. Hatch & Associates

Rug, Persian, Blue Medallion, Honey Color Pendant, Vine, Orange Border, 4 Ft. x 5 Ft. 10 In.
$225

Eldred's

Rug, Persian, Geometric Medallions, Red, Brown, Blue & Ivory, Late 1900s, 6 Ft. x 8 Ft. 6 In.
$780

Eldred's

RUSKIN

Rug, Shag, Midcentury, Abstract, Geometric, Red Ground, 7 Ft. 9 In. x 5 Ft. 7 In.
$246

Clars Auction Gallery

Rug, Turkish, Geometric Shapes, Figures, Borders, Red, Tan, Black, Cream, 1800s, 5 Ft. 9 In. x 3 Ft. 8 In.
$590

Cottone Auctions

Sabino, Vase, Frieze, Archers & Hunting Scene, Opalescent, 16 ½ In.
$492

Stair Galleries

stopped making new pieces in 1933 but continued to glaze and sell the remaining wares until 1935. The art pottery is noted for its exceptional glazes. They also made ceramic "stones" with the famous glaze to be used in jewelry.

Bowl, Eggshell Luster, Pink Iridescent, Band Of Holly, Hemispherical, Footed, c.1911, 7 In. 270
Candlestick, Delphinium Blue Glaze, Impressed Mark, 6 ½ In., Pair 259
Ginger Jar, Lid, Delphinium Blue Luster Glaze, Impressed Marks, 1924, 3 ¾ In. 322
Vase, Lavender, High Fired Lustrous Glaze, Stamped And Dated 1919, 8 x 12 ½ In. 318
Vase, Shouldered, Oval, Crystalline Glaze Vase, Blue Over Yellow, c.1930, 4 ¾ In. 80
Vase, Yellow, Green Grapevine, Impressed Mark, Dated 1905, 6 ½ x 3 ¾ In. 585

RUSSEL WRIGHT

Russel Wright designed dinnerware in modern shapes for many companies. Iroquois China Company, Harker China Company, Sterling China Co., Steubenville Pottery, and Justin Tharaud and Sons made dishes marked *Russel Wright.* The Steubenville wares, first made in 1938, are the most common today. Wright was a designer of domestic and industrial wares, including furniture, aluminum, radios, interiors, and glassware. A new company, Bauer Pottery Company of Los Angeles, is making Russel Wright's American Modern dishes using molds made from original pieces. Pieces are marked *Russel Wright by Bauer Pottery California USA*. Russel Wright dinnerware and other original pieces by Wright are listed here. For more prices, go to kovels.com.

Russel Wright
1948–1950

Russel Wright
1948–1953

Russel Wright
1959–1960

American Modern, Casserole, Lid, Round, Handle, 8 In., 2 Qt. 56
American Modern, Frying Pan, Lid, Light Blue, Cookware 125
Iroquois Casual, Serving Dish, Divided, Avocado Green, 10 x 3 In. 40
Woodfield, Snack Plate & Cup, Raised Leaf Shape, Gray Glaze, 1940s 14

Sabino France

SABINO

Sabino glass was made in the 1920s and 1930s in Paris, France. Founded by Marius-Ernest Sabino (1878–1961), the firm was noted for Art Deco lamps, vases, figurines, and animals in clear, colored, and opalescent glass. Production stopped during World War II but resumed in the 1960s with the manufacture of nude figurines and small opalescent glass animals. Pieces made in recent years are a slightly different color and can be recognized. Only vintage pieces are listed here.

Lamp, Electric, Fish Shape, Opalescent, Bronze Base, Art Deco, Signed, 7 ½ In. 2583
Vase, Frieze, Archers & Hunting Scene, Opalescent, 16 ½ In. ...... *illus* 492

SALESMAN'S SAMPLE, *may be listed in the Advertising or Stove category. Some are considered toys and are listed in the Toy category.*

SALT AND PEPPER SHAKERS

Salt and pepper shakers in matched sets were first used in the nineteenth century. Collectors are primarily interested in figural examples made after World War I. Huggers are pairs of shakers that appear to embrace each other. Many salt and pepper shakers are listed in other categories and can be located through the index at the back of this book.

Amish Couple, Sitting In Rockers, Red, Black, Cast Metal, 1940s, 3 In. 20
Country Boy & Girl, Regal China, Old MacDonald Series 40
Couple, Chinese, Native Costume, Cork Stopper, Porcelain, 3 ½ In. 12
Elsie & Elmer, Borden Cows, Copyright, Porcelain, 4 In. 145
Feet, Red Toenails, Japan 15
Hourglass Shape, White, Gold Letters, Tupperware, 6 In. 45
Lemon, Yellow, Cork Stopper, Japan, 2 x 1 x 1 In. 28
Oval, Black On Black, Santa Clara Pueblo Pottery, c.1945, 2 In. 195
Tree Stumps, Brown, Ceramic, Cork Stopper, 1950s, 3 In. 30

SAMPLER

ABCDE

Samplers were made in America from the early 1700s. The best examples were made from 1790 to 1840 on homemade fabrics. Long, narrow samplers are usually older than square ones. Early samplers just had stitching or alphabets. The later examples had numerals, borders, and pictorial decorations. Those with mottoes are mid-Victorian. A revival of interest in the 1930s produced simpler samplers, using machine-made textiles, usually with mottoes.

Adam & Eve, Angels, Tulip Vine Border, Priscilla Hesell, Aged 18, 1859, 23 x 20 In. 207
Adam & Eve, Floral Border, Elizabeth Brown 1834, Wood Frame, Square, 17 In. 492
Adam & Eve, House, Fruit Basket, Elizabeth Corless, Silk On Linen, 1828, Frame, 29 x 30 In... 1000
Adam & Eve, Trees, Flowers, Sarah Hughes, Age 12, 1821, Frame, 22 x 21 In. 443
Adam & Eve, Verse, Flowers, Elizabeth Losthouse, 1854, Wood Frame, 17 ½ x 21 In. 615
Alphabet, 9 Lines, Vine Border, Mary Leonard, 1808, Frame, 18 ½ x 12 In. 431
Alphabet, Birth Record, Cross Stitch, Gertrude Kyser, 14th Day October, 1800, 18 x 21 In. 325
Alphabet, Family Register, Avis K. Marsh, 1826, Black Wood Frame, 18 x 18 ¾ In. 120
Alphabet, Family Register, Young Family, Floral Borders, Wood Frame, c.1826, 21 x 21 In. 2520
Alphabet, Flower Bouquet, Anne Campbell, 1792, Frame, 23 ¾ x 19 ¾ In. 254
Alphabet, Flowers, Bird, Scenic Reserves, 1849, Wood Frame, 24 x 26 In. 215
Alphabet, House, Birds, Peacocks, Trees, Flowers, A.M. Grigor, Linen, 1866, Frame, 27 x 23 In. . 73
Alphabet, House, Susan L. Hillboro, 1816, Gilt Molded Frame, 8 x 6 In. 106
Alphabet, House, Trees, Olive Engram, Chesterfield, 1823, Frame, 10 x 17 ¾ In. 400
Alphabet, Landscape, Animal Scenes, Cross, Floral Border, 1826, Frame, 15 ½ x 19 ½ In. 156
Alphabet, Numbers, 8-Line Verse, Wreath Like Border, Silk On Linen, 16 x 21 ¾ In. 819
Alphabet, Numbers, Cross-Stitch, Barbara Gibson Aged 8, Frame, 19 x 10 In. 118
Alphabet, Numbers, Family Record, Burdin Barstow, Linen, Green, Early 1800s, 17 x 18 ½ In. . 677
Alphabet, Numbers, Family Record, Emily L. Whiteman, 1840, Frame, 18 ¾ x 19 In. 2214
Alphabet, Numbers, Family Register, Brownbridge, 1836, Square, Frame, 13 In. 236
Alphabet, Numbers, Floral Field, House, Frame, c.1770-80, 18 ½ x 18 ¾ In. .... *illus* 1599
Alphabet, Numbers, House, Jane A. Pendleton, Silk On Linen, 1833, Later Frame, 14 x 16 In. .. 900
Alphabet, Numbers, Houses, Flowering Tree, Martha Ann Dearing, 1819, 17 x 21 In. 870
Alphabet, Numbers, Verse, Border, Ann Brook, 1778, Black Frame, 10 ½ x 8 In. 308
Alphabet, Numbers, Verse, Floral Sprig Border, Lydia M. Irons, Silk On Linen, 1832, 16 x 18 In. 720
Alphabet, Numbers, Verse, Trees, Basket, Border, Harriet Watt, 1826, Frame, 8 x 8 ¾ In. 240
Alphabet, Quaker Verse, Flowers, Birds, Martha Huver, 1818, Frame, 16 x 21 ¾ In. 236
Alphabet, Red, Cream Ground, Mary Anderson, 1790, Oak Frame, 8 ¾ x 7 In. 130
Alphabet, Silk On Linen, Man, Colonial Dress, Crown, God In Heart, 1778, 28 x 11 In. ...*illus* 180
Alphabet, Verse, Adam & Eve, Flowers, Animals, Vine Border, 15 x 15 In. 312
Alphabet, Verse, Flower, Crown, Martha Goulder, 1745, Molded Frame, 17 x 12 In. 369
Alphabet, Verse, Flowers, Fruit Trees, Leah Pughs, Silk On Linen, 1811, 18 ¾ x 16 ¾ In. 360
Alphabet, Verse, Flowers, Sawtooth Borders, Elizabeth Jewett, 1841, Frame, 24 x 24 In. 3120
Alphabet, Verse, House, Trees, Deer, Mary Sutton, Silk On Linen, 1823, Frame, 20 x 19 ½ In. . 1680
Alphabet, Verse, Rose Border, Mary G. Ashley, 1822, Frame, 19 x 14 ¾ In. 330
Alphabet, Wool, House & Gardens, Betsey D. Granger, 1827, Mahogany Frame, 18 ½ x 19 In... 293
Cross-Stich, Animals, Flowers, Birds, Letters, 1854, Frame, 34 ½ x 17 In. 180
Darning, Silk On Linen, 8 Fabric Weave Samples, 1802, 14 ¾ x 14 ¾ In. 480
Family Record, Birds, Squirrels, Flowers, Boulton Family, 1761-1833, Square, 21 In. 106
Family Record, King Family, 1824-72, Lancaster County, Penn., Cherry Frame, 24 x 19 In. 207
House, Strawberry Vines, Almira Sarers, March 7th 1828, Mahogany Frame, 10 x 11 In. 177

Sampler, Alphabet, Numbers, Floral Field, House, Frame, c.1770-80, 18 ½ x 18 ¾ In.
$1,599

Skinner, Inc.

Sampler, Alphabet, Silk On Linen, Man, Colonial Dress, Crown, God In Heart, 1778, 28 x 11 In.
$180

Garth's Auctioneers & Appraisers

Sampler, Verse, Flower Urns, Mary Branson, September 26th 1816, Silk On Linen, 18 x 15 In.
$276

Garth's Auctioneers & Appraisers

Samson, Urn, Hexagonal, Heraldic Ensign, Gilt Figural Finial, 1800s, 18 In., Pair
$660

Brunk Auctions

Samson, Vase, Beaker, Armorial, Hexagonal Base, Late 1800s, 9 ½ In., Pair
$344

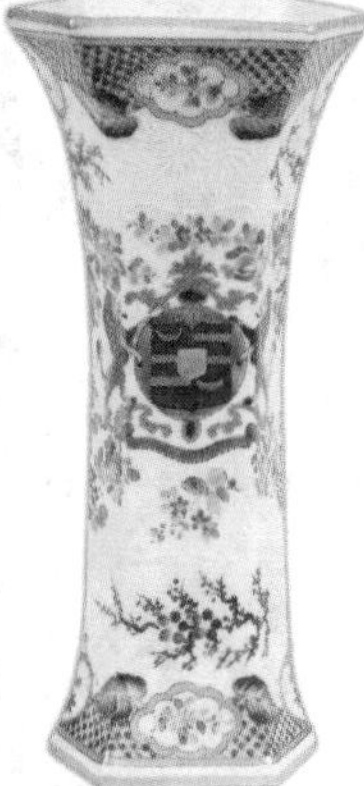

Freeman's Auctioneers & Appraisers

Sandwich Glass, Vase, Amethyst, Tulip, 8-Flute Rim, Octagonal Base, 1850s, 10 In.
$854

Pook & Pook

Mirror Image, Angels, Birds, Crowns, Flowerpots, Elizabeth Mileham, 1837, Square, 10 In..... 266
Tree Of Life, Serpent, Fruit Basket, Animals, Flower & Vine Border, c.1820, 16 x 16 In............. 580
Verse, Altar, Lions, Dogs, Birds, Trees, Vine Border, Ann Richardson, 1828, Frame, 23 x 19 In. 413
Verse, Anne Whitton Aged 11 Years, 1727, Silk On Linen, Frame, 18 x 10 ½ In. 168
Verse, Cats, Parrots, Flowers, Elizabeth Hemming, 1828, Frame, 21 x 17 In............................. 236
Verse, Floral Border, Flower Basket, Ann Louisa Pollard, Silk On Linen, 17 x 19 In.................. 420
Verse, Floral Border, Needlepoint, Charlotte Barnes, 8 Years, 1815, Frame, 12 ½ x 12 ¾ In. 308
Verse, Flower Urns, Mary Branson, September 26th 1816, Silk On Linen, 18 x 15 In. ....*illus* 276
Verse, Flowers, Birds, Trees, Butterfly, Silk On Linen, Gilt Frame, 17 ½ x 15 ½ In.................... 1680
Verse, Flowers, Blue Line Border, Mary A. Fairbairn, Silk On Linen, 1836, Frame, 17 ½ x 17 In.. 2074
Verse, Flowers, Leaves, Martha N. Hewson, Kensington, Silk On Linen, 18 ¾ x 23 In. 3904
Verse, House, Trees, Dog, Alternating Leaves, Flowers, 17 ½ x 16 In. 687
Verse, Lord Of The Lower World, Leaves, Butterflies, Adam & Eve, 20 ½ In. 420
Verse, Pious, Flower Border, Charlotte Amanda Slauson, Silk On Linen, 1838, 17 x 17 In......... 813
Verse, Shepherdess, Dog, Lambs, Trees, Vine Border, Hannah Horton, Aged 11, 1850, 17 In. 177

SAMSON

Samson and Company, a French firm specializing in the reproduction of collectible wares of many countries and periods, was founded in Paris in the early nineteenth century. Chelsea, Meissen, Famille Verte, and Chinese Export porcelain are some of the wares that have been reproduced by the company. The firm used fake marks similar to the real ones on the reproductions. It closed in 1969.

Urn, Hexagonal, Heraldic Ensign, Gilt Figural Finial, 1800s, 18 In., Pair ....*illus* 660
Urn, Lid, 2 Handles, Footed, Shield, Lion, Unicorn, Swags, 7 x 4 ½ x 12 In., Pair...................... 187
Vase, Beaker, Armorial, Hexagonal Base, Late 1800s, 9 ½ In., Pair ....*illus* 344

SANDWICH GLASS

Sandwich glass is any of the myriad types of glass made by the Boston & Sandwich Glass Company of Sandwich, Massachusetts, between 1825 and 1888. It is often very difficult to be sure whether a piece was really made at the Sandwich factory because so many types were made there and similar pieces were made at other glass factories. Additional pieces may be listed under Pressed Glass and in other related categories.

Compote, Clear, Flaring Foot, Pressed Lacy, Hairpin, 1830-40, 5 ⅜ x 10 x 5 In......................... 468
Decanter, Deep Olive, Green, Flared Mouth, Plain Base, Rough Pontil Mark, 1825-35, 8 In. 1872
Dish, Leaf Like Quatrefoil, 4-Petal Blossom, Diamonds, Scallop & Point Rim, c.1830, 7 x 7 In. 761
Inkwell, Opalescent Milk Glass, Painted Flowers, 10 Vertical Ribs, 2 ½ In................................ 360
Lamp, Banquet Style, White Cased Cutback, Grapevine, 3-Footed, Gold Trim, 24 In. 633
Lamp, Medium Teal, 7-Panel Font, Pewter Collar, Whale Oil Burner, c.1850, 3 x 2 ½ In. 3393
Salt, Violet Blue, Basket Of Flowers, Pressed Open, 4-Footed, 1830-40, 2 x 1 ¾ x 3 In. 152
Vase, Amethyst, 6-Petal Rim, Hexagonal Knop, Flared Foot, 1840-60, 11 ½ x 4 x 5 In.............. 1872
Vase, Amethyst, Tulip, 8-Flute Rim, Octagonal Base, 1850s, 10 In. ....*illus* 854

SARREGUEMINES

Sarreguemines is the name of a French town that is used as part of a china mark for Utzschneider and Company, a porcelain factory that made ceramics in Sarreguemines, Lorraine, France, from about 1775. Transfer-printed wares and majolica were made in the nineteenth century. The nineteenth-century pieces, most often found today, usually have colorful transfer-printed decorations showing peasants in local costumes.

Pitcher, Cobalt Blue, Flowers, Leaves, Beaded Rim, 10 In.. 137
Plaque, Painted, Woodcutters, After Menard, Round, Frame, 14 In. Diam................................ 48
Tureen, Duck, Majolica, Basket Weave, Multicolor, 8 ½ x 11 In. 77
Vase, Rectangular Waisted Shape, Carnations, Geometric Borders, Majolica, c.1890 94

SASCHA BRASTOFF

Sascha Brastoff made decorative accessories, ceramics, enamels on copper, and plastics of his own design. He headed a factory, Sascha Brastoff of California, Inc., in West Los Angeles, from 1953 until about 1973. He died in 1993. Pieces signed with the signature *Sascha Brastoff* were his work and are the most expensive. Other pieces marked *Sascha B.* or with a stamped mark were made by others in his company. Pieces made by Matt Adams after he left the factory are listed here with his name.

Ashtray, Alaska Hut, White Ground, 3-Footed, 5 ¾ x 3 In. 39
Ashtray, Green, Copper, Enamel, Flowers, Signed, 1960s, 8 In. 29
Sculpture, Cat Head, Base, Mosaic, Ceramic, Gold, c.1960, 5 x 5 x 8 In. 899

SATIN GLASS

Satin glass is a late-nineteenth-century art glass. It has a dull finish that is caused by hydrofluoric acid vapor treatment. Satin glass was made in many colors and sometimes has applied decorations. Satin glass is also listed by factory name, such as Webb, or in the Mother-of-Pearl category in this book.

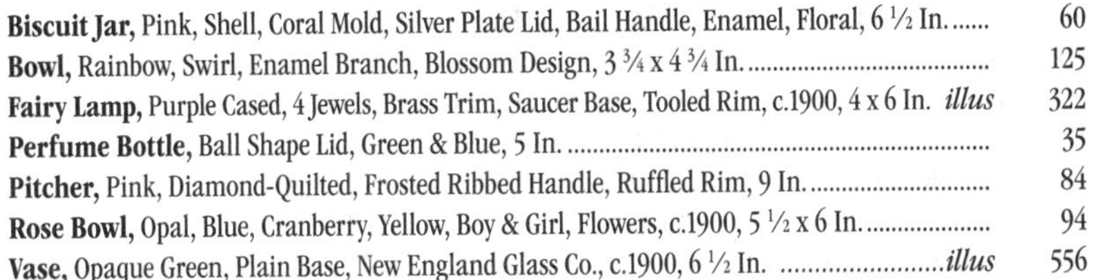

Biscuit Jar, Pink, Shell, Coral Mold, Silver Plate Lid, Bail Handle, Enamel, Floral, 6 ½ In. 60
Bowl, Rainbow, Swirl, Enamel Branch, Blossom Design, 3 ¾ x 4 ¾ In. 125
Fairy Lamp, Purple Cased, 4 Jewels, Brass Trim, Saucer Base, Tooled Rim, c.1900, 4 x 6 In. *illus* 322
Perfume Bottle, Ball Shape Lid, Green & Blue, 5 In. 35
Pitcher, Pink, Diamond-Quilted, Frosted Ribbed Handle, Ruffled Rim, 9 In. 84
Rose Bowl, Opal, Blue, Cranberry, Yellow, Boy & Girl, Flowers, c.1900, 5 ½ x 6 In. 94
Vase, Opaque Green, Plain Base, New England Glass Co., c.1900, 6 ½ In. ....*illus* 556

SATSUMA

Satsuma is a Japanese pottery with a distinctive creamy beige crackled glaze. Most of the pieces were decorated with blue, red, green, orange, or gold. Almost all Satsuma found today was made after 1860, especially during the Meiji Period, 1868–1912. During World War I, Americans could not buy undecorated European porcelains. Women who liked to make hand-painted porcelains at home began to decorate white undecorated Satsuma. These pieces are known today as "American Satsuma."

Bottle, Dragons, Trailing Ribbons, Flames, Flower Sprays, Metallic Ground, 25 x 13 In. 3250
Bowl, Imperial Ship At Sea, Gold Trim, Kinkozan, 2 ½ x 5 ¾ In. ....*illus* 1320
Bowl, Landscape, Figure On Porch, Mountain Sunset, 2 ¾ x 7 ½ In. ....*illus* 138
Charger, Flower, Bamboo, Chrysanthemum Style, c.1900, 2 x 14 ⅝ In. 1968
Dish, Kozan, Stemmed, Lobed, Wavy Rim, Footed, c.1800, 3 ½ x 9 ⅝ In. 62
Figure, Kwannon, Standing, Robe & Headdress, Multicolor, Enamel, 1800s, 20 x 6 x 5 In. 351
Incense Burner, Lid, Figural, Buddha, Dragon Handles, 1800s, 8 ½ x 8 ½ x 6 In. ....*illus* 375
Jar, Lid, Cherry Blossom, Trees, Mountainous Ground, Knop Finial, 5 ½ In. 240
Jar, Pierced Metal Lid, Medallions With Different Designs, 7 ¼ In. ....*illus* 540
Jardiniere, Ormolu Mounts, Dragon Handles, 1900s, 4 ¾ x 16 ½ In. ....*illus* 201
Plate, General & 4 Attendants, Pine Tree At Shore, 9 ½ In. ....*illus* 250
Plate, Immortals, Gilt, Hand Painted, c.1800, 12 x 2 In. ....*illus* 173
Teapot, Lid, Dragon Shape, Tail Handle, Head Spout, 8 x 8 In. 236
Urn, Tapered Lid, Flowers, Lobed, Stepped Foot, Kinkozan, Kyoto, 3 ½ In., Pair ....*illus* 375
Vase, 6 Panels, Blossoming Trees, Gold Trim, Pinched Neck, Flared Rim, 9 ½ In. ....*illus* 688
Vase, Chrysanthemums, Orange, Green, Gilt, High Shoulder, Short Neck, 8 ½ In. 160
Vase, Floral Medallions, Geometrics, Raised Enamels, Gilt Accents, 1920s, 14 x 11 In. ....*illus* 540
Vase, Landscape, Mt. Fuji, Stylized Trees, Clouds, Gold Trim, 7 In. ....*illus* 594
Vase, Long Stick Neck, Elongated Oval Body, Karako, Lord, Woman, Children, 22 ¾ In. ..*illus* 308
Vase, Phoenix, Brocade Bands, Bats, Flowers, Flared Rim, Japan, c.1900, 9 x 10 In. 225
Vase, Scholars, Deities, Dragons, Cranes, Mums, Signed, Ryokuzan, 1800s, 4 ¾ x 5 In. ...*illus* 450
Vase, Trees & Flowers, Gosu Blue Accents, Swollen Form, Petal Rim, 9 In. ....*illus* 420

Satin Glass, Fairy Lamp, Purple Cased, 4 Jewels, Brass Trim, Saucer Base, Tooled Rim, c.1900, 4 x 6 In.
$322

Jeffrey S. Evans & Associates

Satin Glass, Vase, Opaque Green, Plain Base, New England Glass Co., c.1900, 6 ½ In.
$556

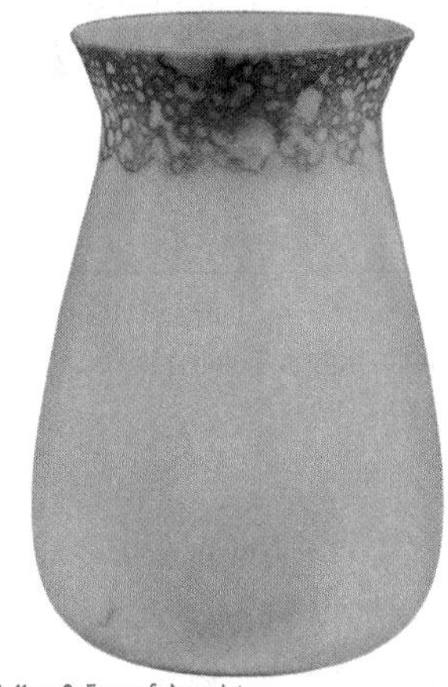

Jeffrey S. Evans & Associates

Satsuma, Bowl, Imperial Ship At Sea, Gold Trim, Kinkozan, 2 ½ x 5 ¾ In.
$1,320

Garth's Auctioneers & Appraisers

TIP

Dishes that can be used in a microwave or conventional oven can be used in a convection oven.

SATSUMA

Satsuma, Bowl, Landscape, Figure On Porch, Mountain Sunset, 2 ¾ x 7 ½ In.
$138

Garth's Auctioneers & Appraisers

TIP
Either Coca-Cola or Tang can be used to remove stains from porcelain.

Satsuma, Incense Burner, Lid, Figural, Buddha, Dragon Handles, 1800s, 8 ½ x 8 ½ x 6 In.
$375

Crescent City Auction Gallery

Satsuma, Jar, Pierced Metal Lid, Medallions With Different Designs, 7 ¼ In.
$540

Garth's Auctioneers & Appraisers

Vase, Urn Shape, Demon Mask Handles, Feggan, Tiger, Deity, Goat, Late 1900s, 28 x 18 In. *illus* 1476
Vase, Warrior, Garden Figure, Butterfly Rim, Signed At Base, 9 ½ In. 130

SATURDAY EVENING GIRLS, *see Paul Revere Pottery category.*

SCALES

Scales have been made to weigh everything from babies to gold. Collectors search for all types. Most popular are small gold dust scales, special grocery scales, and tall figural scales for people to use to check their weight.

Analytical, Chainomatic, Mahogany Case, Drawer, Christian Becker, 19 x 17 x 9 In. 212
Balance, Glass, Brass & Aluminum, Metal Case, Eimer & Amend, c.1900, 19 x 18 x 9 In. *illus* 148
Balance, Henry Troemner, Brass, Arm Marked, 1800s, 30 x 32 In. 608
Candy, Angldile, Springless, Automatic, Headlamp Shape, Green, c.1920, 16 x 11 In. 1170
Candy, Stimpson Computing Co., Silvertone Scoop Pan, Fan Shape Measure, Gilt, 19 In. 275
Hanging, Enterprise, Fish, 30 Lb. Capacity, Pan, Number Markers, c.1915, 25 x 13 In. 82
Postal, Brass & Wood, Balance Type, Set Of Weights, England, 4 ½ x 9 ½ In. 150
Weighing, Advertising Scales Co., Royal Crown Cola, 1 Cent, Bottle, 12 x 22 x 45 In. 9000
Weighing, American Scale Mfg. Co., Character Readings, Fortune, Weight, 1 Cent, c.1950, 54 In. 480
Weighing, Fairbanks, Cast Iron, Squared Wood Post, Black Lacquer, Sliding Measure, 58 In. 12469
Weighing, National Automatic, 1 Cent, Cast Iron, Lollipop, Porcelain Dial, 69 x 17 x 29 In. 1020
Weighing, National Store & Specialty Co., Lancaster, Pa., Red, Metal Pan, 15 x 20 In. 544
Weighing, Pan, Walnut Case, Brass, Marble, Spool Turnings, 1800s, 9 x 2 ½ In. *illus* 108
Weighing, Toledo, Glossy Green, Gold Trim, Brass Pan, 15 x 17 In. 512
Weighing, Toledo, Honest Weight, No Springs, Red, Gold Trim, Metal Pan, 15 x 17 In. 480
Weighing, Watling, Your Weight & Horoscope, Porcelain, Cast Iron Base, 61 x 18 x 23 In. 1020

SCHAFER & VATER

Schafer & Vater, makers of small ceramic items, are best known for their amusing figurals. The factory was located in Volkstedt-Rudolstadt, Germany, from 1890 to 1962. Some pieces are marked with the crown and *R* mark, but many are unmarked.

Dresser Box, Pink Jasperware, Fairy, Cherub, Holding Birds, Flowers On Side, 4 In. 81
Pitcher, Chinese Man Holding Goose, Man's Braid Forms Handle, 6 In. 175
Tobacco Jar, Lid, Devil's Face, Figural, 4 ½ In. 875

SCHEIER POTTERY

Scheier pottery was made by Edwin Scheier (1910–2008) and his wife, Mary (1908–2007). They met while they both worked for the WPA, and married in 1937. In 1939, they established their studio, Hillcrock Pottery, in Glade Spring, Virginia. Mary made the pottery and Edwin decorated it. From 1940 to 1968, Edwin taught at the University of New Hampshire and Mary was artist-in-residence. They moved to Oaxaca, Mexico, in 1968 to study the arts and crafts of the Zapotec Indians. When the Scheiers moved to Green Valley, Arizona, in 1978, Ed returned to pottery, making some of his biggest and best-known pieces.

Bowl, Brown, Glazed, Repeating Figural Motif, c.1960, 8 x 5 In. 625
Dish, Earthenware, Blue, Glazed, Round, Faces, 1960s, 9 $^{3}/_{16}$ x 1 In. 625
Vase, Flared Lip, Short Neck, Bulbous, Light Brown, Triangles, 4 ½ x 6 ½ In. 615
Vase, Stoneware, Brown, Stylized Figures, Sgraffito, c.1950, 15 x 5 ½ In. 2062

SCHNEIDER GLASSWORKS

Schneider Glassworks was founded in 1917 at Epinay-sur-Seine, France, by Charles and Ernest Schneider. Art glass was made between 1918 and 1933. The company went bankrupt in 1939. Charles Schneider and his sons opened a new

Satsuma, Jardiniere, Ormolu Mounts, Dragon Handles, 1900s, 4 ¾ x 16 ½ In.
$201

Blackwell Auctions

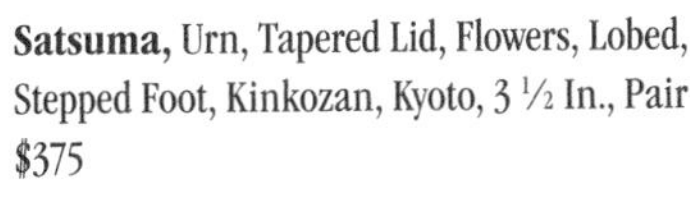

Satsuma, Urn, Tapered Lid, Flowers, Lobed, Stepped Foot, Kinkozan, Kyoto, 3 ½ In., Pair
$375

Garth's Auctioneers & Appraisers

Satsuma, Vase, Floral Medallions, Geometrics, Raised Enamels, Gilt Accents, 1920s, 14 x 11 In.
$540

Ripley Auctions

Satsuma, Plate, General & 4 Attendants, Pine Tree At Shore, 9 ½ In.
$250

Eldred's

Satsuma, Vase, 6 Panels, Blossoming Trees, Gold Trim, Pinched Neck, Flared Rim, 9 ½ In.
$688

Garth's Auctioneers & Appraisers

Satsuma, Vase, Landscape, Mt. Fuji, Stylized Trees, Clouds, Gold Trim, 7 In.
$594

Garth's Auctioneers & Appraisers

Satsuma, Plate, Immortals, Gilt, Hand Painted, c.1800, 12 x 2 In.
$173

Blackwell Auctions

Satsuma, Vase, Long Stick Neck, Elongated Oval Body, Karako, Lord, Woman, Children, 22 ¾ In.
$308

Clars Auction Gallery

Satsuma, Vase, Scholars, Deities, Dragons, Cranes, Mums, Signed, Ryokuzan, 1800s, 4 ¾ x 5 In.
$450

Alderfer Auction Company

Satsuma, Vase, Trees & Flowers, Gosu Blue Accents, Swollen Form, Petal Rim, 9 In.
$420

Garth's Auctioneers & Appraisers

Satsuma, Vase, Urn Shape, Demon Mask Handles, Feggan, Tiger, Deity, Goat, Late 1900s, 28 x 18 In.
$1,476

Locati Auctions

Scale, Balance, Glass, Brass & Aluminum, Metal Case, Eimer & Amend, c.1900, 19 x 18 x 9 In.
$148

Leland Little Auctions

Scale, Weighing, Pan, Walnut Case, Brass, Marble, Spool Turnings, 1800s, 9 x 2 ½ In.
$108

Eldred's

TIP
Store drinking glasses and vases right side up to protect the rims.

Schneider, Ewer, Mottled Blue, Clear Glass, Bulbous Body, Applied Handle, Signed, 14 ½ x 9 ½ In.
$660

Morphy Auctions

Schneider, Vase, Air Trap, Cranberry, Opal Splatter, Signed, 1950s, 6 ⅝ x 4 ½ x 3 ⅝ In.
$263

Jeffrey S. Evans & Associates

Schneider, Vase, Urn Shape, Mottled Cranberry, 2 Loop Handles, Dark Lavender Foot, c.1930, 12 In.
$584

Skinner, Inc.

Scientific Instrument, Chronometer, Rich Hornby, Liverpool, 2-Day, Mahogany Case, Brass, 1830s, 7 x 6 x 6 In.
$1,695

Soulis Auctions

glasswork in 1949. Art glass was made until 1981, when the company closed. See also the Le Verre Francais category.

Ewer, Mottled Blue, Clear Glass, Bulbous Body, Applied Handle, Signed, 14 ½ x 9 ½ In. ..*illus* 660
Ewer, Red Round Foot, Slender Body, Blue Bulbous Top, Applied Handle, 17 x 6 x 4 ½ In. 510
Pitcher, Mottled Glass, Blue, Orange, Yellow, Applied Black Handle, 14 In. 780
Vase, Air Trap, Cranberry, Opal Splatter, Signed, 1950s, 6 ⅝ x 4 ½ x 3 ⅝ In. ....*illus* 263
Vase, Pinched Neck, Amber, Red, Orange, Yellow, Mottled, 1925, 15 In. 910
Vase, Urn Shape, Mottled Cranberry, 2 Loop Handles, Dark Lavender Foot, c.1930, 12 In. *illus* 584

SCIENTIFIC INSTRUMENTS

Scientific instruments of all kinds are included in this category. Other categories such as Barometer, Binoculars, Dental, Medical, Nautical, and Thermometer may also price scientific apparatus.

Barograph, Drum, Brass, Walnut Case, Beveled Glass, Drawer, Lennie, Edinburgh, 8 x 14 x 9 In... 363
Book Press, Cast Iron, Black, Gold Trim, Monogram, c.1890, 12 x 10 In. 8186
Chronometer, Michael Rupp & Co., 2-Day, Roman Numerals, 3-Tier Rosewood Box, c.1900, 7 In.. 1968
Chronometer, Rich Hornby, Liverpool, 2-Day, Mahogany Case, Brass, 1830s, 7 x 6 x 6 In. .*illus* 1695
Chronometer, Salem, Brass, Mahogany Hinged Box, Quartz Movement, 4 x 6 x 6 In. 124
Circumferentor, O. Hanks, Surveyor's Compass, Engraved Brass Dial, c.1840, 5 ½ x 9 In. 1599
Compass, Surveyor's, Julius Hanks, Engraved Silver Dial, Vernier, 1808-25, 6 ½ x 15 In. 2706
Compass, Surveyor's, Star, Sun Rays, Snake, c.1788, 13 In. 2820
Gauge, Koshin-Denki-Kogyo Co. Ltd., Wind Speed, Painted Metal, Wood Handle, Japan, 13 In. 74
Hourglass, Wood Frame, 4 Spindles, Glass Bulbs, Sand, Square Base, 9 In. ....*illus* 148
Lathe, Watchmaker, Rail, Head & Tail Stock, Hand Crank Pulley, Mounted, Later Board, 6 In. *illus* 461
Level, Surveying, Brosset, Brass, Telescope, Tripod, France, Case, 1860, 10 In. 5126
Leveling Rod, Baker, Wood, Brass, Graduated Marks, London, c.1860, 4 Meters 84
Magnifier, Ralph Lauren, Clear Glass, Brass, Adjustable, Marked, 15 x 5 x 4 In. ....*illus* 125
Magnifying Glass, Barley Twist Brass Handle, Whale Ivory Clenched Fist Mount, 1800s, 13 In. 138
Magnifying Glass, Carved, Wood, Green Handle, 2 Parrots, 21 ½ In. 118
Microscope, Bausch & Lomb, Brass, Mirror, Rochester N.Y., 14 ½ x 4 x 8 In., 2 Piece 212
Microscope, Culpeper Type, Monocular, Brass, Mahogany, Ivory Discs, London, c.1780, 26 In. *illus* 1138
Microscope, Leitz, Brass, Black Lacquer, 4 Eyepieces, Case, 1890, 12 In. 1246
Microscope, Verick, Brass, 2 Eyepieces, Japanned Iron Base, Paris, Case, 1880........ 1246
Motor, Electromagnetic, For Rotation Of Geissler Tubes, c.1870, 8 ¾ In. 1175
Orrery, Trippensee Planetarium, Black, White, Brass, Wood, 13 ¾ x 20 x 7 ½ In. ....*illus* 847
Orrery, Trippensee Planetarium, Laing's, Mahogany, Brass Sun, Earth, 1897, 13 x 17 x 7 In. .. 2691
Sand Glass, Carved Oak, 6-Minute, Hexagonal Ends, Barley Twist Spindles, 1800s, 9 ½ In. . *illus* 615
Spyglass, Single Draw, Engraved, Sailcloth Wrap, Sailor's Knot, 1800s, 37 In. 192
Telescope, Astronomical, Brass, 3 Draw, Tripod & Case, 1800s, 6 x 59 x 10 In. 878
Telescope, Brass, 3 Draw, Mahogany, Leather, Tripod Stand, 27 In. 1016
Telescope, Dollond, 3 Draw, Brass & Wood, Late 1800s, 22 In. ....*illus* 144
Telescope, Mahogany, Brass Mounted, Tripod Stand, Walnut Case, England, 1800s, 40 x 9 x 5 In.. 900
Telescope, Parkinson & Frodsham, Brass, Leather, Extends, England, 1860, 16 In. 725
Telescope, Silver Plate, Folding, Adjustable Height Mahogany Stand, 1900s, 21 x 16 x 9 In....... 189
Theodolite, Brunner, Brass, 4 Magnifiers, 2 Telescopes, France, c.1880, 14 In. 506
Transit, Surveyor's, Kolesch & Co., Brass, Bubble Levels, 11 x 8 ½ x 6 In. ....*illus* 182
Transit, Surveyor's, Phelps & Gurley, Silver Dial, Spirit Level, Scope, c.1850, 6 x 9 In. 2952
Transit, Surveyor's, William J Young, Brass, Compass, Scope, c.1850-70, 6 x 9 ¾ In. ....*illus* 885
Vacuum Tube, Crookes, Phosphorescent, Wood, Shaped Glass, Butterfly, c.1910, 14 In. 8313
Waywiser, Joseph Fenn, Wood, Measures Yards, Pole, Mile, Furlong, London, 54 In. 575

SCRIMSHAW

Scrimshaw is bone or ivory or whale's teeth carved by sailors and others for entertainment during the sailing-ship days. Some scrimshaw was carved as early as 1800. There are modern scrimshanders making pieces today on bone, ivory, or plastic. Other pieces may be found in the Ivory and Nautical

Scientific Instrument, Hourglass, Wood Frame, 4 Spindles, Glass Bulbs, Sand, Square Base, 9 In.
$148

Richard Opfer Auctioneering, Inc.

Scientific Instrument, Lathe, Watchmaker, Rail, Head & Tail Stock, Hand Crank Pulley, Mounted, Later Board, 6 In.
$461

Skinner, Inc.

TIP

If you plan to go away on a long trip, put a vase filled with artificial flowers near a lamp where they can be seen from the street. Live flowers last only a few days, so if you can fool a burglar into thinking your flowers are fresh, he will probably pass by and go to a house that appears unoccupied.

S

Scientific Instrument, Magnifier, Ralph Lauren, Clear Glass, Brass, Adjustable, Marked, 15 x 5 x 4 In.
$125

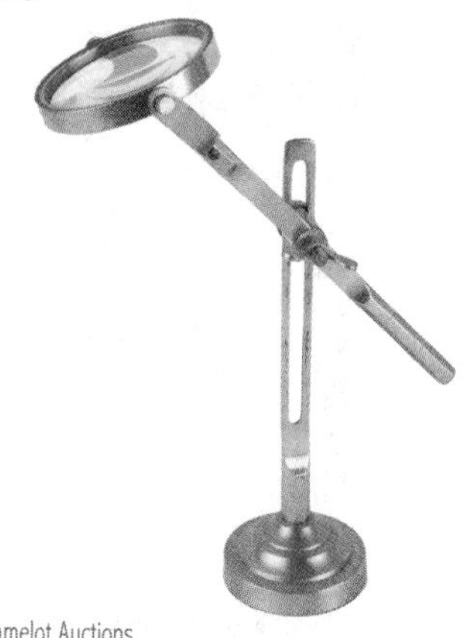

Kamelot Auctions

Scientific Instrument, Microscope, Culpeper Type, Monocular, Brass, Mahogany, Ivory Discs, London, c.1780, 26 In.
$1,138

Freeman's Auctioneers & Appraisers

Scientific Instrument, Sand Glass, Carved Oak, 6-Minute, Hexagonal Ends, Barley Twist Spindles, 1800s, 9 ½ In.
$615

Skinner, Inc.

Scientific Instrument, Telescope, Dollond, 3 Draw, Brass & Wood, Late 1800s, 22 In.
$144

Eldred's

Scientific Instrument, Transit, Surveyor's, Kolesch & Co., Brass, Bubble Levels, 11 x 8 ½ x 6 In.
$182

Fontaine's Auction Gallery

Scientific Instrument, Transit, Surveyor's, William J Young, Brass, Compass, Scope, c.1850-70, 6 x 9 ¾ In.
$885

Bunch Auctions

Scientific Instrument, Orrery, Trippensee Planetarium, Black, White, Brass, Wood, 13 ¾ x 20 x 7 ½ In.
$847

Fontaine's Auction Gallery

Scrimshaw, Bodkin, Whale Ivory, Tapered Shaft, Pearling, 1800s, 2 ¾ In.
$132

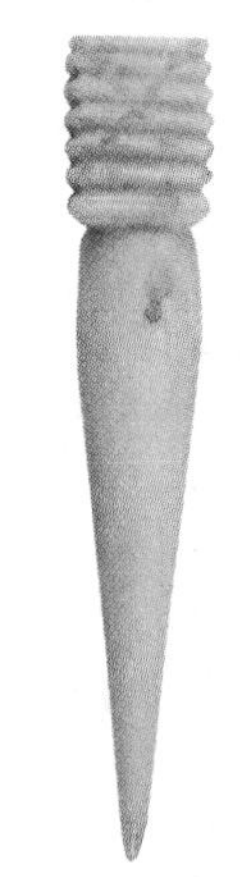

Eldred's

categories. Collectors should be aware of the recent laws limiting the buying and selling of scrimshaw and elephant ivory.

Bodkin, Whale Ivory, Crosshatch, Stepped Carving, Pierced, Tapered Blade, 1850s, 4 ½ In. 100
Bodkin, Whale Ivory, Tapered Shaft, Pearling, 1800s, 2 ¾ In. *illus* 132
Busk, Bone, Heart, Pinwheel, Initials, 1700s, 12 In. 118
Busk, Whalebone, Couple, Heart, Floral Motifs, 1850s, 14 x 1 ⅝ In. 2952
Busk, Whalebone, Rounded End, Carved, Tree, Heart, Bird, H.M.L., 1800s, 12 ½ In. 431
Cribbage Board, Walrus Tusk, Engraved, Eskimo, 1900s, 15 ¾ In. 1320
Dipper, Whale's Tooth, Mounted, Coconut, Mahogany Handle, Carved, 1800s, 16 In. 209
Ditty Box, Whalebone, Mahogany Lid, Vine Swags, Flowers, Fruit, c.1850, 4 x 9 In. *illus* 12000
Footstool, Sperm Whale Vertebrae, White & Brown, 11 ½ x 15 x 17 In. 644
Knitting Needle, Whalebone, Carved Ring, Heart, Faceted Terminal, Pique Inlay, 1800s, 12 In. 625
Knitting Needle, Whalebone, Carved Top, 1800s, 12 ½ In., Pair 148
Pie Crimper, Walrus Ivory, 2 Wheels, Teardrop Hardwood Handle, Geometric Inlay, 7 ½ In. *illus* 375
Pie Crimper, Whalebone, Fluted Wheel, Turned Handle, 1800s, 6 ½ In. 220
Plaque, Baleen, Sailing Ship, Basket, Urn, Compass Rose, Betsey Turner, 1800s, 4 x 7 ½ In. 1230
Pointer, Whalebone, Tuned Handle, Mother-Of-Pearl Top, 1800s, 36 In. 132
Rolling Pin, Whale Ivory Handles & Mounts, Walnut Roller, 1800s, 16 ½ In. *illus* 570
Sheath, Iron, Whaling, Canvas Lid, Wood, 1800s, 10 ½ In. 132
Toothpick Holder, Carved Whalebone, Nude, Pivoting Dagger Shape Blade, Inlay, 1800s, 4 In. 938
Walrus Tusk, 7 Mermaids, Rocks, Seaside, Clouds, M. Cohen, 11 x 3 In. 1080
Walrus Tusk, Man On Sledge, Caribou, Polar Bear & Seal, Marked, Inuit, 1962 819
Walrus Tusk, Multiple Images, Sled Dog, Engraved Nome, Alaska, 1901, 15 In. *illus* 1000
Walrus Tusk, Sailing Ships In Harbor, Snowy Mountain, C. Lehwalder, 1900s, 14 ¾ In. *illus* 2625
Whale's Tooth, British Ship, Attacking, Napoleonic Era, 6 In. 702
Whale's Tooth, Carved, Ship, Depicts, King George III, 1759, 5 ¾ In. 124
Whale's Tooth, Flag Of Our Union, Poseidon, Apollo, 2 Trees, Multicolor, 1800s, 4 In. 1719
Whale's Tooth, Megalodon, Broad Crown, Robust Root, Fossil, 5 x 4 In. *illus* 826
Whale's Tooth, Portrait, Sailing Ship, Ena Brown, 1861, 4 In. 410
Whale's Tooth, Sailor, United States Flag Waving To Ships, Shield, Cannon, 1800s, 5 In. 1046
Whale's Tooth, Scene Of Young Girl, Seated On Boulder, Floral Wreath, 1800s, 6 In. 384
Whale's Tooth, Town Harbor Scene, Sailboats, Paddle Boat, Buildings, c.1815, 6 In. 400

SEG, *see Paul Revere Pottery category.*

SEVRES

Sevres porcelain has been made in Sevres, France, since 1769. Many copies of the famous ware have been made. The name originally referred to the works of the Royal Porcelain factory. The name now includes any of the wares made in the town of Sevres, France. The entwined lines with a center letter used as the mark is one of the most forged marks in antiques. Be very careful to identify Sevres by quality, not just by mark.

Box, Center Reserve, Standing Woman, Gilt Rose Border, c.1900, 2 x 4 ¾ In. 700
Box, Turtle Shape, Hinged Top, Bronze, Cobalt Blue Ground, 1757, 3 ½ x 7 ¾ In. 847
Box, Woman & Child, Landscape, Gilt, Blue Ground, Flowers, 2 ⅜ In. *illus* 140
Inkwell, Lid, Metal Boat Shape, Gilt, Flower, Green, 1900s, 4 x 3 x 6 In. 118
Inkwell, Underplate, Cherub Shape Handles, Painted Reserve, Roses, Daisies, Leaves, 9 x 8 In. 540
Jardiniere, Louis XVI Style, Frolicking Putti, Gilt Ram's Heads, Swags, c.1900, 17 x 18 In. 3600
Lamp, Cobalt Blue, 18th Century Style Figures, Gold Trim, Brass Mounts, 1910s, 35 In., Pair 180
Ornament, Egg Shape, Painted, Gilt, Enamel, Metal Fittings, c.1910, 4 In. 450
Plate, 2 Cherubs, Turquoise Blue Band, Vine Edging, Gilt Rim, c.1840, 9 In., 10 Piece 351
Tureen, Stand, Scattered Loose Bouquet, White Ground, c.1777, 10 ¾ x 12 x 9 ½ In., Pair 2500
Urn, Cobalt Blue, Putti & Flower Scenes, Bacchus Bronze Handles, 11 x 6 ½ In., Pair *illus* 938
Urn, Cream, Winged Putti, Allegorical, Head Handles, Onyx Base, 1800s, 23 x 12 x 8 In. *illus* 1003
Urn, Lid, Bronze Satyr Dore Mount, Cobalt Blue Ground, Flowers, 25 x 13 x 10 In. 2006
Urn, Lid, Cobalt Blue, Courting Scene, Enamel, Gilt Ormolu Trim, c.1850, 25 x 7 ½ In., Pair *illus* 850

TIP
A piece of ribbon can be "pressed" by pulling it across a warm light bulb.

Scrimshaw, Ditty Box, Whalebone, Mahogany Lid, Vine Swags, Flowers, Fruit, c.1850, 4 x 9 In.
$12,000

Eldred's

TIP
When looking at scrimshaw, check the large hole in the tooth. Reproductions are brown, dyed to look old. Real teeth have clean root cavities.

Scrimshaw, Pie Crimper, Walrus Ivory, 2 Wheels, Teardrop Hardwood Handle, Geometric Inlay, 7 ½ In.
$375

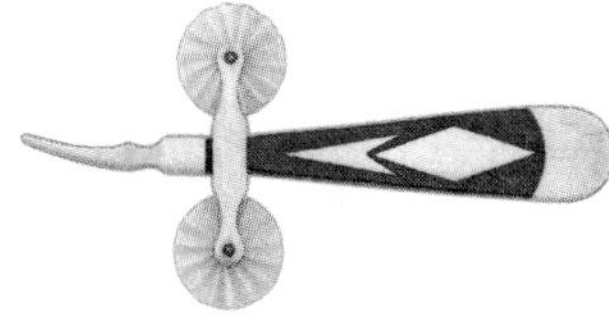

Eldred's

Scrimshaw, Rolling Pin, Whale Ivory Handles & Mounts, Walnut Roller, 1800s, 16 ½ In.
$570

Eldred's

This is an edited listing of current prices. Visit **Kovels.com** to check thousands of prices from previous years and sign up for free information on trends, tips, reproductions, marks, and more.

S

Urn, Lid, Woman, Handles, Gilt, Painted, Cobalt Blue Ground, Metal Mounts, 21 ½ In. 413
Urn, Woman, Blindfolded, Man, Children, Reclining, Trees, A. Maglin, 27 x 14 In. 2375
Vase, Bronze Figural Mount, Hand Painted, Neoclassical, 1800s, 2 x 7 ½ x 5 ½ In. 868
Vase, Lid, Oeil-De-Perdrix, Partridge's Eye, Blue, 1800s, 20 ¾ x 8 In., Pair .... *illus* 3888
Vase, Swan Handles, Gilt, Diamond Pattern, Flowers, Pink, Purple, White, 34 In. 250

SEWER TILE

Sewer tile figures were made by workers at the sewer tile and pipe factories in the Ohio area during the late nineteenth and early twentieth centuries. Figurines, small vases, and cemetery vases were favored. Often the finished vase was a piece of the original pipe with added decorations and markings. All types of sewer tile work are now considered folk art by collectors.

Bank, Pig, Molded Body, Painted Eyes, Early 1900s, 10 In. .... *illus* 123
Figure, Dog, Spaniel, King Charles, Seated, c.1800s, 7 In. .... *illus* 209
Figure, Dog, Spaniel, Seated, Full Body Detail, Brown, c.1900, 13 In. .... *illus* 1169
Figure, Dog, Spaniel, Seated, Sculpted Body Detail, Mounted, Late 1800s, 11 ½ In. 3998
Figure, Dog, Spaniel, Underglaze Black, White Paint, Late 1800s, 12 In. 123
Planter, Tree Stump, Brown, Open Trunk, 4 Smaller Open Trunks, c.1880, 25 x 33 In. ...*illus* 554

SEWING

Sewing, knitting, and weaving equipment of all types is collected, from sewing birds that held the cloth to tape measures, needle books, and old wooden spools. Sewing machines are included here. Needlework pictures are listed in the Picture category.

Awl, Baroque Style, Repousse Flowers & Scrolls, Blank Reserve, c.1890, 4 In. 75
Basket, Lid, Faux Wicker, Plastic Loop Closure, Flower Pincushion, Japan, 10 x 4 x 6 In. 24
Basket, Pink Bag, Wicker Basketry Bottom, Chinese Pekin Beads, Drawstring Closure, 4 x 8 In. 24
Basket, Wicker, Flowered Material On Lid, Tufted Interior, Handle, 4 x 7 x 7 In. 20
Basket, Wicker, Peking Glass Beads & Coins, Red Silk Tassel, 19th Century, 12 In. Diam. 55
Basket, Wicker, Woven, Handle, Victorian, Opens To 17 ½ In. 125
Box, 3 Tiers, Thread Holder, Drawer, Floral Case, Red Border, 1850s, 9 x 7 ½ x 5 ⅜ In. 523
Box, Black Lacquer, Chinoiserie, Dragon Feet, Chinese, 5 ½ x 9 ½ x 12 ½ In. ....*illus* 427
Box, Coromandel Wood, Inlaid, Leaves, Flowers, Central Medallion, c.1810 760
Box, Hinged Lid, Painted, Wall Paper Liner, c.1850, 13 ½ x 9 x 6 ¾ In. 69
Box, Hinged, Painted Pink Flowers, Pincushion, Satin Lined, Japan, 1940s 85
Box, Mahogany, Inlay, Checked Banding, Eagle, Banner, 1800s, 8 x 12 ¾ In. 625
Box, Mahogany, Mother-Of-Pearl Inlay, Red Silk, Lift-Out Tray, 1800s, 4 x 11 x 8 In. 495
Box, Rectangular, Canted Corners, Black Ground, Lift-Out Tray, c.1900, 11 In. 120
Box, Tortoiseshell, Fitted Interior, Silver Plate Feet, England, c.1830, 3 x 7 x 5 In. 1000
Box, Walnut, Round, Fitted Interior, Thread, Needle Storage, 9 x 7 In. 189
Box, Wood, Double Swift On Top, Inlay, Whalebone, Engraved Vine, c.1850, 19 x 14 In. ...*illus* 2040
Cabinet, W.H. Groove, Victorian, Walnut, 2 Drawers, c.1872, 14 ½ x 15 x 7 ½ In. 281
Cabinet, Spool, see also the Advertising category under Cabinet, Spool.
Case, Display, Boye Sewing Needle, Mahogany, Glass Front, Needles, c.1900, 12 x 12 x 7 In. 160
Clamp, Bone, Victorian, 1880s, 3 ½ x 1 In. 50
Compendium, Thimble, Needle Case, Reel, Silver, 3 In. 765
Darner, Plastic, Green, Box, Amerline, 1950s, 5 x 2 In. 25
Darning Egg, Fabric Lined Top, Openwork Body, Bench Clamp, Continental, 1700s, 7 In. *illus* 75
Etui, Spring-Loaded Shell, Medallion, Onyx Base, 1800s, 10 x 5 x 4 In. ....*illus* 400
Hem Gauge, Puffed Top, Silver, c.1910, 4 ¼ In. 75
Machine, Carry, Knobs, Salesman's Sample, Cincinnati, c.1960, 11 ½ x 10 x 10 In. 900
Machine, Cast Iron, Black, Thread Holder, Late 1890s, 11 x 13 x 7 In. ....*illus* 780
Machine, Little Comfort, Black, Hand Crank, 10 x 10 x 13 In. 1320
Machine, Singer Featherweight 221K, Buttonhole Attachments, Instructions, White, 1960s..... 700
Machine, Singer, No. 20, Tabletop, Clamp, Instructions, 1926, 6 ½ In. 120

TIP

Display your collections in a way that fits your lifestyle. Keep small breakables out of the reach of children or pets. Use wax, fishing line, or other barriers to keep small objects on shelves if you live in an area that has earthquakes or even if you live near a train track or highway. Continuous vibrations will make pieces "walk" toward the edge of the shelf and eventually fall off.

Scrimshaw, Walrus Tusk, Multiple Images, Sled Dog, Engraved Nome, Alaska, 1901, 15 In.
$1,000

Cowan's Auctions

Scrimshaw, Walrus Tusk, Sailing Ships In Harbor, Snowy Mountain, C. Lehwalder, 1900s, 14 ¾ In.
$2,625

Eldred's

Scrimshaw, Whale's Tooth, Megalodon, Broad Crown, Robust Root, Fossil, 5 x 4 In.
$826

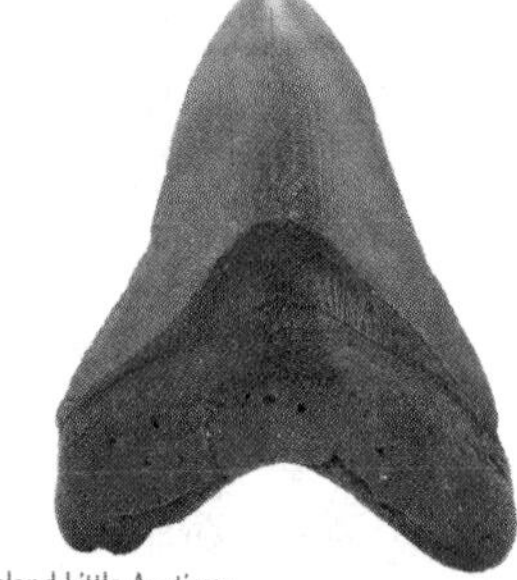

Leland Little Auctions

Sevres, Box, Woman & Child, Landscape, Gilt, Blue Ground, Flowers, 2 3/8 In.
$140

Hindman Auctions

Sevres, Urn, Cobalt Blue, Putti & Flower Scenes, Bacchus Bronze Handles, 11 x 6 1/2 In., Pair
$938

Palm Beach Modern Auctions

Sevres, Urn, Cream, Winged Putti, Allegorical, Head Handles, Onyx Base, 1800s, 23 x 12 x 8 In.
$1,003

Ahlers & Ogletree Auction Gallery

Sevres, Urn, Lid, Cobalt Blue, Courting Scene, Enamel, Gilt Ormolu Trim, c.1850, 25 x 7 1/2 In., Pair
$850

Woody Auctions

Sevres, Vase, Lid, Oeil-De-Perdrix, Partridge's Eye, Blue, 1800s, 20 3/4 x 8 In., Pair
$3,888

Selkirk Auctioneers & Appraisers

Sewer Tile, Bank, Pig, Molded Body, Painted Eyes, Early 1900s, 10 In.
$123

Skinner, Inc.

Sewer Tile, Figure, Dog, Spaniel, King Charles, Seated, c.1800s, 7 In.
$209

Skinner, Inc.

Sewer Tile, Figure, Dog, Spaniel, Seated, Full Body Detail, Brown, c.1900, 13 In.
$1,169

Skinner, Inc.

Sewer Tile, Planter, Tree Stump, Brown, Open Trunk, 4 Smaller Open Trunks, c.1880, 25 x 33 In.
$554

Skinner, Inc.

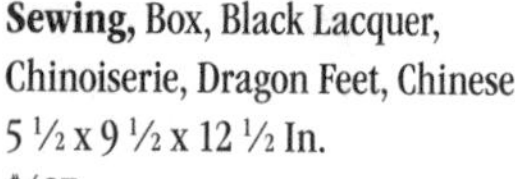

Sewing, Box, Black Lacquer, Chinoiserie, Dragon Feet, Chinese, 5 ½ x 9 ½ x 12 ½ In.
$427

Nadeau's Auction Gallery

Sewing, Box, Wood, Double Swift On Top, Inlay, Whalebone, Engraved Vine, c.1850, 19 x 14 In.
$2,040

Eldred's

Sewing, Darning Egg, Fabric Lined Top, Openwork Body, Bench Clamp, Continental, 1700s, 7 In.
$75

Hindman Auctions

Machine, Singer, Oak, Wrought Iron, Fairmont Trust Company, 1900s .... *illus* 173
Necessaire, Hinged Lid, Silver Inlaid, Tortoiseshell, Fitted Interior, c.1700, 3 ½ In. 406
Needle Case, Book Shape, Velvet, Paper Roses On Lid, Pictures Girl, Dog, c.1800, 3 In. 49
Needle Case, Cylindrical, Harrod's, London, Red, Gold, Turn Top To Dispense Needles, 2 In. .. 165
Needle Case, Punched Design, Silver, Swiss, 1800s, 2 ¾ In. 125
Needle Case, Silver, Chatelaine, Applied Fleur-De-Lis, Leather Sleeve, 3 In. 125
Needle Case, Silver, Punched Design, Swiss, 19th Century, 2 ¾ In. 125
Pattern Book, Lacemaker's, 9 Pages Of Lace Samples, Orders, Early 1900s, 13 ½ x 9 In. 218
Pincushion Dolls are listed in their own category.
Pincushion, Cardboard Box, Block Printed Wallpaper, Silver Accent, 1850s, 4 x 5 ½ In. 406
Pincushion, Cat, Thimble Hat, Flowers, Porcelain, 2 ¾ x 3 ½ In. 10
Pincushion, Donkey, Felt, Straw Hat, Carrot, Baskets On Back, 5 In. 28
Pincushion, Multicolor Beads, Stylized Flowers, Triangular, Germany, c.1880, 3 ⅜ In. 65
Pincushion, Shoe Shape, Carved, Painted, Late 1800s, 3 x 6 In. .... *illus* 738
Pincushion, Shoe Shape, Patterned Fabric, Pink Ribbon Around Edge, 1800s, 3 x 5 ½ In. 50
Pincushion, Silver, Chatelaine, Embossed Roses, Rococo Scrolls, c.1900, 2 In. Diam. 190
Scissors, Folding, Silver Handle, Steel Blades, 4 ½ In. 100
Scissors, Folding, Silver, Marked, W, 3916, 3 In. 100
Scissors, Silver Handles, Curved Metal Blades, Wallace & Sons, 5 In. 65
Scissors, Silver Handles, Flowers, Germany, 4 In. 55
Shears, No. 28, Forged Steel, Chrome Plated Blades, Black Handles, Inlaid, Wiss, c.1965, 9 In. 22
Spool Cabinets are listed here or in the Advertising category under Cabinet, Spool.
Spool Holder, Mixed Wood, Painted, Black, Square, Drawer, 10 In. 147
Swift, Maple, Turned Finial, Graduated Base, Expanding Yarn Winder, c.1870, 22 ½ In. 649
Tape Loom, Cherry, Carved Heart, Handle, Pinwheel, Shaped End, 1774, 24 ½ x 7 ¾ In. *illus* 4920
Tape Loom, Walnut, Carved, Dovetail, 1800s, 11 x 17 In. 800
Tape Measure, Burl, Brass Crank, Carved Heart, Diamond, Whalebone Mount, 1800s, 5 ½ In. 338
Tape Measure, Figural, Pig, Silver, 2 In. 163
Tape Measure, Scottish Terrier, Brown, Tan, Occupied Japan, 2 In. 150
Thimble, 14K Gold, Engraved, Village Scene, ¾ In. 136
Thimble, Georgian, Silver Gilt, Filigree, 1700s, ¾ In. 250
Thimble, Paneled, Geometric Designs, Stippled Edge, Silver, c.1910, ⅞ In. 38
Thimble, Plain Band, Tooled Band, Slanted Scrolls, Silver, c.1900, ¾ In. 20
Thimble, Porcelain, Robin, Flower Spray, c.1880, 1 In. 225
Thimble, Robin, Spray, Bisque, c.1875, 1 ¼ In. 225
Thimble, Sterling Silver, Paneled, Simon Brothers, Size 11, ⅞ In. 27
Thimble, Sterling Silver, Plain Body, Engraved Script W, c.1700, ⅞ In. 75
Thimble, Stylized Fan, Sterling Silver, Ketcham & McDougal, ⅞ In. 41
Thread Winder, Lion's Heads, Bird Feet, Silver, 19th Century, 2 ⅛ In. 270
Yarn Winder, Maple, Molded Elements, Tripod Base, Arris Pad Feet, 1700s, 44 x 26 ½ In. 800
Yarn Winder, Pine, 4 Arms, Splayed Legs, 34 ½ x 18 x 16 In. .... *illus* 83

SHAKER

Shaker items are characterized by simplicity, functionalism, and orderliness. There were many Shaker communities in America from the eighteenth century to the present day. The religious order made furniture, small wooden pieces, and packaged medicines, herbs, and jellies to sell to "outsiders." Other useful objects were made for use by members of the community. Shaker furniture is listed in this book in the Furniture category.

Basket, Bentwood, Oval, Copper Tacks, Swing Handle, Sabbathday Lake, 1900s, 8 x 8 x 10 ¾ In. ... 380
Basket, Round, 2 Notched Bentwood Handles, Blue, New Lebanon, 1800s, 4 x 12 ½ In. 246
Bonnet, Woven, Blue Trim, Custom Stand, Early 1900s, 3 x 2 ⅜ x 3 ½ In. 308
Box, 3-Finger, Oval, Lid, Wood, 3 ½ x 9 ¾ In. .... *illus* 413
Box, Band, Round, Lapped Finger Joints, Metal Tacks, 1863, 1 ½ x 3 In. 82
Bucket, Kerosene, Woodcock & Sawyer, Staves, Grain Paint, Bail Handle, 1860s, 12 x 11 In. *illus* 510
Bucket, Oak Stave Construction, Iron Hoops, White, Inscribed Corn, 1800s, 12 x 11 In. 492
Sewing Caddy, 2-Finger, Oak, Copper Nails, Handle, 4 ¾ x 11 ½ In. 72

Sewing, Etui, Spring-Loaded Shell, Medallion, Onyx Base, 1800s, 10 x 5 x 4 In.
$400

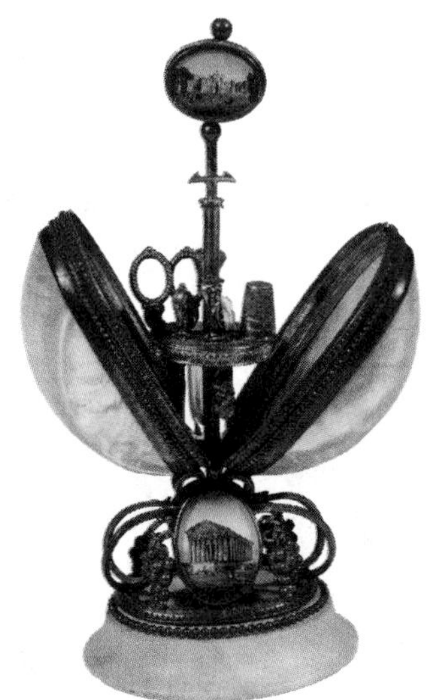

Neal Auction Company

Sewing, Machine, Cast Iron, Black, Thread Holder, Late 1890s, 11 x 13 x 7 In.
$780

Morphy Auctions

Sewing, Machine, Singer, Oak, Wrought Iron, Fairmont Trust Company, 1900s
$173

Selkirk Auctioneers & Appraisers

Sewing, Pincushion, Shoe Shape, Carved, Painted, Late 1800s, 3 x 6 In.
$738

Skinner, Inc.

Sewing, Tape Loom, Cherry, Carved Heart, Handle, Pinwheel, Shaped End, 1774, 24 ½ x 7 ¾ In.
$4,920

Skinner, Inc.

Sewing, Yarn Winder, Pine, 4 Arms, Splayed Legs, 34 ½ x 18 x 16 In.
$83

Bunch Auctions

SHAKER

Shaker, Box, 3-Finger, Oval, Lid, Wood, 3 ½ x 9 ¾ In.
$413

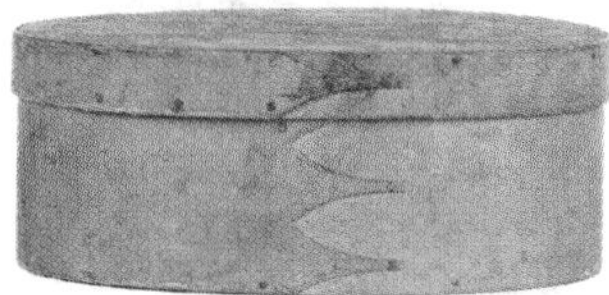

Cottone Auctions

Shaker, Bucket, Kerosene, Woodcock & Sawyer, Staves, Grain Paint, Bail Handle, 1860s, 12 x 11 In.
$510

Garth's Auctioneers & Appraisers

Shaving Mug, Occupational, Fireman, Wagon, Horse, Hook & Ladder, Old English Letters, C.H. Reich, Gilt
$300

Bertoia Auctions

S

Music from the Movies

Watch out for reprints of old movie sheet music. Music before the 1960s was about 50 cents a copy. Now it is almost $3.00. The reprints are usually made to be sold in a store, not to fool the collector, so the price will be shown.

SHAVING MUG

Shaving mugs were popular from 1860 to 1900. Many types were made, including occupational mugs featuring pictures of men's jobs. There were scuttle mugs, silver-plated mugs, glass-lined mugs, and others.

Black Ground, Gilt Rim & Handle, Flowers, Limoges, Morril, 3 ½ In. 30
Occupational, Doctor, D.K. Oliver M.D., Rose, Leaves, Gold Trim, T&V, France, 3 ½ In. 48
Occupational, Fireman, Wagon, Horse, Hook & Ladder, Old English Letters, C.H. Reich, Gilt *illus* 300
Occupational, Railroad, Locomotive, Painted, White Ground, A. Hutchison, 4 x 4 ½ In. 102
Occupational, Tailor, Sadiron, Work Table, Gold Text, 3 ½ In. 226

SHAWNEE POTTERY

Shawnee Pottery was started in Zanesville, Ohio, in 1937. The company made vases, novelty ware, flowerpots, planters, lamps, and cookie jars. Three dinnerware lines were made: Corn, Lobster Ware, and Valencia (a solid color line). White Corn pattern utility pieces were made in 1945. Corn King was made from 1946 to 1954; Corn Queen, with darker green leaves and lighter colored corn, from 1954 to 1961. Shawnee produced pottery for George Rumrill during the late 1930s. The company closed in 1961.

Cookie Jar, Smiley Pig, Clover Bud, Red Neckerchief, Closed Eyes, Cream Ground, 11 In. *illus* 267
Cookie Jar, Winking Owl, Painted, Glazed, c.1937, 11 ½ In. .... *illus* 40
Plate, Salad, Corn King, 7 ⅜ In. 46
Saltshaker, Winnie Pig, Clover, 3 Holes, 3 In. 38
Teapot, Granny Ann, Lavender & Green, 8 x 7 ¾ In. 75
Teapot, Lid, Pink Rose, White Ground, Bud Finial, Ribbed, 6 ½ In. 16

SHEARWATER POTTERY

Shearwater Pottery is a family business started in 1928 by Peter Anderson, with the help of his parents, Mr. and Mrs. G.W. Anderson Sr. The local Ocean Springs, Mississippi, clays were used to make the wares in the 1930s. The company was damaged by Hurricane Katrina in 2005 but was rebuilt and is still in business, now owned by Peter's four children.

Bowl, High Gloss Blue Glaze, Signed JA, James Anderson, 2000, 2 x 4 ¾ In. 95
Plate, Hooded Merganser Ducks, Walter Inglis Anderson, 1960s, 10 In. .... *illus* 2750
Vase, Asian Style Flambe Glaze, Oval, 7 ½ In. 750
Vase, Incised Bird Design, Impressed Circular Mark, Iowa Art Center Sticker, 7 In. 4225
Vase, Melon Shape, Lavender Glaze, Impressed Mark, 6 In. 100

SHEET MUSIC

Sheet music from the past centuries is now collected. The favorites are examples with covers featuring artistic or historic pictures. Early sheet music covers were lithographed, but by the 1900s photographic reproductions were used. The early sheet music pages were larger than more recent sheets, and you must watch out for examples that were trimmed to fit in a twentieth-century piano bench and should be lower priced.

In My Arms, From See Here Private Hargrove, Robert Walker, Donna Reed, 1943 7
Scotland Bells, Waltzes, By Harry J. Lincoln, 2 Women Pictured, 1913 8
That Chinatown Rag, Jack Drislane, Geo. W. Meyer, Intermezzo For Piano 12

SHEFFIELD *items are listed in the Silver Plate and Silver-English categories.*

SHELLEY

Shelley first appeared on English ceramics about 1912. The Foley China Works started in England in 1860. Joseph Ball Shelley joined the company in 1862 and became a partner in 1872. Percy Shelley joined the firm in 1881. The company went through a series of name changes and in 1910 the then Foley China Company became Shelley China. In 1929 it became Shelley Potteries. The company was acquired in 1966 by Allied English Potteries, then merged with the Doulton group in 1971. Shelley is no longer being made. Trio is the name for a cup, saucer, and cake plate set.

Cake Plate, Forget Me Not, Pansy Rose, Pink Ground, Gold Trim, 2 Handles, 10 In. 75
Cup & Saucer, Blue, Dainty, White With Blue Flowers 30
Cup & Saucer, Pink, White Interior, Scalloped Gilt Edge 102
Pitcher, Basin, Light Blue Band, Line Decorations, Diamonds, Fans, c.1935, 13 ¾ In. 75
Plate, Golden Harvest, Wheat Border, 10 ⅞ In. 24
Undertray, For Sugar & Creamer, Hibiscus, Flowers, White Ground, Signed, 8 ½ In. 12

SHIRLEY TEMPLE

Shirley Temple, the famous movie star, was born in 1928. She made her first movie in 1932. She died in 2014. Thousands of items picturing Shirley have been and still are being made. Shirley Temple dolls were first made in 1934 by Ideal Toy Company. Millions of Shirley Temple cobalt blue glass dishes were made by Hazel Atlas Glass Company and U.S. Glass Company from 1934 to 1942. They were given away as premiums for Wheaties and Bisquick. A bowl, mug, and pitcher were made as a breakfast set. Some pieces were decorated with the picture of a very young Shirley, others used a picture of Shirley in her 1936 Captain January costume. Although collectors refer to a cobalt creamer, it is actually the 4 ½-inch-high milk pitcher from the breakfast set. Many of these items have been reproduced and are being sold today.

Badge, Shirley Temple Police, Brass, Shield Shape, Eagle, 1930s, 2 In. 1000
Book, The Poor Little Rich Girl, c.1930 28
Doll, Composition, Sleep Eyes, Mohair Curls, Ideal, Box, 12 In. 288
Doll, Ideal, Composition, Blond Curls, Original Dress, Shoes, Pin, 15 In. 104
Doll, Ideal, Composition, Mohair Wig, Blue Dress, White Netting, Bluebird, 25 In. 36
Doll, Ideal, Composition, Mohair Wig, Little Colonel Costume, Hat, 18 In. 192
Doll, Ideal, Vinyl, Navy & Red & White Check Dress, Box, 1957, 19 In. 132
Doll, Ideal, Vinyl, Tagged Pink & Blue Dress, 1957, 18 ½ In. 125
Doll, Ideal, Vinyl, White & Red Polka Dot Dress, Box, 1973, 20 In. 36
Doll, Ideal, Wardrobe, 3 Dresses, Raincoat, Fitted Box, 1957, 12-In. Doll 192
Paper Dolls, Stand, Dresses, Original Box, Gabriel, 9 In. 41
Photograph, Portrait, Autographed, Love, Shirley Temple, Glossy, 8 x 10 In. 357
Photograph, Shirley & Walt Disney, Oscars, Gelatin, 1939, 9 x 7 In. 250
Pin, Doll's, My Friend Shirley Temple, Red & White, 1 ¼ In. 17
Pin, Doll's, Portrait, World's Darling, Genuine Shirley Temple Doll, 1 ¼ In. 11
Pitcher, Cobalt Blue Glass, Honeycomb, Portrait, Angular Handle, 4 ½ In. 12
Plate, 5 Pictures From Stand Up And Cheer, Multicolor, 1983, 10 ½ In. 5
Purse, Vinyl, Black, Red, Shirley Temple In White, 1952, 3 x 4 In. 35
Water Set, Vaseline Glass, Fluted Sides, Portrait, 3 ½-In. Pitcher, 5 Piece 84

SHRINER, *see Fraternal category.*

SILVER, *Sheffield, see Silver Plate; Silver-English i categories.*

Shawnee, Cookie Jar, Smiley Pig, Clover Bud, Red Neckerchief, Closed Eyes, Cream Ground, 11 In.
$267

Strawser Auction Group

Shawnee, Cookie Jar, Winking Owl, Painted, Glazed, c.1937, 11 ½ In.
$40

Woody Auctions

Shearwater, Plate, Hooded Merganser Ducks, Walter Inglis Anderson, 1960s, 10 In.
$2,750

New Orleans Auction Galleries

S

Silver Flatware Sterling, Acorn, Georg Jensen, 73-Piece Set (Detail)
$2,700

Tremont Auctions

Drying Silver
To keep your silver from spotting when washed in the dishwasher, remove it before the drying cycle. The heat sets the spots.

Silver Flatware Sterling, Chantilly, Gorham, 61-Piece Set (Detail)
$900

Tremont Auctions

Silver Flatware Sterling, Florentine Lace, Reed & Barton, 60-Piece Set (Detail)
$1,000

Tremont Auctions

SILVER FLATWARE

Silver flatware includes many of the current and out-of-production sterling silver and silver-plated flatware patterns made in the past 125 years. Other silver is listed under Silver-American, Silver-English, etc. Most silver flatware sets that are missing a few pieces can be completed through the help of a silver matching service. Three U.S. silver company marks are shown here.

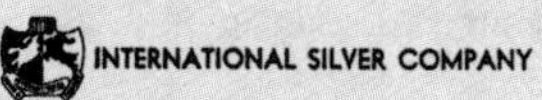

International Silver Co.
1928+

Reed & Barton
c.1915+

Wallace Silversmiths, Inc.
1871–1956

SILVER FLATWARE PLATED

Coronation, Serving Fork, Community 10
Eudora, Luncheon Fork, Towel, 7 In. 12
Fleur De Luce, Cream Ladle, Community, 5 ½ In. 14
Happiness, Pastry Server, W.A. Rogers, c.1914 12

SILVER FLATWARE STERLING

Acorn, Georg Jensen, 73-Piece Set .... *illus* 2700
Burgundy, Baby Set, Fork & Spoon, Reed & Barton, 1948, 4 ½ In. 135
Chantilly, Gorham, 61-Piece Set .... *illus* 900
Chantilly, Serving Spoon, Gorham, 8 ½ In. 56
Florentine Lace, Reed & Barton, 60-Piece Set .... *illus* 1000
Francis I, Cold Meat Fork, Reed & Barton, 7 ⅞ In. 80
Francis I, Salad Set, Fork & Spoon, Reed & Barton, 9 In. 316
Grand Baroque, Wallace, 60-Piece Set .... *illus* 1000
Imperial Queen, Asparagus Server, Whiting, 1893, 10 ⅛ In. .... *illus* 173
Lancaster, Pusher, Baby Food, Gorham, 3 ¾ In. 75
Medallion, Serving Tongs, Gorham, 12 ½ In. .... *illus* 1586
Old Master, Serving Spoon, Towle, 8 ½ In. 85
Shenandoah, Spoon, Wallace 18
Sovereign, Iced Tea Spoon, Gorham, 7 ⅝ In. 34
Strasbourg, Salad Set, Gorham 250

SILVER PLATE

Silver plate is not solid silver. It is a ware made of a metal, such as nickel or copper, that is covered with a thin coating of silver. The letters *EPNS* are often found on American and English silver-plated wares. *Sheffield* is a term with two meanings. Sometimes it refers to sterling silver made in the town of Sheffield, England. Sometimes it refers to an old form of plated silver made in England. Here are marks of three U.S. silver plate manufacturers.

Barbour Silver Co.
1892–1931

J.W. Tufts
1875–c.1915

Meriden Silver Plate Co.
1869–1898

Bottle Coaster, Reticulated, Embossed, Flowers, Leaves, 5 x 7 In., Pair 92
Bowl, Elephant & Palm Tree, Ebony Base, c.1960, 19 ½ x 13 In. 350
Bowl, Figural, Acorn Shape, Oak Leaf, Squirrel, Footed, Middleton, 12 x 12 In. 800
Bowl, Hammered, Cornucopia, Domed Base, Franco Lapini, c.1985, 8 x 13 ¾ In. .... *illus* 281
Box, W.F. Milligan, Bird, Flowers, Mouse Finial, Inscribed Christmas, 1881, 8 x 11 In. 60
Candlesnuffer, Inlaid, Turquoise, Parrot, Leaves, Marked, Emilio Castillo, 12 ½ In. 165

Casket, Vermeil Trim, Panels, Court Scenes, Dragon Feet, Late 1800s, 3 ½ x 7 x 4 ½ In. 156
Centerpiece, Figural, Elkington Style, Palm Trees, Stag, Rockwork Base, 1800s, 24 In. 550
Centerpiece, Oval Bowl, Gadroon, Faux Lion Head Ring Handle, Sheffield, 6 x 14 x 9 In. 832
Cocktail Shaker, Lighthouse Shape, Removable Top, 14 In. 450
Cocktail Shaker, Penguin, Hinged Beak, Ceramic Stopper, Napier Co., 1900s, 12 ½ x 4 In. ... 1416
Cocktail Shaker, Skyscraper, Louis Rice, New York, 1920-22, 11 x 7 x 4 In. .... *illus* 13750
Coffeepot, Birds, Leaves, Lanterns, Gourd Shape, Long Spout, Pairpoint, 11 x 7 In. 45
Epergne, Cherub, Sheaves Of Wheat, Grapevine, 4 Cut Glass Bowls, 20 In. 840
Ice Bucket, Wood Grouse Finial, Hounds, Antler Handles, Wurttemberg Metal Factory, 18 In. . 360
Kettle, Kwami, Flowers, Stand, William Hutton & Son, Early 1900s, 14 ½ x 10 x 6 In. 266
Ladle, Hobstar & Fan Cut Handles, Shell Shape Dippers, Gorham, 13 ½ In., Pair 210
Lamp, 3-Light, Bird & Leaf Design, Disc Feet, Circular Base, 24 x 16 In. 123
Pitcher, Bird Shape Handle, Mother-Of-Pearl, Obsidian Eyes, Los Castillo, 11 ½ In. ....*illus* 531
Pitcher, Water, Art Nouveau, Lid, Gourd Shape Body, Handle, Round Base, Marked Wife, 14 In. 207
Plateau, Beveled, Mirror, Footed, Marked, TB Clark, 18 In. 450
Plateau, Table, Neoclassical Style, Oval, Repousse Ribbon, Ball Feet, Early 1900s, 40 x 18 In. . 840
Samovar, Flower Finial, Lobed Body, Scrolling Leaves, Acanthus, Eagle Spout, 18 x 16 In. 390
Spoon, Souvenir, see Souvenir category.
Stand, Jewelry, Embossed Dog Medallions, Swivel Midsection, Silk Lining, Victorian, 11 In. 150
Teapot, Art Deco, Curved Ribs, Wood Handle & Finial, Ilonka Karasz, c.1928, 5 x 6 In. ...*illus* 1250
Tray, Beaded Rim, Hammered, No. 210 B, Georg Jensen, 8 In. 260
Tray, Hand Chased, Oval, Coat Of Arms, 2 Handles, Sheffield, c.1900, 31 x 21 In. 87
Tureen, Soup, Engraved, Crest, 3-Letter Script, Monogram DRG, England, 11 x 17 x 10 In. 500
Vase, Bud, 3 Turnips, Christofle, France, 1900s, 4 ¼ In. .... *illus* 98
Wine Cooler, Melon Shape, Gadroon Borders, Leafy Handle, Collar, Marked, 9 x 13 In., Pair .. 600

SILVER-AMERICAN

American silver is listed here. Coin and sterling silver are included. Most of the sterling silver listed in this book is subdivided by country. There are also other pieces of silver and silver plate listed under special categories, such as Candelabrum, Napkin Ring, Silver Flatware, Silver Plate, Silver-Sterling, and Tiffany Silver.

Gorham & Co.
1865+

INTERNATIONAL SILVER CO.
International Silver Co.
1898–present

Reed & Barton Co.
1824–2015

Asparagus Server, Bel Chateau, Lunt, 10 In. 92
Basket, Bonbon, Scallop Rim, Handle, Paw Feet, Shreve & Co., 6 ½ x 4 ½ x 5 ½ In. 92
Basket, Pierced Repousse Floral, Rococo Applied Edge, Swing Handle, Gorham, c.1873, 16 x 16 In. *illus* 2006
Bonbon Scoop, Monogram, Leaves, 9 In. .... *illus* 325
Bonbon Scoop, Ornate, Openwork, Bowl & Handle, No. 857, Gorham, 6 ¾ In. 89
Bowl, Boat, Surmounted, Cherub, Oars, Gorham, 1900s, 8 ½ In. 1500
Bowl, Flared Rim, Cornucopia, Reticulated Detail, Mauser, 1892-1913, 3 ⅞ x 14 ¾ In. 900
Bowl, Francis I Pattern, Reed & Barton, 8 In. 156
Bowl, Fruit, Beaded Rim, Footed, S. Kirk & Son Inc., 26 x 10 ⅞ In. 431
Bowl, Gilt Interior, Rococo Handles & Swirls, Openwork Feet, Gorham, 1893, 9 x 14 x 7 In. *illus* 5650
Bowl, Grape & Vine Border, Monogram, Gorham, c.1890, 8 In. 230
Bowl, Lobed Sides, Leaf Rim, Acanthus Leaf, Black, Starr & Frost, c.1900, 2 ⅝ x 8 In. 263
Bowl, Monogram, Renaissance Revival, Marked, Schulz & Fischer, 9 In. 671
Bowl, Monogram Center, Molded Rim, Gorham, 9 ½ x 2 ½ In. 203
Bowl, Ornate, Pierced, Flowers, Footed, Marked Black, Starr & Frost, 7 ½ x 3 ½ In. 180
Bowl, Peaked Rim, Floral Arches, Conforming Foot, Octagonal, Gorham, 1912, 9 ¾ In. 390
Bowl, Pierced Rim, Wreath, Central Monogram, Matthews Co., Early 1900s, 9 In. 120
Bowl, Repousse, Flowers, Kirk, 1 ¾ x 4 In. .... *illus* 246
Bowl, Repousse, Town, Buildings, Flowers, Coin, S. Kirk & Son, 1846-61, 6 x 6 ¾ In. 1280
Bowl, Reticulated Center, Beaded Edge, Gorham, 1916, ¾ x 14 In. 584
Bowl, Round Base, Paul Revere Pattern, Manchester, 4 x 8 In. 144
Bowl, Round, Flares At One End, Allan Adler, Mid-Century Modern, 2 ½ x 12 x 9 ¼ In. 390

Silver Flatware Sterling, Grand Baroque, Wallace, 60-Piece Set (Detail)
$1,000

Tremont Auctions

Silver Flatware Sterling, Imperial Queen, Asparagus Server, Whiting, 1893, 10 ⅛ In.
$173

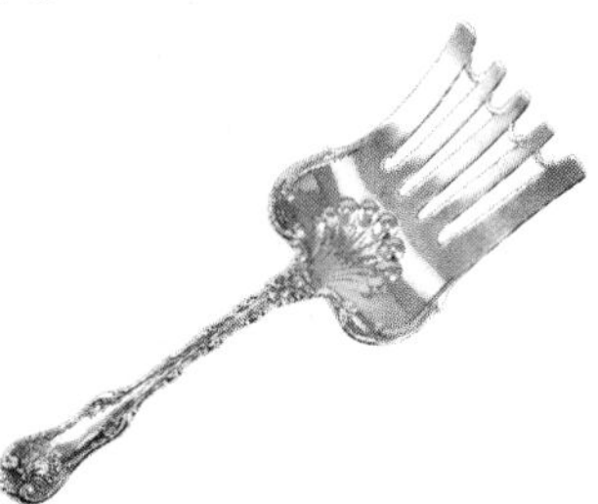

Blackwell Auctions

Silver Flatware Sterling, Medallion, Serving Tongs, Gorham, 12 ½ In.
$1,586

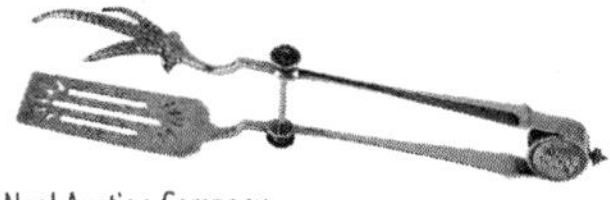

Neal Auction Company

TIP

Experts say you should never put silverware in a dishwasher for several reasons: Eventually the oxidation (black highlights) will disappear, hollow-handled knives are filled with a material that will melt, and if the silver touches stainless steel it will get black spots. Be safe. Wash silver by hand.

Silver Plate, Bowl, Hammered, Cornucopia, Domed Base, Franco Lapini, c.1985, 8 x 13 ¾ In.
$281

Kamelot Auctions

Silver Plate, Cocktail Shaker, Skyscraper, Louis Rice, New York, 1920-22, 11 x 7 x 4 In.
$13,750

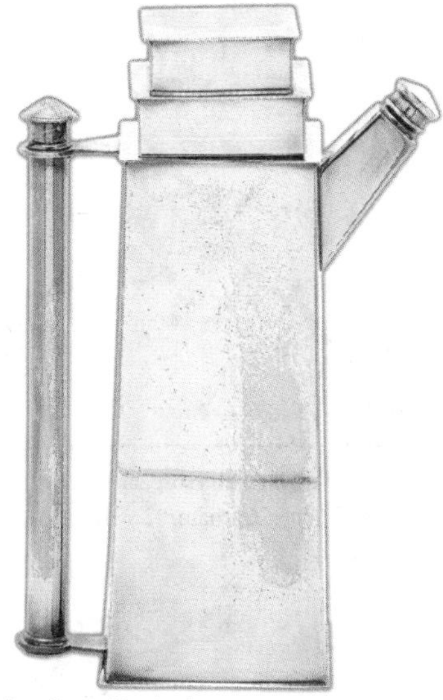

Rago Arts and Auction Center

Silver Plate, Pitcher, Bird Shape Handle, Mother-Of-Pearl, Obsidian Eyes, Los Castillo, 11 ½ In.
$531

Susanin's Auctioneers & Appraisers

Silver Plate, Teapot, Art Deco, Curved Ribs, Wood Handle & Finial, Ilonka Karasz, c.1928, 5 x 6 In.
$1,250

Los Angeles Modern Auctions

Silver Plate, Vase, Bud, 3 Turnips, Christofle, France, 1900s, 4 ¼ In.
$98

Skinner, Inc.

Silver-American, Bonbon Scoop, Monogram, Leaves, 9 In.
$325

Hindman Auctions

Silver-American, Bowl, Gilt Interior, Rococo Handles & Swirls, Openwork Feet, Gorham, 1893, 9 x 14 x 7 In.
$5,650

Soulis Auctions

Silver-American, Bowl, Repousse, Flowers, Kirk, 1 ¾ x 4 In.
$246

Locati Auctions

Silver-American, Basket, Pierced Repousse Floral, Rococo Applied Edge, Swing Handle, Gorham, c.1873, 16 x 16 In.
$2,006

Charleston Estate Auctions

S

Bowl, Shell & Scroll Rim, Towle, 2 x 7 ¾ x 7 ¾ In. 142
Bowl, Vegetable, Lid, Handles, Baldwin & Miller, Inc., New Jersey, 1900, 11 In. 650
Bowl, Vegetable, Scalloped Rim, Engraved, Francis I, Reed & Barton, 1957, 11 ½ x 2 In. 322
Box, Hinged Lid, Art Nouveau, Maiden, Cherubs, Faces Of God, Kerr, c.1890, 2 ½ In. 196
Butter Pat, Flowers, Monogram, Redlich & Co., New York, 3 ⅜ In., 12 Piece 180
Butter, Dome Lid, Medallion Pattern, Removable Finial, No. 393, Gorham, 1873, 6 x 9 In. 1033
Cake Basket, Embossed, Swing Handle, Beaded Edge, Coin, Gorham, 1850s, 3 ¾ x 8 ¾ In. *illus* 308
Cake Basket, Swing Handle, Gadroon, Shell Border, Black, Starr & Frost, 1874, 12 x 15 ⅜ In. 900
Candelabra are listed in the Candelabrum category.
Candlesticks are listed in their own category.
Canister, Chinoiserie, Dome Lid, Monogram, Spiral Feet, c.1893, 5 ½ In. 1476
Case, Traveling, Perfume, Hinged Lid, Lions, Leafy Scrolls, 2 ⅝ x 3 ⅜ x ½ In. 338
Centerpiece, Acorns, Leaves, Footed, Scroll Handles, Dominic & Haff, 10 ½ x 8 ½ x 7 In. *illus* 3422
Centerpiece, Openwork, Embossed, Chased, Flower Grill, Gorham, 1915, 20 In. *illus* 3500
Charger, Flower, Monogram, Hand Chased, Reed & Barton, c.1938, 1 ¾ x 14 In. 527
Charger, Gadroon Rim, Central Monogram, Dunkirk Silversmiths, c.1950, 10 ¾ In. 132
Charger, Rolled Rims, Round, Marked, S. Kirk & Son, 11 In., 8 Piece 2160
Cheese Scoop, Mouse, Cast Figure, Paneled Handle, Egg Shape Terminal, 1800s, 8 ⅝ In. 200
Cheese, Scoop, Lily Of The Valley, Tapered End, Monogram, Whiting, 8 In. 100
Christening Cup, Repousse, Adolphe Himmel, Coin, Marked, Hyde & Goodrich, 3 ⅝ In. 300
Cocktail Shaker, Baluster Body, Curved Handle, Circular Foot, Pineapple Finial, 11 ½ In. 484
Coffeepot, Bird Finial, Engraved, Monogram, Coin, R. & W. Wilson, c.1835, 11 ½ In. 677
Coffeepot, Hinged Lid, Footed, Monogram, Marked, International, 9 ½ x 11 In. 367
Coffeepot, Japanesque Style, Hollow Branch, Twig Handle, Whiting, Late 1800s, 8 ½ In. *illus* 2400
Coffeepot, Lid, Urn Shape, Gooseneck Spout, Footed, Side Handle, 11 ½ In. 313
Coffeepot, Strasbourg, Lid, Scroll Rim, Curved Feet, Shell Knees, Gorham, c.1960, 9 ⅜ In. 410
Coffeepot, Tapered Body, Leaves, Geometric Designs, Charles W. Kennard & Co., 1881, 9 In. 413
Compote, Acanthus Scrolls, Laurel Swags, Stacked Discs, Whiting, 7 ½ x 9 ½ In. 450
Compote, Classical, Shallow Bowl, Inverted Swags, Square Foot, Barbour, c.1930, 2 ½ x 12 In. 248
Compote, Flower, Scalloped Rim, Circular Quadruped Base, S. Kirk & Son, 6 x 9 ½ In., Pair *illus* 1680
Compote, Footed, Organic Stem & Rim, 2 Side Handles, 3 ½ x 8 In. 156
Compote, Gerardus Boyce, Oval, 2 Handles, Flowers, Engraved, c.1830, 15 x 9 ½ x 5 In. 472
Creamer, Beaded Base, Handle, Wide Spout, Coin, Gale & Mosely, c.1830, 7 In. 277
Creamer, Floral Sprays, Circular Base, Handle, S. Kirk & Son, c.1885, 7 In. 246
Creamer, Semi-Oval, Flared Rim, Chased Leaf Accent, Coin, Samuel L. Kirk, 1830s, 5 x 4 In. 152
Cup, Hammered, Engraved Dad, 1967, Alice & Cope, Old Newbury Crafters, 3 In., Pair 142
Dessert Stand, Floral, Reticulated, Octagonal, Monogram, Theodore B. Starr, c.1890, 9 ½ In. *illus* 207
Dish, Leaf Shape, No. 280, Reed & Barton, 1933, 10 In. 165
Dish, Scalloped Edge, Ribbed Interior, Towle, Elizabeth Hanford, 1 ½ x 12 x 8 ½ In. 156
Epergne, 3 Arms, 3 Glass Bowl Inserts, Leaf Shape, Bobeches, Reed & Barton, 20 x 8 x 14 In. 117
Ewer, Gadroon Border, Scroll Handle, Jones, Lows & Ball, Eagle Punch, 1835-41, 13 In. 1800
Ewer, Molded Flowers, Scroll Lip & Handle, Dominick & Haff, 1894, 14 In. 700
Ewer, Pear Shape, Floral, Intertwined Branch Handle, Coin, Mid 1800s, 5 x 9 ½ In. 277
Ewer, Repousse, Grapes, Leaves, Vines, Davis & Galt, 1888-1915, 15 ⅜ In. *illus* 1250
Ewer, Vase Shape, Hinged Lid, Monogram, Stepped Base, Loring Bailey, Early 1800s, 9 ¾ In. 1230
Fish Server, Pierced, Fish, Scrolled Vines, Ivory Handle, Woodcock, 11 x 3 In. *illus* 4410
Fish Server, Strapwork Terminal, Beaded Stem, Blade, Engraved, Wm McGrew, Cincinnati, 1850s *illus* 74
Goblet Set, Water, Tiered Foots, Manchester Silver Co., 6 ¾ In., 6 Piece 944
Goblet, Domed Base, Engraved, Signed, Kirk Stieff, 1958, 6 ½ In., 6 Piece 509
Goblet, Domed Base, Monogram, Hunt Silver Co., c.1935, 7 In., 12 Piece 974
Goblet, Repousse, Flowers, Grape Decoration, Engraved Cartouche, Coin, 1850s, 6 ⅜ In. 200
Goblet, Turned Stem, Inverted Dish Shape Base, Cornelius Wynkoop, c.1730, 5 ¾ In. 2280
Hand Mirror, Handle, Flowers, Gorham, 9 ½ In. 104
Julep Cup, Beaded Rim, Frank Whiting & Co., Early 1900s, 3 ¾ In., 12 Piece 2091
Julep Cup, Rolled Edge Rim, Revere Silver Smiths Inc., 2 x 3 ¾ In. 58
Ladle, 2 Spouts, Engraved Monogram, International, 15 In. 117
Ladle, Applied Lobster, Fish, Turtle, Gilt Bowl, Monogram, Gorham, c.1900, 13 In. 780
Ladle, Beaded Edge, Marked, J. Veal, 1830s, 12 ¾ In. *illus* 308
Ladle, Monogram, Coin, Eagle & Bust Touch Marks, William Mitchell, c.1800, 13 In. *illus* 325
Letter Holder, Art Nouveau, Peacock, Woman, Flowers, Gorham, Early 1900s, 8 x 9 x 4 In. 4484

Silver-American, Cake Basket, Embossed, Swing Handle, Beaded Edge, Coin, Gorham, 1850s, 3 ¾ x 8 ¾ In.
$308

Charlton Hall Auctions

TIP
When polishing silver, first remove all detachable parts like screw-on handles or finials. Rest the silver piece on a cloth in your lap, never on the table or other hard surface. If there are wooden handles or other parts, these should be waxed when the silver is cleaned.

Silver-American, Centerpiece, Acorns, Leaves, Footed, Scroll Handles, Dominic & Haff, 10 ½ x 8 ½ x 7 In.
$3,422

Charleston Estate Auctions

Silver-American, Centerpiece, Openwork, Embossed, Chased, Flower Grill, Gorham, 1915, 20 In.
$3,500

New Orleans Auction Galleries

Silver-American, Coffeepot, Japanesque Style, Hollow Branch, Twig Handle, Whiting, Late 1800s, 8 ½ In.
$2,400

Brunk Auctions

Silver-American, Compote, Flower, Scalloped Rim, Circular Quadruped Base, S. Kirk & Son, 6 x 9 ½ In., Pair
$1,680

Case Antiques

Silver-American, Dessert Stand, Floral, Reticulated, Octagonal, Monogram, Theodore B. Starr, c.1890, 9 ½ In.
$207

Richard D. Hatch & Associates

Silver-American, Ewer, Repousse, Grapes, Leaves, Vines, Davis & Galt, 1888-1915, 15 ⅜ In.
$1,250

Neal Auction Company

Silver-American, Fish Server, Pierced, Fish, Scrolled Vines, Ivory Handle, Woodcock, 11 x 3 In.
$4,410

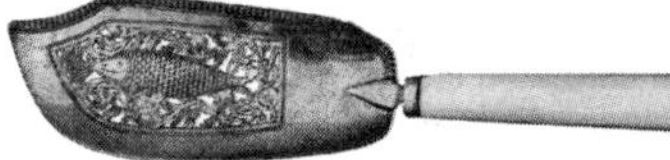

Morphy Auctions

Silver-American, Fish Server, Strapwork Terminal, Beaded Stem, Blade, Engraved, Wm McGrew, Cincinnati, 1850s
$74

Charlton Hall Auctions

Silver-American, Ladle, Beaded Edge, Marked, J. Veal, 1830s, 12 ¾ In.
$308

Charlton Hall Auctions

Silver-American, Ladle, Monogram, Coin, Eagle & Bust Touch Marks, William Mitchell, c.1800, 13 In.
$325

Conestoga Auction Company

Silver-American, Mug, Vase Shape, Floral, Acanthus Leaf Foot, Garret Eoff, c.1840, 4 ¼ In.
$158

Eldred's

Loving Cup, Stepped Base, Engraved, Presented To Hanford MacNider, Wallace, 1940, 15 x 6 In..... 531
Mug, Beaded Rim, Milled Band, Engraved, Gorham, Rhode Island, 1873, 4 In.......................... 98
Mug, Vase Shape, Floral, Acanthus Leaf Foot, Garret Eoff, c.1840, 4 ¼ In. ....*illus* 158
Napkin Rings are listed in their own category.
Pie Server, Openwork, Floral, Olive, Monogram On Reverse, Coin, S.T. Crosby, c.1850, 9 In..... 115
Pipkin, Chippendale, Black, Turned, Ebonized, Hardwood, Handle, Gorham, 1943, 9 In. *illus* 71
Pitcher, Acanthus Leaf, 2 Bands, Stepped Circular Foot, Alfred Welles, Early 1800s, 10 ¾ In.... 702
Pitcher, Baluster Body, C-Scroll Rim, Handle, Footed, Monogram, Early 1900s, 6 ½ In........... 324
Pitcher, Belle Epoque Style, Embossed Flowers, Wide Spout, Redlich & Co., 1900s, 11 In. 1250
Pitcher, Bulbous Body, Footed, Wide Spout, Engraved B, Black, Starr & Frost, 9 x 8 In............. 344
Pitcher, Flowers, Cartouche, Flared Spout, Scroll Handle, J. Kitts, Kentucky, c.1850, 12 In........ 2280
Pitcher, Gold Wash Interior, Garlands, Leafy Handle, Whiting Mfg. Co., c.1900, 11 In. ....*illus* 1053
Pitcher, Helmet Shape, Mt. Vernon Country Club, Baltimore Silversmiths, c.1929, 9 ¾ In...*illus* 277
Pitcher, Semi-Oval Well, Pedestal Base, Engraved, Meriden Brittania Co., 1850s, 11 In. 351
Pitcher, Serpentine Rim, Shaped Handle, Stepped Shoulder, Leafy Banding, Durgin, 8 ½ In.. 400
Pitcher, Tapered, Cylindrical, Monogram, Baldwin & Miller Co., Inc., c.1930, 8 ¾ In. 380
Pitcher, Trophy, American Saddle Horse, Engraved, Lebkuecher & Co., 9 ¾ In. 401
Pitcher, Water, Floral Scroll Rim, Grapevine Handle, Coin, Lewis-Owen, 1850s, 11 ¾ In......... 3500
Pitcher, Water, Grapevine, Footed, Wide Spout, Handle, W.D. Whiting, 9 ½ In. 390
Pitcher, Water, Handle, Jack Boardman & Co., 1900s, 8 In. 300
Pitcher, Water, Oval, Stylized Leaves, Flared Base Rim, Kalo, c.1930, 8 ¾ In. ....*illus* 3900
Pitcher, Water, Repousse, Grapevine, Jenkins & Jenkins, 9 In. 2280
Pitcher, Water, Squat Body, Hammered, Scrolling Vine, Berries Neck & Handle, c.1900, 6 In.. 450
Platter, Chased Leaves, Husk Garland Border, Dominick & Haff, 15 ¾ In. 360
Platter, Oval, Meat, Tree Of Life, Footed, International, 2 x 20 x 13 ½ In. ....*illus* 840
Platter, Oval, Rim, Engraved, Whiting Manufacturing Co., 1916, 18 x 12 ¾ In. 492
Porringer, Bulbous, Scroll Handle, Howard & Co, New York, 1894, 2 x 8 In. ....*illus* 185
Porringer, Circle & Heart Pierced Handle, Marked, John Hastier, 1760s, 6 In........................... 1845
Porringer, Scroll Handle, Coin, Daniel Dupuy, c.1800, 4 In.. 610
Punch Bowl, Art Deco, Flowers, Vine Rim, Domed Base, Mauser Mfg. Co., 1900s, 10 x 20 In.... 6250
Punch Bowl, Domed Foot, Revere Style, Gorham, Rhode Island, 1960, 6 x 11 ½ In. 677
Punch Ladle, Engraved, Armorial Crest, Bright Cut Cartouche, Standish Barry, Baltimore..... 781
Punch Ladle, Henry II, Gilt Wash Bowl, Gorham, 12 ¾ In. 512
Punch Ladle, Medallion, Hotchkiss & Schreuder, 1867, 13 In. ....*illus* 1037
Salt & Pepper, Applied Scroll Rims, Roses, Blackinton & Co., c.1900, 2 In. 200
Salt & Pepper, Urn Shape, Footed, Repousse, Finial, 4 ¾ In. 81
Salver, Ball, Tompkins & Black, Engraved Flowers, Monogram, Coin, 1839-51, 6 In.................. 130
Salver, Card, Repousse, Floral Border, Claw Feet, A.E. Warner, c.1840, 8 x 8 x 13 In. 458
Salver, Circle, Engraved, Ball Feet, Gorham, Early 1900s, 9 In. 338
Salver, Oak Leaf Border, Paw Feet, Coin, Jones, Ball & Poor, c.1850, 15 In. ....*illus* 584
Serving Bowl, Reeded Rim, Angular Handles, Monogram, S. Kirk & Son, 3 ¾ x 9 In. .....*illus* 308
Serving Bowl, Repousse Grape, Leaves Border, Double Walled, Gorham, Late 1800s, 2 x 13 In....... 1560
Serving Bowl, Scalloped Deep Well, Sprays Of Fruit, Repousse, Francis I, 11 ½ In.................. 454
Serving Dish, 2 Handles Lid, Model No. 22, Poole, 1900s, 2 ¾ x 12 In. 350
Serving Fork, 2 Tines, Wallace, c.1909, 6 In.. 47
Serving Ladle, Gold Wash Bowl, Scalloped Rim, Monogram, Gorham, c.1900, 12 In................ 123
Serving Spoon, Hammered, Die Cut Stem, Medallions, Engraved, Wood & Hughes, c.1882, 9 In. *illus* 400
Serving Spoon, Hammered, Rivets, Engraved, C. & G. Carlstrom, Towle, 9 ⅜ In. 154
Serving Spoon, Oyster Shape, Bamboo Stalk Handle, Vermeil Interior, Gorham, 10 In........... 549
Shoehorn, Flowers, Repousse, Pierced End, Initials, Marked, Gorham, c.1900, 6 In. 279
Skewer, Ring Handle, Monogram MB, Paul Revere Jr., Marked Revere, 9 ½ In. 4200
Soup Ladle, Beaded, Monogram W, Coin, Wood & Hughes, c.1850, 12 ½ In. 104
Soup Ladle, Chantilly, Gold Wash Bowl, Monogram W, Gorham, 1895, 10 ½ In. 92
Soup Ladle, Upturned Fiddle, Engraved Armorial, Anthony Rasch, 1820-58, 12 ⅝ In.............. 900
Spoon, Chrysanthemum, Enamel, Gold Wash, Durgin, c.1900, 9 In. 154
Spoon, Straws, Heart Shape, Wallace, 1900s, 8 In., 6 Piece.. 30
Sugar Basket, Swing Handle, Scroll Feet, Monogram, Gorham, 1850s, 3 ½ x 4 ½ In. 154
Sugar Castor, Footed, Floral, Wide Shoulder, Vase Shape Finial, Kirk & Sons, 1880s, 8 ¾ In... 113
Sugar, Dome Lid, Repousse, Urn Shape, S. Kirk & Sons, 1860s, 5 ⅝ x 6 In. 300
Sugar, Lid, Engraved, 2 Handles, Finial, WG Forbes, c.1800, 6 ¾ x 7 ½ In. ....*illus* 502
Sugar Nippers, Engraved, John Ward Gilman, New Hampshire, 1725-1823, 4 ½ In. ....*illus* 3840

Silver-American, Pipkin, Chippendale, Black, Turned, Ebonized, Hardwood, Handle, Gorham, 1943, 9 In.
$71

Leland Little Auctions

TIP
When buying silver with bright cut designs, avoid worn pieces. The best prices are paid for silver with clear, crisp designs.

Silver-American, Pitcher, Gold Wash Interior, Garlands, Leafy Handle, Whiting Mfg. Co., c.1900, 11 In.
$1,053

Jeffrey S. Evans & Associates

Silver-American, Pitcher, Helmet Shape, Mt. Vernon Country Club, Baltimore Silversmiths, c.1929, 9 ¾ In.
$277

Charlton Hall Auctions

Silver-American, Pitcher, Water, Oval, Stylized Leaves, Flared Base Rim, Kalo, c.1930, 8 ¾ In.
$3,900

Brunk Auctions

TIP
Never use lemon-scented dishwashing detergent to wash silver. It leaves spots.

Silver-American, Platter, Oval, Meat, Tree Of Life, Footed, International, 2 x 20 x 13 ½ In.
$840

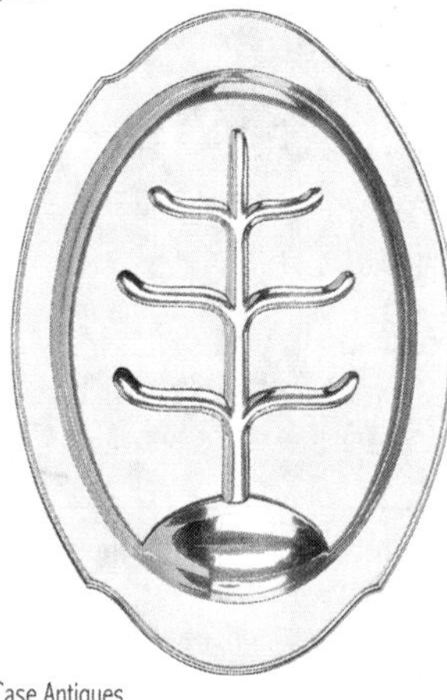

Case Antiques

Silver-American, Porringer, Bulbous, Scroll Handle, Howard & Co, New York, 1894, 2 x 8 In.
$185

Charlton Hall Auctions

Tablespoon, Monogram, Coin, George Hendel, 1802-40, 8 ⅜ In. ...*illus* 295
Tankard, San Francisco Bay Harbor, W.K. Vanderslice, c.1880, 2 x 4 ½ x 3 ½ In. ...*illus* 615
Taperstick, Queen Anne, Octagonal Base, Engraved, Joseph Bird, 1706-07, 3 ⅞ In. ... 1353
Tea & Coffee Set, Coffeepot, Teapot, Sugar & Creamer, Tray, D. Colefish, Gorham... 840
Tea & Coffee Set, Kettle, Stand, Coffeepot, Teapot, Sugar & Creamer, Waste Bowl, Kirk & Sons. 6250
Tea Canister, Japanesque, Applied Tree, Blossom, Whiting, Late 1800s, 4 ¾ x 4 x 4 In. ...*illus* 5400
Tea Set, Chased Dome Lids, Basket Of Flowers, Coin, Wm. Thomson, 9 In., 4 Piece ...*illus* 1342
Teapot, Cushion Shape Body, Shell Borders, Eagle Head Spout, Wood Handle, c.1830, 6 ½ In.. 1476
Teapot, Lid, Urn Finial, Monogram, Eoff & Howell, Early 1800s, 7 In. ... 400
Teapot, Watson Lotus, Gooseneck, Footed, Art Deco, 7 ⅞ In. ... 400
Tongs, Francis I, Fancy Claw Ends, Reed & Barton, 1907, 6 ½ In. ... 207
Tray, Chantilly Duchess, Oval, 2 Handles, Gorham, 25 ½ x 17 In. ...*illus* 1600
Tray, Oblong, Arthur Stone, Marked C, Stamped, Early 1900s, 4 x 20 In. ... 1017
Tray, Openwork Border, Marked, Gorham, Providence, R.I., 1874, 28 In. ... 2750
Tray, Organic Handles, Back Marked 64, Woodside, 13 ¾ In. ... 469
Tray, Oval, Slight Point At Handle, B Monogram On Rim, Shreve & Co., 27 x 17 In. ... 1020
Tray, Plymouth Pattern, 2 Handles, Oval, Monogram, Gorham, 24 ¾ In. ... 1728
Tray, Reticulated Rim, Oval Plateau, Monogram, Shreve & Co., 1892, 14 x 8 In. ... 246
Tray, Scrolling Border, Poppy Blossom, Vine, Open Carved Bone Handles, Gorham, 26 In. ... 5100
Tray, Serving, Oval, Scroll, Leaf Rim, R. Wallace & Sons Mfg. Co., 1950s, 16 x 11 In. ... 380
Tray, Serving, Sculpted Rim, Repousse Rosettes, George W. Shiebler & Co., 1876-1910, 12 In. .. 215
Tray, Square, Round Recessed Area, Floral Japanesque, Gorham, Late 1800s, 7 ½ x 7 ½ In. ... 900
Trinket Box, Tortoiseshell Lid, Inlaid, Footed, Mappin & Webb, 2 ½ In. ... 173
Trophy, Champion Bowling Tournament, Goblet Shape, Scroll, Floral, Inscribed, 1883, 12 In. 1560
Trophy, Conical, Footed, Engraved C.W.F., Watson Co., 8 In. ... 123
Trophy, Engraved Inscription, Footed, Handle, Theodore B. Starr, No. 2892... 375
Trophy, Kentucky State Fair, Antler Handles, 1911, 10 In. ... 1250
Urn, Lid, Stepped Square Base, Shell Corners, Arthur Stone, 16 x 7 In. ...*illus* 7800
Vase, 3 Handles, Bulbous, Wavy Rim, Poppies, Flower, Reed & Barton, 17 In. ... 7865
Vase, Cone Shape, Ruffled Rim, Embossed, Flowers, Footed Base, Shreve & Co., 9 In. ... 215
Vase, Flared, Round Foot, Kalo, c.1920, 18 x 5 In. ... 4375
Vase, Flutter Rim & Repousse, Cherub, Flowers, La Pierre, 1900s, 5 ¾ In. ... 192
Vase, Trumpet, Reticulated Mouth, Foot, Leaves, Engraved, Sweetser Co., N.Y., Early 1900s, 18 In. .. 900
Waste Bowl, Repousse, Footed Shape, Bead Rim, Coin, Peter Krider, c.1850, 5 ⅜ x 5 ⅞ In. ... 250
Wine Coaster, Woodside Pattern 2098, Cast Reticulated, Scroll Border, 7 ⅝ In. ... 250

SILVER-ASIAN

Teapot, Engraved, Gooseneck Spout, 4 Men, Embossed, 1899, 6 ¾ In. ...*illus* 1298

SILVER-AUSTRIAN

Cake Basket, Reticulated Grape, Grape Leaf Border, Vienna, 1827, 8 x 10 ⅜ x 9 In. ... 200
Casket, Enamel Panel, Venus, Cupid, Zodiac, Pierced Ivory, c.1890, 4 ¾ x 8 ½ x 5 In. ...*illus* 7995
Cornucopia, Enamel, Eagle Finial, Mythology, Domed Base, Hermann Bohm, Late 1800s, 7 In. 2583
Platter, Fish, Oval, 2 Handles, Marked Underside, Klinkosch, 22 ½ x 9 ½ In. ... 413
Tray, Oval, Laurel Swags, Medallion, Marked, c.1800, 26 In. ... 677

SILVER-BRAZILIAN

Bird On Ball, Perched, Flowering Branch, Mounted, Openwork, 3 Paw Feet, c.1850, 6 x 4 In... 761

SILVER-BURMESE

Basin, Repousse, Animals, Figural, c.1800, 8 ½ x 13 In. ...*illus* 1125

SILVER-CANADIAN

Tray, Scalloped Edge, Chippendale Style, Engraved, To B.W.K From H.C.G., Birks, 1947, 10 In... 219

SILVER-CHILEAN

Spurs, Hand Stamped Tooling, Engraved, 5 x 2 ½ x 2 In., Pair ...*illus* 82

SILVER-CHINESE

Bowl, Scalloped Rim, 10 Panels, Chrysanthemum, Hung Chong & Co., c.1900, 6 x 9 ¾ In. *illus* 5850
Bowl, Wood, Wide, Shallow Shape, 2 Silver Mounts, Engraved, c.1890, 2 x 4 ½ In. ... 316
Mug, Cylindrical, Bamboo, Scrolled Handle, Font, Shield Engraved, c.1860, 5 ½ In. ...*illus* 840
Platter, Oval, Conforming Handle, Bamboo Stalks, Leafy Sprigs, 18 x 11 ½ In. ... 492
Tankard, Tapered, Repousse, Scenic, Crouching Dragon Handle, Lee Ching, 6 ⅜ x 6 ¾ In. . *illus* 3375
Urn, Art Deco, 2 Side Handles, Burner Base & Feet, c.1930, 14 x 8 x 5 In. ... 819

Silver-American, Punch Ladle, Medallion, Hotchkiss & Schreuder, 1867, 13 In. $1,037

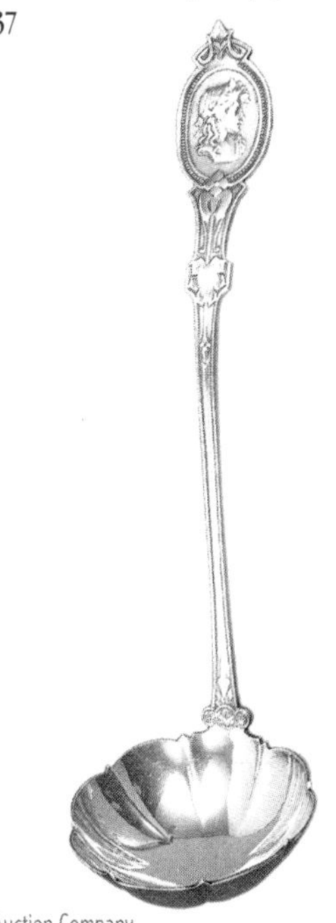

Neal Auction Company

TIP
Keep a piece of white chalk in the drawer with your sterling or plated silver. It retards moisture and slows tarnishing.

Silver-American, Salver, Oak Leaf Border, Paw Feet, Coin, Jones, Ball & Poor, c.1850, 15 In. $584

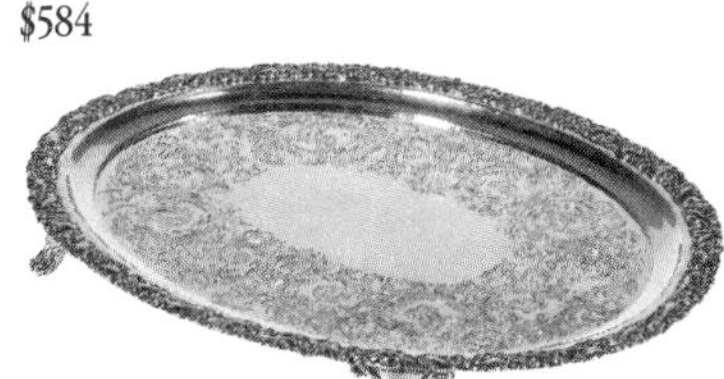

Skinner, Inc.

Silver-American, Serving Bowl, Reeded Rim, Angular Handles, Monogram, S. Kirk & Son, 3 ¾ x 9 In. $308

Charlton Hall Auctions

Silver-American, Serving Spoon, Hammered, Die Cut Stem, Medallions, Engraved, Wood & Hughes, c.1882, 9 In. $400

Charlton Hall Auctions

Silver-American, Sugar, Lid, Engraved, 2 Handles, Finial, WG Forbes, c.1800, 6 ¾ x 7 ½ In. $502

Bunch Auctions

Silver-American, Sugar Nippers, Engraved, John Ward Gilman, New Hampshire, 1725-1823, 4 ½ In. $3,840

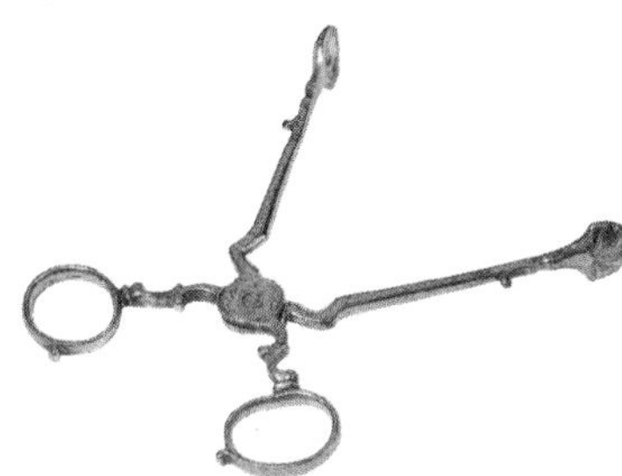

Bourgeault-Horan Antiquarians & Associates, LLC

Silver-American, Tablespoon, Monogram, Coin, George Hendel, 1802-40, 8 ⅜ In. $295

Conestoga Auction Company

Silver-American, Tankard, San Francisco Bay Harbor, W.K. Vanderslice, c.1880, 2 x 4 ½ x 3 ½ In. $615

Clars Auction Gallery

Silver-American, Tea Canister, Japanesque, Applied Tree, Blossom, Whiting, Late 1800s, 4 ¾ x 4 x 4 In. $5,400

Brunk Auctions

Silver-American, Tea Set, Chased Dome Lids, Basket Of Flowers, Coin, Wm. Thomson, 9 In., 4 Piece
$1,342

Neal Auction Company

Silver-American, Tray, Chantilly Duchess, Oval, 2 Handles, Gorham, 25 ½ x 17 In.
$1,600

Neal Auction Company

Silver-American, Urn, Lid, Stepped Square Base, Shell Corners, Arthur Stone, 16 x 7 In.
$7,800

CRN Auctions

Silver-Asian, Teapot, Engraved, Gooseneck Spout, 4 Men, Embossed, 1899, 6 ¾ In.
$1,298

Copake Auctions

Silver-Austrian, Casket, Enamel Panel, Venus, Cupid, Zodiac, Pierced Ivory, c.1890, 4 ¾ x 8 ½ x 5 In.
$7,995

Charlton Hall Auctions

Silver-Burmese, Basin, Repousse, Animals, Figural, c.1800, 8 ½ x 13 In.
$1,125

Hindman Auctions

Silver-Chilean, Spurs, Hand Stamped Tooling, Engraved, 5 x 2 ½ x 2 In., Pair
$82

Cordier Auctions

TIP

Dip polishes remove all the oxidation that blackens crevices in the designs on silver and often leaves the finish looking more like tin than silver.

Silver-Chinese, Bowl, Scalloped Rim, 10 Panels, Chrysanthemum, Hung Chong & Co., c.1900, 6 x 9 ¾ In.
$5,850

Jeffrey S. Evans & Associates

Silver-Chinese, Mug, Cylindrical, Bamboo, Scrolled Handle, Font, Shield Engraved, c.1860, 5 ½ In.
$840

CRN Auctions

SILVER-CONTINENTAL

Basket, Rococo Style, Filigree, Scalloped Glass Liner, Paw Feet, 4 x 10 ¾ x 7 ¾ In. 226
Bowl, Children Playing, Fruit, Lattice Panel, c.1900, 6 ½ In. 173
Casket, Hinged Lid, Neoclassical Style, Flower Baskets, Hoofed Feet, c.1900, 5 x 12 x 8 In. 2340
Cigarette Case, Hinged, Leaves, Engraved, ½ x 3 ¾ x 2 ¾ In. .... *illus* 188
Creamer, Oval, Footed, Chased Anthenion Leaf Band, Helmet Shape Spout, 6 ½ In. .... *illus* 151
Dish, Wavy Openwork, Medallion, Paw Feet, c.1800, 10 ¾ In. 431
Figure, Pheasant Garniture, Full Bodied, Wings, Tail, Feather Details, 5 x 17 In. 400
Gravy Boat, Cartouches & Rocaille Designs, Rococo, 1910s, 7 x 10 In., Pair 1353
Tray, Embossed, Hebrew Writing, Flowers, Shaped Rim, 17 In. 1610
Trinket Box, Hinged Lid, Enamel Genre Scene, Engraved, Bun Feet, c.1900, 2 x 3 ½ x 4 In. 4182
Tureen, Lid, Flower Finial, 2 Handles, Footed, Starburst, 1900s, 8 ½ x 11 In. .... *illus* 625

SILVER-DANISH. Georg Jensen is the most famous Danish silver company.

Georg Jensen
1925–1932

Georg Jensen
1933–1944

Georg Jensen
1945–present

Bowl, Footed, Openwork Floral Base, Hammered, Georg Jensen, 5 x 6 ½ In. 1000
Bowl, Leaves, Berry, Circular Base, Georg Jensen, 1945, 5 ¾ In. 677
Cocktail Shaker, Dome Lid, Baluster Shape, Center Spout, Finial Cap, 1950s, 12 x 8 ⅝ In. .... *illus* 410
Cup, Lion's Head Shape Handle, 2 Bails, 3 Tower Mark, 4 ½ x 5 ½ In. 219
Dish, Lid, Loop Finial, Oval, Scroll Accents, Grann & Laglye, c.1929, 5 x 12 x 9 In. 468
Jug, Bulbous, Wide Spout, Footed, Applied Wood Handle, Grann & Laglye, 1950, 6 In. .... *illus* 138
Pie Server, Heart Shape Handle, Georg Jensen, 1920s, 7 In. 115
Pitcher, Beaded Neck & Foot, Hammer Marked OA, c.1937, 8 In. 277
Pitcher, Grape Clusters, Ebony Handle, Georg Jensen, c.1940, 9 x 7 In. .... *illus* 4500
Salt & Pepper, Blossom, Circular Base, No. 2A, Georg Jensen, 1945, 2 ½ In. 425
Sauceboat, Blossom, Beaded Handle, Round Foot, Georg Jensen, 3 ⅝ x 6 x 2 ⅝ In. .... *illus* 594
Sauceboat, Undertray, Ladle, Beaded Rim, Organic Handles, Stamped, Georg Jensen, 8 In. 2375
Tray, Lid, Finial, Oval, Handles, C.C. Hermann, 6 ½ x 14 ¾ x 8 ⅝ In. .... *illus* 960
Vase, Art Nouveau, Chased Irises, L. Berth, c.1901, 8 ⅝ In. 677

SILVER-DUTCH

Bowl, Brandy, Repousse, Openwork Handles, Circular Gadroon Foot, c.1770, 7 ½ In. .... *illus* 246
Spoon, Apostle, Monogram, Peter Bagijn, c.1633, 7 ¾ In. .... *illus* 1107
Tea Caddy, Hinged Lid, Engraved, Floral Sprays, c.1850, 2 ¾ In. 677
Teapot, Squat, Ribbed Spout, Molded Waist, Bonebakker En Zoon, 1839, 8 In. .... *illus* 288

SILVER-ENGLISH

English sterling silver is marked with a series of four or five small hallmarks. The standing lion mark is the most commonly seen sterling quality mark. The other marks indicate the city of origin, the maker, the year of manufacture, and the king or queen. These dates can be verified in many good books on silver. These prices are partially based on silver meltdown values.

Standard quality mark

City mark – London

Date letter mark

Maker's mark

Sovereign's head mark

Basin, Plain Form & Edge, Push-Up Center, 13 ½ In. 732
Basket, Engraved Crest Of Bird, Swags, William Plummer, George III, 1772, 12 x 13 x 10 In. *illus* 625

Silver-Chinese, Tankard, Tapered, Repousse, Scenic, Crouching Dragon Handle, Lee Ching, 6 ⅜ x 6 ¾ In.
$3,375

Abington Auction Gallery

Silver-Continental, Cigarette Case, Hinged, Leaves, Engraved, ½ x 3 ¾ x 2 ¾ In.
$188

Kamelot Auctions

Silver-Continental, Creamer, Oval, Footed, Chased Anthenion Leaf Band, Helmet Shape Spout, 6 ½ In.
$151

Clars Auction Gallery

Silver-Continental, Tureen, Lid, Flower Finial, 2 Handles, Footed, Starburst, 1900s, 8 ½ x 11 In.
$625

Hindman Auctions

Silver-Danish, Cocktail Shaker, Dome Lid, Baluster Shape, Center Spout, Finial Cap, 1950s, 12 x 8 ⅝ In.
$410

Jeffrey S. Evans & Associates

Silver-Danish, Jug, Bulbous, Wide Spout, Footed, Applied Wood Handle, Grann & Laglye, 1950, 6 In.
$138

Freeman's Auctioneers & Appraisers

Basket, Medallions, Cartouche, Swing Handle, Beaded Rim, Footed, George III, 5 x 4 ¾ In. 540
Basket, Reticulated, Oval Bowl, Beaded Swing Handle, Hester Bateman, George III, 12 ½ In. *illus* 1889
Basket, Swing Handle, Gadroon, Shell Border, Footed, William Eaton, 1813, 10 x 13 x 10 In.... 800
Beaker, Gold Washed Interior, Handle, Chester, Edward VII, 1909, 4 ⅝ In. 281
Beaker, Leaf Accent Rim, Monogram, Marked, DM, 1700s, 3 ¾ In. 461
Bowl, Footed, Flower, Flared Opening, Beaded Rim, 3-Footed, Monogram, 1878, 3 x 5 In. 125
Bowl, Monteith, Reticulated Border, Footed, Initialed R.M. & R.H., 8 x 11 In. ....*illus* 1416
Bowl, Vegetable, Lid, Phoenix Finial, Craddock & Reid, c.1818, 6 x 11 x 9 ½ In., Pair.... 4636
Brandy Warmer, Lid, Hinged Spout, Turned Wood Handle, 1814, 7 ½ x 10 x 4 In. 554
Candelabra are listed in the Candelabrum category.
Candlesticks are listed in their own category.
Card Case, Victorian, Strapwork, Engraved, Monogram LMS, Frederick Marson, 1864, 3 ⅞ x 3 ¾ In. 175
Centerpiece, Figural, Maidens, Laurel Wreaths, Flowers, Cut Glass Bowl, c.1800, 15 In. ..*illus* 4880
Centerpiece, Neoclassical, Cut Glass Dish, Reeded Legs, Emes & Barnard, London, 1813, 10 In. ....*illus* 1800
Cigarette Case, Engine Turned Case, Interior Strap, England, 3 x 4 In. 92
Coffeepot, Dome Lid, Bud & Leaf Finial, Daniel Smith & Rudy Sharp, George III, 11 ¾ In. 1050
Coffeepot, Dome Lid, Wood Scroll Handle, Marked, Thomas Farren, George II, 1733, 9 ½ In. . 1020
Coffeepot, Engraved, Armorial, Victorian Chasing, Fuller White, George II, c.1758, 10 In. 984
Coffeepot, Hinged Lid, Embossed Flowers, Wood Handle, Footed, Edward Feline, 8 In. ....*illus* 431
Compote, Scalloped Edge, Mappin & Webb, London, 1900s, 6 x 9 ¾ In. 170
Cup, Bright Cut Foot, Elongated Stem, Robert Hennell I, George III, 1787, 6 ⅜ In. 313
Cup, Coconut, Carved, Roundel, Lilies, Palm Trees, Hester Bateman, Footed, 1786, 7 In. .*illus* 2006
Cup, Footed, Gilt Wash Interior, London, George III, 1767, 5 In., Pair 500
Dish Cross, Bead Border, Adjustable Arms, William Plummer, Georgian, 1776-1777, 12 ½ In. 580
Dish, Caviar, Lid, Sturgeon, Dolphin Feet, Shell Handles, Hallmark, 1985, 6 x 7 In. ....*illus* 3500
Ewer, Wine, Urn Shape, Robert Makepeace & Richard Carter, 1777-78, 12 In. 1107
Fish Server, Crest On Blade, Engraved, William Eley & William Fern, George III, 1800, 12 In. 188
Fish Slice, Cutwork Blade, Armorial Engraved Bowl & Shield, Thomas James, London, 12 In.. 77
Goblet, Engraved, Armorial, John Parker I & Edward Wakelin, Georgian, 1795, 7 In., 12 Piece 2214
Goblet, Oval Bowl, Gold Wash, Beaded Stem, George III, 1771, 6 In., Pair 400
Iced Tea Spoon, Openwork Bowl, Whiting, Louis XV, c.1891, 8 ⅝ In. 150
Kettle, Stand, Wooden Elements, Mappin & Webb, London, Early 1900s, 11 In. ....*illus* 450
Knife, Reeded Handles, Applied Crest, William Eley & William Fearn, 1816, 8 In., 18 Piece 500
Ladle, Toddy, Baleen Handle, Elizabeth Morley, George III, London, 15 In. 77
Lamp, Weighted, Corinthian Columns, Stepped Base, James Dixon & Sons, c.1903, 36 In., Pair. 1500
Lobster Pick, William Hutton & Sons, Ltd., Sheffield, 1910, 7 ⅝ In., 10 Piece 351
Marrow Scoop, 3 Hallmarks, Lion Passant, Impressed HB, Hester Bateman, c.1777, 8 ⅞ In.... 410
Marrow Scoop, Engraved, Crest On The Reverse, Paul Hanet, George II, 1733, 8 ⅜ In. 250
Muffineer, Finial, Foot Rim, George V, Atkin Brothers, 1926, 7 ½ In. ....*illus* 215
Mug, Bulbous, Leaf Capped Scroll Handle, c.1750, 4 ¾ In. 580
Napkin Rings are listed in their own category.
Pitcher, Engraved, Chased, Thomas Whipham, George II, 1744-45, 7 In. 1722
Pitcher, Footed, Bulbous Body, Marked JW, London, George II, 1752, 7 ⅜ x 8 In. 1875
Platter, Oval, Gadroon & Engraved Crest, George IV, 1823, 19 x 14 In. ....*illus* 1220
Rattle, Coral, Whistle, Repousse, Unite & Hilliard, William IV, 1830-31, 5 ½ In. ....*illus* 154
Salt Cellar, Circular, Corded Rim, Monogram, George III, John Muns, 1763-64, 2 ⅝ In., Pair 492
Saltshaker, Bird Shape, Standing, Wings Spread, Lion Marking, 2 In. ....*illus* 281
Salver, Armorial, Beaded Rim, Scroll Feet, Engraved, 1726, 9 In. 832
Salver, Beaded, Serpentine, Lobed Rim, 4 Ball Feet, Laurel Ribbon, 17 In. 2813
Salver, Engraved Coat Of Arms, Dum Spiro Spero, Edinburgh, George III, 1810, 13 ¾ In. 1003
Salver, Gadroon Rim, Robertson, Walton, Newcastle Hallmark, Regency, 1811, 16 x 12 In. *illus* 2375
Salver, Piecrust Edge, Footed, Thomas Bradbury & Sons, Sheffield, 1929, 12 In. 875
Salver, Round, Molded Border, Cartouche, Scroll Feet, George II, 1730, 18 In. 2460
Salver, Square, Cut Corner, 4-Footed, Chrichton Brothers, London, George V, 1929, 12 In. 684
Salver, Square, Scalloped Edge, Atkin Bros., Sheffield, 1930, 14 x 14 In. 1107
Sauceboat, Footed, Wide Spout, Handle, G, A, T, George III, c.1773, 8 ½ x 4 ¼ x 5 In. 484
Sauceboat, Lion Mask, Leaf Capped Handle, Hair Paw Feet, 1739, 4 ½ x 7 ½ x 4 In., Pair *illus* 3075
Spoon, Anointing, Marked, John Millward Banks, Chester, Edwardian, 5 In. 41
Spoon, Strainer, Armorial Engraved, Handle, George Smith III & William Fearn, London, 12 In.... 189
Spoon, Trifid Rattail, Engraved, John Sutton, William III, 7 ⅜ In. 439
Sugar Basket, Oval, Swing Handle, P. & A. Bateman, George III, 1792, 6 ½ In. 690
Sugar Castor, Lid, Urn Finial, Tripod Feet, J. Collyer Ltd., Birmingham, George V, 6 In. 65

Silver-Danish, Pitcher, Grape Clusters, Ebony Handle, Georg Jensen, c.1940, 9 x 7 In.
$4,500

New Orleans Auction Galleries

Silver-Danish, Sauceboat, Blossom, Beaded Handle, Round Foot, Georg Jensen, 3 ⅝ x 6 x 2 ⅝ In.
$594

Abington Auction Gallery

Silver-Dutch, Bowl, Brandy, Repousse, Openwork Handles, Circular Gadroon Foot, c.1770, 7 ½ In.
$246

Locati Auctions

Silver-Dutch, Spoon, Apostle, Monogram, Peter Bagijn, c.1633, 7 ¾ In.
$1,107

Skinner, Inc.

Silver-Dutch, Teapot, Squat, Ribbed Spout, Molded Waist, Bonebakker En Zoon, 1839, 8 In.
$288

Eldred's

Silver-Danish, Tray, Lid, Finial, Oval, Handles, C.C. Hermann, 6 ½ x 14 ¾ x 8 ⅝ In.
$960

Michaan's Auctions

Silver-English, Basket, Engraved Crest Of Bird, Swags, William Plummer, George III, 1772, 12 x 13 x 10 In.
$625

Susanin's Auctioneers & Appraisers

Silver-English, Basket, Reticulated, Oval Bowl, Beaded Swing Handle, Hester Bateman, George III, 12 ½ In.
$1,889

Clars Auction Gallery

Silver-English, Bowl, Monteith, Reticulated Border, Footed, Initialed R.M. & R.H., 8 x 11 In.
$1,416

Cottone Auctions

Silver-English, Centerpiece, Figural, Maidens, Laurel Wreaths, Flowers, Cut Glass Bowl, c.1800, 15 In.
$4,880

Neal Auction Company

Silver-English, Cup, Coconut, Carved, Roundel, Lilies, Palm Trees, Hester Bateman, Footed, 1786, 7 In.
$2,006

Ahlers & Ogletree Auction Gallery

Silver-English, Kettle, Stand, Wooden Elements, Mappin & Webb, London, Early 1900s, 11 In.
$450

Hindman Auctions

Silver-English, Centerpiece, Neoclassical, Cut Glass Dish, Reeded Legs, Emes & Barnard, London, 1813, 10 In.
$1,800

Case Antiques

Silver-English, Dish, Caviar, Lid, Sturgeon, Dolphin Feet, Shell Handles, Hallmark, 1985, 6 x 7 In.
$3,500

New Orleans Auction Galleries

Silver-English, Muffineer, Finial, Foot Rim, George V, Atkin Brothers, 1926, 7 ½ In.
$215

Charlton Hall Auctions

Silver-English, Coffeepot, Hinged Lid, Embossed Flowers, Wood Handle, Footed, Edward Feline, 8 In.
$431

Stair Galleries

Silver-English, Platter, Oval, Gadroon & Engraved Crest, George IV, 1823, 19 x 14 In.
$1,220

Neal Auction Company

S

Silver-English, Rattle, Coral, Whistle, Repousse, Unite & Hilliard, William IV, 1830-31, 5 ½ In.
$154

Skinner, Inc.

Silver-English, Saltshaker, Bird Shape, Standing, Wings Spread, Lion Marking, 2 In.
$281

Susanin's Auctioneers & Appraisers

Silver-English, Sauceboat, Lion Mask, Leaf Capped Handle, Hair Paw Feet, 1739, 4 ½ x 7 ½ x 4 In., Pair
$3,075

Charlton Hall Auctions

Silver-English, Sugar, 2 Handles, Footed, Peter & Ann Bateman, 2 ¾ In.
$275

Nadeau's Auction Gallery

TIP

You can clean your silver with a paste of baking soda and water. Rub it on, rinse, wipe.

Silver-English, Salver, Gadroon Rim, Robertson, Walton, Newcastle Hallmark, Regency, 1811, 16 x 12 In.

$2,375

New Orleans Auction Galleries

Silver-English, Tankard, Hinged Lid, Engraved Crest, Handle, Walter Brind, George III, 1784, 8 x 7 In.
$1,968

Charlton Hall Auctions

Silver-English, Tea Caddy, Acorn Finial, Monogram, George II, Daniel Smith & Robert Sharp, c.1760, 5 In.
$523

Skinner, Inc.

Silver-English, Tea Caddy, Lid, Oval, Swing Handle, Engraved, Richard Morton, 1700s, 3 ½ x 4 ¾ In.
$1,652

Cottone Auctions

S

SILVER-ENGLISH

Silver-English, Tray, Tea, Rococo, Gadroon Rim, Flowers, Engraved, Daniel Smit, Robert Sharp, 17 x 22 In.
$1,920

Case Antiques

Silver-English, Tureen, Dome Lid, Eagle, Stags, C.F. Kaendler, George II, 1752, 10 x 14 x 9 In.
$31,250

New Orleans Auction Galleries

Silver-English, Urn, Beaded Borders, Finial, Ball Feet, Applied Faucet, Joseph Steward II, 1781, 13 ¾ In.
$615

Brunk Auctions

Sugar Castor, Relief Scrolls, Top Finial, William Hutton & Sons, 1897, 9 x 3 In. 750
Sugar, 2 Handles, Footed, Peter & Ann Bateman, 2 ¾ In. .... *illus* 275
Sugar, Lid, Pear Shape, Spreading Foot, William Plummer, George III, 1764, 3 ⅝ x 6 In. 400
Tankard, Dome Lid, Bulbous, Scroll Handle, Heart Finial, Robert Cox, 1758, 8 In. 1353
Tankard, Dome Lid, Handle, Tapered, George II, 1706, 7 In. 1220
Tankard, Hinged Lid, Engraved Crest, Handle, Walter Brind, George III, 1784, 8 x 7 In. ..*illus* 1968
Tankard, Scroll Handle, Pierced Tab, Floral, Leaf, Joshua Lejeune, c.1750, 7 ½ x 4 ¾ In. 1125
Taperstick, Harlequin, Figural Stem, Beaded Base, Steel & Sons, George V, 1920, 5 ½ In. 338
Tazza, Paul Storr, Chase Swirl Center Top, Beaded, Leaf Base, Scalloped Foot, 4 x 9 In. 3510
Tea Caddy, Acorn Finial, Monogram, George II, Daniel Smith & Robert Sharp, c.1760, 5 In. .... *illus* 523
Tea Caddy, Lid, Oval, Swing Handle, Engraved, Richard Morton, 1700s, 3 ½ x 4 ¾ In. ...*illus* 1652
Tea Strainer, Shaped Handle, Marked, Lion Passant, Pierced Bowl, 6 x 3 In. 163
Teapot, Engraved, Wood Handle, London, 10 In. 649
Teapot, Hinged Lid, Acanthus Leaves, 2 Armorials, Wood Handle, George III, 1767-68, 5 In. 85
Tongs, Tea, Serpent Form Handles, Shell Form Tips, Lion Armorial, Early 1800s, 5 In. 156
Tray, 2 Handles, Footed, Engraved, Henry Chawner, George III, 1792, 3 x 24 x 14 ½ In. 1380
Tray, 2 Handles, Reticulated Rim, Central Monogram, 29 ½ In. 138
Tray, Oval, Reeded Border, Acanthus Handles, Richard Crossley, 1800s, 27 In. 2640
Tray, Tea, Rococo, Gadroon Rim, Flowers, Engraved, Daniel Smit, Robert Sharp, 17 x 22 In. ...*illus* 1920
Trophy, Hunt Cup, Repousse Grapevine, Horses, Dogs, c.1874, 16 In. 2860
Tureen, Dome Lid, Eagle, Stags, C.F. Kaendler, George II, 1752, 10 x 14 x 9 In. .... *illus* 31250
Tureen, Sauce, Oval, Urn Finial, Loop Handle, Hennell, George III, 1807, 5 ½ x 7 ¾ In., Pair.... 1200
Urn, Beaded Borders, Finial, Ball Feet, Applied Faucet, Joseph Steward II, 1781, 13 ¾ In. *illus* 615
Vinaigrette, Oval, Parcel Gilt, Engraved, Monogram, Joseph Willmore, Birmingham, 1 In. *illus* 112
Wine Cooler, Egg, Dart Rim, Grape Leaf Band, Mask Handles, M. Boulton, 1817, 11 In. 7250
Wine Funnel, Clip, Engraved, Charles Lougham, London, George III, 1790, 4 ½ x 3 In. 281
Wine Funnel, Rounded Well, Reeded Band Accent, Long Spout, Shell Clip, c.1819, 5 ½ In. 222

SILVER-FRENCH

Basket, Cartier, Twisted Handle, Woven Silver Body, 11 ½ x 9 ¾ x 8 In. 615
Basket, Openwork, Flowers, Cupids, Swing Handle, Footed, Maison Bloch Eschwege, 14 In. 497
Bowl, Ruffled Rim, Monogram, Marked, Carter, 1900s, 10 In. 344
Box, Lid, Chased Laurel Swags, H. Freres & Cie, c.1800, 4 In. 461
Chocolate Pot, Hinged Lid, Ebony Handle, 1800s, 7 x 8 x 4 In. 154
Cigarette Case, Ribbed Central Register, Black Onyx Clasp, Gilt, 5 In. 158
Coffeepot, Amphora Shape, Dome Lid, Pod Finial, Ebonized Handle, Paw Feet, 1809-19, 12 In. 350
Compote, Round, Faux Marble Enamel Pedestal, Stepped Base, J.E. Puiforcat, 2 ½ x 5 In. 125
Platter, Leaves, Berry, Oval, Paris, Georges Falkenberg, c.1894-1924, 18 x 12 In., Pair 2214
Sauceboat, Bell Flower, Scroll, Attached Underplate, c.1900, 5 x 11 x 6 ¾ In. 600
Serving Dish, Lid, Minerva Head Hallmark, Floral Side Handles, 5 x 12 ⅞ x 7 ¾ In. 761
Sugar Castor, Paneled Style, Cover, Tetard Freres, Early 1900s, 8 ¾ In., Pair .... *illus* 523
Teapot, Napoleon III, Hawk Shape Finial, Water Lilies, Martial Fray, Mid 1800s, 6 ½ In. 468
Teapot, Stand, Impressed Chintz, Blossom Finial, Christofle, France, 16 ½ x 12 ½ In. 390
Tureen, Dome Lid, Flowers, Garland, Figural Busts, Louis Philippe, c.1840, 9 x 10 ½ In. *illus* 7320
Tureen, Dome Lid, Oval, Serpent Handle, Ball Feet, Marked JFI, 1809-19, 9 ½ x 9 x 11 In. 2250

SILVER-GEORGIAN

Coffeepot, Hand Chased, Coat Of Arms, Footed, Flowers, Wood Handle, 1800s, 11 In. 826

SILVER-GERMAN

Bible Cover, Repousse, 3 Archangels, Multicolor Glass Cabochons, 13 Loth, 4 In. 510
Bowl, Embossed, Leaves, Curved Base, Marked, 4 x 7 ¾ In. 123
Bowl, Oval, Reticulated Repousse, Floral Swags, Scrolls, Hanau, c.1900, 11 x 8 ⅝ In. 176
Chalice, Gilt Wash, Hand Engraved, Reticulated, Jewels, G.A. Harblem Jr., 9 In. 2006
Coaster, Cherub, Garlands, Treen Base, Monogram, Koch & Bergfeld, c.1910, 5 In., Pair .*illus* 688
Cocktail Shaker, Squirrel, Glass Eyes, Chain, Ludwig Neresheimer Co., 6 x 12 In. ....*illus* 5000
Compote, Glass Rim, 2 Slender Handles, Hugo Bohm, Early 1900s, 11 In. 461
Dish, Ornate, Pierced, Cherubs, Flowers, Footed, 8 ¾ x 8 ¾ In. 96
Figure, King Arthur, Suit Of Armor, Sword, Shield, L. Neresheimer, Germany, c.1900, 9 ½ In.. 1046
Garniture, Jousting Knights, Full Armor, Lance, Rectangular Base, Armorials, 12 x 12 In. 6563
Salt, Master, Triangular, Ball Feet, J.D. Schleissner & Sohne, 1850, 2 x 3 x 3 In., Pair.......... 468
Sugar, Lid, Reeded Rim, 2 Beast Handles, 3 Curved Legs, Paw Feet, c.1800, 7 x 5 x 3 In. 263
Urn, Lid, Pedestal Foot, Marked 800, c.1900, 8 ¾ In. 275

S

Silver-English, Vinaigrette, Oval, Parcel Gilt, Engraved, Monogram, Joseph Willmore, Birmingham, 1 In.
$112

Leland Little Auctions

Silver-French, Sugar Castor, Paneled Style, Cover, Tetard Freres, Early 1900s, 8 ¾ In., Pair
$523

Charlton Hall Auctions

Silver-French, Tureen, Dome Lid, Flowers, Garland, Figural Busts, Louis Philippe, c.1840, 9 x 10 ½ In.
$7,320

Neal Auction Company

Silver-German, Coaster, Cherub, Garlands, Treen Base, Monogram, Koch & Bergfeld, c.1910, 5 In., Pair
$688

Hindman Auctions

Silver-German, Cocktail Shaker, Squirrel, Glass Eyes, Chain, Ludwig Neresheimer Co., 6 x 12 In.
$5,000

New Orleans Auction Galleries

Silver-German, Wedding Cup, Woman, Swivel, Carved, Gilt Washed Interior, 5 ⅝ In.
$113

Hindman Auctions

S

Silver-Indian, Salver, Hamilton & Co., Gadroon, Leafy Edge, Calcutta, c.1820, 12 ½ In.
$708

Bunch Auctions

Silver-Irish, Sauceboat, Handle, Hoof Feet, Matthew West, Dublin, 1780, 4 ¾ In.
$214

Nadeau's Auction Gallery

Silver-Italian, Pitcher, Bulbous, Openwork Grapevine Handle, Masi & Zaccaro, 7 x 9 In.
$492

Clars Auction Gallery

TIP

Save your old toothbrush to use when polishing silver. It can get the foaming polish in the crevices and then when rinsing it will remove any bits of paste or foam. Do not leave traces of polish to dry. It can damage the piece.

Silver-Italian, Wine Cradle, Chased, Arcanthus, Openwork, Hinged Handle, Buccellati, 7 x 12 In.
$1,342

Neal Auction Company

Silver-Japanese, Box, Copper Inset Lid, Raised Fan, Wood Lined Interior, 1 ½ x 6 x 3 In.
$210

CRN Auctions

Silver-Japanese, Box, Lift Top, Mt. Fuji, Temple Etched On Lid, Stamped, Early 1900s, 1 ½ x 6 In.
$259

Eldred's

Wedding Cup, Woman, Swivel, Carved, Gilt Washed Interior, 5 ⅝ In. .... *illus* 113

SILVER-GREEK

Cup, Gilt, Molded, Animals, Handle, Lalaounis, 3 ½ In., Pair 492

SILVER-HUNGARIAN

Tray, Oval, Reverse Scalloped Edge, Marked, 24 x 17 ½ In. 726
Tray, Scalloped Rim, Rectangular, Marked, 7 x 13 In., Pair 308

SILVER-INDIAN

Salver, Hamilton & Co., Gadroon, Leafy Edge, Calcutta, c.1820, 12 ½ In. .... *illus* 708

SILVER-IRISH

Chalice, Ciborium, Celtic Revival Style, Gilt, Enamel, George V, Edmond Johnson, c.1932, 13 In. 1476
Cream Jug, Charles Marsh, Ireland, c.1821, 4 In. 206
Cup, 2 Handles, Footed, George II, Silversmith, Charles Townsend, 5 ⅜ In. 1170
Cup, Dome Lid, Fluted, Repousse Flower Banding, 16 ½ x 6 ½ In. 2000
Sauceboat, Handle, Hoof Feet, Matthew West, Dublin, 1780, 4 ¾ In. .... *illus* 214

SILVER-ITALIAN

Bowl, Saucer, Hinged Lid, Acorn Finial, Fitted Glass Insert, Buccellati, 1900s, 4 x 8 x 6 In. 750
Dish, Circular, Repousse Rim, Fruits, Braganti, c.1950, 13 In. 240
Ewer, Scrolling Chase, Rosettes, 4 Malachite Cabochons, 12 ½ x 6 ½ x 4 ½ In. 584
Figurine, Frog, Sitting, Stamped Underside, Buccellati, 1 x 2 x 2 In. 500
Gravy Boat, Wide Spout, Loop Handle, Engraved, Flowers, Undertray, 6 In. 523
Nut Dish, Fluted, Scalloped Rim, Footed, Marked, Bulgari, 1900s, 1 ⅝ x 2 ¾ In., Pair 594
Pitcher, Bulbous, Openwork Grapevine Handle, Masi & Zaccaro, 7 x 9 In. .... *illus* 492
Platter, Round Plateau, Grapevine Rim, Masi & Zaccaro, 13 ½ In. 308
Tray, Elephant, Gold Wash Head, Footed, Hand Crafted, Hauy Pouigo, 25 x 15 x 3 ⅜ In. 1188
Wine Coaster, Plateau, Round, Openwork Grapevine Rim, Masi & Zaccaro, 5 ½ In. 215
Wine Cradle, Chased, Arcanthus, Openwork, Hinged Handle, Buccellati, 7 x 12 In. .... *illus* 1342

SILVER-JAPANESE

Bowl, Scalloped Rim, Engraved, Butterflies, Chrysanthemums, Early 1900s, 2 ½ x 7 ¾ In. 308
Box, Copper Inset Lid, Raised Fan, Wood Lined Interior, 1 ½ x 6 x 3 In. .... *illus* 210
Box, Hinged Lid, Ebony, Rectangular, Engraved, Chrysanthemum Bough, c.1935, 6 In. 120
Box, Lift Top, Mt. Fuji, Temple Etched On Lid, Stamped, Early 1900s, 1 ½ x 6 In. .... *illus* 259
Box, Rosewood Line, Gold, Rose, Cormorant, Boat, Basket, Seal, Early 1900s, 5 ½ x 4 x 2 In.... 1192
Jewelry Box, Hinged Lid, Engraved, Flowers, Marked, 3 ¾ x 7 ½ In. 406
Sugar, Gold Washed Interior, Open Handle, Chrysanthemum, c.1900, 6 x 4 ¾ In. .... *illus* 492

SILVER-MEXICAN

Silver objects have been made in Mexico since the days of the Aztecs. These marks are for three companies still making tableware and jewelry.

ChATO CASTiLLO STERLING MEXICO	Matl STERLING MEXICO 925	SANBORN'S STERLING H MADE IN MEXICO
Jorge "Chato" Castillo 1939+	Matilde Eugenia Poulat 1934–1960	Sanborn's 1931–present

Bowl, 2 Handles, Footed, Marked, Owl & Sanborn's, 4 x 10 ½ In. .... *illus* 510
Bowl, Flower Form, Hammered Interior, Marked, Sanborn's, c.1950, 3 ½ x 8 In. 185
Bowl, Oval, Round Footed, Marked, William Spratling, 1962-64, 3 x 12 In. 531
Bowl, Scallop Sides, 3 Ball Feet, Mark, 3 ¾ x 8 In. 275
Bowl, Scalloped Rim, Monogram, Maciel, c.1950, 12 In. 554
Bowl, Shell, Ball Feet, Alfredo Ortega & Sons, Mexico, 18 ½ x 18 In. 1090
Pot, Gold Twist Swing Handle, Bulbous Body, Signed, Tane, 9 x 8 In. .... *illus* 518
Sauceboat, Footed, Molded Rim, Handle, 3 ¾ x 9 x 6 ½ In. 156
Sauceboat, Round Foot, Triple Leaf Shape Handle, 1 ½ x 7 x 4 ½ In. 250
Teapot, Hinged Lid, George III Style, Bulbous, Wooden Handle, Sanborn's, 9 x 7 In. 338

Silver-Japanese, Sugar, Gold Washed Interior, Open Handle, Chrysanthemum, c.1900, 6 x 4 ¾ In.
$492

Locati Auctions

TIP
Wool, felt, rubber, latex, oak, some types of paint, and many types of food will cause your silver to tarnish.

Silver-Mexican, Bowl, 2 Handles, Footed, Marked, Owl & Sanborn's, 4 x 10 ½ In.
$510

CRN Auctions

Silver-Mexican, Pot, Gold Twist Swing Handle, Bulbous Body, Signed, Tane, 9 x 8 In.
$518

Richard D. Hatch & Associates

This is an edited listing of current prices. Visit **Kovels.com** to check thousands of prices from previous years and sign up for free information on trends, tips, reproductions, marks, and more.

S

SILVER-MEXICAN

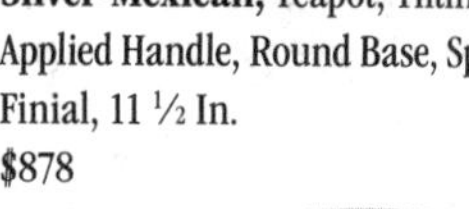

Silver-Mexican, Teapot, Tilting, Applied Handle, Round Base, Spout, Finial, 11 ½ In.
$878

Nadeau's Auction Gallery

TIP
To remove old protective lacquer from a piece of silver, immerse the piece in very hot water for a few hours. This should loosen the lacquer. The process may have to be repeated to get all of the lacquer off. Several commercial lacquer removers are available.

Silver-Russian, Basket, Trompe L'Oeil, Swirl Handle, 2-Headed Eagle Mark, c.1887, 12 ½ In.
$2,583

Skinner, Inc.

Silver-Sterling, Platter, Scalloped Edge, Fish, Oval, 23 ¾ x 11 ⅞ In.
$590

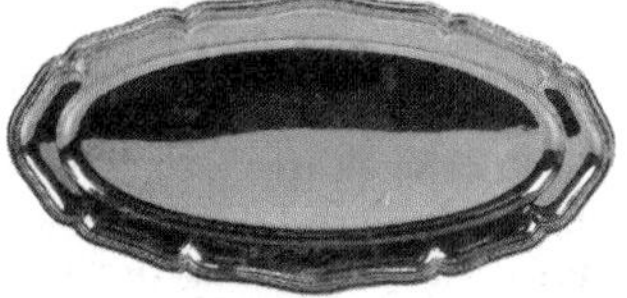

Bunch Auctions

Teapot, Tilting, Applied Handle, Round Base, Spout, Finial, 11 ½ In. .... *illus* 878
Tray, Rectangular, 2 Handles, Glass Insert, Marked, Hecho En, 15 ¾ x 28 ½ In. 1244
Tray, Rectangular, Scrolling Handles, Monogram, c.1960, 20 ½ x 13 In. 738
Tray, Serving, Oval, 2 Shaped Handles, Hecho En Mexico 0925, 1900s, 28 x 23 ¾ x 17 In. 995

SILVER-PERSIAN

Bonbonniere, Melon Shape, Repousse, Chased, Leaves, Hinges, 9 ½ x 8 ¾ In. 3750
Bowl, Scalloped Basin, Pierced, 3 Claw Feet, 5 x 12 ½ In. 1116
Tray, Ornate, Scroll Shape, Botanical Motif, Animals, 16 ½ x 12 In. 1488
Tray, Rectangular, Plateau, Scallop Rim, Handles, Scrolling Vines, Leaves, 12 ½ x 9 In. 615

SILVER-PERUVIAN

Jam Pot, Ladle Finial, Man, Llama, Stonework Ground, Marked, San Judas, 4 ¾ In. 260
Tray, Serving, Oval, Scrolled Leaf, Shell Rim, Camusso, Lima, 1900s, 19 x 13 ¾ In. 585

SILVER-PORTUGUESE

Tray, Lobed Shape, Beaded Rim, Central Coat, Repousse, Coin, 1938, 8 x 8 In. 151
Tray, Rounded Rectangular, Pierced Gallery, 2 Handles, Paw Feet, c.1900, 2 x 21 x 14 In. 1140

SILVER-RUSSIAN

Russian silver is marked with the Cyrillic, or Russian, alphabet. The numbers 84, 88, or 91 indicate the silver content. Russian silver may be higher or lower than sterling standard. Other marks indicate maker, assayer, or city of manufacture. Many pieces of silver made in Russia are decorated with enamel. Faberge pieces are listed in their own category.

Silver–Russian
Silver content numbers

Silver–Russian
1741–1900+

Silver–Russian
1896–1908

Basket, Trompe L'Oeil, Swirl Handle, 2-Headed Eagle Mark, c.1887, 12 ½ In. .... *illus* 2583
Cigarette Case, Niello, Leaves, Arabesques, Marked GK, Late 1800s, 3 ⅜ In. 277
Coffeepot, Lid, Scrolled Handle, Thumb Rest, Ivan Vasilyevich Avdeyev, c.1860, 6 ¾ In. 211
Encrier, Kokoshnik, Serpentine, Nicholas II, Gilt, St. Petersburg, 4 x 4 ⅝ x 4 ⅝ In. 1200
Ladle, Spiral Handle, Scoop, C.K.I., Stepan Levin, c.1874, 7 In. 403
Scoop, Enamel, Vermeil, Leafy, Multicolor Handle, Aleksandr Karpov, c.1887, 5 In. 682
Server, Leaves, Flowers, Scrolled Rim, Footed, Hallmark, 12 In. 554
Sugar Basket, Flowers, Footed, Handle, Marked, Elias Modig, c.1830, 5 ½ x 5 In. 341
Tongs, Enamel, Flowers, Spiral Handle, Aleksandr Karpov, 1889, 5 ½ In. 341
Vase, Bud, Urn Shape, Engraved, Circular Base, Marked, Myuz, 1900s, 4 ½ In. 185

SILVER-SCOTTISH

Creamer, Helmet Style, Handle, Stipple, Edinburgh, 1791, 6 x 5 ½ In. 584
Sauceboat, Peaked Rim, Leaf Handle, 3 Paw Feet, George III, James Weems, 7 In. 504

SILVER-SPANISH

Plate, Colonial, Scalloped Rim, Marked BTON, 6 ½ In., 6 Piece 738

SILVER-STERLING

Sterling silver is made with 925 parts silver out of 1,000 parts of metal. The word sterling is a quality guarantee used in the United States after about 1860. The word was used much earlier in England and Ireland. Other pieces of sterling quality silver are listed under Silver-American, Silver-English, etc.

Bonbon Scoop, Gold Wash, Blue Enamel, Ornate, Openwork, Shallow Bowl & Handle, 5 In. 201
Bowl, Abalone Brickwork Inlay, Blue Topaz, Amethyst, Citrine Gems, Oval, Footed, 6 x 7 In. 345
Bowl, Oval, Ornate, Flowers, Around Rim, Marked, 9 ¼ x 7 x 2 ⅜ In. 84
Bowl, Swan Figure, Serpentine Neck, Plumage, .935 Argentium, 4 ½ x 6 ½ x 3 ¾ In. 308
Bread Plate, Round, Marked, 5 ½ In., 12 Piece 540
Bread Tray, Oblong, Scalloped Rim, c.1950, 11 In. 144

Butter, Cover, WC & Co., Footed, 2 Handles, Crown Finial, Floral, Monogram, 6 ½ x 5 x 5 ½ In. 531
Cake Plate, Renaissance Style, Griffins, Putti, Dolphins, Leafy Scrollwork, c.1910, 11 In. 272
Candelabra are listed in the Candelabrum category.
Candlesticks are listed in their own category.
Compote, Reticulated Edge, Floral Sprays, High Strap Handles, c.1920, 4 x 11 ½ In., Pair 311
Dish, Shell Shape, Engraved Armorial, Marked, E, 1764-65, 5 In., Pair 861
Figure, Owl, Gilt, Blown Glass Eyes, Detailed Feathers, Tail, Stamped F & Son Ltd., 11 x 8 In. 4720
Ladle, Bent Handle, Lily & Vine Motif, Monogram, 11 In. 91
Loving Cup, Filigree, 2 Handles, Monogram, Marked, Christmas 1901, 7 x 9 In. 363
Napkin Rings are listed in their own category.
Pitcher, Art Deco, Footed, Octagonal Panel Shape, Helmet Spout, 11 In. 454
Plaque, Horse, 3 Stallions, Rocky Terrain, Marked Arg. 925, 15 x 21 In. 182
Platter, Scalloped Edge, Fish, Oval, 23 ¾ x 11 ⅞ In. *illus* 590
Punch Bowl, Paul Revere Pattern, Flared Rim, Footed Base, 7 ⅝ x 14 In. *illus* 1560
Sauceboat, Flowers, Undertray, Black Handle, Marked, 1976, 9 x 7 In. 360
Sauceboat, Wide Spout, Shaped Handle, Paw Feet, Constance Leither, 1900s, 3 ½ x 8 x 4 In. 311
Spoon, Souvenir, see Souvenir category.
Tazza, Flower, Filigree, Black, Starr & Frost, Marked, 2 ⅝ x 8 In., Pair 787
Teapot, Curved Handle, Long Neck Spout, Round Lid, Finial, 9 In. 329

SILVER-SWEDISH

Bowl, Scalloped Rim & Base, Footed, Mark, GAD, c.1926, 6 ½ In. 554

SILVER-THAI

Box, Lid, Bulbous, Repousse, Cone Shape Finial, Leaves, 6 x 6 In. 154

SILVER-TURKISH

Bowl, Crowned Monogram Interior, c.1800, 8 ⅜ In. 400

SINCLAIRE

Sinclaire cut glass was made by H.P. Sinclaire and Company of Corning, New York, between 1904 and 1929. He cut glass made at other factories until 1920. Pieces were made of clear glass as well as amber, blue, green, or ruby glass. Only a small percentage of Sinclaire glass is marked with the *S* in a wreath.

Clock, Shelf, Harvest, Engraved Roses, Flower Baskets, Floral Cornucopia, 10 x 7 In. 4160
Pitcher, Cider, Leaves, Fruits, Engraved, Signed, 7 In. 175
Plate, Assyrian, Scalloped Rim, Acid Stamped Signature, 6 ¾ In. 558

SKIING, *see Sports category.*

SLAG GLASS

Slag glass resembles a marble cake. It can be streaked with different colors. There were many types made from about 1880. Caramel slag is the incorrect name for chocolate glass made by Imperial Glass. Pink slag was an American product made by Harry Bastow and Thomas E.A. Dugan at Indiana, Pennsylvania, about 1900. Purple and blue slag were made in American and English factories in the 1880s. Red slag is a very late Victorian and twentieth-century glass. Other colors are known but are of less importance to the collector. New versions of chocolate glass and colored slag glass have been made.

Caramel Slag is listed in the Imperial Glass category.
Blue, Candy Dish, Heart Shape, Crimped Edge, Finger Ring Handle, Fenton, 8 x 6 ½ In. 35
Lamp, Metal Frame, Harbor Scene, Statue Of Liberty, Hollow Base, Edward Miller, 22 In. *illus* 735
Purple, Bottle, Narrow Neck, Bulbous Ribbed Bottom, Screw Opening, 9 In. 22
Purple, Dish, Lion On Nest Cover 44
Purple, Rosary, Silvertone Crucifix, Mary Of Lourdes Image, 14 In. 125
Red, Bell, American Bicentennial, Eagle Finial, 2 Stars, 1776-1976, 6 ½ x 3 In. 34
Yellow, Smoking Stand, Metal Stand, Light-Up Base, 27 x 12 x 9 In. 316

Silver-Sterling, Punch Bowl, Paul Revere Pattern, Flared Rim, Footed Base, 7 ⅝ x 14 In.
$1,560

Case Antiques

Slag Glass, Lamp, Metal Frame, Harbor Scene, Statue Of Liberty, Hollow Base, Edward Miller, 22 In.
$735

Soulis Auctions

Sleepy Eye Repros

Original Sleepy Eye pitchers were made in five sizes. Each was made in one piece. Reproduction pitchers are two pieces, the body and an attached handle.

Sleepy Eye, Sign, Flour, Indian Portrait, Scene Border, Tin Lithograph, 24 x 20 In.
$7,670

Cottone Auctions

Snuffbox, Enamel, Hinged Lid, Circular, Classical Scene, Continental, 1800s, 1 ¾ x 3 In.
$270

CRN Auctions

Soapstone, Carving, Priest, Seated, Wearing Robe, Holding Buddha Figure, Painted, Chinese, 4 In.
$250

Eldred's

Soapstone, Figurine, Luohan, Seated, Beaded Jewels, Velvet Box, c.1800, 2 ½ x 2 x 1 In.
$439

Thomaston Place Auction Galleries

SLEEPY EYE

Sleepy Eye collectors look for anything bearing the image of the nineteenth-century Indian chief with the drooping eyelid. The Sleepy Eye Milling Co., Sleepy Eye, Minnesota, used his portrait in advertising from 1883 to 1921. It offered many premiums, including stoneware and pottery steins, crocks, bowls, mugs, pitchers, and many advertising items, all decorated with the famous profile of the Indian. The popular pottery was made by Weir Pottery Co. from c.1899 to 1905. Weir merged with six other potteries and became Western Stoneware in 1906. Western Stoneware Co. made blue and white Sleepy Eye from 1906 until 1937, long after the flour mill went out of business in 1921. Reproductions of the pitchers are being made today. The original pitchers came in only five sizes: 4 inches, 5 ¼ inches, 6 ½ inches, 8 inches, and 9 inches. The Sleepy Eye image was also used by companies unrelated to the flour mill.

Button, Pinback, 90th Anniversary Jubilee, Indian Profile, 1872-1962, 3 In. 22
Mug, Indian, Teepee, Tent, Blue & White, Handle, Marked, 4 ⅜ In. 30
Pitcher, Indian Chief, Teepees, Tree, Blue, White, 7 ½ In. 75
Sign, Flour, Indian Portrait, Scene Border, Tin Lithograph, 24 x 20 In. .... *illus* 7670
Vase, Indian, Profile, Cattails, Cobalt Blue, Salt Glaze, 8 ¾ x 4 In. 127

SLOT MACHINES *are included in the Coin-Operated Machine category.*

SMITH BROTHERS

Smith Brothers glass was made from 1874 to 1899. Alfred and Harry Smith had worked for the Mt. Washington Glass Company in New Bedford, Massachusetts, for seven years before going into their own shop. They made many pieces with enamel decoration.

Biscuit Jar, Silver Plate Mouth, Cover & Handle, Melon Lobed, White, c.1880, 5 ¼ x 2 ¾ In. 110

SNOW BABIES

Snow Babies, made from bisque and spattered with glitter sand, were first manufactured in 1864 by Hertwig and Company of Thuringia. Other German and Japanese companies copied the Hertwig designs. Originally, Snow Babies were made of candy and used as Christmas decorations. There are also Snow Babies tablewares made by Royal Bayreuth. Copies of the small Snow Babies figurines are being made today, and a line called "Snowbabies" was introduced by Department 56 in 1987. Don't confuse these with the original Snow Babies.

Figurine, Baby, Seated, Painted Face, Kister, 1 ¾ In. 225
Figurine, Baby, Sledding, Brown Painted Sled, Marked Germany, 1 ½ x 1 ⅜ In. 68
Figurine, Child, Carrying Skis, Hertwig 27
Figurine, Elf, Beard, Arm Reaching Out, Sitting On Stump, Germany, 2 In. 34

SNUFF BOTTLES *are listed in the Bottle category.*

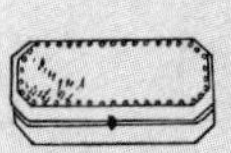

SNUFFBOX

Snuffboxes held snuff. Taking snuff was popular long before cigarettes became available. The gentleman or lady would take a small pinch of the ground tobacco or snuff in the fingers, then sniff it and sneeze. Snuffboxes were made of many materials, including gold, silver, enameled metal, and wood. Most snuffboxes date from the late eighteenth or early nineteenth centuries.

Bone, Wood Caps, Lift Top, Engraved, Geometric, Flowers, 1800s, 4 In. 330
Enamel, Hinged Lid, Circular, Classical Scene, Continental, 1800s, 1 ¾ x 3 In. .... *illus* 270
Gold, 14K, Cabochon Gemstone Clasp, Engraved Inside, Mippi, 3 ¼ x 1 ¾ In. 1416
Porcelain, St. Cloud, Kakiemon Buddha, Silver Base, 2 ½ In. 2583

Portrait, Girl, African Child, Fruit, Monkey, Mounted, Continental, c.1700, 3 In. 677
Silver, George IV, Engine Turned, Engraved R. Myers, John Jones III, London, 1825, 3 ⅞ In..... 163

SOAPSTONE

Soapstone is a mineral that was used for foot warmers or griddles because of its heat-retaining properties. Soapstone was carved into figurines and bowls in many countries in the nineteenth and twentieth centuries. Most of the soapstone collectibles seen today are from Asia. It is still being carved in the old styles.

Carving, Priest, Seated, Wearing Robe, Holding Buddha Figure, Painted, Chinese, 4 In. .*illus* 250
Figurine, Luohan, Seated, Beaded Jewels, Velvet Box, c.1800, 2 ½ x 2 x 1 In. ....*illus* 439
Figurine, Shoushan Luohan, Reclining, Foo Dog, Flowing Robe, Chinese, 1800s, 4 x 3 In. 439
Lamp Base, Carved, Birds & Flowers, Mounted, Brass Base, Chinese, 17 In. ....*illus* 123
Seal, Carved, Old Elephant, 2 Boys Clambering, Bamboo, Deer, Chinese, 8 x 3 In., Pair........... 150

SOFT PASTE

Soft paste is a name for a type of pottery. Although it looks very much like porcelain, it is a chemically different material. Most of the soft-paste wares were made in the early nineteenth century. Other pieces may be listed under Gaudy Dutch or Leeds.

Figurine, Cat, Mantel, White & Black, Glazed, 1700s, 8 ¼ In., Pair... 121
Plate, Queen's Rose, Flowers, Wide Banded Border, 10 In. 153
Sugar, Lid, Sponged Design, Polka Dots, Blue With Purple Centers, Flower Shapes, 5 In. 65

SOUVENIR

Souvenirs of a trip—what could be more fun? Our ancestors enjoyed the same thing and souvenirs were made for almost every location. Most of the souvenir pottery and porcelain pieces of the nineteenth century were made in England or Germany, even if the picture showed a North American scene. In the early twentieth century, the souvenir china business seems to have been dominated by the manufacturers in Japan, Taiwan, Hong Kong, England, and the United States. Souvenir china was also made in other countries after the 1960s. Another popular souvenir item is the souvenir spoon, made of sterling or silver plate. These are usually made in the country pictured on the spoon. Related pieces may be found in the Coronation, Olympics, and World's Fair categories.

Ashtray, Bern, Switzerland, Black Forest, Bear, 3 x 2 x 2 In. 69
Bottle Opener, Dolphin Shape, Florida, Celluloid, Magnet, 6 In. 12
Creamer, Vineyard Haven, Martha's Vineyard, Brown, Tax, Gold Specks, 1900s, 3 ¾ In........... 150
Cup & Saucer, Thousand Islands, St. Lawrence River, Scalloped Rim, England, 1884............. 15
Dutch Shoe, Nijmegan Kronenburgerpark, Porcelain, 3 In... 10
Plate, San Francisco, Chinatown, Good Health, Recipes, 1960s, 8 In. 24
Plate, Washington DC, Capitol Building, Platinum Trim, Japan, 10 ½ In. 25
Spoon, Atlantic City, Pierced Handle, Silver, Watson Co., 5 ⅜ In. 21
Spoon, Helena, Montana, Helmet & Shield, Whiting Mfg., 4 In.. 30
Spoon, Mount Vernon, Ornate, Silver, 1891, 6 In. ....*illus* 28
Spoon, Seattle, Olympic Range From Seattle, Totem Pole Handle, Sterling, 5 In. 70
Trinket Box, Beziers Place De La Citadelle, Eglomise & Ormolu, 2 x 2 x 2 In............................ 199
Tumbler, Saratoga Springs, Sandwich Overlay, Cobalt Cut To Clear, Glass, Leaves, 1850s, 5 In. . 500

SPATTER GLASS

Spatter glass is a multicolored glass made from many small pieces of different colored glass. It is sometimes called End-of-Day glass. It is still being made.

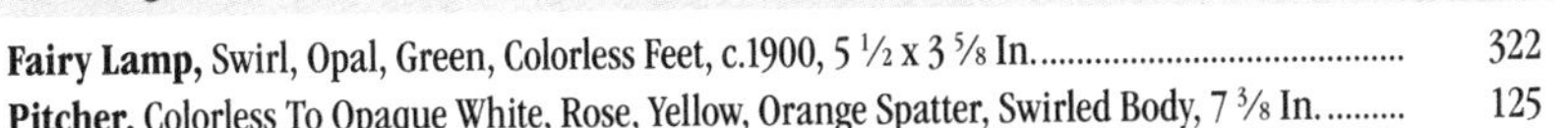

Fairy Lamp, Swirl, Opal, Green, Colorless Feet, c.1900, 5 ½ x 3 ⅝ In.. 322
Pitcher, Colorless To Opaque White, Rose, Yellow, Orange Spatter, Swirled Body, 7 ⅜ In. 125

Soapstone, Lamp Base, Carved, Birds & Flowers, Mounted, Brass Base, Chinese, 17 In.
$123

Stair Galleries

Souvenir Mug

A souvenir mug is decorated or shaped to remind you of a location or event.

Souvenir, Spoon, Mount Vernon, Ornate, Silver, 1891, 6 In.
$28

Hartzell's Auction Gallery Inc.

S

Spatterware, Bowl, Thistle, Shallow, Flower, Leaves, White Ground, 10 ½ In.
$793

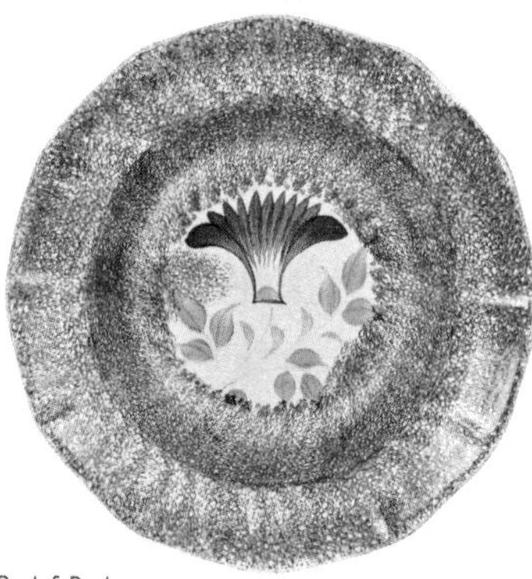

Pook & Pook

Spatterware, Creamer, Rainbow, Red & Green Bands, Loop Handle, 3 ½ In.
$443

Conestoga Auction Company

Spatterware, Cup & Saucer, Rainbow, Red & Yellow Bands, Child's, Saucer, 4 ½ In.
$708

Conestoga Auction Company

TIP
Go outside and try to read your house numbers from the street. If you can't read them, get new, larger ones. Help responding to an emergency must be able to see the numbers in your address.

Spatterware, Mug, Red & Blue, 2 ⅛ In., Child's
$118

Conestoga Auction Company

Prevent Burglaries
Lock your doors and windows. In up to 82 percent of all home burglaries, the burglar enters through a door. Most often the doors were unlocked.

Spatterware, Plate, 6-Point Star, Red, Blue, Green, 8 ½ In.
$325

Conestoga Auction Company

Spatterware, Plate, Dahlia, 6 Petals, Blue Spatter, 9 In.
$325

Conestoga Auction Company

Spatterware, Plate, Rainbow, Red, Green & Blue Bands, 9 ½ In.
$325

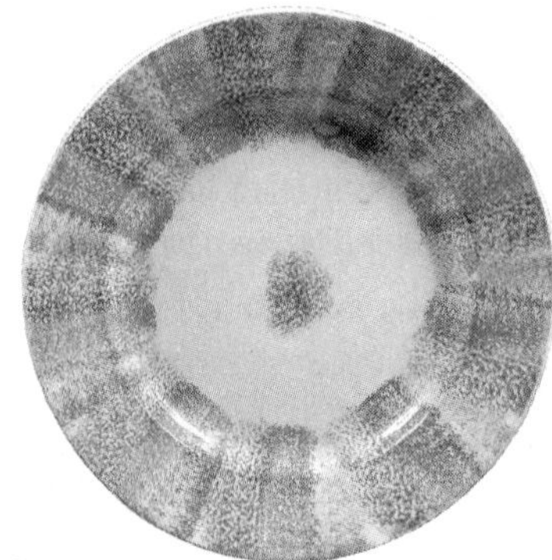

Conestoga Auction Company

Spatterware, Plate, Schoolhouse, Red, Blue & Green Sponged Decoration, 1830s, 8 ½ In.
$878

Jeffrey S. Evans & Associates

TIP
Don't put pottery or porcelain with crazed glaze in the dishwasher. It will crack even more.

Spatterware, Sugar, Lid, 2 Men On Raft, Purple, Footed, Bulbous Body, 4 ½ In.
$976

Pook & Pook

SPATTERWARE

Spatterware and spongeware are terms that have changed in meaning in recent years, causing much confusion for collectors. It is a type of ceramic. Some say that *spatterware* is the term used by Americans, *sponged ware* or *spongeware* by the English. The earliest pieces were made in the late eighteenth century, but most of the spatterware found today was made from about 1800 to 1850. Early spatterware was made in the Staffordshire district of England for sale in America. Collectors also use the word *spatterware* to refer to kitchen crockery with added spatter made in America during the late nineteenth and early twentieth centuries. Spongeware is very similar to spatterware in appearance. Designs were applied to ceramics by daubing the color on with a sponge or cloth. Many collectors do not differentiate between spongeware and spatterware and use the names interchangeably. Modern pottery is being made to resemble old spatterware and spongeware, but careful examination will show it is new.

Bowl, Thistle, Shallow, Flower, Leaves, White Ground, 10 ½ In. .... *illus* 793
Creamer, Rainbow, Red & Green Bands, Loop Handle, 3 ½ In. .... *illus* 443
Creamer, Tulip, Pink, White Flower, Green Leaves, Octagonal, Yellow Sponge Border, 1810s, 5 In.. 1404
Cup & Saucer, Rainbow, Red & Yellow Bands, Child's, Saucer, 4 ½ In. .... *illus* 708
Cup Plate, Rainbow, Red, Sage Green, 4 In. 207
Mug, Red & Blue, Child's, 2 ⅛ In. .... *illus* 118
Pitcher, American Eagle, Shield, Arrows, Blue, Footed, c.1850, 11 ½ In. 110
Pitcher, Peafowl, Multicolor Bird, Red Sponged Border, Heart Shape Leaf, 1830s, 9 ½ In. 556
Pitcher, Rainbow, Blue & Purple, Paneled, Handle, Hexagon Base, 6 ½ In. 130
Plate, 6-Point Star, Red, Blue, Green, 8 ½ In. .... *illus* 325
Plate, Acorn, Red Sponged Border, 12-Sided Rim, Yellow Nuts, Leafy Branch, 1830s, 8 In. 1872
Plate, Dahlia, 6 Petals, Blue Spatter, 9 In. .... *illus* 325
Plate, Dahlia, Paneled, Red & Blue Flower, Green Sprigs, 8 In. 354
Plate, Rainbow, Red, Green & Blue Bands, 9 ½ In. .... *illus* 325
Plate, Schoolhouse, Red & Yellow, White Ground, Blue Spatter Border, Sponged Tree, 9 ⅜ In.. 915
Plate, Schoolhouse, Red, Blue & Green Sponged Decoration, 1830s, 8 ½ In. .... *illus* 878
Plate, Schoolhouse, Red, White Ground, Blue Spatter Border, Sponged Tree, 8 ⅜ In. 130
Platter, Cockscomb, Rose, Multicolor, Octagonal, 1800s, 8 In. 400
Sugar, Lid, 2 Men On Raft, Purple, Footed, Bulbous Body, 4 ½ In. .... *illus* 976
Sugar, Lid, Red, Castle Decoration, 5 ¼ In. 472
Sugar, Lid, Rings, Red, Blue, Green, Drop Ring & Shell Handles, Staffordshire, 5 x 5 In. .*illus* 443
Waste Bowl, Rainbow, Red, Blue & Green Bands, 5 ½ In. .... *illus* 649

SPELTER

Spelter is a synonym for a zinc alloy. Figurines, candlesticks, and other pieces were made of spelter and given a bronze or painted finish. The metal has been used since about the 1860s to make statues, tablewares, and lamps that resemble bronze. Spelter is soft and breaks easily. To test for spelter, scratch the base of the piece. Bronze is solid; spelter will show a silvery scratch.

Sculpture, Boy Playing Violin, Lulli Enfant, Adrien Etienne Gaudez, 20 In. 75
Sculpture, Gull, Green Patina, Wave, Mounted, Marble Base, Signed J. Loriot, 22 x 18 x 9 In... 203

SPINNING WHEEL

Spinning wheels in the corner have been symbols of earlier times for the past 150 years. Although spinning wheels date back to medieval days, the ones found today are rarely more than 150 years old. Because the style of the spinning wheel changed very little, it is often impossible to place an exact date on a wheel. There are different types for spinning flax or wool.

Flax, Carved Heart Details, Bone Finials, Black, Red, 1800s, 48 x 33 In. 120

Spatterware, Sugar, Lid, Rings, Red, Blue, Green, Drop Ring & Shell Handles, Staffordshire, 5 x 5 In.
$443

Conestoga Auction Company

Spatterware, Waste Bowl, Rainbow, Red, Blue & Green Bands, 5 ½ In.
$649

Conestoga Auction Company

Is It Spatterware or Spongeware?

It's easy to tell if it's spatterware or spongeware. Spatterware dishes are decorated with what looks like paint spattered from a brush. Spongeware looks as if the paint was dabbed on with a sponge. Through the years, authors and collectors have jumbled the names until almost all of these types of decoration are lumped under the name *spatterware*, even if the dishes appear to be spongeware. To be correct today, avoid the terms *design spatter*, *stick spatter*, and *cut sponge*. They are all inaccurate names for types of spatterware and spongeware.

Not The Babe

Beware of a baseball that is autographed "Sincerely, Babe Ruth." The Sinclair Oil Company gave signed baseballs as prizes in 1947. The balls were stamped "Sinclair Oil." It is now known that the autograph was signed by a secretary.

Sports, Baseball, Flyer, Bob Feller Candy Bar, Cleveland Indian Star, Frame, 20 x 14 In.
$180

Milestone Auctions

Sports, Baseball, Jersey, Roger Clemens, Houston Astros, All-Star Game, Shadowbox, 44 x 33 In.
$201

Bunch Auctions

Sports, Football, Ball, Autographed, Joe Montana, Cotton Bowl Championship
$248

Charleston Estate Auctions

Mixed Wood, Signed, I.A.M., 1823, 52 In.	23
Mixed Wood, Turned Legs, Pennsylvania, 49 ½ In, 1800s	41
Pine, Oak, Simple Turning, Screw Tension, Large Wheel, c.1810, 55 x 48 x 51 In.	59

SPODE

Spode pottery, porcelain, and bone china were made by the Stoke-on-Trent factory of England founded by Josiah Spode about 1770. The firm became Copeland and Garrett from 1833 to 1847, then W.T. Copeland or W.T. Copeland and Sons until 1976. It then became Royal Worcester Spode Ltd. The company was bought by the Portmeirion Group in 2009. The word *Spode* appears on many pieces made by the factories. Most collectors include all the wares under the more familiar name of Spode. Porcelains are listed in this book by the name that appears on the piece. Related pieces may be listed under Copeland, Copeland Spode, and Royal Worcester.

SPODE

Spode
c.1770–1790

Copeland & Garrett
c.1833–1847

ROYAL WORCESTER SPODE

Royal Worcester Spode Ltd.
1976–present

Bowl, Pattern No. 334, White, Stylized Leaves, Gold Trim, c.1803, 3 x 6 x 3 In.	195
Cake Plate, With Dome, Blue & White Porcelain, 11 x 7 ½ In.	114
Plate, Indented, View Of Bridge Of Salaro, 2 Fishermen On River Bank, Flower Border, 8 In.	65
Platter, Turkey, Farmyard, White, Blue Ground, Floral Borders, 23 ½ x 18 In.	45
Salt & Pepper, Holly, Winter Sprigs, Oval, Footed, 3 In.	19

SPONGEWARE, *see Spatterware category.*

SPORTS, *Cards are listed in the Card category*

SPORTS

Sports equipment, sporting goods, brochures, and related items are listed here. Items are listed by sport. Other categories of interest are Bicycle, Card, Fishing, Sword, Toy, and Trap.

Baseball, Ball, Autographed, Mickey Mantle & Willie Mays, c.1989	345
Baseball, Bat, Powerized, Hillerich & Bradsby, 1960s, 33 ¾ x 2 ¾ In.	29
Baseball, Flyer, Bob Feller Candy Bar, Cleveland Indian Star, Frame, 20 x 14 In. *illus*	180
Baseball, Jersey, Roger Clemens, Houston Astros, All-Star Game, Shadowbox, 44 x 33 In. *illus*	201
Baseball, Plate, Chief Wahoo, Batting, Cleveland Indians Logo, Syracuse China Co., 9 In.	186
Baseball, Sign, Scoreboard, Hanley Beer & Ale, Black Ground, c.1950, 22 ½ x 45 In.	393
Cycling, Medal, Bicycle Racing, Gilt, Bronze, High Wheeler, Boneshaker, Tricycle, 1880, 2 In.	117
Fencing, Helmet, Metal Mesh, Canvas & Leather, 20 x 9 x 9 In.	170
Football, Ball, Autographed, Joe Montana, Cotton Bowl Championship *illus*	248
Golf, Trophy, Bloomington Golf Club, Carved Glass Jar, Silver Lid, Arthur Phillsbury, 1898, 5 In.	173
Golf, Trophy, Leaves & Vine, 2 C-Scroll Handles, Squared Leafy Stem, Whiting, 14 x 12 In. *illus*	2160
Hockey, Jersey, Wayne Gretzky, CCM, Red, Blue, White, Mounted, Shadowbox, 41 x 33 In.	413
Hunting, Cane, Duck Call, Pops Out Of Marsh Grass, Silver Bands, London, c.1900, 36 ½ In.	460
Skiing, Skis, Wood, Metal, Leather, Faber, Canada, 84 In., Pair *illus*	107
Snowshoes, Wood Frame, Leather Harness, Roping, Faber Products, Quebec, 42 In., Pair *illus*	79

STAFFORDSHIRE

Staffordshire , England, has been a district making pottery and porcelain since the 1700s. Thousands of types of pottery and porcelain have been made in the many factories that worked in the area. Some of the most famous factories have been listed separately, such as Adams, Davenport, Ridgway, Rowland & Marsellus, Royal Doulton, Royal Worcester, Spode, Wedgwood, and

Sports, Golf, Trophy, Leaves & Vine, 2 C-Scroll Handles, Squared Leafy Stem, Whiting, 14 x 12 In.
$2,160

Case Antiques

TIP
Save the college sports team schedules you get in the mail or pick up at games or local stores. If any of the players pictured on the schedules become stars, you have a collectible.

Sports, Skiing, Skis, Wood, Metal, Leather, Faber, Canada, 84 In., Pair
$107

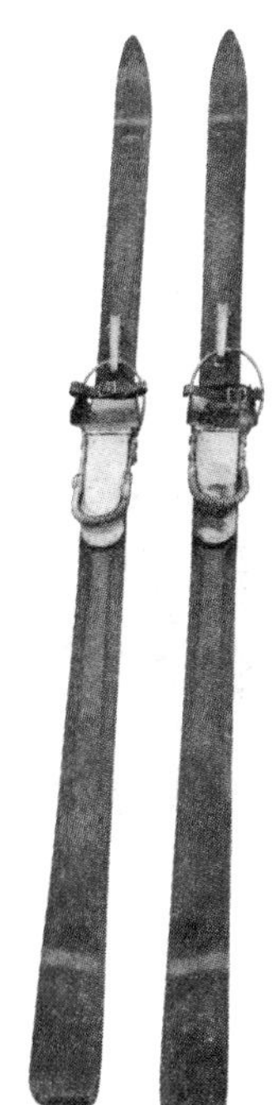

Hartzell's Auction Gallery Inc.

Sports, Snowshoes, Wood Frame, Leather Harness, Roping, Faber Products, Quebec, 42 In., Pair
$79

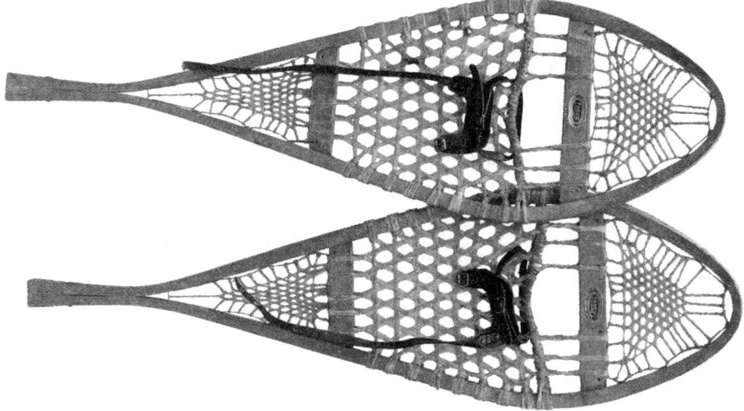

Hartzell's Auction Gallery Inc.

Staffordshire, Bowl, Vegetable, Lid, Ship Of The Line Downs, Dark Blue, Enoch Wood & Sons, 1818-46
$420

Bourgeault-Horan Antiquarians & Associates, LLC

Staffordshire, Bust, John Wesley, Pink Cheeks, Brown, Square Marble Base, England, 1800s, 11 ½ In.
$413

Eldred's

Staffordshire, Dish, Coggled Rim, Dense Yellow Trailed Slip, Dark Brown Ground, c.1780, 13 In.
$3,567

Skinner, Inc.

Staffordshire, Figurine, Dog, Poodle, Seated, Standing Front Legs, 1800s, 9 ½ In., Pair
$293

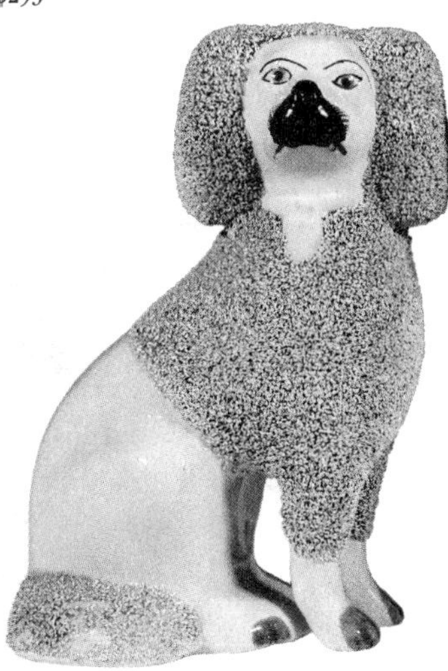

Thomaston Place Auction Galleries

S

Staffordshire, Stirrup Cup, Dog, Hound, Silver Plate Collar, Royale Stratford, England, 1900s, 5 ½ x 2 ¾ In.
$531

Ahlers & Ogletree Auction Gallery

Staffordshire, Stirrup Cup, Fox Head, Glaze, Black Nose & Rim, 5 In.
$236

Strawser Auction Group

Staffordshire, Tureen, Dome Lid, Oval, Historical, Blue & White Transfer, Shugborough, 12 In.
$154

Strawser Auction Group

Staffordshire, Tureen, Lid, Fair Mount, Phila., Blue Transfer, Joseph Stubbs, Burslem, c.1830, 14 x 16 In.
$2,656

Freeman's Auctioneers & Appraisers

Staffordshire, Vase, Lid, Pug Dog, Seated, Brown, Glazed, Rectangular Base, 9 x 10 x 5 ½ In.
$431

Stair Galleries

Stangl, Bird, Hummingbirds, No. 3599D, Double, Brown Oval Base, Paper Label, 10 x 8 ¾ In.
$173

Belhorn Auction Services

Stangl, Bird, Parakeets, No. 3582D, Double, Oval Base, Blue Ink Stamp, 7 x 6 ½ In.
$173

Belhorn Auction Services

Invest in Collectibles

If you invest in collectibles, remember the rules. Buy the best you can, buy perfect items, and care for them so they remain perfect. Provenance (written history) adds to value, as does a signature. Try to spot the trends influenced by news events, such as the death of a celebrity.

Staffordshire, Teapot, Lid, Blue & White, Hunting Dogs & Stags, Footed, 10 ½ In.
$177

Strawser Auction Group

others. Some Staffordshire pieces are listed under categories like Fairing, Flow Blue, Mulberry, Shaving Mug, etc.

Bowl, Vegetable, Lid, Ship Of The Line Downs, Dark Blue, Enoch Wood & Sons, 1818-46 .... *illus* 420
Bust, John Wesley, Pink Cheeks, Brown, Square Marble Base, England, 1800s, 11 ½ In. ..*illus* 413
Canister, Tea, Rectangular, White, Salt Glaze, Molded Tree, c.1750, 3 ½ In. 1476
Coffeepot, Franklin's Tomb, Woman, Sitting, Blue Transfer, 1830s, 10 ½ In. 625
Coffeepot, Lid, Flowers, Blue & White Transfer, Handle, Footed, 1800s, 11 ¾ In. 250
Dish, Coggled Rim, Dense Yellow Trailed Slip, Dark Brown Ground, c.1780, 13 In. ....*illus* 3567
Egg, Boy Playing, Black Transfer, White Ground, Early 1800s, 2 ½ In. 492
Figurine, Dog, Poodle, Seated, Standing Front Legs, 1800s, 9 ½ In., Pair ....*illus* 293
Figurine, Dog, Sitting, Hollow Molded Shape, Gilt Highlights, Glass Eyes, c.1800, 13 In. 177
Figurine, Hen, Multicolor Glaze, Circular Base, Early 1800s, 6 In. 584
Figurine, Lion, Front Paw On Ball, Shaded Brown Glaze, 11 x 12 In. 24
Figurine, Lion, Glass Eyes, Orange & Gold, Black, 10 ¾ x 5 x 9 In., Pair 140
Figurine, Lion, Standing, Light Brown Glaze, Rectangular Base, c.1830, 8 x 9 In., Pair 767
Foot Tub, Light Blue, Garden, Classical Building, People, Handle, 1860s, 7 x 17 ½ x 11 In. 780
Group, Bocage, Figures Seated At Tea, Mounted, Table Base, c.1815-25, 8 x 8 ⅜ In. 1107
Group, Leopard & Cub, Lying Down, Flowers, Green Base, 5 In. 185
Jug, Animals, Black & Turquoise Transfer, Gilt Rim, Inscribed Miss C. Penny, 1876, 7 ½ In. 615
Lamp, Horse & Rider Shape, Electric, Oval Base, 15 In. 308
Lamp, Urn Shape, Purple Transfer, Metal Base, Early 1900s, 21 In. 230
Pipe, Coiled Snake, Boy Masked Bowl, Earthenware, Early 1800s, 6 In. 369
Pitcher, Lafayette At Franklin's Tomb, Wide Spout, Footed, Blue Transfer, 8 In. 336
Plate, Arms Of South Carolina, Floral, Shaped Rim, Blue Transfer, 7 ¼ In. 427
Plate, Blue Transfer Image, Floral Border, Scalloped Rim, England, 1831-46, 8 ¾ In. 293
Plate, Floral, Dark Blue Transfer, Fruit Border, Henshall & Company, England, c.1825, 10 In. 211
Plate, Grand Erie Canal, Blue Transfer, 10 In., Pair 475
Plate, Soup, Bird At Center, Flowers, Salt Glaze, 11 ½ In. 62
Platter, Boston State House, Blue Transfer, Oval, Floral Border, 14 ½ x 19 In. 458
Platter, Lake George, Blue Transfer, Knife Marks, 13 x 16 In. 305
Platter, Landing Of General Lafayette, Blue Transfer, 14 ½ x 19 In. 885
Platter, Landing Of General Lafayette, Well & Tree, Blue Transfer, 14 x 18 ⅜ In. 1708
Platter, Niagara Falls, American Side, Blue Transfer, 11 ¾ x 15 In. 531
Platter, Southwest View Of La Grange, Blue Transfer, Enoch Wood & Sons, c.1840, 18 ¾ In. 431
Sauce, Lid, Dove Shape, Wood, Blown Glass Eggs, England, 1800s, 6 x 9 In., Pair 360
Sauceboat, Oval, Cows & Sheep, Landscape, White, Salt Glaze, c.1760, 7 In. 984
Serving Dish, Hudson River, Blue, Oval, 11 ½ x 8 ¾ In. 427
Stirrup Cup, Dog, Hound, Silver Plate Collar, Royale Stratford, England, 1900s, 5 ½ x 2 ¾ In. .....*illus* 531
Stirrup Cup, Fox Head, Glaze, Black Nose & Rim, 5 In. ....*illus* 236
Teapot, Globular, Translucent Enamel, Engine Turned Body, Lead Glaze, 1765, 6 In. 400
Teapot, Landing Of General Lafayette, Blue Transfer, Footed, Gooseneck Spout, 7 In. 671
Teapot, Lid, Blue & White, Hunting Dogs & Stags, Footed, 10 ½ In. ....*illus* 177
Teapot, Lid, Quatrefoil, Salt Glaze, Scratch Blue, Oak Leaves, c.1750, 5 ½ In. 2829
Teapot, Lid, Reeded Handle & Spout, Green & Yellow, Hexagonal, 1700s, 5 ¾ In. 2829
Teapot, Lid, Stoneware, Bulbous, Dark Maroon Ground, Multicolor Flowers, 1730s, 4 ⅞ In. 439
Toby Jugs are listed in their own category.
Tureen, Dome Lid, Oval, Historical, Blue & White Transfer, Shugborough, 12 In. ....*illus* 154
Tureen, Lid, Fair Mount, Phila., Blue Transfer, Joseph Stubbs, Burslem, c.1830, 14 x 16 In. *illus* 2656
Vase, Lid, Pug Dog, Seated, Brown, Glazed, Rectangular Base, 9 x 10 x 5 ½ In. ....*illus* 431

STANGL POTTERY

Stangl Pottery traces its history back to the Fulper Pottery of New Jersey. In 1910, Johann Martin Stangl started working at Fulper. He left to work at Haeger Pottery from 1915 to 1920. Stangl returned to Fulper Pottery in 1920, became president in 1926, and changed the company name to Stangl Pottery in 1929. Stangl bought the firm in 1930. The pottery is known for dinnerware and a line of bird figurines. Martin Stangl died in 1972 and the pottery was sold to Frank Wheaton Jr. of Wheaton Industries. Production continued until 1978, when Pfaltzgraff Pottery purchased the

Star Wars, Action Figure, Ben Obi Wan Kenobi, Gray Hair, Kenner, Box, 1979, 14 x 10 x 2 ½ In.
$570

Bruneau & Co. Auctioneers

Star Wars, Action Figure, Chewbacca, On Card, Kenner, 12 Back-B, 1978, 9 ¾ x 7 x 1 ½ In.
$393

Bruneau & Co. Auctioneers

Star Wars, Lunch Box, Metal, Return Of The Jedi, Thermos, King-Seeley, 8 ¾ x 7 x 4 In.
$121

Bruneau & Co. Auctioneers

Stein, Porcelain, Bearded Gnomes, 3 Scenes, Multicolor, Simon Peter Gerz, 1900s, 6 ¾ In.
$108

Woody Auctions

Steuben, Bowl, Lid, Rosaline Pink Glass, Applied Alabaster Finial, Signed, F. Carder, 6 In.
$256

Morphy Auctions

Steuben, Bowl, Low Footed, Scroll Feet, Etched Mark, 3 ½ x 11 In.
$344

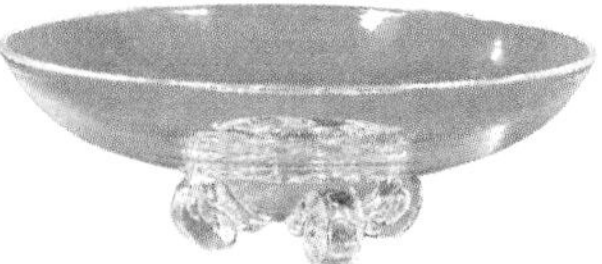

Neal Auction Company

TIP

Doormats at every door catch the dirt and keep it from creating dust and pollution in the house. Shake out, wash, or vacuum the mats frequently.

right to the Stangl trademark and the remaining inventory was liquidated. A single bird figurine is identified by a number. Figurines made up of two birds are identified by a number followed by the letter *D* indicating Double.

Stangl
1926–1930

Stangl
1940s–1978

Stangl
1949–1953

Ashtray, Gold & Silvery Blue, Metallic, 9 x 9 x 2 In. 75
Basket, Terra Rose, Pink & Green, Handle, 6 In. 6
Bird, Chinese Pheasant, No. 3457, Green, Yellow, Red, 15 In. 207
Bird, Hummingbirds, No. 3599D, Double, Brown Oval Base, Paper Label, 10 x 8 ¾ In. ....*illus* 173
Bird, Parakeets, No. 3582D, Double, Oval Base, Blue Ink Stamp, 7 x 6 ½ In. ....*illus* 173
Bird, Penguin, No. 3274, Black, White, Standing, Round Base, Marked, RV, 5 ¾ In. 46
Bird, Running Duck, No. 3432, Green, Brown, 10 In. 58
Bird, White Wing Crossbills, No. 3754D, Double, Red, Black, On Branch, Leaves, 8 ⅝ In. 40
Bird, Willow Ptarmigan, No. 3451, Green, White, 11 In. 276

STAR TREK AND STAR WARS

Star Trek and Star Wars collectibles are included here. The original *Star Trek* television series ran from 1966 through 1969. The series spawned an animated TV series, three TV sequels, and a TV prequel. The first Star Trek movie was released in 1979 and eleven others followed, the most recent in 2016. The movie *Star Wars* opened in 1977. Sequels were released in 1980 and 1983; prequels in 1999, 2002, and 2005. *Star Wars: Episode VII* opened in 2015, which increased interest in Star Wars collectibles. *Star Wars: The Last Jedi* opened in 2017. *Star Wars: Episode IX* was released in 2019. Star Wars characters also appeared in *Rogue One: A Star Wars Story* (2016) and *Solo: A Star Wars Story* (2018). Other science fiction and fantasy collectibles can be found under Batman, Buck Rogers, Captain Marvel, Flash Gordon, Movie, Superman, and Toy.

STAR TREK

Action Figure, Mego, Alien, Talos, 1976, 8 In. 398
Doll, Guinan, Blue Outfit, Serving Tray, 2 Drinking Glasses & Stand, 1995, 9 In. 24
Glass, Collectors, Dr Pepper, U.S.S. Enterprise, 6 ¼ In., 1978 20
Lunch Box, Dome Lid, Mr. Spock & Captain Kirk, 1968, 9 x 7 In. 225

STAR WARS

Action Figure, Ben Obi Wan Kenobi, Gray Hair, Kenner, Box, 1979, 14 x 10 x 2 ½ In. ....*illus* 570
Action Figure, Chewbacca, On Card, Kenner, 12 Back-B, 1978, 9 ¾ x 7 x 1 ½ In. ....*illus* 393
Action Figure, Chewbacca, Unopened, 12-Back Card, Kenner, 1977 944
Action Figure, Jawa, Vinyl Cape, Blaster, Kenner, 1977 1416
Action Figure, Luke Skywalker, Holding Lightsaber, 12-Back Card, Kenner, 1977 1770
Action Figure, Luke Skywalker, X-Wing Pilot, 20-Back Card, Kenner, 1978 236
Action Figure, Ben Obi Wan Kenobi, White Hair, 12-Back Card, Kenner, 1977 1416
Action Figure, Stormtrooper, Holding Blaster, 12-Back Card, Kenner, 1977 1180
Action Figure, Stormtrooper, The Empire Strikes Back, Kenner, 1980, 4 In. 565
Action Figure, Yoda, Snake Around Neck, On Resealed Card, Kenner, 1980 130
Blueprint, Death Star, 1st Generation, Dated 4-27-76, Frame, 29 x 45 In. 1121
Lunch Box, Metal, Return Of The Jedi, Thermos, King-Seeley, 8 ¾ x 7 x 4 In. ....*illus* 121
Photograph, Carrie Fisher, Princess Leia, Signed, 11 x 14 In. 405
Tape Dispenser, Figural, C-3PO, Sigma Ceramics, c.1980, 5 x 7 In. 974
Teapot, Figural, Luke Skywalker On Tuan, Sigma Ceramics, 10 x 10 In. 294
Toy, Imperial Shuttle, White, Battery Compartment, Box, 1984, 20 x 17 x 14 ½ In. 194
Toy, Landspeeder, Die Cast, On Card, Kenner, 1978 561
Toy, Play Set, Death Star Space Station, Accessories, Box, Kenner, 1977 236

Toy, Tie Fighter, Die Cast Metal, 12-Back Card, Kenner, 1978 413
Toy, Tie Fighter, Kenner, Box, 1978 1675

STEINS

Steins have been used by beer and ale drinkers for over 500 years. They have been made of ivory, porcelain, pottery, stoneware, faience, silver, pewter, wood, or glass in sizes up to nine gallons. Although some were made by Mettlach, Meissen, Capo-di-Monte, and other famous factories, most were made by less important German potteries. The words *Geschutz* or *Musterschutz* on a stein are the German words for "patented" or "registered design," not company names. Steins are still being made in the old styles. Lithophane steins may be found in the Lithophane category.

Character, Alligator, E. Bohne & Sohne, Porcelain, ½ Liter 450
Character, Apostle, Pewter, Mounted, Brown Ground, Enamel, Kreussen, 1700s, 5 In. 1230
Character, Apple, Snake Wrap, Porcelain, Inlaid Lid, E. Bohne & Sohne, ⅓ Liter 1320
Character, Berlin Bear, Growling, Tan, Porcelain, Pewter, Schierholz, ½ Liter 2040
Character, Cat, Holds Scroll With German Verse, Pottery, J.W.R., ½ Liter 193
Character, Clown, Exaggerated Grimace, Jester Hat, Pottery, Diesinger, ½ Liter 702
Character, Dog, Multicolor, White Ground, Pewter Lid, c.1750, 10 ½ In. 780
Character, Mushroom, Gnome Handle & Finial, Musterschutz, Schierholz, ½ Liter 900
Character, Rich Man, Portly, Top Hat, Holding Stein, Pottery, Musterschutz, Thwalt, ½ Liter . 102
Character, Soldier, Curly Beard, Navy Blue Uniform, Pottery, Majolica Glaze, ½ Liter 120
Character, Sulky Driver, Porcelain, Face Mask, Eye Protectors, E. Bohne & Sohne, ½ Liter..... 840
Character, Theodore Roosevelt On Elephant, Pottery, Germany, 1 Liter, 12 In. 990
Character, Woman With Baby, Pottery, R. Hanke, Germany, ½ Liter 174
Character, Woman, Masquerade, Porcelain, Musterschutz, Schierholz, ½ Liter 5641
Faience, Castle On Hill, Pewter Lid & Footring, Kolner Walzendrug, c.1785, 6 ½ In. 1742
Faience, Castle, Blue & White, Pewter Lid & Foot, c.1785, 6 ½ In. 180
Faience, Peasant, Flowers, Landscape, Pewter Lid, Thuringen Walzenkrug, 1776, 11 In. 756
Faience, Stag, Leaping, Cartouche, Mottled Ground, Pewter Lid, Germany, c.1900, 7 ½ In. 157
Glass, Amber, Tapered, Scrolling Pewter Overlay & Lid, ½ Liter 90
Glass, Bicycle Rider, Painted, Pewter Lid, ½ Liter 90
Glass, Birds, Leaves, Engraved, Yellow Prunts Around Bottom, Inlaid Lid, ½ Liter 60
Glass, Coat Of Arms, Onoldia Sei's Panier, Student Society, Painted, 1903 On Lid, ½ Liter........ 222
Glass, Crown Over Eagle Crest, Metal Lid, Cased White, Transfer, ½ Liter 96
Glass, Cut, Faceted, Porcelain Inlaid Lid With Gnome, ½ Liter 90
Glass, Drunk Man, Vertical Ribs, Clear & Frosted, Etched, Porcelain Inlaid Lid, ½ Liter 60
Glass, Engraved Decoration, Silver Plate Art Nouveau Mount, W.M.F., ½ Liter 312
Glass, Mundener Radfahrer Club 1885, Blown, Cut, Porcelain Inlaid Lid, ½ Liter 60
Glass, Skier, Transfer, Painted, Pewter Lid, ½ Liter 90
Glass, Stella Berlin 1890, Student Society, Blown, Cut, Porcelain Inlaid Lid, ½ Liter 168
Glass, Trumpeter, Faceted, Painted, Pewter Lid, ½ Liter 204
Mettlach steins are listed in the Mettlach category.
Occupational, Bricklayer, Baurer, Porcelain, Pewter Lid, ½ Liter 60
Occupational, Cabinet Maker, Schreiner, Porcelain, Transfer & Paint, Pewter Lid, ½ Liter..... 102
Occupational, Locksmith, Bauschlosser, Porcelain, Transfer & Paint, Pewter Lid, ½ Liter...... 168
Occupational, Plasterer, Gipser, Constanz 1928, Transfer, Porcelain, Pewter, ½ Liter 168
Occupational, Post Office Worker, Postillion, Munchen, 1916, Porcelain, Pewter, ½ Liter 108
Occupational, Saddle Maker, Sattler, Porcelain, Transfer & Paint, Pewter Lid, 1 Liter 156
Occupational, Tailor, Schneider, Porcelain, Transfer & Paint, Pewter Lid, ½ Liter 192
Occupational, Wagon Builder, Wagner, Porcelain, Transfer & Paint, Pewter Lid, ½ Liter........ 168
Occupational, Wagon Delivery, Fuhrmann, Porcelain, Transfer & Paint, Pewter Lid, ½ Liter 60
Porcelain, Bearded Gnomes, 3 Scenes, Multicolor, Simon Peter Gerz, 1900s, 6 ¾ In. ......*illus* 108
Porcelain, Enamel, Scenes Of Vienna, Musicians, Silver Mount, Cupid Finial, 3 ½ In. 960
Porcelain, Monk Drinking, Shades Of Brown, O'Hara Dial Co., 13 ½ In. 216
Regimental, 1 Comp. Eisenbahn Regt. Nr. 3 Berlin, 1904-06, Epaulet Thumblift, ½ Liter 400
Regimental, 1 Comp. Inft. Regt. Nr. 112, Mulhausen, 1904-06, Roster, Porcelain, ½ Liter....... 120
Regimental, 1 Esc. Ulan Regt., Nr. 17, Oschatz, 1902-05, Saxon Thumblift, ½ Liter 600
Regimental, 2 Esc. Leib. Garde Husar Regt., Potsdam, 1902-05, Roster, Eagle, ½ Liter 510
Regimental, 2 Esk. Bayr. Schwere Reiter Regt., Munchen, Roster, Scenes, Lion, ½ Liter.......... 240

Steuben, Bowl, Ocean Reef, Floating Diatoms, Bronze Base, Michele Oka Doner, 2006, 9 x 15 x 16 In.
$5,938

Abington Auction Gallery

Steuben, Candlestick, Rosaline & Alabaster, Shaped Column, c.1910, 8 In., Pair
$472

Cottone Auctions

Steuben, Compote, Rugby, Engraved Flowers, Footed, Finial, Blue, 1920s, 13 In., Pair
$5,175

Richard D. Hatch & Associates

S

Steuben, Figurine, Owl, Mounted On Base, Signed, 5 ½ In.
$161

Richard D. Hatch & Associates

Steuben, Goblet, Amethyst, Clear, Engraved Lion's Head, Cut Overlay, c.1925, 9 ⅞ x 4 x 3 ⅞ In.
$1,170

Jeffrey S. Evans & Associates

Steuben, Perfume Bottle, Bird Stopper, Round Base, Gold Aurene, Marked, 11 In.
$3,125

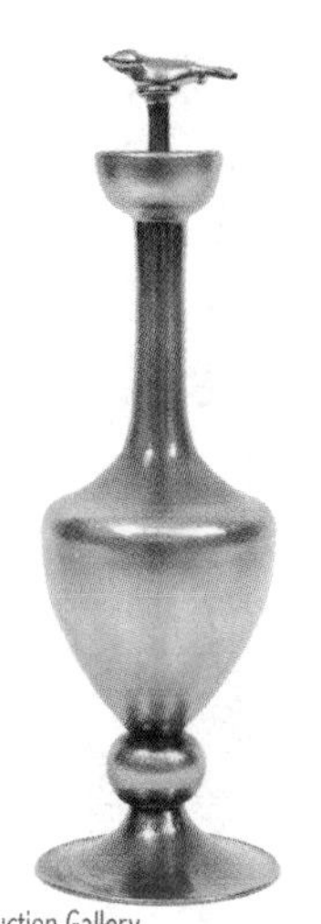

Abington Auction Gallery

Regimental, 3 Battr. Sachs, Dresden, 1908-10, Roster, 4 Scenes, Porcelain, ½ Liter 570
Regimental, 6 Battr. Feld Art. Ludwigsburg, Roster, 2 Scenes, Porcelain, ½ Liter 246
Regimental, 6 Comp. Inft. Regt. Nr. 14, Nurnberg, 1911-13, Roster, Porcelain, ½ Liter 420
Regimental, Cheval Regt., Nurnberg, 1910-13, Roster, 4 Scenes, Horse, Porcelain, ½ Liter 264
Regimental, Skull Form, Meinem Lieben Vater, Danzig, Porcelain, ½ Liter 2761
Regimental, Thorn, Meinen Lieben Vater, Pottery, Scenes, Eagle Thumblift, ½ Liter 114
Stoneware, 4 Relief Rosettes, Salt Glaze, Squat, Swollen, Pewter Lid, c.1640, 5 In. 3721
Stoneware, Apostles All Around, Scroll Bands, Multicolor, Squat, Pewter Lid, 8 In. 132
Stoneware, Coat Of Arms, Incised, Brown Glazes, Pewter Lid & Footring, 1741, 9 In. 930
Stoneware, Deer, Cherubs, Relief, White & Green Glaze, Pewter Lid, Footring, c.1680, 8 In. 1440
Stoneware, Flowers & Hearts, Relief, Red, White & Blue Glaze, Pewter Lid, 1700s, 9 ¾ In. 540
Stoneware, Horizontal Ribs, Yellow & Brown Bands, Pewter Lid & Footring, 1796, 10 In. 342
Third Reich, Airplanes, Stoneware, Relief, Blue, Gray, Engraved Metal Lid, ½ Liter 240
Third Reich, Artillery, Munchen, Roster, Pottery, Pewter Lid, Helmet, Swastika, ½ Liter 240
Third Reich, Munchen, Weihnachten 1935, Stoneware, Pewter Lid, Relief Pilot, ½ Liter 348
Third Reich, Schwere Flak-Stammbatterie, Koblenz, Planes, Artillery, Pottery, ½ Liter 630

STEREO CARD

Stereo cards that were made for stereoscope viewers became popular after 1840. Two almost identical pictures were mounted on a stiff cardboard backing so that, when viewed through a stereoscope, a three-dimensional picture could be seen. Value is determined by maker and by subject. These cards were made in quantity through the 1930s.

Girl & Dog On Blanket, Dawin & Co., 1905 14
Millions Of Trout In Yellowstone River, Adults, Fishing, On Logs 7
One Stick Of Gum For Two, 2 Children, On Log, T.W. Ingersoll, c.1898, 7 x 3 In. 20
The Introduction, 2 Girls, Dog & Cat 12
Uncle Tom & Little Eva, Black Americana, 1896, 7 x 3 In. 25
Want Some Supper Bob?, Hunter, Bear 5

STEREOSCOPE

Stereoscopes were used for viewing stereo cards. The hand viewer was invented by Oliver Wendell Holmes, although more complicated table models were used before his was produced in 1859. Do not confuse the stereoscope with the stereopticon, a magic lantern that used glass slides.

H.C. White, Wood, Aluminum Frame, Glass Lenses, Bennington, Vermont, c.1903 72
ICA Dresden, Germany, c.1895, 5 x 3 x 4 In. 49
Le Taxiphote, Over 300 Glass Slides Of South America, 19 ½ x 11 x 11 In. 594
Unis France, Paris, Tabletop, With Slides Of Paris, French Monuments, 18 x 8 ¾ In. 500

STERLING SILVER, *see Silver-Sterling category.*

STEUBEN

Steuben glass was made at the Steuben Glass Works of Corning, New York. The factory, founded by Frederick Carder and T.G. Hawkes Sr., was purchased by the Corning Glass Company in 1918. Corning continued to make glass called Steuben. Many types of art glass were made at Steuben. Aurene is an iridescent glass. Schottenstein Stores Inc. bought 80 percent of the business in 2008. The factory closed in 2011. In 2014 the Corning Museum of Glass took over the factory and is reproducing some tableware, paperweights, and collectibles. Additional pieces may be found in the Cluthra and Perfume Bottle categories.

Bowl, Aurene, Gold, Ribbed Shape, Scalloped Rim, 5 x 8 ½ In. 615
Bowl, Centerpiece, Dark Blue, Grotesque, Jade, Polished Feet, c.1925, 6 ¾ x 7 x 12 In. 761
Bowl, Centerpiece, Orange, Flat, Turned Out Rim, Aurene, c.1915, 4 x 10 In. 300

Steuben, Vase, Aurene, Blue, Fluted Rim, Shouldered, Signed, 10 ½ x 10 In.
$726

Fontaine's Auction Gallery

Steuben, Vase, Aurene, Gold, Shouldered, Iridescent, Pink To Yellow To Green, Signed, 10 ½ In.
$1,003

Cottone Auctions

Steuben, Vase, Dragon, Acid Cut, Blue Aurene Over Yellow Jade, Droplets, 12 In.
$9,075

Humler & Nolan

Steuben, Vase, Flowers, Mirror Black Acid Cut Back, Alabaster, Round, 7 ½ In.
$944

Cottone Auctions

TIP
Shallow nicks and rough edges on glass can sometimes be smoothed off with fine emery paper.

Steuben, Vase, Iridescent Blue Rim, Bulbous, Verre De Soie, Early 1900s, 12 x 7 ½ In.
$344

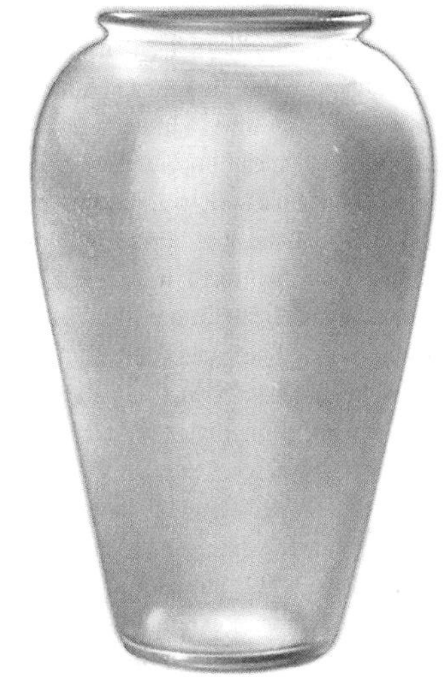

New Orleans Auction Galleries

Steuben, Vase, Jade Green, Swirled, Optic Rib Base & Body, Flared Rim, 4 ¾ x 9 In.
$158

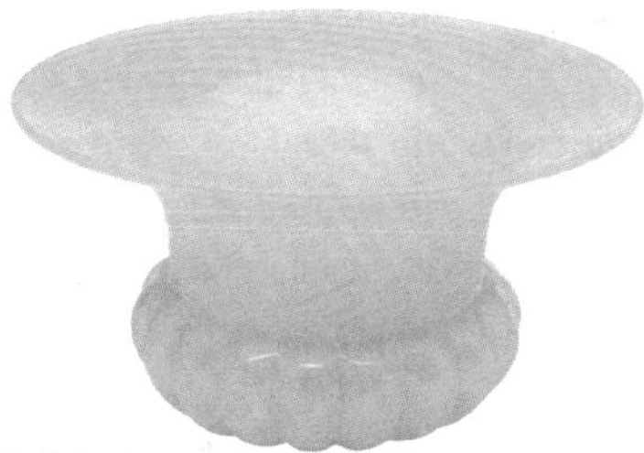

Soulis Auctions

Steuben, Whimsy, Sock Darning Egg, Open Pontil End, Aurene, Gold, 5 ¾ In.
$106

Bunch Auctions

Stevens & Williams, Cup, Green, Yellow, Overlay, Engraved Garland, Floral, Ribbon, Hollow Handles, 8 ¾ In.
$900

Woody Auctions

TIP
Don't keep identification on your key ring. If it is lost, it's an invitation for burglars to visit.

Stevens & Williams, Dish, Green Cut, Rose Overlay, Engraved Floral, Leaf, Gilt Silver Rim, c.1900, 7 In.
$700

Woody Auctions

Stevens & Williams, Pitcher, Cut Glass, Amethyst, Engraved Rosebuds, Silver Spout, Clear Handle, 11 In.
$9,000

Woody Auctions

Stevens & Williams, Pitcher, Ribbed, Blue & White, Clear Applied Handle, Pontil Base, 5 In.
$96

Woody Auctions

Stevens & Williams, Tankard, Stopper, Wheel Cut Overlay, Cranberry Pink Over Yellow, Pinched Body, 10 ¾ In.
$4,235

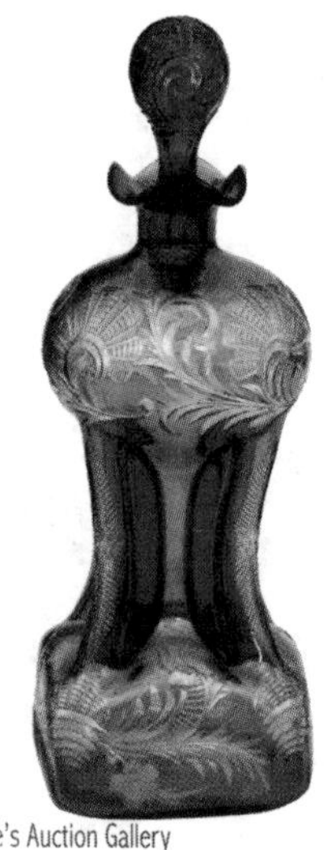

Fontaine's Auction Gallery

Bowl, Clear, Floret, Tri-Lobed Base, Donald Pollard, 1954, 8 In. 140
Bowl, Clear, Shallow Basin, Footed Base, Etched Underside, 4 ¾ x 12 In. 62
Bowl, Jade Green Glass, Acid Etched, Chinese Design, 2 ¾ x 10 In. 625
Bowl, Lid, Rosaline Pink Glass, Applied Alabaster Finial, Signed, F. Carder, 6 In. *illus* 256
Bowl, Low Footed, Scroll Feet, Etched Mark, 3 ½ x 11 In. *illus* 344
Bowl, Ocean Reef, Floating Diatoms, Bronze Base, Michele Oka Doner, 2006, 9 x 15 x 16 In. *illus* 5938
Bowl, Pedestal Base, Nautilus Feet, Signed, 4 ½ In. 115
Candlestick, Rosaline & Alabaster, Shaped Column, c.1910, 8 In., Pair *illus* 472
Candlestick, Teardrop, Baluster, Clear, 8 ¾ x 4 ⅝ In., 4 Piece 800
Chalice, Paneled Sides, Etched Vinery & Leaves, Verre De Soie, 12 x 6 ½ In. 158
Cocktail Shaker, 2 Spouts, Stopper, Round Base, 8 ½ In. 127
Compote, Aurene, Blue, Calcite, Round Foot, 6 x 6 In. 130
Compote, Clear Stem, Molded Rim, Green Base, c.1932, 5 ¾ x 3 In. 250
Compote, Molded, 4-Part Base, Signed, 4 ¾ x 10 In. 80
Compote, Rugby, Engraved Flowers, Footed, Finial, Blue, 1920s, 13 In., Pair *illus* 5175
Decanter, Molded, Stopper, Turned Style, Signed, 10 In. 160
Decanter, Square, Concave Sides, Eagle, Sphere Stopper, 1980s, 10 ¾ x 5 ¾ x 5 In. 439
Figurine, Frog Prince, Crown, Glass, Lloyd Atkins, 6 x 5 ½ In. 791
Figurine, Glass Trout, 18K Gold Lure, Trapped Air Bubbles, Fitted Case, 1970s, 11 In. 720
Figurine, Owl, Mounted On Base, Signed, 5 ½ In. *illus* 161
Figurine, Sea Sprite, Leaping, Signed, George Thompson, c.1952, 9 In. 100
Goblet, Amethyst, Clear, Engraved Lion's Head, Cut Overlay, c.1925, 9 ⅞ x 4 x 3 ⅞ In. *illus* 1170
Lampshade, Blue, Gold Hearts, Vines, Rim, Dome Shape, 10 In. 3600
Paperweight, Excalibur, Glass, Letter Opener, Sword, Gold Grip, 18K, James Houston, 4 ½ x 3 In. 452
Perfume Bottle, Bird Stopper, Round Base, Gold Aurene, Marked, 11 In. *illus* 3125
Perfume Bottle, Teardrop Stopper, Footed, Elongated, Gold Aurene, Early 1900s, 7 ¾ In. 125
Punch Bowl, Clear Center, Applied Teardrop Base, 1950s, 8 x 9 In. 295
Sculpture, 14K Gold Mouse, Sitting On Glass Sliced Cheese Block, 4 x 3 ¾ In. 1540
Sculpture, Clear, Eagle, Spread Wings, Round Base, 5 ½ x 12 ½ In. 341
Sculpture, Glass Prism, Engraved, Wood Base, George Thompson, c.1955, 16 In. 338
Sculpture, Star Stream, Clear, Neil Cohen, Signed, 1988, 5 ½ x 4 ½ In. 277
Sherbet, Cranberry Glass, Medial Band & Base, Pontil Mark, c.1900, 2 ⅞ x 3 ½ In., 10 Piece 129
Tumbler, Lowball, Signed, 3 ⅝ In., 8 Piece 375
Vase, Aurene, Blue, Fluted Rim, Shouldered, Signed, 10 ½ x 10 In. *illus* 726
Vase, Aurene, Blue, Gold & Violet Iridescence, Early 1900s, 10 ½ In. 800
Vase, Aurene, Gold, Glass, Red, Violet Highlights, Iridescent, c.1925, 11 ½ In. 375
Vase, Aurene, Gold, Shouldered, Iridescent, Pink To Yellow To Green, Signed, 10 ½ In. *illus* 1003
Vase, Dragon, Acid Cut, Blue Aurene Over Yellow Jade, Droplets, 12 In. *illus* 9075
Vase, Flowers, Mirror Black Acid Cut Back, Alabaster, Round, 7 ½ In. *illus* 944
Vase, Grotesque, Organic Shape, Clear, Marked, 6 x 13 ½ In. 384
Vase, Iridescent Blue Rim, Bulbous, Verre De Soie, Early 1900s, 12 x 7 ½ In. *illus* 344
Vase, Jade & Alabaster, 2 Side Handles, Footed, 10 In. 288
Vase, Jade Green, Swirled, Optic Rib Base & Body, Flared Rim, 4 ¾ x 9 In. *illus* 158
Vase, Millefiori Flower, White, Gold Iridescent Aurene, Signed, 3 ¾ x 12 ½ In. 4500
Vase, Mirror Black, Celeste Blue, Acid Cut Back, Polished Rim, Cameo, c.1924, 6 ⅝ In. 1170
Vase, Rose Quartz Glass, Floral, Interior Crackle Finish, Fleur-De-Lis Mark, Carder, 8 In. 1063
Vase, Yellow, Wheel Cut, Grapes & Grapevines, c.1915, 9 In. 431
Whimsy, Sock Darning Egg, Open Pontil End, Aurene, Gold, 5 ¾ In. *illus* 106
Wine Cooler, Pedestal Base, Step Cut, Signed, 11 ½ In. 431

STEVENGRAPH

Stevengraphs are woven pictures made like fancy ribbons. They were manufactured by Thomas Stevens of Coventry, England, and became popular in 1862. Most are marked *Woven in silk by Thomas Stevens* or were mounted on a cardboard that tells the story of the Stevengraph. Other similar ribbon pictures have been made in England and Germany.

Bookmark, A Happy Christmas, Poem, Cottage, Trees, Silk, Tassel, 1871, 6 ¾ x 1 In. 35
Bookmark, Home Sweet Home, House, Words & Music, Tassel, 10 x 2 ½ In. 50
Bookmark, Home Sweet Home, Silk, c.1880, 10 ¼ x 2 ½ In. 50

Picture, Called To The Rescue, Boat, Rowers, Rough Sea, Frame, 5 ¾ x 8 ¾ In.	575
Postcard, Hands Across The Sea, RMS Empress Of Britain, Flags, Frame	150

STEVENS & WILLIAMS

Stevens & Williams of Stourbridge, England, made many types of glass, including layered, etched, cameo, cut, and art glass, between the 1830s and 1930s. Some pieces are signed *S & W.* Many pieces are decorated with flowers, leaves, and other designs based on nature.

Basket, Custard Exterior, Pink Interior, Flowers, 2 Applied Handles, 5 x 4 In.	450
Basket, Green Cut, Rose Overlay, Engraved, Flowers, Silver Rim, 2 ¾ x 5 In.	600
Cup, Green, Yellow, Overlay, Engraved Garland, Floral, Ribbon, Hollow Handles, 8 ¾ In. *illus*	900
Decanter, Carved Blossom, Green To Yellow Matte Ground, Clear Handle, Ray Cut Base, 9 ½ In.	6000
Dish, Green Cut, Rose Overlay, Engraved Floral, Leaf, Gilt Silver Rim, c.1900, 7 In. *illus*	700
Pitcher, Cut Glass, Amethyst, Engraved Rosebuds, Silver Spout, Clear Handle, 11 In. *illus*	9000
Pitcher, Ribbed, Blue & White, Clear Applied Handle, Pontil Base, 5 In. *illus*	96
Tankard, Stopper, Wheel Cut Overlay, Cranberry Pink Over Yellow, Pinched Body, 10 ¾ In. *illus*	4235
Vase, White Exterior, Blue Interior, Mottled, Orange Wheat Heads, Bent Ruffled Rim, 9 In. *illus*	96
Wine, Amber, Yellow, Engraved Flowers, Diamond Highlights, Clear Stem, Ray Foot, 8 In.	500

STIEGEL TYPE

Stiegel type glass is listed here. It is almost impossible to be sure a piece was actually made by Stiegel, so the knowing collector refers to this glass as "Stiegel type." Henry William Stiegel, a colorful immigrant to the colonies, started his first factory in Pennsylvania in 1763. He remained in business until 1774. Glassware was made in a style popular in Europe at that time and was similar to the glass of many other makers. It was made of clear or colored glass and was decorated with enamel colors, mold blown designs, or etching.

Perfume Bottle, Bird In Medallion, Flowers, Enamel, 5 ¼ In. *illus*	295
Tumbler, Bird, Heart, Flowers, Enamel, 3 In. *illus*	325

STONE

Stone includes those articles made of stones, coral, shells, and some other natural materials not listed elsewhere in this book. Micro mosaics (small decorative designs made by setting pieces of stone into a pattern), urns, vases, and other pieces made of natural stone are listed here. Stoneware is pottery and is listed in the Stoneware category. Alabaster, Jade, Malachite, Marble, and Soapstone are in their own categories.

Belt Hook, Dragon Head, Curved Shaft, Flat Circular Knob, Chinese, 5 In.	708
Bookends, Geode, Cut To Show Interior Quartz & Agate Bands, 11 x 4 In. *illus*	91
Bookends, Petrified Wood, 6 ½ x 6 In. *illus*	51
Bust, Woman's Head, Carved, White Base, Mounted, Charles Gordon Cutler, 17 In.	468
Figure, Bird, Standing, Wings Spread, Egg Shape, Pink Agate Body, 3 ⅞ x 2 x 2 In. *illus*	281
Figure, Buffalo, Standing, Mounted, Metal Face & Feet, 11 ½ x 17 x 5 ½ In. *illus*	615
Figure, Child, Lying On Stomach, Legs Crouched, Feet Tucked, Wood Stand, Chinese, 3 In.	325
Figure, Dog, Lying Down, Chalcedony, Pink, Gold Mounts, Cabochon Eyes, Case, c.1920, 2 x 4 x 3 In.	644
Figure, Foo Dog, Seated, Carved, Rectangular Base, Chinese, 7 ½ In.	185
Figure, Lion, Seated, Rectangular Base, 20 In., Pair	118
Figure, Maiden, Carnelian, Carved, Attached Teak Stand, Chinese, 5 In.	354
Figure, Mei Jen, Lapis Lazuli, Standing, Long Robe, Holding Flowering Branch, 7 In. *illus*	183
Figure, Monk, Amber, Seated, Holding Sack & Ruyi Scepter, Carved, Chinese, 2 In. *illus*	523
Figure, Mother & Child, Shona, Edward Chiwawa, 20 In.	185
Figure, Olmec Style, Carved, Carrying Burden Basket, 5 ½ In.	512
Figure, Rabbit, Carved, Miniature, Gold & Ruby Eyes, Case, Russia, 3 In.	545
Figure, Tiger, Puddingstone, Quartz Eyes, Sgraffito Stripes, 6 ½ In. *illus*	585
Figure, Woman, Dancing, Limestone, Carved, Octagonal Base, 17 In.	345
Geode, Amethyst, Cathedral, Clear Quartz Inside, 17 x 15 x 7 In.	413

Stevens & Williams, Vase, White Exterior, Blue Interior, Mottled, Orange Wheat Heads, Bent Ruffled Rim, 9 In.
$96

Woody Auctions

Stiegel Type, Perfume Bottle, Bird In Medallion, Flowers, Enamel, 5 ¼ In.
$295

Conestoga Auction Company

Stiegel Type, Tumbler, Bird, Heart, Flowers, Enamel, 3 In.
$325

Conestoga Auction Company

S

Stone, Bookends, Geode, Cut To Show Interior Quartz & Agate Bands, 11 x 4 In.
$91

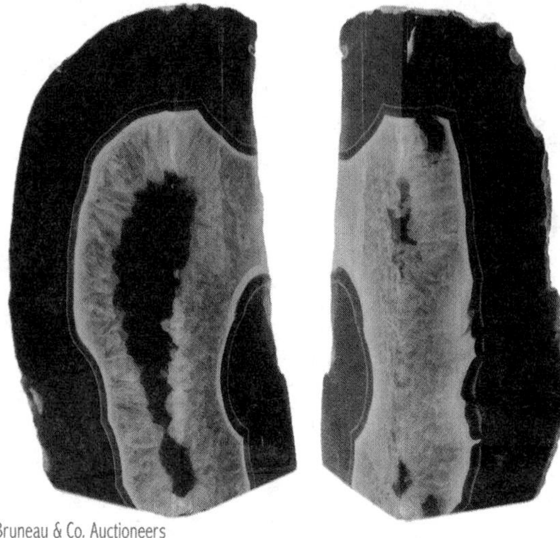

Bruneau & Co. Auctioneers

Stone, Bookends, Petrified Wood, 6 ½ x 6 In.
$51

Hartzell's Auction Gallery Inc.

Stone, Figure, Bird, Standing, Wings Spread, Egg Shape, Pink Agate Body, 3 ⅞ x 2 x 2 In.
$281

Abington Auction Gallery

Stone, Figure, Buffalo, Standing, Mounted, Metal Face & Feet, 11 ½ x 17 x 5 ½ In.
$615

Stair Galleries

Stone, Figure, Mei Jen, Lapis Lazuli, Standing, Long Robe, Holding Flowering Branch, 7 In.
$183

Nadeau's Auction Gallery

Stone, Figure, Monk, Amber, Seated, Holding Sack & Ruyi Scepter, Carved, Chinese, 2 In.
$523

Clars Auction Gallery

Group, 3 Goats, Translucent White, Carved, Wood Stand, Chinese, 3 In. 384
Incense Urn, Lid, Rose Quartz, Dragon Head & Loop Handles, Ogre Mask Feet, 24 In. 549
Inkstone, Petrified Wood, Oval, Seal Script Mark, Chinese, 6 In., Pair 92
Obelisk, Lapis Inlay, Black Onyx, Ball Feet, Raised Plinth, 1900s, 16 In. 1476
Paper Knife, Nephrite, Silver Mounts, Portraits, Male, Female, Inset Gems, Russia, 1900s, 9 In. 1320
Planter, Tree Stump Shape, Limestone, Carved, Concave, Drilled Drains, 23 ½ In. 984
Sculpture, Bodhisattva, Standing, Round Base, Chinese, 1800s, 39 In. .... *illus* 360
Sculpture, Sheep, Epoxy, Bronze Feet & Face, Signed, Francois-Xavier Lalanne, 1990, 34 In. *illus* 237500
Shadowbox, Lighthouse, Shell, Mahogany Frame, 1900s, 15 x 7 ¾ x 10 ½ In. 23
Tazza, Rock Crystal, Gold & Jewel Mount & Stem, Handles, Austria, c.1880, 4 x 4 x 4 ½ In. *illus* 5658
Teapot, Lid, Carnelian, Bulbous Body, Handle, Spout, Finial, Chinese, 6 ½ In. 354
Vase, Carnelian, Carved, Lotus Shape, Flowers, Pods, Chinese, 6 x 8 In. 472

STONEWARE

Stoneware is a coarse, glazed, and fired potter's ceramic that is used to make crocks, jugs, bowls, etc. It is often decorated with cobalt blue decorations. In the nineteenth and early twentieth centuries, potters often decorated crocks with blue numbers indicating the size of the container. A *2* meant 2 gallons. Stoneware is still being made. American stoneware is listed here.

Bank, Chicken Head, Cream Ground, 3 ½ In. .... *illus* 325
Bottle, Dr. Crone's Sarsaparilla Beer, Engraved, 10 In. .... *illus* 106
Bowl, Brown, Glazed, Footed, Edna Arnow, 4 ½ x 7 ⅜ In. 113
Cake Crock, Lid, Cobalt Blue, Incised Lines, Lug Handles, 1850s, 5 ½ x 8 In. 690
Churn, Cobalt Blue, Bird, Molded Rim, 18 In. 630
Churn, Cobalt Blue, Flowers, Ear Handles, Stamped Evan H Stone Pitts Pa., 19 ½ In. 840
Churn, Cobalt Blue, Star Face, Ear Handles, T. Harrington, 1800s, 18 ½ In. .... *illus* 10620
Churn, Dasher, Rounded Top Rim, Slip Glaze, Applied Handle, Albany, 1800s, 8 x 4 ½ In. 197
Churn, Incised Bird On Leaf, Dark Cobalt Blue, 2 Applied Handles, Stamped 5, 1850s, 19 In. 1200
Crock, Blue Floral Spray, 2 Handles, Impressed 4, 4 Gal., 14 ½ In. .... *illus* 266
Crock, Blue, Stenciled, A.P. Donaghho, Parkersburg, W. Va., 4 Gal., 15 In. .... *illus* 424
Crock, Brushed, Applied Handles, Impressed Label, J. Swank, & Co., 1850s, 7 x 10 ½ In. 510
Crock, Cheese, Octagonal Glass Lid, Metal Rod, Reid, Murdoch & Co., 1950s, 7 ½ x 15 In. *illus* 71
Crock, Cobalt Blue Bird On Branch, White's, Utica, 4 Gal., 11 In. .... *illus* 383
Crock, Cobalt Blue Bird, Flat Top, Rounded Rim, Arched Handles, c.1880, 14 In. 263
Crock, Cobalt Blue Bird, Handle, Adam Caire, Po'keepsie NY, 1900s, 9 x 10 ½ In. 207
Crock, Cobalt Blue Bird, Long Tail, O.L. & A.K. Ballard, Vermont, 5 Gal., 13 In. .... *illus* 412
Crock, Cobalt Blue Flower, 2 Handles, Molded Rim, Salt Glaze, 10 ⅜ In. 554
Crock, Cobalt Blue Flower, 3, Slip Trail, Square Rim, Handles, Burger & Lang, c.1875, 10 In. 199
Crock, Cobalt Blue Flower, Freehand, Salt Glaze, Applied Handles, 1850s, 13 ½ In. 240
Crock, Cobalt Blue Flower, Leaves, Folded Rim, Semi-Lunate Handles, C.W. Braun, 12 ½ In. 161
Crock, Cobalt Blue Flowers, 2 Handles, Molded Rim, Pennsylvania, 1800s, 18 In. 519
Crock, Cobalt Blue Flowers, Handle, N. Clark Jr., Athens, N.Y., 1800s, 12 In. .... *illus* 236
Crock, Cobalt Blue Stencil, Folded Lid, Jas Benjamin, Cincinnati, 6 x 8 In. 460
Crock, Cobalt Blue Stylized Leaves, Gray, Salt Glaze, 9 x 5 ½ In. 108
Crock, Cobalt Blue, Bird On Stump, Brady & Ryan, Ellenville, N.Y., 1800s, 11 ½ In. 313
Crock, Cobalt Blue, Eagle, Lug Handles, Conrad, 14 In. 518
Crock, Cobalt Blue, Ear Handles, Molded Rim, N. Clark, Athens, 1800s, 9 x 11 In. 325
Crock, Cobalt Blue, H.F. Behren Grocer, 2217 & 2219 Market Street, Wheeling, W. Va., 1850s, 13 ¾ In. 312
Crock, Cobalt Blue, Leaves, Rolled Rim, Ear Handles, 15 ½ In. .... *illus* 502
Crock, Cobalt Blue, Rounded Rim, Tooled, Williams & Reppert, 1880s, 2 Gal., 11 ¾ x 7 ½ In. 266
Crock, Cobalt Flowers, 2 Handles, Impressed, Burger & Co. Rochester N.Y., 1800s, 14 In. 275
Crock, Cobalt Grape Cluster, Impressed Cowden & Wilcox, Harrisburg, Pa., 1800s, 11 In. 915
Crock, Cobalt Inscription, Molded Rim, 2 Handles, Williams & Reppert, 1800s, 13 ½ In. 336
Crock, Round Lid, Cylindrical, Black Star Logo, SMP & Company, 5 Gal., 13 ½ x 11 In. 509
Dish, Lid, Figural Finial, Tim Mather, Late 1900s, 10 x 12 In. 678
Figure, Angel, Standing, Wood Base, Judy Brady, 4 ½ x 4 ½ In. 53
Figure, Dog, Pug, Lying Down, White, Salt Glaze, c.1770, 6 ⅜ In. 4613
Figure, Dog, Spaniel, Seated, Cobalt Blue, Leash, Collar, Paws, Legs, 1850s, 10 ¾ In. 2040
Figure, Lion, Lying Down, Stepped Oval Base, Brick Clay, 1901, 5 x 11 ½ x 5 ¾ In. 288

Stone, Figure, Tiger, Puddingstone, Quartz Eyes, Sgraffito Stripes, 6 ½ In.
$585

Thomaston Place Auction Galleries

Stone, Sculpture, Bodhisattva, Standing, Round Base, Chinese, 1800s, 39 In.
$360

Selkirk Auctioneers & Appraisers

Stone, Sculpture, Sheep, Epoxy, Bronze Feet & Face, Signed, Francois-Xavier Lalanne, 1990, 34 In.
$237,500

Palm Beach Modern Auctions

S

Stone, Tazza, Rock Crystal, Gold & Jewel Mount & Stem, Handles, Austria, c.1880, 4 x 4 x 4 ½ In.
$5,658

Charlton Hall Auctions

Stoneware, Bank, Chicken Head, Cream Ground, 3 ½ In.
$325

Strawser Auction Group

Stoneware, Bottle, Dr. Crone's Sarsaparilla Beer, Engraved, 10 In.
$106

Copake Auctions

Stoneware, Churn, Cobalt Blue, Star Face, Ear Handles, T. Harrington, 1800s, 18 ½ In.
$10,620

Cottone Auctions

Stoneware, Crock, Blue Floral Spray, 2 Handles, Impressed 4, 4 Gal., 14 ½ In.
$266

Bunch Auctions

Stoneware, Crock, Blue, Stenciled, A.P. Donaghho, Parkersburg, W. Va., 4 Gal., 15 In.
$424

Hartzell's Auction Gallery Inc.

Stoneware, Crock, Cheese, Octagonal Glass Lid, Metal Rod, Reid, Murdoch & Co., 1950s, 7 ½ x 15 In.
$71

Leland Little Auctions

TIP
Put a wide-angle viewer in a solid outside door so you can see who is there before opening the door.

Stoneware, Crock, Cobalt Blue Bird On Branch, White's, Utica, 4 Gal., 11 In.
$383

Cottone Auctions

Stoneware, Crock, Cobalt Blue Bird, Long Tail, O.L. & A.K. Ballard, Vermont, 5 Gal., 13 In.
$412

Conestoga Auction Company

Inkwell, Cylindrical, 3 Quill Holes, Yellow, 1800s, 1 ½ In. ...*illus* 36
Jar, Brushed Cobalt Blue, Oval, Bulbous Body, Applied Handle, J. Bennace, 1850s, 9 ½ In. *illus* 188
Jar, Canning, Brown Glaze, Incised Lines, W. Grinstaff, East Tennessee, c.1900, 7 ¾ In. ... 3240
Jar, Cobalt Blue Flowers, Leaves, Folded Lip, Semi-Lunate Handles, Stamped, Courtland, 11 In. ... 288
Jar, Cobalt Blue, Bee Sting, Folded Lip, Semi-Lunate Handles, 13 x 12 ½ In. ... 196
Jar, Cobalt Blue, Ear Handles, Impressed, C.L. & A.K. Ballard, 1862, 2 Gal., 10 ½ In. ... 360
Jar, Cobalt Blue, Stencil, Gray, H.F. Behrens, c.1900, 8 In. ...*illus* 216
Jar, Dark Brown, Oval, Lug Handles, North Carolina, c.1900, 4 Gal., 14 x 10 ½ In. ...*illus* 540
Jar, Gray, Salt Glaze, Wide Flared Rim, Wm. Hare, Wilmington, Del., 6 In. ... 132
Jar, Lid, Cobalt Blue Flower, 3, Salt Glaze, Incised Shoulder Ring, Baltimore, 1850s, 14 In. ... 164
Jar, Salt Glaze, Inscribed Peach, John Coffman, Rockingham Co., c.1850 ... 4360
Jar, Salt Glaze, Wide Mouth Shape, Square Rim, William H. Crisman, Va., c.1884, 7 ½ In. ... 152
Jar, Storage, Walnut Lid, Strap Handles, Brown, J.M. Hummel, Florence Morgan Co., 16 x 14 In. 2034
Jar, Swirl, Face, 2 Handles, Alkaline Glaze, Signed GKE, Kim Ellington, c.1980, 12 In. ... 380
Jug, Advertising, Brown & White Glaze, J. Ragan & Sons, 8 In. ... 79
Jug, Barrel Shape, Salt Glaze, Center Spout, Vernon Owens, 10 In. ... 354
Jug, Bellarmine, Cartouches, Lion, Crown, Bearded Face, Tan & Mustard Glaze, 9 In. ... 720
Jug, Bellarmine, Molded, Bearded Face, Crest, Handle, 1600s, 10 In. ... 1169
Jug, Bellarmine, Oval Panel, Lion, Bearded Face, Brown Glaze, 1620-50, 8 ⅜ In. ... 480
Jug, Bird Nesting, Tulips, Cobalt Blue Impressed, Cowden & Wilcox, Harrisburg, 1800s, 17 In. ..*illus* 7930
Jug, Blue Bird, Handle, Cream, W Roberts, 3 Gal., 14 In. ... 295
Jug, Brown, Sgraffito Text, C-Scroll Handle, Thixton Millett Co., Owensboro, Ky., 11 x 9 In. ... 230
Jug, Bulbous, Reeded, Manganese Glazed Neck, Molded Crown, GR, Westerwald, 1750s, 7 In. *illus* 738
Jug, Cobalt Blue Arch, Brown Glazed, Tooled Neck, Strap Handle, 1700s, 5 In. ... 277
Jug, Cobalt Blue Beehive & Leaf, Cowden & Wilcox, Harrisburg, Pa., 4 Gal., 17 ½ In. ...*illus* 295
Jug, Cobalt Blue Bird & Leaf, Rolled Rim, Applied Strap Handle, 1800s, 13 In. ... 677
Jug, Cobalt Blue Flower, Rolled Lip, Nichols & Boyton, 1800s, 13 ¾ In. ... 177
Jug, Cobalt Blue Flowers, Bulbous, Lillian & Riedinger, Poughkeepsie, N.Y., 1900s, 12 ½ In. ... 207
Jug, Cobalt Blue Flowers, Bulbous, Samuel L. Pewtress, New Haven, Ct., 11 ½ In. ... 118
Jug, Cobalt Blue Flowers, Stamped Norton & Fenton, Bennington, Vt., 1800s, 4 Gal., 16 In. *illus* 270
Jug, Cobalt Blue Inscription, 2 Handles, Jas. Hamilton & Co., Greensboro, 1800s, 18 In. ..*illus* 580
Jug, Cobalt Blue Leaves, Geometric, C-Scroll Handle, Hamilton & Jones, 2 Gal., 11 ½ x 6 In. ... 207
Jug, Cobalt Blue Leaves, Handle, Molded Rim, A.M. Butler, 11 In. ... 170
Jug, Cobalt Blue Swag & Heart Cartouche, David Morgan, c.1800, 17 x 11 In. ... 4610
Jug, Cobalt Blue, Bulbous Body, Incised, Handle, 1800s, 13 In. ... 620
Jug, Cobalt Blue, F.C. Bender & Son, Pa., ½ Gal., 8 ½ In. ... 367
Jug, Cobalt Blue, Salt Glaze, Hart Fulton, Late 1800s, 2 Gal., 13 x 7 In. ... 164
Jug, Cobalt Blue, Salt Glaze, Painted, E. Kane, Brooklyn, 5 Gal., 17 ½ x 11 In. ... 738
Jug, Coin Bank, Brown Glaze, Strap Handle, Slot For Coins, Memphis, Tenn., 11 x 6 ½ In. ... 570
Jug, Cowden & Wilcox, Cream Salt Glaze, Pennsylvania, c.1890, 9 x 5 In. ... 48
Jug, Face, 2 Profiles, Gina Howell Pottery, West Virginia, Signed, 2001, 12 In. ... 161
Jug, Face, Broken China Teeth, 2 Handles, BB Craig, 16 ½ In. ... 460
Jug, Face, Olive Green Matte Glaze, Stone Eyes, 5 Teeth, Lanier Meaders, 8 x 8 ½ In. ... 7605
Jug, Face, Sour & Bitter, Cobalt Blue, Salt Glaze, Billy Ray Hussey, 1800s, 9 In. ... 366
Jug, Kentucky Whiskey, Glazed, I.W. Harper Nelson Co., 7 x 5 x 5 In. ...*illus* 180
Jug, Oval, Applied Handle, Impressed Label, Charlestown, Hearts, 1810s, 14 ½ In. ... 375
Jug, Oval, Brushed Cobalt Blue, Molded Rim & Handle, Stamped, c.1860, 2 Gal., 13 ½ x 8 In... 207
Jug, Red Devil Mask, White Slip Horns, 2 Spouts, Handle, Michel Bayne, 13 ½ In. ... 165
Jug, Ring Shape, Alkaline Glaze, Arched Handle, Footed, SC Pottery, 1800s, 9 ½ x 8 In. ... 915
Jug, Tan, Blue Script, E. Malin Hoopes, West Chester, Pa., 11 In. ... 1062
Jug, Whiskey, Cobalt Blue Stencils, Handle, Collar Rim, Sullivan Saloon, Tenn., c.1900, 15 In. ..*illus* 1680
Jug, Wood & Wire Handle, Atlantic Coast Dist. Co., c.1815, 10 In. ... 115
Mug, Cobalt Blue, Westerwald, Thread Neck, Rex Medallion, Germany, 1700s, 6 In. ... 263
Mug, Dr. Swett's Original Root Beer, Royal Blue, Brown, Embossed, 6 x 3 ½ x 4 ½ In. ... 90
Pitcher, Blue Floral Spray, Leaves, Round Base, Spout, 2 Gal., 13 In. ... 708
Pitcher, Cobalt Blue Flowers, Bulbous Body, Handle, Pennsylvania, 1800s, 8 ½ In. ... 1098
Pitcher, Cobalt Blue Flowers, Handle, 1800s, 10 In. ...*illus* 180
Pitcher, Cobalt Blue Tulips, Leaves, Tooled Neck & Body, Flared Base, 10 ¾ x 7 ½ In. ... 1125
Platter, White Ground, Flowers, Leaves, Gilt Border, Multicolor, 1838-41, 22 x 17 ½ In. ... 192
Stein, Black Ground, Multicolor Border, Lion's Heads, Couples, Pewter Lid, c.1920, 16 In. ... 150
Tankard, Spiral Body, Applied Handle, Pewter Base, Lid, 7 ½ In. ...*illus* 450

Stoneware, Crock, Cobalt Blue Flowers, Handle, N. Clark Jr., Athens, N.Y., 1800s, 12 In.
$236

Copake Auctions

Stoneware, Crock, Cobalt Blue, Leaves, Rolled Rim, Ear Handles, 15 ½ In.
$502

Copake Auctions

Stoneware, Inkwell, Cylindrical, 3 Quill Holes, Yellow, 1800s, 1 ½ In.
$36

Copake Auctions

This is an edited listing of current prices. Visit **Kovels.com** to check thousands of prices from previous years and sign up for free information on trends, tips, reproductions, marks, and more.

S

Stoneware, Jar, Brushed Cobalt Blue, Oval, Bulbous Body, Applied Handle, J. Bennace, 1850s, 9 ½ In.
$188

Garth's Auctioneers & Appraisers

Stoneware, Jar, Cobalt Blue, Stencil, Gray, H.F. Behrens, c.1900, 8 In.
$216

Selkirk Auctioneers & Appraisers

Stoneware, Jar, Dark Brown, Oval, Lug Handles, North Carolina, c.1900, 4 Gal., 14 x 10 ½ In.
$540

Case Antiques

Stoneware, Jug, Bird Nesting, Tulips, Cobalt Blue Impressed, Cowden & Wilcox, Harrisburg, 1800s, 17 In.
$7,930

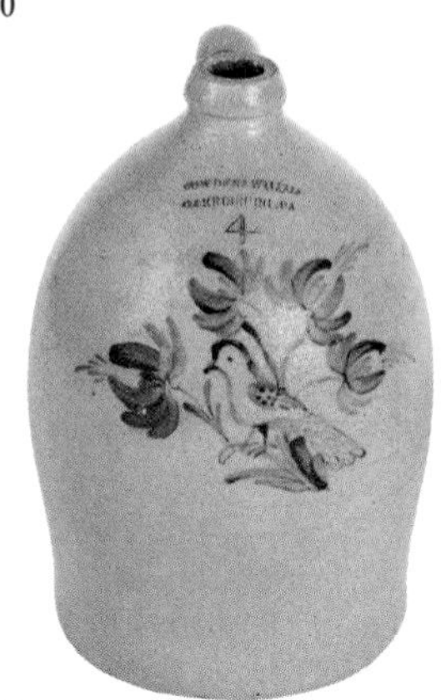

Pook & Pook

Stoneware, Jug, Bulbous, Reeded, Manganese Glazed Neck, Molded Crown, GR, Westerwald, 1750s, 7 In.
$738

Skinner, Inc.

Stoneware, Jug, Cobalt Blue Flowers, Stamped Norton & Fenton, Bennington, Vt., 1800s, 4 Gal., 16 In.
$270

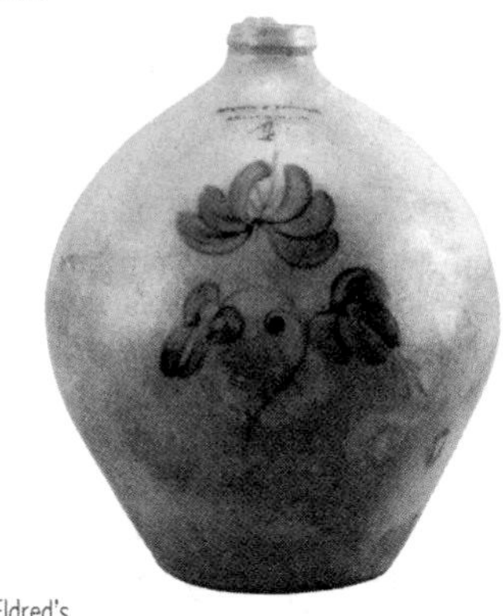

Eldred's

Stoneware, Jug, Cobalt Blue Inscription, 2 Handles, Jas. Hamilton & Co., Greensboro, 1800s, 18 In.
$580

Pook & Pook

Stoneware, Jug, Cobalt Blue Beehive & Leaf, Cowden & Wilcox, Harrisburg, Pa., 4 Gal., 17 ½ In.
$295

Conestoga Auction Company

S

Stoneware, Jug, Kentucky Whiskey, Glazed, I.W. Harper Nelson Co., 7 x 5 x 5 In.
$180

Morphy Auctions

Stoneware, Jug, Whiskey, Cobalt Blue Stencils, Handle, Collar Rim, Sullivan Saloon, Tenn., c.1900, 15 In.
$1,680

Case Antiques

Stoneware, Pitcher, Cobalt Blue Flowers, Handle, 1800s, 10 In.
$180

Eldred's

Stoneware, Tankard, Spiral Body, Applied Handle, Pewter Base, Lid, 7 ½ In.
$450

Milestone Auctions

Stoneware, Vase, Lid, Wheel Thrown, Partial Glaze, Incised Ferns, Signed, Peter Voulkos, Mid-Century, 11 x 4 In.
$3,500

New Orleans Auction Galleries

Stoneware, Water Cooler, Lid, Cobalt Blue Flowers, Embossed, Spigot, Robinson Clay, 3 Gal.
$560

Conestoga Auction Company

Store, Bin, Seed, Oak, 9 Compartments, Rectangular Top, Glass Front, 34 x 45 x 26 In.
$1,003

Bunch Auctions

Store, Bin, Tin, Gold Stencil, Roll Front Opening, Old Black Paint, 1880s, 2 Gal., 24 x 19 x 16 In.
$150

Garth's Auctioneers & Appraisers

Store, Case, Display, Pioneer, Belt Buckles, Wood, Slant Front, Glass, Drawer, 7 x 13 x 9 In.
$240

Rich Penn Auctions

TIP

When you can't decide whether or not to buy a treasure at a show or flea market, remember the classic slogan, "Buy now or cry later."

Store, Cigar Cutter, Guillotine, Oak Frame, Fixed Lower Blade, Sliding Upper Blade, 12 x 4 x 7 In.
$545

Fontaine's Auction Gallery

Store, Cigar Cutter, Stag Horn Handle, Silver Plate Boar's Head Cap, Solingen, 1900s, 7 In.
$819

Thomaston Place Auction Galleries

Store, Mailbox, U.S. Post Office, Metal Front, 17 Lock Boxes, Open Cubbies, 46 x 12 x 14 In.
$780

Rich Penn Auctions

TIP

Get a big mailbox so when you are away your mail will not be seen from the street.

Store, Keg, Beer, Wood, Iron Bands, Kaifer Inc., Pa, 13 x 15 ½ In.
$158

Hartzell's Auction Gallery Inc.

Store, Mannequin, Female, Seated, Crossed Legs, Jointed Waist, Shoulder, 34 x 28 In.
$72

Rich Penn Auctions

Vase, Blue & White, Glazed, Black Rim, c.1950, 10 In. 75
Vase, Cobalt Blue Plume, Freehand, Handle, John L. Smith & Co., 1850s, 2 Gal., 15 In. 408
Vase, Columnar, Mistletoe, Metal Foot Rim, Alexandre Bigot, c.1900, 8 ¾ In. 584
Vase, Crystalline Glaze, Embossed, Flowers, Gres Mougin Nancy, 9 ½ In. 267
Vase, Lid, Wheel Thrown, Partial Glaze, Incised Ferns, Peter Voulkos, Mid-Century, 11 x 4 In. ..*illus* 3500
Water Cooler, Barrel, Cobalt Blue, Brass Spigot, 2 Roulette Bands, 13 x 9 In. 104
Water Cooler, Flowers, T.F. Reppert, Successor To Jas. Hamilton & Co., 1800s, 21 In. 4392
Water Cooler, Lid, Cobalt Blue Flowers, Embossed, Spigot, Robinson Clay, 3 Gal. ....*illus* 560
Water Cooler, Radium Ore Revigator, Lid, White, 15 In. 181

STORE

Store fixtures, cases, cutters, and other items that have no company advertising as part of the decoration are listed here. Most items found in an old store are listed in the Advertising category in this book.

Bin, Coffee, Tin, Tole, Chinoiserie, Slant Hinged Lid, Black Ground, 19 x 18 x 22 In. 153
Bin, Seed, Oak, 9 Compartments, Rectangular Top, Glass Front, 34 x 45 x 26 In. ....*illus* 1003
Bin, Tin, Gold Stencil, Roll Front Opening, Old Black Paint, 1880s, 2 Gal., 24 x 19 x 16 In. *illus* 150
Box, Cinnamon, Country, Little Girl, Fife, Porcelain Knob, 12 x 10 In. 84
Cabinet, Display, Glass, Brass, Hinged Double Doors, 4 Shelves, 20 x 28 x 5 In., Pair 497
Cabinet, Oak Top, Glass Front & Sides, Ornate Bowed Iron Legs, Shelves, 66 x 29 x 18 In. 984
Case, Display, 3 Drawers, Beveled Glass Top, Brass Knob, c.1890, 4 x 9 x 15 In. 537
Case, Display, Castle Showcase Co., Glass Top, Sides, Rolling Doors, 1950s, 44 x 70 x 24 In. 120
Case, Display, Pioneer, Belt Buckles, Wood, Slant Front, Glass, Drawer, 7 x 13 x 9 In. ....*illus* 240
Case, Display, Wood, Glass Sides & 3 Shelves, 24 x 15 x 15 In. 813
Cigar Cutter, Guillotine, Oak Frame, Fixed Lower Blade, Sliding Upper Blade, 12 x 4 x 7 In. *illus* 545
Cigar Cutter, Stag Horn Handle, Silver Plate Boar's Head Cap, Solingen, 1900s, 7 In. ....*illus* 819
Coffee Grinders are listed in the Coffee Mill category.
Counter, Meat, 6 Drawers, 2 Doors, 40 x 92 In. 750
Counter, Pine, 2-Plank Top, Drop Panel Front, Wainscot Finished, Opener, 36 x 20 x 84 In. 593
Counter, Pine, Grain Painted, Yellow, Scrubbed Top, Interior Shelf, 1850s, 31 x 50 x 26 In. 1140
Display, Counter, Brass, 8 Wire Shape Gloves, Star, c.1950, 27 ½ In. 94
Display, Saddlemaker's Horse, 88 x 99 In. 625
Display, Seed Samples, Divided, Wood, Black Stain, Red, Gold, c.1900, 19 x 24 ¾ x 3 ½ In. 136
Display, Window, Flapper Girl, Cut Out, Painted, Yellow, Plywood Base, 15 In. 70
Door Hinges, Iron, Forged, Wood Frame, Salesman's Sample, 23 x 17 In. 125
Egg Crate, Pine, Stenciled, Swing Handle, Alvin J. Bozarth, Boonville, Mo., 13 x 12 x 11 In. 230
Figure, Pig, Smiling, Standing, Dressed As Butcher, Apron, Pottery, c.1970, 20 ½ In. 256
Ice Cream Cone Holder, Glass Cylinder, Metal Lid, Soda Fountain, 14 ½ x 7 In. 300
Keg, Beer, Wood, Iron Bands, Kaifer Inc., Pa, 13 x 15 ½ In. ....*illus* 158
Keg, Wood, Metal Straps, Hinged Lid, Handles, Greif Bros., 17 x 13 In. 72
Mailbox, U.S. Post Office, Metal Front, 17 Lock Boxes, Open Cubbies, 46 x 12 x 14 In. ....*illus* 780
Mannequin, Dress, Wolf Model Form Co., Iron Base, Collapsible, 1963, 63 x 15 In. 127
Mannequin, Female, Seated, Crossed Legs, Jointed Waist, Shoulder, 34 x 28 In. ....*illus* 72
Mannequin, Male Bust, Brown Leather, Wood Stand, 33 In. ....*illus* 679
Rack, Meat, Butcher Shop, Arrows, Heart, Stars, Brass Label, Gus V. Brecht, 1892, 15 x 66 In. .. 2160
Roasted Peanut Warmer, Ko-Pak-Ta, Children Dancing & Jumping, Sunset, Trees, 17 In. 117
Showcase, Oak, Steeple Pediment, Curved Glass, 2 Shelves, Velvet Interior, 40 x 30 x 27 In. 1074
Showcase, Standing, Cherry, Glass Panel Sides, Hinged Door, 1950s, 71 x 25 x 27 In. 189
Sign, Apothecary, Mortar & Pestle, Copper, Gold Leaf, c.1875, 21 In. ....*illus* 3600
Sign, Bootmaker, Tin, 2-Sided, Red, Flange Holder, Late 1800s, 23 x 28 In. 960
Sign, Boots, Iron, Painted, c.1900, 28 ½ x 18 ½ In. 781
Sign, Bowling, Bowling Pin, Red, White, 168 x 8 In. 1125
Sign, Cow, Steak House, Lighted, Black, White, 43 x 63 In. 687
Sign, Fish Market, Painted Pine, Carved, Hanging Chains, 1930s-50s, 67 x 26 x 6 In. ....*illus* 4388
Sign, Groceries, Candy, Cigars, Tobacco, Etc., Tin, Wood Strip Frame, 1910s, 25 x 26 In. 720
Sign, Post Office, Letter Drops, Money Orders, Arrow, Metal, Light-Up, 10 ½ x 20 ½ In. 540
Sign, Rabbit, White, Neon, Die Cut, 64 x 32 x 5 In. 3000
Sign, Ready Made Clothing, 2-Sided, Hanging, Painted, Late 1800s, 24 x 79 ½ In. 1586

Store, Mannequin, Male Bust, Brown Leather, Wood Stand, 33 In.
$679

Copake Auctions

Store, Sign, Apothecary, Mortar & Pestle, Copper, Gold Leaf, c.1875, 21 In.
$3,600

Garth's Auctioneers & Appraisers

Store, Sign, Fish Market, Painted Pine, Carved, Hanging Chains, 1930s-50s, 67 x 26 x 6 In.
$4,388

Thomaston Place Auction Galleries

Store, Sign, Shoe Sale, 1 Cent, Canvas, 2-Sided, Wood Frame, 67 x 17 In.
$295

Copake Auctions

Store, Sign, To Privy, Pointing Hand, Painted, c.1940, 18 In.
$160

Skinner, Inc.

Stove, Cook, Cast Iron, 2 Flat Iron Warmers, Walker & Pratt Co., Boston No. 1, 28 ½ In.
$130

Conestoga Auction Company

TIP

A Sumida vase usually has a swirl on the base, three-dimensional figures of children and animals as decoration, and the vases are often signed in Japanese. Be careful. The orange glaze can be scrubbed off with vigorous cleaning.

Sign, School Books & Supplies, Painted Wood, Rectangular, 22 x 62 In. 325
Sign, Shoe Sale, 1 Cent, Canvas, 2-Sided, Wood Frame, 67 x 17 In. .... *illus* 295
Sign, Soda Fountain, Marked, Cherry, Cast Iron, 20 ½ In. 90
Sign, To Privy, Pointing Hand, Painted, c.1940, 18 In. .... *illus* 160
Spice Box, Tin, Red Ground, Gold Scroll, Lid, Counter, 1880s, 12 x 9 ½ x 9 In. 225
Strawholder, Glass, Cylindrical, Fluted, Stepped Metal Lid, 1910-20, 12 x 4 In. 123
Table, Pine, Rectangular Top, Applied Molded Edge, 6 Turned Legs, c.1910, 30 x 120 x 34 In. .. 472
Tobacco Cutter, Buzz Saw, Embossed Chew, Cast Iron, c.1880, 17 In. 263
Tobacco Cutter, Flat Iron Plug, Black & Red, Painted, Scotten Dillon Co., 16 In. 170

STOVE

Stoves have been used in America for heating since the eighteenth century and for cooking since the nineteenth century. Most types of wood, coal, gas, kerosene, and even some electric stoves are collected. Salesman's samples may be listed here or in Toy.

Cook, Bessie, Cast Iron, Ornate, Nickel Accessories, Doors Open, Salesman's Sample, 12 x 7 In.. 168
Cook, Cast Iron, 2 Flat Iron Warmers, Walker & Pratt Co., Boston No. 1, 28 ½ In. .... *illus* 130
Cook, Great Majestic Junior, Nickel Plated, Cast Iron, Salesman's Sample, 30 In. .... *illus* 1140
Cook, Hanks Junior, Black & Gray, Nickel Plated Trim, Salesman's Sample, 16 x 17 In. .... *illus* 300
Cook, Qualified Range, Enamel, 4 Burners, Salesman's Sample, 16 x 17 In. .... *illus* 210
Cook, Tappan, Eclipse, Steel, White Porcelain, Gas Burners, Salesman's Sample, 18 x 16 In... *illus* 660
Heater, Irons, Boston, Oval Top, Octagonal Waist, Tripod Feet, Magee Furnace Co., 26 x 22 x 17 In.. 254
Heater, Irons, Hexagonal, Cast Iron, Paw Feet, Ofverums Bruk, Holds 6 Irons, Sweden 113
Parlor, Beckwith, Round Oak, Cast Iron, Nickel Trim, Brass Finial, c.1905-08, 55 x 22 In... *illus* 660
Stove Plate, God's Well, Henry Mercer, 1760, 24 x 20 In. 1003

STRETCH GLASS

Stretch glass is named for the strange stretch marks in the glass. It was made by many glass companies in the United States from about 1900 to the 1920s. It is iridescent. Most European stretch glass pieces are blown and may have a pontil mark.

Bowl, Green, 2 ¾ x 10 In. 40
Vase, Green Vaseline Glass, Flared Wavy Edge, 5 ½ x 5 ½ In. 24
Vase, Green, Slanted Oval Mouth, 24 In. 40
Vase, Green, Viking, 24 In. 19

SULPHIDE

Sulphides are cameos of unglazed white porcelain encased in transparent glass. The technique was patented in 1819 in France and has been used ever since for paperweights, decanters, tumblers, marbles, and other type of glassware. Paperweights and Marbles are listed in their own categories.

Glass, Dish, Cameo, Crest, Order Of The Garter, Etched, Scalloped Edge, 6 In. 889
Glass, Plaque, George Washington, Cameo, Oval, Scalloped, Sunburst Back, c.1825, 3 x 3 In... 1178

SUMIDA

Sumida is a Japanese pottery that was made from about 1895 to 1941. Pieces are usually everyday objects—vases, jardinieres, bowls, teapots, and decorative tiles. Most pieces have a very heavy orange-red, blue, brown, black, green, purple, or off-white glaze, with raised three-dimensional figures as decorations. The unglazed part is painted red, green, black, or orange. Sumida is sometimes mistakenly called Sumida gawa, but true Sumida gawa is a softer pottery made in the early 1800s.

Bowl, Pinched Rim, 2 Men On Rim, 1 Man Next To House, 7 ½ In. Diam. 125
Vase, Applied Figures Of Frogs On Bamboo, Blue Ground, 8 In. 152
Vase, Moon Flask, Red, Black, Snow-Capped Mountain, Marked, Signed, 11 ½ x 10 In. 310

Stove, Cook, Great Majestic Junior, Nickel Plated, Cast Iron, Salesman's Sample, 30 In.
$1,140

Rich Penn Auctions

Stove, Cook, Hanks Junior, Black & Gray, Nickel Plated Trim, Salesman's Sample, 16 x 17 In.
$300

Rich Penn Auctions

Stove, Cook, Qualified Range, Enamel, 4 Burners, Salesman's Sample, 16 x 17 In.
$210

Rich Penn Auctions

Stove, Cook, Tappan, Eclipse, Steel, White Porcelain, Gas Burners, Salesman's Sample, 18 x 16 In.
$660

Rich Penn Auctions

Stove, Parlor, Beckwith, Round Oak, Cast Iron, Nickel Trim, Brass Finial, c.1905-08, 55 x 22 In.
$660

Rich Penn Auctions

S

Tea Caddy, Burl, Chestnut, Chest, Dome Lid, Bronze Mounts, Applied Medallions, 7 x 5 ½ x 9 ½ In.
$272

Fontaine's Auction Gallery

Tea Caddy, Chinoiserie, Melon Shape, Stem Finial, 6-Lobed Pewter Container, Early 1800s, 7 ¾ In.
$600

Eldred's

Tea Caddy, Fruitwood, Apple Shape, Hinged Lid, Brass Lock, 1800s, 4 ½ In.
$600

Eldred's

TIP
Have a window or a peephole in every outside door.

SUNBONNET BABIES

Sunbonnet Babies were introduced in 1900 in the book *The Sunbonnet Babies*. The stories were by Eulalie Osgood Grover, illustrated by Bertha Corbett. The children's faces were completely hidden by the sunbonnets. The children had been pictured in black and white before this time, but the color pictures in the book were immediately successful. The Royal Bayreuth China Company made a full line of children's dishes decorated with the Sunbonnet Babies. Some Sunbonnet Babies plates have been reproduced, but they are clearly marked.

Bell, Sunday, Fishing, 3 ¼ In. .... 15 to 20
Figurine, Thursday, Scrubbing, 6 ½ x 4 ¾ In. 20
Pitcher, Wednesday, Mending, 3 ¼ In. 15
Plate, Friday, Sweeping, 7 In. 25

SUNDERLAND LUSTER

Sunderland luster is a name given to a special type of pink luster made by Leeds, Newcastle, and other English firms during the nineteenth century. The luster broth glaze is metallic and glossy and appears to have bubbles in it. Other pieces of luster are listed in the Luster category.

Pitcher, Pink Luster, Little Girl & Angel, Think Of Me, 6 ½ In. 65
Pitcher, Woman In Flowing Dress, Multicolor Enamel, Black Transfer, 1810s, 7 ⅜ In. 129
Rolling Pin, Pink Luster, Ship Sally At Sail, Turned Pine Handles, 17 ¾ In. 80

SUPERMAN

Superman was created by two seventeen-year-olds in 1938. The first issue of Action Comics had the strip. Superman remains popular and became the hero of a radio show in 1940, cartoons in the 1940s, a television series, and several major movies.

Cremation Urn, Metal, Blue, Red Screw Lid, Superman Logo, c.1980, 9 In. 249
Figure, Wood, Composition, Chest Decal, Movable Head, Ideal, 13 In. 1038
Fountain Pen, Plastic, Metal, Red, Blue, Joffe Pen Co., 1947, 5 In. 187
Necktie, Warner Brothers, Hand Made Silk, Korea, 1999, 59 In. 22
Poster, Be My Guest, Palisades Amusement Park, Superman, Hands On Hips, 1968, 42 x 82 In. 2373
Ring, Supermen Of The World, Member, Red, Gold, Superman With Balled Fists, 1940s 7935
Toy, Action Figure, World's Greatest Super-Heroes, Mego, No. 1300, Box, 1972, 8 In. 240
Toy, Superman Lifting Rollover Plane, Tin Litho, Windup, Marx, 1940, 6 ½ x 6 In. 1600

SUSIE COOPER

Susie Cooper (1902–1995) began as a designer in 1925 working for the English firm A.E. Gray & Company. She left to work on her own as Susie Cooper Productions in 1929, decorating white ware bought from other potteries. In 1931 she formed Susie Cooper Pottery, Ltd. and moved her studio to Wood & Sons Crown Works. In 1950 it became Susie Cooper China, Ltd., and the company made china and earthenware. She bought Crown Works in 1959. It became part of the Wedgwood Group in 1966. Wedgwood closed Crown Works in 1979 and Cooper moved her studio to Adams & Sons. In 1986 she moved to the Isle of Man and worked as a free-lance designer. The name *Susie Cooper* appears with the company names on many pieces of ceramics.

A.E. Gray & Co.
c.1925–1931

Susie Cooper
CROWN WORKS
BURSLEM
ENGLAND

Susie Cooper
1932–1956

Susie Cooper
1932–1964

Coffee Set, Coffeepot, Creamer, Sugar, 6 Cups, Stars, Art Deco, Harlequin ... 950
Creamer, Wedding Ring Pattern, Tan, Rust, Green, 1940s, 3 In. ... 20
Cup & Saucer, Dark Red & Cream ... 44
Cup & Saucer, White Gardenia, Blue Interior, Gray Saucer ... 60
Honey Jar, Lid, Underplate, Tan, Brown, Turquoise Rings, 5 x 3 In. ... 95
Plate, Central Bouquet, Blue Border, 9 In. ... 25
Teapot, Art Nouveau Pattern, Brown & Orange Flowers, Leaves, 6 x 4 x 5 In. ... 40

SWASTIKA KERAMOS

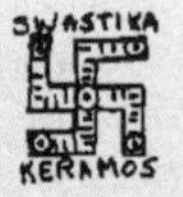

Swastika Keramos is a line of art pottery made from 1906 to 1908 by the Owen China Company of Minerva, Ohio. Many pieces were made with an iridescent glaze.

Vase, Supernatural Winter Forest, Tall Trees, Ruby Color Cloud, 11 ⅞ In. ... 227

SWORDS

Swords of all types that are of interest to collectors are listed here. The military dress sword with elaborate handle is probably the most wanted. A tsuba is a hand guard fitted to a Japanese sword between the handle and the blade. Be sure to display swords in a safe way, out of reach of children.

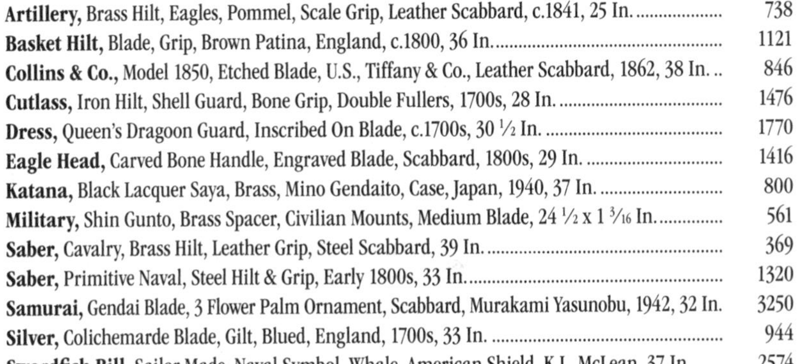

Artillery, Brass Hilt, Eagles, Pommel, Scale Grip, Leather Scabbard, c.1841, 25 In. ... 738
Basket Hilt, Blade, Grip, Brown Patina, England, c.1800, 36 In. ... 1121
Collins & Co., Model 1850, Etched Blade, U.S., Tiffany & Co., Leather Scabbard, 1862, 38 In. ... 846
Cutlass, Iron Hilt, Shell Guard, Bone Grip, Double Fullers, 1700s, 28 In. ... 1476
Dress, Queen's Dragoon Guard, Inscribed On Blade, c.1700s, 30 ½ In. ... 1770
Eagle Head, Carved Bone Handle, Engraved Blade, Scabbard, 1800s, 29 In. ... 1416
Katana, Black Lacquer Saya, Brass, Mino Gendaito, Case, Japan, 1940, 37 In. ... 800
Military, Shin Gunto, Brass Spacer, Civilian Mounts, Medium Blade, 24 ½ x 1 3/16 In. ... 561
Saber, Cavalry, Brass Hilt, Leather Grip, Steel Scabbard, 39 In. ... 369
Saber, Primitive Naval, Steel Hilt & Grip, Early 1800s, 33 In. ... 1320
Samurai, Gendai Blade, 3 Flower Palm Ornament, Scabbard, Murakami Yasunobu, 1942, 32 In. 3250
Silver, Colichemarde Blade, Gilt, Blued, England, 1700s, 33 In. ... 944
Swordfish Bill, Sailor Made, Naval Symbol, Whale, American Shield, K.L. McLean, 37 In. ... 2574

SYRACUSE

Syracuse is one of the trademarks used by the Onondaga Pottery of Syracuse, New York. They also used O.P. Co. The company was established in 1871. The name became the Syracuse China Company in 1966. Syracuse China closed in 2009. It was known for fine dinnerware and restaurant china.

Syracuse China, Corp. 1871–1873

Syracuse China, Corp. 1892–1895

Syracuse China, Corp. 1966–1970

Gardenia, Plate, White, Green, Gardenias, Scalloped Ribbed Border, 10 In. ... 10
Meadow Breeze, Cup & Saucer, Blue & White, Stylized Flowers ... 15
Victoria, Plate, Rose In Center, Rosebud Border, Scalloped Edge, 1949-70, 10 In. ... 18

TAPESTRY, *Porcelain, see Rose Tapestry category.*

TEA CADDY

Tea caddy is the name for a small box made to hold tea leaves. In the eighteenth century, tea was very expensive and it was stored under lock

Tea Caddy, Gilt Lacquer, Bombe Shape, Fitted Compartment, Ivory Finials, Chinese, 1810s, 6 x 11 x 8 In.
$2,760

Eldred's

Tea Caddy, Lacquer, Hinged Lid, Metal Lock Escutcheon, Paw Feet, Octagonal, Chinese, 5 x 8 x 5 In.
$702

Thomaston Place Auction Galleries

TIP

If you live in an old house and the locks are old, check the new types. There have been many improvements, and new locks provide much better security.

Tea Caddy, Mahogany, Sideboard Shape, Brass, 3 Drawers, Carved Backsplash, William IV, 11 x 15 x 7 In.
$960

CRN Auctions

Tea Caddy, Penwork, Lid, Chinoiserie Scene, England, Regency, 8 ½ x 5 ½ x 5 In.
$384

Bunch Auctions

TIP
To get more light in a room and make the room look larger mount a mirror opposite a window.

Tea Caddy, Rosewood, Mother-Of-Pearl Inlay, Handle, Footed, Glass Mixing Bowl, Georgian, 12 x 6 x 6 In.
$196

Richard D. Hatch & Associates

Tea Caddy, Silver, Enamel, Gemstones, Flowers, Russia, 6 x 4 x 4 In.
$2,583

Charlton Hall Auctions

and key. The first tea caddies were made with locks. By the nineteenth century, tea was more plentiful and the tea caddy was larger. Often there were two sections, one for green tea, one for black tea.

Burl, Chestnut, Chest, Dome Lid, Bronze Mounts, Applied Medallions, 7 x 5 ½ x 9 ½ In. *illus* 272
Burl, Coffin Shape, 2 Lidded Compartments, Pad Feet, 1800s, 5 ½ x 7 ¾ x 4 ½ In. 350
Chinoiserie, Black Lacquer, Pewter Lining, Figures In Courtyard, Bail Handles, 7 x 10 x 13 In. 214
Chinoiserie, Melon Shape, Stem Finial, 6-Lobed Pewter Container, Early 1800s, 7 ¾ In. *illus* 600
Coromandel, Decagon Shape, Lidded Compartment, Brass, Shield Escutcheon, 6 ½ x 3 ¾ In. 900
Coromandel, Veneer, Compartment Interior, Lock, 1800s, 5 ½ x 8 ½ x 5 ½ In. 300
Fruitwood, Apple Shape, Hinged Lid, Brass Lock, 1800s, 4 ½ In. *illus* 600
Fruitwood, Apple Shape, Hinged Lid, Turned, 1800s, 4 In. 923
Gilt Lacquer, Bombe Shape, Fitted Compartment, Ivory Finials, Chinese, 1810s, 6 x 11 x 8 In. *illus* 2760
Lacquer, Hinged Lid, Metal Lock Escutcheon, Paw Feet, Octagonal, Chinese, 5 x 8 x 5 In. *illus* 702
Mahogany Inlay, 2 Lids, Lining, England, 1800s, 5 x 7 x 4 In. 246
Mahogany, Coffin Shape, Brass Lion's Mask Ring Handles, Ball Feet, c.1815, 6 x 8 x 4 In. 360
Mahogany, Dome Lid, Hinged, Agate Cabochon Central, Brass, 4 ½ x 8 x 4 ½ In. 283
Mahogany, Federal Flame, Brass Escutcheon, Ball Feet, Late 1700s, 5 ½ x 8 x 5 In. 187
Mahogany, Hinged Lid, 2 Compartments, Mixing Bowl, Brass Trim & Feet, 6 ½ x 11 x 5 ½ In. 127
Mahogany, Hinged Lid, Chippendale, Brass Handle, Ball & Claw Feet, 7 x 11 x 7 In. 1845
Mahogany, Hinged Lid, Georgian, Box, Inlaid, Glass Mixing Bowl, 12 x 6 x 6 In. 161
Mahogany, Lid, Regency Style, Inlaid, Brass Handle, Ball Feet, 6 ¾ x 12 x 6 In. 246
Mahogany, Scalloped Lid, Flowers, Lion's Mask Pulls, Brass Feet, 10 ½ x 7 In. 940
Mahogany, Sideboard Shape, Brass, 3 Drawers, Carved Backsplash, William IV, 11 x 15 x 7 In. *illus* 960
Mother-Of-Pearl, Carved Oval, Taj Mahal On Lid, Brass Ball Feet, 1800s, 6 x 7 ½ x 5 In. 1200
Mother-Of-Pearl, Inlaid Tortoiseshell, Lion Knop, Paw Feet, c.1825, 8 ¾ x 12 x 5 In. 4250
Penwork, Lid, Chinoiserie Scene, England, Regency, 8 ½ x 5 ½ x 5 In. *illus* 384
Rosewood, Coffin Shape, Drop Ring Side Handles, Carved Feet, 1800s, 8 ½ x 13 x 7 ½ In. 761
Rosewood, Lid Panel & Interior, Brass Ball Feet, George IV, c.1820, 7 x 11 x 6 In. 384
Rosewood, Mother-Of-Pearl Inlay, 2 Compartments, Footed, Regency, 6 x 9 x 5 In. 173
Rosewood, Mother-Of-Pearl Inlay, Handle, Footed, Glass Mixing Bowl, Georgian, 12 x 6 x 6 In. *illus* 196
Rosewood, Regency, Brass Inlaid, Lion's Mask Handle, Ball & Claw Feet, c.1810, 8 x 12 x 6 In. 2900
Rosewood, Ring Handles, Bun Feet, Foil Lining, 1850s, 6 x 12 ½ x 5 ½ In. 150
Satinwood, Canted Corner, Oval Burl Panel, Early 1800s, 4 ¾ x 8 ⅜ x 4 ¾ In. 468
Shell, Lid, 2 Compartments, Canted Corners, Bone Bun Feet, Georgia, 4 x 6 x 4 In. 2760
Silver, Dome Lid, Urn Finial, Oval, Bright Cut, Flowers, Hester Bateman, 5 ½ x 5 x 3 ⅝ In. 1287
Silver, Dominick & Haff, Hammered, Dragonfly Motif, N.Y., 1882, 5 x 3 ½ In. 1680
Silver, Enamel, Gemstones, Flowers, Russia, 6 x 4 x 4 In. *illus* 2583
Tortoiseshell, Coffin Shape, 2 Compartments, Ball Feet, George III, 5 x 8 ½ x 5 In. 900
Tortoiseshell, Dome Lid, Tapered Sides, 2 Lidded Compartments, Bail Handle, 1800s, 4 In. 1100
Tortoiseshell, Red, George III, Dome Lid, 2 Compartments, Ball Feet, 1800s, 6 x 6 In. *illus* 3660
Wood, Chamfered Corners, Fluted, Polka Dot Ground, Early 1800s, 5 x 8 x 4 ¾ In. *illus* 637
Wood, Hinged Lid, 2 Compartments, Footed, Regency, 5 ½ x 7 ½ x 4 ½ In. 115

TEA LEAF IRONSTONE

Tea leaf ironstone dishes are named for their decorations. There was a superstition that it was lucky if a whole tea leaf unfolded at the bottom of your teacup. This idea was translated into the pattern of dishes known as "tea leaf." By 1850 at least 12 English factories were making this pattern, and by the 1870s it was a popular pattern in many countries. The tea leaf was always a luster glaze on early wares, although now some pieces are made with a brown tea leaf. There are many variations of tea leaf designs, such as Teaberry, Pepper Leaf, and Gold Leaf. The designs were used on many different white ironstone shapes, such as Bamboo, Lily of the Valley, Empress, and Cumbow.

Bowl, Vegetable, Lid, Berries, 2 Handles, Clementson Bros., c.1885, 10 x 6 ⅝ In. 135
Coffeepot, Lid, Bamboo Painted Handle, Alfred Meakin, England, 9 ½ In. 89
Gravy Boat, Anthony Shaw, 5 ½ x 3 In. 79
Serving Plate, Hexagonal, 2 Handles, Anthony Shaw 38

Sugar, Marked H. Burgess, 6 ½ In. 32

TECO

Teco is the mark used on the art pottery line made by the American Terra Cotta and Ceramic Company of Terra Cotta and Chicago, Illinois. The company was an offshoot of the firm founded by William D. Gates in 1881. The Teco line was first made in 1885 but was not sold commercially until 1902. It continued in production until 1922. Over 500 designs were made in a variety of colors, shapes, and glazes. The company closed in 1930.

Bowl, Green Matte Glaze, Footed, Impressed Marks, 2 x 10 In. ....*illus* 1188
Pitcher, Wishbone, Green Matte Glaze, Handle, Earthenware, Early 1900s, 8 x 5 x 3 In. 469
Vase, Buttressed, Green Matte Glaze, Handles, Marked, 7 In. 345
Vase, Cream Matte Glaze, Flower Form, Earthenware, Terra Cotta, Ill., c.1910, 13 x 6 x 6 In. 875
Vase, Green Matte Glaze, 2 Side Handles, Marked 266, 11 In. 518
Vase, Green Matte Glaze, 4 Buttress Handles, Charcoaling, Impressed Logo, 7 In. 2662
Vase, Green Matte Glaze, Flared Rim, 4 Buttresses Base, 10 ½ x 4 ¾ In. ....*illus* 2260
Vase, Squat, 2 Handles, c.1910, 5 ½ x 4 In. 1625
Vase, Terra-Cotta, Green Matte, Curdled Glaze, Cylindrical, 13 x 5 ½ In. 254

TEDDY BEAR

Teddy bears were named for a president of the United States. The first teddy bear was a cuddly toy said to be inspired by a hunting trip made by President Theodore Roosevelt in 1902. He was praised because he saw a bear cub but did not shoot it. Morris and Rose Michtom started selling their stuffed bears as "teddy bears" and the name stayed. The Michtoms founded the Ideal Novelty and Toy Company. The German version of the teddy bear was made about the same time by the Steiff Company. There are many types of teddy bears and all are collected. The old ones are being reproduced. Other bears are listed in the Toy section.

Farnell, Gold Mohair, Webbed Paw Stitching, 21 In. 840
Ideal, Mohair, Woody, Glass Eyes, 5-Way Jointed, Ribbon, c.1920, 16 In. 59
Mohair, Brown, Stitched Nose, Button Eyes, Germany, 22 In. ....*illus* 118
Mohair, Sitting, Ear Tag, Paper Tags, Strong Museum, 9 In., Pair 90
Steiff, Mohair, Blond, Button Eyes, c.1920, 12 In. 840
Steiff, Mohair, Blond, Glass Eyes, Long Arms, Humpback, Button In Ear, 25 In. 5400
Steiff, Mohair, Blond, Stitched Nose, Script Button, 1960s, 19 In. 210
Steiff, Mohair, Brown, Sewn Mouth & Nose, Head, Legs, Jointed, Glass Eyes, c.1920-30, 5 In. 230
Steiff, Mohair, Cinnamon, Center Seam, Button Eyes, Trailing F Button, 20 In. 6000
Steiff, Mohair, Glass Eyes, Growler, Metal Base, Red & Black Wheels, c.1930, 18 x 23 In. 878
Steiff, Mohair, Golden, Black Stitched Nose, Jointed, Button Eyes, Button In Ear, 14 In. 1440
Steiff, Mohair, Golden, Wood Chip Stuffing, Boot Button Eyes, c.1904, 16 In. 2216
Steiff, Mohair, Long Arms, Humpback, Growler, Button In Ear, 20 In. 660
Steiff, Zoti, Mohair, Curly Blond, Apricot Bib, Jointed, Brown Glass Eyes, 14 In. 1920

TELEPHONE

Telephones are wanted by collectors if the phones are old enough or unusual enough. The first telephone may have been made in Havana, Cuba, in 1849, but it was not patented. The first publicly demonstrated phone was used in Frankfurt, Germany, in 1860. The phone made by Alexander Graham Bell was shown at the Centennial Exhibition in Philadelphia in 1876, but it was not until 1877 that the first private phones were installed. Collectors today want all types of old phones, phone parts, and advertising. Even recent figural phones are popular.

American Bell Telephone Co., Candlestick, Brass, Enamel Dial Ring, 1915-20, 12 x 5 ¾ In... 452
Automatic Electric Co., Pay Phone, Coin Chute, Black, 7 x 5 ½ x 18 In. 228

Tea Caddy, Tortoiseshell, Red, George III, Dome Lid, 2 Compartments, Ball Feet, 1800s, 6 x 6 In.
$3,660

Neal Auction Company

Tea Caddy, Wood, Chamfered Corners, Fluted, Polka Dot Ground, Early 1800s, 5 x 8 x 4 ¾ In.
$637

Eldred's

TIP

If you buy an old teddy bear at a garage sale, bring it home and put it in a plastic bag with some mothballs for a few weeks. Don't let the mothballs touch the bear. The fur and stuffing of old bears attract many types of hungry insects.

Teco, Bowl, Green Matte Glaze, Footed, Impressed Marks, 2 x 10 In.
$1,188

Treadway

Teco, Vase, Green Matte Glaze, Flared Rim, 4 Buttresses Base, 10 ½ x 4 ¾ In.
$2,260

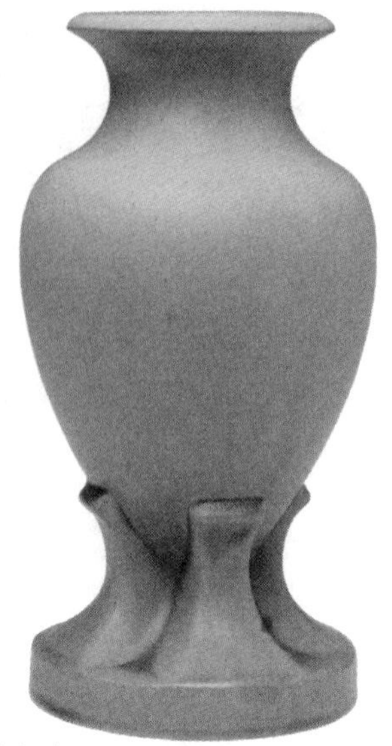

Soulis Auctions

Teddy Bear, Mohair, Brown, Stitched Nose, Button Eyes, Germany, 22 In.
$118

Cottone Auctions

Telephone, L.C. Mayer, Hide-A-Phone, Cover, Euphonia, Bust Of Woman, Hinged, 1917, 13 ¾ In.
$1,088

Auction Team Breker

Telephone, Peel-Connor, Candlestick, Brass, Steel, Electric, 12 ½ In.
$94

Copake Auctions

Telephone, Western Electric, Candlestick, Brass, Bakelite Receiver & Mouthpiece, Coin Box, 12 x 7 In.
$240

Rich Penn Auctions

Telephone, Western Electric, Wall, Oak, Brass, 20 ½ In.
$170

Hartzell's Auction Gallery Inc.

Teplitz, Bust, Woman, Art Nouveau, Bows, Amphora, Signed, Ed. Stellmacher, 14 x 8 ½ x 5 In., Pair
$212

Fontaine's Auction Gallery

Teplitz, Centerpiece, Bulbous, 3 Winged Putti Heads, Pierced Top, Flowers, Insects, Stellmacher, 14 In.
$242

Fontaine's Auction Gallery

Teplitz, Centerpiece, Woman, Reclining, Draped In Sheer Dress, Marked, 19 x 11 In.
$1,353

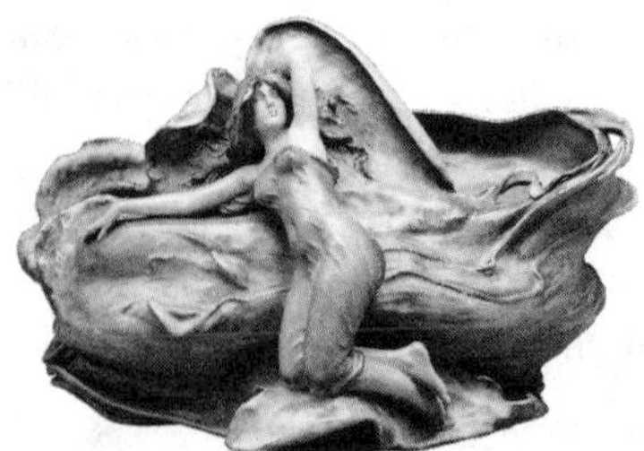

Morphy Auctions

Automatic Electric, Pay Phone, Chrome, Tan, Rotary Dial, Handle, Pay Box, 18 In. 192
Bell System, Pay Phone, Public, Metal, Black, Wall, 23 In. 158
Bell System, Sign, Bell Shape, Cast Aluminum, Wall Mount, 17 ½ x 16 In. 144
Deveau, Candlestick, 6 Buttons, Tapered Shaft, 13 In. 450
Gallows, Fluted Shaft, Nickel Finish, Wood Base, France, 1890s, 14 In. 300
L.C. Mayer, Hide-A-Phone, Cover, Euphonia, Bust Of Woman, Hinged, 1917, 13 ¾ In. ....*illus* 1088
Peel-Connor, Candlestick, Brass, Steel, Electric, 12 ½ In. ....*illus* 94
S.H. Couch Co., Wall, Oak Case, 1910, 13 x 6 ½ In. 106
Sign, Brass, Bronze Plaque, Mounting Holes, Raised Letters, Black Ground, c.1920, 4 x 16 In. .. 90
Wesco Supply, Wall, Fiddle Back, Oak Case, 2 Bells, 9 ½ x 27 In. 156
Western Electric, Candlestick, Brass, Bakelite Receiver & Mouthpiece, Coin Box, 12 x 7 In. *illus* 240
Western Electric, Candlestick, Ringer, Oak Case Box, Brass, Embossed, c.1915, 11 In. 164
Western Electric, Vanity, Oak Finish, Forked Receiver Hook, 1890s, 51 x 26 In. 1800
Western Electric, Wall, Oak, Brass, 20 ½ In. ....*illus* 170
Williams Electric, Tandem, Ornate Walnut Case, Forked Switch Hook, 1890s, 42 In. 690

TELEVISION

Television sets are twentieth-century collectibles. Although the first television transmission took place in England in 1925, collectors find few sets that pre-date 1946. The first sets had only five channels, but by 1949 the additional UHF channels were included. The first color television set became available in 1951.

Normende, Spectra, 1 Color & 3 Monochrome Tubes, White Case, c.1968, 31 x 44 In. 508

TEPLITZ

Teplitz refers to art pottery manufactured by a number of companies in the Teplitz-Turn area of Bohemia during the late nineteenth and early twentieth centuries. Two of these companies were the Alexandra Works founded by Ernst Wahliss, and the Amphora Porcelain Works, run by Riessner, Stellmacher, and Kessel.

Bust, Woman, Art Nouveau, Bows, Amphora, Signed, Ed. Stellmacher, 14 x 8 ½ x 5 In., Pair *illus* 212
Bust, Woman, Art Nouveau, Green Iridescent Shade, Doebrich, Amphora, 14 In. 968
Bust, Woman, Red Hair, Plumed Hat, Flowers, Ruffled Collar, 15 ½ x 5 ½ In. 350
Centerpiece, Bulbous, 3 Winged Putti Heads, Pierced Top, Flowers, Insects, Stellmacher, 14 In. *illus* 242
Centerpiece, Woman, Reclining, Draped In Sheer Dress, Marked, 19 x 11 In. ....*illus* 1353
Ewer, Bulbous, Gilt Devil Handle, Cream Ground, 4 Scroll Legs, Amphora, Signed, 10 ¾ In. 272
Vase, 3 Nudes, Holding Hands, Ruffled Leaves, Mottled Glaze, Amphora, 14 In. ....*illus* 1386
Vase, 3-D Eastern Dragon, Green, Gold, Cream White Ground, Amphora, 14 x 11 x 8 In. 3300
Vase, Bijou, Lady Of The Rhine, Gilt, Ribbed, Multicolor, Amphora, 15 ½ In. 1098
Vase, Climbing Squirrels, Berries, Leaves, Porcelain, Eduard Stellmacher & Co., 19 x 12 In. 340
Vase, Dragon, Gold, Blue & Green Shaded To White, Tapered, Amphora, 14 x 10 In. ....*illus* 9600
Vase, Frog, Fly, Shaded Red Glaze, Gold Trim, Stellmacher, Amphora, Austria, 21 x 9 In. *illus* 5440
Vase, Moths, Spider Webs, Green Iridescent, Jewels, Amphora, RStK, c.1900, 9 ½ In. ....*illus* 3000
Vase, Oval, Portrait, Tiger, Secessionist, Amphora, 8 ⅝ In. ....*illus* 416
Vase, Profile Of Woman, Art Nouveau Style, Eagle Head Helmet, Amphora, 11 ½ In. 787

Teplitz, Vase, 3 Nudes, Holding Hands, Ruffled Leaves, Mottled Glaze, Amphora, 14 In.
$1,386

Morphy Auctions

Teplitz, Vase, Dragon, Gold, Blue & Green Shaded To White, Tapered, Amphora, 14 x 10 In.
$9,600

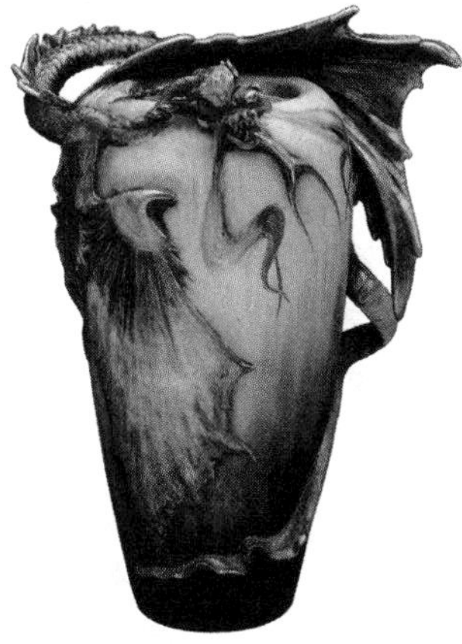

Morphy Auctions

Teplitz, Vase, Frog, Fly, Shaded Red Glaze, Gold Trim, Stellmacher, Amphora, Austria, 21 x 9 In.
$5,440

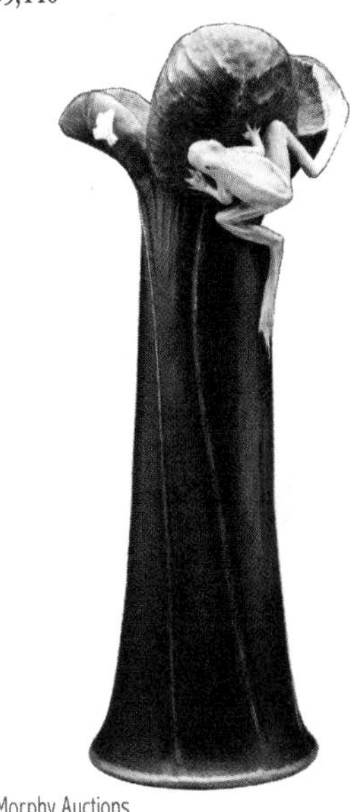

Morphy Auctions

TERRA-COTTA

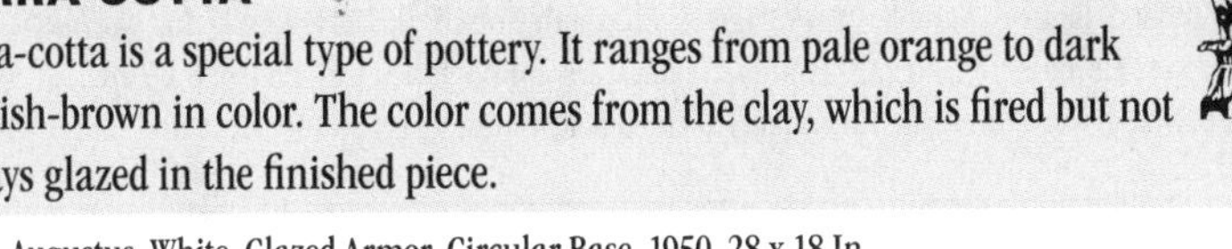

Terra-cotta is a special type of pottery. It ranges from pale orange to dark reddish-brown in color. The color comes from the clay, which is fired but not always glazed in the finished piece.

Bust, Augustus, White, Glazed Armor, Circular Base, 1950, 28 x 18 In. 250
Bust, Elegie, Bronze, Gilt Patina, Signed, Alfred Jean Foretay, c.1900, 21 x 12 x 10 In. 688
Bust, Woman, Head Covering, Low Dress, Marble, Base, Sign, Bouchardon, 27 x 13 ½ In. 300
Desk Weight, Eagle, Spread Wings, Federal, Tray, 5 ½ In. 265
Figurine, Angel, Outspread Wings, Standing, Olen Bryant, 1950s, 24 x 18 ¾ x 9 In. 780
Figurine, Bear, Brown, Seated, Square Base, 21 x 13 x 23 In. ....*illus* 354
Figurine, Blackamoor, Multicolor, Holding Vessel, Ornately Dressed, Painted, c.1900, 24 x 17 x 12 In. .. 767

T

Teplitz, Vase, Moths, Spider Webs, Green Iridescent, Jewels, Amphora, RStK, c.1900, 9 ½ In.
$3,000

Morphy Auctions

Teplitz, Vase, Oval, Portrait, Tiger, Secessionist, Amphora, 8 ⅝ In.
$416

Morphy Auctions

Terra-Cotta, Figurine, Bear, Brown, Seated, Square Base, 21 x 13 x 23 In.
$354

Copake Auctions

Figurine, Drunk, Sleeping, Black Coat, Waistcoat, 7 In. 93
Figurine, Dwarf, Hollowed Tree Trunk, 15 ½ In. 468
Figurine, Mercury, Sitting, Square Base, P. Ipsen, Kjobenhaven, Eneret, 14 In. 502
Figurine, Putto, Basket Of Fruit, Oval Base, c.1900, 15 ½ x 21 ½ x 9 ½ In. 375
Group, Bacchus, Putti Eating Grapes, Flowers, Fruit, Basket, Oval Base, 13 In. 540
Group, Nativity, Holy Family, Animals, Painted, Concepcion Aguilar, 25 x 11 x 12 In. 164
Planter, Raised Floral Garland, Cherub Masks, White Glaze, Square Base, 27 x 19 In. *illus* 217
Planter, Square, Brown, Molded Rim, Footed, Enzo Zago, 15 ½ x 17 ½ x 17 ½ In., 4 Piece 677
Plaque, Visage D'Homme, Stamped Marked, Frame, Pablo Picasso, 23 ½ x 23 ½ In. *illus* 8438
Sculpture, Male Face, Hair & Surrealist Eyes, 10 In. *illus* 369

TEXTILE

Textiles listed here include many types of printed fabrics and table and household linens. Some other textiles will be found under Clothing, Coverlet, Rug, Quilt, etc.

Bedcover, Crewel, Cream, Square Pattern, Geometrics, Blue, Gold, Judy Lennett, Conn., 77 x 81 In. 2160
Bedspread, Crewel, Floral Sprays, Insects, Multicolor Fringe Edge, Quilted, 1800s, 114 x 83 In. 615
Blanket, Mexican, Wool, Blue, Eagle With Snake In Center, Saltillo, 52 x 78 In. 47
Embroidery, 3 Saints, Bishops, Shroud Of Turin, Silk, Frame, 9 ¾ x 14 ½ In. 225
Embroidery, Crane, Flying, Clouds, Dark Blue Ground, Silk, Gold Frame, 1700s, 14 ¾ x 27 In. 182
Flag, 48 Brass State Buttons, Velvet, Inked Notation On Back, Case, Post 1912, 30 x 24 In. *illus* 600
Flag, Alabama, 1st National, 6 Stars, Red, White, Blue, Wool, c.1861, 35 In. 5228
Flag, American Ensign, Wyoming State, Wool, Blue, White, Red, 1870, 52 x 92 In. 240
Flag, American, 13 Stars, 9 Stripes, Hand Sewn, Light Blue Cotton, 1791, 24 x 38 In. *illus* 6000
Flag, American, 13 Stars, Civil War, Frame, 26 ½ x 67 ½ In. *illus* 27600
Flag, American, 13 Stars, Naval Flag, Sewn Wool Bunting, Sewn Grommets, 37 x 67 In. 3600
Flag, American, 36 Stars, Marked Hung At Half Mast At Lincoln's Death, 1865, 86 x 135 In. 1770
Flag, American, 38 Cotton Stars, Wool Bunting, Colorado Statehood, 1877-89, 284 x 142 In. 625
Flag, American, 39 Stars, Unofficial, Frame, 1889, 12 x 23 In. *illus* 236
Flag, American, 45 Stars, Linen, Mounted, Black Ground, Gilt Gesso Frame, c.1900, 23 x 34 In. 677
Flag, American, 48 Stars, Hand Stitched, Cotton, Wool & Felt, 51 x 96 In. 177
Map, British Isles, Oval, Silk, Black Stitching, Giltwood Frame, Ann Field, c.1819, 21 x 17 In. 1053
Needlework, Silk, Eagle, American Flags, Photos, Sailors, Frame, 1924, 29 x 24 In. *illus* 390
Orphrey, Pillar, Metal Thread, Embroidery, Red, Silk Velvet, Frame, 1700s, 70 x 16 In. 1722
Panel, Basket, Overflowing Flowers, Birds, French Knots, Red, Satin, 1700s, 31 ½ x 69 In. 2125
Panel, Embroidery, Silk, Dragons, Clouds & Aquatics, Chinese, Frame, 40 x 21 ½ In., Pair 1243
Panel, Embroidery, Silk, Hanging, Shoulao & Daoist Immortals, Chinese, 204 x 24 In. 3300
Pouch, Crazy Quilt, Patchwork, Embroidery, Green Velvet Edge, Initialed CML, 1885, 7 x 8 In. 168
Scarf, Jewel Tone Blocks, Fleur-De-Lis, Silk, Occupied Japan, 33 x 34 In. 36
Scroll, Painting On Silk, Mountain Landscape, Gold & Black, Japan, c.1900, 46 x 12 ¾ In. *illus* 1680
Table Cover, Silk Threads, Gold Metallic, Floral Medallion, Zardozi, 46 ½ x 42 ½ In. 120
Tapestry, Man In Garden, Holding Whip, Dogs, Fountain, Portico, 1800s, 80 x 90 In. 250
Tapestry, Pheasant, Grooming, Animal, Drinking, Trees, Flowers, Plants, Castle, 54 x 37 In. 875
Tapestry, Pyramids, Hand Woven, Maguey Fiber, After Alexander Calder, 1975, 96 x 72 In. *illus* 16250
Tapestry, Sea Birth, Wool, Woven, Charles L. Madden, France, 1950s, 83 x 65 ½ In. 813
Towel, Embroidery, Needlework, Rows Of Verse, Peacocks, Catherine Derr, 57 x 18 In. 554
Towel, Show, Stitched, Bird, Floral Bouquet, Signed Elisabeth Denlingar, 1831, 55 x 16 In. 150
Towel, Stitched, Figures, Sampler Work, Signed, Elisabeth Gotschall, 1823, 42 x 13 In. *illus* 360
Wall Pocket, Flame Stitch, Zigzag, Triangular Back, Blue, Red, Jane Field, c.1756, 8 x 7 In. 2583
Yardage, Diaperwork, Damask, Horsehair Fabric, Black, 1900s, 434 x 28 In. 410

THERMOMETER

Thermometer is a name that comes from the Greek word for heat. The thermometer was invented in 1731 to measure the temperature of either water or air. All kinds of thermometers are collected, but those with advertising messages are the most popular.

Drink Royal Crown Cola, Tin, Red Ground, Yellow Arrow, 25 x 10 In. 144

Terra-Cotta, Planter, Raised Floral Garland, Cherub Masks, White Glaze, Square Base, 27 x 19 In.
$217

DuMouchelles

Terra-Cotta, Plaque, Visage D'Homme, Stamped Marked, Frame, Pablo Picasso, 23 ½ x 23 ½ In.
$8,438

Abington Auction Gallery

Terra-Cotta, Sculpture, Male Face, Hair & Surrealist Eyes, 10 In.
$369

Clars Auction Gallery

Textile, Flag, 48 Brass State Buttons, Velvet, Inked Notation On Back, Case, Post 1912, 30 x 24 In.
$600

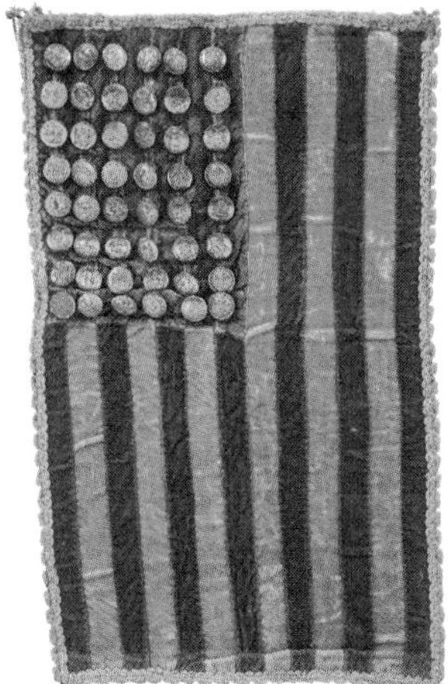

Garth's Auctioneers & Appraisers

Textile, Flag, American, 13 Stars, 9 Stripes, Hand Sewn, Light Blue Cotton, 1791, 24 x 38 In.
$6,000

Brunk Auctions

Textile, Flag, American, 13 Stars, Civil War, Frame, 26 ½ x 67 ½ In.
$27,600

Bourgeault-Horan Antiquarians & Associates, LLC

Textile, Flag, American, 39 Stars, Unofficial, Frame, 1889, 12 x 23 In.
$236

Copake Auctions

T

Textile, Needlework, Silk, Eagle, American Flags, Photos, Sailors, Frame, 1924, 29 x 24 In.
$390

Eldred's

Textile, Scroll, Painting On Silk, Mountain Landscape, Gold & Black, Japan, c.1900, 46 x 12 ¾ In.
$1,680

Eldred's

Textile, Tapestry, Pyramids, Hand Woven, Maguey Fiber, After Alexander Calder, 1975, 96 x 72 In.
$16,250

Rago Arts and Auction Center

Ex-Lax, Chocolated Laxative, Steel, Black Ground & Text, Porcelain, 36 x 8 x 1 In. 293
Mail Pouch, Treat Yourself To The Best, Black, White, Red, Yellow, 38 ½ x 8 In. .... *illus* 295
Mail Pouch Tobacco, Treat Yourself To The Best, Painted Enamel, 38 ½ In. ....*illus* 338
Red Crown Gasoline, Power Mileage, Polarine, Crown, Porcelain, 72 x 19 ½ In.................... 1920
Sun Crest, Bottle, Die Cut, Basket Weave Design, 17 x 5 In. ....*illus* 254
Tums For The Tummy, 3-Sided, Rotating, 10 Cents, Glass Cylinder, Wall Mount, 16 ½ In...... 360
Use Quaker, State Motor Oil, Round, White Ground, Black & Green Text, 12 In. 252

TIFFANY

Tiffany is a name that appears on items made by Louis Comfort Tiffany, the American glass designer who worked from about 1879 to 1933. His work included iridescent glass, Art Nouveau styles of design, and original contemporary styles. He was also noted for stained glass windows, unusual lamps, bronze work, pottery, and silver. Tiffany & Company, often called "Tiffany," is also listed in this section. The company was started by Charles Lewis Tiffany and John B. Young in 1837 in New York City. In 1853 the name was changed to Tiffany & Company. Louis Tiffany (1848–1933), Charles Tiffany's son, started his own business in 1879. It was named Louis Comfort Tiffany and Associated American Artists. In 1902 the name was changed to Tiffany Studios. Tiffany & Company is a store and is still working today. It is best known for silver and fine jewelry. Louis worked for his father's company as a decorator in 1900 but at the same time was working for his Tiffany Studios. Other types of Tiffany are listed under Tiffany Glass, Tiffany Gold, Tiffany Porcelain, Tiffany Pottery, or Tiffany Silver. The famous Tiffany lamps are listed in this section. Tiffany jewelry is listed in the Jewelry and Wristwatch categories. Some Tiffany Studio desk sets have matching clocks. They are listed here. Clocks made by Tiffany & Co. are listed in the Clock category. Reproductions of some types of Tiffany are being made.

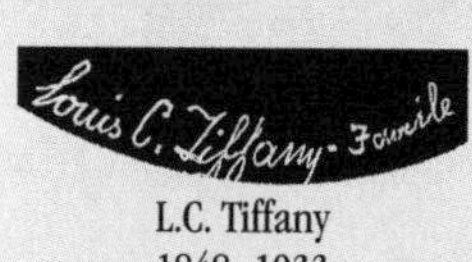

L.C. Tiffany
1848–1933

Tiffany Studios
1902–1919

TIFFANY STUDIOS
NEW YORK.

Tiffany Studios
1902–1922+

Ash Receiver, Bronze, Favrile Glass, Adjustable, Marked, 1651, 36 ½ In. ....*illus* 677
Blotter, Rocker, Zodiac, Bronze, Green Patina, New York, 2 x 5 ½ In. ....*illus* 156
Bookends, Zodiac, Bronze, New York, 6 x 5 In., Pair.. 563
Box, Geometric, Bronze, Hinged Lid, 2 ½ x 6 x 4 In. ....*illus* 960
Candle Lamp, Bronze Base, Ruffled Favrile Shade, Iridescent, Signed, 5 ⅞ In. 726
Candleholder, Bronze, Gimbal, 2 Hinge Assembly, Red-Brown Patina, 5 ½ x 6 ¾ x 4 ¾ In. *illus* 3300
Candleholder, Gold Favrile, Domed Base, Wheel Engraved, 4 x 4 ½ In., Pair 311
Candlestick, Bronze, Favrile Glass, Signed, New York, 22 ½ x 6 In. ....*illus* 3380
Frame, Pine Needle, Favrile Glass, Bronze, Brownish Green Patina, 9 ½ x 8 In. 1770
Frame, Zodiac, Bronze, Embossed, New York, 8 x 7 In... 1188
Inkwell, Abalone Inlay, Bronze Dore, Side Panel, Square, Chamfered Panel, Lid, 3 ¼ In.......... 654
Inkwell, Bronze, Crab Shape, Oyster Shell, Hinged Back, Glass, c.1910, 3 x 7 ¾ In. 7380
Inkwell, Bronze, Green Blown-Out Glass, Red-Brown Patina, Marked, 3 ½ x 4 ½ In................ 4200
Inkwell, Venetian, Bronze, 2 Wells, Marked Tiffany Studios, 2 ½ x 5 x 3 In............................. 188
Inkwell, Zodiac, Bronze, Green Patina, New York, 3 ¾ x 6 ½ In. 313
Lamp Base, 2-Light, Green Favrile Glass, Brass, Round Base, Tiffany Furnaces, 22 In............. 1599
Lamp Base, 4-Light, Bronze, Gold Dore, Art Nouveau, Stick, Marked, 23 ½ In......................... 2040
Lamp Base, Bronze, Weight-Balance, 5 Lily Pad Feet, Slender Shaft, Signed, 55 x 17 x 16 In.... 2700
Lamp Heat Cap, Bronze, Stylized Flower, Acid Etched Cutouts, Brown Patina, Round, 4 ½ In. *illus* 400
Lamp, 3-Light, Geometric, Domed Shade, Geco Turn Switch, 21 ½ x 12 In. 5748
Lamp, 3-Light, Swirling Leaf Style, Leaded Glass Shade, 25 x 18 In. ....*illus* 7800

Textile, Towel, Stitched, Figures, Sampler Work, Signed, Elisabeth Gotschall, 1823, 42 x 13 In.
$360

Garth's Auctioneers & Appraisers

Thermometer, Mail Pouch, Treat Yourself To The Best, Black, White, Red, Yellow, 38 ½ x 8 In., $295

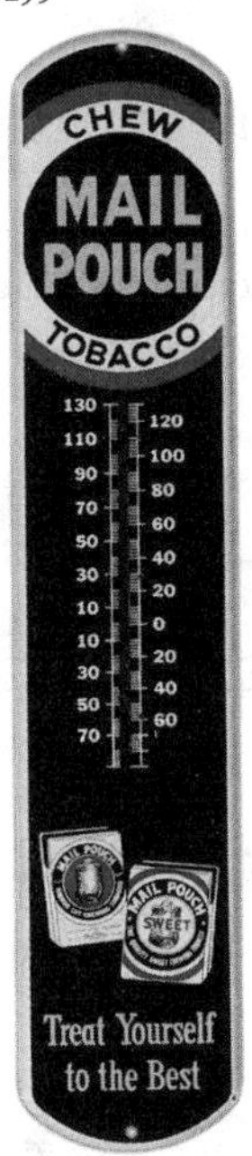

Soulis Auctions

Thermometer, Mail Pouch Tobacco, Treat Yourself To The Best, Painted Enamel, 38 ½ In.
$338

Richard Opfer Auctioneering, Inc.

Thermometer, Sun Crest, Bottle, Die Cut, Basket Weave Design, 17 x 5 In.
$254

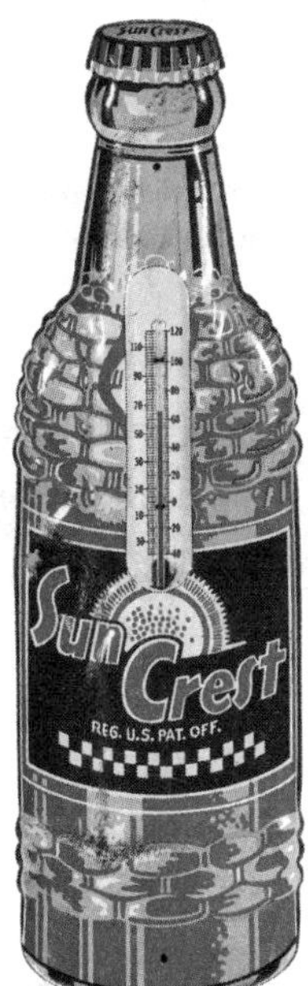

Soulis Auctions

Tiffany, Ash Receiver, Bronze, Favrile Glass, Adjustable, Marked, 1651, 36 ½ In.
$677

Skinner, Inc.

Tiffany, Blotter, Rocker, Zodiac, Bronze, Green Patina, New York, 2 x 5 ½ In.
$156

Treadway

Tiffany, Box, Geometric, Bronze, Hinged Lid, 2 ½ x 6 x 4 In.
$960

CRN Auctions

T

Tiffany, Candleholder, Bronze, Gimbal, 2 Hinge Assembly, Red-Brown Patina, 5 ½ x 6 ¾ x 4 ¾ In.
$3,300

Morphy Auctions

Tiffany, Candlestick, Bronze, Favrile Glass, Signed, New York, 22 ½ x 6 In.
$3,380

Treadway

Tiffany, Lamp Heat Cap, Bronze, Stylized Flower, Acid Etched Cutouts, Brown Patina, Round, 4 ½ In.
$400

Morphy Auctions

Tiffany, Lamp, 3-Light, Swirling Leaf Style, Leaded Glass Shade, 25 x 18 In.
$7,800

Milestone Auctions

Tiffany, Lamp, Aladdin, Bronze, Arabesque, Green Wave Pattern, Damascene Shade, 20 ½ In.
$3,360

Case Antiques

Tiffany, Lamp, Banded Dogwood, Leaded Glass Shade, Bronze, Tiffany Studios, 21 In.
$17,110

Cottone Auctions

Tiffany, Lamp, Desk, Green Translucent Glass Shade, Bronze, Harp Base, Marked, 13 ½ x 9 In.
$1,936

Fontaine's Auction Gallery

Tiffany, Lamp, Frosted, Linenfold Shade, Fancy Heat Cap, c.1908, 6 x 14 In.
$4,095

Jeffrey S. Evans & Associates

Tiffany, Lamp, Geometric, Domed Shade, Butterscotch Leaded Glass, Oil Lamp Base, c.1900, 21 ¾ x 16 In.
$4,000

Neal Auction Company

Lamp, 6-Light, Hanging, Bronze Canopy, Yellow, Green, White, c.1910, 19 x 24 ½ In. ... 38400
Lamp, Aladdin, Bronze, Arabesque, Green Wave Pattern, Damascene Shade, 20 ½ In. ... *illus* 3360
Lamp, Banded Dogwood, Leaded Glass Shade, Bronze, Tiffany Studios, 21 In. ... *illus* 17100
Lamp, Desk, Favrile Glass, Bronze, Footed, New York, c.1910, 12 ½ x 9 ½ x 5 ¾ In. ... 813
Lamp, Desk, Green Translucent Glass Shade, Bronze, Harp Base, Marked, 13 ½ x 9 In. ... *illus* 1936
Lamp, Dragonfly, Cone Shade, Blue Purple, Greenish Blue, Twisted Vine Base, Signed, 26 In... 180000
Lamp, Electric, Domed Shade, Tiffany Style, Jeweled Dragonfly, Leaded Glass, Late 1900s, 16 In. ... 118
Lamp, Favrile Shade, Bronze, Enamel, Square Base, Stamped, 14 ½ x 8 In. ... 8555
Lamp, Frosted, Linenfold Shade, Fancy Heat Cap, c.1908, 6 x 14 In. ... *illus* 4095
Lamp, Geometric, Domed Shade, Butterscotch Leaded Glass, Oil Lamp Base, c.1900, 21 ¾ x 16 In. . *illus* 4000
Lamp, Gold Iridescent Shade, Electrified Candle Insert, Round Base, 12 In. ... 650
Lamp, Hanging, Stalactite Shade, Gold Hooked Feathers, Iridescent Ground, 3 Chains, 25 x 5 In.... 9000
Lamp, Iridescent Swirl, Glass Shade, Green Ribbon, Patinated Bronze, 13 x 9 x 6 In. ... *illus* 6150
Lamp, Kerosene, Urn Shape, Ribbed Legs, Concave Square Base, c.1906, 7 ⅜ x 4 In. ... 556
Lamp, Leaded Shade, Green Striated, Glass, Bronze, Urn Shape Body, 19 ½ x 16 ½ In. ... *illus* 3300
Lamp, Lily, 3-Light, Favrile Glass, Bronze, New York, 8 x 8 In. ... 2500
Lamp, Opaque Glass Shade, Beaded Top Rim, Bronze Base, Urn Style, Lobed Feet, 22 x 15 In. . 2220
Lamp, Student, Glass Shade, Brass, Patinated Bronze Base, 25 In. ... *illus* 1888
Lamp, Textured & Etched Greek Key, Bronze Shade, Marked, 14 x 9 In. ... 1875
Lamp, Zodiac, 1-Light, Turtleback Tiles, Gilt Bronze, 1920s, 14 x 10 ½ In. ... 5940
Letter Rack, Venetian, Bronze, Enamel, Compartment, Carved, 6 x 10 In. ... 488
Pen Tray, Adam, Bronze, Rectangular Shape, Rounded Ends, 9 x 3 In. ... 341
Plate, Bronze, Dish Shape, Reticulated Border, Leafy Scrolls, Blue, Red Enamel, 8 In. ... 945
Sconce, Bronze Dore, 3 Leaded Glass Shades, Oval Panels, Twist Borders, 12 x 7 x 9 In. ... 1089
Smoking Stand, Bronze Dore, Matchbox Holder, Round Base, Marked, 28 x 9 In. ... 484

TIFFANY GLASS

Bottle, Grapes, Favrile, Gold, Pink, Blue, Etched L.C. Tiffany, 9 ½ x 5 In. ... 469
Bowl, Favrile, Blue Scalloped Rim, Signed L.C.T., 3 x 7 In. ... *illus* 688
Bowl, Favrile, Gold, Footed, Ruffled Rim, Signed L.C.T., 8 x 2 ⅝ In. ... 168
Bowl, Favrile, Gold, Shallow Circular Base, Early 1900s, 2 x 7 ⅞ In. ... 160
Candlestick, Favrile, Green, Iridescent, Circular Foot, Pontil, L.C.T., 1900s, 4 ⅝ In., Pair ... 660
Candlestick, Pastel, Violet Sconce, Iridescent Ribbed Stem, Scalloped Base, 1900s, 13 In. ... 185
Cologne Bottle, Bulbous Body, Short Neck, Stopper, Ribbed, Gold Iridescent, 5 ½ In. ... 666
Compote, Blue Feather, Clear Stem & Base, 6 In. ... *illus* 246
Compote, Blue Iridescent, Signed L.C. Tiffany Favrile, 4 x 5 ¾ In. ... 540
Compote, Green, Iridescent, Squat Stem, L.C.T. Favrile, 1900s, 6 In. ... 450
Cordial, Gold Favrile, Flared Rim, Hexagonal Stem, Footed, Early 1900s, 3 ¾ In., Pair ... 246
Goblet, Pale Green, Knop Connector, Applied Rigaree, 1900, 7 x 2 ½ x 2 ⅞ In. ... 644
Jar, Lid, Cylindrical, Square Shoulder, Flaring Lip, Finial, Gold Iridescent, 7 ½ In. ... 726
Paperweight, Bronze, Wave, Inside Panel, Blue Favrile, Signed, 3 ½ x 3 x ½ In. ... 2400
Perfume Bottle, Blue Iridescent, Favrile, Footed, 5 ½ In. ... 177
Perfume Bottle, Gold Iridescence, Bulbous, Long Tapering Neck, Stopper, Flared Rim, 3 ⅞ In. 787
Salt Dip, Blue & Gold, Footed, Favrile, Signed, Engraved, 1 ¾ x 4 In. ... 283
Salt Dip, Gold Iridescent, Ruffled Rim, Signed L.C.T., c.1910, 2 ½ In. ... 125
Salt, Gold Iridescent, Wave Edge, Flower Form, Signed, 2 ¾ In. ... *illus* 161
Shade, Cameo, Favrile, Etched Details, L.C.T. 650, 16 In. ... 4320
Shade, Damascene, Favrile, Signed, New York, 5 x 9 ¾ In. ... 5000
Shade, Dichroic, Pomegranate, Domed, Leaded Glass, Geometric Brick Ground, 6 x 16 In. ... 6655
Toothpick Holder, Iridescent, Bulbous, Dimpled Sides, Flared Rim, 2 In. ... 156
Vase, Blue, Iridescent, Flower Shape, 10 Defined Ribs, Curve Body, Engraved, Signed, 9 In. ... 1133
Vase, Bud Shape, Pulled Feather, Etched, Round Base, Favrile, Foil Label, 9 In. ... 1888
Vase, Bulbous, Gold Iridescent, Slender Neck, Flared Rim, Favrile, 9 x 3 ½ In. ... 622
Vase, Cypriote, Bottle Shape, Red, Iridescent, Early 1900s, 6 In. ... *illus* 861
Vase, Flower Shape, Gold Iridescent, Ribbed, Tapered, Circular Base, Favrile, 6 x 2 ½ In. ... 454
Vase, Flower Shape, Gold Iridescent, Saucer Foot, Green Pulled Feather Body, 15 x 5 ½ In. *illus* 3600
Vase, Gold Iridescent, Flower Form, Bronze Base, Favrile, Signed, 13 ½ In. ... 1029
Vase, Gold Iridescent, Waisted Shape, Bulbous Collar, Tel El Amarna, Favrile, 7 ¾ x 4 ¾ In. ... 2486
Vase, Gold Iridescent, Elongated Body, Fluted Rim, Round Base, 9 ¾ x 5 ¾ In. ... 600

Tiffany, Lamp, Iridescent Swirl, Glass Shade, Green Ribbon, Patinated Bronze, 13 x 9 x 6 In.
$6,150

Clars Auction Gallery

Tiffany, Lamp, Leaded Shade, Green Striated, Glass, Bronze, Urn Shape Body, 19 ½ x 16 ½ In.
$3,300

Morphy Auctions

Tiffany, Lamp, Student, Glass Shade, Brass, Patinated Bronze Base, 25 In.
$1,888

Cottone Auctions

T

Tiffany Lamps
Since about 1970, the phrase "Tiffany lamp" has been misused. You see it in ads and stores to describe modern lamps with stained glass shades. A true Tiffany lamp was made by Louis Comfort Tiffany at his studio from 1891 to 1928.

Tiffany Glass, Bowl, Favrile, Blue Scalloped Rim, Signed L.C.T., 3 x 7 In.
$688

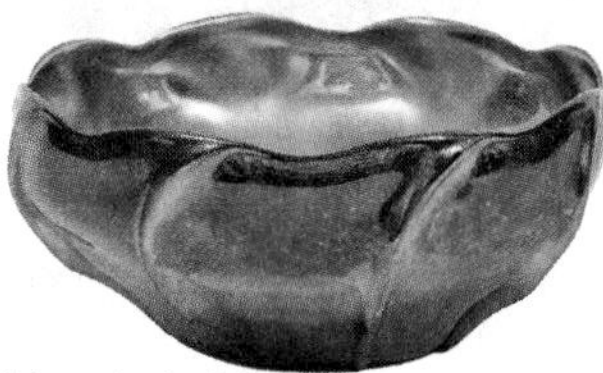

Abington Auction Gallery

Tiffany Glass, Compote, Blue Feather, Clear Stem & Base, 6 In.
$246

Skinner, Inc.

Tiffany Glass, Salt, Gold Iridescent, Wave Edge, Flower Form, Signed, 2 ¾ In.
$161

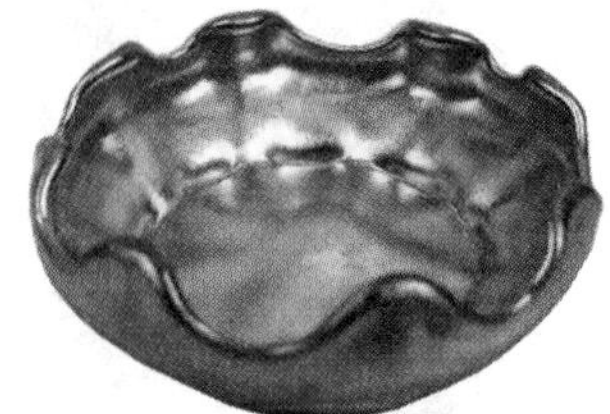

Richard D. Hatch & Associates

Vase, Green Feathers, Gold Ground, Iridescent, Elongated, Signed, 8 In. 561
Vase, Hexagonal Bronze Base, Hexagonal Mouth, Slender, Favrile, Early 1900s, 13 x 3 ½ In. 840
Vase, Jack-In-The-Pulpit, Favrile, Signed L.C. Tiffany, c.1910, 19 ½ In. ....*illus* 5612
Vase, Paperweight, Green Leaves, Stem, White, Orange, Jonquils, Translucent Ground, 8 In. 8470
Vase, Paperweight, Nasturtium, Squat, Vines, Red Opalescent Flower, 1907, 4 ½ x 4 In. ..*illus* 8190
Vase, Ribbed, White, Gold, Amber, Rose Iridescent, Favrile, Signed, L.C. Tiffany, 10 x 4 In. 780
Vase, Trumpet Shape, Gold, Bronze Dore Base, Tiffany Furnaces, Favrile, 1919-28, 15 In. 2583
Vase, Trumpet Shape, Gold, Iridescent, Lobed Body, Ruffled Rim, Favrile, 1900s, 8 ¾ In. 540
Vase, Tulip Shape, Gold, Flared Rim, Scalloped Edge, Stem, Base, Favrile, 13 In. 738

TIFFANY GOLD

Goblet, Iridescent, Scalloped Rim, Circular Base, 7 ¼ In. 213

TIFFANY PORCELAIN

Plate, Gilt, Cobalt Blue Rings, Tiffany & Co., England, 10 In., 12 Piece 484
Plate, Salad, Frank Lloyd Wright, Tiffany & Co., c.1990, 7 ½ In., 5 Piece 177
Vase, Water Lilies, Moss Green, Glazed, Favrile, c.1901, 8 ½ x 3 ½ In. ....*illus* 8125

TIFFANY POTTERY

Pitcher, White Bisque, Molded Tulips, Tiffany & Co., 9 In. 295
Vase, Tulips, White, Embossed, Earthenware, New York, c.1904, 7 x 2 ½ In. 1875

TIFFANY SILVER

Asparagus Tongs, Florentine, Sterling, Monogram, Marked, 1900, 17 ½ In. ....*illus* 1150
Atomizer, Audubon Bird Of Paradise Pattern, Hammered, 3 ⅞ In. 263
Basket, Sweetmeat, Flowers, Loop Handle, Marked, 9 ½ x 8 ½ In. 308
Basket, Swing Handle, Embossed, Flowers, Tiffany Young & Ellis, c.1850, 6 ⅞ x 4 x 7 ½ In. *illus* 325
Bookmark, Zigzag Scribble, Paloma Picasso, Tiffany & Co., 1 ½ In. Diam. 160
Bowl, Fruit, Reticulated Flaring Rim, Initialed GG, c.1912, 2 x 10 In. 303
Bowl, Lobed Body, Acanthus, Flaring Rim, Footed, Tiffany & Co., 5 ½ x 9 In. ....*illus* 660
Bowl, Presentation, Applied Garland, Engraved, Pedestal Base, c.1855, 11 ½ In. 3075
Bowl, Scalloped Rim, Christmas Holly, Fluted Sides, Monogram, New York, 12 In. 2460
Bowl, Shell, Bellflower Border, Monogram, Marked, 1 x 8 ¾ In. 420
Box, Carved Jade Embellishment, Engraved Border, 3 ½ x 2 ⅞ x ¾ In. 938
Candlestick, Bone, Elsa Peretti, For Tiffany & Co., Spain, 15 x 4 ½ In. ....*illus* 2000
Candlestick, Chrysanthemum, Removable Bobeches, Footed, 1902-1907, 10 In., Pair 3750
Candlestick, Gilt, Fluted Shafts, Stepped Square, Columnar, England, c.1961, 11 ¾ In., 4 Piece 2280
Card Holder, Basket Shape, Flowers, Felt Bags, Late 1900s, ¾ In. 1239
Compote, Reticulated, Lattice Rim, Rosettes, Gadrooned Base, Rocaille Feet, 2 ½ x 8 In. 277
Compote, Wheat Sheath Handles, Beading, Engraved, J.C. Moore & Son For Tiffany & Co., c.1860.. 1094
Crumber, Daisy, Stem, Flowerheads, Engraved, 12 In. 246
Cup, Marching Children's Band, Flute, Tambourine, Hand Cart, Trees, 3 ½ x 4 In. 510
Demitasse Pot, Baluster Style, Hinged Lid, Monogram, 9 In. ....*illus* 246
Dish, Flower Shape, Gilt, Scalloped Rim, Marked, Late 1900s, 6 In., Pair 212
Dish, Footed, Spiral, 3 Ball Feet, Marked, Bigelow Kennard & Co., 1 ½ x 4 ⅞ x 5 ⅞ In. 125
Figurine, 3 Circus Acrobats, Colorful Outfits, Ball On Top, Round Base, c.1990, 7 In. ....*illus* 3450
Ice Cream Server, Chrysanthemum, Gold Wash Bowl, Flowering Vine, Monogram, 1880, 10 ⅝ In. 677
Jam Jar, Bucket, Hinged Lid, Rotating Handle, Favrile, c.1910, 6 ½ x 3 ½ In. 930
Kettle, Stand, Oak & Ivy, Openwork, Grosjean & Woodward, 1857, 8 x 9 In. ....*illus* 6000
Mug, Infant, Christening, Floral Band, Leaf Handle, 1933, 3 In. ....*illus* 259
Mug, Reeded Bands, Engraved, New York, c.1875, 3 ¾ In. 338
Party Hat, Triangular, Ball Shape Finial, String, Felt Bag, Marked, Late 1900s, 4 x 4 In. 224
Pie Server, Audubon Pattern, Monogram, 10 In. 472
Pillbox, Pomegranate Shape With Crown Shape Knob, Footed, 1 ¾ In. 236
Pitcher, Art Deco Style, Etched Borders, Paneled, Monogram, c.1907-47, 7 ½ In. 856
Pitcher, Pear Shape, Stepped Base, Scroll Handle, Monogram, 7 ½ In. 840
Plate, Octagonal, Bamboo Shape Border, Marked, 8 ¾ x 9 ½ In. 313
Porringer, Typical Style, Engraved, Dorothy Milburn, New York, 1907-38, 1 ¾ x 7 ⅞ In. *illus* 185
Punch Ladle, Wave Edge, Engraved, Monogram, New York, 1884, 12 In. 338
Ring Tree, Figural, Hand, Art Deco Style, Round Base, Signed, 3 In. 316
Salt & Pepper, Owl, 2 ½ In. 920

T

Tiffany Glass, Vase, Cypriote, Bottle Shape, Red, Iridescent, Early 1900s, 6 In.
$861

Skinner, Inc.

Tiffany Glass, Vase, Flower Shape, Gold Iridescent, Saucer Foot, Green Pulled Feather Body, 15 x 5 ½ In.
$3,600

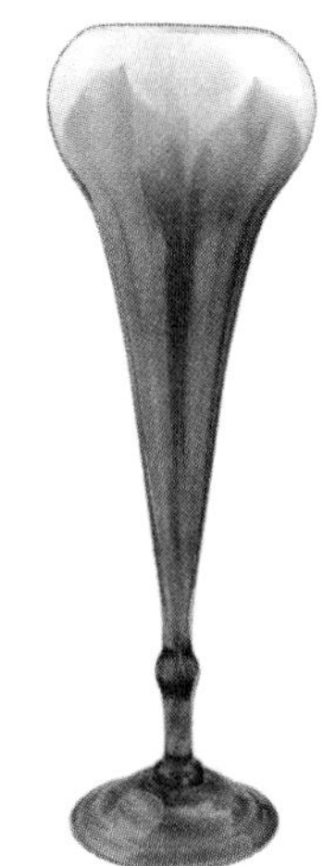

Morphy Auctions

Tiffany Glass, Vase, Jack-In-The-Pulpit, Favrile, Signed L.C. Tiffany, c.1910, 19 ½ In.
$5,612

Neal Auction Company

Tiffany Glass, Vase, Paperweight, Nasturtium, Squat, Vines, Red Opalescent Flower, 1907, 4 ½ x 4 In.
$8,190

Jeffrey S. Evans & Associates

TIP
Use cotton gloves, not latex gloves, when handling silver.

Tiffany Porcelain, Vase, Water Lilies, Moss Green, Glazed, Favrile, c.1901, 8 ½ x 3 ½ In.
$8,125

Rago Arts and Auction Center

Tiffany Silver, Asparagus Tongs, Florentine, Sterling, Monogram, Marked, 1900, 17 ½ In.
$1,150

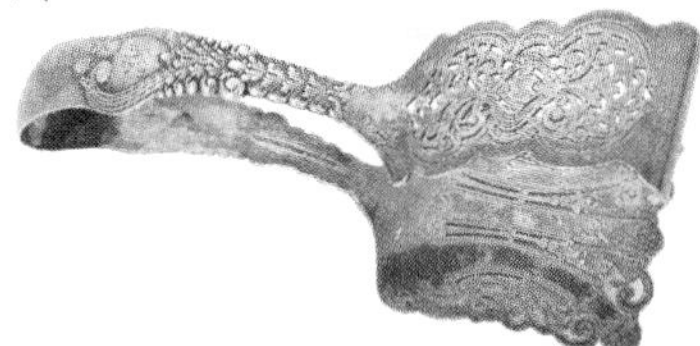

Fontaine's Auction Gallery

Tiffany Silver, Basket, Swing Handle, Embossed, Flowers, Tiffany Young & Ellis, c.1850, 6 ⅞ x 4 x 7 ½ In.
$325

Bunch Auctions

Tiffany Silver, Bowl, Lobed Body, Acanthus, Flaring Rim, Footed, Tiffany & Co., 5 ½ x 9 In.
$660

Case Antiques

Tiffany Silver, Candlestick, Bone, Elsa Peretti, For Tiffany & Co., Spain, 15 x 4 ½ In.
$2,000

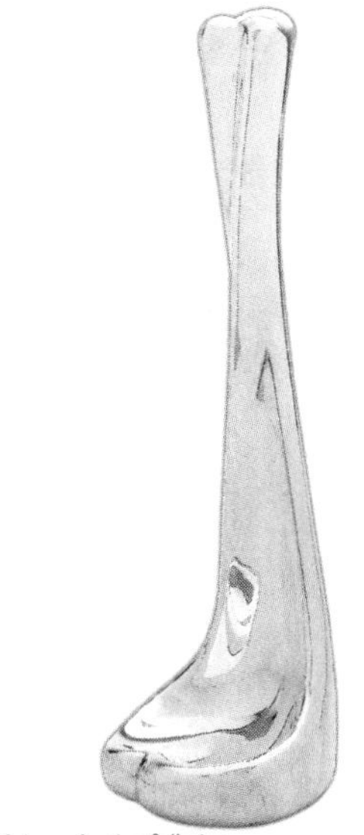

New Orleans Auction Galleries

TIP
Don't display silver on latex paint. It will tarnish quickly.

Tiffany Silver, Demitasse Pot, Baluster Style, Hinged Lid, Monogram, 9 In.
$246

Charlton Hall Auctions

TIP
Polish silver with a soft cloth of cotton or flannel. Rub lengthwise, not in circles to avoid scratching.

Tiffany Silver, Figurine, 3 Circus Acrobats, Colorful Outfits, Ball On Top, Round Base, c.1990, 7 In.
$3,450

Richard D. Hatch & Associates

Tiffany Silver, Kettle, Stand, Oak & Ivy, Openwork, Grosjean & Woodward, 1857, 8 x 9 In.
$6,000

New Orleans Auction Galleries

Tiffany Silver, Mug, Infant, Christening, Floral Band, Leaf Handle, 1933, 3 In.
$259

Richard D. Hatch & Associates

Tiffany Silver, Porringer, Typical Style, Engraved, Dorothy Milburn, New York, 1907-38, 1 ¾ x 7 ⅞ In.
$185

Charlton Hall Auctions

Tiffany Silver, Serving Spoon, Blackberry, Gold Wash, Kidney Shape Bowl, Tiffany & Co., 9 ½ In.
$338

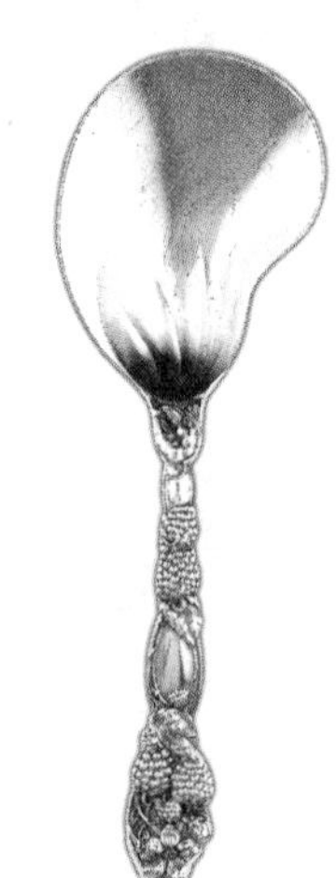

Charlton Hall Auctions

Tiffany Silver, Tray, Square, Hammered Finish, Footed, 8 ½ x 8 ½ In.
$960

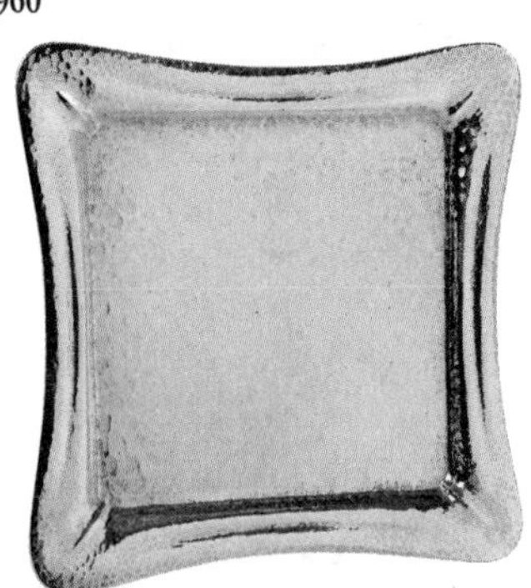

Brunk Auctions

Salt Dip, Greek Key Border, Ram's Heads Feet, c.1850, 3 In., 4 Piece 677
Salt, Master, Gold Wash Bowl Interior, 3 Ram's Head Legs, 1850s, 1 ⅝ x 3 x 3 In., Pair 510
Salver, Reeded Rim, Engraved, New York, 1907-38, 10 In. 308
Serving Bowl, Splayed Rim, Horizontal Ribbed Banding, Footed Base, 1900s, 3 x 5 ½ In. 185
Serving Dish, Rectangular, Curving Ends, Reeded Rim, New York, 1907-38, 1 ¾ x 11 x 6 In. 400
Serving Spoon, Blackberry, Gold Wash, Kidney Shape Bowl, Tiffany & Co., 9 ½ In. .... *illus* 338
Soup, Dish, Pierced, Floral Rim, Ring Feet, Marked, 5 ½ x 5 ½ In. 420
Spoon, Asymmetrical Scoop, Strawberry Pierced Handle, c.1875, 9 ⅝ In. 230
Strainer, Punch, Turned, Hardwood Handle, Marked, 6 In. 271
Taperstick, Foot Rim, Elsa Peretti, c.1920, 7 In. 615
Tazza, Openwork Scrolling Leafy Rim, Fluted Stem, Paulding Farnham, c.1905, 8 ¾ In., Pair 4500
Tea Caddy, Lid, Leaves, Apple, 4 In. 447
Tea Strainer, Openwork Handles, Pierced, c.1900, 5 In. 150
Tray, Round, Engraved Border, Monogram Center, Footed, 1930s, 10 ½ In. 283
Tray, Square, Hammered Finish, Footed, 8 ½ x 8 ½ In. .... *illus* 960
Tureen, Vegetable, Lid, Chrysanthemum, Covered, Footed, 1879, 7 ¾ x 11 ⅜ In., Pair 9000
Vase, Flower Form, Scalloped Rim, Circular Base, Marked, 11 ½ x 6 In. 308
Vase, Trumpet Shape, Flared Rim, Domed Stepped Foot, c.1930, 11 ⅜ x 4 ⅝ In. 1170
Vase, Trumpet, Horizontal Banding, Lid, Engraved, New York, 1907-1938, 12 In. 615
Walking Stick Handle, Engraved Shamrock, c.1890, 36 In. 5175

TIFFIN

Tiffin Glass Company of Tiffin, Ohio, was a subsidiary of the United States Glass Co. of Pittsburgh, Pennsylvania, in 1892. The U.S. Glass Co. went bankrupt in 1963, and the Tiffin plant employees purchased the building and the inventory. They continued running it from 1963 to 1966, when it was sold to Continental Can Company. In 1969, it was sold to Interpace, and in 1980, it was closed. The black satin glass, made from 1923 to 1926, and the stemware of the last 20 years are the best-known products.

Candlestick, Reverse Painted, Exotic Bird & Leaves On Base, 10 In., Pair 45
Cherokee Rose, Iced Tea, 6 ½ In. 36
King's Crown, Cup, Blue & Clear, 2 ½ In. 8

TILE

Tiles have been used in most countries of the world as a sturdy building material for floors, roofs, fireplace surrounds, and surface toppings. The cuerda seca (dry cord) technique of decoration uses a greasy pigment to separate different glaze colors during firing. In cuenca (raised line) decorated tiles, the design is impressed, leaving ridges that separate the glaze colors. Many of the American tiles are listed in this book under the factory name.

Pictorial, Auto Racing, Citroen, Brown, White Enamel, c.1910, 14 x 18 In. 129
Warriors, Imperial Figure, Floral Border, Famille Rose, Wood Frame, 15 x 12 In. 121

TINWARE

Tinware containers for household use have been made in America since the seventeenth century. The first tin utensils were brought from Europe, but by 1798 tin plate was imported and local tinsmiths made the wares. Painted tin is called tole and is listed separately. Some tin kitchen items may be found listed under Kitchen. The lithographed tin containers used to hold food and tobacco are listed in the Advertising category under Tin.

Coffeepot, Embossed Swag Rim, Gooseneck Spout, Footed, Black, 1800s, 10 ¾ In. 305
Coffeepot, Flower, Brass Finial, Gooseneck Spout, 11 In. 177
Coffeepot, Wrigglework, Floral, Footed, Handle, Spout, Lid, 1800s, 11 ¾ In. .... *illus* 793
Mold, Candle, 8 Tubes, Footed, Rectangular Base, 5 x 5 ¾ In. .... *illus* 275

Tinware, Coffeepot, Wrigglework, Floral, Footed, Handle, Spout, Lid, 1800s, 11 ¾ In.
$793

Pook & Pook

Tinware, Mold, Candle, 8 Tubes, Footed, Rectangular Base, 5 x 5 ¾ In.
$275

Pook & Pook

Tinware, Mold, Candle, 12 Tubes, Circular, Hanging, Footed, 1800s, 15 In.
$671

Pook & Pook

This is an edited listing of current prices. Visit **Kovels.com** to check thousands of prices from previous years and sign up for free information on trends, tips, reproductions, marks, and more.

T

Tinware, Top Hat, Anniversary, Band, Base For Display, c.1900, 7 ¾ In.
$761

Jeffrey S. Evans & Associates

Toby Jug, Man, Seated, Green Overcoat, Tricorn Hat, Holding Tankard, Creamware, Late 1700s, 10 In.
$293

Thomaston Place Auction Galleries

Tole, Bin, Flour, Tin, Black Ground, Flowers, Beveled Mirror, Late 1800s, 16 x 10 x 13 ½ In.
$150

Garth's Auctioneers & Appraisers

Tole, Box, Dome Lid, Black Ground, Flowers, Bail Handle, Pennsylvania, 1800s, 5 x 9 In.
$580

Pook & Pook

Tole, Box, Dome Lid, Earthworm Designs, Stenciled Basket Of Fruit, c.1835, 8 x 10 In.
$360

Garth's Auctioneers & Appraisers

Tole, Bucket, Coal, Lid, Black, Flowers, Brass Mask Ring Handles, Late 1900s, 12 x 19 x 11 In.
$59

Leland Little Auctions

Tole, Sign, Painted, Hanging, Gilt, Ocher, Lyre Shape, 2-Sided, 1800s, 22 x 15 In.
$761

Thomaston Place Auction Galleries

Tole, Tea Tray, Wood Stand, Painted, Gilt Rim, X-Stretcher, 19 x 28 x 22 In.
$738

Stair Galleries

Mold, Candle, 12 Tubes, Circular, Hanging, Footed, 1800s, 15 In. .... *illus* 671
Mold, Chocolate, Rabbit, 6 Molds In Frame, Patina, Early 1900s, 16 x 6 x 6 ½ In. 161
Mold, Food, Punched Tin, Shell Bottom, Pennsylvania, 1850s, 3 ½ x 5 x 6 ⅝ In. 439
Sconce, 2-Light, Candle, Punched, Heart, Embossed, 17 In., Pair 236
Top Hat, Anniversary, Band, Base For Display, c.1900, 7 ¾ In. .... *illus* 761

TOBACCO CUTTERS *may be listed in either the Advertising or Store categories.*

TOBACCO JAR

Tobacco jar collectors search for those made in odd shapes and colors. Because tobacco needs special conditions of humidity and air, it has been stored in humidors and other special containers since the eighteenth century. Some may be found in ceramic categories in this book.

Humidor, Benson & Hedges, Plaque On Lid, c.1910, 9 x 12 In. 500
Humidor, Wood, Standing, 2-Part Cabinet, Drawer, Ornate, Rising Sun, Legs, 41 x 19 In. 185
Mahogany, Lid, Finial, Round, Dutch, 8 ¾ In. 198
Porcelain, Landscape Scene, Moriage Trim, 6 ½ In. 62
Stoneware, Blue & White Salt Glaze, Lid, Eckhardt & Engler, Germany, c.1910 85
Wood, Skull, Snake Entwined Through Eyes, Lid, Frog Finial, c.1860, 7 In. 472

TOBY JUG

Toby jug is the name of a very special form of pitcher. It is shaped like the full figure of a man or woman. A pitcher that shows just the top half of a person is not correctly called a toby. It is often called a character jug. More examples of toby jugs can be found under Royal Doulton and other factory names. Some may be found in Advertising in this book.

Cavalier, Feather Hat, Subtle Smile, Burlingtonware, 7 In. 63
Father Neptune, Crown, Seahorse Handle, Lobster Base, Shorter & Sons, 9 ½ In. 68
Gin Woman, Mottled Brown, Tricorn Hat, Apron, Holding Glass, Rockingham, c.1840, 8 In. 143
Judge, Glasses, Blond Curled Hair, Burlingtonware, Shaw & Sons, 1950s, 3 ¾ In. 54
Leprechaun, Green Hat, Roy Kirkham, Staffordshire 80
Man, Seated, Green Overcoat, Tricorn Hat, Holding Tankard, Creamware, Late 1700s, 10 In. *illus* 293
Man, Seated, Holding Mug & Pitcher, Black Hat, Grinning, 6 In. 63
Mr. Pickwick, Green Coat, Rust Vest, Yellow Pants, Black Hat, Raised Arm, 7 ½ In. 125
Mr. Punch & Dog, Both Sitting, Melba Ware, 1950s, 7 x 5 In. 80
Napoleon, Hat, Yellow Shirt, Alfred Evans, 19th Century, 5 ¾ In. 115
Woman, Snuff Taker, Cantankerous Looking, Hand Painted, Oval Base, 1830s, 9 ⅞ In. 468

TOLE

Tole is painted tin. It is sometimes called japanned ware, pontypool, or toleware. Most nineteenth-century tole is painted with an orange-red or black background and multicolored decorations. Many recent versions of toleware are made and sold. Related items may be listed in the Tinware category.

Basket, Scalloped Rim, Loop Handle, Black Ground, Gilt, Late 1800s, 8 x 5 In. 50
Bin, Flour, Tin, Black Ground, Flowers, Beveled Mirror, Late 1800s, 16 x 10 x 13 ½ In. .... *illus* 150
Bin, Lift-Lid, Tin, Black Ground, Flower, J Hall Rohreman & Son, Pa., 1830s, 8 x 6 x 8 In. 225
Bowl, Red Ground, Wire Handles, Lead Liner, Oval, 1800s, 10 ⅞ In. 584
Box, Document, Dome Hinged Lid, Flowers & Leaves, Rectangular, 1800, 5 x 9 x 4 In. 354
Box, Document, Geometric, Lid, Wrought Iron Lock, Early 1800s, 10 x 6 x 5 ½ In. 46
Box, Dome Lid, Black Ground, Flowers, Bail Handle, Pennsylvania, 1800s, 5 x 9 In. .... *illus* 580
Box, Dome Lid, Earthworm Designs, Stenciled Basket Of Fruit, c.1835, 8 x 10 In. .... *illus* 360
Box, Lid, Flowers, Yellow Teardrop, Bail Handle, Hasp, 1830s, 5 ¾ x 8 ¾ x 4 ¾ In. 204
Bucket, Coal, Lid, Black, Flowers, Brass Mask Ring Handles, Late 1900s, 12 x 19 x 11 In. *illus* 59
Canister, Tea, Lid, Chinoiserie, Brown Ground, Gold, 17 x 9 ½ In., Pair 1353
Coal Scuttle, Green Japan, Oval Reserve, Landscape, Fort, Trees, 20 x 18 In. 100

Tole, Teapot, Black Ground, Flowers, Hinged Lid, Applied Handle, c.1830-40, 8 In.
$384

Cowan's Auctions

Toleware

Toleware made in New England, New York, and Pennsylvania had similar designs. Most had black or brown backgrounds, but pieces made in Pennsylvania had a red background and brighter decorations.

Tole, Tray, Central Landscape Scene, Flowers, Grapevine, 1800s, 23 ¾ x 32 x 1 ½ In.
$1,003

Ahlers & Ogletree Auction Gallery

Tole, Tray, Horse, Cart, Peter Hunt Style, Nancy Whorf, Signed Whorf, 13 x 17 ½ In.
$100

Eldred's

Tool, Ax, Broad Blade, Wood Handle, Marked, 6, William Beatty, Chester, Pa., 6 In.
$57

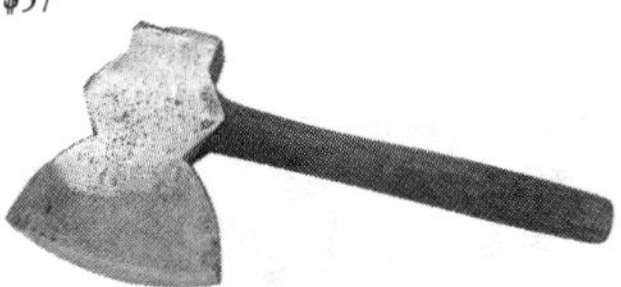

Hartzell's Auction Gallery Inc.

Tool, Hatchel, Painted Pine, Black Geometric, Red Ground, Cover, 1800s, 3 ¾ x 18 In.

$1,098

Pook & Pook

Tool, Saw, T. A. Clark, Maple, Steel Blade, Salesman's Sample, Late 1800s, 3 ½ In.
$295

Copake Auctions

Stanley Tools

Before 1920 there were two companies using the Stanley name. Stanley's Bolt Manufactory in New Britain, Connecticut, was founded in 1843 by brothers Frederick and William Stanley. The company was incorporated in 1852 as The Stanley Works. Augustus, Timothy, and Gad Stanley and Thomas Conklin founded A. Stanley & Company in New Britain in 1854. After mergers they became The Stanley Works in 1920. It is now The Stanley Tools Division of The Stanley Works in New Britain, Connecticut.

Hat Box, Napoleon Hat Shape, Silver Plaque, 8 x 19 x 5 In. 369
Jardiniere, Cherub, Red, 2 Handles, Gold Leafy Border, England, c.1900, 11 x 27 x 18 In. 472
Lamp, Etched Mirror Base, Enameled Metal Flowers, Silk Shade, Italy, c.1920, 19 In., Pair 1770
Match Holder, Wall, Asphaltum Ground, Pinwheel, Leaf, Crimped Edge, 1910s, 7 x 4 ½ In. 351
Sconce, Dark Green, Mirror Reflector Back, Albert Hadley, 15 ½ x 6 ½ x 9 ½ In., 6 Piece 1476
Sign, Painted, Hanging, Gilt, Ocher, Lyre Shape, 2-Sided, 1800s, 22 x 15 In. .... *illus* 761
Tea Tray, Wood Stand, Painted, Gilt Rim, X-Stretcher, 19 x 28 x 22 In. .... *illus* 738
Teapot, Black Ground, Flowers, Hinged Lid, Applied Handle, c.1830-40, 8 In. .... *illus* 384
Tray, Black Ground, Flowers, Cross Bamboo Stretcher, Stand, 19 x 21 x 20 ½ In. 185
Tray, Central Landscape Scene, Flowers, Grapevine, 1800s, 23 ¾ x 32 x 1 ½ In. .... *illus* 1003
Tray, Flowers, Leaves, Black Ground, Hexagonal, 1800s, 6 x 8 ¾ In. 1464
Tray, Horse, Cart, Peter Hunt Style, Nancy Whorf, Signed Whorf, 13 x 17 ½ In. .... *illus* 100
Tray, Red Ground, Leaves, Berries Border, Round, Multicolor, 47 ½ In. 92
Tray, Ribbed Edge, Hitchcock Style, Red, Black Ground, Rectangular 293
Tray, Serving, Stencilwork, Black Lacquer, 2 Servants Fishing, Oval, Late 1800s, 28 x 23 In. 293
Tray, Shipwreck Scene, Tin, Gold Border, Oval, 21 ½ x 28 In. 1170
Tub, Cast Iron Handle, Tin, Leaves, Blue, Red, Yellow, Oval, c.1890, 7 ½ x 18 In. 47

TOM MIX

Tom Mix was born in 1880 and died in 1940. He was the hero of over 300 silent movies from 1910 to 1929, and 25 sound films from 1929 to 1935. There was a Ralston Tom Mix radio show from 1933 to 1950, but the original Tom Mix was not in the show. Tom Mix comics were published from 1942 to 1953.

Book, Big Little Book, Terror Trail, 1932 10
Book, Fighting Cowboy, Whitman Big Little Book, 1935 13
Club Badge, Ralston Straight Shooter, Red & White Checkerboard, Embossed Metal, 1938 380
Creamer, Paneled, Footed, Blue Glass, Portrait, 4 In. 30
Telescope, Ralston Straight Shooter Transfer, 1937, 4 x 1 ½ In. 149

TOOL

Tools of all sorts are listed here, but most are related to industry. Other tools may be found listed under Iron, Kitchen, Tinware, and Wooden.

Ax Blade, Forged Iron, Witch's Foot Symbol, Tapered Socket, Medieval, 14 x 9 In. 984
Ax, Broad Blade, Wood Handle, Marked, 6, William Beatty, Chester, Pa., 6 In. .... *illus* 57
Box, Wood, Tray, Tills, Green, C.I.H., 34 x 13 x 12 In. 91
Candle Dryer, Wood, 6 Folding Arms, Red, Black, Square Base, Pegged Feet, 1880s, 25 x 22 In. 276
Carrier, Wood, Dovetailed, Brown, 9 x 24 x 13 In. 40
Chest, Watchmaker's, Oak, Tabletop, Hinged Lid, 16 Drawers, 8 x 16 x 5 In. 450
Hatchel, Painted Pine, Black Geometric, Red Ground, Cover, 1800s, 3 ¾ x 18 In. .... *illus* 1098
Hay Rake, Wood, Metal, Brass, Salesman's Sample, Marked A.H. 1586, 9 In. 2340
Ladder, Green, 6 Rungs, 19 x 74 In. 35
Ladder, Orchard, Metal, 8 Steps, 9 In. 83
Level, Akron, Eclipse, Brass, Wood, 22 In. 34
Padlock, Keen Kutter, Brass, Red Paint, Key, Logo, c.1906, 5 x 2 In. 102
Plane, Stanley, No. 55, Combination Wood 107
Pulley, Wrought Iron, Wood Handle, 16 x 9 In. 130
Saw, T. A. Clark, Maple, Steel Blade, Salesman's Sample, Late 1800s, 3 ½ In. .... *illus* 295
Scraper, Stanley, Steel, Wide Flat Blade, Short Handle, 3 In. 62
Spade, Blubber, Cast Iron, Wood Pole, 1800s, 46 In. 163
Stump Planter, Burl, Knobby, Hollowed Out, 18 x 15 In. 1020
Sugar Bucket, Lid, Bentwood, Wood Grip, Pine, Maple, Pegs, Copper Brads, 1800s, 6 ½ In. 161
Sugar Bucket, Lid, Wood, 3 Bands, Lehnware Style, Finial, 1800s, 10 ½ x 7 ½ In. 384
Sugar Bucket, Pine Staves, Finger-Lapped Bentwood Bands, Bail Handle, 1850s, 13 x 9 In. 293
Sugar Devil, Cast Iron, Turned Maple Handle, Embossed Shaft, Patd. July 27, 76, 16 In. *illus* 35
Wagon Jack, Conestoga, Wood, Wrought Iron, Punched Design, Iron Gears, Pa., 1881, 20 In. ... *illus* 106
Wheelbarrow, Sammie, Mixed Wood, Carved, Iron Strapping, 1810s, 23 ½ x 61 x 22 In. 780
Workbench, Cabinet Maker's, Elm, Carved, Clamp, Timber Legs, France, 1800s, 31 x 85 x 12 In. *illus* 2250

TOOTHBRUSH HOLDER

Toothbrush holders were part of every bowl and pitcher set in the late nineteenth century. Most were oblong covered dishes. About 1920, manufacturers started to make children's toothbrush holders shaped like animals or cartoon characters. A few modern toothbrush holders are still being made.

Bear, Standing, Brown, White, Foil Label, Victoria Ceramics, Japan, 5 1/4 In. 28
Dog, With Toothache, Tray Holds Toothpaste, Made In Germany, c.1940, 3 3/4 In. 109
Man, Candlestick Maker, 2 Holes, Toothpaste Holder, Japan, 1940s, 5 In. 40

TOOTHPICK HOLDER

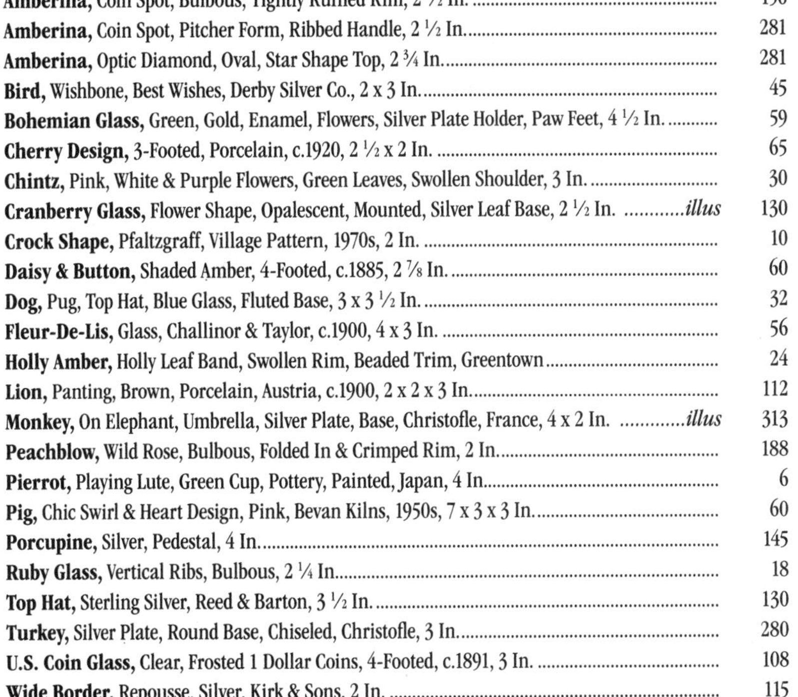

Toothpick holders are sometimes called *toothpicks* by collectors. The variously shaped containers used to hold small wooden toothpicks are made of glass, china, or metal. Most of the toothpick holders are made of Victorian glass. Additional items may be found in other categories, such as Bisque, Silver Plate, Slag Glass, etc.

Amberina, Coin Spot, Bulbous, Tightly Ruffled Rim, 2 1/2 In. 156
Amberina, Coin Spot, Pitcher Form, Ribbed Handle, 2 1/2 In. 281
Amberina, Optic Diamond, Oval, Star Shape Top, 2 3/4 In. 281
Bird, Wishbone, Best Wishes, Derby Silver Co., 2 x 3 In. 45
Bohemian Glass, Green, Gold, Enamel, Flowers, Silver Plate Holder, Paw Feet, 4 1/2 In. 59
Cherry Design, 3-Footed, Porcelain, c.1920, 2 1/2 x 2 In. 65
Chintz, Pink, White & Purple Flowers, Green Leaves, Swollen Shoulder, 3 In. 30
Cranberry Glass, Flower Shape, Opalescent, Mounted, Silver Leaf Base, 2 1/2 In. ....*illus* 130
Crock Shape, Pfaltzgraff, Village Pattern, 1970s, 2 In. 10
Daisy & Button, Shaded Amber, 4-Footed, c.1885, 2 7/8 In. 60
Dog, Pug, Top Hat, Blue Glass, Fluted Base, 3 x 3 1/2 In. 32
Fleur-De-Lis, Glass, Challinor & Taylor, c.1900, 4 x 3 In. 56
Holly Amber, Holly Leaf Band, Swollen Rim, Beaded Trim, Greentown 24
Lion, Panting, Brown, Porcelain, Austria, c.1900, 2 x 2 x 3 In. 112
Monkey, On Elephant, Umbrella, Silver Plate, Base, Christofle, France, 4 x 2 In. ....*illus* 313
Peachblow, Wild Rose, Bulbous, Folded In & Crimped Rim, 2 In. 188
Pierrot, Playing Lute, Green Cup, Pottery, Painted, Japan, 4 In. 6
Pig, Chic Swirl & Heart Design, Pink, Bevan Kilns, 1950s, 7 x 3 x 3 In. 60
Porcupine, Silver, Pedestal, 4 In. 145
Ruby Glass, Vertical Ribs, Bulbous, 2 1/4 In. 18
Top Hat, Sterling Silver, Reed & Barton, 3 1/2 In. 130
Turkey, Silver Plate, Round Base, Chiseled, Christofle, 3 In. 280
U.S. Coin Glass, Clear, Frosted 1 Dollar Coins, 4-Footed, c.1891, 3 In. 108
Wide Border, Repousse, Silver, Kirk & Sons, 2 In. 115

TORQUAY

TORQUAY

Torquay is the name given to ceramics by several potteries working near Torquay, England, from 1870 until 1962. Until about 1900, the potteries used local red clay to make classical-style art pottery vases and figurines. Then they turned to making souvenir wares. Items were dipped in colored slip and decorated with painted slip and sgraffito designs. They often had mottoes or proverbs, and scenes of cottages, ships, birds, or flowers. The Scandy design was a symmetrical arrangement of brushstrokes and spots done in colored slips. Potteries included Watcombe Pottery (1870–1962), Torquay Terra-Cotta Company (1875–1905), Aller Vale (1881–1924), Torquay Pottery (1908–1940), and Longpark (1883–1957).

Cruet, Sailing Ship, Promise Little & Do Much, Cream Color, Blue, Red, 3 1/2 In. 25
Cup & Saucer, Kingfisher, Blue Ground, White Interior, Brown Handle & Underside 65
Eggcup, Laid Today, Sailing Ship, Multicolor 30
Inkwell, Scandy, Dinna Be Aye Ettlin, But Juist Tak An Write, 2 5/8 In. 95

Tool, Sugar Devil, Cast Iron, Turned Maple Handle, Embossed Shaft, Patd. July 27, 76, 16 In.
$35

Conestoga Auction Company

Tool, Wagon Jack, Conestoga, Wood, Wrought Iron, Punched Design, Iron Gears, Pa., 1881, 20 In.
$106

Conestoga Auction Company

Tool, Workbench, Cabinet Maker's, Elm, Carved, Clamp, Timber Legs, France, 1800s, 31 x 85 x 12 In.
$2,250

Crescent City Auction Gallery

Toothpick, Cranberry Glass, Flower Shape, Opalescent, Mounted, Silver Leaf Base, 2 ½ In.
$130

Strawser Auction Group

Toothpick, Monkey, On Elephant, Umbrella, Silver Plate, Base, Christofle, France, 4 x 2 In.
$313

Treadway

Tortoiseshell, Tea Caddy, Hinged Lid, Silvered Mounts, Ivory Trim, Ball Feet, Regency, c.1815, 4 x 5 x 3 In.
$570

Eldred's

Syrup, Blue, Tree, Applied Parrot On Branch, Brown Interior, Applied Handle, 4 In. 45
Vase, Peacock In Tree, Green, Red, Yellow, Blue Ground, 2 Handles, 6 ½ In. 450

TORTOISESHELL

Tortoiseshell is the shell of the tortoise. It has been used as inlay and to make small decorative objects since the seventeenth century. Some species of tortoise are now on the endangered species list, and old or new objects made from these shells cannot be sold legally. There is also a Victorian glass that looks like a tortoise shell and is called tortoiseshell glass.

Cigarette Case, Carved, English Gothic Revival, Silver Plate, Late 1800s, 4 x 3 In. 200
Jewelry Box, Beveled Glass Insert, Ivory Bun Feet, c.1900, 2 x 6 In. 265
Needle Case, Carved Landscapes, Canton, Chinese, 1800s, 6 In. 495
Snuffbox, Buffalo Horn, Inlaid, Pique Work Lid, Early 1900s, 3 In. 180
Tea Caddy, Carved Cameo On Top, Dome Shape, Brass Trim, 5 x 9 x 6 ½ In. 1725
Tea Caddy, Dome Lid, 2 Lidded Compartments, Ball Feet, George III, 5 x 6 ½ x 4 In. 800
Tea Caddy, Hinged Lid, Silvered Mounts, Ivory Trim, Ball Feet, Regency, c.1815, 4 x 5 x 3 In. *illus* 570
Tea Caddy, Lid, George III, 2 Compartments, Ball Feet, c.1810, 5 ¾ x 7 ½ In. .... *illus* 2440
Tea Caddy, Pagoda Shape, Pewter Stringing, Silver Cartouche, Engraved, 6 x 7 x 4 In. 2640
Tea Caddy, Pagoda Shape, Silver Inlay, Mother-Of-Pearl, 7 ½ x 4 ½ In. 1000
Tea Caddy, Serpentine Front, Ball Feet, Ivory Fittings, 5 ½ x 4 In. 1250

TORTOISESHELL GLASS

Tortoiseshell glass was made during the 1800s and after by the Sandwich Glass Works of Massachusetts and some firms in Germany. Tortoiseshell glass is, of course, named for its resemblance to real shell from a tortoise. It has been reproduced.

Bowl, Swirling Pattern, Molded Rim, 6 ½ x 12 ½ In. 72
Powder Jar, Round, Squat, Silver Repousse Lid, c.1900, 2 ½ x 3 In. 80
Snuff Bottle, Globular, Narrow Neck, Pink Coral Stopper, Chinese, 2 ¾ In. 281
Sweetmeat, Gold Mica Accents, Lobed, Silver Plate Lid & Handle, 4 ½ x 5 In. 180
Vase, Tulip Form, 4 Lobes, Enamel Flowers, Footed, c.1890, 7 ½ In. $60

TOTE, *see Purse category.*

TOY

Toy collectors have special clubs, magazines, and shows. Toys are designed to entice children, and today they have attracted new interest among adults who are still children at heart. All types of toys are collected. Tin toys, iron toys, battery-operated toys, and many others are collected by specialists. Penny toys are inexpensive tin toys made in Germany from the 1880s until about 1914. Some salesman's samples may be listed here. Dolls, Games, Teddy Bears, Bicycles, and other types of toys are listed in their own categories. Other toys may be found under company or celebrity names.

Airplane, Acrobats, Crandall's Great Show, 4 Jointed Figures, Bars, Wood, Box, 1867, 10 x 6 In.. 210
Airplane, Biplane, Propeller, Cast Iron Driver, Pressed Steel, Kingsbury, 5 x 16 x 12 In. 360
Airplane, Junkers Ju 87B Stuka, Bomb, Battle Of Britain, Dinky Toys, Box, 2 x 6 ⅝ In. 41
Airplane, Piper Cub, Propeller, Metal, Painted, Yellow, Red, 79 x 48 In. 177
Airplane, Sky Cruiser, 2 Motors, Sky Blue, Silver & Red, Tin, Marx, Box, 19 In. .... *illus* 264
Airplane, Spirit Of St. Louis Type, Copper, Zinc, Glass Windows, 1910s, 18 x 37 In. 1920
Airplane, Tri-Motor, Pressed Steel, Sky Blue, Red, Yellow Propeller, Schieble, 8 x 29 In. ..*illus* 570
Airplane, Yellow, Pilot, Rubber Tires, c.1950, 43 In. .... *illus* 266
Ambulance, Army, M.D. War Dept., Green, Hinged Back Door, Windup, Marx, 14 In. ......*illus* 500
Animal, Monkey, Jocko, Plush, Jointed, Glass Eyes, Felt Ears, Steiff, 1950s, 25 In. 180
Bears are also listed in the Teddy Bear category.

T

Bed, Doll's, Four-Poster, Brass Knob Finial, Angular Headboard, 1850s, 16 ¾ x 9 x 14 In. 492
Bed, Doll's, Four-Poster, Rope, Whale Ivory & Whalebone Inlay, 1800s, 17 x 18 x 13 In. ...*illus* 240
Bed, Doll's, Turned Posts, Scroll Head & Foot Boards, Mattress, 1850s, 17 x 16 x 26 In. 192
Be-Pop, Jivin' Jigger, Figure Dances, Jointed, Tin, Plastic, Windup, Marx, 10 In. 192
Betty Boop & Mickey Mouse, Under Umbrella, Celluloid, 5 ½ In. ....*illus* 425
Bicycles that are large enough to ride are listed in the Bicycle category.
Bicycle, Velocipede, Horse, Wood, Cast Iron, Wheels, Late 1800s, 28 ½ x 34 In. 177
Bird, Flapping Wings, Wood, White, Black & Red Paint, Wheels, Metal Tube, c.1890, 12 In... *illus* 584
Bird, Pigeon, Flying, Propeller Tail, Flaps Wings, Windup, Hook, Gunthermann, 10 In. ..*illus* 800
Blocks, Building, Je Batis, Lithographed, Box Pictures Boy, Blocks, Dog, Box, 12 x 8 In. ..*illus* 40
Boat, Battleship, Armored, 2-Masted, Cannons, Flags, Bing, 19 ½ In. ....*illus* 2250
Boat, Battleship, Maine, Paper On Wood, Cannon, American & English Flags, Bliss, 18 In. 510
Boat, Furnense Line, Tin, White, Black, Red, Windup, Arnold, 18 In. ....*illus* 523
Boat, Sailboat, Wood, 5 Cloth Masts, Movable Rudder, 1900s, 68 x 64 In. ....*illus* 266
Boat, Tugboat, Sea Gull, Paper On Wood, Graphics, 3 Flags, Bliss, 18 In. 720
Boat, Tugboat, Tru-Matic, Red, Blue & Yellow, Pressed Steel, 1940s, 21 ½ x 9 x 16 In. .....*illus* 360
Boy On Tricycle, Bell On Back, Spoke Wheels, Tin Lithograph, Windup, 8 x 9 In. ....*illus* 177
Bus, Double-Decker, Cast Iron, Green Enamel, 4 Nickel Plated Riders, 3 ½ x 8 In. ....*illus* 192
Bus, Double-Decker, Cast Iron, Red Paint, Green Stripe, Rubber Tires, Kenton, 1920s, 6 ½ In.. 720
Bus, Double-Decker, City Bus, Cast Iron, Blue, Orange Stripe, Passengers, Kenton, Box, 7 In.... 4500
Bus, Greyhound Lines, Blue, White, Black Tires, Metal, Buddy L, 16 In. ....*illus* 207
Bus, Seeing New York 899, Driver, 4 Passengers, Cast Iron, Orange Paint, Hubley, 1930, 11 In.. 1560
Camel, Bactrian, Wood, Jointed, Painted Eyes, 2 Humps, Rope Tail, Schoenhut, c.1915, 7 ¾ In.. 152
Cannon, Yankee Boy, Wood, Alligatored Paint, Label, N.O. Fawick Mfg. Co., 9 x 23 In. 192
Car & Trailer, Cord Coupe, Blue, Yellow Top, Wyandotte, 1930s, 24 In. ....*illus* 500
Car, Airflow, Sedan, 1934 Model, Champion, 7 In. ....*illus* 1200
Car, Andy Gump Deluxe Auto, 348 On Front, Cast Iron, Painted, Arcade, 7 In. 4800
Car, Chevrolet, Coupe, Cast Iron, 2-Tone Paint, Arcade, c.1929, 8 In. ....*illus* 660
Car, Chevrolet, Silverado, Black, Battery Operated, 57 x 31 x 29 In. ....*illus* 106
Car, Dodge, Cornet, Convertible, Monaco Hardtop, Brown, Box, 1965, 9 x 2 ½ In. 138
Car, Ford, Mustang GT, Plastic, Orange, Motorized, Box, 1966, 16 In. 219
Car, Ford, Sedan, 4 Door, Driver, Black, Bing, 6 ⅜ In. ....*illus* 300
Car, Ford, Sedan, Die Cast Metal, Blue & Peach, Box, Dinky Toys, Meccano, 4 In. ....*illus* 82
Car, Mercury, Sedan, Metal, Yellow, Whitewall Tires, Zaugg Empire, Box, 1951, 4 ½ In. 35
Car, Packard, Town Car, Aqua, Black, White Tires, Hubley, 11 In. ....*illus* 600
Car, Police Patrol, Driver, 2 Passengers, Cast Iron, Hubley, 12 In. ....*illus* 375
Car, Racing, Thimble Drome Champion, Chromed Aluminum, Motor, Roy Cox, 4 x 10 In. 565
Carousel, 3 Sailors Seated In Swings, Tin Lithograph, Wilhelm Krauss, 10 In. ....*illus* 336
Carousel, Airship, 2 Canopies, 3 Hot Air Balloons, Woman With Flag, Tin, Distler, 17 In. *illus* 1638
Carousel, Racehorses, Multicolor, Tin Lithograph, Brass Ring, Lever, Winner, 12 x 12 In. 71
Carriage, Baby, Tin Lithograph, Penny Toy, 3 ¼ In. ....*illus* 200
Carriage, Doll's, Rattan, Red Paint, Scrolling, 4 Wheels, Ball Finials, 25 x 31 In. ....*illus* 148
Carriage, Doll's, Wood, Painted Details, Fringed Canopy, Metal Wheels, Victorian, 29 x 34 In. 96
Carriage, Doll's, Wood, Painted, Large Spoke Wheels, 1800s, 24 x 33 In. ....*illus* 71
Carriage, Grand Hotel, Tin Lithograph, 4 Wheels, Meier, Penny Toy, 4 ⅞ In. ....*illus* 261
Cart, Horse Drawn, Green, Yellow Wheels, Red Yoke, Black & Gold Mule, 10 x 3 In. 390
Cart, Ox, Cast Iron, Red, Yellow, White, Spoke Wheel, Stevens & Brown, c.1872, 8 ½ In. 620
Cart, Wood, Iron Banded Wheels, Pull Handle, Old Brown Paint, 1800s, 21 ½ x 35 In. ....*illus* 213
Castle, Cardboard, Pressed, Decorated, Tiers, Turret, Oilcloth & Wood Base, Germany, 37 In.. 960
Castle, Fortress, Wood, Painted, Turret, 4 Banners, Bark On Base, Gottschalk, 21 x 24 In. 1800
Cat, Mohair, Black, Standing, Green Glass Eyes, Whiskers, Steiff, 8 x 4 x 13 In. 184
Cat, Mohair, Sitting, Pink Bow, Tag, Susi, Steiff, 5 ¼ In. ....*illus* 169
Cat, Whimsical, Spring Tail, Platform, 4 Wheels, Penny Toy, Distler, 2 ½ In. 300
Chest, Doll's, Rectangular, Wood, Inlaid, 2 Over 3 Drawers, Turned Pulls, 12 x 10 ½ In. 374
Clown, Bisque, Glass Eyes, Black Wood Handle, Musical, c.1900, 9 In. ....*illus* 148
Clown, Disgruntled, Spinning Cane, Bobbing Head, Celluloid, Windup, Occupied Japan, 6 In.. 189
Cradle, Baby, Wood Slats, Held In Frame, Gold Stencil, Salesman's Sample, Pat. Oct '76, 28 In. *illus* 443
Cradle, Doll's, Splint, Woven, Feather Mattress, Maple Rockers, 1800s, 6 ½ x 10 In. 308

Tortoiseshell, Tea Caddy, Lid, George III, 2 Compartments, Ball Feet, c.1810, 5 ¾ x 7 ½ In.
$2,440

Neal Auction Company

Lithographed Tin Toys
Most lithographed tin toys were made between 1870 and 1915, although some were made later. Collectors like animated groups of animals or people, toys that make noise or music, or toys that move. Makers of special interest include Lehmann, Marx, Chein, Unique, Wolverine, and Strauss.

Toy, Airplane, Sky Cruiser, 2 Motors, Sky Blue, Silver & Red, Tin, Marx, Box, 19 In.
$264

Milestone Auctions

Toy, Airplane, Tri-Motor, Pressed Steel, Sky Blue, Red, Yellow Propeller, Schieble, 8 x 29 In.
$570

Morphy Auctions

Toy, Airplane, Yellow, Pilot, Rubber Tires, c.1950, 43 In.
$266

Copake Auctions

Toy, Ambulance, Army, M.D. War Dept., Green, Hinged Back Door, Windup, Marx, 14 In.
$500

Bertoia Auctions

Toy, Bed, Doll's, Four-Poster, Rope, Whale Ivory & Whalebone Inlay, 1800s, 17 x 18 x 13 In.
$240

Eldred's

Battery-Operated Toys

Battery-operated toys were possible after C and D batteries became easily available after World War II. Many of the toys were made in Japan after the war, often using tin from discarded American drink cans left by soldiers.

Toy, Betty Boop & Mickey Mouse, Under Umbrella, Celluloid, 5 ½ In.
$425

Bertoia Auctions

Toy, Bird, Flapping Wings, Wood, White, Black & Red Paint, Wheels, Metal Tube, c.1890, 12 In.
$584

Skinner, Inc.

Toy, Bird, Pigeon, Flying, Propeller Tail, Flaps Wings, Windup, Hook, Gunthermann, 10 In.
$800

Bertoia Auctions

Toy, Blocks, Building, Je Batis, Lithographed, Box Pictures Boy, Blocks, Dog, Box, 12 x 8 In.
$40

Hartzell's Auction Gallery Inc.

Toy, Boat, Battleship, Armored, 2-Masted, Cannons, Flags, Bing, 19 ½ In.
$2,250

Bertoia Auctions

Toy, Boat, Furnense Line, Tin, White, Black, Red, Windup, Arnold, 18 In.
$523

Skinner, Inc.

Toy, Boat, Sailboat, Wood, 5 Cloth Masts, Movable Rudder, 1900s, 68 x 64 In.
$266

Ahlers & Ogletree Auction Gallery

Toy, Boat, Tugboat, Tru-Matic, Red, Blue & Yellow, Pressed Steel, 1940s, 21 ½ x 9 x 16 In.
$360

Morphy Auctions

Toy, Boy On Tricycle, Bell On Back, Spoke Wheels, Tin Lithograph, Windup, 8 x 9 In.
$177

Copake Auctions

Toy, Bus, Greyhound Lines, Blue, White, Black Tires, Metal, Buddy L, 16 In.
$207

Copake Auctions

Toy, Car & Trailer, Cord Coupe, Blue, Yellow Top, Wyandotte, 1930s, 24 In.
$500

Bertoia Auctions

TIP

Don't buy a Fisher-Price toy with a broken part. It's very difficult to find a replacement. The parts that break easily, often the wheels, are the least likely to be available for repairs. Newly made parts are too shiny and new-looking to be suitable.

Toy, Car, Airflow, Sedan, 1934 Model, Champion, 7 In.
$1,200

Bertoia Auctions

Toy, Car, Chevrolet, Coupe, Cast Iron, 2-Tone Paint, Arcade, c.1929, 8 In.
$660

Rich Penn Auctions

Toy, Bus, Double-Decker, Cast Iron, Green Enamel, 4 Nickel Plated Riders, 3 ½ x 8 In.
$192

Soulis Auctions

Tonka Trucks

If you made a line of all the Tonka trucks made in the last fifty years, it would stretch from Los Angeles to Pawtucket, Rhode Island.

Toy, Car, Chevrolet, Silverado, Black, Battery Operated, 57 x 31 x 29 In.
$106

Copake Auctions

TIP
Need a handy screw-driver to open the section that holds batteries in a toy? A penny will work.

Toy, Car, Ford, Sedan, 4 Door, Driver, Black, Bing, 6 3/8 In.
$300

Bunte Auction Services

Toy, Car, Ford, Sedan, Die Cast Metal, Blue & Peach, Box, Dinky Toys, Meccano, 4 In.
$82

Thomaston Place Auction Galleries

Toy, Car, Packard, Town Car, Aqua, Black, White Tires, Hubley, 11 In.
$600

Bertoia Auctions

Toy, Car, Police Patrol, Driver, 2 Passengers, Cast Iron, Hubley, 12 In.
$375

Bertoia Auctions

Toy, Carousel, 3 Sailors Seated In Swings, Tin Lithograph, Wilhelm Krauss, 10 In.
$336

Pook & Pook

Toy, Carousel, Airship, 2 Canopies, 3 Hot Air Balloons, Woman With Flag, Tin, Distler, 17 In.
$1,638

Pook & Pook

Toy, Carriage, Baby, Tin Lithograph, Penny Toy, 3 1/4 In.
$200

Bertoia Auctions

Toy, Carriage, Doll's, Rattan, Red Paint, Scrolling, 4 Wheels, Ball Finials, 25 x 31 In.
$148

Skinner, Inc.

T

Toy, Carriage, Doll's, Wood, Painted, Large Spoke Wheels, 1800s, 24 x 33 In.
$71

Conestoga Auction Company

Toy, Carriage, Grand Hotel, Tin Lithograph, 4 Wheels, Meier, Penny Toy, 4 7/8 In.
$261

Pook & Pook

Toy, Cart, Wood, Iron Banded Wheels, Pull Handle, Old Brown Paint, 1800s, 21 1/2 x 35 In.
$213

Eldred's

TIP

Restoration of an old dollhouse should be restrained. Clean it, repair the structural problems, repaint as little as possible, and redecorate with appropriate old wallpaper fabrics and paint colors.

Toy, Cat, Mohair, Sitting, Pink Bow, Tag, Susi, Steiff, 5 1/4 In.
$169

Hartzell's Auction Gallery Inc.

Toy, Clown, Bisque, Glass Eyes, Black Wood Handle, Musical, c.1900, 9 In.
$148

Cottone Auctions

Toy, Cradle, Baby, Wood Slats, Held In Frame, Gold Stencil, Salesman's Sample, Pat. Oct '76, 28 In.
$443

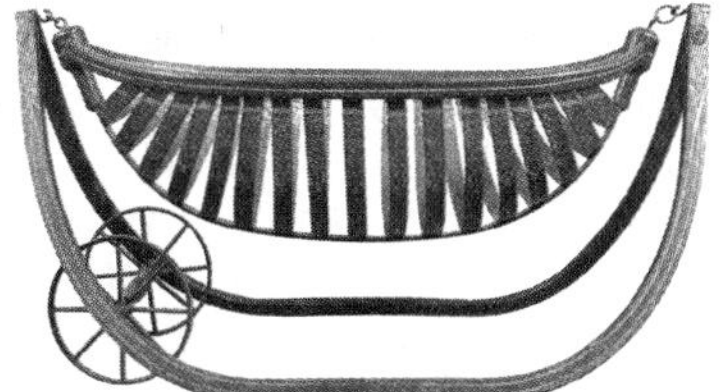

Conestoga Auction Company

Toy, Deep Sea Diver, Tin, Brass Helmet, Air Hose Tube, Bing, 5 In.
$550

Bertoia Auctions

Toy, Dog, Bulldog, Growler, Papier-Mache, Horsehair Collar, Wheels in Paws, 14 x 17 In.
$1,180

Copake Auctions

Toy, Dollhouse, 2 1/2 Story, Wood, White, Green Trim, Maroon Roof, Porch, Steps, 27 x 12 In.
$325

Conestoga Auction Company

T

Toy, Dollhouse, 4 Rooms, Brown, Red, Window Grills, Chimney, 1800s, 38 x 15 x 39 In.
$236

Copake Auctions

Wheels Tell the Age
To determine the age of a Tootsietoy vehicle, look at the wheels. From 1909 to 1932, the wheels were metal and painted black or gold. In the 1933 Tootsietoy catalog, vehicles had either metal wheels or wheels with metal hubs and white rubber tires. Plastic wheels were introduced in the 1950s.

Toy, Ferris Wheel, 6 Swings, Tin, Painted, Composition Riders, Rectangular Base, 10 ¾ In.
$633

Pook & Pook

Dancing Dolls, Cinderella & Prince, Plastic, Battery Operated, Key, Irwin, c.1950, 5 In. 745
Deep Sea Diver, Tin, Brass Helmet, Air Hose Tube, Bing, 5 In. ....*illus* 550
Dog, Bulldog, Growler, Papier-Mache, Horsehair Collar, Wheels in Paws, 14 x 17 In. ....*illus* 1180
Dog, Pug, Lie Lou, Alpaca, Black & Cream, Swivel Head, Tag, Brass Button, 11 ½ In. 204
Dog, Schnauzer, Tessie, Gray Mohair, Brown & White Glass Eyes, Swivel Head, Tag, Steiff, 12 In. 132
Dog, Wood, Carved, Painted, White, Red Spots, Spoke Wheels, Pull Toy, 1800s, 10 x 10 ½ In.... 1845
Dolls are listed in the Doll category.
Dollhouse Furniture, Kitchen Set, Wood, Red & Yellow Paint, Box, 10 Piece........ 163
Dollhouse Furniture, Living Room Set, Wood, Paint, Flocking, Strombecker, Box, 10 Piece .. 118
Dollhouse, 2 Story, Green Roof, 2 Chimneys, Arcade, c.1925, 36 ⅝ x 30 x 37 In........ 222
Dollhouse, 2 Story, Keyhole Cottage, Lithographed Paper Over Wood, Bliss, 16 x 10 In.......... 780
Dollhouse, 2 ½ Story, Wood, White, Green Trim, Maroon Roof, Porch, Steps, 27 x 12 In. *illus* 325
Dollhouse, 4 Rooms, Brown, Red, Window Grills, Chimney, 1800s, 38 x 15 x 39 In. ....*illus* 236
Dollhouse, Cottage, Wood, Paper Lithograph, Paint, Clapboard, Front Opens, 1974, 19 x 10 In. 180
Dollhouse, Plywood, Green Roof, White Sides, Heart, Flowers, Peter Hunt, 39 x 34 x 17 In....... 240
Dollhouse, Wood, 2 Porches, Paper Lithograph, Brick, Stone, Blue Roof, Gottschalk, 18 x 11 In.. 900
Dollhouse, Wood, 3 Story, 6 Rooms, Victorian Style, Real Good Toys, Vermont, 32 x 33 In....... 900
Dollhouse, Wood, Chimney, Thatched Roof Lifts Off, 5 Rooms, R.F. Bernard, 1991, 12 x 19 In. 132
Dresser, Doll's, Bird's-Eye Maple, Mahogany, 2 Drawers, Turned Pulls, 1800s, 15 x 16 x 8 In... 156
Drum Major, Celluloid, Windup, Box, Japan, 11 In. 180
Ferris Wheel, 6 Swings, Tin, Painted, Composition Riders, Rectangular Base, 10 ¾ In. .*illus* 633
Ferris Wheel, Hercules, Multicolor, Tin, Windup, Chein, 16 ½ In.......... 252
Ferris Wheel, Metal, Wood, 6 Cars, Miniature Airplanes, Stencils, Motor, 20 x 16 ⅝ In........... 177
Fire Brigade Band, Painted, 1939 Uniforms, Elastolin, 40 Figures, 2 ¾ In.......... 926
Fire Brigade, Ladder Truck, Station, Tin Lithograph, Friction, Crank, Alps, Japan, c.1955, 7 In. 3464
Fire Station, Wood, Cast Iron Windows, Cloth Roof, Bell Tower, Carpenter, 1890, 26 In. 4500
Fire Truck, City, Fire Dept., Ladder, Hose, Steelcraft, 28 In.......... 748
Fire Truck, Steam Engine, Schoenherr, c.1905, 7 In. ....*illus* 350
Fire Wagon, Fire Chief, Cast Iron, Red Cart, White Horse, Pratt & Letchworth, c.1900, 15 In.... 3000
Fire Wagon, Goat, Mixed Wood Frame, Old Paint, Rubber Tires, 2 Ladders, c.1900, 31 x 50 In. 406
Fire Wagon, Hook & Ladder, 2 Firemen, Red & White, Cast Iron, Pratt & Letchworth, 26 x 4 In. 1320
Fire Wagon, Hook & Ladder, Driver, Horses, Cast Iron, Pratt & Letchworth, c.1900, 23 In. 4500
Fire Wagon, Hose Reel, Driver, Horse, Cast Iron, Pratt & Letchworth, c.1900, 15 In.......... 3900
Fire Wagon, Ladder, Hose No. 4, 2 Men, 2 Horses, Lithographed Paper On Wood, Bliss, 17 In. . 5100
Fire Wagon, Pumper, 3 Horses, Cast Iron, Driver, Hose, Brass Nozzle, c.1915, 8 x 20 In. 410
Fox Hunter, Galloping Horse, Rider With Trumpet, Wood, Leather Bellows, Squeak, 6 In. 1200
Fox, Yes-No, Mohair, Black Glasses, Head Moves When Tail Moves, Schuco, 13 In.......... 900
Fred Flintstone, Riding Purple Dinosaur, Tin, Windup, Marx, Box, 8 In. ....*illus* 420
Games are listed in the Game category.
Gardener, Woman, Walking, Painted, Windup, Moschkowitz, Germany, 8 In. ....*illus* 425
Girl & Baby Carriage, Track With City Graphics, Tin Litho, Windup, Arnold, 1955, 15 In........ 6269
Globe, Attached Sputnik, Flying Saucer, Tin Litho, Windup, M. Seidel, Germany, c.1958, 7 In. . 6095
Gun, Pop Gun, Fires Cork, Double Barrel, Wood & Pressed Steel, Daisy, 21 In. 38
Ham & Sam, Minstrel Team, Piano & Banjo Players, Tin, Windup, Strauss, 7 ⅝ x 7 In. 300
Happy Hippo, Native, Bananas on Pole, Tin, Windup, T.P.S., Japan, Box, c.1950, 6 x 2 In. 333
Horse & Cart, Cast Iron, Ives, c.1890, 9 ½ In.......... 413
Horse & Wagon, Butcher's, Tin, White, Green, Red, 4 Wheels, 11 In. 192
Horse, Black Felt, Wood Platform & Wheels, Pull Toy, 12 ½ x 12 In.......... 106
Horse, Brown, White, Leather Reins, Red Base, 4 Metal Wheels, Pull Toy, 29 x 28 In.......... 523
Horse, Felt Covered, Saddle, Bridle, Painted, Wood Base, Pull Toy, 17 x 17 In. 130
Horse, Papier-Mache, White, Black Detail, Standing On Rolling Platform, 9 ½ x 12 In. 62
Horse, Pine, Horsehair Mane & Tail, Glass Eyes, Leather Reins, Saddle, c.1885, 27 x 11 x 27 In.. 780
Horse, Riding, Burlap Body, Horsehair Tail & Mane, Pedals, Wood Platform, Wheels, 30 In..... 266
Horse, Rocking, Black, Standing, Red, Platform, Wood, 39 In.......... 325
Horse, Rocking, Crandall Type, Cream Body, Leather Ears, Blue Platform, 1910s, 23 x 45 In... 594
Horse, Rocking, Gliding, Wood, Carved, Painted, Leather Saddle, c.1900, 32 x 38 In.......... 153
Horse, Rocking, Horsehair Mane And Tail, Saddle, Wood, Relko, New Zealand, 38 x 61 In........ 640
Horse, Rocking, Velvet Seat, Painted, Red Wood Stand, Early 1900s, 34 x 38 In. 96

SELECTED TOY MARKS WITH DATES USED

Gebruder Bing
1902–1934
Nuremburg, Germany

Gebruder Bing Co.
c.1923–1924
Nuremberg, Germany

F.A.O. Schwarz
1914
New York, N.Y.

Louis Marx & Co.
1920–1977
New York, N.Y.

Ernst Lehmann Co.
1881–c.1947, 1951–2006
Brandenburg, Germany; Nuremburg, Germany

Ernst Lehmann Co.
1915
Brandenburg, Germany

Gebruder Marklin & Co.
1899+
Goppingen, Germany

Nomura Toy Industrial Co., Ltd.
1940s+
Tokyo, Japan

Meccano
1901+
Liverpool, England

Georges Carette & Co.
1905–1917
Nuremburg, Germany

Joseph Falk Co.
1895–1934
Nuremburg, Germany

H. Fischer & Co.
1908–1932
Nuremburg, Germany

Lineol
c. 1906–1963
Bradenburg, Germany

Blomer and Schüler
1919–1974
Nuremberg, Germany

Yonezawa Toys Co.
1950s–1970s
Tokyo, Japan

Toy, Fire Truck, Steam Engine, Schoenherr, c.1905, 7 In.
$350

Bertoia Auctions

Toy, Fred Flintstone, Riding Purple Dinosaur, Tin, Windup, Marx, Box, 8 In.
$420

Milestone Auctions

Toy, Gardener, Woman, Walking, Painted, Windup, Moschkowitz, Germany, 8 In.
$425

Bertoia Auctions

Toy, Horse, Rocking, Wood, Painted, White, Glass Eyes, Saddle, Stand, c.1890, 30 x 37 In.
$175

Eldred's

Toy, Merry-Go-Round, Horses, Swan, Multicolor, Tin, Windup, Chein, Box, 10 x 11 In.
$204

Milestone Auctions

Toy, Motorcycle, Policeman Rider, Sparking, Windup, Gunthermann, Germany, 7 In.
$1,700

Bertoia Auctions

Daughter Anne
In 1952 Anne Odel could take a toy to school if it was no larger than a matchbox. Her father made a die-cast steam roller, the first of the famous Matchbox toys.

Toy, Motorcycle, Rider, Cast Iron, Blue, White Rubber Tires, Kilgore, 4 ¾ x 3 In.
$660

Morphy Auctions

Toy, Motorcycle, Rookie Cop, Multicolor, Tin, Windup, Marx, Box, 8 ½ In.
$390

Milestone Auctions

Horse, Rocking, Wood, Carved, Leather Ears, Saddle, Painted, 20 ½ x 34 In. 256
Horse, Rocking, Wood, Horsehair, Leather Ears, Harness & Saddle, Paint, 1880s, 35 x 51 In. 510
Horse, Rocking, Wood, Painted, Cloth Mane & Tail, Canvas Saddle, 1800s, 31 x 36 In. 354
Horse, Rocking, Wood, Painted, Round Metal Base, Clockwork, 13 x 11 In. 106
Horse, Rocking, Wood, Painted, Saddle, Haddon Rocker's, Oxfordshire, 35 x 42 In. 369
Horse, Rocking, Wood, Painted, White, Glass Eyes, Saddle, Stand, c.1890, 30 x 37 In. *illus* 175
Horse, Trotting, Brown, Metal Wheels, Wood Platform, Pull Toy, 17 x 19 x 7 ½ In. 303
Horse, Wood, Papier-Mache, Saddle, Green, Wheels, Pull Toy, Germany, c.1850, 13 x 4 x 11 In. 259
Humphrey Mobile, Tin, Multicolor, 3 Wheels, Windup, Wyandotte, Box, 9 In. 336
Jonny The Clown, Tips Hat, Tin Lithograph, Windup, Nurnberger, 6 In. 3048
Jumping Jack, Wood, Painted As Harlequin, Jointed Limbs, Erzgebirge, Germany, 13 In. 360
Lion, Nodding, Molded Body, Glass Eyes, Fur Mane, Early 1900s, 8 ½ In. 197
Merry-Go-Round, Horses, Swan, Multicolor, Tin, Windup, Chein, Box, 10 x 11 In. *illus* 204
Merry-Go-Round, Musical, 2 Tiers, Painted, Tin, Windup, Gunthermann, Germany, c.1900, 14 In. 1652
Messe Onkel, Man, Overcoat, Suitcase, Walker, Tin, Windup, Box, MS Brandenburg, c.1955, 6 In. 1662
Motorcycle, Indian, Cast Iron, Yellow Paint, Driver, Hubley Decal On Fender, 9 In. 6000
Motorcycle, Moto-Cross, Runs In Circle, Jump Ramp, Tin Litho, Windup, Huki, Box, 1955, 15 In. 277
Motorcycle, Parcel Post, Harley-Davidson, Driver, Cast Iron, Green, Hubley, c.1930, 9 In. 2700
Motorcycle, Police, Tin Litho, Siren, Electric Light, Friction, Tipp, No. 598, c.1955, 11 In. 276
Motorcycle, Policeman Rider, Sparking, Windup, Gunthermann, Germany, 7 In. *illus* 1700
Motorcycle, Rider, Cast Iron, Blue, White Rubber Tires, Kilgore, 4 ¾ x 3 In. *illus* 660
Motorcycle, Rider, Tin Lithograph, Clockwork, Mettoy, c.1955, 7 ½ In. 5541
Motorcycle, Rider, Tin Lithograph, Tipp, Made In U.S. Zone, Germany, c.1955, 7 ½ In. 2493
Motorcycle, Rookie Cop, Multicolor, Tin, Windup, Marx, Box, 8 ½ In. *illus* 390
Motorcycle, Sidecar, Easter Bunny Delivery, Tin Lithograph, Wyandotte, 6 ½ x 9 x 4 In. 158
Motorcycle, Sidecar, Tin Lithograph, Clockwork, Tipp, U.S. Zone, Germany, 1955, 8 In. 713
Motorcycle, Trick Rider, Tin Lithograph, Technofix, U.S. Zone, Germany, c.1950, 7 In. 1939
Mule, Stuffed, Wood Shavings, Pull Cord, Braying Sound, 1910s, 29 x 29 In. 360
Music Box, Piano, Cast Metal, Marble Top, Windup, 8 x 5 ½ x 4 In. *illus* 24
Music Box, Piano, Wood, Painted Top & Keys, Courting Scene, Putti, Austria, 1900, 27 x 5 In. 544
Nanny With Pram, Walker, Tin Lithograph, Windup, Fritz Voit, Germany, c.1950, 6 In. 370
Paak, Duck & Cart, Ducklings, Tin Litho, Windup, Lehmann, 7 ½ In. 221
Peacock, Standing, Painted, Tin, Windup, Bavaria, 9 ½ In. *illus* 197
Pedal Car, Airplane, Supersonic Jet, Steel, 2 Controls, Murray, c.1950, 44 In. *illus* 1200
Pedal Car, Airplane, U.S. Patrol, Gray, Red, Windshield, Hubcaps, Steel Craft, 27 x 46 In. *illus* 780
Pedal Car, Good Humor Ice Cream Delivery Wagon, Chain Drive, Murray, 24 x 36 In. 1380
Pedal Car, Pressed Steel, Disc Wheels, Red, c.1930, 43 In. *illus* 384
Pedal Car, Roadster, Boat Tail, Pressed Steel, Aqua, White, Upholstery, 24 x 52 In. *illus* 1680
Pedal Car, Stoddard Dayton, Wood, Spoke Wheels, Metal Pedal, 24 x 46 x 20 In. 1560
Pedal Tractor, John Deere, 2-Wheel Trailer, Model 520, Ertl, 63 In. 132
Pedal Tractor, John Deere, Green, Rubber Tires, 24 x 36 x 18 ½ In. *illus* 210
Pedal Tractor, McCormick Farmall, Trailer, Red, Rubber Tires, 29 x 38 x 18 In. 450
Piano, 8 Keys, Wood, Painted, Dancing Women, Putti, Schoenhut, 9 x 7 x 8 In. 34
Play Golf, 9 Holes, Golfer, Green Ground, Tin, Windup, Strauss, 12 In. *illus* 336
Playset, Aerodrome, Diorama, Hangar, 2 Planes, Crew, House, Box, CBJ, Paris, 35 Piece 1320
Playset, Noah's Ark, Hinged Roof, Noah, 35 Animals, Wood, Germany, 18-In. Ark 720
Playset, Village School, Jointed Pupils, Teacher, Books, Paper Pages, Crandall's, Box, 10 In. 540
Playset, Zeppelin Airship, Tin, Ground Crew, Military Figures, Noris, 18 Piece 5400
Plow, Vulcan No. 12, Brass, Aluminum Blade, Salesman's Sample, 22 In. *illus* 930
Pony, Cast Aluminum, Spring Base, Red, Yellow, Black, 32 x 28 In. *illus* 150
Pool Player, Tin, Round Ball Feeder, Windup, Germany, 10 In. *illus* 325
Puppet, Finger, Devil, Composition, Red & Black Head, Cloth Body, 8 In. *illus* 275
Rabbit, Easter Bunny, Brown Fur, Squeaks, Holds Basket, Rectangular Base, 1800s, 8 ½ In. 800
Rabbit, Playing Guitar, Celluloid, Windup, 8 ½ In. 240
Range Rider, Cowboy On Horseback, Rocks, Tin Lithograph, Windup, Marx, 9 ¾ x 11 In. 254
Robot, Blink-A-Gear, Tin, Plastic Limbs, Walks, Eyes Blink, Battery Operated, 15 In. 360
Robot, Lost In Space, Black & Red, Battery Operated, Remco, Box, 14 In. 510
Robot, Rotate-O-Matic Super Astronaut, Blinks & Shoots Gun, Japan, Box, 1960s, 11 ¾ In. 315

Slinky Toy

Richard James invented the Slinky toy in 1945. It was the start of a successful toy company. But in about 1960, James left his wife, Betty, and six children to join a Bolivian religious cult. Betty discovered that her husband had given corporate money to the cult, leaving the firm in debt. She became CEO and made the company a success again by creating dozens of new Slinky toys. Richard James died in 1974. Betty died at age 90 in 2008.

Toy, Music Box, Piano, Cast Metal, Marble Top, Windup, 8 x 5 ½ x 4 In.
$24

Copake Auctions

Toy, Peacock, Standing, Painted, Tin, Windup, Bavaria, 9 ½ In.
$197

Skinner, Inc.

This is an edited listing of current prices. Visit **Kovels.com** to check thousands of prices from previous years and sign up for free information on trends, tips, reproductions, marks, and more.

Toy, Pedal Car, Airplane, Supersonic Jet, Steel, 2 Controls, Murray, c.1950, 44 In.
$1,200

Rich Penn Auctions

Toy, Pony, Cast Aluminum, Spring Base, Red, Yellow, Black, 32 x 28 In.
$150

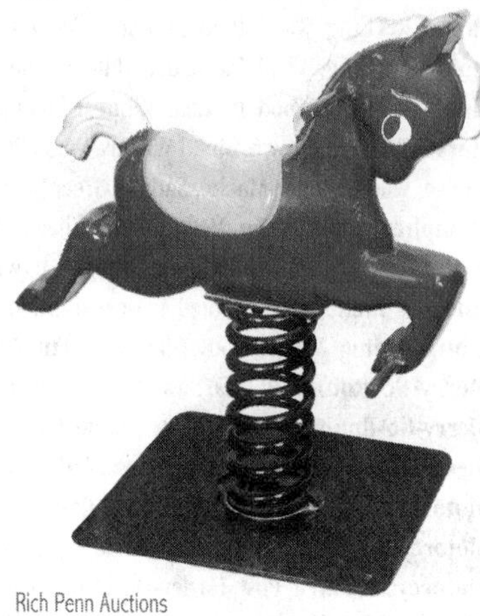

Rich Penn Auctions

Toy, Pedal Car, Airplane, U.S. Patrol, Gray, Red, Windshield, Hubcaps, Steel Craft, 27 x 46 In.
$780

Morphy Auctions

Toy, Pedal Car, Pressed Steel, Disc Wheels, Red, c.1930, 43 In.
$384

Copake Auctions

Toy, Pedal Car, Roadster, Boat Tail, Pressed Steel, Aqua, White, Upholstery, 24 x 52 In.
$1,680

Morphy Auctions

Toy, Pedal Tractor, John Deere, Green, Rubber Tires, 24 x 36 x 18 ½ In.
$210

Morphy Auctions

Toy, Play Golf, 9 Holes, Golfer, Green Ground, Tin, Windup, Strauss, 12 In.
$336

Milestone Auctions

Toy, Plow, Vulcan No. 12, Brass, Aluminum Blade, Salesman's Sample, 22 In.
$930

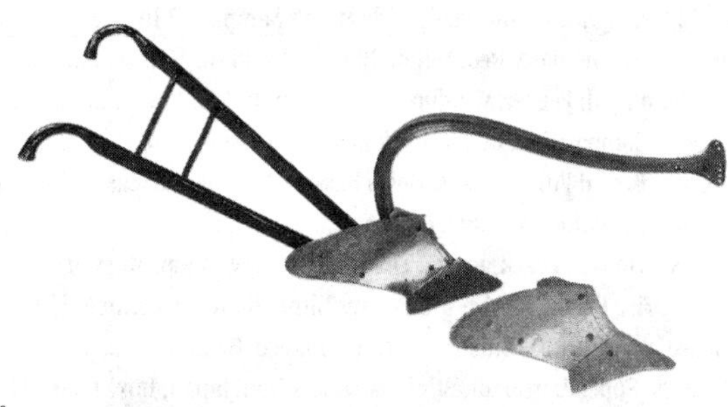

Milestone Auctions

Toy, Pool Player, Tin, Round Ball Feeder, Windup, Germany, 10 In.
$325

Bertoia Auctions

Toy, Puppet, Finger, Devil, Composition, Red & Black Head, Cloth Body, 8 In.
$275

Bertoia Auctions

Toy, Scale, Toledo Computing, Kilgore, Box, 6 In.
$375

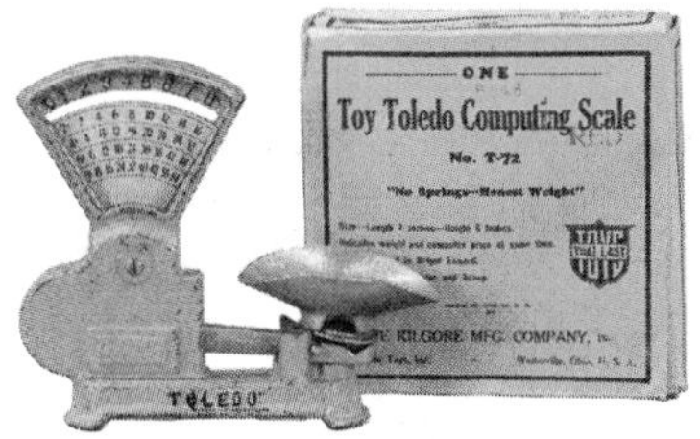

Bertoia Auctions

Toy, Scooter, Wood, Spoke Wheels, Old Red Paint, 1910-20, 52 In.
$177

Copake Auctions

Toy, Sewing Machine, Little Miss, Electric, Thread, Wood Base, Lindstrom
$59

Copake Auctions

Toy, Sled, Bent Oak & Pine, Red, Metal Runners, Larkin, Maine, c.1900, 34 x 13 x 13 In.
$50

Thomaston Place Auction Galleries

Toy, Sled, Fairy, Wood, Iron Runners, 26 ½ In.
$94

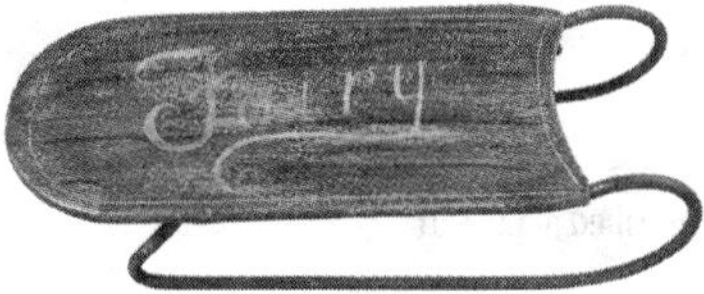

Conestoga Auction Company

Toy, Sled, Runner, Wood, Metal, Painted, 1800s, 14 ½ x 41 ½ In.
$148

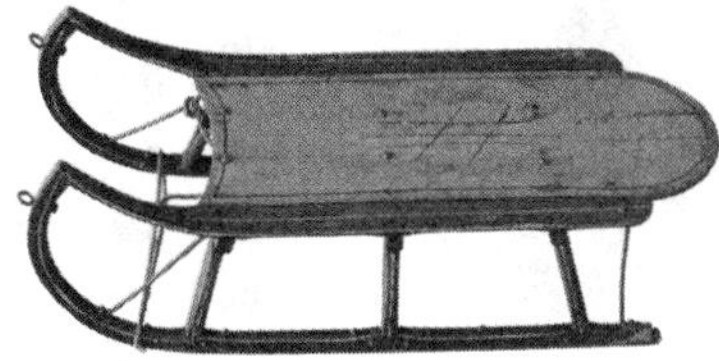

Copake Auctions

Toy, Stove, Cook, Eclipse, Nickel Plated Cast Iron, Accessories, J. & E. Stevens, 15 x 20 In.
$780

Rich Penn Auctions

Toy, Stove, Cook, Lionel No. 455, Range, Oven, Green & Cream Porcelain, c.1930, 33 x 26 In.
$360

Rich Penn Auctions

Toy, Stove, Cook, Utensils, Cast Iron, Doors, 10 x 14 x 8 In.
$106

Copake Auctions

Toy, Tank, Man Inside, Red, Tin, Mechanical, Japan, Inscribed A-12, 6 In.
$116

Clars Auction Gallery

Toy, Taxi, Black, Yellow, Tin, Windup, Door Opens, Gunthermann, Germany, 9 In.
$420

Milestone Auctions

Toy, Train Car, Lionel, Locomotive, 402-E Engine, Light Brown, 6 ½ x 18 x 4 ½ In.
$240

Morphy Auctions

Toy, Train Car, Pullman, Club Car Model, Painted, No. 184, 5 x 14 In.
$269

Clars Auction Gallery

Toy, Trolley, Tin Lithograph, Penny Toy, Meier, Germany, 3 In.
$250

Bertoia Auctions

Robot, Tin Lithograph, Crank, c.1950, 5 In. 308
Rocket Track, Skyway Graphics, Tin Lithograph, Windup, Technofix, Box, c.1955 2771
Roly Poly Clown, Papier-Mache, Blue, Yellow, Green, Orange, Schoenhut, 15 ½ In. 240
Room Box, Bedroom With Living Area, Adobe Style, Electrified, 22 x 11 x 13 In. 132
Room Box, Parlor, Georgian, Paneling, Tapestry Curtains, Accessories, 13 x 28 x 22 In. 3300
Scale, Toledo Computing, Kilgore, Box, 6 In. *illus* 375
Scooter, 3 Wheels, Wood, Steel Handle, 32 ½ In. 35
Scooter, Wood, Spoke Wheels, Old Red Paint, 1910-20, 52 In. *illus* 177
Sewing Machine, Little Miss, Electric, Thread, Wood Base, Lindstrom *illus* 59
Skier, Cross Country, Celluloid Face, Red Checked Jacket, Hat, Windup, Occupied Japan, 4 x 5 In. 295
Skittles Set, Middle Eastern Men, Camel Container, Nodding Head, Germany, 19 In. 4500
Skittles Set, Vegetable People, Head Of Cabbage Storage Container, 14 x 17 In. 8400
Sled, Bent Oak & Pine, Red, Metal Runners, Larkin, Maine, c.1900, 34 x 13 x 13 In. *illus* 50
Sled, Fairy, Wood, Iron Runners, 26 ½ In. *illus* 94
Sled, Iron, Red, Shield Shape Seat, Winter Landscape, Salesman's Sample, 14 x 5 x 5 In. 374
Sled, Runner, Wood, Metal, Painted, 1800s, 14 ½ x 41 ½ In. *illus* 148
Sled, Wood, Iron Runners, Red Paint, Marked, Xmas 1911, 45 In. 91
Sled, Wood, Metal Edged Runner, 48 ½ In. 83
Sled, Wood, Red Ground, Iron Runners, Lou Dillon, 1800s, 39 In. 106
Sleigh, White, Gold, Blue Pinstripes, Upholstered Seat, Late 1800s, 33 x 18 x 41 In. 188
Space Station, Planet-Y, Flying Saucer, Lights, Sounds, Tin Lithograph, Nomura, Box, 1968, 9 In. 762
Stove, Cook, Cast Iron, Accessories, Little Eva, T. Southard, 17 x 14 x 12 In. 182
Stove, Cook, Eclipse, Nickel Plated Cast Iron, Accessories, J. & E. Stevens, 15 x 20 In. *illus* 780
Stove, Cook, Empire Metal Ware Corp, Green, Tin, Electric, c.1930, 14 x 6 x 12 In. 53
Stove, Cook, Lionel No. 455, Range, Oven, Green & Cream Porcelain, c.1930, 33 x 26 In. *illus* 360
Stove, Cook, Steel, Enamel, Pipe, Lid Burner, Towel Bar, Sinhazinha, 1950s, 20 x 17 In. 354
Stove, Cook, Utensils, Cast Iron, Doors, 10 x 14 x 8 In. *illus* 106
Stroller, Doll's, High Wheel, Painted Decoration, Upholstery, 1800s, 28 x 33 x 11 In. 452
Tank, Man Inside, Red, Tin, Mechanical, Japan, Inscribed A-12, 6 In. *illus* 116
Tap, Man Pushing Wheelbarrow, Spoke Wheels, Tin Lithograph, Windup, Lehmann, Box, 6 In. 148
Taxi, Amos 'N' Andy, Fresh Air, Black & Orange, 7 ¾ In. 300
Taxi, Black, Yellow, Tin, Windup, Door Opens, Gunthermann, Germany, 9 In. *illus* 420
Taxi, Li-La Hansom Cab, Driver, Dog, Tin Lithograph, Windup, Lehmann, 1903, 6 In. 531
Teapot, Doll's, Stoneware, Blue & White, Blue Sponge, Bristol, c.1900, 4 In. 293
Teddy Bears are also listed in the Teddy Bear category.
Tenpins, Military, 10 Soldiers, Wood, Painted, Ives, Wood Box, 8 ½-In. Soldiers 1920
Tightrope Walker, Lucky, Spectator Graphics, Tin Lithograph, Windup, Arnold, 1955, 14 ¾ In. 485
Toboggan Run, 2 Sleds, Snow Graphics, Tin Lithograph, Windup, Germany, c.1955, 18 In. 1939
Train Accessory, Marklin, Cattle Loading Ramp, 0 Gauge, 2 Corrals, Railed Sides, 8 In. 510
Train Accessory, Marklin, Central Bahnhof Station, 2 Chimneys, Etched Glass Windows, 14 In. 6000
Train Accessory, Marklin, Clock & Indicator Board, Flippable, 1 & 2 Gauge, French Cities, 10 In. 3000
Train Accessory, Marklin, No. 2526, Tunnel Cut, 1 & 2 Gauge, Hill Turret, Painted, 20 In. 3600
Train Accessory, Marklin, Platform, Awning, Patterned Glass, Beams, c.1900, 12 x 12 In. 9000
Train Accessory, Marklin, Streetlamp Post, 12 In. 660
Train Accessory, Marklin, Switch Tower, 0 Gauge, Brickwork, Shingle Roof, Bell Rings, 8 In. 2160
Train Car, Lionel, Locomotive, 402-E Engine, Light Brown, 6 ½ x 18 x 4 ½ In. *illus* 240
Train Car, Marklin, Baggage, 1 Gauge, 2 Sliding Doors, Doors At Ends, Clerestory Roof, 8 In. 360
Train Car, Marklin, Beer Car, 1 Gauge, Export Brauerei, Lion Logo, Lowernrau, 4 ½ In. 360
Train Car, Marklin, Beer Car, 1 Gauge, Schlitz, Globe & Sash Logo, Hinged Doors, 9 In. 31200
Train Car, Marklin, Beer Wagon, 1 Gauge, Munich Coat Of Arms, Munich Child, 7 In. 1020
Train Car, Marklin, Boxcar, Heinz, 57 Varieties, Tomato Ketchup, 0 Gauge, 7 ½ In. 1200
Train Car, Marklin, Caboose, No. 1835, O Gauge, P.R.R., 90309, c.1904, 4 ½ In. 510
Train Car, Marklin, Coach, No. 2964, Royal Blue Limited, 0 Gauge, Gold Trim, c.1907 9600
Train Car, Marklin, Crane, Crank, 1 Gauge, Enclosed Cabin, Corrugated Roof, c.1908, 5 In. 19200
Train Car, Marklin, Fruit, Ventilated Sides, 1 Gauge, Blue, Gray, 2 Doors, c.1907, 8 ½ In. 8400
Train Car, Marklin, Glass Transport, 1 Gauge, Painted, English Writing, c.1904, 9 In. 840
Train Car, Marklin, Hospital, 1 Gauge, Red Cross, Hinged Roof, Beds, Cabinets, Box, 11 In. 3300
Train Car, Marklin, Poultry Car, 1 Gauge, 4 Gates, Sliding Doors, Chickens, c.1909, 8 ½ In. 3600

Toy, Truck, Concrete Mixer, Decals, Buddy L, Moline Pressed Steel Co., 1929, 14 x 24 In.
$360

CRN Auctions

Toy, Truck, Delivery Van, Strawbridge & Clothier, Tin Lithograph, Box, Santa, 7 ½ In.
$4,500

Bertoia Auctions

Toy, Truck, Delivery, Minic Transport, Express Service, Shell Petrol Can, Triang, 7 ¾ In.
$120

Rich Penn Auctions

Toy, Truck, Lyons' Confectionery, London, Driver, Tin Lithograph, 6 ⅝ x 2 x 3 ½ In.
$1,582

Hartzell's Auction Gallery Inc.

Toy, Truck, Steam Shovel, Pressed Steel, Extended Boom, 4 Wheels, Buddy L, c.1925, 20 In.
$350

Bertoia Auctions

Toy, Truck, Steamroller, Die Cast Metal, Black, Red, Keystone, 1910s, 13 x 21 In.
$300

Garth's Auctioneers & Appraisers

Toy, Truck, Television, American Circus, Clown Driver, Battery Operated, Japan, Box, 9 ½ In.
$500

Bertoia Auctions

Toy, Truck, Tow, Cities Service Gasoline, Metal, Green, White, 18 x 7 In.
$510

Morphy Auctions

Toy, Wagon, Big Show Circus, Lion Inside, Tin Litho, Key Wind, Strauss, 9 In.
$185

Richard Opfer Auctioneering, Inc.

Toy, Wagon, Circus, 2 White Horses, Red Cage, Polar Bear, Cast Iron, Kenton, 6 x 6 ½ In.
$480

Morphy Auctions

Toy, Wagon, Milk, Horse Drawn, Red, White & Black Paint, Cast Iron, c.1920, 13 In.
$180

Eldred's

Toy, Waiter, Wearing Coat & Tails, Tin Lithograph, Windup, Distler, Germany, 6 ½ In.
$650

Bertoia Auctions

Toy, Wheelbarrow, Wood Wheel, Horse, Painted, 1800s, 29 In.
$94

Copake Auctions

TIP

Do not put wax on a wooden toy to preserve it. The wax may yellow and disturb any markings or paper decoration.

Toy, Woman & Dog, Knitting, Dog Pawing, Wood, Squeak, Late 1800s, 4 ½ x 4 In.
$1,599

Skinner, Inc.

Train Car, Marklin, Snowplow Car, No. 1888, Headlamp, 4 Crew Members, c.1906, 5 ½ In...... 1560
Train Car, Marklin, Summer Car, 2 Gauge, Openwork Sides, Faux Curtains, c.1900, 8 In. 7200
Train Car, Marklin, Tram, Electrische Strassenbahn, Lindenau To Leipzig, 0 Gauge, 1904, 7 In.... 12000
Train Car, Pullman, Club Car Model, Painted, No. 184, 5 x 14 In. ....*illus* 269
Train Set, Marklin, Passenger, American Eagle, 1 Gauge, c.1900, Tracks, Box, 4 Piece............ 52800
Train Set, Mother Goose Railroad, Graphics, Jack & Jill Locomotive, Reed, 40 In. 4500
Train Set, New York Central Railroad, Coach, Baggage Car, Locomotive, Wood, Bliss.............. 510
Train Set, Princess, Duke Locomotive, Wood, Painted, Stripes, Reed 660
Train Set, Tantet Et Manon, Exploding, Le Train Catastrophe, 1 Gauge, Friction, 1891, Box.... 3900
Train Set, Tom Thumb Locomotive, 8 Cars, Paper On Wood, Track Base, Box, Germany, 24 In. 4200
Train, Busy Choo, Track, Tin Lithograph, T.P.S., Japan, Box, 1950s, 10 x 6 x 2 In. 125
Train, Engine, Electric Diesel, Wood Base, Track, Lionel, 1947, 14 In.. 374
Train, Keystone Railroad, Die Cast Frame, Walnut Steering Wheels, 1910s, 13 x 26 In. 270
Transformer, Optimus Prime, 4 Missiles, Rifle, Gas Hose, Hasbro, Box, 1985, 10 x 15 In. 393
Trolley, Tin Lithograph, Penny Toy, Meier, Germany, 3 In. ....*illus* 250
Truck, Bell Telephone, Cast Iron, Red Paint, Gold Ladders, Wench Hook, Hubley, 1930, 13 In.. 1920
Truck, Buckeye Ditch Digger, Cast Iron, Painted, Kenton, 9 ½ In. 780
Truck, Circus, Cage, Overland Circus, Driver, Cast Iron, White & Gold, Kenton, 1920s, 9 In. 5100
Truck, Circus, Calliope, Overland Circus, Cast Iron, Yellow, Kenton, 1920s, 9 In....................... 4500
Truck, Concrete Mixer, Decals, Buddy L, Moline Pressed Steel Co., 1929, 14 x 24 In. ....*illus* 360
Truck, Crane, Metal, Cranks, Swivels, Trolley Base, 4 Wheels, Bing, c.1920, 22 x 33 In............ 2494
Truck, Delivery Van, Strawbridge & Clothier, Tin Lithograph, Box, Santa, 7 ½ In. ....*illus* 4500
Truck, Delivery, Minic Transport, Express Service, Shell Petrol Can, Triang, 7 ¾ In. ......*illus* 120
Truck, Dump, Orange, White Rubber Tires, Wyandotte, 12 ½ In. 91
Truck, Dump, Red, Blue Bed, Tin, 7 ½ x 23 In. 219
Truck, Fairfield Ditch Digger, Cast Iron, Paint, Nickeled Chain & Flywheel, Kenton, 10 In........ 1560
Truck, Gasoline, Mack, Driver, Tin, Cast Iron, Green, Arcade, 13 In. 863
Truck, Gasoline, Pressed Steel, Painted, Red, Black Tires, Tonka Toys, 5 x 15 x 6 In. 330
Truck, General Digger, Cast Iron, Red & Green Paint, Rubber Tires, Hubley, c.1930, 10 In........ 420
Truck, Jaeger Cement Mixer, Cast Iron, Blue & Red Paint, Nickeled Wheels, Kenton, 6 In. 780
Truck, Lyons' Confectionery, London, Driver, Tin Lithograph, 6 ⅝ x 2 x 3 ½ In. ....*illus* 1582
Truck, Mail, Metal, Black, Yellow Screened Back, Hard Rubber Tires, Keystone, 26 ½ In.......... 339
Truck, Pickup, Pressed Steel, Green, Flywheel, Friction, Driver, Dayton, 13 In. 300
Truck, Steam Shovel, Pressed Steel, Extended Boom, 4 Wheels, Buddy L, c.1925, 20 In. ...*illus* 350
Truck, Steamroller, Die Cast Metal, Black, Red, Keystone, 1910s, 13 x 21 In. ....*illus* 300
Truck, Tanker, Bengal Gasoline, Tiger, White, 28 x 8 In.. 570
Truck, Tanker, Shell, Aqua, Red, Black Tires, Triang, England, 1946-60, 18 In........................ 180
Truck, Television, American Circus, Clown Driver, Battery Operated, Japan, 9 ½ In. ......*illus* 500
Truck, Tow, Cities Service Gasoline, Metal, Green, White, 18 x 7 In. ....*illus* 510
Truck, Tow, Mack, Red, Green Winch, Metal Wheels, Arcade, 13 In. 3300
Truck, Tow, Service, VW, Blue, Yellow, Tin lithograph, Friction, Tippco, c.1955, 10 In............... 84
Truck, Travel Loader, Pressed Steel, Orange, Black Tires, Adams, Nylint, 30 In., Pair................ 85
Wagon, Big Show Circus, Lion Inside, Tin Litho, Key Wind, Strauss, 9 In. ....*illus* 185
Wagon, Child's, Express, Spoke Wheels, Extended Handle, c.1900, 65 In..................................... 266
Wagon, Child's, Ford Coaster, 100 Year Anniversary Collector Edition, 12 x 15 In. 270
Wagon, Child's, Wood, Red, Spoke Wheels, Pull Handle, 40 x 17 x 15 ½ In................................ 489
Wagon, Circus, 2 White Horses, Red Cage, Polar Bear, Cast Iron, Kenton, 6 x 6 ½ In. ......*illus* 480
Wagon, Delivery, Fancy Goods, Toys, Notions, Horse, Tin, Painted, Stencils, 1870s, 19 In.......... 4800
Wagon, Delivery, Milk, License No. 4, Driver, 2 Horses, Paper On Wood, Reed, 16 ½ In............. 1440
Wagon, Doctor's Cart, Red, Black Canopy, Horse, George Brown, 9 In. 780
Wagon, Goat, Child's, Wood, Painted, Ozark Farm, Wagon, 1800s, 44 In. 413
Wagon, Milk, Horse Drawn, Red, White & Black Paint, Cast Iron, c.1920, 13 In. ....*illus* 180
Wagon, Wood, Green Bench, Iron Rimmed Wheels, 2 Shafts, 38 x 24 x 28 In.............................. 452
Waiter, Wearing Coat & Tails, Tin Lithograph, Windup, Distler, Germany, 6 ½ In. ....*illus* 650
Washing Machine, Columbia Washer, Wood, Iron Wheel, Handle, 1895, 13 x 10 ½ x 20 In..... 403
Water Tower, Pressed Steel, Red, Pull Toy, Buddy L, 32 In.. 960
Wheelbarrow, Wood Wheel, Horse, Painted, 1800s, 29 In. ....*illus* 94
Windmill, Miller & Donkey Rotate, Tin Lithograph, Painted, Steam, 13 ½ In. 744
Woman & Dog, Knitting, Dog Pawing, Wood, Squeak, Late 1800s, 4 ½ x 4 In. ....*illus* 1599

Tramp Art, Altar, Matchstick, Syroco Crucifix, Brass Cup, Candelabra, Lithograph, Last Supper, 24 x 10 In.
$185

Richard Opfer Auctioneering, Inc.

Tramp Art, Clock, Church, Clock Dial, Drawer, Door, Layered, Inlay, Joseph Konieczny, c.1930, 95 In.
$7,380

Skinner, Inc.

T

Tramp Art, Frame, Chip Carved, Hang Ring On Back, 6 x 11 ½ In.
$102

Hartzell's Auction Gallery Inc.

Tramp Art, Mirror, Carved, Flowers, Leaves, Painted, 15 x 12 In.
$338

Skinner, Inc.

Tramp Art, Plant Stand, Wood, Carved Metal Strips, Brads, 36 In.
$74

Richard Opfer Auctioneering, Inc.

Trivet, Wrought Iron, Revolving, Heart, Round, Footed, 1800s, 22 ¾ In.
$336

Pook & Pook

Trunk, Dome Top, Blue Velvet, Woven Geometric Banding, Fringe, France, 1900s, 25 x 30 x 19 In.
$188

Crescent City Auction Gallery

Trunk, Dome Top, Painted, Fruit, Signed, Peter Ompir, 1900s, 24 In.
$148

Conestoga Auction Company

Trunk, Louis Vuitton, Brass Studs, Leather Trim, Top Handle, Monogram, Stand, 14 x 22 x 15 In.
$4,200

CRN Auctions

Trunk, Louis Vuitton, Canvas, Marshall Field & Co., Monogram, 1890s-1900s, 25 ½ x 25 x 25 ¾ In.
$10,625

Hindman Auctions

TIP

Mildew in your old trunk? New cure—special volcanic rocks. They attract and absorb odors.

Trunk, Louis Vuitton, Fitted Interior, Faded Pattern, Leather Handles, 3 Trays, 35 ½ x 20 x 20 In.
$2,125

Hudson Valley Auctions

Trunk, Louis Vuitton, Shoe Bag, Brown, Tan, Zipper, 8 Pockets, Monogram, 1900s, 12 x 18 x 7 In.
$660

Case Antiques

TRAMP ART

Tramp art is a form of folk art made since the Civil War. It is usually made from chip-carved cigar boxes. Examples range from small boxes and picture frames to full-sized pieces of furniture. Collectors in the United States started collecting it about 1970, and examples from other countries, especially Germany, were imported and sold by antiques dealers.

Altar, Matchstick, Syroco Crucifix, Brass Cup, Candelabra, Lithograph, Last Supper, 24 x 10 In. *illus* 185
Box, Chip Carved, Bisected Rectangles, Repeating Triangles, Hinged Lid, 5 x 12 In. 400
Clock, Church, Clock Dial, Drawer, Door, Layered, Inlay, Joseph Konieczny, c.1930, 95 In. *illus* 7380
Comb Box, 3 Tiers, Mirror, Pure & Sweet Cigar Box Drawer, c.1900, 27 x 7 ½ In. 435
Crucifix, Box, Carved Wood, Metal, Tacks, Handles, Beadwork Vignette, Drawer, 25 x 11 In. 197
Dresser, Mirror, Ball & Geometric, 4 Drawers, Carved Feet, 32 ½ x 21 x 12 In. 1243
Frame, Chip Carved, Hang Ring On Back, 6 x 11 ½ In. *illus* 102
Frame, Ship In Bottle, Openworks, Painted, 12 x 15 In. 615
Mirror, Carved, Flowers, Leaves, Painted, 15 x 12 In. *illus* 338
Plant Stand, Wood, Carved Metal Strips, Brads, 36 In. *illus* 74
Planter, Square, Stepped Sides & Base, Green, Painted, Footed, c.1920, 12 ½ x 12 x 12 In. 105

TRAP

Traps for animals may be handmade. One of the most unusual is the mousetrap made so that when the mouse entered the trap, it was hit on the head with a mallet. Other traps were commercially manufactured and often are marked with the name of the manufacturer. Many traps were designed to be as humane as possible, and they would trap the live animal so it could be released in the woods.

Bear, Double Spring, Chain, Ring, Marked American Fur & Trade HBC No. 6, 18 x 44 In. 584
Carrier, Pigeon, Wood, Metal Fittings, Tin Mesh Screen, 10 Cages, 29 x 14 ½ x 20 ½ In. 176
Cricket Cage, Porcelain, Satsuma, Japan, 3 ½ x 6 In. 635
Fish, Basketry, Woven, Handmade, Thailand, 28 x 8 x 8 In. 68
Foothold, Man Trap, Iron, England, 18th Century, 7 x 55 x 12 In. 135

TREEN, *see Wooden category.*

TRENCH ART

Trench art is a form of folk art made by soldiers. Metal casings from bullets and mortar shells were cut and decorated to form useful objects, such as vases. Coins and other things were used to make jewelry.

Ashtray, Copper, Shield Shape, Bullet & Casing Feet, Coins, c.1900, 6 x 5 x 3 In. 145
Bracelet, Coins, 1938, 1942, 1943, Australia, 6 ½ In. 45
Crucifix, Brass Shell Casings, 7 In. 135
Key Ring, Pickekhaube, Central Bullet, Black Tin, Gilt, 2 ½ x 2 ½ In. 129
Letter Opener, Dagger Shape, Etched Saying, Brass Bullet Handle, 6 In. 135
Paperweight, Grenade, Pineapple, 1954, 4 ½ In. 50
Shell Casing, Engraved, Branch Pattern, 6 ¾ In. 68
Spoon, 303 Rifle Cartridge, Silver Plate, 1920s, 5 ¾ In. 149
Tobacco Jar, Brass, Engraved Royal Artillery Grenade Emblem, 4 ¾ x 4 In. 491
Vase, 40 mm Brass Shell Casing, Twist Design, c.1945, 6 In. 99

TRIVET

Trivets are now used to hold hot dishes. Most trivets of the late nineteenth and early twentieth centuries were made to hold hot pressing irons. Iron or brass reproductions are being made of many of the old styles.

Brass, Hearth, Hand Forged Iron, Adjustable Legs, Wing Nuts, Mid 1700s, 7 x 5 ⅜ x 5 In. 94
Brass, Triangular, Cutwork, Fox, Tripod Feet, 5 In. 11

TIP
To be collectible, trunks must be in good condition. Refinishing destroys the trunk's value as an antique. Trunks in poor condition can be refinished to be attractive and useful as pieces of furniture, but they will no longer be of interest to serious trunk collectors.

Trunk, Louis Vuitton, Suitcase, Leather Handle, Brass Hardware, Monogram, c.1950, 18 x 28 x 7 In.
$720

Eldred's

Trunk, Louis Vuitton, Travel Cosmetic Case, Lid, Leather, Light Brown, 9 x 12 ¾ x 8 ¾ In.
$360

Michaan's Auctions

Trunk, Rosewood, Mother-Of-Pearl Inlay, Geometric, Rectangular, 1800s, 17 x 31 x 16 ½ In.
$720

Charleston Estate Auctions

Trunk, Steamer, Chrome, Campaign Style, Brown Leather, Buckle Straps, Ralph Lauren, 17 ½ In.
$1,955

Blackwell Auctions

TIP
To remove the musty smell from an old trunk, try some of the commercial products found in hardware stores. Several new types claim to remove odors by filtering the air.

Tuthill, Bowl, Rex, Cut, Geometric, Clear, 4 x 9 In.
$1,200

Woody Auctions

Typewriter, Coffman, Pocket, Linear Index, Nickel Plated, 1902, 7 ½ x 2 In.
$6,650

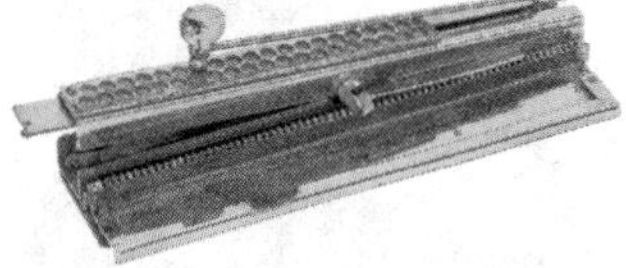

Auction Team Breker

Iron, The Gem, Detachable Handle, Twist Latch, 4 ½ In. 254
Iron, Triangular, Cutwork, Fence, Engraved, Ball Feet, 9 ½ x 6 In. 96
Wrought Iron, Heart Shape, Square Feet, Floyd Co., Va., 1850s, 1 x 6 ½ x 3 ¾ In. 117
Wrought Iron, Revolving, Heart, Round, Footed, 1800s, 22 ¾ In. *illus* 336

TRUNK

Trunks of many types were made. The nineteenth-century sea chest was often handmade of unpainted wood. Brass-fitted camphorwood chests were brought back from the Orient. Leather-covered trunks were popular from the late eighteenth to mid-nineteenth centuries. By 1895, trunks were covered with canvas or decorated sheet metal. Embossed metal coverings were used from 1870 to 1910. By 1925, trunks were covered with vulcanized fiber or undecorated metal. Suitcases are listed here.

Camphorwood, Brassbound & Lockplate, 2 Handles, Chinese, 12 ½ x 30 x 15 In. 527
Camphorwood, Lid Cartouche, Brass Strap, Drop Side Handles, Chinese, 20 x 44 x 22 In. 1170
Camphorwood, Lift Top, Green Leather, Brass Stand & Bail Handles, 1800s, 18 ¾ x 31 x 15 ½ In. 216
Dome Top, Blue Velvet, Woven Geometric Banding, Fringe, France, 1900s, 25 x 30 x 19 In. *illus* 188
Dome Top, Immigrant's, Dovetail Case, Lidded Till, Forged Hardware, 1810s, 20 x 41 x 20 In. 132
Dome Top, Painted, Fruit, Signed, Peter Ompir, 1900s, 24 In. *illus* 148
Dome Top, Pine, Square Nail Construction, Block Printed Wallpaper, Birds, 1886, 13 x 24 In. 330
Dome Top, Red, Blue, Compass Rose, Blue Rope Border, Handles, 1900s, 23 x 40 x 21 ½ In. 96
Hat Box, Round, Leather Handle, Goyard, Monogram, c.1950s, 18 x 20 x 9 ¾ In. 2760
Leather Covered, Black, Brass Tack, 2 Handles, Lock, Key, 1800s, 8 x 20 x 10 In. 101
Leather Covered, Embossed, Crisscrossed Bands, Handles, Locks, Continental, 26 ½ x 38 In. 830
Louis Vuitton, Brass Studs, Leather Trim, Top Handle, Monogram, Stand, 14 x 22 x 15 In. *illus* 4200
Louis Vuitton, Canvas, Marshall Field & Co., Monogram, 1890s-1900s, 25 ½ x 25 x 25 ¾ In. *illus* 10625
Louis Vuitton, Canvas, Trianon Gray, Wood & Metal Strap, Late 1800s, 27 x 45 x 24 In. 2706
Louis Vuitton, Duffel Bag, Keepall Banouliere, Monogram, Leather, 1900s, 12 x 23 x 9 In. 264
Louis Vuitton, Fitted Interior, Faded Pattern, Leather Handles, 3 Trays, 35 ½ x 20 x 20 In. *illus* 2125
Louis Vuitton, Fitted Interior, Tray, Metal Handles, 35 ½ x 20 x 21 In. 7500
Louis Vuitton, Leather, Brass Hardware, Cross Strips, Monogram LV, 12 x 18 x 17 ¾ In. 1375
Louis Vuitton, Shoe Bag, Brown, Tan, Zipper, 8 Pockets, Monogram, 1900s, 12 x 18 x 7 In. *illus* 660
Louis Vuitton, Shoulder Bag, Monogram, Canvas, Cartouchiere, Brown, Strap, 2 Compartments, 30 In. 420
Louis Vuitton, Steamer, Brass Hardware, Wood Slats, c.1910, 21 ¾ x 29 ½ x 19 In. 7605
Louis Vuitton, Steamer, Brown Canvas Exterior, Johne Sloan, Early 1900s, 28 x 48 x 24 In. 360
Louis Vuitton, Suitcase, Brown Monogram, Leather, Gilt Hardware, 1970s, 18 x 27 x 8 In. 2574
Louis Vuitton, Suitcase, Leather Handle, Brass Hardware, Monogram, c.1950, 18 x 28 x 7 In. *illus* 720
Louis Vuitton, Travel Cosmetic Case, Lid, Leather, Light Brown, 9 x 12 ¾ x 8 ¾ In. *illus* 360
Louis Vuitton, Wardrobe, Bracket, 4 Fabric Shoe Compartments, c.1900, 17 x 43 x 21 In. 5400
Pigskin, Red, Gilt, Brass Lock, Iron Handles, Chinese, 1900s, 5 x 10 x 6 In. 72
Pine, 6-Board Construction, Interior Till, Blue, Green, 1860s-80s, 23 x 44 ½ x 21 ½ In. 120
Rosewood, Mother-Of-Pearl Inlay, Geometric, Rectangular, 1800s, 17 x 31 x 16 ½ In. *illus* 720
Seaman's, Carved, Ship, Rope Handles, Marked, Jasen John, 41 ¾ x 20 ½ x 18 In. 207
Steamer, Chevron Canvas, Patinated Locks, 4 Shelves, E. Goyard, 40 ½ x 24 ½ x 21 In. 4997
Steamer, Chrome, Campaign Style, Brown Leather, Buckle Straps, Ralph Lauren, 17 ½ In. *illus* 1955
Storage, Mahogany, Hinged Top, Molded Base, 18 x 31 x 18 In. 176
Travel Case, Doctor's, Leather, Handle, Compartment, Mirror, 1800s, 19 x 12 x 9 In. 148

TUTHILL

Tuthill Cut Glass Company of Middletown, New York, worked from 1902 to 1923. Of special interest are the finely cut pieces of stemware and tableware.

Bowl, Open Petal Pattern, Saw Rim, Signed, 3 x 8 In. 100
Bowl, Primrose & Swirl, Starburst, Engraved Flowers, 3-Footed, 8 ½ In. 115
Bowl, Rex, Cut, Geometric, Clear, 4 x 9 In. *illus* 1200
Compote, Wild Rose Pattern, Engraved Stem & Foot, 7 x 6 ½ In. 150
Dish, Shell Shape, Ribbed, Hobstar, Ruffled Rim, 6 x 6 In. 650

TYPEWRITER

Typewriter collectors divide typewriters into two main classifications: the index machine, which has a pointer and a dial for letter selection, and the keyboard machine, most commonly seen today. The first successful typewriter was made by Sholes and Glidden in 1874.

Coffman, Pocket, Linear Index, Nickel Plated, 1902, 7 ½ x 2 In. *illus* 6650
Draper, Black, Gold Letters, White Keys, c.1898 855
Duplex, Des Moines, Iowa, Double Keyboard, Nickel Plated, 1892 7204
Imperial, Visible Typewriter Mfg. Co., Wisconsin, Sloping Typebar, 1907 *illus* 10391
Lambert Model 3, Lambert Co., N.Y., Single Piece Keyboard, c.1903 1524
Liliput Minima Model A, Index Disc, Lacquered Cast Iron, Germany, 1907 4417
North's Typewriter Mfg., London, Typebar Behind Platen, 1892 12469
Peoples, Index Typewriter, Garvin Machine Co., New York, 1893 1140
Pittsburg Visible No. 10, Pittsburg Writing Machine Co., Interchangeable Bar, 1898 2849
Royal Quiet Deluxe, Gilt Finish, Designed By Henry Dreyfuss, 1948 2494
The Shimer No. 3, Milton, Pa., Black Keys, Carriage Shift, Patented 1891 5542
Travis, Philadelphia Typewriter Co., Typewheel, Patented 1896 10391
Underwood Standard, No. 5, Round Keys, Ruler, Half-Moon Opening, Black, 11 x 12 In. 120
Williams No. 1, Brady Mfg. Co., Brooklyn, Curved 3-Row Keyboard, 1894 8313
Woodstock Electric, G.E. External Motor, Manual Return, c.1925 641

TYPEWRITER RIBBON TIN

Typewriter ribbon tins are now being collected. The lithographed tin containers have been used since the 1870s. Most popular with collectors are tins with pictorial graphics.

American Brand, Hess-Hawkins Co., Brooklyn, NRA Logo 47
Beaver Ribbon, Superb, M.B. Cook Co., Chicago, Ill., Beavers 5
Bucki D & D, Buckeye Ribbon & Carbon Co., Cleveland 30
Caribonum, Purple Box Grade, Gold Trim, London 11
Carter's Guardian, 2 Airplanes, Sky, Carter's Ink Co., Boston, Round 17
Carter's Midnight, Dark Blue, Stars, Galaxy, 2 ½ In. 8
Crystal Brand, J.A. Heale & Co., New York, U.S.A. 90
Elk, Elk's Head Silhouette, Miller, Art Deco Style, Round 10
Herald Square, F.W. Woolworth W Logo, Art Deco Style 13
Keelox Silver Brand, Rochester, N.Y., 2 ¼ In. 3
Monogram Brand, Underwood Corporation, Purple, Silver, Art Deco 8
Panama Standard, Manifold Supplies Inc., Brooklyn 10
The Queen, Crown, Queen Ribbon & Carbon Co., Brooklyn 10
The Webster, Star Brand, F.S. Webster Co., Art Deco Style 15
Type Bar Brand, L.C. Smith & Corona Typewriters, 2 ¾ In. 5 to 10

UMBRELLA

Umbrella collectors like rain or shine. The first known umbrella was owned by King Louis XIII of France in 1637. The earliest umbrellas were sunshades, not designed to be used in the rain. The umbrella was embellished and redesigned many times. In 1852, the fluted steel rib style was developed and it has remained the most useful style.

Bamboo & Lucite Handle, Red Poppy, Tassel, 1950s, 35 In. 95
Brown Plastic Handle, Metal Openwork, Black, 1950s, 33 In. 165
Lucite Handle, Domed Bubble, Clear, Brown Trim, 33 In. 24
Parasol Handle, 14K Gold, Agate, Engraved Etta-Shroyer, 1800s, 8 ¾ In. *illus* 687
Toucan Handle, Yellow & Gray Panels, Aramis Umbrella Co., 34 In. 53
Wood Handle, Brown, Tan, Monogram, Louis Vuitton, 36 In. *illus* 250

Typewriter, Imperial, Visible Typewriter Mfg. Co., Wisconsin, Sloping Typebar, 1907
$10,391

Auction Team Breker

Umbrella, Parasol Handle, 14K Gold, Agate, Engraved Etta-Shroyer, 1800s, 8 ¾ In.
$687

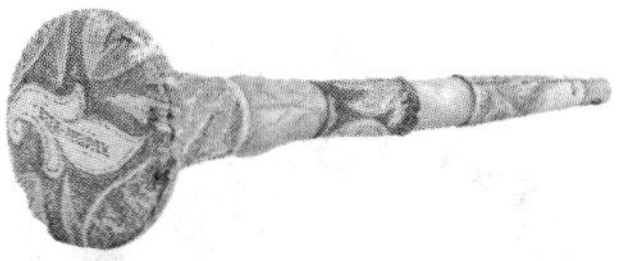

Hindman Auctions

Umbrella, Wood Handle, Brown, Tan, Monogram, Louis Vuitton, 36 In.
$250

Freeman's Auctioneers & Appraisers

TIP

A bed-and-bath type store stocks many of the supplies needed to care for antiques and collectibles. Storage units, cloth hanging bags, repair supplies, gadgets that help in moving furniture, and humidifiers are just a few.

Val St. Lambert, Bucket, Cranberry, Sawtooth Rim, Hobstar Cut Base, c.1908, 6 x 8 In.
$338

Woody Auctions

Val St. Lambert, Cake Stand, Cynthia, 3 Colors, Engraved Flowers, Bull's-Eye, Spokes, c.1925, 4 ¾ x 15 ½ In.
$1,500

Woody Auctions

Val St. Lambert, Cologne Bottle, Cranberry, Clear, Acid Cut, Flowers, Stopper, 5 ¾ In.
$200

Woody Auctions

Val St. Lambert, Decanter, Ariane Pattern, Triangular, Stopper, Cranberry Cut, Ray Base, c.1908, 15 ½ In.
$400

Woody Auctions

Val St. Lambert, Decanter, Cranberry Glass, Cut To Clear, Charles Graffart, c.1930, 6 x 9 In.
$152

Cordier Auctions

Val St. Lambert, Paperweight, Cranberry To Clear, 3-Sided, Diamond, Fan & Bull's-Eye, Hobstar Base, 2 x 4 In.
$200

Woody Auctions

Val St. Lambert, Vase, Cranberry, Slender Shape, Tooled Scalloped Rim, 1890-1910, 5 ½ In., Pair
$424

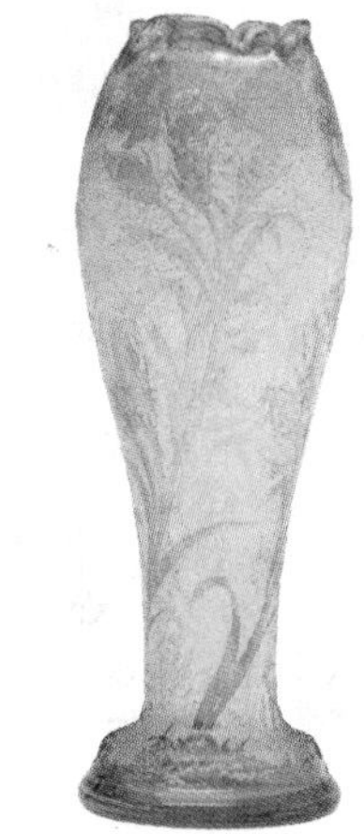

Soulis Auctions

Val St. Lambert, Vase, Yellow Cut To Clear, Ray Cut Base, c.1908, 18 In.
$300

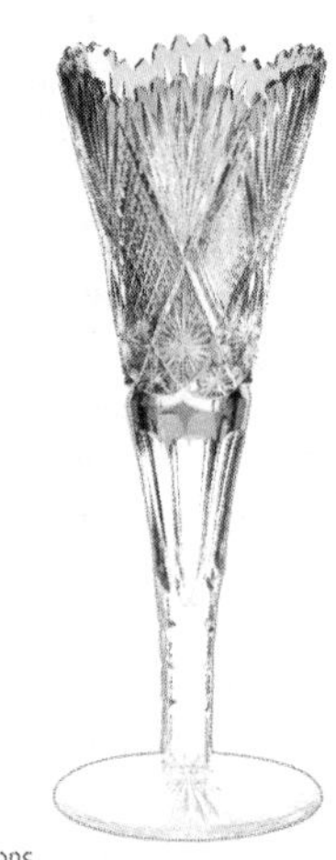

Woody Auctions

Val St. Lambert, Wine, Green Cut To Clear, Notched Hollow Stem, Hobstar Foot, c.1905, 7 ¾ In., Pair
$300

Woody Auctions

UNION PORCELAIN WORKS

Union Porcelain Works was originally William Boch & Brothers, located in Greenpoint, New York. Thomas C. Smith bought the company in 1861 and renamed it Union Porcelain Works. The company went through a series of ownership changes and finally closed about 1922. The company made a fine quality white porcelain that was often decorated in clear, bright colors. Don't confuse this company with its competitor, Charles Cartlidge and Company, also in Greenpoint.

Oyster Plate, 4 Wells, Sauce, Crab Claw, Snail, Mussel, 1881, 9 x 7 In. 250
Oyster Plate, 6 Wells, Crabs, Fish, Seaweed, Seahorse, Round, 9 In. 560
Oyster Plate, 6 Wells, Red Lobster Claw, Frog, Clam Shape, Sauce Shell, 10 ½ In. 354
Oyster Shooter, Sauce Shell, Ribbing Top, 1886, 1 x 4 In. 375

UNIVERSITY CITY POTTERY

University City Pottery, of University City, Missouri, worked from 1909 to 1915. Well-known artists, including Taxile Doat, Adelaide Alsop Robineau, and Frederick Hurten Rhead, worked there.

Vase, Gourd Shape, Celadon, Ivory, Blue Crystalline Glaze, Marked, 1913, 7 ½ In. 27500

UNIVERSITY OF NORTH DAKOTA, *see North Dakota School of Mines category.*

VAL ST. LAMBERT

Val St. Lambert

Val St. Lambert Cristalleries of Belgium was founded by Messieurs Kemlin and Lelievre in 1825. The company is still in operation. All types of table glassware and decorative glassware have been made. Pieces are often decorated with cut designs.

Bucket, Cranberry, Sawtooth Rim, Hobstar Cut Base, c.1908, 6 x 8 In. .... *illus* 338
Cake Stand, Cynthia, 3 Colors, Engraved Flowers, Bull's-Eye, Spokes, c.1925, 4 ¾ x 15 ½ In. ... *illus* 1500
Cologne Bottle, Cranberry, Clear, Acid Cut, Flowers, Stopper, 5 ¾ In. .... *illus* 200
Decanter, Amethyst Cut, Vaseline, Tosca, Stopper, c.1908, 15 In. 2750
Decanter, Ariane Pattern, Triangular, Stopper, Cranberry Cut, Ray Base, c.1908, 15 ½ In. ... *illus* 400
Decanter, Ball Shape Stopper, Cranberry, Triple Notched Handle, Hobstar Base, c.1908, 7 ¾ In. 540
Decanter, Cranberry Glass, Cut To Clear, Charles Graffart, c.1930, 6 x 9 In. .... *illus* 152
Decanter, Pedestal, Balmoral Shape, Yellow To Clear, Stopper, 13 In. 360
Decanter, Pyramid Shape, Amethyst Cut, Stopper, Hobstar Base, c.1908, 17 ¾ In. 600
Goblet, Abbey, Cranberry, Bull's-Eye & Star, Petticoat Foot, c.1920, 6 ½ In. 96
Ice Bucket, Cranberry Cut To Clear, 2 Handles, Hobstar Base, c.1908, 7 In. 225
Paperweight, Cranberry To Clear, 3-Sided, Diamond, Fan & Bull's-Eye, Hobstar Base, 2 x 4 In. *illus* 200
Tankard, Cranberry, Strawberry Diamond, Fan, Ray Cut Base, 13 ¾ In. 225
Tumble-Up, Cranberry Cut To Clear, Hobstar Base, c.1908, 7 In. 800
Vase, Amethyst, Verdi Pattern, Hobstar Foot, c.1908, 11 In. 180
Vase, Copper Overlay, Cobalt Blue Interior, 11 ½ In., Pair 246
Vase, Cranberry, Slender Shape, Tooled Scalloped Rim, 1890-1910, 5 ½ In., Pair .... *illus* 424
Vase, Trumpet Shape, Cranberry Cut To Clear, Ray Cut Base, c.1908, 10 In. 250
Vase, Yellow Cut To Clear, Ray Cut Base, c.1908, 18 In. .... *illus* 300
Wine Cooler, Fancy Cut, Side Handles, Signed, 9 ½ In. 92
Wine Glass, Orange Cut To Clear, Notched Teardrop Stem, Ray Base, 8 In., Pair 175
Wine, Green Cut To Clear, Notched Hollow Stem, Hobstar Foot, c.1905, 7 ¾ In., Pair .... *illus* 300
Wine, Louise, Ray Cut Foot, Cranberry Cut To Clear, c.1906, 4 ½ In. 60
Wine, Saarbrucken, Ruby, Airtrap Notched Stem, Scalloped Hobstar Foot, 7 ¾ In. 120

VALLERYSTHAL GLASSWORKS

Vallerysthal

Vallerysthal Glassworks was founded in 1836 in Lorraine, France. In 1854, the firm became Klenglin et Cie. It made table and decorative glass, opaline, cameo, and art glass. A line of covered, pressed glass animal dishes was made in the nineteenth century. The firm is still working.

Vase, Grapevine Design, Cameo, 9 ½ In. 103

Van Briggle, Bowl, Swirl Leaf, Ming Turquoise Glaze, Marked, Logo, 5 x 6 ½ In.
$63

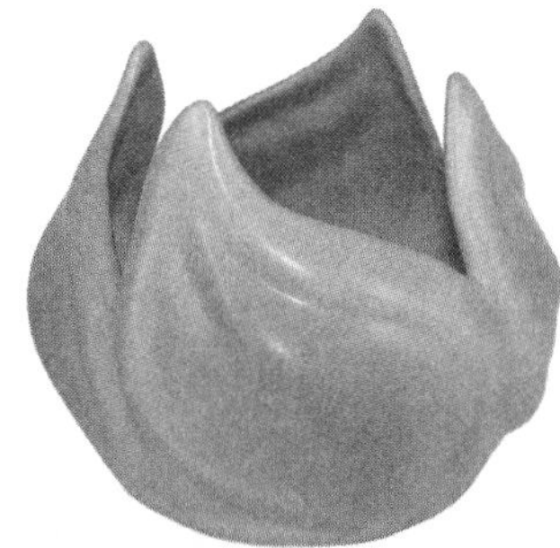

Belhorn Auction Services

TIP
Wear rubber gloves when handling bleaching materials, strong solvents, or other harsh chemicals.

Van Briggle, Figurine, Indian Maiden, Grinding Corn, Ming Turquoise Glaze, 5 x 6 In.
$184

Belhorn Auction Services

Van Briggle, Tile, Green Glaze, Leaves, Frame, 1911, 11 In.
$375

Treadway

U V

Van Briggle, Vase, 3 Indian Heads, Long Braids, Turquoise Glaze, Flaring Base, Round Rim, 12 In.
$340

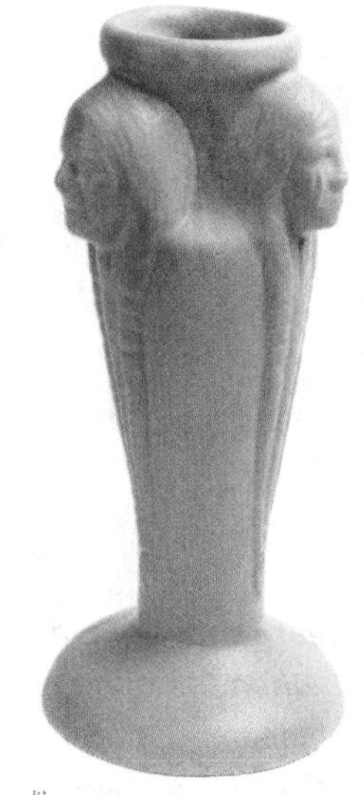

Witherell's

TIP

Keep a "mystery disaster" box. If you find a piece of veneer, an old screw, or even a porcelain rosebud, put it into the box until you are able to make the necessary repairs.

Van Briggle, Vase, Lorelei, Woman, Flowing Hair, Aqua Green Matte Glaze, 10 x 5 ¾ In.
$210

Witherell's

VAN BRIGGLE POTTERY

Van Briggle Pottery was started by Artus Van Briggle in Colorado Springs, Colorado, after 1901. Van Briggle had been a decorator at Rookwood Pottery of Cincinnati, Ohio. He died in 1904 and his wife took over managing the pottery. One of the employees, Kenneth Stevenson, took over the company in 1969. He died in 1990 and his wife, Bertha, and son, Craig, ran the pottery. She died in 2010. The pottery closed in 2012. The wares usually have modeled relief decorations and a soft, matte glaze.

Bowl, Green Glaze, Incised 1902, 4 ¾ x 5 ¾ In. 2500
Bowl, Swirl Leaf, Ming Turquoise Glaze, Marked, Logo, 5 x 6 ½ In. ....*illus* 63
Figurine, Indian Maiden, Grinding Corn, Ming Turquoise Glaze, 5 x 6 In. ....*illus* 184
Lamp, Horse, Brown Glaze, Cream Shade, Butterflies, 16 In. 83
Lamp, Mulberry Glaze, Butterfly Shades, 1950s, 23 x 15 In., Pair 678
Lampshade, Copper, Floral Shape Reserves, Fabric Lining, 7 ½ x 15 In. 4612
Mug, Leaves, Brown, Handle, 4 ½ x 5 In. 1063
Pitcher, Hand Thrown, Lilac Blue, Hand Incised Flowers, Marked, Logo, 8 In. 69
Tile, Green Glaze, Leaves, Frame, 1911, 11 In. ....*illus* 375
Vase, 3 Graces, Nude Figure, Ming Turquoise Glaze, Molded, Logo, 16 ½ In. 426
Vase, 3 Indian Heads, Long Braids, Turquoise Glaze, Flaring Base, Round Rim, 12 In. ....*illus* 340
Vase, 3 Indian Heads, Mountain Craig Glaze, Brown, c.1920, 11 x 5 In. 311
Vase, Lorelei, Woman, Flowing Hair, Aqua Green Matte Glaze, 10 x 5 ¾ In. ....*illus* 210
Vase, Lorelei, Woman, Hair Flows Over Rim, White Matte Glaze, 11 x 5 In. 190
Vase, Narrow Mouth, Stylized Flower Buds, Low Handles, Wide Base, 18 x 8 In. 1625

VASELINE GLASS

Vaseline glass is a greenish-yellow glassware resembling petroleum jelly. Pressed glass of the 1870s was often made of vaseline-colored glass. Some vaseline glass is still being made in old and new styles. The glass fluoresces under ultraviolet light. Additional pieces of vaseline glass may also be listed under Pressed Glass in this book.

Epergne, Opalescent, 3 Hanging Baskets, Mirror Base, 14 ½ x 10 In. 480
Pickle Castor, Silver Plate Frame, Fans, C-Scrolls, Finial, Marked Bersh, 11 In. 180
Pitcher, Opalescent, Reverse Swirl, Ball Shape Stopper, 6 ½ In. 84
Vase, Apple Green, Diamond Cut, Flared Rim, c.1920, 11 ½ In. 275

VENETIAN GLASS, *see Glass-Venetian category.*

VENINI GLASS, *see Glass-Venetian category.*

VERLYS

Verlys glass was made in Rouen, France, by the Societe Holophane Français, a company that started in 1920. It was made in Newark, Ohio, from 1935 to 1951. The art glass is either blown or molded. The American glass is signed with a diamond-point-scratched name, but the French pieces are marked with a molded signature. The designs resemble those used by Lalique.

Dresser Box, Art Deco Raised Butterflies, Blue Satin, Ormolu Center Knob, Signed, 7 In. *illus* 316
Vase, Clear Glass, Frosted, Lovebirds, Footed, 4 ½ x 6 ½ In. 40

VERNON KILNS

Vernon Kilns was the name used by Vernon Potteries, Ltd. The company, which started in 1912 in Vernon, California, was originally called Poxon China. In 1931 the company was sold and renamed Vernon Kilns. It made dinnerware and figurines. It went out of business in 1953. The molds were bought by Metlox, which continued to make some patterns. Collectors search for the brightly colored dinnerware and the pieces designed by Rockwell Kent, Walt Disney, and Don Blanding. For more prices, go to kovels.com.

Fantasia, Figurine, Centaurette, Yellow Hair & Tail, 1940, 18 In. 396
Frontier Days, Plate, Dinner, 1950s, 10 In. 99
Salamina, Plate, Giant Woman Holding Flowers, 2 Birds, c.1935, 9 ½ In. 87
Ultra California, Salt & Pepper, Pink Carnation, c.1940, 2 ⅜ x 2 ¼ In. 32
Ultra California, Serving Bowl, Pink Carnation, c.1940, 8 In. 35

VERRE DE SOIE

Verre de soie glass was first made by Frederick Carder at the Steuben Glass Works from about 1905 to 1930. It is an iridescent glass of soft white or very, very pale green. The name means "glass of silk," and it does resemble silk. Other factories have made verre de soie, and some of the English examples were made of different colors. Verre de soie is an art glass and is not related to the iridescent, pressed, white carnival glass mistakenly called by its name. Related pieces may be found in the Steuben category.

Bowl, Cyprian, Celeste Blue, Footed, Polished Pontil, 2 ½ x 9 ¾ In. 216
Bowl, Dragon, Yellow, White, Orange, Blue, 2 ¼ x 4 In. 1476
Cologne Bottle, Selenium Red Stopper, 4 ¾ In. 156
Salt, Iridescent, 1 ½ x 2 In. 72

VIENNA, *see Beehive category.*

VIENNA ART

VIENNA ART PLATES PAT. FEB. 21ST 1905

Vienna Art plates are round lithographed metal serving trays produced at the turn of the century. The designs, copied from Royal Vienna porcelain plates, usually featured a portrait of a woman encircled by a wide, ornate border. Many were used as advertising or promotional items and were produced in Coshocton, Ohio, by J. F. Meeks Tuscarora Advertising Co. and H.D. Beach's Standard Advertising Co. Some are listed in Advertising in this book.

Plate, Woman, Brown Hair, Red Hat, Green Jewels Border, Kellermeyer's Grocery, 10 In. 85
Plate, Woman, Gold Hat, Brown Hair, Hoop Earrings, Blue Border, H.D. Beach Co., 10 In. 184
Plate, Woman, Long Blond Hair, Gold Border, 9 ½ In. 95

VILLEROY & BOCH POTTERY

V.&B.

Villeroy & Boch Pottery of Mettlach was founded in 1836. The firm made many types of wares, including the famous Mettlach steins. Collectors can be confused because although Villeroy & Boch made most of its pieces in the city of Mettlach, Germany, the company also had factories in other locations. The dating code impressed on the bottom of most pieces makes it possible to determine the age of the piece. Additional items, including steins and earthenware pieces marked with the famous castle mark or the word *Mettlach*, may be found in the Mettlach category.

Vase, Jugenstil, Incised, Blue Cornflowers, Red & Yellow Ground, c.1899, 12 ½ In. 86
Vase, Oval, Mint Green Ground, 2 Nude Male Archers, c.1930, 12 ½ In. .... *illus* 431
Vase, Pedestal, Flared Neck, Incised Band, Infants In Various Activities, c.1885, 12 ½ In. 165

VOLKMAR POTTERY

VOLKMAR Corona N.Y

Volkmar Pottery was made by Charles Volkmar of New York from 1879 to about 1911. He was associated with several firms, including the Volkmar Ceramic Company, Volkmar and Cory, and Charles Volkmar and Son. He was hired by Durant

Verlys, Dresser Box, Art Deco Raised Butterflies, Blue Satin, Ormolu Center Knob, Signed, 7 In.
$316

Richard D. Hatch & Associates

Villeroy & Boch, Vase, Oval, Mint Green Ground, 2 Nude Male Archers, c.1930, 12 ½ In.
$431

Skinner, Inc.

Walrath, Vase, Blue, Stylized White Flowers, Long Stems, Incised, c.1912, 8 ½ In.
$12,500

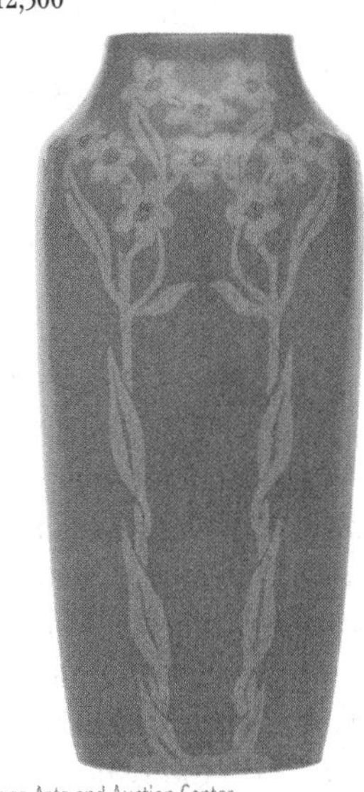

Rago Arts and Auction Center

U V

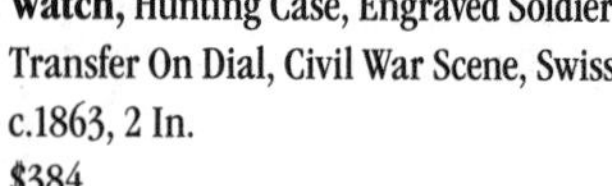

Watch, Hunting Case, Engraved Soldier, Transfer On Dial, Civil War Scene, Swiss, c.1863, 2 In.
$384

Schmitt Horan & Co.

Watch, Open Face, 17 Jewel, 14K Gold, Hinged Back & Bezel, Stem Wind, Swiss, c.1920, Pocket
$708

Schmitt Horan & Co.

Watch, P. Leyland, Open Face, 14K Gold, Engine Turned, Scalloped, Liverpool, c.1820, 2 In.
$1,062

Schmitt Horan & Co.

TIP

If you accidentally drop a vintage watch in water, take it to a professional jeweler immediately. If you can't do that, take the back off the watch and dry it with a hair dryer set on low.

Kilns of Bedford Village, New York, in 1910 to oversee production. Volkmar bought the business and after 1930 only the Volkmar name was used as a mark. Volkmar had been a painter, and his designs often look like oil paintings drawn on pottery.

Vase, Cows, Watering, Landscape, Multicolor, Gilt Bronze Mounts, 17 ¾ In., Pair 1845
Vase, Royal Blue, Bulbous Bottom, Narrow Neck, 7 In. 312

VOLKSTEDT

Volkstedt was a soft-paste porcelain factory started in 1760 by Georg Heinrich Macheleid at Volkstedt, Thuringia. Volkstedt-Rudolstadt was a porcelain factory started at Volkstedt-Rudolstadt by Beyer and Bock in 1890. Most pieces seen in shops today are from the later factory.

Candlestick, Blue, White Cherub & Flowers, 8 In. 454
Figurine, Scantily Clad Woman, Sitting On Chair, Legs Crossed, Hand To Head, 7 In. 5365
Group, Child Chess Players, Marked, Blue Crown, 1920s, 7 x 5 x 5 In. 345
Group, Musical Scene, Women, Man, Colonial Costumes, 15 ½ x 22 x 14 In. 1476

WADE

Wade pottery is made by the Wade Group of Potteries started in 1810 near Burslem, England. Several potteries merged to become George Wade & Son, Ltd., early in the twentieth century, and other potteries have been added through the years. The best-known Wade pieces are the small figurines called Whimsies. They were first were made in 1954. Special Whimsies were given away with Red Rose Tea beginning in 1967. The Disney figures are listed in this book in the Disneyana category.

Ashtray, Horse & Carriage Scene, Olive & Blue Glaze, 6 In. 18
Candleholder, Lion Cub, Tan, Black Base, 1957, 2 x 3 In. 35
Decanter, White & Wine Glaze, Gilt Trim, Oval, Screw Top, Front Tap, W & A Gilbey 24
Figurine, Train Station, Whimsey-On-Why, No. 3, 1 ½ x 1 ½ In. 22
Group, Parakeets, Yellow, Green Tan, On Branch, Marked, c.1939, 7 ½ x 5 x 3 In. 399
Mug, Country Village, Irish Lass, 4 ¼ x 3 ¼ In. 14
Teapot, Genie, Green Turban, Red Waist Vest, Copper Luster, 8 x 10 In. 175

WALL POCKET

Wall pocketswere popular in the 1930s. They were made by many American and European factories. Glass, pottery, porcelain, majolica, chalkware, and metal wall pockets can be found in many fanciful shapes.

Cornucopia Shape, Mahogany, Red Dot, Decoration, Applied Leaves, Mounted, 1800s, 10 x 13 In. 1476
Heart Shape, Painted, Green & Orange Splotch, White Ground, Late 1800s, 10 ½ x 10 In. 492

WALLACE NUTTING *photographs are listed under Print, Nutting. His reproduction furniture is listed under Furniture.*

WALRATH

Walrath was a potter who worked in New York City; Rochester, New York; and at the Newcomb Pottery in New Orleans, Louisiana. Frederick Walrath died in 1920. Pieces listed here are from his Rochester period.

Flower Bowl, Nude, Seated At Center, Blue Glaze, Incised, c.1910, 7 x 6 ⅓ In. 390
Paperweight, Sea Turtle, Dark Green & Black Mottled Glaze, Incised Signature, 4 ½ x 3 In. 300
Vase, Blue, Stylized White Flowers, Long Stems, Incised, c.1912, 8 ½ In. ..... *illus* 12500

WALT DISNEY, *see Disneyana category.*

WALTER, *see A. Walter category.*

WARWICK

Warwick china was made in Wheeling, West Virginia, in a pottery working from 1887 to 1951. Many pieces were made with hand painted or decal decorations. The most familiar Warwick has a shaded brown background. The name *Warwick* is part of the mark and sometimes the mysterious word *IOGA* is also included.

Pitcher, Hibiscus, Brown Tones, 7 ½ In. 50
Tankard, Monk, Eating, Drinking, 12 In. 30
Vase, Flowers, Tapered Brown Edges, 12 x 3 In. 65
Vase, Nasturtium Blossoms, Leaves, Clover Shape, c.1900, 10 ½ x 5 ½ In. 250
Vase, Poinsettia Blossoms, Stick, Red, Brown, 12 In. 79

WATCH

Watches small enough to fit in a man's pocket were important in Victorian times. It wasn't until World War I that the wristwatch was used. All types of watches are collected: silver, gold, or plated. Watches are listed here by company name or by style. Wristwatches are a separate category.

Agassiz, Chronometer, Open Face, Gold Filled, Seconds, 2 In., Pocket 549
American Watch Co., Hunting Case, P.S. Bartlett, 14K Gold, Roman Numerals, Porcelain Dial, 2 In. 1599
Ancre, 14K Gold, Black Hour Numbers, Spade Hands, Sub Seconds Dial, 2 In., Pocket 787
Breitling, Open Face, Chronograph, 18 Jewel, Nickel Case, Black Metal Dial, 1950s 497
Douglas Ralph Samuel, Open Face, 18K Gold, Roman Numerals, Seconds Dial, Pocket 984
E. Howard & Co., Open Face, 14K Gold, Arabic Numeral Porcelain Dial, Sunk Seconds, 2 In... 800
Elgin, 14K Gold, Octagonal, 17 Jewels, Fancy Case, Pocket 344
Elgin, Hunting Case, 14K Gold, 17 Jewel, 1 ⅞ In., Pocket 805
Elgin, Open Face, 21 Jewel, Veritas, Gold Filled Case, Enamel Dial, c.1908, Pocket 234
Gudin, Open Face, Gold Plated, Roman Numerals, Outer No., Paris 4440, 1 ½ In., Pocket 610
Hamilton, Open Face, 17 Jewel, Engraved Silver Plate Fob, Case, c.1930, 3 ¾ x 4 In. 240
Hamilton, Open Face, Railway Special Model 5, 21 Jewel, Gold Filled Case, c.1952, Pocket 234
Hunting Case, Engraved Soldier, Transfer On Dial, Civil War Scene, Swiss, c.1863, 2 In. *illus* 384
James Allan & Co., Enameled Dial, Roman Numerals, Charleston, Chain, 1 ¾ In. 177
Longines, 14K Gold, Pearls, Enamel Face, Woman's, Pocket 311
M.J. Tobias, Hunting Case, Portrait Of Washington, Flowers, 18K Gold, England, 1800s, 2 In.. 1719
Nugent Wells, Hunting Case, 18K, Roman Numerals, Outer Minute Track, Sunk Seconds, 2 In. 1599
Omega, 14K Yellow Gold, Open Face, 17 Jewel, Baton Hour Marker, Pocket, Swiss, 1 ¾ In. 8666
Open Face, 17 Jewel, 14K Gold, Hinged Back & Bezel, Stem Wind, Swiss, c.1920, Pocket ..*illus* 708
Open Face, White Enamel Face, Black Numbers, Engraved, Admiral John Paul Jones, 2 ½ In., Pocket.. 859
P. Leyland, Open Face, 14K Gold, Engine Turned, Scalloped, Liverpool, c.1820, 2 In. ......*illus* 1062
Patek Philippe, Open Face, 18K Gold, Monogram, Sunk Enamel Dial, Pocket ....*illus* 2596
Patek Philippe, Open Face, 18K Gold, Roman Numerals, Outer Minute Track, 2 In. 3075
Patek Philippe, Open Face, 18K Yellow Gold, Silver Dial, Hours, Minutes, Seconds, 1 ¾ In...... 4200
Patek Philippe, Open Face, Stainless Steel, Crown Set, 18 Jewel, 1 ¾ In. 2250
Pendant, Fabr Suisse Einice, Enamel Dial, Putti, Roman Numerals, Floral Fabric, Woman's, 7 In. 144
South Bend, The Studebaker, 21 Jewel, 14K Gold Display Case, Early 1918, 1 ¾ In., Pocket...... 540
Vacheron & Konstantin Geneve, Open Face, 18K, Roman Numerals, Porcelain Dial, 2 In. ... 3198
Waltham, 14K Gold, Roman Numerals, C.W.C. Co., Woman's, 1 ⅜ In., Pocket..........*illus* 339
Waltham, Hunting Case, 14K Gold, Scenic, Roman Numerals, Blue Spade Hand, Pocket.......... 523
Waltham, Open Face, 17 Jewel, 14K Gold, Damascening, Seconds, Box, c.1885, Pocket ....*illus* 20060
Waltham, Open Face, 21 Jewel, 24-Hour Enamel Dial, c.1908, Pocket..........*illus* 222
Watch Holder, House Shape, Peak, Square Door, Circular Opening, Red, 1800s, 5 x 4 ¾ In.... 1599
Watch Holder, Tall Case Clock, Walnut, Whalebone & Walrus Ivory, c.1850, 11 ½ In. .....*illus* 510
William Comyns & Sons Ltd., London, Silver Case, Roman Numerals, 6 ¾ x 5 ¾ x 2 In., Pocket... 484

WATCH FOB

Watch fobs were worn on watch chains. They were popular during Victorian times and after. Many styles, especially advertising designs, are still made today.

Cornucopia, Mother-Of-Pearl, Red Stones, Gold Filled Chain, Victorian, 5 In. 135

Watch, Patek Philippe, Open Face, 18K Gold, Monogram, Sunk Enamel Dial, Pocket
$2,596

Schmitt Horan & Co.

Watch, Waltham, 14K Gold, Roman Numerals, C.W.C. Co., Woman's, 1 ⅜ In., Pocket
$339

Hartzell's Auction Gallery Inc.

Watch, Waltham, Open Face, 17 Jewel, 14K Gold, Damascening, Seconds, Box, c.1885, Pocket
$20,060

Schmitt Horan & Co.

Watch, Waltham, Open Face, 21 Jewel, 24-Hour Enamel Dial, c.1908, Pocket
$222

Jeffrey S. Evans & Associates

Watch, Watch Holder, Tall Case Clock, Walnut, Whalebone & Walrus Ivory, c.1850, 11 ½ In.
$510

Eldred's

Waterford, Bowl, Crystal Kings, Leaf Rim, Vertical, Diamond Cut Bands, Footed, 6 ⅞ x 10 In.
$230

Blackwell Auctions

Edwardian, Carnelian Intaglio Gemstone, Soldier, 14K Gold, 1 ¾ In. 225
Faux Ruby, Baroque Open Work, 10K Gold, 1 In. 160
Hair, Forget-Me-Not, Enamel, Seed Pearls, 9K Gold, ⅞ In. 550
Silver, Rope Chain, Swivel Clasp, Sodalite, c.1900, 24 In. 175

WATERFORD

Waterford type glass resembles the famous glass made from 1783 to 1851 in the Waterford Glass Works in Ireland. It is a clear glass that was often decorated by cutting. Modern glass is being made again in Waterford, Ireland, and is marketed under the name Waterford. Waterford merged with Wedgwood in 1986 to form the Waterford Wedgwood Group. Most Waterford Wedgwood assets were bought by KPS Capital Partners of New York in 2009 and became part of WWRD Holdings. WWRD was bought by Fiskars Group in 2015 and Waterford is now a brand owned by Fiskars.

Bowl, Crystal Kings, Leaf Rim, Vertical, Diamond Cut Bands, Footed, 6 ⅞ x 10 In. .... *illus* 230
Bowl, Hatched, Low, Signed, 3 ½ x 8 In. 68
Bowl, Oval, Sawtooth Rim, Signed, 4 x 13 ¾ x 9 ¾ In. 259
Bowl, Pedestal Base, Diamond Band, Interlocking Swirl Design, 9 ½ x 11 In. 90
Cake Plate, Wheel Cut, Strawberry Diamond, Lismore, 12 ½ In. 89
Champagne, Happiness Pattern, Wheel Cut Glass, Ireland, 2000, 9 In., 6 Piece 325
Claret, Kildare, Clear Wheel Cut Glass, Faceted Stems, 6 ½ In., 24 Piece 472
Decanter, Lismore, Glass, Ball Stopper, Signed, 12 In. 115
Goblet, Lismore, Wheel Cut Glass, Circular Base, Signed, 6 ½ In., 12 Piece 543
Punch Bowl, Laurel Garland, Flared Rim, Footed, Crosshatch, Irish Gothic Font, 1900s, 12 In. 472
Sherbet, Lismore, Wheel Cut Glass, Star, Signed, 3 In., 6 Piece 165
Tumbler, Iced Tea, Uncut Feet, Colleen Short, 1783, 6 ½ In., 8 Piece 472
Vase, Sinclair, Clear Cut, Ruffled Rim, Round Base, Limited Edition, Marked, 13 In. 489
Wine Coaster, Millennium, Vertical Line, Star, Wheat Bundle, Starburst, Sign, 3 ½ x 5 ¼ In. 112

WATT

Watt family members bought the Globe pottery of Crooksville, Ohio, in 1922. They made pottery mixing bowls and tableware of the type made by Globe. In 1935 they changed the production and made the pieces with the freehand decorations that are popular with collectors today. Apple, Starflower, Rooster, Tulip, and Autumn Foliage are the best-known patterns. Pansy, also called Rio Rose, was the earliest pattern. Apple, the most popular pattern, can be dated from the leaves. Originally, the apples had three leaves; after 1958 two leaves were used. The plant closed in 1965. Reproductions of Apple, Dutch Tulip, Rooster, and Tulip have been made. For more prices, go to kovels.com.

Apple, Bowl, 3-Leaf, No. 64, 7 x 4 ¾ In. 42
Apple, Casserole, Tab Handle, No. 18, 2 ½ x 5 In. 60
Apple, Grease Jar, 3-Leaf, No. 1, 5 ½ x 5 In. 240
Apple, Mixing Bowl, 2-Leaf, No. 6 75
Apple, Mug, White Ground, 3 ¾ In. 89
Arches, Mixing Bowl, Pumpkin, No. 9, 9 ½ x 5 In. 35
Cabinart, Pitcher, Lid, Brown & Tan Glaze, Applied Handle, 1940s, 6 In. 24
Cherry, Cookie Jar, Lid, Leaves, Red Flower, No. 21, 7 ½ x 7 In. 200
Pansy, Bowl, Spaghetti, No. 39, 13 x 3 In. 26
Pansy, Pitcher, 2-Leaf, Beige Ground, Purple Flower, 6 ½ x 5 In. 48
Rooster, Ice Bucket, Lid, 5 ¾ x 7 ½ In. 250
Rooster, Ice Bucket, Lid, Yellow Ground, Red, Black, Green, 8 x 7 In. 250
Rooster, Mixing Bowl, No. 65, 5 ¾ x 9 In. 65
Rooster, Pitcher, No. 15 75
Star, Pitcher, No. 17, 7 ½ In. 95
Starflower, Baker, No. 60 38

Starflower, Cookie Jar, Lid, 5-Leaf, No. 21 200
Starflower, Mixing Bowl, Ribbed, No. 4 55
Starflower, Mixing Bowl, Ribbed, No. 5 50
Starflower, Mug, Barrel Shape, No. 501 115
Tear Drop, Bean Pot, Individual, No. 75, 2 ½ x 3 ½ In. 30
Tulip, Pitcher, No. 15, 5 In. 140
Tulip, Pitcher, No. 62, 4 ½ In. 125

WAVE CREST

WAVE CREST WARE

Wave Crest glass is an opaque white glassware manufactured by the Pairpoint Manufacturing Company of New Bedford, Massachusetts, and some French factories. It was decorated by the C.F. Monroe Company of Meriden, Connecticut. The glass was painted in pastel colors and decorated with flowers. The name Wave Crest was used starting in 1892.

Biscuit Jar, Egg Crate, Flowers, Silver Plate Lid, Mounted, 8 x 10 In. 102
Dresser Box, Flowers, Blue, White Ground, Brass Foot, C.F. Monroe, 6 ¾ x 7 ½ In. ....*illus* 288
Dresser Box, Hinged Lid, Round, Swirl Mold, Pink & White Ground, Gilt Feet, 6 x 7 In. ..*illus* 180
Dresser Box, Rectangular, Pink Flowers, Leaves, Gilt Frame Lid, 4 x 6 In. 95
Ewer, White Ground, Flowers & Leaves, Gilt, Woman's Head Handle, 6 ½ In. 130
Glove Box, Yellow, White Tones, Pink Rose, Gilt Metal Feet, 5 ¾ x 9 ¾ In. 350
Jewelry Box, Footed, Metal Bottom, White Ground, Gold Interior, 6 ½ x 7 In. ....*illus* 165
Vase, Urn Shape, Bronze Handles, White Daisies, Signed, 11 In. 374
Vase, White & Cream Ground, Flowers, Enamel, Gilt, Paw Feet, Signed, 10 In. 84

WEAPON

Weapons listed here include instruments of combat other than guns, knives, rifles, or swords and clothing worn in combat. Firearms made after 1900 are not listed in this book. Knives and Swords are listed in their own categories.

Cannon Ball, Gettysburg, Engraved, Wood Base, Edward Woodward, c.1863, 12 Lb. 2829
Cannon, Salute, 70 Bore, Gray Green, Painted, Steel Carriage, c.1915, 25 In. ....*illus* 615

WEATHER VANE

Weather vanes were used in seventeenth-century Boston. The direction of the wind was an indication of coming weather, important to the seafaring and farming communities. By the mid-nineteenth century, commercial weather vanes were made of metal. Many were shaped like animals. Ethan Allen, Dexter, and St. Julian are famous horses that were depicted. Today's collectors often consider weather vanes to be examples of folk art, even though they may not have been handmade.

Arrow & Star, Copper, Tail Feather, Ball Finial, 1800s, 34 In. ....*illus* 1586
Arrow, Copper, Zinc Tip, Gilded, Black Base, Late 1800s, 22 ½ x 36 In. 780
Banner, Boston Style, Reticulated, Spherical Finial, Black Stand, 1800s, 38 ½ x 32 In. 410
Banner, Lyre, Cutout Design, Cast Arrowhead, 37 ½ x 10 In. 384
Bear, Walking, Arrow, Copper, 36 x 16 In. ....*illus* 590
Beaver, Maple Leaf, Sheet Metal, Steel Rod, Stand, Canada, Early 1900s, 28 x 17 In. ......*illus* 4973
Bird, Ceramic, White, Painted, Hinged Directionals, Wood Base, Late 1900s, 26 x 16 x 7 In. 177
Blackhawk, Running, Full Body, Molded Sheet, Copper, Verdigris, Late 1800s, 20 x 26 In. 1230
Butterfly, Pierced, Sheet Metal, Finial, 26 x 21 ½ In. 738
Cockerel, Full Body, Curved Pointed Beak, Molded, Cast Feet, Talons, 15 x 15 x 3 In. 4500
Cockerel, Swelled Body, Copper, Gold Paint, 1800s, 22 In. ....*illus* 1464
Codfish, Copper, Molded, Wood Base, 1900s, 17 x 44 In. 523
Cow, Copper, Molded, Flattened, Full Body, Cast Horns, Verdigris Patina, Late 1800s, 28 In. 1353
Cow, Fiske Type, Queen Of Oneida, Wood Base, Stand, 33 x 22 In. 3540
Cow, Full Body, Copper, Cast Zinc, Iron Head, Harris & Co., Boston, Late 1800s, 23 x 25 In. 5040
Cow, Standing, Full Body, Steel, Silver Paint, Stand, 1800s, 21 ½ x 25 In. 403

TIP

When you open your windows in warm weather, watch out for blowing curtains. They may hit glass or china displayed nearby and cause damage.

Wave Crest, Dresser Box, Flowers, Blue, White Ground, Brass Foot, C.F. Monroe, 6 ¾ x 7 ½ In.
$288

Blackwell Auctions

Wave Crest, Dresser Box, Hinged Lid, Round, Swirl Mold, Pink & White Ground, Gilt Feet, 6 x 7 In.
$180

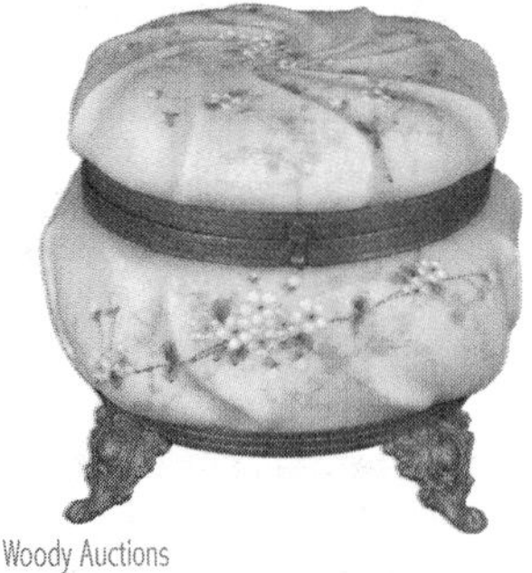

Woody Auctions

Wave Crest, Jewelry Box, Footed, Metal Bottom, White Ground, Gold Interior, 6 ½ x 7 In.
$165

Bunch Auctions

W

TIP

Don't take your car to a flea market if you have another option take your van, truck, or station wagon when you go to a farm auction, flea market, or out-of-town show. You never know when you'll find the dining room table of your dreams.

Weapon, Cannon, Salute, 70 Bore, Gray Green, Painted, Steel Carriage, c.1915, 25 In.
$615

Skinner, Inc.

Weather Vane, Arrow & Star, Copper, Tail Feather, Ball Finial, 1800s, 34 In.
$1,586

Pook & Pook

Weather Vane, Bear, Walking, Arrow, Copper, 36 x 16 In.
$590

Copake Auctions

Weather Vane, Cockerel, Swelled Body, Copper, Gold Paint, 1800s, 22 In.
$1,464

Pook & Pook

Weather Vane, Dog, Hound, Standing, Full Body, Copper, Tail Pointed Back, 1900s, 23 ½ x 36 ½ In.
$1,830

Pook & Pook

Weather Vane, Dog, Poodle, Aluminum, Arrow Directionals, Stand, 21 x 17 In.
$148

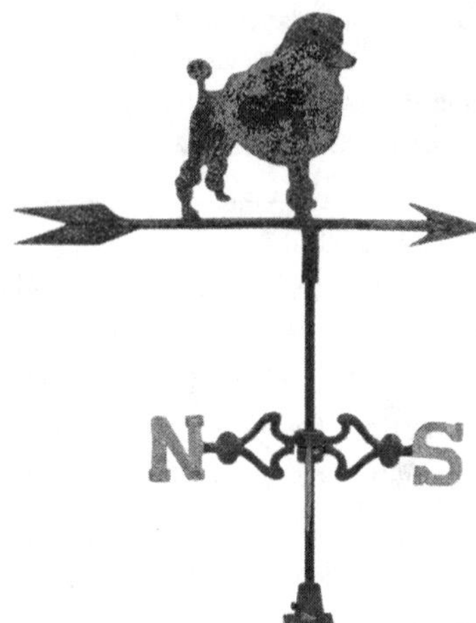

Copake Auctions

Weather Vane, Eagle, On Ball, Copper, Spread Wings, Stand, 19 In.
$354

Copake Auctions

Weather Vane, Fish, Sheet Iron, White, Red, Pierced Scales, Tail, 37 ½ In.
$1,062

Bunch Auctions

Weather Vane, Beaver, Maple Leaf, Sheet Metal, Steel Rod, Stand, Canada, Early 1900s, 28 x 17 In.
$4,973

Thomaston Place Auction Galleries

TIP

Think about security around outdoor fire escapes, skylights, roof doors, bay windows, and windows under second floor windows.

Weather Vane, Horse, Running, Rider, Green Patina, Stand, Signed, A.L. Jewell, 27 x 18 In.
$2,124

Copake Auctions

Weather Vane, Indian Silhouette, Bow, Arrow, Sheet Iron, Painted, c.1900, 43 In.
$1,219

Freeman's Auctioneers & Appraisers

Weather Vane, Pig, Sheet Copper, Flattened, Full Body, Subtle Molded Features, Early 1900s, 27 In.
$1,046

Skinner, Inc.

Weather Vane, Sea Serpent, Pine, Red Paint, Iron Tongue, 1700s, 54 ½ In.
$1,638

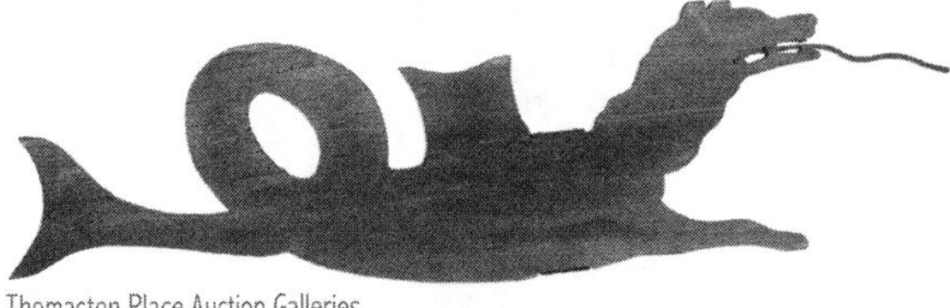

Thomaston Place Auction Galleries

Weather Vane, Seahorse, Cutout, Pierced Eye, Verdigris Patina, Sheet Copper, Stand, Early 1900s, 36 In.
$1,599

Skinner, Inc.

Weather Vane, Statue Of Liberty, Arrow, Feather, Patina, Black Stand, Molded Copper, 27 ½ In.
$1,722

Skinner, Inc.

Webb, Fairy Lamp, Custard, Enamel, Woodbine, Lamp Cup, S. Clarke, c.1900, 3 ¾ x 2 ⅞ In.
$380

Jeffrey S. Evans & Associates

Webb, Jar, Dome Lid, Honey Brown, Carved, Flowerheads, Circular Foot, Cameo, c.1900, 5 In.
$3,998

Skinner, Inc.

Webb, Lamp, Flower, Leaves, Scalloped Edge, Cameo, Burner, Chimney, c.1900, 9 ½ x 2 ¾ In.
$2,340

Jeffrey S. Evans & Associates

Webb, Vase, Butterfly, Floral, Red Ground, Bulbous, Cameo, 7 In.
$3,900

CRN Auctions

Webb, Vase, Flared Rim, Fuchsia Flowers, Leaves, Satin Yellow Ground, Cameo, 4 ½ x 6 In.
$339

Soulis Auctions

Webb, Vase, Rose Pink, White Lily, Butterfly, Ruffled Rim, White Trim, Star Cameo, c.1890, 8 In.
$360

Case Antiques

Dog, Hound, Standing, Full Body, Copper, Tail Pointed Back, 1900s, 23 ½ x 36 ½ In. ..... *illus* 1830
Dog, Pointer, Full Body, Verdigris, Copper, Molded, L.W. Baldwin, Late 1800s, 12 x 32 In. 6765
Dog, Pointing, Verdigris Patina, Copper, 1900s, 14 x 32 In. 660
Dog, Poodle, Aluminum, Arrow Directionals, Stand, 21 x 17 In. .... *illus* 148
Dove, Full Body, Copper, Ball, Mounted, White Pedestal Stand, 1800s, 20 In. 4148
Dove, Sheet Metal, Leafy Twig In Beak, Multicolor, 16 ½ x 32 In. 354
Eagle, On Ball, Copper, Spread Wings, Stand, 19 In. .... *illus* 354
Eagle, On Ball, Full Body, Copper, Spread Wing, Verdigris Patina, c.1900, 16 x 26 ½ In. 875
Fish, Full Body, Pierced Eyes, Metal, Silhouette, Detachable Stand, c.1900, 24 x 24 In. 360
Fish, Sheet Iron, White, Red, Pierced Scales, Tail, 37 ½ In. .... *illus* 1062
Flag, Directional, Polished Steel, Victorian, 15 x 42 x 2 ½ In. 431
Fox, Running, Molded Copper, Patina, Black Stand, 11 x 22 In. 2583
Galleon, Pierced Shape, Applied Verdigris Patina, Sheet Copper, Stand, Early 1900s, 32 In. 984
Horse, Flying, Ring Hoop, Mounted, Gilt Copper, A.L. Jewell & Co., 15 ½ x 31 x 5 ½ In. 10455
Horse, Full Body, Copper, Cast Zinc Head, Wood & Iron Post, Dexter, 1880s, 71 x 33 In. 1500
Horse, Full Body, Copper, Zinc Head, Verdigris Patina, Gilded, Late 1800s, 16 x 27 In. 2280
Horse, Galloping, Jockey, Copper & Zinc, c.1890, 21 x 34 ½ In. 5900
Horse, Jockey, Full Body, Copper, Mixed Metal Cast, Verdigris, 1950s, 29 ½ x 33 In. 1000
Horse, Jockey, Multicolor, Painted, Sheet Metal, Cardinal Directions, Stand, 1900s, 34 In. 344
Horse, Prancing, Hambletonian, Copper, Molded Sheet, Flattened, Stand, Late 1800s, 24 x 24 In. .. 1968
Horse, Rider, Sheet Iron, Full Body, Late 1800s, 29 x 25 In. 244
Horse, Running, Blackhawk, Copper, Bullet Hole, Wood Base, Late 1800s, 17 ½ x 20 In. 1638
Horse, Running, Cast Head, Wood Stand, 28 x 17 In. 915
Horse, Running, Copper, Cast Zinc, c.1900, 26 x 31 In. 938
Horse, Running, Full Body, Black Paint, Wood Base, 32 ½ x 20 In. 94
Horse, Running, Full Body, Sheet Copper, Verdigris Patina, 20 x 32 In. 523
Horse, Running, Jockey, Copper, Verdigris Patina, 17 In. 106
Horse, Running, Rider, Green Patina, Stand, Signed, A.L. Jewell, 27 x 18 In. .... *illus* 2124
Horse, Sulky, Copper, Gilt, Black, Metal Stand, 16 ¾ x 34 x 8 In. 5228
Horse, Sulky, Driver, Harness, Copper, Full Body, Directionals, 21 In. 403
Horse, Sulky, Gilt, Molded, Copper Wire Wheels, Late 1800s-Early 1900s, 21 ½ x 46 x 7 In. 4095
Horse, Trotting, Red, Arrow, Directionals, Steel, Iron, Bronze, 1800s, 9 x 22 In. 104
Indian Silhouette, Bow, Arrow, Sheet Iron, Painted, c.1900, 43 In. .... *illus* 1219
Peacock, Copper, Lead, Mounted On Cupola Roof, Finders, 1960s, 68 x 32 In. 840
Pig, Sheet Copper, Flattened, Full Body, Subtle Molded Features, Early 1900s, 27 In. .... *illus* 1046
Rooster, Copper & Iron, Gilt, Sheet Metal Tail, Custom Stand, c.1900, 22 x 19 x 2 In. 443
Rooster, Copper, Arrow, Directional, Verdigris Patina, Stand, 25 ½ x 21 ½ In. 531
Rooster, Flattened Full Body, Red Comb, Molded Copper, Late 1800s, 20 x 17 In. 1599
Rooster, Full Body, Attached Arrow, Spire, Wrought Iron, 1800s, 69 In. 580
Rooster, Full Body, Copper, Ball, Arrow, Late 1800s, 27 x 31 In. 720
Rooster, Full Body, Iron, Mounted, Square Base, 21 x 14 In. 384
Rooster, Silhouette, Copper, 10 Bullet Strikes, Early 1900s, 17 x 20 In. 468
Rooster, Zinc, Die Press, Cast Iron Directional, Blue Milk Glass Ball, c.1900, 45 x 29 In. 330
Schooner, 2-Masted, Molded, Sheet Copper, Verdigris Surface, Stand, Early 1900s, 28 x 32 In. 1353
Schooner, 2-Masted, Painted Metal Sails, Wire Rigging, Frank Adams, 1950s, 19 ¾ x 34 In. ... 1599
Schooner, 3-Masted, Oak, Iron Fittings, Tin Sail, Wire Rigging, Black Hull, 24 x 69 In. 1404
Schooner, 3-Masted, Painted Pine, Sheet Metal Sails, Frank Adams, c.1930, 24 x 40 In. 1342
Schooner, Wood, Tin, Copper Wire, Martha's Vineyard, Frank Adams, 1930s, 23 x 34 ½ In. 900
Sea Serpent, Pine, Red Paint, Iron Tongue, 1700s, 54 ½ In. .... *illus* 1638
Seahorse, Cutout, Pierced Eye, Verdigris Patina, Sheet Copper, Stand, Early 1900s, 36 In. .. *illus* 1599
Stag, Leaping, Sheet Copper, Full Body, Molded Fur, Jeffrey Nield, c.1990, 27 x 28 In. 2952
Statue Of Liberty, Arrow, Feather, Patina, Black Stand, Molded Copper, 27 ½ In. .... *illus* 1722
Whale, Fins, Green Patina, Directionals, Cast Iron Pole & Base, 1950s, 43 x 24 x 9 ¾ In. 531

WEBB

Webb

Webb glass was made by Thomas Webb & Sons of Ambelcot, England. Many types of art and cameo glass were made by them during the Victorian era. Production ceased by 1991 and the factory was demolished in 1995. Webb Burmese and

Webb, Vase, Round Body, Tapering, Cylindrical Neck, White, Red, Flower, Cameo, 8 In.
$960

Morphy Auctions

Webb Peachblow, Sweetmeat, Enamel, Flowers, Embossed, Silver Plate Lid & Bail, 4 In.
$96

Woody Auctions

Wedgwood, Bottle, Jasperware, Blue, White Flowers, Oval Medallion, Silver Lid, 4 In.
$369

Stair Galleries

This is an edited listing of current prices. Visit **Kovels.com** to check thousands of prices from previous years and sign up for free information on trends, tips, reproductions, marks, and more.

Wedgwood, Bowl, Caneware, Putti, Enamel Blue Interior, Leafy Border, Footed, 7 ⅜ In.
$492

Stair Galleries

Wedgwood, Bowl, Fairyland Luster, Daventry, Nizami, Animals, Flowers, c.1930, 6 ⅝ In.
$2,337

Skinner, Inc.

TIP
Use your phone camera at a flea market. Record things you might want to buy later: Record marks, etc. to look up.

Wedgwood, Bust, Louis XIV, Black Basalt, Long Hair, Mounted, Square Base, 8 In.
$861

Stair Galleries

Webb Peachblow are special colored glasswares of the Victorian era. They are listed at the end of this section. Glassware that is not Burmese or Peachblow is included here.

Fairy Lamp, Custard, Enamel, Woodbine, Lamp Cup, S. Clarke, c.1900, 3 ¾ x 2 ⅞ In. ....*illus* 380
Jar, Dome Lid, Honey Brown, Carved, Flowerheads, Circular Foot, Cameo, c.1900, 5 In. ...*illus* 3998
Lamp, Flower, Leaves, Scalloped Edge, Cameo, Burner, Chimney, c.1900, 9 ½ x 2 ¾ In. ..*illus* 2340
Lamp, Oil, Brass, Clear Glass Chimney, White & Pink Flowers, Cameo, c.1890, 9 In.................. 400
Vase, Butterfly, Floral, Red Ground, Bulbous, Cameo, 7 In. ....*illus* 3900
Vase, Flared Rim, Fuchsia Flowers, Leaves, Satin Yellow Ground, Cameo, 4 ½ x 6 In. ....*illus* 339
Vase, Rose Pink, White Lily, Butterfly, Ruffled Rim, White Trim, Star Cameo, c.1890, 8 In. .*illus* 360
Vase, Round Body, Tapering, Cylindrical Neck, White, Red, Flower, Cameo, 8 In. ....*illus* 960
Wine, Green Overlay, Engraved Fruit Garland, Clear Stem & Foot, c.1920s, 7 ¾ In.................... 330

WEBB BURMESE

Webb Burmese is a shaded Victorian glass made by Thomas Webb & Sons of Stourbridge, England, from 1886. Pieces are shades of pink to yellow.

Bowl, Queen's Burmese, Pink To Yellow Green, Ruffled Edge, 2 x 4 ½ In. 250
Fairy Lamp, Acorn, Ceramic Lamp Cup, Footed Base, Crimped Rim, c.1900, 4 ½ x 5 In.......... 351
Perfume Bottle, Painted, Bamboo Tree, Dragonfly, Flowers, 5 In. 2400
Vase, Hawthorn Pattern, Stick, Bulbous, Ruffled Rim, 3 ¾ In. 112

WEBB PEACHBLOW

Webb Peachblow is a shaded Victorian glass made by Thomas Webb & Sons of Stourbridge, England, from 1885.

Ewer, Sawtooth Rim, White To Pink To Purple, Cascading Gold Vine, 11 ½ In.......................... 469
Plate, Flowering Branches, Butterflies, Piecrust Edge, 8 In. 120
Sweetmeat, Enamel, Flowers, Embossed, Silver Plate Lid & Bail, 4 In. ....*illus* 96
Vase, Bottle Shape, Flying Bird, Flowers, Late 1800s, 7 ⅝ In. 174

WEDGWOOD

Wedgwood, one of the world's most successful potteries, was founded by Josiah Wedgwood, who was considered a cripple by his brother and was forbidden to work at the family business. The pottery was established in England in 1759. The company used a variety of marks, including Wedgwood, Wedgwood & Bentley, Wedgwood & Sons, and Wedgwood's Stone China. A large variety of wares has been made, including the well-known jasperware, basalt, creamware, and even a limited amount of porcelain. There are two kinds of jasperware. One is made from two colors of clay; the other is made from one color of clay with a color dip to create the contrast in design. In 1986 Wedgwood and Waterford Crystal merged to form the Waterford Wedgwood Group. Most Waterford Wedgwood assets were bought by KPS Capital Partners of New York in 2009 and became part of WWRD Holdings. A small amount of Wedgwood is still made in England at the workshop in Barlaston. Most is made in Asia. Wedgwood has been part of Fiskars Group since 2015. Other Wedgwood pieces may be listed under Flow Blue, Majolica, Tea Leaf Ironstone, or in other porcelain categories.

WEDGWOOD & BENTLEY
Wedgwood & Bentley 1769–1780

of ETRURIA ® WEDGWOOD MADE IN ENGLAND & BARLASTON
Wedgwood 1940

W WEDGWOOD ENGLAND 1759
Wedgwood 1998–present

Basket, Pierced Lid, Green Flowers, Leaves, Gilt Rim & Handle, Footed, 4 In. 123
Biscuit Jar, Jasperware, Dark Blue, Maiden, Cherubs, Silver Plate Lid, Swing Handle, 5 In. 115
Bottle, Jasperware, Blue, White Flowers, Oval Medallion, Silver Lid, 4 In. ....*illus* 369
Bowl, Bicentennial, Philadelphia Scene, Bailey, Banks & Biddle, 5 ½ x 12 In............................. 125

Wedgwood, Button, Jasperware, Metal Mount, 1800s
$188

Whitely's Auctioneers

Wedgwood, Cooler, Creamware, Fruit, Lid & Liner, Black Rim, 2 Handles, Ball Shape Feet, 9 ½ In.
$615

Stair Galleries

Wedgwood, Cooler, Lid, Flowers, Handle, Blue, Gilt, 7 ¾ In.
$550

Hindman Auctions

TIP
Use opaque window shades or drapes so the contents of your rooms can't be seen from outside.

Wedgwood, Crocus Holder, Seashell, Seaweed & Coral, Turquoise Interior, Stand, 6 x 12 x 8 ½ In.
$452

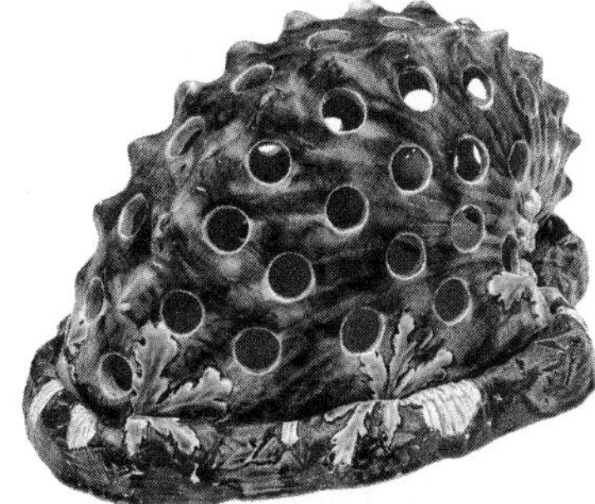

Soulis Auctions

Wedgwood, Dish, Game, Majolica, Oval, Grapevine Festoon, Figural Finial, 5 ½ x 8 x 5 ¾ In.
$396

Soulis Auctions

Wedgwood, Jar, Lid, Canopic, Blue Gray Band, Hieroglyphs, Zodiac Symbols, Egyptian, c.1871, 10 In.
$3,198

Skinner, Inc.

Wedgwood, Jardiniere, Jasperware, Dark Blue Ground, Women, Garden, Garland, Lion's Head Trim, 9 In.
$259

Richard D. Hatch & Associates

TIP
Windows in outside doors should be covered with grillwork or made of unbreakable glass.

Wedgwood, Jug, Caneware, Light Brown, Molded, Enamel, Blue Rim, Bamboo Canes & Leaves, 2 ¾ In.
$738

Stair Galleries

Wedgwood, Mold, Gelatin, Creamware, Oval, Scalloped Rim, Molded Fruit Basket, 12 In.
$431

Stair Galleries

Wedgwood, Plaque, Caneware, Portrait, Heinrich Klaproth, Rosso Antico, Oval, 3 ⅞ In.
$492

Stair Galleries

Wedgwood, Plaque, Jasperware, Portrait, Alexander The Great, White & Blue, Oval, Bentley, 2 In.
$554

Stair Galleries

Wedgwood, Plate, Pearlware, Multicolor, Leaves, White Ground, Yellow, Blue, 1700s, 9 In.
$111

Skinner, Inc.

Wedgwood, Plate, Yellowware, Reticulated, Molded, Mythological Scene, Pegasus & Maiden, 9 In.
$185

Stair Galleries

Wedgwood, Sphinx, Black Basalt, Impressed, c.1842, 9 x 7 In., Pair
$2,560

Neal Auction Company

Wedgwood, Teapot, Lid, Black Basalt, Bamboo Spout & Handle, Reclining Dog Finial, 6 ¾ In.
$431

Stair Galleries

Wedgwood, Teapot, Rosso Antico, Egyptian Designs, Crocodile Finial, c.1805, 4 x 9 x 6 In.
$2,684

Neal Auction Company

Wedgwood, Vase, Caneware, Bamboo Canes, 4 Spouts, Encaustic, Late 1700s, 10 In.
$1,230

Skinner, Inc.

Wedgwood, Vase, Fairyland Luster, Lid, Jeweled Tree With Cat & Mouse, c.1920, 11 In.
$6,150

Skinner, Inc.

Bowl, Black Basalt, Circular, Engine Turned, Footed, Marked, 8 In. 431
Bowl, Caneware, Putti, Enamel Blue Interior, Leafy Border, Footed, 7 3/8 In. .... *illus* 492
Bowl, Dragon Luster, Octagonal, Gilt, Landscape, Diaper Border, c.1920, 8 In. 246
Bowl, Fairyland Luster, Daventry, Nizami, Animals, Flowers, c.1930, 6 5/8 In. .... *illus* 2337
Bust, Louis XIV, Black Basalt, Long Hair, Mounted, Square Base, 8 In. .... *illus* 861
Button, Jasperware, Metal Mount, 1800s .... *illus* 188
Candlestick, Black Basalt, Column, Impressed J, England, c.1890, 11 3/8 In., Pair 475
Canister, Tortoiseshell, Rectangular, Mottled Gray, Green & Yellow, Glazed, c.1760, 4 In. 369
Cann, Saucer, Jasperware, Yellow, Basalt Egyptianesque Design, c.1805, 2 1/2 x 4 3/4 In. 600
Cooler, Creamware, Fruit, Lid & Liner, Black Rim, 2 Handles, Ball Shape Feet, 9 1/2 In. ...*illus* 615
Cooler, Lid, Flowers, Handle, Blue, Gilt, 7 3/4 In. .... *illus* 550
Crocus Holder, Seashell, Seaweed & Coral, Turquoise Interior, Stand, 6 x 12 x 8 1/2 In. ..*illus* 452
Cup, Lid, Jasperware, Lilac & White, Rope Twist Handle, 3 In. 984
Dish, Creamware, Lobed Octagonal, Pink Rim, Flower Center, 10 In. 1107
Dish, Game, Majolica, Oval, Grapevine Festoon, Figural Finial, 5 1/2 x 8 x 5 3/4 In. .... *illus* 396
Ewer, Black Basalt, Neptune Riding Dolphin, Seaweed Swags, Bacchus, 1800s, 16 In., Pair...... 3100
Figurine, Man, Standing On Disc, Sky Plateau II, Glenys Barton, 9 5/8 In. Diam 6150
Flower Frog, Green Hedgehog, c.1875, 6 1/2 In. 530
Jar, Lid, Caneware, Canopic, Egyptian, Zodiac Symbols, Early 1800s, 10 In. 3198
Jar, Lid, Canopic, Blue Gray Band, Hieroglyphs, Zodiac Symbols, Egyptian, c.1871, 10 In. *illus* 3198
Jardiniere, Jasperware, Dark Blue Ground, Women, Garden, Garland, Lion's Head Trim, 9 In. *illus* 259
Jug, Caneware, Light Brown, Molded, Enamel, Blue Rim, Bamboo Canes & Leaves, 2 3/4 In. *illus* 738
Jug, Pearlware, Painted, Flowers, White Ground, Monogram, Blue Rim, 9 In. 369
Ladle, Pearlware, Blue Line Handle & Rim, White Ground, Marked, 10 In. 246
Lamp, Jasperware, 2 Tiers, Lilac Ground, Classical Scene, Bronze Base, Electric, 11 In. 62
Lamp, Oil, Black Basalt, Woman Reading, Late 1800s, 8 1/2 x 7 1/2 x 4 In., Pair 2100
Malfrey Pot, Lid, Fairyland Luster, Willow, Flame, c.1925, 9 3/4 In. 1230
Mold, Gelatin, Creamware, Oval, Scalloped Rim, Molded Fruit Basket, 12 In. .... *illus* 431
Monteith, Creamware, Oval, 2 Handles, Grapevine Border, Scalloped Rim, Marked, 12 3/4 In. . 738
Mug, Caneware, Molded, Bamboo Border, Children, Enamel Leafy Border, Blue Rim, 3 3/8 In. . 554
Pitcher, Jasperware, Blue, White, Portland, Roman Figures, Trees, Cupid, Signed, 8 1/2 In. 182
Plaque, Black Basalt, Frightened Horse, Norman Bates, 9 1/4 x 15 1/2 In. 125
Plaque, Caneware, Portrait, Heinrich Klaproth, Rosso Antico, Oval, 3 7/8 In. .... *illus* 492
Plaque, Jasperware, Medusa, Blue, Gold Frame, Round, c. 1780, 6 In. 600
Plaque, Jasperware, Orestes & Pylades, Temple Of Diana, White Relief, Frame, c.1810, 7 x 23 In. 1968
Plaque, Jasperware, Portrait, Alexander The Great, White & Blue, Oval, Bentley, 2 In. ....*illus* 554
Plate, Caneware, Blue Enamel, Greek Key Border, 8 In. 246
Plate, Pearlware, Multicolor, Leaves, White Ground, Yellow, Blue, 1700s, 9 In. .... *illus* 111
Plate, Yellowware, Reticulated, Molded, Mythological Scene, Pegasus & Maiden, 9 In. ...*illus* 185
Pot, Pierced Lid, Pearlware, Enamel, Brown & Green Bands, 8 In. 861
Sauceboat, Creamware, Shell Shape, Black Printed Transfer, Birds, Domed Base, 7 In. 615
Sphinx, Black Basalt, Impressed, c.1842, 9 x 7 In., Pair .... *illus* 2560
Tankard, Black Basalt, 3 Silver Putti Mounts, Dancing & Playing Cello, 3 3/4 In. 492
Teapot, Lid, Black Basalt, Bamboo Spout & Handle, Reclining Dog Finial, 6 3/4 In. .... *illus* 431
Teapot, Lid, Caneware, Bamboo, Molded Body, 1700s, 5 In. 492
Teapot, Lid, Rosso Antico, Egyptian Designs, Crocodile Finial, Marked, c.1805, 4 x 9 x 6 In. 2200
Teapot, Rosso Antico, Egyptian Designs, Crocodile Finial, c.1805, 4 x 9 x 6 In. .... *illus* 2684
Tray, Leaf Shape, Bird, Brown, Gold Rim, 9 1/2 In. 106
Tray, Rosso Antico, Boat Shape, Swan Handle, Egyptian Design, Satyr, c.1805, 3 1/2 x 10 In. 475
Tureen, Lid & Stand, Creamware, Shaped Handles, Flower Finial, Green Line Rim, 6 1/2 In. 2091
Urn, Lid, Black Basalt, Swags, Sibyl Finial, Impressed Circular, c.1900, 6 1/2 x 5 3/4 In. 700
Vase, Beaker, Rosso Antico, Egyptian Design, Marked RK, c.1805, 6 3/4 x 5 In. 475
Vase, Black Basalt, 2 Handles, Maiden, Anthemion Border, Footed, 6 3/4 In. 2829
Vase, Caneware, Bamboo Canes, 4 Spouts, Encaustic, Late 1700s, 10 In. .... *illus* 1230
Vase, Fairyland Luster, Lid, Jeweled Tree With Cat & Mouse, c.1920, 11 In. .... *illus* 6150
Vase, Hummingbird, Blue Ground, Footed, Luster Bud, Early 1900s, 5 In. 172
Vase, Jasperware, Blue & White, Yellow Ground, Classical Scene, Footed, 2 3/8 In. 185
Vase, Lid, Bone, Snake Handles, Painted, Gold, Enamel, White Ground, Late 1800s, 11 In. .*illus* 738
Vase, Lid, Porphyry, Gilt, Medallion, Basalt Plinth, Wedgwood & Bentley, c.1775, 10 In. ...*illus* 3321

Wedgwood, Vase, Lid, Bone, Snake Handles, Painted, Gold, Enamel, White Ground, Late 1800s, 11 In.
$738

Skinner, Inc.

Wedgwood, Vase, Lid, Porphyry, Gilt, Medallion, Basalt Plinth, Wedgwood & Bentley, c.1775, 10 In.
$3,321

Skinner, Inc.

Weller, Brighton, Figurine, Pheasant, Shades Of Blue, Earth Tone Base, Molded, 7 x 10 1/2 In.
$552

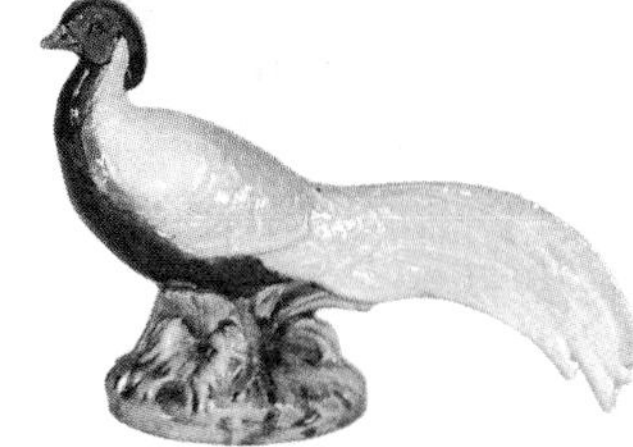

Belhorn Auction Services

W

Weller, Bronze Ware, Vase, Drapery Shape, Impressed, 8 ⅞ In.
$157

Humler & Nolan

Weller, Coppertone, Figurine, Frog, Incised, 3 ¾ In.
$85

Humler & Nolan

Weller, Coppertone, Flower Holder, Frog Holding Water Lily, Marked, 4 In.
$133

Humler & Nolan

TIP

Lock your doors and windows. In 65 percent to 82 percent of all home burglaries, the burglar enters through a door. Most often the doors were unlocked.

WELLER

Weller pottery was first made in 1872 in Fultonham, Ohio. The firm moved to Zanesville, Ohio, in 1882. Artwares were introduced in 1893. Hundreds of lines of pottery were produced, including Louwelsa, Eocean, Dickens Ware, and Sicardo, before the pottery closed in 1948.

LONHUDA

Weller Pottery
1895–1896

LOUWELSA
WELLER

Weller Pottery
1895–1918

Weller Pottery
1920s

Item		Price
Art Nouveau, Vase, Corn Shape, Yellow & Green, 4 ⅝ In.		525
Aurelian, Lamp Base, Oil, Brown Glaze, Floral, Signed On Bottom, 17 ½ x 13 x 13 In.		817
Brighton, Figurine, Pheasant, Shades Of Blue, Earth Tone Base, Molded, 7 x 10 ½ In.	*illus*	552
Bronze Ware, Vase, Drapery Shape, Impressed, 8 ⅞ In.	*illus*	157
Burnt Wood, Vase, Molded Rim, Cylindrical, Brown, 8 ½ In.		63
Camelot, Vase, Bud, Yellow & White Glaze, Marked, 5 In.		562
Coppertone, Beaker, Bright Green Mottled Glaze, c.1975, 6 In.		125
Coppertone, Bowl, Console, Frog, Green, c.1925, 5 ½ x 10 x 6 ¾ In.		226
Coppertone, Bowl, Console, Lily Blossom, 3 x 12 In.		215
Coppertone, Figurine, Frog, Incised, 3 ¾ In.	*illus*	85
Coppertone, Flower Holder, Frog Holding Water Lily, Marked, 4 In.	*illus*	133
Coppertone, Frog, Green & Brown, Marked, 3 ¾ In.		237
Cretone, Vase, Deer, Flowers, White, Black Ground, Hester Pillsbury, Marked, 6 ¾ In.	*illus*	182
Dickens Ware, Jardiniere, Yellow Fuchsia, Glaze, Pinched Neck, 6 In.		106
Dickens Ware, Loving Cup, 3 Handles, Brown, Flowers, c.1900, 5 ½ x 7 ½ In.		90
Dog, Pop-Eye, Figurine, White, Incised, 9 ¾ In.	*illus*	968
Duck, Garden Ornament, Yellow & White, 9 ½ x 12 ½ In.		4500
Eocean, Jardiniere, Hand Painted, Floral, Bulbous Body, 11 x 9 In.		196
Flemish, Pedestal, Cream Ground, Flowers & Parrots, Red & Blue, 1920, 21 ¾ x 10 In.		68
Fru-Russett, Vase, Nude Male, Climbing Tree, Green, Glazed, Incised, c.1904, 16 x 9 In.	*illus*	3750
Glendale, Vase, Embossed Scene, Bird & Nest, 11 ½ x 6 In.	*illus*	311
Glendale, Wall Pocket, 2 Trunk Shape Base, Bird, Nest, Green, Blue, 7 In.	*illus*	219
Hudson, Lamp, Electric, Footed, Blue, Flowers, Marked, 12 x 6 In.		460
Hudson, Vase, Blue & Violet Ground, Flowers, Signed, Dorothy, 5 ½ x 2 ½ In.	*illus*	99
Hudson, Vase, Flowers, Bulbous, 2 Handles, Footed, Blue, Signed, 8 In.	*illus*	207
Hudson, Vase, Light Blue Band Around Top Rim, Flowers, Vine, Marked, 8 x 5 In.	*illus*	345
Hudson, Vase, Pink, Cream, Green, 3 Swans, 13 In.		562
Hudson, Vase, White Flowers, Molded Rim, 1910s-20s, 13 In.		173
Hudson, Vase, Wild Rose, Handles, Sarah Timberlake, 6 ½ In.	*illus*	121
Jardiniere, Grape Clusters, Leaves, Vines, Fluted Rim, Pedestal, 23 ½ In.	*illus*	817
Jardiniere, Peach, Green Matte Glaze, Grapes & Flowers, Footed, 12 ½ x 13 In.	*illus*	226
Lasa, Vase, Pine Trees, Signed, 11 In.	*illus*	121
Lasa, Vase, Scenic View Of Trees On Lake Shore, Hills Background, Signed, 8 In.	*illus*	518
Lebanon, Vase, Men On Camels, 9 In.		1750
Little Bo Peep, Vase, Sheep, Tree, Incised, Dorothy England, Marked, 4 ⅜ In.	*illus*	545
Louwelsa, Vase, Chrysanthemums, Molded Rim, Monogram, 16 x 6 ¾ In.		170
Louwelsa, Vase, Squat, Painted, Rose Branches, Early 1900s, 3 ¾ In.		185
Louwelsa, Vase, Yellow Irises, Glaze, Alfred Haubrich, c.1900, 15 ¾ x 6 In.		311
Muskota, Bowl Holder, Crane Fish, Marked, 10 ¾ x 8 ¾ In.	*illus*	980
Muskota, Figurine, Woman Kneeling, Base, 7 ⅜ In.		175
Pumila, Vase, Water Lily Leaves, Orange Base, 9 ½ In.	*illus*	142
Rhead Faience, Mug, Geisha & Cat, Burgundy, Green, Yellow, 5 In.		281
Roma, Candlestick, Flowers, Pink & Green, 1914, 9 ½ In., Pair		180
Rosemont, Chalice, Flowers & Birds, Black Ground, 9 ⅞ In.		187
Sicardo, Vase, Chrysanthemums, Glazed, c.1905, 20 ½ x 10 ½ In.	*illus*	4225
Sicardo, Vase, Dimple Body, Green Glaze, 2 Organic Shape Handles, 12 ½ x 6 In.		260

Weller, Cretone, Vase, Deer, Flowers, White, Black Ground, Hester Pillsbury, Marked, 6 ¾ In.
$182

Humler & Nolan

Weller, Dog, Pop-Eye, Figurine, White, Incised, 9 ¾ In.
$968

Humler & Nolan

Weller, Fru-Russett, Vase, Nude Male, Climbing Tree, Green, Glazed, Incised, c.1904, 16 x 9 In.
$3,750

Rago Arts and Auction Center

Weller, Glendale, Vase, Embossed Scene, Bird & Nest, 11 ½ x 6 In.
$311

Soulis Auctions

Weller, Glendale, Wall Pocket, 2 Trunk Shape Base, Bird, Nest, Green, Blue, 7 In.
$219

Belhorn Auction Services

Weller, Hudson, Vase, Blue & Violet Ground, Flowers, Signed, Dorothy, 5 ½ x 2 ½ In.
$99

Locati Auctions

Weller, Hudson, Vase, Flowers, Bulbous, 2 Handles, Footed, Blue, Signed, 8 In.
$207

Belhorn Auction Services

Weller, Hudson, Vase, Light Blue Band Around Top Rim, Flowers, Vine, Marked, 8 x 5 In.
$345

Belhorn Auction Services

Weller, Hudson, Vase, Wild Rose, Handles, Sarah Timberlake, 6 ½ In.
$121

Humler & Nolan

W

Weller, Jardiniere, Grape Clusters, Leaves, Vines, Fluted Rim, Pedestal, 23 ½ In.
$817

Fontaine's Auction Gallery

Weller, Jardiniere, Peach, Green Matte Glaze, Grapes & Flowers, Footed, 12 ½ x 13 In.
$226

Soulis Auctions

Weller, Lasa, Vase, Pine Trees, Signed, 11 In.
$121

Humler & Nolan

Weller, Lasa, Vase, Scenic View Of Trees On Lake Shore, Hills Background, Signed, 8 In.
$518

Belhorn Auction Services

Weller, Little Bo Peep, Vase, Sheep, Tree, Incised, Dorothy England, Marked, 4 ⅜ In.
$545

Humler & Nolan

Weller, Muskota, Bowl Holder, Crane Fish, Marked, 10 ¾ x 8 ¾ In.
$980

Belhorn Auction Services

Weller, Pumila, Vase, Water Lily Leaves, Orange Base, 9 ½ In.
$142

Strawser Auction Group

Weller, Sicardo, Vase, Chrysanthemums, Glazed, c.1905, 20 ½ x 10 ½ In.
$4,225

Rago Arts and Auction Center

Weller, Sicardo, Vase, Tapered Conical Shape, Snails Band, Marked, Early 1900s, 5 ¾ In.
$400

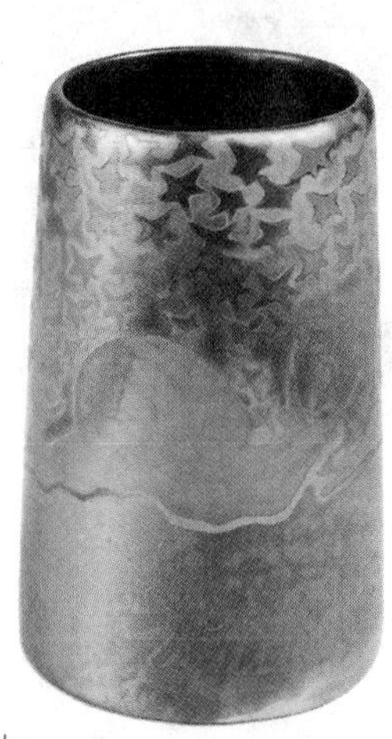

Skinner, Inc.

Sicardo, Vase, Green Glaze, Flowers, Marked, 7 In. 437
Sicardo, Vase, Tapered Conical Shape, Snails Band, Marked, Early 1900s, 5 ¾ In. .... *illus* 400
Silvertone, Vase, Fan Shape, Ruffled Rim, Multicolor, Marked, 7 ¾ In. 150
Silvertone, Vase, Tulip, Ruffled Rim, Stem, Multicolor, 9 ½ In. .... *illus* 115
Vase, Pot Shape, Green & Pink Glaze, Flowers, Signed Leffler, 9 ¾ x 8 ½ In. 688
Zona, Umbrella Stand, Gloss, 6 Maidens, Floral, Boughs Of Ivy, Unmarked, 20 In. .... *illus* 748

WEMYSS

Wemyss ware was first made in 1882 by Robert Heron & Son, later called Fife Pottery, in Scotland. Large colorful flowers, hearts, and other symbols were hand painted on figurines, inkstands, jardinieres, candlesticks, buttons, pots, and other items. Fife Pottery closed in 1932. The molds and designs were used by a series of potteries until 1957. In 1985 the Wemyss name and designs were obtained by Griselda Hill. The Wemyss Ware trademark was registered in 1994. Modern Wemyss Ware in old styles is still being made.

Dish, Cherries, White Ground, Green Border, 12 ½ x 8 ½ In. 99
Figurine, Pig, Cabbage Rose, White Ground 224
Wash Set, Pitcher & Bowl, Cherry Pattern, Robert Heron & Son, Pitcher 6 ½ In. 1800

WESTMORELAND GLASS

Westmoreland glass was made by the Westmoreland Glass Company of Grapeville, Pennsylvania, from 1889 to 1984. The company made clear and colored glass of many varieties, such as milk glass, pressed glass, and slag glass.

Westmoreland Glass
c.1910–c.1929, 1970s

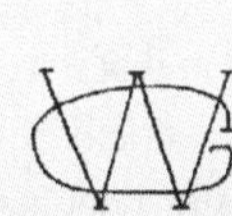
Westmoreland Glass
Late 1940s–1981

Westmoreland Glass
1982–1984

Dolphin, Candlestick, Hexagon Base, Clear, 4 x 4 In., Pair 34
English Hobnail, Compote, Amber, Footed, Ruffled Lip, 4 In. 27
Filigree, Bowl, Pedestal, Frosted Blue Glass, 12 x 12 x 5 In. 135
Humphrey The Camel, Candy Dish, Topaz, Opalescent, Vaseline Glass 180
Jar, Lid, Green Satin Glass, Footed, 6 x 6 x 16 In. 155

WHEATLEY POTTERY

Wheatley Pottery was founded by Thomas J. Wheatley in Cincinnati, Ohio. He had worked with the founders of the art pottery movement, including M. Louise McLaughlin of the Rookwood Pottery. He started T.J. Wheatley & Co. in 1880. That company was closed by 1884. Thomas Wheatley worked for Weller Pottery in Zanesville, Ohio, from 1897 to 1900. In 1903 he founded Wheatley Pottery Company in Cincinnati. Wheatley Pottery was purchased by the Cambridge Tile Manufacturing Company in 1927.

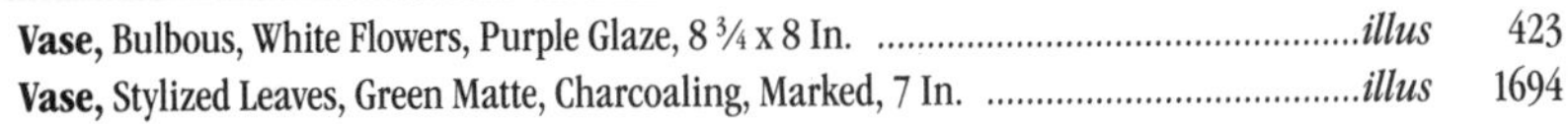
Vase, Bulbous, White Flowers, Purple Glaze, 8 ¾ x 8 In. .... *illus* 423
Vase, Stylized Leaves, Green Matte, Charcoaling, Marked, 7 In. .... *illus* 1694

WILLETS MANUFACTURING COMPANY

Willets Manufacturing Company of Trenton, New Jersey, began work in 1879. The company made belleek in the late 1880s and 1890s in shapes similar to those used by the Irish Belleek factory. It stopped working about 1912. A variety of marks were used, most including the name *Willets.*

Goblet, Grapes & Flowers, Orange, Cream, Gray, Spread Foot, Belleek, 11 x 5 ½ In. 25

Weller, Silvertone, Vase, Tulip, Ruffled Rim, Stem, Multicolor, 9 ½ In.
$115

Apple Tree Auction Center

Weller, Zona, Umbrella Stand, Gloss, 6 Maidens, Floral, Boughs Of Ivy, Unmarked, 20 In.
$748

Belhorn Auction Services

Wheatley, Vase, Bulbous, White Flowers, Purple Glaze, 8 ¾ x 8 In.
$423

Treadway

Wheatley, Vase, Stylized Leaves, Green Matte, Charcoaling, Marked, 7 In.
$1,694

Humler & Nolan

Window, Leaded, Beveled Glass, Medallion, Multicolor Jewel, Central Roundel, 40 x 2 In.
$726

Fontaine's Auction Gallery

TIP
Don't store wooden bowls and other pieces on their sides. This can cause them to warp.

Wood Carving, Avalokitesvara, Seated In Dhyanasana, Multiple Arms, Vietnam, 37 ½ In.
$7,380

Clars Auction Gallery

Mug, Beer, Cream Luster, Cottage & Lake Scene On Band, c.1900, 5 ½ In. 12
Pitcher, Portrait, Draped Nude, Gold Trim, Green Dragon Handle, Belleek, 11 x 5 In. 620
Pitcher, Portrait, Sir John Falstaff, Brown & Green Ground, c.1910, 6 In. 84
Planter, Pansies, Diagonal Ribs, Gilt Dragon Handles, Belleek, c.1920, 9 ½ In. 98
Ramekin, Underplate, Blue Flowers, White Ground, Tightly Ruffled Rim, Belleek, 5 ½ In. 36
Tankard Set, Grapes, Yellow Ground, Belleek, 6 Mugs, Tray, Pitcher 15 ½ In. 136
Tankard, Orange Flowers, Cream To Dark Gray, Bacchus Spout, Dragon Handle, 11 In. 163
Vase, Courting Couple In Cartouche, Green Ground, Gilt Wing Handles, Belleek, 8 In. 84
Vase, Red & Yellow Roses, Mottled Ground, Gold Trim, Oval, Belleek, 12 ½ x 7 In. 155

WILLOW

Willow pattern has been made in England since 1780. The pattern has been copied by factories in many countries, including Germany, Japan, and the United States. It is still being made. Willow was named for a pattern that pictures a bridge, birds, willow trees, and a Chinese landscape. Most pieces are blue and white. Some made after 1900 are pink and white.

Bowl, Vegetable, Georgian Shape, Churchill, England, 8 In. 18
Bowl, Vegetable, Oval, Allertons, England, 9 In. 20
Dish, Lid, John & Co. Crown Pottery, Langton, England, 11 x 9 x 7 In. 88
Gravy Boat, Scalloped Edge, Allertons, England 27
Mug, Handle, NASCO, Japan, 1940s-50s 20
Platter, Impressed 14, c.1900, 14 x 10 ½ In. 75
Tankard, Handle, W.A. Adderley, England 20
Wash Set, Pitcher, Washbasin, Scalloped Edge, Paper Label, Japan, 1950s 175

WINDOW

Window glass that was stained and beveled was popular for houses during the late nineteenth and early twentieth centuries. Some was set in patterns like leaded glass. The old windows became popular with collectors in the 1970s; today, old and new examples are seen.

Leaded, 3 Parts, Cathedral Top, 2 Arched Center Panels, Oak Frame, 69 x 70 In. 787
Leaded, 4 Bull's-Eyes, Red Circle, Green Diamond, Blue Border, 1800s, 48 x 35 x 2 In. 182
Leaded, Beveled Glass, Medallion, Multicolor Jewel, Central Roundel, 40 x 2 In. .... *illus* 726
Leaded, Gothic, Blue Columns, Purple Panels, Arched, 72 x 28 In. 480
Leaded, Peacock, Standing, Blue Body, Mottled Blue, Signed Somers, 44 x 30 x 1 In. 5100
Leaded, Rose, Symmetrical Detail, Slag, Yellow, Lavender, Green, 1910s, 82 ½ In. 780
Leaded, Stained Glass, Mosaic, Central Medallion, Jeweled, 25 x 62 In. 5463
Leaded, Stylized Flowers, Beveled Glass, Multi Jeweled, Lavender Border, 41 ½ x 80 In. 1573
Panel, Leaded & Stained Glass, Multicolor, Portrait Center, 24 x 21 ½ In. 100
Panel, Slag Glass, Arabian Arch, Pressed Rosettes, Oak Frame, 1950s, 56 x 16 In., Pair 540
Panel, Stained, Martin Luther, Otto Von Bismarck, Germany, 18 x 13 ⅜ In. 300
Stained, Art Nouveau, Green, Orange, Maroon, Stripes, Arcs, 31 x 51 In. 370
Stained, Cherub, Anchor, Aldi Filii, 1700s, 15 ½ x 14 ¾ In. 2106
Stained, Cherubs, Centerpiece, Fruit, Flower Urn, Lanterns, Swags, Wood Frame, 61 x 35 In. 620
Stained, Dutch Merchants On Boat, Potatoes, Church, Hand Painted Trim, 32 x 28 In. 207
Stained, Leaded, Tropical Scene, C-Scroll Cartouche, c.1900s, 65 x 48 In. 1188
Stained, St. Cecelia, Playing Pipe, Wilbur Herbert Burnham, 1948, 67 x 16 x 1 ¾ In. 800
Stained, Swan, Mountain Landscape, Grass, River, Pine Frame, c.1950, 67 x 46 In. 1062
Transom, Stained, Multicolor Panels, Blue Border, Painted, Wood Frame, Victorian, 20 x 39 In. 325

WOOD CARVING

Wood carvings and wooden pieces are listed separately in this book. There are also wooden pieces found in other categories, such as Folk Art, Kitchen, and Tool.

Angel, Wings, Gesso, Multicolor, Dotted Flowers, 18 In. 780

Artist's Model, Male, Articulated Joints, 32 x 8 ½ x 3 ½ In. 1300
Avalokitesvara, Seated In Dhyanasana, Multiple Arms, Vietnam, 37 ½ In. *illus* 7380
Bald Eagle Head, Glass Eyes, Feather Detail, Stamped RM, Ron Marino, 1900s, 6 x 8 In. 216
Bald Eagle, Standing, Painted, Mounted, Joseph Moyer, 8 In. *illus* 5368
Blackamoor, Female, Kneeling, Carrying Seashell Basin, Painted, Base, c.1900, 37 x 32 x 2 In. 2520
Bodhisattva, Sitting, Zitan, Carved, Monastic Robes, Lotus Base, Chinese, 12 In. 780
Brushpot, Bamboo, Scholars Playing Go, Bamboo Trees, Clouds, 6 In. 480
Brushpot, Rosewood, Waisted, Cylindrical, Removable Base, 1900s, 8 ½ In. 380
Buddha, Head, Red Lips, Arched Eyebrows, Blue Hair, Chinese, 1900s, 19 x 9 In. 484
Buddha, Standing, Lotus, Dress, Glass Jewels, Plinth Base, Thailand, 61 x 23 x 11 In. 537
Bust, Antheia, Girl, Goddess, Mahogany, 12 x 5 x 19 ½ In. *illus* 944
Bust, Caesar, Laurel Wreath, Breastplate, Black Marble, Socle Base, Italy, 6 ¾ In. 531
Cat, Lying Down, Painted, Black & White, Curled Tail, 14 x 30 x 9 In. 410
Curlew, Glass Eyes, Tail Feather Details, Driftwood Base, Ron Marino, 1900s, 17 x 16 In. 156
Deer Head, Walnut, Antlers, Molded, Mounted On Oak Shield, 26 x 13 x 12 ½ In. 1112
Deer, Teak, Eroded & Textured Surface, Hardwood Stand, Thailand, 1900s, 15 x 10 x 31 In. 450
Dog, Hound, Sitting, Sleepy Eyes, Painted Nails, Square Base, T. Frelinghuysen, 1900s, 30 In. 185
Dog, Pierced With Iron Nails, Metal Fragments, Nkisi Nkondi, Africa, 10 ½ x 22 In. *illus* 256
Dolphin, Plaque, Black, Clark G. Voorhees Jr., 1960s, 17 ¾ In. 1845
Dove, Spread Wings, Feather, Body Details, Hanging, Painted, 1800s, 16 ¾ In. 4920
Duck, Elongated Bill, Buckeye Walnut, 13 x 23 In. 185
Eagle, Bellamy Style, Pine, Spread Wings, Shield, Red, White, Blue Paint, 8 x 27 ½ x 5 In. *illus* 410
Eagle, Gilt, Spread Wings, Mounted, Ball, 1800s, 20 ½ In., Pair 1586
Eagle, Spread Wings, Perched On Root Base, Patina, 47 x 48 x 44 In. 242
Elephant, Ironwood, Applied Eyes & Toes, Wood Tusks, Incised Details, c.1910, 37 x 42 In. *illus* 1250
Fish, Barracuda, Driftwood & Pine Background, Signed, Frank Adamo, 1900s, 18 In. 216
French Horn, Linden, Fumio Yoshimura, Japan, 16 In. *illus* 688
Goblet, Mahogany, Star, Brown, Signed, Sass Goldsmith, Boston, 1800s, 5 ¾ In. 236
Great Horned Owl, Mechanism Flaps Wings, Painted, Mike Borrett, 1900s, 25 In. *illus* 900
Gull, Standing, Wooden Base, Piling, Shell, Signed, Paul S. Moyer III, 15 x 29 x 20 ½ In. 125
Heron, Body Details, Glass Bead Eyes, White, Black, Rectangular Base, Late 1800s, 7 ½ In. 677
Humpback Whale, Glass Eyes, Driftwood Base, Signed, Frank Adamo, 11 x 17 In. 1020
Hunter, Slain Deer Over Shoulder, Black Forest, Late 1700s, 34 x 18 x 11 In. *illus* 6600
Indian Maiden, Cottonwood, Poplar, Knife In Hand, Headdress, Early 1900s, 12 x 3 In. 288
Jesus Christ, Standing, Circular Base, Philippines, c.1900s, 15 In. *illus* 108
Joan Of Arc, Standing, Armor Suit, Torch Light, Multicolor, 1800s, 91 x 22 x 17 In. *illus* 11500
Jungle Scene, Elephants, Monkeys, Vines, Teak, 1900s, 54 x 25 ½ In. 156
Madonna, Standing, Closed Eyes, Varnish, 34 In. 2875
Madonna, Votive Figure, Multicolor, Gilt, Molded Plinth, Painted, Early 1700s, 21 In. 761
Man, Painted, Multicolor, Square Base, 9 ½ In. *illus* 94
Man, Riding Horse, Painted, White, Red & Blue, Rectangular Base, 17 x 14 In. *illus* 102
Man, Standing, Moustache, Left Hand On His Stomach, Square Base, 1800s, 59 In. 4613
Mask, Animal, Staring, Open Mouth, Carved Teeth, Multicolor, Peru, 9 ½ x 11 x 11 In. *illus* 246
Mermaid, Pine, Multicolor, 40 x 16 x 19 In. *illus* 1116
Model, Horse, Striding, Dark Brown, Rectangular Base, 14 x 12 x 4 In. *illus* 313
Parrot, Perched On Swing, Painted, c.1900, 12 In. 1107
Penguin, Standing, Square Base, Painted, Charles Hart Style, 1900s, 9 ¾ In. 594
Plaque, Basket Of Fruit & Vegetables, Painted, 1800s, 10 x 18 In. 5535
Plaque, Chinese Landscape, Central Gilt Eagle, Shield, c.1850-75, 11 ½ x 13 In. 4920
Plaque, Don't Give Up On The Ship, Eagle, Banner, Artistic Carving Company, Boston, 9 x 27 In. 502
Plaque, Eagle, Bellamy Style, Enamel, Gold, Painted, Softwood, Chuck Dorr, 24 In. 380
Plaque, Eagle, Gilt, Feather Details, Spread Wings, George Stapf, 1900s, 30 In. 1845
Plaque, Eagle, Pine, Painted Shield, Gilded, John H. Bellamy, New England, c.1900, 47 In. 1329
Plaque, Eagle, Pine, Spread Wings, Feet Holding 3 Arrows, Painted, 7 x 17 ¾ In. 554
Plaque, Eagle, Spread Wings, Holding Shield, Arrows, Banner, Pine, 1850s, 9 x 24 In. 456
Plaque, Eagle, Spread Wings, Walnut, c.1900, 45 x 14 In. 472
Plaque, Game Birds, Deer, Antlers, Mounted, Black Forest, Late 1800s, 47 x 25 x 10 In. 3250
Plaque, Gilt, Gold, Tin Overlay, Cherubs, Swag, Flower, Early 1900s, 15 x 44 x 1 In. 129
Plaque, Pine, State Of Maine Seal, Sailor, Farmer, Cartouche, Dirigo, 30 x 42 In. *illus* 1638

Wood Carving, Bald Eagle, Standing, Painted, Mounted, Joseph Moyer, 8 In.
$5,368

Pook & Pook

Wood Carving, Bust, Antheia, Girl, Goddess, Mahogany, 12 x 5 x 19 ½ In.
$944

Copake Auctions

Wood Carving, Dog, Pierced With Iron Nails, Metal Fragments, Nkisi Nkondi, Africa, 10 ½ x 22 In.
$256

Neal Auction Company

Wood Carving, Eagle, Bellamy Style, Pine, Spread Wings, Shield, Red, White, Blue Paint, 8 x 27 ½ x 5 In.
$410

Thomaston Place Auction Galleries

Wood Carving, Elephant, Ironwood, Applied Eyes & Toes, Wood Tusks, Incised Details, c.1910, 37 x 42 In.
$1,250

New Orleans Auction Galleries

Wood Carving, French Horn, Linden, Fumio Yoshimura, Japan, 16 In.
$688

Freeman's Auctioneers & Appraisers

TIP
When you open your windows in warm weather, watch out for blowing curtains. They may hit glass or china displayed nearby and cause damage.

Wood Carving, Great Horned Owl, Mechanism Flaps Wings, Painted, Mike Borrett, 1900s, 25 In.
$900

Eldred's

Wood Carving, Hunter, Slain Deer Over Shoulder, Black Forest, Late 1700s, 34 x 18 x 11 In.
$6,600

Brunk Auctions

Wood Carving, Jesus Christ, Standing, Circular Base, Philippines, c.1900s, 15 In.
$108

Eldred's

Wood Carving, Joan Of Arc, Standing, Armor Suit, Torch Light, Multicolor, 1800s, 91 x 22 x 17 In.
$11,500

Stevens Auction Co.

Wood Carving, Man, Painted, Multicolor, Square Base, 9 ½ In.
$94

Copake Auctions

Plaque, Putto, Surrounded By Circular Nimbus, Fluted Accents, 20 x 8 In. 530
Plate Mold, Solid Birch, Turned Treen, c.1830, 2 x 8 ½ In. 211
Puffin, Standing, Tuft, Painted, Signed On Base, Joseph Moyer, 8 ¾ In. 2684
Putti, Heads, Leaves, Painted, Gilt, 1800s, 8 x 12 In. .... *illus* 144
Putto, Baroque, Giltwood, Arms Outstretched, Base, Italy, 1600s-1700s, 22 In. .... *illus* 354
Robin, Painted, Round Base, Signed, R. Mitchell, 6 In. 177
Rooster, Standing, Tin Tail, Painted, Rectangular Base, c.1900, 8 In., Pair 488
Santo, Bishop, Standing, Gilt, Painted, Multicolor, Flat Back, c.1715, 46 In. 1968
Santo, Glass Eyes, White Cassock, Black Shawl, Italy, 1700s, 20 x 8 ½ In. 1000
Santo, St. Anna, Fruitwood, Standing, Holding Bible, Continental, c.1715, 29 ¾ In. 3075
Sconce, Figural Drum, Horns, Arrows, Painted, Spanish Colonial, 30 x 10 ½ x 9 In. 1230
Shoe, Woman's, High Heel, Black, Painted, 19th Century Style, 4 x 9 ½ In. .... *illus* 212
Shorebird, Sanderling, Standing, Driftwood Base, Randy & Elaine Fisher, 1981, 2 ½ x 7 In. 113
Snow Owl, Enamel, Painted, Perched, Beam, Signed, W.T. Baldwin, 27 x 9 x 8 In. 585
Soldier, Standing, Bugle, Multicolor, Painted, Square Base, Syracuse N.Y., 41 In. 384
Sperm Whale, Inscribed Decal, Monogram, Clark Voorhees, 5 ½ x 17 In. .... *illus* 1574
Sperm Whale, Mounted, Pine Backboard, Daniel Bruffee, 12 x 28 ½ In. .... *illus* 510
Sperm Whale, Plaque, Black, Clark G. Voorhees Jr., 1960s, 17 In. 1107
Sphynx, Wood, Gilt, Feathered Wings, Paw Feet, c.1820, 12 x 7 x 15 In., Pair 3630
Toma Maternity, Mother Feeding 2 Children, Africa, 27 In. .... *illus* 81
Whale, Painted, Black, Clark G. Voorhees Jr., 18 In. 2760
Woman, Holding Fan, Painted, Black Base, Asia, 19 ½ In. 138
Woman, Hysterical, Articulated Shoulders, Painted, Pedro Friedeberg, 28 x 15 x 1 ½ In. ... *illus* 938
Woman, Nude, Standing, Light Brown, Stand, 17 ⅝ In. 281
Woman, Seated On Stool, 2 Babies, Breast Feeding, Senufo, Africa, 22 In. .... *illus* 420
Woman, Seated On Stool, Resting, Baule, Africa, 23 In. 303

WOODEN

Wooden wares were used in all parts of the home. Wood was used for many containers and tools. Small wooden pieces are called *treenware* in England, but the term *woodenware* is more common in the United States. Additional pieces may be found in the Advertising, Kitchen, and Tool categories.

Barrel, Lid, Green Highlights, Rope Handle, Stenciled HMS Bounty 1788, 1800s, 18 x 11 In. *illus* 125
Barrel, Oval, Hole, Red Paint, Strap, Oak, 12 ½ x 21 In. 83
Bowl, Ash Burl, Carved Rim Edge, Pennsylvania, 1800s, 5 ½ x 16 In. .... *illus* 1200
Bowl, Green, Round, Patina, 1800s, 11 x 10 ½ x 3 In. 288
Bowl, Pine, Turned, Flat Rim, Blue Paint, Late 1800s, 16 In. 500
Bowl, Turned Ash Burl, Shouldered Lip & Foot, 1800s, 4 ½ x 12 ½ In. 702
Bowl, Turned Ash Leaf Maple, Spherical, Signed Philip Moulthrop, 8 ½ x 11 In. .... *illus* 1440
Bowl, Turned Burl, Rim, Footed Base, Early 1800s, 5 ¾ x 13 In. .... *illus* 1180
Bowl, Turned Burl, Treen, Molded Rim, Grooved Foot, c.1800, 5 x 15 ½ x 16 In. 1755
Bowl, Turned, Red Stain, 1800s, 4 ½ x 14 In. .... *illus* 234
Brush Rest, Scholar's Rock Shape, Carved, Aperture, Chinese, 5 ½ In. .... *illus* 2460
Bucket, Fitted Dome Lid, Pine, Iron Bond, Bowed Side, Chinese, 1900s, 14 x 14 In. 23
Bucket, Pine, Yellow, Stave Construction, Bail Handle, Brown Red Grain, c.1900, 12 In. 120
Bucket, Stave Construction, Lift Lid, Light Green, 1860s, 16 x 15 In. 1440
Bucket, Stave, Iron Band, Horizontal Yellow, Black, Orange, Red, Green, 1800s, 9 x 10 ½ In. .. 2091
Bucket, Yellow, 3 Iron Bands, Swing Bail Handle, Black Stencil, 10 x 12 In. 81
Canteen, Cheese Box, Green, Red Border, Painted, Leather Strap, Early 1800s, 6 x 2 ⅞ In. 492
Canteen, Oval, Iron Band, Flat Bottom, 1800s, 7 x 6 ⅞ x 5 ¾ In .... *illus* 140
Canteen, Red Paint, Cylindrical, Iron Straps, 11 In. 236
Carrier, Oak, Mustard Ground, Divided, Handle, Rectangular, 1800s, 8 x 17 x 10 In. 366
Compote, Round, Turned Stem, Molded Base, 1800s, 8 ½ x 16 ½ In. 384
Cup, Lehnware, Rose, Leaf, Salmon Ground, Red Stem, Green, Blue Base, 3 ⅜ In. .... *illus* 1599
Cup, Presentation, Hunter With Gun, Dog, Walnut, 6 In. 1020
Firkin, Lid, Bentwood Handle, Painted, Brown, c.1800, 11 ½ In. 106
Firkin, Lid, Cedar, Tapered Construction, Handle, Joseph Clark, c.1920s, 5 ½ x 5 ½ In. .. *illus* 390

Wood Carving, Man, Riding Horse, Painted, White, Red & Blue, Rectangular Base, 17 x 14 In.
$102

Hartzell's Auction Gallery Inc.

Wood Carving, Mask, Animal, Staring, Open Mouth, Carved Teeth, Multicolor, Peru, 9 ½ x 11 x 11 In.
$246

Clars Auction Gallery

Wood Carving, Mermaid, Pine, Multicolor, 40 x 16 x 19 In.
$1,116

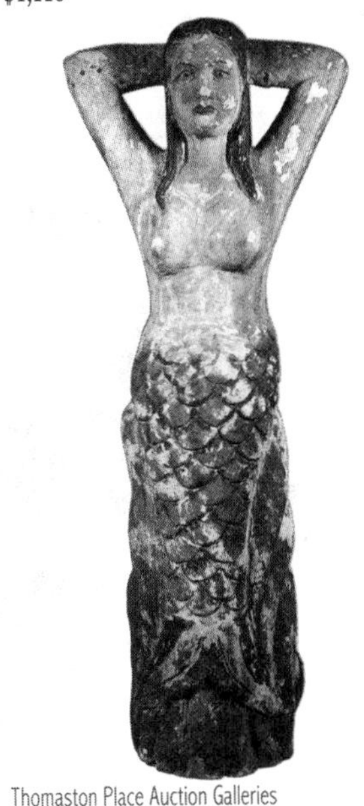

Thomaston Place Auction Galleries

WOODEN

Wood Carving, Model, Horse, Striding, Dark Brown, Rectangular Base, 14 x 12 x 4 In.
$313

Hindman Auctions

Wood Carving, Plaque, Pine, State Of Maine Seal, Sailor, Farmer, Cartouche, Dirigo, 30 x 42 In.
$1,638

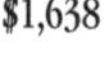

Thomaston Place Auction Galleries

Wood Carving, Putto, Baroque, Giltwood, Arms Outstretched, Base, Italy, 1600s-1700s, 22 In.
$354

Clars Auction Gallery

Wood Carving, Shoe, Woman's, High Heel, Black, Painted, 19th Century Style, 4 x 9 ½ In.
$212

Bunch Auctions

Wood Carving, Sperm Whale, Inscribed Decal, Monogram, Clark Voorhees, 5 ½ x 17 In.
$1,574

Clars Auction Gallery

Wood Carving, Sperm Whale, Mounted, Pine Backboard, Daniel Bruffee, 12 x 28 ½ In.
$510

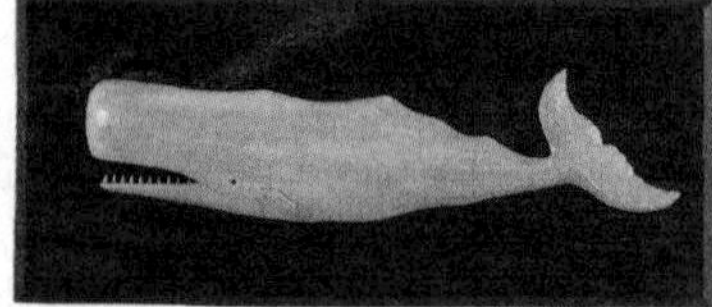

Eldred's

Wood Carving, Toma Maternity, Mother Feeding 2 Children, Africa, 27 In.
$81

Blackwell Auctions

Wood Carving, Woman, Hysterical, Articulated Shoulders, Painted, Pedro Friedeberg, 28 x 15 x 1 ½ In.
$938

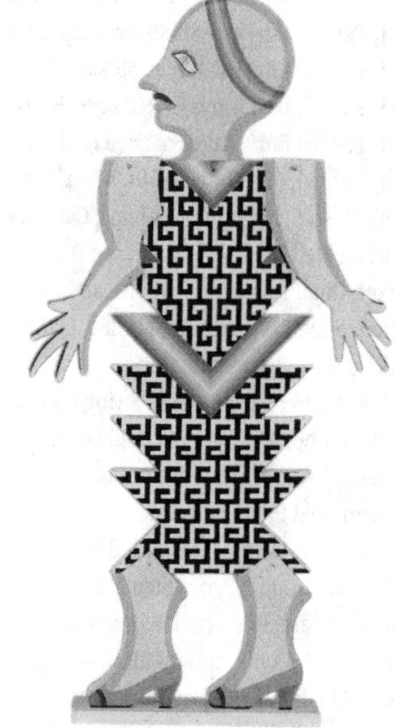

Palm Beach Modern Auctions

Wood Carving, Putti, Heads, Leaves, Painted, Gilt, 1800s, 8 x 12 In.
$144

Eldred's

Wood Carving, Woman, Seated On Stool, 2 Babies, Breast Feeding, Senufo, Africa, 22 In.
$420

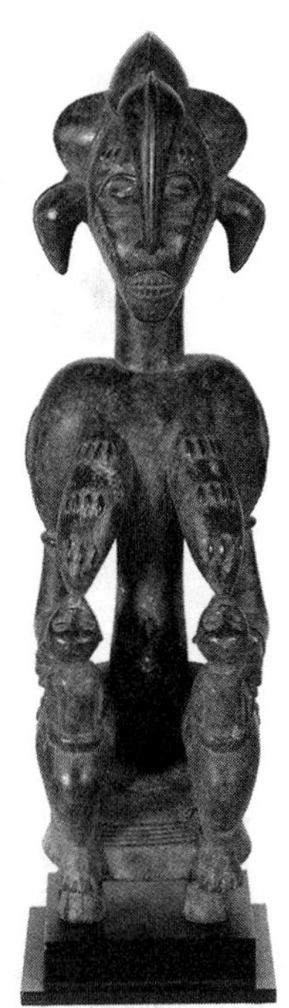

Michaan's Auctions

Wooden, Barrel, Lid, Green Highlights, Rope Handle, Stenciled HMS Bounty 1788, 1800s, 18 x 11 In.
$125

Eldred's

Wooden, Bowl, Ash Burl, Carved Rim Edge, Pennsylvania, 1800s, 5 ½ x 16 In.
$1,200

Case Antiques

Wooden, Bowl, Turned Ash Leaf Maple, Spherical, Signed Philip Moulthrop, 8 ½ x 11 In.
$1,440

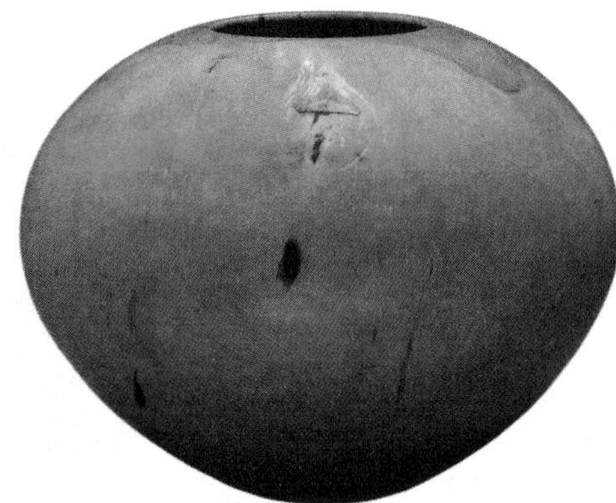

Morphy Auctions

Wooden, Bowl, Turned Burl, Rim, Footed Base, Early 1800s, 5 ¾ x 13 In.
$1,180

Cottone Auctions

Wooden, Bowl, Turned, Red Stain, 1800s, 4 ½ x 14 In.
$234

Skinner, Inc.

Wooden, Brush Rest, Scholar's Rock Shape, Carved, Aperture, Chinese, 5 ½ In.
$2,460

Clars Auction Gallery

Wooden, Canteen, Oval, Iron Band, Flat Bottom, 1800s, 7 x 6 ⅞ x 5 ¾ In
$140

Thomaston Place Auction Galleries

Wooden, Cup, Lehnware, Rose, Leaf, Salmon Ground, Red Stem, Green, Blue Base, 3 ⅜ In.
$1,599

Skinner, Inc.

TIP

Don't use cooking oil to polish furniture, cutting boards, even wooden salad bowls. The oil will eventually become rancid and the wood will have a bad odor and may even be able to contaminate food.

Wooden, Firkin, Lid, Cedar, Tapered Construction, Handle, Joseph Clark, c.1920s, 5 ½ x 5 ½ In.
$390

Eldred's

Wooden, Firkin, Lid, Green, Painted, Swing Handle, Late 1800s, 14 In.
$450

Eldred's

Wooden, Mortar & Pestle, Turned Handle, Green Ground, 1800s, 13 In.
$580

Pook & Pook

Wooden, Peat Bucket, Brassbound, Bail Handle, Band, 1800s, 12 ½ x 12 ¾ In.
$406

Eldred's

Wooden, Scepter, Ruyi, 3 Burl Panels, Chinese, 15 In.
$185

Clars Auction Gallery

Wooden, Sugar, Lid, Treen, Mustard Paint, 5 ¾ In.
$295

Copake Auctions

Wooden, Tray, Oval, Hand Painted, Rooster, Fruits, Hearts, Cream Ground, Peter Hunt, 34 In.
$300

Eldred's

Wooden, Urn, Gilt, Painted, Rose Garlands, Socle Base, Round Plinth, Louis XV, France, 1800s, 23 x 4 In.
$1,062

Ahlers & Ogletree Auction Gallery

Wooden, Tray, Dresser, Rectangular, Rounded Corners, Needlepoint, Beadwork Interior, 11 x 22 In.
$431

Richard D. Hatch & Associates

Firkin, Lid, Green Paint, Tacks, Swing Handle, 1800s, 18 x 11 ½ In. 236
Firkin, Lid, Green, Painted, Swing Handle, Late 1800s, 14 In. ....*illus* 450
Model, Covered Bridge, 16 x 23 x 15 In. 47
Mortar & Pestle, Treen, Maple, Blue, Turned, Urn Shape, Footed, 1810s, 7 ¾ In. 438
Mortar & Pestle, Turned Handle, Green Ground, 1800s, 13 In. ....*illus* 580
Pail, Mahogany, Brass Bands, Fitted Insert, George III, 16 x 14 ¾ In. 1107
Pail, Stave, Iron Band, Painted, Green Sponge, White Ground, Late 1800s, 4 ½ x 5 ½ In. 369
Peat Bucket, Brassbound, Bail Handle, Band, 1800s, 12 ½ x 12 ¾ In. ....*illus* 406
Peat Bucket, Marquise Shape, Brass Lift-Out Liner, Strap, 12 x 14 ½ In. 196
Scepter, Ruyi, 3 Burl Panels, Chinese, 15 In. ....*illus* 185
Sugar, Lid, Treen, Mustard Paint, 5 ¾ In. ....*illus* 295
Tray, Dresser, Rectangular, Rounded Corners, Needlepoint, Beadwork Interior, 11 x 22 In. *illus* 431
Tray, Oval, Hand Painted, Rooster, Fruits, Hearts, Cream Ground, Peter Hunt, 34 In. ......*illus* 300
Tub, Pine, Overlapping Tapering Staves, Ash Handle, 1800s, 15 x 21 In. 800
Urn, Gilt, Painted, Rose Garlands, Socle Base, Round Plinth, Louis XV, France, 1800s, 23 x 4 In. .*illus* 1062
Vase, Burl, Molded Rim, Shouldered, Signed Erico, 14 ½ In. 150
Vase, Loblolly Pine, Spherical, Turned, Philip Moulthrop, Signed, 10 x 12 In. 1800
Vase, Spalted Silver Maple, Philip Moulthrop, c.1990, 5 ¾ x 6 In. ....*illus* 1500

WORCESTER

Worcester porcelains were made in Worcester, England, from 1751. The firm went through many name changes and eventually, in 1862, became The Royal Worcester Porcelain Company Ltd. Collectors often refer to Dr. Wall, Barr, Flight, and other names that indicate time periods or artists at the factory. It became part of Royal Worcester Spode Ltd. in 1976. The company was bought by the Portmeirion Group in 2009. Related pieces may be found in the Royal Worcester category.

Bowl, Lid, Fluted, Bud Finial, Flowers, White & Blue, 5 In. 123
Bowl, Lord Henry Thynne Type, Fluted, Gilt, Scalloped Rim, Flowers, 5 ⅞ In. 92
Jug, Sparrow Beak Spout, Flowers, Blue Crescent, Marked, 4 In. 105
Mug, Sunflowers & Roses, Strap Handle, Marked Cypher C, Dr. Wall, c.1800, 6 In. ....*illus* 270
Plate, Canopic, White Ground, Flowers, Central Medallion, Gilt Rim, 1900s, 9 In., 12 Piece..... 313
Plate, Gilt, Scalloped Rim, Blue Ground, Flowers Center, 7 ½ In. 92
Urn, Lid, Reticulated Egg Shape, 3 Scrolled Feet, Jewels, Grainger, c.1870, 8 x 3 In. ....*illus* 246

WORLD WAR

World War I and World War II souvenirs are collected today. Be careful not to store anything that includes live ammunition. Your local police will tell you how to dispose of the explosives. See also Sword and Trench Art.

WORLD WAR I

Gas Mask, C.W. Steverson, Co. C, 87th Division, Pouch, 1918-1919, 10 x 10 In. ....*illus* 266
Medal, Iron Cross, Metal, 800 Silver Border, Black & White Ribbon, 1 $^{3}/_{16}$ In. ....*illus* 124
Pin, Red Star, 5-Point, Silver Medallion, Cyrillic Writing, Screw Back, 2 x 1 ⅜ In. 30
Poster, Enlist In The Navy, To Arms, Bugle Player, M. Bancroft, c.1917, 41 x 27 In. 250
Poster, For Home & Country, Victory Liberty Loan, Soldier & Family, A. Orr, 1918, 40 In. 188
Poster, I Want You For U.S. Army, Uncle Sam, J.M. Flagg, 1917, 40 x 30 In. 7200
Poster, The First Three!, Portraits, Flag, Red Cross, War Fund, Frame, 1918, 29 x 23 In. ..*illus* 91
Poster, You, Buy A Liberty Bond Lest I Perish, Angry Statue Of Liberty, 40 x 30 In. 813

WORLD WAR II

Binoculars, Big Eye, Naval, Coated Steel, Painted, Pedestal, Nikkon Optics, 21 x 24 x 13 In. *illus* 5265
Cane, Carved, Swastika, Iron Cross, 38 In. 469
Cap, Shako, Police Officer, Green Wool, Leather Trim, Robert Lubftein, Berlin, Size 58 ....*illus* 660
Dress Dagger & Scabbard, Runic SS, Marked RZM, Germany, 15 In. 318
Game, Plonk The Welcome Game, Propaganda, Darts, 16 x 16 In. 350
Goblet, Honor, Luftwaffe, Iron Cross, Eagle, G. Berthold, Metal, Wagner & Sohn, 8 In. 2700
Helmet, German, Metal, Decal, Leather Chin Strap, 6 x 11 In. ....*illus* 502

Wooden, Vase, Spalted Silver Maple, Philip Moulthrop, c.1990, 5 ¾ x 6 In.
$1,500

Rago Arts and Auction Center

Worcester, Mug, Sunflowers & Roses, Strap Handle, Marked Cypher C, Dr. Wall, c.1800, 6 In.
$270

Eldred's

Worcester, Urn, Lid, Reticulated Egg Shape, 3 Scrolled Feet, Jewels, Grainger, c.1870, 8 x 3 In.
$246

Locati Auctions

W

World War I, Gas Mask, C.W. Steverson, Co. C, 87th Div., Pouch, 1918-1919, 10 x 10 In.
$266

Cottone Auctions

World War I, Medal, Iron Cross, Metal, 800 Silver Border, Black & White Ribbon, 1 3/16 In.
$124

DuMouchelles

World War I, Poster, The First Three!, Portraits, Flag, Red Cross, War Fund, Frame, 1918, 29 x 23 In.
$91

Bruneau & Co. Auctioneers

Non-Smoking Hitler
Hitler was the only important World War II leader who didn't smoke.

World War II, Binoculars, Big Eye, Naval, Coated Steel, Painted, Pedestal, Nikkon Optics, 21 x 24 x 13 In.
$5,265

Thomaston Place Auction Galleries

World War II, Cap, Shako, Police Officer, Green Wool, Leather Trim, Robert Lubftein, Berlin, 58 In.
$660

Rich Penn Auctions

World War II, Helmet, German, Metal, Decal, Leather Chin Strap, 6 x 11 In.
$502

Cottone Auctions

World War II, Poster, Buy Defense Bonds, Wood, Carved V, Circular Shield, Tank, Ship, Plane, 49 In.
$780

Bunte Auction Services

World War II, Poster, Buy War Bonds, Uncle Sam, American Flag, Planes, Soldiers, 1942, 59 x 40 In.
$900

Case Antiques

World War II, Poster, Defend Your Country, Enlist Now In The U.S. Army, Uncle Sam, Eagle, 38 x 25 In.
$120

Ripley Auctions

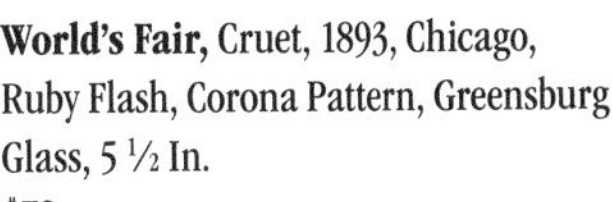

Helmet, Metal, Black, Leather Liner, Runic SS, Swastika Shield, Germany 388
Helmet, Shako, Police, Green, Leather Top & Chin Strap, Aluminum Nazi Insignia 283
Pin, German Iron Cross, 1st Class, Marked 950, 1914 136
Pin, German Iron Cross, 2nd Class, 1939 72
Plaque, Third Reich, Profile Of Hitler's Head, Cast Iron, 12 ½ x 8 ½ In. 450
Poster, Buy Defense Bonds, Wood, Carved V, Circular Shield, Tank, Ship, Plane, 49 In. ...*illus* 780
Poster, Buy War Bonds, Uncle Sam, American Flag, Planes, Soldiers, 1942, 59 x 40 In. ...*illus* 900
Poster, Defend Your Country, Enlist Now In The U.S. Army, Uncle Sam, Eagle, 38 x 25 In. *illus* 120
Poster, Every Fire Is Sabotage, Black & Red Text, Hitler, Tojo, Frame, c.1943, 29 x 23 In. 188
Sword, German Police Officer's, D-Shape Guard, Pommel, Pet. Dan. Krebs, Solingen, 29 In. ... 484

WORLD'S FAIR

World's Fair souvenirs from all of the fairs are collected. The first fair was the Great Exhibition of 1851 in London. Some other important exhibitions and fairs include Philadelphia, 1876 (Centennial); Chicago, 1893 (World's Columbian); Buffalo, 1901 (Pan-American); St. Louis, 1904 (Louisiana Purchase); Portland, 1905 (Lewis & Clark Centennial Exposition); San Francisco, 1915 (Panama-Pacific); Paris (International Exposition of Modern Decorative and Industrial Arts), 1925; Philadelphia, 1926 (Sesquicentennial); Chicago, 1933 (Century of Progress); Cleveland, 1936 (Great Lakes); San Francisco, 1939 (Golden Gate International); New York, 1939 (World of Tomorrow); Seattle, 1962 (Century 21); New York, 1964; Montreal, 1967; Knoxville (Energy Turns the World) 1982; New Orleans, 1984; Tsukuba, Japan, 1985; Vancouver, Canada, 1986; Brisbane, Australia, 1988; Seville, Spain, 1992; Genoa, Italy, 1992; Seoul, South Korea, 1993; Lisbon, Portugal, 1998; Hanover, Germany, 2000; Shanghai, China, 2010; and Milan, Italy, 2015. Memorabilia of fairs include directories, pictures, fabrics, ceramics, etc. Memorabilia from other similar celebrations may be listed in the Souvenir category.

Bank, Mechanical, 1893, Chicago, Goldtone, Oblong Base, Gentleman Seated, J. & E. Stevens. 870
Booklet, 1933, Chicago, Official World's Fair Pictures, Art Deco Building 20
Cruet, 1893, Chicago, Ruby Flash, Corona Pattern, Greensburg Glass, 5 ½ In. ....*illus* 72
Lamp, 1893, Chicago, Columbian Coin, Central Glass Co., Kerosene, 11 ⅜ x 5 ¾ In. 293
Lamp, 1939, New York, Globe, Stars, Ring, Frosted Green Glass, Stepped Base, 11 x 7 In. .*illus* 678
Medal, 1958, Brussels, Bruxelles, Mannekin-Pis, Pictures Boy Statue, Gold 860
Plate, 1904, St. Louis, Festival Hall, Cascade Gardens, Gilt, Westmoreland Glass, 7 In. 31
Poster, 1964, New York, Unisphere, Beams Of Light, D. Klein, 40 x 25 In. 1440
Toy, Tractor Train, New York, 1939, Cast Iron, Arcade, Tin Roof, Decals, 16 In. ....*illus* 660

WPA

WPA is the abbreviation for Works Progress Administration, a program created by executive order in 1935 to provide jobs for millions of unemployed Americans. Artists were hired to create murals, paintings, drawings, and sculptures for public buildings. Pieces are marked *WPA* and may have the artist's name on them.

Figures, Man & Woman, Composition, Cloth Dress & Suit, Base Marked 1880, WPA, 12 In. 90
Plaque, Built By Works Progress Administration 1937, Metal, 6 x 11 In. 344
Woodblock Print, Social Activities In The 30's, Ronald Slayton, Dated 1939, 32 x 16 In. 185
Woodblock Print, Surendorf, State St., Columbia, Calif., Gold Rush Town, 16 x 11 In. 475

WRISTWATCH

Wristwatches came into use during World War I. Wristwatches are listed here by manufacturer or as advertising or character watches. Wristwatches may also be listed in other categories. Pocket watches are listed in the Watch category.

World's Fair, Cruet, 1893, Chicago, Ruby Flash, Corona Pattern, Greensburg Glass, 5 ½ In.
$72

Woody Auctions

World's Fair, Lamp, 1939, New York, Globe, Stars, Ring, Frosted Green Glass, Stepped Base, 11 x 7 In.
$678

Soulis Auctions

World's Fair, Toy, Tractor Train, New York, 1939, Cast Iron, Arcade, Tin Roof, Decals, 16 In.
$660

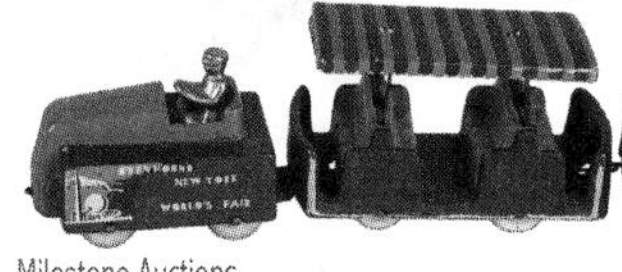

Milestone Auctions

W

Wristwatch, 14K White Gold & Diamond, Woman's
$225

Hudson Valley Auctions

Wristwatch, Girard-Perregaux, 18K Gold, Square Dial, 17 Jewel, Woven, Bracelet, Woman's, c.1950
$1,368

Eldred's

Wristwatch, Hamilton, 14K White Gold, Rectangular Face, Silver Dot Hour Markers, Woman's
$570

Michaan's Auctions

Wristwatch, Movado, 14K Gold, Mesh Bracelet, Roman Numerals, White Dial, Woman's
$732

Nadeau's Auction Gallery

Wristwatch, Omega, Seamaster, Automatic Chronometer, 18K Gold
$2,074

Nadeau's Auction Gallery

Wristwatch, Rolex, 14K White Gold, 17 Round Diamonds, Dress Model, Woman's
$863

Richard D. Hatch & Associates

Wristwatch, Rolex, 18K Gold, Oyster Perpetual, Diamond Dial, Rivet Style Bracelet, Woman's
$6,000

Morphy Auctions

Wristwatch, Rolex, Oyster Perpetual Date, Automatic, Stainless Steel, Woman's, c.1980
$1,265

Blackwell Auctions

W

14K White Gold & Diamond, Woman's ... *illus* 225
Audemars Piguet, Stainless Steel, Square Head, 18 Jewel, Brown Leather Band, Genevieve ... 6435
Baum & Mercier, Tank, 18K Gold, Date Window, Leather Band ... 443
Bertolucci, 18K Gold, Stainless Steel, White Dial, Roman Numeral Marker, Woman's ... 230
Breitling, Chronomat, 18K Gold, Stainless Steel, Black Dial, Gold Numbers, Bullet Band ... 2250
Breitling, Windrider, Crosswind Automatic Chronograph, Stainless Steel Case ... 3000
Brietling, 18K Rose Gold, Chronograph, 17 Jewels, Leather Band ... 2300
Bugatti, Chrome Plated, Metal Head, Black Leather Band, Jean Perret ... 187
Bulgari, Stainless Steel, Chronograph, 22 Jewel, Black Leather Band, Swiss ... 1089
Bulova, 14K White Gold, 17 Jewel, Dot Hour Marker, Arabic Numerals, Woman's ... 308
Bulova, 14K Yellow Gold, Octagon Head, Garnet Dial, Snakeskin Bracelet ... 995
Bulova, 14K Yellow Gold, Round Head, Brown Crocodile Band, Quartz, Accutron ... 585
Citroen, Stainless Steel Head, Black Band, Steering Wheel Case ... 59
Concord, 14K Gold, Tank Style, 2-Tone Dial, Blued Hands, Quartz, Gold Link Bracelet ... 1476
Concord, 14K Yellow Gold, 30 Round Diamonds, Black Dial, Hour Markers, Woman's ... 1150
Ebel, 18K Gold, Stainless Steel Case, Yellow Gold Wave, Gold Bezel, Woman's ... 502
Eterna, 18K Yellow Gold, Square, Applied Baton Hour Markers, Swiss, Woman's ... 1437
Geneve, 18K Yellow Gold, Square Shaped Head, Snakeskin Band, 17 Jewel, Woman's ... 1287
Geneve, Mesh Band, 14K Gold, Diamond Surrounds, Woman's ... 1191
Girard-Perregaux, 18K Gold, Square Dial, 17 Jewel, Woven, Bracelet, Woman's, c.1950 ... *illus* 1368
Gold, 14K Gold, White Face, Quartz Movement, Jordan Bay Valeria ... 1356
Gubelin, 18K Gold, Automatic, Square Case, Dauphine Hands, Gold Mesh Bracelet, c.1960 ... 1599
Hamilton, 14K White Gold, Piping Rock, Silver Dial, Tonneau Shape, c.1929 ... 875
Hamilton, 14K White Gold, Rectangular Face, Silver Dot Hour Markers, Woman's ... *illus* 570
Hamilton, Platinum & Diamond, 17 Jewel, Foldover Clasp, Safety Chain, Woman's, c.1950 ... 1404
Hermes, Medor, Gold Plated, Stainless Steel, Red Band, Box, Pouch, Woman's ... 1102
International Watch Co., 18K, Little Da Vinci, Moon Phase, Chronometer, Leather Band ... 3835
Jacob & Co., 5 Time Zones, Stainless Steel, Mother-Of-Pearl Dial, Quartz, Box ... 2500
LeCoultre, Memovox, 10K Gold Filled, Leather Band, Woman's ... 406
Longines, 14K Gold, Dial Enamel ... 1265
Longines, 14K Yellow Gold, 17 Jewel, Woman's, c.1950 ... 1170
Longines, 18K Gold, Square Case, Stick Dial, 17 Jewel, Woven Bracelet, Woman's ... 976
Movado, 14K Gold, Mesh Bracelet, Roman Numerals, White Dial, Woman's ... *illus* 732
Omega, 14K Yellow Gold, Black Date Dial, Leather Band ... 531
Omega, Seamaster, Automatic Chronometer, 18K Gold ... *illus* 2074
Patek Philippe Calatrava, 18K Gold, Porcelain Dial, Eel Skin Band, Germany ... 8100
Patek Philippe, 18K, Tank Style Case, Silver Split Dial, Gold Dauphine Hands, c.1940 ... 3198
Piaget, 18K White Gold, Rectangular, 17 Jewel, Roman Numeral Marker, Black Band ... 1845
Rolex, 14K White Gold, 17 Round Diamonds, Dress Model, Woman's ... *illus* 863
Rolex, 18K Gold, Oyster Perpetual, Diamond Dial, Rivet Style Bracelet, Woman's ... *illus* 6000
Rolex, Oyster Perpetual Date, Automatic, Stainless Steel, Woman's, c.1980 ... *illus* 1265
Rolex, Oyster Perpetual, Gold, Stainless Steel, 18K, Black Dial, Diamond Marker, Woman's ... 8640
Rolex, Stainless Steel Case, 18K Gold Bezel, Champagne Dial, Datejust, c.1985 ... 2460
Tag Heuer, Stainless Steel, Swiss Automatic, Calibre 60 Movement ... 826
Universal, Mesh Bracelet, 18K Yellow Gold, Roman Numeral Markers, Woman's ... 1244
Wittnauer, 14K Gold, Crosshatch, Hours, Seconds Bit Dial, Leather Band, Box ... 452
Wittnauer, Chronograph, Stainless Steel Round Head, Black Leather Band, Genevieve ... 1053
Wittnauer, Stainless Steel Case, Black Matte Dial, Rotating Bezel, c.1960 ... 1107

YELLOWWARE

Yellowware is a heavy earthenware made of a yellowish clay. It varies in color from light yellow to orange-yellow. Many nineteenth- and twentieth-century kitchen bowls and jugs were made of yellowware. It was made in England and in the United States. Another form of pottery that is sometimes classed as yellowware is listed in this book in the Mocha category.

Bowl, Banded Seaweed, Molded Base, Late 1800s, 5 x 11 ½ In. ... *illus* 120
Bowl, Blue & White Bands, 4 ⅜ x 2 In. ... 40

TIP
Replace a broken watch crystal immediately to avoid letting dust or moisture into the watchworks.

Yellowware, Bowl, Banded Seaweed, Molded Base, Late 1800s, 5 x 11 ½ In.
$120

Eldred's

Yellowware, Figurine, Dog, Spaniel, Curly Coat, Rockingham Glaze, Scalloped Base, 1800s, 10 x 8 x 5 In.
$79

Soulis Auctions

Yellowware, Jar, Lid, Blue Bands, 5 ⅜ x 4 ¼ In.
$79

Hartzell's Auction Gallery Inc.

This is an edited listing of current prices. Visit **Kovels.com** to check thousands of prices from previous years and sign up for free information on trends, tips, reproductions, marks, and more.

Zanesville, Vase, Stoneware, Glossy Black Glaze, Chip At Base, 11 ¾ in.
$46

Belhorn Auction Services

Zsolnay, Vase, Marbleized, Eosin Glaze, 2 Ribbon Handles, 5 Churches Mark, 1897-98, 9 x 5 In.
$2,280

Ripley Auctions

Zsolnay, Vase, Osiris, Lotus Flowers, Bulbous, Cylindrical Neck, Gilt, Pewter Mounts, c.1900, 7 ½ In.
$1,230

Skinner, Inc.

Figurine, Dog, Spaniel, Curly Coat, Rockingham Glaze, Scalloped Base, 1800s, 10 x 8 x 5 In. *.illus* 79
Figurine, Dog, Spaniel, Seated Position, Blue, Brown Splotch, 1800s, 11 In. 369
Figurine, Dog, Whippet, Lying Down, Rectangular Base, Glaze, c.1850, 6 x 10 x 4 ¾ In. 3690
Flask, Potato Shape, Glaze, Signed, E.G., 4 ¾ In. 325
Jar, Lid, Blue Bands, 5 ⅜ x 4 ¼ In. *illus* 79
Teapot, 3 Colors, Scroll Shape, Lid, Handle, Salmon Ground, c.1830, 4 In. 2706

LA MORO

ZANESVILLE

Zanesville Art Pottery was founded in 1900 by David Schmidt in Zanesville, Ohio. The firm made faience umbrella stands, jardinieres, and pedestals. The company closed in 1920 and Weller bought the factory. Many pieces are marked with just the words *La Moro*.

Planter, Green Matte Glaze, 10 x 3 In. 85
Vase, Daffodils, Gloss Aqua, 6-Sided, Marked, c.1920, 9 In. 100
Vase, Gray, Green Splashes, Brown & Black Drip, Shouldered, c.1920, 4 x 5 In. 35
Vase, Ribbed, Turquoise Glaze, 4 x 5 ¼ In. 29
Zanesville, Vase, Stoneware, Glossy Black Glaze, Chip At Base, 11 ¾ in. *illus* 46

ZSOLNAY

Zsolnay pottery was made in Hungary after 1853 and was characterized by Persian, Art Nouveau, or Hungarian motifs. A series of new Zsolnay figurines with green-gold luster finish is available in many shops today. Early Zsolnay was not marked, but by 1878 the tower trademark was used.

Zsolnay Porcelanmanufaktura
1878

Zsolnay Porcelanmanufaktura
1899–1920

Zsolnay Porcelanmanufaktura
1900+

Vase, Figural, 3-D Maiden, Sitting, Iridescent Green Glaze, Art Nouveau, 9 x 5 x 4 ¾ In. 420
Vase, Marbleized, Eosin Glaze, 2 Ribbon Handles, 5 Churches Mark, 1897-98, 9 x 5 In. *...illus* 2280
Vase, Osiris, Lotus Flowers, Bulbous, Cylindrical Neck, Gilt, Pewter Mounts, c.1900, 7 ½ In. *illus* 1230
Vase, Postcards, Figural Women, Long Dresses, Green, Hungary, c.1903, 3 x 4 ¾ In. 1000
Vase, Stick, Gilt Outlined Flowers, Crane, Mottled Brown Ground, 10 ¾ x 5 ½ In. 450

INDEX

This index is computer-generated, making it as complete and accurate as possible. References in uppercase type are category listings. Those in lowercase letters refer to additional pages where pieces can be found. There is also an internal cross-referencing system used in the main part of the book, so if you look for a Kewpie doll in the Doll category, you will be told it is in its own category. There is additional information at the end of many paragraphs about where to find prices of pieces similar to yours.

A

B

E

F

G

H

T

U

V

W

PHOTO CREDITS

We have included the name of the auction house or photographer with each pictured object. This is a list of the addresses of those who have contributed photographs and information for this book. Every dealer or auction has to buy antiques to have items to sell. Call or email a dealer or auction house if you want to discuss buying or selling. If you need an appraisal or advice, remember that appraising is part of their business and fees may be charged.

Abington Auction Gallery
3263 North Dixie Hwy.
Oakland Park, FL 33334
abingtonauctions.com
954-900-4869

Actéon Auction
Hotel Des Ventes De Senlis
63, rue du Faubourg Saint-Martin
60300 Senlis, France
senlis@acteon.auction

Ahlers & Ogletree Auction Gallery
715 Miami Circle, Suite 210
Atlanta, GA 30324
aandoauctions.com
404-869-2478

Alderfer Auction Company
501 Fairgrounds Rd.
Hatfield, PA 19440
alderferauction.com
215-393-3000

American Bottle Auctions
915 28th St.
Sacramento, CA 95816
americanbottle.com
800-806-7722

AntiqueAdvertising.com
P.O. Box 247
Cazenovia, NY 13035
antiqueadvertising.com
315-662-7625

Apple Tree Auction Center
1625 W. Church St.
Newark, OH 43055
appletreeauction.com
704-344-4282

Auction Team Breker
P.O. Box 50 11 19
50971 Köln, Germany
breker.com
207-485-8343 (USA)

Austin Auction Gallery
8414 Anderson Mill Rd.
Austin, TX 78729-4702
austinauction.com
512-258-5479

Belhorn Auction Services
2746 Wynnerock Ct.
Hilliard, OH 43026
belhorn.com
614-921-9441

Bertoia Auctions
2141 DeMarco Dr.
Vineland, NJ 08360
bertoiaauctions.com
856-692-1881

Blackwell Auctions
10900 US Hwy. 19 N
Clearwater, FL 33764
blackwellauctions.com
727-546-0200

Bourgeault-Horan Antiquarians & Associates, LLC
93 Pleasant St.
Portsmouth, NH 03801
bourgeaulthoranauctions.com
603-433-8400

Brinkman Auctions
P.O. Box 559
Wayzata, MN 55391
brinkmanauction.com
763-972-9149

Bruneau & Co Auctioneers
63 4th Ave.
Cranston, RI 02910
bruneauandco.com
401-533-9980

Brunk Auctions
P.O. Box 2135
Asheville, NC 28802
brunkauctions.com
825-254-6846

Bunch Auctions
1 Hillman Dr.
Chadds Ford, PA 19317
bunchauctions.com
610-558-1800

Bunte Auction Services
755 Church Rd.
Elgin, IL, 60123
bunteauction.com
847-214-8423

California Historical Design
1901 Broadway
Alameda, CA 94501
acstickley.com
510-647-3621

Case Antiques
4310 Papermill Dr.
Knoxville, TN 37909
caseantiques.com
865-558-3033

Charleston Estate Auctions
918 Lansing Dr., Suite E
Mt. Pleasant, SC 29464
charlestonestateauctions.com
843-696-3335

Charlton Hall Auctions
7 Lexington Dr.
West Columbia, SC 29170
charltonhallauctions.com
803-779-5678

Christie's
20 Rockefeller Plaza
New York, NY 10020
christies.com
212-636-2000

Clars Auction Gallery
5644 Telegraph Ave.
Oakland, CA 94609
clars.com
510-428-0100

Conestoga Auction Company, a division of Hess Auction Group
768 Graystone Rd.
Manheim, PA 17545
hessauctiongroup.com
717-898-7284

Copake Auction
66 East Main St.
Copake, NY 12516
copakeauction.com
518-329-1142

Cordier Auctions
1500 Paxton St.
Harrisburg, PA 17104
cordierauction.com
717-731-8662

Cottone Auctions
120 Court St.
Geneseo, NY 14454
cottoneauctions.com
585-243-1000

Cowan's Auctions
6270 Este Ave.
Cincinnati, OH 45232
cowanauctions.com
513-871-1670

Crescent City Auction Gallery
1330 St. Charles Ave.
New Orleans, LA 70130
crescentcityauctiongallery.com
504-529-5057

CRN Auctions
57 Bay State Rd.
Cambridge, MA 02138
crnauctions.com
617-661-9582

Crocker Farm, Inc.
15900 York Rd.
Sparks, MD 21152
crockerfarm.com
410-472-2016

Discogs
discogs.com

DuMouchelles
409 E. Jefferson Ave.
Detroit, MI 48226
dumouchelles.com
313-963-6255

Eldred's
P.O. Box 796
1483 Route 6A
East Dennis, MA 02641
eldreds.com
508-385-3116

Fontaine's Auction Gallery
1485 W. Housatonic St.
Pittsfield, MA 01201
fontainesauction.com
413-448-8922

Forsythes' Auctions
206 W. Main St.
Russellville, OH 45168
forsythesauctions.com
937-377-3700

Freeman's Auctioneers & Appraisers
1808 Chestnut St.
Philadelphia, PA 19103
freemansauction.com
215-563-9275

Garth's Auctioneers & Appraisers
P.O. Box 758
Columbus, OH 43216
garths.com
740-362-4771

Glass Works Auctions
102 Jefferson St.
East Greenville, PA 18041
glswrk-auction.com
215-679-5849

GreatCollections.com
17500 Red Hill Ave., Suite 160
Irvine, CA 92614
greatcollections.com
800-44-COINS

Hake's Auctions
P.O. Box 12001
York, PA 17402
hakes.com
717-434-1600

Hartzell's Auction Gallery Inc.
521 Richmond Rd.
Bangor, PA 18013
hartzellsauction.com
610-588-5831

Heritage Auctions
3500 Maple Ave., 17th Floor
Dallas, TX 75219
ha.com
214-528-3500

Hindman Auctions
1338 W. Lake St.
Chicago, IL 60607
hindmanauctions.com
312-280-1212

Hudson Valley Auctions
P.O. Box 432
Cornwall, NY 12518
hudsonvalleyauctions.com
914-213-0425

Humler & Nolan
225 E. Sixth St., 4th Floor
Cincinnati, OH 45202
humlernolan.com
513-381-2041

Hunt Auctions, LLC
256 Welsh Pool Rd.
Exton, PA 19341
huntauctions.com
610-524-0822

Jeffrey S. Evans & Associates
P.O. Box 2638
Harrisonburg, VA 22801
jeffreysevans.com
540-434-3939

Julien's Auctions
8630 Hayden Place
Culver City, CA 90232
juliensauctions.com
310-836-1818

Kamelot Auctions
2220 E. Allegheny Ave.
Philadelphia, PA 19134
kamelotauctions.com
215-438-6990

Leland Little Auctions
620 Cornerstone Ct.
Hillsborough, NC 27278
lelandlittle.com
919-644-1243

Locati Auctions
1425 E. Welsh Rd.
Maple Glen, PA 19002
locatillc.com
215-619-2873

Long Auction Co.
307 Mule Shed
Richmond, KY 40475
longauction.com
859-544-2254

Los Angeles Modern Auctions (LAMA)
16145 Hart St.
Van Nuys, CA 91406
lamodern.com
323-904-1950

Medina Antique Mall
The Medina Antique Mall
2797 Medina Rd.
Medina, OH, 44256
medinaantiquemall.com

Memory Lane Inc.
12831 Newport Ave., Suite 180
Tustin CA 92780
memorylaneinc.com
877-606-5263

Michaan's Auctions
2751 Todd St.
Alameda, CA 94501
michaans.com
800-380-9822

Mile High Card Company
858 W. Happy Canyon Rd., Suite 240
Castle Rock, CO 80108
milehighcardco.com
303-840-2784

Milestone Auctions
38198 Willoughby Pkwy.
Willoughby, OH 44094
milestoneauctions.com
440-527-8060

Morphy Auctions
2000 N. Reading Rd.
Denver, PA 17517
morphyauctions.com
877-968-8880

Nadeau's Auction Gallery
25 Meadow Rd.
Windsor, CT 06095
nadeausauction.com
860-249-2444

Neal Auction Company
4038 Magazine St.
New Orleans, LA 70115
nealauction.com
800-467-5329

New Orleans Auction Galleries
333 St. Joseph St.
New Orleans, LA 70130
neworleansauction.com
504-566-1849

Palm Beach Modern Auctions
417 Bunker Rd.
West Palm Beach, FL 33405
modernauctions.com
561-586-5500

Phillips
450 Park Ave.
New York, NY 10022
phillips.com
212-940-1200

Pook & Pook
463 East Lancaster Ave.
Downingtown, PA 19335
pookandpook.com
610-269–4040

Quittenbaum Kunstauktionen GmbH
Theresienstr. 60
80333 Munich, Germany
quittenbaum.de

Rachel Davis Fine Arts
1301 W. 79th St.
Cleveland, OH 44102
racheldavisfinearts.com
216-939-1190

Rago Arts and Auction Center
333 N. Main St.
Lambertville, NJ 08530
ragoarts.com
609-397-9374

Rich Penn Auctions
P.O. Box 1355
Waterloo, IA 50704
richpennauctions.com
319-291-6688

Richard D. Hatch & Associates
913 Upward Rd.
Flat Rock, NC 28731
richardhatchauctions.com
828-696-3440

Richard Opfer Auctioneering, Inc.
1919 Greenspring Dr.
Timonium, MD 21093
forgegallery.com/opferauction
410-252-5035

Ripley Auctions
2764 E. 55th Pl.
Indianapolis, IN 46220
ripleyauctions.com
317-251-5635

Roland Auctioneers & Valuers
150 School St.
Glen Cove, NY 11542
rolandsantiques.com
212-260-2000

Schmitt Horan & Co.
P.O. Box 162
Windham, NH 03087
schmitt-horan.com
603-432-2237

Seeck Auctions
P.O. Box 377
Mason City, IA 50402
seeckauction.com
641-424-1116

Selkirk Auctioneers & Appraisers
555 Washington Ave., Suite 129
St. Louis, MO 63101
selkirkauctions.com
314-696-9041

Skinner, Inc.
274 Cedar Hill St.
Marlborough, MA 01752
skinnerinc.com
508-970-3000

Sotheby's
1334 York Ave.
New York, NY 10021
sothebys.com
212-606-7000

Soulis Auctions
P.O. Box 17
Lone Jack, MO 64070
dirksoulisauctions.com
816-566-2368

Stair Galleries
549 Warren St.
Hudson, NY 12534
stairgalleries.com
518-751-1000

Stevens Auction Co.
P.O. Box 58
Aberdeen, MS 39730-0058
stevensauction.com
662-369-2200

Strawser Auction Group
200 N. Main St.
P.O. Box 332
Wolcottville, IN 46795
strawserauctions.com
260-854-2859

Susanin's Auctioneers & Appraisers
900 S. Clinton St.
Chicago, IL 60607
susanins.com
312-832-9800

Theriault's
P.O. Box 151
Annapolis, MD 21404
theriaults.com
800-638-0422

Thomaston Place Auction Galleries
51 Atlantic Hwy.
Thomaston, ME 04861
thomastonauction.com
207-354-8141

Toomey & Co. Auctioneers
818 North Blvd.
Oak Park, IL 60301
toomeyco.com
708-383-5234

Treadway
2029 Madison Rd.
Cincinnati, OH 45208
treadwaygallery.com
513-321-6742

Tremont Auctions
615 Boston Post Rd.
Sudbury, MA 01776
tremontauctions.com
617-795-1678

Weiss Auctions
74 Merrick Rd.
Lynbrook, NY 11563
weissauctions.com
516-594-0731

Whitely's Auctioneers
485 S. Federal Hwy.
Dania Beach, FL 33004
whitleysauctioneers.com
954-866-8044

Willis Henry Auctions
22 Main St.
Marshfield, MA 02050
willishenry.com
781-834-7774

Witherell's
300 20th St.
Sacramento, CA 95811
witherells.com
916-446-6490

Wm Morford Auctions
P.O. Box 247
Cazenovia, NY 13035
morfauction.com
315-662-7625

Wolfs Gallery
23645 Mercantile Rd., Suite A
Beachwood, OH 44122
wolfsgallery.com
216 721 6945

Woody Auction
P.O. Box 618
317 S. Forrest St.
Douglass, KS 67039
woodyauction.com
316-747-2694

World Auction Gallery
228 East Meadow Ave.
East Meadow, NY 11554
516-307-8180
worldauctiongallery.com

Wright
1440 W. Hubbard St.
Chicago, IL 60642
wright20.com
312-563-0020

KOVELS

Need ACCURATE and RELIABLE information about antiques & collectibles?

Want the inside scoop on what's hot and what's not? Looking to downsize or settle an estate?

Nationally recognized for their deep knowledge and understanding of the market, Terry Kovel, Kim Kovel, and their team of experts can help you "Identify, Price, Buy, and Sell" — and maybe discover future treasures!

Visit Kovels.com and easily find prices, research marks, delve into identification guides, read the latest news from the antiques and collectibles world, and (last but not least!) enjoy the readers' Q&A.

How is this all accomplished?

Identify – Use our exclusive database to identify marks on pottery, porcelain, silver, and other metals. We guide readers in identifying the age and maker of an item – the first step in determining value. Not sure what you have? Search our Identification Guides written in a clear, precise language for the beginner-to-advanced collector. Even universities rely on our data!

Price – Access prices of more than a million antiques and collectibles, ranging from Colonial-era furniture to folk art to 20th-century toys, pottery, and furnishings. Read in-depth sales reports to see what's selling now – and why!

How to Buy or Sell – Read expert advice on how to get the most for your money, or sell at the best price. Sources include auction houses, clubs, publications, and other experts.

News – Get the latest news on collecting trends. Have a collectibles mystery? Search our extensive digital archive of Kovels' articles. Get the current issue as well as 46 years of information-packed articles from our award-winning publication, *Kovels On Antiques & Collectibles.*

Collectors Corner – Find hundreds of **readers' questions** with answers by Kovels' experts, many with pictures. Plan your next trip to a popular flea market or show by using the **Calendar of Events.** And take advantage of the collective knowledge of the entire Kovels' community of antiques collectors by posting a question, joining a conversation, or starting a thread of your own in the Kovels.com **Forums.**

JOIN NOW AND SAVE 15% ON
ANY ANNUAL MEMBERSHIP
COUPON CODE: **PRICEGUIDE21**

Want weekly antiques and collectibles news delivered to your inbox? Sign up for our free weekly eNewsletter on **KOVELS.COM**.

Learn | **Identify** | **Price**

Are you a DEALER or COLLECTOR who NEEDS to KNOW what's happening?

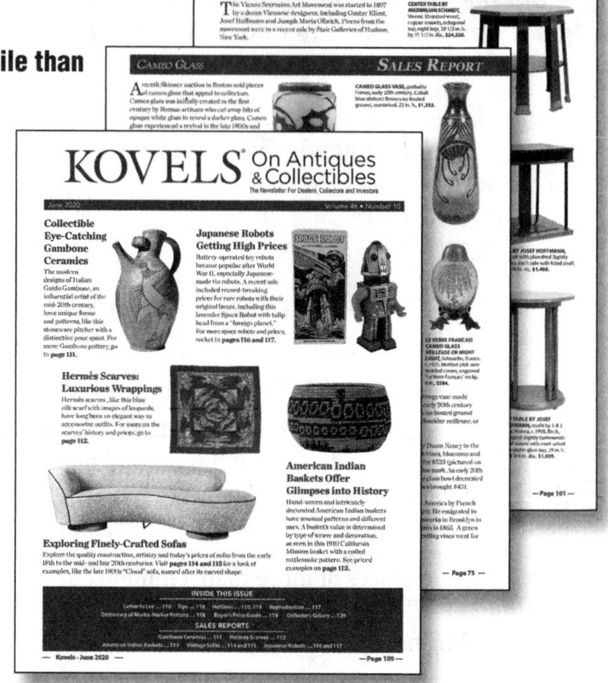

Auctions, trends, and the economy impact prices every year. **Some markets are more volatile than others.**

SUBSCRIBE NOW to our award-winning monthly print newsletter, *Kovels On Antiques & Collectibles.*

This is **THE SOURCE** that helps **COLLECTORS and DEALERS** keep up with the fast-changing world of antique, vintage, and collectible treasures.

- Learn about prices at the latest sales, shows, and auctions.
- Spot tomorrow's emerging trends so you can cash in **TODAY.**
- Discover the true value of dozens of collectibles as prices change month to month.
- Find out how to avoid fakes and frauds and learn about fakes being sold right now!

Become a more successful collector! Try *Kovels On Antiques & Collectibles* print newsletter for just <u>$27 a year</u> (12 issues), a savings of 40% off the regular price!
To subscribe, visit Kovels.com, call, or send this order form to the address below.

Name ____________________
Street ____________________
City __________ State ______ Zip ______
Telephone (____) ________________

☐ MasterCard ☐ Visa ☐ AmEx ☐ Discover ☐ Check *(payable to Kovels)*

Name on Card ____________________
Card No. ____________________
Signature ____________________
Email Address ____________________

KOVELS On Antiques & Collectibles
P.O. Box 292758
Kettering, OH 45429-8758

Or call us at (800) 829-9158 (mention offer **5H20PB53**)

5H20PB53